February 12–16, 2011
San Antonio, Texas, USA

I0047654

Association for
Computing Machinery

Advancing Computing as a Science & Profession

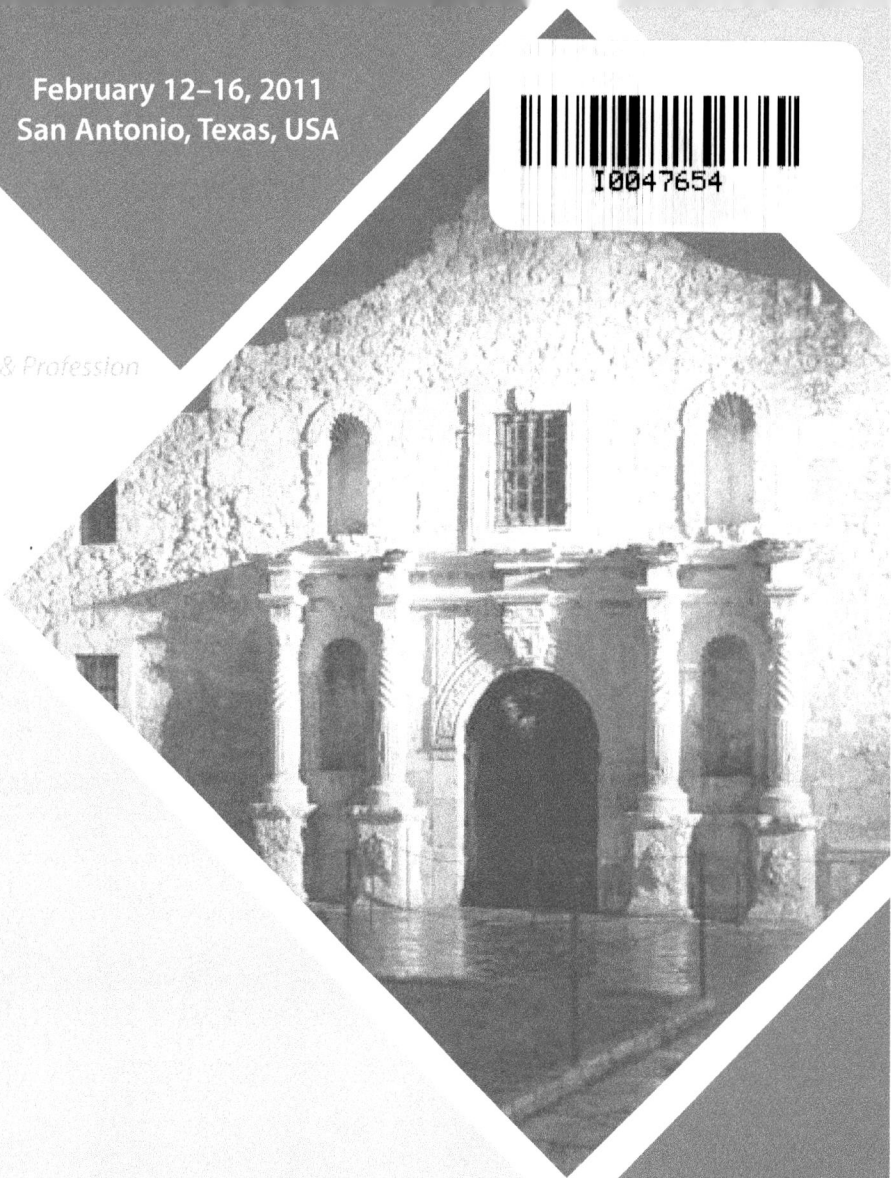

PPoPP'11

Proceedings of the 2011 ACM SIGPLAN Symposium on
Principles and Practice of Parallel Programming

Sponsored by:
ACM SIGPLAN

Supported by:
**Microsoft Research, Qualcomm, National Science Foundation,
Google, and IBM Research**

**Association for
Computing Machinery**

Advancing Computing as a Science & Profession

The Association for Computing Machinery
2 Penn Plaza, Suite 701
New York, New York 10121-0701

ISBN: 978-1-4503-1374-2

Additional copies may be ordered prepaid from:

ACM Order Department
PO Box 11405
New York, NY 10286-1405

Phone: 1-800-342-6626 (US and Canada)
+1-212-626-0500 (all other countries)
Fax: +1-212-944-1318
E-mail: acmhelp@acm.org

Printed in the USA

Chairs' Welcome

It is our great pleasure to welcome you to the *16ᵗʰ ACM Symposium on Principles and Practice of Parallel Programming – PPoPP'11*. PPoPP continues to be the premiere forum where researchers present their work on all aspects of parallelism and concurrency: algorithms and applications, programming models, languages, and environments, system software and runtime systems, and theoretical foundational work. As our industry continues to move toward parallel systems, from large-scale supercomputers to multicore mobile devices, such as smart phones and tablets, research work on concurrency is needed to support developers at all levels of the execution stack.

This year we received 165 completed submissions, close to the conference record high. Because of the large number of submissions, in addition to the 25 program committee members, we formed an external review committee and invited 30 experts in various areas to help out in reviewing papers. In addition, committee members also invited external reviewers, to provide our submitting authors with a total of more than 630 reviews. There was a paper bidding process to match up the expertise of the reviewers and the reviewed papers before papers were assigned to reviewers. An on-line discussion period was conducted among all reviewers of each paper to smooth out the differences among the reviewers before the program committee meeting was held. For the final program, the program committee selected 26 full papers and 13 posters for the program. They span a wide spectrum of areas in parallel programming.

A few years back, the PPoPP Steering Committee recognized the importance of broadening the conference experience through interaction with hardware architects designing parallel systems. This year we continue the collocation with the International Symposium on High-Performance Computer Architecture. Beside encouraging cross-participation in any of the two conference sessions, PPoPP and HPCA will share two keynotes from leading researchers in the area of parallel programming: Jim Larus (Microsoft Research) and Kathryn McKinley (UT Austin), and all the tutorials and workshops.

A conference is successful as long as it presents high quality work. Therefore, our thanks go first to the authors of all submissions: papers and posters, tutorial and workshop proposals, and to the keynote speakers and all the presenters in the conference. We acknowledge that reviewing is hard work and appreciate the efforts of the program committee, the external review committee, and all the external reviewers. We appreciate the commitment and dedication of all members of the organizing committee: Rafael Asenjo, publicity and web; John Cavazos, proceedings; Michael Spear, registration and student support; Karin Strauss, finance; Christoph von Praun, workshops and tutorials; Qing Yi, local arrangements. We thank Keshav Pingali, the PPoPP Steering Committee Chair for his guidance and support; Daniel Jimenez and Shubu Mukherjee, General and Program Chairs of HPCA. We thank ACM SIGPLAN for its ongoing sponsorship and the National Science Foundation, Microsoft Research, Qualcomm Research, IBM Research, and Google for their generous financial support.

Calin Cascaval
PPoPP'11 General Chair
Qualcomm Research, USA

Pen-Chung Yew
PPoPP'11 Program Chair
Academia Sinica, Taiwan and
University of Minnesota, USA

Table of Contents

Session 4: Correctness and Debugging

Session 5: Transactional Memory and Speculative Execution

Session 6: Parallel Applications and Scheduling

Session 7: Parallel Data Structures and Programming Models

Session 8: Programming on GPUs

Posters

16th ACM SIGPLAN Annual Symposium on Principles and Practice of Parallel Programming Organization

General Chair: Calin Cascaval *(Qualcomm Research, USA)*

Program Chair: Pen-Chung Yew *(Academia Sinica, Taiwan and University of Minnesota at Twin Cities, USA)*

Finance Chair: Karin Strauss *(Microsoft Research, USA)*

Registration Chair: Michael Spear *(Lehigh University, USA)*

Publication Chair: John Cavazos *(University of Delaware, USA)*

Local Arrangements Chair: Qing Yi *(University of Texas at San Antonio, USA)*

Publicity and Web Chair: Rafael Asenjo *(University of Malaga, Spain)*

Workshops and Tutorials Chair: Christoph von Praun *(OHM University of Applied Sciences, Nuremberg, Germany)*

Program Committee: George Almasi *(IBM Research, USA)*
Fracois Bodin *(IRISA, France)*
Dhruva Chakrabarti *(HP, USA)*
Albert Cohen *(INRIA, France)*
Luiz DeRose *(Cray Inc., USA)*
Chen Ding *(University of Rochester, USA)*
Alexandra Fedorova *(Simon Fraser University, Canada)*
R. Govindarajan *(Indian Institute of Science, India)*
Bill Gropp *(University of Illinois at Urbana-Champaign, USA)*
Wei-Chung Hsu *(National Chiao-Tung University, ROC)*
Roy Ju *(AMD, USA)*
Mahmut Kandemir *(The Pennsylvania State University, USA)*
Milind Kulkarni *(Purdue University, USA)*
Jaejin Lee *(Seoul National University, Korea)*
John Mellor-Crummey *(Rice University, USA)*
Sam Midkiff *(Purdue University, USA)*
Gopalan Nadathur *(University of Minnesota, USA)*
Santosh Pande *(Georgia Tech, USA)*
Vijaya Ramachandran *(The University of Texas at Austin, USA)*
Lawrence Rauchwerger *(Texas A&M University, USA)*
P. Sadayappan *(Ohio State University, USA)*
Vijay Saraswat *(IBM Research, USA)*
Uzi Vishkin *(University of Maryland, USA)*
Antonia Zhai *(University of Minnesota, USA)*
Hans Zima *(University of Vienna, JPL)*

External Reviewers:

David Abramson
David Bader
Muthu Baskaran
Brad Beckmann
Siegfried Benkner
Jonathan Bentz
Micah Best
James Beyer
Abhinav Bhatele
Sergey Blagodurov
Hans Boehm
Uday Bondhugula
Rajesh Bordawekar
Greg Bronevetsky
Nathan Bronson
Barla Cambazoglu
George Caragea
Gautam Chakrabarti
David Cunningham
Brian Demsky
Stephan Diestelhorst
James Dinan
Julian Dolby
James Edwards
Faith Ellen
Xiaobing Feng
Andrew Gacek
Ben Gaster
Kim Gostelow
Anshul Gupta
Sam Guyer
Lee Howes
Radha Jagadeesan
Troy Johnson
Pramod Joisha
Vivek Kale
Prabhanjan Kambadur
Arkady Kanevsky
Krishna Kavi
Kiyokuni Kawachiya
Darren Kerbyson

Sarfraz Khurshid
Antonio Lain
Akash Lal
Ziyuan Li
Victor Luchangco
Virendra Marathe
Sally McKee
Gokhan Memik
Jose Moreira
Shane Mottishaw
SaiPrasanth Muralidhara
Craig Mustard
Aditya Nori
Ozcan Ozturk
Keshav Pingali
Louis-Noel Pouchet
Kaushik Rajan
Venkatesh-Prasad Ranganath
Atanas Rountev
Norm Rubin
Xipeng Shen
Arrvindh Shriraman
Marc Snir
Jim Sukha
Gabriel Tanase
Keita Teranishi
Vinod Tipparaju
Emina Torlak
Alexandros Tzannes
Eric Van Wyk
Nalini Vasudevan
Kapil Vaswani
Richard Vuduc
Hai Chuan Wang
Michael Whalen
Bob Wisniewski
Felix Wolf
Chia-Lin Yang
Chung Yung
Lingli Zhang
Yoav Zibin

PPoPP 2011 Sponsors & Supporters

Sponsor:

Supporters:

Programming the Cloud

James R. Larus
eXtreme Computing Group
Microsoft Research
Redmond, WA, USA
larus@microsoft.com

Abstract

Client + cloud computing is a disruptive, new computing platform, combining diverse client devices – PCs, smartphones, sensors, and single-function and embedded devices – with the unlimited, on-demand computation and data storage offered by cloud computing services such as Amazon's AWS or Microsoft's Windows Azure. As with every advance in computing, programming is a fundamental challenge as client + cloud computing combines many difficult aspects of software development. Systems built for this world are inherently parallel and distributed, run on unreliable hardware, and must be continually available – a challenging programming model for even the most skilled programmers. How then do ordinary programmers develop software for the Cloud?

This talk presents one answer, Orleans, a software framework for building client + cloud applications. Orleans encourages use of simple concurrency patterns that are easy to understand and implement correctly, building on an actor-like model with declarative specification of persistence, replication, and consistency and using lightweight transactions to support the development of reliable and scalable client + cloud software.

Bio

James Larus is a Director of the eXtreme Computing Group (XCG) in Microsoft Research. Larus has been an active contributor to the programming languages, compiler, and computer architecture communities. Larus became an ACM Fellow in 2006. Larus joined Microsoft Research as a Senior Researcher in 1998 to start and, for five years, led the Software Productivity Tools (SPT) group, which developed and applied a variety of innovative techniques in static program analysis and constructed tools that found defects (bugs) in software. This group's research has both had considerable impact on the research community, as well as being shipped in Microsoft products such as the Static Driver Verifier and FX/Cop and other, widely-used internal software development tools. Larus then became the Research Area Manager for programming languages and tools and started the Singularity research project, which demonstrated that modern programming languages and software engineering techniques could fundamentally improve software architectures. Subsequently, he helped start XCG, which is developing the hardware and software to support cloud computing.

Before joining Microsoft, Larus was an Assistant and Associate Professor of Computer Science at the University of Wisconsin-Madison, where he published approximately 60 research papers and co-led the Wisconsin Wind Tunnel (WWT) research project with Professors Mark Hill and David Wood. WWT was a DARPA and NSF-funded project investigated new approaches to simulating, building, and programming parallel shared-memory computers. Larus's research spanned many areas: including new and efficient techniques for measuring and recording executing programs' behavior, tools for analyzing and manipulating compiled and linked programs, programming languages for parallel computing, tools for verifying program correctness, and techniques for compiler analysis and optimization.

Larus received his MS and PhD in Computer Science from the University of California, Berkeley in 1989, and an AB in Applied Mathematics from Harvard in 1980.

Ordered *vs.* Unordered: a Comparison of Parallelism and Work-efficiency in Irregular Algorithms *

M. Amber Hassaan

Electrical and Computer Engineering
University of Texas at Austin
amber@mail.utexas.edu

Martin Burtscher

Department of Computer Science
Texas State University-San Marcos
burtscher@txstate.edu

Keshav Pingali

Department of Computer Science
University of Texas at Austin
pingali@cs.utexas.edu

Abstract

Outside of computational science, most problems are formulated in terms of *irregular* data structures such as graphs, trees and sets. Unfortunately, we understand relatively little about the structure of parallelism and locality in irregular algorithms. In this paper, we study several algorithms for four such problems: discrete-event simulation, single-source shortest path, breadth-first search, and minimal spanning trees. We show that these algorithms can be classified into two categories that we call *unordered* and *ordered*, and demonstrate experimentally that there is a trade-off between parallelism and work efficiency: unordered algorithms usually have more parallelism than their ordered counterparts for the same problem, but they may also perform more work. Nevertheless, our experimental results show that unordered algorithms typically lead to more scalable implementations, demonstrating that less work-efficient irregular algorithms may be better for parallel execution.

Categories and Subject Descriptors:
D.1.3 [**Programming Techniques**] Concurrent Programming – *Parallel Programming* D.3.3 [**Programming Languages**] Language Constructs and Features – *Frameworks*

General Terms: Algorithms, Languages, Performance

Keywords: Irregular Algorithms, Amorphous Data-parallelism, Parallel Breadth-first Search, Single-Source Shortest Path, Discrete-Event Simulation, Minimal Spanning Tree, Multicore processors, Galois system.

1. Introduction

Over the past two decades, the parallel programming community has acquired a deep understanding of the patterns of parallelism and locality in *regular*, dense matrix algorithms. These insights have led to the development of many languages, tools and techniques that have made it easier to develop high-performance implementations of regular algorithms [5, 14, 26].

Outside of computational science, most problems are *irregular* since the underlying data structures are pointer-based data structures such as trees and graphs. At present, we have few insights into the structure of parallelism and locality in irregular algorithms, and this has stunted the development of techniques and tools for programming these algorithms in parallel [6]. A major complication is that dependences in irregular algorithms are functions of runtime data

values such as the inputs to the program. Therefore, in general, one cannot generate a useful static dependence graph for an irregular algorithm, and it is not possible to come up with asymptotic estimates of parallelism in terms of the size of the problem (in contrast, we can say that there are $O(N^3)$ scalar multiplications that can be done concurrently when multiplying two $N \times N$ dense matrices, for example).

In previous work, we have shown that these problems can be circumvented by taking a *data-centric* view called the *operator formulation of algorithms* in which an algorithm is expressed in terms of its action on data structures [27]. In graph algorithms, the unit of action is the application of an operator to an *active node*, which is a site in the graph where computation needs to be performed. Usually, there are many active nodes in a graph and there may be ordering constraints in the processing of these nodes. In *unordered* algorithms such as Delaunay mesh refinement and preflow-push maxflow computation, active nodes can be processed in any order; in *ordered* algorithms such as event-driven simulation, there is a (partial) order on active nodes that dictates the order in which these nodes must be processed. Applications formulated in this way can be executed in parallel by processing multiple active nodes speculatively [20]. This parallelism, which is called *amorphous data-parallelism* [27], can be exploited by the Galois system, described in more detail in Section 2.

Although many irregular problems can be solved using both ordered and unordered algorithms, the trade-offs between these algorithms are not well understood. In this paper, we study ordered and unordered algorithms for four irregular problems: breadth-first search, discrete-event simulation, minimal spanning tree, and single-source shortest path. This paper makes the following contributions.

- We show that contrary to popular belief, many ordered algorithms exhibit substantial amorphous data-parallelism.
- We find that for the same problem, unordered algorithms have shorter critical paths than ordered algorithms, but may perform more work than ordered algorithms do. Unless care is taken, the amount of additional work may grow with the number of threads used to the execute the program, so it is not always obvious what the best parallel algorithm is for a given problem.
- Fortunately, careful scheduling of computations in unordered algorithms can limit the amount of extra work performed by these algorithms. This allows us to produce scalable parallel implementations of unordered algorithms. However, we do not currently have effective techniques for producing scalable implementations of ordered algorithms.

The rest of this paper is organized as follows. Section 2 reviews amorphous data-parallelism and the Galois and ParaMeter systems. Section 3 describes ordered and unordered algorithms for breadth-first search, single-source shortest path, discrete-event simulation, and minimal spanning tree, and reports measurements of the amount of amorphous data-parallelism in these algorithms. Section 4 dis-

* This work is supported in part by NSF grants 0923907, 0833162, 0719966, and 0702353 and by grants from IBM, NEC and Intel.

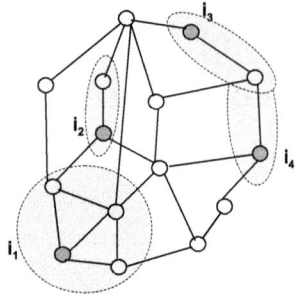

Figure 1. Amorphous data-parallelism in graph algorithms. Dark colored nodes are *Active* nodes and shaded regions are *Neighborhoods*. $i_1, ..., i_4$ are *Activities*

cusses implementation issues for ordered and unordered algorithms. Section 5 presents experimental results obtained by running efficient implementations of unordered algorithms on a multicore processor. Section 6 discusses related work. Section 7 summarizes our conclusions.

2. Amorphous data-parallelism

We use the graph shown in Figure 1 to explain the operator formulation of irregular algorithms, and introduce the Galois system. At each point during the execution of such an algorithm, there are certain nodes or edges in the graph where computation might be performed. Performing a computation may require reading or writing other nodes and edges in the graph. The node or edge on which a computation is centered is called an *active element*, and the computation itself is called an *activity*. It is convenient to think of an activity as resulting from the application of an *operator* (graph transformer) to the active element. The set of nodes and edges that are read or written in performing the activity is called the *neighborhood* of that activity. In Figure 1, the filled nodes represent active nodes, and shaded regions represent the neighborhoods of those active nodes. In some algorithms, activities may modify the graph structure of the neighborhood by adding or removing graph elements. To keep the discussion simple, we assume from here on that active elements are nodes, unless otherwise stated.

In general, there are many active nodes in a graph, so a sequential implementation must pick one of them and perform the appropriate computation. In unordered algorithms, such as the BFS algorithm in Figure 3, the implementation can pick *any* active element for execution. In ordered algorithms, such as the BFS algorithm in Figure 2, there are ordering constraints on the processing of active nodes.

Opportunities for exploiting parallelism in irregular algorithms arise as follows. If there are many active nodes at some point during the computation, each one is a site where a thread can perform computation, *subject to neighborhood and ordering constraints*. When active nodes are unordered, the neighborhood constraints must ensure that the output produced by executing the activities in parallel is the same as the output produced by executing the activities one at a time in some order. For ordered algorithms, this order must be the same as the ordering on active nodes. Given a set of active nodes and an ordering on them, amorphous data-parallelism is the parallelism that arises from simultaneously processing active nodes, subject to these constraints.

2.1 The Galois system

The Galois system is an implementation of these abstractions that enables the exploitation of amorphous data-parallelism on multicore processors [20]. We summarize the main points of this system to make the paper self-contained.

Irregular algorithms can be formulated as iteration over a workset of active nodes. Galois introduces two constructs called *Galois set iterators* for specifying iteration over unordered and ordered sets. These iterators are similar to conventional set iterators, but *they permit new elements to be added to a set while it is being iterated over.*

- **Unordered-set iterator: foreach (e: Set S) do B(e)** The loop body B(e) is executed for each element e of set S in some arbitrary order. The execution may add new elements to S.
- **Ordered-set iterator: foreach (e: OrderedSet S) do B(e)** Similar to the unordered set iterator, except a sequential implementation must choose a minimal element from S in every iteration and the ordering is specified by a user provided comparator.

Note that these iterators have well-defined sequential semantics. In addition, the unordered set iterator expresses the fact that active elements can be processed in any order.

All concurrency control is performed in a library of concurrent data structures similar to the Java collections library, containing concurrent implementations of common data structures like graphs. The library also provides implementations of parallel unordered and ordered sets for implementing Galois set iteration in parallel.

In the baseline execution model, the graph is stored in shared-memory, and active nodes are processed by some number of threads. A free thread picks an arbitrary active element from the workset and speculatively applies the operator to that element, making calls to the graph class API to perform operations on the graph as needed. The neighborhood of an activity can be visualized as a blue ink-blot that begins at the active element and spreads incrementally whenever a graph API call is made that touches new nodes or edges. To ensure that neighborhood constraints are respected, mechanisms similar to those used in thread-level speculation or software transactional memory can be used in principle [7, 9, 16, 29]. Each graph element has an associated logical lock that must be acquired before a thread can access that element. Locks are held until the activity terminates. Lock manipulation is performed by the code in the graph API call, not in the application code. If a lock cannot be acquired because it is already owned by another thread, a conflict is reported to the runtime system, which rolls back one of the conflicting activities. To enable rollback, each graph API method that modifies the graph records *undo* information, *i.e.*, copies of the old data. Like lock manipulation, rollbacks are a service provided by the library and runtime system.

If active nodes are not ordered, the activity terminates when the application of the operator is complete and all acquired locks are released. If active nodes are ordered, active nodes can still be processed in any order, but they must commit in serial order. This can be implemented using a data structure similar to a reorder buffer in out-of-order processors [20]. In this case, locks are released when the activity commits.

2.2 ParaMeter

One measure of amorphous data-parallelism in the execution of an irregular algorithm for a given input is the number of active nodes that can be processed in parallel at each point during the execution *if one had perfect knowledge of neighborhood and ordering constraints*. This is called the *available parallelism* at each step of computation, and a plot showing the available parallelism of an irregular algorithm for a given input is called a *parallelism profile*. Intuitively, this is the parallelism in the execution of the program, assuming that (i) each activity takes one time unit, (ii) there is an unbounded number of processors, and (iii) active nodes are scheduled greedily (neighborhood conflicts between activities of the same priority are resolved by rolling back one of the conflicting activities, chosen at random). In principle, the precise shape of the parallelism profile may depend on how neighborhood conflicts are resolved, but in practice, the parallelism profiles are fairly robust with respect to this choice. The total number of computation steps needed to execute an algorithm for a given input reflects the critical path length in this model.

In this paper, we present parallelism profiles generated by the ParaMeter tool [21]. In studying these profiles, it is important to note that ParaMeter considers conflicts only the abstract data type level; in particular, if the neighborhoods of two activities are disjoint, ParaMeter assumes that there are no conflicts between them. Therefore, these profiles are independent of the concrete representation of the graph.

3. Case studies

This section presents ordered and unordered algorithms for four irregular problems: breadth-first search, single-source shortest-path computation, discrete-event simulation, and minimal spanning tree computation.

3.1 Breadth-First Search

Breadth-first search (BFS) of undirected graphs starts from a *root*, and explores all the neighbors of this node before exploring their neighbors, *etc*. One formulation of BFS is that it computes a value called *level* for each node n such that $level(n)$ is the number of edges on the shortest path from the root to n.

```
1  Graph g = /* read in graph */
2  OrderedWorkSet ows; //ordered by level
3  ows.add(root); //root has level 0
4  foreach (Node n: ows) {
5    int level = n.getLevel() + 1;
6    for (Node m: g.neighbors(n)) {
7      if (m.getLevel() == INF) { //not visited
8        m.setLevel(level);
9        ows.add(m); //add to ows to update neighbors
10 } } }
```

Figure 2. Ordered BFS algorithm

Figure 2 shows pseudocode for the standard BFS algorithm. Initially, the *level* of the root is set to zero, and the *level* of all other nodes is set to ∞ (this can be done while reading in the graph). The algorithm maintains a workset of nodes, *ows*, ordered by *level*. Initially, only the root node *root* is in the workset. Each iteration of the loop removes a node n from the workset and visits the neighbors of n. If a neighbor has not been visited before, *i.e.*, its *level* is infinity, its *level* is set to $level(n)+1$, and it is added to the workset. The algorithm terminates when the workset is empty. This is an *ordered* algorithm because the workset must be processed in a particular order (in this case, in level order).

```
1  Graph g = /* read in graph */
2  WorkSet ws;
3  ws.add(root);
4  foreach (Node n: ws) {
5    for (Node m: g.neighbors(n)) {
6      int level = n.getLevel() + 1;
7      if (level < m.getLevel()) { //can be relaxed
8        m.setLevel(level);
9        ws.add(m); //add to the ws to update neighbors
10 } } }
```

Figure 3. Unordered BFS algorithm

A different algorithm can be obtained by noticing that the *level* of a node is a local minimum in the graph, *i.e.*, the *level* of a node (except for the root) is one higher than the minimum *level* of its neighbors. Hence, the computation of *level* for node n can be described by the following fixpoint system.
Initialization:
$$level(root) = 0; level(k) = \infty, \forall k \ other \ than \ root$$

Fixpoint computation:
$$level(n) = min(level(m) + 1, \forall m \in neighbors \ of \ n)$$

Because of this property, it is possible to process the nodes from the workset in any order, thus yielding an unordered algorithm in which multiple nodes can be processed in parallel. The pseudocode is given in Figure 3. The ordered workset is replaced with an unordered set from which an arbitrary element can be selected. In the unordered algorithm, it may happen that a node is temporarily assigned a *level* that is higher than the final value. However, the *level* will monotonically decrease until it reaches the correct value. Whenever a thread updates the *level* of a node, it adds that node to the workset so that its neighbors can be updated if necessary. The algorithm finishes when the workset is empty. The unordered algorithm may execute more iterations than the ordered algorithm; exactly how many more depends on the scheduling policy implemented in the workset. We discuss this in more detail in Section 5.

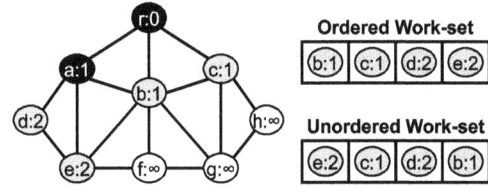

Figure 4. BFS example. The root node r and node a have been processed from the workset (colored black). The nodes in grey are currently active and in the workset. The nodes in the ordered workset are ordered by their level.

The monotonicity of updates in the unordered BFS algorithm enables an important optimization: there is no need to keep undo information for the updates performed by multiple threads on a node as long as the updates are atomic and visible to all the threads. Since only a single value is updated, this update can be implemented efficiently using an atomic primitive like compare-and-swap (CAS), and there is no need to use abstract locks for conflict detection.

3.1.1 BFS: Available parallelism

For our BFS experiments, we used a randomly connected undirected graph containing 4 million nodes and approximately 36.8 million edges. The degree of each node is chosen randomly in the range [10, 20]. Figure 5 shows the parallelism profiles produced by ParaMeter for the unordered and ordered BFS algorithms. The unordered algorithm has a critical path of just eight computation steps, whereas the ordered algorithm has a critical path that is more than 25 times as long. Our implementation of unordered algorithm uses CAS operations instead of abstract locks, which is why ParaMeter does not report any neighborhood conflicts. At every computation step i, all nodes at level i are processed and the nodes at level $i + 1$ become active. Thus, in a graph with average degree d, the available parallelism increases roughly as d^i. In the ordered algorithm, the available parallelism also increases but more slowly because of the ordering constraints and neighborhood conflicts. Nevertheless, there is substantial parallelism even in the ordered version. Both versions perform 4 million iterations (one iteration per node). There is no wasted work performed by the unordered version because the schedule used by ParaMeter ends up being the same as the schedule used by the ordered version; other schedules may perform wasted work.

3.2 Single-Source Shortest Path

The single-source shortest-path problem (SSSP) finds the shortest paths from a given source node to all other nodes in a graph with weighted edges. The edge weights represent the distance between adjacent nodes. SSSP computes a distance $d(n)$ for every node n in

5

(a) Unordered BFS algorithm

(b) Ordered BFS algorithm

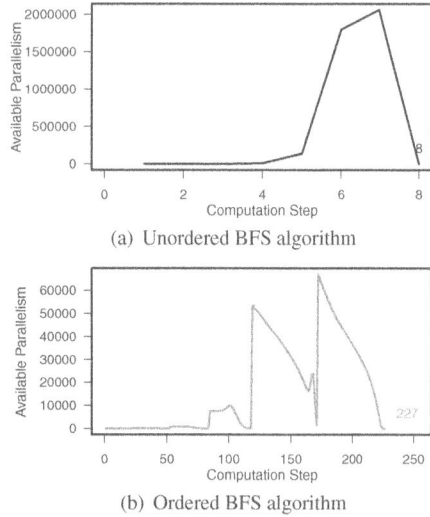

Figure 5. BFS parallelism profiles of a random graph with 4M nodes and approximately 36.8M edges

the graph such that $d(n)$ equals the distance from the source node to n along the shortest path. The distances of all nodes other than the source node are initialized to ∞, and then iteratively reduced to the correct value. BFS can be seen as a special case of SSSP in which all edge weights are 1.

A well-known ordered algorithm for computing SSSP is Dijkstra's algorithm, presented in Figure 6. Conceptually, the algorithm grows a shortest-path subtree of nodes and examines the edges crossing the cut between the nodes in the tree and the rest of the graph. For each edge (n, m) crossing the cut, it adds a pair $< m, distance >$ to the workset, where $distance = d(n) + weight(n, m)$. The workset is ordered by the $distance$ of each pair. Initially, the tree contains only the source node as the root, and the workset contains tuples corresponding to the neighbors of the source node. The algorithm repeatedly removes the pair with the minimum distance from the workset and, if the corresponding node has not already been visited, updates the node's distance and adds $< neighbor, distance >$ pairs to the workset for each of its neighbors. Note that the distance of each node is updated exactly once and that $< node, distance >$ pairs that refer to different nodes can be processed in parallel. However, any change made to the distance of a node must remain speculative until the distance becomes the minimum in the workset because a pair that is processed later may produce a shorter distance for a node than an earlier pair did.

```
1  Graph g = /* read in graph */
2  OrderedWorkSet ows; //ordered by distance
3  for (Node m: g.neighbors(root)) {
4    ows.add(<m, g.edgeWeight(root, m)>);
5  }
6  foreach (Pair <node, dist>: ows) {
7    if (node.getDist() == INF) { // not visited before
8      node.setDist(dist);
9      for (Node m: g.neighbors(node)) { //create tuples
10       if (m.getDist() == INF) { //for unvisited neighbors
11         ows.add(<m, dist + g.edgeWeight(node, m)>);
12  } } } }
```

Figure 6. Dijkstra's ordered SSSP algorithm

To derive the unordered algorithm, we note that shortest distance from the source to each node in the graph can be computed using the following fixpoint system.

Initialization:
$d(root) = 0; d(k) = \infty, \forall k\ other\ than\ root$

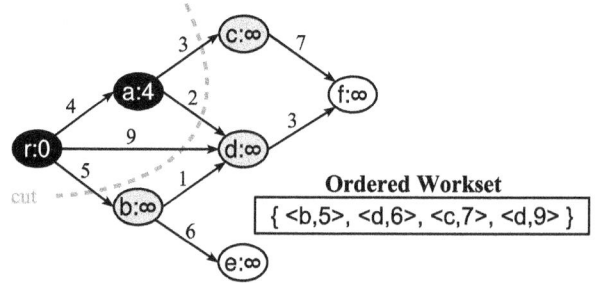

Figure 7. Dijkstra on sample graph. Tuple $< a, 4 >$ has been processed from the workset (shown in black). Tuples corresponding to the edges crossing the cut are in the workset and shown in grey.

Fixpoint computation:
$d(n) = min(d(m)+w(m, n)), \forall m \in incoming\ neighbors\ of\ n$

where $w(m, n)$ is the edge weight, *i.e.*, the distance between m and n. This observation yields an unordered algorithm for SSSP that is essentially the Bellman-Ford algorithm [4, 12, 15]. A node may be updated multiple times, but its distance is guaranteed to decrease monotonically to the correct value. Figure 8 shows the pseudocode for the unordered algorithm based on the fixpoint equation. Initially, the workset contains only the source node. In every step, the algorithm removes a node from the workset and tries to reduce the distance of each outgoing neighbor. If the distance of a neighbor is reduced, this neighbor is added to the workset. Hence, the workset always contains the nodes whose neighbors may need to be updated. The algorithm terminates when no more updates have to be performed. In both the ordered and the unordered algorithms, the neighborhood consists of the neighbors of the node being updated and the node itself.

```
1  Graph g = /* read in graph */
2  WorkSet ws;
3  ws.add(root);
4  foreach (Node n: ws) {
5    for (Node m: g.neighbors(n)) {
6      int dist = n.getDist() + g.edgeWeight(n, m);
7      if (dist < m.getDist()) { // can be relaxed
8        m.setDist(dist);
9        ws.add(m); // add to ws to update neighbors
10  } } }
```

Figure 8. Unordered SSSP algorithm

3.2.1 SSSP: Available parallelism

Figure 9 shows the parallelism profile for the ordered and unordered SSSP algorithms. The input is a directed graph representing the road network of Florida [1]. The graph contains 1.07 million nodes and 2.68 million edges. The edge weights reflect the distances between adjacent locations. Like the unordered BFS implementation, the implementation of the unordered algorithm does not use logical locks. The available parallelism initially increases exponentially because, at each step, all nodes in the workset can be processed in parallel without conflicts. This results in a shorter critical path for the unordered algorithm. The available parallelism drops when the algorithm runs out of nodes to process. Dijkstra's ordered algorithm also shows significant parallelism, almost 20 parallel activities on average, but it has a critical path that is over 30 times longer. Note that it executes roughly 50 times fewer activities than the unordered algorithm (1.34 million compared to 68.06 million). Because active nodes cannot be committed until they become the highest priority nodes in the system, the available parallelism in Dijkstra's algorithm increases slowly and intermittently drops to low values.

(a) Unordered SSSP algorithm

(b) Dijkstra's ordered SSSP algorithm

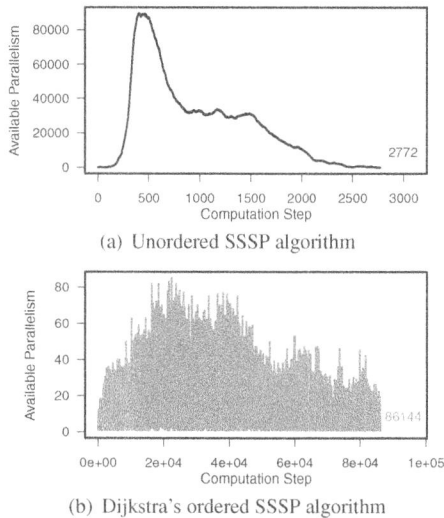

Figure 9. SSSP parallelism profiles of the road network of Florida containing 1.07M nodes and 2.68M edges

3.3 Discrete-Event Simulation

In discrete-event simulation (DES), the goal is to simulate a physical system consisting of one or more processing stations that operate autonomously and interact with other stations by sending and receiving messages. Such a system can be modeled as a graph in which nodes represent processing stations and edges represent communication channels between processing stations along which messages[1] can be sent. In most applications such as circuit or network simulation, a processing station interacts directly with only a small number of other processing stations, so the graph is sparse.

```
1  Graph g = /* read in graph */
2  OrderedWorkSet ows;
3  ows.add(initialEvents); //ordered by timestamp
4  foreach (Event e: ows) {
5    Station s = e.getStation(); // target station
6    List newEvents = s.simulate(e); //newly created
7    ows.add(newEvents); //events are added to the ows
8  }
```

Figure 10. Ordered DES algorithm

Figure 10 shows the pseudocode for the ordered discrete-event simulation algorithm. An ordered workset holds the pending events, ordered by their timestamps. In each step, the earliest message in the workset is removed, and the action of the receiving station is simulated. This may cause other messages to be sent at future times. If so, these messages are added to the workset. In principle, parallelism can be exploited in discrete-event simulation by processing multiple events from the workset concurrently. However, the conditions for non-interference of these activities are fairly complex. In Figure 11, there are two events in the workset for stations A and C, but it may or may not be legal to process them in parallel. If station A processes the event at its input and produces an event with timestamp 3, which is then processed by station B and B produces an event with timestamp 4, that event must be processed by station C before it processes the event with timestamp 5 and there are no opportunities for parallel execution. However, if the event produced by station B has a timestamp greater than 5, it is legal to process the two events, arriving at A and C, in parallel. Whether two events can be processed in parallel at a given point depends on what happens later in the execution.

---

[1] We use the terms *Message* and *Event* interchangeably in this discussion

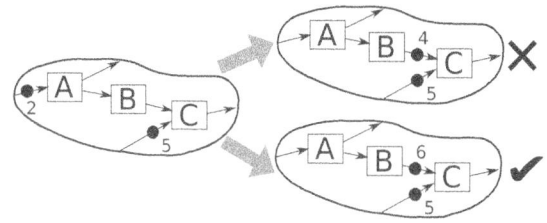

Figure 11. Discrete-event simulation. A, B and C are processing stations. A and C have incoming events with timestamps 2 and 5, respectively. Whether A and C can process events in parallel depends on the events generated by A (and B)

Chandy and Misra [8] proposed an unordered algorithm for DES in which additional messages called NULL messages are sent to permit stations to decide locally whether it is safe to process a given event. In this algorithm, a station can process events only after it has received events on all of its inputs, at which point it determines a set of *Ready Events*. Let T_i be the timestamp of the latest event received on input i of a station. Then the set of Ready Events is $\{Event\ e \mid timestamp(e) \leq min(T_i\ \forall i)\}$. The key observation is that the events received on an input always have monotonically increasing timestamps. A station can therefore safely process all events in the Ready Events set because it will never receive an event with a timestamp lower than $min(T_i)$. A station with a non-empty Ready Events set is called an *active* station. When a station sends a message with timestamp T to one of its neighbors, it also sends a NULL message with timestamp T to its other neighbors. When a station processes an incoming NULL message, it sends out NULL messages (with timestamps incremented by its processing time) to all of its neighbors.

Figure 12 shows the pseudocode for the unordered DES algorithm. The nodes corresponding to active stations are stored in an unordered workset. The call to `simulate()` computes and processes the Ready Events. The outgoing neighbors that have become *active* are added to the workset. The algorithm terminates when there are no active stations left.

```
1  Graph g = /* read in graph */
2  WorkSet ws;
3  ws.addAll(g.readyNodes()); // nodes with initial events
4  foreach (Node n: ws) {
5    Station s = n.getStation();
6    s.simulate(); //process ready events
7    for (Node m: g.neighbors(n)) {
8      if (m.isActive()) //has non-empty ready-events set
9        ws.add(m);
10  } }
```

Figure 12. Chandy-Misra's unordered DES algorithm

3.3.1 DES: Available parallelism

We show the parallelism profile for Chandy-Misra's unordered and the ordered DES algorithms in Figure 13. The input is a 6×6 tree multiplier circuit represented as a directed graph with 688 nodes and 1266 edges; its simulation involves processing 699,621 events. The active elements in the ordered and the unordered algorithms are very different. When a node executes in the unordered algorithm, it processes all the events in its Ready Set, and this is counted as a *single* activity. In the ordered algorithm, the processing of each event is an activity. The unordered algorithm has a critical path that is more than 1000 times shorter than that of the ordered algorithm, and it executes fewer activities (688 compared to 699,621); however, this difference is an artifact of the different notions of activity in the two algorithms. The shape of the available parallelism curve depends on the input. Here, the graph represents a circuit with a small number of inputs and outputs but a substantial amount of circuitry in the "middle". Thus, the available parallelism increases rapidly and then gradually drops off.

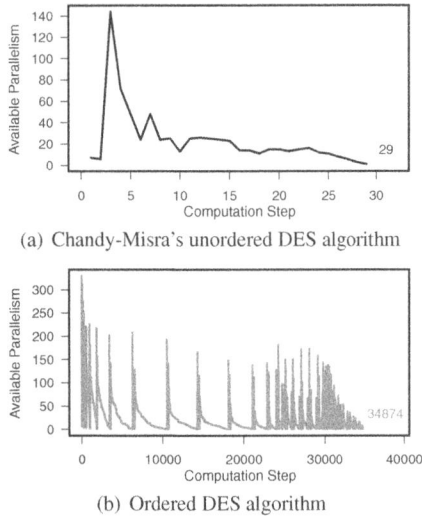

(a) Chandy-Misra's unordered DES algorithm

(b) Ordered DES algorithm

Figure 13. DES parallelism profiles of a 6×6 tree multiplier with 688 nodes and 699,621 events

3.4 Minimal Spanning Tree

MST algorithms compute a minimal-weight spanning tree of a weighted, undirected graph. We study Prim's and Kruskal's algorithms, which are ordered, and Boruvka's algorithm, which is unordered.

```
1  Graph g = /* read in graph */
2  OrderedWorkSet ows; //ordered by weight
3  for (Node m: g.neighbors(root)) {
4    //tuple <node, parent, weight>
5    ows.add(<m, root, g.edgeWeight(root, m)>);
6  }
7  foreach (Tuple <n, parent, weight>: ows) {
8    if (n.getWeight() == INF) { // not visited
9      n.setWeight(weight);
10     n.setParent(parent);
11     for (Node m: g.neighbors(n)) { //create tuples for
12       if (m.getWeight() == INF) { //unvisited neighbors
13         ows.add(<m, n, g.edgeWeight(n, m)>);
14  } } } }
```

Figure 14. Prim's ordered MST algorithm

Prim's algorithm uses an approach similar to Dijkstra's SSSP algorithm. Figure 14 shows the pseudocode. The algorithm starts with a component containing only the root and examines the edges crossing the cut between the component and the rest of the graph. For each examined edge, it adds a tuple $< node, parent, weight >$ to an ordered workset, where the weight of a tuple is the weight of the edge under consideration. (In Dijkstra's algorithm, the weight is the total path weight from the source.) The parallelism in this algorithm is similar to the parallelism in Dijkstra's algorithm. The neighborhood comprises the node of the tuple being processed and its neighbors. Conflicts are resolved based on the weight of the tuple.

Kruskal's algorithm is another ordered MST algorithm. Figure 15 lists the pseudocode. This algorithm begins with an ordered workset containing all edges of the graph sorted by weight. It then removes the edges from the workset and adds them to either an existing MST component or a newly created component, but only if adding the edge does not create a cycle. A cycle would be introduced if the two nodes connected by the edge belong to the same component. The components are managed through a Union-Find data structure, where each node has a link to the representative of

its component. Kruskal's algorithm can process multiple edges in parallel if the nodes comprising each edge belong to different components. The neighborhood of an edge includes its two nodes and the nodes visited during the `findSet()` operation, which follows the links to the representative node.

```
1  Graph g = /* read in graph */
2  OrderedWorkSet ows; //ordered by weight
3  ows.addAll(g.edges());
4  Set mst;
5  foreach (Edge e: ows) {
6    Node rep1 = findSet(e.firstNode())   //find the rep.
7    Node rep2 = findSet(e.secondNode())  //of my component
8    if (rep1 != rep2) { //must be diff. components
9      mst.add(e);
10     union(rep1,rep2); //merge the two components
11  } }
```

Figure 15. Kruskal's ordered MST algorithm

Boruvka's algorithm is an unordered MST algorithm. It is similar to Kruskal's algorithm in that it also creates independent components in parallel. The key insight that allows Boruvka's algorithm to be unordered is that the lightest-weight edge incident upon a node must always be a part of the MST. Figure 16 presents the pseudocode. Initially, each node forms its own MST component and is added to an unordered workset. Then, the algorithm finds the lightest edge leaving a component that does not introduce a cycle and contracts this edge. Contracting involves combining the nodes at either end of the edge into a single component; therefore the neighborhood consists of the these two nodes and their neighbors. The algorithm terminates when there is only one component left.

```
1  Graph g = /* read in graph */
2  WorkSet ws;
3  ws.addAll(g.nodes());
4  Set mst; //will contain the mst edges
5  foreach (Node n: ws) {
6    Edge e = n.lightestEdge();
7    if (e != null) {
8      mst.add(e);
9      Node m = graph.contract(e); //removes cycles
10     ws.add(m); //add the super-node back
11  } }
```

Figure 16. Boruvka's unordered MST algorithm

3.4.1 MST: Available parallelism

Figure 17 shows the parallelism profiles for Boruvka's, Kruskal's, and Prim's MST algorithms. The input is a random undirected graph with 10,000 nodes and 35,605 edges; the edges have random, uniformly distributed integer weights between 1 and 1000. The active elements in the three algorithms are different; they are nodes in Boruvka's algorithm, edges in Kruskal's algorithm, and 3-tuples, corresponding to edges, in Prim's algorithm. The main source of wasted work in Boruvka's algorithm is the nodes left in the workset that have already been merged into other components and are no longer a part of the graph. This is why Boruvka's algorithm executes more than 10,000 activities (19,999 in this particular case). Kruskal's algorithm has the longest critical path, while Boruvka's has the shortest. Both Kruskal's and Boruvka's algorithm are *coarsening* algorithms because they eliminate edges from the graph, which explains why they have similar looking parallelism profiles. This shape is characteristic of other coarsening algorithms as well [27]. Prim's algorithm, on the other hand, is a refinement algorithm because it adds new nodes to the tree, which is why it has a very different parallelism profile.

(a) Boruvka's unordered MST algorithm

(b) Kruskal's ordered MST algorithm

(c) Prim's ordered MST algorithm

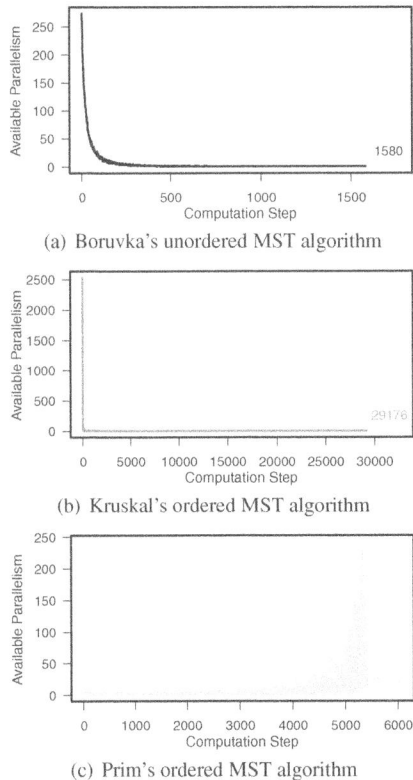

Figure 17. MST parallelism profiles of a random graph with 10,000 nodes and 35,605 edges

4. Implementation

The parallelism profiles in Section 3 demonstrate that there is a significant amount of parallelism in both ordered and unordered irregular algorithms. To study how well this parallelism can be exploited in practice, we implemented these algorithms in the Galois system [20]. In this section, we describe a number of important optimizations for performance.

4.1 Unordered algorithms

We applied the following optimizations to our implementations of unordered algorithms [24].

Work chunking: To reduce the overhead of accessing the workset, we combine the active elements into chunks. This optimization is similar to Chunked Self Scheduling (CSS) [28, 31] and Iteration Coalescing [24]. When a thread accesses the workset, it removes a chunk of active elements instead of just one element. It then iterates over these elements without accessing the workset again. Newly created work is cached locally, and after the entire chunk is processed, this work is added to the global workset. The chunk size can be fixed statically or determined dynamically.

Wasted work reduction: The amount of wasted (and aborted) work depends on the order in which the active elements are processed. However, there is a tradeoff between the cost of reducing such useless work and the overhead incurred by enforcing a processing order. For example, FIFO order eliminates the wasted work on one thread for BFS, but for multiple threads it is costly to enforce strict FIFO order. Therefore, a good tradeoff is to maintain a loose FIFO order in which all threads remove active elements from one end and add to the other. In case of SSSP, we should process the nodes in order of increasing weight to eliminate the wasted work. However, using a priority queue to

implement the workset increases the access time of the workset beyond the benefit of reducing the amount of wasted work.

Removing undo information and conflict detection: SSSP and BFS do not require a conflict detection mechanism because node values decrease monotonically. Conflict detection is needed in DES, but we can apply the *One-Shot* optimization [24] because the neighborhood of every station is statically known to be its outgoing neighbors. A One-Shot implementation first locks the entire neighborhood before making any updates. Thus, an activity will either abort before it made any changes or it is guaranteed to complete successfully. This technique reduces the overhead of the runtime by eliminating the need to keep undo information for the changes made to the graph.

4.2 Ordered algorithms

For ordered algorithms, the main overheads arise from the implementation of ordering constraints.

Commit queue: The executed activities cannot commit until they become the highest priority activities in the system. Therefore, the runtime must keep a record of the executed activities until they commit. A data structure called *Commit Queue* is one way to maintain this information. The Commit Queue must be ordered by the priority of the activities, *i.e.*, the priority of the active element corresponding to an activity. Newly scheduled activities may conflict with already executed activities. Thus, ordered implementations tend to have higher abort ratios.

Sequential commit: Ordered activities can execute in parallel, but they must commit sequentially to ensure correctness. An activity can only commit if it has the highest priority among the executed activities in the commit queue and the pending activities in the workset. If the amount of work per activity is small, as is the case with the ordered algorithms we consider, committing sequentially becomes the main bottleneck. The time to execute an activity needs to be at least $P - 1$ times longer than the time taken by a commit action to keep P threads busy. Note that in unordered algorithms commits can occur in parallel.

Priority-ordered workset: The runtime system needs to know the highest priority element among the pending active elements for two reasons: (i) an executed activity can be committed only if it has highest priority among pending and executing/executed activities, and (ii) to ensure global progress, the highest priority element in the ordered workset needs to be scheduled for execution. Accessing priority queues is usually more expensive than accessing unordered worksets.

In addition, many optimizations that are legal for unordered algorithms are not legal for ordered algorithms. For example, One-Shot optimization cannot be used with ordered algorithms because an activity can be aborted at any point before it is committed, even if it has completed execution and is merely waiting to get to the head of the commit queue.

5. Performance Results

We studied the performance and scaling of our implementations on a Sun UltraSPARC T2 (Niagara 2) Server. This machine has an 8-core processor and 32 GB of main memory. Each core supports 8-way multithreading and has an 8 kB L1 data cache and a 16 kB L1 instruction cache. The 8 cores share a 4 MB L2 cache. We used Sun's 64-bit Hot Spot Java Runtime Environment version 1.6 for our tests. The runtimes reported are the median of five runs in the same JVM instance.

We were unable to obtain a speedup for any of the ordered algorithms discussed in Section 3, so we do not present results for them.

9

5.1 Breadth-First Search

Figure 18 shows the speedups for unordered BFS. We used two randomly generated undirected graphs as input. The large input contains 8 million nodes and 73.6 million edges. The small input contains 4 million nodes and 36.8 million edges. The reported speedups are relative to the ordered sequential algorithm, which uses a FIFO queue. The figure presents results for two implementations:

Fixpoint: The unordered fixpoint code implements the algorithm discussed in Section 3.1 and includes work chunking with a chunk size of 1024 elements. The workset is implemented using a concurrent FIFO queue.

Wavefront: The wavefront code implements a commonly used algorithm that exploits parallelism within a level [3, 22, 34]. It uses two worksets, a current workset containing all nodes at the current level in the graph and a next workset into which all the nodes from the next level are added. Threads only remove nodes from the current workset and update the levels of the unvisited neighbors, which are added to the next workset. After processing an entire level, the threads synchronize at a barrier. We found that work chunking is also necessary for this algorithm to perform well. We used 1024-element chunks.

Both implementations scale well. The fixpoint implementation reaches a speedup of 22 with 32 threads. The wavefront implementation scales slightly better and reaches a speedup of 27 with 32 threads. Scheduling is successful in reducing the amount of wasted work. The fixpoint implementation performs slightly worse because of the cost of the compare-and-swap (CAS) instructions and the complex termination detection. In contrast, termination detection in wavefront is trivial; the parallel computation is terminated when the workset becomes empty.

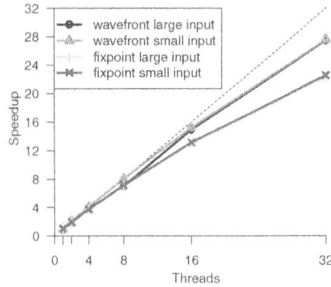

Figure 18. Speedup of the unordered BFS fixpoint and wavefront algorithms; small input = random graph with 4M nodes, 36.8M edges, serial runtime = 21.31 sec.; large input = random graph with 8M nodes 73.6M edges, serial runtime = 45.33 sec.

5.2 Single-Source Shortest Path

Figure 19 shows the speedup results for unordered SSSP. The reported speedups are relative to our sequential implementation of Dijkstra's ordered algorithm, which uses a heap-based priority queue. We used two road networks as inputs [1]. In these inputs, the nodes represent locations and the edge weights represent the distance between adjacent locations. The small input contains the road network of the Western USA and has 6.26 million nodes and 15.1 million edges. The large input contains the road network of the entire USA and has 23.9 million nodes and 57.7 million edges.

Using the FIFO schedule, our Fixpoint SSSP algorithm may perform orders of magnitude of wasted work and is therefore much slower than Dijkstra's algorithm. The Delta Stepping algorithm by Meyer *et al.* [25] essentially offers an efficient schedule for the Fixpoint algorithm. It hashes the nodes into buckets based on their distance label and processes each bucket in parallel in increasing

order. The width of a bucket is controlled by a parameter Δ, which governs the amount of parallelism in each bucket and the number of extra updates. For example, a larger Δ value results in more wasted work but also in increased parallelism per bucket. We found that a Δ value of 400,000 and a chunk size of 128 within a bucket works best for our inputs. We obtain a speedup of 4.4 and 4.7 over Dijkstra's algorithm for the small and large inputs, respectively. The limited scaling arises from the fact that these graphs are very sparse and take little time to process; Madduri *et al.* [23] also noticed poor scalability of these inputs on their implementation of the Delta Stepping algorithm.

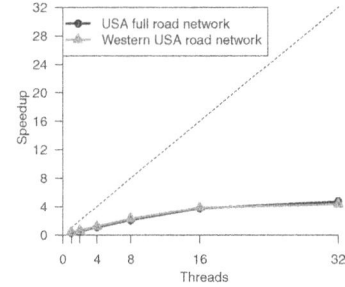

Figure 19. Speedup of the unordered SSSP algorithm; small input = Western USA road network with 6.26M nodes, 15.1M edges, serial runtime = 10.53 sec.; large input = entire USA road network with 23.9M nodes 57.7M edges, serial runtime = 45 sec.

5.3 Discrete-Event Simulation

We implemented the unordered version of the DES algorithm to model logic circuits. We again used two inputs. The small input comprises a 10×10 tree multiplier circuit, which results in 11.68 million events. The large input comprises a 64-bit Kogge-Stone adder circuit, which results in 89.6 million events. The speedup relative to the ordered sequential algorithm is shown in Figure 20. Note that we included the One-Shot optimization described above in our implementation of the unordered algorithm. The small input results in poor scaling, reaching a speedup of 4.5, but the large input scales reasonably and reaches a speedup of 11.3 with 32 threads.

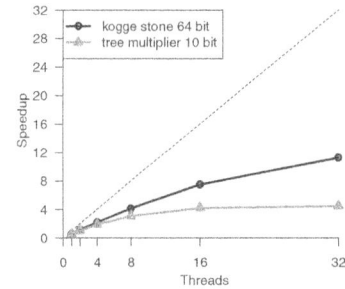

Figure 20. Speedup of the unordered DES algorithm; small input = 10×10 bit tree multiplier, serial runtime = 77.3 sec.; large input = 64-bit Kogge-Stone adder, serial runtime = 409 sec.

5.4 MST Boruvka

Figure 21 shows the speedup results for Boruvka's MST algorithm compared to a sequential implementation of Kruskal's algorithm. We used two inputs for our experiments: The small input is a two dimensional grid of size 1000×1000, where the edges are assigned uniformly random integer weights between 0 and 100. The large input is the road network for Western USA, with 6.26 million nodes and 15.1 million edges. The parallel implementation of Boruvka is slightly different from the pseudocode described in Figure 16. The foreach loop is divided into two phases: (i) *Match* and (ii) *Merge*.

In the Match phase, each node tries to match itself to an unmatched neighbor node on its lightest outgoing edge, thus forming a pair. In the Merge phase, the pair of matched nodes is merged into one bigger component by contracting the selected edge. All the threads either execute the match or the merge phase simultaneously, which eliminates the need for conflict detection and enables the work-chunking optimization. Initially, a large chunk size is chosen; as the execution proceeds, the chunk size shrinks because the number of participating nodes decreases due to edge contractions. The edge contractions have two kinds of effects on the execution:(i) the number of outgoing neighbors of a node increases rapidly, which makes Match and Merge expensive, and (ii) the number of active nodes decreases, limiting the available parallelism towards the end and hence the speedups (*cf.* Figure 17). With 32 threads, we achieve a speedup of 2.7 on the small input and 11.9 on the large input.

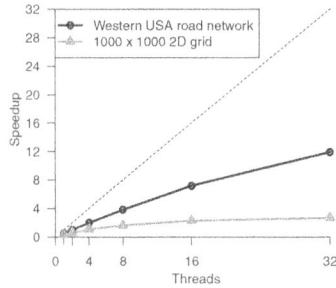

Figure 21. Speedup of Boruvka's MST algorithm; small input = 1000×1000 2D grid, serial runtime = 10.93 sec.; large input = Western USA road network with 6.26M nodes, 15.1M edges, serial runtime = 47.99 sec.

5.5 Wasted work results

In this subsection, we investigate the amount of wasted work executed by our implementations of the unordered algorithms. We used the iteration count of the *foreach* loop as a measure of the work performed. While algorithm specific metrics may be more meaningful, *e.g.*, the number of updates to a node label in BFS and SSSP, the number of iterations correlates with such metrics and applies uniformly to all algorithms considered. Figure 22 shows the number of iterations executed by the unordered implementation relative to the sequential ordered implementation, which does not perform any wasted work. We used the large input for each benchmark to obtain these results. In the BFS Fixpoint and wavefront algorithms, the amount of wasted work is negligible. The one-thread runs of the SSSP Fixpoint algorithm with the Delta Stepping schedule already perform more than 5 times the amount of required work, but the value of the Δ chosen delivers the best scalability for these inputs. Interestingly, the wasted work decreases slightly with the number of threads; due to non-determinism of the parallel execution, the threads deviate slightly from the suggested schedule, which coincidentally results in a more efficient schedule.

In case of DES, the ordered algorithm uses different active elements than the unordered algorithm. Therefore, we plotted the ratio of the number of iterations executed over the number of iterations executed by the one-thread run of the unordered algorithm. Hence, the extra iterations are the iterations aborted due to conflicts, which increase with the number of threads. However, due to the One-Shot optimization, these aborted iterations are cheap and do not significantly hurt parallel performance. Note that the serial unordered implementation performs some wasted work equal to the number of NULL messages processed, which are absent in the ordered algorithm. For Boruvka, we plot the ratio of iterations performed by our parallel implementation to the number of iterations of Kruskal's algorithm. Again, the two algorithms use different types of active el-

ements in the workset. The wasted work represents the number of unsuccessful attempts by a thread to match a node with its neighbor on the lightest outgoing edge (*cf.* Section 5.4). Here, the wasted work increases slightly with the number of threads.

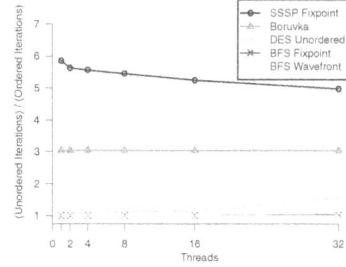

Figure 22. Ratio of iterations performed by the parallel unordered over the sequential ordered implementations for the small inputs

6. Related and Future Work

In the theory community, parallel algorithms for graph problems have been studied using the PRAM model [17, 19]. With the exception of one variant – the so-called Arbitrary CRCW PRAM [30] the PRAM model follows serial semantics, provided (in some PRAM variants) that programmers ensure that multiple processors do not write to the same memory location in a given step. The PRAM model is synchronous and all processors execute instructions in lock-step, so synchronization is inexpensive. In contrast, the Galois execution model is asynchronous because we do not assume anything about the relative speeds of processors. The Explicit Multithreading (XMT) model [32] is an asynchronous extension of the Arbitrary CRCW PRAM variant that exploits independence of order (IOS) semantics in the explicitly parallel sections of the program. Specialized hardware is used to reduce the overhead of creating and managing small threads [33]. In contrast to PRAM and XMT, there are no explicitly parallel constructs in Galois programs. However, the Galois execution model has to contend with small threads as well, and for reducing the overhead of these, the XMT hardware assist would be useful.

There are many parallel implementations of the four irregular problems considered in this paper, but to the best of our knowledge, no previous work has tried to extract common abstractions and lessons from them. In addition to the work cited earlier, we mention some of the most relevant work here. Edmonds *et al.* [13] describe a single-source shortest-path implementation that partitions the graph and employs a separate priority queue for each partition. Their implementation relies on the monotonically decreasing nature of the node values. For SSSP, the issue of wasted work has also been studied. Meyer *et al.* [25] proposed the unordered *Delta Stepping* algorithm, which allows trading off work efficiency for parallelism (and hence scalability) by controlling the Δ parameter *cf.* Section 5.2. Madduri *et al.* [23] describe an efficient implementation of the Delta Stepping algorithm. Bader and Cong [2] and Chung and Condon [11] have discussed parallel implementations of Boruvka's algorithm. Our implementation of Boruvka borrows ideas from this work. *Chaotic relaxation* is an unordered algorithm for iteratively solving linear systems [10].

A common parallelization approach for breadth-first search is a level-based implementation [3, 22, 35], in which all the nodes at a specific level in the graph are processed in parallel. As the neighbors of the nodes in the next level are all assigned the same value, the concurrent updates do not have to be atomic. It would be interesting to design a static analysis that could determine this automatically.

While tradeoffs between unordered and ordered algorithms have been studied in the past, it is not the case that ordered irregular algorithms are necessarily inferior to their unordered counterparts. For example, in the discrete event simulation community, many people use the Time Warp algorithm [18], which is ordered, instead of the Chandy-Misra algorithm [8], which is unordered. Since most ordered algorithms do less work than their unordered counterparts, they may become competitive if we can reduce the overheads of implementing ordering, thus highlighting the need for much better system support for speculative execution of ordered algorithms.

7. Conclusions

This paper studied the theoretically available and practically exploitable amorphous data-parallelism in several ordered and unordered graph algorithms. We found that ordered algorithms had significant available parallelism, with at least ten parallel activities on average even in the worst case. However, this parallelism is hard to exploit because of short loop bodies and the practical difficulties of implementing ordering efficiently. Unordered algorithms have more amorphous data-parallelism and shorter critical paths than ordered algorithms, but they often perform wasted work. Hence, there is a tradeoff between work efficiency and scalability when choosing between ordered and unordered algorithms. Nevertheless, the unordered algorithms are easier to optimize and schedule, which leads to efficient parallel implementations. Hence, our recommendation for parallelization is to convert ordered into unordered algorithms when possible, and control the amount of wasted work by proper scheduling.

References

[1] 9th dimacs implementation challenge - shortest paths. *http://www.dis.uniroma1.it/~challenge9/links.shtml.*

[2] D.A. Bader and G. Cong. Fast shared-memory algorithms for computing the minimum spanning forest of sparse graphs. *Journal of Parallel and Distributed Computing*, 66(11):1366–1378, 2006.

[3] David A. Bader and Kamesh Madduri. Designing multithreaded algorithms for breadth-first search and st-connectivity on the cray mta-2. In *ICPP '06: Proceedings of the 2006 International Conference on Parallel Processing*, pages 523–530, Washington, DC, USA, 2006. IEEE Computer Society.

[4] Richard Bellman. On a routing problem. *Quarterly of Applied Mathematics, 16(1)*, pages 87–90, 1958.

[5] Gianfranco Bilardi, Paolo D'Alberto, and Alexandru Nicolau. Fractal matrix multiplication: A case study on portability of cache performance. In *Algorithm Engineering*, pages 26–38, 2001.

[6] Gianfranco Bilardi, Afonso Ferreira, Reinhard Lüling, and José D. P. Rolim, editors. *Solving Irregularly Structured Problems in Parallel, 4th International Symposium, IRREGULAR '97, Paderborn, Germany, June 12-13, 1997, Proceedings*, volume 1253 of *Lecture Notes in Computer Science*. Springer, 1997.

[7] Brian D. Carlstrom, Austen McDonald, Michael Carbin, Christos Kozyrakis, and Kunle Olukotun. Transactional collection classes. In *PPOPP*, pages 56–67, 2007.

[8] K. Mani Chandy and Jayadev Misra. Distributed simulation: A case study in design and verification of distributed programs. *IEEE Trans. Software Eng.*, 5(5):440–452, 1979.

[9] Philippe Charles, Christian Grothoff, Vijay A. Saraswat, Christopher Donawa, Allan Kielstra, Kemal Ebcioglu, Christoph von Praun, and Vivek Sarkar. X10: an object-oriented approach to non-uniform cluster computing. In *OOPSLA*, pages 519–538, 2005.

[10] D. Chazan and W. Miranker. Chaotic relaxation. *Linear algebra*, 2(199-222), 1969.

[11] Sun Chung and Anne Condon. Parallel implementation of boruvka's minimum spanning tree algorithm. *Parallel Processing Symposium, International*, 0:302, 1996.

[12] Thomas Cormen, Charles Leiserson, Ronald Rivest, and Clifford Stein, editors. *Introduction to Algorithms*. MIT Press, 2001.

[13] Nick Edmonds, Alex Breuer, Douglas Gregor, and Andrew Lumsdaine. Single-source shortest paths with the parallel boost graph library. In *9th DIMACS Implementation Challenge - Shortest Paths*, November, 2006.

[14] Paul Feautrier. Some efficient solutions to the affine scheduling problem: One dimensional time. *International Journal of Parallel Programming*, October 1992.

[15] Jr. Ford, L. R. Network flow theory. Technical Report Report P-923, The Rand Corporation, Santa Monica, Cal, 1956.

[16] Maurice Herlihy and J. Eliot B. Moss. Transactional memory: architectural support for lock-free data structures. In *ISCA*, 1993.

[17] Joseph Ja´ Ja´ . *An Introduction to Parallel Algorithms*. Addison-Wesley Publishing Company, Reading, MA, 1992.

[18] David R. Jefferson. Virtual time. *ACM Trans. Program. Lang. Syst.*, 7(3):404–425, 1985.

[19] Jorg Keller, Cristoph Kessler, and Jesper Traff. *Practical PRAM Programming*. Wiley-Interscience, New York, 2001.

[20] M. Kulkarni, K. Pingali, B. Walter, G. Ramanarayanan, K. Bala, and L. P. Chew. Optimistic parallelism requires abstractions. *SIGPLAN Not. (Proceedings of PLDI 2007)*, 42(6):211–222, 2007.

[21] Milind Kulkarni, Martin Burtscher, Rajasekhar Inkulu, Keshav Pingali, and Calin Cascaval. How much parallelism is there in irregular applications? In *PPoPP*, pages 3–14, 2009.

[22] Charles E. Leiserson and Tao B. Schardl. A work-efficient parallel breadth-first search algorithm (or how to cope with the nondeterminism of reducers). In *SPAA*, pages 303–314, 2010.

[23] Kamesh Madduri, David A. Bader, Jonathan W. Berry, and Joseph R. Crobak. Parallel shortest path algorithms for solving large-scale instances. In *9th DIMACS Implementation Challenge - Shortest Paths*, November, 2006.

[24] Mario Mendez-Lojo, Donald Nguyen, Dimitrios Prountzos, Xin Sui, M. Amber Hassaan, Milind Kulkarni, Martin Burtscher, and Keshav Pingali. Structure-driven optimizations for amorphous data-parallel programs. In *PPoPP*, 2010.

[25] U. Meyer and P. Sanders. δ-stepping: a parallelizable shortest path algorithm. *J. Algs. 49(1)*, pages 114–152, 2003.

[26] http://www.openmp.org/.

[27] Keshav Pingali, Milind Kulkarni, Donald Nguyen, Martin Burtscher, Mario Mendez-Lojo, Dimitrios Prountzos, Xin Sui, and Zifei Zhong. Amorphous data-parallelism in irregular algorithms. regular tech report TR-09-05, The University of Texas at Austin, 2009.

[28] C. D. Polychronopoulos and D. J. Kuck. Guided self-scheduling: A practical scheduling scheme for parallel supercomputers. *IEEE Trans. Comput.*, 36(12):1425–1439, 1987.

[29] Lawrence Rauchwerger and David A. Padua. The LRPD test: Speculative run-time parallelization of loops with privatization and reduction parallelization. *IEEE Trans. Parallel Distrib. Syst.*, 10(2):160–180, 1999.

[30] Yossi Shiloach and Uzi Vishkin. An o(log n) parallel connectivity algorithm. *J. Algorithms*, 3(1):57–67, 1982.

[31] Ten H. Tzen and Lionel M. Ni. Trapezoid self-scheduling: A practical scheduling scheme for parallel compilers, 1993.

[32] Uzi Vishkin, Shlomit Dascal, Efraim Berkovich, and Joseph Nuzman. Explicit multi-threading (xmt) bridging models for instruction parallelism (extended abstract). In *SPAA*, pages 140–151, 1998.

[33] Xingzhi Wen and Uzi Vishkin. Fpga-based prototype of a pram-on-chip processor. In *Conf. Computing Frontiers*, pages 55–66, 2008.

[34] Andy Yoo, Edmond Chow, Keith Henderson, William McLendon, Bruce Hendrickson, and Umit Catalyurek. A scalable distributed parallel breadth-first search algorithm on bluegene/l. In *SC '05: Proceedings of the 2005 ACM/IEEE conference on Supercomputing*, page 25, Washington, DC, USA, 2005. IEEE Computer Society.

[35] Yang Zhang and Eric A. Hansen. Parallel breadth-first heuristic search on a shared memory architecture. In *AAAI-06 Workshop on Heuristic Search, Memory-Based Heuristics and Their Applications*, July 2006.

Programming the Memory Hierarchy Revisited: Supporting Irregular Parallelism in Sequoia *

Michael Bauer
Computer Science Department,
Stanford University
mebauer@cs.stanford.edu

John Clark
Computer Science Department,
Stanford University
jpclark@stanford.edu

Eric Schkufza
Computer Science Department,
Stanford University
eschkufz@cs.stanford.edu

Alex Aiken
Computer Science Department,
Stanford University
aiken@cs.stanford.edu

Abstract

We describe two novel constructs for programming parallel machines with multi-level memory hierarchies: *call-up*, which allows a child task to invoke computation on its parent, and *spawn*, which spawns a dynamically determined number of parallel children until some termination condition in the parent is met. Together we show that these constructs allow applications with irregular parallelism to be programmed in a straightforward manner, and furthermore these constructs complement and can be combined with constructs for expressing regular parallelism. We have implemented spawn and call-up in Sequoia and we present an experimental evaluation on a number of irregular applications.

1. Introduction

For most of the past two decades clusters of single processor machines have been a very popular high-performance computing platform. These machines are typically programmed using a message passing library such as MPI [1] or a partitioned global address space (PGAS) language such as UPC or Titanium [2, 3]. Characteristic of both programming models is that the programmer is presented with a two-level memory hierarchy: memory is divided into a processor's local memory, where accesses are guaranteed to be relatively fast, and the global or remote memory of all the other processors in the cluster, accesses to which are likely to be slow. With the transition to multicore, however, clusters of multicore machines are becoming much more common, and these machines present at least three interesting levels of memory: the individual core, on-

* This work was supported in part by grants from the Department of Energy's Predictive Science Academic Alliance Program (PSAAP), the Army High Performance Research Center (AHPCRC), and a generous grant of time on the Cerillos supercomputer through the Los Alamos National Lab's Institutional Computing Program.

```
void task<inner> matmul( in    float A[M][P],
                         in    float B[P][N],
                         inout float C[M][N] )
{
  // Code to name submatrices of A, B, and C
  // called Ablks, Bblks, and Cblks, respectively
  // block sizes are given by U, V, and X

  // Compute all blocks of C in parallel.
  mappar (int i=0 to M/U, int j=0 to N/V) {
    mapseq (int k=0 to P/X) {
      // Invoke the matmul task recursively
      // on the subblocks of A, B, and C.
      matmul(Ablks[i][k],Bblks[k][j],Cblks[i][j]);
    }
  }
}
void task<leaf> matmul( in    float A[M][P],
                        in    float B[P][N],
                        inout float C[M][N] )
{
  // Compute matrix product directly
  for (int i=0; i<M; i++)
    for (int j=0; j<N; j++)
      for (int k=0; k<P; k++)
        C[i][j] += A[i][k] * B[k][j];
}
```

Figure 1. Dense matrix multiplication in Sequoia.

chip, and global memory. The Roadrunner petaflop supercomputer has four or five memory levels, depending on how one counts [4]. These recent, and likely lasting, changes in machine organization have led to interest in programming models for multi-level memory hierarchies that go beyond the two-level view of memory as simply local or global.

Sequoia is a programming system designed for machines with multi-level memory hierarchies. In previous work, the focus of Sequoia was on regular applications, and the issue of how to program irregular applications was explicitly left open [5]. In this paper we present programming constructs designed to support irregular computations on machines with multi-level memory hierarchies, and we describe an implementation of these ideas as extensions to Sequoia. The extensions are conservative in the sense that Sequoia programs that do not use the new features perform exactly as before. Furthermore, the extensions complement Sequoia's existing support for regular parallel computations, allowing straightforward implementations of programs that require a mix of regular and irregular parallelism.

To set the stage, we briefly describe how a canonical regular application, dense matrix multiply, is implemented in Sequoia. An analysis of the assumptions underlying the constructs used in this example illustrates the limitations of Sequoia for irregular computations.

The key parts of a Sequoia program for matrix multiplication are given in Figure 1. This program defines two *tasks*, `task<leaf> matmul` and `task<inner> matmul`; `task` is a keyword and `matmul` is the task name, which has two implementations called `inner` and `leaf`. A task is the basic unit of computation and locality in Sequoia. Tasks are *isolated*: tasks cannot refer to global variables or take pointer arguments, and so they cannot directly refer to data in use by other tasks. Tasks communicate via parameters passed to and results returned from calls to other tasks. We refer to the caller as the *parent* task and the callee as the *child* (or *sub-*) task. Task parameter passing is copy-in, copy-out (i.e., call-by-value-result [6]).

During compilation, each task in the source program is assigned to a specific memory (and a specific processor) in the target machine. At runtime, all of a task's inputs and storage for its outputs are resident in the assigned memory. When a parent task and its children are assigned to different memories by the compiler, the child task call at runtime results in communication as the task call's arguments are copied to the child task's memory at the start of the task, and the results are copied back to the parent task's memory when the child terminates. Thus, task calls express the movement of data through the memory hierarchy.

Parallelism is expressed via `mappar`, a looping construct that declares each loop iteration can be executed independently of any other. In Figure 1, `task<inner> matmul` uses a `mappar` to compute each submatrix of the output array C in parallel. Inside the `mappar` the analogous, but sequential, `mapseq` construct accumulates the partial results for each subblock of C using a sequence of recursive calls to `matmul` on subblocks of A and B. The recursive call to `matmul` invokes either `task<inner> matmul` or, if we have proceeded far enough in the divide and conquer computation, `task<leaf> matmul`, which is represented here by a naive triply-nested loop. (Which variant is called depends on the number of memory levels of the target machine and is decided in a separate *mapping* phase by either the programmer or the compiler.) A snapshot of the running program for a three-level machine looks like the tree of task invocations shown in Figure 2. The program defines a tree-shaped task hierarchy, with large problems near the root and progressively smaller problems at lower levels of the tree until `task<leaf> matmul` is executed at the leaves of the computation. More background details of Sequoia are discussed in Section 2.

While Sequoia has other important parallel control constructs (e.g., reductions), for the purposes of discussing regular vs. irregular computation, we need only focus on the `mappar` statement in the `inner` variant of `matmul`. An important detail is an implied barrier at the end of the `mappar`: All of the parallel instances of the statement inside the `mappar` must complete before execution continues to the statement after the `mappar`. The example in Figure 1 illustrates two assumptions underlying `mappar`:

1. *The working set of of each subtask is computed in advance.* Task isolation implies that all of the inputs to a task must be known at the time a task is invoked. Furthermore, to guarantee that the child task has sufficient space to complete its computation, at least an upper bound on the size of a task's result must also be known before task invocation.

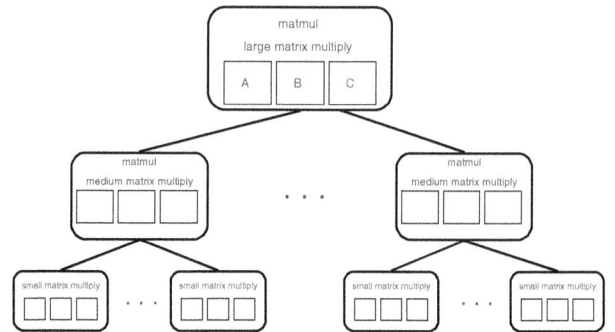

Figure 2. An example task hierarchy for a machine with three levels of memory.

2. *The number of subproblems is computed in advance.* The number of parallel subtasks is fixed on entry to the `mappar`. If the subtasks return results to the parent that represent new parallel work, that work can only be done after the `mappar` is complete.

For our purposes, these two properties can be taken as the definition of a regular parallel computation; we consider a problem where either the number of subproblems is unknown, or the input/output size of the subproblems is unknown in advance, to be irregular. For assumption (1), there are two common situations in which the working set of a task is not known in advance:

- There is a large input data set, but the task only uses a small portion of it, and it is necessary for performance reasons to send the task only that small subset. Unfortunately, the task computes the subset it needs, so the input working set is unknown before task invocation. Algorithms that benefit from caching often have this structure. Effectively, we would like the parent to function as a cache for the child, allowing the child to compute what it needs and then pull additional data from the parent, but isolation prevents this pattern from being expressed directly.

- The output is potentially large relative to the input, so much so that the problem size a task can handle is limited by the size of the output (which must fit in the memory level allocated to the task), not the input. Some search problems where one or a few subtasks may return the entire answer are in this category, as is any problem that has the character of decompressing the input. We would like child tasks to be able to off-load partial results to the parent and then continue executing, thereby enabling children to work on (usually more efficient) larger problem sizes, but again task isolation requires that the entire output is kept at the child and returned on task completion.

The dual problems of unknown input and unknown output size affect not just performance but also how programs are written. Consider a problem in which the input for the natural task one would like to write is unknown. The only way to express this in Sequoia is to write two tasks. The first task A computes the data that is needed and returns an output describing that data request to the parent. The parent then launches a second task B with all of the input data that finishes the job. Essentially, one ends up writing an event-driven system, where events are requests to the parent for more data and the tasks are stages of computation between events. Unfortunately, the problem is even somewhat worse: not only must we program in an event-driven style, but each stage is synchronized by the barrier at the end of a `mappar`, meaning that no type B task can begin until all type A tasks have completed. Of course, if there is more than one unknown input we may need to have more than two stages in our pipeline of events, further compounding the programming problem.

One way to solve this problem is to adopt programming constructs such as threads or the processes in PGAS languages that are not isolated—for example, threads can share arbitrary state with one another. Isolation, however, is a great property to have, as it dramatically simplifies both program reasoning and the compiler scheduling problem in multi-level machines. What we desire is an explicit, but limited, way to "break out" of isolation.

To relax assumption (1) when needed, we propose the ability of child tasks to *call-up* to the parent. That is, just as parents can invoke tasks on the children (a *call-down*), we add the symmetric ability for children to invoke tasks on parents. Call-up violates complete isolation, but it does so explicitly and, as we shall see, has a natural semantics. Note that with call-up child tasks are still isolated from each other; the change is in the relationship of a child task to its parent task.

Turning to assumption (2), consider a situation where the number of parallel subtasks is initially small, but each subtask generates more jobs of the same kind. This is a common pattern; every worklist algorithm has this flavor, where there is a set of jobs to do, and each job may generate new jobs. Using only mappar, a worklist algorithm can only be executed in phases, where all the jobs on the worklist at the beginning of phase i must complete before we can begin executing any of the jobs generated during phase i. If a particular phase has fewer jobs than processors, or about the same number of jobs as processors but the jobs have high variance in execution time, utilization will be unnecessarily low.

To mitigate this problem we would like a parallel control construct that does not fix in advance the number of parallel subtasks it can invoke. We propose *spawn*, a construct that launches an unspecified number of subtasks until some termination condition is met in the parent. Where mappar is analogous to a parallel bounded for loop, spawn is analogous to a parallel while loop.

We stress that for regular or nearly regular computations the constructs provided by the existing Sequoia language are expressive and programs are both very portable and efficient [5, 7, 8]. However, previous work on programming multi-level machines and on Sequoia in particular does not address the problem of programming irregular applications, which is the focus of this paper. Our main contributions are:

- we propose two constructs, *call-up* and *spawn*, for programming irregular applications on hierarchical memory machines (Section 3);

- we give a formal operational semantics for a core calculus including call-up and spawn, showing how these constructs fit into an overall language design (Section 4);

- we evaluate an implementation (Section 5) of our proposal on several irregular applications on a cluster, an SMP, and a cluster of SMPs (Section 6).

Section 7 elaborates on related work, and Section 8 summarizes with a discussion of design alternatives and future work.

2. Hierarchical Memory

Before presenting our proposal, this section gives some additional background on Sequoia. Sequoia requires the programmer to target an abstract parallel machine that is a tree of distinct memory modules, a representation that extends the Parallel Memory Hierarchy [9]. Data transfer between memory modules is conducted via (potentially asynchronous) block transfers. Data transfer occurs at all levels of the hierarchy through task arguments, which may be declared in (read only), out (write only), or inout (a task argument that may be both read and written; see Figure 1 for exam-

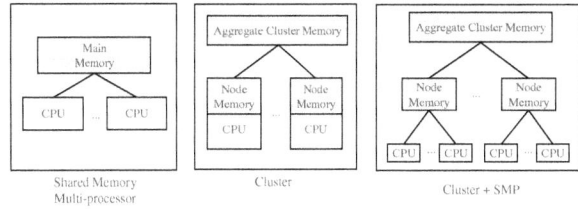

Figure 3. Hierarchical memory machines.

ples). Each task defines a namespace that exists entirely within one memory in the memory hierarchy. Unlike the original Sequoia proposal [5], in our approach there are no restrictions on the computation a task may perform within a level (see Section 3). There may be multiple versions, called *variants* of the same task, allowing, for example, different implementations of the base and inductive cases in divide-and-conquer algorithms (c.f., the inner and leaf versions of matmul in Figure 1).

The computation tree described by a Sequoia program is abstract. Neither the width (the number of parallel subtasks) nor the depth of the tree is specified in the program. The communication protocols used to move data through the machine are also abstracted through parameter passing.

Parallel machines are also modeled as trees. A *machine description* defines for a target machine the number of levels and the number and size of memories at each level, among other details. The tree model provides a simple abstraction for programmers to reason about, but there are important non-tree topologies used in practice, particularly a cluster of nodes where peers in the cluster communicate directly with each other rather than through a parent. Following [5], we model clusters using *virtual levels* that do not correspond to any single physical memory. A cluster virtual level is the sum of all the node memories in the cluster; this forms a distinct address space which is separate from the individual node memories, which are the children of the virtual level. Moving data from the virtual level to a particular child node corresponds to communication across the cluster, as data stored somewhere in the virtual level's physically distributed address space is moved to be local to one node. Figure 3 illustrates three typical hierarchical machines: a shared memory multiprocessor (SMP), a cluster with a virtual level that aggregates all of the local node memories, and a common three-level machine, a cluster of SMPs.

The compilation problem for Sequoia is to map the unbounded, abstract task tree on to the fixed, definite machine tree. A *mapping* assigns tasks in the program to specific levels of the target machine's hierarchy. Mappings are either written by hand in a separate mapping language or are generated automatically by an auto-tuner. Previous work suggests auto-tuning is always preferable [10], but the mappings used in this paper are hand-written. Beyond the mapping, the compiler performs important optimizations such as coalescing data transfers, copy elimination across levels of the memory hierarchy, and software pipelining of compute and communication between adjacent memory levels [7]. The compiler also manages the tedious task of generating and compiling code for each level of the hierarchy; as the machines can be heterogeneous multiple distinct platform compilers may be involved. A simple, portable run-time interface abstracts away the actual communication mechanism between different levels of the memory hierarchy (e.g., MPI calls, DMAs, simple loads and stores to RAM, etc.) [8].

3. Supporting Irregular Applications

This section gives an informal overview of our constructs for irregular parallelism in programs for hierarchical memory machines;

Section 4 presents a more formal treatment. We illustrate our ideas using a simple work-list algorithm, shown in Figure 4. We postpone an explanation of what this example actually does until after we have presented the programming constructs.

Unlike the original Sequoia design, we allow general object-oriented (C++) code in any task at any level of the memory hierarchy. Thus, tasks may create and use objects and build pointer data structures. These are confined to within the task however; arguments to subtasks, with one exception, cannot be pointers or references, or structures (e.g., arrays) that contain pointers or references.

The one exception is that a task may take a *parent object*, indicated using the `parent` type qualifier, as an argument. In Figure 4, the `doWork` method (both `inner` and `leaf` variants) takes a pointer to a worklist object `wl` passed from the calling task (not shown). Parent objects may have no public fields. The only operation permitted on a parent object is to invoke its public methods. A parent object method invocation is a *call-up*: the method executes in the *parent*'s address space, not the address space of the task invoking the parent object method. In Figure 4, in the leaf variant of `doWork` the method invocation `wl->addWork(newWork)` adds `newWork` to the worklist `wl` maintained in the parent task's memory level. Similarly, earlier in the same task the parent method call `wl->getWork(work)` pulls work to do off of the work list stored in the parent. A call-up is synchronous: like a regular function call in a standard language, the child task is suspended until the call-up returns its result from the parent.

Call-up introduces concurrency into the Sequoia programming model, because multiple children may attempt to execute a call-up in the parent's address space simultaneously. We enforce the following simple semantics. During subtask execution the parent blocks, meaning it does not perform any other computation until the subtask returns (or, in the case of a `mappar`, until all of the parallel subtasks return). Thus, while call-ups can modify data structures in the parent's heap, there are no races with the parent's execution. We also require that all call-ups execute atomically in some unspecified order in the parent. That is, concurrent call-ups from multiple children are always serializable in the parent's address space. Call-ups may actually be executed in parallel if there are sufficient resources and it is safe to do so, although our current implementation does not include any such optimization.

Consider the methods `getWork` and `addWork` in Figure 4. These methods are invoked only in a call-up and so always execute in the address space of the parent. (Note that these are `leaf` tasks, which with call-ups no longer means that they execute at the leaves of the machine hierarchy; it only means that these tasks have no subtasks.) Thus, while `getWork` and `addWork` modify the worklist data structure, there is no correctness issue because call-ups are atomic.

The parallel control construct *spawn* takes two arguments: a task call and a termination test. A `spawn` may launch any number of instances of the task call, and it may continue to launch new ones at any time during execution of the `spawn`. Note that every spawned subtask is identical, so `spawn` assumes the use of a call-up to retrieve different data for each subtask. A `spawn` terminates when (1) its termination test (evaluated in the address space of the parent) is true, and (2) all subtasks have terminated. Condition (2) is necessary. Consider the method `doWork` in Figure 4, which spawns worker tasks that add and remove jobs from a worklist, and which terminates when the worklist is empty and there are no worker tasks still executing. The worklist may be empty but if there is a subtask running it may insert one or more new tasks into the worklist; thus, we need to know that subtasks cannot invalidate the termination test, which is done by requiring that all subtasks have completed.

We now briefly explain the worklist example. Initially, `doWork` spawns some number of worker tasks which all receive a pointer to the worklist in the parent's memory through a parent object.

```
void task<inner> Worklist::doWork(parent Worklist* wl) {
  spawn(doWork(wl), wl->isDone());
}
void task<leaf> Worklist::doWork(parent Worklist* wl) {
  // Get work[] (an array of size 1):
  int* work;
  wl->getWork(work);
  int unit = work[0];
  delete [] work;

  // Add work (work[0] new elements, each work[0]-1):
  if ( unit > 1 ) {
    int* newWork = new int[unit];
    for ( unsigned int i = 0; i < unit; i++ )
      newWork[i] = unit-1;
    wl->addWork(newWork);
    delete [] newWork;
  }
}
void task<leaf> Worklist::getWork(out int work[]) {
  work = new int[1];
  if ( list_.empty() ) // If the worklist is empty
    work[0] = 0;       //   send no work.
  else
    work[0] = list_.pop();
}
void task<leaf> Worklist::addWork(in int work[]) {
  for ( unsigned int i = 0; i <= work[0]; i++ )
    list_.push(work[i]);
}
bool task<leaf> Worklist::isDone() {
  return list_.isEmpty();
}
```

Figure 4. A paradigmatic worklist implementation.

Each task `doWork` first gets some work using a call-up of the worklist's `getWork` method, and then adds some number of jobs to the worklist using the worklist's `addWork` method. This example illustrates all of the irregular features discussed in Section 1: the parent acts as a cache for the children, holding the current worklist; the children produce varying amounts of output in the form of new jobs to be placed on the worklist; the `spawn` construct allows new work added to the worklist to be allocated to some child task without the need to first synchronize with all of the children.

There is considerable flexibility in the implementation of `spawn`. First, the runtime system is free to launch as many subtasks as necessary to keep the machine busy. Second, the runtime system can evaluate the termination predicate at any time, including while there are still child tasks running, to gain information about whether it is worthwhile to respawn terminated subtasks or not (the number of times the termination test is evaluated is unspecified, and so the test should be side-effect free). Our current runtime implementation of `spawn` prematurely tests the termination condition as part of a heuristic for determining when to respawn children (see Section 5). In addition, this runtime heuristic could be customized easily by the programmer to match specific applications.

We also enforce two restrictions on call-ups to avoid situations that are undefined or very difficult to compile well. First, a parent object only makes sense so long as the parent task instance that created it is executing; thus, a parent object may be used in any child (and more generally, any descendant) of the creating parent task, but may not escape (i.e., outlive) that parent task. The second restriction is that no call-down may occur within a call-up. That is, a method that is used as a call-up (i.e., invoked by a parent object) may have call-ups in its body but not ordinary task calls (call-downs). Allowing call-downs within call-ups would result in a difficult scheduling problem, as it would no longer be easy to statically determine which tasks might run in parallel. Furthermore, despite considerable experience with `spawn`, we have yet to find an example where allowing a call-down within a call-up would be useful. Both restrictions are easily enforced statically by the type system.

4. Semantics

This section gives a formal treatment of call-up and `spawn`. There is a previously published Sequoia semantics [7] which, unfortunately, is not expressive enough to describe our extensions; the semantics presented here is very different. Like [7], however, our program executions work on *trees of memories*. Also following [7], we model a memory M as a function from names to values, so rather than manipulating addresses we use mnemonic variable names and $M(x)$ looks up the value of variable x in memory M. We use the standard notation $M[x \leftarrow a]$ to denote the memory that is identical to M except that the value a is stored at name x.

A given level of the memory hierarchy has a memory M, zero or more sub-machines $[T_1, \ldots, T_n]$, and two programs P_1 and P_2:

$$
\begin{array}{lcll}
T & := & \langle M, C, P_1, P_2 \rangle & \\
C & := & [T_1, \ldots, T_n] \quad n \geq 0 & \\
P & := & \mathrm{Op}_M(A = f(B)) & \mid \quad \mathrm{If}_M(pred, P_1, P_2) \\
  & \mid & P_1; P_2 & \mid \quad \mathrm{Copy}_{M_i, M_j}(A, B) \\
  & \mid & \mathrm{Mappar}_M(k = start : end, P) & \mid \quad \mathrm{Spawn}_M(P, pred) \\
  & \mid & \mathrm{Up}_M(P) & \mid \quad \texttt{wait} \\
  & \mid & \texttt{resume} & \mid \quad -
\end{array}
$$

The program constructs are purposely limited to a core calculus to keep the semantics small and tractable: standard sequential constructs (primitive operations, if statements, statement sequencing), the Sequoia constructs (copying data between memory levels, `Mappar`, `Spawn`, and a call-up construct `Up`), and three operations needed by the semantics that do not appear in source programs (`wait`, `resume`, and `-`). Note that every operation that uses memory is subscripted with the memory level it accesses; a copy operation is subscripted with two levels, the source and destination memories, which are always adjacent levels in the hierarchy (i.e., parent and child memories). This semantics is at the level of our implementation's intermediate language, after source programs have been desugared and the number of memory levels (depth of the memory tree) and the number of child memories at each level have been made explicit in the program.

For a given *configuration* at a memory level $\langle M, C, P_1, P_2 \rangle$ there may be two programs executing: one *main task* and one call-up from the child memory level. This closely reflects our implementation, which on most platforms implements a memory level using one thread for the main task and another thread to service call-ups. The program "$-$" represents no program—i.e., an idle resource. Two special cases are the configurations $\langle M, C, P, - \rangle$ (or equivalently $\langle M, C, -, P \rangle$) and $\langle M, C, -, - \rangle$. The former represents a memory level with a main task but no active call-ups, the latter represents a memory with no scheduled computation at all; the memory is *idle*. No configuration has a call-up without also having a non-idle main thread.

Notably missing from the core calculus are task calls, which can be emulated by the other constructs. Given a task definition `task f(in a, out b) { P }`, a task call of `f` can be implemented by using copy operations to copy the `in` parameter to the corresponding formal `a` in the child memory, executing the body `P` of `f`, and then copying the `out` parameter back to `b` in the parent memory. For example,

$$\mathrm{Mappar}_{M_i}(\texttt{k} = \texttt{1} : \texttt{n}, \texttt{f}(\texttt{x}[\texttt{k}], \texttt{y}[\texttt{k}])) \equiv$$
$$\mathrm{Mappar}_{M_i}(\texttt{k} = \texttt{1} : \texttt{n}, \mathrm{copy}_{M_{i-1}, M_i}(\texttt{a}, \texttt{x}[\texttt{k}]); \texttt{P}; \mathrm{copy}_{M_i, M_{i-1}}(\texttt{y}[\texttt{k}], \texttt{b}))$$

assuming operations in `P` are suitably annotated to read and write data in memory level M_{i-1}. Call-ups invoked on parent objects can

similarly be expanded into a sequence of primitive operations that copy arguments from the child to the parent memory, execute the body of the call-up, and copy the result back to the child.

Table 1 gives a small step operational semantics for the core calculus. Each rule describes one step of execution: $\langle M, C, P_1, P_2 \rangle \to \langle M', C', P_1', P_2' \rangle$. The first three rules are for familiar statements: primitive operations $A = f(B)$, if statements (only the rule for a predicate that evaluates to *true* is shown; the symmetric rule for *false* is also standard), and statement sequencing. The interesting thing to note about these representative sequential statements is that they take place in one memory level, having no effect on their child memories. Notice that most of the rules work by executing the first statement P_1 in a sequence $P_1; P_2$ and transitioning to a configuration where P_2 remains to be executed. Thus, the rule for statement sequences simply rearranges statement sequences using the associativity of ";" to ensure the first statement is primitive and not itself a statement sequence. To guarantee statements are always part of a sequence (so that some rule will match) we assume programs are initially of the form $P; -$.

The copy operation comes in two flavors: copying data from parent to child and from child to parent. Note that copies in either direction are initiated by the children; on most architectures this is the more efficient arrangement.

A `Mappar` has two cases. If *start* $\leq$ *end* and there is an idle child, a fresh version of the `Mappar` computation can be launched in that child's memory. If *start* > *end*, then the parent implements a barrier: the parent's main task blocks until all children are idle and the parent has no call-up to service, at which point the main task continues to the next statement. A `Spawn` is similar: a `Spawn` can launch a fresh copy of the parallel computation on an idle child, and if all children are idle, the parent has no call-up to service, and the termination predicate is true, the `Spawn` can terminate and the parent's main task moves on to the next statement. The semantics allows a choice when the termination condition evaluates to *true*: the `Spawn` may terminate (assuming the other conditions for termination are also met) or some children may be respawned instead. This semantics allows implementations maximum flexibility, though we expect that implementations will generally not respawn child tasks when the termination condition is *true*.

In summary, the main differences between a `Mappar` and `Spawn` are that the `Mappar` has a fixed number of instances to execute and each child is given a distinct portion of the work at invocation (represented by the value of k in the child memory in the [Mappar] rule), whereas the `Spawn` launches instances until the termination predicate is true. Thus, `Mappar` is like a `for` loop and `Spawn` is akin to a `while` loop.

A call-up `Up(...)` launches a computation on the parent if the parent is not currently executing another call-up (i.e., the parent's configuration is of the form $\langle M, C, P, - \rangle$). The program invoking the call-up (which may be the child's main task or another call-up that the child is handling) must block until the call-up completes, which is the purpose of inserting a `wait` in the child program and a `resume` at the end of the call-up program in the parent. The [Resume] rule restarts the child computation by removing the `wait` when the parent reaches the `resume`. Since only one child can execute at a time, there is always only one `wait` that a `resume` can match.

The [Swap] rule switches the order of the two programs in a configuration. All of the rules execute using only the third component of a configuration, so this rule has the effect of switching the active program between the main task and any call-up awaiting service. It is easy to prove (by induction on the length of an execution) that if a memory level has two programs neither of which is $-$, then the main task is always either at a `Spawn` or a `Mappar`; i.e., call-ups can only happen inside of `Spawn` or `Mappar`. The [Spawn]

17

$$\langle M_i, C, \mathtt{Op}_{M_i}(A = f(B)); P, U \rangle \rightarrow \langle M_i[A \leftarrow f(B)], C, P, U \rangle \qquad \text{[Primitive Op]}$$

$$\frac{M_i(pred) = true}{\langle M_i, C, \mathtt{If}_{M_i}(pred, P_1, P_2); P, U \rangle \rightarrow \langle M_i, C, P_1; P, U \rangle} \qquad \text{[If]}$$

$$\langle M_i, C, (P_1; P_2); P_3, U \rangle \rightarrow \langle M_i, C, P_1; (P_2; P_3), U \rangle \qquad \text{[Sequence]}$$

$$\langle M_i, [\ldots, \langle M_{i-1}^j, C^j, \mathtt{Copy}_{M_i, M_{i-1}}(A, B); P^j, U^j \rangle, \ldots], P, U \rangle \quad \rightarrow$$
$$\langle M_i[A \leftarrow M_{i-1}^j(B)], [\ldots, \langle M_{i-1}^j, C^j, P^j, U^j \rangle, \ldots], P, U \rangle \qquad \text{[Copy Up]}$$

$$\langle M_i, [\ldots, \langle M_{i-1}^j, C^j, \mathtt{Copy}_{M_{i-1}, M_i}(A, B); P^j, U^j \rangle, \ldots], P, U \rangle \quad \rightarrow$$
$$\langle M_i, [\ldots, \langle M_{i-1}^j[A \leftarrow M_i(B)], C^j, P^j, U^j \rangle, \ldots], P, U \rangle \qquad \text{[Copy Down]}$$

$$\frac{start \leq end}{\langle M_i, [\ldots, \langle M_{i-1}^j, C^j, -, - \rangle, \ldots], \mathtt{Mappar}(k = start : end, P_0); P_1, U \rangle \quad \rightarrow}$$
$$\langle M_i, [\ldots, \langle M_{i-1}^j[k \leftarrow start], C^j, P_0; -, - \rangle, \ldots], \mathtt{Mappar}(k = start + 1 : end, P_0); P_1, U \rangle \qquad \text{[Mappar]}$$

$$\frac{start > end \qquad C = [\langle M_{i-1}^1, C^1, -, - \rangle, \ldots, \langle M_{i-1}^n, C^n, -, - \rangle]}{\langle M_i, C, \mathtt{Mappar}(k = start : end, P_0); P_1, - \rangle \rightarrow \langle M_i, C, P_1, - \rangle} \qquad \text{[Barrier]}$$

$$\langle M_i, [\ldots, \langle M_{i-1}^j, C^j, -, - \rangle, \ldots], \mathtt{Spawn}(P_0, pred); P_1, U \rangle \quad \rightarrow$$
$$\langle M_i, [\ldots, \langle M_{i-1}^j, C^j, P_0; -, - \rangle, \ldots], \mathtt{Spawn}(P_0, pred); P_1, U \rangle \qquad \text{[Spawn]}$$

$$\frac{M_i(pred) = true \qquad C = [\langle M_{i-1}^1, C^1, -, - \rangle, \ldots, \langle M_{i-1}^n, C^n, -, - \rangle]}{\langle M_i, C, \mathtt{Spawn}(P_0, pred); P_1, - \rangle \rightarrow \langle M_i, C, P_1, - \rangle} \qquad \text{[Spawn End]}$$

$$\langle M_i, [\ldots, \langle M_{i-1}^j, C^j, \mathtt{Up}(P_0^j); P_1^j, U^j \rangle, \ldots], P, - \rangle \rightarrow \langle M_i, [\ldots, \langle M_{i-1}^j, C^j, \mathtt{wait}; P_1^j, U^j \rangle, \ldots], P, P_0^j; \mathtt{resume} \rangle \qquad \text{[CallUp]}$$

$$\langle M_i, [\ldots, \langle M_{i-1}^j, C^j, \mathtt{wait}; P^j, U^j \rangle, \ldots], \mathtt{resume}, U \rangle \rightarrow \langle M_i, [\ldots, \langle M_{i-1}^j, C^j, P^j, U^j \rangle, \ldots], -, U \rangle \qquad \text{[Resume]}$$

$$\langle M_i, C, P, U \rangle \rightarrow \langle M_i, C, U, P \rangle \qquad \text{[Swap]}$$

$$\frac{\langle M_{i-1}^j, C^j, P^j, U^j \rangle \rightarrow \langle M_{i-1}^{'j}, C^{'j}, P^{'j}, U^{'j} \rangle}{\langle M_i, [\ldots, \langle M_{i-1}^j, C^j, P^j, U^j \rangle, \ldots], P, U \rangle \rightarrow \langle M_i, [\ldots, \langle M_{i-1}^{'j}, C^{'j}, P^{'j}, U^{'j} \rangle, \ldots], P, U \rangle} \qquad \text{[Parallel]}$$

Table 1. Operational semantics.

and [Mappar] rules do not modify the parent memory; thus, there can never be races between a call-up and the parent task. However, it is possible for a copy operation in a child task and a call-up from a different child task to race on an access to the parent's address space. A form of this problem already exists in Sequoia, in that parallel subtasks are forbidden from aliasing out parameters; i.e., two parallel child task calls may not write the same output location [5]. We extend this restriction to cover call-ups as well: no child task may overwrite a parallel child task's input or output arguments, either through out or inout parameters or call-ups. While a suitable static analysis could conservatively check this restriction, our current implementation assumes, but does not enforce, this rule.

Finally, the [Parallel] rule expresses that computation steps can take place in child memories, not just at the parent; this is the rule that models parallel execution at each level of the memory hierarchy.

5. Implementation

A Sequoia runtime sits between two adjacent levels of the memory hierarchy and provides a separate interface for both the parent and the children [8]. We have added two new calls: SpawnChild to the parent interface and CallParent to the child interface. The declarations of these new calls are shown below.

```
SpawnChild(TaskID taskid, ChildID start, ChildID end,
           TerminationID_t termid);
CallParent(ChildID myid, void *parent_ptr,
           CallupID callid);
```

SpawnChild enables a parent task to spawn tasks onto child nodes; CallParent enables a child node to invoke a call-up on a parent object. We briefly discuss the implementation of both methods.

SpawnChild takes a task to spawn, a range of child nodes on which to spawn tasks, and a termination test. The goals of a good implementation are in tension: to both keep the children busy but also to terminate as soon as possible. We employ a simple heuristic to determine whether a task should be respawned on a given child following the completion of the child's task. We say a child has *finished* when its currently assigned task is finished but it has not been evaluated for respawn. A child has *completed* when the runtime system has evaluated the child for respawn and decided not to respawn the child. When a child has finished it is enqueued for possible respawn. The runtime continually dequeues finished children and evaluates whether to respawn them or not. If more than half the of the children have completed, then the runtime does not respawn the child and adds it to the list of completed children. If fewer than half the children have completed, the runtime checks the termination test. If the test is *false* the child and all completed children are respawned (to maintain high utilization); if the test is *true* the child is added to the list of completed children. When all children have completed, the termination test is checked again; if *true* the SpawnChild call terminates; if *false* all children are respawned. We note that other reasonable respawn heuristics exist, and nothing prevents a user from modifying a runtime to include an application-specific heuristic.

When a child invokes CallParent, a task is enqueued at the parent's level. A dedicated thread in the parent pulls the call-up off the queue, executes it, and then sends the results back down to the child. Since call-ups are handled sequentially by a single thread of control at the parent this trivially maintains the atomicity property of call-ups. We see two potential future optimizations for executing call-ups. The first is to leverage the isolation property of tasks to allow the compiler to prove statically when it is safe for call-ups to execute in parallel. The second possibility is to use transactional memory to optimistically execute call-ups in parallel and detect conflicts dynamically.

If a call to CallParent discovers that the parent pointer passed is not local to the current runtime's address space, the runtime will recursively call CallParent on its parent runtime. This will continue passing the call-up up the memory hierarchy until it reaches the runtime containing the object pointed to by the parent pointer. Children can thereby perform call-ups to any of their ancestor levels in the memory hierarchy. By using call-ups to parent pointers at different levels, the programmer has the capability to create hierarchical data caching schemes for deep memory hierarchies.

5.1 Supporting Virtual Levels

Virtual parent levels must implement a distributed shared memory on top of the physically disjoint child memories, usually using MPI. Generally these are the most involved Sequoia runtimes, and present additional challenges for implementing SpawnChild and CallParent. By default, MPI process zero is designated to execute the parent's program and to hold the parent's data (with the exception of distributed arrays). We make two exceptions to this rule to achieve better performance in virtual levels.

The first exception is respawning tasks in a virtual level. If a task is going to be respawned, it should be done so as quickly as possible to keep processors busy, but in a distributed setting the latency of communicating with the parent is significant. We

therefore modify the respawn heuristic described above for virtual levels. The runtime operating at each child node keeps track of the last respawn decision made by the parent. When a child finishes, it locally decides whether to respawn or not using the previous instruction it received. It then communicates to the parent (node 0) that it has finished its task and asks whether to respawn. When the decision from the parent comes back it is cached for determining whether to respawn the next time. This simple form of software pipelining hides the latency of respawn in a distributed environment where the common case is that a task is respawned many times.

The other exception to having node 0 perform all the parent's work is for some call-ups. In the case where a call-up touches only part of a of distributed array that resides on a single node, the runtime passes the call-up to that node for execution. This "owner-computes" optimization is safe because any other call-ups touching the same data will also be sent to the same node and serialized locally. The performance gain that we see from this approach in Section 6.3 is motivation for enhancing our ability to determine when it is safe for call-ups to be performed in parallel. All other call-ups are still handled exclusively by node 0; our runtime assigns a different and lighter load of tasks from a spawn statement to node 0 to allow it devote more resources to servicing call-ups.

6. Applications and Evaluation

We have implemented call-up and spawn in Sequoia++, an extension of Sequoia. In this section, we evaluate the performance of three representative irregular applications written in Sequoia++: a boolean satisfiability solver (SAT), a sparse matrix-vector multiply (SMVM), and a parallel sample sort. We benchmark these applications on a multi-core SMP, a cluster of Opterons, and a cluster of SMPs. The SMP is an 8-node machine, with 128 GB of main memory. Each node in the SMP is a 4-core AMD Opteron, clocked at 2.3 GHz, with a shared 512 Kb L2 cache. The Cerillos cluster at Los Alamos National Labs consists of 360 nodes, connected by InfiniBand. Each node in the cluster consists of two dual-core AMD Opterons, clocked at 1.8 Ghz, with a shared 1024 Kb L2 cache and 8 GB of main memory. For the cluster experiments we use only 1 core of the dual-core chips and a Sequoia cluster runtime; for our cluster of SMP experiments we treat each dual-core chip as a 2 core SMP (running a Sequoia SMP runtime) and the rest of the machine as a cluster of these small SMPs (running a Sequoia cluster runtime).

In our experiments we use the same number of cores (4, 8, 16, or 32) across all three platforms. Figure 5 plots performance of the three applications across the three architectures, and Figure 6 details profiling information displaying the percentage of time spent in each phase of the computation on different memory levels.

6.1 SAT

The satisfiability problem (SAT) is to determine if there is an assignment of true/false to the boolean variables of a propositional formula that makes the formula true. Most parallel SAT solvers decompose the search space by generating partial assignments and delegating the resulting sub-problems to a sequential solver [11]. While the data sizes are small, the solution time of the subproblems is extremely variable, making good load balancing critical.

Our SAT implementation is a worklist algorithm similar to Figure 4. The worklist is initialized with n partial solutions, the complete assignments of the $\log_2 n$ most common variables. We then perform a spawn over the elements in the worklist. Children remove a partial solution from the worklist, and attempt to complete the solution using MiniSat [12]. A child may discover its problem is satisfiable (in which case it uses a call-up to notify the parent) or unsatisfiable (in which case the child simply returns). Another possibility is that the child exceeds a preset time bound, in which

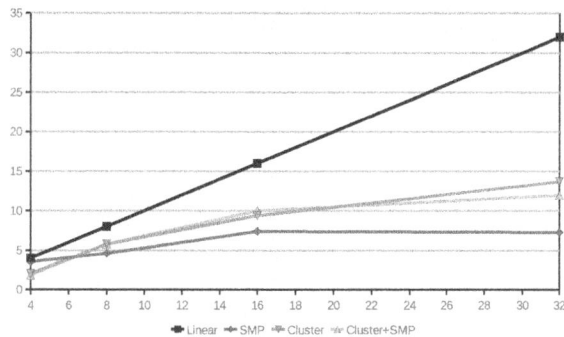

(a) Speedup for SAT.

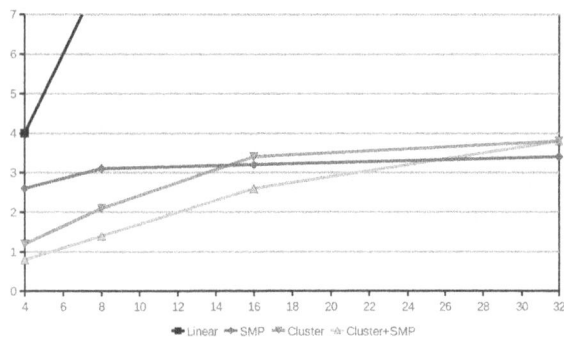

(b) Speedup for SMVM.

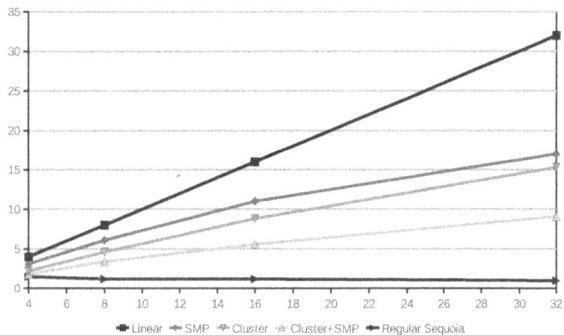

(c) Speedup for sample sort.

Figure 5. Speedup for each application over an optimized, purely sequential algorithm on three different platforms. Figure (c) also contains a line illustrating the speedup achieved by a best-effort sorting implementation using only the regular language features of Sequoia.

case the child splits the problem in two, continuing to work on one of the subproblems and pushing the other one to the parent's worklist using a call-up.

Recently the annual SAT competitions have introduced a track for parallel solvers; the SAT speedups in Figure 6 are averages over runs on all the 2007 contest problems. To date the parallel SAT contest has been held on 4-way SMPs, and our implementation is competitive, achieving a 3.5X average speedup on a 4-core SMP. (Our leaf sequential solver, MiniSat, is regarded as one of the best open source solver, though there are faster closed source and proprietary solvers.) Performance tails off at larger degrees of parallelism (because more of the subproblems represent speculative work that would not be done by the sequential solver), but con-

tinues to improve on the cluster and cluster of SMPs, reaching a maximum of about 14X speedup on 32 processors on the cluster. Interestingly, the SMP does not do so well, topping out at 7.4X speedup on 16 processors. MiniSat caches a significant amount of state and the 4:1 processor-to-L2 cache ratio on the SMP results in more L2 misses than on the cluster and cluster of SMPs where the processor-to-L2 cache ratios are 1:1 and 2:1 respectively. Child tasks spend almost their entire execution performing useful work and less than 1% of their time performing call-ups, indicating that call-ups do not represent a bottleneck to performance for SAT. For brevity, this data is omitted from Figure 6.

6.2 Sparse Matrix-Vector Multiply

Sparse Matrix-Vector Multiplication (SMVM) is a standard kernel used in many scientific applications. Sparse matrices are commonly used to represent large data sets where many of the entries are zero. The distribution of non-zeroes is usually non-uniform, resulting in some parts of the matrix having higher densities of nonzero elements than others. Irregularity in the data representation, and a generally low compute-to-communication ratio, makes SMVM challenging to parallelize. There has been extensive work in optimizing SMVM computations for both sequential [13] and parallel machines with shared [14] and distributed address spaces [15].

In our implementation of SMVM, sparse matrices are represented in the standard compressed-sparse-row format. While other implementations of SMVM attempt to modify the data representation depending on the matrix [15] we do not customize our code for the input matrix. We achieve parallelism in SMVM by dividing the set of dot products that must be computed into chunks. Since each dot product has a variable number of nonzero elements to be multiplied, load balancing is performed in a manner similar to our SAT implementation. We use a `spawn` statement to launch tasks onto the child processors. Children then call-up and retrieve a set of rows on which to operate. Children that complete their rows continue to call-up to get additional dot products to perform. Note that unlike a `mappar`, where iterations are assigned to processors statically by the compiler, the use of `spawn` decides dynamically which dot products will be evaluated on which processors based on load.

As our benchmarks we chose five matrices from the University of Florida Sparse Matrix Library [16]: `atmosmodd`, `nlpkkt80`, `Freescale1`, `ldoor`, and `nlpkkt120`. These matrices come from real-world applications and range in size from 8.8 to 50 million nonzero elements with varying sparsity patterns.

Our reference implementation makes use of the OSKI library for sparse matrix-vector multiplication [13]. OSKI is a purely sequential sparse matrix library capable of dynamically tuning itself for a given matrix at runtime. We set the OSKI library to `ALWAYS_TUNE_AGGRESSIVELY` but we do not include OSKI's tuning time in the reference execution time. This can only make our implementation appear worse, and thus our speedups with respect to OSKI are likely a lower bound on what a user would experience in practice.

In Figure 6, the tightly coupled SMP is able to overcome the parallel overhead at low numbers of processors, but the other two platforms catch up at large machine sizes as memory bandwidth becomes a factor. At 32 processors, all three platforms have approximately the same speedup (a mean of 3.4X-3.8X), which is comparable to the performance of other recent efforts [14, 15]. For example, in [15], speedups (including the time for tuning) range from 2X to 11X with a mean of 4X on 32 nodes. We achieve our best raw performance on the Cluster of SMPs configuration running the `ldoor` matrix multiplication at a sustained rate of 1.57 GFLOPS with 32 child tasks.

The cluster and cluster of SMPs perform better at 32 nodes than the SMP due to additional threads on the SMP being scheduled on

(a) Profile for SMVM.

| □ L2 Call-up Execute | □ L2 Transfer | □ L2 Idle | □ L2 System | ■ L1 Call-up Execute | ■ L1 Transfer | □ L1 Idle |
| □ L1 System | ■ L0 Call-up Wait | ■ L0 Call-up Execute | □ L0 Transfer | □ L0 Child Execute | ■ L0 System | |

(b) Profile for sample sort.

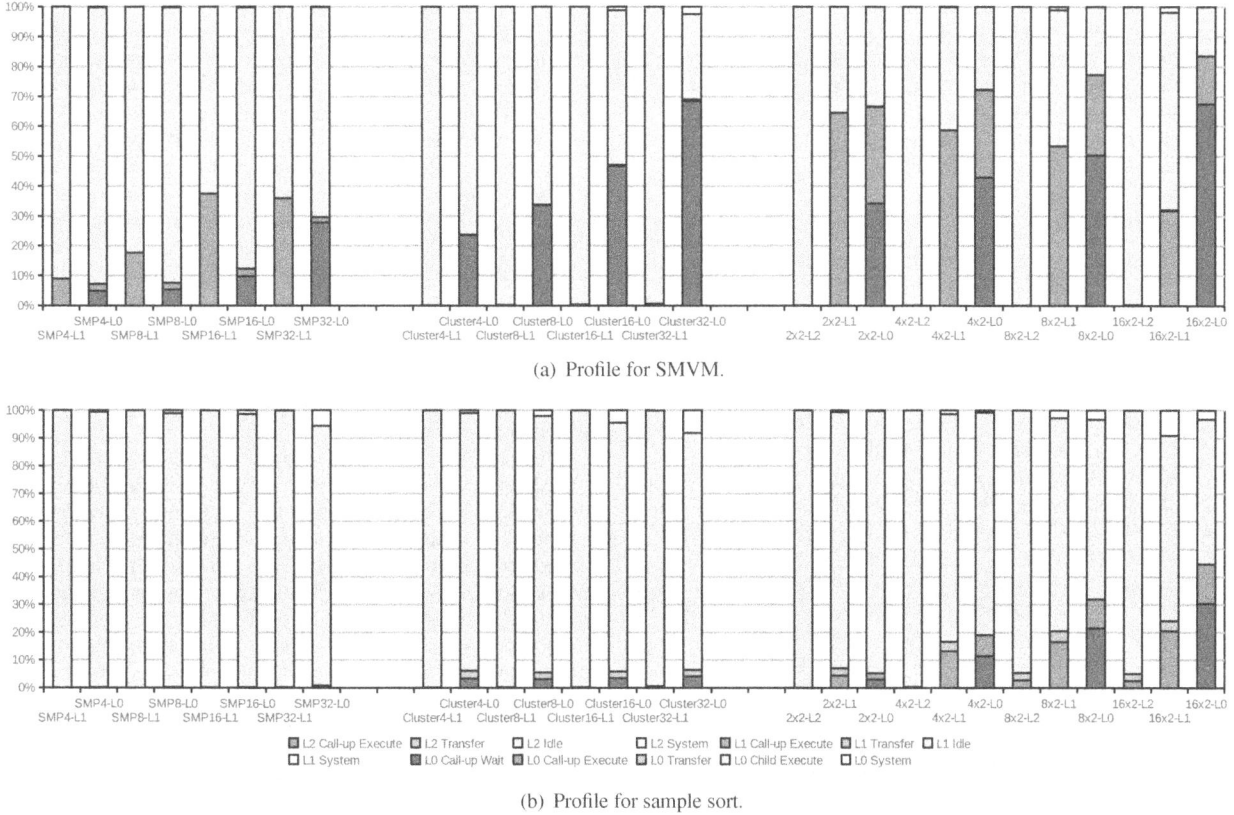

Figure 6. Percentage of time spent in different phases of each computation. Each group of columns corresponds to a different platform and each column to a different memory level within that platform. The `Call-up Execute` component indicates the amount of time spent in useful work performing call-ups while the `Call-up Wait` component indicates the amount of time call-ups from a level spent waiting in a queue before being executed. The `Idle` field indicates time that a parent level spent waiting to handle call-ups while child tasks were executing. The remaining fields are identical to [5].

the same socket and causing higher contention for memory bandwidth. Knowing that memory bandwidth is often the bottleneck for SMVM, we can clearly see in Figure 6 that call-ups are not the performance bottleneck for the SMP configuration as the child tasks spend significant portions of their time performing useful work and no more than 30% of their execution performing call-ups. The same cannot be said for the two cluster configurations as we can see the percentage of time children spend waiting for call-ups to execute increases progressively with the number of leaf-level tasks. On the Cluster of SMPs with 32 leaves, children spend in excess of 67% of their time simply waiting for their call-up to execute. The reason for the increased waiting time is the extra latency to communicate call-ups and their arguments over the network. This additional latency decreases the parent's call-up bandwidth as each call-up now requires additional time to execute. As future research we plan to investigate methods of performing call-ups in parallel.

6.3 Sample Sort

Sample sort is considered to be one of the most efficient comparison-based sorting algorithms for distributed memory architectures [17]. It is a generalization of Quicksort, which recursively decomposes its input into $n > 2$ partitions, and sorts each independently. Because partitions are generated based on pivots randomly selected at runtime, there is no guarantee that partitions will be the same size or require the same time to sort. Sample sort is the most complex of

our three applications and consists of a mix of sequential, regular, and irregular parallel phases:

- **Phase 1** Sequentially select a random subset of the input array as splitters.

- **Phase 2** A `mappar` over the the input array gives subtasks equal-size subsets of input elements; subtasks compute the partition for each element based on the splitters selected in phase 1.

- **Phase 3** In a `spawn` over the input array, subtasks compute the size of the output partitions: they request a subset of the elements, perform a prefix sum over their offsets in the partitions calculated in phase 2, and reduce their results using a call-up. In a second `spawn` children again request a subset of the elements and write them to the appropriate partition using the previously calculated offsets.

- **Phase 4** In a `spawn` over the partitions generated in phase 3, subtasks request a partition from the parent, sort the elements using C++'s STL sort, and write the results back using a call-up.

Our sample sort achieves good absolute performance on all three platforms; at 32 processors performance ranges from 9X speedup on the cluster of SMPs to 17X on the SMP over the sequential C++ STL sorting algorithm; across all platforms leaf task (level 0) utilization is never less than 51% (for the 32 node Cluster of SMP's experiment) indicating that the majority of the execution time is spent performing useful parallel work. We achieve our maximum

21

sorting performance on the SMP machine at a rate of 126 million keys per second with 32 leaf tasks.

As an interesting experiment we also wrote a best-effort sort using only the regular features of Sequoia. The results in Figure 5 show that obtaining good sorting performance is difficult when using only the regular features of Sequoia, indicating the need for additional language features to parallelize irregular code.

7. Related Work

Sequoia is designed to give the programmer explicit control over data locality and communication for programming machines with multi-level memory hierarchies. The language accomplishes this goal through isolated tasks that encapsulate data and control in one level of the hierarchy. Complete isolation is problematic for problems where task working sets are most naturally computed by the tasks themselves, and we have proposed extensions to Sequoia that allow selective exceptions to pure isolated tasks.

The PGAS family of languages, such as Split-C [18], Co-Array Fortran [19], UPC [20], and Titanium [3] present a single program address space with SPMD semantics with one thread per processor. Thus, the threads are not isolated from one another; any thread may reference any accessible data in the global address space, and there is no special problem in expressing irregular algorithms. Currently these languages provide only a two-level memory hierarchy.

More recent parallel language efforts [21–23] support locality cognizant programming through the concept of distributions (from ZPL [24]). While also PGAS languages, these designs also provide more abstract and dynamic notions of *place* (X10) or *locale* (Chapel) than the more static SPMD languages discussed above, and while we are unaware of any studies to confirm it, our intuition is that irregular algorithms should be easier to express in these languages. These are still two-level languages, however.

A recent effort proposes Hierarchical Place Trees (HPT) as a unification of the Sequoia and X10 programming models [25]. Like Sequoia, HPT models machines as a tree of memories. Instead of call-up, however, HPT presents a form of global address space as in X10. At any level of the memory hierarchy, data can be referenced at any ancestor level—while not truly global across the machine, this model allows for tasks to read or write extra data outside of their own locale/place if necessary. This model can be simulated using call-up by writing tasks that are remote *read* and *write* methods for parent levels of the memory hierarchy. We considered extending Sequoia with a model similar to HPT, but ultimately decided that call-up was both more flexible and in many cases more efficient: once we have paid the cost to move to another memory location within the machine, it will often be cheaper to perform a computation locally on the data, rather than simply return the data and perform the computation somewhere else. (For example, in the worklist algorithm adding or removing elements from the worklist involves more than memory references.) The difference in design stems in part from a difference in philosophy about the underlying architectures: if processing elements are only or primarily at the leaves of the memory hierarchy, then HPT is a close match to the machine. However, if interior nodes of the machine tree have their own processors then call-up allows us to take advantage of these to carry out computation at those levels.

Hierarchically Tiled Arrays (HTA) [26] accelerate existing sequential languages with an array data type expressing multiple levels of tiling for locality and parallelism, but also permit arbitrary element access and therefore can directly express at least some irregular algorithms. The HTA approach specifies locality by annotating a data type which is less flexible and less portable than Sequoia's approach of using task composition.

Stream processing languages [27, 28] also build upon a two-tiered memory model [29], choosing to differentiate between on and off-chip storage. Sequoia tasks are a generalization of stream programming kernels. Tasks and kernels share similarities such as isolation, a local address space, and well-specified working sets, but differ in the ability of tasks to arbitrarily nest. Because these languages enforce strong isolation, they have difficulties similar to Sequoia in expressing highly irregular computations.

Sequoia's control flow, when encountering a parallel mapping of subtasks, resembles the thread-less abstraction of concurrency in Cilk [30], X10 [21], Chapel [22], and Fortress [23]. Sequoia's control flow is constrained in comparison to most of these languages since, for example, the calling task cannot proceed until all subtasks complete (similar to the common usage of OpenMP [31] loops). The addition of spawn covers many (perhaps most) of the parallel loop patterns that could not be expressed in Sequoia. Cilk inlets provide a restricted form of call-up, allowing an atomic computation to be performed on the final result of a task (e.g., to perform a reduction across task results).

Previous efforts to model memory hierarchies include the Uniform Memory Hierarchy Model (UMH) [32], which abstracted uniprocessor machines as sequences of memory modules of increasing size. The Parallel Memory Hierarchy Model (PMH) [9] extended this abstraction to parallel architectures by modeling machines as trees of memories. Historically, interest in non-uniform memory access models has been motivated by the analysis of algorithm performance [33, 34]. In Sequoia, hierarchical memory is a fundamental aspect of the programming model, required to achieve both performance and portability across a wide range of architectures. Sequoia has also been influenced by the idea of space-limited procedures [35], a methodology for programming machines modeled using the PMH model.

8. Discussion and Future Work

Sequoia is an attempt to strike a practical balance between performance and portability. In future machines locality is likely to become ever more important, and memory hierarchies are likely to become more complex and diverse—we will have everything from relatively simple two-level multi-core machines to supercomputers with many more levels of memory. The central tenet of Sequoia is that the programmer should have control over and be able to reason about locality and communication. By encapsulating both within a task, and by carefully avoiding any explicit machine dependencies in source programs, Sequoia allows programmers to express locality- and communication-aware algorithms that nevertheless map well to a wide variety of machines.

For regular problems this design works extremely well, but in some sense it cannot work for irregular problems. The fact that the working sets of tasks must be known before task execution is exactly the property that many irregular applications violate, at least if we do not want to write tasks in a low-level event-driven style. Adding parent objects and call-up allow tasks to escape their isolated context and communicate with their parent (and, recursively, any ancestor in the computation tree). The escape from isolation is explicit and tightly constrained, and the semantics are apparently as simple as possible: the only source of concurrency is within the parent's address space, and even then call-ups must execute atomically. Furthermore, the parts of programs that do not use call-up behave exactly as in the original Sequoia design. Thus, call-up and spawn can be seen as providing the missing duals of call-down and mappar, increasing the expressiveness of the language without changing its character or imposing costs when the features are not used.

One alternative to call-ups is to allow tasks access to data in the address space of any ancestor task. As discussed in Section 7 this is the approach adopted by HPT. Call-ups can also only access ancestor memories, but there are some differences between using direct memory references and call-up. First, call-ups provide a concurrency semantics, guaranteeing atomicity of the invoked tasks, while direct memory references have the usual memory model issues around concurrent reads/writes in parallel machines. Second, call-ups can do more than read or write a single piece of data; once we have shifted to another location in the memory hierarchy, we can also perform an arbitrary computation on that data or amortize communication overhead by performing a bulk-transfer of data. A disadvantage of call-up is that access to the memory of remote ancestors must go through multiple recursive call-ups, while a HPT-based system can presumably more directly avoid any overhead in bypassing intermediate levels to go directly to some data more than one level removed in the memory hierarchy.

9. Conclusion

We have introduced *spawn* and *call-up* as new features for expressing irregular parallelism within the Sequoia programming language. We have described the operational semantics for both spawn and call-up within the Sequoia programming model. Our implementations of a series of irregular applications using spawn and call-up have illustrated competitive performance with other parallel codes. We also have demonstrated that spawn and call-up are the dual to the regular constructs already present in Sequoia, giving programmers the tools necessary to parallelize all phases of their code when programming deep memory hierarchies.

Acknowledgments

The authors would like to thank Evan Cox for his work on the implementation of Sequoia++, and the Department of Energy for access to the Cerillos supercomputer at Los Alamos National Labs.

References

[1] M. Snir, S. Otto, S. Huss-Lederman, D. Walker, and J. Dongarra, *MPI-The Complete Reference.* MIT Press, 1998.

[2] W. Carlson, J. Draper, D. Culler, K. Yelick, E. Brooks, and K. Warren, "Introduction to UPC and Language Specification," Center for Computing Sciences, IDA, Technical Report CCS-TR-99-157, 1999.

[3] K. Yelick *et al.*, "Titanium: A high-performance Java dialect," in *Workshop on Java for High-Performance Network Computing*, 1998.

[4] K. Barker *et al.*, "Entering the PetaFLOP era: The architecture and performance of Roadrunner," in *Supercomputing*, 2008.

[5] K. Fatahalian *et al.*, "Sequoia: Programming the Memory Hierarchy," in *Supercomputing*, November 2006.

[6] A. Aho, R. Sethi, and J. D. Ullman, *Compilers: Principles, Techniques, and Tools.* Addison-Wesley, 1986.

[7] T. Knight *et al.*, "Compilation for explicitly managed memory hierarchies," in *Symposium on Principles and Practice of Parallel Programming*, 2007, pp. 226–236.

[8] M. Houston *et al.*, "A portable runtime interface for multi-level memory hierarchies," in *Symposium on Principles and Practice of Parallel Programming*, 2008, pp. 143–152.

[9] B. Alpern, L. Carter, and J. Ferrante, "Modeling parallel computers as memory hierarchies," in *Programming Models for Massively Parallel Computers*, 1993.

[10] M. Ren, J. Y. Park, M. Houston, A. Aiken, and W. Dally, "A tuning framework for software-managed memory hierarchies," in *Int'l Conference on Parallel Architectures and Compilation Techniques*, 2008, pp. 280–291.

[11] Y. Hamadi, S. Jabbour, and L. Sais, "ManySAT: a parallel SAT solver," vol. 6, pp. 245–262, 2008.

[12] N. Eén and N. Sörensson, "An extensible SAT-solver," in *Theory and Applications of Satisfiability Testing*, 2004, pp. 333–336.

[13] R. Vuduc, J. Demmel, and K. Yelick, "OSKI: A library of automatically tuned sparse matrix kernels," in *Inst. of Physics Publishing*, 2005.

[14] A. Buluç *et al.*, "Parallel sparse matrix-vector and matrix-transpose-vector multiplication using compressed sparse blocks," in *Symposium on Parallelism in Algorithms and Architectures*, 2009, pp. 233–244.

[15] S. Lee and R. Eigenmann, "Adaptive runtime tuning of parallel sparse matrix-vector multiplication on distributed memory systems," in *Supercomputing*, 2008, pp. 195–204.

[16] T. A. Davis, "University of florida sparse matrix collection," *NA Digest*, vol. 92, 1994.

[17] N. Leischner, V. Osipov, and P. Sanders, "GPU sample sort," *CoRR*, vol. abs/0909.5649, 2009.

[18] D. Culler *et al.*, "Parallel programming in Split-C," in *Supercomputing*, 1993, pp. 262–273.

[19] R. W. Numrich and J. Reid, "Co-array Fortran for parallel programming," *SIGPLAN Fortran Forum*, vol. 17, no. 2, pp. 1–31, 1998.

[20] W. W. Carlson, J. M. Draper, D. E. Culler, K. Yelick, E. Brooks, and K. Warren, "Introduction to UPC and language specification," UC Berkeley Technical Report: CCS-TR-99-157, 1999.

[21] P. Charles *et al.*, "X10: An object-oriented approach to non-uniform cluster computing," in *Conference on Object Oriented Programming Systems Languages and Applications*, 2005, pp. 519–538.

[22] D. Callahan, B. L. Chamberlain, and H. P. Zima, "The Cascade high productivity language," in *Int'l Workshop on High-Level Parallel Programming Models and Supportive Environments*, 2004, pp. 52–60.

[23] E. Allen, D. Chase, V. Luchangco, J.-W. Maessen, S. Ryu, G. Steele, and S. Tobin-Hochstadt., "The Fortress language specification version 0.707. Technical report," Sun Microsystems, 2005.

[24] S. J. Deitz, B. L. Chamberlain, and L. Snyder, "Abstractions for dynamic data distribution," in *Int'l Workshop on High-Level Parallel Programming Models and Supportive Environments*, 2004, pp. 42–51.

[25] Y. Yan, J. Zhao, Y. Guo, and V. Sarkar, "Hierarchical place trees: A portable abstraction for task parallelism and data movement," in *Workshop on Languages and Compilers for Parallel Computing*, 2009.

[26] G. Bikshandi *et al.*, "Programming for parallelism and locality with hierarchically tiled arrays," in *Symposium on Principles and Practice of Parallel Programming*, 2006, pp. 48–57.

[27] P. Mattson, "A programming system for the Imagine Media Processor," Ph.D. dissertation, Stanford University, 2002.

[28] I. Buck, T. Foley, D. Horn, J. Sugerman, K. Fatahalian, M. Houston, and P. Hanrahan, "Brook for GPUs: Stream computing on graphics hardware," *ACM Trans. Graph.*, vol. 23, no. 3, pp. 777–786, 2004.

[29] F. Labonte, P. Mattson, I. Buck, C. Kozyrakis, and M. Horowitz, "The stream virtual machine," in *Int'l Conference on Parallel Architectures and Compilation Techniques*, September 2004.

[30] R. Blumofe, C. Joerg, B. Kuszmaul, C. Leiserson, K. Randall, and Y. Zhou, "Cilk: An efficient multithreaded runtime system," in *Symposium on Principles and Practice of Parallel Programming*, 1995.

[31] L. Dagum and R. Menon, "OpenMP: An industry-standard API for shared-memory programming," *IEEE Comput. Sci. Eng.*, vol. 5, no. 1, pp. 46–55, 1998.

[32] B. Alpern, L. Carter, E. Feig, and T. Selker, "The uniform memory hierarchy model of computation," *Algorithmica*, vol. 12, no. 2/3, pp. 72–109, 1994.

[33] H. Jia-Wei and H. T. Kung, "I/O complexity: The red-blue pebble game," in *Symposium on Theory of Computing*, 1981, pp. 326–333.

[34] J. S. Vitter, "External memory algorithms," in *Handbook of Massive Data Sets.* Kluwer Academic Publishers, 2002, pp. 359–416.

[35] B. Alpern, L. Carter, and J. Ferrante, "Space-limited procedures: A methodology for portable high performance," in *Int'l Working Conference on Massively Parallel Programming Models*, 1995.

Compact Data Structure and Scalable Algorithms for the Sparse Grid Technique

Alin Murarașu   Josef Weidendorfer   Gerrit Buse   Daniel Butnaru   Dirk Pflüger

Technische Universität München

{murarasu,weidendo,buse,butnaru,pflueged}@in.tum.de

Abstract

The sparse grid discretization technique enables a compressed representation of higher-dimensional functions. In its original form, it relies heavily on recursion and complex data structures, thus being far from well-suited for GPUs. In this paper, we describe optimizations that enable us to implement compression and decompression, the crucial sparse grid algorithms for our application, on Nvidia GPUs. The main idea consists of a bijective mapping between the set of points in a multi-dimensional sparse grid and a set of consecutive natural numbers. The resulting data structure consumes a minimum amount of memory. For a 10-dimensional sparse grid with approximately 127 million points, it consumes up to 30 times less memory than trees or hash tables which are typically used. Compared to a sequential CPU implementation, the speedups achieved on GPU are up to 17 for compression and up to 70 for decompression, respectively. We show that the optimizations are also applicable to multicore CPUs.

Categories and Subject Descriptors D.1.3 [*PROGRAMMING TECHNIQUES*]: Concurrent Programming - Parallel Programming; G.1.2 [*Mathematics of Computing*]: NUMERICAL ANALYSIS - Approximation

General Terms Algorithms, Performance

Keywords Sparse grids, GPU, Performance optimization

1. Introduction

The numerical representation and treatment of functions in higher-dimensional settings suffer the so-called *curse of dimensionality*, the exponential dependency on the number of dimensions. Consider a piecewise d-linear interpolation of a d-dimensional function based on a spatial discretization of the domain of interest, e.g.: spending $\tilde{N}$ grid points in each dimension leads to a full grid with $\tilde{N}^d$ grid points. Thus, the treatment of functions in more than four variables is practically impossible for reasonable discretizations. In applications requiring efficient numerical techniques for multi-dimensional functions – as they occur in computational steering –, this is clearly an obstacle.

Sparse grids enable one to mitigate the curse of dimensionality to some extent, allowing to tackle dimensionalities that are of

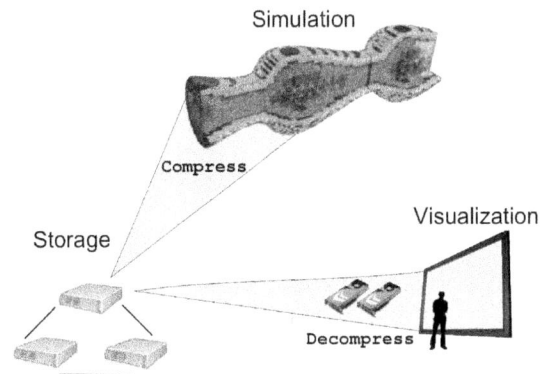

Figure 1: Interactive exploration of multi-dimensional data generated by a previous simulation run, and stored in compressed format.

interest in engineering settings where models depend on a moderate number of variables. They significantly reduce the number of grid points while maintaining similar approximation accuracies as obtained for full grids. Thus, they are well-suited for the representation of higher-dimensional functions, as they provide an efficient compression scheme. Sparse grids, as introduced by Zenger for the solution of partial differential equations in 1990 [1], have meanwhile been employed to a whole range of different applications from fields such as astrophysics, finance, molecular dynamics, or data mining [2, 3].

Our application for sparse grids is the visual and interactive exploration of multi-dimensional data. The idea is that by browsing through the data, new insight into complex phenomena can be gained. However, the sheer size of the data generated by the multi-dimensional and multi-physics simulation under investigation does not only inhibit a smooth interaction with the visualization, but also poses data management challenges.

In order to take advantage of sparse grids in this scenario, two core algorithms need to be implemented efficiently: *hierarchization* and *evaluation*. These methods correspond to a compression step (pre-processing) and a decompression step (online) respectively (see Fig. 1). The more compact data format resulting from the compression step strongly enhances a fast and fluent visualization experience, as bandwidth requirements decrease considerably when forwarding subsets of the data to the visualization system. At the same time visualization algorithms rely heavily on the decompression scheme. The high resolution demands of a smoothly-running visual data exploration application make it a critical component of the whole system. Thus, an extremely efficient and most of all highly scalable implementation becomes crucial.

A first study revealed that the original sparse grid algorithms for compression and decompression, using the usual data structures and parallel implementations for modern multicore CPUs, did not meet the requirements of our application regarding physical size and financial costs. Recent experiences [4] with the potential of GPGPU[1] (general-purpose computation on Graphics Processing Units) suggested that this may allow us to reach our goals by developing alternative data structures and porting the corresponding algorithms.

In this paper, we describe our implementation of compression and decompression for Nvidia GPUs. These are the crucial algorithms of the sparse grid technique for our application. In the later sections, we will focus on *hierarchization* as main part of compression (see Sec. 3), and use *evaluation* as more exact term for decompression. To our knowledge, this is the first space and time efficient implementation of the direct sparse grid technique on GPU architectures.

For such an implementation, the data structure used for storing the sparse grid is of high importance. Usually, trees or hash tables are employed for storing the sparse grid values attributed to grid points at specific coordinates. Typically, much space is needed both for the coordinates in direct or indirect form, and for internal management (e.g. pointers into parts of the data structure). In contrast to this, our approach uses a bijection (*gp2idx*) from the set of points in a sparse grid to a set of consecutive natural numbers (see Sec. 4). Consequently, we are able to store the sparse grid values in a contiguous 1d array without the need for any further strucural information as required in conventional tree- or hash-based approaches. This minimizes the space used, allowing for large sparse grids to be stored in the GPU device memory. But even more importantly, it improves data locality and thus further enhances the scalability of the parallelized implementations of compression and decompression on the GPU. To sum up, the main contributions of this paper are as follows:

- We propose a space efficient data structure for sparse grids (Sec. 4). We compare the memory requirements of our data structure with other data structures typically used for sparse grids. For a 10-dimensional sparse grid with approximately 127 million points, e.g., our data structure consumes up to 30 times less space.

- We present highly efficient and scalable implementations for the compression and decompression algorithms for sparse grids on Nvidia GPUs. The implementations use static workload distribution for parallelization. The compression is up to 17 times faster than the sequential version running on one Intel Nehalem core, the decompression is up to 70 times faster (Sec. 6).

In addition, we measured the performance gain we can get with our compact data structure on standard CPUs with OpenMP parallelization. On a 32-core Opteron machine, a comparison between 1 and 32 cores gives us speedups of 24 for compression and 31 for decompression.

2. The Sparse Grid Technique

Sparse grids help to overcome the curse of dimensionality by reducing the number of grid points from $\mathcal{O}(\tilde{N}^d)$ to $\mathcal{O}(\tilde{N}(\log \tilde{N})^{d-1})$ with only a slightly deteriorated accuracy if the underlying function f is sufficiently smooth. In this section, we briefly describe the technique of sparse grids and introduce the two main principles they are based on, a hierarchical representation of the one-dimensional basis and the extension to the d-dimensional setting via a tensor product approach.

[1] See http://www.gpgpu.org

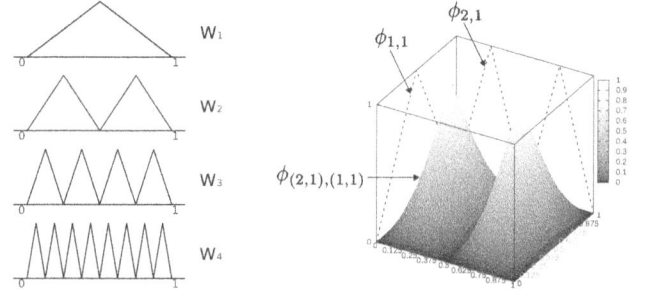

Figure 2: Left: 1d basis functions up to level 4. $V_4 = W_1 \bigoplus \cdots \bigoplus W_4$. Right: 2d basis functions, constructed from two 1d basis functions: $\phi_{(2,1),(1,1)}(x,y) = \phi_{2,1}(x) \cdot \phi_{1,1}(y)$.

2.1 Basis Functions

We consider the representation of a piecewise d-linear function $f_s : \Omega \to \mathbb{R}$ for a certain mesh-width $h_n := 2^{-n}$ with some discretization level n. For reasons of simplicity, we restrict ourselves to the domain $\Omega := [0,1]^d$. To obtain the approximation f_s of some function f, we discretize Ω and employ basis functions ϕ_i which are centered at the grid points stemming from the discretization. f_s is thus provided as a weighted sum of N basis functions, $f_s := \sum_{j=1}^{N} \alpha_j \phi_j$, with coefficients α_j.

We use the standard one-dimensional hat function, $\phi(x) = \max(1 - |x|, 0)$, from which we derive one-dimensional hat basis functions by dilatation and translation,

$$\phi_{l,i}(x) := \phi(2^l x - i),$$

which depend on a level l and an index i, $0 < i < 2^l$. The basis functions are centered at grid points $x_{l,i} = 2^{-l}i$ at which we interpolate f and have local support. Introducing the hierarchical index sets

$$I_l := \{i \in \mathbb{N} : 1 \leq i \leq 2^l - 1, i \text{ odd}\}$$

we obtain a set of hierarchical subspaces W_l spanned by the corresponding basis $\Phi_l := \{\phi_{l,i}(x), i \in I_l\}$. See Fig. 2 (left) for the basis functions up to level 4. Note that we restrict ourselves to functions that are zero on the boundary of Ω to keep the descriptions as simple as possible; adding the two basis function $\phi_{0,0}$ and $\phi_{0,1}$ on level 0 would allow to treat non-zero boundary values.

The hierarchical basis functions are then extended to d dimensions via a tensor product approach and are defined as

$$\phi_{\underline{l},\underline{i}} := \prod_{t=1}^{d} \phi_{l_t, i_t}(x_t),$$

where $\underline{l}$ and $\underline{i}$ are multi-indices, uniquely indicating level and index of the underlying one-dimensional hat functions for each dimension; see Fig. 2 (right). The basis

$$\Phi_{W_{\underline{l}}} := \left\{ \phi_{\underline{l},\underline{i}}(\underline{x}) : i_j = 1, \ldots, 2^{l_j} - 1, i_j \text{ odd}, j = 1, \ldots, d \right\}$$

span subspaces $W_{\underline{l}}$. As in the one-dimensional setting, all basis functions for a certain $\underline{l}$ belong to a regular grid, have pairwise disjoint, equally sized supports, and cover the whole domain.

2.2 Full and Sparse Grids

We can now formulate the space of piecewise linear functions V_n on a full grid with mesh-width h_n for a given level n as a direct sum of $W_{\underline{l}}$,

$$V_n = \bigoplus_{|\underline{l}|_\infty = n} W_{\underline{l}}, \qquad |\underline{l}|_\infty := \max_{1 \leq t \leq d} l_t.$$

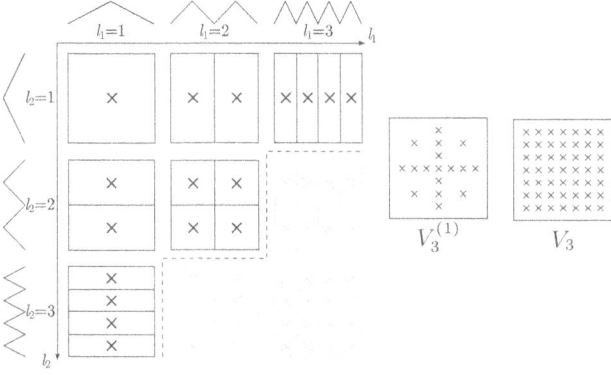

Figure 3: The two-dimensional subspaces $W_{\underline{l}}$ up to $l = 3$ ($h_3 = 1/8$) in each dimension. The optimal a priori selection of subspaces is shown in black (left), leading to a sparse grid of level $n = 3$ for the sparse grid space $V_3^{(1)}$ (middle). In comparison to the corresponding full grid V_3 (right) using the grey subspaces as well, the benefit of using sparse grids can be clearly seen.

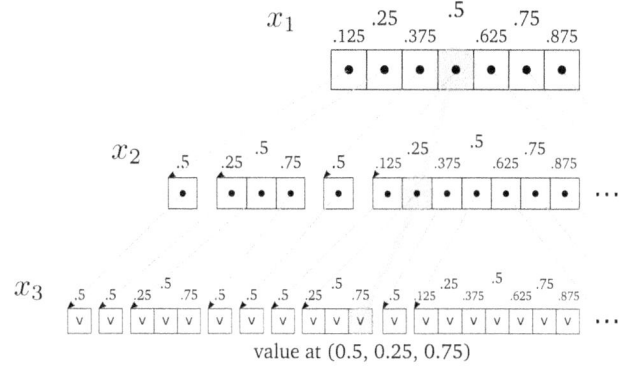

value at (0.5, 0.25, 0.75)

Figure 4: The prefix tree data structure for a regular sparse grid of level $n = 3$ representing grid points by coordinates. The arrays contain the one-dimensional substructures (essentially binary trees), each level corresponding to one dimension. The access to grid point with $\underline{l} = (1, 2, 2)$ and $\underline{i} = (1, 1, 3)$ or equivalent coordinates $(0.5, 0.25, 0.75)$ is indicated in gray.

The hierarchical subspace splitting allows to select those subspaces (or subgrids, respectively) that contribute most to the approximation. This can be done by an a priori *selection* [2], resulting in the sparse grid space $V_n^{(1)}$,

$$V_n^{(1)} = \bigoplus_{|\underline{l}|_1 \leq n+d-1} W_{\underline{l}}, \qquad |\underline{l}|_1 := \sum_{t=1}^{d} l_t.$$

Figure 3 shows the selection of subspaces and the resulting regular (i.e. non-adaptive) sparse grid for $n = 3$, i.e. the sparse grid space $V_3^{(1)}$, as well as the corresponding full grid for V_3.

2.3 Data Structures

Typical data structures for sparse grids are either hash-based or tree-based. The former ones map a grid point to an index which is then used to access a vector of coefficients, as this reduces the memory requirements and especially simplifies implementations considerably; for references, see the section on related work.

The latter ones aim to replicate the hierarchical structure of sparse grids, storing a pointer-based tree-like structure. If the full parent-child relationship is realized, this requires $\mathcal{O}(dN)$ storage, as each grid point has $2d$ child nodes in general. A more memory efficient data structure is considering each dimension d in a fixed order and storing binary trees of $d - 1$-dimensional trees, which reduces the memory requirements. Figure 4 shows this concept for a regular sparse grid of level $n = 3$ in three dimensions, replacing the one-dimensional binary trees by arrays. Thus, the data structure is essentially a prefix tree or trie, storing the common prefix for multiple grid point coordinates only once. Of course, pointer-based data structures are not well-suited for GPUs.

3. The Sparse Grid Operations

To compress a general function represented on a full grid, we select only the function values at grid points also contained in a sparse grid. We can then express the problem of representing a function on a sparse grid as the problem of computing the hierarchical coefficients $\alpha_{\underline{l},\underline{i}}$, which is called hierarchization. Decompression (interpolation) refers to evaluating f_s anywhere inside the domain. In this section, we present algorithms for both hierarchization and interpolation as they are usually used. They reflect the recursive na-

ture of the sparse grid's structure, clearly illustrating the difficulties of porting them to GPUs.

3.1 *Hierarchization* – Computing Hierarchical Coefficients

Algorithm 1 shows the one-dimensional implementation of the hierarchization operation. This is the basic building block. To perform the full multi-dimensional hierarchization two levels of complexity are added. First, for a fixed dimension d the one-dimensional hierarchization is performed starting from all grid points with $l_d = 1$ and $i_d = 1$ in dimension d. Second, the previous procedure is applied unchanged to all the remaining dimensions, one after another, working on updated values from the previous steps.

Algorithm 1 1d recursive hierarchization

1: **func** *hierarchize1d(gp, leftVal, rightVal, level)* :

2: **if** *level* < *maxLevel* **then**
3:     *hierarchize1d(gp.leftChild, leftVal, gp.value, level + 1)*
4:     *hierarchize1d(gp.rightChild, gp.value, rightVal, level + 1)*
5: **end if**
6: *gp.value* ← *gp.value* − (*leftVal* + *rightVal*)/2

This procedure can be illustrated with the help of Fig. 5 (left): if the horizontal dimension (x_1) is first picked for hierarchization, *hierarchize1d* starts from all points on the main vertical sparse grid axis. From each of those, Alg. 1 is executed in the horizontal direction. Next, we hierarchize in the vertical dimension (x_2), starting from all grid points on the horizontal main axis. One important observation is the lack of locality of the *hierarchize1d* function (Fig. 5 (right)) with negative impact on cache efficiency.

3.2 *Evaluation* – Interpolating Between Grid Points

Interpolation directly applies to the evaluation of the sparse grid function. For visualization, we will have to be able to evaluate our sparse grid function at arbitrary locations in our domain: we have to perform d-linear interpolations.

As introduced in Sec. 2, each point of the sparse grid has a corresponding hierarchical coefficient with an associated multi-dimensional basis function. Evaluating the sparse grid function at an arbitrary point $x \in [0, 1]^d$ implies retrieving a subset of the grid's hierarchical coefficients, multiplying them with the corresponding basis function values and adding up the products. This is

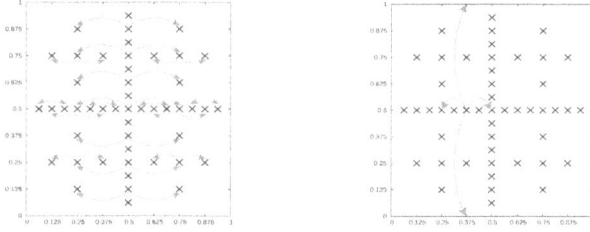

Figure 5: Left: Sparse grid traversal during hierarchization in the x_1-direction. Right: Shows the hierarchical parents (dependencies) for a grid point.

Algorithm 2 1d recursive evaluation

1: **func** *evaluate1d(gp, x, level)* :

2:    $res \leftarrow basis(gp, x) \cdot gp.value$
3:    **if** $level < maxLevel$ **then**
4:      **if** x left of gp **then**
5:        $res \leftarrow res + evaluate1d(gp.leftChild, x, level + 1)$
6:      **else**
7:        $res \leftarrow res + evaluate1d(gp.rightChild, x, level + 1)$
8:      **end if**
9:    **end if**
10:   **return** res

---

shown for the one-dimensional case in Alg. 2. After the contribution of the current point is calculated in line 2, the algorithm descends recursively and collects the contributions of all other points in the same dimension. In line 4 an optimization is made based on the fact that not all points contribute to the interpolation (too far away from the desired interpolation point). For a multi-dimensional representation the algorithm becomes more complicated due to the basis function evaluation. A recursion also in dimensions is necessary to first evaluate the multi-dimensional basis functions. Only afterwards, the resulting value can be multiplied with the hierarchical coefficient and summed up.

4. A Compact Data Structure

In this section we present a space efficient data structure for regular sparse grids. In contrast to the inherent hierarchical nature of sparse grids, our data structure is flat which makes it more suitable for iterative algorithms and thus the GPU architecture. Its key component is a bijection called *gp2idx* that perfectly maps level-index-vector pairs (i.e. $(\underline{l}, \underline{i})$) to consecutive integer indices. Using *gp2idx*, all hierarchical coefficients of a regular sparse grid can be efficiently stored and accessed in a 1d array. We explain how to modify the classic *hierarchization* and *evaluation* algorithms in order to fully benefit from our data structure, also in terms of parallel usage. We can overcome the simplifying assumptions we make in our data structure, mainly the representation of zero boundary multi-dimensional functions, by extending our approach in a very natural way. This aspect is discussed at the end of the section.

Note that for the remainder of this work we are not following the common notation and start counting levels and level vector components from 0.

4.1 Storage Scheme

When interpolating functions on a regular grid it is obvious not to store the grid points' coordinates explicitly but only the function values and mesh widths. Retrieving data from a multi-dimensional array as well as recalculating coordinates via a multi-index are simple and cheap tasks. Due to their structure, this is not as straightfor-

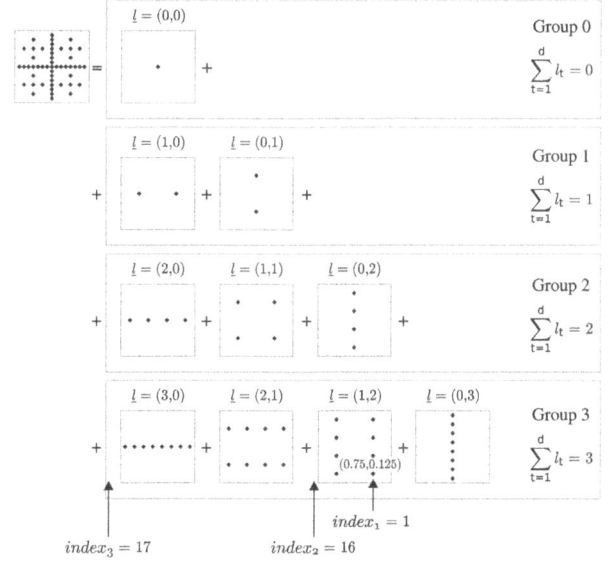

Figure 6: All subspaces of a 2d sparse grid are stored consecutively in memory from top to bottom, left to right. The value at grid point $\underline{l} = (1, 2)$, $\underline{i} = (3, 1)$ (coordinates $(0.75, 0.125)$) can be found at position 34 ($= index_1 + index_2 + index_3$) in a plain 1d array.

ward for sparse grids. Many applications thus need to store those multi-indices together with the data, the hierarchical coefficients, as key-value pairs (e.g. in a hash map). With our composite map *gp2idx* that bijectively maps a sparse grid's points to consecutive integer indices we are able to eliminate the need for storing any keys.

Figure 6 illustrates how we can decompose a sparse grid into a set of regular grids, the so-called subspaces, and group them with respect to their levels. The reason behind is that all subspaces $\underline{l}$ on level $n = |\underline{l}|_1$ contain the same number of hierarchical coefficients. With our modified level vector notation this number can directly be computed as $2^{|\underline{l}|_1}$.

The image also demonstrates that finding the hierarchical coefficient associated with level-index-vector pair $(\underline{l}, \underline{i})$ can be divided into computing three separate indices:

- $index_3$: number of coefficients associated with levels $l' < |\underline{l}|_1$
- $index_2$: number of coefficients in the subspaces that precede subspace $\underline{l}$ in its corresponding level group
- $index_1$: index of the coefficient in subspace $\underline{l}$ identified by $\underline{i}$.

Computing $index_1$ is simple as it comes down to identifying the position of one element in a regular grid. But before we can determine the offsets $index_2$ and $index_3$ we need to discuss the number of subspaces on level n. This is done in the next subsection.

4.2 An Optimal Index Map, *gp2idx*

The challenging part about defining a map from level-index-vector pairs to integer indices without gaps is counting the subspaces of a level. Consider the set

$$\mathcal{L}_n^d = \{\underline{l} \in \mathbb{N}_0^d \,\big|\, |\underline{l}|_1 = n\} \qquad (1)$$

of level vectors of level n in d dimensions. Determining its cardinality $\mathcal{S}_n^d$ is known as the problem of integer partitioning, where a positive integer is divided into d positive integer summands. Using

---
Algorithm 3 Recursive level vector enumeration, $enumerate(d, n)$

1: **if** $d = 1$ **then**
2:     **output** n
3: **else**
4:     **for** $k = 0$ to n **do**
5:         **output** $concatenate(enumerate(d - 1, \, n - k), \, k)$
6:     **end for**
7: **end if**

Algorithm 4 Iterator increment function, $next(\underline{l})$

1: $\underline{r} \leftarrow \underline{l}$
2: $t \leftarrow 0$
3: **while** $\underline{l}[t] = 0$ **do**
4:     $t \leftarrow t + 1$
5: **end while**
6: $\underline{r}[t] \leftarrow 0$
7: $\underline{r}[0] \leftarrow \underline{l}[t] - 1$
8: $\underline{r}[t + 1] \leftarrow \underline{l}[t + 1] + 1$
9: **return** $\underline{r}$
---

combinatorial mathematics the number can be written as

$$\mathcal{S}_n^d = C_{d-1+n}^{d-1} = \binom{d - 1 + n}{d - 1} = \binom{d - 1 + n}{n}. \quad (2)$$

Concerning $index_3$, we can now compute it via the formula

$$index_3 = \sum_{j=0}^{n-1} \mathcal{S}_j^d \cdot 2^j$$

which counts the total number of hierarchical coefficients stored for all levels $l' < n$.

To be able to determine $index_2$ we introduce a recursive enumeration scheme (see Alg. 3) that induces an order on the elements of $\mathcal{L}_n^d$. For simplicity we now generally assume $d \geq 2$. Our algorithm starts with the last component l_d of a level vector $\underline{l}$ and sets it one after another to values $k \in \{0, \ldots, n\}$. For each of these values it recursively descends into $enumerate(d-1, n-k)$ in order to enumerate the elements of $\mathcal{L}_{n-k}^{d-1}$ in the first $d - 1$ components of $\underline{l}$. The recursion stops once only the first component is left. It is clear that $enumerate$ only returns valid level vectors and that no combination is omitted. Next, we observe that the enumeration starts with $first(d, n)$ and ends with $last(d, n)$ defined as

$$first(d, n) := (n, 0, \ldots, 0)^T, \quad last(d, n) := (0, \ldots, 0, n)^T. \quad (3)$$

Recursion is not supported on the GPU so we change the enumeration to an iterator scheme, in which we compute a unique successor $next(\underline{l}) = \underline{r}$ for each $\underline{l} \in \mathcal{L}_n^d \setminus \{last(d, n)\}$. Take the smallest index t with component $m = l_t \neq 0$. It holds that we currently see $last(t + 1, m)$ in the first $t + 1$ components of $\underline{l}$. From the recursive definition it is then clear that the next change must happen on the recursion level above. Here we increase the loop variable k in line 4 of Alg. 3 by one and return the value $concatenate(enumerate(t + 1, \, m - 1), \, k)$ in line 5. This has two effects:

1. By increasing k we set $r_{t+1} := l_{t+1} + 1$.

2. We recursively initialize the first $t + 1$ components of $\underline{r}$ with $first(t+1, m-1)$. Compared to $\underline{l}$ this only requires two changes in $\underline{r}$: Setting $r_t := 0$ and $r_0 := m - 1$ as for all components $r_j, 0 < j < t$ we have $r_t = l_t = 0$.

Algorithm 4 implements these steps in an iterative function $next$. Note finally that all trailing components $r_j, j > t + 1$ remain unchanged, and that the special case of $t = 0$ is treated automatically if lines 6 and 7 of the algorithm are executed in this order.

Based on this order induced on the level vectors we now define the function $subspaceidx$ as follows

$$subspaceidx(\underline{l}) = \sum_{t=1}^{d-1} \binom{t + \sum_{j=0}^{t} l_j}{t} - \binom{t + \sum_{j=0}^{t-1} l_j}{t}. \quad (4)$$

It is constructed such that it maps all elements $\underline{l} \in \mathcal{L}_n^d$ to a consecutive integer index starting from 0. We prove this by showing that $b - a = 1$ holds for images $a = subspaceidx(\underline{l})$ and $b = subspaceidx(next(\underline{l}))$ with $\underline{l} \neq last(d, n)$. Still we assume $d \geq 2$.

Proof. In order to understand the effect of $next$ on the index a we focus on the differing components of $\underline{l}$ and $\underline{r} = next(\underline{l})$. As we can see clearly in lines 6–8 of Alg. 4 these are at indices $\{0, t, t + 1\}$ with $t = min_{j \in \{0, \ldots, d-1\}}\{l_j \neq 0\}$.

We note that the index of the sum in $subspaceidx$ starts at 1. Therefore only the changes in the vector components t and $t + 1$ are important for $subspaceidx$. About these we know $r_t = 0$ and $r_{t+1} = l_{t+1} + 1$ while their contributions to $b = subspaceidx(\underline{r})$ have the form

$$b_{\underline{r}, \{t, t+1\}} = \underbrace{\left[\binom{(t+1) + (l_t + l_{t+1})}{t + 1} - \binom{(t+1) + (l_t - 1)}{(t+1)} \right]}_{\text{summand for } t + 1}.$$

For a the corresponding summands look like this

$$a_{\underline{l}, \{t, t+1\}} = \underbrace{\left[\binom{(t+1) + (l_t + l_{t+1})}{(t+1)} - \binom{(t+1) + l_t}{(t+1)} \right]}_{\text{summand for } t + 1}$$
$$+ \underbrace{\left[\binom{t + l_t}{t} - \binom{t + 0}{t} \right]}_{\text{summand for } t}.$$

Computing the difference and using $\binom{t+l_t}{t} + \binom{t+l_t}{(t+1)} = \binom{(t+1)+l_t}{(t+1)}$ gives us

$$b - a = b_{\underline{r}, \{t, t+1\}} - a_{\underline{l}, \{t, t+1\}} = \binom{t}{t} = 1.$$

In the special case $t = 0$ the "summand for t" does not exist. $b - a$ then degenerates to $\binom{l_t}{1} - \binom{l_t - 1}{1} = l_t - (l_t - 1) = 1$.

With the fact that $subspaceidx(first(d, n)) = 0$ and the knowledge that the $next$ function returns a unique successor for any $\underline{l} \in \mathcal{L}_n^d \setminus \{last(d, n)\}$ the proof is complete. $\square$

Now we have the means to also compute $index_2$ and integrate this part into the composite index map $gp2idx$ that maps each grid point to an integer index. The final algorithm for $gp2idx$ is shown in Alg. 5. It runs in $\mathcal{O}(d)$ time if we apply two optimizations. First, the repeated expensive calculation of the binomial coefficient via $binomial$ can be avoided. We use a small $n \times d$ lookup matrix called $binmat$ to do so, n being the maximum level in the grid. $binmat$ can be initialized in $\mathcal{O}(n \cdot d)$ time and because of the binomial coefficient's symmetry property we can even reduce it to half its size. Second, the computation of $index_3$ in lines 13 to 16 of the algorithm would also rather be implemented as an $\mathcal{O}(1)$ lookup operation than as an $\mathcal{O}(|\underline{l}|_1)$ loop.

Using basic rules of combinatorial mathematics we can furthermore reduce the number of lookups in $binmat$ in lines 8–10 to one per iteration.

4.3 Impact on Initial Algorithms

The $gp2idx$ bijection eliminates the need to store coordinates, or equivalent $(\underline{l}, \underline{i})$, for matching hierarchical coefficients to their

Algorithm 5 The optimal index map, $gp2idx(\underline{l}, \underline{i})$

1: $index_1 \leftarrow 0$
2: **for** $t = 0$ to $d - 1$ **do**
3:     $index_1 \leftarrow index_1 \cdot 2^{\underline{l}[t]} + (\underline{i}[t] - 1)/2$
4: **end for**

5: $sum \leftarrow \underline{l}[0]$
6: $index_2 \leftarrow 0$
7: **for** $t = 1$ to $d - 1$ **do**
8:     $index_2 \leftarrow index_2 - binomial(t + sum, t)$
9:     $sum \leftarrow sum + \underline{l}[t]$
10:    $index_2 \leftarrow index_2 + binomial(t + sum, t)$
11: **end for**
12: $index_2 \leftarrow index_2 \cdot 2^{sum}$

13: $index_3 \leftarrow 0$
14: **for** $s = 0$ to $sum - 1$ **do**
15:    $index_3 \leftarrow index_3 + binomial(d - 1 + s, d - 1) \cdot 2^s$
16: **end for**

17: **return** $index_1 + index_2 + index_3$

corresponding basis functions. Besides the minimal memory consumption, there are also other benefits from using the bijective function $gp2idx$, its inverse $idx2gp$ and the *next* iterator. We modified the algorithms for hierarchization and evaluation presented in Sec. 3 in order to fully benefit from our data structure.

In Alg. 6 the hierarchical coefficients are stored in a 1d array, *rawStorage*. The coefficients in this array can be traversed in the order of their dependencies. The groups of subspaces or regular grids are updated in descending order of the refinement level, starting with the largest $|\underline{l}|_1$ and finishing with the smallest. This ensures that updating a coefficient does not break the dependencies of other coefficients. It is worth mentioning that, compared to Alg. 1, the new hierarchization algorithm is no longer recursive, thus becoming better suited for GPUs.

Algorithm 6 Multi-dimensional hierarchization based on $gp2idx$

1: Initialize *rawStorage* with corresponding values from the full grid
2: **for** $t = 0$ to $d - 1$ **do**
3:     **for** $j = numOfGridPoints - 1$ downto 0 **do**
4:         $(\underline{l}, \underline{i}) \leftarrow idx2gp(j)$
5:         $val_1 \leftarrow rawStorage[gp2idx(leftParent(\underline{l}, \underline{i}, t))]$
6:         $val_2 \leftarrow rawStorage[gp2idx(rightParent(\underline{l}, \underline{i}, t))]$
7:         $rawStorage[j] \leftarrow rawStorage[j] - (val_1 + val_2)/2$
8:     **end for**
9: **end for**

Another advantage lies in a reduced number of cache misses caused when accessing hierarchical coefficients. Since $gp2idx$ and $idx2gp$ operate on a small matrix of size $d \cdot n$, *binmat*, the number of cache misses triggered by their execution can be considered 0. Accordingly, cache misses only occur when referencing coefficients in the *rawStorage* array, and we therefore expect to have at most one miss per coefficient access. This even applies for the worst case scenario of random access.

The j loop can be parallelized using static decomposition which represents another positive aspect for GPUs. However, minor modifications must be applied to Alg. 6 so that the groups of subspaces are updated correctly, without destroying the semantics of sequential execution. Specifically, a global barrier must be executed after each group of subspaces is updated in descending order, from the largest $|\underline{l}|_1$ to the smallest.

In its new form, *evaluation* (Alg. 7) is also iterative, thus GPU compatible. We can see that neither $gp2idx$ nor $idx2gp$ are used. Traversing all valid combinations for $\underline{l}$ is done using the *next* function and the definitions for the *first* and *last* subspaces in a group.

The number of cache misses is minimal, generated by line 15. Cache exploitation can be improved by observing that it is advantageous to execute the loops from lines 3 and 5 on multiple evaluation points, i.e. blocking is performed on the set of evaluation points and each block is processed after the j and $\underline{l}$ loops. The optimization is based on the fact that a subspace containing the coefficients with the same $\underline{l}$ is needed by all the evaluations and is already present in cache.

Algorithm 7 Multi-dimensional evaluation based on *next* iterator

1: $res \leftarrow 0$
2: $index_2 \leftarrow 0$
3: **for** $j = 0$ to $n - 1$ **do**
4:     $\underline{l} \leftarrow first(d, j)$
5:     **for** $k = 1$ to C_{d-1+j}^j **do**
6:         $prod \leftarrow 1$
7:         $index_1 \leftarrow 0$
8:         **for** $t = 0$ to $d - 1$ **do**
9:             $div \leftarrow 2^{-\underline{l}[t]}$
10:           $index_1 \leftarrow index_1 \cdot 2^{\underline{l}[t]} + \lfloor coords[t]/div \rfloor$
11:           $left \leftarrow \lfloor coords[t]/div \rfloor \cdot div$
12:           $right \leftarrow left + div$
13:           $prod \leftarrow prod \cdot basis(left, right, coords[t])$
14:         **end for**
15:         $prod \leftarrow prod \cdot rawStorage[index_1 + index_2]$
16:         $res \leftarrow res + prod$
17:         $\underline{l} \leftarrow next(\underline{l})$
18:         $index_2 \leftarrow index_2 + 2^j$
19:     **end for**
20: **end for**
21: **return** res

The evaluation operation is embarrassingly parallel provided that each thread performs evaluation for its private set of multi-dimensional points in the domain.

4.4 An Extendable Context

One of our assumptions was that the functions to be represented using the sparse grid technique are zero-boundary functions. The application can be easily modified in order to cope with non-zero boundaries whereas our data structure requires a more complex extension. This extension is based on the observation that the boundary of a d-dimensional sparse grid is composed of lower-dimensional, zero-boundary sparse grids for which we already have an efficient data structure.

Let C_n^k be the number of k-combinations from a set of n elements. The number of $d - j$-dimensional sparse grids in the boundary is $2^j \cdot C_d^{d-j}$. One can verify this formula by simply counting the projections of a sparse grid in lower-dimensional planes as depicted in Fig. 7. Storing the boundary as a 1d contiguous array implies determining for any point on the boundary the first index of its corresponding sparse grid in the 1d array. This can be achieved by grouping the sparse grids according to their dimensionality. The number of sparse grids in the group corresponding to dimensionality j is $2^{d-j} \cdot C_d^j$. An ordering function has to be defined in order to find the correct sparse grid within a group. Next, $gp2idx$ can be used.

5. Sparse Grids on GPUs

In this section we describe the architecture of Nvidia GPUs and the CUDA programming model. We continue with our implementation of sparse grid compression and decompression on GPUs. Since it has a minimal memory footprint, our data structure is a good fit for GPUs which have a relatively small amount of RAM. Moreover, our implementation is optimized for the best exploitation of computational resources on GPUs.

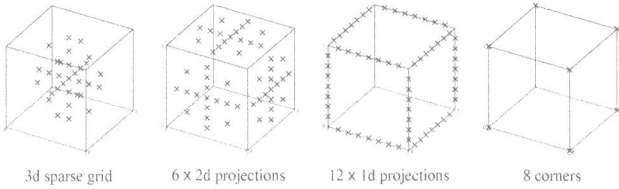

Figure 7: 3d sparse grid with non-zero boundary. The boundary of a 3d sparse grid is composed of lower-dimensional sparse grids.

5.1 GPU Architecture

In contrast to CPUs which use the die space for complex control logic and large caches, GPUs devote a higher percentage of transistors to floating point units. GPUs provide massive parallelism and deliver better performance than CPUs especially for applications with regular access patterns, e.g. dense matrix operations [5].

In the following we focus on the C1060 model of Nvidia Tesla [6]. This is a high-end GPU which contains 30 8-way SIMD units called by Nvidia Streaming Multiprocessors (SM). In Nvidia terminology, each way is called a Scalar Processor (SP). C1060 supports up to 1024 thread contexts in hardware per SM [7]. Each thread is generally executed on one of the 8 ways of the SIMD unit. One of the main characteristics of Nvidia GPUs is multithreading which offers the possibility to hide the latency originating from various instructions, especially the latency caused by loads from and stores to RAM, by executing a large number of threads (up to 30720 on a Tesla) concurrently with a low cost per context switch.

Nvidia GPUs are SIMD based architectures. Each SM control unit creates, manages and executes synchronously the threads in groups of 32 called warps. Every instruction is broadcasted synchronously to all the active threads in a warp. Branching may cause threads in the same warp to follow different execution paths. This type of behavior of the threads inside a warp is called diverge. It has the potential to severely reduce the performance of a GPU application, up to a factor of 32.

GPUs have their own dedicated RAM, global memory, which is in the order of several Gigabytes, e.g. C1060 has 4 GB of DDR3 memory. For performance, GPUs are also equipped with multiple fast memories on the chip: constant cache, texture cache and shared memory [8]. The properties of these fast memories vary in terms of latency, bandwidth and usage. The constant cache is a read-only cache and, according to [9], its level-1 has the lowest latency among the memories on the GPU. The texture cache is a read-only memory used for optimizing the bandwidth rather than latency, i.e. its latency is comparable with the one of the global memory. Finally, the shared memory is a low latency, read-write memory, is private per SM and controlled explicitly by the programmer.

5.2 GPU Programming

The Compute Unified Device Architecture (CUDA) is one of the available frameworks for programming Nvidia GPUs. From a programming point of view, a CUDA application has a CPU and a GPU part. The main responsibilities of the CPU part are: allocating memory on the GPU, transferring data to and from the GPU over PCI Express and launching the GPU program called kernel. A kernel cannot contain recursive functions. Each instance of a kernel in execution is a thread. Besides being packed in warps, the threads are also grouped in blocks of threads. This grouping is important as only the threads inside a block can synchronize via barriers (_syncthreads) and share data from the shared memory. Each thread has a 2d block identifier (*blockIdx*) and a 3d thread identifier (*threadIdx*). Combining the block and the thread identifiers offers

the means to uniquely identify a thread on the GPU and to assign its part from the workload to be computed on the GPU.

A first optimization for GPU programs consists of the proper exploitation of multithreading. This is equivalent to maximizing the number of active threads and can be achieved by reducing the register file and shared memory consumption per thread. Second, efficient use of the memory hierarchy can provide a substantial speedup to GPU applications. This optimization includes at least: enabling coalesced accesses to global memory in order to reduce the number of memory transactions, using the fast memories on-chip and reducing the number of bank conflicts caused by accessing the shared memory. Third, divergent branches can serialize the execution of the threads composing a warp. To improve the performance, the number of divergent branches needs to be minimized. Note that these are the optimizations which proved to be relevant to our application and they represent only a subset of the optimizations applicable to CUDA applications. For a detailed list of optimizations we refer the reader to [7].

5.3 GPU Implementation of Sparse Grid Operations

The implementation of the hierarchization algorithm (Alg. 6) has minimal memory consumption. Moreover, the parallelization is based on statically decomposing the set of grid points for which the hierarchical coefficients are computed. Both minimal memory consumption and static workload distribution are factors that enable an efficient implementation of hierarchization on Nvidia GPUs. The decomposition is done such that each thread block is responsible for updating one subspace or regular grid of coefficients. In order to avoid breaking dependencies between coefficients, the subspace groups depicted in Fig. 6 are updated in descending order of $|\underline{l}|_1$. In other words, the update of group j must finish before group $j-1$ can be updated. The necessary barriers are enforced by the CPU program by launching the hierarchization kernel multiple times, each time for updating another group of subspaces. With respect to efficient use of fast memory, $\underline{l}$ and $\underline{i}$ are placed in shared memory. Accessing global memory for the subspaces to be updated are optimized for coalescing. However, accesses to dependencies or parents as shown in Fig. 5 (right) cannot be packed, thus representing the main source of uncoalesced accesses and branch divergence.

Finding the best implementation of hierarchization on GPU implies determining the fastest way to compute the bijection *gp2idx* which in turn relies heavily on the *binmat* matrix. Since *binmat* is a read-only matrix containing the binomial coefficients, it is compatible with all the fast memories available on the GPU. However, the texture cache is not a true candidate as our goal is to obtain low latency access to *binmat* rather than high bandwidth. In this context, three options were considered: computing the binomial coefficients on the fly in $\mathcal{O}(n)$, accessing *binmat* from shared memory and placing *binmat* in constant cache. Experiments revealed that computing on the fly makes hierarchization approximately 4 times slower than when shared memory or constant cache are used. If *binmat* is stored in constant cache, hierarchization is slightly faster than the version based on placing *binmat* in shared memory, confirming the GPU memory benchmarking results presented in [9].

For the evaluation algorithm (Alg. 7), the parallelization scheme relies on statically decomposing the set of multi-dimensional points for which function values are to be computed. This approach is embarrassingly parallel and makes sense since the number of interpolation points is typically around 10^5 or more, thus fully utilizing the GPU computational resources. More precisely, each thread performs interpolation for one multi-dimensional point in the domain. Shared memory is used for storing $\underline{l}$ and *coords*. Furthermore, copying *coords* from global memory to shared memory satisfies the coalescing requirements. Note also that divergent branching inside a warp is minimized in this approach.

Data Structure	Time	Non-seq. Refs.
Standard STL map	$\mathcal{O}(d \cdot log(N))$	$\mathcal{O}(log(N))$
Enhanced STL map	$\mathcal{O}(d + log(N))$	$\mathcal{O}(log(N))$
Enhanced STL hash_table	$\mathcal{O}(d)$	$\mathcal{O}(1)$
Prefix tree	$\mathcal{O}(d)$	$\mathcal{O}(d)$
Our data structure	$\mathcal{O}(d)$	$\mathcal{O}(1)$

Table 1: Time complexities and number of non-sequential memory references for accessing a value from a grid point. N is the total number of sparse grid points.

All the arrays from hierarchization and evaluation are private to each thread, have length d and are stored in shared memory. Consequently, the pressure on shared memory is linearly dependent on d and can decrease the number of active threads, i.e. it reduces the benefits of multithreading. In order to decrease the shared memory consumption per thread, we set $\underline{l}$ as an array shared between all threads inside the same thread block. Only the master thread (thread 0) from the thread block modifies $\underline{l}$, and all the threads in the block read $\underline{l}$. Although this adds synchronization via the __syncthreads device function, the improvements over the versions without block shared $\underline{l}$ cannot be ignored, i.e. this results in 1.62 times faster hierarchization and 1.59 times faster evaluation.

6. Results

For all evaluations in this section, we use sparse grids with refinement level 11.

6.1 Comparison of Data Structures

First, we compare the memory consumption of various data structures for sparse grids. Table 1 shows the structures taken into consideration and their access properties. The number for non-sequential references gives a hint regarding locality of accesses, i.e. the number of cache misses to be expected on standard CPUs.

The first three data structures use the C++ Standard Template Library (STL) [10]. "Standard STL map" consumes space for keys linearly to the number of dimensions. "Enhanced STL map" and "enhanced STL hash table" use our gp2idx function. Memory consumption is reduced by storing the result of gp2idx as key, i.e. it is constant with regard to dimensionality. The "prefix tree" data structure is the classical tree-based data structure using pointers, as described in Sec. 2.3. As it can be seen in Fig. 8, our data structure uses the smallest amount of main memory. Moreover, "prefix tree"

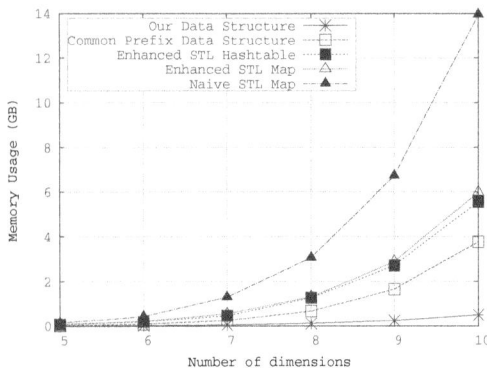

Figure 8: Memory consumption of a sparse grid.

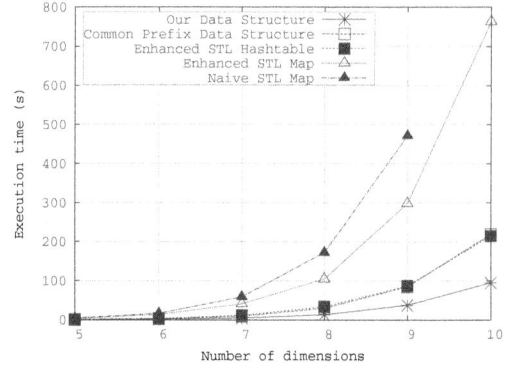

(a) Runtime for sequential hierarchization.

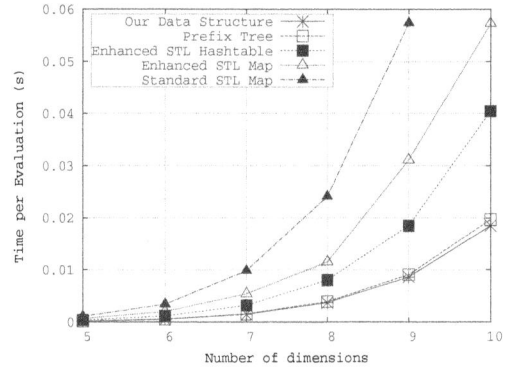

(b) Runtime for sequential evaluation.

Figure 9: Sequential runtimes on i7-920.

follows, showing that its compression scheme is superior to using gp2idx in conjunction with an STL hash table or map.

6.2 Performance Measurements

As experimental setup, the following hardware was used:

- a 4-core, single-socket Nehalem i7-920 with 24 GB of DDR3 1066 MHz memory,
- a Tesla C1060 with 4 GB of DDR3 800 MHz 512 bit memory,
- a 32-core, 8-socket AMD Opteron 8356 machine with 256 GB of DDR2 667 MHz main memory,
- an 8-core, dual-socket Nehalem E5540 supporting 16 simultaneous threads with 24 GB of DDR3 1066 MHz memory.

There are three implementations of our application that we considered in our tests: the sequential C++ version which provides the base for speedup numbers, the CUDA version implemented using the CUDA SDK [11], and a version for x86 multicore systems based on OpenMP 3.0. The CPU versions are optimized with respect to cache and SSE. The tasking concept was applied for parallelizing the recursive algorithms for both hierarchization and evaluation shown in Sec. 3. The number of points in the sparse grids used in our tests was in the range of [2047, 127574017], corresponding to level 11 sparse grids with dimensionalities between 1 and 10.

First, we did runtime measurements with sequential C++ versions of the sparse grid operations using the different data structures on the i7-920 system. Our data structure gives the best execution times for both sequential hierarchization and evaluation as depicted in Fig. 9a and Fig. 9b. The prefix tree has similar execution time for hierarchization as the enhanced STL hash table. This is

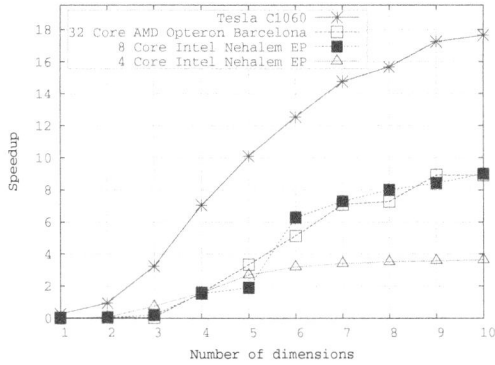

(a) Hierarchization on GPU and multicore CPU.

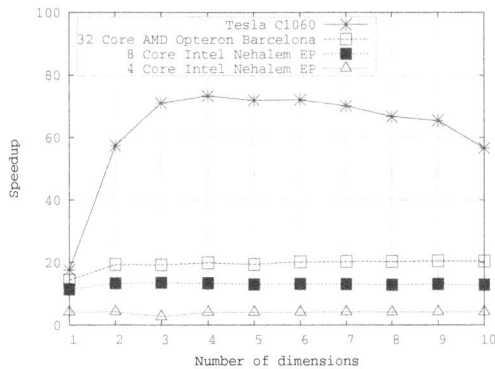

(b) Evaluation on GPU and multicore CPU.

Figure 10: Performance on GPU and CPU.

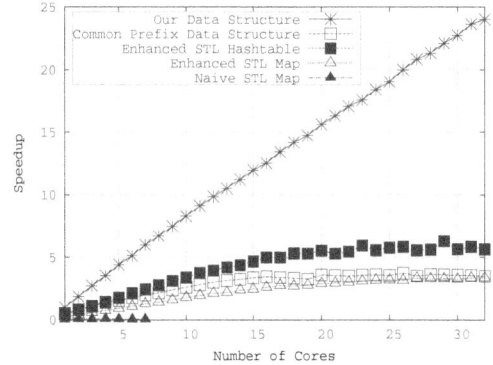

(a) Hierarchization scalability.

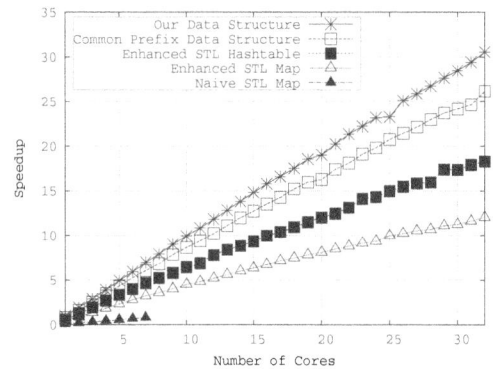

(b) Evaluation scalability.

Figure 11: Scalability on CPU.

due to good cache locality for accessing the children of grid points. For evaluation, its performance is very close to the performance obtained with our data structure. This also happens because the cache is exploited properly. Once a hierarchical coefficient is found, the next needed one – corresponding to a higher refinement level – resides in the same coefficient array at the bottom of the structure. Hence, the next hierarchical coefficient is already loaded in cache.

With regard to the sequential runtimes on the i7-920 system, we provide speedup numbers of implementations using our data structure in Fig. 10a and Fig. 10b. Most important for our application are the Tesla C1060 results corresponding to the GPU implementations. We see that these versions of the sparse grid operations are superior to the ones on x86 multicore architectures. The execution time of hierarchization is reduced by approximately a factor of 2 compared to the fastest multicore architectures considered in our tests whereas evaluation is roughly 3 times faster than the best performance on multicore CPUs. Evaluating a function represented as a sparse grid at 10^5 points leads to an efficient usage of the parallel resources as all the multicore architectures are able to offer constant speedup independent of the number of dimensions. The speedup on the GPU is expected to decrease when the number of dimensions is greater than 10. This is due to the increasing pressure on the shared memory inside an streaming multiprocessor. More exactly, each GPU thread requires shared memory space that depends linearly on the number of dimensions. If the number of dimensions grows over a certain value, this limits the number of threads that can be executed concurrently on one streaming processor, thus reducing any potential for latency hiding.

Finally, we measured the scalability achievable with our data structure on the Opteron system. Regarding parallel hierarchiza-

tion, the tree and hash table data structures saturate the connection to main memory, thus limiting the scalability as shown in Fig. 11a when the number of processors is greater than 15. Another cause for the reduced scalability for these data structures can be linked to the use of tasks necessary for the dynamic decomposition of the workload. Evaluation is not memory bound and this can be seen in Fig. 11b. The memory connection is not saturated and does not block the scalability. The prefix tree provides the best speedup from all the tree and hash table data structures. This happens because of better cache locality when accessing the hierarchical coefficients required by the evaluation operation.

7. Related Work

The power of sparse grids has already been exploited for a whole range of different types of problems, see [2, 3]. Depending on the requirements of the respective application, different types of data structures have been considered. Typically, hash-based realizations of the data structure are employed (see [12, 13] for discussions). They provide a reasonable trade-of by reducing the memory requirements in contrast to pointer-based approaches. Yet, they keep the access structures as flexible as possible and suitable for adaptive refinement. To meet harsh requirements such as minimal storage space, flexibility can be traded for efficiency. Note that data structures for sparse grids are ongoing research [14, 15].

Parallelizations of sparse grid methods have typically been achieved by employing the so-called combination technique [16], which obtains an approximation of the sparse grid solution by a superposition of partial solutions obtained on several smaller, but anisotropic full grids. Obtaining the independent partial solutions can be parallelized trivially. Furthermore, due to the regular structure of the full partial grids, each partial solution can be vectorized in a straightforward manner [17]. The benefit of employing vectorization on GPUs is evident [18, 19]. However, grid points and corresponding function values have to be replicated across multiple full grids. Thus, higher memory requirements have to be met.

Our approach requires minimal storage at the cost of computing a cache-efficient mapping from a grid point to the position of its corresponding coefficient or function value in a linear ordering of the sparse grid points. To the best of our knowledge, this is the first time that a direct sparse grid implementation on a GPU has been achieved.

In general, there are multiple data structures, hash tables and trees, developed to cope with the problem of storing and retrieving efficiently multi-dimensional data [20]. Such data structures can also be used for storing the points required by the sparse grid technique. However, they rely on storing information about multi-dimensional coordinates. Therefore, our performance expectations for these data structures are similar to the results provided in Sec. 6. In our approach based on *gp2idx*, we do not store any coordinates. Nevertheless, we emphasize that our solution does not address the sparsity problem in all types of grids. In contrast to the work mentioned above and to the best of our knowledge, there is no other data structure in the context of the sparse grid technique with smaller memory footprint than our data structure.

An approach for enabling complex data structures on GPUs is presented in [21]. Although the proposed solution was published before the release of CUDA, some of its concepts are still valid. For instance, the authors describe the procedure for handling iterators in parallel on GPUs. Moreover, copying a pointer based data structure between different memory spaces is another issue addressed by the authors. The paper shows that it is feasible to operate with complex data structures on GPUs but the inefficiencies related to memory consumption and access time are still present.

8. Conclusion

In this paper we focus on identifying problems and offering solutions for successfully porting the sparse grid technique to Nvidia GPUs. Our motivation is a computational steering application in which compressing and decompressing multi-dimensional data plays a crucial role. In their original form, sparse grid compression and decompression are based on recursion and complex data structures like trees and hash tables. As GPUs do not support recursion and do not favor trees or hash tables, we propose a data structure that eliminates these limitations as the main optimization.

Our data structure is based on a bijection that maps a multi-dimensional sparse grid to a 1d continuous array. Therefore, it minimizes memory consumption. Furthermore, it enables us to replace the recursive compression and decompression operations by iterative algorithms, fully compatible with GPUs. We obtain impressive speedup numbers on the GPU. Consequently, our sparse grid implementation is both space and time efficient.

As a next step, we plan to tune our application for Nvidia GPUs based on the Fermi architecture [22]. We expect that the two-level cache, 64 KB level-1 per SM and 768 KB shared level-2 could be beneficial for both sparse grid operations. Another point of interest for us will be the integration of our data structure into other applications that rely on the sparse grid technique for representing higher-dimensional functions.

Acknowledgement

This publication is based on work supported by Award No. UK-C0020, made by King Abdullah University of Science and Technology (KAUST).

References

[1] C. Zenger. Sparse grids. In Wolfgang Hackbusch, editor, *Parallel Algorithms for Partial Differential Equations*, volume 31 of *Notes on Numerical Fluid Mechanics*, pages 241–251. Vieweg, 1991.

[2] H.-J. Bungartz and M. Griebel. Sparse grids. *Acta Numerica*, 13(-1):147–269, 2004.

[3] D. Pflüger. *Spatially Adaptive Sparse Grids for High-Dimensional Problems*. Dissertation, Institut für Informatik, Technische Universität München, February 2010.

[4] H. Hacker, C. Trinitis, J. Weidendorfer, and M. Brehm. Considering GPGPU for HPC Centers: Is it Worth the Effort? In *Proceedings of "Facing the Multicore-Challenge 2010"*, volume 6310 of *LNCS*. Springer, 2010.

[5] V. Volkov and J. Demmel. Benchmarking GPUs to tune dense linear algebra. In *SC*, page 31, 2008.

[6] E. Lindholm, J. Nickolls, S. F. Oberman, and J. Montrym. NVIDIA Tesla: A Unified Graphics and Computing Architecture. *IEEE Micro*, 28(2):39–55, 2008.

[7] NVIDIA. *CUDA Programming Guide 2.2.1*, 2009.

[8] S. Ryoo, C. I. Rodrigues, S. S. Baghsorkhi, S. S. Stone, D. B. Kirk, and W. W. Hwu. Optimization principles and application performance evaluation of a multithreaded GPU using CUDA. In *PPOPP*, pages 73–82, 2008.

[9] H. Wong, M. M. Papadopoulou, M. Sadooghi-Alvandi, and A. Moshovos. Demystifying gpu microarchitecture through microbenchmarking. In *ISPASS*, pages 235–246, 2010.

[10] Hewlett-Packard Company. *Standard Template Library Programmer's Guide*, 1994.

[11] NVIDIA. CUDA SDK. http://developer.nvidia.com/object/cuda_2_2_downloads.html.

[12] M. May and T. Schiekofer. An Abstract Data Type for Parallel Simulations based on Sparse Grids. In A. Bode, J. Dongarra, T. Ludwig, and V. Sunderam, editors, *Proceedings of the Third European PVM Conference*, volume 1156 of *Lecture Notes in Computer Science*, pages 59–67. Springer Verlag, 1997.

[13] M. Griebel. Adaptive sparse grid multilevel methods for elliptic PDEs based on finite differences. *Computing*, 61(2):151–179, 1998.

[14] C. Feuersänger. Dünngitterverfahren für hochdimensionale elliptische partielle Differentialgleichungen. Diplomarbeit, Institut für Numerische Simulation, Universität Bonn, 2005.

[15] S. Dirnstorfer. Adaptive numerische Quadratur höherer Ordnung auf dünnen Gittern. Diplomarbeit, Fakultät für Informatik, Technische Universität München, 2000.

[16] M. Griebel. The Combination Technique for the Sparse Grid Solution of PDE's on Multiprocessor Machines. *Parallel Processing Letters*, 2:61–70, 1992.

[17] M. Griebel. A parallelizable and vectorizable multi-level algorithm on sparse grids. In *Parallel algorithms for partial differential equations*, Notes Numer. Fluid Mech. 31, pages 94–100. Vieweg, Wiesbaden, 1991.

[18] C. Teitzel, M. Hopf, and T. Ertl. Scientific visualization on sparse grids. Technical report, Universitt Erlangen-Nrnberg, Lehrstuhl fr Graphische Datenverarbeitung (IMMD IX), 2000.

[19] A. Gaikwad and I. M. Toke. GPU based sparse grid technique for solving multidimensional options pricing PDEs. In *WHPCF '09: Proceedings of the 2nd Workshop on High Performance Computational Finance*, pages 1–9, New York, NY, USA, 2009. ACM.

[20] V. Gaede and O. Günther. Multidimensional Access Methods. *ACM Comput. Surv.*, 30(2):170–231, 1998.

[21] A. E. Lefohn, S. Sengupta, J. Kniss, R. Strzodka, and J. D. Owens. Glift: Generic, efficient, random-access GPU data structures. *ACM Trans. Graph.*, 25(1):60–99, 2006.

[22] NVIDIA. NVIDIA's Next Generation CUDA Compute Architecture: Fermi. White paper, 2009.

A Domain-Specific Approach To Heterogeneous Parallelism

Hassan Chafi   Arvind K. Sujeeth   Kevin J. Brown
HyoukJoong Lee   Anand R. Atreya   Kunle Olukotun

Pervasive Parallelism Laboratory
Stanford University

{hchafi, asujeeth, kjbrown, hyouklee, aatreya, kunle}@stanford.edu

Abstract

Exploiting heterogeneous parallel hardware currently requires mapping application code to multiple disparate programming models. Unfortunately, general-purpose programming models available today can yield high performance but are too low-level to be accessible to the average programmer. We propose leveraging domain-specific languages (DSLs) to map high-level application code to heterogeneous devices. To demonstrate the potential of this approach we present OptiML, a DSL for machine learning. OptiML programs are implicitly parallel and can achieve high performance on heterogeneous hardware with no modification required to the source code. For such a DSL-based approach to be tractable at large scales, better tools are required for DSL authors to simplify language creation and parallelization. To address this concern, we introduce Delite, a system designed specifically for DSLs that is both a framework for creating an implicitly parallel DSL as well as a dynamic runtime providing automated targeting to heterogeneous parallel hardware. We show that OptiML running on Delite achieves single-threaded, parallel, and GPU performance superior to explicitly parallelized MATLAB code in nearly all cases.

Categories and Subject Descriptors D.1.3 [*Programming Techniques*]: Concurrent Programming – Parallel programming; D.3.4 [*Programming Languages*]: Processors – Code generation, Optimization, Run-time environments

General Terms Languages, Performance

Keywords Parallel Programming, Domain-Specific Languages, Dynamic Optimizations

1. Introduction

Current industry trends favor chip multiprocessors consisting of simpler cores[18, 28] as well as heterogeneous systems consisting of general-purpose processors, SIMD units and accelerator devices such as GPUs[4, 30]. Existing applications can no longer take advantage of the additional compute power available in these new and emerging systems without a significant parallel programming effort. Writing parallel programs, however, is not straightforward because in contrast to the familiar and standard *von Neumann* model for sequential programming, a variety of incompatible parallel pro-

gramming models are available, each with their own set of trade-offs. Emerging heterogeneous systems further complicate this challenge as each accelerator vendor usually provides a distinct driver API and programming model to interface with the device.

It is not realistic to expect the average programmer to deal with all this complexity. Moreover, exposing the programmer directly to the various models supported by each compute device will ultimately be detrimental to application portability, forward scalability and maintenance. As new system configurations emerge, applications will constantly need to be rewritten to take advantage of any new capabilities. It is essential to develop appropriate abstractions so that programmers can write high-level code and not worry about low-level details that negatively impact productivity. Thus, there is a need for parallel heterogeneous programming models that target average programmers who are not interested in becoming parallel/heterogeneous programming experts. This *mass market* parallel heterogeneous programming model should be driven by the following goals:

- **Productivity**: the application developer can, ideally, write programs without having to use any explicit parallel or heterogeneous constructs.

- **Performance**: the application should achieve good performance without sacrificing productivity. The system metric should be performance per man-hour.

- **Portability and Forward Scalability**: the application should leverage the varying amount of compute resources across different systems, both existing and emerging. The forward scalability goal manifests itself across two dimensions: the number of a particular compute resource and the diversity of compute resource types.

There has been a resurgence in research aimed at simplifying parallel programming [9] and delivering on these goals. This paper describes key elements of an ongoing effort to create a development environment that uses a domain-specific approach to solve the issues relating to heterogeneous parallelism. The components of this environment are shown in Figure 1. The environment consists of four main components: applications composed of multiple domain-specific languages (DSLs), DSLs embedded in the Scala programming language [2], a Scala-based framework that simplifies the parallelization of DSLs and a runtime for DSL parallelization and mapping to heterogeneous architectures.

A domain-specific approach to parallel programming can address all of the goals of a *mass market* parallel heterogeneous programming model. A domain-specific language is a computer programming language of restricted expressiveness focused on a particular domain[34]. DSLs are in widespread use in a variety of domains and are becoming more popular. Examples of widely used DSLs are TeX and LaTeX for typesetting academic papers, SQL

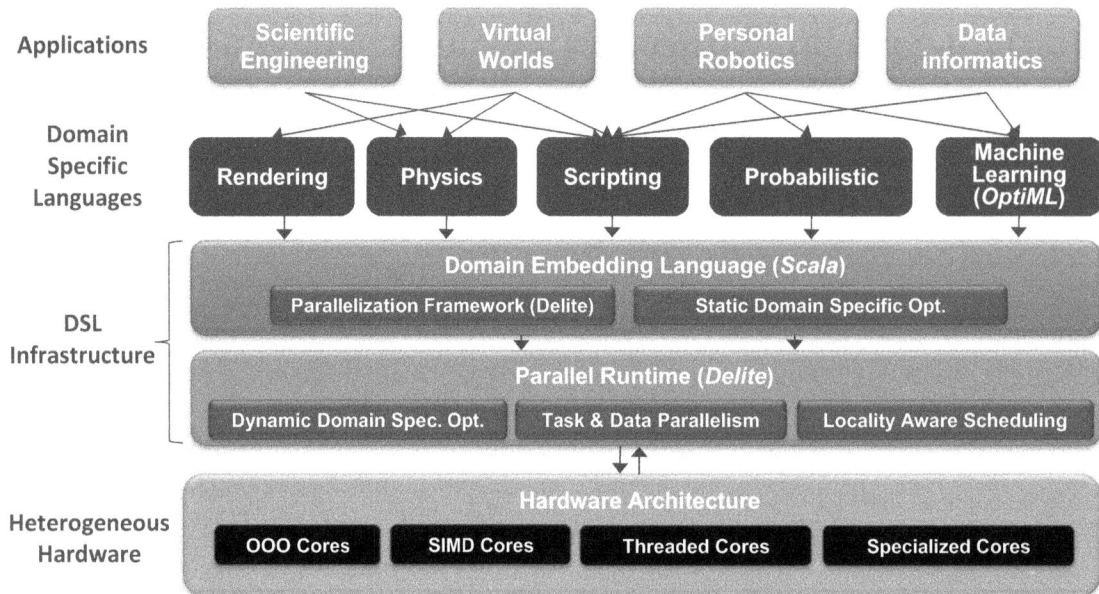

Figure 1: An environment for domain-specific programming of heterogeneous parallel architectures.

for database querying, Rails for web application development and VHDL for hardware design. OpenGL can also be viewed as a DSL. By exposing an interface for specifying polygons and the rules to shade them, OpenGL created a high-level programming model for real-time graphics decoupled from the hardware or software used to render it, allowing for aggressive performance gains as graphics hardware evolves. The use of DSLs can provide significant gains in the productivity and creativity of application developers, the portability of applications, and application performance. We exploit this trend towards DSLs and propose an approach to parallel heterogeneous programming that hides the complexity of the underlying machine behind a collection of DSLs. A programmer using one or more of these DSLs writes her programs using domain-specific notation and constructs. The programs appear sequential and all parallelism and use of the heterogeneous machine resources is implicit. DSLs raise the level of abstraction and can provide a sequential model which satisfies the *productivity* goal.

An additional benefit of using a domain-specific approach is the ability to use domain knowledge to apply static and dynamic optimizations to a program written using a DSL. Most of these domain-specific optimizations would not be possible if the program was written in a general-purpose language. General-purpose languages are limited when it comes to optimization for at least two reasons. First, they must produce correct code across a very wide range of applications. This makes it difficult to apply aggressive optimizations. Compiler developers must err on the side of correctness. Second, because of the general-purpose nature needed to support a wide range of applications (e.g. financial, gaming, image processing, etc.), compilers can usually infer little about the structure of the data or the nature of the algorithms the code is using. DSLs on the other hand, with their expressive power and knowledge of the domain's data structures and algorithms make such optimizations feasible. This makes DSLs a good choice to deliver on our *performance* goal. In order to validate this approach, we are developing multiple DSLs that span a variety of domains. In this paper, we present OptiML, a DSL aimed at machine learning. We provide an overview of OptiML in Section 2.

Since interesting applications might leverage a variety of DSLs, it is critical to not only simplify the development of DSLs by creating a shared infrastructure, but also to allow these DSLs to interoperate. Our current approach is to embed these DSLs in a common embedding language. Scala, our choice for the embedding language, provides features that simplify this task [10, 16]. This approach should be applicable to any sufficiently expressive embedding language.

The ability to easily embed DSLs simplifies the task of a DSL developer. However, assistance in parallelizing and targeting heterogeneous resources is also needed. Delite, our framework and runtime for building and executing parallel DSLs provides facilities that allow DSL developers to easily parallelize their DSLs. Using Delite, a DSL developer implicitly exposes task level parallelism by enabling a run-ahead model, similar to recent proposals [13, 19], across each invocation of the DSL's operations. Delite also allows the developer to express data-level parallelism available within DSL operations. Using such a runtime allows us to deliver on our *portability and forward scalability* goal. We provide details of the Delite framework and runtime in Section 3. Our specific contributions are:

- We present OptiML, a DSL for machine learning, which provides implicitly parallel domain-specific abstractions. We show that such a DSL can be used to simplify programming heterogeneous parallel systems.

- We show how domain knowledge can aid in extracting implicit parallelism, and demonstrate the benefits of using domain-specific optimizations to further enhance the performance of some machine learning applications.

- We introduce Delite, a framework and runtime to simplify building and executing implicitly parallel DSLs. We show how we use Delite to implement and parallelize OptiML.

- We provide experimental results demonstrating the benefits of using DSLs as a means of simplifying heterogeneous parallel programming. We demonstrate that in most cases, OptiML running on Delite outperforms explicitly parallelized MATLAB code on a set of common machine learning applications executing on a combination of CMP and GPU resources.

2. OptiML: A DSL for Machine Learning

In this section, we introduce a DSL written using Delite that will serve as a running example for the rest of this paper. OptiML is a DSL for machine learning, a popular and growing domain. Machine learning (ML) is generally concerned with learning patterns from data and applying the learned models to tasks such as regression, classification, clustering, and estimation. ML is a particularly good domain for studying parallelism: it is at the core of several emerging applications (e.g. collaborative filtering, object recognition), it contains applications and datasets that are time-bound in practice, and it has both regular and irregular parallelism at varying granularity.

Most machine learning kernels use linear algebra operations and prominently feature vectors and matrices. MATLAB is one of the most commonly used languages for ML applications and incorporates some of the same features that make a DSL appealing. MATLAB increases productivity by providing an easy syntax for manipulating and using vectors and matrices, and improves performance by providing fast, optimized implementations of linear algebra operations and common algorithms. While it is effective as a language for linear algebra, it is intended to be general and applicable across many application domains. By using a DSL specifically targeted at machine learning, it is possible to capture higher level information that can be used to increase productivity, improve performance, and expose more parallelism.

To accomplish these goals, OptiML exploits the following key aspects of machine learning:

- Many algorithms are iterative and/or solve constrained optimization problems. These algorithms have kernels with a fixed structure that are executed repeatedly many times.

- Most applications operate on large datasets, and many of these datasets contain significant redundancy (e.g. network traffic traces). This implies that some data points in a training set may not always be essential.

- Many algorithms are probabilistic and can acceptably trade-off accuracy for performance.

- Kernels contain large amounts of data parallelism at varying granularity.

- Most algorithms are limited by low arithmetic intensity and therefore memory bandwidth. Most accesses are either streaming (disjoint) or reductions.

Figure 2 shows a side-by-side comparison of a simple ML application written in OptiML and MATLAB. Since most machine learning users are already familiar with MATLAB, OptiML uses MATLAB-like syntax and compares favorably in terms of conciseness and productivity. OptiML inherits Scala's static type safety and type inference, as well as its tooling and IDE support. OptiML is optimized to perform well inside a JVM environment in a way that is transparent to the user; extreme care is taken to avoid boxing of primitives and patterns that reduce the effectiveness of JIT optimizations. Furthermore, the DSL includes native versions of heavyweight operations (e.g. matrix multiplication) that use JNI to call an underlying BLAS wrapper. In addition to fast sequential performance, Section 4 shows that OptiML can provide parallel performance comparable to or better than equivalent MATLAB implementations. While OptiML programs can achieve good performance with a simple imperative style, MATLAB programs usually require explicit vectorization or parallelization to achieve the best performance. This problem is compounded by the fact that usually either vectorization or parallelization must be chosen, and the trade-off between them is not obvious.

OptiML is implemented as an embedded DSL within Scala. The current version consists of a compiler plugin and a library. The compiler plugin allows OptiML to support user-supplied anonymous functions as parameters to operations. If an anonymous function depends on or mutates another data structure, this dependency must be registered with the runtime. The compiler plugin inspects closures inside OptiML applications and extracts dependencies, wrapping them in an object that is dynamically passed on to the runtime. The plugin can also statically check that OptiML programs obey the restricted semantics of its control structures, described later.

The library provides implementations of implicitly parallel ML-specific data and control structures. OptiML programs operate on the high-level mutable types `Vector[T]` and `Matrix[T]`, regardless of their underlying implementation (array-based, views, sparse, etc.). OptiML also provides data types that encode semantic information, such as `TrainingSet`, `TestSet`, `Image`, `IndexVector`, etc. Most of these structures are wrappers around matrices or vectors, but their use allows the DSL to identify additional parallelization or optimization opportunities. For example, most applications operate on training sets in a streaming fashion, and training sets are usually very large. OptiML can exploit this information when deciding whether an operation is worth parallelizing or shipping to a heterogeneous device such as a GPU. These domain-informed decisions are communicated to the Delite runtime using the interfaces described in Section 3.3.2. Although not currently supported, future versions of OptiML will have direct support for irregular structures that occur in ML, such as graphs.

In addition to these data structures, OptiML provides concise and flexible control structures. OptiML's control structures hide implementation details and expose coarse-grained parallelism inside applications. Although most operations in OptiML can be executed in parallel, this often results in fine-grained parallelism that does not scale well (e.g. vector addition). These domain specific control abstractions allow intuitive application code that is already decomposed into scalable operations. OptiML can dynamically check the size of the operation (e.g. the number and type of elements being summed) to determine whether it should submit a sequential or parallel operation to Delite. A summary of supported control structures is provided in the pseudocode snippets of Listing 1.

```
1   // sum: implemented as a parallel tree-reduce
2   val ans = sum(begin, end){ i =>
3     <ith value to sum>   }
4
5   // vector construction: implemented as a parallel map
6   val my_vector = (0::end) { i =>
7     <ith value of my_vector>   }
8
9   // untilconverged: implemented sequentially, but can
10  // be parallelized dynamically using optimizations
11  untilconverged(x, threshold) { x =>
12    <new value of x>   }
13
14  // gradient descent: implemented sequentially using
15  // stochastic, or in parallel using batch g.d.
16  gradient(trainingSet, alpha, threshold) {
17    <hypothesis function, takes a training sample and
18     returns a scalar>   }
```

Listing 1: Pseudocode snippets demonstrating OptiML control structures.

The control structures listed here support efficient parallelism in our current set of example applications. Two of these structures, sum{...} and (0::end){...} employ restricted semantics that

```
1   // x : TrainingSet[Double]
2
3   val m = x.numRows
4   val n = x.numCols
5
6   val (y_zeros, y_ones, mu0_num, mu1_num) = sum(0,m) { i =>
7     if (x.labels(i) == false) {
8       (1, 0, x(i), 0)
9     else {
10       (0, 1, 0, x(i))
11     }
12   }
13
14  val phi = 1./m * y_ones
15  val mu0 = mu0_num / y_zeros
16  val mu1 = mu1_num / y_ones
17
18  val sigma = sum(0,m) { i =>
19    if (x.labels(i) == false) {
20      ((x(i)-mu0).trans).outer(x(i)-mu0)
21    }
22    else {
23      ((x(i)-mu1).trans).outer(x(i)-mu1)
24    }
25  }
```

(a) OptiML code

```
1   % x: Matrix
2   % y: Vector
3
4   m = length(y);
5   n = size(x, 2);
6   y_ones = 0;
7   y_zeros = 0;
8   mu0_num = zeros(1,n);
9   mu1_num = zeros(1,n);
10
11  for i=1:m
12    if (y(i) == 0)
13      y_zeros = y_zeros + 1;
14      mu0_num = mu0_num + x(i,:);
15    else
16      y_ones = y_ones + 1;
17      mu1_num = mu1_num + x(i,:);
18    end
19  end
20
21  phi = 1/m * y_ones;
22  mu0 = mu0_num / y_zeros;
23  mu1 = mu1_num / y_ones;
24
25  sigma = zeros(n, n);
26  for i=1:m
27    if (y(i) == 0)
28      sigma = sigma + (x(i,:)-mu0)'*(x(i,:)-mu0);
29    else
30      sigma = sigma + (x(i,:)-mu1)'*(x(i,:)-mu1);
31    end
32  end
```

(b) MATLAB code

Figure 2: Side-by-side comparison of OptiML and MATLAB code for Gaussian Discriminant Analysis (GDA).

benefit parallelism; all accesses inside their closures must be disjoint (i.e. only access the ith element of any data structure). This allows them to be trivially parallelized using chunking and for locality to be preserved within the chunks. Because this corresponds to the great majority of ML use-cases, we have not found this restriction to be unduly constraining. A general-purpose language or compiler might provide constructs with similar restrictions (e.g. *parfor*), but cannot provide practical guidance on when to use them or require that they be used.

Finally, OptiML currently supports two dynamic, domain-specific optimizations. We evaluate the benefit of these optimizations in Section 4. We briefly describe them below:

- **Relaxed Dependencies:** in some iterative applications, there is limited data parallelism. However, when the algorithm is robust to minor perturbations, dependencies can be relaxed to provide more task parallelism at the cost of a marginal loss in accuracy. OptiML supports a run-time configurable relaxation percentage. *untilconverged* is an example of a relaxable operation; if it is relaxed, some number of iterations are allowed to run in parallel and intentionally race. OptiML relaxes operations by not registering the dependency with Delite.

- **Best Effort Computations:** in the same vein as relaxed dependencies, it is not strictly necessary to execute every computation to achieve acceptable results in ML. To exploit this, OptiML provides data structures with "best effort" semantics. The semantics are defined in the DSL by various policies that the DSL user can choose from. This optimization can reduce total execution time and sequential overhead in some applications, resulting in better single-threaded performance as well as scaling.

We are developing a prototype version of OptiML using polymorphic embedding with Scala[10]. Polymorphic embedding allows a library to directly analyze and transform programs written using the library. This will remove the need for a compiler plugin and allow future versions of OptiML to perform static optimizations as well.

3. Delite: A Framework for Parallelizing DSLs

Constructing a new DSL is a difficult process in general. Delite significantly simplifies this process by providing a shared framework and runtime to implement and execute implicitly parallel DSLs. Each DSL that utilizes the Delite framework inherits the Delite execution model which provides the capability of executing on heterogeneous hardware.

3.1 A deferred execution model

Delite's execution model enables implicit parallelization of applications by providing facilities for deferral of method execution. Each method invocation can be packaged as a Delite op and submitted to the Delite runtime. Ops encode their immediate dependencies which allows the runtime to build a dynamic execution graph.

To illustrate the steps in execution, consider the simple application code snippet written using OptiML shown in Figure 3. The application thread executes sequentially (Figure 3a). However, each call to the *plus* and *times* methods returns immediately after submitting its op to the runtime. These ops encode any dependencies on other data objects. A Matrix proxy (this object implements the Matrix interface but has no valid data elements) is returned as the result of the method invocation (Figure 3b). The application is oblivious to the fact that computation is deferred and "runs-ahead" allowing more ops to be submitted. The submitted ops form a dynamic task graph (Figure 3c). Given a program's task graph, the runtime system is able to target a variety of parallel architectures automatically (Figure 3d). Independent parts of the task graph are scheduled to run in parallel and data movement is minimized with a

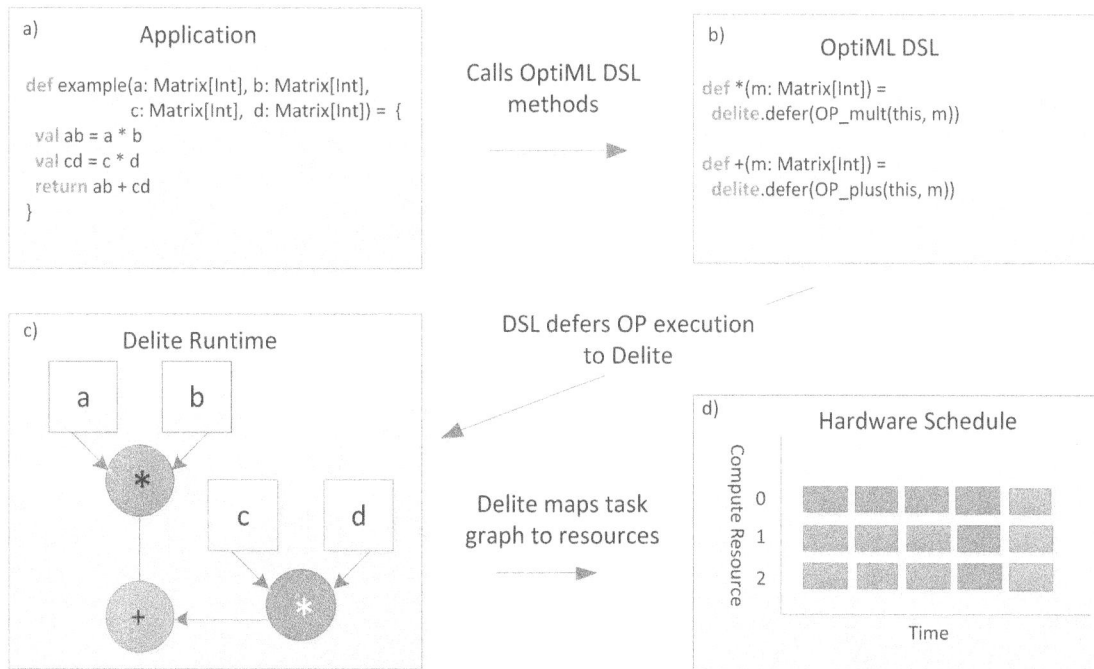

Figure 3: Delite application execution overview.

scheduling algorithm that takes communication costs into account. Therefore, Delite automatically provides implicit task parallelism for each DSL at the operation granularity that the DSL defines. Furthermore, data-parallel tasks can be further decomposed into multiple independent tasks yielding more parallelism.

Each Delite op returns a proxy, which unlike most implementations of futures, is *transparent* to the caller. The proxy has the same return type as a concrete result, and can be used interchangeably with other proxies and concrete instances. This allows a DSL user to write code that is oblivious to the underlying execution model. Figure 4 shows the Delite class diagram for the Vector object in the OptiML DSL. A Scala `trait` is similar to a Java interface. Here, `Vector[T]` is the only type the DSL user interacts with. In this example the data reference in `VectorImpl` will initially be null upon creation and the VectorImpl object acts as a proxy. Once the op responsible for the creation of the proxy completes execution, the VectorImpl object acts as a concrete instance with its data reference set to the concrete array containing the result. The force method inherited by Vector and all other DSL types enforces synchronization when required, preventing data from being accessed before it exists. If a proxy result is required (e.g. due to a control dependency) but is not yet ready, the proxy is implicitly forced to execute and return a concrete result.

3.2 A framework for creating implicitly parallel DSLs

Delite allows DSL authors to integrate a DSL into the Delite runtime by providing a framework of extendable types and interfaces, the most important of which are the Delite op archetypes.

3.2.1 Delite ops

When defining a Delite op, the DSL author specifies its dependencies and the return type of the proxy. Listing 2 shows how a simple op can be written to subtract two vectors. Its input arguments, v1 and v2 (which may themselves be proxies), are added as dependency edges on the task graph when this op is submitted to the runtime. Although this op can be written in a data-parallel man-

```
1  protected[optiml] case class OP_-[A]
2    (v1: Vector[A], v2: Vector[A])
3    extends DeliteOP_SingleTask[Vector[A]](v1,v2) {
4
5    def task = {
6      if (v1.length != v2.length)
7        throw new IndexOutOfBoundsException
8      val result = Vector[A](v1.length)
9      for (k <- 0 until v1.length){
10       result(k) = v1(k) - v2(k)
11     }
12     result
13   }
14 }
```

Listing 2: An example sequential op in the OptiML DSL.

ner, for this example we use a simple sequential implementation by extending `DeliteOP_SingleTask`. This type can be used for any sequential task and requires only a *task* method, which will be invoked by Delite when the op is executed. Data-parallel ops have a richer interface that simplifies data decomposition and parallel execution; these are described in Section 3.2.2.

The DSL author is free to package work into Delite ops however he or she deems best. So far we've focused on how a method call can be naturally translated into an op, but there are other possibilities. The *sum* control structure in OptiML creates two Delite ops, one to generate all the temporary results and another to perform the final summation.

3.2.2 Data-parallel operations

Delite exposes data-parallelism by providing support for various data decomposition patterns. The framework provides data-parallel op archetypes as classes that can be extended. Some of the currently supported archetypes include `op_map`, `op_reduce` and `op_zipWith`. Each op operates on a `DeliteCollection`, which is a `trait` that each collection-based DSL type implements. This

39

```
┌─────────────────────────────────────┐
│    trait DeliteDSLType[T]            │
├─────────────────────────────────────┤
│ final def force: T = { ... }         │
└─────────────────────────────────────┘
                  ▲
┌─────────────────────────────────────┐
│    trait DeliteCollection[T]         │
├─────────────────────────────────────┤
│ def size: Int                        │
│ def chunk(start: Int,                │
│           end: Int) : Iterator[T]    │
│ def dc_apply(n: Int) : T             │
│ def dc_update(n: Int, x: T)          │
└─────────────────────────────────────┘
                  ▲
┌─────────────────────────────────────┐
│    trait GPUableCollection[T]        │
├─────────────────────────────────────┤
│ def gpu_data: Array[T]               │
│ var shipToGPU: Boolean = true        │
└─────────────────────────────────────┘
                  ▲
┌─────────────────────────────────────┐
│    trait Vector[T]                   │
├─────────────────────────────────────┤
│ def length: Int                      │
│ def size = length                    │
│ def +(v: Vector[T]) =                │
│   delite.defer(OP_plus(this, v))     │
│ def *(v: Vector[T]) =                │
│   delite.defer(OP_times(this, v))    │
└─────────────────────────────────────┘
                  ▲
┌─────────────────────────────────────┐
│    class VectorImpl[T]               │
├─────────────────────────────────────┤
│ var data: Array[T] = null            │
│ def length = data.length             │
│ def gpu_data = data                  │
│ def dc_apply(n: Int) = data(n)       │
│ def dc_update(n: Int, x: T) {        │
│   data(n) = x                        │
│ }                                    │
└─────────────────────────────────────┘
```

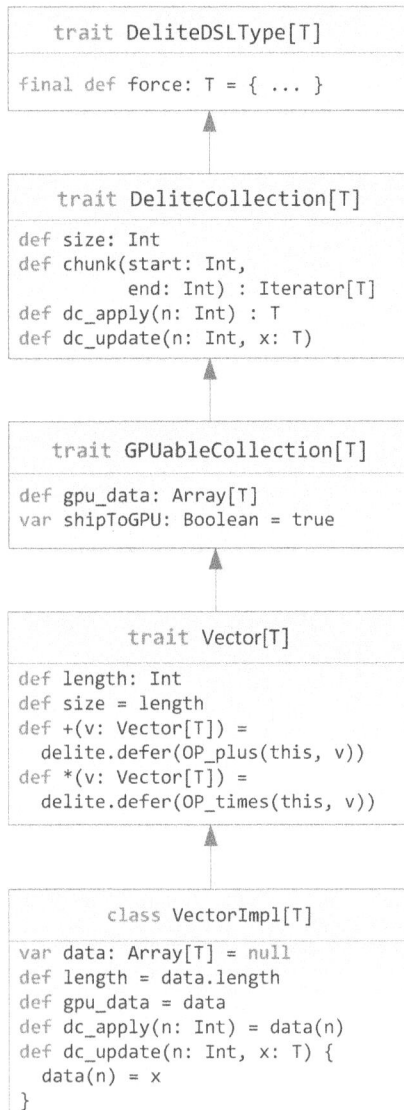

Figure 4: Class diagram of the OptiML Vector class.

```
16  protected[optiml] case class OP_-[A]
17    (val collA: Vector[A], val collB: Vector[A],
18     val out: Vector[A])
19    extends DeliteOP_ZipWith2[A,A,A,Vector] {
20
21    def func = (a,b) => a - b
22  }
```

Listing 3: An example data-parallel op in the OptiML DSL.

trait and its implementation for OptiML's Vector is shown in Figure 4. The DSL author provides data-parallel ops by extending one of the archetypes in a very similar manner as a sequential task. In the data-parallel case, however, rather than providing the task to be executed, the DSL author simply provides the function to be performed. Listing 3 shows how the same subtraction op from Listing 2 can be written to obtain automated data-parallel execution.

Delite is responsible for sizing and scheduling the chunks of a DeliteCollection, allowing the runtime to adapt the needs of the application to the available resources in the system. DeliteCollection provides Delite with a flat, uniform interface to the elements of arbitrary data structures. This allows the DSL author to encode domain-specific decompositions. Specifically, the DSL author must implement a *size* and *chunk* method for the collection. As the name implies, *size* is the total number of elements of the collection. *chunk* takes two indices and returns an iterator over the requested range. The DSL author is free to construct the iterator in any way, and can therefore optimize the decomposition for locality without Delite knowing anything about the underlying data structure. For array-based collections, Delite maximizes performance by iterating over the array elements directly utilizing flat read and write methods (*dc_apply* and *dc_update*) that the DSL author implements. In addition, primitive array-based collections can choose to implement the GPUableCollection interface which allows Delite to manage shipping the op's corresponding CUDA kernel to the GPU. The details of Delite's GPU support are discussed in Section 3.3.2. All data-parallel ops in Delite maintain the illusion of atomic execution, so the DSL author does not need to worry about the case of a partially complete data-parallel operation.

3.2.3 Handling side effects

In the preceding discussion of the Delite execution model we have implicitly assumed all ops are functionally pure (side-effect free). However, Delite also allows ops that mutate the state of DSL objects. Delite deals with the possibility of side effects and potential race conditions by restricting, tracking and isolating mutating operations. First, ops are restricted to only mutate the state of DSL objects. This restriction combined with the fact that all op inputs are either primitives (immutable) or DSL objects prevents data consumed by ops to be mutated arbitrarily. Next, any op that mutates data or has side effects must explicitly declare the object(s) it is going to mutate. The DSL author provides this information using the op interface in essentially the same way as declaring inputs. Finally, using these declarations Delite adds the anti-dependencies created by these mutating ops as it builds up the task graph and enforces sequential correctness at execution time by honoring these additional edges in the task graph. This mechanism allows Delite to support fast, mutating ops and avoid costly copy-by-value operations.

3.2.4 Assisting GPU code generation

In order for the Delite runtime to target a GPU device automatically, the DSL must provide a corresponding CUDA kernel for each op that the DSL wants to be shipped to the GPU. In the case of regular operations this task is simplified by automatic code generation from Scala code to CUDA code. This is feasible due to restricted semantics: the op must use disjoint memory accesses that allow it to be transformed into a data-parallel operation in a straightforward way. The DSL author can mark each op for which he or she wishes Delite to generate a CUDA kernel using the @GPU annotation. A compiler plugin is then used to map the regular Scala code to CUDA. For ops that are irregular or benefit greatly from hand optimization, the DSL author must provide an appropriate CUDA kernel.

3.3 A heterogeneous parallel runtime

We now turn our attention to how Delite executes ops on heterogeneous parallel hardware. The current version of Delite supports execution on multiple CPUs and a GPU in a single machine. We plan to expand to supporting clusters in the near future as well as other accelerators as they become available.

3.3.1 Scheduling

Delite schedules ops to run from the window of currently deferred ops, honoring the dependencies and anti-dependencies present in the task graph. Ops are scheduled using a low-cost clustering heuristic in order to minimize communication costs among ops as well as scheduling overhead. Data-parallel ops are submitted to the runtime as a single op and later split into the desired number of op chunks. The number of chunks is chosen at scheduling time based on the size of the collection and the availability of hardware resources in the system. When scheduling op chunks, the locality concern of the scheduler is modified to consider the dependencies among individual chunks of the op input and output data structures rather than the objects as a whole. Scheduled ops are enqueued to run on the selected resource and perform a final safety check immediately before executing to ensure all dependencies and anti-dependencies have been satisfied at that time.

3.3.2 Supporting GPU execution

Unlike other environments such as MATLAB which require non-trivial user effort to explicitly mark operations and data structures that should be shipped to the GPU, Delite schedules onto CPU and GPU resources in a way that is completely transparent to the user, allowing a single version of the application source code to target either execution environment. The DSL author determines which ops are appropriate for the GPU and implements an additional interface that allows Delite to manage shipping the op to the GPU. The DSL author provides a CUDA kernel for each op as described in Section 3.2.4. The interface also allows the DSL author to disable GPU execution of the op when desired (e.g., when the dataset is very small). The GPU manager can override this hint when locality concerns dictate that poor computation performance is preferable to high communication cost.

In order to support automated GPU execution, Delite implements a memory manager for each GPU device in addition to all the facilities it provides for CPU execution. The entire main memory of the device is pre-allocated at startup and then managed as a cache by Delite at run-time. When ops are scheduled for execution onto the GPU, Delite ships the corresponding CUDA kernel to the GPU device and automatically injects the required memory transfers if all of the op's inputs are not currently in the device cache. All data transferred to the device remains there for reuse until the CPU requires a result. Ops that merely produce temporary results may never return data back to the CPU. This optimization fits naturally into our model of DSL objects that only contain valid data upon requirement. When data created by or mutated by the GPU is required by the CPU, the GPU memory manager automatically transfers the appropriate data back to the CPU main memory. Finally, if the CPU performs a mutating operation the GPU cache copy (if one exists) is invalidated.

4. Experimental Analysis

In this section, we present performance results for a set of machine learning applications written in OptiML and running on Delite. Each application is written without any explicit parallelization. We compare our results to reference implementations written in MATLAB, including GPU implementations that use either MATLAB 7.11's beta support or AccelerEyes's Jacket [3]. We also show how each application scales on a highly threaded system and analyze what limits the application's scalability. We conclude by showing the impact of the domain-specific optimizations described in Section 2 on performance.

4.1 Methodology

We implemented four versions of each application: an OptiML version, a MATLAB version, a MATLAB version using MATLAB 7.11's GPU constructs, and a MATLAB version using Jacket's GPU constructs. We use the same OptiML application code to run on multiple CPUs or on a combination of CPU+GPU; we use a run-time configuration option to enable or disable shipping OptiML ops that have corresponding GPU kernels to the GPU device. The MATLAB versions are algorithmically identical to the OptiML versions, but we make a reasonable effort to vectorize and parallelize the MATLAB code. For MATLAB parallelization, we used the parallel computing toolbox (specifically the *parfor* construct). When both vectorization and parallelization are possible for a particular loop, we choose whichever method yields the fastest running time at the highest processor count. For the GPU version of the MATLAB applications, we offloaded all GPU-supported operations that were computationally intensive. Jacket supports more operations than MATLAB, such as matrix and vector indexing, and we took advantage of those.

We present results on two machines with significantly different characteristics. The performance and optimization experiments are run on a Dell Precision T7500n with two quad-core Intel Xeon X5550 2.67 GHz processors. Each core has 2-way hyperthreading for a total of 16 hardware thread contexts. It has 24GB of RAM and an NVIDIA GTX 275 GPU. This system is representative of currently available high performance client machines. The scalability experiments are run on a Sun UltraSPARC T2+ with four 8-core 1.16 GHz processors. Each core has 8-way multithreading for a total of 256 hardware threads. It has 128 GB of RAM. Although the T2+'s single-threaded performance is much slower than the X5550's, its large number of hardware threads and greater memory bandwidth make it much more suited for studying scalability at high thread counts.

We ran our experiments using Sun's Java SE Runtime Environment 1.6.0_16-b01 and the HotSpot 64-bit server VM with default options. For each experiment we time the computation part of the application, ignoring initialization steps. We run each application, including initialization steps, 10 times to warm up the JIT and smooth out fluctuations due to GC. We report the average time of the last five executions. Table 1 presents the applications used in our study. These applications all come from the machine learning domain.

4.2 Performance comparison

We begin by comparing the performance of the various versions of our machine learning applications running on the Intel-based system. The results of this experiment are shown in Figure 5. The figure shows execution time normalized to the OptiML version running in sequential mode without any Delite overheads (OptiML ops are not deferred in this case, but instead are executed as they are encountered). We discuss issues relating to the scalability of each application in the next subsection. Single-threaded performance of the OptiML version of our applications is better than MATLAB in most cases. The MATLAB parallel constructs use MPI, which adds significant overhead. To measure the impact of these parallel overheads on single-threaded performance, we have written and run sequential MATLAB versions of our applications and found that OptiML, including Delite overheads, matches or exceeds sequential MATLAB performance. Although MATLAB scripts are interpreted, linear algebra operations utilize native BLAS libraries under the hood. Therefore in applications that are largely composed of matrix and vector operations, such as RBM, the single-threaded MATLAB version performed comparably to a C implementation also calling BLAS functions as well as to the OptiML implementation. Applications requiring more loops, conditionals, and pointer

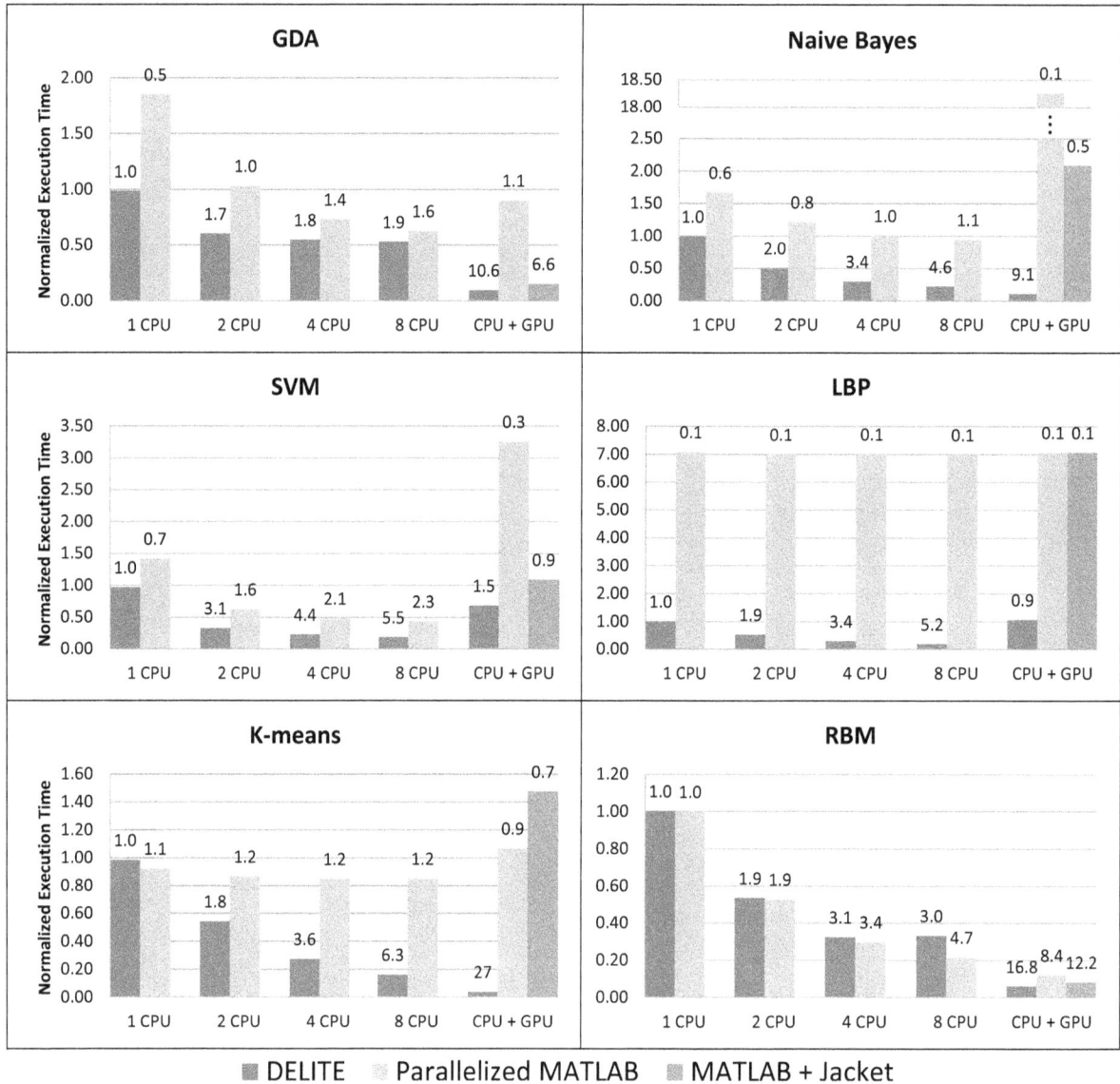

GDA

Naive Bayes

SVM

LBP

K-means

RBM

■ DELITE   ▨ Parallelized MATLAB   ▨ MATLAB + Jacket

Figure 5: Execution time of the various versions of our applications normalized to OptiML running in sequential mode. Speedup numbers are reported on top of each bar.

chasing, such as LBP, exhibited worse single-threaded performance in MATLAB compared to OptiML largely due to interpretive overheads.

In all applications except for RBM, OptiML outperforms the explicitly parallelized MATLAB versions. RBM has several fine-grained vector operations for which MATLAB uses highly optimized BLAS implementations. We are adding support for more fine-grained BLAS implementations within OptiML to close the gap. The parallel MATLAB version of k-means exhibited poor performance at all thread counts, so we opted to use a vectorized version instead. This is an example of the difficult and unclear trade-offs required to get scalable performance with MATLAB. LBP is an example of an application that is not well-suited to MATLAB. One possible implementation that exploits parallelism required a great degree of pointer indirection which is slow in MATLAB. Our chosen implementation removes pointer indirection by storing messages in a single shared array. This yields better performance but

eliminates the ability to parallelize the application safely using *par-for*.

We now compare the performance of our applications running on a combination of CPU and GPU resources. GDA and RBM achieve good speedups compared to the CPU-only version. This is due to two factors: first, these applications do not require frequent synchronization between the CPU and GPU. Second, they use large matrices with regular memory access patterns. SVM is similar except that the CPU and GPU must exchange data on every iteration of the convergence loop, resulting in significantly worse performance. The Delite GPU manager (with input from the DSL) dynamically determines which ops should be shipped to the GPU to maximize the overall performance. This determination is at the granularity of individual operations. This results in improved performance by avoiding the overhead of executing small kernels on the GPU. In contrast, the MATLAB and Jacket GPU implementations require the application to explicitly specify which data struc-

NAME	DESCRIPTION	PERFORMANCE COMPARISON INPUT	SCALABILITY TEST INPUT
Gaussian Discriminant Analysis (GDA)	Generative learning algorithm for modeling the probability distribution of a set of data as a multivariate Gaussian	1,200x1,024 matrix	1,200x512 matrix
Loopy Belief Propagation (LBP)	Graph-based inference algorithm using message-passing	23,768 edges 3,630 nodes	23,768 edges 3,630 nodes
Naive Bayes (NB)	Fast, low-work supervised learning algorithm for classification	25,000x1,448 matrix	12,000x1,448 matrix
K-means Clustering (K-means)	Unsupervised learning algorithm for finding similar clusters in a dataset	262,144x3 matrix	25,000x100 matrix
Support Vector Machine (SVM)	Optimal margin classifier, implemented using the Sequential Minimal Optimization (SMO) algorithm	800x1,448 matrix	800x1,448 matrix
Restricted Boltzmann Machine (RBM)	Stochastic recurrent neural network, without connections between hidden units	2,000 Hidden Units 2,000 Dimensions	2,000 Hidden Units 2,000 Dimensions

Table 1: Applications used for experimental analysis.

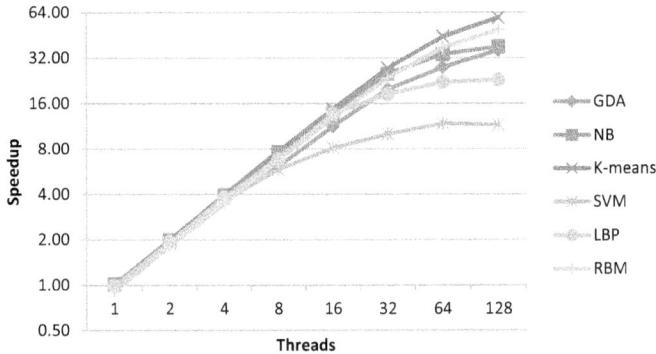

Figure 6: Scalability of our selected OptiML applications running in a highly threaded system. Speedup is measured relative to OptiML running in sequential mode.

tures reside on the GPU; all subsequent operations on GPU data structures must occur on the GPU. NB and k-means contain loops with regular memory access patterns that can easily be translated to CUDA kernels. This results in substantially improved performance over the MATLAB implementations, which only ship individual MATLAB operations. Finally, LBP is a low dimensional, highly irregular graph algorithm and is not easily mapped to GPUs.

4.3 Scalability study

Figure 6 shows the result of running our OptiML applications in a highly threaded environment. The UltraSPARC T2+ has a total of 64 integer ALUs and 32 floating point units. Hence, most of the applications are limited to a maximum speedup of around 64. Most applications also suffer from low arithmetic intensity, which as we noted earlier is a characteristic of the machine learning domain, leading to sub-linear speedups. We next look at what limits each application's scalability in detail:

Gaussian Discriminant Analysis (GDA): GDA scaling is limited in two ways. While algorithmically the program is both very parallel and regular, low arithmetic intensity causes the memory system to become a bottleneck. Additionally, the final reduction

phase in the application causes greater serial overhead at high thread counts.

Naive Bayes (NB): NB also suffers from low arithmetic intensity. It simply streams through a large dataset and collects some statistics. This amounts to very little computation and while we stream through chunks of the dataset in parallel, we are ultimately limited again by the memory system.

K-means Clustering: k-means, unlike many of our applications, has high arithmetic intensity. The algorithm is limited by the number of clusters and the dimensionality of the training data. We chose a representative dataset containing a large number of training samples and clusters which results in good scalability.

Loopy Belief Propagation (LBP): LBP is a graph-based algorithm characterized by irregular computation. Delite uses dynamically load-balanced tasks for the parallel work, which provides much better performance than a static schedule. However, LBP is limited by the fact that a single node in the graph can become a bottleneck if it has a significant portion of the total number of messages to be sent in an iteration.

Support Vector Machine (SVM): Our SVM implementation is a simplified version of a widely used algorithm called Sequential Minimal Optimization (SMO). SMO is an iterative algorithm with loop carried dependencies across iterations. Within each iteration, there is limited fine grained data-parallelism that does not scale well. Beyond 32 threads, SVM runs out of parallel work and is limited by Amdahl's law.

Restricted Boltzmann Machine (RBM): RBM is similar to SVM in that it is iterative with dependencies carried across iterations. However, each iteration is dominated by large matrix multiplications and thus RBM exhibits good scalability.

4.4 The benefit of domain-specific optimizations

In Section 2, we described two domain-specific optimizations that OptiML supports: best effort computation and relaxed dependencies. Figure 7 shows the improved performance that results from applying these optimizations to k-means and SVM. For k-means, we used a converging best effort policy that dropped distance calculations that were unchanged in the previous n iterations. We show results for three different values of n, each of which results in a different trade-off between performance and accuracy. The error we report is the average percentage difference in the final cluster locations. For this experiment, we clustered a 262144 pixel RGB image, and the best effort optimization drastically reduces computation time with only minor differences in the discovered clusters.

As we mentioned in the previous section, the SMO implementation of SVM has inter-loop dependencies that prevent parallelization across iterations. In this experiment, we used a smaller training set with less available data parallelism. However, we enabled the relax dependency optimization in OptiML, which allows two iterations to run in parallel inside the *untilconverged* implementation (note that no changes are required in the application code). This optimization is able to improve performance despite unprotected races to shared state because the algorithm is probabilistic and relatively robust to this kind of manipulation. The iterations frequently access disjoint parameters and SMO is ultimately able to complete faster with less than a 1% loss in classification accuracy.

5. Related Work

Delite builds upon a variety of previously published work in domain-specific languages and parallel programming:

Domain-specific languages and optimizations: A good starting point for those interested in domain-specific languages is an annotated bibliography by Deursen et al.[34]. Mernik et al.[26] propose a pattern-based framework to help with deciding whether or not to invest in developing a domain-specific language and how to

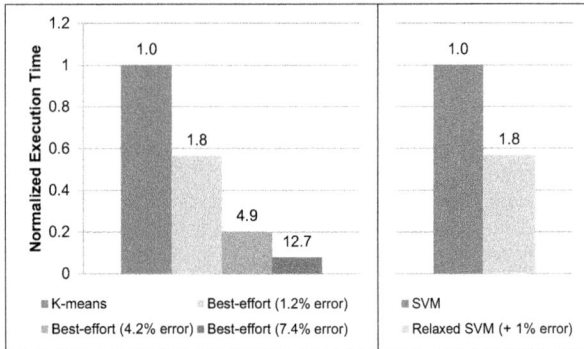

Figure 7: The impact of domain-specific optimizations on k-means and SVM at 8 threads. Execution time is normalized to the 8 thread version without optimization shown in Figure 5. Speedup numbers are reported on top of each bar.

go about doing so. We adopt DSLs mainly for the AVOPT pattern: domain specific analysis, verification, optimization, parallelization, and transformation. Frameworks for developing domain-specific languages have also been proposed[14, 21]. These frameworks mostly help authors develop external DSLs and provide tools that help in the construction and transformation of an abstract syntax tree. We adopt an approach similar to that presented by Hudak[17] and embed our DSLs directly into a host language. Previous work has also shown the benefit of using domain knowledge to enhance the performance of applications: Menon et al demonstrate the benefits of applying high level transformations to MATLAB code[25] and show performance gains in both interpreted and compiled code. Guyver et al[15] presents a mechanism for annotating library methods with domain-specific knowledge which yields significant improvement in performance. CodeBoost[5] allows for user-defined rules that are used to transform the program using domain knowledge. In contrast, Delite allows DSL developers to encode dynamic domain-specific optimizations.

Heterogeneous programming: There have been proposals to help programmers target heterogeneous systems. Some proposals such as EXOCHI[35] and OpenCL[32] provide abstractions that allow the programmer to explicitly manage and target any available accelerator. This approach reduces the ad hoc nature of directly using vendor drivers and APIs for each device. Merge[22] builds on top of EXOCHI by providing a framework for associating a kernel variant with a particular accelerator and shifting the responsibility of selecting the appropriate kernel to the runtime. These proposals however, are still too low level for a *mass market* programming model. Nevertheless, we believe that such proposals are extremely useful when used by the runtime to dispatch work to the different heterogeneous devices. Harmony[13], a recent proposal, reasons about the whole program by building a data dependency graph and then scheduling independent kernels to run in parallel. Harmony can also automatically select from different variants of each deferred kernel. However, Harmony does not apply any domain-specific transformations or perform automatic data-decomposition of the program kernels.

Data-parallel programming models and libraries: This approach to parallel programming hides the complexity of the underlying system by only exposing the programmer to a data-parallel API. Examples of this approach include RapidMind[23], PeakStream[29], and Accelerator[31]. These APIs mostly consist of vector and array primitives which map well to SIMD-based accelerators and work well for many algorithms. However, they are inadequate for parallel algorithms that are irregular and require

a more general task-based decomposition. Delite is informed by these previous proposals in the way it handles data-parallel ops. Dryad[19], a distributed execution engine for very coarse-grained data-parallel operations, targets clusters. Delite is similar in that it translates an application to an execution graph prior to mapping it to particular system configuration. Unlike Delite, Dryad applications need to explicitly construct this execution graph. DryadLINQ[20] attempts to overcome the complexity of execution graph construction and allows a programmer to write LINQ[24] programs that are automatically translated to a Dryad execution graph. In this case, LINQ could be considered as the DSL and Dryad as the runtime. Delite differentiates itself by adding facilities for authoring implicitly parallel DSLs, targets finer grained on-chip parallelism and exploits task parallelism.

Parallel programming languages: Parallel programming languages focus on two main categories: explicit and implicit parallelism. Explicitly parallel languages rely on the programmer to identify parallel work; notable examples include Parallel Haskell[33], Cilk[7], X10[12] and Chapel[11]. Requiring programmers to explicitly parallelize their code may have an adverse effect on the productivity goal, and it is often difficult to achieve scalable performance using explicit constructs. Languages that support implicit parallelization often rely on data-parallel operations on parallel collections. These include NESL[6], High Performance Fortran[1], X10 and Chapel. One could also argue that stream programming languages such as Brook[8] and to some extent CUDA[27] are data-parallel languages with streams being synonymous to a parallel collection of records. OptiML provides the same facilities, but uncovers coarse-grained parallelism using domain knowledge and adds implicit task parallelism through Delite.

6. Conclusion

With the increasing dominance of heterogeneous parallel systems, applications must be able to leverage parallelism to improve performance. To enable average application developers to exploit parallelism, a *mass market* parallel programming model should shield these developers from parallel programming complexity. To achieve this, we proposed a domain-specific approach to parallel programming that provides application developers with familiar, high-level semantics while still delivering high performance and scalability through implicit task and data parallelism. DSLs also allow domain-specific knowledge to be leveraged to optimize program execution and data decomposition. Finally, DSL methods are a convenient abstraction for targeting heterogeneous platforms since they can be translated to different target processing nodes.

As an example of this approach, we introduced OptiML, a DSL for machine learning. OptiML is built using Delite, a framework and runtime that simplifies developing implicitly parallel DSLs that target heterogeneous platforms. We demonstrated how domain knowledge can be used to extract parallelism and to optimize application code. We presented results showing that OptiML can outperform explicitly parallelized MATLAB on a set of common machine learning applications. Using a single version of application source code, running on a combination of CMP and GPU resources, OptiML exhibits robust speedups and scalability up to 59x on 128 threads. OptiML compares favorably to MATLAB, achieving average (geometric mean) performance improvements of 3.4x on 8 cores and 5.1x on GPU (MATLAB + Jacket).

7. Acknowledgments

This research was sponsored by the Department Of Energy (DOE) through Sandia order 942017, the Army under contract AHPCRC W911NF-07-2-0027-1 and the Defense Advanced Research Project Agency (DARPA) through Oracle order 630003198. The views and conclusions contained in this document are those of the authors and should not be interpreted as representing the official policies, either expressed or implied, of the Defense Advanced Research Projects Agency, the Department of Energy, the Army or the U.S. Government. Additional funding provided by the Stanford Pervasive Parallelism Laboratory affiliates program which is supported by NVIDIA, Oracle/Sun, AMD, and NEC.

References

[1] High Performance Fortran. http://hpff.rice.edu/index.htm.

[2] Scala. http://www.scala-lang.org.

[3] AccelerEyes. Jacket. http://www.accelereyes.com/products/jacket.

[4] AMD. The Industry-Changing Impact of Accelerated Computing. Website. http://sites.amd.com/us/Documents/AMD_fusion_Whitepaper.pdf.

[5] O.S. Bagge, K.T. Kalleberg, M. Haveraaen, and E. Visser. Design of the CodeBoost transformation system for domain-specific optimisation of C++ programs. In *Source Code Analysis and Manipulation, 2003. Proceedings. Third IEEE International Workshop on*, pages 65–74, Sept. 2003.

[6] Guy E. Blelloch. Programming parallel algorithms. *Commun. ACM*, 39(3):85–97, 1996.

[7] Robert D. Blumofe, Christopher F. Joerg, Bradley C. Kuszmaul, Charles E. Leiserson, Keith H. Randall, and Yuli Zhou. Cilk: an efficient multithreaded runtime system. In *PPOPP '95: Proceedings of the fifth ACM SIGPLAN symposium on Principles and practice of parallel programming*, pages 207–216, New York, NY, USA, 1995. ACM.

[8] Ian Buck, Tim Foley, Daniel Horn, Jeremy Sugerman, Kayvon Fatahalian, Mike Houston, and Pat Hanrahan. Brook for GPUs: Stream computing on graphics hardware. *ACM TRANSACTIONS ON GRAPHICS*, 23:777–786, 2004.

[9] Bryan C. Catanzaro, Armando Fox, Kurt Keutzer, David Patterson, Bor-Yiing Su, Marc Snir, Kunle Olukotun, Pat Hanrahan, and Hassan Chafi. Ubiquitous parallel computing from Berkeley, Illinois, and Stanford. *IEEE Micro*, 30(2):41–55, 2010.

[10] Hassan Chafi, Zach DeVito, Adrian Moors, Tiark Rompf, Arvind Sujeeth, Pat Hanrahan, Martin Odersky, and Kunle Olukotun. Language virtualization for heterogeneous parallel computing. In *Onward!*, 2010.

[11] B.L. Chamberlain, D. Callahan, and H.P. Zima. Parallel Programmability and the Chapel Language. *Int. J. High Perform. Comput. Appl.*, 21(3):291–312, 2007.

[12] Philippe Charles, Christian Grothoff, Vijay Saraswat, Christopher Donawa, Allan Kielstra, Kemal Ebcioglu, Christoph von Praun, and Vivek Sarkar. X10: an object-oriented approach to non-uniform cluster computing. *SIGPLAN Not.*, 40(10):519–538, 2005.

[13] Gregory F. Diamos and Sudhakar Yalamanchili. Harmony: an execution model and runtime for heterogeneous many core systems. In *HPDC '08: Proceedings of the 17th international symposium on High performance distributed computing*, pages 197–200, New York, NY, USA, 2008. ACM.

[14] Rickard E. Faith, Lars S. Nyland, and Jan F. Prins. Khepera: A system for rapid implementation of domain specific languages. In *In Proceedings USENIX Conference on Domain-Speci Languages*, pages 243–255, 1997.

[15] Samuel Z. Guyer and Calvin Lin. An annotation language for optimizing software libraries. In *PLAN '99: Proceedings of the 2nd conference on Domain-specific languages*, pages 39–52, New York, NY, USA, 1999. ACM.

[16] Klaus Havelund, Michel Ingham, and David Wagner. A case study in DSL development: An experiment with Python and Scala. In *The First Annual Scala Workshop at Scala Days 2010*, 2010.

[17] Paul Hudak. Building domain-specific embedded languages. *ACM Comput. Surv.*, page 196.

[18] Intel. From a Few Cores to Many: A Tera-scale Computing Research Review. Website. http://download.intel.com/research/platform/terascale/terascale_overview_paper.pdf.

[19] Michael Isard, Mihai Budiu, Yuan Yu, Andrew Birrell, and Dennis Fetterly. Dryad: distributed data-parallel programs from sequential building blocks. In *EuroSys '07: Proceedings of the 2nd ACM SIGOPS/EuroSys European Conference on Computer Systems 2007*, pages 59–72, New York, NY, USA, 2007. ACM.

[20] Michael Isard and Yuan Yu. Distributed data-parallel computing using a high-level programming language. In *SIGMOD '09: Proceedings of the 35th SIGMOD international conference on Management of data*, pages 987–994, New York, NY, USA, 2009. ACM.

[21] Ken Kennedy, Bradley Broom, Arun Chauhan, Rob Fowler, John Garvin, Charles Koelbel, Cheryl McCosh, and John Mellor-Crummey. Telescoping languages: A system for automatic generation of domain languages. *Proceedings of the IEEE*, 93(3):387–408, 2005. This provides a current overview of the entire Telescoping Languages Project.

[22] Michael D. Linderman, Jamison D. Collins, Hong Wang, and Teresa H. Meng. Merge: a programming model for heterogeneous multi-core systems. In *ASPLOS '08*, New York, NY, USA, 2008. ACM.

[23] Michael D. McCool, Kevin Wadleigh, Brent Henderson, and Hsin-Ying Lin. Performance evaluation of GPUs using the RapidMind development platform. In *SC '06: Proceedings of the 2006 ACM/IEEE conference on Supercomputing*, page 181, New York, NY, USA, 2006. ACM.

[24] Erik Meijer, Brian Beckman, and Gavin Bierman. LINQ: Reconciling object, relations and XML in the .NET framework. In *SIGMOD '06: Proceedings of the 2006 ACM SIGMOD International Conference on Management of Data*, pages 706–706, New York, NY, USA, 2006. ACM.

[25] Vijay Menon and Keshav Pingali. A case for source-level transformations in MATLAB. In *PLAN '99: Proceedings of the 2nd conference on Domain-specific languages*, pages 53–65, New York, NY, USA, 1999. ACM.

[26] Marjan Mernik, Jan Heering, and Anthony M. Sloane. When and how to develop domain-specific languages. *ACM Comput. Surv.*, 37(4):316–344, 2005.

[27] NVIDIA. CUDA. http://developer.nvidia.com/object/cuda.html.

[28] Kunle Olukotun, Basem A. Nayfeh, Lance Hammond, Kenneth G. Wilson, and Kunyung Chang. The case for a single-chip multiprocessor. In *ASPLOS '96*.

[29] PeakStream. The PeakStream platform: High productivity software development for multi-core processors. technical report, 2006.

[30] G. C. Sih and E. A. Lee. A compile-time scheduling heuristic for interconnection-constrained heterogeneous processor architectures. *IEEE Trans. Parallel Distrib. Syst.*, 4(2):175–187, 1993.

[31] David Tarditi, Sidd Puri, and Jose Oglesby. Accelerator: using data parallelism to program GPUs for general-purpose uses. In *ASPLOS-XII: Proceedings of the 12th international conference on Architectural support for programming languages and operating systems*, pages 325–335, New York, NY, USA, 2006. ACM.

[32] The Khronos Group. OpenCL 1.0. http://www.khronos.org/opencl/.

[33] P. W. Trinder, H.-W. Loidl, and R. F. Pointon. Parallel and distributed Haskells. *J. Funct. Program.*, 12(5):469–510, 2002.

[34] Arie van Deursen, Paul Klint, and Joost Visser. Domain-specific languages: an annotated bibliography. *SIGPLAN Not.*, 35(6):26–36, 2000.

[35] Perry H. Wang, Jamison D. Collins, Gautham N. Chinya, Hong Jiang, Xinmin Tian, Milind Girkar, Nick Y. Yang, Guei-Yuan Lueh, and Hong Wang. Exochi: architecture and programming environment for a heterogeneous multi-core multithreaded system. In *PLDI '07: Proceedings of the 2007 ACM SIGPLAN conference on Programming language design and implementation*, pages 156–166, New York, NY, USA, 2007. ACM.

Copperhead: Compiling an Embedded Data Parallel Language

Bryan Catanzaro

University of California, Berkeley

catanzar@cs.berkeley.edu

Michael Garland

NVIDIA Research

mgarland@nvidia.com

Kurt Keutzer

University of California, Berkeley

keutzer@cs.berkeley.edu

Abstract

Modern parallel microprocessors deliver high performance on applications that expose substantial fine-grained data parallelism. Although data parallelism is widely available in many computations, implementing data parallel algorithms in low-level languages is often an unnecessarily difficult task. The characteristics of parallel microprocessors and the limitations of current programming methodologies motivate our design of Copperhead, a high-level data parallel language embedded in Python. The Copperhead programmer describes parallel computations via composition of familiar data parallel primitives supporting both flat and nested data parallel computation on arrays of data. Copperhead programs are expressed in a subset of the widely used Python programming language and interoperate with standard Python modules, including libraries for numeric computation, data visualization, and analysis.

In this paper, we discuss the language, compiler, and runtime features that enable Copperhead to efficiently execute data parallel code. We define the restricted subset of Python which Copperhead supports and introduce the program analysis techniques necessary for compiling Copperhead code into efficient low-level implementations. We also outline the runtime support by which Copperhead programs interoperate with standard Python modules. We demonstrate the effectiveness of our techniques with several examples targeting the CUDA platform for parallel programming on GPUs. Copperhead code is concise, on average requiring 3.6 times fewer lines of code than CUDA, and the compiler generates efficient code, yielding 45-100% of the performance of hand-crafted, well optimized CUDA code.

Categories and Subject Descriptors D.3.4 [*Programming Languages*]: Processors – Code generation, Compilers; D.3.2 [*Language Classifications*]: Parallel languages; D.1.3 [*Concurrent Programming*]: Parallel Programming

General Terms Algorithms, Design, Performance

Keywords Python, Data Parallelism, GPU

1. Introduction

As the transition from sequential to parallel processing continues, the need intensifies for high-productivity parallel programming tools and methodologies. Manual implementation of parallel programs using efficiency languages such as C and C++ can yield high performance, but at a large cost in programmer productivity, which some case studies show as being 2 to 5 times worse than productivity-oriented languages such as Ruby and Python [15, 25]. Additionally, parallel programming in efficiency languages is often viewed as an esoteric endeavor, to be undertaken by experts only. Without higher-level abstractions that enable easier parallel programming, parallel processing will not be widely utilized. Conversely, today's productivity programmers do not have the means to capitalize on fine-grained, highly parallel microprocessors, which limits their ability to implement computationally intensive applications. To enable widespread use of parallel processors, we need to provide higher level abstractions which are both productive and efficient.

Although the need for higher-level parallel abstractions seems clear, perhaps less so is the type of abstractions which should be provided, since there are many potential abstractions to choose from. In our view, nested data parallelism, as introduced by languages such as NESL [4], is particularly interesting. Nested data parallelism is abundant in many computationally intensive algorithms. It can be mapped efficiently to parallel microprocessors, which prominently feature hardware support for data parallelism. For example, mainstream x86 processors from Intel and AMD are adopting 8-wide vector instructions, Intel's Larrabee processor used 16-wide vector instructions, and modern GPUs from NVIDIA and AMD use wider SIMD widths of 32 and 64, respectively. Consequently, programs which don't take advantage of data parallelism relinquish substantial performance, on any modern processor.

Additionally, nested data parallelism as an abstraction clearly exposes parallelism. In contrast to traditional auto-parallelizing compilers, which must analyze and prove which operations can be parallelized and which can not, the compiler of a data-parallel language needs only to decide which parallel operations should be performed sequentially, and which should be performed in parallel. Accordingly, nested data parallel programs have a valid sequential interpretation, and are thus easier to understand and debug than parallel programs that expose race conditions and other complications of parallelism.

Motivated by these observations, Copperhead provides a set of nested data parallel abstractions, expressed in a restricted subset of the widely used Python programming language. Instead of creating an entirely new programming language for nested data parallelism, we repurpose existing constructs in Python, such as map and reduce. Embedding Copperhead in Python provides several important benefits. For those who are already familiar with Python, learning Copperhead is more similar to learning how to use a Python package than it is to learning a new language. There is no need to learn any new syntax, instead the programmer must learn only what subset of Python is supported by the Copperhead language and runtime. The Copperhead runtime is implemented as a standard Python extension, and Copperhead programs are invoked through the Python interpreter, allowing them to interoperate with the wide variety of existing Python libraries for numeric computation, file manipulation, data visualization, and analysis. This makes Copperhead a productive environment for prototyping, debugging, and implementing entire applications, not just their computationally intense kernels.

Of course, without being able to efficiently compile nested data parallel programs, Copperhead would not be of much use. To this end, the Copperhead compiler attempts to efficiently utilize modern parallel processors. Previous work on compilers for nested data parallel programming languages has focused on flattening transforms to target flat SIMD arrays of processing units. However, today's processors support a hierarchy of parallelism, with independent cores containing tightly coupled processing elements. Accordingly, the Copperhead compiler maps nested data parallel programs to a parallelism hierarchy, forgoing the use of flattening transforms. We find that in many circumstances, this is substantially more efficient than indiscriminate application of the flattening transform.

The current Copperhead compiler targets CUDA C++, running on manycore Graphics Processors from NVIDIA. We generate efficient, scalable parallel programs, performing within 45-100% of well optimized, hand-tuned CUDA code. Our initial implementation focus on CUDA does not limit us to a particular hardware platform, as the techniques we have developed for compiling data-parallel code are widely applicable to other platforms as well. In the future, we anticipate the development of Copperhead compiler backends for other parallel platforms. Additionally, the compiler techniques we propose are suitable for compiling other data parallel languages, such as NESL and Data Parallel Haskell.

2. Related Work

There is an extensive literature investigating many alternative methods for parallel programming. Data parallel approaches [2, 3, 13] have often been used, and have historically been most closely associated with SIMD and vector machines, such as the the CM-2 and Cray C90, respectively. Blelloch *et al.* designed the NESL language [4], demonstrating a whole-program transformation of nested data parallel programs into flat data parallel programs. The flattening transform has been extended to fully higher-order functional languages in Data Parallel Haskell [7]. In contrast to these methods, we attempt to schedule nested procedures directly onto the hierarchical structure of the machines we target.

The CUDA platform [23, 26] defines a blocked SPMD programming model for executing parallel computations on GPUs. Several libraries, such as Thrust [14], provide a collection of flat data parallel primitives for use in CUDA programs. Copperhead uses selected Thrust primitives in the code it generates.

Systems for compiling flat data parallel programs for GPU targets have been built in a number of languages, including C# [28], C++ [21, 22], and Haskell [19]. Such systems typically define special data parallel array types and use operator overloading and metaprogramming techniques to build expression trees describing the computation to be performed on these arrays. The Ct [11] library adopts a similar model for programming multicore processors. However, these systems have not provided a means to automatically map nested data parallel programs to a hierarchically nested parallel platform.

Rather than providing data parallel libraries, others have explored techniques that mark up sequential loops to be parallelized into CUDA kernels [12, 20, 30]. In these models, the programmer writes an explicitly sequential program consisting of loops that are parallelizable. The loop markups, written in the form of C pragma preprocessor directives, indicate to the compiler that loops can be parallelized into CUDA kernels.

There have also been some attempts to compile various subsets of Python to different platforms. The Cython compiler [9] compiles a largely Python-like language into sequential C code. Clyther [8]

takes a similar approach to generating OpenCL kernels. In both cases, the programmer writes a Python program which is transliterated into an isomorphic C program. Rather than transliterating Python programs, PyCUDA [18] provides a metaprogramming facility for textually generating CUDA kernel programs, as well as Python/GPU bindings. Theano [29] provides an expression tree facility for numerical expressions on numerical arrays. Garg and Amaral [10] recently described a technique for compiling Python loop structures and array operations into GPU-targeted code.

These Python/GPU projects are quite useful; in fact Copperhead's runtime relies on PyCUDA. However, to write programs using these tools, programmers must write code equivalent to the *output* of the Copperhead compiler, with all mapping and scheduling decisions made explicit in the program itself. Copperhead aims to solve a fairly different problem, namely compiling a program from a higher level of abstraction into efficiently executable code.

3. Copperhead Language

A Copperhead program is a Python program that imports the Copperhead language environment:

```
from copperhead import *
```

A Copperhead program is executed, like any other Python program, by executing the sequence of its top-level statements. Selected procedure definitions within the body of the program may be marked with the Copperhead decorator, as in the following:

```
@cu
def add_vectors(x, y):
    return map(lambda xi,yi: xi+yi, x, y)
```

This @cu decorator declares the associated procedure to be a Copperhead procedure. These procedures must conform to the requirements of the Copperhead language, and they may be compiled for and executed on any of the parallel platforms supported by the Copperhead compiler. Once defined, Copperhead procedures may be called just like any other Python procedure, both within the program body or, as shown below, from an interactive command line.

```
>>> add_vectors(range(10), [2]*10)
[2, 3, 4, 5, 6, 7, 8, 9, 10, 11]
```

The @cu decorator interposes a wrapper object around the native Python function object that is responsible for compiling and executing procedures on a target parallel platform.

Copperhead is fundamentally a data parallel language. It provides language constructs, specifically map, and a library of primitives such as reduce, gather, and scatter that all have intrinsically parallel semantics. They operate on 1-dimensional arrays of data that we refer to as *sequences*.

3.1 Restricted Subset of Python

The Copperhead language is a restricted subset of the Python 2.6 language. Every valid Copperhead procedure must also be a valid Python procedure. Portions of the program outside procedures marked with the @cu decorator are normal Python programs that will be executed by the standard Python interpreter, without any restrictions imposed by the Copperhead runtime or compiler. The Copperhead language supports a very restricted subset of Python in order to enable efficient compilation.

Copperhead adopts the lexical and grammatical rules of Python. In summarizing its restricted language, we denote expressions by E and statements by S. We use lower-case letters to indicate identifiers and F and A to indicate function-valued and array-valued expressions, respectively.

3.1.1 Expressions

The most basic expressions are literal values, identifier references, tuple constructions, and accesses to array elements.

$$E \; : \; x \mid (E_1, \, \ldots, \, E_n) \mid A[E]$$
$$\mid \textbf{True} \mid \textbf{False} \mid \text{integer} \mid \text{floatnumber}$$

The basic logical and arithmetic operators are allowed, as are Python's `and`, `or`, and conditional expressions.

$$\mid E_1 + E_2 \mid E_1 < E_2 \mid \textbf{not} \; E \mid \ldots$$
$$\mid E_1 \; \textbf{and} \; E_2 \mid E_1 \; \textbf{or} \; E_2 \mid E_1 \; \textbf{if} \; E_p \; \textbf{else} \; E_2$$

Expressions that call and define functions must use only positional arguments. Optional and keyword arguments are not allowed.

$$\mid F(E_1, \, \ldots, \, E_n) \mid \textbf{lambda} \; x_1, \, \ldots, \, x_n : \; E$$

Copperhead relies heavily on `map` as the fundamental source of parallelism and elevates it from a built-in function (as in Python) to a special form in the grammar. Copperhead also supports a limited form of Python's list comprehension syntax, which is de-sugared into equivalent `map` constructions during parsing.

$$\mid \textbf{map}(F, \, A_1, \, \ldots, \, A_n)$$
$$\mid [E \; \textbf{for} \; x \; \textbf{in} \; A]$$
$$\mid [E \; \textbf{for} \; x_1, \, \ldots, \, x_n \; \textbf{in} \; \textbf{zip}(A_1, \, \ldots, \, A_n)]$$

In addition to these grammatical restrictions, Copperhead expressions must be *statically well-typed*. We employ a standard Hindley-Milner style polymorphic type system. Static typing provides richer information to the compiler that it can leverage during code generation, and also avoids the run-time overhead of dynamic type dispatch.

3.1.2 Statements

The body of a Copperhead procedure consists of a *suite* of statements: one or more statements S which are nested by indentation level. Each statement S of a suite must be of the following form:

$$S \; : \; \textbf{return} \; E$$
$$\mid x_1, \, \ldots, \, x_n \; = \; E$$
$$\mid \textbf{if} \; E: \; \text{suite} \; \textbf{else}: \; \text{suite}$$
$$\mid \textbf{def} \; f(x_1, \, \ldots, \, x_n): \; \text{suite}$$

Copperhead further requires that every execution path within a suite must return a value, and all returned values must be of the same type. This restriction is necessary since every Copperhead procedure must have a well-defined static type.

All data in a Copperhead procedure are considered immutable values. Thus, statements of the form `x = E` bind the value of the expression `E` to the identifier `x`; they *do not* assign a new value to an existing variable. All identifiers are strictly lexically scoped.

Copperhead does not guarantee any particular order of evaluation, other than the partial ordering imposed by data dependencies in the program. Python, in contrast, always evaluates statements from top to bottom and expressions from left to right. By definition, a Copperhead program must be valid regardless of the order of evaluations, and thus Python's mandated ordering is one valid ordering of the program.

Because mutable assignment is forbidden and the order of evaluation is undefined, the Copperhead compiler is free to reorder and transform procedures in a number of ways. As we will see, this flexibility improves the efficiency of generated code.

3.2 Data Parallel Primitives

Copperhead is a data parallel language. Programs manipulate data sequences by applying aggregate operations, such as `map`, or `reduce`. The semantics of these primitives are implicitly parallel:

```
@cu
def spmv_csr(vals, cols, x):
    def spvv(Ai, j):
        z = gather(x, j)
        return sum(map(lambda Aij, xj: Aij*xj, Ai, z))

    return map(spvv, vals, cols)
```

Figure 1. Procedure for computing Ax for a matrix A in CSR form and a dense vector x. Underlined operations indicate potential sources of parallel execution.

they may always be performed by some parallel computation, but may also be performed sequentially.

Table 1 summarizes the main aggregate operations used by the examples in this paper. They mirror operations found in most other data parallel languages. With two minor exceptions, these functions will produce the same result regardless of whether they are performed in parallel or sequentially. The `permute` primitive is the primary exception. If the `indices` array given to `permute` contains one or more repeated index values, the resulting sequence is non-deterministic since we guarantee no particular order of evaluation. The other exception is `reduce`. If given a truly commutative and associative operation, then its result will always be identical. However, programs often perform reductions using floating point values whose addition, for instance, is not truly associative. These problems are commonly encountered in general parallel programming, and are not unique to Copperhead.

To demonstrate our use of these operators, Figure 1 shows a simple Copperhead procedure for computing the sparse matrix-vector product (SpMV) $y = Ax$. Here we assume that A is stored in Compressed Sparse Row (CSR) format—one of the most frequently used representation for sparse matrices—and that x is a dense vector. The matrix representation simply records each row of the matrix as a sequence containing its non-zero values along with a corresponding sequence recording the column index of each value. A simple example of this representation is:

$$A = \begin{bmatrix} 1 & 7 & 0 & 0 \\ 0 & 2 & 8 & 0 \\ 5 & 0 & 3 & 9 \\ 0 & 6 & 0 & 4 \end{bmatrix} \quad \begin{array}{l} \text{vals} = [[1,7],[2,8],[5,3,9],[6,4]] \\ \text{cols} = [[0,1],[1,2],[0,2,3],[1,3]] \end{array}$$

The body of `spmv_csr` applies a sparse dot product procedure, `spvv`, to each row of the matrix using `map`. The sparse dot product itself produces the result y_i for row i by forming the products $A_{ij}x_j$ for each column j containing a non-zero entry, and then summing these products together. It uses `gather` to fetch the necessary values x_j from the dense vector x and uses `sum`, a convenient special case of `reduce` where the operator is addition, to produce the result.

This simple example illustrates two important issues that are a central concern for our Copperhead compiler. First, it consists of a number of potentially parallel aggregate operations, which are underlined. Second, these aggregate operators are nested: those within `spvv` are executed within an enclosing `map` operation invoked by `spmv_csr`. One of the principal tasks of our compiler is to decide how to schedule these operations for execution. Each of them may be performed in parallel or by sequential loops, and the nesting of operations must be mapped onto the hardware execution units in an efficient fashion.

4. Compiler

The Copperhead compiler is a source-to-source compiler responsible for converting a suite of one or more Copperhead procedures

`y = replicate(a, n)`	Return an n-element sequence whose every element has value `a`.
`y = map(f, x1, ..., xn)`	Returns sequence `[f(x1[0], ..., xn[0]), f(x1[1], ..., xn[1]), ...]`.
`y = zip(x1, x2)`	Return sequence of pairs `[(x1[0],x2[0]), (x1[1],x2[1]), ...]`.
`y = gather(x, indices)`	Produce sequence with `y[i] = x[indices[i]]`.
`y = permute(x, indices)`	Produce `y` where `y[indices[i]] = x[i]`.
`s = reduce(⊕, x, prefix)`	Computes `prefix` $\oplus$ `x[0]` $\oplus$ `x[1]` $\oplus$ ... for a commutative and associative operator $\oplus$.
`y = scan(f, x)`	Produce `y` such that `y[0]=x[0]` and `y[i] = f(y[i-1], x[i])`. Function `f` must be associative.

Table 1. Selected data-parallel operations on sequences.

```
# lambda0 :: (a, a) → a
def lambda0(Aij, xj):
    return op_mul(Aij, xj)

# spvv :: ([a], [Int], [a]) → [a]
def spvv(Ai, j, _k0):
    z0 = gather(_k0, j)
    tmp0 = map(lambda0, Ai, z0)
    return sum(tmp0)

# spmv_csr :: ([[a]], [[Int]], [a]) → [a]
def spmv_csr(vals, cols, x):
    return map(closure([x], spvv), vals, cols)
```

Figure 2. SpMV procedure from Figure 1 after transformation by the front end compiler.

into a code module that can execute on the target parallel platform. We have designed it to support three basic usage patterns. First is what we refer to as JIT (Just-In-Time) compilation. When the programmer invokes a @cu-decorated function either from the command line or from a Python code module, the Copperhead runtime may need to generate code for this procedure if none is already available. Second is batch compilation, where the Copperhead compiler is asked to generate a set of C++ code modules for the specified procedures. This code may be subsequently used either within the Copperhead Python environment or linked directly with external C++ applications. The third common scenario is one where the compiler is asked to generate a collection of variant instantiations of a Copperhead procedure in tandem with an autotuning framework for exploring the performance landscape of a particular architecture.

In the following discussion, we assume that the compiler is given a single top level Copperhead function—referred to as the "entry point"—to compile. It may, for instance, be a function like spmv_csr that has been invoked at the Python interpreter prompt. For the CUDA platform, the compiler will take this procedure, along with any procedures it invokes, and produce a single sequential *host* procedure and one or more parallel *kernels* that will be invoked by the host procedure.

4.1 Front End

After parsing the program text using the standard Python ast module, the compiler front end converts the program into a simplified abstract syntax tree (AST) form suitable for consumption by the rest of the compiler. It applies a sequence of fairly standard program transformations to: lift all nested lambdas and procedures into top level definitions, make closures explicit, convert all statements to single assignment form with no nested expressions, and infer static types for all elements of the program. Programs that contain syntax errors or that do not conform to the restricted language outlined in Section 3 are rejected.

For illustration, Figure 2 shows a program fragment representing the AST for the Copperhead procedure shown in Figure 1. Each procedure is annotated with its most general polymorphic type, which we determine using a standard Hindley-Milner style

type inference process. Lexically captured variables within nested procedures are eliminated by converting free variables to explicit arguments—shown as variables _k0, _k1, etc.—and replacing the original nested definition point of the function with a special closure([k_1, ..., k_n], f) form where the k_i represent the originally free variables. In our example, the local variable x was free in the body of the nested spvv procedure, and is thus converted into an explicit closure argument in the transformed code. Single assignment conversion adds a unique subscript to each local identifier (e.g., z_0 in spvv), and flattening nested expressions introduces temporary identifiers (e.g., tmp_0) bound to the value of individual sub-expressions. Note that our single assignment form has no need of the ϕ-functions used in SSA representations of imperative languages since we disallow loops and every branch of a conditional must return a value.

4.2 Scheduling Nested Parallelism

The front end of the compiler carries out platform independent transformations in order to prepare the code for scheduling. The middle section of the compiler is tasked with performing analyses and scheduling the program onto a target platform.

At this point in the compiler, a Copperhead program consists of possibly nested compositions of data parallel primitives. A Copperhead procedure may perform purely sequential computations, in which case our compiler will convert it into sequential C++ code. Copperhead makes *no attempt* to auto-parallelize sequential codes. Instead, it requires the programmer to use primitives that the compiler will *auto-sequentialize* as necessary. Our compilation of sequential code is quite straightforward, since we rely on the host C++ compiler to handle all scalar code optimizations, and our restricted language avoids all the complexities of compiling a broad subset of Python that must be addressed by compilers like Cython [9].

Copperhead supports both flat and nested data parallelism. A flat Copperhead program consists of a sequence of parallel primitives which perform purely sequential operations to each element of a sequence in parallel. A nested program, in contrast, may apply parallel operations to each sequence element. Our spmv_csr code provides a simple concrete example. The outer spmv_csr procedure applies spvv to every row of its input via map. The spvv procedure itself calls gather, map, and sum, all of which are potentially parallel. The Copperhead compiler must decide how to map these potentially parallel operations onto the target hardware: for example, they may be implemented as parallel function calls or sequential loops.

One approach to scheduling nested parallel programs, adopted by NESL [4] and Data Parallel Haskell [7] among others, is to apply a flattening (or vectorization) transform to the program. This converts a nested structure of vector operations into a sequence of flat operations. In most cases, the process of flattening replaces the nested operations with segmented equivalents. For instance, in our spmv_csr example, the nested sum would be flattened into a segmented reduction.

The flattening transform is a powerful technique which ensures good load balancing. It also enables data parallel compilation for flat SIMD processors, where all lanes in the SIMD array work in lockstep. However, we take a different approach. Flattening transformations are best suited to machines that are truly flat. Most modern machines, in contrast, are organized hierarchically. The CUDA programming model [23, 24], for instance, provides a hierarchy of execution formed into four levels:

1. A *host thread* running on the CPU, which can invoke
2. Parallel *kernels* running on the GPU, which consist of
3. A grid of *thread blocks* each of which is comprised of
4. Potentially hundreds of *device threads* running on the GPU.

The central goal of the Copperhead compiler is thus to map the nested structure of the program onto the hierarchical structure of the machine.

Recent experience with hand-written CUDA programs suggests that direct mapping of nested constructions onto this physical machine hierarchy often yields better performance. For instance, Bell and Garland [1] explored several strategies for implementing SpMV in CUDA. Their Coordinate (COO) kernel is implemented by manually applying the flattening transformation to the spmv_csr algorithm. Their other kernels represent static mappings of nested algorithms onto the hardware. The flattened COO kernel only delivers the highest performance in the exceptional case where the distribution of row lengths is extraordinarily variable, in which case the load balancing provided by the flattening transform is advantageous. However, for 13 out of the 14 unstructured matrices they examine, applying the flattening transform results in performance two to four times slower than the equivalent nested implementation.

Experiences such as this lead us to the conclusion that although the flattening transform can provide high performance in certain cases where the workload is extremely imbalanced, the decision to apply the transform should be under programmer control, given the substantial overhead the flattening transform imposes for most workloads.

Our compiler thus performs a static mapping of nested programs onto a parallelism hierarchy supported by the target parallel platform.

Returning to our spmv_csr example being compiled to the CUDA platform, the map within its body will become a CUDA kernel call. The compiler can then chose to map the operations within spvv to either individual threads or individual blocks. Which mapping is preferred is in general program and data dependent; matrices with very short rows are generally best mapped to threads while those with longer rows are better mapped to blocks.

Because this information is data dependent, we currently present the decision of which execution hierarchy to target as a compiler option. The programmer can arrange the code to specify explicitly which is preferred, an autotuning framework can explore which is better on a particular machine, or a reasonable default can be chosen based on any static knowledge about the problem being solved. In the absence of a stated preference, the default is to map nested operations to sequential implementations. This will give each row of the matrix to a single thread of the kernel created by the call to map in spmv_csr.

4.3 Synchronization Points and Fusion

The compiler must also discover and schedule synchronization points between aggregate operators. We assume that our target parallel platform provides a SPMD-like execution model, and therefore synchronization between a pair of parallel operations is performed via barrier synchronization across parallel threads. Similarly, a synchronization point between a pair of operators that have been marked as sequentialized implies that they must be implemented with separate loop bodies.

The most conservative policy would be to require a synchronization point following every parallel primitive. However, this can introduce far more synchronization, temporary data storage, and memory bandwidth consumption than necessary to respect data dependencies in the program. Requiring a synchronization point after every parallel primitive can reduce performance by an order of magnitude or more, compared with equivalent code that synchronizes only when necessary. In order to produce efficient code, our compiler must introduce as few synchronization points as possible, by fusing groups of parallel primitives into single kernels or loop bodies.

In order to determine where synchronization points are necessary, we need to characterize the data dependencies between individual elements of the sequences upon which the parallel primitives are operating. Consider an aggregate operator of the form $x = f(y_1, \ldots, y_n)$ where x and the y_i are all sequences. Since the elements of x may be computed concurrently, we need to know what values of y_i it requires.

We call the value $x[i]$ *complete* when its value has been determined and may be used as input to subsequent operations. The array x is complete when all its elements are complete.

We categorize the bulk of our operators into one of two classes. The first class are those operators which perform induction over the domain of their inputs. This class is essentially composed of permute, scatter, and their variants. We cannot in general guarantee that any particular $x[i]$ is complete until the entire operation is finished. In other words, either the array x is entirely complete or entirely incomplete.

The second class are those operators which perform induction over the domain of their outputs. This includes almost all the rest of our operators, such as map, gather, and scan. Here we want to characterize the portion of each y_j that must be complete in order to complete $x[i]$. We currently distinguish three broad cases:

- *None*: $x[i]$ does not depend on any element of y_j
- *Local*: completing $x[i]$ requires that $y_j[i]$ be complete
- *Global*: completing $x[i]$ requires that y_j be entirely complete

With deeper semantic analysis, we could potentially uncover more information in the spectrum between local and global completion requirements. However, at the moment we restrict our attention to this simple classification.

Each primitive provided by Copperhead declares its completion requirements on its arguments (none, local, global) as well as the completion of its output. Completing the output of class 1 operators requires synchronization, while the output of class 2 operators is completed locally. The compiler then propagates this information through the body of user-defined procedures to compute their completion requirements. For example, a synchronization point is required between a class 1 primitive and any point at which its output is used, or before any primitive that requires one of its arguments to be globally complete. We call a sequence of primitives that are not separated by any synchronization points a *phase* of the program. All operations within a single phase may potentially be fused into a single parallel kernel or sequential loop by the compiler.

4.4 Shape Analysis

Shape analysis determines, where possible, the sizes of all intermediate values. This allows the back end of the compiler to statically allocate and reuse space for temporary values, which is critical to obtaining efficient performance. For the CUDA backend, forgoing shape analysis would require that every parallel primitive be executed individually, since allocating memory from within a CUDA kernel is not feasible. This would lead to orders of magnitude lower performance.

Our internal representation gives a unique name to every temporary value. We want to assign to each a *shape* of the form $\langle [d_1, \ldots, d_n], s \rangle$ where d_i is the array's extent in dimension i and s is the shape of each of its elements. Although Copperhead currently operates on one-dimensional sequences, the shape analysis we employ applies to higher dimensional arrays as well. The shape of a 4-element, 1-dimensional sequence [5,4,8,1] would, for example, be $\langle [4], \text{Unit} \rangle$ where $\text{Unit}=\langle [], \cdot \rangle$ is the shape reserved for indivisible types such as scalars. Nested sequences are not required to have fully determined shapes: in the case where subsequences have differing lengths, the extent along that dimension will be undefined, for example: $\langle [2], \langle [*], \text{Unit} \rangle \rangle$. Note that the dimensionality of all values are known as a result of type inference. It remains only to determine extents, where possible.

We approach shape analysis of user-provided code as an abstract interpretation problem. We define a shape language consisting of Unit, the shape constructor $\langle D, s \rangle$ described above, identifiers, and shape functions extentof(s), elementof(s) that extract the two respective portions of a shape s. We implement a simple environment-based evaluator where every identifier is mapped to either (1) a shape term or (2) itself if its shape is unknown. Every primitive f is required to provide a function, that we denote f.shape, that returns the shape of its result given the shapes of its inputs. It may also return a set of static constraints on the shapes of its inputs to aid the compiler in its analysis. Examples of such shape-computing functions would be:

```
gather.shape(x, i) = ⟨extentof(i), elementof(x)⟩
zip.shape(x1, x2)  = ⟨extentof(x1),
                      (elementof(x1),elementof(x2))⟩
                   with extentof(x1)==extentof(x2)
```

The gather rule states that its result has the same size as the index array i while having elements whose shape is given by the elements of x. The zip augments the shape of its result with a constraint that the extents of its inputs are assumed to be the same. Terms such as extentof(x) are left unevaluated if the identifier x is not bound to any shape.

To give a sense of the shape analysis process, consider the spvv procedure shown in Figure 2. Shape analysis will annotate every binding with a shape like so:

```
def spvv(Ai, j, _k0):
    z0 :: ⟨extentof(j), elementof(_k0)⟩
    tmp0 :: ⟨extentof(Ai), elementof(Ai)⟩
    return sum(tmp0) :: Unit
```

In this case, the shapes for z_0, tmp_0, and the return value are derived directly from the shape rules for gather, map, and sum, respectively.

Shape analysis is not guaranteed to find all shapes in a program. Some identifiers may have data dependent shapes, making the analysis inconclusive. For these cases, the compiler must treat computations without defined shapes as barriers, across which no fusion can be performed, and then generate code which computes the actual data dependent shape before the remainder of the computation is allowed to proceed.

Future work involves allowing shape analysis to influence code scheduling: in an attempt to better match the extents in a particular nested data parallel problem to the dimensions of parallelism supported by the platform being targeted. For example, instead of implementing the outermost level of a Copperhead program in a parallel fashion, if the outer extent is small and the inner extent is large, the compiler may decide to create a code variant which sequentializes the outermost level, and parallelizes an inner level.

```
struct lambda0 {
    template<typename T_Aij, typename T_xj >
    __device__ T_xj operator()(T_Aij Aij, T_xj xj)
        { return Aij * xj; }
};

struct spvv {
    template<typename T_Ai,
             typename T_j,
             typename T_k0 >
    __device__ typename T_Ai::value_type
    operator()(T_Ai Ai,
               T_j j,
               T_k0 _k0) {
        typedef typename T_Ai::value_type _a;
        gathered<...> z0 = gather(_k0, j);
        transformed<...> tmp0 =
            transform<_a>(lambda0(), Ai, z0);
        return sequential::sum(tmp0);
    }
};

template<typename T2>
struct spvv_closure1 {
    T2 k0;
    __device__ spvv_closure1(T2 _k0) : k0(_k0) { }

    template<typename T0, typename T1>
    __device__ typename T0::value_type
    operator()(T0 arg0, T1 arg1) {
        return spvv()(arg0, arg1, k0);
    }
};

template<typename _a > __global__
void spmv_csr_phase0(nested_sequence<_a, 1> vals,
                     nested_sequence<int,1> cols,
                     stored_sequence<_a> x,
                     stored_sequence<_a> _return) {
    int i = threadIdx.x + blockIdx.x*blockDim.x;

    if( i < vals.size() )
        _return[i] = spvv_closure1<stored_sequence<_a> >
                        (x)(vals[i], cols[i]);
}
```

Figure 3. Sample CUDA C++ code generated for spmv_csr. Ellipses (...) indicate incidental type and argument information elided for brevity.

4.5 CUDA C++ Back End

The back end of the Copperhead compiler generates platform specific code. As mentioned, we currently have a single back end, which generates code for the CUDA platform. Figure 3 shows an example of such code for our example spmv_csr procedure. It consists of a sequence of function objects for the nested lambdas, closures, and procedures used within that procedure. The templated function spmv_csr_phase0 corresponds to the Copperhead entry point.

Not shown here is the Copperhead generated C++ host code that invokes the parallel kernels. It is the responsibility of the host code to marshal data where necessary, allocate any required temporary storage on the GPU, and make the necessary CUDA calls to launch the kernel.

We generate templated CUDA C++ code that makes use of a set of sequence types, such as stored_sequence and nested_sequence types, which hold sequences in memory. Fusion of sequential loops and block-wise primitives is performed through the construction of compound types. For example, in the `spvv` functor shown above, the calls to `gather`, and `transform` perform no work, instead they construct `gathered_sequence` and `transformed_sequence` structures that lazily perform the appropriate computations upon dereferencing. Work is only performed by the last primitive in a set of fused sequential or block-wise primitives. In this example, the call to `seq::sum` introduces a sequential loop which then dereferences a compound sequence, at each element performing the appropriate computation. When compiling this code, the C++ compiler statically eliminates all the indirection present in this code, yielding machine code which is as efficient as if we had generated the fused loops directly.

We generate fairly high level C++ code, rather than assembly level code, for two reasons. Firstly, existing C++ compilers provide excellent support for translating well structured C++ to efficient machine code. Emitting C++ from our compiler enables our compiler to utilize the vast array of transformations which existing compilers already perform. But more importantly, it means that the code generated by our Copperhead compiler can be reused in external C++ programs. We believe that an important use case for systems like Copperhead is to prototype algorithms in a high-level language and then compile them into template libraries that can be used by a larger C++ application.

5. Runtime

Copperhead code is embedded in standard Python programs. Python function decorators indicate which procedures should be executed by the Copperhead runtime. When a Python program calls a Copperhead procedure, the Copperhead runtime intercepts the call, compiles the procedure, and then executes it on a specified execution place. The Copperhead runtime uses Python's introspection capabilities to gather all the source code pertaining to the procedure being compiled. This model is inspired by the ideas from Selective, Embedded, Just-In-Time Specialization [6].

The Copperhead compiler is fundamentally a static compiler that may be optionally invoked at runtime. Allowing the compiler to be invoked at runtime matches the no-compile mindset of typical Python development. However, the compiler does not perform dynamic compilation optimizations specific to the runtime instantiation of the program, such as treating inputs as constants, tracing execution through conditionals, etc. Forgoing these optimizations enables the results of the Copperhead compiler to be encapsulated as a standard, statically compiled binary, and cached for future reuse or incorporated as libraries into standalone programs which are not invoked through the Python interpreter.

Consequently, the runtime compilation overhead we incur is analogous to the build time of traditional static compilers, and does not present a performance limitation. The Copperhead compiler itself typically takes on the order of 300 milliseconds to compile our example programs, and the host C++ and CUDA compilers typically take on the order of 20 seconds to compile a program. Both of these overheads are not encountered in performance critical situations, since Copperhead's caches obviate recompilation. The actual runtime overhead, compared with calling an equivalent C++ function from within C++ code, is on the order of 100 microseconds per Copperhead procedure invocation.

For each Copperhead procedure, the CUDA runtime generates a host C++ function which coordinates the launch and synchronization between multiple parallel phases, as well as allocates data for temporary results. Copperhead uses PyCUDA [18] and CodePy [17] to provide mechanisms for compiling, persistent caching, linking and executing CUDA and C++ code. The Copperhead runtime uses Thrust [14] to implement fully parallel versions of certain data parallel primitives, such as `reduce` and variations of `scan`.

5.1 Places

In order to manage the location of data and kernel execution across multiple devices, the Copperhead runtime defines a set of *places* that represent these heterogeneous devices. Data objects are created at a specific place. Calling a Copperhead procedure will execute a computation on the current target place, which is controlled utilizing the Python `with` statement.

Currently we support two kinds of places: CUDA capable GPUs and the native Python interpreter. Copperhead is designed to allow other types of places, with corresponding compiler back ends to be added. For instance, multi-core x86 back end would be associated with a new place type.

To faciliate interoperability between Python and Copperhead, all data is duplicated, with a *local* copy in the Python interpreter, and a *remote* copy which resides at the place of execution. Data is lazily transferred between the local and remote place as needed by the program.

5.2 Data Structures

Copperhead adopts a common technique for representing arbitrarily nested sequences as a flat sequence of data, along with a descriptor sequence for each level of nesting. The descriptor sequences provide the necessary information to build a view of each subsequence, including empty subsequences.

In addition to supporting arbitrarily nested sequences, Copperhead also allows programmers to construct uniformly nested sequences, which support the important special case where the shape is completely defined. For such sequences, a set of strides and lengths are sufficient to describe the nesting structure - descriptor sequences are not required. Uniformly nested sequences also allow the data to be arbitrarily ordered: when the programmer creates a uniformly nested sequence, they either specify the data ordering or provide a tuple of strides directly. This allows the programmer to express data layouts analogous to row- and column-major ordering for doubly nested sequences, as well as their analogues for more deeply nested sequences. The programmer may provide the strides directly, which allows the subsequences to be aligned arbitrarily. This can provide important performance benefits when data access patterns with standard nested sequences are not matched well to the processor's memory hierarchy.

We have seen have seen two to three fold performance improvements by using the correct nested data structure type. Future work may investigate autotuning over alignments and data layouts.

6. Examples

In this section, we investigate the performance of Copperhead code in several example programs. As we compare performance, we compare Copperhead compiled code to published, well-optimized, hand-crafted CUDA implementations of the same computation. Our compiler can't apply all the transformations which a human can, so we don't expect to achieve the same performance as well-optimized code. Still, we aim to show that high-level data parallel computations can perform within striking distance of human optimized efficiency code.

The Copperhead compiler and runtime is freely available at `http://code.google.com/p/copperhead`.

6.1 Sparse Matrix Vector Multiplication

Continuing with the Sparse Matrix Vector Multiplication example, we examine the performance of Copperhead generated code for three different SpMV kernels: compressed sparse row, vector compressed sparse row, and ELL. The CSR kernel is generated by compiling the Copperhead procedure for CSR SpMV onto the standard parallelism hierarchy, which distributes computations along the outermost parallelism dimension to independent threads. Data parallel operations are sequentialized into loops inside each thread. For the CSR kernel, each row of the matrix is then processed by a different thread, and consequently, adjacent threads are processing widely separated data. On the CUDA platform, this yields suboptimal performance for most datasets.

The vector CSR kernel improves on the performance of the CSR kernel by mapping to a different parallelism hierarchy: one where the outermost level distributes computations among independent thread blocks, and subsequent data parallel operations are then sequentialized to block-wise operations. As mentioned earlier, the Copperhead programmer can choose which hierarchy to map to, or can choose to autotune over hierarchies. In this case, mapping to the block-wise hierarchy improves memory performance on the CUDA platform, since adjacent threads inside the same thread block are processing adjacent data, allowing for vectorized memory accesses.

The ELL representation stores the nonzeros of the matrix in a dense M-by-K array, where K bounds the number of nonzeros per row, and rows with fewer than K nonzeros are padded. The array is stored in column-major order, so that after the computation has been mapped to the platform, adjacent threads will be accessing adjacent elements of the array. For example:

$$A = \begin{bmatrix} 1 & 7 & 0 & 0 \\ 0 & 2 & 8 & 0 \\ 5 & 0 & 3 & 9 \\ 0 & 6 & 0 & 4 \end{bmatrix} \quad \begin{array}{l} \texttt{vals = [[1,2,5,6],[7,8,3,4],[*,*,9,*]]} \\ \texttt{cols = [[0,1,0,1],[1,2,2,3],[*,*,3,*]]} \end{array}$$

ELL generally performs best on matrices where the variance of the number of non-zeros per row is small. If exceptional rows with large numbers of non-zeros exist, ELL will perform badly due to the overhead resulting from padding the smaller rows.

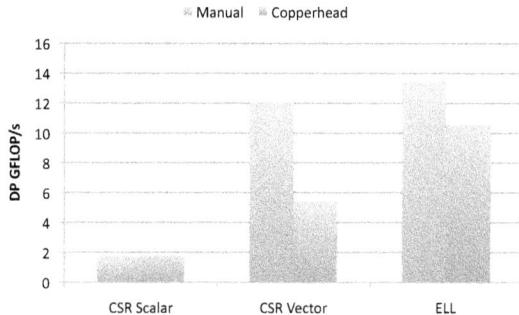

Figure 4. Average Double Precision Sparse Matrix Vector Multiply Performance

We compare against Cusp [1], a C++ library for Sparse Matrix Vector multiplication, running on an NVIDIA GeForce GTX 480 GPU. We use a suite of 8 unstructured matrices which were used by Bell and Garland [1], and which are amenable to ELL storage. Copperhead generated code achieves identical performance for the scalar CSR kernel, and on average provides 45% and 79% of Cusp performance for the vector CSR and ELL kernels, respectively.

Our relatively low performance on the vector CSR kernel is due to a specialized optimization which the Cusp vector CSR implementation takes advantage of, but the Copperhead compiler does not: namely the ability to perform "warp-wise" reductions without synchronization, packing multiple rows of the SpMV computation into a single thread block. This optimization is an important workaround for the limitations of today's CUDA processors, but we consider it too special purpose to implement in the Copperhead compiler.

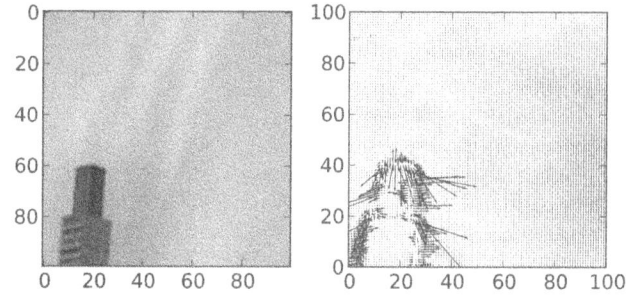

Figure 5. Left: closeup of video frame. Right: gradient vector field for optical flow

6.2 Preconditioned Conjugate Gradient Linear Solver

The Conjugate Gradient method is widely used to solve sparse systems of the form $Ax = b$. We examine performance on a preconditioned conjugate gradient solver written in Copperhead, which forms a part of an fixed-point non-linear solver used in Variational Optical Flow methods [27]. Figure 5 was generated using the `matplotlib` Python library, operating directly from the Copperhead solver, highlighting the ability of Copperhead programs to interoperate with other Python modules, such as those for plotting.

Conjugate gradient performance depends strongly on matrix-vector multiplication performance. Although we could have used a preexisting sparse-matrix library and representation, in this case we know some things about the structure of the matrix, which arises from a coupled 5-point stencil pattern on a vector field. Taking advantage of this structure, we can achieve significantly better performance than any library routine by creating a custom matrix format and sparse matrix-vector multiplication routine. This is an ideal scenario for Copperhead, since the productivity gains enable programmers to write custom routines that take advantage of special knowledge about a problem, as opposed to using a prebuilt library.

In addition to writing a custom sparse-matrix vector multiplication routine, practically solving this problem requires the use of a preconditioner, since without preconditioning, convergence is orders of magnitude slower. We utilize a block Jacobi preconditioner. Figure 6 shows the Copperhead code for computing the preconditioner, which involves inverting a set of symmetric 2x2 matrices, with one matrix for each point in the vector field, as well as applying the preconditioner, which involes a large number of symmetric 2x2 matrix multiplicaitons.

We implemented the entire solver in Copperhead. The custom SpMV routine for this matrix runs within 10% of the hand-coded CUDA version, achieving 49 SP GFLOP/s on a GTX 480, whereas a hand-tuned CUDA version achieves 55 SP GFLOP/s on the same hardware. Overall, for the complete preconditioned conjugate gradient solver, the Copperhead generated code yields 71% of the custom CUDA implementation.

6.3 Quadratic Programming: Nonlinear Support Vector Machine Training

Support Vector Machines are a widely used classification technique from machine learning. Support Vector Machines classify multi-dimensional data by checking where the data lies with respect to a decision surface. Nonlinear decision surfaces are learned via a Quadratic Programming optimization problem, which we implement in Copperhead.

We make use of the Sequential Minimal Optimization algorithm, with first-order variable selection heuristic [16], coupled with the RBF kernel, which is commonly used for nonlinear SVMs.

```
@cu
def vadd(x, y):
    return map(lambda a, b: return a + b, x, y)
@cu
def vmul(x, y):
    return map(lambda a, b: return a * b, x, y)
@cu
def form_preconditioner(a, b, c):
    def det_inverse(ai, bi, ci):
        return 1.0/(ai * ci - bi * bi)
    indets = map(det_inverse, a, b, c)
    p_a = vmul(indets, c)
    p_b = map(lambda a, b: -a * b, indets, b)
    p_c = vmul(indets, a)
    return p_a, p_b, p_c
@cu
def precondition(u, v, p_a, p_b, p_c):
    e = vadd(vmul(p_a, u), vmul(p_b, v))
    f = vadd(vmul(p_b, u), vmul(p_c, v))
    return e, f
```

Figure 6. Forming and applying the block Jacobi preconditioner

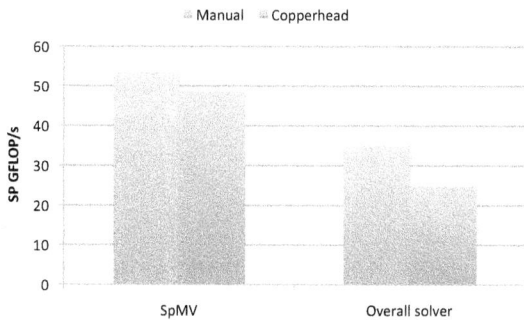

Figure 7. Performance on Preconditioned Conjugate Gradient Solver

Computationally, this is an iterative algorithm, where at each step the majority of the work is to evaluate distance functions between all data points and two active data points, update an auxiliary vector and then to select the extrema from data-dependent subsets of this vector. More details can be found in the literature [5]. Space does not permit us to include the Copperhead code that implements this solver, but we do wish to point out the RBF kernel evaluation code, shown in Figure 9, is used both on its own, where the compiler creates a version that instantiates the computation across the entire machine, as well as nested as an inner computation within a larger parallel context, where the compiler fuses it into a sequential loop.

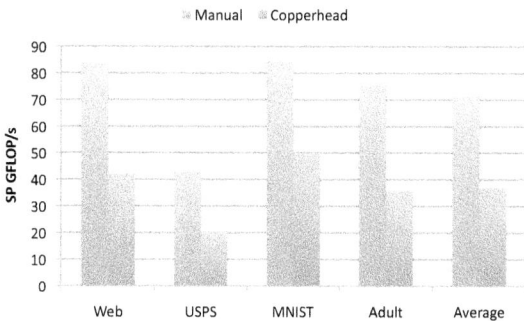

Figure 8. Support Vector Machine Training Performance

```
@cu
def norm2_diff(x, y):
    def el(xi, yi):
        diff = xi - yi
        return diff * diff
    return sum(map(el, x, y))
@cu
def rbf(gamma, x, y):
    return exp(-gamma * norm2_diff(x,y))
```

Figure 9. RBF Kernel evaluation

We compare performance against GPUSVM, a publically available CUDA library for SVM training. Figure 8 shows the throughput of the Copperhead implementation of SVM training over four datasets. On average, the Copperhead implementation attains 51% of hand-optimized, well tuned CUDA performance, which is quite good, given the Copperhead implementation's simplicity. The main advantage of the hand coded CUDA implementation on this example compared to the Copperhead compiled code is the use of on-chip memories to reduce memory traffic, and we expect that as the Copperhead compiler matures, we will be able to perform this optimization in Copperhead as well, thanks to our existing shape analysis, which can inform data placement.

6.4 Productivity

Productivity is difficult to measure, but as a rough approximation, Table 2 provides the number of lines of code needed to implement the core functionality of the examples we have put forth, in C++/CUDA as well as in Python/Copperhead. On average, the Copperhead programs take about 4 times fewer lines of code than their C++ equivalents, which suggests that Copperhead programming is indeed more productive than the manual alternatives.

Example	CUDA & C++	Copperhead & Python
Scalar CSR	16	6
Vector CSR	39	6
ELL	22	4
PCG Solver	172	79
SVM Training	429	111

Table 2. Number of Lines of Code for Example Programs

7. Future Work

There are many avenues for improving the Copperhead runtime and compiler. The first set involves improving the quality of code which the compiler emits. For example, the compiler currently does not reorder parallel primitives to increase fusion and reduce synchronization. The compiler also does not attempt to analyze data reuse and place small, yet heavily reused sequences in on-chip memories to reduce memory bandwidth, nor does it attempt to take advantage of parallelism in the dataflow graph or parallel primitives. Another avenue for future work involves broadening the scope of programs which can be compiled by the Copperhead compiler, such as supporting multi-dimensional arrays, adding new data parallel primitives, and supporting forms of recursion other than tail recursion.

We also intend to create other back-ends for the Copperhead compiler, in order to support other platforms besides CUDA. Some potential choices include support for multicore x86 processors and OpenCL platforms.

8. Conclusion

This paper has shown how to efficiently compile a nested data parallel language to modern parallel microprocessors. Instead of using flattening transforms by default, we take advantage of nested parallel hardware by mapping data parallel computations directly onto the hardware parallelism hierarchy. This mapping is enabled by synchronization and shape analyses, which which we introduce. Instead of creating a new data parallel language, we have embedded Copperhead into a widely used productivity language, which makes Copperhead programs look, feel and operate like Python programs, interoperating with the vast array of Python libraries, and lowering the amount of investment it takes for a programmer to learn data parallel programming.

We then demonstrated that our compiler generates efficient code, yielding from 45 to 100% of the performance of hand crafted, well-optimized CUDA code, but with much higher programmer productivity. On average, Copperhead programs require 3.6 times fewer lines of code than CUDA programs, comparing only the core computational portions.

Large communities of programmers choose to use productivity languages such as Python, because programmer productivity is often more important than attaining absolute maximum performance. We believe Copperhead occupies a worthwhile position in the tradeoff between productivity and performance, providing performance comparable to that of hand-optimized code, but with a fraction of the programmer effort.

9. Acknowledgments

Research partially supported by Microsoft (Award #024263) and Intel (Award #024894) funding and by matching funding from U.C. Discovery (Award #DIG07-10227). Additional support comes from Par Lab affiliates National Instruments, NEC, Nokia, NVIDIA, Samsung, and Sun Microsystems. Bryan Catanzaro was supported by an NVIDIA Graduate Fellowship.

References

[1] N. Bell and M. Garland. Implementing sparse matrix-vector multiplication on throughput-oriented processors. In *SC '09: Proc. Conference on High Performance Computing Networking, Storage and Analysis*, pages 1–11. ACM, 2009.

[2] G. E. Blelloch. *Vector models for data-parallel computing*. MIT Press, Cambridge, MA, USA, 1990. ISBN 0-262-02313-X. URL http://www.cs.cmu.edu/~guyb/papers/Ble90.pdf.

[3] G. E. Blelloch. Programming parallel algorithms. *Commun. ACM*, 39 (3):85–97, 1996.

[4] G. E. Blelloch, S. Chatterjee, J. C. Hardwick, J. Sipelstein, and M. Zagha. Implementation of a portable nested data-parallel language. *Journal of Parallel and Distributed Computing*, 21(1):4–14, Apr. 1994.

[5] B. Catanzaro, N. Sundaram, and K. Keutzer. Fast Support Vector Machine Training and Classification on Graphics Processors. In *Proceedings of the 25th International Conference on Machine Learning*, pages 104–111, 2008.

[6] B. Catanzaro, S. Kamil, Y. Lee, K. Asanović, J. Demmel, K. Keutzer, J. Shalf, K. Yelick, and A. Fox. SEJITS: Getting Productivity and Performance With Selective Embedded JIT Specialization. Technical Report UCB/EECS-2010-23, EECS Department, University of California, Berkeley, 2010.

[7] M. M. T. Chakravarty, R. Leshchinskiy, S. P. Jones, G. Keller, and S. Marlow. Data parallel Haskell: a status report. In *Proc. 2007 Workshop on Declarative Aspects of Multicore Programming*, pages 10–18. ACM, 2007.

[8] Clyther. Clyther: Python language extension for opencl. http://clyther.sourceforge.net/, 2010.

[9] Cython. Cython: C-extensions for python. http://cython.org/, 2010.

[10] R. Garg and J. N. Amaral. Compiling python to a hybrid execution environment. In *GPGPU '10: Proc. 3rd Workshop on General-Purpose Computation on Graphics Processing Units*, pages 19–30. ACM, 2010.

[11] A. Ghuloum, E. Sprangle, J. Fang, G. Wu, and X. Zhou. Ct: A Flexible Parallel Programming Model for Tera-scale Architectures. Technical Report White Paper, Intel Corporation, 2007.

[12] T. D. Han and T. S. Abdelrahman. hiCUDA: a high-level directive-based language for GPU programming. In *GPGPU-2: Proc. 2nd Workshop on General Purpose Processing on Graphics Processing Units*, pages 52–61. ACM, 2009.

[13] W. D. Hillis and J. Guy L. Steele. Data parallel algorithms. *Commun. ACM*, 29(12):1170–1183, 1986. ISSN 0001-0782.

[14] J. Hoberock and N. Bell. Thrust: A parallel template library, 2009. URL http://www.meganewtons.com/. Version 1.2.

[15] P. Hudak and M. P. Jones. Haskell vs. Ada vs. C++ vs. Awk vs...an experiment in software prototyping productivity. Technical Report YALEU/DCS/RR-1049, Yale University Department of Computer Science, New Haven, CT, 1994.

[16] S. S. Keerthi, S. K. Shevade, C. Bhattacharyya, and K. R. K. Murthy. Improvements to Platt's SMO Algorithm for SVM Classifier Design. *Neural Comput.*, 13(3):637–649, 2001. ISSN 0899-7667.

[17] A. Klöckner. Codepy. http://mathema.tician.de/software/codepy, 2010.

[18] A. Klöckner, N. Pinto, Y. Lee, B. Catanzaro, P. Ivanov, and A. Fasih. Pycuda: Gpu run-time code generation for high-performance computing. *CoRR*, abs/0911.3456, 2009.

[19] S. Lee, M. M. T. Chakravarty, V. Grover, and G. Keller. GPU kernels as data-parallel array computations in Haskell. In *Workshop on Exploiting Parallelism using GPUs and other Hardware-Assisted Methods (EPAHM 2009)*, 2009.

[20] S. Lee, S.-J. Min, and R. Eigenmann. OpenMP to GPGPU: a compiler framework for automatic translation and optimization. In *Proc. 14th ACM SIGPLAN Symposium on Principles and Practice of Parallel Programming*, pages 101–110. ACM, 2009.

[21] M. McCool. Data-parallel programming on the Cell BE and the GPU using the RapidMind development platform. In *Proc. GSPx Multicore Applications Conference*, Nov. 2006.

[22] M. D. McCool, Z. Qin, and T. S. Popa. Shader metaprogramming. In *Proc. Graphics Hardware 2002*, pages 57–68. Eurographics Association, 2002.

[23] J. Nickolls, I. Buck, M. Garland, and K. Skadron. Scalable parallel programming with CUDA. *Queue*, 6(2):40–53, Mar/Apr 2008.

[24] *NVIDIA CUDA C Programming Guide*. NVIDIA Corporation, May 2010. URL http://www.nvidia.com/CUDA. Version 3.1.

[25] L. Prechelt. Are Scripting Languages Any Good? A Validation of Perl, Python, Rexx, and Tcl against C, C++, and Java. In *Advances in Computers*, volume 57, pages 205 – 270. Elsevier, 2003.

[26] J. Sanders and E. Kandrot. *CUDA by Example: An Introduction to General-Purpose GPU Programming*. Addison-Wesley, July 2010. ISBN 978-0-13-138768-3.

[27] N. Sundaram, T. Brox, and K. Keutzer. Dense Point Trajectories by GPU-accelerated Large Displacement Optical Flow. In *European Conference on Computer Vision*, pages 438–445, September 2010.

[28] D. Tarditi, S. Puri, and J. Oglesby. Accelerator: using data parallelism to program GPUs for general-purpose uses. *SIGARCH Comput. Archit. News*, 34(5):325–335, 2006.

[29] Theano. Theano: A python array expression library. http://deeplearning.net/software/theano/, 2010.

[30] M. Wolfe. Implementing the PGI accelerator model. In *Proc. 3rd Workshop on General-Purpose Computation on Graphics Processing Units*, pages 43–50. ACM, 2010.

OoOJava: Software Out-of-Order Execution

James C. Jenista   Yong hun Eom   Brian Demsky

Department of Electrical Engineering and Computer Science
University of California, Irvine
Irvine, CA 92697
{jjenista, yeom, bdemsky}@uci.edu

Abstract

Developing parallel software using current tools can be challenging. Even experts find it difficult to reason about the use of locks and often accidentally introduce race conditions and deadlocks into parallel software. OoOJava is a compiler-assisted approach that leverages developer annotations along with static analysis to provide an easy-to-use deterministic parallel programming model. OoOJava extends Java with a task annotation that instructs the compiler to consider a code block for out-of-order execution. OoOJava executes tasks as soon as their data dependences are resolved and guarantees that the execution of an annotated program preserves the exact semantics of the original sequential program. We have implemented OoOJava and achieved an average speedup of $16.6\times$ on our ten benchmarks.

Categories and Subject Descriptors   D.1.3 [*Concurrent Programming*]: Parallel programming

General Terms   Algorithms, Languages, Performance

1. Introduction

Mainstream processors currently ship with as many as twelve cores and processors with as many as 1,000 cores will become commonplace within a few years [5]. Software development tools lag behind hardware platforms; developing parallel software using current tools is both difficult and error-prone. They require developers to reason carefully about the interactions of many parallel threads to write correct software — a task which even the best developers find extremely difficult. Experience shows that applications written using existing models are prone to both races and deadlocks.

Deterministic programming models have been recognized to simplify developing parallel code by eliminating race conditions [4]. Deterministic parallel programming systems exist today that strive to take sequential code with parallelization annotations and generate a parallel implementation with the same behavior but better performance. However, much of this work either limits the structure of the code that can be parallelized (loops only) [9], constrains the usage of data structures [2, 20], requires extensive annotations [4, 24], or only guarantees determinism under unchecked conditions (disjoint data structures) [11, 22, 28].

Hardware has long extracted unstructured parallelism from sequential instruction streams through out-of-order execution [29]. Processors dynamically extract dependences between sequential instructions and then execute the instructions out-of-order while preserving the dependences. This paper leverages the same proven techniques at a coarser granularity to parallelize software.

OoOJava provides a deterministic parallel programming model by extending sequential Java with a single annotation, a task, to instruct the compiler to consider a code block for out-of-order execution. OoOJava executes tasks as soon as their data dependences are resolved and guarantees that the execution of an annotated program preserves the exact semantics of the *serial elision*, the sequential program obtained by removing all annotations. The annotations affect program performance but never correctness.

This basic approach has been known for some time. We leverage a new extension to pointer analysis, disjoint reachability analysis [17], to augment our modified approach to effects [19]. OoOJava uses the results of disjoint reachability analysis to generate a handful of lightweight comparisons that allow it to safely dynamically extract parallelism even when the heap accesses cannot be statically determined to be disjoint. We combine this with a new value forwarding approach that is analogous to register renaming and eliminates write-after-write and write-after-read hazards for variables. These techniques allow OoOJava to parallelize a wide range of programs while requiring few changes to sequential code.

This paper makes the following contributions:

- **OoOJava:** It presents a deterministic parallel programming model that extends Java with the task annotation while preserving the program's sequential semantics. Because of OoOJava's similarity to Java, developers will likely find it easy to use.

- **Dependence Analysis:** OoOJava uses static analysis to discover variable and heap dependences.

- **Software-Based Out-of-Order Execution:** Processors execute instructions out-of-order to extract fine-grained, unstructured parallelism. OoOJava adapts out-of-order execution techniques to parallelize code blocks in its software runtime and guarantees that the execution respects all dependences.

- **An Implementation and Evaluation:** We have implemented OoOJava and evaluated its performance on ten benchmarks.

The remainder of the paper is organized as follows. Section 2 presents an example. Section 3 presents an overview of our approach. Section 4 presents our approach to managing variable dependences. Section 5 presents our approach to managing heap dependences. Section 6 discusses various aspects of our system. Section 7 evaluates the approach on several benchmark applications. Section 8 discusses related work; we conclude in Section 9.

2. Example

We present a compiler example to illustrate OoOJava. Figure 1 presents the `typeCheckAndFlatten` method that begins compiling a set of methods. Consider this method without the `task` keyword or the associated curly braces. The loop retrieves the abstract syntax tree (AST) associated with a method in Line 5, type checks the AST in Line 7, and flattens the AST into a control flow graph (CFG) in Line 8. If different loop iterations operate on dif-

```
 1  public void typeCheckAndFlatten () {
 2    Iterator <MethodDesc> methodsItr=allMethods.iterator ();
 3    while ( methodsItr.hasNext () ) {
 4      MethodDesc m = methodsItr.next ();
 5      AST ast = m2ast.get ( m );
 6      task par {   // Parallelizable task
 7        ast.typeCheck ();
 8        CFG cfg = ast.flatten ();
 9      }
10      task seq {   // Sequential task
11        m2cfg.put ( m, cfg );
12      }
13    }
14    m2cfg.serializeToDisk ();
15  }
```

Figure 1. Compiler Example

ferent AST's and the AST's do not share mutable data, Lines 7 through 8 from different iterations can run in parallel. However, the loop iterations are not completely independent. Line 11 stores the CFG for every loop iteration into the same hashtable and therefore has a dependence on itself from the previous loop iteration.

OoOJava extends the sequential programming model with the task annotation that hints to the compiler that it can decouple the annotated block of code from the parent thread's execution. A task is declared with the keyword `task`, followed by a name for the task and a pair of braces enclosing the block. Task names have no semantic meaning but are useful for communicating feedback about dependences between tasks to the developer. Tasks do not introduce a new variable scope — variables declared in a task can be accessed outside of the task. A task must have a single exit.

In our example, we enclosed Lines 7 and 8 in the task `par` to decouple their execution from the main thread. An instance of the task `par` can be safely executed in parallel if the variable `ast` references a different object than it does in previous iterations, and the objects in the AST that are updated are only reachable from one `AST` object. Parallelizing this loop poses a problem for most automatic parallelization systems — it is difficult to statically determine that different loop iterations access different `AST` objects.

Line 11 poses a challenge for parallelization — it has a dependence on the result of flattening the AST and a sequential dependence on itself from the previous loop iteration. We enclose Line 11 in the task `seq` to allow the main thread to continue past this statement to dispatch other task instances. The sequential dependence will force all instances of `seq` to execute serially.

3. Execution Model

OoOJava's execution model is inspired by out-of-order processors. An out-of-order processor takes as input an instruction stream. When the processor *issues* the next instruction in the stream, it records any dependences of the instruction on previously issued instructions. The processor *dispatches* an instruction to an available functional unit when the instruction's dependences are resolved. A completed instruction *retires* by updating the processor's state.

Similarly, when a thread reaches the definition of a task, it allocates a record for the task and makes a runtime count of all outstanding dependences the task has on its sibling tasks. The thread then issues the task and skips to the end of the task declaration to immediately resume executing its own code. OoOJava dispatches a task when its dependences are fully resolved. When a task finishes execution, it waits for all of its children to retire before it retires.

Tasks can be nested and there is an implicit top-level task for the main method. Tasks in OoOJava form a tree at runtime. A parent is responsible for issuing its children and managing the dependences among its children and itself.

A key component to our approach is conservatively extracting dependences between tasks to ensure that parallel execution pre-serves the behavior of the program's serial elision. Program dependences can take two forms: control dependences and data dependences. OoOJava handles control dependences implicitly by constraining a task to have a single exit. One implication is that a task should not throw an exception that it does not catch. Section 6 discusses the constraints OoOJava places on exceptions in more detail.

A task may have a data dependence on another task through a variable or through conflicting heap accesses to the same object. Different dynamic instances of the same task access the same variables. Like register renaming in out-of-order hardware, a critical component of parallelization is to eliminate write-after-write and write-after-read hazards on variables by forwarding values directly to the consuming task. Section 4 presents our analysis for extracting variable dependences and our strategy for respecting them.

OoOJava structures task dependence relations to minimize overheads. Nested task annotations can generate dynamic trees of tasks. If we allow dependences between arbitrary tasks in the hierarchy then the maintenance of dependences becomes a global problem and a potential bottleneck. OoOJava restricts task dependence relations to be only parent-child or sibling-sibling in nature. OoOJava enforces this structure by attributing a child's dependences to its parent and only retiring a task after all of its children have retired. This structure simplifies the management of dependences by localizing the problem; a parent manages the dependences between itself and its children. Moreover, it allows our implementation to parallelize dependence tracking and therefore supports scaling to systems with a large number of cores.

4. Variable Dependences

A task has a variable dependence on a second task if it reads a variable that was last written by the second task. In the example from Section 2, task `seq` reads the value of the variable `cfg` that the most recent instance of task `par` wrote. Therefore, the task `seq` has a variable dependence on the most recent instance of the task `par` for the variable `cfg`'s value. The variable dependence analysis statically extracts variable dependences between tasks.

4.1 Variable Dependence Analysis

Variable dependence analysis abstracts the source of a variable's current value with a variable source tuple that consists of (1) the name of the task that produced the value, (2) which instance of that task, relative to the most recent dynamic instance, produced the value, and (3) which variable it wrote the value to. Variable source tuples are useful as they statically characterize how the program's execution propagates values in variables between tasks.

To be more precise, the variable source for the variable $v_1 \in V$ has the form $\langle t, g, v_2 \rangle \in S \subseteq T \times G \times V$. The combination of a task $t \in T$ and an age $g \in G$ of that task (i.e. how many instances of that task have been issued between the source instance and the current program point) together statically specify a dynamic instance of a task. To bound the analysis, g is taken from the set $G = \{0, 1, \ldots, k\}$, where a variable source with $g = k$ means an instance with an unknown age and $g = 0$ means the most recent instance. The variable $v_2 \in V$ specifies which variable at the exit of the task given by t and g contains the relevant value. A variable source provides a complete abstract address for the variable's value.

Each task has a set of in-set variables and a set of out-set variables. A task's in-set variables are variables read by the task that were written to before it began executing. Similarly, out-set variables are variables a task writes values to that may be read outside of that task. Our analysis calculates in-set and out-set variables by examining variable sources at a task's enter and exit points. In the example, task `par` has the in-set $\{ast\}$ and the out-set $\{cfg\}$ while task `seq` has the in-set $\{m2cfg, m, cfg\}$. Task in-sets and out-sets combined with variable source tuples provide the necessary information to route the values of variables between tasks.

	Example Code	M at the exit of the line
4	`MethodDesc m = methodsItr.next();`	$\{\langle \mathtt{m}, \langle \mathtt{main}, 0, \mathtt{m}\rangle\rangle\}$
5	`AST ast = m2ast.get( m );`	$\{\langle \mathtt{m}, \langle \mathtt{main}, 0, \mathtt{m}\rangle\rangle, \langle \mathtt{ast}, \langle \mathtt{main}, 0, \mathtt{ast}\rangle\rangle\}$
6	`task par {`	$\{\langle \mathtt{m}, \langle \mathtt{main}, 0, \mathtt{m}\rangle\rangle, \langle \mathtt{ast}, \langle \mathtt{main}, 0, \mathtt{ast}\rangle\rangle\}$
7	`ast.typeCheck();`	$\{\langle \mathtt{m}, \langle \mathtt{main}, 0, \mathtt{m}\rangle\rangle, \langle \mathtt{ast}, \langle \mathtt{main}, 0, \mathtt{ast}\rangle\rangle\}$
8	`CFG cfg = ast.flatten();`	$\{\langle \mathtt{m}, \langle \mathtt{main}, 0, \mathtt{m}\rangle\rangle, \langle \mathtt{ast}, \langle \mathtt{main}, 0, \mathtt{ast}\rangle\rangle, \langle \mathtt{cfg}, \langle \mathtt{par}, 0, \mathtt{cfg}\rangle\rangle\}$
9	`}`	$\{\langle \mathtt{m}, \langle \mathtt{main}, 0, \mathtt{m}\rangle\rangle, \langle \mathtt{cfg}, \langle \mathtt{par}, 0, \mathtt{cfg}\rangle\rangle\}$
10	`task seq {`	$\{\langle \mathtt{m}, \langle \mathtt{main}, 0, \mathtt{m}\rangle\rangle, \langle \mathtt{cfg}, \langle \mathtt{par}, 0, \mathtt{cfg}\rangle\rangle\}$
11	`m2cfg.put( m, cfg );`	$\{\langle \mathtt{m}, \langle \mathtt{main}, 0, \mathtt{m}\rangle\rangle, \langle \mathtt{cfg}, \langle \mathtt{par}, 0, \mathtt{cfg}\rangle\rangle\}$
12	`}`	$\{\}$

Figure 2. Example for Variable Dependence Analysis

4.1.1 Example

Figure 2 presents the results of the variable dependence analysis on the main loop from the example; for brevity we limit the variables analyzed to `m`, `ast`, and `cfg`. The left column of the figure shows the code and the right column shows the relevant variable source entries in the set M at the exit of the line. When a statement writes to a variable, it generates variable source tuples with the current task instance as the source task. For example, after Line 8 writes to the variable `cfg`, the set M gains the tuple $\langle \mathtt{cfg}, \langle \mathtt{par}, 0, \mathtt{cfg}\rangle\rangle$. This tuple indicates that the current value of the variable `cfg` was computed by the `par` task, that the current instance of this task produced the value, and it is available in that task instance's `cfg` variable. This result will expose a variable dependence of task `seq` on task `par`. The fact that the variable `cfg` maps to the tuple $\langle \mathtt{par}, 0, \mathtt{cfg}\rangle$ informs the compiler that task `seq` must obtain the value of `cfg` from the most recent instance of task `par`.

4.1.2 Abstract Domains

The analysis is structured as a standard forward dataflow analysis. There is a set L for each program point of the live variables at the entrance to that program point. The analysis computes a mapping $M \subseteq V \times S$ at each program point. The relation M maps a variable to the set of variable source tuples that describe the possible sources of the variable's value. At program entry, M is empty.

The mapping M forms a lattice. The partial order ($\sqsubseteq$) is defined by the subset relation ($\subseteq$); join ($\sqcup$) is set union ($\cup$); bottom ($\perp$) is the empty set ($\emptyset$); and top ($\top$) is the maximally full set. The lattice M has a finite height because both the set of live variables and the set of variable source tuples are finite.

4.1.3 Program Representation

To simplify the transfer functions we decompose program statements into simple operations: variable reads denoted $\mathrm{rd}(\mathtt{x})$, variable writes denoted $\mathrm{wr}(\mathtt{x})$, and copy statements. For example, the analysis views method invocations as a read of every argument followed by a write to the return value. Finally, the entry and exit points of tasks are relevant; for task t the analysis recognizes $\mathrm{enter}(t)$ and $\mathrm{exit}(t)$.

4.1.4 Transfer Functions

Figure 3 presents the transfer functions for the variable dependence analysis, each of the form $M' = (M - \text{KILL}) \cup \text{GEN}$. We define the convenience function $M(\mathtt{x}) = \{s \mid \langle \mathtt{x}, s\rangle \in M\}$.

Write Statement: When a statement writes to a variable the enclosing task becomes the new source of that variable's value. The GEN set for the statement $\mathrm{wr}(\mathtt{x})$ creates the tuple $\langle \mathtt{x}, \langle t, 0, \mathtt{x}\rangle\rangle$, indicating that the current value of $\mathtt{x}$ was written to by most recent instance of the task t and was stored in the variable $\mathtt{x}$ at the exit of task t. Writing a new value to a variable removes the old values of that variable. Therefore, the KILL set for the statement $\mathrm{wr}(\mathtt{x})$ removes all of the previous sources for the variable $\mathtt{x}$.

Read Statement: Our compiler implements several optimizations to reduce the overhead of communicating values between tasks through variables. The transfer functions for statements that

st	$M' = (M - \text{KILL}) \cup \text{GEN}$
$\mathrm{wr}(\mathtt{x})$	$\text{KILL} = \{\mathtt{x}\} \times M(\mathtt{x})$
	$\text{GEN} = \{\langle \mathtt{x}, \langle t_{\mathrm{curr}}, 0, \mathtt{x}\rangle\rangle\}$
$\mathrm{rd}(\mathtt{x})$	Single child sources:
	If $M(\mathtt{x}) = \{\langle t_{\mathrm{child}}, g, v_1\rangle, \ldots, \langle t_{\mathrm{child}}, g, v_m\rangle\} \wedge$
	$\qquad t_{\mathrm{child}}$ is a child of t_{curr}
	$\quad Y = \{\forall y \in L \mid \exists w_1, \ldots, w_k,$
	$\qquad M(y) = \{\langle t_{\mathrm{child}}, g, w_1\rangle, \ldots,$
	$\qquad \langle t_{\mathrm{child}}, g, w_k\rangle\}\}$
	$\text{KILL} = \{\langle y, s\rangle \mid \forall y \in Y, \forall s \in M(y)\}$
	$\text{GEN} = \{\langle y, \langle t_{\mathrm{curr}}, 0, y\rangle\rangle\} \mid \forall y \in Y\}$.
	Mixed sources case:
	If $M(\mathtt{x}) = \{\langle t_{\mathrm{child}}, g_1, v_1\rangle, \langle t_2, g_2, v_2\rangle, \ldots\} \wedge$
	$\qquad t_{\mathrm{child}}$ is a child of t_{curr}
	$\text{KILL} = \{\mathtt{x}\} \times M(\mathtt{x}),$
	$\text{GEN} = \{\mathtt{x}\} \times \{\langle t_{\mathrm{curr}}, 0, \mathtt{x}\rangle\}$.
	No child sources case:
	$\qquad \text{KILL} = \text{GEN} = \emptyset$
$\mathtt{x} = \mathtt{y}$	$\text{KILL} = \{\mathtt{x}\} \times M(\mathtt{x})$
	$\text{GEN} = \{\langle t, g, v\rangle \in M(\mathtt{x}) \mid t \text{ is a child of } t_{\mathrm{curr}}\} \cup$
	$\quad \{\langle t_{\mathrm{curr}}, 0, \mathtt{x}\rangle \mid \langle t, g, v\rangle \in M(\mathtt{x}) \wedge$
	$\quad \neg t \text{ is a child of } t_{\mathrm{curr}}\}$
$\mathrm{enter}(t_{\mathrm{curr}})$	$\text{KILL} = \{\langle t, g, w\rangle \mid \forall \langle t, g, w\rangle \in M \wedge t = t_{\mathrm{curr}}\}$
	$\text{GEN} = \{\langle t, g \oplus 1, w\rangle \mid \forall \langle t, g, w\rangle \in M \wedge t = t_{\mathrm{curr}}\}$
	$g_1 \oplus g_2 = \begin{cases} g_1 + g_2 & \text{if } g_1 + g_2 < k, \\ k & \text{otherwise.} \end{cases}$
$\mathrm{exit}(t_{\mathrm{curr}})$	$Z = \{z \in L \mid M(z) = \{\langle t, g, v\rangle, \ldots\} \wedge$
	$\quad (t \text{ is a child of } t_{\mathrm{curr}} \vee t = t_{\mathrm{curr}})\}$
	$\text{KILL} = \{\langle z, s\rangle \mid \forall z \in Z, \forall s \in M(z)\}$
	$\text{GEN} = \{\langle z, \langle t_{\mathrm{curr}}, 0, z\rangle\rangle \mid z \in Z\}$.

Figure 3. Transfer Functions for Variable Dependence Analysis (t_{curr} denotes the currently executing task)

read from variables must account for these optimizations. If a statement reads from a variable whose value was written by a child task of the current task, the statement must stall (wait) for the child task to complete and then copy the value from the child. If the compiler can statically determine the exact child task instance the statement reads from, it can optimize the code to eliminate future dynamic checks by copying the values for all other variables that it can determine were written to by the same child task. The single child source rule gives the transfer function for this case. The KILL part of the transfer function for the single child source for $\mathrm{rd}(\mathtt{x})$ kills the variable sources for all variables with the same source as the variable $\mathtt{x}$. The GEN part of the transfer function replaces the variable sources for these variables with new sources for the current task to indicate that the variables' values are currently available.

If the compiler determines that a variable may contain a value written to by a child task but cannot statically determine the exact

59

instance, it can only copy the value for that variable. The mixed source rule gives the transfer function for this case. The KILL part of the transfer function for the statement $\mathrm{rd}(\mathtt{x})$ removes the old variable sources for the variable $\mathtt{x}$. The GEN part of the transfer function for the statement $\mathrm{rd}(\mathtt{x})$ adds a new source for the current task to indicate that the variable $\mathtt{x}$'s value is currently available.

If none of the sources for a variable's value is a child, then the value is currently available and the read has no effect on variable sources. The transfer function for this case does not change M.

Copy Statement: The variable dependence analysis uses a separate transfer function for the copy statement $\mathtt{x} = \mathtt{y}$ rather than decomposing it into the combination of a read and a write statement, because the analysis can utilize the semantics of a copy to potentially eliminate stalls. The key observation is that copy statements do not immediately need the value of a variable and therefore can be lazily evaluated. Our compiler leverages this observation to delay stalls for copy statements when possible. This optimization can allow the program to possibly issue more tasks and improve parallelism or even eliminate the stall completely if the variable is overwritten. The transfer function for the copy statement copies the abstract variable sources from $\mathtt{y}$ to $\mathtt{x}$ if the variable $\mathtt{y}$ includes a child task source. Otherwise, the variable's value is currently available and it operates the same as the transfer function for $\mathrm{wr}(\mathtt{x})$.

Enter Statement: When a source from a task flows across a back edge and reaches the enter statement for the same task, OoOJava must perform some bookkeeping. The problem is that variable sources name a dynamic instance of a task; at the creation of a new instance of a task, previous instances of the same task age by one. The transfer function for the statement $\mathtt{enter}(t_{\mathrm{curr}})$ in Figure 3 increments the age of previous variable sources from t_{curr}. The analysis becomes finite by bounding the age by k; a variable source with the age k is interpreted as an unknown age.

Exit Statement: Recall the discussion in Section 3 of the design decision to simplify the management of task dependence relations by attributing a child task's dependences to its parent. An implication of this decision is that the transfer function for an exit statement must reflect that a parent task becomes the source for all of its children's values. The transfer function for the $\mathtt{exit}(t_{\mathrm{curr}})$ statement finds variables with at least one child source and changes such variables to have exactly one source, the current task instance. The compiler generates code to copy the values from the child tasks to the current task. Other variable's sources remain unchanged.

4.1.5 Virtual Reads

We introduce virtual reads to simplify the runtime management of variable dependences. Consider the following problem: which task is the source of a variable when a later task conditionally writes to that variable? We want to avoid the overhead of searching through a series of tasks at runtime to find a variable's value.

Our solution is to treat a conditional write to a variable as a virtual read. The variable dependence analysis identifies this case in the $\mathtt{exit}(t_{\mathrm{curr}})$ transfer function: it occurs when a live variable at the task exit has a mixture of sources that are from both (1) outside of the current dynamic task instance and (2) from inside the current instance and its children. The transfer function forces such a task to require the variable's value before starting to execute and therefore when the task exits, it has the variable's value.

4.2 Code Generation

We next describe how the compiler uses the results of the variable dependence analysis to generate code. We divide code generation for accessing a variable $\mathtt{x}$ within task t_{curr} into three categories based on $M(\mathtt{x})$ at the relevant program point:

Immediate Access: When all of the sources in $M(\mathtt{x})$ are from the current task t_{curr}, its ancestors, or their siblings, the variable stores a currently available value. Therefore, the compiler simply generates normal code to access the variable $\mathtt{x}$ immediately.

Optimized Stall: When all of the sources in $M(\mathtt{x})$ are from a single instance of a child t_{child} with an age less than k, then the compiler statically knows which dynamic task instance will provide the value for variable $\mathtt{x}$. In this case the generated code should stall the current task until t_{child} retires and copy the value of $\mathtt{x}$ before generating a normal access to $\mathtt{x}$. If the same task is statically known to be the source of other variables, the compiler generates code to also read those values. This optimization avoids the overhead of extra dynamic checks for future accesses to those variables.

Dynamic Tracking: Otherwise, the analysis cannot track the variable's source statically. In this case, the compiler identifies the points in the control flow graph at which the sources for the variable became unknown statically. At these points, the compiler inserts code to dynamically track which task generates the variable's value. The compiler must also handle the case in which it is statically unknown whether the variable's value is currently available — in this case the code tracks (1) whether the variable has a value, (2) the actual value if it is available, and (3) the source of the value if the value is not currently available. Code is placed just prior to the variable access to check whether the value is available or whether to stall for the task instance that will provide the value.

To complete code generation for variable accesses, the compiler generates bookkeeping code at the exit statement of each task. As mentioned in our discussion of the task exit transfer function, a parent becomes the source for the values of its children, so the compiler generates code to stall a task until all of its children have retired. Then the task copies the values from the children to itself and makes them available for other tasks to access.

At each task entrance, the compiler generates code to issue the task. Each task maintains a count of its unresolved dependences. This count is updated using atomic operations. The issue code iterates over all of the sibling tasks that the issued task depends on. If the sibling task has not retired, the newly issued task is added to its forwarding list. When the sibling task retires, it decrements the dependence count of all tasks on its forwarding list. When the dependence count reaches zero, the task is dispatched for execution. The dependence count includes both heap dependences and variable dependences; Section 5.4.4 discusses the heap contributions.

5. Heap Dependence Analysis

Heap dependences have long posed a challenge to automatically parallelizing code that manipulates data structures. OoOJava reasons about a heap access in terms of the *heap root* used to reach the accessed heap object; a heap root is an object referenced by a live variable through which deeper heap references are obtained. Heap roots occur in two contexts: a heap root is either referenced by a variable in the in-set of a task, or it is the first object along a heap path accessed by a parent task after the exit of a child task. In the latter case, we refer to the parent statement that accesses the variable as a potential *stall site* because the parent task may have to stall there for a child task to complete.

Two tasks can only have a heap dependence when both of the following two conditions are true. The first condition is that one task writes to a field f of an object allocated at site a and a second task either reads or writes to the field f of an object allocated at site a. We call the pair of accesses potentially conflicting accesses and objects allocated at site a potentially conflicting objects. The second necessary condition is that there must exist a potentially conflicting object that is reachable from the heap roots of both tasks that perform the potentially conflicting accesses.

5.1 Heap Dependence Overview

We next present a straightforward dynamic approach for preserving heap dependences. We will later extend this basic approach with the static analysis that OoOJava uses to make this approach efficient.

5.1.1 Naïve Dynamic Approach

OoOJava uses an effects analysis extension to a standard pointer analysis to report all possible heap accesses a task may execute. Effects are reported as a 4-tuple consisting of (1) the heap root used to access the affected object, (2) the allocation site of the affected object, (3) the effect type (read or write), and (4) the affected field.

In the example from Section 2, the effects analysis would report write effects to objects in the AST due to the call to the `typeCheck` method at Line 7. The analysis would also report read effects to the objects in the AST due to the calls to both the `typeCheck` method at Line 7 and the `flatten` method at Line 8. In both cases, the task `par` reached the affected objects through the AST object referenced by the `ast` in-set variable.

In many cases, the compiler can statically determine that two effects cannot conflict. However, statically checking that the updates to the ASTs do not conflict is difficult because two instances of the task `par` may both write to the same AST objects. We next describe a dynamic approach that can rule out such conflicts.

To issue an instance p of task `par`, the system would dynamically check for conflicts between p and all instances of tasks that have not retired: take, for example, an earlier instance p_0 of the task `par`. The runtime would traverse the heap reachable from the in-set variable `ast` to identify all concrete objects that the effects can apply to; the dynamic check would use the allocation site information to prune the set of objects that an effect could apply to. If this dynamic check shows that there are no conflicting accesses between the instance p and all previous non-retired task instances to the same object, then it is safe to immediately dispatch p. One potential concern is that a data structure may not yet contain all objects that it will when the task is supposed to run. However, in this case there will be a conflict detected on some existing object that will eventually reference the additional objects.

This dynamic approach can incur significant overhead for large data structures. In the next section, we describe how OoOJava uses static analysis to eliminate these overheads.

5.1.2 Optimization

The key insight behind OoOJava is to use reachability results from static analysis combined with simple dynamic checks to make the previous approach practical. For example, if we can determine (1) that all affected objects in an AST are only reachable from at most one AST object through static analysis and (2) that different instances of the task `par` operate on different AST objects through a dynamic check, then there is no conflict between the tasks.

We introduce an effects analysis in Section 5.2 to discover a set of effects that conservatively summarizes the heap effects of a task. Section 5.3 presents an overview of the approach to reachability analysis that we use to statically compute the reachability of objects from the heap roots in the effects. Section 5.3.2 presents rules for determining whether two effects conflict. Finally, Section 5.4 describes how OoOJava efficiently implements the dynamic checks to preserve all heap dependences between tasks.

5.2 Effects Analysis

OoOJava uses heap effects to conservatively abstract the read and write heap accesses a task may perform.

5.2.1 Abstract Domains

OoOJava represents an effect with the 4-tuple $\langle h, a^{\text{aff}}, o, f \rangle \in U \subseteq H \times A \times O \times F$, where h is the heap root used to access the affected object, $a^{\text{aff}} \in A$ is the allocation site of the affected object, $o \in O = \{\text{read}, \text{write}, \text{strong}\}$ is the operation, and $f \in F$ is the affected field.

Recall that the analysis uses two different types of heap roots. The first type of heap root abstracts the objects referenced by a task's in-set variables. The second type abstracts objects referenced by live variables after the exit of a child task. Formally, a heap root

h is given by the tuple $\langle st, v, a \rangle \in H \subseteq ST \times V \times A$, where st is either a stall site or the entrance to a task, v is the stall site variable or in-set variable, and a is the allocation site of the object referenced by v at location st.

The analysis assumes the presence of a pointer analysis. Our implementation uses the underlying pointer analysis for disjoint reachability analysis, but for the purposes of this discussion many available pointer analyses may serve. We assume the pointer analysis abstracts objects with a set of heap nodes $n \in N$ and heap references with a set of edges $e \in E \subseteq V \times N \cup N \times F \times N$. We define helper functions $E(\mathtt{x}) = \{\langle \mathtt{x}, n \rangle \in E\}$ and $E(\mathtt{x}, \mathtt{f}) = \{\langle n, \mathtt{f}, n' \rangle \in E \mid \langle \mathtt{x}, n \rangle \in E\}$. We also assume that the pointer analysis provides a function $\mathcal{A}$ that maps a heap node to an allocation site. Though we assume a heap node only abstracts objects allocated at one site, modifications to support pointer analyses in which heap nodes abstract objects allocated at multiple sites are straightforward. The analysis computes at each program point the mapping $R \subseteq E \times H$ from an edge to the heap roots that were used to reach the edge's target object.

The analysis also computes at each program point a set of variables $\mathcal{L}$ that the application may have to stall for before accessing the object they reference. These stalls occur if the variable references a heap root leading to a potentially conflicting object.

The mapping R and set $\mathcal{L}$ both form lattices. The partial order ($\sqsubseteq$) is defined by the subset relation ($\subseteq$); join ($\sqcup$) is set union ($\cup$); bottom ($\bot$) is the empty set ($\emptyset$); and top ($\top$) is the maximally full set. The lattices have finite heights because their domains are finite.

The analysis generates a set of effects U for the program. Note that there is only one set of effects for the entire program.

5.2.2 Example

We present the calculation of R and then U for the task `par` as an example of the effects analysis. Assume `Hashtable` objects, `AST` objects and `TreeNode` objects in our running example are allocated at program points a_{HT}, a_{AST} and a_{TN}, respectively.

At the task entrance in Line 6 of Figure 1 the effects analysis maps the edge $\langle \mathtt{ast}, n_{\text{AST}} \rangle$ to a new heap root $\langle \mathtt{par}, \mathtt{ast}, a_{\text{AST}} \rangle$. Deeper heap references acquired through in-set variable `ast` will map to the same heap root.

At the invocation of the `typeCheck` method in Line 7 of Figure 1 the analysis will propagate the heap root for the argument edge $\langle \mathtt{ast}, n_{\text{AST}} \rangle$ in the main context to the parameter edge $\langle \mathtt{this}, n_{\text{AST}} \rangle$ in the `typeCheck` method context, as shown in Figure 5(a). Figure 4 lists the `typeCheck` method. Line 104 in Figure 4 initializes the variable `tmp` that will be used to traverse `TreeNode` objects; the effects analysis maps this new heap reference to the heap root of the reference it is obtained from, namely $\langle \mathtt{par}, \mathtt{ast}, a_{\text{AST}} \rangle$. Figure 5(a) gives the complete mappings in R after analyzing the `typeCheck` method.

The second pass of the effects analysis will compute the program effects. Line 104 in Figure 4 reads the `root` field of the object referenced by `this`. At this program point, R maps the edge $\langle \mathtt{this}, n_{\text{AST}} \rangle$ to the heap root $\langle \mathtt{par}, \mathtt{ast}, a_{\text{AST}} \rangle$, so this heap root will be the first element of the new effect generated at this statement. The second element of the effect

```
101   public class AST {
102     ...
103       public void typeCheck() {
104         TreeNode tmp = this.root;
105         while (...) {
106           tmp.type = ...;
107           tmp = tmp.children[...];
108           ...
```

Figure 4. Listing of the `typeCheck` method invoked in Figure 1.

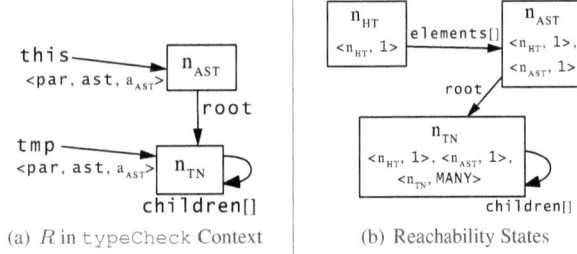

(a) R in `typeCheck` Context   (b) Reachability States

Figure 5. Examples for Heap Dependence Analysis

is the allocation site for the object affected by this read, given by $\mathcal{A}(n_{\text{AST}}) = a_{\text{AST}}$. The latter elements of the effect are the heap access operation and the affected field, making the effect $\langle\langle\texttt{par}, \texttt{ast}, a_{\text{AST}}\rangle, a_{\text{AST}}, \texttt{read}, \texttt{root}\rangle$ that is added to U at this program point. We can interpret this effect as a read of the `root` field of an object allocated at site a_{AST}, and the local heap reference was obtained through a heap root object allocated at a_{AST} and referenced by the in-set variable `ast` of task `par`. Line 106 adds the effect $\langle\langle\texttt{par}, \texttt{ast}, a_{\text{AST}}\rangle, a_{\text{TN}}, \texttt{write}, \texttt{type}\rangle$ to U, which is a write to the `type` field of a `TreeNode` object and associated with the same heap root as the previously discovered effect. Similarly, Line 107 adds the effect $\langle\langle\texttt{par}, \texttt{ast}, a_{\text{AST}}\rangle, a_{\text{TN}}, \texttt{read}, \texttt{children}[]\rangle$.

5.2.3 Transfer Functions

We decompose the effects analysis into two passes. The first pass computes the mapping R from edges to the heap roots used to access the edges' target objects. The second pass then uses the mapping R to compute the application's set of effects U.

Figure 6 presents the transfer functions for computing the mapping R from reference edges in the points-to graph to heap roots. The analysis introduces new heap roots into points-to graphs at two classes of statements: (1) task enter statements and (2) statements of a parent task that may have to stall to avoid heap conflicts with a child task. These statements create new heap roots for the corresponding variable's edges. Heap roots are then subsequently propagated to newly created references because we are interested in determining which heap root was used to access an affected object.

The heap roots analysis uses a supporting analysis to precompute which variables may require stalls to access. This analysis is relevant for sections of a task following the exit of a child task. This analysis computes the set of variables $\mathcal{L}$ for which accesses to the objects referenced by these variables may require the generation of a stall. Figure 6 presents the transfer functions for computing the set $\mathcal{L}$. At the exit of a child task, the set $\mathcal{L}$ contains all live variables that reference objects. At the entrance of a task, the set $\mathcal{L}$ is empty because all data structures can be accessed without needing to stall for child tasks. The transfer functions for $\mathcal{L}$ remove a variable at a statement that reads the variable and therefore serves as a potential stall site for the data structure referenced by the variable.

Figure 7 presents the transfer functions for computing heap effects. Load statements and store statements are the only statements that operate on object fields in the heap and therefore are relevant for collecting effects. These transfer functions record for each field access: the heap root that was used to reach the affected object, the allocation site of the affected object, the operation, and the field that the statement accessed. The analysis accumulates effects into a global set U. The effects analysis treats array operations as normal field accesses on a special array field. Section 5.3.2 discusses the reasons for the strong update rule.

5.2.4 Interprocedural Extension

We next present the interprocedural extension to the effects analysis. The pointer analysis we used handles method calls by tak-

st	$R' = (R_a - \text{KILL}) \cup \text{GEN}$
x = ...	$\text{KILL} = \{\forall\langle e, h\rangle \in R \mid e \in E(\texttt{x})\}$
x = new	$R_a = R$
	$\text{GEN} = \emptyset$
	$\mathcal{L}' = \mathcal{L}\backslash\{\texttt{x}\}$
x = y	$R_a = R$
	$\text{GEN} = \{\langle\langle\texttt{x}, n\rangle, h\rangle \mid \forall\langle\texttt{y}, n\rangle \in E, \langle\langle\texttt{y}, n\rangle, h\rangle \in R\}$
	$\mathcal{L}' = \{v \in V \mid (v \in \mathcal{L} \wedge v \neq \texttt{x}) \vee (\texttt{y} \in \mathcal{L} \wedge v = \texttt{x})\}$
x = y.f	$R_a = R \cup \{\langle\langle\texttt{x}, n\rangle, \langle\texttt{st}, \texttt{y}, \mathcal{A}(n)\rangle\rangle \mid \forall\langle\texttt{y}, n\rangle \in E, \texttt{y} \in \mathcal{L}\}$
	$\text{GEN} = \{\langle\langle\texttt{x}, n'\rangle, h\rangle \mid \forall\langle n, \texttt{f}, n'\rangle \in E(\texttt{y}, \texttt{f}),$
	$\quad (\langle\langle n, \texttt{f}, n'\rangle, h\rangle \in R_a \vee \langle\langle\texttt{y}, n\rangle, h\rangle \in R_a)\}$
	$\mathcal{L}' = \mathcal{L}\backslash\{\texttt{x}, \texttt{y}\}$
x.f = y	$R_a = R \cup \{\langle\langle\texttt{x}, n\rangle, \langle\texttt{st}, \texttt{x}, \mathcal{A}(n)\rangle\rangle \mid \forall\langle\texttt{x}, n\rangle \in E, \texttt{x} \in \mathcal{L}\}$
	$\quad \cup \{\langle\langle\texttt{y}, n'\rangle, \langle\texttt{st}, \texttt{y}, \mathcal{A}(n')\rangle\rangle \mid \forall\langle\texttt{y}, n'\rangle \in E, \texttt{y} \in \mathcal{L}\}$
	$\text{KILL} = \emptyset$
	$\text{GEN} = \{\langle\langle n, \texttt{f}, n'\rangle, h\rangle \mid \forall\langle\texttt{x}, n\rangle \in E, \forall\langle\texttt{y}, n'\rangle \in E,$
	$\quad \langle\langle\texttt{y}, n'\rangle, h\rangle \in R_a\}$
	$\mathcal{L}' = \mathcal{L}\backslash\{\texttt{x}, \texttt{y}\}$
enter(t_{curr})	$R_a = R$
	$\text{KILL} = \{\langle e, \langle\texttt{st}, v, \mathcal{A}(n)\rangle\rangle \mid \texttt{st} \text{ is a stall site}\}$
	$\text{GEN} = \{\langle\langle v, n\rangle, \langle t_{\text{curr}}, v, \mathcal{A}(n)\rangle\rangle \mid v \text{ is an in-set variable for}$
	$\quad t_{\text{curr}} \wedge \langle v, n\rangle \in E\}$
	$\mathcal{L}' = \emptyset$
exit(t_{curr})	$R_a = R$
	$\text{KILL} = \{\langle e, \langle\texttt{st}, v, \mathcal{A}(n)\rangle\rangle \mid \texttt{st} \text{ is a stall site} \vee v \text{ is an in-set}$
	$\quad \text{variable for the current instance of } t_{\text{curr}}\}$
	$\text{GEN} = \emptyset$
	$\mathcal{L}' = V$

Figure 6. Transfer Functions for Computing Heap Roots

st	$U' = U \cup GEN$
x=y.f	$\text{GEN} = \{\langle h, \mathcal{A}(n), \texttt{read}, \texttt{f}\rangle \mid \forall\langle\texttt{y}, n\rangle \in E,$
	$\quad \langle\langle\texttt{y}, n\rangle, h\rangle \in R\}$
weak x.f=y	$\text{GEN} = \{\langle h, \mathcal{A}(n), \texttt{write}, \texttt{f}\rangle \mid \forall\langle\texttt{x}, n\rangle \in E,$
	$\quad \langle\langle\texttt{x}, n\rangle, h\rangle \in R\}$
strong x.f=y	$\text{GEN} = \{\langle h, \mathcal{A}(n), \texttt{write}, \texttt{f}\rangle \mid \forall\langle\texttt{x}, n\rangle \in E,$
	$\quad \langle\langle\texttt{x}, n\rangle, h\rangle \in R\} \cup \{\langle h, n, \texttt{strong}, *\rangle \mid$
	$\quad \forall\langle\texttt{x}, n_0\rangle \in E, \forall n \in N, \langle\langle\texttt{x}, n_0\rangle, h\rangle \in R\wedge$
	$\quad n\text{'s reachability decreases}\}$

Figure 7. Transfer Functions for Effects

ing a snapshot of the portion of the caller's heap reachable by the callee just prior to the method invocation and labeling the heap elements with predicates—these predicates are initially tautologies. For example, the predicate for an edge $\langle n_1, f, n_2\rangle$ is that the edge $\langle n_1, f, n_2\rangle$ existed in the caller. Then the heap contexts for all of a method's callers are merged. The predicates serve to preserve analysis precision by preventing the erroneous propagation of edges from one caller to another. The interprocedural extension also adds predicates to heap roots: heap root predicates specify that a given edge in the caller had the given heap root. There is a special predicate for heap roots created in the current method context — the analysis uses this predicate to determine which heap roots to prune at task exits (in the case of recursive tasks).

5.2.5 Basic Effect Conflict Elimination

OoOJava considers a task to have a heap dependence on an earlier task when an effect of one task conflicts with an effect of the other. Consider a task t_0 with the effect $\langle h_0, a_0^{\text{aff}}, o_0, f_0 \rangle$ and a task t_1 with the effect $\langle h_1, a_1^{\text{aff}}, o_1, f_1 \rangle$:

1. If $a_0^{\text{aff}} \neq a_1^{\text{aff}}$, then there is no conflict because the objects must be different if they were allocated at different sites.
2. If $o_0 = o_1 = \texttt{read}$, then there is no conflict because reads do not conflict.
3. If $f_0 \neq f_1$, then there is no conflict because the two effects access different fields.

When these rules cannot eliminate a conflict, OoOJava will consider reachability to possibly eliminate the conflict or generate a simple dynamic check for the conflict.

5.3 Reachability-based Conflict Detection

Disjoint reachability analysis is a new static analysis that conservatively extracts reachability properties between heap objects. OoOJava uses these reachability properties to generate lightweight dynamic checks that can rule out conflicts. When OoOJava cannot eliminate a conflict between two effects using the basic conflict detection rules, it uses disjoint reachability analysis to compute the reachability from the heap nodes that correspond to the allocation sites in the effects' heap roots. Section 5.3.1 presents an overview of disjoint reachability analysis. Section 5.3.2 presents the reachability-based conflict detection rules that OoOJava uses to eliminate the possibility of conflicts between effects when the basic conflict resolution rules cannot.

5.3.1 Disjoint Reachability Analysis

Existing heap analyses have primarily either used equivalence classes of objects (e.g. TVLA [25]) or access paths [12] to reason about heap references. Disjoint reachability analysis combines aspects of both approaches — it combines an abstraction that decomposes the heap into static regions with reachability annotations that provide access path information. Choi et al. used a combination of storage and paths for alias analysis [8], however that approach focuses only on reachability from variables and cannot express disjoint reachability relations among an unbounded number of objects, which is a useful property to know about highly parallel programs.

Disjoint reachability analysis extends a standard pointer analysis with reachability states. An object's reachability state conservatively characterizes the set of objects that can possibly reach the given object through heap references. Disjoint reachability analysis is demand-driven — it only computes reachability from objects of interest to the compiler. OoOJava uses the results from the effects analysis to generate a set of allocation sites of interest.

A reachability state is a set of heap node-arity pairs with the constraint that no two pairs have the same heap node. The arity element of the pair is taken from the set $\{0, 1, \texttt{MANY}\}$. A reachability state that abstracts the reachability of an object o that includes the pair $\langle n_1, \mu \rangle$ means that at most μ objects abstracted by heap node n_1 have paths through the heap to object o. The arity 0 means exactly zero, 1 means at most one, and MANY means any number of objects. We omit reachability tuples with arity 0.

The analysis associates a set of reachability states S_n with each heap node n in the points-to graph. For each object o that is abstracted by heap node n there is a reachability state $s \in S_n$ that conservatively abstracts the reachability of o.

The analysis also associates a set of reachability states S_e with each edge $e \in E$ in the points-to graph. Reachability states associated with an edge characterize the reachability of the objects reachable from that edge. Intuitively, these reachability states provide a precise way to propagate reachability changes through the heap abstraction. For each object o and for each sequence of references $r_1; r_2; ...; r_j$ in the heap that form a path to o, there is a reachability

```
1  x = new SharedObj();   // objs abstracted by n1
2  y = new Foo();         // objs abstracted by n2
3  z = new Bar();         // objs abstracted by n3
4  if ( ... ) {
5    y.f = x;             // obj in n2 reaches obj in n1
6  } else {
7    z.b = x;             // obj in n3 reaches obj in n1
8  }
```

Figure 8. Code Fragment for Reachability Example

state $s \in S_e$ that conservatively abstracts the reachability of object o in the set of reachability states for each edge $e_1; e_2; ...; e_j$, where each edge e_i abstracts reference r_i. A complete presentation of disjoint reachability analysis is available in a technical report [17].

Figure 8 presents an example to illustrate disjoint reachability analysis. At the exit of Line 8 the reachability states set for heap node n_1, which abstracts the shared objects in this example, only includes $[\langle n_2, 1 \rangle]$ and $[\langle n_3, 1 \rangle]$. This reachability states set shows that a shared object from allocation site 1 cannot be reachable from both an object from site 2 and site 3 at this program point. If that were possible (by moving Line 7 to just after Line 5, for instance), then the reachability state $[\langle n_2, 1 \rangle, \langle n_3, 1 \rangle]$ would be present in the reachability states set associated with n_1 at the exit of Line 8.

5.3.2 Reachability-based Effect Conflict Elimination

In the running example presented in Section 2 we noted that a necessary condition for safely executing instances of task par in parallel is to ensure two given instances do not have heap dependences, specifically with respect to objects in an AST. Assume, as previously in the effects analysis example, that AST objects are allocated at the same site and are summarized in the points-to graphs by heap node n_{AST}. Next assume that an AST object serves as a data structure root object for a collection of TreeNode objects summarized by n_{TN}. Disjoint reachability information associated with n_{TN} is critical to OoOJava for deciding when to safely execute instances of task par. If the set of reachability states associated with n_{TN} includes a state with reachability tuple $\langle n_{\text{AST}}, \texttt{MANY} \rangle$ then a given TreeNode object may be reachable from any number of AST header objects, and therefore we cannot be certain whether any two instances of par might access a common TreeNode object.

However, Figure 5(b) presents the points-to graph of our running example, annotated with reachability states, and we find only $\langle n_{\text{AST}}, 1 \rangle$, meaning a given TreeNode object is reachable from at most one AST object. If a dynamic check determines two instances of par have references to distinct AST objects then we can be sure they access disjoint sets of TreeNode objects, and therefore are safe to execute concurrently.

If the basic conflict detection rules cannot eliminate a possible conflict between two effects, the results of disjoint reachability analysis may rule out a conflict by stating whether the effects of the tasks in question operate on disjoint sets of objects or not.

Consider the two effects: $\langle \langle st_0, v_0, a_0^{\text{root}} \rangle, a^{\text{aff}}, o_0, f \rangle$ and $\langle \langle st_1, v_1, a_1^{\text{root}} \rangle, a^{\text{aff}}, o_1, f \rangle$. OoOJava inspects the set of reachability states S for each heap node associated with a^{aff} to decide whether the effects conflict:

1. If $a_0^{\text{root}} \neq a_1^{\text{root}} \wedge \forall s \in S. s \cap (\{\langle a_0^{\text{root}}, 1 \rangle, \langle a_0^{\text{root}}, \texttt{MANY} \rangle\} \times \{\langle a_1^{\text{root}}, 1 \rangle, \langle a_1^{\text{root}}, \texttt{MANY} \rangle\}) \neq \emptyset$, then there is no conflict. If there is no reachability state that contains both heap roots, then the two heap roots cannot access the same object allocated at allocation site a^{aff} and therefore the effects do not conflict.
2. If $a_0^{\text{root}} = a_1^{\text{root}} \wedge \forall s \in S. s \cap \{\langle a_0^{\text{root}}, \texttt{MANY} \rangle\} = \emptyset$, then the compiler can generate a simple dynamic check to eliminate the possibility of a conflict. If $a_0^{\text{root}} \neq a_1^{\text{root}}$ at runtime, then there is no conflict. We call conflicts that can be eliminated by a dynamic check *fine-grained conflicts*.

3. If neither basic nor reachability-based conflict detection eliminates a conflict, we say the effects have a *coarse-grained conflict*.

It is important to note that reachability states are not generally comparable between different program points. However, if there is no strong update, and therefore no decrease in reachability information, on any control path from one program point to another, then it is safe to compare reachability states at different times. The effects analysis adds `strong` to the domain of possible effects and generates a strong update effect whenever a write effect decreases the reachability state obtained at that same program point. Effects of type `strong` always conflict with other effects on the same affected object allocation site and result in a coarse-grained conflict.

5.4 Code Generation

OoOJava assembles all effect conflicts between tasks (including an instance of a task with previous instances of itself) into a heap effect conflict graph, discussed in Section 5.4.1. A set of heap dependence queues implements the conflict graph efficiently at runtime. Section 5.4.2 discusses the queue properties and Section 5.4.3 gives the algorithm for finding a minimal set of heap dependence queues that covers the conflict graph. Section 5.4.4 presents the process for generating code to issue a task by inserting it into relevant heap dependence queues.

5.4.1 Conflict Graphs

OoOJava generates conflict graphs from the results of the effects analysis and the disjoint reachability analysis. There is a conflict graph for each task that summarizes the heap dependences between that task and its child tasks. There is a node in a conflict graph for each heap root. There are two types of edges in the conflict graph: coarse-grained edges indicate that the corresponding code blocks cannot be reordered and fine-grained edges indicate that the code blocks can only be reordered if the corresponding heap roots refer to different objects. Without loss of generality, whenever there is both a fine-grained and coarse-grained edge between the same two nodes, we drop the fine-grained edge because the ordering constraints of the coarse-grained edge dominate.

5.4.2 Heap Dependence Queues

OoOJava compiles each conflict graph into a set of heap dependence queues that enforce the conflict graph's ordering constraints. Each heap dependence queue accepts the following types of entries: read, write-fine, write-coarse, parent-read, parent-write-fine, parent-write-coarse, and self-conflicting-coarse. Figure 9 illustrates the ordering constraints that a single heap dependence queue enforces between entries of different types. A dashed edge indicates a fine-grained ordering constraint that accesses associated with the heap roots of the corresponding types can be only reordered if the heap roots refer to different objects. A solid edge indicates a coarse-grained ordering constraint that accesses associated with the heap roots of the corresponding types can never be reordered.

5.4.3 Compiling the Conflict Graph into Queues

We formulate compiling a conflict graph into a set of heap dependence queues as a graph covering problem. Each edge in the conflict graph must be enforced by an edge in a heap dependence queue's constraint graph. The compiler maps nodes in the conflict graph to nodes in the heap dependence queues. An edge in the conflict graph is enforced by the heap dependence queue if the edge's endpoints in the conflict graph map to nodes in a heap dependence queue with the same type of edge between them.

Figure 10 presents a greedy algorithm for heuristically covering the conflict graph with a minimal set of heap dependence queues. The algorithm covers edges in the conflict graph until the given heap dependence queue cannot cover any more edges; the process repeats until it covers every conflict edge in the conflict graph.

Line 2 creates a new heap dependence queue. Lines 3-13 cover the fine-grained edges in the conflict graph that the heap depen-

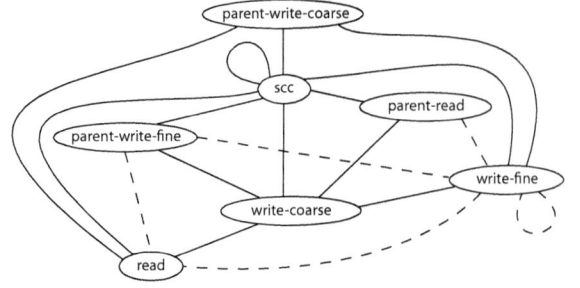

Figure 9. Heap Dependence Queue Ordering Constraints

$\text{Cover}(\text{conflict graph } C = (V, V_p, E, E_f, E_c))$
1. Set of covered edges $E' \leftarrow \emptyset$
2. create new queue $q \leftarrow (rd = \emptyset, wr = \emptyset, crs = \emptyset, par\_rd = \emptyset,$
   $\qquad\qquad par\_wr = \emptyset, par\_crs = \emptyset, scc = \emptyset)$
3. if $\exists (u, v) \in E_f \setminus E'$ then
4. $\quad U \leftarrow U \cup \{u\}$
5. $\quad$ while $U \neq \emptyset$ remove u from U
6. $\qquad$ if $(u, u) \in E \wedge \forall x.\text{QCovFine}(q, x) \implies (u, x) \in E$ then
7. $\qquad\quad E' \leftarrow E' \cup \{(u, x) \mid \forall v \in V, \text{QCovFine}(q, v)\}$
8. $\qquad\quad U \leftarrow U \cup \{v \mid (u, v) \in E_f \setminus E'\}$
9. $\qquad\quad$ if $u \in V_p$ then $par\_wr \leftarrow par\_wr \cup \{u\}$ else $wr \leftarrow wr \cup \{u\}$
10. $\qquad$ else if $(u, u) \notin E \wedge \forall x.\text{QCovFnWr}(q, x) \implies (u, x) \in E$ then
11. $\qquad\quad E' \leftarrow E' \cup \{(u, v) \mid \forall v \in V, \text{QCovFnWr}(q, v)\}$
12. $\qquad\quad U \leftarrow U \cup \{v \mid (u, v) \in E_f \setminus E'\}$
13. $\qquad\quad$ if $u \in V_p$ then $par\_rd \leftarrow par\_rd \cup \{u\}$ else $rd \leftarrow rd \cup \{u\}$
14. else $\exists (u, v) \in E_c \setminus E'$
15. $\quad$ if $(u, u) \in E_c$ then $scc \leftarrow \{u\}$
16. $\quad$ else if $u \in V_p$ then $par\_rd \leftarrow \{u\}$ else $rd \leftarrow \{u\}$
17. $U \leftarrow \{u \mid \forall (u, v) \in E_c \setminus E', \text{QCovFine}(v)\}$
18. while $U \neq \emptyset$ remove u from U
19. $\quad$ if $u \in V_p \wedge \forall x.\text{QCovFnCh}(q, x) \implies (u, x) \in E_c$ then
20. $\qquad E' \leftarrow E' \cup \{(u, v) \mid \forall v \in V, \text{QCovFnCh}(q, v)\}$
21. $\qquad U \leftarrow U \cup \{v \mid (u, v) \in E_f \setminus E'\}$
22. $\qquad par\_crs \leftarrow par\_crs \cup \{u\}$
23. $\quad$ else if $u \notin V_p \wedge (u, u) \notin E_c \wedge \forall x.\text{QCovFine}(q, x) \implies (u, x) \in E_c$ then
24. $\qquad E' \leftarrow E' \cup \{(u, v) \mid \forall v \in V, \text{QCovFine}(q, v)\}$
25. $\qquad U \leftarrow U \cup \{v \mid (u, v) \in E_c \setminus E'\}$
26. $\qquad crs \leftarrow crs \cup \{u\}$
27. $\quad$ else if $u \notin V_p \wedge (u, u) \in E_c \wedge \forall x.\text{QCov}(q, x) \implies (u, x) \in E_c$ then
28. $\qquad E' \leftarrow E' \cup \{(u, v) \mid \forall v \in V, \text{QCov}(q, v)\} \cup \{(u, u)\}$
29. $\qquad U \leftarrow U \cup \{v \mid (u, v) \in E_c \setminus E'\}$
30. $\qquad scc \leftarrow scc \cup \{u\}$
31. $Q \leftarrow Q \cup \{q\}$
32. if $\exists e \in E.e \notin E'$ then goto 2 else return Q

$\text{QCov}((rd, wr, crs, par\_rd, par\_wr, par\_crs, scc), u) =$
$\quad (u \in rd \vee u \in wr \vee u \in crs \vee u \in par\_rd \vee u \in par\_wr \vee$
$\quad u \in par\_crs \vee u \in scc)$

$\text{QCovFine}((rd, wr, crs, par\_rd, par\_wr, par\_crs, scc), u) =$
$\quad (u \in rd \vee u \in wr \vee u \in par\_rd \vee u \in par\_wr)$

$\text{QCovFnWr}((rd, wr, crs, par\_rd, par\_wr, par\_crs, scc), u) =$
$\quad (u \in wr \vee u \in par\_wr)$

$\text{QCovFnCh}((rd, wr, crs, par\_rd, par\_wr, par\_crs, scc), u) =$
$\quad (u \notin V_p \wedge (u \in rd \vee u \in wr))$

Figure 10. Conflict Graph Covering Algorithm

dence queue will enforce. Line 3 checks for an uncovered fine grained edge. If an uncovered fine-grained edge is discovered, Line 4 adds one of its endpoints to the set U. The loop in Line 5 removes a node from the set U and the rest of the loop attempts to map the conflict graph node to a node in the heap dependence graph. Lines 6-9 try to map a node to a write node in the heap dependence queue, and Lines 10-13 try to map a node to a read node. A constraint on mapping a node in the conflict graph to a node in the heap dependence queue is that the mapping will not introduce a new ordering constraint that is not present in the conflict graph. Lines 6 and 10 verify that the mapping preserves this constraint.

Lines 14-16 perform the initial mapping of a node to a queue if there was no fine-grained edge to cover. Line 17 computes the set of nodes that serve as end-points to coarse-grained edges that are incident to nodes mapped to the current queue. Lines 18-30 then cover coarse-grained edges in the conflict graph by mapping conflict graph nodes to the current heap dependence queue.

5.4.4 Implementation

We next discuss the code OoOJava generates to issue a task. There is a record for each task that maintains a count of the task's unresolved dependences, including variable and heap dependences, as previously mentioned in Section 4.2.

OoOJava first generates code to forward or copy the values of in-set variables to the new task. OoOJava next generates code to preserve heap dependences. This code adds the newly issued task to each of the relevant heap dependence queues as determined by the conflict graph compilation algorithm.

OoOJava uses a similar code generation strategy for stall sites. At a stall site, a task adds itself to each heap dependence queue as determined by the conflict graph compilation algorithm. It then waits to be notified by the heap dependence queue.

A potential issue arises with the read and write-fine states — it is possible that the value of the pointer in a variable will be forwarded by another task and the value is unknown when the task is issued. In this case, the heap dependence queue must maintain the total ordering of this task until it determines the actual value of the variable. It can then safely allow reorderings of the task.

The heap dependence queue manages heap dependences to determine which tasks may be safely executed out-of-order. Heap dependence queues are designed to provide constant-time operations. Heap dependence queues are implemented internally as a linked-list of hashtables for fine-grained entries (read, write-fine, parent-read, and parent-write-fine), vectors for coarse-grained entries (write-coarse and parent-write-coarse), and single entries for self-conflicting coarse-grained entries (self-conflicting-coarse).

Consecutive sequences of fine-grained entries in a heap dependence queue are grouped into a hashtable. The hash keys are unique object IDs that persist across garbage collections, and in the case of collisions, tasks are placed in a linked-list for the bin which preserves their execution order. Hash collisions can cause false dependences — we size the hashtable to be large enough that false collisions do not significantly limit parallelism relative to the number of cores. This hash-based strategy enables OoOJava to respect fine-grained heap dependences with constant time operations.

Any consecutive sequence of coarse-grained entries inserted into the heap dependence queue are grouped into one list element. No fine-grained conflicts inserted into the heap dependence queue before or after coarse-grained elements may be reordered across the coarse-grained elements.

All entries except parent entries remain in the queue after the corresponding task dispatches and are removed only when that task retires. A special property of parent entries is that they can be removed from the heap dependence queues as soon as their conflict is resolved. The observation is that a parent entry cannot conflict with later child tasks as they have not been dispatched.

The self-conflicting-coarse entry may never be reordered with any other entries. Therefore, each task inserted with type self-conflicting-coarse is a single element in the heap dependence queue and nothing may be reordered across it.

6. Discussion

At this point, we have not discussed parallelizing programs that perform I/O. We present one strict and one relaxed strategy for handling I/O in OoOJava. The strict strategy is to serialize all I/O operations in the program. In this strategy, every I/O operation is serialized and the trace of I/O operations will match the serial elision. The strict strategy prohibits parallelism when unrelated tasks access disjoint sets of file descriptors.

We can relax our I/O strategy to expose additional parallelism if the application satisfies the following two conditions: (1) the developer annotates whether different file descriptors may access the same file and (2) external programs do not depend on the exact ordering of accesses across different files. This strategy is straightforward to implement in OoOJava — simply model native methods that implement file operations as writing to a special field in the file descriptor object. We expect that the relaxed strategy is sufficient for the correct behavior of many programs and has the potential to expose significantly more parallelism.

OoOJava can be extended to safely support applications that combine threads and tasks. The basic idea is that threaded programs could call into libraries that are implemented using tasks. In this model, the developer is responsible for using locks to ensure that the threaded parts of the program do not concurrently modify data structures accessed by tasks. OoOJava would then analyze the task part of the program in isolation assuming a maximally aliased heap at entry. Before exiting the task part of the program, the parent thread would stall until all tasks retire.

Parallelization requires revisiting Java's exception model. It is helpful to divide exceptions into two categories: expected exceptions that developers write handlers for and unexpected exceptions that cause an application to simply exit. Expected exceptions that are caught inside the same task do not pose an issue for OoOJava. As a result, the common use of exceptions to recover from expected error conditions is largely unaffected by OoOJava.

Nearly all Java statements can potentially throw some type of unexpected exception (null pointer exception, array bound exceptions, division by zero). Developers typically do not write exception handlers for such exceptions and simply allow them to halt the program. Precisely handling such exceptions requires support for rollback because an application may execute past a task that later throws an uncaught exception. OoOJava gives such exceptions imprecise semantics to improve performance.

It is of course possible to efficiently support imprecise try-catch blocks that enclose a large number of dynamic tasks. Such blocks catch the exceptions of all enclosed tasks, but allow the enclosed tasks to be executed out-of-order. Such a block is implemented by simply waiting until all enclosed tasks have retired.

7. Evaluation

We have implemented OoOJava and evaluated it on a 1.9 GHz 24-core AMD Magny-Cour Opteron with 16 GB of memory. Our compiler generates C code which is then compiled by GCC. We enabled all optimization in GCC and classic compiler optimizations in our compiler. Our implementation and benchmarks are available available at http://demsky.eecs.uci.edu/compiler.php. We report times averaged over 10 runs.

7.1 Benchmarks

We selected a diverse set of benchmarks to provide an interesting cross-section of application behaviors and a variety of algorithmic structures and ported them to OoOJava. We took Crypt, RayTracer, MonteCarlo, and SOR from the Java Grande Benchmark suite [27]. We took both KMeans and Labyrinth from the STAMP benchmark suite [7] to explore benchmarks with irregular parallelism. We took Power from the JOlden benchmark suite [6] and MergeSort from DPJ suite [4]. We took Tracking from SD-VBS [30].

7.2 Performance Discussion

Figure 11 presents the measured speedups and lines of code including libraries for each benchmark. We report speedups relative to sequential versions compiled using our compiler's Java frontend.

Benchmark	Measured Speedup	Lines
MonteCarlo	27.69×	5,669
Power	20.21×	1,846
Tracking	20.17×	4,747
RayTracer	20.00×	2,832
Crypt	17.69×	2,035
Moldyn	13.87×	2,299
KMeans	13.81×	3,220
MergeSort	12.72×	1,895
Labyrinth	11.12×	4,315
SOR	8.79×	2,740

Figure 11. Speedups on Benchmarks (Higher is Better)

RayTracer computes rows of a scene in parallel while the initial scene set-up and per-row checksum operations it executes must be serialized; the speedup of 20.00× indicates OoOJava is able to efficiently execute RayTracer across the available cores.

Tracking extracts motion information from a sequence of images. We targeted the most computationally expensive stage of the algorithm and obtained a 20.17× speedup.

KMeans, Moldyn, and Power execute many iterations of a parallel computation followed by a sequential computation. Though the repeated sequential portions of these benchmarks limit available parallelism, the speedups for these benchmarks are still significant. Our version of KMeans is 1.96× faster than the parallelized TL2 version included in the STAMP benchmark suite even though our version incurs significant additional overheads to implement array bounds checks. With array bounds checking disabled, our version is 3.37× faster than the parallelized TL2 version.

Crypt consists of an encryption phase and a decryption phase, both of which are followed by a sequential reconstruction of the full message. OoOJava effectively extracted parallelism in this benchmark and achieved a 17.69× speedup.

The MergeSort taken from DPJ implements a sequential merge operation. This sequential code has a non-trivial overhead and limits parallelism at all levels of recursion.

Labyrinth employs a speculative strategy in a deterministic environment. Each iteration launches a set of independent parallel routing computations, some of which may compute conflicting routes. In series, compatible routes are added to the master solution and conflicting routes are rescheduled for the next parallel iteration. Both the sequential computation and conflicts between routes limit available parallelism. OoOJava achieved a speedup of 11.12× for this speculative algorithm. Our version is 1.67× faster than the parallelized TL2 version included in the STAMP benchmark suite even though our version incurs significant additional overheads to implement array bounds checks. With array bounds checks disabled, OoOJava is 1.80× faster than the parallelized TL2 version.

The speedup for SOR is limited because the benchmark is memory bandwidth-limited. Tasks access a large amount of data relative to the computation requiring significant memory bandwidth. We confirmed this by measuring the average execution of the parallel tasks for a 24-worker implementation and a 2-worker implementation of SOR. The body of parallel tasks for this benchmark perform no synchronization or system calls, so differences in execution time can only be attributed to the memory system. For 24 workers the average execution of the parallel task is 683,927 processor cycles and for 2 workers, 245,242 processor cycles.

The speedup for MonteCarlo reflects that the individual simulations are independent and that there is much parallelism.

We measured the task dispatch overhead in processor cycles for a microbenchmark that issues 500,000 lightweight tasks. The average time over ten executions taken to dispatch a task was 1692.3 processor cycles. For comparison, we also conducted this experiment on an 8-core Intel Nehalem Xeon and observed that the average of 10 profiled executions was 735.7 processor cycles.

To quantify the overhead of our research compiler, we compared the generated code against the OpenJDK JVM 14.0-b16 and GCC 4.1.2. The sequential version of Crypt compiled with our compiler ran 4.6% faster than on the JVM. We also developed a C++ version compiled with GCC and found our compiler's version ran 25% slower than the C++ version. Our compiler implements array bounds checking; with array bounds checking disabled, the binary from our compiler runs only 5.4% slower than the C++ binary. We used the optimization flag -O3 for the C++ version as well as for the underlying C code generated by our compiler. This is in close agreement with more extensive experiments on six benchmarks that measured an average overhead for our compiler with array bounds checks disabled of 4.9% relative to GCC [33].

7.3 Parallelization Discussion

We typically began our parallelization efforts by using a profiler to identify computationally intensive sections of code. From there we manually inspected the hot spots and added task annotations to expose expected parallelism. The reported dependences informed us when the annotations did not result in the implementation we expected. In this way we incrementally parallelized a benchmark until the implementation matched our expectation of the available parallelism in the benchmark's core algorithms. Parallelization efforts typically required on the order of one to two dozen line changes. We changed the most lines in Labyrinth and Crypt. The lines we added to Crypt break the message into sub-problems.

Labyrinth was more challenging. The original version of Labyrinth from STAMP intentionally used data races to read a shared map for route planning and then later used safe reads to verify that a planned route was valid. We modified Labyrinth to maintain the same basic speculative algorithm, but in a safe, easy-to-debug, deterministic form. Our modified version uses rounds of parallelized route planning followed by sequential code to apply the routes from the previous parallel round. Our version is both much simpler to debug and faster than the original STAMP version.

Our experience porting RayTracer demonstrated the value of OoOJava's developer feedback. We enclosed the work for each row of pixels in a task and expected its instances to have no dependences; OoOJava reported the instances had conflicting accesses to a global scratch pad object. To remove this dependence, we simply moved the allocation of the scratch pad object into the task.

8. Related Work

Parallel functional languages [20] can offer strong correctness guarantees for parallel applications. However, these languages place onerous restrictions on the mutation of data structures, and therefore make it difficult to efficiently express many algorithms.

Kendo [21] addresses challenges of developing parallel software by enforcing deterministic interleavings for the widely used explicit thread and lock model. Models that generate parallel implementations from sequentially expressed code, like OoOJava, make reasoning about program behavior easier for the programmer.

Coarse-grained or macro-dataflow languages [10, 15] compose several sequential operations together to construct larger granularity code segments for dataflow execution. OoOJava can be viewed as a combined dynamic-static approach to translating imperative code into macro-dataflow code.

Deterministic, speculative models [3, 13, 31, 32] offer simple programming models, but incur potentially significant dynamic overheads to support recovery from mis-speculation and to dynamically check for potential conflicts. Static analysis enables OoOJava to parallelize applications without incurring these overheads.

Several non-speculative models including OpenMP [9], Cilk [22], or JCilk [11] rely upon correct developer annotations.

66

Annotation errors can cause these models to produce incorrect results. Annotation errors in OoOJava never affect correctness.

Other systems require extensive developer annotations to avoid unchecked access to data structures [4, 24] or additional code to create serialization sets [1]. OoOJava requires minimal annotations, which will likely improve developer productivity.

StarSs dynamically schedules function invocation when a function's operands are available [14]. StarSs avoids heap dependence analysis by restricting superscalar functions to pass-by-value and not allowing data structures with pointers to be passed. StarSs restricts superscalar execution to functions to avoid variable hazards; OoOJava's variable analysis and value forwarding allow tasks to be freely used wherever it is convenient.

OoOJava addresses parallelism opportunities that can be difficult for similar systems to take advantage of. For example, OpenMP, Cilk, and StarSs require explicit synchronization before accessing the results of parallel computations. Cilk with *inlets* and OpenMP with *reductions* do support limited aggregation of results in a parallel loop, however the aggregation operations in these systems do not necessarily execute in the same order as prescribed by the serial elision which would break non-commuting operations. Moreover, neither OpenMP nor Cilk can schedule an arbitrary chain of out-of-order computations, while OoOJava can.

OoOJava differs from inspector-executor approaches [23, 26] in that it supports complex object-oriented data structures, uses the results of static analysis to avoid inspecting nearly all memory accesses, and does not require a runtime preprocessing phase.

Decoupled software pipelining (DSWP) [16] maps memory operations in a loop that may conflict to the same thread of a software pipeline. While this approach simplifies the necessary heap analysis, it limits parallelism — at most one thread can write to a statically identified heap region. In contrast, OoOJava can execute instances of write instructions across many cores. OoOJava also uses a sophisticated heap dependence analysis that can determine that some write statements of a loop are conflict-free where DSWP cannot. DSWP extracts very fine-grained parallelism compared to OoOJava; the techniques are likely synergistic.

In an earlier position paper [18] we explored an out-of-order software model without providing technical details. In this current work we describe in detail the necessary analysis and runtime support to implement OoOJava and present a complete evaluation.

9. Conclusion

For parallel programming to become mainstream, parallel programming tools must become easy to use. We presented an approach to parallel programming that uses annotations to suggest parallelization of a sequential program. OoOJava automatically handles the details of implementing the parallelization and guarantees that the parallel version has the same behavior as the original sequential version. We have successfully parallelized ten applications and achieved significant speedups. Moreover, we found that parallelizing applications with OoOJava was straightforward and required only minor modifications to our benchmark applications.

Acknowledgments

This research was supported by the National Science Foundation under grants CCF-0846195 and CCF-0725350. We would like to thank the anonymous reviewers for their helpful comments.

References

[1] M. D. Allen, S. Sridharan et al. Serialization sets: A dynamic dependence-based parallel execution model. In *PPoPP*, 2009.

[2] P. Bellens, J. Perez et al. CellSs: a programming model for the Cell BE architecture. *SC*, 2006.

[3] E. D. Berger, T. Yang et al. Grace: Safe multithreaded programming for C/C++. In *OOPSLA*, 2009.

[4] R. L. Bocchino, Jr., V. S. Adve et al. A type and effect system for deterministic parallel Java. In *OOPSLA*, 2009.

[5] S. Borkar. Thousand core chips: A technology perspective. In *DAC*, 2007.

[6] B. Cahoon and K. S. McKinley. Data flow analysis for software prefetching linked data structures in Java. In *PACT*, 2001.

[7] C. Cao Minh, J. Chung et al. STAMP: Stanford transactional applications for multi-processing. In *IISWC*, 2008.

[8] J.-D. Choi, M. Burke et al. Efficient flow-sensitive interprocedural computation of pointer-induced aliases and side effects. In *POPL*, 1993.

[9] L. Dagum and R. Menon. OpenMP: An industry-standard API for shared-memory programming. *IEEE Comput. Sci. Eng.*, 1998.

[10] K. Dai. Code parallelization for the LGDG large-grain dataflow computation. In *CONPAR 90 - VAPP IV*, 1990.

[11] J. S. Danaher, I.-T. A. Lee et al. The JCilk language for multithreaded computing. In *SCOOL*, 2005.

[12] A. Deutsch. Interprocedural may-alias analysis for pointers: Beyond k-limiting. In *PLDI*, 1994.

[13] C. Ding, X. Shen et al. Software behavior oriented parallelization. In *PLDI*, 2007.

[14] Y. Etsion, F. Cabarcas et al. Task superscalar: An out-of-order task pipeline. In *MICRO*, 2010.

[15] C. Huang and L. V. Kale. Charisma: Orchestrating migratable parallel objects. In *HPDC*, 2007.

[16] J. Huang, A. Raman et al. Decoupled software pipelining creates parallelization opportunities. In *CGO*, 2010.

[17] J. C. Jenista, Y. Eom et al. Disjoint reachability analysis. Tech. Rep. UCI-ISR-10-4, University of California, Irvine, 2010.

[18] J. C. Jenista, Y. Eom et al. OoOJava: An out-of-order approach to parallel programming. In *HotPar*, 2010.

[19] P. Jouvelout and D. Gifford. The FX-87 interpreter. In *ICCL*, 1988.

[20] H.-W. Loidl, F. Rubio et al. Comparing parallel functional languages: Programming and performance. *HOSC*, 2003.

[21] M. Olszewski, J. Ansel et al. Kendo: Efficient deterministic multithreading in software. In *ASPLOS*, 2009.

[22] K. H. Randall. *Cilk: Efficient Multithreaded Computing*. Massachusetts Institute of Technology, 1998.

[23] L. Rauchwerger, N. M. Amato et al. Run-time methods for parallelizing partially parallel loops. In *ICS*, 1995.

[24] M. C. Rinard, D. J. Scales et al. Jade: A high-level, machine-independent language for parallel programming. *Computer*, 1993.

[25] M. Sagiv, T. Reps et al. Parametric shape analysis via 3-valued logic. *TOPLAS*, 2002.

[26] J. H. Saltz and R. Mirchandaney. Run-time parallelization and scheduling of loops. *TC*, 1991.

[27] L. A. Smith, J. M. Bull et al. A parallel Java Grande benchmark suite. In *SC*, 2001.

[28] J. Subhlok and B. Yang. A new model for integrated nested task and data parallel programming. In *PPoPP*, 1997.

[29] R. M. Tomasulo. An efficient algorithm for exploiting multiple arithmetic units. *IBM J. of Res. Dev.*, 1967.

[30] S. K. Venkata, I. Ahn et al. SD-VBS: The San Diego Vision Benchmark Suite. In *IISWC*, 2009.

[31] C. von Praun, L. Ceze et al. Implicit parallelism with ordered transactions. In *PPoPP*, 2007.

[32] A. Welc, S. Jagannathan et al. Safe futures for Java. In *OOPSLA*, 2005.

[33] J. Zhou and B. Demsky. Bamboo: A data-centric, object-oriented approach to multi-core software. In *PLDI*, 2010.

SpiceC: **Scalable** *p*arallelism **via** *i*mplicit *c*opying **and** *e*xplicit **Commit**

Min Feng   Rajiv Gupta   Yi Hu

University of California, CSE Department, Riverside

{mfeng, gupta, yihu}@cs.ucr.edu

Abstract

In this paper we present an approach to parallel programming called SpiceC. SpiceC simplifies the task of parallel programming through a combination of an intuitive computation model and SpiceC directives. The SpiceC parallel computation model consists of multiple threads where every thread has a *private space* for data and all threads share data via a *shared space*. Each thread performs computations using its private space thus offering isolation which allows for speculative computations. SpiceC provides easy to use SpiceC compiler directives using which the programmers can express different forms of parallelism. It allows developers to express high level constraints on data transfers between spaces while the tedious task of generating the code for the data transfers is performed by the compiler. SpiceC also supports data transfers involving dynamic data structures without help from developers. SpiceC allows developers to create clusters of data to enable parallel data transfers. SpiceC programs are portable across modern chip multiprocessor based machines that may or may not support cache coherence. We have developed implementations of SpiceC for shared memory systems with and without cache coherence. We evaluate our implementation using seven benchmarks of which four are parallelized speculatively. Our compiler generated implementations achieve speedups ranging from 2x to 18x on a 24 core system.

Categories and Subject Descriptors D.3.3 [*Language Constructs and Features*]: Concurrent programming structures

General Terms Language, Design, Performance

Keywords Compiler directives, Multicores, Speculation

1. Introduction

Shared memory parallel systems have been widely used because they offer a single view of the memory thereby making parallel programming easier. Developers do not have to be aware of the location of data. With the increase in number of cores on a chip, exploiting parallelism becomes crucial to improving the application performance on shared memory processors. A few shared memory parallel programming models, e.g. OpenMP [9] and Threading Building Blocks (TBB) [25], have been proposed to facilitate the development of parallel applications on shared memory multiprocessors. However, with the advent of manycore processors and new forms of parallelism, developers need a new programming model to further exploit parallelism.

A shared memory programming model must support multiple forms of parallelisms for successfully handling a wide range of applications. DOALL parallelism and its extensions have been widely used in many applications. Existing shared memory parallel programming models can be easily used to write DOALL loops. However, to be able to exploit parallelism when cross-iteration dependences may be present, a shared memory programming model must support more forms of parallelisms such as DOACROSS and pipelining. Sometimes cross-iteration dependences that are present statically are found to rarely manifest at runtime. To aggressively exploit dynamic parallelism in such loops, a shared memory programming model must provide convenient ways for developers to express speculative parallelism. The compiled programs must be able to detect misspeculation and perform recovery as needed.

Nowadays, a shared memory programming model should be able to adapt to different types of shared memory multiprocessors. As multiprocessors transition from multicores to manycores, the scalability of traditional cache coherence protocols, such as snoopy- or directory-based protocols, becomes a problem. Although significant efforts have recently been put to develop scalable cache coherence, we are still looking for new solutions to the cache coherence problem due to the technological parameters and constraints of existing manycore multiprocessors [1, 3]. Recently, Intel Labs has created their new Tera-scale multiprocessor – "Single-chip Cloud Computer (SCC)" which is a 48-core processor without support for cache coherence. Other similar manycore processors may be created in the future. Therefore, in the long term, a shared memory programming model should support not only multicore processors with cache coherence but also manycore processors without cache coherence.

This paper presents a new programming model, called SpiceC (*S*calable *p*arallelism via *i*mplicit *c*opying and *e*xplicit Commit), which addresses three issues – programmability, versatility, and performance portability. To make programming easier, SpiceC uses programming style similar to OpenMP [9]. Developers do not write new parallel programs but simply add SpiceC directives into the text of a sequential program. SpiceC does not require developers to explicitly write communication between threads. To ensure that programmers can easily reason about their programs, a form of *sequential consistency* is employed. SpiceC is versatile as it supports multiple forms of parallelism: DOALL, DOACROSS, pipelining, and speculative parallelism. Parallel computation, misspeculation check, and misspeculation recovery are all expressed via high level primitives. SpiceC achieves portability as it does not necessarily require either cache coherence or message passing. It can be implemented on any multicore or manycore system that has a logical shared memory with or without cache coherence. Besides, SpiceC allows developers to create *clusters* of data to enable commits on different clusters to be performed in parallel.

We have implemented the SpiceC model. We have the same implementation for systems with or without cache coherence but apply different optimizations to improve the performance on different systems. We evaluate our implementation on a 24-core machine using seven benchmarks from SPEC2000, PARSEC, and Mediabench. These benchmarks are parallelized using DOALL, DOACROSS, pipelining, and speculative parallelism. Our implementation achieves 6x-18x speedup for these benchmarks using optimizations designed for systems with cache coherence and 2x-18x speedup using optimizations designed for systems without cache coherence.

The remainder of the paper is organized as follows. Section 2 first illustrates the design of SpiceC model with program examples and then describes its implementation details. Section 3 presents the evaluation of SpiceC model. Section 4 discusses the related works and Section 5 concludes this paper.

2. SpiceC: Design and Implementation

The *SpiceC* computation model represents a simple view of a parallel computation that serves as the basis for the programmer interface as well as corresponding implementation. In this model a parallel computation consists of multiple threads where each thread maintains a *private space* for data. In addition, a *shared space* is also maintained that holds shared data and provides a means for threads to communicate data to each other. A thread cannot access the private space belonging to other threads. Each thread carries

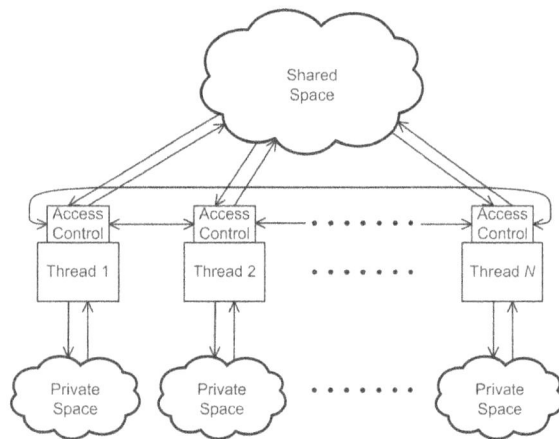

Figure 1. SpiceC Computation Model.

out its computation as follows: using *copying* operations it transfers data to its private space from shared space; it *operates* on the data in private space and produce results that are also written to the private space; and finally the thread affects the transfer of results to shared space using a `commit` operation thus allowing all threads to see the computed results. Thus, in this model, a thread performs its computation in *isolation* from other threads. Associated with each thread is an *access control* module which manages all accesses a thread makes to shared space. The access control modules of different threads perform actions on the shared space in coordination with each other.

A variable in shared space may be accessed by a thread by simply referring to it. A thread's first access to a shared space variable results in an image of that variable being created in its private space and this image is initialized by *copying* the value of the variable from shared space to private space. After copying, all subsequent

accesses to the variable, including both read and write accesses, refer to the variable's image in the private space. In other words, the thread can manipulate the value of the variable in isolation, free of contention with other threads. Most importantly, the above semantics is enforced automatically by the implementation of SpiceC model – the programmer simply refers to the variable by its name without having to distinguish between first or subsequent accesses. Therefore we refer to the above copying as *implicit copying* as it is automatically performed without help from the programmer. There will be times when the private space of a thread will need to be cleared and so updated values of shared data can be accessed from shared space. The clearing of private space, like its setup through copying, is also *implicit*. The private space of a thread is cleared at program points that correspond to boundaries of *code regions* (e.g., iteration boundaries of parallel loops, boundaries separating pipeline stages, synchronization points).

When a thread has finished a block of computation and wishes to expose its results to other threads, it performs an *explicit commit* operation. This results in the transfer of variable's values from private space to shared space. The programmer is provided with an Application Programming Interface (API) using which he/she can specify points in the program where the values of variable's need to be committed to shared space. SpiceC supports two types of `commit` operations. The first type of `commit` operation simply copies all copied variables to the shared space after acquiring the write permission to the shared space. The second type of `commit` operation checks for *atomicity violation* before committing, that is, it checks to see if any of the copied variables was updated by another thread after being copied into the private space of the committing thread. An *atomic commit* enables programmers to express speculative computations with little effort.

Next we briefly describe how the design of SpiceC addresses the following issues: Programmability (i.e., reducing the burden of parallel programming), Versatility (i.e., providing means to program different types of parallelism), and Performance Portability (i.e., programs deliver performance on different platforms without having to rewrite them).

Programmability. The complexity of parallel programming hinders developers from using it. To make programming easier, SpiceC uses programming style similar to OpenMP [9]. Developers do not write new parallel programs but simply add *SpiceC directives* into the text of a sequential program. Parallelism is exploited by the compiler based upon the directives. SpiceC model can be used to cause selected portions of the code to be executed in parallel while the remaining code remains serial.

To ensure that the programmer can easily reason about a program, a form of *sequential consistency* is employed as follows. In SpiceC, the *copy* and *commit* operations naturally divide code in parallel regions into chunks. These chunks can be executed with atomicity and in isolation as specified by developers. Sequential consistency is then enforced by the software at the coarse grain level of chunks. For performance, the compiler can freely reorder instructions within a chunk without the risk of violating coarse grain sequential consistency.

SpiceC removes the need to explicitly specify communication between threads. The work of *copying* and *commit* is done by the compiler and the implementation of supporting API functions. Developers only need to insert *commit* calls in their codes. This greatly reduces developer burden of programming explicit communication in a message-passing model such as Message Passing Interface (MPI). For example, in a message-passing model, developers need to write the following three functions to transfer a linked list from a thread to another: the first converting the linked list to a binary string, the second transferring the string to another thread, and the last for reconstructing the linked list from the string. In SpiceC, after a thread commits the linked list, other threads can access it as any other shared space variable. Developers do not need to write any special code to handle the linked list.

Although dynamic data structures are widely used in programs, they are not well supported by existing parallel programming models. It is challenging to parallelize programs with dynamic data structures using OpenMP [30]. Developers must either explicitly decompose the dynamic data structures into chunks and store pointers to these chunks in an array or use the "omp single nowait" clause. Furthermore, it is impossible for OpenMP to parallelize a program with irregular access patterns of dynamic data structures without a major rewriting of the original program [30]. In MPI, dynamic data structures need be managed by the programmer, which requires a lot of tedious programming. For example, to transfer a binary tree between threads, developers must manually convert it into a string at the source node and do the reverse conversion at the destination node. SpiceC model does not require developers to explicitly manage dynamic data structures since the compiler and/or the runtime system handles the copying and commits of dynamic data structures automatically.

Versatility. To efficiently parallelize applications, we support multiple forms of parallelism: DOALL, DOACROSS, pipelining, and speculative parallelism. It is difficult to use existing parallel programming model to implement some forms of parallelism while ensuring correctness and delivering high performance. For example, speculation must be expressed using low level primitives in existing languages [22]. Speculative computation, misspeculation check, and misspeculation recovery must be programmed by the user which can be a non-trivial programming exercise. In contrast SpiceC supports high level primitives and developer only needs to specify the parallelism and the coarse-grained dependences in the program. Compilers and runtime systems take care of the tedious part of parallel code generation.

SpiceC provides other benefits to parallel program developers. First, since a thread only updates variables in its private space before committing, it is easy to reverse the computation by simply discarding the content in the private space. In addition, the *commit* operation provided by SpiceC can check atomicity violation at runtime before committing. This makes it easy for developers to write programs with speculative parallelism. Secondly, parallel programming is error-prone. In SpiceC, an error in one thread does not affect other threads until it is committed. Therefore, it is easy to realize *fault tolerance* in SpiceC model. For example, developers can capture all fatal exceptions in thread T and reset T when exceptions happen. This enables other threads to continue operating even in the presence of errors in T.

Performance Portability. SpiceC can be implemented on any multicore or manycore system that has a logically shared memory with or without cache coherence. The portability of SpiceC makes it attractive alternative for developers who want their programs deployed on multiple platforms. Moreover, since current cache coherence protocols may not scale to manycore systems [1, 3], SpiceC makes it possible to scale shared-memory programs (e.g., OpenMP programs) to manycore systems.

Writes to shared memory often turn into performance bottlenecks for the program since they are serialized to enforce the sequential semantics of the program. SpiceC allows developers to create *clusters* of data. Commits to different *clusters* can be performed in parallel even if there is user-specified dependency among them. This increases the scalability of SpiceC especially for manycores where there may be hundreds of threads writing to the shared space. SpiceC pays a performance penalty for conducting checks on copy operations. Therefore, we have developed optimizations for reducing the number of copy checks and the time overhead of each copy check.

2.1 Programming Interface

SpiceC aims to provide a portable standard for writing parallel programs while hiding the complexity of parallel programming from developers. This section presents directives supported by SpiceC. SpiceC compiler directives enable the programmer to mark and parallelize a section of code that is meant to be run in parallel just as is the case in OpenMP [9]. A compiler directive in C/C++ is called a pragma (pragmatic information). Compiler directives specific to SpiceC model in C/C++ start with `#pragma SpiceC`. Table 1 shows the compiler directives supported by SpiceC.

`#pragma SpiceC parallel` is used to specify the parallel region of the program. The parallel region must be a loop, written in `for`, `while`, or `do ... while` form. Developers must specify in what form of parallelism the parallel region is to be executed. SpiceC supports three types of parallelism: DOALL, DOACROSS, and pipelining.

`#pragma SpiceC subregion` is used to specify a subregion in the parallel region. Developers can assign a name to the subregion and specify the execution order of different instances of the subregion or different subregions. By default, the whole loop body of the parallel region is one subregion.

`#pragma SpiceC commit` is used to call the `commit` operation, which commits all variables that are updated in the subregion to the shared space. Developers can specify whether to perform *atomicity* check before the commit operation. If the atomicity check fails, the subregion is re-executed. Developers can also specify the execution order of the `commit` operation which can be used to enforce the sequential semantics the parallel region.

`#pragma SpiceC barrier` is used to insert a barrier in the parallel region. In SpiceC model, each thread clears its private space when it encounters a barrier. Developers can optionally specify which variables to clear to enable avoidance of unnecessary copying overhead.

2.1.1 Code Regions & Types of Parallelism

In this section we illustrate the use of directives in marking code regions and expressing different forms of parallelism. We present examples written in SpiceC that show how different forms of parallelism can be expressed with little effort by the programmer.

Explicit parallel code in SpiceC. Figure 2 shows an example of explicit parallel code written in SpiceC that illustrates how shared space may be used by threads to communicate values to each other. The parallel code is executed by two threads. It is divided into two phases. In the first phase the two threads calculate values of variables a and b respectively. The programmer does not specify that a and b are to be copied into the private spaces – they are automatically copied upon their first uses. At the end of the first phase, a and b need to be committed into the shared space so that their new values are accessible to other threads. The programmer need not identify a and b in the commit operation – this is handled automatically which makes it easy to use. In other words, developer only specifies "when" to commit but need not specify "what" to commit. At the barrier, the two threads clear variable a and b in their private spaces and wait for each other. When both threads reach the synchronization point, they continue their computation and copy the value of a and b from the shared space again when they are used. Developers may or may not specify which variables to clear at the barrier. If variables are not specified at the barrier, the entire private spaces are cleared.

Directive	Description
#pragma SpiceC parallel [parallelism]	specify a program region that is meant to run in parallel using SpiceC model
#pragma SpiceC subregion [name] [order]	specify a subregion in the parallel region that is executed under the order specification
#pragma SpiceC commit [check_type] [order]	perform commit operation with specified check and order
#pragma SpiceC barrier [for_variable (variables)]	clear variables from private space

Table 1. Compiler directives implemented by SpiceC

```
#pragma SpiceC parallel {
    int tid = spicec_get_thread_id();
    if (tid == 0)
        a = calculate_a();
    else
        b = calculate_b();
    #pragma SpiceC commit
    #pragma SpiceC barrier for_variable(a,b)
    if (tid == 0)
        c = calculate_c(a,b);
    else
        d = calculate_d(a,b);
}
```

Figure 2. Communicating parallel threads written in SpiceC.

```
#pragma SpiceC doall {
    for(i=0;i<nodes;i++)
        nodes[i].cluster = closest_cluster(nodes[i], clusters);
    #pragma SpiceC commit
} //implicit barrier

#pragma SpiceC doall {
    for(i=0;i<clusters;i++)
        clusters[i].mean = calculate_mean(clusters[i], nodes);
    #pragma SpiceC commit
}
```

Figure 3. K-means clustering algorithm written in SpiceC.

```
#pragma SpiceC doacross {
    for(i=0;i<n;i++) {
        #pragma SpiceC subregion R1 order_after(ITER-1, R1)
        {
            job = read_stream(input_buffer);
            #pragma SpiceC commit
        }
        #pragma SpiceC subregion R2 no_order
        {
            decode(job);
            #pragma SpiceC commit
        }
        #pragma SpiceC subregion R3 order_after(ITER-1, R3)
        {
            write_stream(output_buffer, job);
            #pragma SpiceC commit
        }
    }
}
```

Figure 4. A typical stream decoder written in SpiceC.

DOALL Parallelism in SpiceC. Figure 3 shows a K-means clustering program written in SpiceC. This program looks very similar to an OpenMP program. Without the directives, the program can still be compiled as a sequential program. The K-means clustering algorithm has two steps: the first step assigns each node to the cluster with the closest mean and the second step calculates the new means to be the centroid of the nodes for each cluster. We specify the parallelization of each step using DOALL parallelism. `Commit` operations are inserted at the end of each parallel region. By using DOALL, workloads are divided and assigned among the threads at the beginning of the parallel region. No execution order is specified in this example. Therefore each thread executes fully in parallel with other threads. All threads join at the end of the parallel region, which acts as a implicit barrier.

DOACROSS Parallelism in SpiceC. Figure 4 shows a typical stream decoding program written in SpiceC model. The program repeatedly does the three steps: read a stream from the input buffer, decode the stream, and write the stream back to the output buffer. There are two cross-iteration dependences in the loop. In each iteration, the `read_stream` function reads a stream from the input buffer and moves the input buffer pointer to the next stream. Therefore, the `read_stream` in the current iteration depends on itself in the previous iteration. Similarly, `write_stream` also has cross-iteration dependence on itself. To parallelize this program, we specify the loop as DOACROSS parallelism. By using DOACROSS,

consecutive iterations are assigned to different threads to allow them to be executed in parallel. The loop is divided into three subregions with each step forming one subregion. We specify that subregion R1/R3 in the current iteration can only be executed after R1/R3 in the previous iteration finishes. The keyword "ITER" used in the SpiceC pragmas refers to the current iteration and "ITER-1" refers to the preceding iteration. No execution order is specified for R2 since it does not have cross-iteration dependence.

DOACROSS Speculative Parallelism in SpiceC. Figure 5 shows the kernel of benchmark telecomm-CRC32 in MiBench suite. The program calculates 32-bit CRC for each file in the file list and put the results into the `error` variable. The update of `error` depends on the value of `error` from previous iterations. Therefore, the subregion R2 has a cross-iteration dependence on itself. However, since the function `calculate_crc` usually returns 0 that represents success in real runs, the cross-iteration dependence is rarely manifested. We can parallelize the program by *speculating* on the absence of the dependence. We parallelize the program using DOACROSS parallelism. The loop body is divided into two subregions. The subregion R1 is executed sequentially since there is a cross-iteration dependence due to variable i. The subregion R2 is executed in parallel but the commit operation in R2 is performed sequentially to ensure the sequential semantics of the loop. Before the commit operation, an atomicity check is performed to detect if the cross-iteration dependence occurred. If the dependence is detected, then the whole subregion R2 is re-executed. Otherwise, R2 can commit its results safely.

Pipelined Parallelism in SpiceC. Figure 6 shows the same stream decoder as shown in Figure 4. But in this example, we parallelize it using pipelined parallelism. We still divide the loop body into three subregions. Each subregion is a stage of the pipeline. By using pipelining, each subregion is executed in one thread, similar to Decoupled Software Pipelining [24]. In this program, the subregion R2 needs data from R1 and R3 needs data from R2. Therefore, we

```
error=0;
i=0;
#pragma SpiceC doacross {
    while(i<n) {
        #pragma SpiceC subregion R1 order_after(ITER-1, R1) {
            string = read_file(file[i++]);
            #pragma SpiceC commit
        }
        #pragma SpiceC subregion R2 no_order {
            ret = calculate_crc(string);
            if (ret != 0)
                error |= ret;
            #pragma SpiceC commit \
                        atomicity_check order_after(ITER-1, R2)
        }
    }
}
```

Figure 5. Kernel of benchmark telecomm-CRC32.

specify R2 to be executed after R1 and R3 after R2. In this case, we do not need to specify the cross-iteration execution order (e.g., R1 in the current iteration should be executed after R1 in the previous iteration) since it is ensured by the very nature of pipelining. Unlike the model of producer and consumer, SpiceC model commits data to the same place every time. Therefore, subsequent commit may overwrite the value from previous commit. To avoid this problem, we expand the scalar variable job into an array and make each iteration compute using different memory locations.

```
#pragma SpiceC pipelining {
    for(i=0;i<n;i++) {
        #pragma SpiceC subregion R1 {
            job[i] = read_stream(input_buffer);
            #pragma SpiceC commit
        }
        #pragma SpiceC subregion R2 order_after(ITER, R1) {
            decode(job[i]);
            #pragma SpiceC commit
        }
        #pragma SpiceC subregion R3 order_after(ITER, R2) {
            write_stream(output_buffer, job[i]);
            #pragma SpiceC commit
        }
    }
}
```

Figure 6. Stream decoder parallelized using pipelining parallelism.

2.1.2 Dynamic Data Structures

In this section we present examples written in SpiceC that show how programs with dynamic data structures can be parallelized with little effort by the programmer. We also illustrate the use of data clusters for improving the performance of commits.

Copy and commit of dynamic data structures. Figure 7 shows an example of binary tree insertion that uses linked dynamic data structures to represent the tree structure. Each iteration of the loop either updates the root node or performs a node insertion in the left/right subtree. Since two iterations may go through the same path and update the same node, the loop has a cross-iteration dependence. However, since most iterations usually insert nodes at the bottom of the tree, it is unlikely that two iterations will insert leaf nodes at the same place. Therefore the cross-iteration dependence is rarely manifested. We can parallelize the program by *speculating*

on the absence of the dependence on the dynamic data structures. We specify the program to be parallelized by using DOACROSS parallelism. The loop body just contains one subregion – R1. The subregion R1 is executed in parallel but the commit operation in R1 is performed sequentially to ensure the sequential semantics of the loop. Similar to use of static variables in SpiceC model, developers do not need to manually write code for copying and committing of dynamic data structures. Developers only need to specify when to commit the dynamic data structures, which makes using dynamic data structures a lot easier. A dynamic data object is automatically copied into the private space when it is accessed for the first time and committed back to the shared space when the commit operation is called. This makes it easy to write speculative parallel programs with dynamic data structures.

```
#pragma SpiceC doacross {
    for(i=1;i<n;i++) {
        # pragma SpiceC subregion R1 {
            ret = compare(nodes[i], tree.root);
            if ( ret < 0 ) {
                insert_node(nodes[i], tree.root.left);
            }
            else if (ret > 0) {
                insert_node(nodes[i], tree.root.right);
            }
            else if (ret == 0) {
                update_node(nodes[i], tree.root);
            }
            # pragma SpiceC commit \
                        atomicity_check order_after(ITER-1, R1)
        }
    }
}
```

Figure 7. Binary tree insertion using linked dynamic data structures.

Data clusters and parallel commits in SpiceC. To increase the scalability of our implementation, we allow developers to specify what data clusters a subregion reads and writes. If the clusters used by a subregion are not written by its precedent subregions, the subregion is allowed to commit even though its precedent subregions have not finished their commits. Thus, out-of-order commits of subregions are possible.

Figure 8 shows the same binary tree insertion as shown in Figure 7. But in this example, we use clusters to improve the performance of commits. Since the tree is represented by a dynamic data structure, commits could be lengthy due to copying of dynamic data structures at runtime. In this example, the programmer specifies execution order of commits, that is, commits must be executed in sequential order to ensure the program's original semantics. In this case, the serialized commits could significantly harm the performance of the parallelized program if a lot of dynamic data structures need to be committed. To enable parallel commits, we define three clusters – root, left, and right before entering the parallel region. We explicitly use read_cluster, write_cluster, and readwrite_cluster API calls in subregion R1 to dynamically specify which clusters are actually read or written at runtime. When no more clusters will be accessed in the current region, we use the finalize_cluster API call to tell other threads which clusters are read/written by the current thread, although it is unknown which variables will be read/written in the current thread. The commit operations in the example check what clusters are read/written in the subregion and can be performed in advance when no preceding iterations write to the same clusters. In this case, the commit operations only need to wait for the `finalize_cluster` API calls in the preceding iterations. Since the `finalize_cluster` API is called at an early stage of the subregion, the commits can be performed out of order. This increases the scalability of the `commit` mechanism. In this form of cluster use, developers do not need to explicitly specify which variables belong to each cluster. They only need to bear that information in mind and insert `read_cluster`, `write_cluster`, or `readwrite_cluster` API calls where corresponding variables are used. This makes clusters easy to program. Our cluster definition is also flexible enough to achieve any mapping from variables to clusters. For example, developers can divide an array into several clusters and insert `read_cluster` calls if certain parts of array are read.

```
cluster root = initialize_cluster();
cluster left = initialize_cluster();
cluster right = initialize_cluster();
#pragma SpiceC doacross using_clusters {
    for(i=1;i<n;i++) {
        # pragma SpiceC subregion R1 {
            read_cluster(root);
            ret = compare(nodes[i], tree.root);
            if ( ret < 0 ) {
                readwrite_cluster(left);
                finalize_cluster();
                insert_node(nodes[i], tree.root.left);
            }
            else if (ret > 0) {
                readwrite_cluster(right);
                finalize_cluster();
                insert_node(nodes[i], tree.root.right);
            }
            else if (ret == 0) {
                write_cluster(root);
                finalize_cluster();
                update_node(nodes[i], tree.root);
            }
            # pragma SpiceC commit \
                        atomicity_check order_after(ITER-1, R1)
        }
    }
}
```

Figure 8. Example of using clusters to improve the performance of commits.

2.2 Implementation of SpiceC

This section describes the implementation of SpiceC on shared-memory systems with or without cache coherence. The core components of the SpiceC prototype implementation consist of: a source-to-source translator and a user-level runtime library. The translator analyzes the loops and SpiceC directives and translates them to C/C++ codes. The analysis is done by extending ROSE [23], which is an open source compiler infrastructure to build source-to-source code translator. We translate `#pragma parallel` into pthread library calls for creating and managing threads. The parallel region is wrapped into a function. Branch statements are used for assigning iterations or subregions to threads. The runtime library implements the `copy` and `commit` operations as well as thread synchronization operations.

In our implementation of SpiceC, all accesses to the shared space are managed by the *access control* runtime system. The access control runtime system makes sure that all variables are copied and committed properly in the parallel region and the copy and commit operations strictly follow the user-specified execution order. To make sure that every variable is copied and committed prop-

erly, the access control runtime system maintains metadata for each variable. Each variable has *metadata* in both shared and private spaces. In the shared space, we record the version of each variable for atomicity check. In a private space, metadata includes its shared space address, its type/size, whether they have been copied into the private space, and its version when it is copied. For fast access of dynamic data structures, we also extend pointers to contain partial metadata of the data structures they point to. We have the same basic implementation for shared memory systems with and without cache coherence while using different optimizations based on the presence of cache coherence. More details of access control are described as we elaborate on the implementations of copy and commit operations. It should be noted that although we implement the *copy* and *commit* operations in a user-level runtime library, they can also be implemented by the operating system kernel at page level. This could accelerate the `copy` and `commit` operations of shared data structures and avoid some of the runtime overhead associated with address translation of pointers.

2.2.1 Copy Operation

In SpiceC, shared variables are copied into the private space before being used. The implementation details of copy operation are given as follows.

Memory allocation in private spaces. For all global and stack variables that could be accessed in the parallel region, memory is allocated in every private space at compile time. This saves time in comparison to dynamically allocating memory for them at runtime. For shared dynamic data structures, we cannot allocate memory at compile time because they are instantiated at runtime. In our implementation, a thread dynamically allocates memory for shared dynamic data structures in its private space when they are used.

Data copying and access checks. In SpiceC, the variables are copied from the shared space to a thread's private space only when they are actually used in the thread. Since we do not want to repeatedly perform the copy operations for the same variables in an iteration, the copy operations are only implicitly performed at the first use of each variable. Therefore we need to check whether a shared variable has been copied into the private space when it is used at runtime. This can result in high runtime overhead if we place a check at every use of a shared variable. For better performance, we eliminate the redundant checks in the following ways: (1) if a shared variable is used in every control-flow path of the parallel region, we copy its value at the beginning of the parallel region and eliminate all checks for it; and (2) if a use of shared variable is dominated by another use or define of the same variable in every path of the parallel region, we eliminate the check at this use. Besides, we do not put checks for variables declared or created inside the parallel region.

Metadata. To support the checks, every global/stack variable has 1-bit metadata in each private space to indicate whether its value has been copied into the private space. The metadata are allocated in thread local storage at the compiler time. Every thread resets the metadata in its private space at the beginning of each subregion. When a global/stack variable is used, the thread needs to check its 1-bit metadata. If its metadata is one, the variable has already been copied into the private space. If its 1-bit metadata is zero, the thread then copies the variable into its private space and sets the 1-bit metadata to one.

Dynamic data structures are always referenced via pointers. When we dereference a pointer, we must not only check whether the dynamic data structure has been copied into the private space but also locate its private copy if it has been copied. To enable fast checks for dynamic data structures, we extended the current pointer representation. An extended pointer has four fields: `shared` space address of the data structure, `private space address` of the data structure, `thread ID`, and `iteration ID`. In the sequential region of the program, only shared space address field is used. When dereferencing an extended pointer in the parallel region, we first check whether the `private space address` field is valid (i.e., whether the dynamic data structure has a copy in the private space at the specified address). This is done by checking whether the pointer's `thread ID` and `iteration ID` fields match the current thread and iteration. If they match, the private space address is valid and we can directly use it. Otherwise, the private space address stored in the pointer is invalid. In this case, we need to check whether the pointed data structure has been copied into the private space due to the dereference of other pointers. On systems with cache coherence, we use `heap prefix` proposed in our prior work [28] to solve this problem. `Heap prefix` is the metadata of the data structure and located adjacent to the data structure in the shared space. It contains the location information of the data structure in each private space. Since the shared space address in a pointer is always valid, we can quickly locate the `heap prefix` by using the shared space address. On systems without cache coherence, we do not use `heap prefix` because `heap prefix` is located in the shared space which is not cachable and thereby very slow to access. Instead every thread places the metadata related to itself in its private space and uses a hash function to locate it [26]. For example, the metadata of dynamic data structure A's copy in thread i is stored in thread i's private space. When thread i refers to A using a pointer with invalid private space address field, it hashes the shared space address stored in the pointer to locate A's metadata in the private space. After checking the metadata, we know if the data structure has been copied. If it has not been copied, we need to copy it from the shared space to the private space, update its metadata, and make the `private space address` field of the pointer point to the newly created private copy. If the data structure has been copied, we only need to update the extended pointer according to the metadata.

We use an example to illustrate the copy operation for dynamic data structures. In Figure 7, *root.left* is a pointer to the left child of the root. When thread T1 executes iteration I1, it first copies the root node and the new node into its private space. Assume that the new node is inserted as the left child of the root. Therefore, T1 updates *root.left* to point to the new node and commits the root node back to the shared space at the end of the subregion. Later on, when another thread T2 executes iteration I2, it also first copies the root node and the new node into its private space. When T2 dereferences *root.left* for the first time, it does not know if the left node has been copied into its private space due to the dereference of other pointers. T2 first tries to locate its private copy of the left child. A fast way to locate the private copy is to use the *root.left*'s `private space address` field. However, the `private space address` field is invalid since it points to T1's private space. The `thread ID` and `iteration ID` fields of *root.left* do not match T2 and I2. T2 then checks the metadata (i.e., heap prefix or hash table) of the left child and finds that the left child has not been copied. Finally, T2 copies the left child into its private space and updates the metadata and the `private space address`, `thread ID`, and `iteration ID` fields of *root.left*.

2.2.2 Commit Operation

In SpiceC, all copied variables need to be committed to the shared space after a subregion is finished. To realize this, when a variable is copied to the private space, it is appended to a link list in the private space. Besides, all dynamic data structure instantiated in the subregion are also appended to the link list. When `commit` is called, it scans the link list and copies all variables in the list to the

shared space. If developers do not want a locally created dynamic data structure to be committed, they must *free* it before committing.

When a dynamic data structure and its pointers in the private space are committed to the shared space, all these pointers need to be redirected to the shared copy of the dynamic data structure. This usually results in high runtime overhead for searching the pointers and translating the addresses. In our implementation, we do not need to alter the pointers when committing them. Our extended pointer contains two address fields: one for shared space address and the other for private space address, similar to `double pointer` proposed in our prior work [28]. The shared space address field always contains the shared space address of the data structure no matter in which space the pointer is. When we assign a pointer to another pointer, we copy both address fields. We use the shared space address field of a pointer when we refer to the shared copy of the data structure. Therefore, we do not need to translate the addresses when committing pointers. For example, in Figure 7, when a thread accesses the root node, it copies the root node into its private space. Later on, when the thread accesses the left child of the root via the pointer *root.left*, it copies the left child into its private space and makes the `private space address` field of *root.left* point to the private copy of the left child. If somehow the thread needs to commit the root node and its left child, it only needs to copy them back to the shared space. No address translation is required for *root.left* since its `shared space address` field always points to the left node in the shared space.

In SpiceC, developers can specify whether to perform an atomicity check before a commit operation. If the atomicity check fails, the subregion needs to be re-executed and all content in the private space is discarded. The atomicity check scans the link list of the copied variables to see if any of them have been updated in the shared space by other threads since being copied into current thread's private space. To support the atomicity check, each variable has a version number in the shared space. The version number is incremented when the variable is committed by a thread. When a thread copies a variable, it also copies its version number. When performing atomicity checks for a variable, the thread compares its version numbers in both space. If the numbers are different, then the variable must have been committed by other threads after being copied. Version numbers are only maintained when there is at least one commit operation requiring atomicity check in the parallel region. Our implementation also provides value-based atomicity check, which compares variables' values instead of their version numbers to ignore silent dependences. Value-based atomicity check could be time-consuming if the sizes of variables are very large.

We allow two `commits` to execute in parallel if they are non-check `commits` with no order specification. On systems with cache coherence, the cache coherence mechanism will handle the situation where two commits update different sets of variables that share the same cache lines. On systems without cache coherence, the shared space is usually non-cachable. Therefore, we do not need to worry about cacheline-level sharing. As long as two `commits` update different sets of variables, they will not cause coherence problem. If two `commits` may update the same set of variables, developers should specify the check type or execution order to avoid data race.

2.2.3 Relaxed copy/commit model

The programs written in SpiceC model are portable across CMP machines with or without cache coherence. However, in some cases, `copy` and `commit` operations are unnecessary and may incur higher overhead compared to directly accessing the shared space. To improve the performance of SpiceC in these cases, we relax the copy/commit model by allowing the threads to directly access the shared space.

On systems with cache coherence, since the shared space is cachable and fast to access, we prefer to directly access the shared space if copy and commit operations are unnecessary. We relax the copy/commit model in the following cases. (1) If a subregion uses non-check commit without any order specification, we allow the subregion to directly operate on the shared space since it has no dependence with any other part of program that is executed simultaneously. (2) Read-only variables do not need to be committed even in the subregions where copy and commit operation are required. Therefore, we only copy a variable when it is to be written. When a variable is to be read, we only record its version number in its `heap prefix` for atomicity check. In this way, we reduce the copy/commit overhead for read-only variables.

On systems without cache coherence, shared space is usually non-cachable to avoid consistency problem. Directly accessing the shared space is much slower than accessing the private spaces which is cachable. Therefore, we make copy of every variable that is to be accessed in the private space to make subsequent accesses to the same variable faster. We do not relax copy/commit model on systems without cache coherence since it is better for performance.

2.2.4 Synchronization

In SpiceC model, developers can specify the execution order for subregions and commits. Depending on the system configuration, our implementation uses different synchronization mechanisms to ensure the specified execution order.

On systems with cache coherence, we use busy-waiting algorithms to ensure the execution order. A flag is set after each subregion is finished. Before a subregion or commit is executed, we check the flags of the subregions which it is waiting for. If the flags are set, then we continue the execution. Busy-waiting algorithms achieve low wake-up latency and hence yield good performance [20].

Systems without cache coherence usually provide hardware support for message-passing interface (MPI) to enable fast communication between cores. Therefore we use MPI to ensure the execution order. At runtime, for every iteration or subregion, we know the thread that will execute it. Since the execution order is explicitly specified in the code, a thread can know which thread is waiting for it at runtime. Therefore, after a thread finishes a subregion, it can send signal to the waiting thread.

2.2.5 Loop Execution

Next we describe how we execute loops with different forms of parallelism. For loops with DOALL parallelism, the workloads are distributed among the threads at the beginning of the loop. For example, for a DOALL loop with n iterations, thread i will execute the loop from iteration $n/m * i$ to $n/m * (i+1) - 1$, where m is the total number of threads. For loops with DOACROSS parallelism, each thread executes one iteration at a time. After committing an iteration, a thread fetches another iteration by executing the loop index. Loop index is always executed in sequential order. We do not allow loop index to depend on any part of loop body. If loop index does depend on loop body, developers need to move it into the loop body and specify the execution order or check type for it. For example, a DOACROSS loop is executed by m threads. Thread i only executes iteration $m * j + i$, where $j \in \{0, 1, 2, \ldots\}$. Thread i begins to execute iteration $m * j + i$ only after it finishes iteration $m * (j-1) + i$ and thread $i-1$ finishes the index part of iteration $m * j + i - 1$. For loops with pipelining parallelism, each thread is dedicated to execute one subregion, as in [24]. For example, a pipelining loop contains m subregions. Thread i executes the i-th subregion for every iteration.

Processors	4×6-core 64-bit AMD Opteron 8431 Processor (2.4GHz)
L1 cache	Private, 128KB for each core
L2 cache	Private, 512KB for each core
L3 cache	Shared among 6 cores, 6144KB
Memory	32GB RAM

Table 2. Dell PowerEdge R905 Machine details.

3. Evaluation

This section evaluates our initial implementations of SpiceC model. We have two implementations with different optimizations: (1) the first is designed for shared-memory systems with cache coherence using relaxed copy/commit model and busy-waiting synchronization; and (2) the second is designed for shared-memory systems without cache coherence using strict copy/commit model and message passing synchronization. The experiments are conducted on a 24-core DELL PowerEdge R905 machine. Table 2 lists the machine details. The machine runs Ubuntu Server v10.04. We report results for both implementations on the machine. Since the machine has hardware support for cache coherence, accessing the shared space on it is faster than that on a system without cache coherence. Therefore, the performance reported for the second implementation is higher than the actual performance on a system without cache coherence. We use the machine for evaluating the second implementation because we currently do not have a manycore machine with message passing hardware instead of cache coherence.

3.1 Benchmarks

SpiceC was applied to benchmarks selected from PARSEC, SPEC CPU2000, MediaBench, and MiBench suites. For the benchmark CRC32 and `bzip`, we applied two different forms of parallelism. For some of the benchmarks, we unrolled their loops to increase the workload of each iteration. Table 3 shows the details of the benchmarks.

Benchmarks using DOALL. `Streamcluster` was developed to solve online clustering problem. It is from the PARSEC suite and thereby has a manually parallelized version. We took its serial version and added SpiceC directives to it. There are 9 loops that can be parallelized using DOALL. Among them, three loops need to compute sums of large arrays of values. For the three loops, we did very simple modifications to realize parallel sum reduction.

`Fluidanimate` was designed to simulate an incompressible fluid for interactive animation purposes. It is also from the PARSEC suite. Its serial version requires manually partitioning workloads for parallelization. We took its pthread version and replaced all pthread calls with SpiceC directives. In the pthread version, there are a lot of lock operations for synchronization. In the SpiceC version, we removed all these lock operations, which makes the program easier to understand.

Benchmarks using DOACROSS. The CRC32 program computes the 32-bit CRC used as the frame check sequence in Advanced Data Communication Control Procedures (ADCCP). Its kernel is shown in Figure 5. In each iteration, it first reads data from a file, then calculates CRC based on the data, and finally summarizes the error code into variable "error". In the experiments, we parallelized it in two ways. One way to parallelizing it is applying non-speculative DOACROSS. We need to divide the loop body into three subregions – input, computation and output. Input and output subregions need to be executed in order since there are cross-iteration dependences in them. Computation subregion can executed in parallel. The other way of parallelizing it is using speculation as shown in Figure 5.

`Bzip2` is a tool used for lossless, block-sorting data compression and decompression. In the experiments, we parallelized its

76

Benchmark	Function	LOC	Parallelism	Speculation?	Using Cluster?	% of Runtime	# of Dir.
streamcluster	pkmedian & pspeedy & pFL	300	DOALL	No	No	88%	21
fluidanimate	RebuildGrid & ComputeForces & ProcessCollisions & AdvanceParticles	206	DOALL	No	No	96%	16
CRC32	main	15	DOACROSS	No	No	100%	7
			DOACROSS	Yes	No	100%	5
256.bzip2	compressStream	127	DOACROSS	Yes	Yes	99%	17
			pipelining	No	No	99%	7–19
197.parser	batch_process	1183	DOACROSS	Yes	Yes	99%	15
ferret	do_query	84	pipelining	No	No	99%	13–25
mpeg2enc	dist1	91	pipelining	Yes	No	56%	13-21

Table 3. Benchmark details. From left to right: benchmark name, function where the parallelized loops are located, lines of code in the function, type of parallelism exploited, whether speculation is used, whether cluster is used, percentage of total execution time taken by the parallelized loops, and number of directives used for parallelization.

compression part. There are many superfluous cross-iteration dependences on global variables in bzip2. To remove these dependences, we made many global variables local to each iteration and replicate buffers for each iteration. We used two ways of parallelizing bzip2: using DOACROSS and using pipelining. For the DOACROSS version, we still divided the loop body into three subregions – input, compression, and output. Cross-iteration dependences in input and output subregions are enforced by specifying execution order for them. Cross-iteration dependences in compression subregions rarely manifest at runtime. Therefore, we run compression subregion in parallel and use atomicity check at commit to ensure the dependence. To enable parallel commits, we use two data clusters: one for variables where cross-iteration dependences may occur and the other for all other variables. For pipelining version, we need to carefully divide the loop body into stages. We inlined several functions in the loop and moved some parts of loop around to make the stages balanced.

`Parser` is a syntactic parser of English based on link grammar. We used speculative DOACROSS to parallelize parser. The problem with parser is that we need to speculate on dependences for many variables, including control variables which is a set of global variables and dictionary structures which is a set of linked dynamic data structures. This causes the commit operations to become bottlenecks for the parallelized program. To solve this problem, we partitioned the variables into four clusters: global control variables, dynamic data structures, error counter, and other variables. We inserted `read_cluster` and `write_cluster` calls at the places where corresponding variables are used.

Benchmarks for pipelining. `Ferret` is a tool used for content-based similarity search of feature-rich data. In the PARSEC suite, this program is parallelized using a 6-stage pipeline. We parallelized its serial version using two different forms of pipeline: a 6-stage pipeline and a more fine-grained 14-stage pipeline. To realize the pipelining, we inlined several functions but did not move any statements.

`Mpeg2enc` is a MPEG video encoder. We parallelized a loop in function "dist1" using a 5-stage pipeline and a 9-stage pipeline. Loop exits are required to be speculated to achieve parallelization.

3.2 Performance with Relaxed Model

This section presents the results of the first implementation that uses relaxed copy/commit model and busy-waiting synchronization. Figure 9(a) shows the speedups of benchmarks with DOALL and DOACROSS parallelisms. As we can see, the performance of most benchmarks scales well over the number of threads, except for `streamcluster`. The performance of `streamcluster` goes down when the number of threads exceeds 20. This is because we parallelized `streamcluster` on inner loops. As the number of threads increases, the overhead of creating and joining threads gets higher

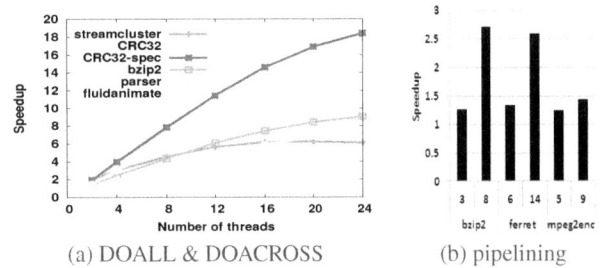

(a) DOALL & DOACROSS   (b) pipelining

Figure 9. Speedup with relaxed model.

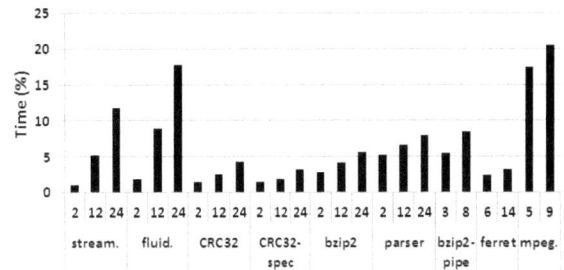

Figure 10. Parallelization overhead with relaxed model.

while the workload for each thread shrinks. We only show results of 2, 4, 8, and 16 threads for `fluidanimate` because it can only take power of 2 as thread number. CRC32 achieves the highest speedup among all the benchmarks. This is because most part of the program can be executed in parallel. Its speculative version performs better than the non-speculative version since the misspeculation rate is only around 0.1%. `Parser` and `bzip2` achieves moderate speedup. Their misspeculation rates are 0.92% and 0.5% respectively. Most performance loss is due to atomicity checks.

Figure 9(b) shows the speedups of benchmarks with pipelining parallelism. The number under each bar indicates the number of threads used. We only show the results of certain numbers of threads since it is hard to breakdown the program into arbitrary number of stages. Their speedups are between 1.2x and 2.8x, much less than the speedups achieved by DOALL and DOACROSS. For `bzip2` and `ferret`, their poor performance is mainly due to the unbalanced workloads. For `mpeg2enc`, a significant performance loss is due to its high misspeculation rate which is around 16%.

Figure 10 shows the average parallelization overhead on each thread. The number under each bar indicates how many threads are used when calculating the overhead. The overhead includes time spent on synchronization, copy/commit, atomicity check, and misspeculation recovery. As we can see, parallelization over-

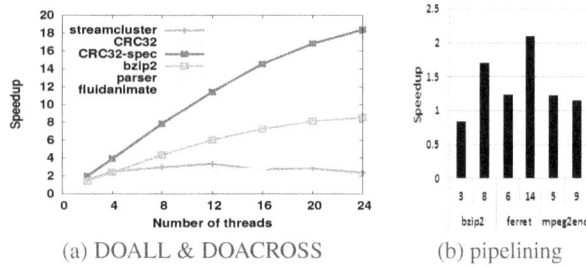

(a) DOALL & DOACROSS   (b) pipelining

Figure 11. Speedup with strict model.

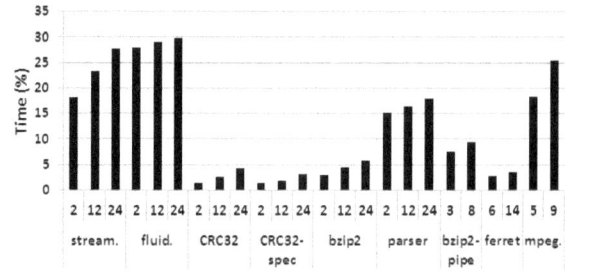

Figure 12. Time overhead with strict model.

head increases with the number of threads. `streamcluster` and `fluidanimate` has higher overhead since we parallelized them on more fine-grained level. The overhead of `mpeg2enc` is mainly due to high misspeculation rate. `Parser` has moderate overhead, which is caused by the atomicity check for dynamic data structures. A significant overhead of `bzip2` using pipelining is synchronization due to unbalanced workloads. The rest benchmarks have relatively low parallelization overhead.

3.3 Performance with Strict Model

This section presents the results of the second implementation that uses strict copy/commit model and message passing synchronization. Figure 11(a) shows the speedups of the benchmarks with DOALL and DOACROSS parallelism. Similar to results in the previous section, the performance of most benchmarks scales well with the number of threads, except for `streamcluster`. We can see that `CRC32` and `bzip2` are not affected much by using strict copy/commit model. `CRC32` still achieves highest speedup since it has very few variables that require copying. `Bzip2` needs to copy only a few more variables using the strict model. Therefore, its performance does not degrade much. The performance of `Streamcluster` and `fluidanimate` are greatly degraded by use of the strict model. The major part of performance loss is due to the large amount of data that needs to be copied. `Streamcluster` and `fluidanimate` respectively require 98MB and 163MB memory space at runtime. Using the strict model, they need to dynamically copy/commit most of the data in each parallel region. Since the parallelization is done at fine-grained level, the copy and commit overhead is significant compared to the computation workload assigned to each thread. Therefore, `streamcluster` and fluidanimate show loss of performance using the strict model. `Parser` also takes a moderate performance hit using the strict model. This is because many dynamic data structures need to be copied even though they are read-only. Figure 11(b) shows the speedups of the benchmarks with pipelining parallelism. `Bzip2` loses performance because some buffers need to be copied between subregions. `Mpeg2enc` is parallelized at very fine-grained level. The extra copy and commit overhead significantly drags down its performance. `Ferret` is only slightly affected by using the strict model. Its workload is well partitioned so that there is not much data requiring copy and commit.

Figure 10 shows the average parallelization overhead on each thread when using the strict model. The number under each bar indicates how many threads are used when calculating the overhead. As we can see, parallelization overhead increases in the strict model. `Streamcluster` and `fluidanimate` incur up to 30% overhead due to extra copy and commit operations. `Parser`'s overhead using 24 threads goes from 8% up to 18% which significantly degrades its performance. `Mpeg2enc`'s overhead with the 9-stage pipeline increases by 5%, which is significant compared to each stage's workload.

4. Related Work

Many programming models have been proposed to write parallel programs for multiprocessors. OpenMP [9] is probably the most widely used programming model for parallelizing sequential programs on shared-memory systems. Similar to SpiceC, OpenMP also uses compiler directives to express shared-memory parallelism. OpenMP gives developers a simple interface to parallelize their programs. Compared to SpiceC, OpenMP lacks the following features. (1) *Native support for various forms of parallelism.* For example, to write a pipelining program using OpenMP, developers have to manually transform their loop layouts, which is sometimes very tricky. (2) *Native support for speculative parallelism.* Chung et al. [7] use transactional memory in OpenMP loops to realize speculative parallelization. However, there is still no convenient way for developers to select which dependence to speculate. (3) *Support for dynamic data structures.* To parallelize programs with dynamic data structures using OpenMP, developers must modify the original program using "omp single nowait" or explicitly decompose the dynamic data structures into chunks. For irregular access patterns of dynamic data structures, it is impossible to use OpenMP without rewriting the original program [30]. (4) *Support for shared-memory systems without cache coherence.* OpenMP needs to be extended to efficiently parallelize programs for such systems. OpenMP assumes that every thread can access the shared memory with minimum latency [9], which is not the case on systems without cache coherence.

Threading Building Blocks (TBB) [25] is another programming model used to parallelize programs for shared-memory systems. Instead of using compiler directives, TBB provides a set of threadsafe containers and algorithms to allow developers to easily write parallel programs. To use TBB, developers need to wrap their codes using the containers provided by TBB. Like OpenMP, TBB does not support speculative parallelism. To parallelize a loop with cross-iteration dependences, developers need to manually use low level primitives to handle the dependences.

Single Program Multiple Data (SPMD) is another programming model to achieve parallelism. Message passing interface (MPI) [13] is currently the de facto standard for SPMD. Using MPI, developers need to explicitly write parallel programs, including manually distributing workloads among threads and handling all communications and synchronizations between threads. Since developers can fully control their programs in MPI, MPI is good for optimizing performance and managing data locality. Partitioned global address space (PGAS) is a parallel programming model which tries to combine the performance advantage of MPI with the programmability of a shared-memory model. It includes Unified Parallel C [8], Co-Array Fortran [11], Titanium [14], Chapel [4] and X10 [5]. Unified Parallel C, Co-Array Fortran, and Titanium use SPMD style and try to improve the programmability of SPMD. Chapel and X10 extend PGAS to allow each node to execute multiple tasks from a task pool and invoke work on other nodes.

There are a few other programming interfaces proposed to improve parallel programming. Sequoia [12] is a memory hierarchy aware parallel programming model. In Sequoia, developers explicitly control the movement and placement of data at all levels of the machine memory hierarchy to make parallel programs bandwidth-efficient. Hierarchically Tiled Array (HTA) [2] accelerates sequential OO languages by using an array to express multiple levels of tiling for locality and parallelism. Prabhu et al. [22] proposed two language constructs to enable developers to express value speculation parallelism in producer and consumer model. Mehrara et al. [19] proposed a low-cost software transactional memory for writing speculative parallel programs. A runtime system is proposed in [16–18, 21] to exploit the data parallelism in irregular applications. They support speculative parallelism but developers must provide code to perform rollback once speculation fails. Bamboo [31] is a data-oriented programming languages for manycore processors.

Software-based thread level speculation (TLS) techniques have been proposed for automatically parallelizing sequential programs [10, 15, 27–29]. They are all based on state separation, i.e., the results of speculative computations are stored in a separate space other than the non-speculative space. Behavior oriented parallelization (BOP) [10, 15] uses OS-assisted techniques for copying data between spaces. Tian et al. [28] proposed a set of optimizations for copying dynamic data structures between spaces.

Concurrent aggregates [6] allow developers to group objects into an aggregate, upon which hierarchical abstraction is built. Since each aggregate contains multiple objects, it can receive multiple message at the same time. This increases maximum message rate between levels in the hierarchy. SpiceC allows developers to group variables into clusters to enable simultaneous commits of different variable clusters.

5. Conclusion

This paper proposes the SpiceC shared memory parallel programming model that is designed to exploit multiple forms of parallelism and can be ported across shared memory multiprocessors that may or may not support cache coherence. The SpiceC model provides a set of compiler directives, which can be easily used to parallelize sequential programs. We describe the implementation of SpiceC model for shared memory systems with and without cache coherence. In the experiments, we parallelize seven benchmarks by inserting SpiceC directives without much modification to the serial codes. The parallelized benchmarks achieve 2x-18x speedups on a 24-core machine.

References

[1] M. Azimi, N. Cherukuri, D. N. Jayasimha, A. Kumar, P. Kundu, S. Park, I. Schoinas, and A. S. Vaidya. Integration challenges and tradeoffs for tera-scale architectures. *Intel Technology Journal*, 11(3): 173–184, 2007.

[2] G. Bikshandi, J. Guo, D. Hoeflinger, G. Almasi, B. B. Fraguela, M. J. Garzarn, D. Padua, and C. V. Praun. Programming for parallelism and locality with hierarchically tiled arrays. In *PPoPP*, pages 48–57, 2006.

[3] K. D. Bosschere, W. Luk, X. Martorell, N. Navarro, M. OBoyle, D. Pnevmatikatos, A. Ramirez, P. Sainrat, A. Seznec, P. Stenstrom, and O. Temam. High-performance embedded architecture and compilation roadmap. In *Transactions on HiPEAC*, volume 1, pages 5–29, 2007.

[4] B. L. Chamberlain, D. Callahan, and H. P. Zima. Parallel programmability and the chapel language. *International Journal of High Performance Computing Applications*, 21(3):291–312, 2007.

[5] P. Charles, C. Grothoff, V. Saraswat, C. Donawa, A. Kielstra, K. Ebcioglu, C. von Praun, and V. Sarkar. X10: an object-oriented approach to non-uniform cluster computing. In *OOPSLA*, 2005.

[6] A. A. Chien and W. J. Dally. Concurrent aggregates. In *PPoPP*, pages 187–196, 1990.

[7] J. Chung, H. Chafi, C. Minh, A. McDonald, B. Carlstrom, C. Kozyrakis, and K. Olukotun. The common case transactional behavior of multithreaded programs. In *HPCA*, pages 266–277, 2006.

[8] U. Consortium. UPC language specifications, v1.2. *Lawrence Berkeley National Lab Tech Report LBNL-59208*, 2005.

[9] L. Dagum and R. Menon. Openmp: An industry-standard api for shared-memory programming. *IEEE computational science & engineering*, 5(1):46–55, 1998.

[10] C. Ding, X. Shen, K. Kelsey, C. Tice, R. Huang, and C. Zhang. Software behavior oriented parallelization. In *PLDI*, 2007.

[11] Y. Dotsenko, C. Coarfa, and J. Mellor-Crummey. A multi-platform co-array fortran compiler. In *PACT*, 2004.

[12] K. Fatahalian, D. R. Horn, T. J. Knight, L. Leem, M. Houston, J. Y. Park, M. Erez, M. Ren, A. Aiken, W. J. Dally, and P. Hanrahan. Sequoia: Programming the memory hierarchy. In *SC*, 2006.

[13] W. Gropp, E. Lusk, and A. Skjellum. *Using MPI: Portable Parallel Programming with the Message Passing Interface*. The MIT Press, 1994.

[14] P. Hilfinger, D. Bonachea, K. Datta, D. Gay, S. Graham, B. Liblit, G. Pike, J. Su, and K. Yelick. Titanium language reference manual. *U.C. Berkeley Tech Report, UCB/EECS-2005-15*, 2005.

[15] K. Kelsey, T. Bai, C. Ding, and C. Zhang. Fast track: A software system for speculative program optimization. In *CGO*, 2009.

[16] M. Kulkarni, K. Pingali, B. Walter, G. Ramanarayanan, K. Bala, and L. P. Chew. Optimistic parallelism requires abstractions. In *PLDI*, pages 211–222, 2007.

[17] M. Kulkarni, K. Pingali, G. Ramanarayanan, B. Walter, K. Bala, and L. P. Chew. Optimistic parallelism benefits from data partitioning. In *ASPLOS*, pages 233–243, 2008.

[18] M. Kulkarni, M. Burtscher, R. Inkulu, K. Pingali, and C. Cascaval. How much parallelism is there in irregular applications? In *PPoPP*, 2009.

[19] M. Mehrara, J. Hao, P.-C. Hsu, and S. Mahlke. Parallelizing sequential applications on commodity hardware using a low-cost software transactional memory. In *PLDI*, pages 166–176, 2009.

[20] J. M. Mellor-Crummey and M. L. Scott. Algorithms for scalable synchronization on shared-memory multiprocessors. *ACM Trans. Comput. Syst.*, 9(1):21–65, 1991.

[21] M. Mendez-Lojo, D. Nguyen, D. Prountzos, X. Sui, M. A. Hassaan, M. Kulkarni, M. Burtscher, and K. Pingali. Structure-drive optimization for amorphous data-parallel programs. In *PPoPP*, 2010.

[22] P. Prabhu, G. Ramalingam, and K. Vaswani. Safe programmable speculative parallelism. In *PLDI*, pages 50–61, 2010.

[23] D. Quinlan. Rose: Compiler support for object-oriented framework. In *CPC*, 2000.

[24] R. Rangan, N. Vachharajani, M. Vachharajani, and D. I. August. Decoupled software pipelining with the synchronization array. In *PACT*, 2004.

[25] J. Reinders. *Intel threading building blocks: outfitting C++ for multi-core processor*. O'Reilly Media, 2007.

[26] M. F. Spear, L. Dalessandro, V. J. Marathe, and M. L. Scott. A comprehensive strategy for contention management in software transactional memory. In *PPoPP*, 2009.

[27] C. Tian, M. Feng, and R. Gupta. Copy or discard execution model for speculative parallelization on multicores. In *MICRO*, 2008.

[28] C. Tian, M. Feng, and R. Gupta. Supporting speculative parallelization in the presence of dynamic data structures. In *PLDI*, pages 62–73, 2010.

[29] C. Tian, M. Feng, and R. Gupta. Speculative parallelization using state separation and multiple value prediction. In *ISMM*, 2010.

[30] T.-H. Weng, R.-K. Perng, and B. Chapman. Openmp implementation of SPICE3 circuit simulator. *Int. J. Parallel Program.*, 35(5):493–505, 2007.

[31] J. Zhou and B. Demsky. Bamboo: a data-centric, object-oriented approach to many-core software. In *PLDI*, 2010.

Inferring Ownership Transfer for Efficient Message Passing

Stas Negara   Rajesh K. Karmani   Gul Agha

University of Illinois at Urbana-Champaign

{snegara2,rkumar8,agha}@illinois.edu

Abstract

One of the more popular paradigms for concurrent programming is the Actor model of message passing; it has been adopted in one form or another by a number of languages and frameworks. By avoiding a shared local state and instead relying on message passing, the Actor model facilitates modular programming. An important challenge for message passing languages is to transmit messages efficiently. This requires retaining the pass-by-value semantics of messages while avoiding making a deep copy on sequential or shared memory multicore processors. A key observation is that many messages have an *ownership transfer* semantics; such messages can be sent efficiently using pointers without introducing shared state between concurrent objects. We propose a conservative static analysis algorithm which infers if the content of a message is compatible with an ownership transfer semantics. Our tool, called SOTER (for *Safe Ownership Transfer enablER*[1]) transforms the program to avoid the cost of copying the contents of a message whenever it can infer the content obeys the ownership transfer semantics. Experiments using a range of programs suggest that our conservative static analysis method is usually able to infer ownership transfer. Performance results demonstrate that the transformed programs execute up to an order of magnitude faster than the original programs.

Categories and Subject Descriptors   D.2.0 [*Software*]: SOFTWARE ENGINEERING—General

General Terms   Languages, Performance

Keywords   Actors, Message Passing, Ownership Transfer, Static Analysis

1. Introduction

The arrival of computing platforms such as multicores and clouds have brought a disruption in the field of computer programming: mainstream developers need to write and maintain parallel programs. It has been argued that the thread based model makes the task of parallel programming unnecessarily more difficult (e.g., see [14]). The alternative, message passing as in the Actor programming model, is gaining increased interest among researchers

---

[1] Soter is also the name of the Greek god of safety, deliverance, and preservation from harm.

as well as practitioners. Actors are concurrent, autonomous entities that encapsulate local state and communicate using messages. There are two important advantages of using actors. First, the code is more modular: because the state of different concurrent objects is isolated, compositional reasoning is facilitated. Second, an actor program is portable without modification across sequential processors, shared memory multicore architectures, message passing multicore architectures, as well as clusters.

Some of the well known languages and frameworks that incorporate Actor-oriented programming include Erlang, E, Scala Actors library, SALSA, ActorFoundry, Microsoft's Asynchronous Agents Library and Axum. (For a brief survey, see [10, 12]). A number of significant applications have been written using the Actors model: these include open source applications such as Twitter's message queuing system and Lift Web Framework, and commercial applications such as the image processing application in MS Visual Studio 2010 and Vendetta's game engine. In fact, MPI processes are also a special case of Actors where some of the dynamic aspects of actors are restricted. MPI has been widely used in the High-Performance Computing (HPC) community to write programs.

When actors reside in different nodes of a message passing multicore architecture, or of a networked computers, message passing provides a natural implementation. However, even on a single core, programmers want to divide their code into logical units or objects. Actors add concurrency to objects. The *grain size* of an actor corresponds to the work load generated by an actor and its memory footprint. The most intuitive decomposition of an application often leads to actors that are much smaller than the processing and memory capacity of a node. This means that many actors may time share on a single node. Sending messages between actors on the same node corresponds to a *pass-by-value* semantics [3].

Pass-by-value requires making a deep copy of message contents before the message is sent out with a fresh copy. Such copying can severely degrade performance: deep nested object oriented structures need to be serialized and deserialized to make a fresh copy. The performance penalty is the major source of inefficiency in implementations of Actor programs [10] as well as MPI programs [1]. The issue gains particular urgency with the adoption of message passing paradigm for multicore chips (with shared memory).

An important observation is that many message passing programs tend to have simple structure where messages have an *ownership transfer* semantics, i.e. an actor hands off an object or data stream to another actor by passing it in a message [9]. If such cases can be identified in Actor programs, performance may be significantly enhanced [10]. This problem is closely related to the problem of ensuring *safe yet efficient message passing* [24].

One approach to efficient messaging is to send pointers for all message contents by default, and ask the programmer to explicitly make a copy if required [8]. If the programmer is not careful, this approach breaks Actor *encapsulation* by introducing shared state between actors, thereby reducing it to shared state programming. A complimentary approach is to require the programmer to annotate message contents which can be sent by reference (pointer) safely, thus explicitly declaring ownership transfer of such objects. A deep copy for remaining message contents may be provided automatically at runtime [10]. Note that both these approaches require the programmer to reason about messages in terms of a dual semantics – pass-by-value and ownership transfer. We believe this creates confusion: for example, the best practices section [15] of the Asynchronous Agents Library documentation suggests sending pointers for large data structures in messages; however, the walk through examples [16, 17] create copies even though it would be safe in these cases to send pointers.

A recent proposal is to ask programmers to use a novel type system to annotate message content. Specifically, variants of *ownership types* have been proposed for Kilim and Scala [7, 24]. The programming model for Singularity operating system [5] also proposes a simple type system based on object capabilities for exchange of objects between different concurrent processes. We believe such type systems may be rather restrictive and cumbersome for ordinary programmers. More importantly, the question is whether requiring such type declarations can be justified for the improved performance they offer: if we could get comparable performance through automatic inference, the answer would be no.

In this paper, we explore the effectiveness of a simpler alternative: we develop and apply a static analysis method to determine the cases where messages contents can be safely passed by reference. Such an analysis relieves the programmer of the burden of using a complicated type system, or of reasoning in terms of a dual semantics for message passing. Although a sound static analysis is necessarily conservative, if it works for a large number of cases, it may be justified by a sufficient performance improvement. We evaluate the effectiveness of our static analysis method by comparing it with explicit annotations done by advanced undergraduate and graduate student programmers.

We describe the design and implementation of a custom static analysis algorithm for Actor programs written using the JVM based frameworks. The algorithm employs a novel *live variable analysis* along with *context-sensitive call graph creation* and *field-sensitive points-to analysis*. Note that the fastest known interprocedural dataflow algorithm [21] does not scale for a small Actor program, given the library calls and the size of the library code. However, we are able to exploit the *sparsity* of message sending sites (relative to the rest of computation) to design a custom interprocedural live variable analysis. Our analysis splits the expensive interprocedural analysis into two phases of intraprocedural analysis: a standard *local live variable analysis* followed by a *forward data-flow analysis*. This enables the algorithm to scale to large Actor programs, albeit by trading some precision. We show that our algorithm is sound, i.e. whenever our algorithm selects an object to be sent by reference, it does not introduce a race between two actors. We also show that the algorithm terminates.

Evaluating the effectiveness of our algorithm poses some difficulty. While there are many JVM-based Actor frameworks [10], we do not have a large base of open source code in these frameworks. However, we were able to use a variety of programs written in *ActorFoundry* [2], a JVM-based Actor framework developed at Illinois. These programs include examples from the ActorFoundry distribution, benchmarks used in [12, 13], "hard" synthetic programs written to test our analysis, and programs written by advanced Computer Science students in the project-oriented Software Engineering course at Illinois. While the programs we use are all relatively small, each of the analyses includes the ActorFoundry framework which is approximately 38.7K lines of code.

Experimental results suggest that our analysis is fast and successfully identifies majority of the places where message contents

can be sent by reference. Interestingly, these include many places which were missed by programmers who were providing manual annotations. Therefore, it is a reasonable conjecture that the precision trade off of our proposed analysis is not a significant liability. Experimental results also suggest that the transformation resulting from our algorithm can improve performance of actor programs by up to an order of magnitude in some cases.

We also adapted our implementation to analyze *Scala* actor programs [8]. In Scala, message contents are sent by reference; hence we adapted SOTER to check the safety of sending messages, instead of using it to improve execution efficiency. Our tests result in two important observations. First, SOTER is able to prove the correctness for most message passing sites, and report warnings for other sites. Second, we note that the bytecode generated for Scala programs as well as for the Scala library itself tends to be much larger, as much as $10x$ larger than that for ActorFoundry. The results suggest that our algorithm scales linearly in the size of the bytecode.

We believe that our results suggest that compiler writers should focus on developing more effective inference mechanisms to optimize message passing, and this may be sufficiently effective so that programming language designers need not burden the programmer with added complexity of type systems for the purpose of improving efficiency of message passing.

2. Illustrative Actor Language

We now describe the syntax and semantics of *ActorFoundry*, which will be used to present the motivating examples for this study. ActorFoundry is syntactically similar to Java and in fact is implemented as a Java-based Actor library [2]. In the ActorFoundry, an Actor behavior is defined using a class definition which extends `Actor`. An Actor definition can include zero or more public methods annotated with `@message`, which specify the messages that an actor instance can receive. The method body is executed when an actor instance receives a corresponding message.

Upon receiving a message, an actor can create new actors (using the `create()` method and passing the name of an Actor definition), send messages to other actors (using the `send()` method) and update its local state. Messages are sent asynchronously, i.e. the sending actor does not wait for the message to arrive or be processed at the destination. A send can take an arbitrary number of arguments, which correspond to the arguments of the corresponding method in the destination actor class. Message parameters and return types should be serializable. Blocking messages can also be sent using the `call()` method, which is syntactic sugar [3, 10].

2.1 Semantics

Consider an ActorFoundry program *P*. *P* includes a set of actor definitions used to create actors. Note that there is no shared state among these actors. An actor has a local state comprising of primitives and objects. Each actor also has an unbounded queue in which it receives its messages. We assume that at the beginning of execution the message queue of every actor is empty. An actor and one of its messages is selected as the program's entry point (by the programmer). The ActorFoundry runtime first creates an instance of the initial actor, say *a_init*, and then sends the initial message *msg_init* to it. This action appends the contents of the message *msg_init* to the message queue of actor *a_init*.

Every actor initially tries to dequeue a message from its message queue; if the message queue is empty, the actor blocks and waits for the next message to arrive. If the queue is non-empty, the actor *non-deterministically* removes a message from its own queue. The non-determinism in picking a message models the asynchrony associated with message passing in actors. Each actor executes the following steps in a loop: remove a message from the queue, 'decode' the message, execute the corresponding method (which may update the actor's local state, create new actors and send new messages).

An actor executing a `create` method produces a new instance of an actor. We assume that the new actor is assigned a fresh identifier. An actor communicates with other actors it knows about by sending asynchronous messages using the `send` method (and blocking messages using `call`). An actor may also throw an exception during the processing of a message. A program terminates when there are no pending messages in the system.

3. Illustrative Example

We present a couple of examples to illustrate the problem of identifying messages that transfer ownership, as well as to motivate the different techniques we use to solving the problem. Figure 1 presents a code fragment of a `RefMessenger` actor in ActorFoundry: a `RefMessenger` actor can receive two types of messages, `store` and `transfer` (lines 3 and 6); in response to message `transfer`, it sends two messages `compute` to the actor that is bound to `relayActor` by calling the method `relayPrint` (lines 8-9). We would like to check whether a `RefMessenger` actor transfers the ownership of `item` to the `relayActor` at line 13, which would make it safe to pass by reference the object `data` to `relayActor` (through the call at line 8). In order to answer this question, we perform a static points-to analysis; the analysis detects all objects that may "escape" to `relayActor` through the message at line 13. We also perform a static live variable analysis in order to check whether, after sending the message at line 13, an "escaped" object may be accessed by the `RefMessenger` actor. Both these analyses are interprocedural and are performed on a call graph, a directed graph that represents calling relationships between procedures (subroutines) in a program. We address the particularities of call graph construction in Section 3.3.

```
1   public class RefMessenger extends Actor {
      ...
2     StringBuffer localName = null;
3     @message public void store(String name) {
4       localName = new StringBuffer(name);
5     }
6     @message public void transfer() {
7       StringBuffer data = new StringBuffer("Hi ");
8       relayPrint(data);
9       relayPrint(localName);
10      data.append(localName);
11    }
12    void relayPrint(StringBuffer item) {
13      send(relayActor, "compute", item);
14    }
15  }
```

Figure 1. A simplified version of `RefMessenger` example in ActorFoundry.

3.1 Points-to Analysis

Points-to analysis establishes which pointers may point to which memory locations. The *points-to graph* can tell that the two variables, `data` and `item`, point to the same `StringBuffer` object allocated at line 7. This graph is a result of interprocedural points-to analysis, where allocated objects are represented as nodes denoted with s_i:T, where i shows the line number where the object is allocated, and T represents its type.

Any object that may be pointed by variable `item` may escape to `relayActor` through the message at line 13 (Figure 1). Thus, performing an interprocedural points-to analysis enables detection of the fact that the object s_7:StringBuffer has escaped. But this analysis is not sufficient to answer the question whether this object is accessed by the `RefMessenger` actor after having escaped (sent)

to `relayActor`. We employ a live variable analysis in order to answer the latter question.

3.2 Live Variable Analysis

A *live variable analysis* of a program is a dataflow analysis that calculates the set of variables that may be read before being written to in the program. An interprocedural live variable analysis performed on the code fragment in Figure 1[2] detects that variable `data` is live after the call to method `relayPrint` at line 8 completes, because its value is read and modified at line 10. Although the scope of the variable `data` is limited to the method `transfer`, and is not visible inside the method `relayPrint`, the object it points to is live throughout method `relayPrint`, including the program point right after the message to actor `relayActor` is sent (line 13). We require an interprocedural analysis to detect the escaping of the object pointed to by variable `data`, because its intraprocedural counterpart treats every method in isolation and misses the fact that the object is live in method `relayPrint`.

In Section 3.1 we established that the variable `data` points to the object s_7:StringBuffer, and that this object escapes to actor `relayActor`. Live variable analysis shows that this object is live in actor `RefMessenger` after escaping to actor `relayActor`. Consequently, we conclude that it is *not* safe to pass the variable `item` by reference, because passing it by reference would result in sharing the object s_7:StringBuffer between the `RefMessenger` actor and `relayActor`.

3.3 Call Graph Construction

The construction of a *call graph* has a significant impact on both the precision and the speed of interprocedural analysis. Our approach is based on the *open systems* design, i.e. we do not assume any information about the outside world while analyzing a particular actor. Thus we need to consider all possible messages that an actor can receive from the outside world.

Consider the `RefMessenger` actor in Figure 1. The actor can receive two types of messages, `store` and `transfer`. The execution of `RefMessenger` actor starts when it receive either one of them, and hence the methods `store` and `transfer` serve as two separate entry-points. Our analysis recognizes that they are received by the same instance of `RefMessenger`. This enables us to handle code such as that given in Figure 1 where the instance field `localName` is initialized in one message handler (line 4) but escapes in another one (line 13, through the call at line 9). Our analysis correctly detects that the object s_4:StringBuffer escapes to actor `relayActor` at line 13.

Context sensitivity plays an important role in call graph construction. A context-insensitive analysis produces more imprecise and smaller call graph compared to a context-sensitive analysis. In a context-insensitive call graph, every invoked method, distinguished by its signature, is represented with a single node regardless of the context in which this method is invoked.

Consider the code example from Figure 2 and its context-insensitive call graph. Were we use this call graph for our points-to analysis, we would decide that linked list `l1` has to be passed to actor `myActor` by value because there are objects that `l1` transitively points to that are live after the program point where `l1` is passed to actor `myActor` (line 7). Although this decision is safe (i.e., it does not produce a data race), it is too conservative and misses an opportunity for optimization.

---

[2] Static analysis performed directly on Java source code serves only for the demonstration purposes. SOTER performs both points-to and live variable analises on a low-level intermediate representation (IR) in a static single assignment (SSA) form.

```
1  public class TestActor extends Actor {
      ...
2    @message public void test(){
3      LinkedList<A> l1 = new LinkedList<A>();
4      LinkedList<A> l2 = new LinkedList<A>();
5      l1.add(new A(1));
6      l2.add(new A(2));
7      send(myActor, "process", l1);
8      l2.add(new A(3));
9    }
10 }
```

Figure 2. A code example, whose analysis is highly affected by context-sensitivity of the call graph.

An example of a context-sensitive call graph is a graph that distinguishes invocations of the same method on different receiver instances. Such a call graph would have many more nodes than its context-insensitive counterpart. However it provides much better precision. A *receiver instance context call graph* has two distinct nodes for method add of class LinkedList<A>: one node represents invocations on the linked list l1, and another node represents invocations on the linked list l2. The corresponding points-to graph shows that linked lists l1 and l2 transitively point to non-intersecting sets of instances of class A, and, consequently, an analysis based on such points-to graph would correctly decide to pass linked list l1 to actor myActor by reference (line 7 in Figure 2).

For our static analysis, we construct a receiver instance context call graph in order to exploit the better precision such a call graph offers. Although a context-sensitive call graph is much bigger, it is also considerably sparser than a context-insensitive call graph. As a result, Andersen's points-to analysis performed on a context-sensitive call graph does not take much longer as demonstrated in [22]. For the final step of our analysis, namely the live variable analysis, we describe a custom interprocedural algorithm that scales well for large programs.

4. Static Analysis Algorithm

We describe our static analysis using a simple, illustrative actor program presented in Figure 3. The program consists of four classes, the last two of which specify actor behavior:

1. Class MutableValue is a wrapper around an integer value. The value is assigned when an instance of class MutableValue is created and may be changed during the lifetime of this object.

2. Class ValueHolder holds a MutableValue as a field and provides method getMutableValue to access the encapsulated object. Instances of class ValueHolder are passed between actors. In ActorFoundry, objects between actors are passed by copy, which is implemented using serialization/deserialization of objects. Therefore, both ValueHolder and MutableValue classes implement the java.io.Serializable interface.

3. Class SumActor specifies an actor that can receive message sum with two arguments of type ValueHolder. This message computes the sum of two integer values of MutableValue fields of the arguments, stores this sum in the MutableValue field of the second argument, and then prints it to the console.

4. Class ExecutorActor specifies an actor that can receive message boot. The message handler creates an instance of SumActor and several instances of MutableValue and ValueHolder, and then sends two sum messages to the created SumActor.

4.1 Call Graph Construction

In the first step of our analysis, we construct the program's call graph. It requires identifying all messages that actors of this pro-

```
public class MutableValue implements java.io.Serializable{
  private int value;
  public MutableValue(int value){
    this.value = value;
  }
  public int getValue(){
    return value;
  }
  public void setValue(int value){
    this.value = value;
  }
}

public class ValueHolder implements java.io.Serializable{
  private MutableValue mv;
  public ValueHolder(MutableValue mv){
    this.mv = mv;
  }
  public MutableValue getMutableValue(){
    return mv;
  }
}

public class SumActor extends Actor{
  @message public void sum(ValueHolder vh1, ValueHolder vh2){
    int val = vh1.getMutableValue().getValue();
    MutableValue mv = vh2.getMutableValue();
    mv.setValue(mv.getValue() + val);
    System.out.println("Sum:" + mv.getValue());
  }
}
```

```
1  public class ExecutorActor extends Actor{
2    @message
3    public void boot(Integer val)
4            throws RemoteCodeException{
5      MutableValue mv = new MutableValue(val);
6      ValueHolder vh = new ValueHolder(mv);
7      execute(vh);
8      System.out.println("val:" + mv.getValue());
9    }
10   private void execute(ValueHolder vh)
11           throws RemoteCodeException{
12     ActorName sumActor = create(SumActor.class);
13     add(sumActor, vh);
14   }
15   private void add(ActorName sumActor, ValueHolder vh3){
16     MutableValue mv1 = new MutableValue(1);
17     MutableValue mv2 = new MutableValue(2);
18     ValueHolder vh1 = new ValueHolder(mv1);
19     ValueHolder vh2 = new ValueHolder(mv2);
20     send(sumActor, "sum", vh1, vh2);
21     send(sumActor, "sum", vh2, vh3);
22   }
23 }
```

Figure 3. A running example of an actor program. Import statements are omitted due to space considerations.

gram can receive, since these serve as entry-points in the constructed call graph. The call graph for the program in Figure 3 has two entry-points: one for message sum of SumActor and another one for message boot of ExecutorActor.

Figure 4 shows a fragment of the constructed call graph that starts from the entry-point for message boot. We have omitted the part of the call graph that starts from the entry-point for message sum: it does not present any interesting case for our analysis because the functionality of this message does not involve sending messages to other actors. Moreover, we do not show calls to methods that are not defined within the code of class ExecutorActor (e.g. framework calls that are inside the body of methods create and send), and calls that construct the output String at line 8. The omitted parts do not affect the analysis, and have been omitted in order to simplify the presentation.

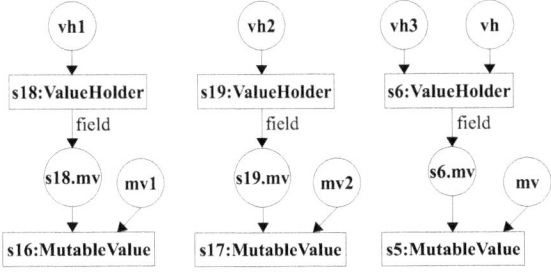

Figure 5. Filtered points-to graph for the code fragment from Figure 3.

4.2 Points-to Analysis

We use a receiver instance context call graph to perform *flow-insensitive* Andersen's points-to analysis [4]. Figure 5 illustrates a fragment of the resulting points-to graph for the code from Figure 3. This fragment is relevant to our analysis: it presents objects that escape to the actor `sumActor` (lines 20 and 21) and pointers that point to them directly or indirectly. Our points-to analysis is *field-sensitive*, i.e. it distinguishes instance fields of different instances of the same class. This allows us to distinguish instance field `mv` of different instances of `ValueHolder` as shown in Figure 5, where every instance field `mv` is represented with a separate pointer, whose name prefix corresponds to the name of the containing `ValueHolder` instance (`s18.mv`, `s19.mv`, `s6.mv`).

4.3 Live Variable Analysis

To detect objects that may be accessed after being passed to other actors, we perform an interprocedural live variable analysis. Even the fastest, polynomial time algorithms for this analysis that are precise, for example the algorithm in [21], can effectively handle only small size programs as shown in [23]. Because any actor program is analyzed together with the ActorFoundry framework, which is a relatively large 38.7KLOCs software, we cannot employ such algorithms (e.g. applying an implementation of the algorithm from [21] we ran out of memory even for the smallest actor programs). In order to be able to handle programs of such a large scale, we elaborate a custom algorithm which conservatively assumes that every instance field is live as long as the containing object is live. The key idea behind our approach is to split an interprocedural analysis into two intraprocedural phases. Our evaluation (Section 5) shows that this algorithm scales well for large programs.

We first present an overview of our algorithm; in Section 4.4, we describe its properties, including soundness and termination. Figure 6 shows an overview of our algorithm. The algorithm takes as input the receiver instance context call graph, *callGraph*, and the results of points-to analysis, *pointstoGraph*, for a given program. The output of the algorithm, *passByValue*, specifies for each argument of every message passing site in the program, whether it needs to be copied. For a particular argument *arg* of a call site *cs* the value of *passByValue[cs,arg]* is *true* when *arg* needs to be copied, and *false* when it is safe to pass *arg* by reference.

The initialization of our algorithm (lines 1-14 in Figure 6) computes the set of all message passing sites in a program, *passingCallSites*, and the set of all call graph nodes, *passingNodes*, that contain at least one message passing site. Also, it initializes all entries of *passByValue* to *false*. The algorithm visits each call site of every call graph node. For every visited call site *cs*, the procedure *isMessagePassingCallSite(cs)* returns *true* if *cs* involves sending a message to another actor (and thus, may escape objects), and *false* in the contrary case. If a call site *cs* may send messages, it is added to *passingCallSites* (line 8) and its containing call graph node is added to *passingNodes* (line 7). In ActorFoundry call sites

input: *callGraph, pointstoGraph*
output: *passByValue*
1 *passingNodes* = ∅;
2 *passingCallSites* = ∅;
3 foreach (Node *n*: *callGraph*){
4   *callSites* = getContainedCallSites(*n*);
5   foreach (CallSite *cs*: *callSites*){
6   if (isMessagePassingCallSite(*cs*)){
7   *passingNodes* = *passingNodes* ∪ *n*;
8   *passingCallSites* = *passingCallSites* ∪ *cs*;
9   foreach (Argument *arg*: *cs*){
10   *passByValue[cs,arg]* = *false*;
11   }
12   }
13   }
14 }
15 *reachingNodes* =
       transitiveClosure(*callGraph, passingNodes*);
16 *callSiteLiveVariables* =
       computeLiveVariables(*reachingNodes*);
17 *nodeLiveVariables* =
       propagateLiveVariables(*reachingNodes*,
                              callSiteLiveVariables);
18 foreach (CallSite *cs*: *passingCallSites*){
19   Node *n* = getContainingNode(*cs*);
20   *liveObjects* = ∅;
21   *liveVariables* =
           callSiteLiveVariables[cs] ∪ *nodeLiveVariables[n]*;
22   foreach (LiveVariable *var*: *liveVariables*){
23   *liveObjects* = *liveObjects* ∪
                   getPointedObjects(*pointstoGraph, var*);
24   }
25   foreach (Argument *arg*: *cs*.getArguments()){
26   *escapedObjects* =
               getPointedObjects(*pointstoGraph, arg*);
27   if ((*escapedObjects* ∩ *liveObjects*) ≠ ∅){
28   *passByValue[cs,arg]* = *true*;
29   }
30   }
31 }

Figure 6. Overview of our algorithm for interprocedural live variable analysis.

that may send messages to other actors are calls to methods `send`, `call`, and `create` of class `Actor`. For the program in Figure 3 the set *passingCallSites* contains call sites at lines 12, 20, and 21. And the set *passingNodes* includes call graph nodes that contain these call sites. In Figure 4 these are `executorActor.add` node for call sites at lines 20 and 21, and `executorActor.execute` node for call site at line 12.

The algorithm then computes *reachingNodes* (line 15 in Figure 6) - the set of all call graph nodes that can reach *passingNodes*. The *reachingNodes* is computed by the procedure *transitiveClosure*, which takes the *callGraph* and the *passingNodes* as arguments. Figure 7 shows the procedure *transitiveClosure*, which computes all reaching nodes, *reachingNodes*, that can reach the initial set of nodes, *initNodes*, as a transitive closure of *initNodes* in a particular call graph *callGraph*. The nodes in *reachingNodes* are the only nodes in the call graph, from which the control flow may reach message passing call sites. So, *reachingNodes* contains all call graph nodes that are relevant to our analysis. For our example program *reachingNodes* includes the following nodes from Figure 4: `executorActor.add`, `executorActor.execute`, and `executorActor.boot`.

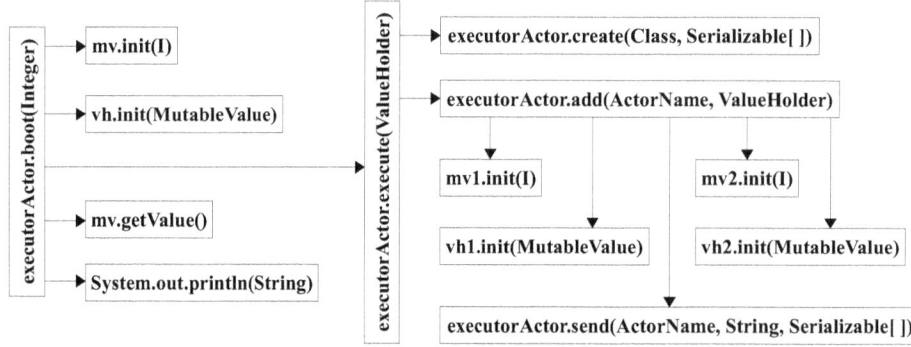

Figure 4. Filtered call graph for the code fragment from Figure 3.

procedure *transitiveClosure*
input: *callGraph, initNodes*
output: *reachingNodes*
1   *reachingNodes* = ⊘;
2   foreach (Node *n*: *initNodes*){
3   *workList* = {*n*};
4   while (*workList* ≠ ⊘){
5   *workNode* = pop(*workList*);
6   if (*workNode* ∉ *reachingNodes*){
7   *reachingNodes* = *reachingNodes* ∪ *workNode*
8   *callers* = getCallers(*callGraph, workNode*);
9   append(*workList, callers*);
10   }
11   }
12 }
13 return *reachingNodes*;

Figure 7. Collecting all call graph nodes that reach *initNodes*.

procedure *computeLiveVariables*
input: *reachingNodes*
output: *callSiteLiveVariables*
1   foreach (Node *n*: *reachingNodes*){
2   *OUT* = performLocalLiveVariableAnalysis(*n*);
3   *callSites* = getContainedCallSites(*n*);
4   foreach (CallSite *cs*: *callSites*){
5   if (isMessagePassingCallSite(*cs*) OR
6   (getCalledNode(*cs*) ∈ *reachingNodes*)){
7   *callSiteLiveVariables[cs]* = *OUT[cs]*;
8   }
9   }
10 }
11 return *callSiteLiveVariables*;

Figure 8. Performing local live variable analysis for *reachingNodes* and storing its relevant part in *callSiteLiveVariables*.

Next, our algorithm applies a standard intraprocedural live variable analysis to collect local variables that are live just after the relevant call sites (line 16 in Figure 6). A call site is relevant to our analysis if it is either a message passing call site or is represented as a node in the set *reachingNodes*. Figure 8 presents procedure *computeLiveVariables* that takes as input *reachingNodes* and returns *callSiteLiveVariables* which specifies the set of live variables at the program point just after a relevant call site.

For every node *n* from *reachingNodes*, procedure *computeLiveVariables* performs a standard local live variable analysis (line 2) that calculates the set of live variables for every program point in the analyzed node *n*. In order to reduce the memory consumption, we keep the results only for the program points that are relevant to our analysis, i.e. those program points that are just after relevant call sites (lines 4-9). Relevant call sites and the corresponding sets of live variables for the example program shown in Figure 3 are as follows: line 7 - {mv}; line 12 - {sumActor, vh}; line 13 - {}; line 20 - {sumActor, vh2, vh3}; line 21 - {}.

As we demonstrated in Section 3.2, if a variable *var* is live at the program point just after a call site that represents a call of some call graph node *n*, then it is live in node *n* as well. We call such variable *var* a *node live variable* for node *n*, because it is live at every program point inside node *n*. If node *n* contains other call sites, which represent calls of other call graph nodes, then variable *var* is live in those nodes too and so on. This propagation of variable *var* is a forward data-flow problem defined on the nodes of the underlying call graph. Our algorithm uses procedure *propagateLiveVariables* to compute node live variables for every node from *reachingNodes* (line 17 in Figure 6).

Figure 9 shows procedure *propagateLiveVariables* that propagates live variables forward in the call graph. It takes as input *reachingNodes* and the sets of live variables for all relevant call sites, *callSiteLiveVariables*. The output of this procedure is *nodeLiveVariables*, which specifies for every node from *reachingNodes* the set of node live variables. The initialization part of the procedure (lines 1-8) defines for every node *n* from *reachingNodes* initial values for sets *IN[n]* and *OUT[n]*, which represent correspondingly the set of node live variables at the entry and at the exit of node *n*. Both initial entry and exit sets are a union of all live variables from all call sites that call node *n* (lines 2-7). The computation part of the procedure (lines 9-17) is a fixed-point algorithm for a forward data-flow problem, where the transfer function is identity (line 15), and the meet operator is union (line 13). Procedure *getPredecessors* (line 11) returns a set of call graph nodes that immediately precede the given node. For *reachingNodes* and *callSiteLiveVariables* shown previously for our code example in Figure 3, procedure *propagateLiveVariables* computes the following *nodeLiveVariables*: executorActor.boot - {}, executorActor.execute - {mv}, executorActor.add - {mv}.

In the end (lines 18-31 in Figure 6), our algorithm computes for every call site *cs* from *passingCallSites* the set of all live variables, *liveVariables*, as a union of local live variables for call site *cs* and node live variables of the call graph node that contains call site *cs* (line 21). Next, we use *pointstoGraph* to compute the set of all live objects (lines 22-24). Then, for every argument *arg* of call site *cs* we compute all objects that *arg* points to, which is the set of objects that may escape to other actors (line 26). Finally, if the intersection of the objects that are live after call site *cs*, *liveObjects*, and the objects that may escape, *escapedObjects*, is not empty, we mark that *arg* should be passed by value (lines 27-29).

For the example program in Figure 3, our algorithm establishes that: call site at line 20 – argument vh1 can be passed by reference, argument vh2 should be passed by value; call site at line 21 – argument vh2 can be passed by reference, argument vh3 should

```
procedure propagateLiveVariables
input: reachingNodes, callSiteLiveVariables
output: nodeLiveVariables
1  foreach (Node n: reachingNodes){
2    IN[n] = ∅;
3    callSites = getCallingCallSites(n);
4    foreach (CallSite cs: callSites){
5      IN[n] = IN[n] ∪ callSiteLiveVariables[cs];
6    }
7    OUT[n] = IN[n];
8  }
9  do{
10   foreach (Node n: reachingNodes){
11     predecessors = getPredecessors(n);
12     foreach (Node pred: predecessors){
13       IN[n] = IN[n] ∪ OUT[pred];
14     }
15     OUT[n] = IN[n];
16   }
17 } while (changes to any OUT occur);
18 foreach (Node n: reachingNodes){
19   nodeLiveVariables[n] = OUT[n];
20 }
21 return nodeLiveVariables;
```

Figure 9. Propagating live variables through *reachingNodes*.

be passed by value. Argument vh2 of the call site at line 20 should be passed by value, because variable vh2 is live at the program point right after the call site at line 20. Argument vh3 of the call site at line 21 should be passed by value, because according to the points-to graph in Figure 5, it transitively points to the object *s5:MutableValue*, which is live, as it is the same object node live variable *mv* of node executorActor.add points to.

4.4 Discussion

Our interprocedural live variable analysis consists of two related but distinct phases. In the first phase, we perform a standard intraprocedural live variable analysis for a subset of call graph nodes. Specifically, as shown above, we consider only those nodes of the call graph that are relevant to our analysis. Program statements of a call graph node are translated into an intermediate representation (IR) in a static single assignment (SSA) form, where every variable is assigned exactly once. Such representation significantly reduces both the time and the complexity of intraprocedural live variable analysis. In the second phase, we solve a forward data-flow problem defined on the nodes of the constructed call graph. For this problem we do not consider the internal control flow of the call graph nodes. As a result, this analysis is just like a regular intraprocedural analysis, except that we use call graph nodes instead of basic blocks and call edges instead of control flow edges.

Figure 10 illustrates our two-phase approach. In the first phase (marked with number 1) we perform intraprocedural live variable analysis on the control flow graphs of individual call graph nodes. In the second phase (marked with number 2) we propagate live variables forward in the call graph, disregarding the internal control flow of the call graph nodes. Splitting an interprocedural analysis into two phases, both of which are intraprocedural by nature, makes our algorithm fast and scalable for large programs as demonstrated in Section 5. The trade off is the reduced precision of our analysis. Although our analysis conservatively assumes that every instance field is live as long as the containing object is live, the evaluation results presented in Section 5 show that it is able to detect the majority of optimization opportunities for a variety of actor programs.

Complexity. Our algorithm consists of a standard Andersen's points-to analysis, followed by a standard intraprocedural live vari-

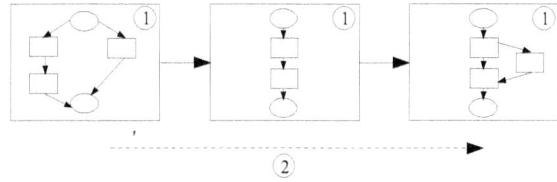

Figure 10. Two phases of our live variable analysis. In the first phase (marked with number 1) we consider internal control flow graphs of individual call graph nodes for the classical intraprocedural live variable analysis. In the second phase (marked with number 2) we propagate live variables forward in the call graph, disregarding the internal control flow of the call graph nodes.

able analysis for a subset of call graph nodes n, and a forward data flow problem for live variable propagation. The last two phases are intraprocedural by nature and have a comparable complexity. Hence, the complexity of our algorithm is $O($ complexity of Andersen's points-to analysis $+(n+1)*$ complexity of the intraprocedural live variable analysis).

Soundness. An argument *arg* of a message passing call site *cs* in a call graph node *n* is marked by our algorithm to be passed by value, if *arg* transitively points to at least one object *o* that is live after message passing call site *cs* (lines 18-31 in Figure 6). Considering that the employed Andersen's points-to analysis is sound, it is sufficient to demonstrate that our interprocedural live variable algorithm does not miss any objects that are live after some message passing call site. If there is a live object *o* then there should be at least one live variable *var* that transitively points to *o*. There are three kinds of variables that can be live after some message passing call site *cs* in a call graph node *n*:

- Variable *var* is a local variable in the call graph node *n*. Such variable is detected as live at the program point right after the message passing call site *cs* in the first phase of our algorithm, where we perform a standard intraprocedural live variable analysis.

- Variable *var* is a local variable in an immediate or a transitive caller node of the call graph node *n*. The second phase of our algorithm propagates such variable to the call graph node *n*, and variable *var* becomes a node live variable for node *n*.

- Variable *var* is an instance field of the class whose method is represented with the call graph node *n*. Our algorithm conservatively assumes that every instance field is live as long as the containing object is live. In this case, the containing object for variable *var* is object this in the method represented with the node *n*. Object this is always live in any instance method, and so *var* is live as well.

Thus, if variable *var* is live after some message passing call site, our algorithm detects this regardless of the kind of *var*. Consequently, all objects variable *var* points to are detected as live, including object *o*.

Termination. Observe that the first phase of our algorithm performs a standard intraprocedural live variable analysis for a subset of call graph nodes, *reachingNodes*. An intraprocedural live variable analysis for a call graph node terminates, and the number of nodes in a call graph is finite. Thus, the first phase terminates. In the second phase of our algorithm, we solve a data-flow problem using a fixed-point algorithm (lines 9-17 in Figure 9). For every node *n* from the set of nodes *reachingNodes* the set *OUT[n]* of node live variables never shrinks. Considering that the number of variables in a program is finite and the number of call graph nodes is finite, the fixed-point algorithm eventually reaches a point, when *OUT[n]* does not change for any node $n \in reachingNodes$, and terminates.

Thus, the second phase terminates. Both phases of our algorithm terminate and so, our algorithm terminates.

5. Implementation and Evaluation

SOTER is a Java implementation of the static analysis described in Section 4. SOTER uses IBM T. J. Watson Libraries for Analysis (WALA) framework [25] that provides a flow-insensitive Andersen's points-to analysis and an infrastructure for implementing data-flow analysis. Our analysis algorithm is language-independent. The current implementation takes Java bytecode as input, and thus can be easily extended to handle programs in any language or framework that compiles to Java bytecode (e.g. Kilim, Jetlang, SALSA). We initially implemented support for ActorFoundry [2]. Later, we extended SOTER to support Scala [8] programs, which took only a couple of weeks of part-time effort. SOTER's source code as well as ActorFoundry and Scala subject programs can be found at http://osl.cs.uiuc.edu/soter

We performed all experiments on a 4-core 2.4GHz, 3GB RAM machine. Any ActorFoundry actor program is analyzed together with ActorFoundry framework, a relatively large software, whose bytecode size is 726KB. Any Scala program is analyzed together with Scala library, whose bytecode size is 13MB. In the worst case our analysis took around 78 seconds.

The goal of the evaluation is to assess the effectiveness and usefulness of SOTER. To achieve this goal, we applied SOTER on a variety of ActorFoundry and Scala actor programs.

5.1 ActorFoundry

For ActorFoundry actor programs, we would like to answer two questions:

- **Effectiveness:** How many opportunities to safely pass a message contents by reference are detected by SOTER in comparison to the total number of such opportunities and to what fairly sophisticated programmers can manually achieve?

- **Usefulness:** What is the performance improvement achieved by SOTER?

Table 1 presents results that assess the effectiveness of SOTER. Each row displays data for a particular actor program, whose name appears in the second column. The first column reflects the general category of an actor program.

These categories include programs from the ActorFoundry distribution, 'Benchmarks' refers to the programs used in an earlier study [12, 13], 'Synthetic' category is attributed to actor programs written specifically to test our analysis, and 'Real world' programs are those written by advanced students in the Software Engineering course in Computer Science at Illinois. All presented actor programs except those from **Synthetic** category were written without the knowledge of a tool such as ours. The third column, **LOC**, shows the number of lines of code in the program (not counting comments and blank lines). The fourth column, **Bytecode size**, displays the size of the analyzed bytecode for every program. Although the size of the programs may seem relatively small, they represent a wide variety of programmers and purpose. Moreover, these programs are written on top of an Actor library. A library encapsulates much of the functionality required to express an actor program, and therefore the actor code itself has a smaller size than it would have without a library-based approach.

The fifth column, **Passed arguments**, represents the total number of message passing call site arguments present in the code of an actor program. The following two columns show correspondingly the number of arguments that could be safely passed by reference, having an ideal understanding of the analyzed program[3], and the number of arguments that SOTER reports as safe to be passed by reference. The next column, **Human misses**, presents the number of arguments that are safe to be passed by reference, which are missed by developers (advanced CS students at Illinois), who manually optimized the program. N/A in this column means that the program is not manually optimized. The following column displays the effectiveness of SOTER, i.e. the ratio of detected opportunities to safely pass arguments by reference to the total number of such opportunities.

SOTER is quite effective: on average it is able to detect around 71% of available optimization opportunities. Also, it detects some opportunities missed by developers. The last column shows how long it takes SOTER to analyze the corresponding actor program. Our analysis is quite fast: for ActorFoundry actor programs it does not exceed 24 seconds.

Table 2 shows the performance improvement achieved by SOTER by comparing the execution time of actor programs before and after application of SOTER. We exclude actor programs whose execution time is too small to base our evaluation on. For the majority of actor programs evaluated, SOTER speeds up the execution more than twice, and for two of them, by more than an order of magnitude. The last column reflects the execution time of actor programs, where all arguments that could be safely passed by reference having an ideal understanding of the actor program are indeed passed by reference. Note that for the majority of actor programs, the ideal execution time and the execution time after applying SOTER are very close. However, for some actor programs, there is still considerable room for improvement even after applying SOTER, which is mainly due to the conservatism of our static analysis. We discuss possible extensions of our analysis in Section 7.

5.2 Scala

For Scala actor programs, we assess effectiveness of SOTER in the same way as for ActorFoundry (Section 5.1), and present our results in Table 3. We divided our Scala subject programs into two categories: those that are manually annotated for Scala message passing safety according to a type system proposed by Haller et al. [7] (annotated), and the rest (unannotated). Column **Total by ref.** reflects both the total number of message passing call site arguments present in the code of an actor program and the number of message arguments passed by reference, because in Scala all messages are sent by reference. Table 3 shows that SOTER automatically proves safety of passing by reference of a significant part of annotated message arguments, as well as completely checks the correctness of 3 unannotated programs. Overall effectiveness of SOTER is around 84%.

Since in Scala all messages are sent by reference, SOTER can not improve performance any further. Instead, the usefulness of SOTER for Scala actor programs is to check automatically whether it is indeed safe to pass message arguments by reference.

According to Table 3, SOTER is able to prove the correctness of passing message arguments by reference in the majority of cases. This strongly suggests that ownership transfer is a common idiom, and SOTER is able to infer it automatically in most cases. In the rest of cases, SOTER generates a warning for the programmer to check the correctness manually. We also note that the size of Scala programs and library is almost an order of magnitude larger than those of ActorFoundry, and the results suggest that SOTER scales almost linearly for Scala programs.

---

[3] Note that complete knowledge of the semantics of the analyzed program yields far better results than any possible static analysis.

Table 1. The effectiveness of SOTER on different ActorFoundry actor programs. Size of ActorFoundry library, AFL=726KB.

Category	Program	LOC	Bytecode size (KB)	Passed arguments	Ideal by ref.	SOTER by ref.	Human misses	SOTER/Ideal ratio	Analysis time (sec)
ActorFoundry distribution	threadring	43	4.0 + AFL	7	7	7	1	100%	3.4
	concurrent	204	11.3 + AFL	12	12	7	N/A	58%	3.8
	copymessages	80	8.4 + AFL	19	18	10	5	56%	12.5
	performance	126	12.6 + AFL	14	14	12	N/A	86%	3.6
	pingpong	62	6.4 + AFL	9	9	8	N/A	89%	3.5
	refmessages	20	3.3 + AFL	3	3	2	2	67%	3.3
	rpcping	65	7.7 + AFL	9	9	9	N/A	100%	3.4
	sor	320	22.7 + AFL	36	36	18	10	50%	3.8
Benchmarks	chameneos	187	13.6 + AFL	12	12	4	1	33%	3.5
	fibonacci	53	8.8 + AFL	28	28	24	N/A	86%	3.5
	leader	81	7.0 + AFL	12	12	2	N/A	17%	3.4
	philosophers	77	9.5 + AFL	6	6	6	N/A	100%	3.3
	pi	73	8.4 + AFL	6	6	4	N/A	67%	3.4
	shortestpath	126	7.4 + AFL	59	59	52	N/A	88%	3.5
Synthetic	quicksortCopy	76	5.3 + AFL	3	3	3	N/A	100%	12.5
	quicksortCopy2	92	5.3 + AFL	8	8	6	N/A	75%	12.4
Real world	clownfish	700	48.8 + AFL	87	87	59	N/A	68%	24.0
	rainbow_fish	591	47.7 + AFL	68	68	67	N/A	99%	3.6
	swordfish	615	37.1 + AFL	83	83	13	N/A	16%	4.1
	threadfin	471	27.8 + AFL	101	101	98	N/A	97%	12.8

Table 2. The performance improvement achieved by SOTER.

Program	Parameters	Execution time (ms) Before	Execution time (ms) After	Improvement	Speed up	Ideal execution time (ms)
threadring	504 actors, 1 mil passes	25870	1880	92.7%	13.76	1880
concurrent	601 actors	187510	15990	91.5%	11.73	1390
copymessages	31810 actors, 10000 elements	7730	3710	52.0%	2.08	610
sor	6402 actors, 80 x 80 matrix	76960	61620	19.9%	1.25	5890
chameneos	14 actors, 100000 rendezvous	56890	36640	35.6%	1.55	1620
leader	30001 actors	14050	8190	41.7%	1.72	7380
philosophers	60001 actors, 30000 philosophers	9550	1380	85.5%	6.92	1380
pi	3002 actors, 30000 intervals	4210	3890	7.6%	1.08	3880
quicksortCopy	200002 actors, 100000 elements	24660	4530	81.6%	5.44	4530
quicksortCopy2	200002 actors, 100000 elements	16320	4870	70.2%	3.35	3580

Table 3. The effectiveness of SOTER on different Scala actor programs. Size of Scala library, SL=13MB.

Category	Program	LOC	Bytecode size (KB)	Total by ref.	SOTER by ref.	SOTER/Total ratio	Analysis time (sec)
annotated	RayTracer	693	247.1 + SL	3	2	67%	77.9
	RayTracer2	688	253.3 + SL	3	2	67%	75.7
unannotated	Leader	91	35.1 + SL	10	10	100%	21.2
	ShortestPath	99	32.6 + SL	3	2	67%	25.7
	Fibonacci	69	30.2 + SL	4	4	100%	21.1
	QuickSortCopy	83	40.0 + SL	4	2	50%	22.3
	DiningPhilosophers	78	56.4 + SL	5	5	100%	21.7

6. Related Work

The problem of safe yet efficient message passing has attracted much interest among researchers recently. Erlang, which has been around for more than 20 years, uses only immutable types in messages. However, immutable objects can have a severe performance penalty as every update to the object involves copying data values or pointers. This increases space and time complexity of implementing immutable types, specially for large data structures. We discuss more recent proposals based on type systems below.

6.1 Type Systems

Various type systems have been proposed to control aliasing in ways which makes it safe and efficient to share objects. These include variants of Linear types, Ownership types and recently Universe Types [19]. A detailed summary and comparison has been presented in [7]. We briefly mention three systems which are proposed specifically for message passing. The Singularity Operating System is architected essentially using actors [9]. Messages are not allowed to have internal aliasing, but are exchanged using a special exchange heap [5]. Kilim [24] proposes a variant of Linear Types combined with an interprocedural shape analysis. The type system is quite restrictive in terms of shapes of message objects (tree shaped) and may not be easily understandable by programmers. Recently a type system based on uniqueness and capabilities has been proposed for Scala Actors [7]. This system allows richer message structures and the examples in the paper show that it requires fewer annotations.

An inherent difficulty with type systems is that programmers have to annotate their code and this puts varying degree of overhead on them. However, the type systems do provide guidance on what properties to analyze and infer in order to guarantee other properties like ownership.

6.2 Inferring Ownership and other Types

In order to ease this burden, mechanisms have been proposed to infer some of the aforementioned types. Specifically, techniques to infer Universe Types have been proposed in [11, 20]. These techniques are based on a static analysis and a SAT solving step. The techniques are augmented with a dynamic analysis in [6]. In [18], a static analysis based on Andersen's points-to analysis is proposed to infer the ownership of heap objects.

Note that these methods only infer ownership but do not deal with transfer of ownership. Actors on the other hand have the ownership of their state by construction, and we are interested in cases when the ownership is transferred to other actors.

7. Discussion and Future Work

Our preliminary results suggest that an inexpensive but conservative static analysis method can infer ownership transfer so that it may identify most places where messages can be sent efficiently by passing pointers instead of making a deep copy. The results suggest that much of the efficiency of message passing programs executed on shared memory multicores may be regained without requiring programmers to deal with the complexity of type annotations or to reason about a dual message passing semantics. In fact, our experimental results suggest that programmers may often be able to do no better.

SOTER currently does not identify safe read-read sharing. In cases where the entire program is available (closed systems), identifying such sharing would enable further optimizations. Our analysis also does not extend to cases of false sharing where different segments of a large data structure are accessed by different actors, possibly at different times. In this case, our static analysis may improve the efficiency of a dynamic analysis framework which checks the safety of such sharing. However, we believe that as languages and frameworks evolve to be more Actor-oriented, data structures themselves will be designed and implemented as collections of actors, thus avoiding problems created by passing large data structures. Such actor collections will enable concurrency while enforcing the consistency required by the abstract data type defined by the collection.

Acknowledgments

The authors would like to thank the anonymous reviewers for their detailed and useful feedback, and members of the development teams of the Axum and Orleans projects at Microsoft for useful discussions leading to this work. We would like to acknowledge the assistance of Philipp Haller in obtaining Scala programs, and Samira Tasharofi, Steven Lauterburg, and others for providing actor programs.

References

[1] Panel on A single programming model for clusters and multiprocessor nodes: Dream, nightmare, reality, or vision at UIUC, 2009.

[2] ActorFoundry. ActorFoundry homepage. http://osl.cs.uiuc.edu/af, 1998-2010.

[3] G. Agha, I. A. Mason, S. Smith, and C. Talcott. A Foundation for Actor Computation. *Journal of Functional Programming*, 7(01):1–72, 1997.

[4] L. O. Andersen. *Program Analysis and Specialization for the C Programming Language*. PhD thesis, University of Copenhagen, DIKU, 1994.

[5] M. Fähndrich, M. Aiken, C. Hawblitzel, O. Hodson, G. Hunt, J. R. Larus, and S. Levi. Language support for fast and reliable message-based communication in singularity os. *SIGOPS Oper. Syst. Rev.*, 40 (4):177–190, 2006.

[6] A. Fuerer. Combining run-time and static universe type inference. Master's thesis, ETH Zurich, 2007.

[7] P. Haller and M. Odersky. Capabilities for Uniqueness and Borrowing. In *Proceedings of the European Conference on Object Oriented Programming (ECOOP)*, 2010.

[8] P. Haller and M. Odersky. Actors that unify threads and events. In *COORDINATION*, 2007.

[9] G. C. Hunt and J. R. Larus. Singularity: Rethinking the software stack. *SIGOPS Oper. Syst. Rev.*, 41(2):37–49, 2007. doi: http://doi.acm.org/10.1145/1243418.1243424.

[10] R. K. Karmani, A. Shali, and G. Agha. Actor frameworks for the JVM platform: A comparative analysis. In *Proceedings of the 7th International Conference on the Principles and Practice of Programming in Java*, 2009.

[11] N. Kelleberger. Static universe type inference. Master's thesis, ETH Zurich, 2005.

[12] S. Lauterburg, M. Dotta, D. Marinov, and G. Agha. A framework for state-space exploration of Java-based actor programs. In *24th IEEE/ACM International Conference on Automated Software Engineering, ASE 2009*. IEEE, 2009.

[13] S. Lauterburg, R. K. Karmani, D. Marinov, and G. Agha. Evaluating ordering heuristics for dynamic partial-order reduction techniques. In *Fundamental Approaches to Software Engineering (FASE) with ETAPS*, 2010.

[14] E. A. Lee. The problem with threads. *Computer*, 39(5):33–42, 2006. doi: http://doi.ieeecomputersociety.org/10.1109/MC.2006.180.

[15] Microsoft Corporation. Best Practices in the Asynchronous Agents Library - Do Not Pass Large Message Payloads by Value. http://msdn.microsoft.com/en-us/library/ff601928.aspx, 2010.

[16] Microsoft Corporation. Asynchronous Agents Library Walkthrough: Creating an Agent-Based Application. http://msdn.microsoft.com/en-us/library/dd504791.aspx, 2010.

[17] Microsoft Corporation. Asynchronous Agents Library Walkthrough: Creating a Dataflow Agent. http://msdn.microsoft.com/en-us/library/dd504791.aspx, 2010.

[18] A. Milanova. Static Inference of Universe Types. In *Intl. Workshop on Aliasing, Confinement and Ownership in Object-Oriented Programming*, 2008.

[19] P. Müller and A. Rudich. Ownership transfer in universe types. In *OOPSLA '07: Proceedings of the 22nd annual ACM SIGPLAN conference on Object-oriented programming systems and applications*, pages 461–478, 2007.

[20] M. Niklaus. Static universe type inference using a SAT-solver. Master's thesis, ETH Zurich, 2006.

[21] T. Reps, S. Horwitz, and M. Sagiv. Precise interprocedural dataflow analysis via graph reachability. In *POPL '95: Proceedings of the 22nd ACM Symposium on Principles of Programming Languages*, pages 49–61, 1995.

[22] M. Sridharan and S. J. Fink. The complexity of Andersen's analysis in practice. In *SAS '09: Proceedings of the 16th International Symposium on Static Analysis*, pages 205–221, Berlin, Heidelberg, 2009. Springer-Verlag.

[23] M. Sridharan, S. J. Fink, and R. Bodik. Thin slicing. In *PLDI '07: Proceedings of the 2007 ACM SIGPLAN conference on Programming language design and implementation*, pages 112–122, New York, NY, USA, 2007. ACM. doi: http://doi.acm.org/10.1145/1250734.1250748.

[24] S. Srinivasan and A. Mycroft. Kilim: Isolation typed actors for Java. In *Proceedings of the European Conference on Object Oriented Programming (ECOOP)*, 2008.

[25] WALA. WALA Static Analysis Library. http://wala.sourceforge.net/.

All-Window Profiling and Composable Models of Cache Sharing

Xiaoya Xiang   Bin Bao   Tongxin Bai
Chen Ding

Computer Science Department
University of Rochester
Rochester, NY 14627
{xiang,bao,bai,cding}@cs.rochester.edu

Trishul Chilimbi

Microsoft Research
One Microsoft Way
Redmond, WA 98052
trishulc@microsoft.com

Abstract

As multi-core processors become commonplace and cloud computing is gaining acceptance, more applications are run in a shared cache environment. Cache sharing depends on a concept called footprint, which depends on all cache accesses not just cache misses. Previous work has recognized the importance of footprint but has not provided a method for accurate measurement, mainly because the complete measurement requires counting data access in all execution windows, which takes time quadratic in the length of a trace.

The paper first presents an algorithm efficient enough for off-line use to approximately measure the footprint with a guaranteed precision. The cost of the analysis can be adjusted by changing the precision. Then the paper presents a composable model. For a set of programs, the model uses the all-window footprint of each program to predict its cache interference with other programs without running these programs together. The paper evaluates the efficiency of all-window profiling using the SPEC 2000 benchmarks and compares the footprint interference model with a miss-rate based model and with exhaustive testing.

Categories and Subject Descriptors   C.4 [*Performance of systems*]: Modeling techniques; D.2.8 [*Metrics*]: Performance measures

General Terms   measurement, performance

Keywords   data footprint, cache interference, reuse distance, composable models

1.   Introduction

A basic question in multi-core processor design is whether to use partitioned or shared cache. Partitioned cache can be wasteful when only one program is running. Shared cache is risky since programs interfere with each other.

Current multi-core processors use a mix of private and shared cache. Intel Nehalem has 256KB L2 cache per core and 4MB to 8MB L3 cache shared by all cores. IBM Power 7 has 8 cores,

PPoPP'11   February 12–16, 2011, San Antonio, Texas, USA.
Copyright © 2011 ACM 978-1-4503-0119-0/11/02. . . $10.00

with 256KB L2 cache per core and 32MB L3 shared by all cores. Cache sharing becomes a significant factor. The performance of a program may change drastically depending on what other programs are running.

Cache sharing models can be loosely divided into on-line and off-line types. On-line models are used to minimize the interference among programs that are currently being executed on a given machine. Off-line models do not improve performance directly but can be used to understand the causes of interference and to predict its effect before running the programs (so they may be grouped to reduce interference). An off-line model has three advantages over on-line analysis:

- *All data accesses, not just cache misses.* To be efficient, on-line models consider just cache misses in select execution periods. Cache interference, as we will show, depends on more than just cache misses. An off-line model can measure the effect of all data accesses in an execution.

- *"Clean-room" statistics.* An off-line model measures the characteristics of a single program unperturbed by other programs. Such "clean-room" metrics avoids the chicken-egg problem when programs are analyzed together: the interference depends on the miss rate of co-running programs, but their miss rate in turn depends on the interference.

- *Composable models.* The clean-room, off-line models of individual programs can be composed to predict the interference in any program group. There are 2^P co-run combinations for P programs. The composable model makes 2^P predictions using P clean-room single-program runs rather than 2^P parallel runs. This property helps in model validation—errors cannot as easily cancel each other (and be hidden) by accident when each model is used in making 2^{P-1} predictions.

To accurately model cache sharing, we collect all-window statistics. In an execution of n run-time instructions, the number of different, non-empty windows is $\binom{n}{2} = \frac{n*(n+1)}{2}$ or $O(n^2)$. What's more, it takes $O(n)$ to count all data access in a window. There had been no prior solution that could measure such all-window statistics for large-scale traces.

The first part of this work is an algorithmic advance that makes all-window profiling possible. We use three techniques to reduce the cost of all-window analysis. The first is to count by footprint sizes rather than window sizes. The second is to use relative precision in footprint sizes. The third is to use trace compression. As a result, the new algorithm can count a large number of windows in

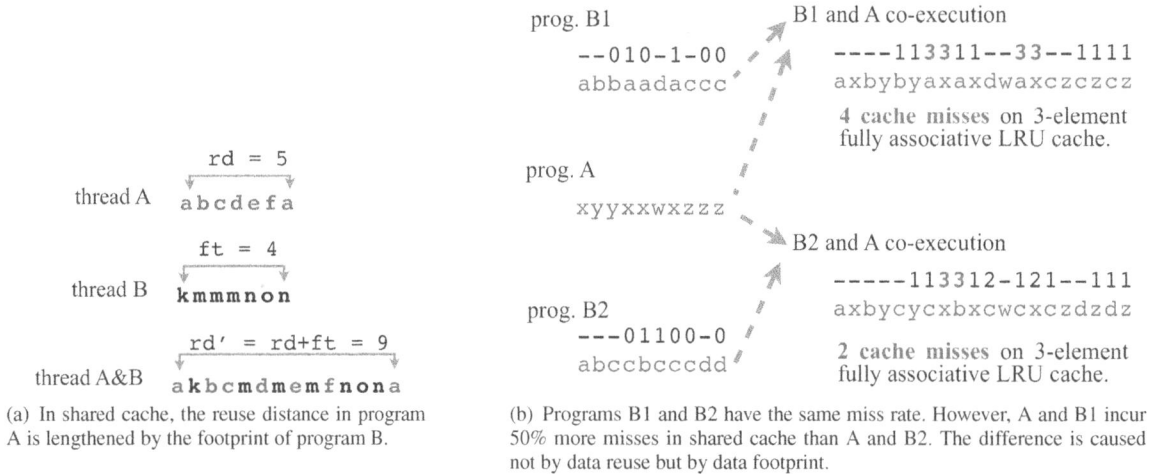

rd = 5

thread A `abcdefa`

ft = 4

thread B **kmmmnon**

rd' = rd+ft = 9

thread A&B `a`**k**`b`**m**`c`**m**`d`**m**`e`**n**`f`**o**`n`**n**`a`

(a) In shared cache, the reuse distance in program A is lengthened by the footprint of program B.

prog. B1
```
--010-1-00
abbaadaccc
```

prog. A
```
xyyxxwxzzz
```

prog. B2
```
---01100-0
abccbcccdd
```

B1 and A co-execution
```
----113311--33--1111
axbybyaxaxdwaxczczcz
```
4 cache misses on 3-element fully associative LRU cache.

B2 and A co-execution
```
-----113312-121--111
axbycycxbxcwcxczdzdz
```
2 cache misses on 3-element fully associative LRU cache.

(b) Programs B1 and B2 have the same miss rate. However, A and B1 incur 50% more misses in shared cache than A and B2. The difference is caused not by data reuse but by data footprint.

Figure 1. Example illustrations of cache sharing.

a single step. The asymptotic cost is reduced from $O(n^3)$ to significantly below $O(n \log n)$.

Based on all-window profiling, the second part of this work gives a algorithm to compute the circular effect between cache interference and program miss rate. We model the effect using an recursive equation, solve it using an iterative algorithm, and prove the convergence.

The third part of the work is an evaluation of all-window footprint in 14 SPEC2K benchmark programs, with traces as long as 100 billion data accesses. We show, for the first time as far as we know, the footprint distribution in up to a sextillion (10^{21}) windows. We show the quantitative difference between footprint and miss rate. In addition, we predict cache interference using the composable model and compare footprint-based prediction with one based on miss rate and one on exhaustive testing.

The rest of the paper is organized is as follows. Section 2 gives the background especially the asymmetrical effect of cache sharing. Section 3 describes the new algorithm for measuring all-window footprints. Section 4 develops the composable model of cache sharing. Section 5 evaluates all-window profiling and the composable model on SPEC 2K benchmarks. Section 6 discusses possible uses of the new algorithm. Finally, the last two sections discuss related work and summarize.

2. Background on Off-line Cache Models

Reuse windows and the locality model For each memory access, the temporal locality is determined by its reuse window, which includes all data access between this and the previous access to the same datum. Specifically, whether the access is a cache (capacity) miss depends on the reuse distance, the number of distinct data elements accessed in the reuse window. The relation between reuse distance and the miss rate has been well established [14, 19, 28]. The capacity miss rate can be defined by a probability function involving the reuse distance and the cache size. Let the test program be A.

$$P(\text{capacity miss by A alone})$$
$$= P(\text{A's reuse distance} \geq \text{cache size})$$

Footprint windows and the cache sharing model Off-line cache sharing models were pioneered by Chandra et al. [8] and Suh et al. [25] for a group of independent programs and extended for multi-threaded code by Ding and Chilimbi [11], Schuff et al. [20],

and Jiang et al. [16] Let A, B be two programs share the same cache but do not shared data, the effect of B on the locality of A is

$$P(\text{capacity miss by A when co-running with B})$$
$$= P((\text{A's reuse distance + B's footprint}) \geq \text{cache size})$$

Given an execution window in a sequential trace, the *footprint* is the number of distinct elements accessed in the window. The example in Figure 1(a) illustrates the interaction between locality and footprint. A reuse window in program A concurs with a time window in program B. The reuse distance of A is lengthened by the footprint of B's window.

Footprint, locality, and the miss rate An implication of the cache sharing model is that cache interference is asymmetric if locality and footprint are different metrics of a program. A program with large footprints and short reuse distances may disproportionally slowdown other programs while experiencing little to no slow down itself. This is confirmed in our experiments. In one program pair, the first program shows near 85% slowdown while the other program shows only 15% slowdown.

Locality is determined by data access in reuse windows. There are up to n reuse windows in a trace of n data accesses. Footprint is determined by data access in all windows. There are $\binom{n}{2} = \frac{n*(n+1)}{2}$ footprint windows. Therefore, measuring footprint is computationally a much harder problem than measuring locality.

The conventional metric of cache performance is miss rate. The miss rate is defined for all windows but it measures only the number of misses not the total amount of data access. In particular, it does not count if an accessed datum is already in cache. The error may be large for shared cache, whose sizes are 4MB to 32MB in size on today's machines. In fact, neither reuse distance nor footprint can be determined by counting cache misses alone. Furthermore, the miss rate is machine dependent and needs to be measured for each cache configuration.

Miss rate $\neq$ cache interference Figure 1(b) shows three short program access streams. Programs B1 and B2 have the same set of reuse distances and hence the same capacity miss rate. However when running with program A, B1 causes twice as many capacity misses as B2. It shows that locality alone does not fully determine cache interference. Reuse distances and cache misses are not sufficient. We need to know data footprint.

In general when considering the interference by program B on program A, it is necessary to know B's footprint in windows of all sizes since the size of A's reuse windows can be arbitrary. This requires all-window footprint analysis, which we show next. A similar algorithm may be used to collect other types of all-window statistics such as all-window miss rates or all-window thread interleaving [10].

3. All-Window Footprint Analysis

Let n be the length of a trace and m the number of distinct data in the trace. We consider so-called "on-line" profiling, which traverses the trace element by element but does not store the traversed trace. Instead it stores a record of the history. The naive algorithm works as follows. At each element, it counts the footprint in all the windows ending at the current element. There are $O(n^2)$ windows in the trace. The naive algorithm counts each of them. The cost is $O(n^2)$. This does not include the cost of measuring the footprint in each window, which is up to n in size. In the rest of this section, we describe four techniques to reduce this complexity. In the title, we refer to each algorithm by the main idea and the asymptotic complexity.

3.1 Footprint Counting: The NM Algorithm

Assume that the first i accesses of a trace refer to m_i data. There are i windows ending at the ith element and i footprints from these windows. The i footprints have at most m_i different sizes. The first idea to reduce the cost is counting by m_i footprint sizes rather than by i windows. For each size, we count all footprints of this size in a single step. The cost for counting all footprints is $O(m)$ per access instead of $O(n)$. Instead of counting $O(n^2)$ windows one by one as in the naive algorithm, the NM algorithm counts the $O(n^2)$ windows in $O(nm)$ steps.

In the example in Figure 2, consider the second access of b (before "l"). It is the 6th access in the trace, so there are 6 windows ending there. However, only 3 distinct elements are accessed, so the 6 footprints must have one of the 3 sizes. Indeed, the footprint size of the 6 windows is 1,2,3,3,3,3 respectively.

$$aabacb \mid acadaadeedab$$

Windows ending at the second b
$$b, \; cb, \; acb, \; bacb, \; abacb, \; aabacb$$

Figure 2. There are 3 different footprint sizes for the 6 windows ending at the second b. The 6 footprints are counted in 3 steps by the NM algorithm.

To count windows by footprint sizes, we represent a trace as follows. At each point, we store the position of the last access of each datum seen so far. Then, all windows between a consecutive pair of last accesses have the same footprint and are counted in one step. For example in Figure 2, there is no other last access before access 4 (the last access of a), so the four windows, starting at 1 to 4 and ending at 6, have the same footprint and can be measured in one step. A method based on last accesses has previously been used by Bennett and Kruskal to measure reuse distance [2].

3.2 Relative Precision Footprint: The NlogM Algorithm

The use of large cache is affected mostly by large footprints. For a large footprint, in most cases we care about only the first few digits

not the exact footprint. The second idea is to measure footprints in approximate sizes, in particular, in a relative precision such as 99% or 99.9%. The number of different footprint sizes becomes $O(\log m)$ instead of m.

To maintain a relative position, we store the last-access information of a trace in a *scale tree* structure developed by Zhong et al. [28] In a scale tree, each (constant-size) tree node represents a window in the trace. The number of nodes depends on the required precision. Asymptotically, a scale tree has $O(\log m)$ nodes [28]. If we consider last accesses as markers in the trace, the precise NM algorithm uses m markers, while the relative precision algorithm uses $O(\log m)$ markers. Hence, the cost is reduced to NlogM. The idea of the NlogM algorithm was first described in a 2-page poster paper without a complete algorithm in PPOPP 2008 [10].

3.3 Trace Compression: The CKM Algorithm

The third idea is to analyze windows ending within a group of elements in a cost similar to analyzing windows ending at a single element. A user sets a threshold c. The trace is divided into a series of k intervals called *footprint intervals*. Each interval has c distinct elements (except for the last interval, which may have fewer than c distinct elements). This is known as trace compression. It has been used by Kaplan et al. to shorten a trace while still preserving the miss rate behavior [17]. In footprint analysis, it allows us to traverse the trace interval by interval rather than element by element. The length of the trace is reduced from n to k. Next we describe the concepts and the algorithm and show that this use of compression does not lose precision in footprint analysis.

Definition *The footprint interval.* Given a start point x in a trace and a constant c, the footprint interval is the *largest time window* from x that contains accesses to exactly c distinct data elements.

Figure 3 (b) shows an example trace and its division into footprint intervals. The division is unique. It maximizes the length of each interval in order to minimize the number intervals. We define the length of an interval as the number of elements it has. In this example, the length is 9 for the first interval I_1 and 8 for the second interval I_2.

We denote the series of footprint intervals by I_i, data accesses by π, the first access s and the number of footprint intervals K. The trace partition is:

$$I(\pi, s, c) = \cup_{i=1}^{K} I_i$$

where $\forall i$, I_i is a footprint interval of size c; and $\forall i \neq j$, I_i and I_j do not overlap.

Windows contained within a footprint interval have a footprint size between 1 and c and can be easily measured. The more difficult question is how to measure the footprint of a window that spans more than one interval. To show the algorithm, we first introduce some new terms. Assuming the current point is the start of the current interval, we define

Definition NEXT-FIRST-ACCESSES, the first accesses to distinct data after the current point.

Definition PREVIOUS-LAST-ACCESSES, the last accesses to distinct data before the current point.

Definition SUB-INTERVALS. The current interval is divided by the next-first-accesses into sub-intervals.

Definition PAST-PARTITIONS. The trace before the current point is divided by the previous-last-accesses into past partitions.

Figure 3 shows for the first element in the second interval, the 3 next-first-accesses, the 3 previous-last-accesses, the 3 sub-intervals, and the 3 past partitions. A past partition may span multiple intervals.

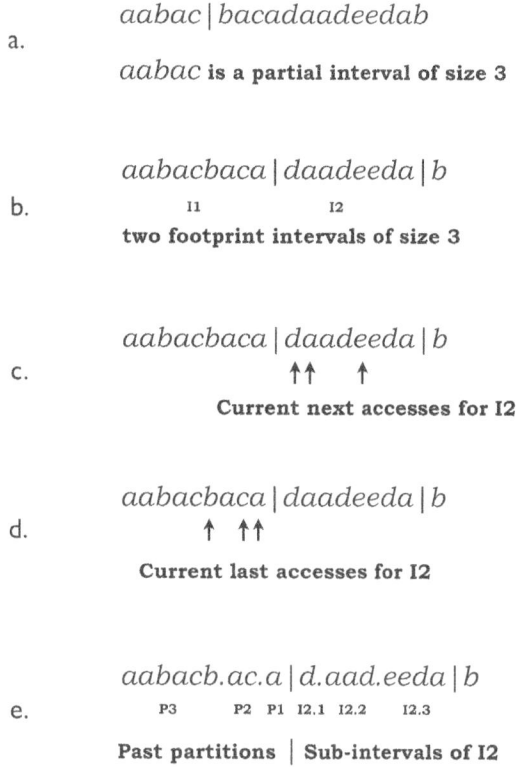

a.

$$aabac \mid bacadaadeedab$$

$aabac$ **is a partial interval of size 3**

b.

$$aabacbaca \mid daadeeda \mid b$$

$I1 \qquad\qquad I2$

two footprint intervals of size 3

c.

$$aabacbaca \mid daadeeda \mid b$$

↑↑ ↑

Current next accesses for I2

d.

$$aabacbaca \mid daadeeda \mid b$$

↑ ↑↑

Current last accesses for I2

e.

$$aabacb.ac.a \mid d.aad.eeda \mid b$$

P3   P2 P1 I2.1 I2.2   I2.3

Past partitions │ Sub-intervals of I2

Figure 3. Illustrations of the definitions used in the CKM algorithm

To count distinct footprint sizes in all windows, it is sufficient to count between sub-interval and past partition markers, as is stated by the following theorem. Note that the footprint count for windows spanning multiple intervals is precise regardless of the choice of c.

Theorem 3.1. *All windows starting within the same past-partition and ending within the same sub-interval have the same footprint.*

Proof Suppose a time window starts from the past-partition p and ends at the sub-interval s. Suppose the successive data accesses within p are $p_a, p_{a-1}, ..., p_1$ and the successive data accesses within s are $s_1, s_2, ..., s_b$. By definition, the previous-last-access in p is p_1. The next-first-access in s is s_1. Let w^* be the window from p_1 to s_1. Let the footprint of w^* be fp^*.

Fix the start position at p_1 and consider the window $w1$ that ends at s_2. Since each sub-interval has only one next-first-access, s_2 is not a first access and does not add to the footprint. The footprint of $w1$ is fp^*. Similarly, we see that all windows starting at p_1 and ending at $s_i, i = 2, ..., b$ have the footprint fp^*.

Now let's fix the end position at s_1 and consider the window $w1$ that starts at p_2. Since each past-partition has only one previous-last-access, p_2 cannot be a previous-last-access and therefore does not add to the size of the footprint. The footprint of $w1$ is fp^*. Similarly, we see that all windows starting at $p_a, ..., p_2, p_1$ and ending at s_1 have the footprint fp^*. Composing these two cases, we have the stated conclusion. ∎

By Theorem 3.1, the measurement of all-window footprints is reduced to measuring the footprint in windows between every past partition and every sub-interval. The number of past-partitions is up to m. The number of sub-intervals is c. Therefore, the number of distinct footprints for windows ending at each footprint interval is at most cm. Since the number of the footprint intervals is k, the time cost is then $O(ckm)$, hence the CKM algorithm.

We define the *compression factor* as $\frac{n}{k}$, which is the length of the trace over the number of intervals. The compression factor is minimal when $c = 1$ and $k = n$ and maximal when $c = m$ and $k = 1$. When c increases from 1 and m, the compression factor changes monotonically, as shown by the following lemma.

Lemma 3.2. *k is a non-increasing function of c.*

Proof Suppose e_i is the end position of footprint interval $I_i, i = 1, ..., k$. We will prove by induction on i that e_i will never move backward when c is increased to $c*$.

In the base case, I_1 starts at the beginning of the trace, and e_1 moves only forward in time when c is increased. Therefore, the start position of I_2 does not move backwards.

Suppose start position of $I_i, i \geq 2$ does not move backwards, and the next interval starting with the new start position and ending with previous e_i has a footprint of no more than c. As a result, the new e_i will only move forward in time when c is increased to c^*. ∎

3.4 Putting It All Together: The CKlogM Algorithm

We combine the relative precision NlogM algorithm and the trace compression CKM algorithm as follows. Instead of using previous-last-accesses in the CKM algorithm, we use the the relative precision footprint sizes described in Section 3.2. The approximation divides the past trace into $O(\log m)$ past partitions. The number of next-first-accesses is still c, and the number of intervals is k. The total cost becomes $O(ck \log m)$, hence the CKlogM algorithm.

3.5 Comparison with Previous Footprint Analysis

Direct counting Agarwal et al. counted the number of cold-start misses for all windows starting from the beginning of a trace [1]. In time-sharing systems, processes are switched at regular intervals. The cached data of one process may be evicted by data brought in by the next process. Thiebaut and Stone computed what is essentially the single-window footprint by dividing a trace by the fixed interval of CPU scheduling quantum and taking the average amount of data access of each quantum [26]. It became the standard model for studying multi-programmed systems in 1990s (e.g. [12]). These methods are simple and effective as far as only a linear number of windows are concerned.

If we fix the window size m, there are $n - m$ windows of this size. We call them sliding windows. A hardware counter can quickly count consecutive, non-overlapping windows. There are $\frac{n}{m}$ (assuming m divides n) non-overlapping windows, which is a subset of sliding windows. If we use the average of non-overlapping windows to estimate the average of sliding windows, we have a sampling rate $\frac{1}{m}$. Sampling at this low rate (for large m) may be accurate, but we cannot tell for sure unless we have all-window results to compare with.

Iterative generation Two recent methods by Suh et al. [25] and Chandra et al. [8] derived the footprint from an iterative relation involving the miss rate. Consider a random window w_t of size t being played out on some cache of infinite size. As we increase t, the footprint increases with every cache miss. Let $E[w_t]$ be the expected footprint of w_t, and $M(E[w_t])$ be the probability of a miss at the end of w_t. For window size $t + 1$, the footprint either increments by one or stays the same depending on whether $t + 1$ access is a cache miss, as shown by the following equation:

$$E[w_{t+1}] = E[w_t](1 - M(E[w_t])) + (E[w_t] + 1)M(E[w_t])$$

To be precise, the term $M(E[w_t])$ requires simulating sub-traces of all size t windows, which is impractical. Suh et al. simplified the relation into a differential equation and made the assumption of linear window growth when window sizes were close [25]. Chandra et al. computed the recursive relation bottom up [8]. Neither method places a bound on how the estimate may deviate from the actual footprint. In addition, their approach produces the average footprint, not the distribution.

The distribution is important. Considering two sets of footprints, A and B. One tenth of A has size $10N$ and the rest has size 0. All of B has size N. A and B have the same average footprint N but their different distribution can lead to very different types of cache interference.

Sampling and statistical inference Beyls and D'Hollander used hold-and-sample and reservoir sampling to profile reuse time [5]. As part of a continuous program optimization framework, Cascaval et al. sampled TLB misses to approximate reuse distance [6]. Recently, Schuff et al. used sampling to measure reuse distance on shared cache [20]. These methods are based on sampling.

Two techniques by Berg and Hagersten (known as StatCache) [3] and by Shen et al. [22, 23] were used to infer cache miss rate from the distribution of reuse times. Let each access represented by a random variable X_i, which is assigned 1 if the access i is a miss and 0 otherwise. Let accesses i, j be two consecutive accesses to some data. The reuse time is $j - i$. Let $P(k)$ be the probability that a cache block is replaced after k misses. The following equation holds

$$E[X_j] = P(X_{i+1} + X_{i+2} + \ldots + X_{j-1})$$

With the goal of inferring number of cache misses in every interval, the analysis problem is one of all-window statistics. However, there can be $O(n)$ variables in the equation. To produce an estimate, Berg and Hagersten assumed constant miss rate over time and random cache replacement [3]. Shen et al. assumed a Bernulli process and LRU cache replacement [22, 23] (and later used a similar model to analyze multi-threaded code [16]). While both methods are shown to be accurate and effective for miss rate prediction, the accuracy of the all-window statistics has not been verified. One can easily construct two example executions that have arbitrarily different footprints while showing the same reuse times. The two methods do not guarantee a precision for the miss-rate estimate.

In a poster paper, Ding and Chilimbi described two solutions: linear sampling and all-window measurement [10]. The sampling rate of linear sampling is $1/n$, where n is the length of the trace, which can be too low to be statistically meaningful. The second technique is equivalent to the *NlogM* algorithm in this paper, which is too slow as we will show in Section 5.

4. Cache Interference Prediction and Ranking

Shared cache is a dynamic system. The interaction between active programs is likely non-linear since the cause and effect form a loop. The memory access of one program affects the performance of its peers, whose effect "feed back" to itself. In this section we first express this relation in an equation system and then present our solution.

Let programs 1 and 2 of infinite length run on shared cache. Let their speed be cpi_1, cpi_2 when running alone, as measured by cycles per instruction. When they execute together, let the change in their speeds be δ_1, δ_2. If we assume uniform speed change, an original time window of size t in an individual execution will take

time $t\delta_1$ in program 1 and $t\delta_2$ in program 2. We call this effect *execution dilation* and the term δ_i the dilation factor of program i.

If we know execution dilation, we can compute its effect on cache sharing by matching for example each reuse window of size t in program 1 with a footprint window of size $t\frac{cpi_1\delta_1}{cpi_2\delta_2}$. From this matching, we can compute the relative increase in the number of capacity misses in shared cache.

$$x_1 = \frac{P\left[d_1 + f_2\left(t(d_1)\frac{cpi_1\delta_1}{cpi_2\delta_2}\right) \geq C\right]}{P[d_1 \geq C]} \tag{1}$$

where d_1 is a reuse distance of program 1, $t(d_1)$ is the size of reuse window of d_1 when program 1 is running alone, $f_2(x)$ is the footprint of program 2 in a window of size x, and c is the size of shared cache. The relative increase in shared-cache misses for program 2 is similarly computed as x_2.

To connect caching effect with execution time, we need a timing model. An accurate model is highly unlikely to exist given the complexity of modern computers. For example, the penalty of a cache miss on an out-of-order issue processor depends on the parallelism with surrounding instructions, the overlapping with other memory accesses, and the choice of hardware or software prefetching. Instead of looking for an accurate model, we use a simple model that can capture some first-order effect in the relation between cache misses and execution time.

We use a linear model, $T = T^n n + T^p m^p + T^s m^s$, where T is the execution time, n is the number of instructions, m^p is the number of private-cache misses, m^s is the number of shared-cache misses, and T^n, T^p, T^s are the average cost of an instruction, a private-cache miss, and a shared-cache miss. Of the 6 factors, n, m^p, m^s are trace specific, and T^n, T^p, T^s are machine specific. The values of T^n, T^p, and T^s are learned by linear regression given the linear model and a set of measured execution times and predicted L1 and L2 cache misses from SPEC2K benchmarks. The product of $T^n n$ can be viewed as the execution time when all data access are cache hits. The other two factors, $T^p m^p, T^s m^s$, are the penalty from cache misses. We make the simplifying assumption that all misses have the same penalty. A similar assumption was used by Marin and Mellor-Crummey [18].

The following equation combines the cache model and the time model to produce the dilation factor for program i ($i = 1, 2$)

$$\frac{T^n n_i + T^p m_i^p + T^s m_i^s x_i}{T^n n_i + T^p m_i^p + T^s m_i^s} = \delta_i \tag{2}$$

Substituting x_i with its equation, we have two recursive equations of two unknowns, δ_i. The formulation can be extended to p programs by changing the equation for x_i to

$$x_i = \frac{P\left[d_i + \Sigma_{j \neq i} f_j\left(t(d_i)\frac{cpi_i\delta_i}{cpi_j\delta_j}\right) \geq C\right]}{P[d_i \geq C]} \tag{3}$$

and generating p equations with p unknowns.

We solve the recursive equations using an iterative method. We first set δ_i to be 1, use the equations to compute the new value of δ_i', and repeat until all δ_i stops changing ($|\delta_i' - \delta_i| < \varepsilon \delta_i$).

To analyze the convergence property of the solution, consider the 2-program run case. We symbolize x_i in Equation 3 as a function $x_i(\frac{\delta_1}{\delta_2})$. Substituting this function into Equation 2 for δ_1, δ_2 and putting one over the other we have

$$\frac{\frac{T^n n_1 + T^p m_1^p + T^s m_1^s x_1\left(\frac{\delta_1}{\delta_2}\right)}{T^n n_1 + T^p m_1^p + T^s m_1^s}}{\frac{T^n n_2 + T^p m_2^p + T^s m_2^s x_2\left(\frac{\delta_1}{\delta_2}\right)}{T^n n_2 + T^p m_2^p + T^s m_2^s}} = \frac{\delta_1}{\delta_2} \tag{4}$$

If we represent the left-hand size as a function F, the equation becomes $F(\frac{\delta_1}{\delta_2}) = \frac{\delta_1}{\delta_2}$. Following theorem ensures the convergence of our iteration model.

Theorem 4.1. $\exists \delta_1, \delta_2$, such that $\frac{\delta_1}{\delta_2} = F(\frac{\delta_1}{\delta_2})$.

Proof Let $r = \frac{\delta_1}{\delta_2}$. According to the definition of F, we have the following 3 statements immediately.

- $y = F(r)$ is non-decreasing. Notice, when r increases $x_1(r)$ increases while $x_2(r)$ decreases.
- $F(0_+) = C1 > 0$, where C1 is constant.
- $F(\text{inf}) = C2 < \text{inf}$, where C2 is constant.

Let $r_1 = max\ S_1$, where $S1 = \{r | \forall s \leq r, F(s) \geq s\}$, $r_2 = min\ S_2$, where $S2 = \{r | \forall s < r, F(s) \geq s, F(r) \leq r\}$. Obviously $r_1 \leq r_2$. we claim $r_1 = r_2$.

Assume $r_1 \neq r_2$ by contradiction. According to the definition of $r_1, F(r_1) \geq r_1$, which means $F(r_1) \notin S_1$. According to the definition of $r_2, F(r_1) \in S_2$, which means $F(r_1) \geq r_2$. Because $F(r_2) \leq r_2$, we have $F(r_1) \geq F(r_2)$, which contradicts the assumption that $F(r)$ is non-decreasing. Since $r_1 = r_2$ by definition, we conclude $F(r_1) = r_1$. ■

Interference is a complex relation. To run n programs on a machine with p processors, there are $\binom{n}{p}$ choices of co-execution. With the asymmetrical effect of cache sharing, every program in every set may have a different interference. Our model, which we call, *PAW* (Profiling of All-Window footprints) model or *PAW* prediction, can be used to predict the interference and rank co-run choices so that a user can choose program combinations that have least interference. *PAW* statistics, locality and footprint, are machine independent. To make prediction, *PAW* requires two items of information from the target machine: the sequential running time of each program and the size of the shared cache. The process does not need any parallel testing.

5. Evaluation

5.1 Experimental Setup

We have tested 14 SPEC2K benchmarks, which include all programs that we could compile and run. Other programs have compilation errors due to either our configuration setup or the benchmark code. Each of the successful tests is compiled using a modified GCC 4.1 compiler with "-O3" flag. The compiler is modified to instrument each memory access and generate the data access trace when the program runs. The reuse distance analysis is the relative-accuracy approximation algorithm [28]. The precision is set to 90%. Since profiling is machine-dependent, we use a Linux cluster for profiling different benchmarks in parallel to save time. Each node has two 3.2GHz 64-bit Intel Xeon processors with 1MB L2 cache each and 6GB physical memory total. We use a set of newer machines for cache-interference tests. Each has a 2.0GHz Intel Core Duo processor with two cores sharing 2MB L2 cache and 2GB memory.

5.2 All-window Footprint

Figure 4 shows the full distribution of all-window footprint in 4 of the 15 benchmarks. While every program has a different looking footprint, we choose these 4 because they demonstrate the range of variations. Each graph shows window size, measured in number of data accesses with exponential scale, in the x-axis and footprint, measured in bytes, in the y-axis. It's worth to note, since our measurements are based on 64-byte blocks the footprint sizes are always multiples of 64. At each window size, each graph shows five footprint numbers: the minimal size min, the maximal size max,

the median, and the two footprints whose size is higher than 90% and 10% of footprints. We connect the points into a line, so each distribution is drawn with five curves. In probability terms, a point (x, y) on the n% curve indicates that a window of x data accesses has n% chance to have a footprint smaller than y.

The footprint distribution shows highly summarized information about program data usage. For example, every point $< x, y >$ in the min curve shows the minimal footprint in all windows of size x is y. As a sanity check, a reader can verify that the minimal and the maximal footprints are monotone functions of the window size. The monotonicity should hold in theory but in an observation, it is not guaranteed if we sample a set of windows rather than measure all windows.

All-window footprint shows the characteristics of the working sets in a program. *Gzip* has constant-size median working sets for windows from 1 million to 256 million accesses, shown by Figure 4(a). In compression or decompression, the same data buffers are repeatedly used for each chunk of the input or output file. Constant-size working sets are a result of complete data reuse. *Bzip2* creates larger auxiliary data structures in order to improve compression ratio over a larger scope. Its working sets increase in size with the length of the execution window. The rate of increase, however, gradually decreases, as shown by Figure 4(b).

Shown in Figure 4(c), *Equake* has the clear streaming access pattern because its working set size increases linearly with the execution window length. In fact, it shows the most rapid growth, resulting in the largest footprint among all programs we have tested. 90% of footprints increase from 8KB to 8MB when window size increases from 30K to 32M data accesses. Its footprint interferes with many other programs when running in shared cache. Twolf in Figure 4(d) shows the smallest variation in footprint size. 80% of windows have nearly the same size footprint. These examples show that applications have different characteristics in their footprint distribution.

5.3 Comparison with Miss Count

It is interesting to consider the relation between the number of misses in a window and the footprint of the window. On average, the number of misses is the miss rate times the window size. Therefore, the average miss count grows linearly. It is unbounded if a program executes forever. The footprint is bounded by the size of program data. The growth cannot be always linear.

This difference is shown in the example of *Gzip* result in Figure 5. The miss count should be in the unit of 64-byte blocks. The figure shows it in bytes growing linearly from 2^{-9} byte to 2^{26} (83MB or 1.3 million misses) for window sizes ranging from 1 access to 18 billion. For the same window sizes, the footprint grows from 64 bytes (1 block) to 83MB. This difference leads to different predictions of cache interference. We compare the accuracy of these predictions next.

5.4 Prediction of Program Interference

For interference we run our test set of 15 programs on a dual-core machine mentioned earlier. There are $\binom{15}{2} = 105$ ways of pairing two of the 15 programs to share cache, 455 ways of choosing 3, and 1365 ways of choosing 4. We use all-window profiling on each of 15 programs in a sequential run and use the composable model to rank cache interference of co-run choices. The ranking is based on the predicted slowdown (the geometric mean in each group).

There are two questions about the prediction. The first is how accurate the model is in predicting the cache interference. It can be evaluated by measuring the change in the miss rate when programs are run together. The second is how useful the model is in predicting the performance of shared cache. It can be evaluated by measuring the change in the actual execution time. We show re-

Distribution of all-window footprint

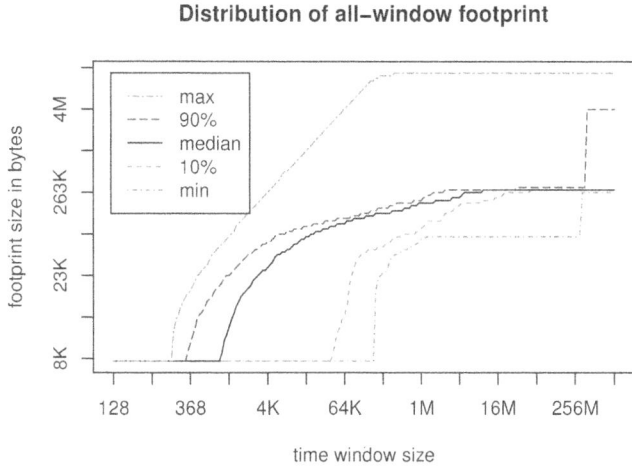

(a) **Gzip** has constant-size median working sets for windows from 1 million to 256 million accesses.

Distribution of all-window footprint

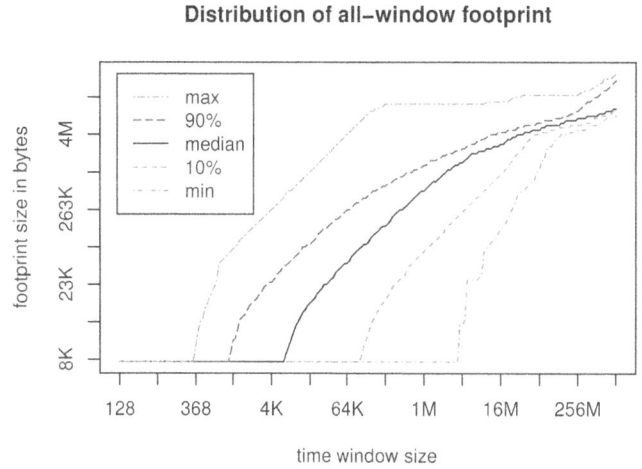

(b) **Bzip2** has a larger working set than *Gzip* for windows larger than 256 thousand accesses.

Distribution of all-window footprint

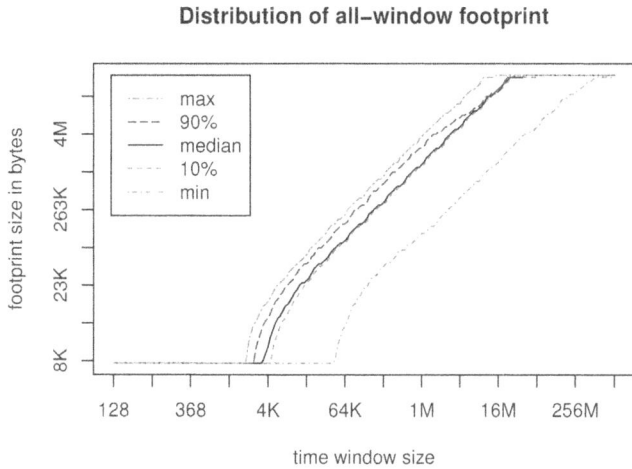

(c) **Equake** has a streaming access pattern. The footprint increases linearly with the window size.

Distribution of all-window footprint

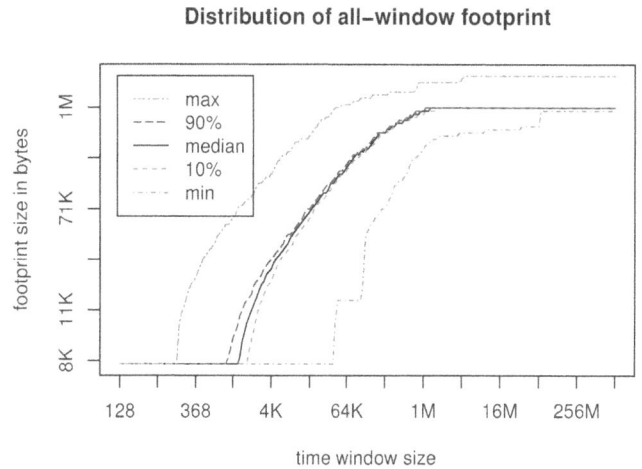

(d) **Twolf** shows a narrow distribution —80% windows of the same length have nearly the same footprint.

Figure 4. The distribution of all-window footprint shows the characteristics of the working set in 4 SPEC benchmarks.

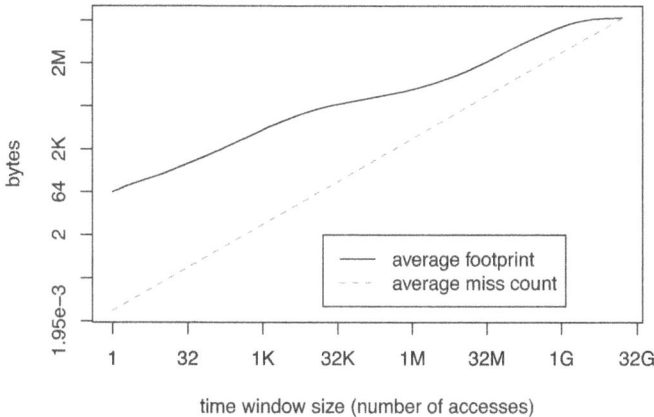

Figure 5. Comparison of linear miss count growth and non-linear footprint growth in *Gzip*.

sults that answer the second question. To measure the interference, we run a pair of programs long enough and take the average slow down, following the method used in [27].

We evaluate the prediction by plotting an *interference-ranking graph*. Figure 6(a) shows two sets of results. The first is the actual slowdown of the program pairs ordered by the footprint-based prediction. The second is the slowdown when program pairs are ordered by results from all-pair testing. The second one is a monotone curve, which is the ideal result for a prediction method. The data points of the footprint-based prediction are connected into a line. It is not monotone, but it is generally the case that program pairs with a higher rank have a greater slowdown than program pairs with a lower rank. The method ranks high interference pairs better than it ranks low interference pairs. This can be attributed to the simple execution-time model. When the cache effect becomes significant, the footprint model shows its strength. In practical use, users are more concerned with large degradations.

Figure 6(b) shows the effect of miss-rate based predictor in comparison with the ideal result. The prediction is obtained by using the miss count instead of the footprint. The miss count is computed from the average miss rate, which is computed using the

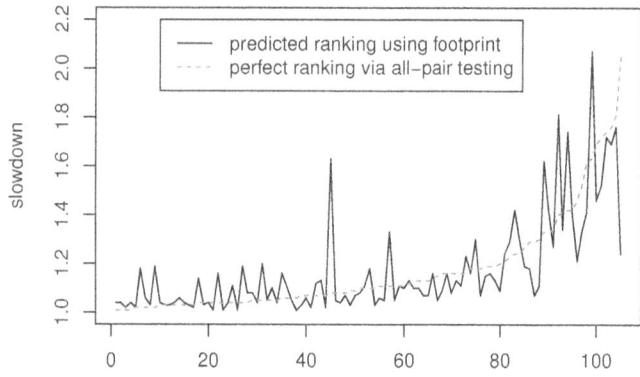

(a) Footprint-based interference ranking compared to exhaustive testing. The y-axis shows the slowdown (quadratic mean) by the xth program pair.

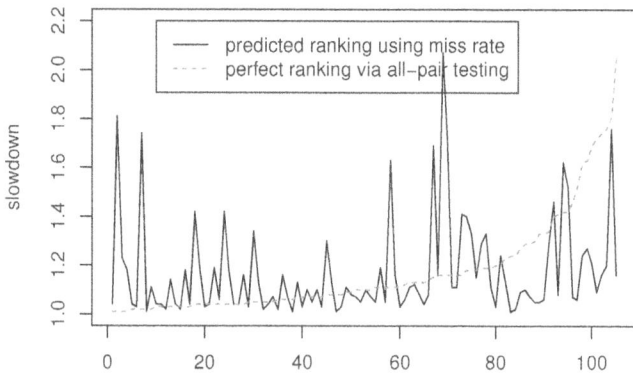

(b) Miss-rate based interference ranking compared to exhaustive testing. The y-axis shows the slowdown (quadratic mean) by the xth pair.

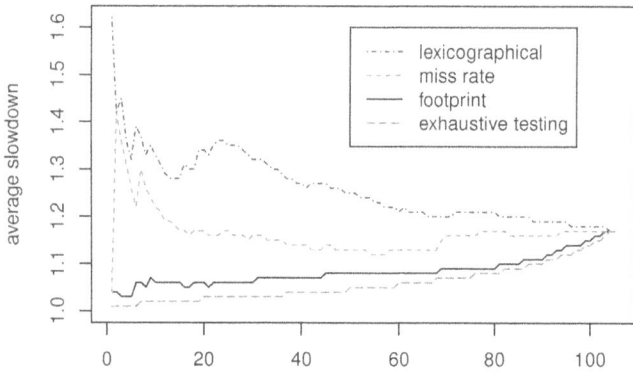

(c) Cumulative mean interference by 4 ranking methods. The y-axis shows the average slowdown (quadratic mean) for the first x pairs.

Figure 6. All-window footprint predicts the performance effect of all-pair cache sharing better than the miss rate does.

reuse distance in the sequential run. Miss rate may significantly underestimate the cache footprint. As an example, the pair, art and twolf, has the second lowest total miss rate (miss per second) in their sequential run, but when running together, art causes twolf to run 91% slower while itself actually runs 6% faster (we do not have an explanation for the speedup). Overall, the high-interference pairs (on the right half of the graph) do not show a rising trend, indicating the ranking fails to predict in co-run slowdown.

Figure 6(c) shows the cumulative mean slowdown of groups 1 to x at each point. The ideal result, based on the ranking from exhaustive measurement, increases from 1% slowly until near the end when it quickly rises to 17%. This is because most programs do not interfere significantly but for the few that do, they interfere badly. The mean slowdown for the first 85 pairs is less than 10%, but the next 20 pairs raise the average of all 105 pairs to 17%.

Footprint-based ranking shows a similar result to the ideal ranking. The cumulative mean slowdown is 6% and 3% respectively for the prediction and the ideal for the first 25 pairs and 8% and 5% for the first 50 pairs. The two curves move closer after the 62th pair. The difference in their average slowdown is no more than 2%. If we take the first 25 pairs, the cumulative slowdown in miss-rate based ranking is 17%, which is near 3 times the 6% cumulative slowdown by footprint. As a basis for comparison, Figure 6(c) also shows the effect of random ranking, which does not consider the effect of cache interference. Random ranking is obtained by ranking co-run pairs according to the lexicographic order of their program names.

5.5 Efficiency

Measurement speed We have tested 26 reference inputs of the 14 benchmark programs that we could compile. For brevity, Table 1 shows results for one reference input (the first one in the test order) of each benchmark. The programs are listed by the increasing order of their SPEC benchmark number, from 164 for *gzip* to 300 for *twolf*.

prog.	N (10^9)	M (10^3)	K (10^6)	N/K (10^3)	CKlogM Refs/sec (10^6)
gzip	24	232	7.2	3.4	1.9
vpr	41	159	6.9	5.9	2.9
gcc	16	360	2.3	7.3	3.5
mesa	31	28	1.8	17.5	8.4
art	30	11	12	2.4	1.7
mcf	14	315	27	0.50	0.3
equake	108	167	7.6	14.2	6.5
crafty	41	7.5	25	1.7	1.3
ammp	4.7	51	2.6	1.8	1.1
parser	78	102	21	3.7	1.9
gap	68	787	3.6	19.0	7.3
vortex	31	196	3.0	10.4	4.9
bzip2	42	530	7.8	5.4	2.4
twolf	106	12	48	2.2	1.8
median	36	162	7.4	4.6	**2.1**
mean	45	211	12.5	6.8	**3.3**

Table 1. Measurement speed by CKlogM ($C = 128$) for the reference input of 14 SPEC2K benchmarks. The speed closely correlates with the average interval length (N/K). The average speed is 3.3 million references per second.

The size of the execution is measured by the length of the data access trace and the number of data cache lines the program touched, shown in the second and third columns of the table. The size of each data cache line is 64-byte. The number of intervals,

98

K, and the average length of each interval, N/K, are shown next. Finally, the last column shows the measurement speed in the unit of million references per second.

The length of the traces range from 4 billion to 108 billion, the size of data ranges from 7 thousand to 787 thousand, the number of intervals ranges from 1.8 million to 48 billion, the average interval length ranges from 504 to 19 thousand, and the measurement speed ranges from 264 thousand data accesses per second to 8.4 million accesses per second. If we measure in terms of the number of windows measured, the speed ranges from 10^{15} (a quadrillion) windows per second to nearly 10^{18} (a quintillion) windows per second.

The speed closely correlates with the average interval length. The average length of k means that in a random time window, 128 distinct data elements are accessed by each k accesses. When the length is 500, the measurement speed is less than 300 thousand accesses per second. However, when the length is 19,000, the speed becomes 7.3 million accesses per second. The average length is determined by the length of the trace and the number of intervals. Hence the cost of the algorithm is determined by the number of intervals, K, more than any other factor.

Comparison between CKlogM and NlogM The NlogM algorithm was the first to attempt complete all-window measurement [10]. Here we compare NlogM with CKlogM for $C = 128$ and $C = 256$. Table 2 shows the result of 12 SPEC2K benchmarks (that the NlogM method could finish analyzing), including the length of the trace, the size of data, the measurement time by NlogM, and the speedup numbers by CKlogM for two Cs. We have to use test inputs because it takes too long for NlogM to measure larger inputs. The measurement time ranges from 414 seconds for *mcf* to 4 hours for *parser* by NlogM and from 3 and 2 seconds for *twolf* to 18 and 17 minutes for *ammp* by CKlogM when $C = 128$ and $C = 256$. The largest reduction is a factor of 316 for *twolf* from 10 minutes to 2 seconds. The smallest reduction is a factor of 8 for *mcf* from 7 minutes to 53 seconds.

prog.	N	M	NlogM time [sec]	CKlogM C=128 time (speedup)	CKlogM C=256 time (speedup)
gzip	804M	9K	12K	328(35)	246(47)
vpr	298M	5K	4K	84(49)	41(90)
gcc	255M	15K	4K	37(102)	19(198)
mesa	173M	25K	2.6K	10(259)	9(288)
art	1.0B	5K	12K	119(104)	108(114)
mcf	40M	5K	414	52(7.8)	41(10)
equake	342M	40K	5K	42(126)	33(161)
crafty	935M	8K	15K	739(20)	187(78)
ammp	818M	51K	13K	1129(12)	1036(13)
parser	929M	24K	14K	142(101)	98(147)
gap	277M	147K	5K	30(168)	20(252)
vortex	2087M	65K	–	537(N/A)	283(N/A)
bzip2	3029M	60K	–	660(N/A)	565(N/A)
twolf	76M	309	631	3(210)	2(316)
median	320M	12K	5178	47(**101**)	41(**131**)
mean	497M	28K	7343	201(**100**)	153(**142**)

Table 2. Time comparison for the test input of 14 SPEC 2K benchmarks. On average (excluding Vortex and Bzip2 for which *NlogM* does not finish), the measurement time is reduced from 2 hours per program to 73 and 52 seconds when $C = 128$ and 256 respectively.

The average statistics is shown at the bottom of Table 2. On average across 12 benchmarks, the length of the trace is half billion

memory accesses and the size of data is 28 thousand words. The average measurement time of NlogM is two hours. The average reduction by CKlogM is a factor of 100 to 73 seconds when $C = 128$ and a factor of 142 to 52 seconds when $C = 256$. In other words, *CKlogM reduces the average measurement time from two hours to one minute.*

5.6 Relation between c and Measurement Speedup

We define the *speedup factor* by $\frac{N}{CK}$. Intuitively, a larger c produces a greater speedup. However, this is not true. We have measured all power-of-two c values for all our tests and studied the relation between c and the potential speedup. When the speedup numbers for different c were drawn as a curve, we have observed variations in terms of whether a curve has a single peak or whether the shape changes when a program is run with different inputs. Figure 7 show the speedup factor for 4 programs whose footprint we have shown in Figure 4. The highest speedup is in tens of thousands for bzip2 and gzip, one hundred thousand for equake, and (too large to shown in the figure) 1.6 million for twolf.

N/CK Speedup Factor

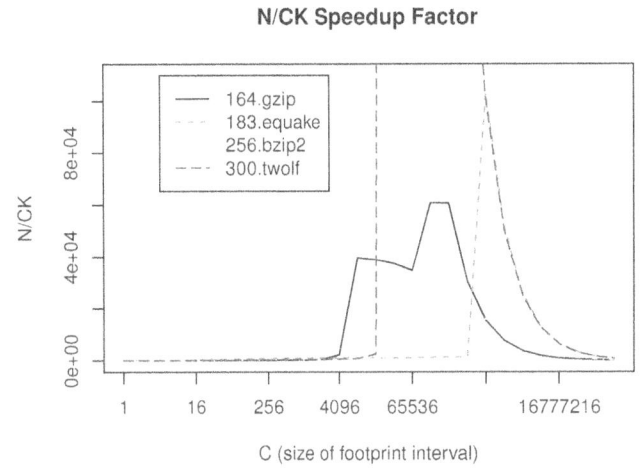

Figure 7. $\frac{N}{CK}$ gives the speedup factors for 4 SPEC CPU2000 benchmarks. The speedup factors for twolf are as high as 1.6 million but are not shown above 100K in order to make other numbers easy to see.

6. Potential Uses of All-window Profiling

The new algorithm and the accurate modeling of cache sharing may have a number of uses:

- *footprint-based program optimization.* Traditionally, the way to improve memory performance is to improve program locality. For shared cache, we may reduce the interference by reducing the size of program footprint even if the locality stays unchanged. All-window footprint can aid footprint-oriented techniques in two ways. The first is to identify "hot" spots in a program and help program tuning. For example, a tool can identify loops and functions in a program that have the largest footprint or a footprint larger than 90% of the windows of the same size. Second, all-window analysis can be used to fully evaluate the effect of a footprint-oriented program transformation.

- *sampling vs. all-window statistics.* Statistics such as the miss rate may differ depending on two factors, which windows are chosen to measure the miss rate, and how large the windows are. All-window analysis can be used to determine whether the miss rate is uniform as a function of window sizes - whether the miss rate in small windows is the same as the miss rate in large windows. Similarly, it can determine whether the miss behavior in a subset of windows is similar to the miss behavior in all windows. In addition, On-line techniques may use the miss rate to approximate the footprint. Accurate footprint results can be used to calibrate approximation methods and determine their effectiveness and limitations.

- *cache vs. other resources.* Cache sharing is only one factor in performance. Others include the sharing of memory interface and the CPU scheduler [30]. An accurate estimate of cache interference can help us determine how important cache sharing is when compared against other factors, and how useful and portable a cache model may be in performance prediction.

- *working set characterization.* Working set is an important metric in workload characterization. It helps to have the full distribution of working-set size in all windows not just the average. With the distribution, we can evaluate statistically how good the average is as an estimate for an execution window.

- *batch scheduling.* The composable model may help ahead-of-time co-run scheduling. If a workload has a fixed number of program-input pairs, a batch scheduler can use the type of ranking results shown in Section 5.4 to choose which sub-group of tasks to start on the next available multi-core computer.

7. Related Work

We have discussed in Section 3.5 related work in footprint analysis. Next we review related techniques in modeling shared cache performance.

Cache sharing Chandra et al. modeled cache sharing between independent applications and gave the framework that we use in this paper [8]. Cache sharing in multi-threaded code is affected by two additional factors: data sharing and thread interleaving. The effect can be characterized by extending the concept of reuse distance [20, 21] or inferred using a composable model [11, 16]. Previous methods did not measure footprint precisely and did not model the circular interaction. The techniques in this paper measure the all-window footprints with a guaranteed precision and use an iterative algorithm to compute the circular interference among co-run applications.

Zhang et al. used a conflict graph to show the asymmetrical effect of cache sharing [27]. They did not explain the causes, which we model as the combined effect of footprint and locality.

Program co-scheduling Many techniques have been developed for selecting applications to run on shared cache. Snavely and Tullsen devised a scheduler that generates and evaluates a set of random schedules in the sampling phase and picks the best one for the remaining execution [24]. Fedorova et al. suspended program execution when needed to ensure a set of programs have equal share of cache [13]. The technique is based on the assumption that if two programs have the same frequency of cache misses, they have the same amount of data in cache. The two techniques are dynamic and do not need off-line profiling. However, on-line analysis may not be accurate and cannot predict interference in other program combinations.

Jiang et al. formulated the problem of optimal co-scheduling and showed that although the problem is NP-hard, an approximation algorithm can yield a near-optimal solution [15]. As inputs, their solution requires accurate prediction of co-run degradation. They gave a prediction method based on statistical inference of application footprint [16]. As discussed in Section 3.5, the result from statistical inference does not have a precision guarantee. The all-window analysis and the composable model can provide the needed

prediction, with an accuracy similar to exhaustive testing (as shown in Section 5.4).

Zhuravlev et al. defined a metric called *Pain* to estimate the performance degradation due to cache sharing [30]. The degree of pain that application A suffers while it co-runs with B is affected by A's cache sensitivity, which is proportional to the expectation of its reuse distance distribution, and B's cache intensity, which is measured by the number of last level cache accesses per million instructions. The pain of A-B co-scheduling is estimated as the sum of the pains of A and B. Pain is a composable model. It differs from *PAW* in the notion of cache intensity. It is defined using a single window size. In computing B's interference of A, *PAW* considers all window sizes in B since a reuse window in A may have an arbitrary length.

Trace and static analysis Measuring footprint requires counting distinct data elements. The problem has long been studied in measuring various types of stack distances. A review of measurement techniques for reuse distance (LRU stack distance) can be found in [28]. Kaplan et al. studied the problem of optimal trace compression–to generate the shortest possible trace that still preserves same LRU behavior in large cache [17]. Our footprint measurement is similar in that both methods use intervals as the basic unit in analysis. More recently, Zhou studied random cache replacement policy and gave a one-pass deterministic trace-analysis algorithm to compute the average miss rate (instead of simulating many times and taking the average) [29]. Reuse distance can be analyzed statically for scientific code [4, 7] and recently MATLAB code [9]. The static techniques also compute the footprint in loops and functions. Unlike profiling whose results are usually input specific, static analysis can identify and model the effect of program parameters. These techniques are concerned with only reuse windows and cannot measure the footprint in all execution windows, which is the problem we have solved in this paper.

8. Summary

We have presented the first accurate all-window footprint analysis. The new algorithm uses footprint counting, relative precision approximation, and trace compression to reduce the asymptotic cost to $O(CK\log M)$. We have successfully measured all-window footprints in the SPEC2K benchmark suite in its full-length executions. It is the first time such complete measurement is made. The results show that applications differ in their footprints in terms of not just the size but also the relation with time and the compactness of the distribution. The previous fastest accurate method could only measure these programs on their test input, for which the new algorithm reduces the profiling time from 2 hours to 1 minute. The all-window analysis measures a quadrillion to nearly a quintillion footprints per second.

We have also presented an iterative algorithm to compute the non-linear, asymmetrical effect of cache sharing and developed a tool for ranking program co-run choices without parallel testing. The ranking is close to that from exhaustive parallel testing, reducing performance slowdown by as much as a factor of 3 compared to miss-rate based ranking.

Acknowledgments

We would like to thank Xiao Zhang for help with the experimental setup. The presentation has been improved by the suggestions from Xipeng Shen, Santosh Pande, and the systems group at University of Rochester especially Kai Shen. Xiaoya Xiang and Bin Bao are supported by two IBM Center for Advanced Studies Fellowships. The research is also supported by the National Science Foundation (Contract No. CCF-0963759, CNS-0834566, CNS-0720796).

References

[1] A. Agarwal, J. L. Hennessy, and M. Horowitz. Cache performance of operating system and multiprogramming workloads. *ACM Transactions on Computer Systems*, 6(4):393–431, 1988.

[2] B. T. Bennett and V. J. Kruskal. LRU stack processing. *IBM Journal of Research and Development*, pages 353–357, 1975.

[3] E. Berg and E. Hagersten. Statcache: a probabilistic approach to efficient and accurate data locality analysis. In *Proceedings of the IEEE International Symposium on Performance Analysis of Systems and Software*, pages 20–27, 2004.

[4] K. Beyls and E. D'Hollander. Generating cache hints for improved program efficiency. *Journal of Systems Architecture*, 51(4):223–250, 2005.

[5] K. Beyls and E. D'Hollander. Discovery of locality-improving refactoring by reuse path analysis. In *Proceedings of HPCC. Springer. Lecture Notes in Computer Science Vol. 4208*, pages 220–229, 2006.

[6] C. Cascaval, E. Duesterwald, P. F. Sweeney, and R. W. Wisniewski. Multiple page size modeling and optimization. In *Proceedings of the International Conference on Parallel Architecture and Compilation Techniques*, St. Louis, MO, 2005.

[7] C. Cascaval and D. A. Padua. Estimating cache misses and locality using stack distances. In *International Conference on Supercomputing*, pages 150–159, 2003.

[8] D. Chandra, F. Guo, S. Kim, and Y. Solihin. Predicting inter-thread cache contention on a chip multi-processor architecture. In *Proceedings of the International Symposium on High-Performance Computer Architecture*, pages 340–351, 2005.

[9] A. Chauhan and C.-Y. Shei. Static reuse distances for locality-based optimizations in MATLAB. In *International Conference on Supercomputing*, pages 295–304, 2010.

[10] C. Ding and T. Chilimbi. All-window profiling of concurrent executions. In *Proceedings of the ACM SIGPLAN Symposium on Principles and Practice of Parallel Programming*, 2008. *poster paper*.

[11] C. Ding and T. Chilimbi. A composable model for analyzing locality of multi-threaded programs. Technical Report MSR-TR-2009-107, Microsoft Research, August 2009.

[12] B. Falsafi and D. A. Wood. Modeling cost/performance of a parallel computer simulator. *ACM Transactions on Modeling and Computer Simulation*, 7(1):104–130, 1997.

[13] A. Fedorova, M. Seltzer, and M. D. Smith. Improving performance isolation on chip multiprocessors via an operating system scheduler. In *Proceedings of the International Conference on Parallel Architecture and Compilation Techniques*, 2007.

[14] M. D. Hill and A. J. Smith. Evaluating associativity in CPU caches. *IEEE Transactions on Computers*, 38(12):1612–1630, 1989.

[15] Y. Jiang, X. Shen, J. Chen, and R. Tripathi. Analysis and approximation of optimal co-scheduling on chip multiprocessors. In *Proceedings of the International Conference on Parallel Architecture and Compilation Techniques*, pages 220–229, 2008.

[16] Y. Jiang, E. Z. Zhang, K. Tian, and X. Shen. Is reuse distance applicable to data locality analysis on chip multiprocessors? In *Proceedings of the International Conference on Compiler Construction*, pages 264–282, 2010.

[17] S. F. Kaplan, Y. Smaragdakis, and P. R. Wilson. Flexible reference trace reduction for VM simulations. *ACM Transactions on Modeling and Computer Simulation*, 13(1):1–38, 2003.

[18] G. Marin and J. Mellor-Crummey. Cross architecture performance predictions for scientific applications using parameterized models. In *Proceedings of the International Conference on Measurement and Modeling of Computer Systems*, pages 2–13, 2004.

[19] R. L. Mattson, J. Gecsei, D. Slutz, and I. L. Traiger. Evaluation techniques for storage hierarchies. *IBM System Journal*, 9(2):78–117, 1970.

[20] D. L. Schuff, M. Kulkarni, and V. S. Pai. Accelerating multicore reuse distance analysis with sampling and parallelization. In *Proceedings of the International Conference on Parallel Architecture and Compilation Techniques*, 2010.

[21] M. Schulz, B. S. White, S. A. McKee, H.-H. S. Lee, and J. Jeitner. Owl: next generation system monitoring. In *Proceedings of the ACM Conference on Computing Frontiers*, pages 116–124, 2005.

[22] X. Shen and J. Shaw. Scalable implementation of efficient locality approximation. In *Proceedings of the Workshop on Languages and Compilers for Parallel Computing*, pages 202–216, 2007.

[23] X. Shen, J. Shaw, B. Meeker, and C. Ding. Locality approximation using time. In *Proceedings of the ACM SIGPLAN-SIGACT Symposium on Principles of Programming Languages*, pages 55–61, 2007.

[24] A. Snavely and D. M. Tullsen. Symbiotic jobscheduling for a simultaneous multithreading processor. In *Proceedings of the International Conference on Architectural Support for Programming Languages and Operating Systems*, pages 234–244, 2000.

[25] G. E. Suh, S. Devadas, and L. Rudolph. Analytical cache models with applications to cache partitioning. In *International Conference on Supercomputing*, pages 1–12, 2001.

[26] D. Thiébaut and H. S. Stone. Footprints in the cache. *ACM Transactions on Computer Systems*, 5(4):305–329, 1987.

[27] X. Zhang, S. Dwarkadas, and K. Shen. Towards practical page coloring-based multi-core cache management. In *Proceedings of the EuroSys Conference*, 2009.

[28] Y. Zhong, X. Shen, and C. Ding. Program locality analysis using reuse distance. *ACM Transactions on Programming Languages and Systems*, 31(6):1–39, Aug. 2009.

[29] S. Zhou. An efficient simulation algorithm for cache of random replacement policy. In *Proceedings of the IFIP International Conference on Network and Parallel Computing*, pages 144–154, 2010. Springer Lecture Notes in Computer Science No. 6289.

[30] S. Zhuravlev, S. Blagodurov, and A. Fedorova. Addressing shared resource contention in multicore processors via scheduling. In *Proceedings of the International Conference on Architectural Support for Programming Languages and Operating Systems*, pages 129–142, 2010.

ULCC: A User-Level Facility for Optimizing Shared Cache Performance on Multicores

Xiaoning Ding *

The Ohio State University

dingxn@cse.ohio-state.edu

Kaibo Wang

The Ohio State University

wangka@cse.ohio-state.edu

Xiaodong Zhang

The Ohio State University

zhang@cse.ohio-state.edu

Abstract

Scientific applications face serious performance challenges on multicore processors, one of which is caused by access contention in last level shared caches from multiple running threads. The contention increases the number of long latency memory accesses, and consequently increases application execution times. Optimizing shared cache performance is critical to significantly reduce execution times of multi-threaded programs on multicores. However, there are two unique problems to be solved before implementing cache optimization techniques on multicores at the user level. First, available cache space for each running thread in a last level cache is difficult to predict due to access contention in the shared space, which makes cache conscious algorithms for single cores ineffective on multicores. Second, at the user level, programmers are not able to allocate cache space at will to running threads in the shared cache, thus data sets with strong locality may not be allocated with sufficient cache space, and cache pollution can easily happen.

To address these two critical issues, we have designed ULCC (User Level Cache Control), a software runtime library that enables programmers to explicitly manage and optimize last level cache usage by allocating proper cache space for different data sets of different threads. We have implemented ULCC at the user level based on a page-coloring technique for last level cache usage management. By means of multiple case studies on an Intel multicore processor, we show that with ULCC, scientific applications can achieve significant performance improvements by fully exploiting the benefit of cache optimization algorithms and by partitioning the cache space accordingly to protect frequently reused data sets and to avoid cache pollution. Our experiments with various applications show that ULCC can significantly improve application performance by nearly 40%.

Categories and Subject Descriptors   D.1.3 [*Programming Techniques*]: Concurrent Programming—Parallel programming

General Terms   Algorithms, Design, Performance

Keywords   Multicore, Cache, Scientific Computing

1. Introduction

Multicore processors have been widely used in all kinds of computing platforms from laptops to large supercomputers. According to the recently announced Top 500 supercomputer list, by June 2010, 85% of these supercomputers have been equipped with quad-core processors and 5% use processors with six or more cores [27]. However, application programming is facing a new performance challenge on multicore processors caused by the bottleneck of the memory system (e.g. [19, 33]). On a multicore processor, the last level cache space and the bandwidth to access memory are usually shared and contended among multiple computing cores. The contention for the shared cache increases the amount of accesses to off-chip main memory, and the contention for memory bandwidth increases the queuing delay of memory accesses. The accumulated contention in the cache and the memory bus significantly delays the execution time due to inefficient management of the shared cache at runtime. Optimizing the performance of shared last level caches can reduce both slow memory accesses and memory bandwidth demand, which has become a critical technique to address the performance issue in multicore processors.

Cache optimization at the user level has been one of the most effective methods to improve execution performance for scientific applications on the platforms with single-core processors. A large number of research projects have been carried out to restructure algorithms and programming with cache optimization (e.g. [5, 8, 12, 20, 28–31]). However, cache optimization in multicore processors faces two new challenges due to architectural changes in the memory hierarchy.

One important factor for cache conscious programming is the available cache size for given data sets in order to fully utilize the cache with minimum misses [33]. However, on multicores, due to access dynamics to shared caches, the available cache space size for each thread can be hardly predicted, particularly when an application is programmed in a MPMD model (multiple programs co-run on the same set of processors). Let's take a blocking algorithm for linear systems as an example. In such an algorithm, the block size is an important factor affecting performance, and an unsuitable block size causes extra cache misses, leading to poor execution performance. An optimal block size is usually a function of the available cache space size for blocking. On a single-core processor the last level cache is not shared, and the available space for blocking is determined by the cache size. However, on a multicore platform, a last level cache is shared among multiple threads co-running on multiple cores. How much cache space a thread can occupy is determined by dynamic access patterns of the thread and other threads sharing the cache with it. Thus, it is difficult for a programmer to determine the available cache space for each thread to make effective blocking actions. In practice, a sub-optimal block size may be selected, causing mediocre or even poor performance.

Another major source of poor performance in a multicore processor is last level cache pollution, which is a more serious problem than that on a single-core processor because multiple tasks are affected. Cache pollution is incurred when a thread accesses a sizable

---

* Currently working at Intel Labs Pittsburgh.

data set with weak locality (i.e. data with infrequent reuses or without reuses), and consequently replaces data sets with strong locality (i.e. data with frequent reuses in the cache). For threads running on single-core processors, because of the private cache architecture, a thread can only pollute the cache on one core (processor) and cannot affect threads running on other cores (processors). However, on a multicore processor, because of the shared cache architecture, a thread can pollute the whole shared cache and affect all the other threads sharing the cache. Furthermore, on a multicore processor, multiple threads may access weak locality data sets simultaneously and evict strong locality data sets very quickly.

Due to the above serious concerns, it is highly desirable for programmers to distinguish weak locality data sets from strong locality data sets and explicitly specify different space allocation priorities to them in shared caches on multicore processors. In other words, a strong locality data set should be protected by allocating it with sufficient space, while a weak locality data set must be carefully watched by giving it limited space. Unfortunately, programmers lack necessary system support to make effective allocation actions even though the programmers are very knowledgeable about the locality strength of each data set.

To address these two critical issues, we present ULCC (User Level Cache Control), a software runtime library that enables programmers to explicitly manage space sharing and contention in last level caches by making cache allocation decisions based on data locality strengths. With the functions provided by ULCC, programmers can hand-tune their programs to optimize the performance of last level caches on multicores. Unlike database applications or server applications, whose access patterns are dynamic and sometimes determined by the distribution of their data or requests, most scientific applications have regular and consistent access patterns. Thus, scientific application programmers can determine the sizes and locality strengths of data sets based on their algorithms in the programming stage. With the locality information and our effective support from ULCC, programmers can make effective decisions and enforce a necessary cache space allocation for their programs that can facilitate cache optimization in the programming stage and ensure that strong locality data stay in the cache during executions.

We make three major contributions in this paper. First, we have carefully designed ULCC as a runtime library to enable user level cache controls for application programming. We provide a set of functions in ULCC to support different programming models, such as MPI, OpenMP, and pthread, to tightly couple our ULCC implementation with commonly used programming interfaces. With these functions, ULCC allows programmers to manage cache space allocation flexibly and effectively while it hiding most complexity of the cache structure on multicore architecture and ULCC implementation details. Thus, programmers can focus on analyzing their algorithms and planning optimal cache space allocation; while ULCC can focus on helping users making full utilization of cache space with least overhead. Second, we have implemented a prototype of ULCC at the user level based on operating system support. Though ULCC relies on the page coloring technique [15], it does not require OS kernel modifications. This makes ULCC highly portable. Finally, we have tested ULCC with extensive experiments as to its effectiveness in improving the performance of scientific programs. We have also evaluated the overhead of ULCC. Our experiments show that ULCC can effectively and significantly improve execution performance with negligible overhead.

The remainder of the paper is organized as follows. In Section 2, we introduce the motivation and the background information of ULCC. Then in Section 3 we present the overall structure of ULCC, the design of its key components, and the implementation based on the Linux system. We present our experience with ULCC in

Section 4. Finally, we discuss related works in Section 5, and conclude the paper in Section 6.

2. Motivation and Background

In this section, with a motivating example, we illustrate the challenges a programmer may encounter in cache optimization. We show how ULCC works to help the programmer address the challenges, and explain the underlying techniques ULCC relies on to achieve this goal.

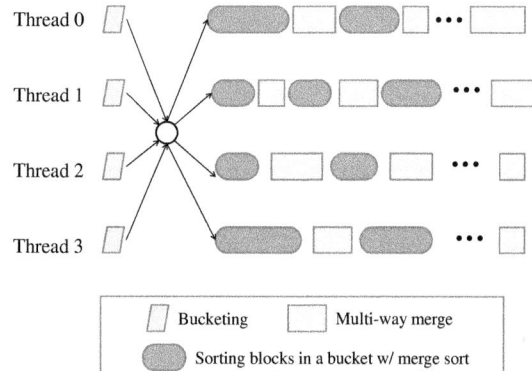

Figure 1. An application sorting a large array with multiple threads

The example program sorts elements in a large array with four threads in parallel on a quad-core processor. The program first rearranges the elements into a number of buckets according to the values of their keys in a way similar to bucket sort. Then it sorts the elements in every bucket with merge sort. To improve cache efficiency, optimizations including blocking and multi-way merging are applied as suggested in [13]. For each bucket, a thread first partitions the elements into blocks. Then it sorts the blocks one by one with merge sort. When a thread sorts a block, it uses a sorting buffer to store the intermediate results of merge sort. The buffer has the same size as the block size, and is reused for sorting different blocks. The block size should be adjusted to guarantee that sorting each block does not incur extra memory accesses after the block has been loaded into the last level cache. After all the blocks have been sorted, the thread merges the sorted blocks in one pass with a multi-way merging by constructing a full binary tree structure. Therefore, after the buckets are ready, each thread repeatedly selects an unsorted bucket, sorts the blocks in it, and merges the sorted blocks, as illustrated in Figure 1.

When the program runs on a quad-core X5355 processor in which there are two pairs of cores and cores in each pair share an L2 cache, the interference caused by cache contention and cache pollution can significantly slowdown its execution. Cache pollution happens when one thread is sorting blocks and the other thread sharing the same L2 cache with it is merging sorted blocks. Most of the data accessed by merging, including the sorted blocks and the buffer saving the final results, will not be reused. Accessing them means loading them into the L2 cache and evicting the to-be-reused data, e.g. the block being sorted and the sorting buffer.

Cache space contention happens when both threads sharing the same L2 cache work on sorting blocks. For the threads sharing the same L2 cache, if the aggregated size of their sorting buffers and the blocks they are sorting exceeds the L2 cache size, severe cache contention will occur. To quickly sort the elements in each block, the total size of the blocks being sorted and sorting buffers should fit into the last level cache. However, cache contention still happens when a thread finishes sorting a block and starts to work on another block. Loading the new block into the L2 cache evicts the to-be-reused data in sorting buffers and the block being sorted by the other thread. This causes further performance degradation, as we will show in Section 4.

With the support from ULCC, the program can separate the cache space used by different threads and reserve separate cache space slots in the last level cache for each block being sorted and the sorting buffer for each thread, in order to avoid cache pollution and cache contention. Thus, each thread can carry out merge sort block by block without suffering interference from other threads or from its own block switching. With this method, the performance of the program can be improved by over 20%.

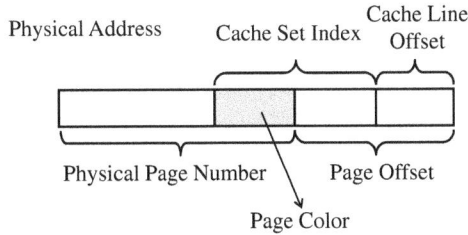

Figure 2. Physical address in the page coloring technique

ULCC enforces a user demanded cache allocation based on the page coloring technique. The page coloring technique was proposed for operating systems to reduce cache misses through careful mapping between virtual pages and physical pages for single-core [9] and multicore processors [15]. The logic of the page coloring technique is shown in Figure 2. Memory management in operating systems uses the most significant bits of a physical address as the physical page number. When the address is used in a cache lookup operation, some bits in the middle of the address (*cache set index* in the figure) are used to determine the cache set to look up. There are several common bits between the cache set index and the physical page number. These bits are referred to as page color. The page coloring technique assigns a page color to every physical page and cache set. Thus, it divides a cache into multiple non-overlapping bins (denoted as cache colors) and separates physical pages into disjoint groups based on their colors. Each cache color or physical page group corresponds to a page color, and the physical pages in the same color are mapped to the cache sets in the same color. By manipulating the mapping between virtual pages and physical pages, the page coloring technique can control how the data sets in application virtual spaces are mapped to cache sets, i.e. how the cache space is allocated among the data sets. In the above example, a ULCC supported program changes the layout of its data on physical space, such that threads sharing the same L2 cache visit data on physical pages in different colors, and physical pages for blocks and physical pages for sorting buffers are in different colors.

3. Overall Structure and Design of ULCC

ULCC first provides application programmers with an easy-to-use interface to specify how cache space should be allocated among their data sets for efficient use of the last level caches on multicores. Then, in the execution of a program, it enforces a cache space allocation by changing the mapping between virtual pages of the program and physical pages. In this section, we explain how ULCC achieves these objectives. We first introduce the general structure of ULCC. Then we describe its interface and key components.

As shown in Figure 3, in the top layer of ULCC is a set of library functions for programmers to specify desired cache space allocation. We will introduce how an application uses these functions in

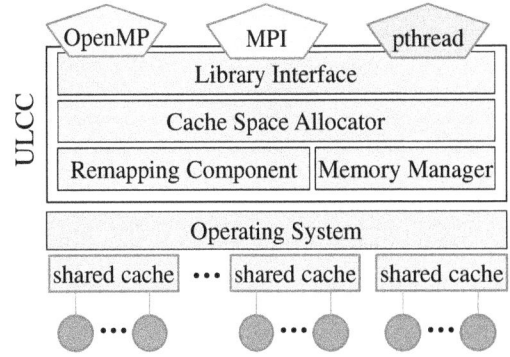

Figure 3. The overall structure of ULCC

Section 3.1. The *Cache Space Allocator* (Section 3.2) in the middle layer manages and selects cache colors in the shared caches on a multicore platform to make cache space allocation more efficient. Actual cache space allocation is realized by the *Remapping Component*, which allocates physical pages in the colors selected by the *Cache Space Allocator* and remaps virtual pages over to these physical pages. We will describe this component in Section 3.3. The last component, *Memory Manager* (Section 3.4) reduces the overhead incurred by allocating pages in desired colors. It pre-allocates, manages, and garbage collects physical pages in different colors. When some physical pages in specific colors are required by the *Remapping Component*, the *Memory Manager* can check the physical pages it manages and release the physical pages in the desired colors to satisfy the requirements quickly.

3.1 Interface

ULCC provides a number of functions as its interface. With these functions, an application can affect cache space allocation by first defining some cache space slots and then specifying the mapping between data sets and cache slots (i.e. which data set will use which cache slot). To effectively allocate last level cache space among its data sets, the application should specify the cache usage for the data sets in its major data structures (e.g. data sets that account for most accesses). The ULCC interface designs the functions using the following rules.

- ULCC hides most of the complexity of the cache structure on a multicore architecture.

Based on this rule, ULCC allows an application to describe its desired cache allocation in a general way without dealing with machine-dependent details, such as cache colors, associativity, or which cores share the same last level cache. There are three reasons for using this rule: i) Letting programmers explicitly deal with those structural factors unnecessarily increases their burden because the cache structure can be complex on a platform with multiple processors. ii) This rule provides underlying components with more opportunities and space for performance optimization. For example, without specifying cache colors in the program, the *Cache Space Allocator* can have multiple choices on cache colors and choose the ones that can achieve better performance. iii) An application may run on different platforms. Even on the same platform, the amount of available resources for the application may vary across different runs. For example, on a computer with four dual-core processors (each with a shared last level cache), a four-thread application may use two processors or four processors in different runs. Hiding detailed cache structure decouples the application implementation from hardware architecture or configuration variations. Thus application programs can be highly portable.

- The interface allows programs to pass necessary information for underlying components to allocate cache space efficiently. For example, when ULCC allocates cache space for a data set, it needs to know which threads will access the data set so that it only allocates cache space on the processors running the threads.

- The interface needs to maintain high flexibility for a program to describe how cache space will be allocated among its data sets. Through the interface, a program makes cache space requests, such as how much cache space a data set can use, which data sets can share the same cache space slot and which cannot.

```
/****** MASTER THREAD ********/
...
ULCC_Init(Num_Processors);
/*Available cache space size in KB for the application*/
Space_Avail_App=ULCC_Available_Space_App();
/*Cache space in KB for each thread on average*/
Average_Space=Space_Avail_App/Num_Threads;
...
fork slave threads;
wait for slave threads to complete;
ULCC_Exit();
...
/****** SLAVE THREAD ******/
/*Define a cache space slot*/
Cache_Slot_ID = ULCC_Cache_Slot(Average_Space, private);
/*Define a set of threads*/
TG = ULCC_Thread_Group(NULL, My_Thread_ID);
/*Create a data set to use the cache space slot*/
Data_Set = ULCC_Data_Set(TG);
/*Include data in address ranges from Addr1
to Addr2 and from Addr3 and Addr4 into data set*/
ULCC_More_Data(Data_Set, Addr1, Addr2);
ULCC_More_Data(Data_Set, Addr3, Addr4);
/*Do the actual cache space allocation on the processor
that the thread runs on */
ULCC_Allocate(Data_Set, Cache_Slot_ID);
...
```

Figure 4. An example illustrating ULCC function usages

We use Figure 4 to illustrate how a program specifies the desired cache allocation with ULCC functions. The program creates a master thread and a number of slave threads. With ULCC functions, the program evenly partitions the available last level cache space among the slave threads, and in each slave thread it remaps the data set accessed by the thread to the corresponding partition to avoid inter-thread interference in shared caches.

As shown in the *MASTER THREAD* part, the program initiates ULCC by specifying the number of processors the application will run on. The *ULCC_Init* function initializes the ULCC data structures for the application and makes connection to the *Memory Manager*. Then the program gets the size of the available cache space the application can use by calling *ULCC_Available_Space_App*, which calculates the size based on the cache structure of the target platform and the number of processors the application uses. After that, the program calculates the size of the cache space that each slave thread can use.

In the *SLAVE THREAD* part, to allocate cache space, a thread first calls *ULCC_Cache_Slot* to define a cache space slot by specifying the properties of the slot, including the size and whether it is "private" or "shared". "Private" slot is usually for strong locality data. The slot is dedicated to the data sets that are associated with it by the program calling *ULCC_Allocate* with its slot ID (*Cache_Slot_ID* returned by the *ULCC_Cache_Slot* function). When the slot is shared by multiple data sets with strong localities (by calling *ULCC_Allocate* multiple times with the same *Cache_Slot_ID*), the application should guarantee that the data sets time-share the slot without causing much contention (e.g. by visiting data set *A* and then visiting data set *B*). *Cache Space Allocator* in ULCC ensures that "private" cache slots are non-overlapping to

secure the cache space for the strong locality data sets. By contrast, a "shared" slot is for weak locality data, and ULCC tries to reuse the cache colors that are already allocated for other weak locality data to make full use of the space in last level caches, as we will explain in the next subsection.

After the cache slot is defined, the thread defines a data set to be mapped to the slot. To define a data set, the thread calls ULCC functions to provide information including which threads access the data set and which data are included in the data set. After that, the thread calls *ULCC_Allocate* to inform the *Cache Space Allocator* to allocate cache colors and *Remapping Component* to change physical pages holding the corresponding virtual pages. If the data set will be accessed by multiple threads (defined in the argument of *ULCC_Data_Set*), ULCC allocates cache space of the specified size on all the processors that the threads run on.

For streaming data with weak spacial locality and randomly-accessed data with weak temporal locality, loading them into caches on accesses causes cache pollution. Making these data non-cacheable can improve performance. Thus ULCC allows a program to mark a data set noncacheable by calling the *ULCC_Allocate* function with the second argument set to *NULL*.

3.2 Cache Space Allocator

The *Cache Space Allocator* (briefly *Allocator*) is in charge of managing cache colors. When an application requests some cache space for a data set, the *Allocator* decides which cache colors should be allocated to fulfill the request. The *Allocator* makes the decision in two steps. It first decides how many cache colors should be allocated on each shared cache in the first step. Then it decides which colors should be selected in the second step.

As we have explained in the previous subsection, a program does not prescribe specific colors when it requests cache space. Thus, the *Allocator* has opportunities to improve performance in both steps. In the first step, the *Allocator* aims to maximize cache space utilization and prevent space under-utilization. In the second step, the *Allocator* selects cache colors carefully to reduce the subsequent overhead incurred by ULCC enforcing the cache space allocation.

To efficiently manage and allocate cache colors, the *Allocator* maintains a data structure for bookkeeping the allocation of its colors, for each shared cache on a multicore platform. The data structure marks the status of a cache color to be either *unspecified*, *shared*, or *private*. The cache colors under *unspecified* status are not allocated yet. Cache colors under *shared* status are for weak locality data and can be shared by the weak locality data sets in different threads or even different applications. Because weak locality data lack reuses, the sharing will not cause pollution or contention. Instead, the sharing can minimize the cache space for weak locality, and thus can maximize the cache space for strong locality data to get better performance. The *private* status of cache colors means that the colors are reserved for the exclusive use of some strong locality data sets. Not sharing the colors secures the space for these data sets to avoid cache contention or pollution in these colors. The ULCC interface allows applications to use the "shared" or "private" flag in function *ULCC_Cache_Slot* to denote whether the cache space to be allocated is for weak locality data or strong locality data, and the *Allocator* sets the allocated cache colors accordingly.

In the first step, assuming a cache slot with size S is to be allocated to a data set with size S_d and the size of each cache color is S_c, the *Allocator* calculates the number of cache colors that should be allocated on a shared cache, which is S/S_c. To prevent under-utilization of cache space, it only allocates the colors in the shared caches on the cores that access the data set, based on the processor affinity information of the threads. For example, an application will allocate 256KB cache space for a data set. Each cache color is 64KB. If the data set will be accessed by four threads running on two dual-core processors (each with a shared cache), the *Allocator* decides that ULCC allocates 4 cache colors in each of the two shared caches.

If the cache space to be allocated is of "private" type, the *Allocator* continues with the second step to select cache colors. If the cache space to be allocated is of "shared" type, the *Allocator* examines the status of the cache colors in the shared caches. If there are already cache colors under the "shared" status, the *Allocator* will try to "reuse" these colors for the data set. Thus fewer cache colors can be allocated. In the above example, if the application specifies the 256KB cache space as "shared" and there is already a cache color in color 0 having been marked as "shared" in each shared cache, the ULCC reuses the cache color and allocates another 3 cache colors in each shared cache.

In the second step, the *Allocator* carefully selects colors to reduce the subsequent overhead incurred by ULCC enforcing the cache space allocation. To enforce the cache space allocation, the *Remapping Component* (to be discussed in section 3.3) needs to acquire physical pages in the selected colors and use these physical pages to hold the virtual pages of the designated data set. Acquiring the physical pages in a certain color may become more difficult and incur higher overhead when such physical pages become scarce in memory. Thus it is desirable that the *Allocator* carefully selects cache colors to minimize this overhead, especially when the data set is large.

To achieve this objective, ULCC maintains an array to record the number of physical pages in each color that are available in the *Memory Manager*. The array is shared by *Allocator* and *Memory Manager*. When a number of cache colors are to be allocated, the *Allocator* first calculates the average number (N) of physical pages that are needed in each color, which is $S_d \times S_c / S$. Then it searches the array and looks for the colors with more physical pages than N. The *Allocator* does not select colors with fewer physical pages than N. The reason is that if these colors are selected the *Memory Manager* would not satisfy the physical page allocation requirements with existing pre-allocated physical pages and it may take a long time or may even be impossible for the *Memory Manager* to acquire more physical pages. If the cache slot is "private", among the colors with more physical pages than N, the *Allocator* selects the noncontinuous colors (e.g. colors 0, 3, 7, 9, instead of colors 0, 1, 2, 3) with the fewest physical pages. The *Allocator* does not select colors with much more physical pages than N because the extra physical pages in these colors become underutilized if there are no other data sets being mapped to the colors. The reason why the *Allocator* chooses noncontinuous colors is to take advantage of the *Memory Manager* to accelerate physical page allocation as we will explain later.

3.3 Remapping Component

The *Remapping Component* adjusts the mappings between virtual pages and physical pages to implement actual cache space allocation. It first acquires physical pages in the desired colors corresponding to the allocated cache colors. Then it copies the data set to the newly acquired pages to prevent data loss if the data set has been initialized. Finally, it maps the virtual pages holding the data set to the newly acquired physical pages. To prevent page swapping from changing the physical pages used by the data set, ULCC locks these pages and makes them memory-resident.

To acquire the physical pages in desired colors, the *Remapping Component* first allocates a bunch of physical pages by *malloc*-ing some virtual memory space and writing a byte into each page in the space. Then the *Remapping Component* determines the physical page numbers and the colors of these pages. In the current ULCC

implementation under Linux, the *Remapping Component* determines the physical page number of a page through the *pagemap* interface, which allows an application to examine its page table at the user level. The color of a page is equal to the physical page number modulo the number of cache colors of a shared cache. In a system without *pagemap* support, e.g. FreeBSD, Solaris, or Windows, ULCC can use a kernel module or a pseudo-device driver carrying out virtual-to-physical address translation to get physical page numbers. After the *Remapping Component* has selected the pages in the desired colors, it releases unneeded physical pages.

To map the virtual pages holding a data set to the physical pages in the desired colors, the current ULCC implementation makes *mremap()* system calls in Linux system. System call *mremap()* expends or shrinks a memory space, or moves a memory space to another address by changing the mapping between virtual pages and physical pages. On the systems where *mremap()* is not available, ULCC changes the page mappings by creating a shared memory segment and remapping the virtual pages holding the data set to the physical pages in the shared memory segment with *mmap()* system calls. After the virtual pages holding the data set have been remapped over to the physical pages, subsequent accesses to the data set will only use the cache space in the desired colors.

3.4 Memory Manager

The *Memory Manager* is a stand-alone process, independent of the applications using ULCC. It pre-allocates, manages, and garbage-collects physical pages to facilitate the allocation of physical pages in the colors required by the *Remapping Component*.

The *Memory Manager* is started as a system service before users run any ULCC-supported applications. When it is started, it first acquires a number of physical pages (e.g. 1/2 of the available physical pages on the system). It organizes the pages into different lists based on their colors, with pages in the same color on the same list. When a ULCC-supported application requires physical pages in specific colors, it notifies the *Memory Manager*. The *Memory Manager* releases some of the physical pages it manages that are in required colors to satisfy the application. Because the *Allocator* usually allocates noncontinuous colors, the released pages are not continuous in physical memory space. Thus the buddy system managing free physical pages in OS kernel puts the physical pages at the head of the free list, which is the place the OS first tries to allocate physical pages from. This makes it much easier for the application to acquire the physical pages in the required colors. After the *Memory Manager* has released the physical pages, the application immediately begins requesting physical pages from the OS and quickly obtains the physical pages the *Memory Manager* just released to satisfy its requirements. ULCC maintains the information on the mappings between data sets and the cache colors. Thus when the memory space holding a data set is released, the ULCC also notifies the *Memory Manager* to garbage-collect the physical pages for future use.

The *Memory Manager* sleeps for most of the time, and is awakened occasionally when a ULCC-supported application requests or releases physical pages. The pages it manages are seldom accessed. To avoid OS page swapping removing these pages, the *Memory Manager* pins them into memory. However, this may increase the memory pressure on the system. To solve this problem, the *Memory Manager* periodically wakes up and checks the amount of free memory in the system. If the amount of free memory is below a threshold, it proactively releases a part of the memory it holds.

4. Experiments and Case Studies

In this section, we explore a few case studies and present the experiment results based on the ULCC implementation on a Linux system. We aim to answer the following questions specifically.

- **The usability of ULCC**: Is it easy for a programmer to determine desirable cache allocation based on data locality analysis? Can a programmer easily enforce the cache allocation with the support of ULCC?

- **The performance of ULCC**: How much performance improvement can an application achieve by using ULCC?

- **The overhead of ULCC**: How much overhead does ULCC incur?

4.1 Experiment Setup and Workloads

We carried out our experiments on a Dell PowerEdge 1900 workstation with two 2.66GHz quad-core Xeon X5355 processors. Each X5355 processor has two pairs of cores and cores in each pair share a 4MB, 16-way set associative L2 cache. Thus there are 64 cache colors in each shared L2 cache and each cache color corresponds to 64KB of cache space. Each core has a private 32KB L1 instruction cache and a private 32KB L1 data cache. Both adjacent-line prefetching and stride prefetching are enabled on the processors. The workstation has 16GB physical memory with eight 2GB dual-ranked Fully Buffered DIMMs (FB-DIMM). The operating system is 64-bit Red Hat Enterprise Linux AS release 5. The Linux kernel is 2.6.30. The compiler is gcc 4.1.2. The C language library is glibc 2.5. We used pfmon [6] to collect performance statistics such as L2 cache misses.

As case studies, we selected two computational kernels (*MergeSort* [13] and *MatMul* [12]) implemented with pthread and two scientific programs (*CG* and *LU*) from an OpenMP implementation of NAS benchmarks [1]. The *MergeSort* is described in Section 2. The *MatMul* implements a matrix multiplication algorithm similar to that described in paper [12] but with multiple threads. Each program has two implementations. One is the original program that is designed to optimize cache performance for single-core systems with techniques such as blocking and padding. The other is the improved program with ULCC support to reduce cache contention and pollution for its execution on multicore systems. We run each program four times with one thread, two threads, four threads, and eight threads, respectively. Because we were targeting the performance of shared last level caches, for two-thread executions, we used two cores sharing the same L2 cache, and for four-thread executions, we used a pair of cores sharing the same L2 cache on each processor. In each program, we used *sched_setaffinity* to pin each thread to a computing core.

4.2 Case Studies

In this section, we use several case studies to illustrate how programmers identify data sets with different localities, determine desired cache space, and use ULCC to enforce cache allocation. We show the performance improvements for both single-thread executions and executions with multiple threads of the selected programs.

- **MergeSort**

In the experiment, we used the program to sort ten million data elements in an array. Each data element has an integer key and a 56-byte content. To avoid severe cache contention, we selected the block size such that the total size of a block and a sorting buffer was equal to the L2 cache size in single-thread execution and equal to half of the L2 cache size in executions with multiple threads.

The major data structures in the program include the original array to be sorted, sorting buffers, the binary trees used by multiway merging, and the destination array to save final results. Among them, the original array is divided into blocks and data elements in each block are accessed multiple times before they are sorted. Elements in a sorting buffer are accessed multiple times when the program sorts each block until all the blocks have been sorted in each bucket. Nodes in a binary tree are repeatedly used in each

multi-way merging. Data sets in these data structures have strong localities. Each element in the destination array is written only once. Thus, the destination array has weak locality. After a block has been sorted, the elements in it are accessed for only one more time in the multi-way merging. Thus elements in it become weak locality data.

To avoid cache contention and cache pollution, the program can protect strong locality data structures with ULCC by securing sufficient cache space for them. Specifically, for the single-thread execution, the program allocates half of the L2 cache space to the original array (i.e. the blocks) and the other half of the L2 cache space to the sorting buffer. When the program is doing multiway merge, both the original array and destination array have weak locality. Thus they can share the cache space allocated to the original array. Though the binary tree has strong locality, the program lets it share the cache space with the sorting buffer because they are accessed in different execution phases and do not compete with each other for cache space. Similarly, in the execution with multiple threads, for each thread, the program allocates 1/4 of an L2 cache space to the buckets sorted by the thread and the part of destination array saving its sorting results, and allocates another 1/4 of an L2 cache space to the sorting buffer and the binary tree used by the thread.

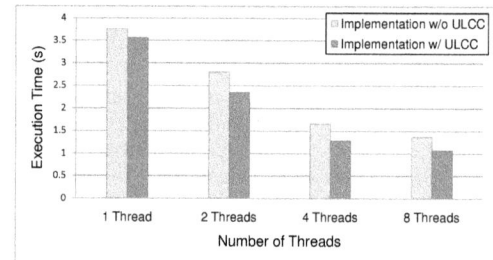

Figure 5. The execution times of *MergeSort* implementations with and without ULCC as the number of threads is varied from one to eight.

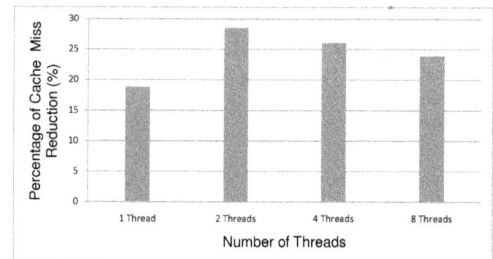

Figure 6. The percentages of miss reduction of *MergeSort* with ULCC enforcing the desired cache allocation.

For this program, we show the execution times[1] for both its implementations with and without ULCC in Figure 5 where we vary the number of threads from one to eight. In Figure 6, we show what percentage of L2 cache misses can be reduced by enforcing the above cache allocation. The figures clearly show the effectiveness of delicate user-controlled cache space allocation with ULCC. Even one thread on a single processor can still get performance improvement (execution time reduced by 5.4%) through reducing

---

[1] We only consider the time spent on sorting the data elements. Thus the time spent on initializing the data array is not included.

L2 cache misses with ULCC optimizing the cache space allocation among its data structures. The reason is that even with a single thread in the program, switching blocks would also evict part of the space previously occupied by the sorting buffer from the L2 cache if the program does not use ULCC to separate the cache space for the original array and the cache space for the sorting buffer. With more threads in the same execution, due to the cache sharing, cache contention and cache pollution further degrades performance. Thus, in these cases cache optimizations supported by ULCC achieve better performance. For example, ULCC reduces the execution time by 22.7% when four threads are used.

- **MatMul**

The *MatMul* program multiplies two double precision matrices A and B, and produces the product matrix C. The size of each matrix is 2048×2048. To achieve necessary data reuses in L2 caches, the matrix multiplication is carried out block by block. For the block a on the ith block row and jth block column of matrix A, it is multiplied with all the blocks on the jth block row of matrix B, and the results are accumulated into the blocks on the ith block row of matrix C. Before the program finishes the computation with block a, it is desirable that the data in a can be kept in the cache. However, without a dedicated space for block a, the data in it may be repeatedly evicted from the cache before its next use every time the program switches blocks in matrix B and matrix C, even with a rather small block size. To reduce the chance that the data in each block of matrix A is evicted from the last level cache prematurely, we set the block size to 360×360 (about 1MB) for the single-thread executions and 256×256 (512KB) for other executions.

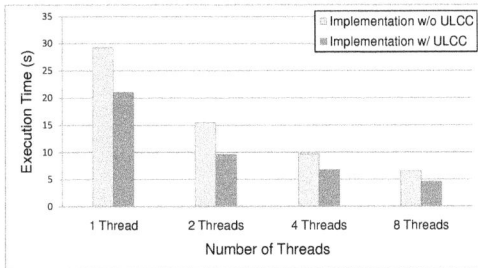

Figure 7. The execution times of *MatMul* implementations with and without ULCC as the number of threads is varied from one to eight.

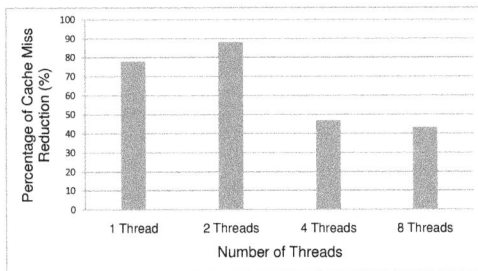

Figure 8. The percentages of miss reduction of *MatMul* with ULCC enforcing the desired cache allocation.

Figure 7 compares the execution times of the original implementation and the implementation that allocates dedicated cache space for the blocks in A leveraging the ULCC support. Though the block size is much smaller than the L2 cache size, the extra cache misses caused by data in blocks of matrix A being evicted from L2 caches can still degrade the performance of *MatMul* by over 30%. With ULCC, the program allocates a 1MB cache space to matrix A,

and allocates the remaining cache space to matrices B and C, for the single-thread execution. In the cases with multi-thread executions, for each thread, the program allocates a 512KB cache space to the part of matrix A it uses. The remaining cache space is shared by matrices B and C. With the dedicated cache space, each block in A is protected after it is loaded into an L2 cache. This significantly reduces L2 cache misses, as shown in Figure 8, and avoids performance degradation.

- **NAS LU**

NAS LU benchmark uses symmetric successive over-relaxation (SSOR) to solve a block lower triangular-block upper triangular system resulting from an unfactored implicit finite-difference discretization of the Navier-Stokes equations in three dimensions by splitting it into block lower and upper triangular systems. In the experiments, we run the benchmark with input class A.

Among the major data structures of the application, the data structures for the three dimensional field variables and residuals (arrays *frct*, *flux*, *u*, and *rsd*) have weak locality. They are referenced with a looping access pattern, and their sizes far exceed the L2 cache size. In each time-step iteration, they are accessed only a few times. By contrast, arrays a, b, c, and d have strong locality. Their sizes are relatively small and fit into an L2 cache. In each time-step iteration, they are repeatedly accessed multiple times for each z plane. Accessing the data structures for the field variables and the residuals causes cache pollution because it flushes the data in arrays a, b, c, and d from L2 caches. To avoid cache pollution, with ULCC, the program allocates dedicated L2 cache space to arrays a, b, c, and d. This also keeps the arrays away from interference incurred by the application accessing other data structures.

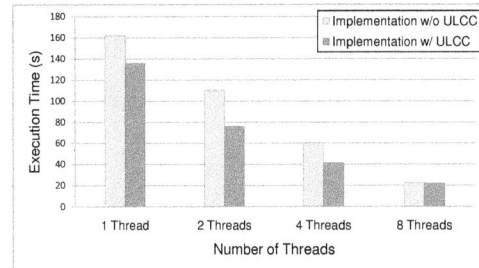

Figure 9. The execution times of *LU* implementations with and without ULCC as the number of threads is varied from one to eight.

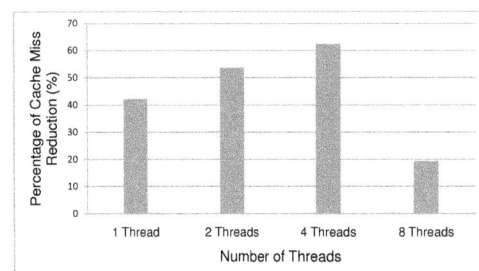

Figure 10. The percentages of miss reduction for *LU* with ULCC enforcing the desired cache allocation.

Figure 9 shows the execution times for the implementation without ULCC and the implementation with ULCC as the number of threads is varied from one to eight. Figure 10 shows the percentages of L2 cache miss reduction through the cache optimization. For the execution with two threads and the execution with four threads, the cache optimization supported by ULCC reduces L2 cache misses by 54% and 62% respectively, and reduces the execution times by 31% and 32% respectively.

For the execution with eight threads, cache optimization cannot achieve as much performance improvement as it does for the executions with fewer threads. This is because arrays a, b, c, and d are split among the threads in LU, and each thread only accesses a portion of elements in each array. In the eight-thread execution, each thread accesses a smaller portion of the data in these arrays than it does in the executions with fewer threads. Consequently, data elements in these arrays become less likely to be evicted from L2 caches by the accesses to weak locality data sets in the eight-thread execution than they do in the executions with fewer threads.

For single-thread execution, the cache optimization helps to reduce the execution time by 16%, which is less than that of the execution with two threads. This is because cache pollution with a single thread is not as intensive as that with two threads sharing the same L2 cache.

- **NAS CG**

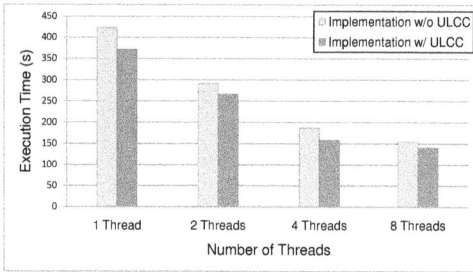

Figure 11. The execution times of CG implementations with and without ULCC as the number of threads is varied from one to eight.

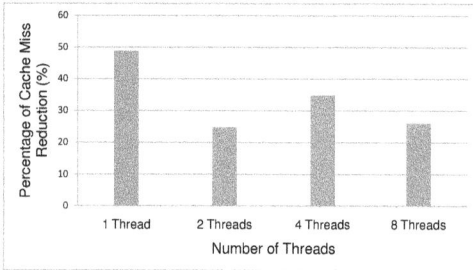

Figure 12. The percentages of miss reduction for CG program with ULCC enforcing the desired cache allocation.

The CG benchmark spends most of its execution time on multiplying a sparse matrix and a dense vector. The non-zero elements in the matrix are stored in array a, and the vector is stored in array p. The program uses another array $colidx$ to hold the column indexes for the non-zero elements in the matrix. Thus, for each element $a[k]$ in a, there is an element $colidx[k]$ in $colidx$ storing its column number in the matrix.

When the program calculates the product vector, for each non-zero element $a[k]$ in the matrix, the program visits array $colidx$ to get the column index $colidx[k]$ of the element, and multiplies $a[k]$ with the $colidx[k]$-th element in the vector, i.e. $p[colidx[k]]$. Thus, during the matrix-vector multiplication, elements in a and $colidx$ are visited only once. However, elements in p are repeatedly visited because the matrix have multiple rows. Obviously, a and $colidx$ are weak locality data structures, and p is a strong locality data structure.

The implementation with ULCC limits the cache space for a and $colidx$ by allocating only a minimum number of cache colors

to these arrays. Thus accessing these arrays will not evict the data in array p from L2 caches. As shown in Figure 11 and Figure 12, the above cache optimization reduces L2 cache misses by 25% to 50%, and reduces the execution times by 8% to 16% accordingly (input class is C). Among the executions with different number of threads, cache optimization reduces the number of cache misses in the single-thread execution by the largest percentage, but it cannot reduce the execution time by the largest percentage. This is because in a single-thread execution the L2 cache space is dedicated to one thread. Thus the miss rate of a single-thread execution is lower than that of multi-thread executions, and reducing cache misses does not have as much impact on execution time as it does for multi-thread executions.

4.3 Experiments to Measure Overhead

To optimize cache performance with ULCC support, an application has to pay some overhead for acquiring physical pages in desired colors, copying data, and changing the mapping between virtual pages and physical pages. In this subsection, we measure the overhead. We show that with the *Memory Manager*, the overhead can be significantly reduced to a level comparable to that of memory allocation, which is negligible for scientific applications.

We used a micro-benchmark to measure the overhead. The benchmark allocates a cache slot to a 32MB data set with ULCC functions and measures the time. We run the benchmark multiple times, each time with a different cache slot size selected from 64KB to 2MB. Figure 13 shows the times measured with the benchmark. To highlight the benefit of using *Memory Manager*, we show the times for the ULCC implementations with and without *Memory Manager*.

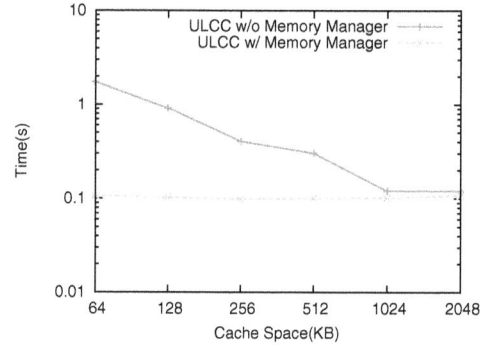

Figure 13. The overhead of ULCC implementations with and without *Memory Manager*. Both axises are in log scale.

As Figure 13 shows, without *Memory Manager*, ULCC may incur some overhead that is non-negligible for short-running applications. For example, it takes nearly 2 seconds to allocate a 64KB cache space to the 32MB data set. The main reason is that without the *Memory Manager*, the *Remapping Component* must spend long time to acquire a large number of physical pages, from which it selects physical pages in the required colors to finish remapping. For example, when ULCC allocates 64KB cache space in a selected cache color for the data set, it needs to acquire and examine $32MB \times 64 = 2GB$ of physical memory (64 is the total number of cache colors in a shared L2 cache) on average to fulfill its requirements (i.e. 32MB physical memory in the selected color). According to our measurement, acquiring 2GB physical memory takes about 1.6 seconds, while copying the data set into the selected 32MB physical space takes only 0.02 second and adjusting the mapping between the corresponding virtual pages and the physical pages takes only 0.03 second. Fewer physical pages are needed when the benchmark allocates larger cache space to the same data set. For example, if 512KB cache space (corresponding to 8 cache colors) is being allocated to the data set, only 256MB physical memory on average is needed to get 32MB physical memory in the required colors. which takes much less time. Thus, a trend we have observed is that the time spent on allocating cache space for the data set decreases significantly when the size of the cache space increases.

The *Memory Manager* can reduce overhead significantly, especially when the size of the allocated cache space is small. The reason is that with *Memory Manager*, a ULCC-supported application does not need to acquire so much physical memory to obtain enough physical pages in desired colors. With the pre-allocated physical pages and the knowledge of their colors, the *Memory Manager* can "pass" physical pages in the required colors to the *Remapping Component* without the overhead incurred by acquiring extra physical pages. With the *Memory Manager*, the *Remapping Component* can also reduce the overhead incurred by page remapping. Without *Memory Manager*, the physical pages are mapped one by one to the virtual space of the data set, and mapping each physical page requires a *mremap()* call. By contrast, with the *Memory Manager*, most physical pages obtained by the *Remapping Component* are continuous in virtual space. The physical pages continuous in virtual space can be mapped together with one *mremap* call.

To compare ULCC with the design from direct OS kernel support, we also modified the Linux kernel to allocate free physical pages in the colors required by user level applications. We found that ULCC with *Memory Manager* incurs comparable overhead to that of OS kernel support. The overhead is also comparable to that of allocating physical pages regardless of their colors and copying the data set to the newly allocated pages. For example, it takes ULCC 0.1 second to allocate 256KB cache space to a 32MB data set, while it takes Linux operating system 0.03 second to allocate 32MB memory regardless of page colors, and it takes 0.02 second to copy 32MB data to the newly allocated memory space. These experiments show that the overhead incurred by ULCC is reasonable, especially for scientific applications whose execution times are usually long.

In most cases, a programmer can specify the desired cache allocation at the beginning of the program when the data structures in the program have not been initialized or allocated with physical space. Thus when the program allocates cache space to the data structures, there is no need to copy any data over to the newly allocated physical space. At the same time, because the physical space for the data structures has been allocated by ULCC, there is no need for OS to allocate physical space when the data structures are being initialized. Thus ULCC incurs much less overhead in these cases.

5. Related Work

Our work is related to the following research areas: cache conscious program design and library design to improve the productivity of parallel programming and efficiency of parallel programs, cache partitioning to provide each of the running threads with a chunk of dedicated cache space to avoid interference from other co-running threads, and sophisticated scheduling policies for multicore or SMT (Simultaneous MultiThreading) processors to co-schedule threads that can efficiently use the shared resources in multicore/SMT processors.

5.1 Cache Conscious Program Design and Library Design

As a major method to improve application performance in high performance computing, restructuring algorithms and programs to make an efficient use of CPU caches has been intensively studied [5, 12, 20, 28, 30, 32]. Common techniques exploit data access locality by rearranging computing operations to improve temporal locality, such as strip mining [28], loop interchange, blocking [12], or reorganizing data layout for better spacial locality [5]. Libraries that implement dense linear algebra operations in a cache conscious way, such as BLAS [3], LAPACK [2], and ATLAS [29], have been extensively used for performance programming.

However, the approaches above are designed for single-core systems, and cannot address the cache contention and pollution problems in shared caches on multicore processors. Addressing these problems requires a high degree of synergy between the programs themselves and different system components. ULCC provides programmers with an easy-to-use interface to address the problems effectively, while it hides and takes over the tasks of dealing with complex structures and operations from the users.

There are other libraries or runtime systems that facilitate parallel programming, such as PVM and MPI. However, they don't handle cache optimizations. ULCC can be an important supplement to them.

5.2 Cache Partitioning

Cache partitioning has been confirmed to be an effective approach to address cache contention and pollution problems. Various hardware cache partitioning solutions have been proposed, which allocate a chunk of dedicated cache space (partition) for each running thread and dynamically adjust the sizes of the partitions according to the cache requirements of the threads [10, 17, 21, 24]. Due to the extra complexity and chip overhead to implement cache partitioning in hardware, hardware supported cache partitioning has not been available in commercial multicore processors. Thus several studies use software approaches to separate the cache space used by different running threads with the page coloring technique in operating systems [14–16, 25, 34]. Recent research results have confirmed that separating cache space used by data with different localities reduces cache misses because it avoids cache pollution incurred by weak locality data [18, 23].

However, there are no facilities for programmers to use to control directly the cache space allocation among the data structures in a program. Existing work focuses on automatically detecting access patterns with profiling or with hardware support, and lacks enough flexibility needed by programmers to leverage their insightful understanding of the program to enforce the cache allocation they desire. In addition, existing work focuses on single node system and relies on heavy modification of operating system key components. Their solutions cannot be portably used in existing high performance computing environments. Thus a portable and flexible facility like ULCC addresses this concern to enable programmers to exploit fully the benefits from optimizing cache space allocation.

5.3 Multicore/SMT-aware Scheduling

Threads co-running on an SMT or a multicore processor share and compete for the shared resources on the processor such as functional units, shared caches, and memory bus. How the shared resources can be efficiently used becomes a critical issue. As one of the major approaches to address this issue, scheduling has been focused on by a large number of papers [4, 7, 11, 22, 26, 35].

These papers focus on general systems such as desktop systems and server systems where scheduling plays an important role. However, scientific applications usually require only basic scheduling functions, and in most cases, for better performance scientific applications statically map threads to computing cores by setting their affinities.

6. Conclusion

We have proposed and implemented a user level facility called ULCC that enables programmers to control explicitly cache space allocation among the data structures in their programs to maximize the utilization of shared last level caches on multicore processors by reducing cache pollution and cache contention. ULCC provides an easy-to-use interface for programmers to specify the desired cache allocation without having efforts to deal with complex structures and operations in the memory hierarchies on the systems with multiple multicore processors. In ULCC, the *Cache Space Allocator* efficiently allocates cache colors to fulfill the requirements of a program. The *Remapping Component* enforces the desired cache space allocation by adjusting the mapping between virtual pages and physical pages with existing operating system support. Thus ULCC does not require modifications in operating system kernels. To minimize the overhead of ULCC, the *Memory Manager* preallocates, manages, and garbage-collects physical pages, so that the *Remapping Component* can acquire physical pages in desired colors and adjust the mappings quickly.

The benefits to users for achieving high performance and high throughputs may come from ULCC in two ways. First, ULCC-based programming secures sufficient cache space for data structures with strong locality, and limits cache space for data structures with weak locality. Second, ULCC can further help users to adjust block sizes to maximize throughputs. Our experiments have shown the effectiveness of ULCC with various applications. We will further refine and optimize ULCC for its wide usage in application communities.

7. Acknowledgments

The authors thank the anonymous reviewers for their constructive comments and suggestions. They thank Bill Bynum for reading the paper and for his suggestions. They also thank Hao Wang, Feng Chen, and Rubao Lee for helpful discussion. This research was supported by National Science Foundation under grants CNS0834393 and CCF0913150.

References

[1] NAS parallel benchmarks in OpenMP. URL http://phase.hpcc.jp/Omni/benchmarks/NPB/index.html.

[2] E. Anderson, Z. Bai, J. Dongarra, A. Greenbaum, A. McKenney, J. Du Croz, S. Hammerling, J. Demmel, C. Bischof, and D. Sorensen. LAPACK: A portable linear algebra library for high-performance computers. In *SC '90*, pages 2–11, 1990.

[3] L. S. Blackford, J. Demmel, J. Dongarra, I. Duff, S. Hammarling, G. Henry, M. Heroux, L. Kaufman, A. Lumsdaine, A. Petitet, R. Pozo, K. Remington, and R. C. Whaley. An updated set of basic linear algebra subprograms (blas). *ACM Trans. Math. Softw.*, 28(2):135–151, 2002.

[4] S. Chen, P. B. Gibbons, M. Kozuch, V. Liaskovitis, A. Ailamaki, G. E. Blelloch, B. Falsafi, L. Fix, N. Hardavellas, T. C. Mowry, and C. Wilkerson. Scheduling threads for constructive cache sharing on CMPs. In *SPAA'07*, pages 105–115, 2007.

[5] T. M. Chilimbi, M. D. Hill, and J. R. Larus. Cache-conscious structure layout. In *PLDI '99*, pages 1–12, 1999.

[6] HP Corp. Perfmon project. URL http://www.hpl.hp.com/research/linux/perfmon.

[7] Y. Jiang, X. Shen, J. Chen, and R. Tripathi. Analysis and approximation of optimal co-scheduling on chip multiprocessors. In *PACT'08*, pages 220–229, 2008.

[8] D. Kang. Dynamic data layouts for cache-conscious factorization of DFT. In *IPDPS '00*, page 693, 2000.

[9] R. E. Kessler and M. D. Hill. Page placement algorithms for large real-indexed caches. *ACM Trans. Comput. Syst.*, 10(4), 1992.

[10] S. Kim, D. Chandra, and Y. Solihin. Fair cache sharing and partitioning in a chip multiprocessor architecture. In *PACT'04*, pages 111–122, 2004.

[11] R. Knauerhase, P. Brett, B. Hohlt, T. Li, and S. Hahn. Using OS observations to improve performance in multicore systems. *IEEE Micro*, 28(3):54–66, 2008.

[12] M. D. Lam, E. E. Rothberg, and M. E. Wolf. The cache performance and optimizations of blocked algorithms. In *ASPLOS '91*, pages 63–74, 1991.

[13] A. LaMarca and R. E. Ladner. The influence of caches on the performance of sorting. In *SODA '97*, pages 370–379.

[14] R. Lee, X. Ding, F. Chen, Q. Lu, and X. Zhang. MCC-DB: minimizing cache conflicts in muli-core processors for databases. In *VLDB'09*.

[15] J. Lin, Q. Lu, X. Ding, Z. Zhang, X. Zhang, and P. Sadayappan. Gaining insights into multicore cache partitioning: Bridging the gap between simulation and real systems. In *HPCA '08*, pages 367–378, Salt Lake City, UT, 2008.

[16] J. Lin, Q. Lu, X. Ding, Z. Zhang, X. Zhang, and P. Sadayappan. Enabling software multicore cache management with lightweight hardware support. In *SC'09*, 2009.

[17] C. Liu, A. Sivasubramaniam, and M. Kandemir. Organizing the last line of defense before hitting the memory wall for CMPs. In *HPCA'04*, pages 176–185, 2004.

[18] Q. Lu, J. Lin, X. Ding, Z. Zhang, X. Zhang, and P. Sadayappan. Soft-OLP: Improving hardware cache performance through software-controlled object-level partitioning. In *PACT '09*, pages 246–257, 2009.

[19] S. K. Moore. Multicore is bad news for supercomputers. pages 213–226, 2008.

[20] M. Penner and V. K. Prasanna. Cache-friendly implementations of transitive closure. In *PACT '01*, page 185, Barcelona, Spain, 2001.

[21] M. K. Qureshi and Y. N. Patt. Utility-based cache partitioning: A low-overhead, high-performance, runtime mechanism to partition shared caches. In *MICRO'06*, pages 423–432, 2006.

[22] A. Snavely, D. M. Tullsen, and G. Voelker. Symbiotic jobscheduling with priorities for a simultaneous multithreading processor. In *SIGMETRICS'02*, pages 66–76.

[23] L. Soares, D. Tam, and M. Stumm. Reducing the harmful effects of last-level cache polluters with an OS-level, software-only pollute buffer. In *MICRO '08*, pages 258–269, 2008.

[24] G. E. Suh, L. Rudolph, and S. Devadas. Dynamic partitioning of shared cache memory. *J. Supercomputing*, 28(1), 2002.

[25] D. Tam, R. Azimi, L. Soares, and M. Stumm. Managing shared l2 caches on multicore systems in software. In *WIOSCA '07*, 2007.

[26] D. Tam, R. Azimi, and M. Stumm. Thread clustering: sharing-aware scheduling on SMP-CMP-SMT multiprocessors. In *EuroSys'07*, pages 47–58, 2007.

[27] TOP500.Org. URL http://www.top500.org/lists/2010/06.

[28] A. Wakatani and M. Wolfe. A new approach to array redistribution: Strip mining redistribution. In *PARLE '94*, pages 323–335, 1994.

[29] R. C. Whaley and J. Dongarra. Automatically tuned linear algebra software. In *SC '98*, 1998.

[30] M. Wolfe. Iteration space tiling for memory hierarchies. In *PP '89*, pages 357–361, Philadelphia, PA, 1989.

[31] M. Wolfe. More iteration space tiling. In *SC '89*, pages 655–664, 1989.

[32] L. Xiao, X. Zhang, and S. A. Kubricht. Improving memory performance of sorting algorithms. *ACM J. Exp. Algorithmics*, 5:2000, 2000.

[33] K. Yotov, T. Roeder, K. Pingali, J. Gunnels, and F. Gustavson. An experimental comparison of cache-oblivious and cache-conscious programs. In *SPAA '07*, pages 93–104, 2007.

[34] X. Zhang, S. Dwarkadas, and K. Shen. Towards practical page coloring-based multicore cache management. In *EuroSys'09*, pages 89–102, 2009.

[35] S. Zhuravlev, S. Blagodurov, and A. Fedorova. Addressing shared resource contention in multicore processors via scheduling. In *ASPLOS '10*, pages 129–142, 2010.

ScalaExtrap: Trace-Based Communication Extrapolation for SPMD Programs *

Xing Wu

North Carolina State University
xwu3@ncsu.edu

Frank Mueller

North Carolina State University
mueller@cs.ncsu.edu

Abstract

Performance modeling for scientific applications is important for assessing potential application performance and systems procurement in high-performance computing (HPC). Recent progress on communication tracing opens up novel opportunities for communication modeling due to its lossless yet scalable trace collection. Estimating the impact of scaling on communication efficiency still remains non-trivial due to execution-time variations and exposure to hardware and software artifacts.

This work contributes a fundamentally novel modeling scheme. We synthetically generate the application trace for large numbers of nodes by extrapolation from a set of smaller traces. We devise an innovative approach for topology extrapolation of single program, multiple data (SPMD) codes with stencil or mesh communication. The extrapolated trace can subsequently be (a) replayed to assess communication requirements before porting an application, (b) transformed to auto-generate communication benchmarks for various target platforms, and (c) analyzed to detect communication inefficiencies and scalability limitations.

To the best of our knowledge, rapidly obtaining the communication behavior of parallel applications at arbitrary scale with the availability of timed replay, yet without actual execution of the application at this scale is without precedence and has the potential to enable otherwise infeasible system simulation at the exascale level.

Categories and Subject Descriptors   D.1.3 [*Programming Techniques*]: Concurrent Programming—Parallel programming; D.4.8 [*Operating Systems*]: Performance—Modeling and prediction

General Terms   Measurement, Performance

Keywords   High-Performance Computing, Message Passing, Tracing, Performance Prediction

1. Introduction

Scalability is one of the main challenges for scientific applications in HPC. A host of automatic tools have been developed by both academia and industry to assist in communication gathering and analysis for MPI-style message passing [7]. Most of these tools either obtain lossless trace information at the price of poor scalability [13] or preserve only aggregated statistical trace information to limit the size of trace files as in mpiP [22]. Recent work on communication tracing and time recording made a breakthrough in this realm. ScalaTrace introduced an effective communication trace representation and compression algorithm [14]. It managed to preserve the structure and temporal ordering of events, yet maintains traces in a space-efficient representation. However, ScalaTrace needs to be linked to the original application and executed on a high-performance computing cluster of a *given number of compute nodes* to obtain a trace. Due to the often long application execution times and limited availability of cluster resources for large numbers of nodes, obtaining the trace information of a large-scale parallel application remains costly.

An alternative to obtaining communication traces is to model and predict application behavior [9, 10]. Generally, this approach takes a number of machine and application parameters as input. It utilizes a set of formulae to assess the impact of scaling on the system characteristics and predict performance in terms of wall-clock runtime of an application. Similarly, this approach provides only overall statistics for an application on a particular architecture. Without a detailed application trace, more sophisticated static analysis is impossible. In addition, measuring the system and application performance parameters is also non-trivial given the complexity of supercomputers and large-scale scientific applications.

Contributions: This paper contributes a set of algorithms and techniques to extrapolate full communication traces and execution times of an application at larger scale with information gathered from smaller executions. Since extrapolation is based on analytical processing of smaller traces with mathematical transformations, this approach can be performed on a single workstation, much in contrast to analysis or visualization of large traces in contemporary tools (*e.g.*, Vampir Next Generation [3]). It thus enables, for the first time, the instant generation of trace information of an application at arbitrary scale without necessitating time-consuming execution. Specifically, we extrapolate two aspects of the application behavior, namely the (1) communication trace events with parameters and (2) timing information resembling computation. The extrapolation of the communication trace is based on the observation that, in many regular SPMD stencil and mesh codes, communication parameters and communication groups are related to the sizes and dimensions of the communication topology. Thus, extrapolation of communication traces becomes feasible with the detection of communication topologies and the analysis of communication parameters to infer evolving patterns. The extrapolation of timing information involves a process of analytical modeling. In order to mitigate timing fluctuations under scaling, we employ statistical methods. Such extrapolations are facilitated by ScalaTrace's compression scheme that preserves application structure. In contrast, extrapolation with

---

* We would like to thank the Juelich Supercomputing Centre for giving us access to their Blue Gene/P system.

other trace formats, such as OTF [11], would be far more tedious and time/space consuming as structure is neither established across nodes nor retained after binary-level compression.

This trace extrapolation approach has been implemented in the ScalaExtrap tool, which we utilize to evaluate our extrapolation approach with a microbenchmark and several NAS Parallel Benchmark codes [1]. We utilize up to 16,384 nodes of a 73,728-node IBM Blue Gene/P supercomputer to generate communication traces for extrapolation and verification. Experiments were performed to assess both the correctness of communication extrapolation and the accuracy of the timing extrapolation. Experimental results demonstrate that our topology detection algorithm is capable of identifying and characterizing stencil/mesh and collective communication patterns. Upon topology detection, the communication trace extrapolation algorithm correctly extrapolates all communication events, parameters and communication groups at an arbitrary target size for both stencil/mesh point-to-point and collective communication. The experiments also demonstrate that the extrapolation of timing information resembles the running time of the original parallel application. Compared to the running time of the original application, the accuracy of replay times of the corresponding extrapolated trace is, in the majority of cases, higher than 90%, sometimes as high as 98%. Given the difficulty of extrapolating application execution time with only the time information obtained from several small executions, our approach achieves unprecedented accuracy that is sufficient for modeling, procurement and analysis tasks.

Overall, this work explores the potential to extrapolate communication behavior of parallel applications. Several novel algorithms for communication topology detection and communication trace extrapolation are introduced. Experimental results demonstrate that rapid generation of an application's trace information at arbitrary size is entirely possible, which is unprecedented. In contrast to tedious and application-centric model development, our approach opens new opportunities for automatically deriving communication models, facilitating communication analysis and tuning at any scale. Our work further enables system simulation at extreme scale based on a single file, concise communication trace representation. More specifically, HPC simulation tools (e.g., Dimemas or SST [12, 19, 21]), which currently cannot operate at petascale levels, could benefit by utilizing our extrapolated single-file traces that are just 10s of megabytes in size. Benchmark generation is important for cross-platform performance analysis due to its standard and portable source code and the platform-independent nature. Our work enables code generation at extreme scale by providing large traces that are otherwise unavailable. Furthermore, by contributing a set of detection techniques of communication patterns, our work has the potential to enable the generation of flexible and stand-alone programs that can be executed with arbitrary numbers of nodes and any possible input.

This paper is structured as follows. Section 2 summarizes related work on ScalaTrace with respect to its ability to support extrapolation. Section 3 provides a detailed introduction to the algorithms designed for extrapolation. Sections 4 and 5 present the experimental framework and results. Section 6 discusses the limitations of this work and uncovers future challenges. Section 7 contrasts this work with prior research. Section 8 summarizes this work.

2. Overview of ScalaTrace

Our work utilizes the publicly available ScalaTrace infrastructure [14]. ScalaTrace is an MPI trace-gathering framework that generates near constant-size communication traces for a parallel application regardless of the number of nodes while preserving structural information and temporal ordering. ScalaTrace utilizes the MPI profiling layer (PMPI) to intercept MPI calls of HPC programs. Extended regular section descriptors (RSDs) are used to record the parameters and information of a single MPI event nested in a loop. Power-RSDs (PRSDs) recursively specify RSDs nested in multiple loops. For example, for the 4-point stencil code shown in Figure 1, *RSD1: <MPI_Irecv, (NORTH, WEST, EAST, SOUTH)>* and *RSD2: <MPI_Isend, (NORTH, WEST, EAST, SOUTH)>* denote the alternating send/receive calls to/from the 4 neighbors, and *PRSD1: < 1000, RSD1, RSD2, MPI_Waitall>* denotes the a loop with 1000 iterations. In the loop's body, RSD1, RSD2, and a following MPI_Waitall are called sequentially. During application execution, ScalaTrace performs intra-node compression, which captures the loop structure on-the-fly and represents MPI events in such a compressed manner. Local traces are combined into a single global trace upon application completion, i.e., within the PMPI interposition wrapper for MPI_Finalize. The key approaches to achieve near-constant inter-node compression are the location-independent encoding and communication group encoding schemes detailed in the following.

```
neighbor[] = {NORTH, WEST, EAST, SOUTH};
for(i=0; i<1000; i++) {
    for(j=0; j<4; j++) {
        MPI_Irecv(neighbor[j]);
        MPI_Isend(neighbor[j]);
    }
    MPI_Waitall();
}
```

Figure 1. Sample Stencil Code for RSD and PRSD Generation

- *Location-independent encoding:* Communication end-points in SPMD programs differ from one node to another. By encoding endpoints *relative* to the index of an MPI task on a node, a location independent denotation is created that describes the behavior of large node sets. In a stencil/mesh topology, only few of such distinct sets/groups tend to exist. Location-independent encoding not only opens up opportunities for inter-node compression to unify endpoints across different computational nodes but also enables extrapolation.

- *Communication group encoding:* Similarity in communication patterns is recognized to succinctly denote sets/groups of nodes with common behavior. In a topological space, a communication group refers to a subset of nodes that have identical communication patterns. With this encoding scheme, a communication group is represented as a *rank list*. Using the EBNF metasyntax, a *rank list* is represented as $< dimension\ start\_rank\ iteration\_length\ stride\ \{iteration\_length\ stride\} >$, where $dimension$ is the dimension of the group, $start\_rank$ is the rank of the starting node, and the $iteration\_length\ stride$ pair is the iteration and stride of the corresponding dimension. As an example, consider the row-major grid topology in Figure 2. The shaded nodes form a communication group. This group is represented as *ranklist <2 6 3 5 3 1>*, where the tuple indicates that this communication group is a 2-dimensional area starting at node 6 with 3 iterations of stride 5 in the y-dimension and 3 iterations of stride 1 in the x-dimension, respectively. Since this encoding scheme takes node placement into account, it naturally reflects the spatial characteristics of a communication group.

We exploit these representations as a foundation for extrapolating communication topology.

Besides communication tracing, ScalaTrace also preserves the timing information of a parallel application in a scalable way [18]. Along with the intra-node and inter-node compression processes, "delta" times representing the computation between communication events are recorded and compressed. For the purpose of scala-

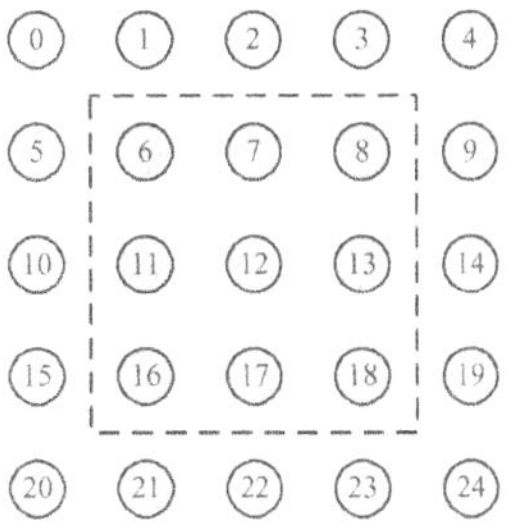

Figure 2. Ranklist Representation for Communication Group

bility, delta times of a single MPI function call across multiple loop iterations are not recorded one by one. Instead, histograms with a fixed number of bins for delta times are dynamically constructed to provide a statistical view. Delta times are distinguished by not only the call context of recorded events, but also by their path sequence, which addresses significant variation of delta times caused by path differences, *e.g.*, within entry/exit paths of a loop.

Finally, ScalaReplay is a replay engine operating on the application traces generated by ScalaTrace. It interprets the compressed application trace on-the-fly and issues MPI communication calls accordingly. During replay, all MPI calls are triggered over the same number of nodes with their original parameters (e.g., message payload size) but a randomly generated message content. This ensures comparable bandwidth requirements on communication interconnects. ScalaReplay emulates computation events in the original application by sleeping so that the communication contention characteristics are maintained during replay. In general, the replay engine can be utilized for rapid prototyping and tuning, as well as to assess communication needs of future platforms for large-scale procurements in conjunction with system simulators (Dimemas/SST) [12, 19, 21]. In this work, we use ScalaReplay to verify the correctness of extrapolation results, which will be discussed later in this paper.

3. Communication Extrapolation

This work focuses on the extrapolation of communication traces and execution times. The respective design is subsequently implemented in a novel tool, ScalaExtrap. The challenge of communication trace extrapolation is to determine how the communication parameters change with node and problem scaling. The main idea is to identify the relationship between communication parameters and the characteristics of the communication topology, *i.e.*, typically the sizes of each dimension. As a simple example, in Figure 2, assume *node 0* communicates with *node 4*, *i.e.*, a node at distance of 4. If we can identify that the topological communication space is a grid consisting of 25 nodes with 5 nodes per row, we know that *node 0* actually communicates with the upper-right node. Therefore, when there are 1024 = 32×32 nodes, we can safely infer that *node 0* communicates with *node 31*, which is still the upper-right node.

Characterizing a communication pattern from one or more traces is non-trivial nonetheless. Without the knowledge of a given node assignment scheme and topology, identifying the communication pattern provided by a trace file is equivalent to solving the graph isomorphism problem, which is known to be NP hard [24]. Therefore, instead of attempting to find a universal solution, we constrain our work to applications where

1. nodes are numbered in a row-major fashion and

2. communication is performed in stencil/mesh point-to-point manner or via collectives involving all MPI tasks.

In essence, our communication trace extrapolation algorithm first identifies the nodes at the "corner" of a topological space. It then

calculates the sizes of each dimension of the topological space accordingly. Upon acquiring the topology data, we represent the communication parameters, *e.g.*, the destination rank of MPI_Send, as a function of the known topology data and their undetermined coefficients. In order to calculate these coefficients, we correlate multiple traces and construct a set of linear equations. Finally, we employ Gaussian Elimination to solve the set of equations. With the fixed coefficients, we can extrapolate the value of the desired communication parameter by simply substituting the topology data with their values at the desired problem size. Since the set of linear equations is constructed with the matching values of a communication parameter across traces of different node sizes, we further assume that

1. target applications are SPMD programs and

2. communication traces are compressed perfectly at both intra-node level and inter-node level so that the traces obtained from different node sizes are structurally identical (which only becomes feasible due to ScalaTrace's structure-preserving trace compression).

The second aspect of this work concerns the extrapolation of program execution time. In the input trace files, computation time and communication time between (and optionally during) MPI communication events are preserved statistically with histograms. When analyzing the corresponding delta time, scaling trends can be identified across different number of nodes. Therefore, statistical curve fitting methods are utilized to model an evolving trend and extrapolate the execution time to a desired target size. In order to eliminate outliers, we further introduce several confidence coefficients to statistically determine the best extrapolated value under such constraints.

3.1 Topology Identification

Topology identification is the basis of communication trace extrapolation. In order to identify a topology, it is important to find the nodes at the corner or on the boundary of a topological space, which we call *critical nodes*. We devised a three-step approach to identify the communication topology.

1. We create an adjacency list of communication endpoints for each node and group nodes according to their adjacency lists.

2. We identify critical nodes by analyzing the adjacency lists.

3. We calculate the sizes of each dimension (x, y, and z) of the communication topology.

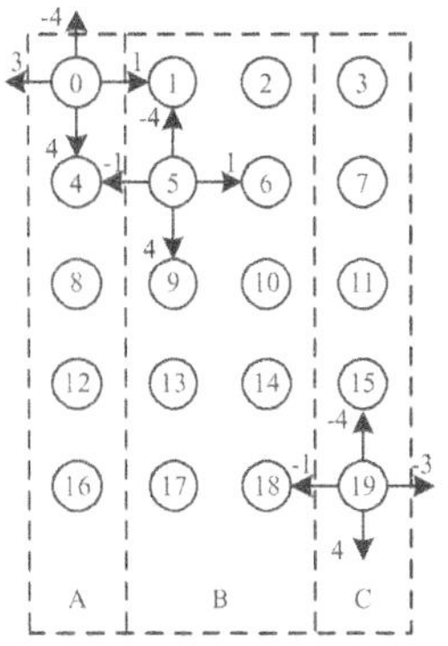

Figure 3. Topology Detection

First, our algorithm traverses the input trace to construct communication adjacency lists for each node. According to the relative positions (encodings) of all the communication endpoints of each node, nodes with same endpoint patterns are placed into the same group. Figure 3 illustrates an example of a 2D mesh topology. In this example, nodes on the boundaries communicate with nodes at the opposite side in a wrap-around manner while the internal nodes communicate with their immediate neighbors. Note that wrapping around in the vertical direction does not lead to different endpoint encoding. Therefore, the nodes are divided in to three groups (A, B, and C) with group sizes 5, 10, and 5, respectively.

Next, we analyze the adjacency list of each node to identify the critical nodes. Exploiting the row major constraint, we scan all nodes sequentially to identify loop structures with respect to communication adjacency list patterns. The underlying rationale is that critical nodes define a topology. Between corresponding critical nodes, communication patterns emerge repeatedly. According to the length of a loop structure, the sizes of the groups consist of critical nodes, *i.e.*, *critical groups*, are calculated as

$$critical\ group\ size = \frac{n}{length\ of\ loop},$$

where n denotes the number of nodes engaged in MPI communication. For example, in Figure 3, each row has the same group distribution (A B B C) and is thus identified as a single iteration of the loop structure. Since the length of such a loop iteration is 4, the size of the *critical groups* (group A and C) is $20/4 = 5$. Having obtained the size of the critical groups, we then associate critical nodes with groups by matching sizes of critical groups.

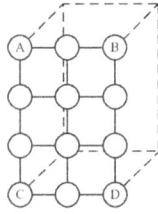

Figure 4. Boundary Size Calculation

Finally, we calculate the sizes of each dimension. Again exploiting the row-major constraint, in a d-dimensional topological space, the number of nodes at the *d-th* dimension is the total number of nodes. The number of nodes at the *i-th* ($i < d$) dimension, n_i, is the inclusive range of numbers of nodes between *node 0* (*1st* critical node) and the 2^i-*th* critical node. Once we have determined the number of nodes at each dimension, the boundary size of the *i-th* dimension, s_i, is calculated as

$$s_i = \frac{n_i}{n_{i-1}}$$

For example, in the 3D topology of Figure 4, the number of nodes in the *1st* dimension, $n_1=3$, is the number of nodes between A and B inclusively, the number of nodes in the second dimension, $n_2=12$, is the number of nodes between A and D, and the number of nodes in the third dimension n_3 is the total number of nodes. Hence, we have

$$\begin{cases} x = s_1 = n_1/n_0 = 3 \\ y = s_2 = n_2/n_1 = 4 \\ z = s_3 = n_3/n_2 \end{cases}$$

3.2 Extrapolation of Communication Traces

The extrapolation of communication traces consists of the extrapolation of both communication groups and communication parameters to indicate who communicates and how they communicate. The extrapolation algorithm is based on the observation that, in regular SPMD stencil/mesh codes, *strong scaling* (increasing the number of nodes under a constant input size) linearly increases/decreases the value of communication parameters and the topological sizes.

Given several data points, a fitting curve can be constructed to extrapolate the growth rate of the communication parameters and the topology information (the sizes of each dimension) of the communication groups.

Specifically, in an n-dimensional Cartesian space, the coordinates of node X and Y are $(X_1, X_2, ..., X_n)$ and $(Y_1, Y_2, ..., Y_n)$, where X_i and $Y_i \in [0, S_i - 1]$ and S_i is the size of the *i-th* dimension of the topological space ($1 \le i \le n$). Assuming the locations of node X and Y differ only in the *i-th* dimension, the distance between X and Y in the *i-th* dimension is $d_i = X_i - Y_i$. With the assumption of linear correlation between topology size and communication parameters, $d_i = X_i - Y_i = a_i \times S_i + b_i$, where a_i and b_i are two constants. Furthermore, with the row-major node placement assumption, the rank of an arbitrary node $A(A_1, A_2, ..., A_n)$ is

$$Rank_A = \sum_{i=1}^{n} A_i \prod_{j=1}^{i-1} S_j.$$

Therefore, $d_i{}'$, the rank distance between X and Y, is

$$d_i{}' = (X_i - Y_i) \times \prod_{j=1}^{i-1} S_j = (a_i \times S_i + b_i) \times \prod_{j=1}^{i-1} S_j$$

In general, for two arbitrarily selected nodes M and N, their rank distance d' is the sum of their rank distances in each dimension,

$$
\begin{aligned}
d' &= d_0{}' + d_1{}' + ... + d_n{}' \\
&= \sum_{i=1}^{n} (N_i - M_i) \prod_{j=1}^{i-1} S_j = \sum_{i=1}^{n} (a_i \times S_i + b_i) \prod_{j=1}^{i-1} S_j \\
&= a_n \prod_{j=1}^{n} S_j + \sum_{i=1}^{n-1} (a_i + b_{i+1}) \prod_{j=1}^{i} S_j + b_1 = \sum_{i=0}^{n} c_i \prod_{j=1}^{i} S_j,
\end{aligned}
$$

where $c_n = a_n$, $c_0 = b_1$, and $c_i = a_i + b_{i+1}(1 \le i \le n - 1)$.

In order to extrapolate the rank of a communication endpoint (src/dest), which is defined by the rank distance between nodes, we need to identify how the topology information is related to the communication parameter. We construct a set of linear equations to solve c_i ($1 \le i \le n-1$). In general, for an n-dimensional topology, $n+1$ input traces are needed to solve $n+1$ coefficients. We employ Gaussian Elimination to solve the equations. Once the values of $c_i (1 \le i \le n - 1)$ are determined, a fitting curve for the given parameter is established. In order to extrapolate the same parameter for a larger execution, we utilize the known coefficients and specify the topology information at the target task size. The desired value is then calculated accordingly.

As an example, in a 2D space, the bottom-right node in Figure 5 communicates with its *EAST* neighbor in a wrap-around manner. In order to extrapolate the rank of the communication endpoint, three input traces with dimensions 4×4, 5×5, and 6×6 are used to construct the set of linear equations shown in Figure 6, and $c_2 = 1$, $c_1 = -1$, and $c_0 = 1$ are obtained as the values of the coefficients. To extrapolate a 10×10 mesh, we re-construct the equation with coefficients and topology information assigned. Subsequently, the target value V is calculated as $V = c_2 \times 10 \times 10 + c_1 \times 10 + c_0 = 91$.

Besides the communication parameters, communication groups are also extrapolated. The topological space of an application can be partitioned into several communication groups according to the communication endpoint pattern of each node. Under *strong scaling*, partitions tend to retain their position within the topological space but change their sizes for each dimension accordingly. For example, Figure 7 shows the distribution of 9 communication groups of a 2D stencil code. Despite the changing problem size, groups *A*, *C*, *G*, and *I* always represent corner nodes, groups *B*, *D*,

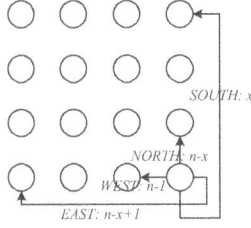

Figure 5. Generic Representation of Communication Endpoints

$$\left\{ \begin{array}{l} c_2 \times 4 \times 4 + c_1 \times 4 + c_0 = 13 \\ c_2 \times 5 \times 5 + c_1 \times 5 + c_0 = 21 \\ c_2 \times 6 \times 6 + c_1 \times 6 + c_0 = 31 \end{array} \right.$$

Figure 6. Set of Equations for Communication Endpoint Extrapolation

F, and H are always the boundaries, and group E contains the remaining (interior) nodes.

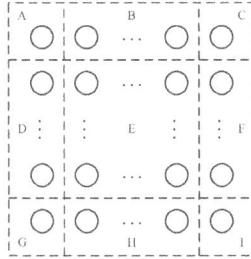

Figure 7. Distribution of Communication Groups of a 2D Stencil Code

This opens up the opportunity to extrapolate communication groups of the same application at arbitrary size. In order to extrapolate, we represent communication groups as *rank lists*, which effectively specifies the starting node and the dimension sizes of a group. Since the dimension sizes are defined by the distances between nodes (vertices), we again utilize a set of linear equations to establish the relation between the topology information of communication groups and the task sizes. Extrapolation is performed for the *start_rank*, *iteration_length*, and *stride* fields of the rank list. The output rank list reflects the communication group at the target size. For example, for the topology shown in Figure 7, when the total number of nodes is 16, the rank list of group E, as defined in Section 2, is $<2\ 5\ 2\ 4\ 2\ 1>$, *i.e.*, a 2D space starting from *node 5* with x- and y-dimensions of size 2. Similarly, the rank lists of group E at sizes 25 and 36 are $<2\ 6\ 3\ 5\ 3\ 1>$ and $<2\ 7\ 4\ 6\ 4\ 1>$, respectively. We can thus construct the set of linear equations for each field in the rank list to derive a generic representation of the rank list as:

$$<2 \quad x+1 \quad x-2 \quad x \quad x-2 \quad 1>.$$

Subsequently, assuming that we want to extrapolate for size 10×10, let x be 10, which yields the output rank list $<2\ 11\ 8\ 10\ 8\ 1>$ that precisely matches the *rank list* representation of communication group E at this problem size.

By combining the extrapolation of both communication groups and communication parameters, we are capable of extrapolating the communication trace for a given application at arbitrary topological sizes.

3.3 Handling Dynamic Load Balancing

The extrapolation of communication traces requires the input traces to be structurally identical so that the corresponding RSDs can be matched across different traces. Being structurally identical requires the traces to have the same number of RSDs and the matching RSDs should be generated by the same MPI event in the original application, though the values of the communication parameters and the loop information can be different.

However, the NPB code IS (Integer Sort) [1] results in structurally different traces due to an inherent dynamic workload balancing scheme. Specifically, in IS, each node first sorts their local elements into buckets, then calls MPI_Alltoallv to distribute the buckets to different nodes. Since the bucket sizes are determined by the randomly generated elements, the message sizes of MPI_Alltoallv are different in each iteration both within and across nodes. In addition, to create different program behavior, IS changes the values of several elements every iteration, so the parameters for MPI_Alltoallv keep changing across timesteps. As a result, the compression of MPI_Alltoallv fails for both intra- and inter-node phases, which leads to structurally different traces.

In fact, MPI_Alltoallv supports different message volumes between different node pairs (in contrast to MPI_Alltoall). Compression based on identical parameter values across nodes rarely succeeds. Therefore, we decided to improve *ScalaTrace* to trade precision for a higher degree of abstraction that allows more aggressive trace compression and ultimately enables extrapolation. We observe that the total volume of data exchanged by MPI_Alltoallv across all nodes for each synchronous call represents the topology boundary data. This boundary data volume is constant across all nodes. Thus, we aggregate mismatched parameters, such as message payload sizes, across all nodes. We subsequently record the average value (per node) instead of actual parameter values, which diverges only slightly from the average value. Note that this improvement is not just a customization for extrapolation of IS but rather results in improved compression of *any* application with similar usage patterns of MPI_Alltoallv. Given a constant overall input data size, the message size of MPI_Alltoallv in IS follows an inverse-proportion relationship relative to the number of nodes. (A similar behavior is also observed for FT.) We consequently enhanced ScalaTrace with the ability to detect and handle curve fitting for inverse-proportional relations, *e.g.*, for message sizes. Utilizing this methodology, we are able to obtain perfectly compressed communication traces for IS, which enables extrapolation through ScalaExtrap.

3.4 Handling Unique Communication Patterns

While the above extrapolation algorithm applies to stencil/mesh topologies, which characterize communication of a large number of parallel applications, we also observed a more complex communication pattern that required explicit communication information for extrapolation. As an example, consider the communication topology of NPB CG in Figure 8. The primary communication pattern is repeated across each row. For a single node, both the amount and the distance of endpoints changes with the number of nodes. Specifically, when there are a total of $n = x^2 (x = 1, 2, 4, ...)$ nodes, each node will have lgx communication endpoints with distance

$$d = (-1)^{\lfloor \frac{r}{2^i} \rfloor} \times 2^i,$$

where $0 \leq i \leq lgx$ and r is the rank of the node. Moreover, there is a secondary communication pattern along the diagonals in which nodes at symmetric positions communicate.

In order to detect the communication topology of CG, we improved the topology detection algorithm so that communications originating from different locations in the source code are differen-

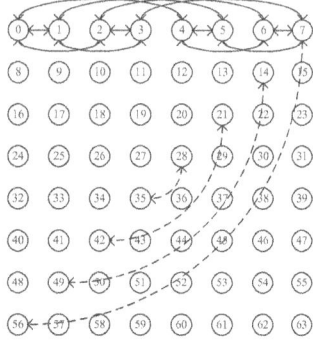

Figure 8. CG Communication Topology

tiated by their distinct call stacks. This enables us to handle applications with multiple interleaved communication topologies. Without the interference of diagonal communication, the loop detection process is able to identify the primary row-wise communication pattern and thus calculate the boundary sizes $x = y = \sqrt{n}$. The communication pattern of CG, however, is not linearly correlated with the topology sizes (which is beyond the scope of this work). We thus manually provide information to facilitate the extrapolation. In future work, we plan to enhance ScalaExtrap to support user-plugins that specify communication patterns. With this functionality, unique communication patterns can be analyzed by ScalaExtrap exploiting its extrapolation capability.

3.5 Extrapolation of Timing Information

Besides the communication traces, we also extrapolate the timing information of the application. ScalaTrace preserves the "delta" time for each communication event and for the computation between two communication events. For a single MPI function call across multiple loop iterations, *i.e.*, for a RSD, the delta times are recorded in multi-bin histograms. These histograms contain the overall average, minimum, and maximum delta time, the distribution of the delta execution times represented as histogram bins, and the average, minimum, and maximum delta time for each histogram bin. To extrapolate timing information, we utilize curve fitting to capture the variations in trends of the delta times with respect to the number of nodes, *i.e.*, $t=f(n)$, where t is the delta execution time and n is the total number of nodes. Hence, the target delta time t_e is calculated as $t_e = f(n_e)$, where n_e is the total number of nodes at a given problem size. While we can extrapolate only the aggregated average delta time per RSD, to restrain the statistics of delta time, extrapolation is performed for each field of a histogram. Currently, we implemented four statistical models based on curve fitting for each extrapolation. We use a deviation-based metric to determine the best of these models to fit to a given curve.

1. Constant: This method captures constant time, *i.e.*, $t=f(n)=c$. Before calculating the constant time, the input time t_o with the largest absolute value of deviation is excluded from the input times to mitigate the influence of outliers (which can be caused by either unstable system state or an empty bin). Subsequently, the average value of the remaining input times reflects the constant time c, and $d_1=std.$ *dev./average* is used to evaluate this fitting curve among the remaining values.

2. Linear: This method captures linearly increasing/decreasing trends, *i.e.*, $t=f(n)=an+b$. We use the least-squares method to fit the curve. In order to avoid mis-classifications, such as a constant time relationship as a linear relationship with a near-zero slope, we define a threshold slope $s_{min}=0.2$ such that $\forall a < s_{min}\ t=f(n)=b$. For curve evaluation, $d_2 = \sqrt{residual}/average$ is used, where *average* refers to the average value of the estimated running times.

3. Inverse Proportional: This method captures inverse-proportional trends, *i.e.*, $t=f(n)=k/n$. We observe this trend in the NAS Parallel Benchmark IS, where MPI_Alltoallv dynamically rebalances the per-node workloads even though the collective workload over all nodes is constant. Let t_i be the input times, n_i be the corresponding number of nodes, and $k_i = t_i \times n_i$. We extrapolate the constant k as the average value of k_i. Again, we exclude the outlier k_o, which has the largest absolute value within the deviation. To evaluate this fitting curve, we calculate the standard deviation of k_i and then divide by the average value of k_i, *i.e.*, $d_3=std.$ *dev./average* is used for comparison.

4. Inverse Proportional + Constant: This method captures the execution time consisting of an inverse proportional phase and a constant phase, *i.e.*, $t=f(n)=k/n+c$. Instead of directly extrapolating t, we utilize the least-squares method to extrapolate $t' = tn = cn + k$ and use $d_4 = \sqrt{residual}/average$ for the curve evaluation. With an extrapolated c and k, t is subsequently calculated as $t = t'/n = k/n + c$.

Having obtained the deviations for each curve-fitting process, we compare the values to determine the curve that best fits. For a closer approximation, we define a threshold value $d_t = 0.05$, such that if and only if $d_{min} + d_t < d_i$ holds for all d_i other than d_{min} will the corresponding candidate curve be selected as the fitting curve. Otherwise, the extrapolation for the current field is postponed until we have processed all the fields in the same histogram. Since every field in the histogram should have the same variation trend, we finalize the pending extrapolation according to the decisions of the remaining fields.

4. Experimental Framework

Our extrapolation methodology for communication traces was implemented as the ScalaExtrap tool that generates a synthetic trace for a freely selected number of nodes. The extrapolation is based on traces obtained from application instrumentation with ScalaTrace on a cluster. For both base traces generation and results verification, we use a subset of JUGENE, an IBM Blue Gene/P with 73,728 compute nodes and 294,912 cores, 2 GB memory per node, and the 3D torus and global tree interconnection networks. We performed experiments with (a) one MPI task per node and (b) one per core. We report the results for the former because this configuration provides more memory per MPI task, which enables larger scale runs. Nonetheless, configurations (a) and (b) show equally accurate and correct results.

The extrapolation process is run on a single workstation and requires only 1 or 2 seconds, irrespective of the target number of nodes for extrapolation. This low overhead is due to the linear time complexity of our algorithm with respect to the total number of MPI function calls in an application. Results from extrapolation are subsequently compared to traces and runtimes of an application at the same scale, where runtimes for extrapolated traces are obtained via ScalaReplay (see Section 2).

We conducted extrapolation experiments with the NAS Parallel Benchmark (NPB) suite (version 3.3 for MPI) with class D and E input sizes [1]. We report our extrapolation results for BT, EP, FT, CG, LU, and IS. These benchmarks have either a stencil/mesh communication pattern or collective communication, both of which are applicable to our extrapolation algorithm. Among these benchmarks, IS originally exhibited imperfect compression resulting in non-scalable trace sizes due to its dynamic load re-balancing via workload exchange through the MPI_Alltoallv communication collective. In order to utilize our extrapolation techniques, we enhanced ScalaTrace such that minor differences in MPI_Alltoallv parameters caused by load re-balancing are eliminated as explained in Section 3.3. The communication trace extrapolation for CG is facilitated by manually specifying the communication pattern as a plugin function (see Section 3.4). The extrapolation of timing information does not require any extra information.

5. Experimental Results

Experiments were conducted with respect to two aspects, namely the correctness of communication traces and the accuracy of timing information, both for extrapolations under strong scaling, *i.e.*, when varying the number of nodes. Notice that strong scaling is actually a *harder* problem under extrapolation as it tends to affect communication parameters such as message volume size. In contrast, weak scaling (increasing the number of nodes and problem sizes at the same rate) is easier as it tends to preserve message volumes sizes irrespective of the number of nodes.

5.1 Correctness of Communication Trace Extrapolation

We first evaluated our communication trace extrapolation algorithm with microbenchmarks and the NPB BT, EP, FT, CG, LU, and IS codes. We assessed the ability to retain communication semantics across the extrapolation process for these benchmarks at the target scale. The microbenchmarks perform regular stencil-style/torus-style communication in topological spaces from 1D to 3D. The NPB programs exercise both collective and point-to-point communication patterns. We verified the extrapolation results in multiple ways.

1. The extrapolated trace file T_{e_0} was compared with the trace file obtained from an actual execution at the same scale T_{target} on a per-event basis (Exp1 in Figure 9).

2. The extrapolated trace T_{e_0} was replayed such that aggregate statistical metrics about communication events could be compared to those of a corresponding original application run at the same problem size and node size (Exp2 in Figure 9).

3. After extrapolation, traces T_{e_1}, T_{e_2}, ..., T_{e_i} were collected in a sequence of replays to obtain a fixed point in the trace representation (Exp3 in Figure 9).

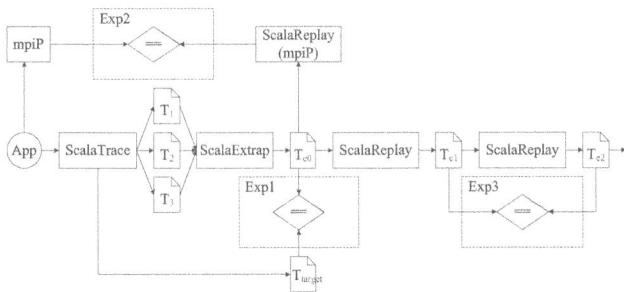

Figure 9. Correctness of Trace Extrapolation and Replay

First, the per-event analysis of trace files showed that extrapolated MPI parameters and communication groups perfectly matched those of the application trace for all benchmarks except one (Exp1 in Figure 9). In BT, the message volume of non-blocking point-to-point sends and receives *approximates* an inverse-proportional relationship with respect to the number of nodes. However, it diverges slightly from an inverse-proportional approximation for extrapolating the message volume due to integer division (discarding the remainder) inherent to the source code. This inaccuracy is later amplified in the extrapolation process and results in message volumes that are about 13% smaller than the actual ones at a given scaling factor in the worst case. As imprecisions remain localized to certain point-to-point messages, this effect is shown to be contained in that resulting timings are deemed

accurate within the considered tolerance range for extrapolation experiments (see timing results below). Such imprecisions have no side-effect on semantic correctness (causal order) of trace events whatsoever. Overall, the results of static trace analysis show that our synthetically generated extrapolation trace is equivalent to the trace obtained from actual execution of the same application at the same scaling level.

Second, we replayed the extrapolated trace T_{e_0} to assess if the MPI communication events are fully captured (see Exp2 in Figure 9). For this experiment, ScalaReplay is linked with mpiP [22], which yields frequency information of each MPI call distinguished by call site (using dynamic stackwalks). During replay, all MPI function calls recorded in the synthetically generated extrapolation trace were executed with the same number of nodes and their original payload size. For comparison, we instrumented the original application with mpiP and executed it at extrapolated sizes (problem and node sizes). We compared the *Aggregate Sent Message Size* reported by mpiP between the original application and the replayed extrapolated trace. Results show that the total send volumes of these experiments are identical, except for *MPI_Isend* in BT as discussed above. We also compared the total number of MPI calls recorded in the mpiP output files. The results allowed us to verify that the number of communication events in the actual and extrapolated traces match, *i.e.*, the correctness of communication trace extrapolation is preserved.

Third, we evaluated the correctness of ScalaReplay by replaying the generated trace file in sequence until a fixed point is reached (see Exp3 in Figure 9). The fixed point approach is a well established mathematical proof method that establishes conversion, in this case of the trace data. In this experiment, instead of instrumenting ScalaReplay with mpiP, we interposed MPI calls through ScalaTrace again. As ScalaReplay issues MPI function calls, ScalaTrace captures these communication events and generates a trace file for it, just as would be done for any other ordinary MPI application. We start by replaying the extrapolated trace file T_{e_0} and obtain a new trace T_{e_1}. This trace differs from T_{e_0} in that call sites of the original program have been replaced by call sites from ScalaReplay. This affects not only stackwalk signatures but also the structure of trace files due to the recursive approach of replaying trace files in place over their internal (PRSD) structure without decompressing it. We then replay trace T_{e_1} to obtain another trace T_{e_2} and so on for T_{e_i}. We then compare pairs of trace files $T_{e_i}, T_{e_{i+1}}$. If two such traces match, a fixed point has been reached. In these experiments, we verified that pairs of trace files, baring syntactical differences, are semantically equivalent to each other. In other words, ScalaReplay neither adds nor drops any communication events during replay, *i.e.*, by obtaining a fixed point it was shown that all MPI communication calls are preserved during replay.

5.2 Accuracy of Extrapolated Timings: Timed Replay

We further analyzed the timing information of extrapolated traces for the NPB BT, EP, FT, CG, and IS codes with a total number of nodes of up to 16,384. For CG, EP, and FT, we used class D input sizes. For BT, class E was used so that a sufficient workload is guaranteed at 16,384 nodes. For IS, we modified the input size to adapt it for 16,384 nodes (the original NPB3.3-MPI provides only class D problem size and supports a maximum of 1024 nodes). These problem sizes and node sizes were decided based on the memory constraints (for some benchmarks, memory constraints compel us to generate the base traces already at large scales, which in turn leaves fewer target sizes for evaluation) and the availability of computational resources to assess the effects and limitations of our timing extrapolation approach.

In this set of experiments, we first generated 4 trace files for each benchmark as the extrapolation basis. From these base traces,

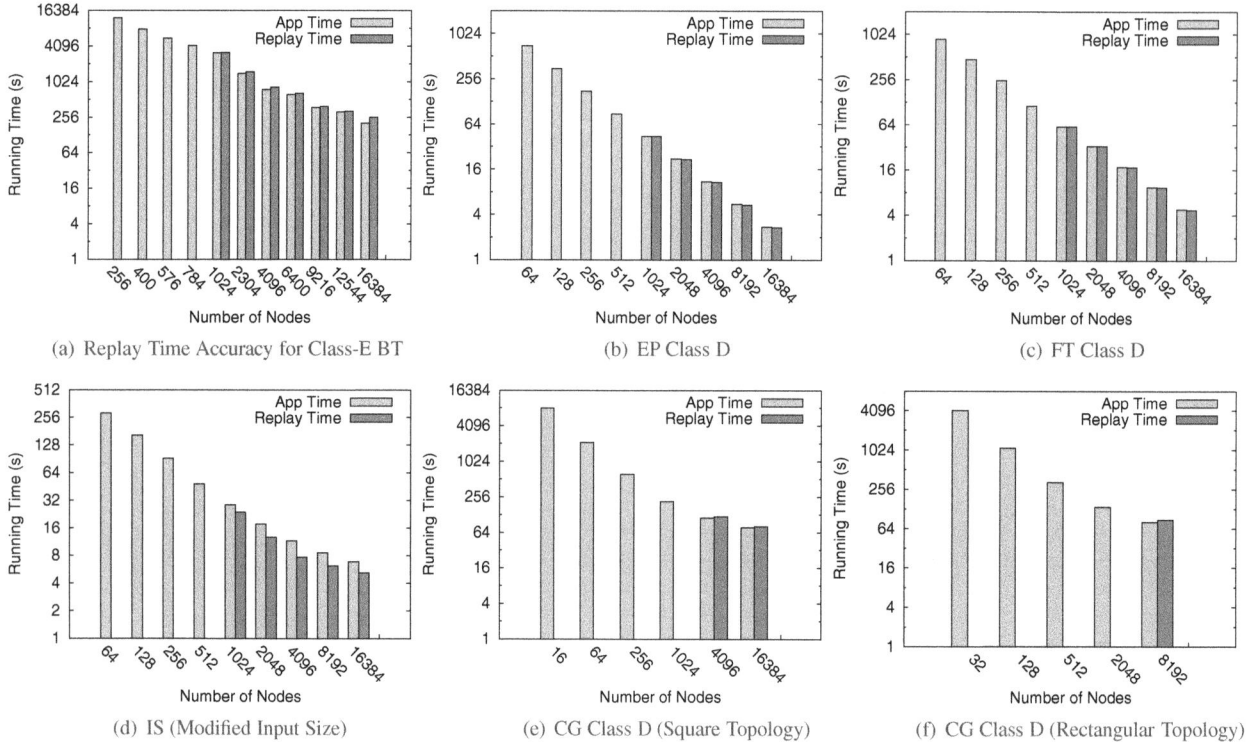

(a) Replay Time Accuracy for Class-E BT   (b) EP Class D   (c) FT Class D

(d) IS (Modified Input Size)   (e) CG Class D (Square Topology)   (f) CG Class D (Rectangular Topology)

Figure 10. Replay Time Accuracy for Benchmarks

an extrapolated trace was constructed next using ScalaExtrap, including extrapolated delta time histograms. We then assess the timing accuracy by replaying the extrapolated traces. During replay, ScalaReplay parses the timing histograms of the computation periods in the trace files. It simulates computation by sleeping to delay the next communication event by the proper amount of time. In this context, the effect of load imbalance is preserved by ScalaTrace. The timing histogram records not only *min, max, avg, std.dev* values, but also the *frequency* for each timing bin, and these statistics are also extrapolated by ScalaExtrap. During replay, the sleeping time is generated according to these statistics and the unbalanced timing behavior is thus reproduced. Communication is simply replayed with the same extrapolated end points and payload sizes but a random message payload. We do not impose any delays on communication as published results indicate better accuracy with just delays for computation only [14], which we also confirmed. In this experiment, ScalaReplay is linked to neither ScalaTrace nor mpiP to avoid additional overhead caused by the instrumentation layer of these tools. Hence, the output of ScalaReplay in this experiment is the total time to replay a trace. For each extrapolated trace, we run the corresponding application at the same problem size and record its overall execution time for comparison.

Figure 10 depicts the extrapolation accuracy of BT, EP, FT, IS, and CG, respectively, for a varying number of nodes. We show the extrapolation results of CG in separate figures because they have different communication topologies and thus a different extrapolation basis. As shown in Figure 10, the timing extrapolation accuracy is generally higher than 90%, sometimes even higher than 98%, where accuracy is defined as

$$Accuracy = \frac{|Replay\ Time\ -\ App\ Time|}{App\ Time}.$$

For BT, we observed slightly lower accuracy when the total number of nodes approaches 16,384. At such sizes the computational workload becomes so small that the influence of non-deterministic fac-

tors, such as system overheads or performance fluctuation of MPI collectives caused by different process arrival patterns [6], become dominant. Compared to the other benchmarks, IS shows a constantly lower accuracy (66%-83%). Two reasons may explain this phenomenon: (a) Although IS dynamically rebalances the workload across all nodes, the execution time of the application's sorting algorithm on each process still takes a different amount of time. Hence, collective MPI calls take unpredictable time to synchronize as the arrival times of processes at collectives varies significantly due to load imbalance. Since the degree of imbalance is determined by randomly determined delta times from histograms, it is difficult to predict/extrapolate this behavior. (b) Source code analysis shows that the most computationally intensive code section in IS consists of two phases, namely (i) an inverse-proportional phase (runtime is inverse-proportional to the number of nodes), and (ii) a relatively short constant phase (runtime does not change significantly with node sizes). When the node size is small, the inverse-proportional phase almost solely determines the computation time. As a result, our algorithm fails to uncover a small constant factor that contributes to timing for larger node sizes. ScalaExtrap instead treats it as a pure inverse-proportional timing trend. Without the short constant factor in the timing curve, the extrapolated runtime drops slightly faster than the real runtime leading to a constantly shorter replay time. However, since we are able to capture the dominating inverse-proportional timing trend, we still obtained an acceptable timing prediction accuracy.

In large, minor inaccuracies during replay stem from imprecise curve fitting for the extrapolation of computation times. For the simulation of communication duration, ScalaReplay depends only on the communication parameters such as end points and payload sizes, which are shown to be correctly extrapolated in Section 5.1. Overall, the extrapolated timing information precisely reflects the runtime of the original application at the target problem size and node size.

6. Discussion and Future Work

This work explored the extrapolation of the communication behavior of parallel applications, which is unprecedented. For the extrapolation of communication traces, the detection of communication topology is vital but non-trivial. We currently focus on stencil/mesh topology with nodes arranged in a row-major fashion. While a large amount of parallel applications fall into this category, we observed more complex communication topologies that are hard to detect with a generic approach, which thus limits the applicability of this work. In future work, we plan to support user plugins so that the extrapolation of complicated and unique communication patterns can be facilitated by user-supplied information.

Extrapolation of timing information of parallel applications is another objective of this work. Currently, we capture four categories of the most commonly seen timing trend. However, the prediction of more complicated timing trends, *e.g.*, the detection of the combination of multiple types of timing trends, may require more sophisticated algorithms.

7. Related Work

ScalaTrace is an MPI trace-gathering framework that generates near constant-size communication traces for a parallel application regardless of the number of nodes while preserving structural information and temporal ordering [14, 18] (see Section 2. Our extrapolation work builds on the trace representation of ScalaTrace.

Xu *et al.* construct coordinated performance skeletons to estimate application execution time in new hardware environments [23, 24]. They detect dominant communication topologies by comparing an application communication matrix against a predefined set (library) of reference patterns. In this work, complicated communication patterns, such as the NAS benchmark CG, are handled by manually provided specifications of the new patterns. Moreover, the graph spectrum analysis and graph isomorphism tests utilized in this work lack scalability in terms of time complexity and thus limit the applicability of this work at large sizes. Most significantly, their work does not capture all communication events.

Zhai *et al.* collect MPI communication traces and extract application communication patterns through program slicing [26]. This work utilizes a set of source code analysis techniques to build a program slice that only contains the variables and code sections related to MPI events, and then executes the program slice to acquire communication traces. While removing the computation in the original application enables a fast and cheap trace collection, it also causes the loss of temporal information that is essential for characterizing the application runtime behavior. In addition, the lack of trace compression limits its feasibility for large-scale application tracing. Based on the FACT framework, Zhai *et al.* employ a deterministic replay technique to predict the sequential computation time of one process in a parallel application on a target platform [25]. The main idea is to use the information recorded in the trace to simulate the execution result of MPI calls when there is actually only one MPI process, and utilize the deterministic data replay to simulate the runtime of the computation phases on the target platform. While this approach manages to predict the computation time, it fails to capture the communication related effects. In addition, this work focuses on cross-platform performance prediction but cannot predict the application performance on a cluster that is larger than the available host platform.

Dimemas is a discrete-event-based network performance simulator that uses Paraver traces as input [15]. It simulates the application behavior on the target platform with specified processor counts and network latency. However, Dimemas simulations are infeasible for peta-/exascale simulations due to a lack of hardware resources to generate the input trace and the sheer size of traditional application traces. Our work, in contrast, focuses on the trace extrapolation for larger platforms that applications have not yet been ported to or even future platforms (exascale). The extrapolated traces can then be either replayed with ScalaReplay (former case) or used as the input trace for simulators (Dimemas/SST) in the latter case for performance prediction.

Preissl *et al.* extract communication patterns, *i.e.*, the recurring communication event sets, from MPI traces [16]. They first search for repeating occurrences of identical events in the trace of each individual process and then iteratively grow them into global patterns. The output of this algorithm can be used to identify potential bottlenecks in parallel applications. Preissl *et al.* further utilize the detected communication patterns to automate source code transformations such as automatic introduction of MPI collectives [17]. Our method, in contrast, focuses on the spatial aspect of communication events, *i.e.*, the identification and extrapolation of communication topology.

Eckert and Nutt [4, 5] extrapolate traces of parallel shared-memory applications. They take as input the traces collected on an existing architecture and extrapolate them to a target platform with different architectural parameters, without re-executing the original application. This work analyzes the causal event stream. It focuses on the correctness of the extrapolated trace given the existence of program-level non-determinism, *e.g.*, the interleaving of events or modifications in the actual set of events caused by moving the trace across different architectures. In contrast, our work is based on deterministic application execution. We also preserve the causal ordering of communication events but our focus is on the communication behavior at arbitrary problem sizes.

Performance modeling has traditionally taken the approach of algorithmic analysis, often combined with tedious source code inspection and hardware modeling for floating-point operations per second, memory hierarchy analysis from caches over buses to main memory and interconnect topology, latency and bandwidth considerations. In particular, Kerbyson *et al.* present a predictive performance and scalability model of a large-scale multidimensional hydrodynamics code [9]. This model takes application, system, and mapping parameters as input to match the application with a target system. It utilizes a multitude of formulae to characterize and predict the performance of a scientific application. Snavely *et al.* model and predict application performance by 1) characterizing a system with machine profiles, namely single processor performance and network latency and bandwidth, 2) collecting the operations in an application to generate application signatures, and 3) mapping signatures to profiles to characterize performance [2, 21]. İpek *et al.* follow a completely different approach by utilizing artificial neural networks (ANNs) to predict the performance when application configuration varies [8]. This approach employs repeated sampling of a small number of points in the design space that are statistically determined through SimPoint [20]. Only these points are then simulated and results are utilized to teach the ANNs, which are subsequently utilized to predict the performance for other design points. In contrast, our work explores the potential of extrapolating the application runtime according to its evolving trend across increasing problem sizes. Since this method requires neither measurement of performance metrics nor intense computation, it provides a simple and highly efficient approach to study the effect of scaling across a large numbers of compute nodes. In contrast to all of the above approaches, our ScalaExtrap does not just simulate communication behavior at scale but allows such behavior to be observed in practice through replaying on a target platform with large numbers of nodes, even if the corresponding application itself has not been ported yet.

8. Conclusion

Scalability is one of the main challenges of scientific applications in HPC. Advanced communication tracing techniques achieve lossless trace collection, preserve event ordering and encapsulate time in a scalable fashion. However, estimating the impact of scaling on communication efficiency is still non-trivial due to execution time variations and exposure to hardware and software artifacts.

This work contributes a set of algorithms and analysis techniques to extrapolate communication traces and execution times of an application at large scale with information gathered from smaller executions. The extrapolation of communication traces depends on an analytical method to characterize the communication topology of an application. Based on the observation that problem scaling increases/decreases communication parameters and topology at a certain rate, we utilize a set of linear equations to capture the relation between communication traces for changing number of nodes between traces and extrapolate communication traces accordingly. For the extrapolation of timing information, we utilize curve fitting approaches to model trends in delta times over traces with varying number of nodes. Statistical methods are further employed to mitigate timing fluctuations under scaling. Experiments were conducted using an implementation through our ScalaExtrap tool and with the NAS Parallel Benchmark suite. We utilized up to 16,384 nodes of a 73,728-node IBM Blue Gene/P. Experimental results show that our algorithm is capable of extrapolating stencil/mesh and collective communication patterns. Extrapolation of timing information is further shown to provide good accuracy.

We believe that extrapolation of communication traces for parallel applications at arbitrary scale is without precedence. Without porting applications, communication events can be replayed and analyzed in a timed manner at scale. This has the potential to enable otherwise infeasible system simulation at the exascale level.

References

[1] D. H. Bailey, E. Barszcz, J. T. Barton, D. S. Browning, R. L. Carter, D. Dagum, R. A. Fatoohi, P. O. Frederickson, T. A. Lasinski, R. S. Schreiber, H. D. Simon, V. Venkatakrishnan, and S. K. Weeratunga. The NAS Parallel Benchmarks. *The International Journal of Supercomputer Applications*, 5(3):63–73, Fall 1991.

[2] D.H. Bailey and A. Snavely. Performance modeling: Understanding the present and predicting the future. In *Euro-Par Conference*, August 2005.

[3] H. Brunst, D. Kranzlmüller, and W. Nagel. Tools for Scalable Parallel Program Analysis - Vampir NG and DeWiz. *The International Series in Engineering and Computer Science, Distributed and Parallel Systems*, 777:92–102, 2005.

[4] Z. Eckert and G. Nutt. Trace extrapolation for parallel programs on shared memory multiprocessors. Technical Report TR CU-CS-804-96, Department of Computer Science, University of Colorado at Boulder, Boulder, CO, 1996.

[5] Zulah K. F. Eckert and Gary J. Nutt. Parallel program trace extrapolation. In *International Conference on Parallel Processing*, pages 103–107, 1994.

[6] Ahmad Faraj, Pitch Patarasuk, and Xin Yuan. A study of process arrival patterns for MPI collective operations. In *International Conference on Supercomputing*, pages 168–179, June 2007.

[7] W. Gropp, E. Lusk, N. Doss, and A. Skjellum. A high-performance, portable implementation of the MPI message passing interface standard. *Parallel Computing*, 22(6):789–828, September 1996.

[8] Engin İpek, Sally A. McKee, Rich Caruana, Bronis R. de Supinski, and Martin Schulz. Efficiently exploring architectural design spaces via predictive modeling. In *ASPLOS-XII: Proceedings of the 12th international conference on Architectural support for programming languages and operating systems*, pages 195–206, 2006.

[9] D. Kerbyson, H. Alme, A. Hoisie, F. Petrini, H. Wasserman, and M. Gittings. Predictive performance and scalability modeling of a large-scale application. In *Supercomputing*, November 2001.

[10] Darren J. Kerbyson and Adolfy Hoisie. Performance modeling of the blue gene architecture. In *JVA '06: Proceedings of the IEEE John Vincent Atanasoff 2006 International Symposium on Modern Computing*, pages 252–259, 2006.

[11] A. Knüpfer, R. Brendel, H. Brunst, H. Mix, and W. E. Nagel. Introducing the open trace format (OTF). In *International Conference on Computational Science*, pages 526–533, May 2006.

[12] Jesús Labarta, Sergi Girona, and Toni Cortes. Analyzing scheduling policies using dimemas. *Parallel Computing*, 23(1-2):23–34, 1997.

[13] W. E. Nagel, A. Arnold, M. Weber, H. C. Hoppe, and K. Solchenbach. VAMPIR: Visualization and analysis of MPI resources. *Supercomputer*, 12(1):69–80, 1996.

[14] M. Noeth, F. Mueller, M. Schulz, and B. R. de Supinski. Scalatrace: Scalable compression and replay of communication traces in high performance computing. *Journal of Parallel Distributed Computing*, 69(8):969–710, August 2009.

[15] V. Pillet, J. Labarta, T. Cortes, and S. Girona. PARAVER: A tool to visualise and analyze parallel code. In *Proceedings of WoTUG-18: Transputer and occam Developments*, volume 44 of *Transputer and Occam Engineering*, pages 17–31, April 1995.

[16] Robert Preissl, Thomas Köckerbauer, Martin Schulz, Dieter Kranzlmüller, Bronis R. de Supinski, and Daniel J. Quinlan. Detecting patterns in mpi communication traces. In *ICPP '08: Proceedings of the 2008 37th International Conference on Parallel Processing*, pages 230–237, Washington, DC, USA, 2008. IEEE Computer Society.

[17] Robert Preissl, Martin Schulz, Dieter Kranzlmüller, Bronis R. Supinski, and Daniel J. Quinlan. Using mpi communication patterns to guide source code transformations. In *ICCS '08: Proceedings of the 8th international conference on Computational Science, Part III*, pages 253–260, Berlin, Heidelberg, 2008. Springer-Verlag.

[18] P. Ratn, F. Mueller, Bronis R. de Supinski, and M. Schulz. Preserving time in large-scale communication traces. In *International Conference on Supercomputing*, pages 46–55, June 2008.

[19] Arun F Rodrigues, Richard C Murphy, Peter Kogge, and Keith D Underwood. The structural simulation toolkit: exploring novel architectures. In *Poster at the 2006 ACM/IEEE Conference on Supercomputing*, page 157, 2006.

[20] Timothy Sherwood, Erez Perelman, Greg Hamerly, and Brad Calder. Automatically characterizing large scale program behavior. In *ASPLOS-X: Proceedings of the 10th international conference on Architectural support for programming languages and operating systems*, pages 45–57, 2002.

[21] A. Snavely, L. Carrington, N. Wolter, J. Labarta, R. Badia, and A. Purkayastha. A framework for performance modeling and prediction. In *Supercomputing*, November 2002.

[22] J. Vetter and M. McCracken. Statistical scalability analysis of communication operations in distributed applications. In *ACM SIGPLAN Symposium on Principles and Practice of Parallel Programming*, 2001.

[23] Qiang Xu, Ravi Prithivathi, Jaspal Subhlok, and Rong Zheng. Logicalization of mpi communication traces. Technical Report UH-CS-08-07, Dept. of Computer Science, University of Houston, 2008.

[24] Qiang Xu and Jaspal Subhlok. Construction and evaluation of coordinated performance skeletons. In *International Conference on High Performance Computing*, pages 73–86, 2008.

[25] J. Zhai, W. Chen, and W. Zheng. Phantom: predicting performance of parallel applications on large-scale parallel machines using a single node. In *ACM SIGPLAN Symposium on Principles and Practice of Parallel Programming*, pages 305–314, 2010.

[26] J. Zhai, T. Sheng, J. He, W. Chen, and W. Zheng. Fact: fast communication trace collection for parallel applications through program slicing. In *Supercomputing*, pages 1–12, 2009.

How's the Parallel Computing Revolution Going?

Kathryn S. McKinley
The University of Texas at Austin

Abstract

Two trends changed the computing landscape over the past decade: (1) hardware vendors started delivering chip multiprocessors (CMPs) instead of uniprocessors, and (2) software developers increasingly chose managed languages instead of native languages. Unfortunately, the former change is disrupting the virtuous-cycle between performance improvements and software innovation. Establishing a new parallel performance virtuous cycle for managed languages will require scalable applications executing on scalable Virtual Machine (VM) services, since the VM schedules, monitors, compiles, optimizes, garbage collects, and executes together with the application. This talk describes current progress, opportunities, and challenges for scalable VM services. The parallel computing revolution urgently needs more innovations.

Categories & Subject Descriptors: B.8.2

General Terms: Languages, Performance, Measurement, Experimentation.

Keywords: Managed Languages, Multicore.

Bio

Professor McKinley holds an Endowed Professorship in the Department of Computer Science at The University of Texas at Austin. She received her Ph.D. from Rice University working with Ken Kennedy. Her research interests include compilers, memory management, runtime systems, programming languages, security, reliability, and architecture. She and her collaborators have produced tools based on their research that are in wide research and industrial use: the DaCapo Java Benchmarks, TRIPS Compiler, Hoard memory manager, MMTk garbage collector toolkit, and the Immix mark-region garbage collector. McKinley has graduated fourteen PhD students and is currently supervising five. Her service includes program chair for ASPLOS'04, PACT '05, and PLDI '07; co-Editor-in-Chief of ACM Transactions on Programming Language Systems (TOPLAS) (2007-2010); and CRA-W board member (2009-present). McKinley received an NSF CAREER award, IBM Faculty awards, outreach awards, and best paper awards. She is an IEEE Fellow and an ACM Fellow.

Thread Contracts for Safe Parallelism*

Rajesh K. Karmani P. Madhusudan Brandon M. Moore

University of Illinois at Urbana-Champaign

{rkumar8,madhu,bmmoore}@illinois.edu

Abstract

We build a framework of thread contracts, called ACCORD, that allows programmers to annotate their concurrency co-ordination strategies. ACCORD annotations allow programmers to declaratively specify the parts of memory that a thread may read or write into, and the locks that protect them, reflecting the concurrency co-ordination among threads and the reason why the program is free of data-races. We provide *automatic* tools to check if the concurrency co-ordination strategy ensures race-freedom, using constraint-solvers (SMT solvers). Hence programmers using ACCORD can both formally state and prove their co-ordination strategies ensure race freedom.

The programmer's implementation of the co-ordination strategy may however be correct or incorrect. We show how the formal ACCORD contracts allow us to automatically insert *runtime* assertions that serve to check, during testing, whether the implementation conforms to the contract.

Using a large class of data-parallel programs that share memory in intricate ways, we show that natural and simple contracts suffice to document the co-ordination strategy amongst threads, and that the task of showing that the strategy ensures race-freedom can be handled efficiently and automatically by an existing SMT solver (Z3). While co-ordination strategies can be proved race-free in our framework, failure to prove the co-ordination strategy race-free, accompanied by counter-examples produced by the solver, indicates the presence of races. Using such counterexamples, we report hitherto undiscovered data-races that we found in the long-tested `applu_l` benchmark in the Spec OMP2001 suite.

Categories and Subject Descriptors D.1.3 [*PROGRAMMING TECHNIQUES*]: Concurrent Programming—Parallel programming; D.2.4 [*SOFTWARE ENGINEERING*]: Software/Program Verification—Programming by contract; F.3.1 [*LOGICS AND MEANINGS OF PROGRAMS*]: Specifying and Verifying and Reasoning about Programs

General Terms Reliability, Verification

Keywords concurrent contracts, constraint solvers, data-races, testing

* This work was funded partly by the Universal Parallel Computing Research Center at the University of Illinois at Urbana-Champaign, sponsored by Intel Corp. and Microsoft Corp., and NSF Career Award #0747041.

1. Introduction

Perhaps the most generic error in shared-memory concurrent programs is that of a data-race— two concurrent accesses to a memory location, where at least one of them is a write. The primary reason why data-races must be avoided is that memory models of many high-level programming languages do not assure sequential consistency in the presence of data-races [16]. In some cases, like the new semantics of $C++$, the semantics of programs is *not even defined* when data-races are present [5, 7]. Consequently, data-races in high-level programming languages are almost always (if not always) symptomatic of bugs in the program, and are best avoided by mainstream programmers. However, there is no really acceptable shared-memory programming paradigm today that allows programmers to write certifiably race-free code.

ACCORD:

While there have been several attempts to build new shared-memory programming languages that avoid races by design (see Guava [4] and DPJ [6] for example), we propose in this work to instead work with the languages that are currently available, but provide an *annotation framework*, similar to code contracts for sequential programs [17, 18], that allows a programmer to express the concurrency co-ordination strategy amongst threads, and prove them race-free.

Intuitively, a programmer's attempt to parallelize a piece of sequential code consists of two phases:

(a) to come up with a *co-ordination strategy* of the computation amongst threads (for example, deciding what parts of the memory each thread will work on, the locks they will employ to have mutually exclusive access to data, etc.), and

(b) to *implement* the co-ordination strategy in terms of real code.

Unfortunately, the results of the first phase often remain undocumented. A diligent programmer may spell out the strategy in comments written in a natural language, but often the strategy is lost in the code.

In this paper, we propose a *formal annotation language* called ACCORD (Annotations for Concurrent Co-ORDination), using which the programmer can express the concurrent co-ordination strategy. We postulate that doing this has multiple benefits in ensuring correctness. First, we propose automatic solutions to the problem of checking whether the strategy is correct (i.e. ensures race-freedom). Second, we propose automatic insertion of assertions in a program that can be used during testing to check if the program conforms to the annotated co-ordination strategy.

The philosophy behind ACCORD specifications is to document *memory-access contracts* between threads. When several threads are spawned at a point, an ACCORD annotation expresses two aspects of the sharing strategy: (a) the set of memory locations that each thread T will read and write to *without* mutexes such as locks, and (b) the memory locations that each thread T will access only when possessing an associated lock. These read/write regions can be *conservative*, in that the programmer can specify a superset of the regions actually touched, as long as the annotations are sufficient to argue that the program is race-free. The key idea is that such thread contracts are extremely natural to write (indeed, the programmers clearly know this when they come up with the co-ordination strategy, even before they write the code), and moreover, is sufficient to argue and establish that the strategy ensures race-freedom.

In this paper, we are primarily concerned with highly parallel programs written for speed (as opposed to programs that are inherently concurrent, like client-server programs). Examples of popular shared-memory programming languages in this domain are OpenMP, Cilk, and TBB. The Accord annotation framework works for a restricted class of *array-based* parallel programs that employ fork-join parallelism. Such programs are the most commonly used paradigm for writing shared-memory parallel programs. For instance, OpenMP primarily allows fork-join parallelism and most programs written in OpenMP tend to work by partitioning arrays in intricate ways to exploit parallelism, and moreover the forked threads seldom *communicate* in any way until the join-point. The restriction to fork-join parallelism allows for a much simplified syntax of annotations to express the co-ordination strategy that is both intuitive as well as easy to write.

Accord specifications are written both at *forking* points of threads as well as *function boundaries*. Annotations at function boundaries describe also the read and write regions and the locking strategy in the function, and are useful for modular reasoning and testing.

Verifying co-ordination strategies: The idea of writing Accord annotations is that it captures formally the concurrency co-ordination strategy between threads, and hence is amenable to analysis. In particular, an important question to ask is whether the annotated co-ordination strategy is adequate to ensure race-freedom; we call this the *annotation adequacy check*.

Our primary contribution in this paper is to show that annotation adequacy for many array-based fork-join programs can be proved automatically using *constraint solvers*. Intuitively, proving whether the co-ordination strategy ensures race-freedom reduces to the problem of verifying whether two threads are allowed by the strategy to simultaneously access a variable, with one of the accesses being a write. This can be compiled into a constraint satisfaction problem (often using integer arithmetic constraints, uninterpreted functions, and array theories) and hence can be handled by constraint solvers based on SMT-solving technology (such as the solver Z3, from Microsoft Research [10]). Furthermore, consistency checks of various Accord annotations at different points in the program (such as checking if the read/write sets of an parallel loop is a superset of the read/write sets of an inner loop or a function called within) can also be posed as constraints that state the inclusion of regions, and can be verified using an SMT solver.

Expressing the co-ordination strategy formally and using automatic static-checking to show that the strategy maintains concurrency safety and is internally consistent goes a long way in writing correct programs.

Compiling co-ordination strategy to assertions for testing: The documentation of the co-ordination strategy using a formal syntax also serves as a *specification* of the code implementing the strategy. We show in this paper that we can automatically transform an annotated parallel program to one with assertions that tests whether the threads conform to the co-ordination strategy expressed as Accord annotations. The function-level annotations allow us to modularly check the Accord annotations at runtime against the local regions defined for the function (given that the consistency of

the annotations has been checked). This allows us to check whether the program meets the co-ordination strategy during the *testing* of the program on test inputs. Any violations during such tests would indicate that the co-ordination strategy hasn't been implemented correctly in the program.

Experience and Evaluation: We have applied our framework over several non-trivial *data-parallel algorithms* that employ fork-join concurrency with extremely intricate sharing of data.

The first suite of programs include simple matrix multiplication routines, a race-free implementation of quicksort that uses parallel rank computation to partition an array with respect to a pivot, the successive over-relaxation (SOR) program that uses an intricate checker-board separation of a 2D-array combined with barriers, and an LU Factorization program. Our second suite includes benchmarks from the Java Grande Forum benchmark suite [27]. This includes a Montecarlo algorithm that uses locks as well as separation to achieve race-free parallelism and sparse matrix multiplication, where the concurrent sharing strategy is dynamically determined using *indirection arrays*. We also include in our suite buggy variants of the above correct programs, which at first glance seem correct but have subtle errors.

On a third suite of benchmarks, we examine large programs written in OpenMP and annotate them to prove race-freedom. These examples comprise thousands of lines of code, but require very little annotation (at most 37 for a program), and are sufficient to capture the co-ordination strategy in sufficient detail to argue why it ensures race-freedom. While annotating these programs, we found one that couldn't pass our verification tools, which led us to find subtle data-races in a Spec OMP2001 benchmark called applu_l that has escaped detection for more than 10 years (the NAS benchmark suite, however, seems to have a correct version).

Our experience has been that Accord specifications are extremely *natural* to write by the programmer (we wrote annotations for large programs that we didn't even write), and it captures the sharing strategy directly using a simple declarative language. Furthermore, the automatic constraint-solvers such as Z3 can easily and efficiently prove that the co-ordination strategies imply race-freedom. As programmers, we found we gained considerable confidence that the program is free of data-races by knowing the co-ordination strategies ensured race-freedom and that the program conformed to the co-ordination strategy in the testing phase.

In summary, our proposal is that programmers formally write, using a succinct declarative notation, the co-ordination strategy they are implementing. Doing this allows the effective use of analyses tools: one that proves that the co-ordination strategy indeed does ensure race-freedom, and the other that, during the testing phase, checks if the program implements the co-ordination strategy. We believe that this greatly helps in writing race-free code, and through experience on annotating a large suite of programs, we show that correct programs have succinct annotations that can be proved to ensure race-freedom, and that failure to provide verifiable annotations leads to finding bugs.

2. An Illustrative Example

In this section, we provide an overview of Accord approach using a simple example. Listing 1 shows the implementation of parallel matrix multiplication algorithm in an imperative, C-like language (ignoring the `reads`, `writes`, `where` clauses for now). The program takes two matrices $A[m, n]$ and $B[n, p]$ as input, and computes the product as $C[m, p]$.

Accord ***contract for read and write sets*** Lines 3-5 and 8-9 are Accord annotations. The annotation has a `reads` clause (line 8) and a `writes` clause (line 9) that declaratively specify, for every parallel iteration of the `foreach` statement at line 7, the set of memory locations that are read and written by the iteration, respectively. For each iteration k, the read and write annotations specify the locations that the thread corresponding to iteration k will access. Note that the annotation is allowed to refer to all program variables that are in scope. This feature allows a simple and succinct annotation for this program.

Listing 1 Fully parallel implementation of matrix multiplication

```
1  void mm (int[m,n] A, int[n,p] B) {
2    foreach (int i := 0; i < m; i:=i+1)
3      reads A[i,$x],B[$x,$y],C[i,$y] writes C[i,$y]
4      where 0 <= $x and $x < n
5        and 0 <= $y and $y < p
6      for (int j := 0; j < n ; j:=j+1)
7        foreach (int k := 0; k < p; k:=k+1)
8          reads A[i,j],B[j,k],C[i,k]
9          writes C[i,k] {
10         C[i,k] := C[i,k] + (A[i,j] * B[j,k]);
11 } }   }
```

Observe that the annotation at lines 3–5 also introduce *auxiliary variables* ($x and $y); these are *implicitly universally quantified*. This annotation also demonstrates the usage of a `where` clause. A `where` clause constrains (specifies bounds for) the variables in the `reads` and `writes` clauses. This annotation declares that the parallel computation corresponding to index i can read $A[i,\$x]$, $B[\$x,\$y]$ and $C[i,\$y]$, and write to $C[i,\$y]$, *for any values of $x and $y* that satisfy the condition: $0 \leq \$x < n$ and $0 \leq \$y < p$.

Notice that the annotation for this program is a simple and natural way to declare the co-ordination (sharing strategy) among threads, and indeed, the programmer ought to have this separation of memory in mind when reasoning about race-freedom. While the sharing strategy in this program is not hard (and static analysis tools can synthesize them for this example), the strategy is often very complex in larger examples: the regions can be complex (defined using complex arithmetical and logical constraints), they can be dictated by data stored in arrays (like in parallelism using indirection arrays), can be predicated by conditions that change the sharing strategy (for example, code may decide to handle certain instances using parallelism while others are handled sequentially when there is little parallelism to exploit), etc. Moreover, in order to see that the sharing strategy ensures race-freedom, we may *require* properties of data computed just before the fork-point: for example, in programs that parallelize using indirection arrays, the annotation may say that each thread i writes to $B[A[i]]$, and we may need to know that the array $A[]$ has *distinct* values in order to realize that the forked threads will not cause races. The latter condition is captured using a `requires` clause in the ACCORD annotations.

Proving the co-ordination strategy ensures race-freedom (annotation adequacy) We *automatically* generate a logical formula from the annotation (not the program) that serves as a verification condition for checking whether the co-ordination strategy ensures race-freedom. Specifically, the formula is a conjunction of two subformulas: (a) there exist no two threads such that one of them reads and the other writes to the same location, and (b) there exist no two threads such that both write to the same location (see §5 for details on generating the formula). The negation of such a formula is provided to a constraint-solver, like the SMT solver Z3. A similar check is done to ensure that all locations protected under locks are protected under a uniform lock amongst all threads. If the formula can be satisfied, there is a race allowed by the annotation. Otherwise, the co-ordination strategy expressed in the annotation

ensures race-freedom, and if the program satisfies the annotation, it would be race-free as well.

For example, consider the outer-most loop at line 2 in Listing 1. Here we present the race freedom condition for two write accesses only. Two threads, corresponding to say indices i_1 and i_2 can access $C[i_1,\$y]$ and $C[i_2,\$y]$, provided $y satisfies the `where` clause. We hence form a constraint that asks whether there are two *distinct* i_1 and i_2 that may result in writing to the same position in C:

$$\exists i_1,i_2,\$y. \; (\; i_1 \neq i_2 \wedge \$y \geq 0 \wedge \$y < p \wedge i_1 = i_2 \wedge \$y = \$y \;)$$

It is evident that this formula cannot be satisfied. This is verified by feeding the formula to Z3. Hence, there is no race among the threads spawned at line 2, as long as the threads conform to the specified contract.

An example with a data race A natural question a programmer may wonder about is whether the middle loop in the algorithm in Listing 1 can be parallelized. If the *for* loop at Line 6 is changed to *foreach* loop, its annotation would look like: `reads` $A[i,j], B[j,\$y], C[i,\$y]$ `writes` $C[i,\$y]$. The annotation adequacy phase will however fail.

Transforming the program to test if it conforms to the co-ordination strategy (testing annotation correctness): While the verification that the co-ordination strategy ensures race-freedom gives some degree of assurance, we still do not know whether the program itself adheres to this strategy. In other words, we would like to be able to check whether the program satisfies its ACCORD specification, i.e. we want to verify whether the set of memory locations that may be accessed by a thread is contained in the set of memory locations specified in its annotation.

In order to answer this question, we propose to transform the formal ACCORD specification to *assertions* in the parallel program, so that checking these assertions at runtime during testing will in effect check whether the program meets the co-ordination strategy. ACCORD annotations of functions allow us to insert these assertions locally, checking whether the accesses at any point in the program are in accordance with the read and write regions specified by the local annotation in scope.

For example, we can transform the program in Listing 1 such that every access to a shared variable by a thread is preceded by a check that verifies that the access conforms to its ACCORD annotations. In general, this will require *storing* the values of variables at the fork-points, and inserting appropriate assertions in the code using these memoized variables. The parallel program with assertions corresponding to Listing 1 is given (on page 8) in Listing 6.

3. Parallel Programs

We define a simple parallel programming language, given by the following grammar, that resembles an imperative language like C, but with only boolean and integer types, and their multi-dimensional arrays, and with parallel-loop constructs and locks. The language also has the ACCORD annotation language built in.

$$
\begin{aligned}
\langle pgm \rangle & ::= \langle decl \rangle^* \langle fun \rangle^* \\
\langle fun \rangle & ::= \langle type \rangle \; f(\langle decl \rangle^*)[\textbf{requires } \langle \phi \rangle] \langle \textbf{annot} \rangle^* \{\langle stmt \rangle\} \\
\langle stmt \rangle & ::= \langle decl \rangle \mid \langle loc \rangle := \langle expr \rangle \mid \\
& \quad \textbf{if } \langle bexpr \rangle \textbf{ then } \langle stmt \rangle \textbf{ else } \langle stmt \rangle \mid \\
& \quad \textbf{skip} \mid \textbf{return} \langle expr \rangle \mid \langle stmt \rangle ; \langle stmt \rangle \mid \\
& \quad \textbf{while } \langle bexpr \rangle \; do \; \{\langle stmt \rangle\} \mid \langle parstmt \rangle \mid \\
& \quad \textbf{for}(\langle type \rangle i := \langle expr \rangle ; \langle bexpr \rangle ; \langle stmt \rangle)\{\langle stmt \rangle\} \mid \\
& \quad \textbf{synchronized} \; (l)\{\langle stmt \rangle\} \\
\langle parstmt \rangle & ::= \textbf{thread} \langle \textbf{annot} \rangle^* \{\langle stmt \rangle\} \\
& \quad \mid \textbf{foreach}(\langle type \rangle i := \langle expr \rangle ; \langle bexpr \rangle ; \langle stmt \rangle) \\
& \quad [\textbf{requires } \langle \phi \rangle] \langle \textbf{annot} \rangle^* \{\langle stmt \rangle\} \\
& \quad \mid \textbf{par } [\textbf{requires } \langle \phi \rangle]\{\langle parstmt \rangle \textbf{ with } \langle parstmt \rangle\}
\end{aligned}
$$

$\langle loc \rangle \quad ::= i \mid i[\langle aexpr \rangle^*]$

$\langle expr \rangle \quad ::= \langle aexpr \rangle \mid \langle bexpr \rangle \mid f(\langle expr \rangle^*)[\texttt{requires } \langle \phi \rangle]$

$\langle bexpr \rangle \quad ::= \texttt{true} \mid \texttt{false} \mid \langle aexpr \rangle \langle rop \rangle \langle aexpr \rangle \mid$
$\qquad\qquad \langle bexpr \rangle \texttt{ or } \langle bexpr \rangle \mid \langle bexpr \rangle \texttt{ and } \langle bexpr \rangle \mid \texttt{not } \langle bexpr \rangle$

$\langle \phi \rangle \qquad ::= \texttt{forall } i \texttt{ in } [\langle aexpr \rangle, \langle aexpr \rangle].\langle \phi \rangle \mid$
$\qquad\quad \texttt{exists } i \texttt{ in } [\langle aexpr \rangle, \langle aexpr \rangle].\langle \phi \rangle \mid$
$\qquad\quad \langle \phi \rangle \texttt{ and } \langle \phi \rangle \mid \langle \phi \rangle \texttt{ or } \langle \phi \rangle \mid \texttt{not } \langle \phi \rangle \mid \langle bexpr \rangle$

$\langle aexpr \rangle \quad ::= c \in \mathbb{N} \mid \langle loc \rangle \mid \langle aexpr \rangle \langle aop \rangle \langle aexpr \rangle$

$\langle decl \rangle \quad ::= \langle type \rangle i$

$\langle type \rangle \quad ::= \texttt{int} \mid \texttt{bool} \mid \texttt{lock} \mid$
$\qquad\qquad \texttt{int}[\langle aexpr \rangle^*] \mid \texttt{bool}[\langle aexpr \rangle^*]$

$\langle \textbf{annot} \rangle ::= (\texttt{reads} \mid \texttt{writes})\langle region \rangle [\texttt{under lock } l^*]$
$\langle \textbf{region} \rangle ::= \langle loc \rangle [\texttt{where } \langle \phi \rangle]$

i, f, l are identifiers
$\langle aop \rangle$: arithmetic operators, like $+, -, *, /, \%$ (modulo), etc.
$\langle rop \rangle$: relational operators on numbers, like $<, =$, etc.

A program has a sequence of global variable declarations followed by a list of functions. Each function has a return type, a name and a declaration of local variables followed by a sequence of statements, where statements include assignments, conditionals, sequential loops, synchronized blocks, or parallel statements. A parallel statement can be a foreach loop, which forks a separate thread for executing each different iteration of the loop. We assume foreach loops specify a lower bound, an upper bound, and a stride, which is similar to Fortran loops. All the threads spawned at this point must finish before the subsequent statement is executed. Hence foreach loops implicitly give fork-join parallelism. (Note that the runtime may actually schedule these parallel iterations on system threads in any manner; all that is assured is the causal dependence of the tasks and the fork- and join-points.) A parallel statement can also be defined using the with construct, which is a parallel composition operator that executes two statements in parallel. The language allows expressing nested fork-join parallelism.

The synchronized (l) block statement allows accesses the block to execute under a lock l. Note that this syntax allows *nested locking* only and furthermore, given any point in a function of the program, we can syntactically determine the set of locks that have been acquired since the beginning of the function.

The foreach construct can be optionally augmented with an *annotation* ($\langle annot \rangle$). Such a parallel-loop annotation declares, for each thread spawned at this point, the set of memory locations it will access (read and write). A write access is considered stronger than a read access; therefore if a location is both read and written to, it only needs be specified as a write annotation. An optional where clause specifies bounds for the variables in the reads and writes clauses. The under lock clause expresses that a memory location is accessed only when the prescribed lock is held by the executing thread. The annotation language also has a requires clause that allows making general assumptions on the state of the program variables when the forking happens. These are *pre-conditions* that the programmer asserts they know at the forking-point and are needed to argue why the co-ordination strategy is race-free (for example, this clause may say that the values in the array A[] are all distinct, in a program with parallelism using indirection arrays). The where and requires clauses are allowed to have *bounded quantifiers* to state properties about entire arrays, etc. However, we require that all auxiliary variables mentioned in the clause are quantified. The bounded range of the quantification is required to test the property at runtime.

Function declarations can also be annotated with read/write regions (the memory locations read and written by the function). For nested parallel blocks, we require that the outer parallel loop's

annotation declares access to program variables (without holding any locks) that are used in inner blocks' annotation. Although the annotation language describes the general syntax, we abuse the notation a bit by grouping locations and regions in our examples (e.g. reads x, y stands for reads x reads y).

The annotation language has no *execution semantics*; it is solely designed to help the programmer annotate the precise parts of the memory accessed by each thread, along with the assumptions it makes, in order to argue that the strategy results entails race-freedom.

Let us assume that there is a main function, where the program starts, and that there are no calls to this function. Let us also assume that foreach loop indices (and other variables mentioned in the loop declaration) are never modified in the loop body. Notice that we do not support any form of aliasing in our language nor do we allow throwing exceptions. Handling aliasing in our framework can be achieved, and will basically proceed through an integrated static region-based alias analysis. However, in our current framework we require that parameters of a function do not alias. Exception handling can also be achieved in our framework by ensuring that an exception in one thread does not abort the execution of parallel threads. However, these will make the exposition of our thesis too complex, and we delegate this to future work.

Semantics The semantics of a program is the natural one: assignments, conditionals, loops etc. have the normal semantics; calls to functions are call-by-value. Assignments occur *atomically* even if they read multiple shared variables and write to a shared variable; it turns out that this is not unreasonable, as if we can prove a program race-free under these semantics, then the program with non-atomic assignments would also be race-free.

There is an implicit *barrier* at the end of the foreach loop and the with construct. The semantics ensures that all threads complete before the next statement is executed. The semantics of synchronized blocks is that the specified lock is acquired and released at the start and end of the block respectively.

An execution is hence a partial order of events that respects the above rules for the foreach and with constructs (i.e. events across the fork or across a barrier are ordered in the right way) and the locking mechanism, and furthermore is *sequentially consistent* (i.e. events in one thread must respect the program order).

Data Race Two operations in an execution that are *not* acquisitions or releases of locks are said to be in *conflict* if they access the same memory location and at least one of them is a write. A program has a *data-race* if there is some *sequentially consistent* execution which has two operations in conflict that are not ordered (in other words, there is a sequentially consistent execution after which two conflicting operations are enabled). A program is *data-race free* if it has no data-races.

The above definition of data-races using an ideal sequentially consistent semantics is the standard one (see [2] for instance). Note that races on locks are not considered data-races. Programming languages such as Java and C++ have similar semantics and definition of data-races; furthermore, the memory model of these languages assures us that if the program is data-race free (according to the sequentially-consistent memory model as above), the actual memory model will ensure sequential consistency. This seemingly circular definition (data-races are defined using the sequentially consistent model and lack of data-races ensures the weak memory model assures sequential consistency) is standard and known as the *data-race freedom guarantee* (DRF guarantee). Our goal is to write programs with annotations that we can prove data-race free, and hence assure sequential-consistency in any memory model that has a DRF-guarantee.

4. ACCORD Annotations for Parallel Programs

In this section, we present several examples of data-parallel programs and annotate them using ACCORD contracts. The programs illustrate the expressiveness and succinctness of our annotation language. The suite includes a modified version of the successive over-relaxation (SOR) algorithm, a fully parallel quicksort algorithm (with parallel partitioning and sorting) [21], a parallel implementation of the MonteCarlo simulation program (only the parallel component) from the Java Grande benchmark suite [27], and a sparse matrix multiplication routine with parallelism using indirection arrays. Note that the programs have been annotated by the authors.

4.1 Successive Over-Relaxation with Red-Black Ordering

Successive over-relaxation (SOR) is a variant of the Gauss-Siedel method for solving a linear system of equations, which results in faster convergence. The elements in the equation matrix can be reordered in such a way that alternate elements are marked as red and black (hence the name red-black ordering), giving a checker board pattern. Importantly, in each iteration of SOR all the red elements can be updated in parallel while reading the black elements, followed by a barrier and then an update of the black elements while reading the red elements, thus avoiding races.

Listing 2 shows a parallel implementation of the routine that is executed in each iteration of the SOR algorithm. The program takes a matrix $A[m, n]$ as input, and updates the elements in the matrix A. This code expresses very fine-grained parallelism since all elements of one kind (red or black) are updated in parallel.

Listing 2 Successive Over-Relaxation with Red-Black Ordering

```
1  void sor (int[m,n] A, int w) {
2
3    //update red
4    foreach (int id := 1; id < m; id:=id+1)
5      reads A[id,$j],A[id-1,$j],A[id+1,$j],
6        A[id,$j-1],A[id,$j+1] writes A[id,$j]
7      where 0 <= $j and $j < n and ((id+$j) % 2 = 0){
8
9      foreach(int k := 2-(id%2); k < n; k := k+2){
10       reads A[id,k], A[id-1,k], A[id+1,k],
11         A[id,k-1], A[id,k+1]
12       writes A[id,k]
13       requires ((id + k) % 2 = 0) {
14
15       A[id,k] := (1 - w) * A[id,k] + w * 0.25 *
16         (A[id-1,k]+A[id+1,k]+A[id,k-1]+A[id,k+1]);
17     } }
18
19   //update black
20   ...
21  } } }
```

The `foreach` loop at line 4 divides the matrix among threads in a row-wise fashion. In each iteration of this loop, the red elements in a given row are read and written, while the adjacent black elements are read only. In a checker board pattern, a simple way to check the membership of each element is to test whether the sum of its indices (x, y) is odd or even, which can be expressed using arithmetic constraints (an element (x, y) is red iff $(x + y)\%2 = 0$). As Listing 2 suggests (lines 5-7), ACCORD annotations can express such a sharing strategy by allowing complex modulo arithmetic constraints in the `where` clause. Also note that the annotation uses an *auxiliary* variable $\$j$, which is free, to specify the columns that will be accessed by a thread.

The inner `foreach` loop (line 9), which further divides the elements in a row among threads, is annotated similarly. The only difference is that the natural way to write this annotation is to use the two loop variables to specify the memory locations read and written by each thread (id and k). The second outer loop (beginning at line 20 and not shown here) is similar to the first loop except that it reads both red and black elements, and updates black elements only.

4.2 Quicksort

We implement a race-free, fully parallel algorithm for quicksort [21]. While many parallel implementations of quicksort only exploit the inherent divide-and-conquer parallelism, our implementation performs the partitioning of the array around a pivot in parallel as well, using a parallel rank (prefix sum) algorithm.

Listing 3 shows our implementation. The main function takes an array $A[n]$ and sorts its contents by recursively calling itself. Due to limited space, we have not shown the functions *rel_pos_rec* and *write_pos_rec*, which exhibit a similar recursive parallelism.

Listing 3 Quicksort algorithm with parallel partitioning.

```
1  void qsort (int[n] A, int i, int j) reads i, j
2    writes A[$k] where (i <= $k and $k < j) {
3    if (j-i < 2) return;
4    int pivot := A[i]; //first element
5    int p_index := dyn_partition(A, pivot, i, j);
6    // swap 1st element and element at p_index
7
8    par requires p_index >= i and p_index < j {
9    thread writes A[$k] where (i<=$k and $k<p_index)
10     { qsort(A, i, p_index); }
11   with
12   thread writes A[$k] where (p_index<$k and $k<j)
13     { qsort(A, p_index + 1, j); }
14   }
15  }
16
17  int dyn_partition(int[n] A,int pivot,int i,int j)
18    reads i, j, pivot
19    writes A[$k] where (i<=$k and $k< j) {
20
21    int[n] temp, B;
22    int smalls := rel_pos_rec(A,temp,pivot,i,j);
23    write_pos_rec(A,B,temp,pivot,i,j,0,smalls);
24    A := B;
25    return smalls;
26  }
```

In addition to being a complex program, it highlights some interesting features of our annotation language. The `thread` statement can be annotated (lines 9 and 12), similarly to the `foreach` statement, and the annotation specifies the set of memory locations read and written by the thread. This example also requires annotating functions (lines 2 and 18-19). Function annotations, which include `reads` and `writes` clauses, are important as they give local read and write regions that can be used for modularly testing the program against the annotations. The quicksort program also shows that recursive partitioning can be handled by our annotation language in addition to iterative partitioning of data.

4.3 MonteCarlo Simulation

MonteCarlo is a multi-threaded benchmark from the Java Grande suite. It uses Monte Carlo techniques to find the price of a product based on the price of an underlying asset. The given code sequentially generates N tasks, each with a different parameter. During the parallel phase, these tasks are divided among a group of threads in a block fashion. At the end of processing each task, the corresponding thread writes the simulation result back into a list of results, which is *shared among the threads*. The accesses are protected by a lock. After the parallel phase, the results are reduced in a sequential fashion.

Listing 4 Simplified version of the MonteCarlo simulation code from Java Grande.

```
1  void main(int[nTasks] tasks) {
2    int slice := (nTasks+nThreads −1)/nThreads;
3
4    foreach (int i:=0;i<nThreads;i:=i+1)
5      reads next under lock gl,tasks[$k]
6      writes next,results[$j] under lock gl
7      where (i*slice)<= $k and $k<((i+1)*slice) {
8
9      int ilow := i*slice;
10     int iupper := (i+1)*slice;
11     if (i = nThreads −1) iupper := nTasks;
12
13     for(int run:=ilow; run<iupper; run:=run+1){
14       int result := simulate(tasks[run]);
15
16       synchronized (gl) {
17         next := next + 1;
18         results[next] := result;
19       }
20 } } }
```

Listing 4 shows a simplified version of the program for illustration. Some functions have not been shown due to limited space. The main function takes an array $tasks[n]$ as input and processes each element within the array using parallel threads. Note the program acquires a lock at line 16 before writing to the shared variables $next$ and $results$, and then releases the lock implicitly at line 19.

4.4 Sparse Matrix Multiplication

In Listing 5, we show the simplified core of the Sparse Matrix Multiplication program from the Java Grande suite. The annotation on lines 7-8 specifies that each thread writes to $yt[row[\$j]]$, hence the answer to whether the loop is race-free depends on the runtime contents of the indirection array $row[]$. The subsequent pre-condition (lines 10-14) specifies a property of this array which helps in firmly establishing the race-freedom of the loop. We conjecture that such a complex strategy is in the programmer's mind during the design or implementation of the algorithm, but is hard to statically infer automatically. By declaring it using ACCORD's annotation language makes it easier to reason about the race-freedom of the program.

5. Annotation Adequacy: Generating Non-interference Conditions

The annotation adequacy phase in ACCORD checks whether the contract implies race-freedom, i.e. whether *any* program that satisfies the contract is race-free. We construct a verification condition from the annotation which is then checked by Z3, an SMT solver from Microsoft Research. The verification condition is constructed such that it is satisfiable if the annotations are insufficient to prevent a memory race at some particular memory location. Hence, if the condition is satisfied, then a satisfying solution gives *valuable debugging information*: two threads and a memory location involved, and a program state sufficient for both thread annotations to grant simultaneous access to the location. On the other hand, if the conditions are unsatisfiable then no two concurrent threads that satisfy the annotation can race.

The verification condition is constructed in two parts. One part checks the regions written to by one thread are disjoint from the

Listing 5 Simplified version of the Sparse Matrix Multiplication code from Java Grande.

```
1  void sparsematmult(int nThreads,
2             int[] yt, int[] x, int[] val,
3             int[m] row, int[n] col,
4             int[] lowsum, int[] highsum) {
5    foreach (int id = 0; id < nThreads; id:=id+1)
6
7      reads x[col[$j]], val[$j] writes yt[row[$j]]
8      where $j >= lowsum[id] and $j < highsum[id]
9
10     requires (forall $t1 in [0,nThreads −1],
11       $t2 in [0,nThreads −1]. (t1 != t2 implies
12       (forall $x1 in [lowsum[$t1],highsum[$t1]−1],
13       $x2 in [lowsum[$t2],highsum[$t2]−1].
14         row[$x1] != row[$x2] ))) {
15
16     for (int i=lowsum[id]; i<highsum[id]; i:=i+1){
17       yt[ row[i] ] += x[ col[i] ] * val[i];
18 } } }
```

regions read or written by any other thread created in the same parallel construct. Thus no data race involves sibling threads. The next part checks that the regions declared for a function call or parallel statement are subsets of the regions declared for the surrounding thread. By induction up to a common ancestor, this ensures no two threads which might execute concurrently can have a data race.

5.1 Non-interference with a parallel statement

Consider a parallel loop of the form: foreach(int i:=1, cond(i), i:=i+1) with a requires formula ψ, a set of read annotations R and a set of write annotations W. Given an annotation a in one of these sets, let $arr(a)$ be the array mentioned in the annotation (scalar variables are treated as 0-dimensional arrays), and $locks(a)$ be the set of locks on the annotation (which may be empty). The annotation is parameterized over the loop index i; $a(i)$ is the formula describing the region for iteration i. The array indices are formal parameters of this formula. It may include program variables, however, any other variables must be quantified.

We treat par blocks similarly to a foreach loop with the index ranging from 1 to 2, with appropriately adapted annotations.

Let $Conforms(A, \vec{x}, \varphi)$, abbreviated $[\![A[\vec{x}] \in \varphi]\!]$, be the formula that expresses that access to the location $A[\vec{x}]$ is allowed by the annotation φ. The formula is simply *false* if the A is not the array mentioned in the annotation, otherwise the formula is formed by replacing the formal parameters in the boolean expression in φ with the corresponding expressions in $\vec{x}$.

For instance, consider the writes annotation for C on line 3 in Listing 1. Then, for a parallel iteration with loop-index i_1,
$[\![C[i, k] \in (C[x, y] \text{ where } 0 \le x \wedge x < n \wedge 0 \le y \wedge y < p)]\!]$
$= (0 \le i \wedge i < n \wedge 0 \le k \wedge k < p)$.

We are now ready to define the constraint that is satisfiable iff the annotation on a single parallel foreach construct allows a race between child threads. Consider a foreach loop with read annotations R, write annotations W, and a requires clause ψ. Then we generate the following constraint:

$$\psi \wedge \exists i, j, \vec{x}. \, [\, (i \ne j) \wedge$$

$$\bigvee_{\substack{A \in arr(R) \cup arr(W)}} \left(\bigvee_{\substack{w \in W, a \in R \cup W \\ arr(w) = arr(a) \\ locks(w) \cap locks(a) = \emptyset}} [\![A[\vec{x}] \in w(i)]\!] \wedge [\![A[\vec{x}] \in a(j)]\!] \right)]$$

The formula asserts that there is a single location which two distinct iterations i and j either both write into, or one of them writes to and the other reads from, without holding some common locks. For each parallel block, the above formula is constructed, translated into the SMT-LIB[23] syntax accepted by Z3, and then checked. This formula is satisfiable iff the annotation permits races.

5.2 Checking inclusion of nested annotations

The previous section describes the check that the regions described in the annotations for each thread created by a parallel statement are disjoint. However, we also want the the annotations at various levels in a program be *consistent* with each other. Apart from ensuring the sanity of the annotations, this check is important for the testing phase, as we can simply check whether the program at any point reads and writes to the region specified in the annotation immediately surrounding the access. This check is done by writing a formula which can be satisfied only if there is some location which may be accessed under the child annotations but not the parent's annotation.

If the child statement is a function call the function annotation will be written in terms of the formal parameters of the function. The actual parameters in the call statement need to be substituted for the actual parameters before checking inclusion. Also, function annotations may give the surrounding context if we are checking a child statement which is not lexically within any parallel construct.

One complication is that a program variable may be mentioned in both sets of annotations, but have different values at the two different points. This can be handled by substituting fresh variables for free variables corresponding to program variables that may be modified. In particular, we prohibit assignments to the index of a `foreach` loop, so these variables may be shared. To handle locks, we find the set L of additional locks held at the child statement, and refer to it while constructing the verification condition.

The check will be described for the most general case, which is a pair of nested `foreach` loops. A function annotation can be treated as if it came from a loop with a single iteration, whose annotation does not mention the loop index.

Inclusion fails if access to some location is granted by one of the child's annotations, but not by any of the parent's annotations. Let R_p and W_p be the read and write annotations for the parent, R_c and W_c be the read and write annotations for the child, and ψ_c and ψ_p be the requires formula for the child and parent. Note the child annotations may be parameterized over an inner and an outer thread index. The formula for checking read annotations is

$$\exists i, j, \vec{x}.\, [\, \psi_c \wedge \psi_p \wedge$$
$$\bigvee_{r \in R_c} [\![arr(r)[\vec{x}] \in r(i,j)]\!] \wedge \neg\Big(\bigvee_{\substack{p \in R_p \cup W_p \\ arr(p)=arr(r) \\ locks(p) \subseteq L \cup locks(r)}} [\![arr(r)[\vec{x}] \in p(i)]\!] \Big)]$$

and for write annotations

$$\exists i, j, \vec{x}.\, [\, \psi_c \wedge \psi_p \wedge$$
$$\bigvee_{w \in W_c} [\![arr(w)[\vec{x}] \in w(i,j)]\!] \wedge \neg\Big(\bigvee_{\substack{p \in W_p \\ arr(p)=arr(w) \\ locks(p) \subseteq L \cup locks(w)}} [\![arr(w)[\vec{x}] \in p(i)]\!] \Big)]$$

If the parent annotations contain no existentially quantified auxiliary variables, this formula contains no nested quantifiers. Otherwise, negating membership in the parent regions produces universal quantifiers. This can be avoided if auxiliary variables are only used on annotations for function or parallel statements which contain no function calls or parallel statements. In our experiments, all inclusion checks resulted in formulas with only existential quantification, and can thus be handled reliably by an SMT solver.

6. Transforming Programs for Testing Against Annotations

While the previous phase ensures that the co-ordination strategy ensures race-freedom, it does not ensure that the program itself implements the strategy correctly. The objective of this section is to describe how to transform a parallel program with ACCORD annotations to one with assertions, such that on any test run, the assertions check whether the program correctly implements the co-ordination strategy.

Note that testing tools can, of course, check whether executions have data-races or not. However, the testing that we are achieving here is more general— we are checking whether the executions meet the *co-ordination strategy*. Therefore, even if a certain run does not exhibit data-races, the run could still violate the declared co-ordination strategy, and thus hint at the presence of data-races in other executions in the program.

For example, consider a forking point that creates two threads T_1 and T_2, and consider an execution where T_1 writes to x, followed by a lock-protected access to y, and then T_2 does a lock-protected access to y followed by a write to x. In this execution, there is no data-race, as the lock-protected accesses to y make the accesses to x causally ordered (and an accurate testing tool that keeps track of the happens-before relation will not detect the race). However, there is no way to annotate the threads in any way such that the annotation implies race-freedom and the execution satisfies the annotation (indeed, such an annotation cannot allow T_1 and T_2 to both write to x without being under a common lock).

The transformation of the parallel program to one with assertions is done by specializing the annotation to each thread and translating them to runtime assertions which are then inserted in the thread body.

We do not give a formal description of how the assertions are inserted, but go through the main components and insertion procedures. First, note that in a function, we need to check whether the accesses in the function correspond to only the annotation of the function, and need not check whether the annotation of a caller of the function is also satisfied. This is primarily because of the fact that our inclusion checks ensure that the annotations of the function define subregions of the regions defined by any caller. Similarly, inside nested parallel loops, we need to check accesses against only the annotations at the innermost parallel loop.

Next, in order to check the `requires` clauses in the annotation, note that they allow only *bounded* quantification over ranges, and hence can be checked using a series of nested loops that range over the domains. We can then insert assertions that check if the specified pre-condition holds.

Finally, turning to the accesses, one complication that arises is that an access to an array $A[\vec{x}]$ may be within an annotation a, but the program variables used in a may have changed before the access. We hence insert, at the point of the annotation, assignments to new variables that *cache* the value of the program variables at the annotation site. These variables never get modified, and are used at the access points to check if the indices $\vec{x}$ satisfy the conditions demanded by the annotations. More precisely, for every access to $A[\vec{x}]$, we first figure out statically the set L of locks acquired since the beginning of the `foreach` loop or function immediately surrounding this access. If the access is a read access we insert an assertion that checks the following formula, where R and W are the enclosing set of read and write annotations, and i is the index of the enclosing loop (replace $p(i)$ with p if the access is not surrounded by a loop).

$$\bigvee_{\substack{p \in R \cup W \\ arr(p)=A, locks(p) \subseteq L}} [\![A[\vec{x}] \in p(i)]\!]$$

In this expression, the program variables are replaced by the cached program variables to build the assertion (and bounded quantification in `where` clauses are converted to loops). Similarly, for a write access to $A[\vec{x}]$, insert an assertion that checks the following formula.

$$\bigvee_{\substack{p \in W \\ arr(p)=A, locks(p) \subseteq L}} [\![A[\vec{x}] \in p(i)]\!]$$

Consider the matrix multiplication program given in Listing 1. The transformed program with assertions is given in Listing 6. The first three assertions (lines 7-9) correspond to the first annotation and the accesses to A, B and C, while the last three assertions (lines 11-13) correspond to the second annotation.

Listing 6 Transformed parallel program with assertions corresponding to the parallel implementation of matrix multiplication in Listing 1

```
1
2  void mm (int[m,n] A, int[n,p] B) {
3    foreach (int i := 0; i < m; i:=i+1) {
4      n':=n; p':=p;
5      for (int j := 0; j < n ; j:=j+1)
6        foreach (int k := 0; k < p; k:=k+1) {
7          assert(i=i and 0<=j and j<n');
8          assert(0<=j and j<n' and 0<=k and k<p');
9          assert(i=i and 0<=k and k<p');
10
11          assert(i=i and j=j);
12          assert(j=j and k=k);
13          assert(i=i and k=k);
14
15          C[i,k] := C[i,k] + (A[i,j] * B[j,k]);
16  } }    }
```

Races in the transformed program: The transformed program P' could have data-races. However, we argue that this does not interfere with checking whether the original program P satisfies its annotations.

First, let us assume that in any annotation, the variables mentioned in the annotation are included in the read-set defined by the immediately surrounding annotation. Let us also assume that the annotation adequacy phase passes, and hence we know that if P satisfies its annotations, then it is race-free.

Next, note that P satisfies its annotations iff P' satisfies its assertions on all sequentially consistent runs. This follows from the fact that we have introduced assertions precisely to check the annotations.

We now want to argue that P satisfies its annotation iff P' satisfies its assertions in any run on a memory model with a DRF guarantee.

First, we argue that if P satisfies its annotations, then P' will be race-free. This is easy to see; P' reads from variables mentioned in the annotation which are already covered by the surrounding read annotation, and hence P' accesses only variables that are allowed by the annotation of P, which ensures race-freedom. Hence P' is race-free, and hence we can run P' on any memory model with a DRF guarantee, which will result only in sequentially consistent runs, and hence satisfy all its assertions.

Conversely, if a run of P' (on a DRF memory model) fails an assertion, then either the run is sequentially consistent or not. In the former case, we know that P also does not meet its annotation on a sequentially consistent run. In the latter case, by the DRF guarantee P' must not be race-free, and hence by the argument above P cannot satisfy its annotations.

Hence, we can test whether P satisfies its annotations by testing P' on any memory model that has a DRF guarantee.

7. Evaluation

In this section, we describe our experience in augmenting parallel programs with ACCORD in order to check race-freedom. We provide statistics of annotation burden and show that the ACCORD annotations are minimal and do not put an undue burden on the programmer, and that the annotation language can express the sharing in complex and realistic programs. We evaluated over three suites of benchmarks, which we describe below.

Suite 1: Apart from the examples that we have described in sections §2 and §4 (matrix multiplication, SOR, and QuickSort), we also annotated and checked parallel LU Factorization (LuFact).

Suite 2: This includes four programs from the Java Grande Forum (JGF) benchmark suite: `montecarlo` (MonteCarlo simulation), `series` (which computes Fourier coefficients of a function), `moldyn` (an N-body code modeling interacting particles) and `sparsematmult`. These programs are parameterized by the number of threads: during execution, the threads divide the data among themselves by computing a non-linear formula over the total number of threads and the size of the data. This formula forms the region of computation for each thread.

Suite 3: The last suite of benchmarks is part of the Spec OMP2001 Suite (v3.2), consisting of fairly large programs written in OPENMP. It was significantly harder to understand and annotate the co-ordination strategy in these programs, though the number of annotations required were only a small fraction of the code.

We were able to annotate all these programs and check them for race-freedom using ACCORD. Table 1 presents the results of our evaluation. The name and the code size of our benchmarks are given in the first two columns. Some benchmarks also require annotating functions that are called from parallel blocks for modular reasoning. Note that these are considerably larger programs (up to 2586 LOC and up to 33 fork-join loops).

Annotations The next five columns (labeled *Annotations*) of Table 1 provide information about the annotations required for these programs. The fourth column records the number of total `reads` and total `writes` clauses required to annotate each program. The number of `where` and `lock` clauses in each program are listed in the next column. The last column under *Annotations* lists the number of pre-conditions in the program.

The annotation statistics show that the additional burden on the programmer incurred in writing ACCORD annotations is not much, especially in the larger programs. These results and our experience suggest that the annotations themselves are a natural way to express the parallel co-ordination strategy. We tested the annotations for several of these programs by transforming the parallel program to include assertions (as described in Section 6), and by executing them on test inputs. We believe ACCORD annotations can simplify both manual and automatic reasoning significantly.

Checking Annotation Adequacy: As discussed earlier, we generate a verification condition which is fed to Z3 in order to prove that the annotations imply race-freedom. The columns under the adequacy phase in Table 1 show the results of checking constraints generated for non-interference between sibling threads. Note that we did not find nested parallel blocks in any of the programs.

The first column in the adequacy phase gives the logic used to prove whether the verification condition is satisfiable. We use the SMT_LIB notation [23]. Note that most programs are proved race-free using linear integer constraints. Proving the SOR, `wupwise_l` and `applu_l` program requires non-linear integer arithmetic. The

Table 1. Summary of results from evaluating ACCORD.

	Lines of code	# Parallel Loops/Function Annotation	Annotations				Adequacy phase			Proven Race Free?
			# reads/writes clauses	# where clauses	# lock clauses	# Pre cond.	Logic used	Time taken	Success? (Yes/No)	
MatMult	25	2	2/2	1	0	0	QF_LIA	<1s	Yes	Yes
MatMult (buggy)	30	3	3/3	1	0	0	QF_LIA	<1s	No	No
SOR	45	4	4/4	4	0	2	QF_NIA	<1s	Yes	Yes
Quicksort	100	-	4/7	9	0	0	QF_LIA	<1s	Yes	Yes
LuFact	35	1	1/1	1	0	0	QF_LIA	<1s	Yes	Yes
LuFact (buggy)	35	1	1/1	1	0	0	QF_LIA	<1s	No	No
montecarlo-jgf	255	1	1/1	1	1	0	QF_UFLIA+MA	<1s	Yes	Yes
sparsematmult-jgf	50	1	1/1	1	0	1	AUFLIA	<1s	Yes	Yes
series-jgf	800	1	1/1	1	0	0	QF_UFLIA+MA	<1s	Yes	Yes
moldyn-jgf	1300	6	5/6	6	0	0	QF_LIA	<1s	Yes	Yes
wupwise_l	1029	16	14/14	0	1	4	QF_NIA	<1s	Yes	Yes
swim_l	275	12	12/12	0	0	0	QF_LIA	<1s	Yes	Yes
mgrid_l	722	22	21/20	0	0	0	QF_LIA	<1s	Yes	Yes
applu_l	2586	33/4	30/34	4	0	0	QF_NIA	<1s	No	No (8)
gafort_l	691	9/4	12/13	0	1	1	QF_LIA	<1s	Yes	Yes
art_l	1594	5/7	12/11	1	1	0	QF_LIA	<1s	Yes	Yes

QF_LIA - Quantifier Free Linear Integer Arithmetic, **QF_NIA** - Quantifier Free Non-Linear Integer Arithmetic, **AUFLIA** - Arrays and Linear Integer Arithmetic with Uninterpreted Functions, **QF_UFLIA+MA** - Quantifier Free Linear Integer Arithmetic with Uninterpreted Functions and Multiplication Axioms

verification condition for certain benchmarks includes multiplication and division, which Z3 is unable to handle. Therefore, we use a linear integer arithmetic with uninterpreted functions (UF), and model multiplication as an uninterpreted function with basic axioms that capture its properties. This allowed us to prove the race-freedom property of MonteCarlo, series and sparsematmult.

The next column reports the time taken by Z3 per parallel loop (the time taken is minimal), and whether the annotations implied race-freedom. The last column reports whether ACCORD could prove the program to be race-free. For both buggy programs, the annotation adequacy check failed i.e., Z3 is able to prove the existence of a data-race, given the verification condition generated from the program annotations. While we intentionally introduced a race in the matrix multiplication algorithm (see §2), the data-race in the LU Factorization was an unintended bug in our implementation. The data-race occurs due to an overlap between a read set and a write set (of different threads) due to a subtle boundary condition.

Finally, and surprisingly, we also discovered a set of (eight) previously unknown data-races in the applu_l benchmark from the Spec OMP2001 suite, which has been available as a benchmark for more than 10 years. The bugs have been reported and duly acknowledged. Seven of these data-races have a similar bug pattern, which is triggered only under certain interleavings (the bug is caused because of the removal of a barrier between two for-each loops using a nowait clause). This further strengthens our claim that annotating programs with ACCORD can help discover bugs due to complex sharing strategies.

8. Related Work

There is a rich literature on using type analysis in order to ensure race-freedom [3, 4, 6, 8, 12, 13, 20]. Ownership types that statically enforce object-level encapsulation, combined with *effect* systems that capture computational effects, have been used to define nested regions, separate them, and ensure race-freedom. These systems have been extended for locks to statically ensure deadlock-freedom. The Deterministic Parallel Java language [6] combines types and effects to give the user the ability to give distinct names for regions, including nested regions, specify read and write effects on regions by parallel threads, and by ensuring disjointness of regions, ensure race-freedom and even determinacy.

The main difference between our work and that of type systems is that our annotations allow *dynamic* and *complex logical parti-tioning* of the heap into different regions. It would be very hard to type check, for example, the Successive Over-Relaxation (SOR) example. The regions in SOR are *dynamic* (due to the phases) and even within a phase, the regions are not nested and are instead specified using logical constraints (*row + col* is even/odd). Realizing such a program using static types or type annotations, even with dynamic ownership, is quite challenging, unless the program is rewritten using different data-structures or using copying data between different structures that have different regions. The complexity of course comes at a price— our analyses tackle an undecidable problem (while usually type-analysis is often decidable and fast), and we trade this in order to be able to express complex separation constraints. We instead rely on the emerging class of software verification and SMT solver technology to be effective in practice.

SharC [3] is a type system that assigns different kinds of sharing modes to objects, and these are enforced using a combination of static and dynamic techniques (dynamic techniques kick in when the static analyses fail). The work in [14] proposes contracts which allow fractional permissions, which can be verified using an SMT solver. These approaches deal with objects that are shared among different threads during their lifetime, and employ mutual exclusion synchronization primitives such as locks for correct behavior. In this paper, we need annotations for sharing complex sub-regions that are logically defined and dynamically evolve, and hence the mechanisms proposed in the above work do not suffice. However, combining our annotations with the annotations above to handle static simple region separation and locks would be interesting.

There is some recent work [15] that proposes *inferring* the read and write regions from loop-free (SPMD) CUDA [1] programs, and using SMT solvers to check whether these regions do not intersect. Note that CUDA programs are recursion free and function pointer free. We believe that such an inference may be very hard for larger programs with complex control and data structures. We have instead proposed annotation mechanisms that the user can write for a fairly general purpose programming language.

Separation logic [24] is a Hoare logic for reasoning about heap structures, especially separation, and hence is very relevant as a means of annotation to separate threads. Separation logic has been primarily used to separate dynamic heaps using recursion. When moving to programs with dynamic data, we certainly envisage using logics for separation.

There is a rich literature on *checking* concurrent programs for data-races, a posteriori, with no extra user annotations, using static analysis, testing and model-checking: lock-set based algorithms as in Eraser [25], vector-clock based algorithms [26], hybrid algorithms [22, 29], Goldilocks [11], and static-analysis algorithms [9].

Data-race-freedom or the similar property of non-interference has also been the focus of parallel compilers community under the broader problem of dependency analysis for loops and operations over arrays [28]. The primary motivation in their work is to automatically extract parallelism. We believe manual annotations go a long way in simplifying the problem (for instance, kernels like sparse matrix). In addition, we use sophisticated theorem provers to prove race-freedom. However, we believe that techniques from the auto-parallelization community can help in inferring many simple ACCORD annotations.

9. Discussion and Future Work

Race-freedom is a generic correctness condition for concurrent programs and, given that languages like the next version of C++ consider programs with races erroneous and do not even offer semantics for them, there is an urgent need for software engineering techniques to ensure programs are race-free.

We have, in this paper, proposed a mechanism by which a programmer can formally express the intended concurrency co-ordination strategy, for array-based programs with fork-join parallelism working over complex read/write regions. Expressing the co-ordination strategy formally allows us to check automatically if the strategy ensures race-freedom and also allows automatic insertion of assertions to test if the program conforms to the strategy. We believe that the ACCORD thread contracts and the accompanying reasoning mechanisms presented in this paper are elegant in capturing *complex* region separation for data-parallel programs to prove race-freedom.

The ACCORD annotations programmers write can have benefits other then ensuring race-freedom. There is a promising line of work that suggests that the annotations can make programs run faster— for instance, information about the separation of data can be made available through the compiler to the underlying architecture in order to provide efficient runtime execution mechanisms. The new architecture framework DeNovo being developed at Illinois aims to utilize precisely this kind of separation information and assurance of race-freedom to build simple cache-coherence and faster runtime architectures [19].

The ACCORD language proposed here is a first step towards building a language that can express concurrency co-ordination strategies. ACCORD has currently several limitations— the language cannot handle read/write regions of dynamically allocated heaps, and cannot handle non-fork-join parallelism. These are not inherent limitations to our approach; for example, there are simple mechanisms, such as the inductively-defined nested regions in DPJ [6], or separation logic annotations that can express regions of the dynamic heap. In fact, in ongoing work, we are pursuing an extension of the work presented in this paper with researchers working on DPJ [6], to design a more general and full-fledged annotation language, with associated static-checking and testing mechanisms.

References

[1] NVIDIA CUDA programming guide version 3.0. *http://www.nvidia.com/cuda*, 2010.

[2] S. Adve, M. Hill, B. Miller, and R. Netzer. Detecting data races on weak memory systems. In *The 18th Annual International Symposium on Computer Architecture, 1991.*, pages 234–243, 1991.

[3] Z. Anderson, D. Gay, R. Ennals, and E. Brewer. SharC: checking data sharing strategies for multithreaded c. In *PLDI '08*, pages 149–158. ACM New York, NY, USA, 2008.

[4] D. F. Bacon, R. E. Strom, and A. Tarafdar. Guava: A dialect of java without data races. In *OOPSLA '00*. ACM Press, 2000.

[5] P. Becker. Working draft, standard for programming language C++. Technical report, ISO/IEC JTC 1, Information Technology, Subcommittee SC 22, 2010.

[6] R. Bocchino and V. A. et al. A type and effect system for deterministic parallel java. In *OOPSLA '09*. ACM, 2009.

[7] H.-J. Boehm and S. V. Adve. Foundations of the c++ concurrency memory model. In *PLDI '08*, New York, NY, USA, 2008. ACM.

[8] C. Boyapati and M. Rinard. A parameterized type system for race-free java programs. In *OOPSLA '01*, pages 56–69. ACM, 2001.

[9] J.-D. Choi, K. Lee, A. Loginov, R. O'Callahan, V. Sarkar, and M. Sridharan. Efficient and precise datarace detection for multithreaded object-oriented programs. In *PLDI '02*, pages 258–269, 2002.

[10] L. de Moura and N. Bjørner. Z3: An efficient smt solver. In *Tools and Algorithms for the Construction and Analysis of Systems*, volume 4963/2008 of *LNCS*, pages 337–340. Springer Berlin, April 2008.

[11] T. Elmas, S. Qadeer, and S. Tasiran. Goldilocks: a race and transaction-aware java runtime. In J. Ferrante and K. S. McKinley, editors, *PLDI '07*, pages 245–255. ACM, 2007.

[12] C. Flanagan and M. Abadi. Object types against races. In *CONCUR*, volume 1664 of *LNCS*, pages 288–303. Springer, 1999.

[13] C. Flanagan and S. N. Freund. Type-based race detection for java. In *PLDI '00*, pages 219–232, New York, NY, USA, 2000. ACM.

[14] K. R. Leino and P. Müller. A basis for verifying multi-threaded programs. In *ESOP '09*, pages 378–393, Berlin, Heidelberg, 2009. Springer-Verlag.

[15] R. Lublinerman and S. Tripakis. Checking equivalence of spmd programs using non-interference. Technical Report UCB/EECS-2009-42, EECS Department, University of California, Berkeley, Mar 2009.

[16] J. Manson, W. Pugh, and S. Adve. The Java memory model. In *POPL '05*, pages 378–391. ACM New York, NY, USA, 2005.

[17] B. Meyer. Applying "design by contract". *Computer*, 25(10):40–51, 1992. ISSN 0018-9162. doi: http://dx.doi.org/10.1109/2.161279.

[18] Microsoft Corporation. Code Contracts. *http://research.microsoft.com/en-us/projects/contracts/*, 2008-10.

[19] Parallel@Illinois. Denovo: Rethinking hardware for disciplined parallelism. *http://rsim.cs.illinois.edu/denovo/*, 2008-10.

[20] P. Permandla, M. Roberson, and C. Boyapati. A type system for preventing data races and deadlocks in the java virtual machine language: 1. In *LCTES '07*, page 10, New York, NY, USA, 2007. ACM.

[21] D. Powers. Parallelized Quicksort and Radixsort with Optimal Speedup. In *Proceedings of the International Conference on Parallel Computing Technologies, 1991.*, pages 167–176, 1991.

[22] E. Pozniansky and A. Schuster. Efficient on-the-fly data race detection in multithreaded c++ programs. In *PPoPP '03*, pages 179–190, New York, NY, USA, 2003. ACM.

[23] S. Ranise and C. Tinelli. The smt-lib standard: Version 1.2. 2006.

[24] J. Reynolds. Separation logic: A logic for shared mutable data structures. In *Logic in Computer Science, 2002. Proceedings.*, pages 55–74, 2002.

[25] S. Savage, M. Burrows, G. Nelson, P. Sobalvarro, and T. Anderson. Eraser: A dynamic data race detector for multithreaded programs. *ACM Transactions on Computer Systems (TOCS)*, 1997.

[26] D. Schonberg. On-the-fly detection of access anomalies. In *PLDI '89*, pages 285–297. ACM New York, NY, USA, 1989.

[27] L. A. Smith and J. M. Bull. A multithreaded java grande benchmark suite. In *In Proceedings of the Third Workshop on Java for High Performance Computing*, pages 97–105, 2001.

[28] M. J. Wolfe. *High Performance Compilers for Parallel Computing*. Addison-Wesley Longman Publishing Co., Inc., Boston, MA, USA, 1995. ISBN 0805327304.

[29] Y. Yu, T. Rodeheffer, and W. Chen. Racetrack: efficient detection of data race conditions via adaptive tracking. *SIGOPS Oper. Syst. Rev.*, 39(5):221–234, 2005.

GRace: A Low-Overhead Mechanism for Detecting Data Races in GPU Programs

Mai Zheng, Vignesh T. Ravi, Feng Qin, and Gagan Agrawal

Dept. of Computer Science and Engineering
The Ohio State University
2015 Neil Ave, Columbus, OH, USA
{zhengm, raviv, qin, agrawal}@cse.ohio-state.edu

Abstract

In recent years, GPUs have emerged as an extremely cost-effective means for achieving high performance. Many application developers, including those with no prior parallel programming experience, are now trying to scale their applications using GPUs. While languages like CUDA and OpenCL have eased GPU programming for non-graphical applications, they are still explicitly parallel languages. All parallel programmers, particularly the novices, need tools that can help ensuring the correctness of their programs.

Like any multithreaded environment, data races on GPUs can severely affect the program reliability. Thus, tool support for detecting race conditions can significantly benefit GPU application developers. Existing approaches for detecting data races on CPUs or GPUs have one or more of the following limitations: 1) being ill-suited for handling non-lock synchronization primitives on GPUs; 2) lacking of scalability due to the state explosion problem; 3) reporting many false positives because of simplified modeling; and/or 4) incurring prohibitive runtime and space overhead.

In this paper, we propose GRace, a new mechanism for detecting races in GPU programs that combines static analysis with a carefully designed dynamic checker for logging and analyzing information at runtime. Our design utilizes GPUs memory hierarchy to log runtime data accesses efficiently. To improve the performance, GRace leverages static analysis to reduce the number of statements that need to be instrumented. Additionally, by exploiting the knowledge of thread scheduling and the execution model in the underlying GPUs, GRace can accurately detect data races with no false positives reported.

Based on the above idea, we have built a prototype of GRace with two schemes, i.e., GRace-stmt and GRace-addr, for NVIDIA GPUs. Both schemes are integrated with the same static analysis. We have evaluated GRace-stmt and GRace-addr with three data race bugs in three GPU kernel functions and also have compared them with the existing approach, referred to as B-tool. Our experimental results show that both schemes of GRace are effective in detecting all evaluated cases with no false positives, whereas B-tool reports many false positives for one evaluated case. On the one hand, GRace-addr incurs low runtime overhead, i.e., 22-116%, and low space overhead, i.e., 9-18 MB, for the evaluated kernels. On the

other hand, GRace-stmt offers more help in diagnosing data races with larger overhead.

Categories and Subject Descriptors C.1.2 [*Processor Architectures*]: Multiple Data Stream Architectures; C.4 [*Performance of Systems*]: Reliability, availability, and serviceability; D.2.5 [*Software Engineering*]: Testing and Debugging

General Terms Algorithm, Design, Reliability

Keywords CUDA, Concurrency, Data Race, GPU, Multithreading

1. Introduction

1.1 Motivation

Starting from the last 4-5 years, parallel computation has become essential for taking full advantage of Moore's law. Prior to that, chip designers delivered increases in clock rates and instruction-level parallelism, and enabled single-threaded code to be executed faster. This changed trend is probably best reflected in the cost effectiveness and popularity of GPUs. Through a large number of simple (in-order execution) cores, GPUs achieve very high peak performance with low costs and modest power requirements.

Today, a variety of non-graphical applications are being developed on GPUs by programmers, scientists, and researchers around the world [1], spanning different domains, including computational biology, cryptography, financial modeling, and many others. On the one hand, GPUs are becoming part of the high-end systems. For example, in the list of top 500 supercomputers released in May 2010, two of the top seven systems were based on GPUs. On the other hand, a single GPU attached to a desktop or a laptop is being used by application developers who never used parallel machines in the past.

Sustaining the trend towards application acceleration using GPUs or GPU-based clusters will require advanced tool support [33]. Though CUDA [1] and OpenCL [23] have been quite successful, they are both explicitly parallel languages, and pose a programming challenge for those lacking prior parallel programming background. As we stated above, it is common for today's desktops and laptops to have low and medium-end GPUs, making a highly parallel environment accessible and affordable to application developers that never used clusters or SMPs in the past. Developing correct and efficient parallel programs, however, is a formidable challenge for this group of users. Similarly, when developing high-end applications for a cluster of GPUs, a hybrid programming model combining Message Passing Interfaces (MPI) and CUDA must be used, making the code hard to write, maintain, and test even for very experienced parallel programmers. Recently, a number of efforts have been initiated with the goal of automatic code generation for GPUs [26, 31, 40, 44], but these efforts are still in early stages.

PPoPP'11, February 12–16, 2011, San Antonio, Texas, USA.
Copyright © 2011 ACM 978-1-4503-0119-0/11/02...$10.00

Any multithreaded program involves the risk of *race conditions*. A data race occurs when two or more threads access the same memory location concurrently, and at least one of the accesses is a write [39]. As GPUs obtain high performance with a large number of concurrent threads, race conditions can very easily manifest [7, 27]. Once a race condition has occurred, it can lead to program crashes, hangs, or silent data corruption [28]. Besides the fact that many GPU programmers may lack parallel programming experience, another reason for data races can be programmers' unawareness of implicit assumptions made in third-party kernel functions. For example, one assumption a kernel function developer may make while aggressively optimizing shared memory use in a GPU program is *"the maximal number of threads per block will be 256"*. A user of this kernel may be unaware of such an assumption, and may launch the kernel function with 512 threads. This is likely to create overlapped memory indices among different threads and lead to data races.

Many approaches have been developed for detecting data races in multithreaded programs that run on CPUs. These approaches can be classified into three categories: lockset based methods [9, 39], happens-before based techniques [12, 34, 37], and hybrid schemes combining these two [35, 38, 43]. Lockset based methods maintain a set of locks that protect each shared variable and report a data race if a lockset is empty. Happens-before based techniques maintain the Lamport happens-before relation [25] between different accesses to each shared variable by tracking synchronization events and report a data race if there is no strict order between two accesses to a shared variable. While effective in detecting data races for CPU programs, these approaches are mostly inapplicable to GPU programs. This is because GPU programs only use barriers for synchronization instead of locks, which makes lockset based methods obsolete. Furthermore, GPU programs typically have simple happens-before relation through barriers, which makes existing happens-before based techniques unnecessarily expensive.

Recently, two approaches [7, 27] have been proposed to detect data races in GPU programs. PUG [27], proposed by Li *et al.*, symbolically models GPU kernel functions and leverages Satisfiability Modulo Theories (SMT) solvers to detect data races. While effective in finding subtle data races, PUG may also report false positives due to its approximation of the models. Furthermore, the state explosion of thread interleavings remains a problem for PUG, even though partial order reduction methods can mitigate the problem to some degree.

Boyer *et al.* proposed a dynamic tool to detect data races by tracking all accesses to shared variables at runtime [7]. More specifically, for each access to a shared variable, the tool reports a data race if other threads have accessed the same shared variable after last synchronization call. While the tool can detect data races, it incurs prohibitive (several orders of magnitude) runtime overhead since it is designed for execution only in the emulation mode. Even though it may be ported to real GPUs, the runtime overhead is expected to be very large. This is because the tool accesses the device memory at least tens of thousands of times for each shared memory access from a kernel function. Additionally, as we will show later, this tool can report many false positives since it does not consider all details of GPU thread scheduling.

As we stated above, one of the examples of race conditions we have observed arises when a third party kernel is incorrectly used by an application developer. Detecting such race conditions requires low-overhead mechanisms that only incur modest overheads, suitable for an application development environment. While the overheads for any tool that performs runtime logging will clearly be too high for a production run of the application, our target is to keep slowdowns comparable to those of versions compiled with the debugging (-g -G) option. Second, the mechanisms must report very few (or preferably none) false positives so that they can guide programmers to quickly fix the data races.

1.2 Our Contributions

In this paper, we propose a low-overhead technique, called GRace, for accurately detecting data races in GPU programs. GRace exploits the advantages of both static analysis (i.e., no runtime overhead) and dynamic checking (i.e., accurate detection). The main idea is to first detect data races and prune addresses that cannot cause data races by statically analyzing the program. For other memory accesses, GRace instruments the corresponding statements to check data races during program execution.

Our idea is based on the observation that many memory accesses in GPU kernel functions are regular and therefore the memory addresses can be pre-determined at compile time. For example, the statement "$Array[tid] = 3$" assigns 3 to the array element indexed with current thread id. Based on this observation, GRace statically detects, or prunes the possibility of, data races for a majority of the memory accesses. This step is expected to significantly reduce the number of statements that need to be monitored by dynamic checking and therefore improve the overall performance of GRace.

Certainly static analysis may not determine all memory accesses in GPU programs. For example, a memory index that depends on user input data cannot be determined at compile time. In this case, GRace instruments the corresponding statements and detects data races at runtime.

Unlike previous work [7], GRace's dynamic checking mechanism is aware of GPU architecture and runtime systems, i.e., memory hierarchy and thread scheduling. By exploiting memory hierarchy, particularly the programmer controlled shared memory, GRace temporarily stores memory access information in GPU's shared memory, which is much faster than GPU's device memory. As a result, GRace can efficiently detect part of data races via faster memory accesses. Similarly, GRace is aware of thread scheduling mechanism and execution model. Therefore, GRace does not report false positives in our experiments.

In summary, we have made the following contributions on detecting data races in GPU programs.

- **Combining static analysis and dynamic checking.** Our proposed GRace utilizes static analysis for improving the performance of a dynamic data race detection tool for GPU programs. Our experimental results show that GRace can efficiently detect data races and benefits significantly from static analysis.

- **Exploiting GPU's thread scheduling and execution model.** We have identified the key difference between data race detection on GPU and that on CPU, which lies in GPU-specific thread scheduling and the execution model. By exploiting the difference, GRace can detect data races more accurately in GPU programs than existing work. Furthermore, we have explored two designs of GRace, including GRace-stmt with more helpful bug diagnostic information, and GRace-addr with lower runtime and space overhead.

- **Exploiting GPU's memory hierarchy.** By leveraging low-latency memory in GPU, GRace detects data races more efficiently. Users can decide whether to enable such feature or not based on their own needs.

- **Implementing and evaluating a prototype of GRace.** We have implemented a prototype of GRace and evaluated it with three GPU kernel functions, including two well-known data-mining algorithms and one used in the previous work in this area. Specifically, we have evaluated the functionality and performance of GRace, as well as benefits from utilizing static analysis and exploiting GPU architecture and runtime systems.

```
1  __device__ void sample_kernel(int* result)
2  {
3      extern __shared__ int s_array[];
4      int tid = threadIdx.x;
5      ...
6      s_array[ tid ] = tid;
7      result[ tid ] = s_array[ tid + 1 ] * tid;
8  }
```

Figure 1. An example of data race in a GPU kernel function.

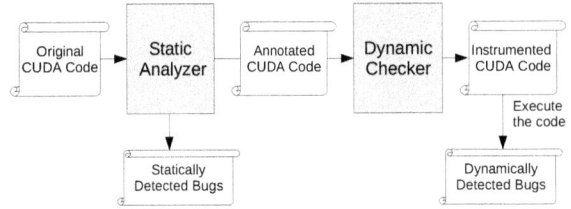

Figure 2. GRace overview. Two shaded blocks are the components of GRace.

2. Background: GPU and Data Race in GPU Programs

2.1 An Example of Data Race on GPU Programs

Figure 1 shows an example of data race in a GPU kernel function. Line 6 writes data to the shared memory address with the index of tid and Line 7 reads the data from the shared memory address with the index of $tid + 1$. This kernel function will be executed by all the threads. It will appear that Threads i and $i + 1$ incurs a data race since Thread i reads the shared memory address $s\_array[i + 1]$ at line 7 and Thread $i + 1$ writes the same shared memory address at line 6. However, this is not true for all pairs of threads due to GPU's thread scheduling and the SIMD execution within a warp of threads.

All threads within a warp are scheduled together on one multiprocessor, and executed in the SIMD fashion. Thus, threads within a warp can only cause data races by executing the same instruction. On the contrary, threads across different warps can have data races by executing the same or different instructions. Therefore, in the above case, Threads i and $i + 1$ have a data race only if they belong to different warps. This implies that only threads at the boundary of two consecutive warps incur data races. Without such a detailed knowledge of thread scheduling and execution model of GPUs, a tool can easily report many false positives. This, in turn, can make it very hard for a programmer to debug the application.

2.2 GPU Architecture and SIMD Execution Model

A modern Graphical Processing Unit (GPU) architecture consists of two major components, the processing component and the memory component. The processing component in a typical GPU is composed of a certain number of streaming multiprocessors. Each streaming multiprocessor, in turn, contains a set of simple cores that perform in-order processing of the instructions. To support general purpose computations on GPUs, different vendors releases their proprietary software development kits, runtime support, and APIs. These releases include CUDA (from NVIDIA) [1], Stream SDK (from AMD) [2], and OpenCL (from Khronos group) [23]. To achieve high performance, a large number of threads, typically a few thousands, are launched. These threads execute the same operation on different sets of data. A block of threads are mapped to and executed on one streaming multiprocessor. Furthermore, threads within a block are divided into multiple groups, termed as *warp* in CUDA, and *wavefront* in stream SDK and OpenCL. Each warp or wavefront of threads are co-scheduled on a streaming multiprocessor and execute the same instruction in a given clock cycle (SIMD execution). The number of threads/work-items in a warp or a wavefront varies with the design choice. For example, on NVIDIA Tesla cards, the warp size is 32, while the wavefront size on ATI Radeon is 64. The APIs also provide an explicit barrier synchronization mechanism across threads within a block. However, there is no explicit synchronization between blocks, which are implicitly synchronized at the completion of kernel execution.

The memory component of a modern GPU typically contains several layers. One is the *host memory*, which is available on the CPU main memory. This is essential as any general purpose GPU

computation can only be launched from the CPU. The second layer is the *device memory*, which resides on the GPU card. This represents the global memory on a GPU and is accessible across all streaming multiprocessors. The device memory is interconnected with the host through a PCI-Express. This interconnectivity enables DMA transfer of data between host and device memory. Note that any access to device memory is of high latency and hence expensive. A scratch memory, which is programmable and of high-speed access, is available privately to a streaming multiprocessor. The scratch memory is termed as *shared memory* on NVIDIA cards and *local data store* on AMD cards. Registers and local memory that is private to each simple core in a streaming multiprocessor is also available.

On NVIDIA GPUs, the size of the shared memory on each multiprocessor was 16 KB till recently (up to the Tesla cards). The latest GPUs from NVIDIA (Fermi) have a slightly different design (with a 64 KB *cache*). This cache can be partitioned into either a 48 KB programmable cache (like shared memory on older cards) and a 16 KB L1 (hardware-controlled) cache, or a 16 KB programmable cache and a 48 KB L1 cache.

For simplicity, we use the terms from NVIDIA to describe our work in the rest of this paper.

3. GRace Design and Implementation

3.1 Design Challenges and GRace Overview

It is challenging to design a low overhead, accurate dynamic data race detector for GPU programs. More specifically, there are three key design challenges which we list below:

How to handle a large number of shared memory accesses in GPU programs? Typically, a GPU kernel function launches thousands of threads to achieve the best use of available cores and for masking latencies. As a result, a running GPU kernel issues a large number of shared memory accesses from many threads concurrently. We need to monitor all of these memory accesses and check possible data races for each pair of memory accesses from different threads. This can easily involve a prohibitive runtime overhead, which is also the key limitation of the previous work in this area [7].

How to detect data races in GPU programs accurately? As we explained in the previous section, GPU runtime systems typically schedule a warp (or wavefront in stream SDK and OpenCL) of threads to run together on a GPU processor. The threads within a warp execute the same instruction in a given clock cycle (SIMD model). As a result, different instructions are executed sequentially by all the threads within a Warp and thereby cannot cause any data races. Without distinguishing threads based on warps, a detection method can easily introduce false positives.

How to handle slow device memory in GPUs? Detecting data races at runtime requires monitoring and storing a large number of memory accesses. The best choice is to store these data in device memory since it is much larger than shared memory, and also faster than the host memory. However, even the device memory is much slower than the shared memory. As a result, data race detection for each memory access is expected to be very slow if all profiling data is stored in device memory.

To address the above challenges, GRace exploits static analysis, knowledge of GPU-specific thread scheduling, and the memory hierarchy. As shown in Figure 2, GRace consists of two major components: Static Analyzer and Dynamic Checker. More specifically, Static Analyzer first detects certain data races and also prunes memory access pairs that cannot be involved in data races. Other memory access statements, which are neither determined as data races nor pruned by the Static Analyzer, are instrumented by the Dynamic Checker. It then efficiently detects data races at runtime by leveraging both shared memory and device memory.

To detect a data race, both Static Analyzer and Dynamic Checker check one synchronization block at a time. A *synchronization block* contains all the statements between a pair of consecutive synchronization (barrier) calls. The reason for checking one synchronization block at a time is that memory accesses across different synchronization blocks are strictly ordered and therefore they cannot cause data races. In the case of no explicit synchronization calls, the end of a kernel function is the implicit synchronization point.

GRace currently only considers data races in shared memory accesses from GPU kernel functions. In our experience, race conditions are more likely on shared memory accesses, since the use of a small shared memory is aggressively optimized in kernel functions. For example, variables that are updated frequently and/or updated by different threads are usually stored in shared memory. To detect races in device memory, our proposed static analysis (Section 3.2) and exploitation of thread scheduling knowledge (Section 3.3.1) are still applicable since these techniques are irrelevant to the locations where races occur.

It should be noted that the latest NVIDIA cards are also supporting a traditional L1 cache. However, it is expected that experienced GPU programmers, particularly those developing kernels, will continue to use and aggressively optimize shared memory even on newer cards. This is because a programmer controlled cache can provide better reuse, especially when a developer has a deep understanding of the application and the architecture.

3.2 Static Analyzer

In this subsection, we describe the algorithm for static analysis. The goal of our static analysis is to resolve as many memory references as possible, and determine if they could be involved in a data race or not. After our static analysis phase, only the memory references that cannot be resolved completely, or the memory references that could conflict with another access that cannot be resolved, are instrumented. Another key goal of our static analysis is to help further reducing the overhead of dynamic instrumentation. To achieve this goal, our static analysis determines whether the same address is accessed across iterations and/or threads. If so, dynamic checker can perform the instrumentation for only certain threads and/or iterations so that the runtime and space overheads are drastically reduced.

Our overall analysis algorithm for a synchronization block is shown in Algorithm 1. The kernel code within a synchronization block may contain nested loops. However, we assume that there is no unstructured control-flow, i.e. the loops are explicit, and are not created with the use of a *goto* statement. We perform the following, if the address can be statically determined. All memory accesses are transformed into a linear constraint in terms of the *thread id* (tid) and loop iterator(s) (I). Also, the constraints are parameterized with the range of values that tid and I can possess. We consider all pairs of left-hand-side memory accesses to examine the possibility of *write-write* race conditions. Similarly, we consider all pairs comprising a left-hand-side and a right-hand-side memory accesses, to

---

Algorithm 1 Static Analyzer

```
 1: for each synchronizationblock do
 2:     for each pair of write − write and read − write accesses
        do
 3:         if static_determinable(sh_mem_addr) then
 4:             lin_constraints[] = gen_constraints(sh_mem_addr,
                tid, iter_id)
 5:             add_params_to_constraints(tid, iter_id,
                    max_thread_id, max_iteration)
 6:             soln_set[] = constraint_solver(lin_constraints[])
 7:             if empty(soln_set[]) then
 8:                 No data race
 9:             else
10:                 Extract conflicting tid_x, tid_y from soln_set[]
                        and report inter/intra warp data races
11:             end if
12:         else
13:             Mark the pair of accesses as 'Montior at Runtime'
14:             for each of the two accesses do
15:                 if check_loop_invariant(sh_mem_addr) then
16:                     Mark as loop invariant
17:                 end if
18:                 if check_thread_invariant(sh_mem_addr) then
19:                     if is_write(sh_mem_addr) then
20:                         Report Intra-warp data races
21:                     else
22:                         Mark as thread invariant
23:                     end if
24:                 end if
25:             end for
26:         end if
27:     end for
28: end for
```

---

evaluate the possibility of a *read-write* race condition. Integer programming (*linear constraint solver*) is used to determine the existence of combination of tid and I for which the shared memory addresses accessed by distinct threads can be identical. A conflict could be intra-warp only if the conflict arises between the threads with identifiers from $i*warpSize$ to $(i+1)*warpSize-1$, where $0 \le i < warpNum$. Similarly, a conflict may lead to *inter-warp* race if the conflict arises between threads with identifiers that are across different warps.

If the address can not be determined at compile time, we mark for analysis at runtime (for Dynamic Checker). After this, all such pairs have been determined, we next consider how the overheads of dynamic instrumentation can be reduced. Towards this, we determine if an address potentially involved in a conflict is invariant across threads. If so, the address needs to be recorded during execution of only one thread. Moreover, we can only have an *inter-warp* race in this condition, as race condition must arise with execution of a different instruction by another thread. Otherwise, within an instruction, if the write access (which is thread invariant) is not protected by atomic operation we report an intra-warp data race.

Also, if a memory access expression is invariant across iterations of one or more loops in which this memory access is enclosed, it only needs to be recorded during one iteration of the loop. We later demonstrate the benefits of these optimizations in the experimental results section.

Now, we consider a case study with *Co-clustering* [8], a popular data mining algorithm. Co-clustering considers clustering along two dimensions, i.e., original points can be viewed as being in a two dimensional array. We use a GPU implementation of this code that was aggressively optimized for shared memory use in a recent

```
1   void rowClusterCount(float* data, int numRow, int numRowCluster,
        int numColCluster, int numCol, float* Acompressed, float*
        rowQuality4Compressed, int* rowCL, int* colCL, int* rowCS_l)
2   {   //Args of kernel are in device memory

        //Declaration of shared memory arrays
3       extern __shared__ float s_float[];
4       float* Acomp = s_float;
5       float* rowQual = s_float + numColCluster * numRowCluster;
6       float* rowCS = s_float + numColCluster * numRowCluster +
                        numRowCluster;
7       float* sh_rowCL = s_float + numColCluster * numRowCluster +
                          numRowCluster + numRowCluster;

        /* Omitting other declarations and shared memory initialization */

        //Computation and reduction on shared memory
8       for (int r = 0; r < numRow; r += rowcluster_THREADS *
            rowcluster_BLOCKS)
9       {
10        for (int rc = 0; rc < numRowCluster; rc++)
11        {
12          if (rowCS[rc] > 0)
13          {
14            for (int c = 0; c < numCol; c++)
15            {
16              tempDistance += data[(r+n_index)*numCol+c] *
                                Acomp[rc*numRowCluster + colCL[c]];
17              tempDistance = -2*tempDistance + rowQual[rc];
18            }
29          }
20        }
21        sh_rowCL[r+tid] = minCL;
22      }
23  }
```

Figure 3. A simplified code of Co-clustering kernel.

study [32]. A simplified portion of this GPU kernel code is shown in Figure 3. From the code, we can see that there are four arrays declared in the shared memory (lines 3-7) and there is one nested *for* loop (lines 8-22). Looking into the memory accesses within those four arrays on shared memory, three of those arrays (*rowCS* at line 12, *Acomp* at line 16, and *rowQual* at line 17) are read-only and the last one (*sh_rowCL* at line 21) is write only. Thus, there are three pairs of memory addresses that needs to be analyzed for data races. Next, for each of the three pairs of memory addresses, we need to generate linear constraints. These linear constraints are created as a function of *tid* and *loop index*. Note that, all the four shared memory arrays point to the base address of *s_float* with some offsets. Thus, this offset translation is also accounted for when formulating the linear constraints. Additionally, we also provide some ranges for the parameters that are in the linear constraints. For example, let us consider *rowCS[rc]*. First, rowCS is translated based on its offset from the base address of *s_float*. Then, the constraint is generated with *rc* as an unknown. However, the range of values that *rc* can take is known from the loop initialization. Thus, this range will be parameterized into the constraint. The other variables in the subscript, *numColCluster* and *numRowCluster* are constants taken from the user input. Once a constraint is developed and parameterized, it is fed into the linear constraint solver. The solution output is analyzed to detect any inter/intra data races. It turns out, in this example, there cannot be any data races between reads on *rowCS* and writes to *sh_rowCL*, and between reads on *rowQual* and writes to *sh_rowCL*.

A specific case arises with respect to a variable like *Acomp* where the subscript variable contains *indirect accesses* (*colCL[c]*). In this case, the static analysis cannot resolve the memory access, and we mark the address to be instrumented by the dynamic checker. Since this memory access can have a conflict with *sh_rowCL*, it is also marked for instrumentation.

It appears that our static analysis can at most reduce the accesses to be instrumented from four to two. However, static analysis can extract other information that can be used by the dynamic checker.

Algorithm 2 Intra-warp Race Detection
_____
1: **if** $accessType$ is $read$ **then**
2:      Stop execution of this algorithm
3: **end if**
4: **for** $targetIdx = 0$ to $warpSize - 1$ **do**
5:      $sourceIdx \leftarrow tid \% warpSize$
6:      **if** $sourceIdx \neq targetIdx$ **then**
7:          **if** $warpTbl[sourceIdx] = $
                $warpTbl[targetIdx]$ **then**
8:              Report a Data Race
9:          **end if**
10:     **end if**
11: **end for**
_____

For example, accesses to *Acomp* are invariant across all the threads in the block. Thus, it is sufficient to monitor *Acomp* for only one thread. Furthermore, *Acomp* needs to be monitored only once in the outer loop, i.e., when $r = 0$, since accesses to *Acomp* are invariant across iterations of the loop.

3.3 Dynamic Checker

Dynamic Checker detects data races at runtime. Given a GPU kernel function, the Dynamic Checker instruments every memory access statement that is annotated by Static Analyzer. At runtime, the inserted code after these memory access statements records information of the memory access and detects *intra-warp* data races, which are caused by the same statement from multiple threads within a warp. Furthermore, Dynamic Checker instruments every synchronization call to detect *inter-warp* data races, which are caused by the same or different statements from multiple threads across different warps. Note that the profiling and checking code will be executed only by one thread and/or at one iteration if Static Analyzer determines the memory address is invariant across threads and/or loop iterations.

By separating intra-warp and inter-warp races, GRace improves detection accuracy, i.e., no false positives caused by different instructions from intra-warp threads accessing the same address. Another benefit of this separation is that GRace can perform fast intra-warp race detection after each memory access and delay the slow inter-warp race detection to each synchronization call. Furthermore, GRace can utilize a small chunk of shared memory to temporarily store memory accesses from a warp of threads and thereby speed up intra-warp race detection.

3.3.1 Intra-warp Race Detection

GRace maintains a table, called warpTable, to store memory access information from every statement executed by each warp of threads. More specifically, after each instrumented memory access in the kernel function, GRace records the access type (read or write) and the memory addresses accessed by all the threads within a warp into the corresponding warpTable. A warpTable has one address entry for each thread, which allows all the threads within a warp to write the accessed memory addresses into the table in parallel.

After recording one warp of memory accesses in a warpTable, GRace performs intra-warp race detection as described by Algorithm 2. More specifically, it first checks whether the access type is read (line 1). If yes, the checking process stops (line 2) since it is impossible to have races only through reads. Otherwise, GRace scans the table (line 4) to check whether two threads access the same memory address (line 5-7). If so, GRace reports a data race with the executed statement and racing thread ids (line 8). All threads within a warp execute the above steps in parallel. Note that GRace requires no explicit synchronization between updating a warpTable and detecting intra-warp races since both operations will be executed se-

Algorithm 3 Inter-warp Race Detection by GRace-stmt

1: **for** $stmtIdx1 = 0$ to $maxStmtNum - 1$ **do**
2:    **for** $stmtIdx2 = stmtIdx1 + 1$ to $maxStmtNum$ **do**
3:       **if** $BlkStmtTbl[stmtIdx1].warpID =$
        $BlkStmtTbl[stmtIdx2].warpID$ **then**
4:          Jump to line 15
5:       **end if**
6:       **if** $BlkStmtTbl[stmtIdx1].accessType$ is $read$ **and**
        $BlkStmtTbl[stmtIdx2].accessType$ is $read$ **then**
7:          Jump to line 15
8:       **end if**
9:       **for** $targetIdx = 0$ to $warpSize - 1$ **do**
10:          $sourceIdx \leftarrow tid \% warpSize$
11:          **if** $BlkStmtTbl[stmtIdx1][sourceIdx] =$
           $BlkStmtTbl[stmtIdx2][targetIdx]$ **then**
12:            Report a Data Race
13:          **end if**
14:       **end for**
15:    **end for**
16: **end for**

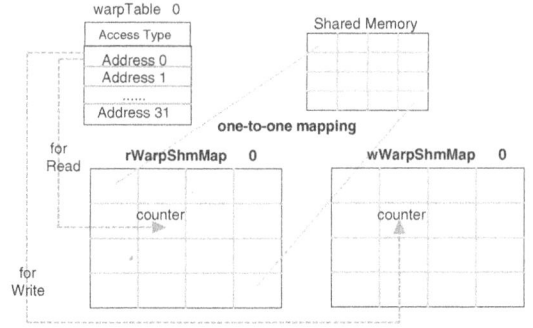

Figure 4. Data structures of a rWarpShmMap and a wWarpShmMap. Each Warp-ShmMap or BlockShmMap entry is corresponding to one shared memory address in one-to-one mapping. Each address stored in a warpTable is used as the index to increase the corresponding counter in the rWarpShmMap and rBlockShmMap, or wWarpShmMap and wBlockShmMap, depending on the access type. Note that rBlockShmMap and wBlockShmMap are not shown here due to space limit.

quentially (SIMD) by all threads within a warp. This is important because inserted synchronization may lead to deadlock if the statement is a conditional branch executed by a subset of threads within a warp.

After performing intra-warp race detection, GRace transfers memory access information from the warpTable, fully or partially, to device memory for future inter-warp race detection, which is discussed in Section 3.3.2. As a result, GRace can recycle the warpTable for next memory access and race detection for the same warp of threads. This design choice keeps the memory footprint of intra-warp race detection minimal. Our experimental results have shown that typically 1 KB can hold the warpTables for all the warps on Tesla C1060 (More details in Section 5). Thus, GRace only incurs 6% space overhead for 16 KB shared memory in Tesla cards. With the trend of increasing size of shared memory, the relative space overhead will become even smaller. For example, the latest release of GPU chip, Fermi, gives the option of having 48 KB shared memory, which reduce the relative space overhead of our approach to 2%. If running legacy GPU kernel functions that assume 16 KB shared memory, GRace can enjoy plenty of shared memory. The extreme case is that a kernel function uses up shared memory for its own benefits. In such case, GRace can store the warpTables in device memory and performs intra-warp race detection there.

3.3.2 Inter-warp Race Detection

GRace periodically detects inter-warp races after each synchronization call. More specifically, GRace transfers the memory access information from a warpTable to device memory after each intra-warp race detection. After each synchronization call, GRace identifies inter-warp races by examining memory accesses from multiple threads that are across different warps. After detecting inter-warp races at one synchronization call, GRace reuses the device memory for next synchronization block.

By exploring the design space along two dimensions, i.e., accuracy of bug reports and efficiency of bug detection, we propose two inter-warp detection schemes. One scheme organizes memory access information by the executed program statements. This scheme reports data races with more accurate diagnostic information while incurring time and space overheads that are quadratic and linear with regard to the number of executed statements, respectively. The other scheme organizes memory access information by shared memory addresses. This scheme incurs constant time and

space overhead while reporting aggregated diagnostic information on data races. We present both schemes in the rest of this section.

The statement-based scheme (GRace-stmt). This scheme of GRace (referred to as GRace-stmt) literally stores all the memory addresses that have been accessed from all the threads in device memory and identifies two threads from different warps for accessing the same memory address. More specifically, GRace-stmt maintains a BlockStmtTable in device memory for the threads from all the warps that can access the same shared memory. Each entry of the BlockStmtTable stores all the content of a warpTable (all memory addresses accessed from one statement executed by a warp of threads) and the corresponding warp ID. Essentially, GRace-stmt organizes a BlockStmtTable by memory access statements from all the threads.

At each synchronization call, GRace-stmt scans the entire BlockStmtTable and identifies inter-warp data races as described in Algorithm 3. More specifically, GRace-stmt checks two Block-StmtTable entries at a time throughout the entire table (line 1-2). For each pair of the entries, GRace-stmt checks both the warp IDs and access types (line 3-8). If the warp IDs are the same or both access types are read, GRace-stmt skips this pair since any pair of memory accesses from both entries cannot cause inter-warp data races. Otherwise, GRace-stmt utilizes a warp of threads in parallel to check whether there are two addresses, one from each entry, are the same (line 9-14). Once the same addresses are found, GRace-stmt reports a data race (line 12).

On the one hand, GRace-stmt provides accurate diagnostic information about a detected race, including the pair of racing statements (i.e., the indexes of the BlockStmtTable entries), the pair of racing threads (i.e., the indexes of both memory addresses in the BlockStmtTable entries), and racing memory address. This is very helpful for developers to quickly locate the root cause and fix the data race. On the other hand, the algorithm complexity of GRace-stmt is quadratic with regard to the number of BlockStmtTable entries, i.e., the number of instrumented statements that are executed. Furthermore, the space overhead incurred by GRace-stmt is linear to the number of BlockStmtTable entries. Although this indicates that GRace-stmt may not be scalable, it is expected to perform well with a small number of statements being instrumented and executed (See our experimental results in Section 5).

The address-based scheme (GRace-addr). This scheme of GRace (referred to as GRace-addr) stores summarized information of the memory addresses that have been accessed from all the threads and detects data races based on the summarized information. More specifically, GRace-addr maintains two tables for each warp, one

Algorithm 4 Inter-warp Race Detection by GRace-addr

1: **for** $idx = 0$ to $shmSize - 1$ **do**
2:    **if** $wBlockShmMap[idx] = 0$ **then**
3:       Jump to line 15
4:    **end if**
5:    **if** $rWarpShmMap[idx] = 0$ **and**
      $wWarpShmMap[idx] = 0$ **then**
6:       Jump to line 15
7:    **end if**
8:    **if** $wWarpShmMap[idx] \leq wBlockShmMap[idx]$ **and**
      $wWarpShmMap[idx] > 0$ **then**
9:       Report a Data Race
10:    **else if** $wWarpShmMap[idx] = 0$ **then**
11:       Report a Data Race
12:    **else if** $rWarpShmMap[idx] \leq$
      $rBlockShmMap[idx]$ **then**
13:       Report a Data Race
14:    **end if**
15: **end for**

---

for read access from threads within the warp (referred to as rWarp-ShmMap) and the other for write access (referred to as wWarpShmMap). Additionally, for all the warps that can access the same shared memory, GRace-addr maintains two tables, one for read access from all such warps of threads (referred to as rBlockShmMap) and the other for write access (referred to as wBlockShmMap). Each entry in any of these tables maps to one shared memory address linearly. Specifically, each entry stores a counter that records the number of accesses to the corresponding shared memory address from all the threads within a warp (for rWarpShmMap or wWarpShmMap) or across all warps (for rBlockShmMap or wBlockShmMap). Figure 4 shows the data structures of rWarpShmMap and wWarpShmMap, which are the same as rBlockShmMap and wBlockShmMap.

After performing each intra-warp race detection, GRace-addr transfers memory access information in the warpTable to the corresponding rWarpShmMap and rBlockShmMap for read, or to the corresponding wWarpShmMap and wBlockShmMap for write. More specifically, GRace-addr scans through the warpTable and, for each warpTable entry, adds one to the value of the corresponding counter in the rWarpShmMap and rBlockShmMap, or wWarpShmMap and wBlockShmMap. Essentially, these tables keep the number of accesses to each shared memory address for different warps, individually and aggregately.

At each synchronization call, GRace-addr detects inter-warp races as described in Algorithm 4. More specifically, GRace-addr scans through all the counters stored in the rWarpShmMap and the wWarpShmMap for each warp in parallel (line 1). For each shared memory address, GRace-addr first rules out the cases of all read accesses (line 2-4) and no accesses from the local (or current) warp (line 5-7). Then GRace-addr detects data races of write-write conflict, i.e., writes from both local and remote warps (line 8-9), followed by read-write conflict, i.e. read from local warp and write from remote warp (line 10-11). Lastly, GRace-addr detects data races of write-read conflict, i.e., write from local warp and read from remote warp (line 12-13).

On the one hand, the time and space complexities of the GRace-addr algorithm are linear to the size of shared memory, which is constant for a given GPU. Therefore, GRace-addr is scalable in terms of the number of instrumented statements, although it may not be a better choice for a kernel with a small number of instrumented statements. On the other hand, GRace-addr provides aggregated information about a data race, which is less accurate than GRace-stmt. For example, GRace-addr reports racing memory

address and the pairs of racing warps instead of racing statements or racing threads. However, the bug information provided by GRace-addr is still useful. For example, programmers can narrow down the set of possibly racing statements based on a racing memory address reported by GRace-addr. Similarly, programmers can derive racing threads based on the ranges of reported racing warps.

4. Evaluation Methodology

Our experiments were conducted using a NVIDIA Tesla C1060 GPU with 240 processor cores (30×8), a clock frequency of 1.296 GHz, and 4 GB device memory. This GPU was connected to a machine with two AMD 2.6 GHz dual-core Opteron CPUs and 8 GB main memory. We have implemented the prototype of GRace. Static Analyzer utilizes the linear constraint solver [16], and Dynamic Checker is built on CUDA SDK 3.0. Note that we do not see any particular difficulty to port GRace to other GPU environments such as stream SDK or OpenCL.

We have evaluated GRace with three applications, including Co-clustering [8] (referred to as co-cluster), EM clustering [10] (referred to as em), and scan code [7] (referred to as scan). Among these applications, co-cluster and em are both clustering (data mining) algorithms. We have used GPU implementations of these applications that were aggressively optimized for shared memory use in a recent study [32]. scan is the simple code used in previous work on GPU race detection [7].

In developing GPU *kernels* for co-cluster and em, i.e. in creating GPU implementations of the main computation steps, certain implicit assumptions were made. For example, co-cluster assumes that the initialization values of a particular matrix should be within a certain range, whereas em assumes that the maximum thread number within a block is 256. If these kernels are used by another application developer, these assumptions may be violated, and data races can occur. We create invocations of these kernels in ways such that race conditions were manifested. Additionally, to trigger data races in scan, we remove the first synchronization call as was done in the previous work on GPU race detection [7].

We have designed four sets of experiments to evaluate the key aspects of GRace:

- The first set evaluates the functionality of GRace in detecting data races of GPU kernel functions. We compare GRace with the previous approach [7], referred to as B-tool in this paper, in terms of reported number of races and false positives. In this set, we use bug-triggering inputs and parameters to trigger data races.

- The second set evaluates the runtime overhead incurred by GRace in terms of execution time of kernel functions. We also compare GRace with B-tool. Additionally, we evaluate the space overhead caused by GRace and compare it with B-tool. In this set, we use normal inputs and parameters to launch the kernel functions so that data races do not occur.

- The third set evaluates the benefit of Static Analyzer. We measure the instrumented statements and memory accesses statically and dynamically in two configurations, i.e., with Static Analyzer and without Static Analyzer. Furthermore, we compare the runtime overhead of GRace with and without Static Analyzer.

- The fourth set evaluates the benefit of shared memory. We measure the runtime overhead of GRace in two configurations, i.e., warpTables stored in shared memory and warpTables stored in device memory.

Note that all the above experiments evaluate two inter-warp detection schemes GRace-stmt and GRace-addr, both with the same intra-warp detection scheme and the same Static Analyzer.

Apps	GRace-stmt				GRace-addr				B-tool		
	R-Stmt#	R-Mem#	R-Thd#	FP#	R-Stmt#	R-Mem#	R-Wp#	FP#	R-Stmt#	RP#	FP#
co-cluster	1	10	1,310,720	0	-	10	8	0	-	1	0
em	14	384	22,023	0	-	384	3	0	-	200,445	45,870
scan	3 pairs of racing statements are detected and all addresses are resolved by Static Analyzer								-	Err*	Err*

Table 1. Overall effectiveness of GRace for data race detection. We compare the detection capability of GRace-stmt and GRace-addr with that of B-tool, the tool proposed by previous work [7]. R-Stmt is pairs of conflicting accesses, R-Mem is memory address invoked in data races, R-Thd is pairs of threads in race conditions, R-Wp is pairs of racing warps. FP means false positives, and RP means the race number reported by B-tool. '-' means the data is not reported by the scheme. * B-tool leads to an error when running with scan on the latest versions of CUDA and Tesla GPUs, because of hardware and software changes.

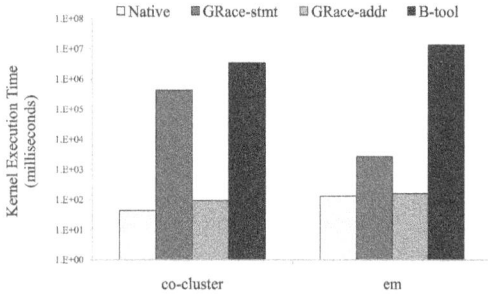

Figure 5. Runtime overhead of GRace. Note that the y-axis is on a logarithmic scale.

Apps	GRace-stmt		GRace-addr		B-tool
	ShM	DM	ShM	DM	Mem*
co-cluster	1.1 KB	43 MB	1.1 KB	9 MB	257 MB
em	1.1 KB	0.8 MB	1.1 KB	18 MB	514 MB

Table 2. Space overhead of GRace. ShM means shared memory, DM is device memory, and Mem is (host) memory. * B-tool is running in emulation mode, which does not require shared memory or device memory.

5. Experimental Results

5.1 Overall Effectiveness

Table 1 demonstrates the overall effectiveness of GRace. Specifically, we evaluate three schemes, including GRace-stmt, GRace-addr, and the previous work B-tool [7]. For GRace-stmt and GRace-addr, we measure four metrics, including the number of pairs of racing statements, the number of memory addresses involved in data races, the number of pairs of threads or warps in race conditions, and the number of false positives within the reported pairs of threads or warps. For B-tool, we present the number of data races reported by the tool. Unlike GRace-stmt or GRace-addr, B-tool reports a data race whenever the current thread accesses a memory address where other threads have conflicting accesses before. It does not report pairs of statements, threads, or warps involved in race conditions. For the kernel functions, we use bug-triggering parameters or inputs to trigger the data races. For co-cluster, we launch 8 blocks with 256 threads per block. For em, we launch 8 blocks with 320 threads per block. For scan, we do not execute it since Static Analyzer detects the races and does not annotate any statement for runtime checking.

As shown in Table 1, both GRace-stmt and GRace-addr can effectively detect data races. For example, among the reported data races, there are no false positives for both GRace-stmt and GRace-addr. On the contrary, B-tool generates 45,870 false positives, among the reported 200,445 data races for em. GRace-stmt and GRace-addr are accurate because both schemes leverage the knowledge of GPU's thread scheduling and SIMD execution model. As a result, GRace does not check memory accesses issued from different instructions that are executed by different threads within a warp, which are the sources of false positives reported by B-tool. Due to B-tool's incorrect use of inserted synchronization calls for the instrumentation code, it could not be run for scan on the new hardware and software.

Table 1 indicates that GRace-stmt provides more accurate information about data races than GRace-addr and B-tool do. Since GRace-stmt logs memory accesses at the program statement level, it can report the pair of racing statements once a bug is found. On the contrary, GRace-addr and B-tool cannot report the pair of statements involved in a race, since they do not keep information of the statements that have accessed the conflicting memory ad-

dresses before. Furthermore, GRace-addr reports only the pairs of racing warps, which are coarser-grained than what is available from GRace-stmt and B-tool. However, diagnostic information provided by GRace-addr is still useful to locate the root causes. For example, based on memory addresses involved in a race and the corresponding pair of racing warps, programmers can narrow down the search range of possible statements and threads responsible for the data race and further identify the root causes.

Table 1 further shows that Static Analyzer not only reduces runtime overhead of dynamic checking, can it also detect data races. For example, Static Analyzer detects the data races in scan and resolves all memory addresses. Therefore, it totally eliminates the overhead of running Dynamic Checker for this application.

5.2 Runtime Overhead

We measure the execution time for co-cluster and em in four configurations: executing the kernels on GPU natively without any instrumentation, executing the kernels with GRace-stmt on GPU, executing the kernels with GRace-addr on GPU, and executing the kernels with B-tool in the device emulation mode provided by the CUDA SDK. We run B-tool in emulation mode as it is not designed to run on an actual GPU [7]. For both kernels, we use *normal inputs*, i.e. those that do not trigger data races, for these experiments. Note that GRace does not have runtime overhead for scan since the Static Analyzer did not annotate any statements.

Figure 5 shows that GRace-addr and GRace-stmt incur lower runtime overhead than the B-tool. For example, GRace-addr and GRace-stmt slow down em by 22% and 19 times, respectively. On the contrary, B-tool incurs several orders of magnitude higher runtime overhead, i.e. slowing down em by 103,850 times. There are several reasons for the big performance gap between GRace and B-tool. First, GRace-addr and GRace-stmt utilize static analysis to significantly reduce the number of memory accesses that need to be checked dynamically. Second, both GRace-addr and GRace-stmt delay inter-warp race detection to synchronization calls, while B-tool checks data races for each memory access, which requires scanning of four bookkeeping tables after each memory access. Third, emulation mode further adds to the slow-down.

Figure 5 also indicates that GRace-addr is significantly more efficient than GRace-stmt. For example, GRace-addr slows down em and co-cluster by 22% and 116%, respectively, while GRace-stmt slows down em and co-cluster by 19 times and 9,862 times, respectively. This is mainly because GRace-addr's inter-warp race detection algorithm runs in a constant amount of time, i.e. it does not depend on the execution number of instrumented statements. Whereas, the complexity of GRace-stmt's inter-warp race

Apps	w/o Static Analyzer				with Static Analyzer			
	Static #		Dynamic #		Static #		Dynamic #	
	Stmt	MemAcc	Stmt	MemAcc	Stmt	MemAcc	Stmt	MemAcc
co-cluster	8	8	10,524,416	10,524,416	2	2	41,216	41,216
em	7	13	19,070,976	54,460,416	7	13	20,736	10,044

Table 3. Benefits from Static Analyzer, which applies to both GRace-stmt and GRace-addr. Stmt means statements and MemAcc means memory access. Static# means the number of instrumented statements or memory accesses at compile time. Dynamic # means the number of instrumented statements or memory accesses that are executed at program runtime.

Apps	Native (ms)	GRace-stmt (ms)		GRace-addr (ms)	
		w/o SA	w/ SA	w/o SA	w/ SA
co-cluster	43.5	Abt*	429,502	10,889	93.9
em	130	Abt*	2,655	47,861	158

Table 4. Runtime overhead of GRace-stmt and GRace-addr with and without applying Static Analyzer. SA means Static Analyzer. * Jobs for GRace-stmt without Static Analyzer were terminated after several hours due to out of memory.

Apps	GRace-stmt (ms)		GRace-addr (ms)	
	w/o ShM	w/ ShM	w/o ShM	w/ ShM
co-cluster	433,056	429,502	120.8	93.9
em	2,764	2,655	158.5	158.3

Table 5. Runtime overhead of GRace-stmt and GRace-addr with and without utilizing shared memory. ShM means shared memory.

detection algorithm is quadratic with respect to the execution number of instrumented statements. Both GRace-addr and GRace-stmt use the same intra-warp race detection method, whose complexity is linear with respect to the number of dynamic memory accesses. Note that, intra-warp race detection, which is performed in shared memory, is much faster than inter-warp race detection, which is performed in device memory.

Overall, we can see that GRace-addr's runtime overheads are very modest, making it suitable for invocation by an end-user, who is testing a full application. If a race condition is detected in a specific kernel, the user can trigger GRace-stmt, and collect more detailed information to help debugging the application.

5.3 Space Overhead

Table 2 presents the memory space overheads incurred by GRace-stmt, GRace-addr, and B-tool. GRace-addr incurs much smaller space overhead than B-tool. For example, GRace-addr requires around 9 MB and 18 MB for co-cluster and em, respectively, while B-tool requires 257 MB and 514 MB for the two kernels, respectively. The reason is that B-tool maintains two bookkeeping tables for each thread, where each table is four times the size of the shared memory, and another two tables for each block. Unlike B-tool, GRace-addr maintains two bookkeeping tables for each warp, which has 32 threads in our platform, and two tables for each block. Therefore, GRace-addr incurs a factor of 28 less space overhead than B-tool.

Table 2 shows that GRace-stmt incurs lower space overhead than GRace-addr when the execution number of instrumented statements is small. For example, GRace-stmt requires 0.8 MB for em, while GRace-addr needs 18 MB for the same kernel function. This is because the space required by GRace-stmt increases linearly with the execution number of instrumented statements, while the space required by GRace-addr depends on the number of warps and the size of shared memory. Therefore, we can choose GRace-stmt for detecting data races in kernel functions where the instrumented statements are expected to execute for only a few times.

5.4 Benefits from Static Analysis

To evaluate benefits from static analysis, we use four metrics, which are the number of instrumented statements, the number of instrumented shared memory accesses (one statement could result in multiple memory accesses), the number of dynamically-executed instrumented statements, and the number of dynamically-executed instrumented shared memory accesses. Note that the above numbers are aggregated from all the threads within a block.

Table 3 shows that GRace benefits significantly from static analysis, which applies to both GRace-stmt and GRace-addr in the same way. For example, Static Analyzer reduces the number of

statements and memory accesses that need to be instrumented for co-cluster from 8 to 2. More importantly, the execution numbers of instrumented statements and memory accesses for both co-cluster and em are drastically reduced, which in turns reduces the runtime overhead for GRace.

There are three main sources for the runtime overhead reduction. The first one is memory accesses that are statically determined as races or involving in no races. GRace does not need to instrument such memory accesses. The second source is memory addresses that are invariant across threads. In this case, GRace requires only one thread to instrument and check data races for relevant memory accesses. This, for example, reduces the total number of co-cluster's dynamic execution of instrumented memory accesses by a factor of 256. The third one is memory addresses that are invariant to loop iterators. This means GRace only needs to instrument the relevant memory accesses for one iteration. This helps particularly with em, where we reduce the total number of dynamic execution of instrumented memory accesses by a factor of 5,422.

Table 4 further indicates the benefits from static analysis. It shows the runtime overhead incurred by GRace-stmt and GRace-addr with and without applying Static Analyzer. For example, GRace-addr incurs 302 times overhead for em when Static Analyzer is not used, while the slowdown is only by 22% when Static Analyzer is used.

5.5 Benefits from Shared Memory

To evaluate benefits from shared memory, we run the kernels with two versions of GRace-stmt and GRace-addr, respectively. One version logs memory accesses for a warp, and detects intra-warp races, in shared memory. The second version performs logging and detection for intra-warp races in the device memory.

Table 5 shows that shared memory improves the performance of race detection for both GRace-stmt and GRace-addr. For example, GRace-addr in shared memory slows down co-cluster by 116%, while slowing down the same kernel by 177% with device memory only. This is an expected result, since shared memory is much faster than the device memory.

Table 5 also shows that the performance gains for different applications or different race detection schemes varies. For example, performance improvement caused by shared memory for GRace-addr on em is negligible, while the improvement for GRace-addr on co-cluster is 22%. This is mainly because shared memory is only used for intra-warp race detection for both GRace-addr and GRace-stmt, and inter-warp race detection is still in device memory. As a result, the benefit from shared memory becomes more pronounced with larger number of instrumented statement being executed.

6. Related Work

GRace is related to previous studies on data race detection, bug detection for parallel and distributed programs, tool development for GPU programming, and optimizations of GPU programs. Due to space limit, this section briefly describes these studies.

Data race detection. Besides the dynamic race detection techniques discussed in previous section [9, 12, 34, 35, 37–39, 43], researchers proposed static methods for data race detection, including static lockset algorithm [13] and race type-safe systems [6, 18]. Without runtime information, static methods may generate many false positives. Additionally, researchers also proposed to detect data races using model checking [20], which has the limitation of state explosion problem in general. Furthermore, happens-before relation has also be applied to detect races in OpenMP programs [22]. Unlike these approaches, our work focuses on detecting races in GPU programs, which have different characteristics to deal with. To manage race or contention of shared resources, new OS schedulers have been proposed [17].

Bug detection for parallel and distributed programs. Many approaches monitor program execution to detect bugs in parallel and distributed programs [11, 15, 19, 21, 24, 29, 41, 42]. Various techniques [36, 45] have been proposed to reduce the cost of program monitoring. Additionally, interactive parallel debuggers [3–5, 14, 30] help programmers to locate the root causes of software bugs in parallel programs by collecting, aggregating, and visualizing program runtime information. Our work can be integrated with these debuggers to help programmers quickly identify root causes.

Tool development for GPU programming. In the area of general purpose computing on GPUs, there have been numerous application development studies on GPUs over the last 3-4 years. We only focus on efforts on tool development for GPU programming. As we stated earlier, there have been two very distinct efforts on race detection for GPUs [7, 27]. In addition, there has been one recent effort on performance measurement on CUDA programs [33]. Malony *et al.* have developed TAUcuda, which captures CUDA performance events in profile and trace forms. The distinct feature of this tool is that it does not require instrumentation, i.e., neither the source code nor the binary code is modified. However, it is based on an experimental version of CUDA driver, which is not widely available. This tool is also not designed for race detection.

Optimizations of GPU programs. There have been many efforts on optimizations of GPU programs and code generation for GPU programs [26, 31, 40, 44, 46], but none of them have focused on program correctness issues.

7. Conclusions

In this paper, we have presented GRace, a low-overhead approach for detecting data races in GPU programs. GRace first utilizes static analysis to prune memory accesses that are either definitely involved in data races, or can never be in any data race. After this, GRace instruments the unresolved memory accesses for detecting intra-warp and inter-warp data races, exploiting the knowledge of the GPU architecture and the execution model. Furthermore, to detect inter-warp data races, we have explored two designs, i.e. GRace-stmt with more accurate bug diagnostic information, and GRace-addr with lower runtime and space overhead.

We have built a prototype of GRace and have evaluated GRace with three data race bugs in three GPU kernel functions. We have also compared both schemes of GRace, i.e., GRace-stmt and GRace-addr, with an existing dynamic method, B-tool. Our experimental results have shown that both GRace-stmt and GRace-addr can detect data races effectively and efficiently without reporting

any false positives, while B-tool slows down the program significantly and can report many false positives. Furthermore, the experimental results have demonstrated that GRace-addr incurs low runtime (22-116%) and space overhead (9-18 MB), while being able to detect race conditions in target programs. The only limitation is that it provides less accurate bug reports. GRace-stmt, in comparison, incurs larger runtime (19-9,862 times) and space (0.8-43 MB) overheads, while providing more accurate bug reports. Moreover, the experimental results have indicated the benefits of the use of static analysis and careful use of memory hierarchy at runtime, for both GRace-stmt and GRace-addr.

Overall, as GRace-addr's runtime overheads are very modest, it is suitable for an end-user to test a full application. GRace-stmt can be invoked when a race condition is detected in a specific kernel, and can provide more detailed information for debugging.

8. Acknowledgments

The authors would like to thank the anonymous reviewers for their invaluable feedback. We appreciate the useful discussion with Wenjing Ma, Xin Huo, Wenbin Zhang and Zhezhe Chen. This work was supported in part by an allocation of computing time from the Ohio Supercomputer Center, and by the NSF grants #CCF-0833101 and #CCF-0953759 (CAREER Award).

References

[1] CUDA Community Showcase. http://www.nvidia.com/object/cuda_apps_flash_new.html.

[2] ATI Stream Technology. http://www.amd.com/stream.

[3] D. H. Ahn, B. R. de Supinski, I. Laguna, G. L. Lee, B. Liblit, B. P. Miller, and M. Schulz. Scalable temporal order analysis for large scale debugging. In *Proceedings of the ACM/IEEE Conference on Supercomputing (SC)*, 2009.

[4] D. C. Arnold, D. H. Ahn, B. R. de Supinski, G. Lee, B. P. Miller, and M. Schulz. Stack trace analysis for large scale debugging. In *Proceedings of the 21st IEEE International Parallel and Distributed Processing Symposium (IPDPS)*, 2007.

[5] S. M. Balle, B. R. Brett, C.-P. Chen, and D. LaFrance-Linden. Extending a traditional debugger to debug massively parallel applications. *J. Parallel Distrib. Comput.*, 64(5), 2004.

[6] C. Boyapati, R. Lee, and M. Rinard. Ownership types for safe programming: preventing data races and deadlocks. In *Proceedings of the International Conference on Object Oriented Programming, Systems, Languages and Applications (OOPSLA)*, 2002.

[7] M. Boyer, K. Skadron, and W. Weimer. Automated dynamic analysis of CUDA programs. In *Proceedings of the Third Workshop on Software Tools for MultiCore Systems (STMCS)*, 2008.

[8] H. Cho, I. S. Dhillon, Y. Guan, and S. Sra. Minimum sum-squared residue co-clustering of gene expression data. In *Proceedings of the 4th SIAM International Conference on Data Mining (SDM)*, 2004.

[9] J.-D. Choi, K. Lee, A. Loginov, R. O'Callahan, V. Sarkar, and M. Sridharan. Efficient and precise datarace detection for multithreaded object-oriented programs. In *Proceedings of the ACM SIGPLAN Conference on Programming language design and implementation (PLDI)*, 2002.

[10] A. Dempster, N. Laird, and D. Rubin. Maximum Likelihood Estimation from Incomplete Data via the EM Algorithm. *Journal of the Royal Statistical Society*, 39(1):1–38, 1977.

[11] J. DeSouza, B. Kuhn, B. R. de Supinski, V. Samofalov, S. Zheltov, and S. Bratanov. Automated, scalable debugging of MPI programs with Intel Message Checker. In *Proceedings of the 2nd International workshop on Software engineering for high performance computing system applications (SE-HPCS)*, 2005.

[12] A. Dinning and E. Schonberg. An empirical comparison of monitoring algorithms for access anomaly detection. In *Proceedings of the ACM*

SIGPLAN Annual Symposium on Principles and Practice of Parallel Programming (PPoPP), 1990.

[13] D. Engler and K. Ashcraft. Racerx: effective, static detection of race conditions and deadlocks. In *Proceedings of the ACM Symposium on Operating Systems Principles (SOSP)*, 2003.

[14] Etnus, LLC. TotalView. http://www.etnus.com/TotalView.

[15] C. Falzone, A. Chan, E. Lusk, and W. Gropp. A portable method for finding user errors in the usage of MPI collective operations. *International Journal of High Performance Computing Applications*, 21(2):155–165, 2007.

[16] P. Feautrier. Parametric integer programming. *RAIRO Recherche Opérationnelle*, 22(3):243–268, 1988.

[17] A. Fedorova, S. Blagodurov, and S. Zhuravlev. Managing contention for shared resources on multicore processors. *Commun. ACM*, 53(2): 49–57, 2010.

[18] C. Flanagan and S. N. Freund. Type-based race detection for java. In *Proceedings of the ACM SIGPLAN Conference on Programming Language Design and Implementation (PLDI)*, 2000.

[19] Q. Gao, F. Qin, and D. K. Panda. DMTracker: Finding bugs in large-scale parallel programs by detecting anomaly in data movements. In *Proceedings of the ACM/IEEE Annual Conference on Supercomputing (SC)*, 2007.

[20] T. A. Henzinger, R. Jhala, and R. Majumdar. Race checking by context inference. In *Proceedings of the ACM SIGPLAN Conference on Programming Language Design and Implementation (PLDI)*, 2004.

[21] T. Hilbrich, B. R. de Supinski, M. Schulz, and M. S. Müller. A graph based approach for MPI deadlock detection. In *Proceedings of the 23rd International Conference on Supercomputing(ICS)*, 2009.

[22] M.-H. Kang, O.-K. Ha, S.-W. Jun, and Y.-K. Jun. A tool for detecting first races in openmp programs. In *Proceedings of the International Conference on Parallel Architectures and Compilation Techniques (PACT)*, 2009.

[23] Khronos Group. OpenCL: The Open Standdard for Heterogeneous Parallel Programming. http://www.khronos.org/opencl, 2008.

[24] B. Krammera, K. Bidmona, M. S. Muller, and M. M. Rescha. MARMOT: An MPI analysis and checking tool. In *Parallel Computing (PARCO)*, 2003.

[25] L. Lamport. Time, clocks, and the ordering of events in a distributed system. *Commun. ACM*, 21(7):558–565, 1978.

[26] S. Lee, S.-J. Min, and R. Eigenmann. OpenMP to GPGPU: A Compiler Framework for Automatic Translation and Optimization. In *Proceedings of the ACM SIGPLAN Annual Symposium on Principles and Practice of Parallel Programming (PPoPP)*, 2009.

[27] G. Li and G. Gopalakrishnan. Scalable SMT-based verification of GPU kernel functions. In *Proceedings of the ACM SIGSOFT International Symposium on the Foundations of Software Engineering (FSE)*, 2010.

[28] S. Lu, S. Park, E. Seo, and Y. Zhou. Learning from mistakes: a comprehensive study on real world concurrency bug characteristics. In *Proceedings of the International Conference on Architectural Support for Programming Languages and Operating Systems (ASPLOS)*, 2008.

[29] G. Luecke, H. Chen, J. Coyle, J. Hoekstra, M. Kraeva, and Y. Zou. MPI-CHECK: A tool for checking Fortran 90 MPI programs. *Concurr. Comput. Pract. Exp.*, 15(2), 2003.

[30] S. S. Lumetta and D. E. Culler. The mantis parallel debugger. In *SIGMETRICS Symposium on Parallel and Distributed Tools (SPDT)*, 1996.

[31] W. Ma and G. Agrawal. A translation system for enabling data mining applications on GPUs. In *Proceedings of the International Conference on Supercomputing(ICS)*, 2009.

[32] W. Ma and G. Agrawal. An Integer Programming Framework for Optimizing Shared Memory Use on GPUs. In *Proceedings of International Conference on High Performance Computing(HiPC)*, 2010.

[33] A. D. Malony, S. Biersdorff, W. Spear, and S. Mayanglambam. An experimental approach to performance measurement of heterogeneous parallel applications using cuda. In *Proceedings of the International Conference on Supercomputing (ICS)*, 2010.

[34] R. H. B. Netzer and B. P. Miller. Improving the accuracy of data race detection. In *Proceedings of the ACM SIGPLAN Annual Symposium on Principles and Practice of Parallel Programming (PPoPP)*, 1991.

[35] R. O'Callahan and J.-D. Choi. Hybrid dynamic data race detection. In *Proceedings of the ACM SIGPLAN Annual Symposium on Principles and Practice of Parallel Programming (PPoPP)*, 2003.

[36] J. Odom, J. K. Hollingsworth, L. DeRose, K. Ekanadham, and S. Sbaraglia. Using dynamic tracing sampling to measure long running programs. In *Proceedings of the ACM/IEEE Annual Conference on Supercomputing (SC)*, 2005.

[37] D. Perkovic and P. J. Keleher. Online data-race detection via coherency guarantees. In *Proceedings of the USENIX Symposium on Operating Systems Design and Implementation (OSDI)*, 1996.

[38] E. Pozniansky and A. Schuster. Efficient on-the-fly data race detection in multithreaded C++ programs. In *Proceedings of the ACM SIGPLAN Annual Symposium on Principles and Practice of Parallel Programming (PPoPP)*, 2003.

[39] S. Savage, M. Burrows, G. Nelson, P. Sobalvarro, and T. Anderson. Eraser: a dynamic data race detector for multithreaded programs. *ACM Trans. Comput. Syst.*, 15(4):391–411, 1997.

[40] N. Sundaram, A. Raghunathan, and S. Chakradhar. A framework for efficient and scalable execution of domain-specific templates on GPUs. In *Proceedings of the IEEE International Parallel and Distributed Processing Symposium (IPDPS)*, 2009.

[41] J. S. Vetter and B. R. de Supinski. Dynamic software testing of MPI applications with Umpire. In *Proceedings of the ACM/IEEE Conference on Supercomputing (SC)*, 2000.

[42] S. Yang, A. R. Butt, Y. C. Hu, and S. P. Midkiff. Trust but verify: monitoring remotely executing programs for progress and correctness. In *Proceedings of the ACM SIGPLAN Annual Symposium on Principles and Practice of Parallel Programming (PPoPP)*, 2005.

[43] Y. Yu, T. Rodeheffer, and W. Chen. Racetrack: efficient detection of data race conditions via adaptive tracking. In *Proceedings of the ACM Symposium on Operating Systems Principles (SOSP)*, 2005.

[44] S. zee Ueng, M. Lathara, S. S. Baghsorkhi, and W. mei W. Hwu. CUDA-lite: Reducing GPU Programming Complexity. In *Proceedings of the International Workshop on Languages and Compilers for Parallel Computing (LCPC)*, 2008.

[45] A. Zhai, G. He, and M. Heimdahl. Hardware and compiler support for dynamic software monitoring. In *Proceedings of the International Workshop on Runtime Verification (RV)*, 2009.

[46] E. Z. Zhang, Y. Jiang, Z. Guo, and X. Shen. Streamlining gpu applications on the fly: thread divergence elimination through runtime thread-data remapping. In *Proceedings of the International Conference on Supercomputing (ICS)*, 2010.

Cooperative Reasoning for Preemptive Execution

Jaeheon Yi   Caitlin Sadowski   Cormac Flanagan

Computer Science Department
University of California at Santa Cruz
Santa Cruz, CA 95064
{jaeheon,supertri,cormac}@cs.ucsc.edu

Abstract

We propose a *cooperative methodology* for multithreaded software, where threads use traditional synchronization idioms such as locks, but additionally document each point of potential thread interference with a "yield" annotation. Under this methodology, code between two successive yield annotations forms a *serializable transaction* that is amenable to sequential reasoning.

This methodology reduces the burden of reasoning about thread interleavings by indicating only those interference points that matter. We present experimental results showing that very few yield annotations are required, typically one or two per thousand lines of code. We also present dynamic analysis algorithms for detecting *cooperability violations*, where thread interference is not documented by a yield, and for *yield annotation inference* for legacy software.

Categories and Subject Descriptors   F.3.1 [*Logics and Meanings of Programs*]: Specifying and Verifying and Reasoning about Programs–*specification techniques*; D.2.4 [*Software Engineering*]: Software/Program Verification–*reliability*; D.2.5 [*Software Engineering*]: Testing and Debugging–*monitors*

General Terms   Languages, Algorithms, Verification

Keywords   Atomicity, Yield Annotation, Cooperability, Parallelism, Concurrency

1. Cooperative Concurrency

The widespread adoption of multi-core processors necessitates a software infrastructure that can effectively exploit multiple threads of control. Unfortunately, several decades of experience has demonstrated that developing reliable multithreaded software is problematic at best. We argue the difficulties of multithreaded programming are chiefly due to its *preemptive semantics*: between any two instructions of one thread, interleaved instructions of a second thread could change the state of shared variables, thus influencing the subsequent behavior and correctness of the first thread. We refer to this situation as an *interference point*.

Preemptive semantics fails to identify the interference points that actually impact the behavior of a program: all program points must be considered as potential interference points, until excluded

PPoPP'11,   February 12–16, 2011, San Antonio, Texas, USA.
Copyright © 2011 ACM 978-1-4503-01190-0/11/02...$10.00

through careful analysis. The pervasive presence of potential interference points invalidates traditional sequential reasoning. To illustrate this difficulty, consider the statement "x++". Under sequential semantics, "x++" is a simple increment operation, but under preemptive semantics, "x++" becomes a *potentially non-atomic read-modify-write*.

To address this problem, we propose a *cooperative methodology* for developing multithreaded software. The central idea behind this methodology is that all thread interference should be explicitly documented with a "yield" annotation. A program is *cooperable* if it satisfies this constraint. Yield annotations are purely for documentation purposes and have no run-time effect. Consequently, this cooperative methodology does not constrain the programmer's ability to use a variety of synchronization idioms (locks, barriers, semaphores, etc) to achieve appropriate parallelism and performance.

The key benefit of explicit yield annotations is that they divide the execution of every thread into *transactions*, each consisting of the sequence of instructions between two successive yield annotations. Since thread interference occurs only at yield annotations, each transaction is serializable and behaves *as if* it is executing serially, without interleaved instructions of other threads. Consequently, the code inside each transaction is amenable to sequential reasoning.

More generally, *sequential reasoning is correct by default*. That is, cooperability guarantees that any section of code unbroken by yield annotations exhibits sequential behavior. In the presence of explicit yield annotations, sequential reasoning naturally generalizes into *cooperative reasoning*, which accounts for explicitly marked thread interference.

Cooperative concurrency decomposes the difficult problem of verifying correctness of a multithreaded program into two simpler subproblems:

1. verifying that the program is cooperable, *i.e.*, that yields document all thread interference;

2. and verifying that the program is correct using cooperative reasoning.

To address subproblem 1, we present COPPER, a dynamic analysis that detects *cooperability violations*: undocumented interference points. COPPER observes the execution trace of the target program, and uses a graph-based algorithm to verify that this observed trace is serializable. In particular, it reports an error if the yield annotations are not sufficient to capture all thread interference.

We present evidence that subproblem 2 is much simpler than verification under traditional preemptive semantics. We propose *interference density* as a metric capturing the difficulty of program reasoning, where the interference density of a program under a particular semantics is the number of interference points per line of code under that semantics. Experimental results show that the inter-

	Transaction	Yield
Compile-time analysis	Atomicity	**Cooperability**
Run-time enforcement	Transactional Memory	Automatic Mutual Exclusion

Figure 1. Alternatives to preemptive semantics: one may analyze or enforce either transactions or yields (transactional boundaries).

ference density for the cooperative semantics is at least an order of magnitude lower than for the preemptive or atomic semantics: typically 0.17% of source code lines require yield annotations. Additionally, we present anecdotal evidence that applying cooperability to legacy programs reveals bugs. Across 14 benchmark programs, we found 20 cooperability violations that reflect errors in the code. Finally, a recently completed user study demonstrated that yield annotations are associated with a statistically significant improvement in the ability of programmers to identify synchronization defects [29].

When writing new code, a programmer will co-design the algorithm, its synchronization code, and its yield annotations. For large legacy applications, however, manually writing yield annotations is rather tedious. To address this problem, we present SILVER, a dynamic analysis for inferring yield annotations. If an operation would violate cooperability by causing undocumented thread interference, SILVER automatically inserts an implicit yield right before that operation, thus avoiding the cooperability violation. Due to test coverage issues inherent in any dynamic analysis, SILVER may under-approximate the set of required yields. Nevertheless, we found the inferred yield annotations to be extremely helpful.

Atomicity, Transactional Memory, and AME. Several prior techniques have been proposed for controlling thread interference. Figure 1 summarizes the most closely related proposals, divided along two orthogonal dimensions: whether transactions are analyzed or enforced, and whether one specifies transactions (atomic blocks) or transactional boundaries (yields):

- An atomic block is a code fragment that behaves *as if* it executes serially. While atomicity permits sequential reasoning inside each atomic block, preemptive reasoning is still required outside atomic blocks, and so atomicity requires both kinds of reasoning. In contrast, cooperative reasoning is uniformly applicable to all code under our proposed methodology.

- Transactional memory offers an *enforcement* model of execution for transactions, where the runtime system guarantees that atomic blocks satisfy serializability. However, finding a robust semantics for transactional memory has proven elusive, while performance issues hold back widespread adoption.

- Automatic mutual exclusion (AME) inverts transactional memory by executing all code in a single transaction, unless otherwise specified. We are inspired by AME's feature of safety by default but are focused on analysis not enforcement, since enforcement mechanisms may not be appropriate for legacy programs. Current AME implementations leverage transactional memory implementations, with the problems listed above.

Section 8 contains a more detailed comparison with related work.

Cooperability for Legacy Programs. We believe that our proposed cooperative methodology is well-suited for ongoing maintenance of legacy programs. Understanding legacy programs is often

difficult, due to poor documentation and programmer churn. We provide a low-cost migration path for enabling cooperative reasoning in legacy programs: SILVER can provide the initial yield annotations to achieve cooperability, while COPPER can verify cooperability upon subsequent modification.

Note that the inferred yield annotations do not affect the execution semantics of a program. This analysis approach to cooperative semantics distinguishes it from other approaches based on enforcement, such as transactional memory, which explicitly change the execution behavior: transitioning to an enforcement-based approach is potentially much more disruptive, and may unintentionally change the behavior of sensitive legacy applications. Instead, our approach enables cooperative reasoning while retaining the same preemptive execution behavior.

Contributions. The key contributions of this paper are:

- We propose a cooperative methodology for developing multi-threaded software.

- We present dynamic analyses for detecting cooperability violations (Section 4) and for inferring yield annotations (Section 5).

- We describe the implementation of these algorithms (Section 6).

- We show that cooperability results in a substantially lower interference density than preemptive semantics or atomicity (Section 7.1).

- We show that across 14 benchmarks, our analyses revealed 20 cooperability violations that are real errors (Section 7.2).

2. Motivating Example

We illustrate the benefits of cooperability using the `Buffer` class defined in Figure 2, which implements a single-element FIFO queue. The class provides blocking `dequeue` and `enqueue` methods, which busy-wait when necessary, along with a `nonBlockingDequeue` method, which returns `null` if the queue is empty.

The three columns on the right side of Figure 2 describe where thread interference may occur under the preemptive, atomic, and cooperative semantics, respectively. The preemptive column "P" emphasizes that, in the absence of any analysis, almost every line of code in the `Buffer` class has the potential for concurrent threads to make arbitrary modifications to the program state. Clearly, any attempt to reason about the behavior of this class needs to begin with understanding and limiting where thread interference may occur.

The atomicity column "A" illustrates that the two methods `main` and `nonBlockingDequeue` are not vulnerable to thread inference, since they are atomic. The busy-waiting methods `enqueue` and `dequeue` are not atomic and so are still vulnerable to pervasive thread interference.

We could use syntactic atomic statements to limit where interference may occur in these methods but this approach is unsatisfactory due to the static scope of atomic blocks and their awkward interaction with other control constructs. For example, in the following version of `dequeue`, the atomic blocks clutter the code but are still inadequate; for example, they suggest that interference may occur between the initialization of `elem` and the loop test:

```
Object dequeue() {
  Object elem; atomic { elem = null; }
  while (atomic { elem == null }) {
    atomic { elem = dequeueNonBlocking(); }
  }
  atomic { return elem; }
}
```

Figure 2: Example Program `Buffer`

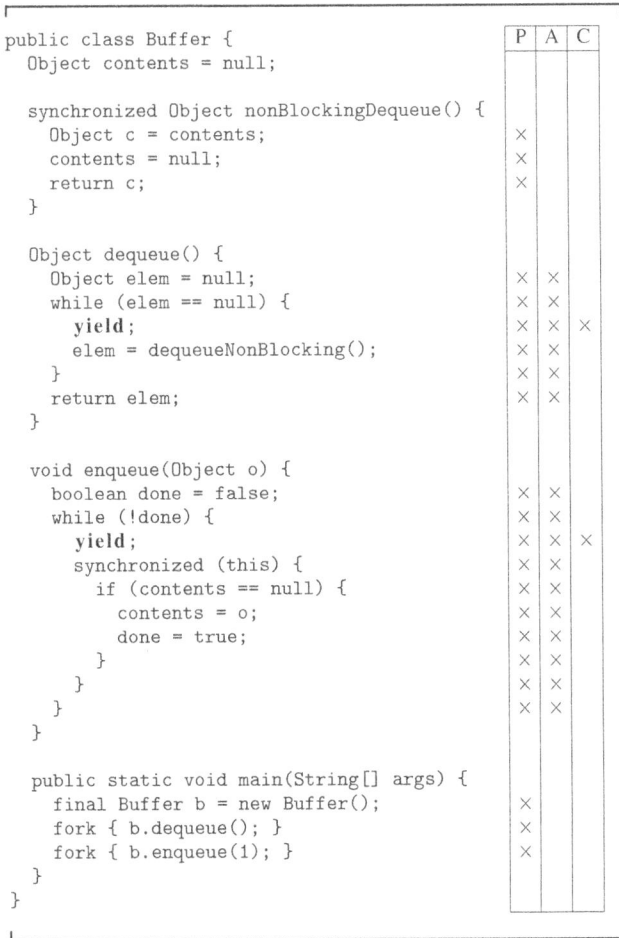

```
public class Buffer {                              | P | A | C |
  Object contents = null;                          |   |   |   |

  synchronized Object nonBlockingDequeue() {       |   |   |   |
    Object c = contents;                           | × |   |   |
    contents = null;                               | × |   |   |
    return c;                                      | × |   |   |
  }                                                |   |   |   |

  Object dequeue() {                               |   |   |   |
    Object elem = null;                            | × | × |   |
    while (elem == null) {                         | × | × |   |
      yield;                                       | × | × | × |
      elem = dequeueNonBlocking();                 | × | × |   |
    }                                              | × | × |   |
    return elem;                                   | × | × |   |
  }                                                |   |   |   |

  void enqueue(Object o) {                         |   |   |   |
    boolean done = false;                          | × | × |   |
    while (!done) {                                | × | × |   |
      yield;                                       | × | × | × |
      synchronized (this) {                        | × | × |   |
        if (contents == null) {                    | × | × |   |
          contents = o;                            | × | × |   |
          done = true;                             | × | × |   |
        }                                          | × | × |   |
      }                                            | × | × |   |
    }                                              | × | × |   |
  }                                                |   |   |   |

  public static void main(String[] args) {         |   |   |   |
    final Buffer b = new Buffer();                 | × |   |   |
    fork { b.dequeue(); }                          | × |   |   |
    fork { b.enqueue(1); }                         | × |   |   |
  }                                                |   |   |   |
}                                                  |   |   |   |
```

Instead of syntactic scoping, one could use `atomic_begin` and `atomic_end` statements to delimit atomic blocks, but this approach is also unsatisfactory. Again taking the `dequeue` example, the first `atomic_begin` and last `atomic_end` statement suggest interference before and after the method call:

```
Object dequeue() {
  atomic_begin;
  Object elem = null;
  while (elem == null) {
    atomic_end;
    atomic_begin;
    elem = dequeueNonBlocking();
  }
  return elem;
  atomic_end;
}
```

If we move these statements to the call sites for dequeue, the nonlocal scoping is awkward. Another problem is that these atomic statements are easy to abuse and misplace; for example, one might put code in between two transactions.

The final cooperative semantics column "C" of Figure 2 shows how yield annotations can precisely and naturally specify thread interference points in both atomic and non-atomic methods. For atomic methods, the absence of yield annotations precludes thread interference. For the two non-atomic methods, interleaved steps of other threads may cause thread interference, but this interference

appears *as if* it happens only at the start of each busy-waiting loop, as documented by the yield annotation. Thus, the cooperative semantics needs to consider only one point of thread interference, in contrast to the preemptive or atomic semantics that permit thread interference at all points in these non-atomic methods.

The notion of cooperability also helps detect concurrency errors. For example, consider the following erroneous version of `dequeue`, which busy-waits until the queue is non-empty, and then calls `nonBlockingDequeue`:

```
Object dequeue() {
  while (contents == null) { yield; }
  return nonBlockingDequeue();
}
```

Our analysis would detect that this code is not cooperable, since there is an additional thread interference point at the end of the `while` loop that needs to be explicated via the following additional yield annotation.

```
Object dequeue() {
  while (contents == null) { yield; }
  yield;
  return dequeueNonBlocking();
}
```

This yield annotation now clarifies to the programmer that the buffer state may change between the loop test (`contents == null`) and the call to `dequeueNonBlocking`, and so helps highlight the semantic error in the code, whereby a concurrent thread could remove the buffer contents before `dequeueNonBlocking` is called. In comparison, method-level atomicity would not reveal this error, since the `dequeue` method is intentionally non-atomic.

3. Defining Cooperative Semantics

In order to present our dynamic analyses, we start by formalizing the notion of cooperability in terms of execution traces.

3.1 Core Operations

We are interested in analyzing a running program; an *operation* is the basic entity of analysis during program execution and represents the execution of a single atomic instruction. Our dynamic analyses recognize a concise language of access and synchronization operations: threads t and u may read and write shared variables x, acquire and release mutual exclusion locks m, wait for and notify other threads, and fork a new thread or join (wait) on another thread's completion. These operations represent a core subset of the operations observed during program execution. Volatile variables are simply treated as shared variables in our analyses. Additionally, a yield operation indicates when a yield annotation is seen in the program. These core operations are represented by the grammar:

$$op ::= read(t, x, v) \quad | \ write(t, x, v)$$
$$| \ acquire(t, m) \quad | \ release(t, m)$$
$$| \ prewait(t, m) \quad | \ postwait(t, m) \ | \ notify(t, m)$$
$$| \ fork(t, u) \quad | \ join(t, u)$$
$$| \ yield(t)$$

Some operations are implicitly accompanied by a yield operation. For example, a wait call on lock m releases that lock, waits for another thread to notify m, and then re-acquires m. The execution of a wait call is represented with two operations: $prewait(t, m)$ releases lock m and implicitly may yield to another thread; and $postwait(t, m)$ re-acquires m. Similarly, the *join* operation is preceded by an implicit yield operation, since the joining thread intentionally blocks until the joinee thread completes.

It is straightforward to add atomic block annotations, such as `atomic_begin` and `atomic_end`, to the core language [38]. This extension increases expressivity; *e.g.*, methods may be declared as atomic. However, we omit this extension for clarity of presentation.

3.2 Conflicting Operations

While an operation is the most basic element of analysis, we are more interested in the relationship between operations. Each operation modifies the *program state*, which captures the value of all variables and locks in the running program (including the instruction counter for each thread) at a single point in time.

Two operations that occur in sequence *conflict* if the resulting state may differ when the operations are reordered. There are several kinds of conflicts: writes to a variable conflict with other accesses (reads or writes) to that variable; operations on a lock (acquire, release, prewait, postwait, notify) conflict with each other; forking or joining a thread conflicts with all operations of the target thread; and operations by the same thread conflict with each other. Two operations *commute* if they do not conflict. Either ordering of a commuting pair of operations results in the same state.

A *trace* is a sequence of operations that captures an execution of a running program. We say that two traces are *equivalent* if one can be obtained from the other by applying some number of commutations on adjacent operations in the trace.

The *happens-before* relation [22] orders conflicting operations: we say that a *happens-before* b, or $a < b$, if a and b conflict, and a occurs before b in the trace. The happens-before relation is transitively closed and is a partial order. We use the happens-before relation to characterize how an operation may influence subsequent operations in a trace.

3.3 Preemptive and Cooperative Semantics

A *scheduling semantics* defines the policy for when a context switch may occur in a program. We formalize two scheduling semantics: preemptive and cooperative.

A *preemptive* semantics is one where a context switch may occur after any operation in a trace. Preemptive semantics is the default execution semantics for multithreaded programs. In this semantics, a yield does not influence context switching and thus is a no-op.

Alternatively, in a *cooperative* semantics, context switching may occur either at a yield operation or at thread termination. The yield operations observed for a single thread, in conjunction with the thread's start and end, delimit sequences of operations; each sequence is a *transaction*. A *serial* trace is thus a sequence of transactions. We relate preemptive and serial traces as follows: a trace, perhaps preemptively scheduled, is *serializable* if it is equivalent to a serial trace.

Figure 3 illustrates this notion of a serial trace. In particular, trace A is preemptive and arbitrarily interleaves the operations of the two threads. By repeatedly swapping adjacent commuting operations, however, we can transform trace A into the equivalent trace B. For example, Thread 2's accesses to `done` are local, and thus commute with any operation by Thread 1. The resulting trace B is serial, since it is a sequence of transactions. We then say that the original trace A is serializable, since it is equivalent to the serial trace B.

We say a program is cooperable if it only generates serializable traces. This notion of cooperable programs significantly simplifies reasoning about program correctness. In particular, even though a cooperable program can execute with preemptive semantics on modern multicore hardware, we may use the simpler cooperative semantics to understand the program's behavior. Furthermore, cooperability violations often reveal synchronization errors that result in unintended thread interference (Section 7.2).

Figure 3: Trace of `Buffer.main`

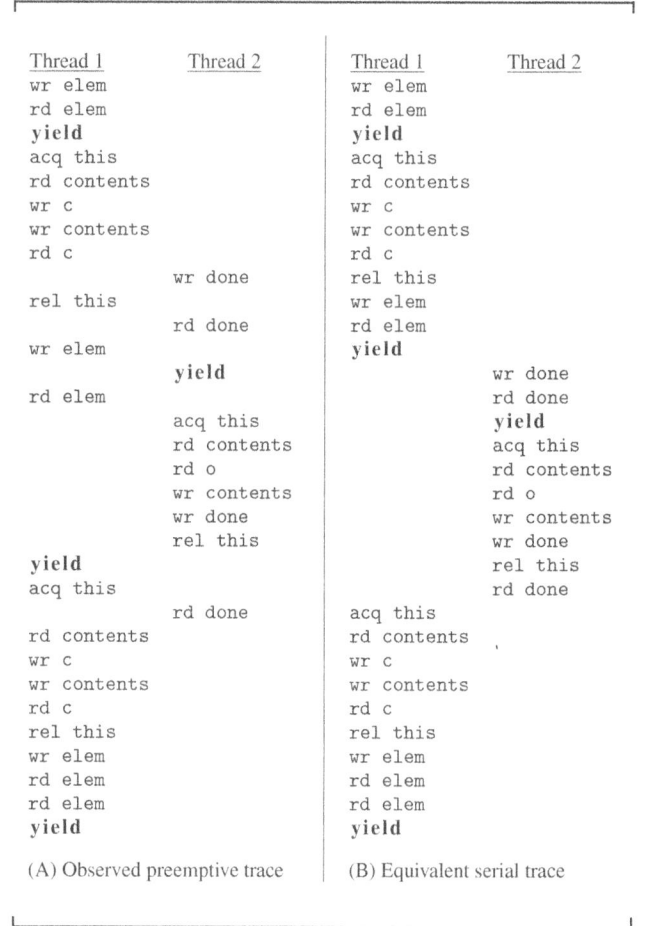

Thread 1	Thread 2	Thread 1	Thread 2
wr elem		wr elem	
rd elem		rd elem	
yield		**yield**	
acq this		acq this	
rd contents		rd contents	
wr c		wr c	
wr contents		wr contents	
rd c		rd c	
	wr done	rel this	
rel this		wr elem	
	rd done	rd elem	
wr elem		**yield**	
	yield		wr done
rd elem			rd done
	acq this		**yield**
	rd contents		acq this
	rd o		rd contents
	wr contents		rd o
	wr done		wr contents
	rel this		wr done
yield			rel this
acq this			rd done
	rd done	acq this	
rd contents		rd contents	
wr c		wr c	
wr contents		wr contents	
rd c		rd c	
rel this		rel this	
wr elem		wr elem	
rd elem		rd elem	
rd elem		rd elem	
yield		**yield**	
(A) Observed preemptive trace		(B) Equivalent serial trace	

4. Cooperability Checking

This section presents a dynamic analysis, called COPPER, for detecting cooperability violations by observing a program trace. Conceptually, our analysis maintains a graph structure representing the happens-before relation on transactions, where each node corresponds to some transaction. We abuse terminology slightly to say that transaction e_1 *happens-before* transaction e_2 if e_1 contains an operation that happens-before an operation in e_2. Our analysis checks for a *cycle* between transactions e_1 and e_2, where e_1 happens-before e_2, yet also e_2 happens-before e_1. This type of situation may occur, for example, when operation a in e_1 happens-before an operation b in e_2, and b happens-before an operation c in e_1. Such a cycle implies that the trace is not equivalent to any serial trace, since this cyclic ordering prevents one transaction from being commuted to occur entirely before the other. Our analysis for checking cooperability reports exactly this situation: a *cooperability violation*.

In order to precisely describe and discuss our analysis, we formalize the analysis state as follows. The domain Txn is a set of transactions or nodes in our analysis. Sometimes there does not exist an transaction to refer to, for example, the transaction of the last write for a variable that has not yet been written. We use $\bot$ to denote this situation, and use $Txn_\bot = Txn \cup \{\bot\}$. Our analysis state has 5 components:

- $\mathcal{C}_t$: Txn identifies the current transaction for each thread t. Initially, every thread t starts with a fresh transaction.

- $\mathcal{U}_m$: $Txn_\perp$ identifies the last transaction to release (or unlock) each lock m. Initially, every lock m is not held so $\mathcal{U}_m = \perp$.

- $\mathcal{R}_{x,t}$: $Txn_\perp$ identifies the last transaction of a thread t that reads each variable x. Initially, $\mathcal{R}_{x,t} = \perp$.

- $\mathcal{W}_x$: $Txn_\perp$ identifies the last transaction that wrote to each variable x. Initially, $\mathcal{W}_x = \perp$.

- $\mathcal{H} \subseteq Txn \times Txn$ tracks the transaction-based happens-before relation. For efficiency, transitive edges are not explicitly added to $\mathcal{H}$, and so $\mathcal{H}^*$, the transitive closure of $\mathcal{H}$, represents the happens-before relation on transactions. Initially, we have $\mathcal{H} = \varnothing$.

We present the COPPER algorithm for checking cooperability in Figure 4. COPPER is shown as a function `analyze` that processes each successive operation in a trace, and which has cases for each type of operation. The algorithm is designed to maintain each component in the analysis state for the purpose of accurately tracking the happens-before relation on transactions. In particular, we monitor the $\mathcal{H}$ component for a cycle. Whenever COPPER encounters an operation that conflicts with a previous operation, it tries to add the necessary happens-before edge between transactions to $\mathcal{H}$. Since the happens-before relation is lifted from operations to transactions and the algorithm checks for cycles in this relation, we must take care not to accidentally add self-edges. We use the binary $\uplus$ operator to add a set of edges $E \subseteq Txn_\perp \times Txn_\perp$ to the happens-before graph $\mathcal{H}$ in a safe manner:

$$\mathcal{H} \uplus E \stackrel{\text{def}}{=} \mathcal{H} \cup \{(n_1, n_2) \in E \mid n_1 \neq n_2,\ n_1 \neq \perp,\ n_2 \neq \perp\}$$

Three types of operations start a new transaction: *yield*, *prewait*, and *join*. The `analyze` case for *yield* creates a fresh node n, adds the appropriate intrathread edge to $\mathcal{H}$, and updates $\mathcal{C}_t$ with the fresh node. The `analyze` cases for *prewait* and *join* contain a call to `analyze`($yield(t)$) that reflect their implicit yield annotations.

Three types of operations may introduce a cycle in the happens-before graph: *read*, *write*, and *acquire*. These operations all can cause thread interference by racing to access a shared variable or acquire a lock. Figure 5 shows the function `addInEdges`(t, N), which adds an edge from each node $n \in N$ to $\mathcal{C}_t$, and also checks for and handles cooperability violations. When adding an edge that would create a cycle, `addInEdges` detects this situation and does not add that edge, in order to preserve the acyclicity of $\mathcal{H}$; instead, it reports a cooperability violation.

The `analyze` case for $read(t, x, v)$ adds a happens-before edge from $\mathcal{W}_x$, the last transaction to write to x, to the current transaction, via a call to `addInEdges`. Next, $\mathcal{R}_{x,t}$ is updated with the current transaction $\mathcal{C}_t$, reflecting the last read operation of x by t.

Similarly, the `analyze` case for $write(t, x, v)$ adds happens-before edges from $\mathcal{W}_x$ and $\mathcal{R}_{x,t'}$ to $\mathcal{C}_t$, because the write operation conflicts with the prior write and also all prior reads. Next, $\mathcal{W}_x$ is updated with the current transaction $\mathcal{C}_t$, reflecting the last write operation of x.

The `analyze` case for $acquire(t, m)$ processes the happens-before edge between the last release of m and the current acquire operation by t. The corresponding case for $release(t, m)$ simply stores the last transaction that released m.

As discussed in Section 3.1, a *prewait* operation can be viewed as a *release* followed by a *yield*, and a *postwait* operation reacquires the released lock. The `analyze` case for *notify* is a no-op, since *notify* does not release the lock.

The `analyze` case for $fork(t, u)$ adds a happens-before edge from the forking thread t to the first transaction of the forked thread u, which is always fresh. Similarly, the case for $join(t, u)$ adds a

Figure 4: COPPER Cooperability Checking Algorithm

```
analyze yield(t):
  fresh n
  H ← H ⊎ {(C_t, n)}
  C_t ← n

analyze read(t, x, v):
  addInEdges t {W_x}
  R_{x,t} ← C_t

analyze write(t, x, v):
  addInEdges t {W_x}
  addInEdges t {R_{x,t'} | t' ∈ Tid}
  W_x ← C_t

analyze acquire(t, m):
  addInEdges t {U_m}

analyze release(t, m):
  U_m ← C_t

analyze prewait(t, m):
  analyze release(t, m)
  analyze yield(t)

analyze postwait(t, m):
  analyze acquire(t, m)

analyze notify(t, m):
  no-op

analyze fork(t, u):
  H ← H ⊎ {(C_t, C_u)}

analyze join(t, u):
  analyze yield(t)
  H ← H ⊎ {(C_u, C_t)}
```

Figure 5: `addInEdges` for Detecting Cooperability Violations

```
addInEdges t N =
  if cycle in H ⊎ {(n, C_t) | n ∈ N}
     report cooperability violation
  else
     H ← H ⊎ {(n, C_t) | n ∈ N}
  endif
```

happens-before edge from the last transaction of the joinee thread u to the current transaction of t, the joining thread. However, since we model *join* using an implicit yield, the case includes a call to `analyze`($yield(t)$).

5. Yield Inference

A cooperability checker is useful for verifying that an execution trace is serializable and that thread interference is documented via yield annotations. For legacy programs, however, such yield annotations may not exist, and manually annotating such programs imposes a burden. SILVER, our yield inference algorithm, alleviates this annotation burden.

The SILVER algorithm mostly behaves identically to the COPPER checking algorithm, until a cooperability violation appears. We

151

Figure 6: addInEdges for Inferring Yield Annotations

```
addInEdges t N =
  if cycle in H ⊎ {(n, C_t) | n ∈ N} then
    insert a yield just before the current operation
    analyze yield(t)
  endif
  H ← H ⊎ {(n, C_t) | n ∈ N}
```

have modularized these two algorithms so that their difference is isolated to the function addInEdges. Figure 6 presents the SILVER version. When the analysis of a particular operation would cause a cooperability violation and associated cycle in the happens-before graph, this function automatically inserts a yield operation right before the current operation *op*. This new yield operation means that *op* now executes in a fresh transaction, and precludes the potential for incoming edges (from nodes in *N* to that fresh transaction) from forming a cycle.

It is trivial to make any program cooperable: simply add enough yields to the program. Too many yields, however, are counterproductive and noisy. SILVER counteracts noise by minimizing the number of yield annotations inferred, adding one only when necessary. Although we have not yet formalized this notion of minimality, our experiments demonstrate that SILVER infers a small number of yield annotations.

6. Implementation

We implemented the COPPER cooperability checker and SILVER yield inference algorithm using the ROADRUNNER framework [14] for dynamic analysis of multithreaded Java programs. ROADRUNNER dynamically instruments the target bytecode of a program during load time. The instrumentation code creates a stream of events for field and array accesses, synchronization operations, thread fork/join, etc., and the COPPER and SILVER tools operate on this event stream as it is created.

The implementation closely follows the analysis. The happens-before relation on transactions H is represented by a list of ancestor transactions: if transaction e_1 happens-before transaction e_2, then e_2's ancestor set will contain e_1. The ancestor sets are transitively closed, making cycle detection an $O(1)$ operation.

Scaling the implementation to handle realistic benchmark programs is a key challenge, especially for memory usage. One problem is object churn, where short-lived transactions are created and then immediately thrown away. Object churn puts pressure on the garbage collector, and may adversely impact performance. Instead, SILVER and COPPER statically allocate a set of transaction objects. Every transaction starts free, is inUse when referenced in the analysis, and becomes free when no longer referenced. Reference counting of in-edges determines when an inUse transaction becomes free: since a completed transaction with no in-edges will never incur additional in-edges in the future, such transactions are ineligible to form a cycle and may be marked as free.

Scalability could also suffer if too many transactions are inUse simultaneously, saturating the statically allocated set of transactions. The use of weak references solves this issue in practice by allowing significantly more transactions to be considered free earlier in the trace. In particular, a transaction n referred to by W_x, $R_{x,t}$ or U_m can be involved in a cycle only if some transaction in C_t or H refers to n. Our implementation requires reference counting only for C_t and H, and otherwise uses weak references for W_x, $R_{x,t}$ and U_m.

7. Evaluation

This section compares the number of interference points for cooperability versus preemptive semantics and atomicity, and evaluates the effectiveness of cooperability at finding synchronization defects. We also briefly discuss the performance of our analysis tools.

We used a collection of multithreaded Java benchmarks ranging in size from 1,000 to 50,000 lines of code. These benchmarks include: colt, a library for high performance computing [36]; hedc, a warehouse webcrawler for astrophysics data [36]; raja, a raytracer program [17]; elevator, a real-time discrete event simulator [36]; mtrt, a raytracer program from the SPEC JVM98 benchmark suite [32]; and several benchmarks (crypt, lufact, moldyn, montecarlo, raytracer, series, sor, sparse) from the Java Grande set [20] (configured with four threads and the base data set). Included is a large reactive benchmark: jigsaw, W3C's web server [33], coupled with a stress test harness.

Excluding the Java standard libraries, all classes loaded by benchmark programs were instrumented. In all experiments, we used a fine granularity for array accesses, with a distinct shadow object for each element in an array. We ran these experiments on a machine with 12 GB memory and eight cores clocked at 2.8 GHz, running Mac OS X 10.6.1 with Java HotSpot Server VM 1.6.0.

We report the *loaded lines of code* (LLOC) for each benchmark in Column 3 of Figure 7, a line count of Java source files that have actually been loaded by the JVM. The loaded lines of code provide a more accurate impression of a program's size as compared to raw line count, which may include vast amounts of dead code.

7.1 Interference Density

Cooperability greatly reduces the number of interference points in a program, compared to atomicity or preemptive semantics. To substantiate this claim, we collected data about our benchmark set to compare the number of interference points for three distinct semantics:

- In preemptive semantics, every access to a shared variable and every lock acquire is a potential point of interference. We count the number of syntactic program locations corresponding to access and acquire operations seen in the trace. We note that this count already excludes many operations that do not cause interference, such as operations on local variables, lock releases, method calls, etc.

- In *atomic semantics*, a context switch may occur only outside an atomic block; thus, in this semantics, we count thread interference points that occur outside atomic methods. The knowledge of which methods are non-atomic is obtained *a priori* by running an atomicity checker [16]. In addition, when in a non-atomic method, we also count every call to an atomic method, since thread interference may occur just before such a call.

- In cooperative semantics, we report the number of yield annotations inferred by SILVER on unannotated code.

To collect this data, we ran SILVER on unannotated code to obtain a complete set of yield annotations sufficient to guarantee serializability for the observed trace. Because SILVER is a dynamic analysis, it may infer only a subset of the necessary yield annotations for the program. In practice, we find that the inferred yield annotations are a fairly precise underapproximation: COPPER typically verifies subsequent runs over this set of inferred yields. Also, a quick experiment shows that the number of additional yield annotations inferred in later executions diminishes significantly (Figure 8). Note that due to scheduling nondeterminism, COPPER may observe a sufficiently different trace than SILVER, and thus may occasionally report a new cooperability violation.

Program	Thread Count	Size (LLOC)	Preemptive		Atomic		Cooperative		Intended Yields	Errors
			Points	Density	Points	Density	Points	Density		
sparse	4	712	196	27.53%	49	6.88%	1	0.14%	1	0
sor	4	721	134	18.59%	49	6.80%	4	0.55%	3	1
series	4	811	90	11.10%	31	3.82%	1	0.12%	1	0
crypt	7	1083	252	23.27%	55	5.08%	2	0.18%	2	0
moldyn	4	1299	737	56.74%	64	4.93%	4	0.31%	4	0
elevator	5	1447	247	17.07%	54	3.73%	3	0.21%	1	2
lufact	4	1472	242	16.44%	57	3.87%	4	0.27%	4	0
raytracer	4	1862	355	19.07%	65	3.49%	4	0.21%	3	1
montecarlo	4	3557	377	10.60%	41	1.15%	2	0.06%	1	1
hedc	6	6409	305	4.76%	76	1.19%	4	0.06%	3	4
mtrt	5	6460	695	10.76%	25	0.39%	2	0.03%	1	1
raja	2	6863	396	5.77%	45	0.66%	1	0.01%	1	0
colt	11	25644	601	2.34%	113	0.44%	16	0.06%	16	0
jigsaw	77	48674	3415	7.02%	550	1.13%	52	0.11%	34	10
Total/Averages		107014	8042	16.50%	1274	3.11%	100	0.17%		

Figure 7. Interference Points and Interference Density Under Preemptive, Atomic, and Cooperative Semantics

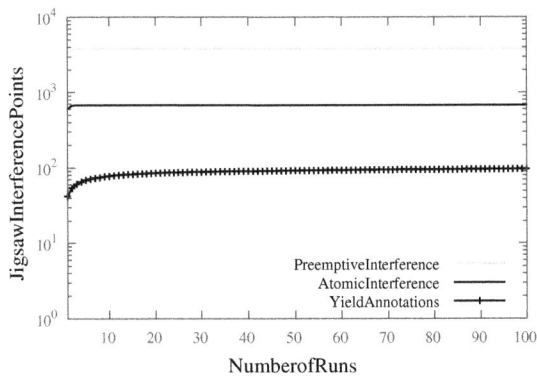

Figure 8. The yield annotations inferred by SILVER for `jigsaw` are stable over multiple runs.

In order to quantify the relative frequency of interference points, we use *interference density*, the number of interference points per loaded line of code. Interference density provides a way to compare the amount of interference across different benchmarks.

Our results are listed in Figure 7, which compares the number of interference points and interference density across our benchmark set according to the three semantics. For preemptive semantics, the interference density ranges from at least 2% to over 50%, and gives a measure of the high cost of reasoning about programs in a preemptive manner. For atomic semantics, the interference density drops by roughly an order of magnitude, but can still reach almost 7% of loaded lines of code, implying that 1 out of every 14 lines must be scrutinized to understand the effects of thread interference, even with method-level atomicity annotations.

For cooperative semantics, the interference density drops by a further order of magnitude as compared with atomic semantics. Indeed, cooperative interference density never rises above 0.6% for our benchmark set, implying that fewer than 6 lines per *thousand* impact the meaning and understandability of a program with respect to nondeterministic scheduling. These results show that cooperability significantly reduces the number of thread interference points to consider in multithreaded programs, as compared to prior techniques. Put differently, yield annotations are relatively rare, and thus do not degenerate into noise.

7.2 Defect Detection

Legacy programs can be difficult to understand, and are often sensitive to change. A set of *intended* yield annotations for such a program assists in understanding thread interference without perturbing preemptive executions. Furthermore, given a legacy program with intended yield annotations, cooperability violations correspond to likely bugs.

Our analysis approach to cooperative semantics can be contrasted with other approaches based on enforcement, such as automatic mutual exclusion, which explicitly change the execution semantics. Transitioning to an enforcement-based approach is potentially disruptive, and may unintentionally change the execution behavior for legacy applications.

To evaluate the effectiveness of cooperability at finding and understanding bugs, we first ran SILVER on our benchmark set and by manual inspection distilled a set of intended yields from the inferred yield annotations, as shown in Column 10 of Figure 7. These intended yields can differ from the inferred ones, due to the choice of yield annotation placement. We then ran COPPER on the resulting yield-annotated program and inspected the results; Column 11 summarizes the number of code bugs that we detected, a number of which reflect known race conditions and destructive atomicity violations.

sparse, series, crypt, raja. The intended thread interference in these programs are all due to the implicit yielding before a join.

sor. For the `sor` benchmark, SILVER reports four yield annotations. One is caused by a join's implicit yield. The other three yield annotations are inferred near code intended to act as a barrier. Of these three, two are intended, while the remaining yield annotation actually reflects an error in the barrier implementation. The barrier in `sor` fails to synchronize accesses to individual non-volatile array elements, and introduces nondeterminism into `sor`.

moldyn, lufact. All of the inferred yield annotations for `moldyn` and `lufact` are situated in barrier code. After manually adding yield annotations before and after barrier operations, COPPER verified the serializability of the observed traces.

elevator. SILVER inferred several yield annotations that implicate two methods as non-atomic (`claimUp` and `claimDown`), both of which have known destructive atomicity violations.

Program	Base Time (ms)	Slowdown			Base Memory (MB)	Memory Overhead		
		EMPTY	VELODROME	COPPER		EMPTY	VELODROME	COPPER
colt	16108	0.8	0.8	0.8	34	2.1	3.1	3.9
crypt	321	6.9	20.0	20.8	34	3.7	12.6	13.3
lufact	358	4.5	7.6	7.9	24	1.9	3.1	4.0
moldyn	806	8.8	12.2	12.9	23	2.0	2.8	3.8
montecarlo	1220	5.0	10.6	11.2	116	5.2	8.4	8.0
mtrt	498	7.6	9.4	9.7	48	2.4	4.1	4.5
raja	420	6.0	7.6	7.4	34	1.7	2.2	2.8
raytracer	770	5.4	23.9	16.5	32	1.4	1.9	2.6
series	1111	1.7	2.1	2.1	22	1.9	2.6	3.6
sor	465	3.9	11.3	21.7	35	1.7	3.1	3.7
sparse	457	6.1	16.3	16.9	36	1.8	3.6	4.3
Average		5.2	11.1	11.6		2.3	4.3	5.0

Figure 9. Time and Space Overheads for EMPTY, VELODROME, and COPPER.

raytracer. This program needs four yield annotations for ensuring cooperability: two are in barrier code, one is an implicit yield associated with a join, and one corresponds to a known destructive race on JGFRayTracerBench.checksum1.

montecarlo. SILVER inferred two yield annotations, corresponding to a join and a racy variable access.

hedc. The hedc benchmark has four racy variables, some of which cause erroneous behavior. After adding a set of intended yields to the program, COPPER issued thread interference reports corresponding to the four racy variables.

mtrt. SILVER reported the implicit yield on a join and inferred a yield annotation for a known racy variable access.

colt. We believe that all the inferred yield annotations in the colt benchmark are intentional.

jigsaw. For the jigsaw yield annotations, five are caused by waits, and 29 are interference points induced by acquire operations. The remaining 18 inferred yield annotations are caused by 8 racy variables and 2 destructive atomicity violations. For example, thread interference just before a call to updateStatistics() in org.w3c.jigsaw.http.httpd could result in slightly outdated statistics information. Thread interference between checking whether log is null and accessing log in org.w3c.jigsaw.-http.CommonLogger could cause a null pointer exception, if the shutdown method runs concurrently.

While finding bugs in code is clearly important, relating how such bugs interact with the rest of the program is just as important for understanding and fixing them. A maintenance strategy based on cooperability improves over existing analyses by providing a richer context for understanding bugs. COPPER's reports cohesively connect race conditions and atomicity violations: thread interference is often caused by a race on a variable or lock, while the call stack at the interference point informs us which methods are non-atomic due to that race.

As an additional data point regarding the benefits of cooperability, we recently conducted a user evaluation on the effectiveness of cooperability for highlighting concurrency bugs [29]. We found that for 2 out of 3 sample programs, yield annotations were associated with a statistically significant improvement in bugs found, compared to un-annotated programs. This study demonstrates the potential of cooperability to significantly improve understanding of thread interference.

7.3 Performance

Figure 9 reports on the performance of our analyses. We compare with the VELODROME atomicity checker [16]. VELODROME is a good choice for comparison, since COPPER and VELODROME check related properties, and both use similar cycle-based techniques. For each of the compute-bound benchmarks, we report on the running time and memory usage of that benchmark (without instrumentation), and on the slowdown and memory overhead incurred by ROADRUNNER when running with the EMPTY tool (which just measures the instrumentation overhead but performs no dynamic analysis); with VELODROME; and with COPPER. We used an implementation of FASTTRACK [13], a modern precise race detector, to filter out non-racy accesses for COPPER and VELODROME; these accesses form the majority of operations in a trace.

The results show that COPPER has an acceptable slowdown and memory overhead for this type of dynamic analysis, and exhibits a similar performance profile to VELODROME. The average slowdown for COPPER was 11.6x, as compared with a slowdown for VELODROME of 11.1x. Similarly, the average memory overhead for COPPER was 5.0x, as compared with a memory overhead for VELODROME of 4.3x. The SILVER inference algorithm exhibits performance similar to the COPPER checking algorithm, which is unsurprising since the two algorithms are closely related.

8. Related Work

Cooperability The notion of cooperability was partly inspired by recent work on automatic mutual exclusion, which proposes ensuring mutual exclusion by default [18, 1]. A major difference is in the meaning of a yield annotation: automatic mutual exclusion *enforces* a yield at runtime, while COPPER *checks* that such a yield annotation guarantees an equivalent serial trace. In prior work, we presented a type and effect system for cooperability [38], which is complementary to the dynamic analysis approach explored in this paper. Kulkarni *et al.* explore *task types*, a data-centric method for obtaining *pervasive atomicity* [21], a notion closely related to cooperability. In their system, threading and data sharing are made explicit via task types, and a combination of type checking and runtime monitoring guarantee correct sharing between threads.

Cooperative semantics have been explored in various settings; for example in high scalability thread packages [35] and as alternative models for structuring concurrency [3, 4, 9]. TIC, a cooperative extension of transactional memory [31], uses a wait construct to suspend a transaction and allow conditional interference. Jalbert and Sen focus on simplifying buggy traces by minimizing context switches, which can be understood as providing an equivalent (buggy) trace under a cooperative scheduler [19]. Our work on cooperability is complementary to this work: serializable traces are already partially simplified since context switches need only be considered at yield annotations.

Race Freedom A data race is a well-known situation where two threads simultaneously access a shared variable without synchronization, and at least one thread is writing to that variable. Races often reflect incorrect synchronization, and the absence of races guarantees that a program's behavior can be understood *as if* it is executing on a sequentially-consistent memory model [2].

A large amount of literature has been devoted to finding and fixing data races in an efficient manner: see, for example [13, 27, 8]. However, race-free programs may still exhibit unintended thread interference, because race freedom is a low-level property dealing with memory accesses. That is, higher-level semantic notions of thread non-interference are not addressed by race freedom.

Recent work by Matsakis and Gross address the notion of time in a type system by making execution *intervals* and the happens-before relation between intervals [24] explicit. This approach increases the annotation burden in favor of increased precision and modularity in statically analyzing for data races.

Atomicity A variety of tools have been developed to detect atomicity violations, both statically and dynamically. Static analyses for verifying atomicity include type systems [15, 30] and techniques that look for cycles in the happens-before graph [11]. Compared to dynamic techniques, static systems provide stronger soundness guarantees but typically involve trade-offs between precision and scalability.

Dynamic techniques analyze a specific executed trace at runtime. Artho *et al.* [5] develop a dynamic analysis tool to identify one class of "higher-level races" using the notion of view consistency. Wang and Stoller describe several dynamic analysis algorithms [37]. Sen and Park [26] develop a tool called AtomFuzzer which attempts to schedule an atomicity violation into exhibiting a real error. The closest atomicity analysis is VELODROME [16], which uses a cycle-based algorithm with transactions as nodes. Farzan and Madhusudan [12] provide space complexity bounds for a similar analysis.

Software transactional memory [23] is a concurrency programming model proposed as an alternative to lock-based concurrency, where the runtime system ensures the atomic execution of transactions. Some recent work has been devoted to addressing the semantic difficulties of software transactional memory [31] and making it compatible with lock-based programming [34]. The relationship between atomicity and transactional memory is analogous to that between cooperability and automatic mutual exclusion: software transactional memory enforces the atomic execution of transactions, while atomicity guarantees that atomic blocks always execute as if in such a transaction.

Deterministic Parallelism As other researchers have begun to realize limits of atomicity, there has been renewed focus on checking for deterministic parallelism. SingleTrack [28] goes beyond the notion of atomicity to check serializability of multithreaded transactions which are also verified to be free of internal conflicts (thus guaranteeing determinism at the transaction level). Deterministic Parallel Java [7] introduces a type system to guarantee determinism by default. Burnim et al. present an assertion-based mechanism for checking determinism where bridge assertions can be used to relate different executions of the same program [10]. Enforcement schemes for determinism also exist [25, 6].

9. Future Work

One interesting topic for future work is to explore more expressive yield annotations. For example, a join could yield only to the joinee thread. This way, the use of fork/join parallelism for deterministic computations would not involve the creation of yield annotations. Alternatively, our analysis could be extended to support annotations of data or methods as yielding.

A semantics with both yield and atomic annotations would allow atomic methods to be specified at the interface level and yield annotations to pinpoint why code is not atomic. We feel that this semantics would combine the strengths of each type of annotation.

When inferring yield annotations, there are multiple choices of where to insert a yield annotation, and another area of future work is to insert yield annotations higher in the call stack, for example, at a call to a synchronized method. We are still investigating which annotation placement is the most useful to infer.

Inspired by the results of our prior user study, we would like to investigate some of these upcoming design decisions through more user studies. Also, we are exploring the development of program logics for cooperability, perhaps extending Hoare logic, to help clarify the benefits of cooperative reasoning.

References

[1] M. Abadi and G. Plotkin. A model of cooperative threads. In *Symposium on Principles of Programming Languages (POPL)*, 2009.

[2] S. V. Adve and K. Gharachorloo. Shared memory consistency models: A tutorial. *IEEE Computer*, 29(12):66–76, 1996.

[3] A. Adya, J. Howell, M. Theimer, W. J. Bolosky, and J. R. Douceur. Cooperative task management without manual stack management. In *Annual Technical Conference*. USENIX Association, 2002.

[4] R. M. Amadio and S. D. Zilio. Resource control for synchronous cooperative threads. In *International Conference on Concurrency Theory (CONCUR)*, 2004.

[5] C. Artho, K. Havelund, and A. Biere. High-level data races. In *International Conference on Verification and Validation of Enterprise Information Systems (ICEIS)*, 2003.

[6] E. D. Berger, T. Yang, T. Liu, and G. Novark. Grace: Safe multithreaded programming for C/C++. In *Object-Oriented Programming, Systems, Languages, and Applications (OOPSLA)*, 2009.

[7] R. L. Bocchino, Jr., V. S. Adve, D. Dig, S. Adve, S. Heumann, R. Komuravelli, J. Overbey, P. Simmons, H. Sung, and M. Vakilian. A type and effect system for Deterministic Parallel Java. In *Object-Oriented Programming, Systems, Languages, and Applications (OOPSLA)*, 2009.

[8] M. D. Bond, K. E. Coons, and K. S. McKinley. PACER: Proportional detection of data races. In *Conference on Programming Language Design and Implementation (PLDI)*, 2010.

[9] G. Boudol. Fair cooperative multithreading. In *International Conference on Concurrency Theory (CONCUR)*, 2007.

[10] J. Burnim and K. Sen. Asserting and checking determinism for multithreaded programs. In *International Symposium on Foundations of Software Engineering (FSE)*, 2009.

[11] A. Farzan and P. Madhusudan. Causal atomicity. In *Computer Aided Verification (CAV)*, 2006.

[12] A. Farzan and P. Madhusudan. Monitoring atomicity in concurrent programs. In *Computer Aided Verification (CAV)*, 2008.

[13] C. Flanagan and S. N. Freund. FastTrack: Efficient and precise dynamic race detection. In *Conference on Programming Language Design and Implementation (PLDI)*, 2009.

[14] C. Flanagan and S. N. Freund. The RoadRunner dynamic analysis framework for concurrent programs. In *Program Analysis for Software Tools and Engineering (PASTE)*, 2010.

[15] C. Flanagan, S. N. Freund, M. Lifshin, and S. Qadeer. Types for atomicity: Static checking and inference for Java. *Transactions on Programming Languages and Systems (TOPLAS)*, 30(4):1–53, 2008.

[16] C. Flanagan, S. N. Freund, and J. Yi. Velodrome: A sound and complete dynamic atomicity checker for multithreaded programs. In *Conference on Programming Language Design and Implementation (PLDI)*, 2008.

[17] E. Fleury and G. Sutre. Raja, version 0.4.0-pre4. Available at http://raja.sourceforge.net/, 2007.

[18] M. Isard and A. Birrell. Automatic mutual exclusion. In *Workshop on Hot Topics in Operating Systems (HOTOS)*, 2007.

[19] N. Jalbert and K. Sen. A trace simplification technique for effective debugging of concurrent programs. In *International Symposium on Foundations of Software Engineering (FSE)*, 2010.

[20] Java Grande Forum. Java Grande benchmark suite. Available at http://www.javagrande.org, 2008.

[21] A. Kulkarni, Y. D. Liu, and S. F. Smith. Task types for pervasive atomicity. In *Object-Oriented Programming, Systems, Languages, and Applications (OOPSLA)*, 2010.

[22] L. Lamport. Time, clocks, and the ordering of events in a distributed system. *Communications of the ACM*, 21(7):558–565, 1978.

[23] J. R. Larus and R. Rajwar. *Transactional Memory*. Synthesis Lectures on Computer Architecture. Morgan & Claypool Publishers, 2006.

[24] N. D. Matsakis and T. R. Gross. A time-aware type system for data-rrace protection and guaranteed initialization. In *Object-Oriented Programming, Systems, Languages, and Applications (OOPSLA)*, 2010.

[25] M. Olszewski, J. Ansel, and S. Amarasinghe. Kendo: efficient deterministic multithreading in software. In *International Conference on Architectural Support for Programming Languages and Operating Systems (ASPLOS)*, 2009.

[26] C.-S. Park and K. Sen. Randomized active atomicity violation detection in concurrent programs. In *International Symposium on Foundations of Software Engineering (FSE)*, 2008.

[27] P. Ratanaworabhan, M. Burtscher, D. Kirovski, B. Zorn, R. Nagpal, and K. Pattabiraman. Detecting and tolerating asymmetric races. In *Symposium on Principles and Practice of Parallel Programming (PPoPP)*, 2009.

[28] C. Sadowski, S. N. Freund, and C. Flanagan. SingleTrack: A dynamic determinism checker for multithreaded programs. In *European Symposium on Programming (ESOP)*, 2009.

[29] C. Sadowski and J. Yi. Applying usability studies to correctness conditions: A case study of cooperability. In *Onward! Workshop on Evaluation and Usability of Programming Languages and Tools (PLATEAU)*, 2010.

[30] A. Sasturkar, R. Agarwal, L. Wang, and S. D. Stoller. Automated type-based analysis of data races and atomicity. In *Symposium on Principles and Practice of Parallel Programming (PPoPP)*, 2005.

[31] Y. Smaragdakis, A. Kay, R. Behrends, and M. Young. Transactions with isolation and cooperation. In *Object-Oriented Programming, Systems, Languages, and Applications (OOPSLA)*, 2007.

[32] Standard Performance Evaluation Corporation. SPEC benchmarks. http://www.spec.org/, 2003.

[33] The World Wide Web Consortium. Jigsaw Web Server. Available from http://www.w3.org/Jigsaw/, 2009.

[34] T. Usui, Y. Smaragdakis, R. Behrends, and J. Evans. Adaptive locks: Combining transactions and locks for efficient concurrency. In *Parallel Architectures and Compilation Techniques (PACT)*, 2009.

[35] R. Von Behren, J. Condit, F. Zhou, G. Necula, and E. Brewer. Capriccio: scalable threads for internet services. *ACM SIGOPS Operating Systems Review*, 37(5):281, 2003.

[36] C. von Praun and T. Gross. Static conflict analysis for multi-threaded object-oriented programs. In *Conference on Programming Language Design and Implementation (PLDI)*, 2003.

[37] L. Wang and S. D. Stoller. Accurate and efficient runtime detection of atomicity errors in concurrent programs. In *Symposium on Principles and Practice of Parallel Programming (PPoPP)*, 2006.

[38] J. Yi and C. Flanagan. Effects for cooperable and serializable threads. In *Workshop on Types in Language Design and Implementation (TLDI)*, 2010.

Communicating Memory Transactions

Mohsen Lesani   Jens Palsberg

UCLA Computer Science Department
University of California, Los Angeles, USA
{lesani, palsberg}@cs.ucla.edu

Abstract

Many concurrent programming models enable both transactional memory and message passing. For such models, researchers have built increasingly efficient implementations and defined reasonable correctness criteria, while it remains an open problem to obtain the best of both worlds. We present a programming model that is the first to have opaque transactions, safe asynchronous message passing, and an efficient implementation. Our semantics uses tentative message passing and keeps track of dependencies to enable undo of message passing in case a transaction aborts. We can program communication idioms such as barrier and rendezvous that do not deadlock when used in an atomic block. Our experiments show that our model adds little overhead to pure transactions, and that it is significantly more efficient than Transactional Events. We use a novel definition of safe message passing that may be of independent interest.

Categories and Subject Descriptors D.1 [**Programming Techniques**]: D1.3 Concurrent Programming – Parallel programming

General Terms Languages, Design, Algorithms

Keywords Transactional Memory, Actor

1. Introduction

1.1. Background

Multi-cores are becoming the mainstream of computer architecture, and they require parallel software to maximize performance. Therefore, researchers sense the need for effective concurrent programming models more than ever before. We expect a concurrent programming model to provide means for both isolation and communication: concurrent operations on shared memory should be executed in isolation to preserve consistency of data, while threads also need to communicate to coordinate cooperative tasks. The classical means of programming isolation and communication is locks and condition variables [16]. Locks protect memory by enforcing that the memory accesses of blocks of code are isolated from each other by mutual exclusion. Condition variables allow threads to communicate: a thread can wait for a condition on shared memory locations and the thread that satisfies the condition can notify waiting threads. However, development and maintenance of concurrent data structures by fine-grained locks is notoriously hard and error-prone, and lock-

based abstractions do not lend themselves well to composition. We need a higher level of abstraction.

A promising isolation mechanism to replace locks is memory transactions because they are easy to program, reason about, and compose [12]. The idea is to mark blocks of code as atomic and let the runtime system guarantee that these blocks are executed in isolation from each other. Researchers have developed several implementations [5][13], semantics [1][24][15], and correctness criteria [10][24] for memory transactions. In particular, we prefer to work with memory transactions that satisfy a widely recognized correctness criterion called opacity [10]. To complement memory transactions, which communication mechanism should replace condition variables? We want the addition of a communication mechanism to preserve opacity while adding little implementation overhead to pure transactions. Let us review the strengths and weaknesses of several known mechanisms.

1.2. Synchronizers, retry, and punctuation

Luchango and Marathe were the first to consider the interaction of memory transactions and they introduced synchronizers. A synchronizer encapsulates shared data that can be accessed simultaneously by every transaction that synchronizes (i.e. requests access) to it. The transactions that synchronize on a synchronizer (that is either read from or write to it) all commit or abort together. Additional concurrency control mechanisms are needed to protect the shared data against race conditions [20]. The work is recently extended to transaction communicators [22].

To enable a transaction to wait for a condition, Harris and Fraser introduced guarded atomic blocks [11], and Haskell added the "retry" keyword [12]. On executing "retry", Haskell aborts and then retries the transaction. Later, Smaragdakis et al. [28] established the need for transactional communication. They showed that neither of the previous mechanisms supports programming of a composable barrier abstraction: if used in an atomic block, the barrier deadlocks. In contrast to Haskell's "retry", Smaragdakis et al. [28] and also Dudnik and Swift [7] advocated that the waiting transaction should be committed rather than aborted. They observed that if the transaction is aborted, all its writes are discarded, while if it is committed, its writes will be visible to other transactions, thereby enabling the transaction to leave information for other transactions before it starts waiting.

Dudnik and Swift used their observation as the basis for designing transactional condition variables [7]; their model allows no nesting of atomic blocks. Smaragdakis et al. [28] used their observation as the basis for designing TIC which enables programming of a barrier abstraction that won't deadlock even if it is used in an atomic block. TIC splits ("punctuates") each transaction into two transactions; this may violate local invariants and therefore requires the programmer to provide code for reestablishing the local invariants. TIC executes that code at the point of the split, that is, after wait is called and before the first half of the transaction is committed. As explained in [28], TIC breaks isolation and therefore doesn't satisfy opacity.

1.3. Message Passing

A dual approach to providing means for isolation and communication is to begin with a message passing model such as Actors [2] and Concurrent ML (CML) [26], and then add an isolation mechanism. Examples of such combinations include Stabilizers [30], Transactional Events (TE) [6], and Transactional Events for ML (TE for ML) [8].

In Stabilizers, threads can communicate by sending and receiving synchronous messages on channels. The programmer can mark locations of code as stable checkpoints. If a thread encounters a transient fault, it calls "stabilize", which causes the run-time system to revert back the current thread, and all threads with which it has transitively communicated, to their latest possible stable checkpoints. In summary, Stabilizers support program location recovery but not atomicity and isolation as explained in [30].

Inspired by CML and Haskell STM, TE provides the programmer with a sequencing combinator to combine two events such as synchronous sends and receives into one compound event. The combination is an all-or-nothing transaction in the sense that executing the resulting event performs either both or none of the two events. The sequencing combinator enables straightforward programming of: (1) a modular abstraction of guarded (conditional) receive (this is not possible in CML), (2) three-way-rendezvous (a generalization of barrier) (this is not possible with pure memory transactions [6]), and (3) memory transactions (by representing each location as a server thread). TE supports the completeness property, namely: if there exists an interleaving for a set of compound events such that their sends and receives are matched to each other, the interleaving is guaranteed to be found. While the completeness property can terminate some scheduler-dependent programs, scheduler-independence is the well known property expected from concurrent algorithms. More importantly, finding such an interleaving is NP-hard [6] and can be implemented with an exponential number of run-time search threads [6]. Our experiments show that the performance penalty can be excessive.

TE supports all-or-nothing compound events but it prevents any shared memory mutation inside compound events. In follow-up work on TE, the authors of TE in ML [8] explain that encoding memory as a ref server is inefficient. They extend TE to support mutation of shared memory in compound events. TE for ML logically divides a compound event into sections called chunks. Chunks are delimited by the sends and receives of the compound event. The semantics of TE for ML breaks the isolation of shared memory mutations of a compound event at the end of its chunks. At these points (i.e. before sends and receives), the shared memory mutations that are done in the chunk can be seen by chunks of other synchronizing events. Similar to the punctuation in TIC, chunking breaks isolation and thus doesn't satisfy opacity.

1.4. Our Approach

The above review shows that previous work has problems with either nesting of atomic blocks, opacity, or efficiency. Our goal is to do better. In this paper, we present Communicating Memory Transactions (CMT) that integrates memory transactions with a style of asynchronous communication known from the Actor model. CMT is the first model to have opaque transactions, safe asynchronous message passing, and an efficient implementation. We use a novel definition of safety for asynchronous message passing that generalizes previous work. Safe communication means that every committed transaction has received messages only from committed transactions. To satisfy communication safety, CMT keeps track of dependencies to enable undo of message passing in case a transaction aborts. We show how to program three fundamental communication abstractions in CMT, namely synchronous queue, barrier, and three-way rendezvous. In particular we show that our barrier and rendezvous abstractions do not deadlock when used in an atomic block. To enable an efficient implementation, CMT does not satisfy the completeness property [8] found in TE. Based on the transactional memory implementations TL2 [5] and DSTM2 [13], we present two efficient implementations of CMT. We will explain several subtle techniques that we use to implement the semantics. Our experiments show that our model adds little overhead to pure transactions, and that it is significantly more efficient than Transactional Events.

In Section 2 we discuss five CMT programs. In Section 3 we recall the optimistic semantics of memory transactions by Koskinen, Parkinson, and Herlihy [15], and in Section 4 we give a semantics of CMT as an extension of the semantics in Section 3. In Section 5 we explain our implementation of CMT, and in Section 6 we show our experimental results.

2. Examples

The goal of this section is to give examples of CMT programs and give an informal discussion of the semantics of CMT. In particular, we will illustrate the notions of communication safety, dependency and collective commit. We use the following syntax: to delimit parallel sections of the program, $\|$ is used. *ch send e* sends the result of expression *e* to channel *ch*. $x := ch$ *receive* receives a message from channel *ch* and assigns it to the thread local variable x. To provide means of programming abstractions, macro definitions are allowed: *let macroName(params) t*. The body term *t* of the macro is inlined with *params* at the call sites.

Let us start with a simple example: a server thread that executes a transaction in response to request messages from a client thread.

```
{ // Client              { // Server
  atomic                   atomic
    ch send unit             x := ch receive
} ||                       }
```

The server transaction receives the tentative message from the client transaction and mutates memory according to the message. If the client transaction aborts, the message that it has sent is invalid. Therefore, the server transaction should commit only if the client transaction is committed. In other words, the communication is safe under the condition that a receiving transaction is committed only if the sender transaction is committed. We say that the receiving transaction depends on the sender transaction. If the sender aborts the receiver should abort as well. The abortion is propagated to depending transactions. If a receive is executed on a channel that is empty or contains an invalid message (a message sent by an aborted transaction), the receive suspends until a message becomes available.

Consider the two-way rendezvous abstraction that can swap values between two threads. (Rendezvous is a generalization of barrier that swaps values in addition to time synchronization.)

```
let rendezvous(sc_1,rc_1,sc_2,rc_2)     let swap(x,sc,rc,v)
  atomic                                  sc send v;
    x_1 := sc_1 receive;                  x := rc receive
    x_2 := sc_2 receive;
    rc_1 send x_2;
    rc_2 send x_1;
```

158

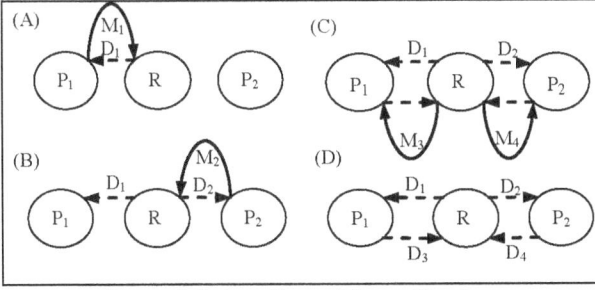

Figure 1. Interactions of 2-way Rendezvous

Consider the following program that employs the above abstractions. Each abstraction is inlined at its call sites and its parameters are substituted with passed arguments. Columns represent parallel parts of the program. (To discuss the interaction of transactions, the parties call *swap* inside atomic blocks.)

```
{ // Party₁              { // Rendezvous        { // Party₂
  atomic                   rendezvous(            atomic
    // code before           ch₁, ch₂,              // code before
    swap(                    ch₃, ch₄)              swap(
      x, ch₁, ch₂, unit);  } ||                      x, ch₃, ch₄, unit);
    // code after                                   // code after
} ||                                              }
```

Figure 1 shows the steps of execution of the above program. Solid arrows show messages and dashed arrows show dependencies. $Party_1$ sends a tentative $Message_1$ to Rendezvous. Rendezvous receives $Message_1$ and becomes dependent on $Party_1$ (Figure 1.A). The same happens for $Party_2$ (Figure 1.B). At this point, Rendezvous is dependent on both parties.

Assume that $Party_2$ aborts. The abortion is propagated to Rendezvous by $Dependency_2$. Rendezvous is also aborted and retried. On the retry, it receives $Message_1$ again. But as $Message_2$ is invalid, the second receive suspends. This means that Rendezvous repeats Figure 1.A again. It effectively ignores the aborted transaction of $Party_2$ and waits for another.

When $Party_2$ is retried, Figure 1.B is repeated. At this time, Rendezvous has received request messages from both parties. It tentatively sends swapped messages back to both $Party_1$ and $Party_2$. The parties are released from suspension and receive the messages. They get dependent on Rendezvous (Figure 1.C). At this time, parties and Rendezvous are interdependent (Figure 1.D).

Assume that $Party_2$ aborts in the code after *swap*. Dependencies propagate abortion to Rendezvous and then to $Party_1$. In other words, if one of the parties aborts, the Rendezvous and all the other parties are aborted and retried. This is the expected behavior: as $Party_2$ is aborted, the value that it has swapped with $Party_1$ is invalid. Therefore, $Party_1$ should be aborted as well. (This also matches the semantics expected from the barrier. As $Party_2$ aborts, it is retried. This means that it will reach the barrier again. By the semantics of the barrier, no party should pass the barrier when there is a party that has not reached the barrier. Thus, as $Party_2$ will reach the barrier, $Party_1$ should not have passed it. Therefore, $Party_1$ should be aborted as well.)

Finally, the transactions of Rendezvous, $Party_1$ and $Party_2$ reach the end of the atomic blocks. As they are interdependent, each of them can be committed only if the others are committed. If each of them obliviously waits until its dependencies are resolved, deadlock happens. As will be explained in the following sections, interdependent transactions are recognized as a cluster and transactions of a cluster are collectively committed.

In contrast to an implementation using Haskell retry, calling *swap* inside a nested atomic block does not lead to a deadlock. In

Synchronous Queue	Barrier	3-way Rendezvous
The abstractions:	The abstractions:	The abstractions:
let syncSend(	*let barrier(*	*let rendezvous(*
sc, rc, v)	*bc₁, pc₁,*	*sc₁, rc₁,*
sc send v;	*bc₂, pc₂)*	*sc₂, rc₂,*
rc receive	*atomic*	*sc₃, rc₃)*
let syncReceive(	*bc₁ receive;*	*atomic*
x, sc, rc)	*bc₂ receive;*	$x_1 := sc_1$ *receive;*
$x := sc$ *receive;*	*pc₁ send unit;*	$x_2 := sc_2$ *receive;*
rc send unit	*pc₂ send unit*	$x_3 := sc_3$ *receive;*
	let await(bc, pc)	rc_1 *send* $\langle x_2, x_3 \rangle$;
The program:	*bc send unit;*	rc_2 *send* $\langle x_1, x_3 \rangle$;
{ // Sender	*pc receive*	rc_3 *send* $\langle x_1, x_2 \rangle$;
syncSend(		*let swap(x, sc, rc, v)*
x, ch_0, ch_1)	The program:	*sc send v;*
} || { // Receiver	{ // Barrier	$x := rc$ *receive*
syncReceive(	*barrier(*	
x, ch_0, ch_1)	$ch_1, ch_2,$	The program:
}	ch_3, ch_4)	{ // Rendezvous
	} || { // Party₁	*rendezvous(*
	await(ch₁, ch₂)	$ch_1, ch_2,$
	} || { // Party₂	$ch_3, ch_4,$
	await(ch₃, ch₄)	ch_5, ch_6)
	}	} || { // Party₁
		swap(
		$x, ch_1, ch_2,$ *unit)*
		} || { // Party₂
		swap(
		$x, ch_3, ch_4,$ *unit)*
		} || { // Party₃
		swap(
		$x, ch_5, ch_6,$ *unit)*
		}

Figure 2: CMT Programs

addition, in contrast to TIC and TE for ML, opacity of transactions is satisfied.

Similar to Two-way Rendezvous, the abstractions for Synchronous queue, Barrier and Three-way rendezvous can be programmed in CMT as shown in Figure 2. Please note that it is assumed that these basic abstractions are used only once. For example, the basic barrier abstraction is not a cyclic barrier. For the three-way rendezvous, we assume that *e* can be pairs of the form $\langle e, e \rangle$. Implementations of Barrier with Haskell retry, TIC and TE for ML and an implementation of CMT can be seen in the technical report [17] section 15.1. Implementations of Synchronous Queue and Rendezvous can be seen in the technical report [17] sections 15.2 and 15.3.

3. Memory Transactions

We now recall the optimistic semantics of memory transactions by Koskinen, Parkinson, and Herlihy [15]. Their semantics is the starting point for our semantics of CMT in Section 4. TL2 is an implementation that realizes this semantics.

Note: we have fixed a few typos in the syntax, semantics and definition of moverness after personal communication with the authors of [15].

3.1. Syntax

A configuration is a triple of the form $\langle \mathcal{T} \cdot \sigma_{sh} \cdot \ell_{sh} \rangle$. (To simplify reading of long configurations, "·" is used to separate elements of configurations.) $\mathcal{T}$ represents the set of threads. σ_{sh} denotes the shared store that contains objects. ℓ_{sh} is a log of pairs $\langle \tau^{cmt}, \ell_\tau \rangle$: each committed transaction τ^{cmt} and the operations it has performed ℓ_τ. $\mathcal{T}$ is a set of elements of the form $\langle \tau, s, \sigma_\tau, \overline{\sigma_\tau}, \ell_\tau \rangle$. τ is

OCMD
$$\langle\langle\tau, c; s, \sigma_\tau, \overline{\sigma_\tau}, \ell_\tau\rangle, \mathcal{T} \cdot \sigma_{sh} \cdot \ell_{sh}\rangle \xrightarrow{\perp}_o \langle\langle\tau, s, [\![c]\!]\sigma_\tau, \overline{\sigma_\tau}, \ell_\tau\rangle, \mathcal{T} \cdot \sigma_{sh} \cdot \ell_{sh}\rangle \qquad \tau \neq \perp$$

OBEG
$$\langle\langle\perp, beg; s, \sigma_\tau, \overline{\sigma_\tau}, []\rangle, \mathcal{T} \cdot \sigma_{sh} \cdot \ell_{sh}\rangle \xrightarrow{\langle\tau, beg\rangle}_o \langle\langle fresh(\tau), s, snap(\sigma_\tau, \sigma_{sh}), \sigma_\tau[stmt \mapsto "beg; s"], []\rangle, \mathcal{T} \cdot \sigma_{sh} \cdot \ell_{sh}\rangle$$

OAPP
$$\langle\langle\tau, x := o.m; s, \sigma_\tau, \overline{\sigma_\tau}, \ell_\tau\rangle, \mathcal{T} \cdot \sigma_{sh} \cdot \ell_{sh}\rangle \xrightarrow{\langle\tau, o.m\rangle}_o \langle\langle\tau, s, \sigma_\tau[o \mapsto ([\![o]\!]\sigma_\tau).m, x \mapsto rv(([\![o]\!]\sigma_\tau).m)], \overline{\sigma_\tau}, \ell_\tau :: ("o.m")\rangle, \mathcal{T} \cdot \sigma_{sh} \cdot \ell_{sh}\rangle \quad \tau \neq \perp$$

OCMT
$$\dfrac{\forall \langle\tau^{cmt}, \ell_{\tau'}\rangle \in \ell_{sh}: \tau^{cmt} > \tau \Rightarrow \ell_\tau \triangleright \ell_{\tau'}}{\langle\langle\tau, end; s, \sigma_\tau, \overline{\sigma_\tau}, \ell_\tau\rangle, \mathcal{T} \cdot \sigma_{sh} \cdot \ell_{sh}\rangle \xrightarrow{\langle\tau, cmt\rangle}_o \langle\langle\perp, s, zap(\sigma_\tau), zap(\sigma_\tau), []\rangle, \mathcal{T} \cdot merge(\sigma_{sh}, \ell_\tau) \cdot \ell_{sh} :: \langle fresh(\tau^{cmt}), \ell_\tau\rangle\rangle} \quad \tau \neq \perp$$

OABT
$$\langle\langle\tau, s, \sigma_\tau, \overline{\sigma_\tau}, \ell_\tau\rangle, \mathcal{T} \cdot \sigma_{sh} \cdot \ell_{sh}\rangle \xrightarrow{\langle\tau, abt\rangle}_o \langle\langle\perp, [\![stmt]\!]\overline{\sigma_\tau}, \overline{\sigma_\tau}/stmt, \overline{\sigma_\tau}, []\rangle, \mathcal{T} \cdot \sigma_{sh} \cdot \ell_{sh}\rangle \qquad \tau \neq \perp$$

$$snap(\sigma_\tau, \sigma_{sh}) = \sigma_\tau[o \mapsto [\![o]\!]\sigma_{sh}] \quad \forall o \in objects(P) \qquad merge(\sigma_{sh}, [\,]) = \sigma_{sh}$$
$$zap(\sigma_\tau) = \sigma_\tau[o \mapsto \perp] \quad \forall o \in objects(P) \qquad merge(\sigma_{sh}, ("o.m") :: \ell_\tau) = merge(\sigma_{sh}[o \mapsto ([\![o]\!]\sigma_{sh}).m], \ell_\tau)$$

Figure 3: Optimistic Semantics of Memory Transactions

the transaction identifier (or $\perp$ that denotes that the code is executing outside transactions). Transaction identifiers are assumed to be ordered by the time that they are generated. s is the statement to be executed by the thread. Statements have the following syntax:

$s \to i; s \mid i$ *Statement*
$i \to beg \mid end \mid x := o.m \mid c \mid skip$ *Instruction*

beg and *end* denote the start and end of transactions. We use *atomic s* as a syntactic sugar for *beg; s; end*. $o.m$ denotes calling method m on shared object o. Commands (reading and writing) that are applied to thread-local state are represented by c. σ_τ is the transaction-local store of objects. $\overline{\sigma_\tau}$ is the backup store that stores states of (thread-local) objects before the transaction is started. It is used to recover state when the transaction aborts. The statement before the transaction is started is also backed up in $\overline{\sigma_\tau}$. The pattern $\overline{\sigma_\tau}; stmt \mapsto s$ denotes a back up store that maps the backed up statement to s. ℓ_τ is the ordered log of operations that has been performed by the transaction. The initial configuration is of the form $Conf_0^o = \langle\mathcal{T}_0 \cdot \sigma_{sh_0} \cdot []\rangle$. $\mathcal{T}_0$ is $\mathcal{T}_0 = \{T_1, ..., T_n\}$ where $T_i = \langle\perp, P_i, \sigma_{sh_0}, \sigma_{sh_0}; stmt \mapsto \perp, []\rangle$. $\{P_{i=1..n}\}$ are the parallel segments of the program. σ_{sh_0} is the store where every object is mapped to its initial state i.e. $\sigma_{sh_0} = \{\forall o \in objects(P).o \mapsto init(o)\}$. $M[k \mapsto v]$ denotes assigning value v to key k in map M. $[\![k]\!]M$ represents value of key k in map M.

3.2. Operational Semantics

The semantics [15] is shown in Figure 3. The semantics is a labeled transition system. The syntax supports nested atomic blocks. We can transform a program with nested atomics into an equivalent program with only top-level atomics by simply removing all inner atomics. Hence, it is sufficient that the semantics supports only top-level atomics.

We will now explain the five rules in Figure 3. The *OCMD* rule applies the statement to the local store. $[\![c]\!]\sigma_\tau$ denotes application of the command c to the local store σ_τ. The *OBEG* rule starts a new transaction. A *fresh* transaction identifier is generated. $fresh(\tau)$ generates unique and increasing transaction identifiers τ. The current store and also the current statement are stored in the backup store. A snapshot of the current state of objects is taken from the shared store to the local store. The *OAPP* rule executes a method. The method is applied to the local store and is logged in the local log. rv represents the returned value. As defined by [15], read and write operations on memory locations are special cases of method call. The *OCMT* rule checks that the methods of the

current transaction are right movers with respect to the methods of the transactions that have been committed since the current transaction has started. Right moverness ensures that tentative execution of a transaction can be committed even though other transactions have committed after it started. Please refer to the appendix for a detailed definition of right moverness. If the methods of the transaction satisfy the moverness condition, the transaction is committed. The methods of the local log are applied to the shared store. The local log is also saved with a *fresh* id in the shared log. This is used to check moverness while later transactions are committing. The *OABT* reduction aborts the transaction. The store and the statement that were saved in the backup store when the transaction was starting are restored.

3.3. Properties

The semantics satisfies opacity which is a correctness condition for memory transactions [10]. We say that a sequence of labels $l_1, ... l_n$ is given by $\to_o$ started from $Conf_1^o$ if there are configurations $Conf_{i=2..n}^o$ such that for each $i \in \{1..n-1\}: Conf_{i=1}^o \xrightarrow{l_i}_o Conf_{i=n+1}^o$.

THEOREM 1 (Opacity). Every sequence of labels $\langle\tau, beg\rangle$, $\langle\tau, o.m\rangle$, $\langle\tau, abt\rangle$ and $\langle\tau, cmt\rangle$ given by $\to_o$ started from $Conf_0^o$ is opaque (Proposition 6.2 of [15]).

4. Communicating Memory Transactions

We now present the syntax and semantics of CMT. The semantics adds a core message passing mechanism to the semantics presented in the previous section.

4.1. Syntax

The syntax is extended as follows:

$s \to i; s \mid i$ *Statement*
$i \to beg \mid end \mid x := o.m \mid c \mid skip$ *Instruction*
$\mid ch \, send \, e \mid x := ch \, receive$

ch send e sends the result of expression e to channel *ch*. $x := ch \, receive$ receives a message from channel *ch* and assigns it to the thread local variable x. We assume that messages are primitive values.

The configuration of the semantics in section 3 is augmented with the following elements: $\mathcal{M}$, $\mathcal{C}$ and $\mathcal{D}$. Therefore a configuration is a tuple of the form $\langle\mathcal{T} \cdot \sigma_{sh} \cdot \ell_{sh} \cdot \mathcal{M} \cdot \mathcal{C} \cdot \mathcal{D}\rangle$. $\mathcal{M}$

CMD	
	$\langle\langle\tau, c; s, \sigma_\tau, \overleftarrow{\sigma_\tau}, \ell_\tau\rangle, \mathcal{T} \cdot \sigma_{sh} \cdot \ell_{sh} \cdot \mathcal{M} \cdot \mathcal{C} \cdot \mathcal{D}\rangle \xrightarrow{\perp} \langle\langle\tau, s, [\![c]\!]\sigma_\tau, \overleftarrow{\sigma_\tau}, \ell_\tau\rangle, \mathcal{T} \cdot \sigma_{sh} \cdot \ell_{sh} \cdot \mathcal{M} \cdot \mathcal{C} \cdot \mathcal{D}\rangle \qquad \tau \neq \perp$

BEG
$$\mathcal{M}' = \mathcal{M} \cup \{\tau \mapsto \mathbf{r}\}$$
$$\langle\langle\perp, \text{beg}; s, \sigma_\tau, \overleftarrow{\sigma_\tau}, [\,]\rangle, \mathcal{T} \cdot \sigma_{sh} \cdot \ell_{sh} \cdot \mathcal{M} \cdot \mathcal{C} \cdot \mathcal{D}\rangle \xrightarrow{\langle\tau, \text{beg}\rangle} \langle\langle\text{fresh}(\tau), s, \text{snap}(\sigma_\tau, \sigma_{sh}), \sigma_\tau[\text{stmt} \mapsto \text{"beg}; s\text{"}], [\,]\rangle, \mathcal{T} \cdot \sigma_{sh} \cdot \ell_{sh} \cdot \mathcal{M}' \cdot \mathcal{C} \cdot \mathcal{D}\rangle$$

APP
$$\langle\langle\tau, x := o.m; s, \sigma_\tau, \overleftarrow{\sigma_\tau}, \ell_\tau\rangle, \mathcal{T} \cdot \sigma_{sh} \cdot \ell_{sh} \cdot \mathcal{M} \cdot \mathcal{C} \cdot \mathcal{D}\rangle \xrightarrow{\langle\tau, o.m\rangle}$$
$$\langle\langle\tau, s, \sigma_\tau[o \mapsto ([\![o]\!]\sigma_\tau).m, x \mapsto rv(([\![o]\!]\sigma_\tau).m)], \overleftarrow{\sigma_\tau}, \ell_\tau :: (\text{"}o.m\text{"})\rangle, \mathcal{T} \cdot \sigma_{sh} \cdot \ell_{sh} \cdot \mathcal{M} \cdot \mathcal{C} \cdot \mathcal{D}\rangle \qquad \tau \neq \perp$$

CMT
$$\text{Cluster}(\{\tau_{i=1..n}\}, \mathcal{M}, \mathcal{D})$$
$$\forall\tau_{i=1..n}\forall\langle\tau^{cmt}, \ell_{\tau'}\rangle \in \ell_{sh} : \tau^{cmt} > \tau_i \Rightarrow \ell_{\tau_i} \unrhd \ell_{\tau'} \qquad \forall\tau_{i=1..n}\forall\tau_{j=1..i-1} : \ell_{\tau_i} \unrhd \ell_{\tau_j}$$
$$\mathcal{M}' = \mathcal{M}[\tau_i \mapsto \mathbf{c}]_{i=1..n}$$
$$\langle\langle\tau_i, \text{end}; s_i, \sigma_{\tau_i}, \overleftarrow{\sigma_{\tau_i}}, \ell_{\tau_i}\rangle_{i=1..n}, \mathcal{T} \cdot \sigma_{sh} \cdot \ell_{sh} \cdot \mathcal{M} \cdot \mathcal{C} \cdot \mathcal{D}\rangle \xrightarrow{\langle\tau_1,\text{cmt}\rangle...\langle\tau_n,\text{cmt}\rangle}$$
$$\langle\langle\perp, s_i, \text{zap}(\sigma_{\tau_i}), \text{zap}(\sigma_{\tau_i}), [\,]\rangle_{i=1..n}, \mathcal{T} \cdot \text{merge}(\sigma_{sh}, \{\ell_{\tau_{i=1..n}}\}) \cdot \ell_{sh} :: \text{seq}(\langle\text{fresh}(\tau_i^{cmt}), \ell_{\tau_i}\rangle_{i=1..n}) \cdot \mathcal{M}' \cdot \mathcal{C} \cdot \mathcal{D}\rangle \qquad \forall\tau_{i=1..n} : \tau_i \neq \perp$$

ABT
$$\mathcal{M}' = \mathcal{M}[\tau \mapsto \mathbf{a}]$$
$$\langle\langle\tau, s, \sigma_\tau, \overleftarrow{\sigma_\tau}, \ell_\tau\rangle, \mathcal{T} \cdot \sigma_{sh} \cdot \ell_{sh} \cdot \mathcal{M} \cdot \mathcal{C} \cdot \mathcal{D}\rangle \xrightarrow{\langle\tau, \text{abt}\rangle} \langle\langle\perp, [\![\text{stmt}]\!]\overleftarrow{\sigma_\tau}, \overleftarrow{\sigma_\tau}/\text{stmt}, \overleftarrow{\sigma_\tau}, [\,]\rangle, \mathcal{T} \cdot \sigma_{sh} \cdot \ell_{sh} \cdot \mathcal{M}' \cdot \mathcal{C} \cdot \mathcal{D}\rangle \qquad \tau \neq \perp$$

Send
$$\mathcal{C}' = \mathcal{C}[ch \mapsto \langle\tau, v\rangle]$$
$$\langle\langle\tau, ch \text{ send } v; s, \sigma_\tau, \overleftarrow{\sigma_\tau}, \ell_\tau\rangle, \mathcal{T} \cdot \sigma_{sh} \cdot \ell_{sh} \cdot \mathcal{M} \cdot \mathcal{C} \cdot \mathcal{D}\rangle \xrightarrow{\langle\tau, ch \text{ send}\rangle} \langle\langle\tau, s, \sigma_\tau, \overleftarrow{\sigma_\tau}, \ell_\tau\rangle, \mathcal{T} \cdot \sigma_{sh} \cdot \ell_{sh} \cdot \mathcal{M} \cdot \mathcal{C}' \cdot \mathcal{D}\rangle \qquad \tau \neq \perp$$

Receive
$$\mathcal{C}(ch) = \langle\tau', v\rangle \qquad \mathcal{D}' = \mathcal{D} \cup \{\tau \curvearrowright \tau'\}$$
$$\langle\langle\tau, x := ch \text{ receive}; s, \sigma_\tau, \overleftarrow{\sigma_\tau}, \ell_\tau\rangle, \mathcal{T} \cdot \sigma_{sh} \cdot \ell_{sh} \cdot \mathcal{M} \cdot \mathcal{C} \cdot \mathcal{D}\rangle \xrightarrow{\langle\tau, ch \text{ receive}\rangle} \langle\langle\tau, s, \sigma_\tau[x \mapsto v], \overleftarrow{\sigma_\tau}, \ell_\tau\rangle, \mathcal{T} \cdot \sigma_{sh} \cdot \ell_{sh} \cdot \mathcal{M} \cdot \mathcal{C} \cdot \mathcal{D}'\rangle \qquad \tau \neq \perp$$

$$
\begin{array}{rcl}
\text{snap}(\sigma_\tau, \sigma_{sh}) & = & \sigma_\tau[o \mapsto [\![o]\!]\sigma_{sh}] \quad \forall o \in \text{objects}(P)\\
\text{zap}(\sigma_\tau) & = & \sigma_\tau[o \mapsto \perp] \quad \forall o \in \text{objects}(P)
\end{array}
$$

$$\text{Cluster}(\{\tau_{i=1..n}\}, \mathcal{M}, \mathcal{D}) = \forall i \in \{1 \ldots n\} : \begin{bmatrix} \forall\tau : ((\tau_i \curvearrowright \tau) \in \mathcal{D}) \Rightarrow \\ \begin{pmatrix} (\mathcal{M}(\tau) = \mathbf{c}) \text{ or} \\ (\exists j \in \{1 \ldots n\} : \tau = \tau_j) \end{pmatrix} \end{bmatrix}$$

$$
\begin{array}{rcl}
\text{merge}(\sigma_{sh}, [\;]) & = & \sigma_{sh}\\
\text{merge}(\sigma_{sh}, (\text{"}o.m\text{"}) :: \ell_\tau) & = & \text{merge}(\sigma_{sh}[o \mapsto ([\![o]\!]\sigma_{sh}).m], \ell_\tau)\\
\text{merge}(\sigma_{sh}, \{\}) & = & \sigma_{sh}\\
\text{merge}(\sigma_{sh}, \{\ell_{\tau_{i=1..n}}\}) & = & \text{merge}(\text{merge}(\sigma_{sh}, \{\ell_{\tau_{i=1..n-1}}\}), \ell_{\tau_n})\\
\text{seq}(f(i)_{i=1..n}) & = & f(1) :: \cdots :: f(n)
\end{array}
$$

Figure 4: CMT Semantics

maps each transaction id to the state of the transaction. The state of a transaction can be either $\mathbf{r}$ (running), $\mathbf{c}$ (committed), or $\mathbf{a}$ (aborted). A committed transaction has finished successfully, while an aborted transaction has stopped execution and had its tentative effects discarded. $\mathcal{C}$ is a partial function that maps channels ch to pairs of the form $\langle\tau, v\rangle$ where τ is the sender transaction and v is the current value of the channel. To guarantee communication safety, we track dependencies between transactions. $\mathcal{D}$ is the transaction dependency relation that is a set of elements of the form $\tau \curvearrowright \tau'$. Transaction τ is dependent on transaction τ', i.e. $\tau \curvearrowright \tau'$, if τ receives a message that is sent by τ'. The dependency to τ' is said to be resolved, if τ' is committed. The initial configuration is $\text{Conf}_0 = \langle\mathcal{T}_0 \cdot \sigma_{sh_0} \cdot [\,] \cdot \emptyset \cdot \emptyset \cdot \emptyset\rangle$. $\mathcal{T}_0$ and σ_{sh_0} are defined as the prior semantics.

4.2. Operational Semantics

The rules **CMD**, **APP** are not changed other than the addition of $\mathcal{M} \cdot \mathcal{C} \cdot \mathcal{D}$ to both sides of the rules. The two rules **BEG** and **ABT** have a small change. They set the state of the transaction in $\mathcal{M}$ to running $\mathbf{r}$ and aborted $\mathbf{a}$, respectively.

The **Send** rule sends a message on a channel. The mapping $\mathcal{C}$ is updated to map the channel to the pair $\langle\tau, v\rangle$ where τ is the id of the current transaction and v is the sent value. The id of the sender transaction that is saved here is retrieved later when the message is received to record a dependency from the receiver to the sender. In CMT, each channel can hold a single value, while our implementation supports an arbitrary number of messages, as explained in section 5.

The **Receive** rule receives a message from a channel. If there exists a value in the channel, the value is received and the dependency of the current transaction to the sender transaction is added to $\mathcal{D}$. The condition that the sender transaction is not aborted can be added as an optimization.

The semantics in Figure 4 supports transactions that can send and receive. It is straightforward to extend the semantics to allow code executing outside transactions to send and receive.

The **CMT** rule encodes the collective commitment of a cluster. A set of transactions are committed if they satisfy the following two conditions.

To respect dependencies, the first condition is that only transactions of clusters are committed where Cluster is defined as follows. A set of transactions that have reached the end of their atomic blocks (called terminated) is a cluster iff any unresolved dependencies of them are to each other. The transactions that are considered in the **CMT** rule have already reached the end of their atomic blocks. It is checked that their dependencies are either to other transactions of the set or to committed transactions.

It is notable why the following simple commitment condition is not used instead: a transaction that has reached the end of its atomic block is committed only if all its dependencies are already resolved. It is straightforward that this condition directly translates to communication safety. But it can lead to deadlock. For example, if two transactions receive messages from each other, they are interdependent. As mentioned for the example of Section 2, if each transaction in a dependency cycle obliviously waits until its dependencies are resolved, it may wait forever. In classical distributed transactions [18][3], all receives happen at the beginning of sub-transactions. Therefore, the dependencies form a tree and hierarchical commit and two phase commit protocol (2PC) can be employed. In CMT receives can happen in the middle of transactions; thus, the dependencies can in general form a cyclic graph. A commitment condition is needed that guarantees communication safety and also allows commitment of transactions with cyclic dependencies. It is also notable that in contrast to edges in DB read-write dependence graphs [9] that represent serialization precedence of source to the sink transaction, edges in the message dependence graphs represent commit dependence of source to the sink transaction. The former cannot be cyclic but the latter can.

The second condition is the moverness of transactions of the cluster with respect to each other. In the basic commit rule, the moverness condition was that methods of the committing transaction are right movers with respect to methods of the recently committed transactions. In addition to that, as we commit a set of transactions, we need to check that there is an order of them where methods of each transaction in the order are right movers with respect to method of earlier transactions in the order. (Note that this order is not necessarily the causal order of sends and receives.) If the conditions are met, the local logs of the transactions are applied to the shared store, the local logs are stored in the shared log with *fresh* ids, and the state of the transactions are set to committed $\mathbb{c}$ in $\mathcal{M}$.

4.3. Properties

4.3.1. Opacity

The semantics of Figure 4 extends the semantics of Figure 3 with communication semantics while preserving the opacity of transactions. This enables programmers to reason locally about the consistency of data in each atomic block.

THEOREM 2 (Opacity). Every sequence of labels $\langle \tau, \text{beg} \rangle$, $\langle \tau, o.m \rangle$, $\langle \tau, \text{abt} \rangle$ and $\langle \tau, \text{cmt} \rangle$ given by $\rightarrow$ started from $Conf_0$ is opaque.

High-level proof idea: Please refer to the technical report [17] section 10.1 for the formalization and the proof (29 pages). We reduce opacity for CMT to opacity for the semantics in Section 3. We show that for every sequence L of labels $\langle \tau, \text{beg} \rangle$, $\langle \tau, o.m \rangle$, $\langle \tau, \text{abt} \rangle$ and $\langle \tau, \text{cmt} \rangle$ that can be obtained from transitions of $\rightarrow$, there is a sequence of transitions of $\rightarrow_o$ that yield a sequence of labels L' that is the same as L other than addition of calls to a definite new object. By THEOREM 1, L' is opaque. We show that removing all calls to an object from a sequence of labels preserves opaqueness of the sequence. Therefore, as L' is opaque, L is opaque. ∎

4.3.2. Communication Safety

Assume that a transaction τ_r receives a message m that is tentatively sent by another transaction τ_s. Receiving m and using its value is a part of the computation of τ_r. Therefore, validity of the computation of τ_r relies on validity of m. If τ_s finally aborts, m becomes invalid and τ_r should be prevented from committing. This means that the receiving transaction τ_r should not commit before the sending transaction τ_s is committed. The notion is formalized as the following correctness condition:

DEFINITION 1 (Communication). The communication relation for an execution is the set of receiver and sender transaction pairs in the execution.

Suppose $Exec = Conf_0 \overset{l_0}{\rightarrow} Conf_1 \overset{l_1}{\rightarrow} ... \overset{l_{n-1}}{\rightarrow} Conf_n$. We define
$Comm(Exec) = \{ \tau_r \frown \tau_s \mid \exists i, j, ch: \ 0 \le i < j < n,$
$\qquad\qquad\qquad l_i = (\tau_s, ch\ send), l_j = (\tau_r, ch\ receive)$
$\qquad\qquad\qquad \forall k: (i < k < j) \Rightarrow (\forall \tau: l_k \ne (\tau, ch\ send)) \}$

Intuitively, τ_s is the last sender on ch before τ_r receives.

DEFINITION 2 (Unsafe execution) A configuration $Conf_0$ can execute to an unsafe configuration iff there is an execution
$\qquad Exec = Conf_0 \overset{l_0}{\rightarrow} Conf_1 \overset{l_1}{\rightarrow} ... \overset{l_{n-1}}{\rightarrow} Conf_n$, where
$\qquad Conf_n = \langle \mathcal{T}_n \cdot \sigma_{sh_n} \cdot \ell_{sh_n} \cdot \mathcal{M}_n \cdot \mathcal{C}_n \cdot \mathcal{D}_n \rangle$,
$\qquad \exists \tau_r, \tau_s: \ \mathcal{M}_n(\tau_r) = \mathbb{c}$
$\qquad\qquad\quad \tau_r \frown \tau_s \in Comm(Exec)$
$\qquad\qquad\quad \mathcal{M}_n(\tau_s) \ne \mathbb{c}$

THEOREM 3: Communication Safety: An initial configuration $Conf_0$ cannot execute to an unsafe configuration.

Please refer to the technical report [17] section 10.2 for the proof (16 pages).

High level proof idea: The first step is to prove $\mathcal{D}_n = Comm(Exec)$ and thereby show that all members of $Comm(Exec)$ stem from the *Receive* rule. Next we prove that when τ_r *receive*s a message from τ_s, τ_r is running, and we notice that the *Receive* rule adds $\tau_r \frown \tau_s$ to $Comm(Exec)$. Later in the execution, τ_r may want to commit, and now the $\tau_r \frown \tau_s$ in $Comm(Exec)$ forces the *CMT* rule to ensure that τ_r only commits if either τ_s has already committed, or τ_r and τ_s commit together as members of the same cluster. ∎

Our notion of communication safety generalizes a correctness criterion in [8]; let us explain why. Both TE and TE for ML support synchronous message passing. A high-level nondeterministic semantics "defines the set of correct transactions". In the high-level semantics, a set of starting transactions are stepped as follows: if there is a sequence of sub-steps that can match all the sends and receives of the transactions to each other, the transactions are committed together in single step. A low-level semantics is also defined that specifies stepping of the search threads that find the matching. It is proved that the low-level semantics complies with the high-level semantics. This essentially means that if a set of transactions are committed in the low-level semantics, each of them has communicated with transactions that are also committed at the same time. Our approach supports asynchronous messages. When a transaction sends a message, the message is enqueued in the recipient channel. Therefore, when a transaction is committing, there may not be matched receivers for the messages that it has sent but definite senders have sent the messages that it has received. Therefore, communication safety defines the condition that sender transactions are committed.

5. Implementation

We will now explain how we have implemented the calculus in Section 4 as the core functionality of a Scala [25] library called Transactors. Transactors integrate features of both memory transactions and actors. A transactor is an abstraction that consists of a thread and a channel that is called its mailbox. A mailbox is essentially a queue that can hold an arbitrary number of messages. Similar to the actor semantics [2], the messages in the mailbox are unordered. The thread of a transactor can perform the following operations both outside and inside transactions: reading from and

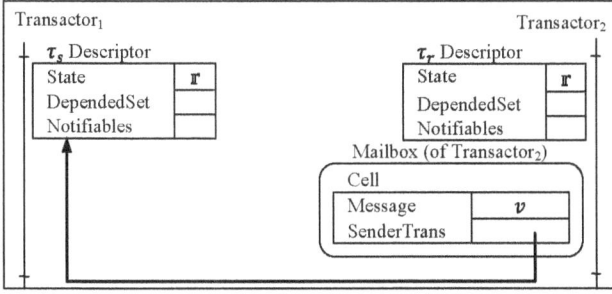

Figure 6. Sending

writing to shared memory and also sending messages to other transactors and receiving messages from its mailbox.

Recall that the starting point for Section 4 was Section 3 with its semantics of memory transactions. Similarly, the starting point for our implementation of the semantics in Section 4 is TL2, which implements Section 3's semantics of memory transactions. We explain how we have extended TL2 with an implementation of the new concepts in Section 4. In particular, we will explain about data structures that are built when messages are sent and received, the mechanism that notifies waiting transactions, cluster search and collective commit. (Our technique can work for other implementations of the semantics in Section 3 as well. In the technical report [17] section 13 we will explain how we have extended the implementation of DSTM2 in much the same way as we extended TL2. The pseudo codes of these two implementations can be found in the technical report [17] sections 12 and 14.)

In TL2, all memory locations are augmented with a lock that contains a version number. Transactions start by reading a global version-clock. Every read location is validated against this clock and added to the read-set. Written location-value pairs are added to the write-set. At commit, locks of locations in the write-set are acquired, the global version-clock is incremented and the read-set is validated. Then the memory locations are updated with the new global version-clock value and the locks are released.

In the implementation of transactors, the read and write procedures remain unchanged. As will be explained in subsection for the implementation of the **CMT** rule, we adapt the commit procedure to perform collective commitment of a cluster.

Each transaction has a descriptor that is a data structure that stores information regarding that transaction. This information includes the state of the transaction and a set that holds references to descriptors of depended transactions. Transactions change state as shown in Figure 7. Compared to the semantics in Section 4, the possible states of a transaction also include terminated. A transaction is terminated if it has reached the end of its atomic block and is not committed or aborted yet. The transaction descriptor also contains a set of notifiables and a message backup set that will be explained as we proceed.

In terms of $\mathcal{M}$ and $\mathcal{D}$ from the semantics, the descriptor of each transaction τ stores its state, $\mathcal{M}(\tau)$, and a set that holds references to descriptors of each τ' that $\tau \curvearrowright \tau' \in \mathcal{D}$. The mailboxes of transactors correspond to channels of $\mathcal{C}$. The semantics in Section 4 has seven rules. Two of those rules, **CMD** and **APP**, make no changes to the transaction map, channels, and dependencies. In the following five subsections we will explain how we implement the other five rules.

5.1. Starting a Transaction

We begin with the **BEG** rule. The rule changes M to $\mathcal{M}' = \mathcal{M} \cup \{\tau \mapsto r\}$. When a transaction τ is started, a new transaction

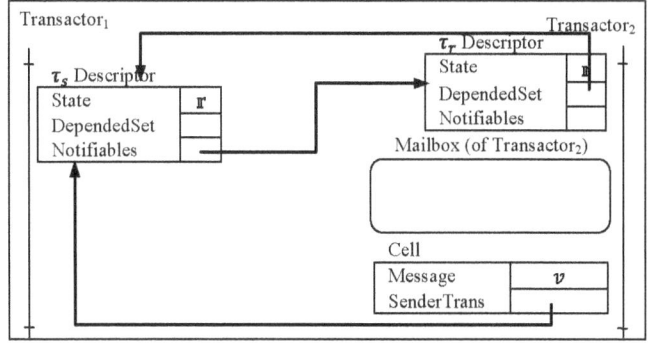

Figure 5. Receiving

descriptor with the running state r is created and stored in a thread local variable. (Later, to get the descriptor of the current transaction, this thread local variable is checked. If the variable has no value, the execution is outside atomic blocks and otherwise, the value is the descriptor of the current transaction.) The global version-clock is read and the body of the atomic block is started.

5.2. Sending and Receiving a Message

Next we consider the **Send** rule. The rule changes $\mathcal{C}$ to $\mathcal{C}' = \mathcal{C}[ch \mapsto (\tau, v)]$. When a message v is being sent, a new cell containing the message is enqueued to the mailbox. As the **Send** rule defines, besides the message, the sender transaction τ saves a reference to the descriptor of itself in the new cell. If the recipient transactor has been suspended inside a transaction to receive a message, it is resumed. If the send is being executed outside transactions, a reference to a dummy transaction descriptor that is always committed is saved as the sender transaction in the cell and if the recipient transactor has been suspended to receive a message (inside or outside a transaction), it is desuspended. Figure 6 depicts relations of data structures while a message is being sent.

Next we consider the **Receive** rule. The rule requires that $\mathcal{C}(ch) = (\tau_s, v)$ and changes $\mathcal{D}$ to $\mathcal{D}' = \mathcal{D} \cup \{\tau_r \curvearrowright \tau_s\}$. When a receive is being executed, cells of the mailbox are iterated. The reference to the descriptor of the sender transaction τ_s is obtained from each cell. The state of τ_s is read from its descriptor and the state of the message v of the cell is determined according to the state of τ_s. We use the terminology that (1) if the sender is committed, then the message is stable; and (2) if the sender is aborted, then the message is invalid. (3) if the sender is running or terminated, then the message is tentative. As any transaction that receives an invalid message should finally abort, invalid messages are dropped. This is the optimization that was mentioned for the **Receive** rule. Thus, if the receive is being executed inside a transaction, a stable or tentative message is required to be taken from the mailbox. As executions that are outside transactions cannot be aborted, tentative messages can not be given to receives that are executed outside transactions. Therefore, a stable message is required for receives that are outside transactions. Cells are iterated and any invalid message is dropped until a required message is found. The thread suspends if a required message is not found until one becomes available. To track dependencies, if

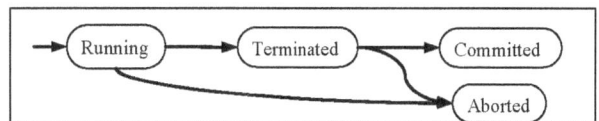

Figure 7. State transitions of a transaction

the found message is tentative, a reference to the descriptor of τ_s is added to the depended set of the descriptor of the current transaction τ_r. The depended sets of descriptors constitute a dependency graph. We say that τ_1 is adjacent to τ_2 if the descriptor of τ_2 is in the depended set of the descriptor of τ_2.

Figure 5 depicts data structures and their relations while a message is being received. Assume that a transaction τ_s has sent a message v that is received by another transaction τ_r. Assume that τ_s is running and τ_r is being terminated. As τ_r has an unresolved dependency, it cannot be committed yet. Therefore, the thread running τ_r goes to the waiting state until τ_s aborts or commits. Hence, when τ_s is aborted or committed, it should notify τ_r. Notification is done by notifiables. When τ_r is receiving the tentative message v, the reference to the descriptor of τ_s is obtained from the cell that contains v and a reference to the descriptor of τ_r is subscribed to it as a notifiable. On abortion or commitment of a transaction (τ_s), all its registered notifiables are notified.

When a transaction aborts, its effects should be rolled back. The messages that it has received from its mailbox should be put back. Therefore, to track messages that are received inside a transaction, when a message is being received, the cell that the message is obtained from is added to a backup set in the transaction descriptor (not shown in the figures). The set is iterated when the transaction is being aborted and any cell that is not invalid is put back to the mailbox.

5.3. Abortion

Next, we consider the *ABT* rule. The rule changes $\mathcal{M}$ to $\mathcal{M}' = \mathcal{M}[\tau \mapsto a]$. A transaction τ may deterministically abort as the result of resolution of a shared memory conflict. When τ is aborting, its state is set to aborted in its descriptor. Any cell of its backup set that is not invalid is put back to the mailbox. In addition, to wake up waiting transactions, τ propagates abortion to dependent transactions. Assume that $\{\tau_{r_{i=1..n}}\}$ is the set of transactions that are dependent on τ and $\{N_{i=1..n}\}$ is the set of notifiables that reference descriptors of $\{\tau_{r_{i=1..n}}\}$. τ notifies each N_i. The notification makes an abort event for τ_{r_i} if it is waiting. Finally, after notification, τ restarts its atomic block as a new transaction. On abortion of each τ_{r_i}, the same situation recurs, i.e. each of them notifies its own notifiables. Therefore, abortion of τ is propagated to transactions that are (transitively) dependent on τ. Note that by an implicit traversal of notifiable objects, abortion is propagated in the reverse direction of dependencies. The traversal avoids infinite loops by terminating at previously aborted transaction descriptors.

5.4. Termination and Commitment

Termination Every transaction that reaches the end of its atomic block sets the state of its descriptor to terminated. Then, the cluster search is started from the descriptor of the current transaction to check if it is possible to commit the transaction at this time. If the cluster search succeeds in finding a cluster, the transactions of the cluster are collectively committed and the atomic block returns successfully. Cluster search and collective commit are explained in the next subsection. If the cluster search cannot find a cluster at this time, the thread running the transaction goes to the waiting state. There are three different events that wake up a transaction from the waiting state:

- An Abortion event is raised when the transaction is notified of abortion of a depended transaction. On this event, the transaction starts abortion as explained above.
  A Dependency Resolution event: As will be explained in the collective commit procedure, a transaction that commits

notifies all of the transactions that are dependent on it about the dependency resolution. On this event, as a dependency of the current transaction is known to be resolved, it may be able to commit; therefore, the cluster search is retried.

- A Commitment event is raised when the transaction is notified of that it is committed by the cluster search and collective commit that is started from another transaction. On this event, the notifiables that are registered to the descriptor of transaction are notified of the dependency resolution. The atomic block returns successfully.

Commitment Next, we consider the *CMT* rule. The rule has the condition that the set of transactions should be a cluster $\mathsf{Cluster}(\{\tau_{i=1..n}\}, \mathcal{M}, \mathcal{D})$ and also two moverness conditions $\forall \tau_{i=1..n} \forall \langle \tau^{cmt}, \ell_{\tau'} \rangle \in \ell_{sh} : \tau^{cmt} > \tau_i \Rightarrow \ell_{\tau_i} \rhd \ell_{\tau'}$ and $\forall \tau_{i=1..n} \forall \tau_{j=1..i-1} : \ell_{\tau_i} \rhd \ell_{\tau_j}$. If the rule is applied, it changes $\mathcal{M}$ to $\mathcal{M}' = \mathcal{M}[\tau_i \mapsto c]_{i=1..n}$. According to the first condition, to commit a transaction, the dependency graph should be searched for a cluster containing the transaction. If the cluster search succeeds in finding a cluster, the collective commit algorithm is executed on the found cluster to check moverness conditions.

Cluster Search: A cluster is a set of terminated transactions whose dependencies are all to members of that same cluster or to committed transactions. A cluster search inputs a terminated transaction τ, and outputs either the smallest cluster that contains τ, or reports that no such cluster exists, or reports that τ must abort. We are looking for the smallest cluster because in a later phase we will have to order them, which is a time-consuming task. The smallest cluster is necessarily a strongly connected component (SCC) so we do cluster search with Tarjan's algorithm [29] for identifying SSCs. The idea is to gradually expand a candidate set of transactions containing τ until the candidate set is a cluster or the algorithm reports that no such clusters exists or that tau must abort. Specifically, if we have a candidate set and a dependency $\tau_r \curvearrowright \tau_s$, where τ_r is a member of the candidate set, then the cluster search does a case analysis of τ_s. If τ_s is:

- Terminated: we add τ_s to the candidate set.
- Committed: we do nothing, since the dependency is resolved.
- Running: we report that no such cluster exists.
- Aborted: we report that τ must abort.

If the Tarjan algorithm finds only one SCC, a cluster containing τ is found. On the other hand, if more than one SCC is found, the last SCC (that contains τ) is dependent on other SCCs. It is not a cluster before the other SCCs commit. Therefore, we report that no such cluster exists. (If more than one SCC is found, it is still possible to commit them. They can be committed in the order that they are found by Tarjan algorithm. This is because, the first SCC that is found is a cluster and also any SCC in the found sequence will be a cluster if the SCCs before it in the sequence are committed. But for simplicity, the current transaction waits for other SCCs to finalize.)

After the cluster search, we take one of three actions depending on the output. (1) if a cluster containing τ is found, then we commit all the transactions in the cluster; (2) if the result is that no such cluster exists, then we cache that information to avoid needlessly doing the search again before the graph changes: the thread running τ goes to the waiting state; and (3) if the result is that τ must abort, then we abort τ.

Although a transaction may wait after termination to be notified by other transactions, the implementation satisfies finalization, the progress property that we define as follows. We define that a transaction is finalized iff it is aborted or committed.

We define that a transaction is settled iff it is terminated and it is not transitively dependent on a running transaction. The finalization property is that every settled transaction is eventually finalized.

Collective Commit: To commit a set of transactions, it should be checked that there exists an order of commitment of the transactions where earlier transactions in the order do not invalidate later transactions in the order. This check corresponds to the condition $\forall \tau_{i=1..n} \forall \tau_{j=1..i-1} : \ell_{\tau_i} \rhd \ell_{\tau_j}$ that requires an order of transactions where operations of later transactions in the order are right movers in respect to operations of earlier transactions. In TL2, a write to a location invalidates a read from the same location. Therefore, an order is required where for each location, the reading transaction comes before the writing transaction. This condition is implemented as follows. A graph of transactions is made where a transaction τ_r has an edge to transaction τ_w if the read set of τ_r has an intersection with the write set of τ_w. If there is a cycle in the graph, a desired order does not exist. In this case, the current transaction starts abortion. Otherwise, it is possible to commit the transactions of the cluster together. Note that a pure write (writing to a location without reading it) does not conflict with another pure write and any order of commitment is valid for them. The lock for each location in the write sets of all the transactions is acquired. The global counter is incremented and is read as the write version. The read set of each transaction in the cluster is validated. This validation corresponds to the condition $\forall \tau_{i=1..n} \forall \langle \tau^{cmt}, \ell_{\tau'} \rangle \in \ell_{sh} : \tau^{cmt} > \tau_i \Rightarrow \ell_{\tau_i} \rhd \ell_{\tau'}$. If one of the locks cannot be acquired or a read set is not validated, the acquired locks are released and the current transaction is aborted. Otherwise, collective commit can be done. The write sets of the transactions are written to memory with the write version. The acquired locks are released. The state of the descriptor of each transaction is set to committed. Each transaction other than τ_s is notified of commitment. This notification makes a Commitment event. Each transaction that is committed sends dependency resolution notification to all notifiables $\{N_{i=1..n}\}$ that are registered to its descriptor. Each N_i references a receiving transaction τ_{r_i}. The notification makes a Dependency Resolution event for τ_{r_i} if it is waiting. When a transaction is committed, the messages that it has sent become stable. Therefore, they can be received by receives that are executed outside transactions. Each transaction that is committed desuspends the transactors that it has sent a message to and are suspended on receives that are executed out of transactions.

6. Experimental Results

6.1. Benchmarks and Platform

We experiment with three benchmarks: A server benchmark and two benchmarks from STAMP [23]. We adopt the Server benchmark that is independently explained by [20] as the Vacation Reservation, by [14] as the Server Loop programming idiom and by [21] as the Job Handling system. A server thread handles requests from client threads. Each request should appear to be handled atomically i.e. the handling code of the server is a transaction. In addition, the request of the client thread may be sent inside a transaction. The transaction of a client may request the service multiple times. We experiment with two instances of this benchmark.

The service can simply be provision of unique ids [14]. A generic function (`serverLoop`) is offered in [14] to create servers. Employing Transactors, we provide a generic class (`Server`) that can be extended to create servers. The pseudo code of `Server` can be found in the technical report [17] section 15.4.

We compare the message passing performance of our two implementations of Transactors with the implementation of TE for ML on a Server instance that generates unique ids. To the best of our knowledge, TE for ML is the closest semantics with similar goals. (We programmed and tried to conduct comparisons on other cases such as barrier, but the implementation of TE for ML took a very long time or deadlocked on these cases.)

As a tangible application of this programming idiom, consider a web application with two tiers: the application logic tier and the database tier. The system may be organized such that separate threads run the two tiers. The case study in [4] showed that to speed up handling future requests, the application logic tier may cache some of the data that it sends to the database tier. The application tier updates the cached data in the data structures and the database tier updates the data in the database. Although the updates are performed by different threads, they should be done atomically; either both or none should be seen by other threads.

We adopt the method suggested by [4] to unify memory and database transactions. The approach benefits form handlers that are registered to be run at different points of the transaction lifecycle. We extended our library to support registration of handlers for both of the implementations. We experiment with the authorship database scheme from [4]. We consider inserting a new paper info including its authors. Using our library, we define application logic transactor and database server transactor. The application logic transactor starts a transaction, sends an update request to the database server transactor, performs updates to the data structures and finishes the transaction after receiving an acknowledge message from the database server transactor. Upon receipt of a request, the database server transactor, executes a transaction comprised of queries to update data in the database and sends back an acknowledge message. The two transactions are interdependent and are collectively committed. (Note that if writing to the database is only to maintain a log for later accesses, the application logic transactor does not need to wait for the acknowledge message. In this case, only the database transaction is dependent on the application logic transaction and therefore, the application logic transaction can commit before the database transaction is done.) We study the overhead of cluster search and collective commit on this case.

To study the overhead of transactions supported by Transactors over pure transactions, we have adopted Kmeans clustering and Genome sequencing benchmarks from the Stanford transactional benchmark suite [23] and have programmed them in Scala using our Transaction and Transactors libraries.

The experiments are done on Intel(R) Core(TM)2 Duo CPU T7250 @2.00GHz and Linux 2.6.31-21-generic #59-Ubuntu. Scala version is 2.7.7.final (Oracle Java HotSpot(TM) Server VM, Java 1.6.0_17). TE for ML patch is on OCaml 3.08.1. Oracle MySQL version is 14.14 distribution 5.1.41. The database connector is MySQL Connector/J v.5.1.13. All the reported numbers are after warmup and are averages of results from repeated experiments. All the raw numbers are available in the technical report [17] section 16.

6.2. Measurements

Message Passing Performance The first experiment compares the performance of the unique id generator server in Transactors and in TE for ML over different number of repetitions of the client transaction. The same thread repeats the client transaction. (New threads are not launched for each repetition.) In this experiment, the number of requests of the client transaction is constant (equal to 2). Performance ratio represents the

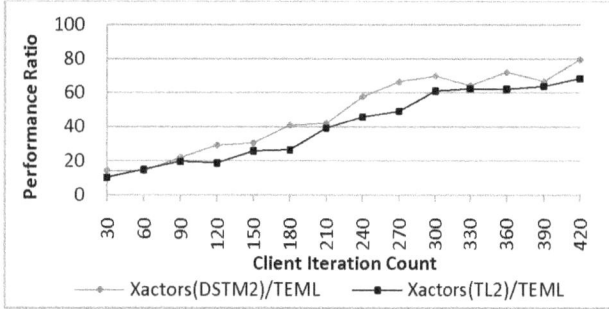
Figure 8. Server – Performance over Client Iteration Count

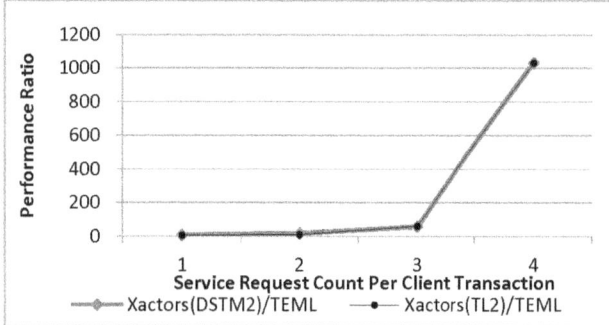
Figure 9. Server – Performance over Service Request Count

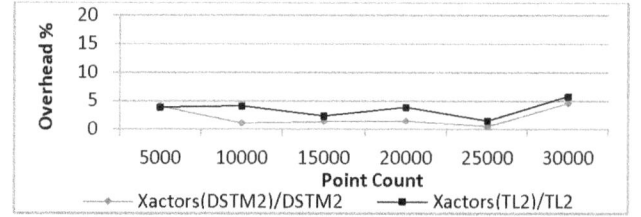
Figure 10. Kmeans Clustering – Performance Overhead

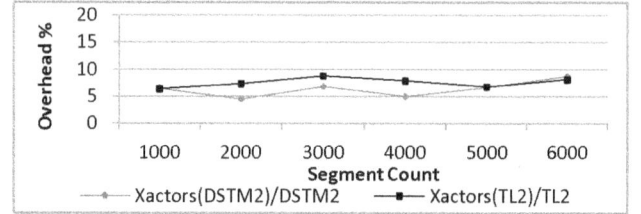
Figure 11. Genome Sequencing – Performance Overhead

communication, there is an overhead. We study this overhead on Kmeans clustering and Genome sequencing benchmarks. Each of our implementations of Transactors is based on an implementation of memory transactions. We compare the performance of each implementation of Transactors over the implementation of the memory transactions that it is based on. The performance overhead for the Kmeans and Genome cases over different input sizes is shown respectively in Figure 10 and Figure 11. The experiments show that the overhead is below ten percent.

6.3. Assessment

Message Passing Performance   In the first experiment, the performance ratio increases with the number of client iterations. This is because Transactors use a constant number of threads. On the other hand in TE for ML, to support the completeness property, when a thread receives on a channel, every message that has been sent to the channel should be tried by a search thread. As the messages that are sent to a channel increase, the number of search threads for a receive statement increases and affects performance.

In the second experiment, in the executions with more requests in the client transaction, more messages are sent to the server channel. As mentioned for the first experiment, in TE for ML, increase in the number of messages that are sent to a channel affects performance of receive statements on the channel. Furthermore, for clients that send more requests, more `chooseEvt` statements are executed at the server thread. The number of search threads that reach a `chooseEvt` statement are doubled to try each branch. In effect, the exponential number of search threads aggravates the performance of TE for ML.

As mentioned before, TE for ML is inherently inefficient as its semantics requires finding the successful matching which is NP-hard. The measurements indicate that Transactors provide up to a thousand times faster communication than TE for ML.

Overhead of Cluster Search and Collective Commit   The overhead in the implementation based on DSTM2 is relatively low. The overhead of the collective commit procedure in the implementation based on TL2 is relatively high due to the time consuming procedure of checking existence of an order of commitment that respects moverness. This procedure is the hot spot to be optimized.

Overhead over Pure Transactions   In our implementations, special care is devoted to optimization of the paths that are passed

performance of Transactors divided by the performance of TE for ML. The two lines in Figure 8 show the performance ratio of the two implementations of Transactors over the implementation of TE for ML. The performance ratio increases with the number of client iterations.

The second experiment compares the performance of the server case over different number of requests of the client transaction. In this experiment, the number of repetitions of the client transaction is constant (equal to 40). Figure 9 shows the performance ratio of each of the implementations of Transactors over the implementation of TE for ML. As the number of requests increase, the performance ratio grows fast. (The two curves overlap at this scale.)

Overhead of Cluster Search and Collective Commit   In this experiment, the application logic transactor maintains the set of papers and the map of each author to her set of papers. Upon addition of a new paper, the application logic transactor updates the papers set and the author-to-papers map. The database transactor inserts a row to the Paper table, gets the unique id assigned to the paper and for each author, inserts a row to the PaperAuthor table. We measure the time of the application logic transaction for insertion of a paper with four authors. Table 1 shows the percent of time that is spent in the cluster search and collective commit procedures.

Overhead over Pure Transactions   Atomic blocks of Transactors provide opacity just like atomic blocks of basic memory transactions. Therefore, Transactors can be used wherever basic transactions are used. But as Transactors support

Table 1. Percent of Total Time Spent in Cluster Search and Collective Commit

	Cluster Search	Collective Commit
Xactors (DSTM2)	2.5	8.6
Xactors (TL2)	3.6	19.3

by transactions that do not send or receive messages. The measurements suggest that Transactors add less than ten percent overhead to non-communicating transactions.

7. Conclusion

This paper presents CMT that defines the semantics of transactional communication. The usefulness of CMT is shown by expressing three fundamental communication idioms. It is proved that the semantics satisfies opacity and communication safety. The semantics is implemented on top of two implementations of memory transactions. The experiments show that the implementations provide considerably efficient communication and add low overhead to non-communicating transactions.

8. References

[1] Abadi, M., Birrell, A., Harris, T., and Isard, M. 2008. Semantics of transactional memory and automatic mutual exclusion. SIGPLAN Not. 43, 1 (Jan. 2008), 63-74.

[2] Agha, Gul A. ACTORS: A Model of Concurrent Computation in Distributed Systems. MIT Press, Cambridge, Massachusetts, 1986.

[3] Aguilera, M. K., Merchant, A., Shah, M., Veitch, A., and Karamanolis, C. 2007. Sinfonia: a new paradigm for building scalable distributed systems. In Proc. of SOSP '07. 159-174.

[4] Dias, R. J. and Lourenco, J. M.. 2009. Unifying Memory and Database Transactions. In Proc. of Euro-Par '09

[5] Dice, D., Shalev O., and Shavit N. Transactional locking II. In DISC'06, volume 4167 of Lecture Notes in Computer Science. Springer, 2006.

[6] Donnelly, K. and Fluet, M. 2008. Transactional events. J. Functional Programming. 18, 5-6 (Sep. 2008), 649-706.

[7] Dudnik P. and Swift, M. M. Condition Variables and Transactional Memory: Problem or Opportunity? In Proc. of TRANSACT'09.

[8] Effinger-Dean, L., Kehrt, M., and Grossman, D. 2008. Transactional events for ML. In Proc. of ICFP '08. 103-114.

[9] Gray J. Reuter A. 1992. Transaction Processing: Concepts and Techniques (1st ed.). Morgan Kaufmann Publishers Inc., San Francisco, CA, USA.

[10] Guerraoui, R. and Kapalka, M. 2008. On the correctness of transactional memory. In Proc. of PPoPP '08. 175-184.

[11] Harris, T. and Fraser, K. 2003. Language support for lightweight transactions. SIGPLAN Not. 38, 11 (Nov. 2003), 388-402.

[12] Harris, T., Marlow, S., Peyton-Jones, S., and Herlihy, M. 2005. Composable memory transactions. In Proc. of PPoPP '05. 48-60.

[13] Herlihy, M., Luchangco, V., and Moir, M. 2006. A flexible framework for implementing software transactional memory. In Proc. of OOPSLA '06. 253-262.

[14] Kehrt, M., Effinger-Dean L., Schmitz M., Grossman D. Programming Idioms for Transactional Events. PLACES 2009.

[15] Koskinen, E., Parkinson, M., and Herlihy, M. 2010. Coarse-grained transactions. In Proc. of POPL '10. 19-30.

[16] Lampson, B. W. and Redell, D. D. 1980. Experience with processes and monitors in Mesa. Commun. ACM 23, 2 (Feb. 1980), 105-117.

[17] Lesani, M. and Palsberg J. Communicating Memory Transactions. Technical report, 2010. http://www.cs.ucla.edu/~lesani/papers/CommMemTrans.pdf

[18] Lipton, R. J. 1975. Reduction: a method of proving properties of parallel programs. Commun. ACM 18, 12 (Dec. 1975), 717-721.

[19] Liskov, B. 1988. Distributed programming in Argus. Commun. ACM 31, 3 (Mar. 1988), 300-312.

[20] Luchangco, V. and Marathe, V. J. Transaction Synchronizers. In Proc. of SCOOL'05.

[21] Luchangco, V. and Marathe, V. J. You are not alone: breaking transaction isolation. In Proc. of IWMSE '10. 50-53.

[22] Luchangco, V. and Marathe, V. J. Transaction Communicators: Enabling Cooperation Among Concurrent Transactions. In Proc. of PPoPP'11.

[23] Minh, C. C., Chung, J., Kozyrakis, C., Olukotun K. STAMP: Stanford Transactional Applications for Multi-Processing. In Proc. of IISWC '08.

[24] Moore, K. F. and Grossman, D. 2008. High-level small-step operational semantics for transactions. In Proc. of POPL '08. 51-62.

[25] Odersky, M. The Scala Language Specification. 2010. Programming Methods Laboratory. EPFL.

[26] Reppy, J. H. 1999 Concurrent Programming in ML. Cambridge University Press.

[27] Scott, M. L. Sequential specification of transactional memory semantics. In Proc. of TRANSACT'06.

[28] Smaragdakis, Y., Kay, A., Behrends, R., and Young, M. 2007. Transactions with isolation and cooperation. In Proc. of OOPSLA '07. 191-210.

[29] Tarjan, Robert, 1971. Depth-first search and linear graph algorithms. In Proc. of the 12th Annual Symposium on Switching and Automata Theory (13-15 Oct. 1971)., 114-121.

[30] Ziarek, L., Schatz, P., and Jagannathan, S. 2006. Stabilizers: a modular checkpointing abstraction for concurrent functional programs. In Proc. of ICFP '06. 136-147.

9. Appendix

The semantics uses a notion of right moverness [18] that we define here. Let Σ denote all the possible states of the store σ_{sh}. Let R denote the set of registers. For each $r \in R$, let $M_r = \{read, write\}$ denote the set of methods of r. For $r \in R$, $\sigma_1, \sigma_2 \in \Sigma$ and $m \in M_r$, let $\sigma_1 \xrightarrow{v \leftarrow r.m} \sigma_2$ denote the state transition from σ_1 to σ_2 by calling m on r that returns value v. Right moverness is defined as follows:

$$\forall r_1, r_2 \in O, m_1 \in M_{r_1}, m_2 \in M_{r_2}:$$
$$r_1.m_1 \rhd r_2.m_2 \equiv \forall \sigma_1, \sigma_2, \sigma_3, \sigma_4 \in \Sigma:$$
$$\left(\left(\sigma_1 \xrightarrow{v_1 \leftarrow r_1.m_1} \sigma_2 \text{ and } \sigma_1 \xrightarrow{v_2 \leftarrow r_2.m_2} \sigma_3 \xrightarrow{v'_1 \leftarrow r_1.m_1} \sigma_4 \right) \Rightarrow (v_1 = v'_1) \right)$$

According to the above definition, the right moverness relations are:

$$\forall r_1, r_2 \in R, m_1, m_2 \in M_R: (r_1 \neq r_2) \Rightarrow (r_1.m_1 \rhd r_2.m_2)$$
$$r.read \rhd r.read$$
$$r.write \rhd r.read$$
$$r.write \rhd r.write$$

Note that $r.read \rhd r.write$ is not correct.

Now we define right moverness for sequences of method calls. Let l denote a sequence of method calls on registers R (that is $l = v_1 \leftarrow r_1.m_1, ..., v_n \leftarrow r_n.m_n$). Let $l_1 :: l_2$ denote the concatenation of the two sequences l_1 and l_2. Let $l[i]$ denote the ith method call in the sequence l. Let $l[1..i]$ denote the sequence of the first i method calls in the sequence l. Let $\sigma_1 \rightarrow \sigma_2$ denote multiple step transitions by l. That is if $l = v_1 \leftarrow r_1.m_1, ..., v_n \leftarrow r_n.m_n$ then $\sigma_1 \xrightarrow{l} \sigma_n \Leftrightarrow \sigma_1 \xrightarrow{v_1 \leftarrow r_1.m_1} \sigma_2 ... \sigma_{n-1} \xrightarrow{v_n \leftarrow r_n.m_n} \sigma_n$. Lifted right moverness is defined as follows: If $l_1 = v_1 \leftarrow r_1.m_1, ..., v_n \leftarrow r_n.m_n$ and l_2 are two sequences of methods then

$$l_1 \rhd l_2 \equiv \forall i = 1..n: \forall \sigma_1, \sigma_2, \sigma_3, \sigma_4, \sigma_5 \in \Sigma:$$
$$\left(\left(\sigma_1 \xrightarrow{l_1[1..i-1]} \sigma_2 \xrightarrow{v_i \leftarrow r_i.m_i} \sigma_3 \text{ and } \sigma_1 \xrightarrow{l_2 :: l_1[1..i-1]} \sigma_4 \xrightarrow{v'_i \leftarrow r_i.m_i} \sigma_5 \right) \Rightarrow (v_i = v'_i) \right)$$

Note that although $r.read \rhd r.write$ is not correct, $r.write, r.read \rhd r.write$ is correct.

Transaction Communicators: Enabling Cooperation Among Concurrent Transactions

Victor Luchangco

Oracle Labs
victor.luchangco@oracle.com

Virendra J. Marathe

Oracle Labs
virendra.marathe@oracle.com

Abstract

In this paper, we propose to extend transactional memory with *transaction communicators*, special objects through which concurrent transactions can communicate: changes by one transaction to a communicator can be seen by concurrent transactions before the first transaction commits. Although isolation of transactions is compromised by such communication, we constrain the effects of this compromise by tracking dependencies among transactions, and preventing any transaction from committing unless every transaction whose changes it saw also commits. In particular, mutually dependent transactions must commit or abort together, and transactions that do not communicate remain isolated. To help programmers synchronize accesses to communicators, we also provide special *communicator-isolating transactions*, which ensure isolation even for accesses to communicators. We propose language features to help programmers express the communicator constructs.

We implemented a novel communicators-enabled STM runtime in the Maxine VM. Our preliminary evaluation demonstrates that communicators can be used in diverse settings to improve the performance of transactional programs, and to empower programmers with the ability to safely express within transactions important programming idioms that fundamentally require compromise of transaction isolation (e.g., CSP-style synchronous communication).

Categories and Subject Descriptors   D.1.3 [*Programming Techniques*]: Concurrent Programming

General Terms   Design, Languages, Performance

Keywords   Transactional Memory, Communication

1. Introduction

Multicore systems are making shared-memory multiprocessors ubiquitous, requiring concurrent programs to exploit their potential. But today's software engineers are ill equipped to write correct concurrent programs: the collection of tools and methodologies for cost-effective development of reliable concurrent programs is sparse. One fundamental problem is maintenance of the shared mutable state, used by threads to communicate in a shared-memory program. To ensure the integrity of this communication, various mechanisms have been devised for threads to synchronize their access to this shared state.

PPoPP'11, February 12–16, 2011, San Antonio, Texas, USA.
Copyright © 2011 ACM 978-1-4503-0119-0/11/02...$10.00

Transactional memory (TM) is a promising technology for facilitating concurrent programming by enabling shared-memory multiprocessors to be programmed in the transactional style, which has been so successful in database systems: A thread may execute a block of code as a *transaction*, which may either *commit*, in which case its effects become visible to other threads, or *abort*, in which case its effects are discarded. In a conventional database system, the only effects of consequence are those on the database. TM extends this protection to memory accesses.

A TM system ensures that transactions are *isolated*; that is, each transaction appears to execute without its operations being interleaved with operations of other threads. Furthermore, committed transactions appear to execute one at a time in some order, which we call the *transaction order*. We say the transaction order *explains* the execution.

Isolation can greatly simplify concurrent programming because it supports modular reasoning: a programmer can consider each transaction separately, rather than having to consider all the possible interleavings of its operations with the operations of other transactions. However, isolation also limits the applicability of transactions [16] because isolated transactions are incompatible with barriers, condition variables, and other common synchronization mechanisms and programming idioms that require communication among transactions while they are *active* (i.e., not yet committed or aborted). We believe that for transactional programming to reach its full potential, it must work with such techniques for programming concurrent systems.

Consider, for example, a system that processes client jobs that should appear to be handled atomically. Processing some of these jobs may involve accessing a database, and these accesses should themselves appear atomic. The system may be organized as illustrated in Figure 1, with the threads handling client jobs separate from those with direct access to the database, so that a thread handling a job that requires access to the database must place a request to do so into a queue; the request will be handled by a database thread. In such a system, a thread handling a job cannot simply execute the job in a single transaction: if the job requires access to the database, the thread handling the job must communicate with the database thread that handles its request. Nor can the thread simply break the job into two transactions, one to handle the part before the request and the other to handle the part after getting the result: if the transaction for the second part aborts, then the effects of the first transaction, and of the database thread that satisfied the request, should be discarded as well. c

In this paper, we propose *transaction communicators*, special objects through which concurrent transactions can communicate: changes to a communicator by one transaction can be seen by other transactions before the first transaction commits. Such communication compromises isolation because a transaction may see the effects of other transactions that have not committed (and indeed,

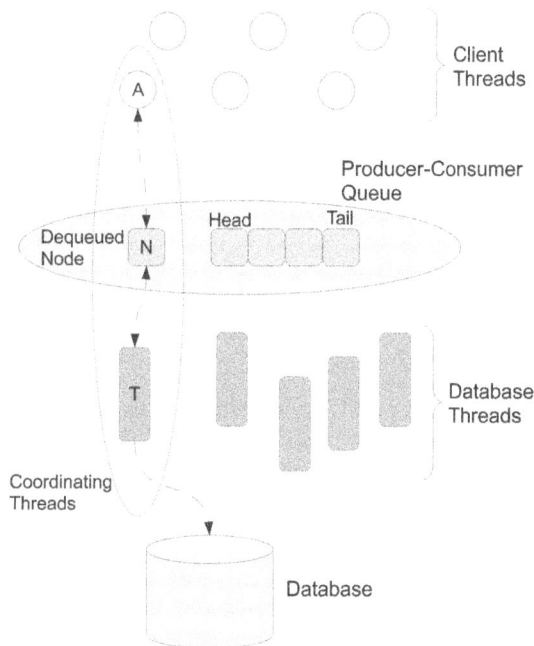

Figure 1. An example scenario where transactions may need to communicate with each other.

might abort rather than commit). We limit the impact of this compromise by preventing a transaction from committing unless every transaction whose effects it has seen also commits. Thus, two transactions that each see effects of the other transaction must either both commit or both abort. If they commit, they occupy the same position in the transaction order. Transactions that do not communicate (i.e., do not access any communicator) remain isolated.

Transaction communicators reintroduce a problem that transactions are intended to eliminate: the possibility of unsynchronized conflicting access to shared state. Although this problem is greatly reduced within transactions (such conflicts can occur only on communicators, which should be relatively rare and must be explicitly declared), programmers must synchronize access to communicators. To help programmers maintain a transactional style of programming, we provide a special *communicator-isolating transaction* that ensures isolation even for accesses to communicators.

We implemented a library-based prototype communicators-enabled STM runtime in the Maxine VM [21]. Although this prototype implementation imposes some restrictions on the use of communicators and does not include compiler support for language-level constructs, it embodies all the core ideas of communicators and also allows us to perform some preliminary experiments.

In summary, this paper makes the following contributions:

- We present the transaction communicator, a novel abstraction that permits restricted compromise of isolation of transactions to enable useful collaboration among them.

- We illustrate how to use communicators with several examples presented in a simple extension of Java with constructs to express atomic blocks and communicators.

- We describe a novel STM runtime infrastructure, in the Maxine VM, that supports communicators.

- We present preliminary evaluation of communicators to demonstrate their use in enabling interesting transaction communication idioms and in improving performance of TM applications.

2. Transaction Communicators

As described above, some useful synchronization patterns may require communication among concurrent transactions. In this paper, we propose the *transaction communicator*, a special object that enables desirable communication but limits the impact of the resulting compromise of isolation: Updates to a communicator by a transaction are visible to other transactions accessing the communicator, even before the updating transaction commits, but a transaction that sees the effects of another transaction must not commit unless that other transaction commits, nor precede the other transaction in the transaction order. Thus, communicators induce dependencies among concurrent transactions. In contrast to ordinary transactional memory, mutually dependent transactions induced by cyclic dependencies on communicators may commit, provided that they all commit. In this case, they all occupy the same position in the transaction order.

To guarantee this semantics, before a transaction T can commit, it must check whether all the transactions it depends on (i.e., those transactions whose effects it has observed) have already committed. If so, then T can also commit. Otherwise, T must wait until all the uncommitted transactions it depends on are ready to commit (if any of them abort, then T must also abort). Because there may be a cycle of dependencies in the set of transactions attempting to commit, the transactions cannot simply commit one at a time. Rather, the system must detect such cycles and commit all the transactions in any such cycle together.

In every other way, the semantics of transactions are unchanged. In particular, a transaction that sees the effects of another transaction on a non-communicator object must be ordered strictly after the other transaction. Thus, mutually dependent transactions that make conflicting accesses on non-communicator objects cannot be committed. Also, no committed transaction may see the effects of an aborted transaction.[1]

More precisely, instead of a total order of the committed transactions[2] to explain the execution, we require only a total order of "super-transactions", each consisting of one or more committed transactions that have no conflicting accesses on non-communicator objects. Every committed transaction must be in exactly one super-transaction. The super-transactions must appear to execute one at a time in the "super-transaction order", but the operations of transactions within the same super-transaction may appear to be interleaved in any way consistent with the sequential semantics of each transaction.

Note that based on only non-communicator accesses, transactions within a super-transaction commute. Thus, any total order of the transactions consistent with the super-transaction order explains the non-communicator accesses of the execution. That is, looking only at the operations on non-communicator objects, the transactions appear to be isolated. (Of course, doing the transactions in that order may have yielded different results for communicator operations, which may in turn have resulted in different operations on non-communicator objects being invoked.)

3. Communicator-Isolating Transactions

Because operations on communicators within transactions are visible to other transactions, transactions must synchronize access to communicators to use them effectively. Although it is possible to

---

[1] We do not specify the guarantees for aborted transactions, as there are several possibilities (e.g., [6, 9, 14]), and the choice is orthogonal to the issues addressed in this paper.

[2] We do not consider nested transactions for now because when transactions execute sequential code, as we implicitly assume in this paper, committed nested transactions can simply be *flattened* into the enclosing transaction.

use locks to do so, we prefer to maintain and encourage the transactional style by providing a new kind of transaction that also isolates accesses to communicators. We call these *communicator-isolating transactions* (CITs). The semantics is straightforward: All operations within a CIT, including accesses to communicators, appear to execute together without interleaving with operations of any other thread. Thus, a CIT can be used within an ordinary transaction to synchronize access to communicators, making it easy, as we illustrate in Section 4, to construct communicators of various data types using simple read/write communicators.

CITs isolate communicator accesses and ordinary transactions do not, so we cannot simply flatten a CIT nested within an ordinary transaction into its parent: when the nested CIT commits, its effects on communicators—but not its effects on non-communicator objects—must be made visible. (A CIT within a CIT, and an ordinary transaction within an ordinary transaction, can be flattened because no effects are made visible when the nested transaction commits.[3])

4. Illustrations

In this section, we illustrate the utility of transaction communicators (and CITs) with three examples. The first two examples show how use read-write communicators (i.e., communicators that support only read and write operations) to implement exchanger and queue communicators. The last example shows how a communicator can be used to improve scalability by turning transactional conflicts into dependencies.

We present pseudocode for these examples in an extension to the Java programming language with support for atomic blocks and read-write communicators in the form of specially designated fields.[4] Specifically, to an extension of Java with support for atomic blocks [10], we add two keywords: txcomm designates a field that ordinary transactions can use to communicate (i.e., the field is a read-write communicator), and txcommatomic designates a block of code that should be executed in a CIT. Note that a txcomm modifier on a reference declaration does *not* imply that the referenced object pointed to is a communicator. Transactions cannot communicate through that object unless it has one or more txcomm fields of its own.

4.1 Exchangers

Exchanger is a class of the Java concurrency library package whose instances serve as rendezvous points for threads to meet and exchange data objects. An *exchange* operation invoked within a transaction cannot complete successfully without violating isolation. In this section, we describe a simple communicator-based version of Exchanger, shown in Figure 2, that can be used by transactions.

The Exchanger declares two txcomm buffers (buf1 and buf2). A transaction that invokes the exchange method attempts to populate one of the two buffers and return the contents of the other.

The exchange method contains two txcommatomic blocks. The first is executed by all transactions to check and populate an available buffer (i.e., one that contains the value null). If neither buffer is available, the method simply returns null. The second txcommatomic block is executed only by the transaction that populated buf1. This block gets the second buffer's value and resets the values of both buffers. In each case, we use a txcommatomic block to provide atomic access to the two buffers.

```
class Exchanger {
    txcomm Object buf1;
    txcomm Object buf2;
    public exchange(Object myBuf) {
        Object otherBuf = null;
        txcommatomic {
            if (buf1 == null) {
                // populate the first buffer slot
                buf1 = myBuf;
            } else {
                if (buf2 == null) {
                    // second buffer slot available
                    buf2 = myBuf;
                    // return the buffer in first slot
                    return buf1;
                } else {
                    // both slots occupied, return null
                    return null;
                }
            }
        }
        // spin-wait for the second buffer to be populated
        while (true) {
            txcommatomic {
                if (buf2 != null) {
                    // second buffer finally populated
                    otherBuf = buf2;
                    buf1 = null;
                    buf2 = null;
                    return otherBuf;
                }
            }
        }
    }
}
```

Figure 2. Communicator-based exchanger

As is clear from the pseudocode, enforcing the dependencies is completely transparent to the programmer. Transactions that conduct an exchange on an instance of Exchanger become mutually dependent. A transaction T that observes that it cannot participate in an exchange (because both buffers of the exchanger are already populated), also depends on the transactions that last populated those buffers (i.e., the exchanging transactions), so if either of those two transactions aborts, then all three (including T) must abort. However, the exchanging transactions do not depend on T since neither sees any update by T. Because of this asymmetric dependency, the exchanging transactions need not abort if T does (perhaps because it could not participate in an exchange).

4.2 Producer-consumer queues

The producer-consumer queue is a widely used data structure that permits buffered communication between concurrent threads. We now present a communicator-based implementation (Figure 3) that can be used by transactions to communicate, as, for example, in the job-processing application described in the introduction.

The data structure consists of a simple linked list with head and tail references. A producer enqueues a new item by adding a node to the tail; a consumer dequeues an item by taking it from the node pointed to by the head. Threads/processes can concurrently access the producer-consumer queue. One particularly interesting part of the producer-consumer interaction appears in the boundary cases where the queue is either empty, or full (in case of bounded queues). When a consumer requests an item from the queue, if the queue is empty, some implementations force the consumer to *wait* for some producer to enqueue an item in the queue. Similarly, when a producer attempts to enqueue an item in a full queue, the producer may be forced to wait for a consumer to dequeue an item from the queue. In both cases, coordination between the producer and the consumer becomes crucial to avoid unnecessary unbounded waiting for both.

---

[3] Flattening is not always possible in systems that support user-visible aborts, but this issue is orthogonal to those discussed in this paper.

[4] We advocate a language extension rather than a library because of the limitations imposed by library-based STM systems in delivering the programmability promise of TM [5].

171

```
class ProducerConsumerQueue {
    txcomm Node head = null;
    txcomm Node tail = null;
    public void produce(Object data) {
        Node myNode = new Node(data);
        txcommatomic {
            if (tail == null) {
                head = tail = myNode;
            } else {
                tail.next = myNode;
                tail = myNode;
            }
        }
    }
    public Object consume() {
        Node node;
        while (true) {
            txcommatomic {
                if (head != null) {
                    // queue is not empty, do the dequeue
                    node = head;
                    if (head.next == null) {
                        // dequeuing last node
                        head = tail = null;
                    } else {
                        head = head.next;
                    }
                    return node.data;
                }
            }
        }
    }
}
class Node {
    txcomm Object data;
    txcomm Node next;
    public Node(Object data) {
        this.data = data;
    }
}
```

Figure 3. Communicator-based producer-consumer queue

Figure 3 illustrates a communicator-based unbounded producer-consumer queue. The head and tail fields of the queue, as well as the data and next fields of the node class are declared with the txcomm modifier. The producer uses a single txcommatomic block to enqueue a node in the queue. The consumer spin-waits on an empty queue, and uses a txcommatomic block to dequeue a node from the queue if the queue is not empty.

Each txcommatomic block is designed to avoid establishing unnecessary dependencies between transactions. For example, the producer checks the value of the tail field to determine if the queue is empty, whereas the consumer checks the value of the head field to do so. If the producer had checked head to see if the queue is empty, the check would have created a dependency on the last consumer (which modified head). We observe that, while designing a communicator-based data structure, the programmer should be careful to avoid extraneous dependencies between transactions due to access of txcomm fields. Tools to improve on this programmability aspect of communicators are a subject of future work.

4.3 Maintaining the size of a concurrent collection

Many collection implementations maintain a size field containing the number of items currently in the collection. Because this field is modified by each operation that inserts or deletes an item in the collection, it can be a contention bottleneck for the collection, severely restricting the scalability of transactional applications that use it. Communicators can be used to transform "low-level" memory conflicts on the size field into dependencies, improving scalability by reducing the number of transactions that must abort or wait.

Figure 4 presents an implementation of a concurrent red black tree (much of the pseudocode elided for clarity) as a canonical ex-

```
class RedBlackTree {
    // fields
    ...
    // the size of the collection
    txcomm int size;
    // insert method
    boolean insert(Item item) {
        atomic {
            if (!lookup(item)) {
                // item not present, insert logic here
                ...
                // now increment the size of the collection
                txcommatomic {
                    size++;
                }
                return true;
            }
            return false;
        }
    }
    // delete method
    boolean delete(Item item) {
        atomic {
            if (lookup(item)) {
                // item present, delete logic here
                ...
                // now decrement the size of the collection
                txcommatomic {
                    size--;
                }
                return true;
            }
            return false;
        }
    }
}
```

Figure 4. Concurrent red-black tree with communicator size field

ample of a concurrent collection with a size field. The size field is implemented as a communicator (i.e., declared as a txcomm field), and is modified only inside txcommatomic blocks. This implementation essentially converts potential transactional conflicts on accesses to the size field into transactional dependencies, thereby improving scalability. We support our claim with some performance analysis in Section 7.

5. Discussion

5.1 Accessibility of communicators

As described above, communicators may be accessed directly within ordinary transactions. Although we can imagine a system in which they may even be accessed nontransactionally, allowing such access raises many well-known issues related to simultaneous transactional and nontransactional access [4]. We envision that communicators will be used sparingly to enable the kinds of communication patterns among transactions illustrated in Section 4, and so it is better to avoid those difficult issues by simply forbidding nontransactional access of communicators.

One might even argue that communicators should only be accessed within CITs, to avoid the problem of unsynchronized access to them. Indeed, for expedience, our prototype implementation (Section 6) only supports such access. However, allowing direct communicator access within ordinary transactions, particularly for read-only operations, eliminates some syntactic clutter. Of course, multiple such "naked" accesses to communicators are not guaranteed isolation—CITs are necessary to enforce such isolation.

5.2 Tracking dependencies

The exact dependencies induced by operations on communicators are subtle. For example, a transaction that reads a value depends on

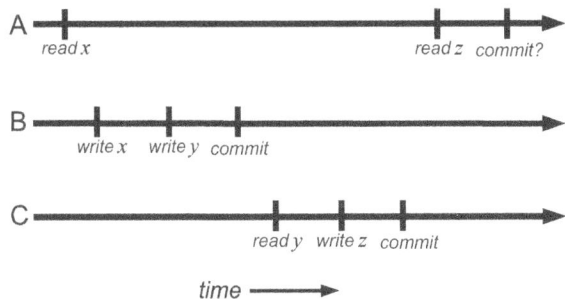

Figure 5. Execution illustrating the need for proper validation of communicators accessed by communicating transactions: x is a communicator; y and z are not. Transaction A must not commit: if it did, it must be ordered before or together with B (it sees the value of x prior to B's write), and after C (it sees the value C wrote in z), but B must be ordered before C (C sees the value B wrote).

the transaction that wrote that value, but writing to a communicator does not make the writing transaction depend on any other transaction, because the writer does not "see" any effects. Thus, we need only track *true* read-after-write dependencies, not *anti-* (write-after-read) and *output* (write-after-write) dependencies. We do not even need to track all read-after-write dependencies: a read sees only the effects of the most recent write, not those that precede it. And if the value it reads has been written more than once, then the transaction reading the value can commit as long as any of the transactions that wrote the value also commit. Determining a minimal set of dependencies is difficult (if not impossible).

Fortunately, it is not necessary to determine a minimal set of dependencies: as in dependence-aware STMs [3, 18], maintaining more dependencies than necessary may cause more transactions to abort, but preserves the semantics of committed transactions. The cost of more precise tracking of dependencies should be weighed against the benefit of aborting fewer transactions. We simply need to ensure that any extra dependencies do not interfere with progress guarantees by forming a cycle of dependent transactions that cannot be committed (for example, by having transactions that conflict on non-communicator objects).

5.3 Respecting the super-transaction order

Although a transaction may see changes to a communicator by other transactions in the same super-transaction, it must not see any changes by transactions in different super-transactions. Consider, for example, the execution depicted in Figure 5. When transaction A attempts to commit, the committed value of x is neither the value that A read nor a value written by a transaction in the same super-transaction as A (C must be ordered after B and before A and they cannot be in the same super-transaction as either because it accesses common non-communicator objects with each). Thus, A must abort.

We can guarantee this semantics by checking, when a transaction validates, that no other transaction has committed a change to a communicator it has read (i.e., the same check made for non-communicator objects). Alternatively, we could enforce anti-dependencies: a transaction cannot commit unless and until every transaction it has an anti-dependency on also commits.

5.4 Transaction conflicts

Concurrent accesses of communicators by transactions create dependencies between those transactions. In contrast, concurrent accesses of ordinary shared objects, where at least one access is a write, lead to conflicts between transactions, which in turn lead to transaction stalls and aborts. It is important to address the in-

teraction of such transaction conflicts with communicator-enabled "transaction cooperation". Specifically, what happens when transactions that access communicators conflict?

A naive approach to handling conflicts is to simply stall or abort one of the conflicting transactions, as is often done in ordinary TM systems without communicators. However, when transactions may communicate, this approach may lead to deterministic livelocks. For example, one transaction may wait for an item to be produced by another (using a communicator-based queue, for example), and the producer may require an acknowledgment from the consumer (using another communicator). Thus, the producer and consumer are necessarily mutually dependent. If they also conflict on some non-communicator object, then they can never both commit, and so they will inevitably livelock (or deadlock, if the system stalls them both indefinitely). Therefore, we need a more sophisticated approach to handle such conflicts.

We believe that such deterministic conflicts between communicating transactions are a result of *programming error*, much as if a lock-based program allowed a deadlock. A pro-active solution would be to let the system provide the programmer with appropriate feedback to help diagnose and fix the error. When a transaction detects a conflict with a transaction that it depends on,[5] the system could throw a special CooperatorConflictException. This solution returns the responsibility of handling such "dependency-violating" conflicts to the programmer, where, we believe, it belongs. In most cases, we think the programmer will be able to identify the error and find a workaround, or else identify that the conflict as a nondeterministic event, which will eventually go away if the transaction is aborted and retried.

5.5 Programmability issues

Communicators allow cooperation between concurrent transactions by enabling programmers to build specialized transaction communication channels. However, communication channels are typically a *means*, not the *end*, of passing data between transactions; the communicating transactions are actually interested in the data that is communicated.

For instance, consider a typical producer-consumer interaction: The producer usually creates the data (which may include writing to the data) that it passes to the consumer. The consumer then reads (and possibly writes) the data it received from the consumer. If the data were an ordinary shared object, this programming pattern would lead to deterministic conflicts between the producer and the consumer transactions. To enable such interactions between concurrent transactions, communicated data objects must also be communicators. We expect that this will not be a problem in most cases: the communicated data objects will likely be immutable, in which case there is no danger of conflicts, or small objects with scalar fields.

When complex structures are communicated between transactions, the programmer must ensure that access of these structures will not lead to deterministic conflicts between the communicating transactions. Although this may be doable in select cases, in general, such sharing patterns would be too difficult for the programmer get right (avoid deterministic conflicts). Thus, we advocate that programmers use communicators to communicate just simple or immutable data objects. We believe that this simple guideline—enforced either by programming discipline (our current approach), or by the compiler and runtime system (a subject of future research)—will go a long way in making communicators an acceptable TM programming abstraction.

---

[5] We are assuming abort-on-exception semantics for our TM system.

173

6. Implementation

We now describe the STM we developed to evaluate communicators. We developed this STM in the Maxine VM [21], a freely available, open-source VM written almost exclusively in Java. The base STM follows earlier STM implementations for managed-code environments [1, 11]: It is object-based: transaction conflicts are detected at the granularity of Java objects. However, speculative writes are logged at the level of primitive types (e.g., references, ints, floats, etc.) for each field of an object. Transactions write in place, locking any object that they write. A transaction maintains an *undo log* with the previous values of speculatively overwritten values to be restored in case the transaction aborts. Reads are "invisible": a transaction maintains a *read set* to ensure consistency, but it does not access other transactions' read sets, and cannot determine what locations they have read. For simplicity, we only support flat nesting of transactions, except for communicator-isolating transactions nested within ordinary transactions, which must not be flattened to preserve semantics, as discussed in Section 3.

6.1 The STM runtime

Our STM is *library-based*: we have not modified the compiler to support the language-level constructs discussed in Section 2. Thus, we must manually add the instrumentation that a compiler would do automatically. For example, we must use beginTransaction and commitTransaction methods to delimit atomic blocks, and must explicitly "open" transactional objects before they can be accessed. Although this results in messier and more error-prone coding [5], it is simpler to implement and more flexible for the kind of preliminary experimentation we want to do. In particular, we can support multiple variants and extensions simultaneously without having to modify the compiler.

In addition to per-object metadata, we maintain a *transaction descriptor* that represents a transaction. The transaction descriptor contains fields that record its status (i.e., whether it has committed or aborted or is still active), its read set, its write set, and its undo log. (The write set is used to detect conflicts at object granularity; the undo log tracks speculative writes at fied granularity.) To support communicators, we introduce two new status values, Protected and Validated, which are used in the commit protocol described in Section 6.4. We also maintain separate read sets and undo logs for the communicators the transaction has accessed, and a list of transactions it depends on (depList).

To implement txcomm fields, we provide a communicator class for each primitive type (e.g., TxCommObject for reference types, TxCommInt for integer types, etc.), which the programmer uses to declare communicators. For example, the declaration

    txcomm int count;

is written in our communicator-enabled STM as:

    TxCommInt count;

6.2 Communicator-isolating transactions (CITs)

We implement a communicator-isolating transaction (CIT) as a closed nested transaction within an ordinary transaction. In addition to performing the usual locking/logging/validation/etc. operations on ordinary shared object accesses, a CIT performs similar operations on communicator accesses (using special get and set methods of the communicators) to guarantee their isolation from concurrent CITs (recall that in our implementation, communicators can be accessed only from CITs). The separate read and write sets and undo log for communicator accesses are used in this context. In particular, a CIT acquires exclusive ownership of all the communicators it writes, and shares (with concurrent CITs) read-only accesses to communicators by making these reads "invisible" to concurrent writer CITs, and validating the reads (using the communicator read set) when the CIT attempts to commit. This behavior is like that of

closed nested transactions, with a key difference: when a CIT commits, it releases the exclusive ownership of all the communicators it modified (note that we implement flat nesting semantics for CITs nested within other CITs; thus the inner CIT's commit essentially becomes a nop). This enables subsequent communicator accesses, potentially done by concurrent transactions, to "see" the updates of the CIT. A committing CIT merges its communicator undo log entries in the enclosing (parent) transaction to enable rollback in case the transaction aborts.

6.3 Tracking depedencies

To track dependencies, each communicator has a lastWriter field, which points to the transaction that most recently wrote it. A transaction that accesses a communicator adds that communicator's last writer to its depList. Thus, our implementation tracks output dependencies as well as true dependencies.

To avoid the potential bad behavior exhibited in Figure 5, we maintain two version numbers: writeVersion, which every transaction that writes the communicator increments and stores in its write set; and commitVersion, which a committing transaction updates with the version number it stored in its write set (provided that the number in its write set is greater than the current commitVersion). When a transaction first reads a communicator, it also reads and logs the communicator's writeVersion in its communicator read set. Then, during its final validation (when it is committing), the transaction compares the commitVersion of each communicator that it read with the writeVersion that the transaction logged for that communicator in its communicator read set, and aborts if the former is greater than the latter. This check permits a reader of a communicator to commit only if no subsequent writer of that communicator has committed. This has the effect of indirectly tracking some anti-dependencies between transactions.

6.4 Transaction commits and aborts

To detect cycles of dependent transactions, we use two new status values, Protected and Validated, in the commit protocol. When a transaction T attempts to commit, it first switches its status to Protected. From this point on, no other thread may abort T directly. However, T must abort itself if its read set is not valid or if some transaction it depends on aborts.

After becoming Protected, T constructs the set S of all transactions it directly or indirectly depends on as follows: Starting with the transactions in its depList, remove any that are Committed, and for any Protected or Validated transaction A in S, add the transactions in A's depList. (A's depList will not change after this because A has begun its commit protocol.) If any transaction in S is Aborted then T also aborts.

When all transactions in S are either Protected or Validated (and their depLists have been added to S), then T validates its read set. If the validation fails, then T aborts. Otherwise, T changes its status to Validated, and waits for all the transactions in S to be Validated. (As before, committed transactions are removed from S, and T must abort if any transaction in S aborts.) When all transactions in S are Validated, T changes its status to Committed. Because our STM writes in place, nor further clean-up is needed.

When a transaction T aborts, we must roll back its speculative writes. For any object that only T has written, this is straightforward, because T stored the value it overwrote in its undo log. However, if T wrote a communicator, its abort may lead to a cascade of aborts by other transactions that directly or indirectly depend on T, and several of these transactions may have written the same communicator. In this case, we must be careful to restore the correct value. To that end, we implemented the following conservative solution: T waits for the transaction that wrote the communicator immediately before T—we call that transaction T's *predecessor*—to either commit or abort. If T's predecessor commits, then T restores the value written by the predecessor. On the other hand, if T's predecessor aborts, T should not do its rollback (which would restore the value written by its aborted predecessor).

7. Evaluation

We now describe our experience using communicators in three benchmarks. The first benchmark is a transactional red-black tree with a size field that contains the number of nodes in the tree. This benchmark illustrates how communicators can improve scalability by transforming transaction conflicts into dependencies. The second benchmark was inspired by a specific component (to be elaborated later) of SPECjbb2005 [20], an industry-standard JVM evaluation benchmark. This benchmark illustrates the use of communicators to enable parallelism in large transactions. The third benchmark is a variant of the job-processing example from Section 1. This benchmark illustrates communicators as enablers of explicit synchronous communication between concurrent transactions. Our results also give insight into the performance characteristics of our implementation. Together, they demonstrate that communicators are an effective tool for helping programmers express a diverse range of programming idioms that were impossible to express, or required specialized solutions (e.g., open nesting [17], irrevocability [23], etc.).

Our experiments were conducted on a multiprocessor system consisting of eight 2.8GHz Quad-Core AMD Opteron™ chips. Thus, the system supports 32 hardware threads.

7.1 Red-black tree with size field

Concurrent collections are frequently used in parallel programs, and TM runtimes are often evaluated on concurrent collections such as red-black trees and hash tables. However, the collection implementations do not accurately reflect versions used in real systems, which support a size() operation that returns the number of items currently in the collection. Typically a collection implementation maintains a size field, which is modified appropriately when items are inserted into or deleted from the collection. Accesses to the size field of a collection may significantly increase contention between transactions performing insert/delete operations even on disjoint regions in the collection.

Figure 6 illustrates our point: The red-black tree with an ordinary size field does not scale beyond 4 threads—updates to size quickly become a contention bottleneck, and throughput drops significantly as the number of threads increases. In these tests, we used the Polite contention manager [12], which employs exponential backoff before aborting the conflicting transaction. We believe that no contention manager will perform significantly better because updates to size become a serialization bottleneck.

Making the size field a communicator (much like in the code in Figure 4—no other fields or objects are communicators, so transactional accesses of non-size fields of the red-black tree and its nodes are subject to ordinary TM conflict detection and management policies) dramatically improves performance: This implementation scales much better, deteriorating in performance only slightly after peaking with about 10 threads. The communicators infrastructure imposes a latency cost of approximately 15% at low thread counts, but this loss is more than made up for by scalability as the number of threads increases.

7.2 Emulating intra-transaction concurrency

Concurrency within transactions has been advocated by researchers as a means to improve performance of large transactions [22]. Communicator can be used to emulate large transactions with internal concurrency, and thereby achieve the same performance improvements, by combining several transactions into super-transactions.

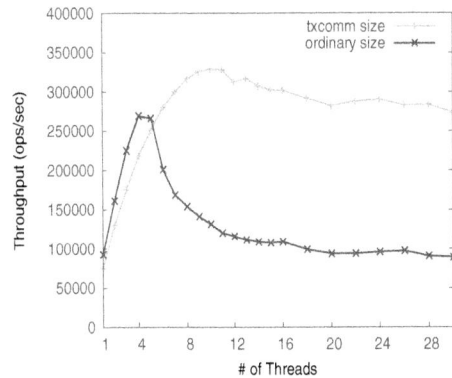

Figure 6. Throughput results of test runs on Red-Black implementations that contain the size field. The ordinary size graph depicts the throughput in the case where the size field is an ordinary shared object. The txcomm size graph depicts the throughput in the case where the size field is a implemented as a communicator. In both implementations, the red-black tree can contain up to 128K nodes, and usually averages to about 64K nodes. Each thread repeatedly executes one of the insert/delete/lookup operations on the red-black tree, with a 10%/10%/80% distribution respectively. Each operation of the tree is executed in a transaction. The performance numbers reported here were averaged over 3 runs of 30 seconds each.

For example, communicators can be used to emulate master-slave parallelism within a transaction: A master transaction initiates slave transactions to do computations on their respective data partitions (shared data is partitioned between the slave transactions), and then waits for all the slaves to finish. (In the communicators-based equivalent of master-slave parallelism, programmers must be careful to avoid any overlap in the data partitions that may lead to deterministic conflicts between the slaves.) We demonstrate this potential with a benchmark inspired by our observation of SPECjbb2005, an industry-standard benchmark used to evaluate server-side JVMs. It emulates a 3-tier client/server application. The tiers are for input selection, middle tier business logic, and backend computation that represents a database in the form of a set of Java collections (TreeMaps and HashMaps).

The application simulates a store-management system, in which the store consists of a group of warehouses (each controlled by a distinct thread), and each warehouse contains an inventory of different types of items, a customer pool, a supplier pool, etc. Seven types of SPECjbb "transactions" represent typical activities that appear in such applications: new orders, stock updates, customer updates, etc. One of these transactions—the DeliveryTransaction—does bulk deliveries for all possible outstanding orders within a warehouse. This is a big transaction: it walks through the entire HashMap of new orders, fulfilling any outstanding orders it encounters. Although this transaction is executed infrequently (about 3% of the SPECjbb transactions are deliveries), it consumes a large portion of the application's running time (approximately 50% in our experiments). We believe that such heavyweight operations are a good target for intra-transaction concurrency.

To that end, we have developed a benchmark that mimics just the delivery transaction of SPECjbb. The benchmark consists of a pre-populated, 32K entry, hash table. A transaction (not the SPECjbb "transaction") can invoke an enumeration operation on the hash table, which walks through all the items in the table and randomly updates their values. The hash table is split into disjoint partitions, each of which is processed by a slave transaction.

```
class MasterSlaveCoordinator {
    // flag used by the master to instruct the slaves
    // to process their data partitions
    txcomm boolean go;
    // the count indicating how many slaves have
    // completed their task
    txcomm int slavesDone;
}
```

Figure 7. The master instructs the slaves to process their hash table partition by setting the go flag. Each slave increments the slavesDone counter once it has processed its hash table partition, and then attempts to commit. The master transaction spin-waits for the slavesDone counter to become equal to the total number of slaves, and then attempts to commit. All coordination is done within nested txcommatomic blocks.

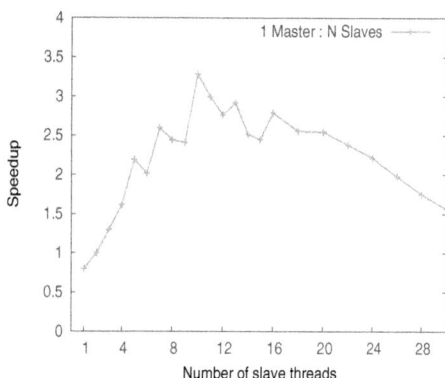

Figure 8. Speedup (over single-threaded transaction runs) results of our intra-transaction concurrency improvement benchmark. The performance results were averaged over 3 test runs. The hash table used had a maximum capacity of 32K entries, with the table being approximately half full at all times of the test runs.

After initializing the hash table (to about half the capacity of 32K), the master thread repeatedly runs enumeration transactions (we ran a total of 50,000 transactions for each test). In the non-concurrent version, the master thread itself invokes the enumeration. In the concurrent version, the master instructs its slaves to process their respective hash table partitions, and then waits for all the slaves to finish. The coordination between master and slaves uses two communicators, shown in Figure 7.

Figure 8 shows the speedup of our communicator-based solution over the single-threaded version. The cost of using communicators, as seen in the 1-slave configuration, is approximately 20%. As the number of threads increases, our parallelized version delivers up to 3.2x speedup, with throughput peaking with 10 threads, before slowly deteriorating. Figure 9 shows that this deterioration is caused by the increasing costs of enforcing dependencies between transactions: The cost of the commit protocol, fueled by the complex transaction dependencies, increases significantly with more slave transactions. With 4 slaves, over 40% of the time is spent in the commit protocol. With 28 slaves, only 15% of the time is spent in doing useful work, and most of the remaining time (about 65%) is spent in the commit protocol. This highlights the need to improve the commit protocol in our system. Note that virtually no transaction aborts in this benchmark (less than 0.5% time is spent in aborted transactions).

7.3 A client-server application

We developed a simple variant of the job-processing example from Section 1, in which a client requests a server to execute a task,

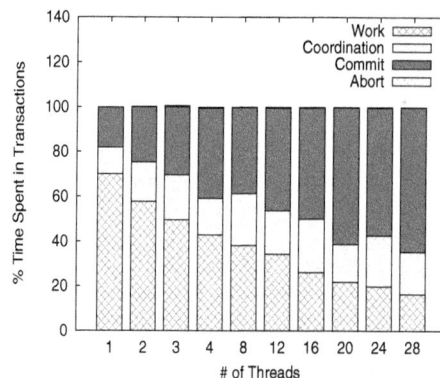

Figure 9. Distribution of percentage of time spent in a transaction. Work refers to the amount of time spent doing real work (enumerating through the hash table partitions); Coordination refers to the time spent in coordination between the master and the slave threads; Commit refers to the time spent committing the interdependent transactions together; and Abort refers to the time spent executing transactions that eventually abort.

and the server returns a response. The request and response occur through communicators, so the client and server operations appear to happen together, as a super-transaction. Shared data is partitioned between client and server transactions. All client transactions access a shared client-side hash table, and all the server transactions access a shared server-side hash table. Local computations are simulated using idle spin loops. Client and server threads are paired together during initialization, and communication happens only between these pairs.

Each client thread repeatedly executes client-side transactions. A client-side transaction (i) executes an operation (insert, delete, or lookup) on the client-side hash table, (ii) posts a request to the server-side transaction (this request instructs the server-side to execute an operation on the server-side hash table), (iii) does some local computation (including a 100-microsecond idle loop), (iv) waits for the response from the server-side, and finally, (v) based on the response (which is a success/failure flag), executes another operation on the client-side hash table.

Each server thread also repeatedly executes server-side transactions. A server-side transaction (i) waits for a request from the client-side, (ii) does some local computation (a 100-microsecond loop), (iii) performs the requested operation on the server-side hash table, and finally (iv) posts the response of the hash table operation.

The data structure used by the client and server transactions to communicate is depicted in Figure 10.

Unlike previous benchmarks, there is no obvious implementation to compare against: Without communicators, client and server transactions cannot communicate. One alternative approach to the problem is to use *irrevocable* transactions [23], where a client-side transaction becomes irrevocable when it posts a request, and instead of using transactions, server-side threads use alternate synchronization mechanisms (e.g., locks) to ensure atomicity of the server-side operations. Thus the client-side transaction, after it becomes irrevocable, can interact with a server-side thread. Although workable, irrevocability does not scale. Furthermore, replacing transactions with a different synchronization mechanism on the server-side may be a nontrivial endeavor. Nonetheless, we compare this alternative with our client-server benchmark.

Figure 11 shows the throughput results of our benchmark with 1 through 16 client theads (and the same number of server threads). Clearly the irrevocability-based solution does not scale and our

```
class ClientServerAnchor {
  // request type: insert, delete, lookup
  txcomm int requestType;
  // request hash table key
  txcomm int requestKey;
  // response: indicates the success/failure of
  // requested operation
  txcomm boolean response;
  // flag to indicate if the client request is ready
  txcomm boolean clientRequestReady;
  // flag to indicate if the server response is ready
  txcomm boolean serverResponseReady;
}
```

Figure 10. The client places its request in the requestType and requestKey fields (which means that it wants the server transaction to execute the operation of type requestType for the key requestKey on the server-side hash table). The client signals the server to proceed by setting the clientRequestReady flag. Similarly the server transaction places its response in the anchor's response field, and signals the client by setting the serverResponseReady flag.

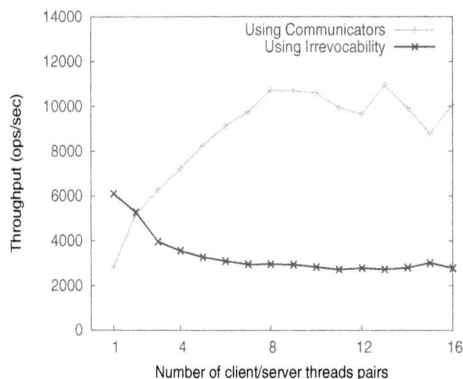

Figure 11. Throughput results of the client-server application. Results are averaged over 3 test runs, each running for 30 seconds.

communicator-based solution scales well (by a factor of almost 4). However, the irrevocability-based solution outperforms our communicator-based solution in single-thread runs (by a factor of about 2), because of the high overheads associated with the coordination of operations on communicators, and the high-latency commit operation. Furthermore, the server-side hash table in the irrevocability-based solution is the high-performance concurrent HashMap from the java.util.concurrent package, which is much faster than our transactional hash table.

Notice that the transactions for which we present performance results here are quite big (more than 100 microseconds long). We experimented with shorter transactions as well and found that the coordination/commit overhead for communicators was too high for our approach to outperform the irrevocability-based approach, again emphasizing the need for to improve the performance of our communicator infrastructure.

8. Related work

The idea of relaxing isolation to allow concurrent transactions to cooperate was embodied in our earlier work on *synchronizers* [16]. However, synchronizers enforced bidirectional dependencies between communicating transactions, which introduced several difficulties. For instance, a set of transactions about to commit could be forced to abort by another transaction that belatedly reads or writes a synchronizer that the transactions accessed. As a result, idioms such as synchronous exchange channels (exchangers) cannot

be easily implemented with synchronizers. Suggested workarounds place a significant burden on the programmer.

Tracking dependencies among transactions is not original to our work. Rather, it has been proposed as a way to reduce aborts in transactional memory implementations [3, 18]. However, those systems maintain isolation, so transactions with cyclic dependencies must all abort, whereas with communicators, such transactions may commit (as long as they all commit).

Transactional events [7] enable composition of synchronous communication between threads by adding transactional all-or-nothing semantics to sequences of communication events. The communication messages are sent by threads via "event synchronization transactions". The fates of such synchronously communicating transactions are joined in that they commit or abort together. Composing synchronous communication operations significantly simplifies idioms such as 3-way synchronous operations. Transactional events appear to be similar to synchronizers, though their use is targeted toward a smaller problem domain—composition of multiple synchronous send/receive operations to simplify otherwise complex synchronous communication protocols.

Accesses to communicators, particularly when done within a nested txcommatomic block, can be viewed as a form of *open nesting* [2, 17], because updates made to txcomm fields within the txcommatomic block become visible to concurrent transactions once the txcommatomic block commits, even if the outer atomic block has not yet committed. However, there is a crucial difference: we track dependencies between transactions due to communicator accesses, and the system ensures that a transaction cannot commit unless all transactions that it depends on also commit. Furthermore, if the transaction for the outer atomic block aborts, the effects of the nested txcommatomic transaction are also rolled back. In contrast, the effects of a committed open-nested transaction are not rolled back; instead, the programmer must provide "compensating actions" to reverse these effects.

The TIC model [19] also attempts to enable cooperation between concurrent transactions by introducing the Wait primitive that "punctuates" the calling transaction. Punctuation breaks the isolation of a transaction by splitting it into two distinct transactions, one before and one after the Wait call. To address the violated isolation, TIC proposes several new constructs and type system extensions to "expose" the violation to the calling contexts, and to help the programmer restore program invariants broken during such violations. This model of punctuation and restoration is somewhat similar to open nesting and compensating actions, albeit with better type system support. However, the complete lack of isolation between the two halves of a punctuated atomic block can present significant programmability challenges in some contexts (e.g. the job scheduling problem from Figure 1). Dudnik and Swift [8] take a similar punctuate-on-wait approach in their condition variable proposal. They do not, however, support mechanisms to propagate punctuation information and enable restoration of broken program invariants, as TIC does.

Recently, and independently, Lesani and Palsberg developed *transactors* [15], which combines the actor model with transactions. Transactors can send and receive messages within transactions, which create dependencies between transactions by different actors. As with communicators, transactions cannot commit unless the transactions they depend on commit, and cyclic dependencies require all transactions in the cycle to commit or abort together.

9. Conclusion

Although transactional memory is a promising mechanism to help address the challenge of writing concurrent programs, we believe that the scope of transactional programming will be limited unless it works with commonly used programming idioms and concurrency control techniques that are incompatible with isolation of transactions. To that end, we have presented transaction communicators, which enable programmers to have concurrent transactions communicate in a controlled fashion, sufficient to enable programming idioms such as CSP-style synchronous communication [13], producer-consumer interactions, etc.

Our preliminary evaluation demonstrates that communicators can be useful in a wide range of settings—to alleviate contention bottlenecks, to break down and parallelize large transactions, and to perform explicit inter-transaction communication. We believe that communicators open a new research frontier for transactional programming. In addition to the programming idioms explored in this paper, we expect to find many more useful and interesting ways of programming TM applications using communicators (e.g., condition variables, enforcing transaction ordering, etc.).

Acknowledgments

We are grateful to the Maxine team for their technical support, to Dhruva Chakrabarti and the anonymous reviewers for their many helpful questions and suggestions.

References

[1] A.-R. Adl-Tabatabai, B. T. Lewis, V. Menon, B. R. Murphy, B. Saha, and T. Shpeisman. Compiler and Runtime Support for Efficient Software Transactional Memory. In *Proceedings of the ACM SIGPLAN Conference on Programming Language Design and Implementation*, pages 26–37, 2006.

[2] K. Agrawal, C. E. Leiserson, and J. Sukha. Memory Models for Open-Nested Transactions. In *Proceedings of the ACM SIGPLAN Workshop on Memory Systems Performance and Correctness*, 2006.

[3] U. Aydonat and T. Abdelrahmen. Serializability of transactions in software transactional memory. In *TRANSACT*, 2009.

[4] C. Blundell, E. C. Lewis, and M. Martin. Deconstructing Transactions: The Subtleties of Atomicity. In *the 4th Annual Workshop on Duplicating, Deconstructing, and Debunking*, 2005.

[5] L. Dalessandro, V. J. Marathe, M. F. Spear, and M. L. Scott. Capabilities and Limitations of Library-Based Software Transactional Memory in C++. In *2nd ACM SIGPLAN Workshop on Languages, Compilers and Hardware Support for Transactional Computing*, 2007.

[6] S. Doherty, L. Groves, V. Luchangco, and M. Moir. Towards formally specifying and verifying transactional memory. *Formal Aspects of Computing*, To appear. Earlier version appeared in Refine 2009.

[7] K. Donnelly and M. Fluet. Transactional Events. In *Proceedings of the 11th ACM SIGPLAN International Conference on Functional Programming*, pages 124–135, 2006.

[8] P. Dudnik and M. M. Swift. Condition Variables and Transactional Memory: Problem or Opportunity? In *Proceedings of the 4th ACM SIGPLAN Workshop on Transactional Computing*, 2009.

[9] R. Guerraoui and M. Kapalka. *Principles of Transactional Memory*. Morgan Claypool, 2010.

[10] T. Harris and K. Fraser. Language Support for Lightweight Transactions. In *Proceedings of the 18th Annual ACM SIGPLAN Conference on Object-Oriented Programing, Systems, Languages, and Applications*, pages 388–402, 2003.

[11] T. Harris, M. Plesko, A. Shinnar, and D. Tarditi. Optimizing Memory Transactions. In *ACM SIGPLAN 2006 Conference on Programming Language Design and Implementation*, pages 14–25, June 2006.

[12] M. Herlihy, V. Luchangco, M. Moir, and W. N. Scherer III. Software Transactional Memory for Dynamic-sized Data Structures. In *Proceedings of the 22nd Annual Symposium on Principles of Distributed Computing*, pages 92–101, 2003.

[13] C. Hoare. *Communicating Sequential Processes*. Prentice Hall, 1985.

[14] D. Imbs, J. R. Gonzalez de Mendivil, and M. Raynal. Brief announcement: Virtual world consistency: A new condition for STM systems. In *Proceedings of the 28th Annual ACM Sympoisium on Principles of Distributed Computing*, 2009.

[15] M. Lesani and J. Palsberg. Communicating Memory Transactions. In *Proceedings of the 16th ACM SIGPLAN Symposium on Principles and Practice of Parallel Programming*, 2011.

[16] V. Luchangco and V. J. Marathe. Transaction Synchronizers. In *Proceedings of the Workshop on Synchronization and Concurrency in Object-Oriented Languages*, 2005.

[17] J. E. B. Moss. *Nested Transactions: An Approach to Reliable Distributed Computing*. PhD thesis, Massachusetts Institute of Technology, 1981.

[18] H. E. Ramadan, I. Roy, and E. Witchel. Dependence-Aware Transactional Memory for Increased Concurrency. In *Proceedings of the 41st Annual IEEE/ACM International Symposium on Microarchitecture*, pages 246–257, 2008.

[19] Y. Smaragdakis, A. Kay, R. Behrends, and M. Young. Transactions with Isolation and Cooperation. In *Proceedings of the 22nd Annual ACM SIGPLAN Conference on Object Oriented Programming Systems and Applications*, pages 191–210, 2007.

[20] Standard Performance Evaluation Corporation (SPEC). SPECjbb2005 Java Server Benchmark. http://www.spec.org/jbb2005/.

[21] The Maxine Virtual Machine. http://research.sun.com/projects/maxine/.

[22] H. Volos, A. Welc, A.-R. Adl-Tabatabai, T. Shpeisman, X. Tian, and R. Narayanaswamy. NePaLTM: Design and Implementation of Nested Parallelism for Transactional Memory Systems. In *The 23rd European Conference on Object-Oriented Programming*, pages 123–147, 2009.

[23] A. Welc, B. Saha, and A.-R. Adl-Tabatabai. Irrevocable Transactions and Their Applications. In *Proceedings of the 20th Annual Symposium on Parallelism in Algorithms and Architectures*, pages 285–296, 2008.

Lock-free and Scalable Multi-Version Software Transactional Memory *

Sérgio Miguel Fernandes   João Cachopo

IST / INESC-ID

{Sergio.Fernandes,Joao.Cachopo}@ist.utl.pt

Abstract

Software Transactional Memory (STM) was initially proposed as a lock-free mechanism for concurrency control. Early implementations had efficiency limitations, and soon obstruction-free proposals appeared, to tackle this problem, often simplifying STM implementation. Today, most of the modern and top-performing STMs use blocking designs, relying on locks to ensure an atomic commit operation. This approach has revealed better in practice, in part due to its simplicity. Yet, it may have scalability problems when we move into many-core computers, requiring fine-tuning and careful programming to avoid contention.

In this paper we present and discuss the modifications we made to a lock-based multi-version STM in Java, to turn it into a lock-free implementation that we have tested to scale at least up to 192 cores, and which provides results that compete with, and sometimes exceed, some of today's top-performing lock-based implementations.

The new lock-free commit algorithm allows write transactions to proceed in parallel, by allowing them to run their validation phase independently of each other, and by resorting to helping from threads that would otherwise be waiting to commit, during the write-back phase. We also present a new garbage collection algorithm to dispose of old unused object versions that allows for asynchronous identification of unnecessary versions, which minimizes its interference with the rest of the transactional system.

Categories and Subject Descriptors   D.1.3 [*Programming Techniques*]: Concurrent Programming—Parallel programming

General Terms   Algorithms, Transactions, Scalability

Keywords   Transactional Memory, Multi-Version Concurrency Control, Lock-Free Synchronization, Garbage Collection

1. Introduction

Since the seminal work on Transactional Memory [12] and Software Transactional Memory (STM) [19], there has been a boom in related research, which has led to several proposals for STM

* This work was partially supported by FCT (INESC-ID multiannual funding) through the PIDDAC Program funds and the RuLAM project (PTDC/EIA-EIA/108240/2008).

implementations, each with their own set of characteristics. One such implementation is the Java Versioned Software Transactional Memory (JVSTM) [3], which was specifically designed to optimize the execution of read-only transactions. In the JVSTM, read-only transactions have very low overheads, and they never contend against any other transaction. In fact, read-only transactions are wait-free [11] in the JVSTM.

JVSTM's design goals stem from the observation and development of real-world domain-intensive web applications. These applications have rich and complex domains, both structurally and behaviorally, leading on one hand to very large transactions, but having also a very high read/write ratio. These characteristics have been observed over several years of use of the JVSTM in the FénixEDU project in a production environment [4]. This web application executes concurrent transactions to process the user requests, and the number of read-only transactions represents, on average, over 95% of the total number of transactions executed.

The design of the JVSTM allows it to excel in read-intensive workloads [2], but raises doubts on its applicability to other types of workloads, where writes dominate. Even though during the execution of a write-transaction reads and writes of transactional locations are wait-free, the commit of these transactions serialize on a global lock, thereby having the potential of impairing severely the scalability of a write-intensive application.

In this paper we address this problem by presenting and discussing the implementation of a new scalable and efficient commit algorithm for the JVSTM that is able to maintain the exact same properties for reads, as before. This new commit algorithm allows commits to proceed in parallel during the validation phase, and resorts to helping from threads that would otherwise be waiting to commit, during the write-back phase. We evaluate the new algorithm with four benchmarking applications, and show it to scale well up to 192 parallel transactions, when tested on a machine with a little over 200 cores.

In the following section we give an overview of the key aspects of the JVSTM that are relevant to understand the new commit algorithm. Then, in Section 3 we describe the new algorithm, followed by a description, in Section 4, of the asynchronous garbage collection mechanism for old versions, which we developed to address a scalability problem in the existing code. In Section 5 we present a performance evaluation. Section 6 provides a discussion on properties of the algorithms and related work. We conclude in section 7.

2. JVSTM overview

JVSTM is a word-based STM that supports transactions using a Multi-Version Concurrency Control (MVCC) method. Each transactional location uses a Versioned Box (VBox) [3] to hold the history of values for that location, as exemplified in Figure 1. A VBox instance represents the identity of the transactional location, and

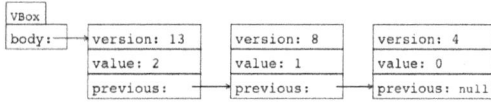

Figure 1. A transactional counter and its versions.

contains a body with the list of versions. Each element (VBoxBody) in the history contains a version number, the value for that version, and a reference to the previous state of that versioned box.

A transaction reads values in a version that corresponds to the most recent version that existed when the transaction began. Thus, reads are always consistent and read-only transactions never conflict with any other, being serialized in the instant they begin, i.e., it is as if they had atomically executed in that instant. Conversely, write-only transactions are serialized at commit-time (when the changes are atomically made visible) and, thus, they never conflict as well. Read-write transactions (write transactions for short) require validation at commit-time to ensure that values read during the transaction are still consistent with the current commit-time, i.e., values have not been changed in the meanwhile by another concurrent transaction.

During a transaction, the JVSTM records each transactional access (either a read or a write) in the transaction's local log (in the read-set or in the write-set, respectively). During commit, if the transaction's read-set is valid, then its write-set is written-back, producing a new version of the values, which will be available to other transactions that begin afterwards. The following pseudo-code in Figure 2 summarizes the commit algorithm of write transactions (the commit of read-only transactions simply returns).

The global lock provides mutual exclusion among all committing write transactions, which ensures atomicity between validating the read-set and writing-back the write-set. Also, the version number is provided by a unique global counter that changes only inside the critical region. The commit operation sets a linearization point when it updates the global counter. After that point, the changes made by the transaction are visible to other transactions that start. When a new transaction starts, it reads that number to know which version it will use to read values.

Also, observe that a read from a transactional location is usually very fast, for the following reasons: (1) No synchronization mechanism is required to read from a VBox. The only (lock-free) synchronization point occurs at the start of the transaction, when it reads the most recent committed version number; (2) the list of versions is always ordered by decreasing version number. The commit operation keeps the list ordered, because it always writes to the head of the list a version number that is higher than the previous head version; and (3) the required version tends to be at the head of the list, or very near to it. If it is not at the head, then it is because after this transaction started, another transaction has already committed and written a new value to that same location (recall the expected low number of write transactions, and that a transaction always starts in the most recent version available).

```
commit() {
  GLOBAL_LOCK.lock();
  try {
    if (validate()) {
      int newTxnumber = globalCounter + 1;
      writeBack(newTxNumber);
      updateGlobalCounter(newTxNumber);
    }
  } finally { GLOBAL_LOCK.unlock(); }
}
```

Figure 2. The global lock-based commit algorithm.

2.1 Deletion of old versions

To keep the list of versions in each VBox from growing indefinitely, versions are kept only for as long as any transaction may require them. JVSTM ensures forward progress and transactions always start from the most recent version available. As older transactions finish (or restart due to conflict), older versions may become unused, because they become logically inaccessible, and should be removed. When a write transaction commits, all values that it writes replace logically the older values, from the point of view of transactions that start henceforth. Thus, these older values can be removed, if there is no transaction running in a version older than the version just committed.

To identify which versions are no longer accessible and to manage garbage collection of old versions the JVSTM uses the *Active Transactions Record* [2]. This structure holds a list of transaction records deemed to be *active*, in a singly-linked list of records, with each record holding a reference to the next most recent record. Each record keeps information about a write transaction that already committed, namely the commit version and the values that were written (as references to the VBoxBody instances created during the commit). A record also has a counter of how many transactions are running in the record's version. When a new transaction starts, it atomically increments the counter on the most recent record. When a transaction finishes, it decrements the same counter and checks if it has reached zero. A record is considered active if the counter is positive or there is an older record that is active.

When a record becomes inactive and there is already a newer record[1], versions produced by the newer record make older versions inaccessible. At this point, older versions are removed by setting the field previous in each VBoxBody in the newer record to null. This process is dubbed "cleaning the record". Notice that a version v_1 is never lost, unless there is a transaction that writes a newer version v_2 to the same VBox. In such case, v_1 may be removed, only if the record referring to it becomes inactive.

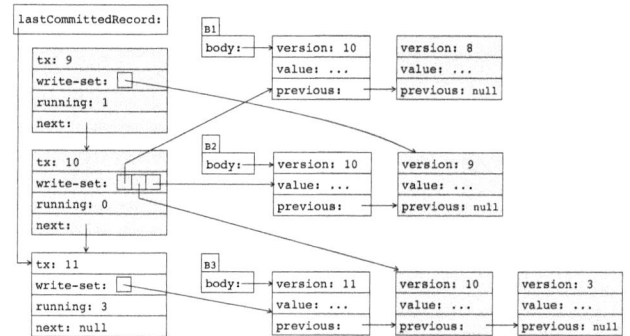

Figure 3. An example snapshot of the Active Transactions Record.

Figure 3 provides an example scenario, in which there are three active records representing the commits of versions 9, 10, and 11. There are also three transactional locations managed by VBoxes B1, B2, and B3. Transaction 9 wrote to B1, transaction 10 wrote to all three locations, and transaction 11 (the most recent write transaction to commit) wrote to B3. Currently, there are four running transactions: One that started in version 9, and three that started in version 11. When the transaction running in version 9 finishes, it will decrement the running counter to zero. After this occurs, record 9 is identified as inactive, and record 10 is cleaned. This is accomplished by setting to null the previous field in all VBoxBodies with

---

[1] A newer record ensures that new transactions will start in a more recent version and not re-activate this record.

180

version number 10. Now, record 10 also is identified as inactive, and record 11 is cleaned. After both records are cleaned, the objects shown in gray can be garbage collected.

2.2 The need for a new commit algorithm

In many cases, the time spent by a write transaction in the critical region at commit time is very short when compared to the time it takes to actually execute an entire transaction. Moreover, the JVSTM was initially developed to support read-heavy applications, in which the number of read-only transactions corresponds to more than 95% of the total number of transactions executed. The other 5% seldom overlap in time, even more so, if we only consider the time of the commit operation. These facts put together justified the use of the global-lock approach, with good performance results. Nevertheless, there are reasons to implement an alternate solution.

The rate of execution of write transactions affects performance. Locks do not scale. Different applications have different workloads regarding read and write operations and may execute many write transactions in a short period of time, especially in the case of CPU-intensive applications. This may highly increase the probability of having more than one write transaction trying to commit concurrently. Whereas this may not be an issue for machines with a small number of cores, many-core machines are an emerging reality and the number of cores available at an affordable price is growing. Thus, it is reasonable to assume that in a many-core machine the high contention on the global lock will degrade performance significantly.

Contention in multi-processing increases the probability of restarts due to conflicts, and reduces the overall throughput. It is easy to understand that when more transactions run concurrently, the probability of conflicts increase. But it is not so obvious that this situation may be aggravated when running N transactions in less that N processors.

As we saw, a write transaction has a conflict if some value that it read was already changed when it tries to commit. So, intuitively, the probability of conflict increases with the length of the transaction and the number of concurrent transactions, but it should not depend on the number of available processors, because having less processors should slow down all transactions proportionally and, thus, maintain the probability of having transactions committing during the execution of another transaction. Yet, this intuition is valid only if all transactions proceed without interference. Once a transaction may have to wait for a lock, things change.

The JVSTM's commit operation uses a fair locking policy. This means that each transaction will obtain the lock in the order that it was requested. When a write transaction (T_1) commits, it tries to get the lock. If another transaction (T_0) already has it, then T_1 has to wait. The more transactions there are, then the less processor time T_0 will have to finish and release the lock. Thus, there is a higher probability that other write transactions ($T_2, \ldots, T_n$) will queue up for the lock as well, because they will be given processor time to execute, whereas T_1 is still waiting. Suppose that when T_1 finally gets the lock, it fails validation, releases the lock, and restarts. Releasing the lock and restarting is generally much faster than committing T_2, thus T_1 will typically restart with the version number of T_0's commit (the most recent at the time of restart). So, in practice, the length of T_1, during which other transactions may commit and therefore conflict with T_1, has effectively increased from its normal executing length by the amount of time that it had to wait for the lock.

This occurs because the re-execution of T_1, on average, will see more transactions committing than its first execution. It is not certain that using an unfair lock would reduce the probability of

restarts, simply because then $T_2, \ldots, T_n$ would still be able to get ahead of T_1 in the race to commit.

3. Lock-free commit algorithm

In this section we describe a new commit algorithm that we developed to replace the existing lock-based implementation. Conceptually, the algorithm contains the same steps as before: (1) validate the read-set; (2) write-back the write-set; and (3) make the commit visible to other transactions. In the following sections we explain how each step is accomplished in the new algorithm.[2]

3.1 Validation

In the lock-based commit algorithm, validation explicitly checks that the most recent version of each value in the read-set is still the same version that was read during the transaction (*snapshot validation*). The insight is that validation can also be performed incrementally by checking the write-sets of all transactions that have committed versions greater than the one this transaction started with (*delta validation*). Suppose that transaction T started in version v_1. For any transaction T_i that committed a version greater than v_1, if any element in the write-set of T_i is in the read-set of T, then T cannot commit, because of a conflict.

Of course that, without exclusion in the validation step, while T is validating itself, other transactions can also be validating themselves to commit as well. We need to order the commits in such a way that each transaction can finish validation and be sure that it is valid to commit.

To do so, we use and extend the functionality of the Active Transactions Record that already exists in the JVSTM. The Active Transactions Record holds a list of transaction records, each containing information about a write transaction that has already committed. To support the delta validation, we extend this list to also include valid, but not yet fully committed records. Thus, a transaction that can get an entry in this list effectively establishes its commit order (and, as such, its commit version). The code depicted in Figure 4 shows how a transaction concurrently validates its read-set in a lock-free way.

```
validateCommitAndEnqueue() {
  ActiveTxRecord lastValid = this.activeTxRecord;
  do {
    lastValid = validate(lastValid);
    this.commitTxRecord = new ActiveTxRecord(lastValid.txNumber+1,
                                             this.writeSet);
  } while (!lastValid.trySetNext(this.commitTxRecord));
}
```

Figure 4. The lock-free validation algorithm.

Each write transaction has two transaction records: The `active-TxRecord`, which points to the record that represents the version in which the transaction started; and, the `commitTxRecord`, which is the record that is created to represent the transaction's own commit. To be valid, a transaction needs to check for an empty intersection between its read-set and the write-set of each record, from the `activeTxRecord` onward. This is what the `validate` method does: It checks all records from the `lastValid` onward and it returns the last successfully validated record (or throws a `CommitException` if validation fails at any point). Next, the new `commitTxRecord` is created with an incremented commit version number, and the transaction's write-set. The `trySetNext` is a *compare-and-set* operation (CAS) that atomically sets the `commitTxRecord` as the next valid record after the `lastValid`. This is a tentative operation that

---

[2] For clarity, we omit minor code details, and simplify syntax. The full code is available at http://groups.ist.utl.pt/esw-inesc-id/git/jvstm.git.

only succeeds if the next record is still unset. Otherwise, this means that another transaction has won the race for that position, in which case validation resumes from the last known valid record. Thus, commit order is defined by the order in which transaction records enter the Active Transactions Record list. All transactions that are in the process of committing must obtain a position in this list, after validating themselves. Even if not all transactions are already written-back, being in this list enables future committing transactions to check their validity against all those that are already queued for a sure commit.

Notice that this validation algorithm is lock-free, because even though a single transaction may continuously fail to get a commit position, this implies that the transactional system as a whole must be making progress, i.e., other transactions are in fact validating and queueing their commit records. Additionally, if no commits occur between the start and commit of a transaction, then validation is not necessary, because that transaction's `activeTxRecord` is the most recent one and is already valid, so the committing transaction only needs to queue up its commit record.

3.2 Write-back

After a successful validation, a transaction obtained a commit version, which is represented by the commit record that was placed in the commit queue. Figure 5, shows an example of a possible state of the Active Transactions Record. Transactions 9 and 10 have already committed[3], whereas transactions 11 to 13 are valid but not yet written-back. At this time, any new transaction, will start in version 10, because it is the last committed version. We also show the two transaction records in use by transaction 12 (thus, assuming that transaction 12 started before transaction 10 committed).

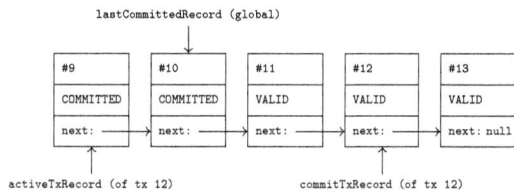

Figure 5. The Active Transactions Record is extended to hold write transactions that are valid but not yet written-back.

Writing-back consists in adding a new `VBox` body to the corresponding `VBox`, for each value in the write-set of the transaction, with the version obtained during validation. Taking into account that each value is written to a different location, each write can be done in parallel. One could even consider the concurrency between any two valid transactions that need to write-back values to different locations, but this is not so simple: Within each `VBox` we need to maintain the list of versions ordered, to keep the reads fast. If two valid transactions try to commit different values to the same location, then they need to be ordered according to their commit version. This poses a difficulty, because it is expensive to compute whether the write-sets of valid transactions intersect. This problem did not exist in the lock-based version, simply because only one transaction could be in the write-back phase, at any given time.

The easiest way to ensure that write-backs to the same location are performed in order is to write-back only one transaction at a time, beginning with the oldest valid transaction that is yet uncommitted. Each valid transaction will help the oldest valid transaction to write-back, up to, and including, itself. This way, instead of blocking, transactions waiting to commit can be helpful and increase the overall write-back throughput. This behavior is shown in the code depicted in Figure 6.

---

[3] The commit status of a write transaction is given by its commit record.

```
// in class Transaction:
ensureCommitStatus() {
  ActiveTxRecord recToCommit = lastCommittedRecord.getNext();
  while (recToCommit.txNumber <= this.commitTxRecord.txNumber) {
    if (!recToCommit.isCommitted()) {
      WriteSet writeSet = recToCommit.getWriteSet();
      writeSet.helpWriteBack(recToCommit.txNumber);
      finishCommit(recToCommit);
    }
    recToCommit = recToCommit.getNext();
  }
}

// in class WriteSet:
helpWriteBack(int newTxNumber) {
  int finalBucket = random.nextInt(this.nBuckets);
  int currBucket = finalBucket;
  do {
    if (!this.bucketsDone[currBucket].get()) {
      this.bodiesPerBucket[currBucket] =
                 writeBackBucket(currBucket, newTxNumber);
      this.bucketsDone[currBucket].set(true);
    }
    currBucket = (currBucket + 1) % this.nBuckets;
  } while (currBucket != finalBucket);
}

List writeBackBucket(int bucket, int newTxNumber) {
  List newBodies = new LinkedList();
  for (BucketEntry be : this.buckets[bucket]) {
    VBoxBody newBody = be.vbox.commit(be.value, newTxNumber);
    newBodies.add(newBody);
  }
  return newBodies;
}

// in class VBox:
VBoxBody commit(Object newValue, int txNumber) {
  VBoxBody currHead = this.body;
  VBoxBody existingBody = currHead.getBody(txNumber);

  if (existingBody == null) {
    VBoxBody newBody = new VBoxBody(newValue, txNumber, currHead);
    existingBody = CASbody(currHead, newBody);
  }
  return existingBody;
}

VBoxBody CASbody(VBoxBody expected, VBoxBody newBody) {
  if (compareAndSwapObject(this, VBox.bodyOffset, expected,
                           newBody)) {
    return newBody;
  } else {
    return this.body.getBody(newBody.version);
  }
}
```

Figure 6. Algorithm for concurrent write-back with support for helping from other committing transactions.

After validation, transactions run the `ensureCommitStatus` method. This method starts by accessing the globally available `lastCommittedRecord` to get the next record to commit. After each iteration, it is guaranteed that the transaction corresponding to `recToCommit` has been committed. To share the work among concurrent helping transactions we split the values to write-back into several buckets, of approximately the same size each. The write-set itself holds the buckets, so `ensureCommitStatus` delegates the write-back operation to the write-set, configuring it with the version number to use.

The `helpWriteBack` method picks a random[4] bucket to start, and then iterates through each bucket once. For each bucket, it checks whether that bucket is already written-back, by checking

---

[4] There is one instance of the randomizer class per thread, to eliminate contention on the random number generator.

182

the `bucketsDone` array. This array contains an `AtomicBoolean` for each bucket that indicates whether the values in the corresponding bucket are already written back. Any helping transaction may find that some buckets are already written-back, if some other transaction has helped. For those buckets that are not yet written-back, this helping transaction will attempt to write each value to its respective `VBox`, and mark the bucket as done. The `writeBackBucket` method, iterates through the elements of the bucket invoking `commit` on each `VBox` with the value and version to commit.

The `commit` method handles the creation of the new `VBoxBody` and inserts it at the head of the list of bodies. Due to concurrency in the write-back operation, more than one thread can attempt to write-back to the same `VBox`. As such, the `commit` operation starts by searching (via the `getBody` method) whether there is already a `VBoxBody` with the required version. If it does not exist, then the new `VBoxBody` is created and `CASBody` attempts to install it. This operation tries to replace the `VBox`'s current `body` with the new one with a single CAS attempt. If it succeeds, it returns the new head of the list. It if fails, then it is because a concurrent helping transaction succeeded, in which case it looks up the required `VBoxBody` to return. So, `commit` always returns the written-back `VBoxBody`. These bodies are collected in the `newBodies` list that is stored in the `bodiesPerBucket` array in the position corresponding to the bucket being written-back. In Section 4 we will explain how these lists are used by the garbage collection algorithm to eliminate old versions.

Finishing a commit requires publicizing the changes globally, and it can be done only after all values are in place. According to the Java Memory Model [14], any write to memory performed before a volatile write of a given location x will necessarily be seen by other threads, as long as they first perform a volatile read of x. The setting of each `AtomicBoolean` in the `bucketsDone` array entails volatile write semantics, thus when another thread sees that a bucket is done (issuing a volatile read), it will surely be able to see the values of that bucket written-back.

At the end of `helpWriteBack` the helper transaction can be sure that all buckets of this write-set are written-back, because either this transaction did it or checked that another transaction did it. So, the helper is sure that the helped transaction can be safely committed.

The write-back phase is wait-free, because any transaction that enters this phase is certain to finish it in a bounded number of steps, in spite of other threads executing any other code concurrently. The number of iterations performed in `ensureCommitStatus` is clearly bounded, because there is a finite number of records between the `lastCommittedRecord` and the transaction's own `commitTxRecord`, which was already enqueued in the validation phase. The number of buckets is fixed per write-set and the `helpWriteBack` method only iterates them once. The CAS to set the new `VBoxBody` may fail, but in that scenario the written-back value is already there, so the operation does not have to be retried. Also, when the CAS fails, finding the written-back value to return is a limited search, because the list of versions only grows at the head, and the search is performed in the opposite direction.

3.3 Finishing a commit

All transactions that help to write-back another have to try to finish that transaction, because no transaction really knows whether it was the first one to fully complete the write-back. Nevertheless, after the write-back operation is completely finished, making the changes globally visible is a trivial operation with two steps: (1) set the commit flag in the commit record; and, (2) set the global `lastCommittedRecord` to be the record just committed. This is done in the `finishCommit` method, as shown in Figure 7.

In this new version of the commit algorithm, the linearization point is step (1), which sets a volatile boolean variable to `true`. Updating the global reference to the last committed record is just a

```
finishCommit(ActiveTxRecord recToCommit) {
  recToCommit.setCommitted();
  lastCommittedRecord = recToCommit;
}
```

Figure 7. Finishing a commit and publishing changes.

helping operation to reduce the search effort of new transactions. The `finishCommit` operation has no synchronization, so it is possible that thread interleaving causes some late thread to actually set the `lastCommittedRecord` reference back to a previously committed record, when there is already a more recent committed record. For this reason, whenever a new transaction begins, it obtains the most recent version from the `lastCommittedRecord`, and then it iterates forward, looking for the most recent committed record. Recall that a record enters the list immediately after validation succeeds, whereas in the lock-based algorithm, the list was only updated in mutual exclusion, after each successful commit.

3.4 Validation revisited

As mentioned in Section 3.1, validation of a transaction T can be performed in two different ways: (1) A snapshot validation atomically checks if T's read-set is still up to date with the current global state (this corresponds to the original validation used in the lock-based commit); and (2) a delta validation incrementally checks each write-set committed since T started and looks for an intersection with T's read-set (the validation that we introduced in the new commit algorithm).

Either validation technique has advantages and shortcomings, performance-wise. Snapshot validation depends solely on the size of the read-set. The time it takes to validate a read set is proportional to its size. Conversely, delta validation is independent of the size of the read-set. This holds true as long as the lookup function that searches whether any given element is contained in the read-set can be executed in constant time. Delta validation depends on the size and number of all the other write-sets committed while the transaction executed.

From our experience, read-sets are, on average, several times larger than write-sets, although this difference is highly dependent on each application's read and write patterns. So, delta validation will tend to perform better when the average size of a read-set to validate is greater than the average size of the list of write-sets to iterate multiplied by their average write-set size. Whereas the size of the write-set is application dependent, the length of the write-set list to iterate grows with the number of write transactions. As the number of concurrent transactions increases, so does the cost of delta validation. To tackle this problem we have made a modification to the validation procedure, in which we mix the two techniques. This is presented in the code in Figure 8.

```
validate() {
  ActiveTxRecord lastSeenCommitted = helpWriteBackAll();
  snapshotValidation();
  validateCommitAndEnqueue(lastSeenCommitted);
}
```

Figure 8. The mixed validation.

Before any actual validation takes place, a transaction helps to write-back all pending commits already queued. The `helpWrite-BackAll` method is similar to the `ensureCommitStatus` method, except that it helps to commit all queued records and it returns the last one that it helped to commit. Then a snapshot validation is performed. Notice that there is no synchronization and, therefore, it is possible that concurrent commits occur. However, the list of committed versions for each transactional location surely contains at least all the commits up to the version of the `lastSeenCommitted` record. Thus, snapshot validation, at least, validates up to that point.

Still, if validation succeeds, we must check for any newer commits and ensure a valid commit position. So, we run the delta validation, but this time only from the `lastSeenCommitted` record onwards. The `validateCommitAndEnqueue` method is adjusted to receive the starting record, instead of defaulting to `activeTxRecord`.

Even though this algorithm may be slower for a low number of transactions, it will scale much better, because it keeps the list of write-sets to check small. Moreover, the initial step in which the transaction helps to write-back, is not wasted work, as this would have to be done by some transaction anyway.

Taking into account the progress guarantees of each phase of the commit algorithm, we can conclude that this algorithm is lock-free.

4. Asynchronous elimination of old versions

The existing garbage collection (GC) mechanism for old versions that we describe in Section 2.1 is already lock-free, so we could use it and still claim that the JVSTM with our new commit algorithm was lock-free. However, during our tests we have found that the existing algorithm contains a bottleneck in the atomic counters of the Active Transactions Record. In this section we will present the problem with the original GC and describe the replacement that we developed.

The problem is that the shared counters used in the Active Transactions Record, simply do not scale when used intensively. The following factors contribute to the bottleneck: (1) very short transactions, (2) read-dominated workloads, and (3) increased number of concurrent transactions in many-core machines. Given that every transaction increments/decrements these counters at the beginning/end, the more transactions there are, the more concurrent updates there will be to the counters, which is worsened when all transactions can run in parallel. Also, if the transactions are short, the percentage of time spent beginning and finishing is larger, when compared to the rest of the time. Most importantly, in a scenario where read-only transactions prevail, most transactions will be using the same version, thus trying to modify the same counter. We verified by experience that the current GC of old versions, causes a performance degradation in read-dominated scenarios, when there are above 20 parallel short transactions running.

Taking this into account, we developed a new algorithm to eliminate unused versions, which runs in a separate thread, still uses the Active Transactions Record, but does not require the records to have any counters at all.

```
class TxContext {
  volatile ActiveTxRecord oldestRequiredRecord;
  WeakReference<Thread> ownerThread;
}
```

Figure 9. The `TxContext` data structure keeps a per-thread registry of the oldest record required.

Instead, there is, as shown in Figure 9, a per-thread transaction context (`TxContext`) that holds a reference to the transaction record currently in use by the thread's running transaction. Each context is stored in a thread-local variable. Then there is a globally accessible list of all existing contexts and the GC task repeatedly iterates through this list, identifying which is the oldest record in use and cleaning all records up to the oldest in use. Each context also contains a `WeakReference` to the thread that created it (`ownerThread`). This is to allow the GC to detect when a thread has died, so that it can remove unnecessary contexts from the global list. In the rest of

this section we present the details for the lock-free GC implementation.

Adding a new `TxContext` to the global list is a simple add operation on a non-blocking list. This only needs to be done once for every new thread that starts a transaction for the first time. Afterwards, each thread reuses its own context. Whenever a new transaction starts, it determines its version, and sets the corresponding `ActiveTxRecord` in the context's `oldestRequiredRecord`. When a transaction finishes (either with a commit or abort) it sets the record to `null`.

Due to the concurrency between the GC algorithm and the start of a new transaction, after setting the `oldestRequiredRecord` a transaction must check again whether there is a newer record, and, if so, upgrade to it, simply by setting it as the `oldestRequiredRecord`. This double-check sequence is required to ensure that the GC task never removes a record that may be in use by a transaction. Notice that a write transaction that commits will mark its `commitTxRecord` as committed, before setting the `oldestRequiredRecord` to `null`. This ensures that, if the GC task decides that a record is inaccessible, then new transactions will have to see the newer record, and use it. The GC's main algorithm is shown in Figure 10.

```
run() {
  while(true) {
    ActiveTxRecord rec = findOldestRecordInUse();
    cleanUnusedRecordsUpTo(rec);
  }
}

ActiveTxRecord findOldestRecordInUse() {
  ActiveTxRecord alreadyCommitted = lastCommittedRecord;

  ActiveTxRecord minRequiredRec_1 = getOldestRecord();
  if (minRequiredRec_1 == null) {
    return alreadyCommitted;
  }

  ActiveTxRecord minRequiredRec_2 = getOldestRecord();
  return (minRequiredRec_2 != null) ?
         minRequiredRec_2 : minRequiredRec_1;
}
```

Figure 10. The new GC algorithm.

The GC is launched in a *daemon* thread that runs an infinite loop: It finds the oldest record in use and then cleans all records up to that record. The algorithm to find the oldest record in use leverages on the following property: Apart from changing to `null`, the `oldestRequiredRecord` for each context never changes backwards, i.e., after being set to a record R_a it cannot be changed later in time to another record R_b, such that R_b.txNumber $<$ R_a.txNumber. This property ensures the GC that once a transaction has set a record R in its context it will never access another record older than R, which is guaranteed, because a transaction always starts on the latest committed record. With this in mind, the `findOldestRecordInUse` method starts by reading the current `lastCommittedRecord`. Should the search fail to find any other record, it is safe to clean up to the `alreadyCommitted` record.

Then it performs two passes over the list of contexts to get the oldest record of each pass. The `getOldestRecord` method (not shown) returns the record with the lowest `txNumber` from the list, or it returns `null` if it does not find any record in the list of contexts. If the first pass returns `null`, then the `alreadyCommitted` record is the safest point to clean up to, and the method returns. Otherwise, a second pass is executed to ensure that, due to concurrency, it did not miss a thread that was starting a transaction with a record older than `minRequiredRec_1`, which could occur for any context C_i read before reading the context C_{min} that contained the identified `minRequiredRec_1`[5]. For this reason, the second invocation of `getOldestRecord` only needs to check the contexts up to C_{min}. For clarity, this optimization is not shown in the code in Figure 10. After the second pass, if a record older than `minRequiredRec_1` was found then that record is returned; otherwise `minRequiredRec_1` is the oldest.

Additionally, the `getOldestRecord` method also removes from the global list of contexts any context that is no longer associated with a thread. It does so when the `WeakReference` in the `ownerThread` becomes `null`.

After identifying the oldest record in use, the GC task cleans every record from the last one cleaned to the oldest in use. Cleaning a record requires an iteration over all the `VBoxBody` instances created by the commit of that record's transaction, and setting the field `previous` in each `VBoxBody` to `null`. The list of `VBoxBody` instances to iterate is stored in the `bodiesPerBucket` array, which was produced during the write-back phase of the commit, and is accessible through the record. The `cleanUnusedRecordsUpTo` method uses a pool of worker threads to do the actual cleaning work, handing off one record to clean to each thread in the pool.

The algorithm that we presented here does not use counters to keep information about which records are still required. Conversely, it may not eliminate old versions as fast as the previous version and cause memory to be kept for a bit longer than necessary. Overall, it requires more memory to maintain the data structures for the GC.

The biggest improvement provided is that contention is virtually eliminated when starting and finishing a transaction. The only cost that a transaction incurs is related to the cache coherence mechanisms, due to possible invalidations and cache misses that can occur when reading and writing to the shared variables (namely `lastCommittedRecord` and `oldestRequiredRecord`), which is negligible when compared to the previous overhead of atomically updating the counters.

As a side effect, we benefit from transactions that run faster, because now the transaction's thread does not have to spend time doing maintenance cleaning before returning after a commit.

5. Performance evaluation

Our goal is to evaluate the scalability of our lock-free implementation. Additionally, we intend to compare it with some of the top-performing STM implementations, which are blocking. Direct comparison is usually difficult for several reasons, such as the use of different programming languages, customized execution environments, lack of common benchmarks, and others. Fortunately, thanks to the DeuceSTM project [13], there are Java implementations of both the TL2 [6] and the LSA [17] algorithms that can be used out-of-the-box. Therefore, in this section, we present a comparison between TL2 and LSA running in DeuceSTM version 1.3.0, and the lock-free JVSTM.

JVSTM requires each transactional location to have an indirection handler (`VBox`) to the actual data. DeuceSTM does not assume a versioned model, and expects each transactional location to contain the data itself: It does not support the required indirection. As such, we chose not to implement JVSTM in DeuceSTM. Although technically feasible, it would require us to subvert design choices of either DeuceSTM or JVSTM, which we believe would make the comparison less fair. This decision can have significant effects on performance depending on application-specific logic that executes within a transaction, as we will see ahead.

For this evaluation, we considered four benchmarks that are often used to evaluate STM implementations. Three of them are

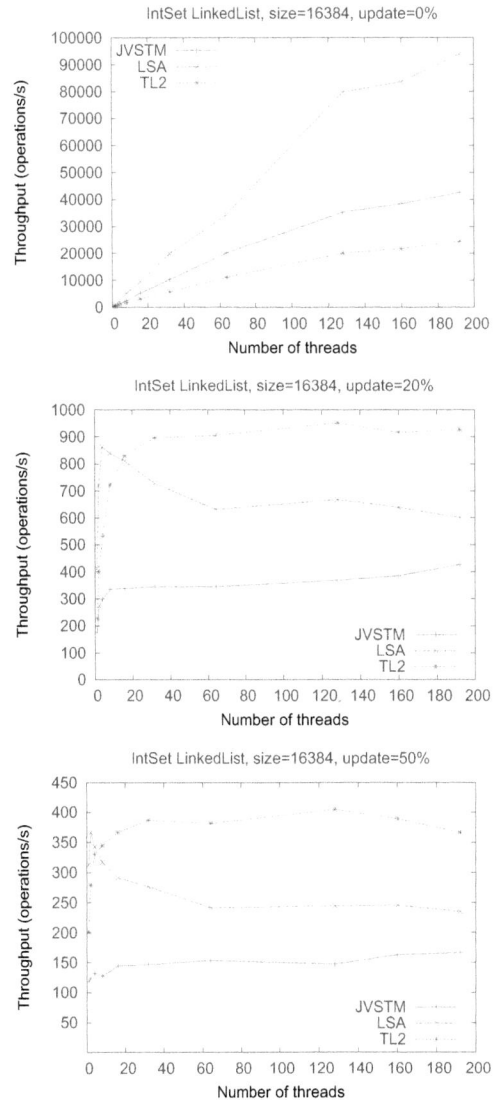

Figure 11. The linked list benchmark.

micro-benchmarks that correspond to three different implementations of integer sets, namely using a linked list, a skip list, and a red-black tree. The common `IntSet` interface supports three operations: insertion, deletion, and search. The fourth benchmark is STMBench7 [10], which simulates the workload of a real-world object-oriented application. This benchmark implements a shared data structure, consisting of a set of graphs and indexes, which models the object structure of complex applications. It supports many different operations, varying from simple to complex. All four benchmarks measure the throughput as the number of operations executed per second. All tests used the runtime optimization for read-only transactions that allows them to skip read-set validation.

The micro-benchmarks were executed on an Azul Systems' Java Appliance with 208 cores, running a custom Java HotSpot(TM) 64-Bit Tiered VM (1.6.0_07-AVM_2.5.0.5-5-product). We run tests up to 192 concurrent transactions. Sadly, we were not able to use the same infrastructure to run the STMBench7. The reason for this is related to the way DeuceSTM works, and the requirements to run it with the STMBench7. In brief, DeuceSTM works by

---

[5] In this case the context C_i must have had `null` in its `oldest-RequiredRecord`.

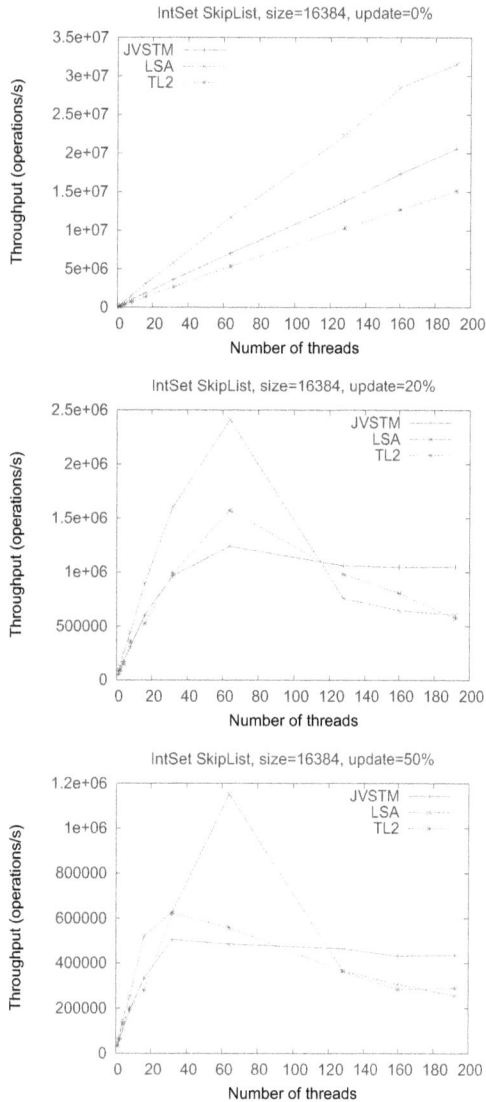

Figure 12. The skip list benchmark.

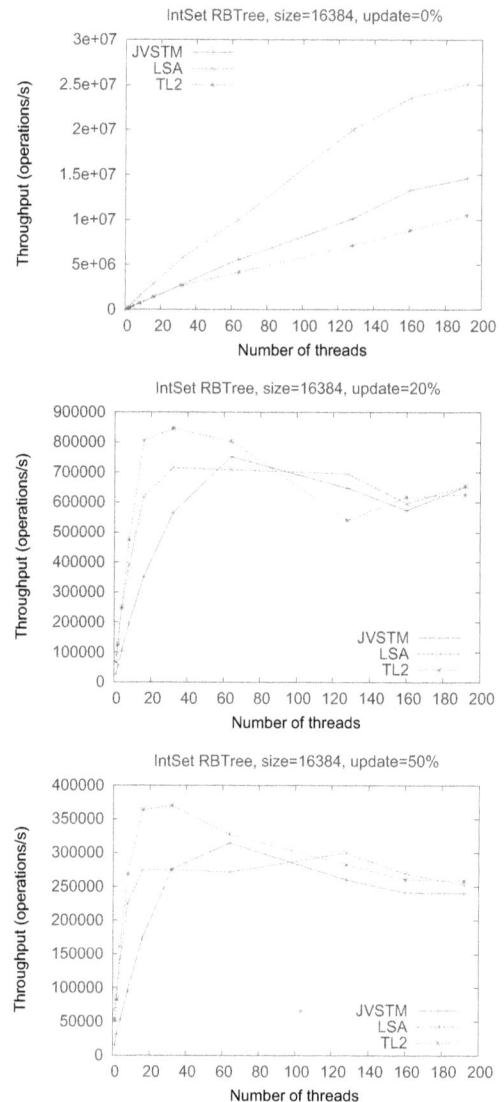

Figure 13. The red-black tree benchmark.

instrumenting the Java bytecode that runs within a transaction. In STMBench7's case, this meant that we had to pre-instrument the Java Runtime classes and start the JVM with the modified runtime (with `-Xbootclasspath/p:deuce_rt.jar` or similar). However, this did not work properly on Azul's Appliance, failing during the execution of the benchmark. For this reason we resorted to another machine with two quad-core Intel Xeon CPUs E5520 with hyper-threading, resulting in 8 cores and 16 hardware threads. We tested using Java HotSpot(TM) 64-Bit Server VM (1.6.0_20-b02) with up to 16 concurrent transactions.

5.1 IntSet micro-benchmarks

For the micro-benchmarks we used a fixed size set with 16K elements in all tests, and changed the ratio of updates. We tested with read-only transactions (only searches, 0% updates), then 20% updates, and, finally 50% updates. The write operations alternated between insertions and deletions, so that the total size of the set was constant over time.

Figures 11, 12, and 13 show the results for the three implementations when running from 1 up to 192 parallel transactions. In

all read-only tests our implementation outperforms TL2, and does worse than LSA. As expected, given the absence of conflicts, all implementations steadily increase the throughput as the number of threads increases, albeit at different rates.

Considering updates, changing the ratio of write-transactions from 20% to 50% reduces the overall throughput in all cases, but does not influence the performance of each STM relative to the others. In general, memory accesses within write transactions are more expensive for JVSTM than DeuceSTM, because, whenever reading any location, JVSTM needs to access the transaction's local write-set first, to search for a transaction-local write, whereas DeuceSTM just gets the value from memory after cheaply ensuring that it is still valid. To a large extent this accounts for the reason why JVSTM does not achieve a higher maximum throughput in write transactions. JVSTM performs the worst in the linked list benchmark, showing approximately 30% of the throughput of LSA and 50% of the throughput of TL2. In the skip list benchmark, JVSTM starts off from behind, but as it keeps a sustained throughput it overtakes the other implementations beyond approximately 120 threads. The throughput of LSA and TL2 spikes at around 60 threads (more no-

STMBench7 (read-dominated workload)

STMBench7 (write-dominated workload)

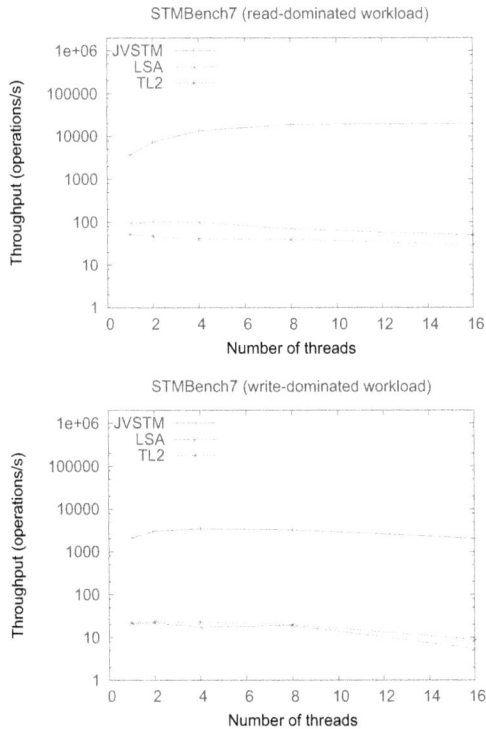

Figure 14. The STMBench7 benchmark.

ticeable in LSA), but then degrades quickly, most probably due to lock contention. In the red-black tree benchmark, all STMs perform similarly, tending to stabilize approximately on the same throughput from 60 threads onward. Overall, our implementation maintains a sustained performance over a growing number of parallel transactions, whereas the lock-based versions have higher throughput but then break for higher thread counts.

For these three micro-benchmarks the amount of code executed within each transaction is very small, and the transactions only need to manipulate the set's data structure. This causes the transactional locations managed by either STM to be the same. The next benchmark will provide a different setting.

5.2 STMBench7 benchmark

The transactions in STMBench7 vary, spanning from simple to complex manipulations of the objects, with this benchmark performing much more application logic than the micro-benchmarks. We tested with three workloads: read-dominated, read-write and write-dominated, which correspond to an increasing number of write operations. In all three cases the structural modifications and long traversals were disabled. We present the results for this benchmark in Figure 14. Here, notice that the vertical axes use a logarithmic scale. Given the space restrictions, we omit the results for the read-write workload, which are identical to the write-dominated workload. The JVSTM completely dominates the results, showing a throughput hundredfold that of LSA and TL2. As before, throughput decreases when increasing the percentage of writes.

Over-instrumentation is most likely the main reason why Deuce-STM looses performance in STMBench7. Each transaction of STMBench7 contains much more application logic that does computation with the data read than the micro-benchmarks do. Over-instrumentation results from DeuceSTM not being able to tell what is important for the transaction and what is not (e.g. access to values local to a transaction). In JVSTM, it is up to the programmer to

identify the transactional memory locations (by wrapping them in VBoxes), which allows for a much finer control of what needs to be transactional.

There are additional reasons that contribute for this huge gap in performance. For one, the fact that with JVSTM we can provide transactional implementations for the containers required by the benchmark, whereas DeuceSTM needs to instrument the entire Java Runtime. Another reason it that STMBench7 executes many conflicting operations that manipulate the same shared objects. This necessarily causes contention when validating object accesses, either during a transaction or at commit time, and transactions may have to spend time waiting for a lock until they can decide whether they performed valid accesses. Conversely, our lock-free implementation does not prevent forward progress of the system as a whole, and allows for fast restarts in case of conflict, because validation is performed completely in parallel.

6. Discussion and related work

Even though the initial proposals for STMs used nonblocking designs (from lock-free to obstruction-free), their implementation presented large overheads, making them less performing in practice than simpler blocking designs [7]. So, most, if not all, of the most recent and current top-performing STMs block some threads to ensure exclusive access to some critical region during certain operations (e.g., TL2 [6], RingSTM [20], TinySTM [8], NOrec [5], McRT-STM [18]), typically the commit operation.

The original JVSTM followed a similar approach, using a global lock to ensure exclusive access to the commit operation of write transactions. Unlike other approaches, however, in the JVSTM read-only transactions do not use any locks, and they are wait-free. Using a single global lock has the advantage of being simple to implement and very fast when the lock is uncontended, but has the disadvantage, as we discussed already, of preventing concurrent commits that could proceed in parallel because the committing transactions accessed unrelated data.

STMs such as TL2 allow such concurrent commits by acquiring locks for all the transactional locations accessed by the transaction (and later releasing them once the commit is concluded), but this approach has overheads that are typically proportional to the size of the read-set (R) plus the size of the write-set (W). Another problem of these blocking designs is the duration of the critical region, which depends on what needs to be done within that region. The original JVSTM validates the transaction and does the write-back of the write-set with the lock held, thereby spending time that is proportional to $R + W$ in the critical region. Likewise for TL2 that needs to validate the transaction after acquiring the locks. The LSA algorithm proposed in [17] can be applied to either blocking or non-blocking STMs. We found an implementation that is obstruction-free [1], whereas the one available in DeuceSTM is actually blocking.

Our new commit algorithm allows for concurrent commits without incurring into the overheads of acquiring locks. In our design, validation is lock-free and is performed by each thread individually, racing for a position in the commit queue. The write-back phase imposes ordered writes among the committing transactions, with transactions that have a lower version number having to be committed first, but a transaction does not block waiting for other transactions to finish. Instead, transactions help to write-back other transactions that are ahead of them, thus accelerating the commit of older transactions. The write-back phase follows a wait-free algorithm.

NOrec [5] uses a lock-free validation mechanism similar to ours, but it does not allow any concurrent commits, thus limiting scalability. RingSTM [20], on the other hand, supports concurrent commits, but only insofar as the write-sets do not overlap. If this occurs, the committing transactions have to write-back serially, and there is no helping mechanism installed.

The design of our helping mechanism allows us to dispense with more expensive locking behavior, because it maintains the sequential ordering of the write-back of all valid transactions. Besides, it maintains intact the properties of the original JVSTM design in what regards read-only transactions, as well as the behavior of reads and writes to transactional locations during the execution of a transaction. There are other proposed STM designs that include helping mechanisms, but they incur performance penalties in the reads. In [9] a transaction that reads may need to help other transactions that are writing to that location, before it can know the value. In [15] the entire read-set is validated every time a new record is accessed.

To the best of our knowledge, our commit algorithm is unique in this regard, being the first to use helping to reduce the time of the commit of a transaction, by doing the commit of a single transaction concurrently by as many cores as those available to commit on the system.

The problem of garbage collecting unused versions is seldom addressed in the context of STMs, perhaps because the most common STMs do not support multi-versioning. In [16] the authors show that no STM can be optimal in the number of previous versions kept. In fact, JVSTM may keep more versions than are actually required. Such can occur, e.g., when a long-running transaction is still running with an old version, and there have already been many updates to the same object. This will cause JVSTM to keep many versions of the same location, until the old transaction finishes and allows for record cleaning, whereas, in fact, the only versions required could simply be the oldest and the newest versions of the object, because no other transaction was running at the moment. However, and contrary to what is stated in [16], JVSTM is MV-permissive, because it keeps all versions that any running transaction may require. This holds true for both the previous garbage collection algorithm and the new one.

7. Conclusion

In face of the widespread growth of parallel computational power, the concern for the development of scalable applications is gaining relevance. In this paper we have presented a new scalable and efficient lock-free commit algorithm for the JVSTM, which shows performance comparable to, and sometimes better than, other top-performing blocking STMs. We have also presented a new lock-free algorithm for the garbage collection of unused versions, which eliminates the contention that existed in the shared counters used by the previous garbage collector.

Because we had access to a test machine with a high number of real cores, we were able to obtain results that provide high levels of confidence about the real scalability of the algorithms. We are confident on their ability to scale to an even higher number of cores and we expect, in the future, to be able to experimentally confirm this assumption. Regarding the effects on the overall performance of applications, there were mixed results especially among the micro-benchmarks, showing that execution patterns and domain-specific logic can have a great influence on the outcome.

Acknowledgments

We wish to thank Azul Systems and Dr. Cliff Click for giving us access to the hardware on which we could run some of the tests presented in this paper. We also acknowledge the reviewers' insightful comments, which have helped us to improve the final version of the paper.

References

[1] LSA-STM project home page. http://tmware.org/lsastm.

[2] J. Cachopo. *Development of Rich Domain Models with Atomic Actions*. PhD thesis, Instituto Superior Técnico, Universidade Técnica de Lisboa, 2007.

[3] J. Cachopo and A. Rito-Silva. Versioned boxes as the basis for memory transactions. *Sci. Comput. Program.*, 63(2):172–185, 2006.

[4] N. Carvalho, J. Cachopo, L. Rodrigues, and A. Rito-Silva. Versioned transactional shared memory for the FénixEDU web application. In *WDDDM '08: Proceedings of the 2nd workshop on Dependable distributed data management*, pages 15–18, New York, NY, USA, 2008. ACM.

[5] L. Dalessandro, M. F. Spear, and M. L. Scott. NOrec: Streamlining STM by abolishing ownership records. In *PPoPP '10: Proc. 15th ACM Symp. on Principles and Practice of Parallel Programming*, jan 2010.

[6] D. Dice, O. Shalev, and N. Shavit. Transactional locking II. In *DISC '06: Proc. 20th International Symposium on Distributed Computing*, pages 194–208, sep 2006. Springer-Verlag Lecture Notes in Computer Science volume 4167.

[7] R. Ennals. Efficient software transactional memory. Technical Report IRC-TR-05-051, Intel Research Cambridge Tech Report, Jan 2005.

[8] P. Felber, C. Fetzer, and T. Riegel. Dynamic performance tuning of word-based software transactional memory. In *PPoPP '08: Proc. 13th ACM SIGPLAN Symposium on Principles and practice of parallel programming*, pages 237–246, feb 2008.

[9] K. Fraser and T. Harris. Concurrent programming without locks. *ACM Trans. Comput. Syst.*, 25(2):5, 2007.

[10] R. Guerraoui, M. Kapalka, and J. Vitek. Stmbench7: A benchmark for software transactional memory. In *EuroSys '07: Proceedings of the 2nd ACM SIGOPS/EuroSys European Conference on Computer Systems 2007*, pages 315–324, New York, NY, USA, 2007. ACM.

[11] M. Herlihy. Wait-free synchronization. *ACM Trans. Program. Lang. Syst.*, 13(1):124–149, 1991.

[12] M. Herlihy and J. E. B. Moss. Transactional memory: architectural support for lock-free data structures. In *ISCA '93: Proceedings of the 20th annual international symposium on Computer architecture*, pages 289–300, New York, NY, USA, 1993. ACM.

[13] G. Korland, N. Shavit, and P. Felber. Noninvasive concurrency with Java STM. In *MultiProg 2010: Third Workshop on Programmability Issues for Multi-Core Computers*, 2010.

[14] J. Manson, W. Pugh, and S. V. Adve. The Java memory model. In *POPL '05: Proceedings of the 32nd ACM SIGPLAN-SIGACT symposium on Principles of programming languages*, pages 378–391, New York, NY, USA, 2005. ACM.

[15] V. J. Marathe and M. Moir. Toward high performance nonblocking software transactional memory. In *PPoPP '08: Proceedings of the 13th ACM SIGPLAN Symposium on Principles and practice of parallel programming*, pages 227–236, New York, NY, USA, 2008. ACM.

[16] D. Perelman, R. Fan, and I. Keidar. On maintaining multiple versions in STM. In *PODC '10: Proceedings of the 29th ACM symposium on Principles of Distributed Computing*, July 2010.

[17] T. Riegel, P. Felber, and C. Fetzer. A lazy snapshot algorithm with eager validation. In *Proceedings of the 20th International Symposium on Distributed Computing, DISC 2006*, volume 4167 of *Lecture Notes in Computer Science*, pages 284–298. Springer, Sep 2006. ISBN 3-540-44624-9.

[18] B. Saha, A.-R. Adl-Tabatabai, R. L. Hudson, C. C. Minh, and B. Hertzberg. McRT-STM: A high performance software transactional memory system for a multi-core runtime. In *Proceedings of the 11th Symposium on Principles and Practice of Parallel Programming*, pages 187–197. ACM Press, 2006.

[19] N. Shavit and D. Touitou. Software transactional memory. In *Proceedings of the 14th Annual ACM Symposium on Principles of Distributed Computing*, pages 204–213. ACM Press, 1995.

[20] M. F. Spear, M. M. Michael, and C. von Praun. RingSTM: scalable transactions with a single atomic instruction. In *SPAA '08: Proc. twentieth annual symposium on Parallelism in algorithms and architectures*, pages 275–284, jun 2008.

Enhanced Speculative Parallelization Via Incremental Recovery

Chen Tian, Changhui Lin, Min Feng, Rajiv Gupta

University of California, CSE Department, Riverside, CA 92521

{tianc, linc, mfeng, gupta}@cs.ucr.edu

Abstract

The widespread availability of multicore systems has led to an increased interest in speculative parallelization of sequential programs using software-based thread level speculation. Many of the proposed techniques are implemented via *state separation* where non-speculative computation state is maintained separately from the speculative state of threads performing speculative computations. If speculation is successful, the results from speculative state are committed to non-speculative state. However, upon misspeculation, *discard-all* scheme is employed in which speculatively computed results of a thread are discarded and the computation is performed again. While this scheme is simple to implement, one disadvantage of *discard-all* is its inability to tolerate high misspeculation rates due to its high runtime overhead. Thus, it is not suitable for use in applications where misspeculation rates are input dependent and therefore may reach high levels.

In this paper we develop an approach for *incremental recovery* in which, instead of discarding all of the results and reexecuting the speculative computation in its entirety, the computation is restarted from the earliest point at which a misspeculation causing value is read. This approach has two advantages. First, the cost of recovery is reduced as only part of the computation is reexecuted. Second, since recovery takes less time, the likelihood of future misspeculations is reduced. We design and implement a strategy for implementing incremental recovery that allows results of partial computations to be efficiently saved and reused. For a set of programs where misspeculation rate is input dependent, our experiments show that with inputs that result in misspeculation rates of around 40% and 80%, applying incremental recovery technique results in 1.2x-3.3x and 2.0x-6.6x speedups respectively over the discard-all recovery scheme. Furthermore, misspeculations observed during discard-all scheme are reduced when incremental recovery is employed – reductions range from 10% to 85%.

Categories and Subject Descriptors D.3.4 [*Programming Languages*]: Processors—Compilers, Optimization

General Terms Performance, Languages, Design, Experimentation

Keywords Speculative Parallelization, Incremental Recovery, Multicore Processors

PPoPP'11, February 12–16, 2011, San Antonio, Texas, USA.
Copyright © 2011 ACM 978-1-4503-0119-0/11/02...$10.00

1. Introduction

Exploiting loop level parallelism is critical to improving the performance of sequential applications on multicore processors. However, many sequential loops cannot be parallelized via static analysis based parallelization techniques due to the presence of cross-iteration dependences. However, it has been observed that in many applications such dependences, although potentially present, rarely manifest themselves at runtime and thus despite the presence of cross-iteration dependences these loops are a significant source of parallelism [5, 15, 37]. To exploit such parallelism, speculative parallelization has been proposed that employs *thread level speculation* (TLS) to optimistically extract and exploit parallelism. The compiler first assumes the absence of cross-iteration dependences so that the sequential loops can be optimistically parallelized. When the speculatively parallelized program is executed, the runtime system or specialized hardware is used to detect misspeculation (i.e., manifestation of ignored dependences) and recover from it. While hardware based TLS has been extensively researched, the specialized hardware structures (e.g., versioning cache [8], versioning memory [7] etc.) on which such techniques rely have not been incorporated in commercial multicore processors. On the other hand, software-based TLS has also drawn attention of researchers and the advantage of this approach is that it can be used to take advantage of multicore systems available today.

Software TLS uses runtime systems to detect misspeculations and recover from them. However, the overhead imposed by the runtime system must be reduced so that benefits of parallelism can be realized. Many of the prior works on software TLS rely on *state separation* where non-speculative computation state is maintained separately from speculative state of threads that perform speculative computation and thus recovery from misspeculation can be performed by simply *discarding* speculative state [5, 13, 35–38]. All of these works have demonstrated the benefits of software TLS for applications in which misspeculation events are infrequent (typically a few percent). As misspeculation rate rises, the benefits of parallelism quickly evaporate due to the high recovery cost. This is a serious problem in context of applications where the misspeculation rate is *input dependent* as illustrated next.

We identified five applications in which the misspeculation rate is input dependent. Figure 1 shows the performance of these five programs for inputs which result in low (around 1%), medium (around 40%), and high (around 80%) misspeculation rates. The speedups are measured in comparison to execution time of the sequential version of the application and it is for the case where 4 cores are available for executing speculative threads. As we can see, for medium and high misspeculation rates mostly execution slow down is observed (i.e., speedup is less than 1). While prior works have applied speculative parallelization to these applications, they have only considered inputs with low misspeculation rates to illustrate the benefits. However, since the performance is a function of input characteristics, it is unclear as to whether or not employing

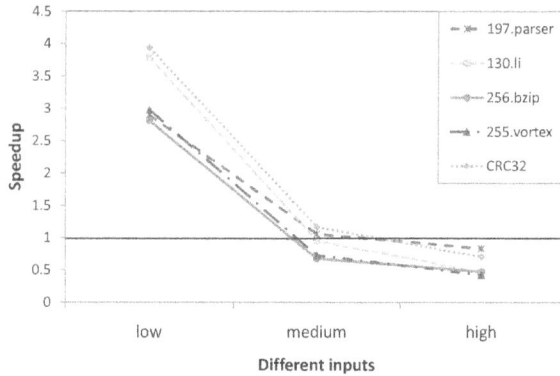

Figure 1. Misspeculation Rate vs. Performance.

speculative parallelization would result in benefit or loss. To overcome this problem, in this paper, we develop an approach which performs well even when misspeculation rates are medium to high. Thus, speculative parallelization can be applied no matter the nature of inputs.

The fundamental reason for the performance loss is that when a misspeculation occurs, all speculatively computed results are assumed to be incorrect and hence discarded. Thus, recovery is expensive as the speculative computation must be repeated in its entirety. We will refer to this strategy as *discard-all*. Some other works employ rollback to recover from misspeculation [15, 18, 21]. The rollback cost is minimized by having the programmer exploit application specific knowledge in providing the rollback code. While state separation has been fully automated, the rollback approach relies on the programmer to provide rollback code. *The goal of this paper is to extend the fully automated approach of state separation so that it can handle high misspeculation rates.*

We have observed that although *discard-all* strategy is simple to implement, it is also wasteful. To recover from misspeculation, it is often necessary to only reexecute part of the computation. This is because while many values may be speculatively read by the speculative computation, the misspeculation may be caused by only some or even by only one of these values. Therefore a significant part of the computation need not be reexecuted, only part of the computation that is dependent on the misspeculation causing value needs to be rexecuted. Based on this observation, this paper presents an approach for *Incremental Recovery* that mitigates the performance loss caused by misspeculation recovery. The *incremental recovery* strategy has two advantages. First, the cost of recovery is reduced as only part of the computation is reexecuted. Second, since recovery takes less time, the likelihood of future misspeculations is reduced. While the benefits of *incremental recovery* are clear, designing an efficient implementation of this strategy is a challenge. We develop an implementation of *incremental recovery* as a natural extension of state separation which allows results of partial computations to be efficiently saved and reused. Our experiments show that *incremental recovery* often yields speedups where *discard-all* produces slowdowns. The key contributions of this work are:

- We demonstrate that there are two benefits of incremental recovery. First, the cost of recovery is lower as only part of the speculative computation needs to be reexecuted when a misspeculation is encountered. Second, faster recovery reduces the likelihood of future misspeculations. We observe that both these factors play a significant role in performance improvement.

- We present the design and implementation of an efficient software based incremental recovery algorithm that allows partial results of a speculative computation to be saved and reused

upon misspeculation. The key feature of this implementation is that it simply extends the use of state separation that is already used to implement thread level speculation.

- For a set of programs, our experiments show that even with inputs that result in high misspeculation rates of around 40% and 80%, applying incremental recovery technique can achieve 1.2x-3.3x and 2.0x-6.6x speedups respectively in comparison to the discard-all recovery scheme. Misspeculations during discard-all are reduced by 10% to 85% by incremental recovery.

The rest of the paper is organized as follows. Section 2 describes background on state separation based thread level speculation. Section 3 provides an overview of our approach for incremental recovery. Section 4 develops an efficient implementation of incremental recovery. The experimental results are presented in Section 5. Sections 6 and 7 discuss related work and present conclusions.

2. Background

State Separation. Many prior research works have used State Separation for realizing software based TLS (SS-TLS) [5, 13, 35–38]. State separation causes the non-speculative state of the computation to be maintained separately from the speculative states of parallel computations being performed speculatively (e.g., loop iterations). The first implementation of state separation proposed in [5, 13] creates processes to perform speculative computations – since each process has its own address space, state separation is achieved. Another implementation of state separation, CorD, was proposed by us in [37] and further used in [35, 36, 38]. In this implementation multiple threads that operate is separate portions of the application's address space are used. In addition to parallel threads that perform speculative computations, a main thread is used to coordinate their activities. In particular, the main thread assigns speculative computations to parallel threads, speculatively *copies-in* data into the memories allocated to parallel threads, checks for misspeculations, and if no misspeculation occurs it *copies-out* the speculatively computed results from memories of parallel threads to the memory allocated to hold the non-speculative computation state. Figure 2 summarizes how state separation is achieved in CorD. In this paper we build upon the thread based CorD model because thread based parallelization involves less runtime overhead than process based implementation of state separation.

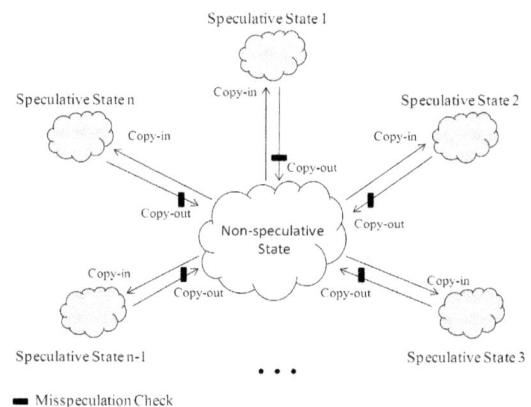

Figure 2. Computation State Under SS-TLS.

Discard-all Recovery. The advantage of using state separation to support speculative execution is the low overhead of handling misspeculations. Since each thread has its own space, updates to the same variable by different threads are performed on its copies in

190

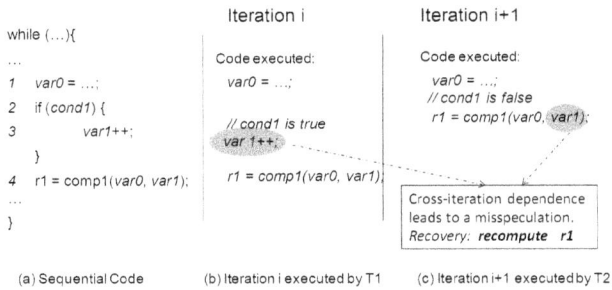

Figure 3. An Example Of Misspeculation Detection And Recovery Using Discard-all In SS-TLS.

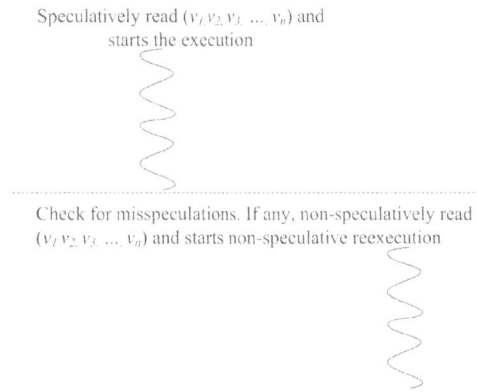

Figure 4. Discard-all Recovery in SS-TLS.

different spaces, and thus non-speculative state memory is not affected by any of the parallel threads. Once a misspeculation is detected, the speculatively computed results can be simply discarded and recomputed. Figure 3 illustrates the above using an example. In Figure 3(a) we can see that the sequential loop has a possible cross-iteration dependence due to variable *var1* (dependence is between lines 3 and 4). Suppose this loop is speculatively parallelized and executed by two threads T1 and T2. If *var1* is updated in iteration *i*, the value of *var1* used by T2, which is executing iteration *i+1*, is wrong, because T2 optimistically assumes no cross-iteration dependences will manifest themselves. This dependence leads to a misspeculation and can be captured by the SS-TLS runtime system. To recover from this misspeculation, the system only needs to ask T2 to *discard* the value of *r1* that was speculatively computed, and now non-speculatively reexecute the entire iteration with the latest value of *var1*.

3. Incremental Recovery

Motivation. In SS-TLS, recovery from misspeculations is achieved by discarding all speculatively computed results. This process is shown in Figure 4. Before starting speculative execution of a computation (e.g., a loop iteration), the input values or *live-ins* needed for its execution are speculatively read from non-speculative state and copied into the speculative state for the thread. The reads of values $(v_1, v_2, v_3, \ldots v_n)$ are speculative because the values are read while execution of one or more earlier iterations is in progress; if any of these values is changed by these earlier iterations, then misspeculation occurs. After reading, the computation is performed and then the misspeculation check is executed. If the check fails, misspeculation occurs. To recover from misspeculation, the values of *live-ins* are now read again, this time non-speculatively, and the entire computation is repeated. This strategy for recovery is called *discard-all* as all results computed are discarded and computation is performed again in its entirety. It should be noted that even if the misspeculation occurs due to *any* one of the live-ins, *all* results are discarded. While this approach is simple to implement, discarding all speculatively computed results is a suboptimal solution. It is possible that a subset of speculatively computed results may be correct and thus there may not be a need to perform the entire computation again. Discarding all results can be very wasteful, especially when the misspeculation rate is relatively high because the cost of recovery begins to add up. However, under the above model we lack the ability to identify the part of the computation that need not be reexecuted.

It is worth noting that one update by a thread may cause multiple misspeculations. If *n* parallel threads are simultaneously executing *n* consecutive loop iterations, then misspeculation can occur in *n-1* threads due to a cross-iteration dependence between the first iteration and *n-1* later iterations. In other words, the first thread may update the value of a variable that acts as a live-in variable

for *n-1* later iterations. This is another reason why the overhead of misspeculation can accumulate to significantly high levels leading to net slowdowns from parallelization as opposed to speedups.

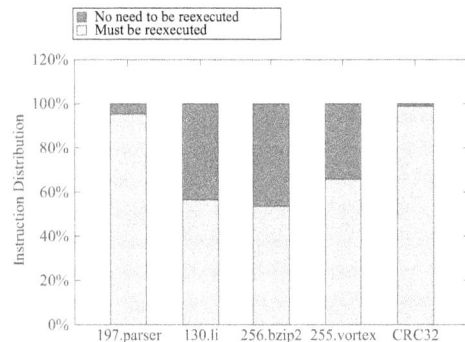

Figure 5. Wasteful Work by Discard-all Recovery.

Figure 5 shows the total waste during the recoveries from a misspeculations for five programs. The waste is measured in terms of the number of instructions. In particular, when a live-in variable is updated in an iteration, we measure the average percentage of instructions that are directly or indirectly dependent upon the updated value within the next iteration. Since an update of a live-in variable usually leads to misspeculations, these instructions have to be reexecuted during the recovery. The remainder of the instructions are the ones that do not depend upon any updated value. Therefore, there is no need to reexecute them. From the figure, we can see that over 40% instructions are not affected when a live-in variable is updated in the preceding iteration. In the case of `197.parser` and `CRC32`, less than 5% instructions are affected. This means the results calculated by more than 95% instructions are still correct even if a cross-iteration dependence arises and it is unnecessary to reexecute the entire iteration.

Our Approach. Motivated by the above study we explore the design of an incremental recovery scheme. There are two key characteristics that must be considered in designing a recovery scheme:

1. First is the *granularity* at which reuse is supported – the finer the granularity the greater is the amount of reuse that can be achieved; and

2. Second is the *complexity* of the scheme that identifies what subset of computation can be reused during recovery.

As the granularity becomes finer, the degree of reuse increases but so does the complexity of identifying subcomputation that can be reused. An incremental recovery scheme that works at the granularity of a single instruction will provide maximum reuse but will have the highest complexity. On the other extreme is the *discard-all* scheme which the simplest but does not allow any reuse.

Next we present our approach that balances the granularity and complexity. Therefore it allows significant amount of computation to be reused during recovery while at the same time it lends itself to an efficient implementation. As shown in Figure 6, we delineate the computation into many sections according to the points at which the *earliest reads* of the *live-ins* are encountered. In the figure we assume that the first speculative read of v_i appears before the first speculative read of v_{i+1} for all i. Therefore, the live-ins $(v_1, v_2, \cdots v_n)$ cause the computation to be divided into $n + 1$ sections. Now let us assume that of all the values among $(v_1, v_2, \cdots v_n)$ that cause misspeculation, v_i is the one that is read the earliest. In this case we can be sure that the entire computation performed by the sections of code preceding the first read of v_i can be reused. Thus, the recovery can be performed by simply repeating the execution of code starting from the point at which v_i was first read. If v_i happens to be v_1, the reuse achieved is minimum. On the other hand, if v_i happens to be v_n, the reuse is the maximum.

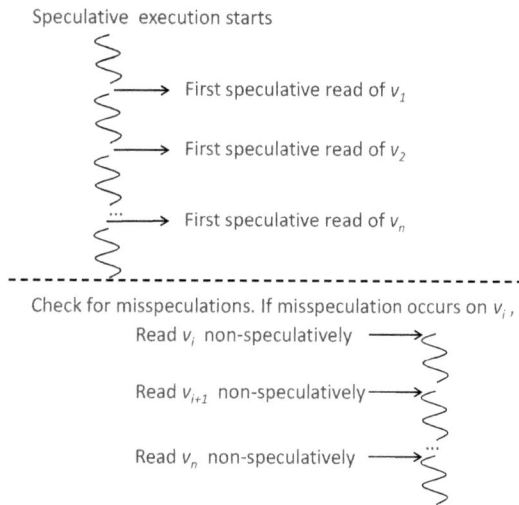

Figure 6. Incremental Recovery in SS-TLS.

To implement the above strategy, we must address the problem of implementing *computation reuse*. The approach we take restores the speculative state of a parallel thread to the point at which it must begin execution during recovery. For example, in Figure 6, the speculative state must be restored to the point that immediately precedes the instruction that represents the *first read* of v_i. We can implement this restoration simply by using the capability of state separation that is already available as follows. At each point that represents a potential first read of a speculative value, i.e. a value from $(v_1, v_2, \ldots v_n)$, we create a new version of the speculative state. In other words, the speculatively computed results generated by each of the executed sections of code in Figure 6 are separated from each other. The misspeculation check is performed in the order the first reads are performed and the first read that causes misspeculation is found. The state prior to this point is available and serves as the basis for performing execution of recovery code.

Thus the key idea we use is to decouple the creation of a parallel thread that performs speculative execution from the creation of the speculative space that it uses for saving results. At each point which represents a first read of a speculative value, a *new version* or *copy* of the speculative space is created. Figure 7 illustrates the idea. Figure 7 shows a parallel thread that creates three speculative spaces

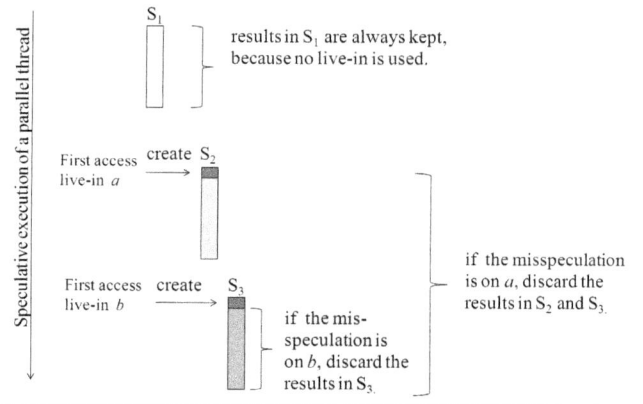

Figure 7. Decoupling Space Allocation From Thread Creation.

S_1, S_2, and S_3 instead of just one space during the speculative execution. Space S_2 is created when the first access of live-in variable a is encountered, and S_3 is created when the first access of live-in variable b is encountered. If a misspeculation is found to have occurred due to a, the results stored in S_2 and S_3 are discarded and recomputed using the correct value of a. However, if the misspeculation is caused by b, only the results in S_3 are recomputed. The results in S_1 are only computed once and are never discarded during recovery because the computation does not use any speculative variable.

Impact of Incremental Recovery on Misspeculation Rate. So far we have discussed one direct benefit of incremental recovery, i.e. reusing previously performed computation to reduce the code reexecuted during recovery. Besides this benefit, the incremental recovery technique has another advantage – it reduces the misspeculation rate. In SS-TLS, variables modified by a parallel thread are stored in the corresponding speculative state. Prior works have shown that copy-in operation of a variable should be performed when the variable is about to be modified, since it can avoid unnecessary copying [36]. If the access to a variable is a read, then the parallel thread can directly read the value from non-speculative state. This is known as copy-on-write scheme, and has been discussed and used in most existing SS-TLS systems [5, 36, 37]. When such scheme is combined with our incremental recovery technique, misspeculation rates can be reduced. Figure 8 illustrates the reason.

Figure 8(a) shows the original recovery scheme. Suppose two iterations i and j are executed in parallel and variable *var* is speculatively updated in iteration i and used in j. Further assume the update to *var* is incorrect due to the presence of some other cross-iteration dependence (step 1). As a result, a misspeculation is detected for the thread that is executing iteration i (step 2). To recover, this thread has to recompute everything including the value of *var* (step 3) and then commit the correct results (step 5). If the value of *var* is ever read by the thread executing iteration j before the results of iteration i are committed (step 4), then a misspeculation certainly occurs (step 6).

Figure 8(b) shows the situation where incremental recovery is used. The thread executing iteration i still encounters a misspeculation and has to recompute the value of *var*. However, during the recovery if we only recompute the values that were incorrectly computed earlier, then the recovery time is smaller and the results can be committed much faster (step 4). Consequently, the chance of reading the correct value of *var* in a later iteration is significantly increased (step 5) and the misspeculation that had happened before can now be avoided as shown (step 6).

(a) Without Incremental Recovery   (b) With Incremental Recovery

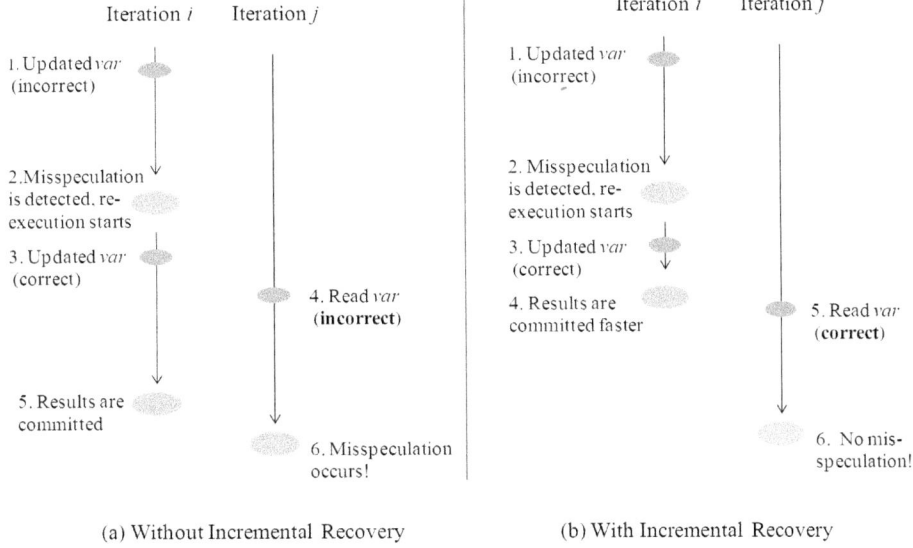

Figure 8. The Effect Of Reducing Misspeculation Rate.

4. Realization of Incremental Recovery

4.1 Creating Multiple Subspaces

Previous section shows that to decouple the space allocation from thread creation, a new subspace must be created when a speculative value is first read. There are different ways to create subspaces. One simple scheme is to dynamically allocate a contiguous memory region (e.g., through *malloc* call) as shown in Figure 9(a). However, repeated allocation of subspaces may cause allocation to eventually fail when the size of subspace is very large. This is because the memory allocator may not find a free memory chunk of the requested size. This situation gets worse with the increase in the number of parallel threads.

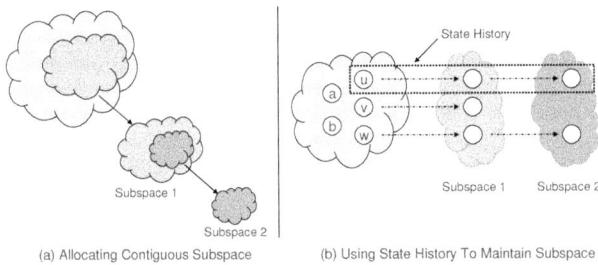

(a) Allocating Contiguous Subspace   (b) Using State History To Maintain Subspace

Figure 9. Allocating A Subspace.

To address this problem, we propose to maintain subspaces by using the *state history* for each variable. In particular, the state of an individual variable in a particular subspace is represented as a pair of a *space identifier* (SID) and the variable's value. A SID is a unique integer assigned to each subspace created by the same thread. The states of each variable are linked together in ascending order of space creation time as shown in Figure 9(b). With this scheme, each subspace is not physically contiguous any more. Updating a variable in a different subspace can be simply implemented by adding a (SID, value) pair into this variable's state history. For example, in Figure 9(b), variable u and w have two different values in subspaces 1 and 2 respectively while v is only updated in subspace 1. Thus, subspace 1 is the one that contains all the three variables, subspace 2 only contains u and w. Since the values of variables a and b are not affected by speculative values, these variables do not exist in any subspace. The benefit of this approach is that the memory allocated is greatly reduced. Moreover, the memory allocation requests are now at the granularity of variable's size and hence more variables can be handled.

Since each subspace is identified by a SID, each thread maintains a thread local variable *current* SID (CSID) to represent the latest subspace that has been created. When a speculative value is first read, a new subspace is created. The creation can be simply implemented as an increment of CSID. All variables that are defined directly or indirectly using a speculative value are copied into the new subspace. These operations are implemented through live-in access checks and statement transformations as shown in Figure 10.

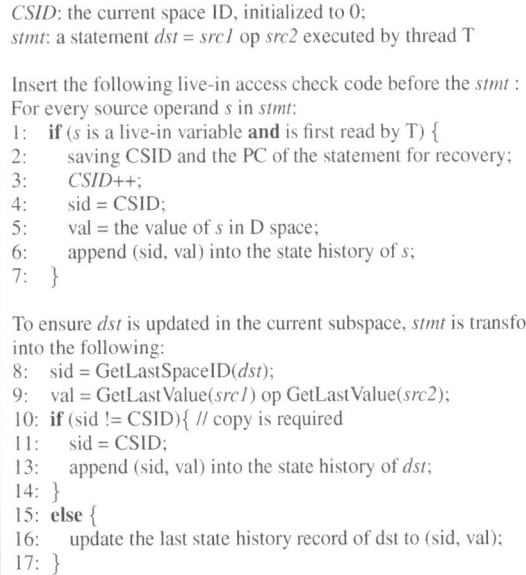

CSID: the current space ID, initialized to 0;
stmt: a statement *dst = src1 op src2* executed by thread T

Insert the following live-in access check code before the *stmt* :
For every source operand *s* in *stmt*:
1:   **if** (*s* is a live-in variable **and** is first read by T) {
2:      saving CSID and the PC of the statement for recovery;
3:      *CSID*++;
4:      sid = CSID;
5:      val = the value of *s* in D space;
6:      append (sid, val) into the state history of *s*;
7:   }

To ensure *dst* is updated in the current subspace, *stmt* is transformed into the following:
8:   sid = GetLastSpaceID(*dst*);
9:   val = GetLastValue(*src1*) op GetLastValue(*src2*);
10: **if** (sid != CSID){ // copy is required
11:     sid = CSID;
13:     append (sid, val) into the state history of *dst*;
14: }
15: **else** {
16:     update the last state history record of dst to (sid, val);
17: }

Figure 10. Live-in Access Checks And Statement Transformation.

From Figure 10, one can see that the live-in access check code is inserted preceding each statement. For each source operand that

193

is a live-in variable and is first read by a speculative thread T (line 1), a new subspace is created by incrementing *CSID* by 1 (line 3). As a result, each subspace corresponds to a speculative use of one live-in variable, and later created space has a larger space ID. The old CSID and the PC of current statement are stored and are used if the recovery is needed at this point (line 2). The live-in variable is also copied into this new subspace by appending the pair of CSID and the variable's value in the non-speculative state into its state history (lines 4-6). Thus, the ID of the subspace created for a live-in variable and the speculatively-read value of the live-in are always stored in the first record of this live-in variable's state history.

To update the destination operand *dst*, its subspace ID is first computed (line 8) and the updated value is computed using the latest values of its sources operands (line 9). Since the update has to be performed on the current subspace, the space ID of *dst* is compared with CSID (line 10). If they are different, the *(sid, val)* pair is appended into *dst*'s state history. Otherwise, the last record in the state history is updated with the new pair *(sid, val)*. Function *GetLastSpaceID()* and *GetLastValue()* are auxiliary functions which retrieve the space ID and value respectively from the last record in a variable's state history.

Besides the live-in access checks and statement transformation performed during speculative execution, a mechanism also needs to be developed to identify the live-in variables that are accessed during speculative execution. This is important because the values of live-in variables are the ones that require validation and copy-out operations after parallel threads finish their executions. Therefore, a *live-in table* is maintained for each parallel thread to track the live-ins accessed by the thread. The table has 3 fields as shown below.

NonSpecAddr	SpecAddr	WriteFlag

When a live-in variable is first accessed by a parallel thread T, an entry for this variable is created in the table. The *NonSpecAddr* field and *SpecAddr* field contain the live-in variable's non-speculative address and speculative address respectively. The *WriteFlag* field shows whether the live-in has been ever updated during speculative execution. Once a write access to this variable is encountered, this field is set to true. Subspaces and the live-in table are maintained during the speculative execution; they are crucial for performing the misspeculation detection and copy-out operations which will be described in the next two subsections.

4.2 Handling Speculative Results

After a parallel thread finishes its task, the main thread needs to perform misspeculation check to validate the speculatively computed results. If the speculation succeeds, the results are copied back to the non-speculative state. Otherwise, recovery procedure is initiated so that the correct values can be recomputed. In our approach, the results computed by parallel threads are handled in the same order as the order in which the tasks assigned to them were created. The in-order result-handling ensures the updates to non-speculative state memory is consistent with the sequential program semantics.

A misspeculation occurs if a speculatively read live-in variable has been updated during an earlier speculative task. On the other hand, if a parallel thread updates a live-in variable, then all other parallel threads that are using this variable to perform later tasks should be considered as failed because they are using an incorrect value. Based on this idea, a scheme is developed for the main thread to perform the copy-out operations and misspeculation checks. This scheme is presented in Figure 11.

Copy-out. Each parallel thread has a flag *SpecFail* indicating if its speculation has failed. When a parallel thread finishes its speculative task and the main thread determines that it is this thread's turn to commit its results, this flag is examined. If the flag indicates that no misspeculation occurred (line 1), the main thread

---

```
T.LTable: live-in table of a parallel thread T;
T.SepcFail: the flag indicating a failed speculation of T;
T.FailedAt[ ]: the live-in variables which cause the
speculation of thread T to fail;

1:    if (T.SpecFail != True) {
2:        foreach entry e in T.Ltable {
3:            if (e.WriteFlag == True) {
4:                val = GetLatestValue(e.SpecAddr);
5:                CopyBack(e.NonSpecAddr, val);
6:                foreach thread t executing a later speculative task {
7:                    if (e.NonSpecAddr is in the t.LTable ){
8:                        t.SpecFail = True;
9:                        add e.NonSpecAddr into t.FailedAt[ ] ;
10:                   } //endif
11:               } //end foreach
12:           }//end if
13:       }//end for each
14  }
15: else { //recovery
16:       pc = GetRecoveryPC(T.FailedAt[ ]);
17:       sid = GetRecoverySpaceID(T.FailedAt[ ]);
18:       ask thread T to reexecute from instruction pc using
              the latest values of live-in variables, and
              the values stored in the latest subspace whose SID
              is no more than sid for none-live-in variables ;
      }
```

Figure 11. Misspeculation Checks And Recovery.

starts to copy back the results. Specifically, the main thread goes through this parallel thread's live-in table (line 2) and identifies the modified live-in variables (line 3). The *WriteFlag* of a live-in variable is set when an access to this variable is a write. For each modified live-in variable, the main thread finds its latest value (line 4) and copies the value to the non-speculative state (line 4). The non-speculative address of a live-in variable is available as it is stored in the live-in table when the live-in variable is first accessed.

Misspeculation Check. The misspeculation check is performed by executing lines 6 to 11. In particular, when a live-in variable is committed, the main thread searches the live-in table of all other threads that are executing later speculative tasks. If this variable is found in another thread *t*'s live-in table (line 7), then thread *t* is using a stale value because the value of this variable has just been updated. As a result, the *SpecFail* flag of *t* is set to *true* (line 8). This variable identified by its non-speculative address is also added into another thread attribute *FailedAt* (line 9). The variables stored in *FailedAt* are used to identify the starting point of reexecution during the misspeculation recovery. Note that the use of *WriteFlag* ensures that multiple writes to a live-in variable within one task will not cause later tasks to be recovered multiple times.

Recovery. If the *SpecFail* flag of a thread *t* is set to *True*, then reexecution is required for recovery. The *FailedAt* attribute of *t* indicates which live-in variables caused the speculation to fail. Since, when each live-in variable is first read, the instruction address of the read and the space ID before the read are recorded (Figure 10, line 2), the main thread can retrieve these two values of the first accessed live-in variable by calling another two auxiliary functions *GetRecoveryPC* and *getRecoverySpaceID* (lines 16-17). These two values determine the starting point of the reexecution. The main thread now asks thread *t* to reexecute from instruction *pc*. During the reexecution, the latest value of every live-in variable is used. For other variables, their values stored in the latest subspace whose SID is no greater than *sid* are used. This can be done by searching for the state history of each variable. In this way, the reexecution is consistent with the sequential semantics and all incorrect speculatively computed results are simply discarded. More importantly, all

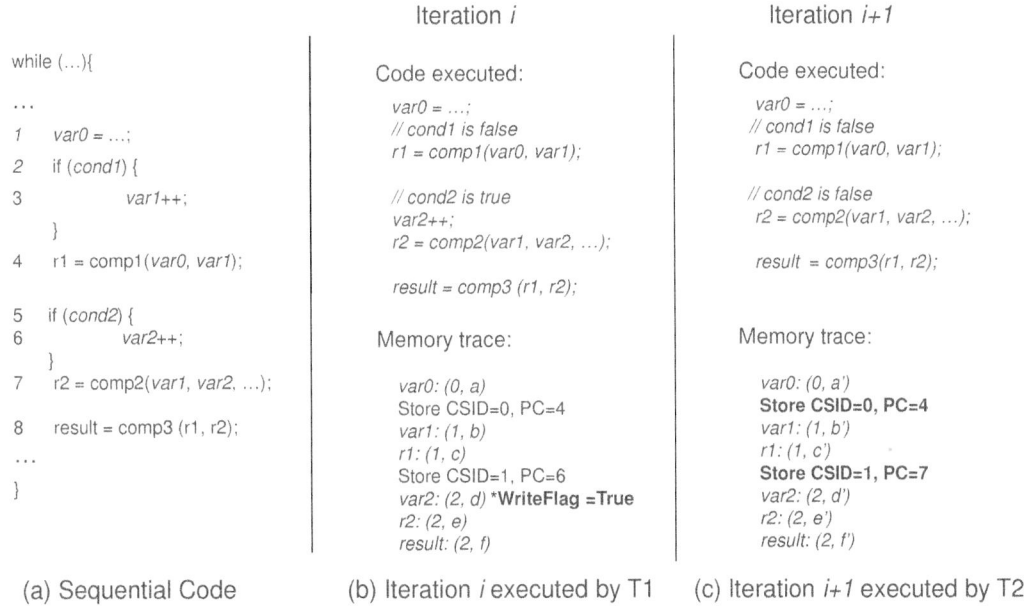

Figure 12. An Example Of Recovery.

correct speculatively computed results are reused because they are stored in different subspaces.

Figure 12 shows an example. Figure 12(a) shows the sequential code where two live-in variables *var1* and *var2* can be observed. Consider iteration *i* and *i+1*, which are speculatively executed by threads *T1* and *T2* in parallel. The executed code and memory operations for these two threads are shown in figures (b) and (c) separately. During *T1*'s execution, *T1* updates *var2*, and hence, the *WriteFlag* of this variable is set to true. When the main thread performs the misspeculation check, it searches for all other threads that are currently using *var2* and sets the corresponding flag *Spec-Fail* to true (Figure 11). In this example, *T2.SpecFail* is set to true and *var2* is added to *T2.FailedAt*. When the main thread examines *T2*'s results, it realizes that *T2*'s speculation has failed because of *var2*. Hence, it retrieves the CSID and PC of the recovery point that corresponds to *var2* (CSID=1 and PC=7 in this case), and sends the latest value of *var2* to *T2*. With such information, *T2* now can start the incremental recovery. In particular, it reexecutes the code from the instruction whose PC is 7, and uses the latest value of *var2* and the value stored in space 1 for all other variables.

Handling Exceptions. In certain situations, executing different loop iterations in parallel may cause the program to exhibit abnormal behavior. For instance, suppose an integer variable *var* is 0 initially. In the first iteration, it is updated to some integer that is larger than 0 and then used as a divisor in the second iteration. If these two iterations are speculatively executed in parallel, the thread executing the second iteration will throw a floating point exception, which will terminate the program. To solve this problem, all signals that lead to an abnormal termination are captured and handled by customized signal handlers. In these handlers, *SpecFail* flag of the corresponding parallel thread is set to true and recovery point is set to the beginning of the task. Therefore, during the recovery, the parallel thread can reexecute its task with the latest values of all live-in variables and exceptions will not take place any more. This exception handling mechanism guarantees that the parallelized application is strictly consistent with the sequential version.

5. Experiments

5.1 Experimental Setup

To study the effectiveness of our techniques we identified five benchmarks shown in Table 1 for which misspeculation rate is input dependent. The first three columns of the table give the name, lines of source code, number of live-in variables for these programs. Note that the outermost loops in these benchmarks can be speculatively parallelized. Exploiting such parallelism when certain inputs are used yields good speedups, especially for program CRC32 [37]. Thus, CRC32 is selected in addition to the four SPEC programs for comparison to previous work. For each benchmark in our experiments, three different inputs were used which give rise to cross-iteration dependences and thus misspeculations at a low ($< 1\%$), medium (around 40%), and high (around 80%) frequency as shown by the last three columns. Experiments were conducted using these different inputs to evaluate the effectiveness of incremental recovery and its comparison to *discard-all* recovery.

Name	LOC	# of Live-ins	Cross-iteration Dep. Frequency		
			low	medium	high
197.parser	9.7K	8	1%	49.3%	82.4%
130.li	7.8K	6	2%	40%	80%
256.bzip2	2.9K	9	0.5%	38.2%	79.2%
255.vortex	49.3K	11	0.5%	43.2%	81.3%
CRC32	0.2K	1	1%	40%	80%

Table 1. Benchmark Description.

In the experiments, the parallel version of every benchmark program is generated through a source-to-source transformation. Specifically, to support the space and thread decoupling scheme, every basic type in C (e.g., int, char etc.) is redefined as a new class in C++. The class contains not only the original type, but also the type of state history in parallel spaces. When a variable is declared to be of a class base type, its non-speculative storage is allocated during the compilation and its state history for each thread is created and dynamically maintained as shown in Figure 10. The parallel threads are created and controlled using a template similar to

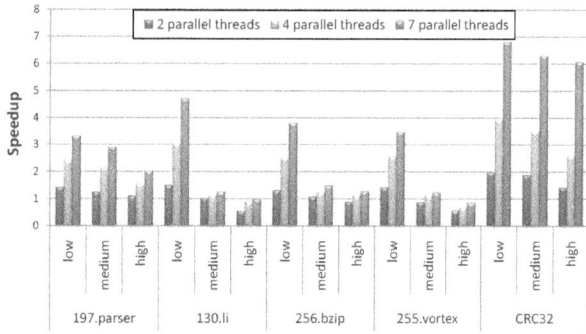

Figure 13. Speedups: Incr. Recovery vs. Sequential Execution.

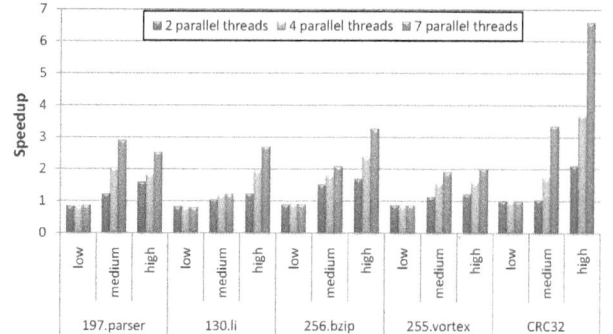

Figure 14. Speedups: Incremental Recovery vs. Discard-all.

one described in [37], but written in C++. The runtime system that detects the misspeculation and handles the speculatively computed result described in this paper was also implemented in C++.

All the experiments were conducted under CentOS 4 OS running on a *dual quad-core* Xeon machine with 16GB memory. Each core runs at 3.0 GHz. Since there are a total of 8 cores on this system, we measured the performance when 2, 4, and 7 speculative threads are created in addition to the main thread that coordinates the activities of the parallel threads.

5.2 Performance Results

5.2.1 Speedups over Sequential Execution

The first experiment conducted measured the speedups resulting from speculative parallelization that employs incremental recovery for different inputs and different number of parallel threads. Figure 13 shows the speedups when using 2, 4, and 7 speculative threads in comparison to executions of sequential versions of the applications. As we can see, for each benchmark, on any given input, the performance of the benchmark improves as the number of parallel threads spawned increases. When 7 threads are executed on input-low, all benchmarks obtained the best speedups which range from 3.3 to 6.8.

When input-medium and input-high are used, performance gains can still be observed in most cases, but these gains drop dramatically for 130.li, 255.vortex and 256.bzip. Especially when running on input-high, the first two benchmarks experience slowdowns as misspeculations more than wipe out the benefits of parallelism. However, for 197.parser and CRC32, speedups can be observed even when input-high is used. In these two programs, only a small number of instructions need to be reexecuted when a misspeculation occurs and hence the performance is not limited by the misspeculation rate. The highest speedups achieve on input-medium and input-high are 2.9 and 2.0 for 197.parser, 6.3 and 6.1 for CRC32 respectively.

5.2.2 Comparison With Discard-All Scheme

Speedup Comparison. Next we show the advantage of incremental recovery over discard-all. The speedups of incremental recovery based speculative parallelization over discard-all based speculative parallelization are shown in Figure 14. We observe that for all benchmarks running with input-medium and input-high, incremental recovery has much better performance than discard-all scheme. It brings more benefit when more threads are used. As shown in Figure 14, the speedups observed when 7 threads are used, range from 1.2x (130.li) to 3.3x (CRC32) for input-medium and from 2.0x (255.vortex) to 6.6x (CRC32) for input-high.

The reason is that the misspeculation rates become higher when more threads are used, which significantly slows down the parallelized version that uses the discard-all scheme. In contrast, when

incremental recovery is applied, only part of the speculatively computed results need to be recomputed and the overhead of recovery is greatly reduced. As a result, incremental recovery can still speed up the sequential program in most cases as shown in Figure 13. It is worth noting that for 255.vortex and 130.li running with input-high, Figure 13 indicates that incremental recovery technique cannot speed up the sequential executions. However, the performance of the original parallelized version is even worse. That explains why the speedups are still obtained in this experiment.

In the case of input-low, the performance of using incremental recovery is worse than the original scheme. The performance loss is about 15% on an average. This is because of the overhead of the recovery system. In particular, every load or store has to be performed on a state history — a list of the pairs of space ID and value. This is more expensive than operating on a single value. The results of the experiment shows that incremental recovery is much more effective if the misspeculation rate is very high and the discard-all scheme is better otherwise.

Misspeculation Comparison. Another reason for incremental recovery technique performing better on input-medium and input-high is that it reduces the number of misspeculations. In our scheme, copy-on-write scheme is applied (see Figure 10), and using incremental recovery technique can increase the chance of a later iteration reading the correct values of the variables that are modified in an earlier iteration as discussed in section 3. The reason is that our technique allows the recovery to be performed faster and thus it speeds up the result-committing stage of every thread. Experiments were conducted to measure this effect. In particular, the misspeculation rate is collected for both incremental recovery technique and the discard-all technique. The misspeculation rate reduction is then computed based on these two numbers and the results are shown in Figure 15. Note that the comparisons are only made on input-medium and input-large.

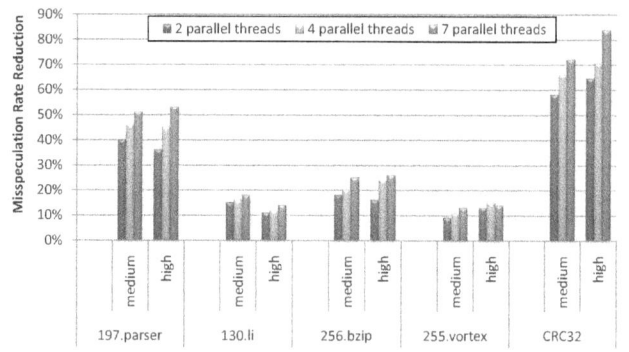

Figure 15. Misspeculation Rate Reductions.

From the figure, one can see that for `197.parser` and CRC32, up to 50% and 85% misspeculations are respectively eliminated. As mentioned earlier, in these two programs, only one statement, which defines the live-in variable, needs to be recomputed during the recovery. With incremental recovery technique, the live-in variable can be committed faster, which increases the chance of later threads getting the correct version. As a result, performance of these two benchmarks is significantly improved by our technique (see Figure 13). For other programs, the number of reexecuted statements during the recovery is far greater, and hence the observed misspeculation reduction is around 20% for `256.bzip`, 10% for `130.li`, and 10% `255.vortex` on an average.

Recovery Time Comparison. To further understand the difference between the speculative execution with and without incremental recovery technique, we conducted another experiment to measure the fraction of time that is spent in recovery mode (i.e., reexecution of previously failed tasks) during the speculative execution. We used seven parallel threads in this experiment and the fraction numbers are averaged across all parallel threads. Figure 16 shows the results.

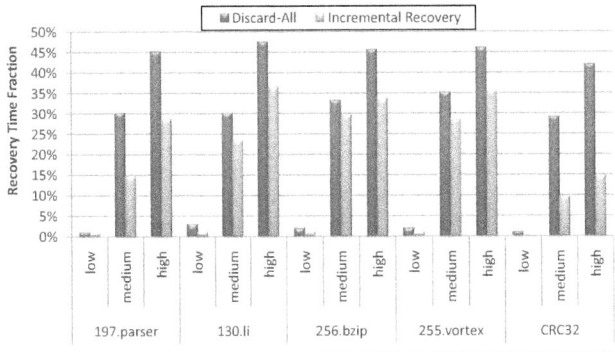

Figure 16. Recovery Time Comparison.

From the figure, we can see that for `input-low`, less than 2% of the execution time of each parallel thread is spent on recovery during both executions. Thus, incremental recovery does not provide any benefit. However, when `input-medium` is used, difference can be noticed. With incremental recovery, the fraction of time spent in recovery ranges from about 10%(CRC32) to 28% (`255.voertex`). With discard-all scheme, this number is around 30% for all benchmarks. This implies that very high misspeculation rates are encountered during the parallel executions of these benchmarks and about one third of the time is spent on reexecutions. For `input-high`, recovery takes about 45% of the execution time of each thread when the original discard-all scheme is used in the parallelization. With incremental recovery, however, each thread of parallelized `197.parser` and CRC32 spent less than 30% of time on recovery. In other programs, these numbers are around 35%, which are still smaller than discard-all scheme.

Finally, recall that benefit of incremental recovery over discard-all is due to two reasons – reduction in computation and reduction in misspeculation rate. We breakdown the contributions of these two factors in Figure 17. As we can see, although majority of the savings result from computation reduction, when misspeculation rates are high, significant savings result from reduction in misspeculation rate.

5.3 Overhead Analysis

Execution Time Breakdown. The execution time spent by each parallel thread can be broken down into three different categories: *communication*, *recovery*, and *speculative computation*. Figure 18 shows the results. They are measured and averaged across all seven

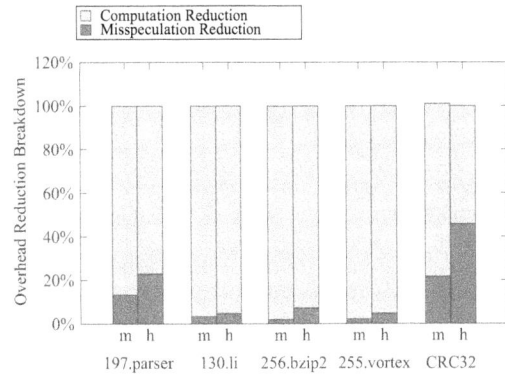

Figure 17. Breakdown: Reuse and Misspeculation Reduction.

parallel threads. As we can see, the time spent on the communication is only a small portion for all programs regardless of the input. This implies that all parallel threads are busy performing computations. For all parallelized programs running on `input-low`, each thread spends most of the time on speculative execution. When the input changes, more misspeculations take place, and thus more time is spent on the recovery. In the case of `256.bzip2`, `130.li` and 255.vortex running on `input-high`, about 35% of the time is spent on reexecuting the speculative computation.

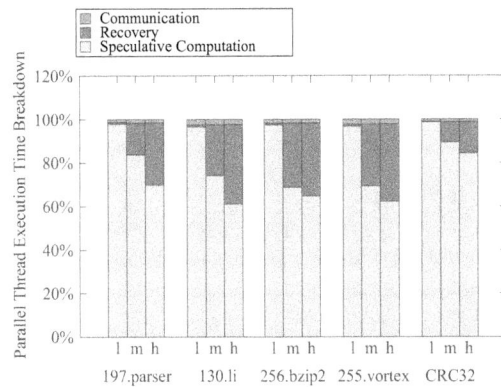

Figure 18. Time Breakdown: Speculative Threads.

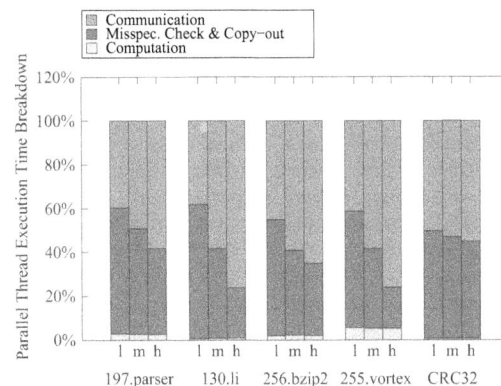

Figure 19. Time Breakdown: Main Thread.

Figure 19 shows the time breakdown for the main thread. Three categories are considered: *communication*, *misspeculation checks & copy-out*, and *computation*. Different from parallel threads, the main thread spent a large portion of the execution time on communication. Another significant portion is spent on misspeculation checks and committing results. When different inputs are used to create more misspeculations, one can observe that communication time increases, because parallel threads fail more often. As a result, the main thread has to spend more time on waiting for the correct results to be produced.

Space Overhead. Maintaining multiple spaces for one thread consumes more space. An experiment is conducted to monitor the peak value of memory consumption. The memory used by the corresponding sequential program is considered as the baseline. Figure 20 shows the space overhead. As expected, using more threads consumes more space because each variable accessed by a parallel thread takes more memory space in this technique. When 7 parallel threads are used, the largest overhead is observed which ranges from 3.2 to 5.1 across all benchmarks. Note that the data in this figure is for `input-high` only because the space overhead is not sensitive to the misspeculation rate.

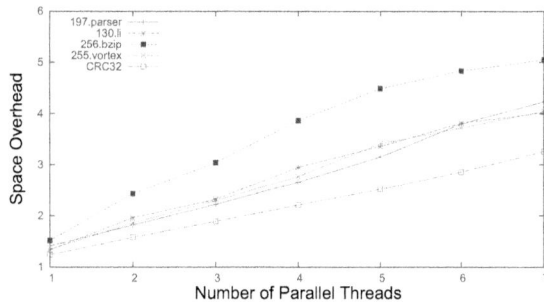

Figure 20. Space Overhead.

6. Related Work

A great deal of research has been carried out on hardware TLS [6, 10, 14, 19, 31, 33]. While the compiler is responsible for speculatively parallelizing sequential code, hardware is provided to handle the difficult tasks of detecting and handling misspeculations. Specialized hardware structures are used, such as special buffers [10, 23], versioning cache [8], or versioning memory [7]. Unfortunately, none of these features are available in commercial multicore processors of today. Therefore an attractive alternative avenue of optimistically extracting parallelism from programs is based upon a purely software realization of TLS.

Most of the software TLS systems use state separation to support speculations [2, 3, 5, 9, 13, 26–28, 35–38]. To identify speculatively parallelizable loops, some of these works rely on static analysis [2, 3, 9, 26], some require the complete trace of a program to perform the parallelization [27, 28], and others use profiling technique to gather certain types of runtime information. As already described, Ding *et al.* proposed using processes to achieve state separation [5, 13] while in our prior work on CorD we proposed thread based state separation [37].

In recent work we proposed the use of multiple value predictions to reduce high misspeculation rate [35]. The idea is to predict the values of live-in variables that frequently cause misspeculations. However, its applicability is determined by the prediction accuracy. Moreover, due to the creation of multiple speculative versions for the same loop iteration, this work requires much more processor resources – one core per version. Thus, it is even more wasteful than discard-all as it always discards the results of all versions except the correct one. Our work, on the other hand, reduces the cost of misspeculation recovery and thus is far less expensive.

Instead of state separation, Kulkarni *et al.* proposed a rollback based speculative parallelization technique [15–18, 21]. They introduce two special constructs that users can employ to identify

speculative parallelism. When speculation fails, user supplied code is executed to perform rollback. In other words, users must define the reverse computation in their programs. While the above work requires help from the programmer, our approach accomplishes the same tasks automatically.

Software pipelining is another parallelization technique that has been greatly studied [1, 12, 25, 34, 39]. Different from DO-ALL parallelization, these techniques partition each loop iteration into several pipeline stages and each stage is executed on a different core. While some of them focus on multicore processors [25, 39], others target stream and graphic processors [1, 12, 34]. Hardware versioning memory is used to separate non-speculative and speculative results.

Transactional memory (TM) [4, 11, 22] has been an active area of research. It is designed to enforce the atomicity of shared memory accesses in parallel programs and cannot be directly used to parallelize sequential programs due to several reasons [20]. First, STM needs special mechanisms to avoid or resolve dead-lock and live-lock situations. Second, STM aims at achieving good throughput and fairness. This requires STM to consider the priorities of transactions [32]. Besides, STM internally uses locks to prevent data races [33] and barriers to ensure strong atomicity [29, 30] and in-order commit [20]. This results in high runtime overhead for STM while providing a convenience for programmers writing parallel applications. Mehrara *et al.* proposed customized STM for speculative parallelization [20]. Their work assumes dependent variables can be identified at compile time and requires a set of special registers to track such variables. Raman *et al.* also proposed the use of multi-threaded transactions to support speculative execution [24]. However, their work focuses on applying transactions on software pipelining parallelization instead of DO-ALL parallelization.

7. Conclusion

In this paper we presented an *incremental recovery* technique to reduce the overhead of misspeculation recovery in an existing implementations of SS-TLS. The key idea was to decouple the creation of each parallel thread from the creation of speculative memory spaces. Use of multiple spaces during speculative execution allows the speculatively computed results to be stored and reused when a misspeculation occurs. Our experiments show that for a set of programs with inputs causing around 40% and 80% misspeculation rates, applying incremental recovery technique can achieve 1.2x-3.3x and 2.0x-6.6x speedups respectively in comparison to the discard-all recovery scheme used in prior works.

Acknowledgments This work is supported by NSF grants CCF-0963996, CCF-0905509, CNS-0751961, and CNS-0810906 to the University of California, Riverside.

References

[1] I. Buck. *Stream computing on graphics hardware.* PhD thesis, Stanford, CA, USA, 2005.

[2] M. Cintra and D. R. Llanos. Toward efficient and robust software speculative parallelization on multiprocessors. In *PPoPP '03: Proceedings of the ninth ACM SIGPLAN symposium on Principles and practice of parallel programming*, pages 13–24, 2003.

[3] M. H. Cintra and D. R. L. Ferraris. Design space exploration of a software speculative parallelization scheme. *IEEE Trans. Parallel Distrib. Syst.*, 16(6):562–576, 2005.

[4] P. Damron, A. Fedorova, Y. Lev, V. Luchangco, M. Moir, and D. Nussbaum. Hybrid transactional memory. In *ASPLOS-XII*, pages 336–346, 2006.

[5] C. Ding, X. Shen, K. Kelsey, C. Tice, R. Huang, and C. Zhang. Software behavior oriented parallelization. In *PLDI '07: Proceedings*

of the 2007 ACM SIGPLAN conference on Programming language design and implementation, pages 223–234, 2007.

[6] M. Franklin and G. S. Sohi. Arb: A hardware mechanism for dynamic reordering of memory references. *IEEE Transactions on Computers*, 45(5):552–571, 1996.

[7] M. J. Garzarán, M. Prvulovic, J. M. Llabería, V. Viñals, L. Rauchwerger, and J. Torrellas. Tradeoffs in buffering speculative memory state for thread-level speculation in multiprocessors. *Transactions on Architecture and Code Optimization*, 2(3):247–279, 2005.

[8] S. Gopal, T. N. Vijaykumar, J. E. Smith, and G. S. Sohi. Speculative versioning cache. In *HPCA '98: Proceedings of the 4th International Symposium on High-Performance Computer Architecture*, pages 195–205, 1998.

[9] M. Gupta and R. Nim. Techniques for speculative run-time parallelization of loops. In *Supercomputing '98: Proceedings of the 1998 ACM/IEEE conference on Supercomputing (CDROM)*, pages 1–12, Washington, DC, USA, 1998. IEEE Computer Society.

[10] L. Hammond, M. Willey, and K. Olukotun. Data speculation support for a chip multiprocessor. In *ASPLOS-VIII: Proceedings of the eighth international conference on Architectural support for programming languages and operating systems*, pages 58–69, 1998.

[11] M. Herlihy and J. E. B. Moss. Transactional memory: Architectural support for lock-free data structures. In *ISCA'93: Proceedings of the 20th Annual International Symposium on Computer Architecture*, pages 289–300, 1993.

[12] U. J. Kapasi, S. Rixner, W. J. Dally, B. Khailany, J. H. Ahn, P. Mattson, and J. D. Owens. Programmable stream processors. *Computer*, 36(8):54–62, 2003.

[13] K. Kelsey, T. Bai, C. Ding, and C. Zhang. Fast track: A software system for speculative program optimization. In *CGO '09: Proceedings of the 2009 International Symposium on Code Generation and Optimization*, pages 157–168, 2009.

[14] V. Krishnan and J. Torrellas. The need for fast communication in hardware-based speculative chip multiprocessors. In *PACT '99: Proceedings of the 1999 International Conference on Parallel Architectures and Compilation Techniques*, pages 24–33, 1999.

[15] M. Kulkarni, M. Burtscher, R. Inkulu, K. Pingali, and C. Casçaval. How much parallelism is there in irregular applications? In *PPoPP '09: Proceedings of the 14th ACM SIGPLAN symposium on Principles and practice of parallel programming*, pages 3–14, 2009.

[16] M. Kulkarni, P. Carribault, K. Pingali, G. Ramanarayanan, B. Walter, K. Bala, and L. P. Chew. Scheduling strategies for optimistic parallel execution of irregular programs. In *SPAA*, pages 217–228, 2008.

[17] M. Kulkarni, K. Pingali, G. Ramanarayanan, B. Walter, K. Bala, and L. P. Chew. Optimistic parallelism benefits from data partitioning. In *ASPLOS XIII*, pages 233–243, 2008.

[18] M. Kulkarni, K. Pingali, B. Walter, G. Ramanarayanan, K. Bala, and L. P. Chew. Optimistic parallelism requires abstractions. In *PLDI '07: Proceedings of the 2007 ACM SIGPLAN conference on Programming language design and implementation*, pages 211–222, 2007.

[19] P. Marcuello and A. González. Clustered speculative multithreaded processors. In *ICS '99: Proceedings of the 13th international conference on Supercomputing*, pages 365–372, 1999.

[20] M. Mehrara, J. Hao, P.-C. Hsu, and S. Mahlke. Parallelizing sequential applications on commodity hardware using a low-cost software transactional memory. In *PLDI '09: Proceedings of the 2009 ACM SIGPLAN conference on Programming language design and implementation*, pages 166–176, 2009.

[21] M. Méndez-Lojo, D. Nguyen, D. Prountzos, X. Sui, M. A. Hassaan, M. Kulkarni, M. Burtscher, and K. Pingali. Structure-driven optimizations for amorphous data-parallel programs. In *PPoPP '10: Proceedings of the 14th ACM SIGPLAN symposium on Principles and practice of parallel programming*, pages 3–14, 2010.

[22] M. J. Moravan, J. Bobba, K. E. Moore, L. Yen, M. D. Hill, B. Liblit, M. M. Swift, and D. A. Wood. Supporting nested transactional memory in logtm. In *ASPLOS-XII*, pages 359–370, 2006.

[23] M. Prvulovic, M. J. Garzarán, L. Rauchwerger, and J. Torrellas. Removing architectural bottlenecks to the scalability of speculative parallelization. In *ISCA '01: Proceedings of the 28th annual international symposium on Computer architecture*, pages 204–215, 2001.

[24] A. Raman, H. Kim, T. R. Mason, T. B. Jablin, and D. I. August. Speculative parallelization using software multi-threaded transactions. In *ASPLOS '10: Proceedings of the fifteenth edition of ASPLOS on Architectural support for programming languages and operating systems*, pages 65–76, New York, NY, USA, 2010. ACM.

[25] E. Raman, G. Ottoni, A. Raman, M. J. Bridges, and D. I. August. Parallel-stage decoupled software pipelining. In *CGO '08: Proceedings of the 2008 International Symposium on Code Generation and Optimization*, pages 114–123, 2008.

[26] L. Rauchwerger and D. A. Padua. The lrpd test: Speculative run-time parallelization of loops with privatization and reduction parallelization. *IEEE Trans. Parallel Distrib. Syst.*, 10(2):160–180, 1999.

[27] P. Rundberg and P. Stenstrom. Low-cost thread-level data dependence speculation on multiprocessors. In *In Fourth Workshop on Multithreaded Execution,Architecture and Compilation*, 2000.

[28] P. Rundberg and P. Stenström. An all-software thread-level data dependence speculation system for multiprocessors. *J. Instruction-Level Parallelism*, 3, 2001.

[29] F. T. Schneider, V. Menon, T. Shpeisman, and A.-R. Adl-Tabatabai. Dynamic optimization for efficient strong atomicity. In *OOPSLA '08: Proceedings of the 23rd ACM SIGPLAN conference on Object-oriented programming systems languages and applications*, pages 181–194, 2008.

[30] T. Shpeisman, V. Menon, A.-R. Adl-Tabatabai, S. Balensiefer, D. Grossman, R. L. Hudson, K. F. Moore, and B. Saha. Enforcing isolation and ordering in stm. In *PLDI '07: Proceedings of the 2007 ACM SIGPLAN conference on Programming language design and implementation*, pages 78–88, 2007.

[31] G. Sohi, S. E. Breach, and T. N. Vijaykumar. Multiscalar processors. In *ISCA '95: Proceedings of the 22nd annual international symposium on Computer architecture*, pages 414–425, 1995.

[32] M. F. Spear, L. Dalessandro, V. J. Marathe, and M. L. Scott. A comprehensive strategy for contention management in software transactional memory. In *PPoPP '09: Proceedings of the 14th ACM SIGPLAN symposium on Principles and practice of parallel programming*, 2009.

[33] J. G. Steffan, C. B. Colohan, A. Zhai, and T. C. Mowry. A scalable approach to thread-level speculation. In *ISCA '00: In Proceedings of the 27th Annual International Symposium on Computer Architecture*, pages 1–12, 2000.

[34] W. Thies, V. Chandrasekhar, and S. Amarasinghe. A practical approach to exploiting coarse-grained pipeline parallelism in c programs. In *MICRO 40: Proceedings of the 40th Annual IEEE/ACM International Symposium on Microarchitecture*, pages 356–369, 2007.

[35] C. Tian, M. Feng, and R. Gupta. Speculative parallelization using state separation and multiple value prediction. In *ISMM '10: Proceedings of the 2010 International Symposium on Memory Management*, 2010.

[36] C. Tian, M. Feng, and R. Gupta. Supporting speculative parallelization in the presence of dynamic data structures. In *PLDI '10: Proceedings of the 2010 ACM SIGPLAN conference on Programming language design and implementation*, pages 63–73, 2010.

[37] C. Tian, M. Feng, V. Nagarajan, and R. Gupta. Copy or discard execution model for speculative parallelization on multicores. In *MICRO '08: Proceedings of the 2008 41st IEEE/ACM International Symposium on Microarchitecture*, pages 330–341, 2008.

[38] C. Tian, M. Feng, V. Nagarajan, and R. Gupta. Speculative parallelization of sequential loops on multicores. *International Journal of Parallel Programming*, 37(5):508–535, 2009.

[39] N. Vachharajani, R. Rangan, E. Raman, M. J. Bridges, G. Ottoni, and D. I. August. Speculative decoupled software pipelining. In *PACT '07: Proceedings of the 2007 International Conference on Parallel Architectures and Compilation Techniques*, pages 49–59, 2007.

Lifeline-based Global Load Balancing

Vijay Saraswat

IBM TJ Watson Research Center
vijay@saraswat.org

Prabhanjan Kambadur

IBM TJ Watson Research Center
pkambadu@us.ibm.com

Sreedhar Kodali

IBM Systems and Technology Group
srkodali@in.ibm.com

David Grove

IBM TJ Watson Research Center
groved@us.ibm.com

Sriram Krishnamoorthy

Pacific Northwest National Laboratory
sriram@pnl.gov

Abstract

On shared-memory systems, Cilk-style work-stealing [5] has been used to effectively parallelize irregular task-graph based applications such as Unbalanced Tree Search (UTS) [24, 28].

There are two main difficulties in extending this approach to distributed memory. In the shared memory approach, thieves (nodes without work) constantly attempt to asynchronously steal work from randomly chosen victims until they find work. In distributed memory, thieves cannot autonomously steal work from a victim without disrupting its execution. When work is sparse, this results in performance degradation. In essence, a direct extension of traditional work-stealing to distributed memory violates the *work-first principle* underlying work-stealing. Further, thieves spend useless CPU cycles attacking victims that have no work, resulting in system inefficiencies in multi-programmed contexts. Second, it is non-trivial to detect *active distributed termination* (detect that programs at all nodes are looking for work, hence there is no work). This problem is well-studied and requires careful design for good performance. Unfortunately, in most existing languages/frameworks, application developers are forced to implement their own distributed termination detection.

In this paper, we develop a simple set of ideas that allow work-stealing to be efficiently extended to distributed memory. First, we introduce *lifeline graphs*: low-degree, low-diameter, fully-connected directed graphs. Such graphs can be constructed from k-dimensional hypercubes. When a node is unable to find work after w unsuccessful steals, it quiesces after informing the outgoing edges in its lifeline graph. Quiescent nodes do not disturb other nodes. A quiesced node is reactivated when work arrives from a lifeline, and itself shares this work with those of its incoming lifelines that are activated. Termination occurs precisely when computation at all nodes has quiesced. In a language such as X10,

such passive distributed termination can be detected automatically using the **finish** construct – no application code is necessary.

Our design is implemented in a few hundred lines of X10. On the binomial tree described in [26], the program achieve 87% efficiency on an Infiniband cluster of 1024 Power7 cores, with a peak throughput of 2.37 GNodes/sec. It achieves 87% efficiency on a Blue Gene/P with 2048 processors, and a peak throughput of 0.966 GNodes/s. All numbers are relative to single core sequential performance. This implementation has been refactored into a reusable *global load balancing framework*. Applications can use this framework to obtain global load balance with minimal code changes.

In summary, we claim: (a) the first formulation of UTS that does not involve application level global termination detection, (b) the introduction of lifeline graphs to reduce failed steals (c) the demonstration of simple lifeline graphs based on k-hypercubes, (d) performance with superior efficiency (or the same efficiency but over a wider range) than published results on UTS. In particular, our framework can deliver the same or better performance as an unrestricted random work-stealing implementation, while reducing the number of attempted steals.

Categories and Subject Descriptors   D.1.3 [*Concurrent Programming*]: Parallel Programming

General Terms   Algorithms, Design

Keywords   UTS, global load balancing, distributed computing, X10, work-stealing, parallel programming

1. Introduction

The emergence of new architectures that emphasize distributed memory — clouds and commodity clusters, P7, and Blue Gene – provides significant new opportunities for application developers. New application areas such as business analytics, data mining are presented with unparalleled opportunities to deal efficiently with large workloads. However, these exciting opportunities bring new challenges for parallel system designers.

The APGAS programming model [30] provides a useful and convenient framework for stating these problems and their solutions. The parallel system is viewed as a collection of *places*. Data is partitioned across the places with support for selective replication. In addition to remote data access through one-sided communication primitives, *activities*

PPoPP '11   February 12–16, 2011, San Antonio, Texas, USA.
Copyright © 2011 ACM 978-1-4503-0119-0/11/02...$10.00

can be launched on remote places. This allows complementary approaches to move the data or the computation as they match the application domain (e.g., linear algebra vs tree traversal). The APGAS framework also subsumes other newer programming models such as Map-Reduce [8]. Map-Reduce frameworks such as Hadoop allow parallel processing of large files using user-defined map and reduce operations. However, it is challenging to rewrite well-established parallel algorithms to fit the map-reduce model.

A fundamental problem in achieving the promise of scale-out computing in such a programming model is the *global load-balancing problem*. Many problems can be conceptualized in terms of distributed task collections, with dependences between them expressed as data or control dependences. In this paper, we focus on task collections with no dependences. In addition, the tasks encapsulate all data needed for their processing and do not take advantage of the global address space.

Dynamically load balancing such a computation assumes these tasks to be mobile — they can be executed anywhere and do not exhibit affinity to a place. This paper presents a solution to the global load balancing problem for such a task collection.

This problem has been studied in the context of shared-memory systems. In a typical design, the tasks to be processed at each place are placed in a deque. The worker at a given place processes tasks from the top, while thieves steal from the bottom of the deque. Workers continues to processes it local tasks until they run out of work. Thieves attempt to minimize their idle time by looking for work to steal. If T_1 is the time to run a program with one worker and T_∞ is the time required to run the same program with an infinite number of workers, then T_p, the time to run this program with P workers is $T_1/P + T_\infty$. Simultaneously, the space required to run a program with P workers is bounded by $P \times S(1)$, where $S(1)$ is the space required to run the program with one worker. This approach is usually referred to as "work-stealing".

Although work-stealing appears simple at the outset and has attractive space and time bounds, efficient parallelization of applications using the work-stealing scheduler requires careful engineering. The key factor in getting optimal performance in a work-stealing scheduler is reducing the critical path overhead; that is, a worker busy with work must continue with this work and not be interrupted to help a thief. Implementations, such as Cilk's "THE" protocol [15] have been carefully designed so that a worker thread does not pay more than the cost of a volatile write in all those cases where it is not a victim. In fact, the THE protocol also ensures that victims do not pay the cost of locking and unlocking the deque unless there is a single task to be wrestled for. However, if the worker is a thief, it has to acquire a lock before stealing a task from the victim. In this scheduling scheme, contention arises when: (1) multiple thieves try to steal from the same victim, (2) there is a single task on the victim's deque, or (3) both.

In a distributed memory setting, local and remote data accesses incur different costs — the cost of communication cannot be ignored. Additionally, different communication operations might incur very different costs (eg., lock operations vs data access). While lock contention can be expensive in shared memory machines, it has been shown to dramatically impact parallel efficiency at scale in distributed memory contexts [11]. On many architectures, the operations involved in stealing work are not supported in hardware. As a result,

steals interrupt the remote worker, incurring additional cost. In particular, the time to process a given set of tasks depends not just on the tasks being processed, but potentially also on the number interruptions due to incoming steal requests.

One central problem is termination detection [4, 9, 10, 14]. In the usual formulation, computation must terminate once it is the case that *every* worker is looking for work; for then no worker has work. In the shared memory case, this can be implemented with a simple barrier algorithm. When a worker finishes its work, it checks into the barrier. If it finds it is the last worker to check into the barrier, it signals termination to all other workers. Otherwise it looks for work randomly, periodically checking to see if termination has been signaled (and terminating if it is). If it finds work, it checks out of the barrier before claiming the work, thus guaranteeing correctness.

As the number of workers scales, repeatedly checking into and out of the barrier can cause performance problems, and more scalable algorithms have to be designed. [26] proposes that workers enter the barrier only when they are "nearly certain" that there is no work in the system. This heuristic decision is made as follows. The worker randomly selects a victim. If the victim has no work, the thief moves to the next worker. Once it completes a circuit of all workers it makes the decision that there is likely no work in the system and enters the barrier. These additional traversals are of size $O(P)$ and can increase the latency to termination.

On scale out, the single location can become a bottleneck. Instead a combining tree must be used [11]. A node forwards a termination signal only when it has processed all its work. The algorithm involves phases of signaling up and down the tree. In the up phase, each node signals its parent for successful termination only if such a decision is reported by this node and its children. In the down phase, each node forwards the signal to its children and exit task processing if a terminate signal was received. The root of the tree broadcasts a terminate signal through its children only if its children and itself voted for termination. When a victim of a steal since the last vote becomes idle, it votes not to terminate. Thus termination is successfully detected by the root node only when all nodes participate in the up phase with no steals since the last up phase. This results in multiple termination detection phases during the computation, which is also slowed down due to active stealing by the nodes.

We contrast the problem with the (somewhat dual) *passive termination detection problem* in X10. In X10 any activity may spawn ("push") more activities on any node in the system. A **finish** operator must detect when all activities spawned within its scope have terminated. In contrast with the active version of the problem, worker threads at each place are passive, they wait for the arrival of messages containing work rather than actively searching for work themselves.

X10 implements a particular version of *vector counts* to detect passive termination. Each worker maintains a vector of counts, one per place.[1] This vector tracks how many asyncs this place has created remotely, and how many asyncs have terminated at this place. Once a place has quiesced (there is no activity running at that place), it sends its vector to the place that spawned the finish. This place simply sum-reduces the count (component-wise). Termination is detected once (and only once) the reduced vector is zero. For computations in which a place spawns computations at only a few other places, say bounded by a constant z, only vectors of

---

[1] This vector is usually very sparse and is maintained sparsely.

size z need to be communicated between places. Note that these design does not involve speculative waves of termination detection, rather it simply monotonically accumulates a set of vector counts, until the set reduces to zero.

When attempting to solve the UTS problem in X10 the natural question is whether **finish** can be used to implement UTS termination detection.

The central contribution of this paper is that it can. We show that global work stealing can be elegantly formulated as a simple X10 program using **async**, **at** and **finish**. The details are in the next section, we summarize the basic principles here.

Initially one **async** is launched at every place, under the control of a single **finish**. The termination of this **finish** will signal global termination. These asyncs will initially attempt to look for work by guessing a random id, and looking for work at the place with that id. This can be done using the **at** operator, without spawning any new asyncs. Now in "pure" work-stealing, if the async did not find any work at this victim, it will continue looking for work at other victims. This leads immediately to the active termination detection problem: when should the async know to stop looking for work, because there is no work?

Our key insight is to perform such random steals at most w times, where w is some pre-determined bound. If no work has been found after w attempts, the async *terminates*. However, before it does so, it establishes one or more *lifelines*. A lifeline is simply another place. Establishing a lifeline means checking if that place has work, and if so performing a steal, as usual. But if that place does not have work then the id of the thief is recorded at that place as an "incoming" lifeline. Since that place does not have any work, it must itself, recursively, have established a lifeline. Once a place finds some work, it checks to see if any incoming lifelines have been recorded. If so, it *distributes* a portion of its work to this lifeline q, and clears it. Distribution is performed by spawning an async at place q, which *re-initiates* activity at q. Now it can be seen that there is no more work left to do precisely when all the asyncs in the system have terminated – and this condition will, of course, be detected by the single top-level **finish**.

1.1 Lifeline graphs

While the lifeline scheme is correct, it may not be efficient. How are lifelines determined? A natural possibility is that a lifeline is simply another place chosen at random. But it is easy to see this would not work. Place p may randomly choose to make q its lifeline, and simultaneously q could choose to make p its lifeline. As a result both places will be dead – they will not have any running activity and will never get one. Hence throughput and scalability will suffer. A good lifeline graph must have the property that as long as there is a place which has work, there must be a path from that place to every other place in the system.

Another alternative is to base the lifeline graph on a permutation with cycle of length P. For instance, each place p can be mapped to place $(p + 1)\%P$. This guarantees that the only cycle is of length P: thus a place will be involved in a cycle only if all places are involved in it, i.e. only when there is no work.

This scheme is correct and works reasonably well for small P. The problem is that it takes on the average $P/2$ hops for work to reach a place from another place. During this time the target place is idle.

An alternative would be to consider the fully connected graph, with an edge from every vertex to every other vertex.

While this ensures that tasks have to take only one hop to reach an idle worker, it creates the problem that tasks at one site have to be divided up into many pieces, one for each incoming lifeline. Workers with tasks on their hand may waste cycles moving tasks to their (many!) incoming lifelines, instead of executing them.

We are interested therefore in (directed) graphs that have the following properties. (a) Each vertex must has bounded out-degree. (b) The graph must be connected, (c) The graph must have a low diameter (there should be short paths from every vertex to every other vertex).

A parametric family of graphs that satisfy this property are the *cyclic hypercubes* defined as follows. Choose a radix h and a power z such that $h^{z-1} < P \leq h^z$ (P is the number of processes/places). Each vertex p is represented as a number in base h with z digits. It has an outgoing edge to every vertex a distance $+1$ from it in the Manhattan distance (in modulo h arithmetic). That is, the vertex p labeled $(a_1, \ldots, a_z)$ has an outgoing edge to every vertex q such that for some $i \in 1..z$, $q = (a_1, \ldots, (a_i + 1)\%h, \ldots, a_z)$. In two dimensions ($z = 2$), we have a square of size h^2 with all the elements in a row connected in a cycle, and all the elements in a column connected in a cycle.

In such a graph the average number of hops for work to travel from one place to another is $(h \times z)/2$.

One final point is worth mentioning. Usually $P < h^z$, and so P must be embedded in a graph with h^z nodes. Care must be taken to ensure that each place is connected to the next node in that dimension that represents a real, distinct place. This may mean that in a particular dimension a node has no neighbor (i.e. it has less than z lifelines). It is not difficult to show that for every $P > 1$ every node must have at least one neighbor.

1.2 Results

The lifeline scheme has been implemented in X10. The core implementation for binomial trees (presented in the next section) is around 150 lines of code (not counting the implementation of SHA1Rand). [2] The full implementation – with libraries for w-adic numbers, support for geometric trees, command-line processing, timing, data-collection and comments – is about 1500 lines.

The same code has been timed on three different platforms – a small x86-Infiniband cluster (Triloka), a Blue Gene/P machine and a Power7-Infiniband cluster. On the 157 billion node binomial tree reported on in [26], the implementation shows an efficiency of 87% for 1024 cores on BG/P (483.2 vs 0.54 M Nodes/sec), and 86% for 1024 cores on Power7 (2371 vs 2.7 M Nodes/sec), and 94% for 128 cores on x86 (253.4 vs 2.1 M Nodes/sec). All comparisons are with sequential performance. These numbers contrast with the 80% efficiency reported in [26] on 1024 cores of an x86 cluster. [11] reports 99% efficiency at 8192 cores as compared to a baseline of 512 cores on an x86 cluster. These results involved dedication of 1 out of the 8 cores in each SMP node to assist in work stealing. As compared to the approach in this paper, which utilizes all available cores to perform work, the effective efficiency reported in [11] is 87%. The efficiency numbers reported here are over a larger range of process counts (sequential run vs 128 and 1024 cores, thus $128x$ and $1024x$) as compared to $8k/512 = 16x$ as reported in [11].

---

[2] Due to space constraints, we refer you to [25, 26] for the exact description of both binomial and geometric trees.

On a larger binomial tree, of size 416b, the implementation shows an efficiency of 87% for 2048 cores of BG/P (966.11 vs 0.54 MNodes/sec).

We have also benchmarked the implementation on a geometric tree of size 109B. The implementation shows an efficiency of 89% (1683 vs 1.85 M Nodes/sec) on the Power7 cluster and an efficiency of 92% (357.6 vs 0.38 M Nodes/sec) on the Blue Gene/P cluster. [3]

1.3 Rest of this paper

In the next section we present the scheme in more detail, illustrating with the relevant fragments of X10 code. The code is released under the Eclipse Public Licence and is available from the X10 repository on Sourceforge.[4]

We present the results in more detail in Section 3. Finally in Section 4 we discuss more details of related work.

2. Basic lifeline scheme

We now present the basic scheme by discussing the actual X10 code for the implementation.

To understand the presentation below the following characteristics of X10 must be kept in mind.

- An **async**(p) S statement launches an activity at place p. This activity executes S and terminates. The invoking activity continues immediately, without waiting for the newly created activity to terminate.

- An **at**(p) S statement executes statement S synchronously at place p. That is, the execution of the activity is suspended until S terminates. An **at**(p) e expression evaluates e at p and returns the result.

- A **finish** S statement executes statement S and waits until all activities created during its execution have themselves (recursively) terminated. These activities may be launched at the current place or some remote place.

- The implementation below assumes each place is running a single worker, and workers are not dynamically created.[5]

- Therefore user code must explicitly call Runtime.probe() to service incoming (synchronous or asynchronous) requests. It is up to user code to determine the frequency of polling. (See below for a further discussion of this point.)

- Incoming messages are processed only at specific places in user code, namely calls to Runtime.probe() in the user code or to remote operation invocations (i.e., the asynchronous **async**(p) S operation or synchronous **at**(p) S). At this point zero or more incoming messages (**async**'s, **at**'s) may be processed.[6]

- Since all data-structures are touched by a single worker thread, no locks are needed to guarantee atomicity or mutual exclusion.

---

[3] Let Th_s and Th_p be the throughputs achieved for a program when run serially and in parallel with P processors, respectively. Then, we define efficiency as $Th_p/(Th_s \times P)$.

[4] https://x10.svn.sf.net/svnroot/x10/benchmarks/trunk/UTS.

[5] The programmer ensures this by executing the program with the environment variables X10_NUM_THREADS and X10_STATIC_THREADS set to appropriate values.

[6] X10 supports the bodies of incoming **async**'s and **at**'s may themselves perform network operations, including Runtime.probe(). Thus user code must be written in such a way that it is prepared to handle incoming messages recursively.

- Like Cilk, we use deques to store unexecuted tasks; the owning process operates on the shallow end of the deque (using it as a stack), whereas responses to stealing and lifeline requests operate on the deep end of the deque. This is important even in the absence of multiple threads (i.e., contention) because it promotes cache reuse — there is a greater chance that unexecuted tasks that have just been spawned are not stolen and hence are still in cache.

- If no user code is running at a place, the X10 worker continues to run and will process incoming messages until a termination signal is received from place 0.

The code below uses a deque, implemented as a circular buffer. The deque supports push() and pop() operations on one end and a steal(i) operation at the other end (the parameter i specifies the number of elements to remove).

The design satisfies the following invariants:

- At any time, at most one activity runs in a given place.

- At any time, at most one message has been sent on an outgoing lifeline (and hence at most one message has been received on an incoming lifeline).

First, an object is created at each place. This object maintains information about the state of the execution at that place (e.g. counters). This object is referenced through a place local handle, st(). This handle may be freely communicated from place to place. At any place P, the object associated with this handle at that place may be obtained by simply applying st() to the empty argument list, that is, evaluating st()[7]

Specifically the object maintains the following information:

- various parameters associated with the tree being constructed. Of particular interest are: (a) nu, the maximum number of tasks that will be popped for execution from the dequeue before distribution and polling, (b) w, the maximum number of random steals made before turning to lifeline steals, (c) z, the dimensionality of the lifeline graph, (d) k, the number of items to steal at a time ($k = 0$ for "steal half").

- the **Boolean** control variable active that is true *iff* a user-activity is running at the place.

- the **Boolean** control variable noLoot which is used to record whether loot (number of stolen tasks) has arrived asynchronously.

- the array lifelinesActivated contains a **Boolean** per place. lifelinesActivated(p.id) is true only if this place has activated the outgoing lifeline to p, and has not yet received loot in return. In principle only z values need to be recorded; the current implementation keeps an array of P booleans.

- a stack thieves that records which incoming lifelines have been activated. The size of this stack is bounded by z.

Launching work. Computation is initiated from place 0. The given root node is expanded one level; this will typically cause tasks to be added to the deque. Then an **async** is spawned at each place (other than 0). The async is given an initial apportionment of loot; this may be empty. Finally the current activity continues by processing its own deque, after

---

[7] Effectively one may think of a place local handle as a handle to a distributed array of elements; at any place, the id of that place may be used to access the element of the array stored at that place.

marking itself as active. Once it has finished processing its stack, it terminates.

```
def main (st:PLH, rootNode:TreeNode) {
 finish {
    processBinomialRoot (b0, rootNode, deque);
    val lootSize = stack.size()/Place.MAX_PLACES;
    for (var pi:Int=1 ; pi<P ; ++pi) {
      val loot = deque.steal(lootSize);
      async (Place(pi))
        st().launch(st, true, loot, 0);
    }
    active=true;
    processDeque(st);
    active=false;
 }
}
```

When an activity is launched at a place p from place s, it first resets the (local) **Boolean** flag lifelinesActivated(s) at p (thus enabling code running at p to establish a new lifeline back to s at a future point in time). It then checks to see if an activity is already running (is active true?). If so, it simply processes the loot and terminates. Otherwise it becomes "the" activity at this place. After processing its loot, it determines whether there are any incoming lifelines, and if so distributes work through those lifelines. Finally it processes all the elements remaining on its deque until the deque is empty (note this could take a long time). It then terminates. (Note that launch is invoked at place either by the main activity or through the distribution mechanism – see distribute below.)

```
def launch(st:PLH, init:Boolean,
   loot:ValRail[TreeNode], depth:Int, source:Int) {
   lifelinesActivated(source) = false;
   if (active) {
     noLoot = false;
     for (r in loot) processSubtree(r);
   } else {
     active=true;
     for (r in loot) processSubtree(r);
     if (depth > 0)
       distribute(st, depth+1);
     processDeque(st);
     active=false;
}}
def processSubtree (node:TreeNode) {
   ++nodesCounter;
   binomial (q, m, node, deque);
}
```

Local work execution. The deque is processed in a loop until empty. Each time around in the loop, at must nu items are processed from the deque. The network is then probed to handle incoming messages. If some thieves have registered themselves, loot is distributed. When the deque becomes empty, an attempt is made to steal from other workers. If no loot is found[8] the activity terminates, otherwise it resumes processing the deque.

```
def processDeque(st:PLH) {
   while (true) {
     var n:Int = min(deque.size(), nu);
     while (n > 0) {
       for ((count) in 0..n−1)
         processSubtree(deque.pop());
```

---
[8] note that loot may arrive synchronously through the call to attemptSteal() or it could arrive asynchronously through an incoming distribution, discussed below

```
       Runtime.probe();
       val numThieves = thieves.size();
       if (numThieves > 0)
         distribute(st, 1, numThieves);
       n = min(deque.size(), nu);
     }
     val loot = attemptSteal(st);
     if (null != loot)
       processLoot(loot, false);
     else {
       if (! noLoot) {
         noLoot=true;
         continue;
       }
       else
         break;
}}}
```

We use a command line parameter (n) to control the frequency of polling. This can affect the performance of the program. Frequent polling incurs overhead and comes in the way of the worker executing real work. Infrequent polling means that steal requests from thieves are not processed quickly, thereby stalling thieves. In practice we have found n=511 or n=1023 gives good results for most UTS workloads.

Distributions. A distribution is made to an incoming lifeline only if there is enough work. Work is popped from the deep-end of the deque. To distribute work, an async is launched at the target place. Note that this async is governed by the single **finish** in main().

```
def distribute(st:PLH, depth:Int) {
   val n = thieves.size();
   if (n > 0)
     distribute(st, 1, n);
}
def distribute(st:PLH, depth:Int, var n:Int) {
   val lootSize= deque.size();
   if (lootSize > 2) {
     n = Math.min(n, lootSize−2);
     val s = lootSize/(n+1);
     for ((i) in 0..n−1) {
       val thief = thieves.pop();
       val loot = deque.steal(s);
       async (Place(thief))
         st().launch(st, false, loot, depth);
     }
   }
}
```

Various modifications are possible and will be explored in future work. Instead of dividing the current set of tasks evenly among all the recipients, the donor could randomly select one of the thieves and send it a portion of the loot (depending on the value of k). This would be a dual to random work-stealing – here work is "pushed" to places that have indicated earlier that they needed work (note they may no longer need work, since some other lifeline may have supplied them).

Another important consideration is that as the code is written it copies the items out of the deque one at a time for each target destination. An alternative would be for the activity to block off portions of the deque and trigger asynchronous DMA's to transfer the loot to the destination. This may result in better performance, particularly at high z's, and in cases where the size of the deque can grow large.

Stealing. To make a steal, an activity randomly guesses another place, and uses the **at** operation to retrieve loot from that place. It tries this at most w times, also breaking immediately if loot arrives asynchronously, for example because it is being distributed on a lifeline.

If no loot is received during this phase, the activity tries its lifelines one after the other, returning as soon as loot is found. Care is taken to ensure that a request is not made of an outgoing lifeline if a request has already been made of that lifeline and no loot has been received from it so far. The difference between the stealHandler() invocations in the direct steal phase and in the lifeline phase is the second argument: this is set to **true** only in the lifeline phase.

```
def attemptSteal(st:PLH):ValRail[TreeNode] {
  if (Place.MAX_PLACES == 1) return null;
  for (var i:Int=0; i<w && noLoot; i++) {
    var q_:Int = 0;
    val p=here.id;
    while((q_= myRandom.nextInt(Place.MAX_PLACES))== p) ;
    val q = q_;
    val loot = at (Place(q)) st().stealHandler(p,false);
    if (loot != null) return loot;
  }
  if (! noLoot) return null;
  for (var i:Int=0;
         (i<myLifelines.length()) && noLoot
         && 0<=myLifelines(i);
         ++i) {
    val L:Int = myLifelines(i);
    if (!lifelinesActivated(L) ) {
      lifelinesActivated(L) = true;
      val loot = at(Place(L)) st().stealHandler(p, true);
      if (null!=loot) {
        lifelinesActivated(L) = false;
        return loot;
      }}}
  return null;
}
```

A try at a steal is handled by examining the size of the deque. If the deque has enough tasks, then they are popped from the deque and returned. Otherwise if isLifeLine is set, the place making the try is recorded in the thieves stack (used during distribution).

```
def stealHandler(p:Int, life:Boolean):ValRail[TreeNode] {
  val length = deque.size();
  val numSteals = k==0u ? (length >=2u ? length/2u : 0u)
   : (k < length ? k : (k/2u < length ? k/2u : 0u));
  if (numSteals==0u) {
    if (life)
      thieves.push(p);
    return null;
  }
  return deque.steal(numSteals);
}
```

This is a very simple scheme and different from the implementation used in [26] and the implementation described in [11]. [26] implements steals as follows. Each worker polls periodically. When it receives a steal request, it determines the amount of loot to release and removes it logically from the deque (without copying it out). It returns a remote reference to the loot. The thief then initiates a separate DMA to retrieve the loot. This DMA request is handled purely by the network adapter without disrupting the worker. Thus the worker does not need to spend time copying the loot, and avoids polluting its cache. [11] keeps an extra helper thread on the side to perform the control operations necessary for stealing. Data is also transfered by DMA where possible.

X10 has idioms for expressing DMA transfer to remote locations. However for the trees we are considering, the loot to be transferred is rarely more than a few hundred elements, and stealing is relatively infrequent. For such systems it is not clear that the more elaborate implementation wins.[9] In future work we plan to implement DMA steals and evaluate the trade-off on various examples within the context of a unified implementation.

Consistent with the results reported in [26], we have found that "steal half" works best for binomial trees. This is not surprising given that the binomial tree is such that each node has the same potential to generate work. Stealing half leads to more rapid diffusion of work through the system. This is in contrast to the fixed-function geometric tree in which nodes higher in the tree have a much greater potential to generate work than nodes lower in the tree. For such systems steal-half gives poor performance and fixed-size steals are better. In particular for the geometric trees we have investigated, we have found that stealing 7 items at a time works well.

3. Results and Analysis

The results presented in this paper were obtained by compiling the program with the 2.0.5 version of the X10 compiler.

All speedups are reported with respect to the performance of a sequential implementation of UTS. The sequential program is iterative and uses the same deque data-structure used by the parallel program to record the nodes of the tree being constructed. It does not have any parallel overheads associated with it – specifically it does not invoke the probe operation. However, because sequential runtimes for large trees can be very large, we reduced the size of the input on which the sequential program was run. Table 1 gives a detailed description of the trees used to test the sequential performance of UTS on our test machines.

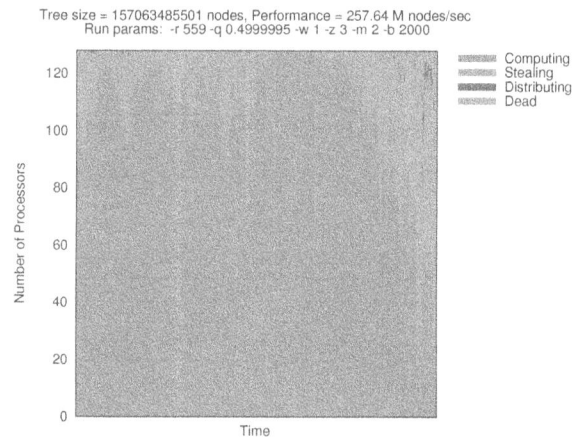

Figure 1. States of the compute nodes during the execution of X10's UTS application execution over time for a BINOMIAL tree of size 157 billion nodes. The results were collected on IBM's Triloka Linux cluster. Each node attempted 1 random steal (the parameter w) before resorting to one of its 3 lifelines (the parameter z).

---

[9] We instrumented our implementation and determined that the worker was spending less than 0.01% of its compute time in copying this data. This analysis did not account for cache misses due to pollution.

Machine	Tree type	t	r	b	m	q	a	d	Tree size	MNodes/sec
Triloka	BINOMINAL	0	559	2000	2	0.49995	—	—	57354859	2.104
ANL-BG/P	BINOMINAL	0	559	2000	2	0.4995	—	—	2859057	0.54
P7HV32	BINOMIAL	0	42	20000	6	0.166666665	—	—	510009729	2.7
P7HV32	GEOMETRIC	1	0	4	—	—	3	10	6700654	1.85
IBM-BG/P	GEOMETRIC	1	0	4	—	—	3	10	6700654	0.37

Table 1. As sequential execution (*not* parallel execution on 1 node) of UTS for very large trees requires excessive machine time, the sequential performance of UTS on various machines for both BINOMIAL and GEOMETRIC trees was measured using smaller trees. The command-line parameters used to generate the trees for sequential benchmarking are shown in this table. For a full explanation of the meaning of the command-line parameters to UTS, please refer to [24]. ANL-BG/P and IBM-BG/P are abbreviations for the Blue Gene/P clusters at Argonne National Laboratory and IBM T.J. Watson Research Center,respectively.

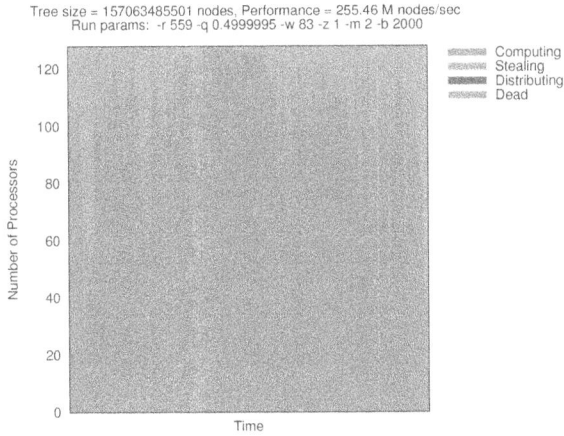

Figure 2. States of the compute nodes during the execution of X10's UTS application execution over time for a BINO-MIAL tree of size 157 billion nodes. The results were collected on IBM's Triloka Linux cluster. Each node attempted 83 random steals (the parameter w) before resorting to its single lifeline (the parameter z).

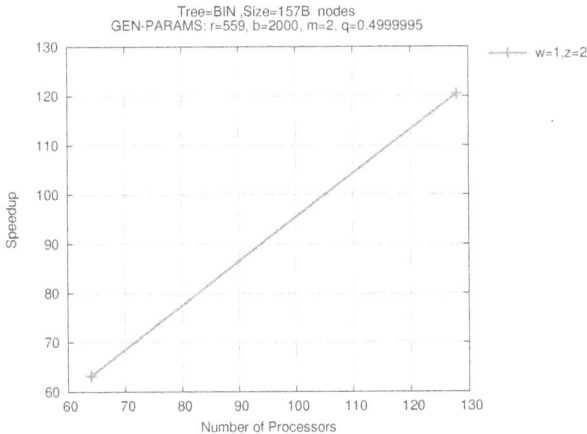

Figure 4. UTS speedup achieved for a 157 billion node BI-NOMIAL tree on Argonne National Lab's Blue Gene/P cluster. The speedup shown is based on the sequential performance of UTS, which is 0.54 million nodes per second. The parameter w indicates the number of random steals attempted before resorting to lifelines. The parameter z indicates the number of lifelines for each compute node. The UTS revision number used was 15277.

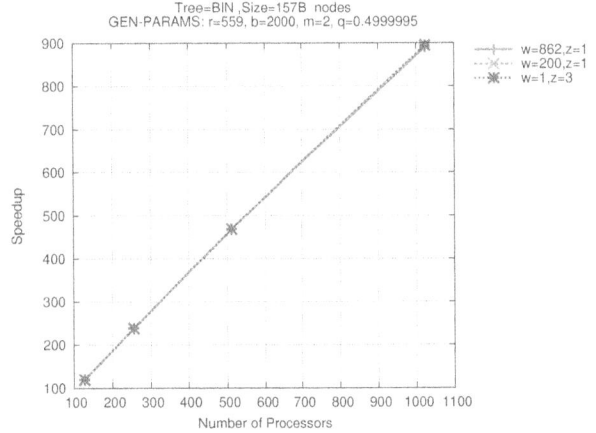

Figure 3. UTS speedup achieved for a 157 billion node BI-NOMIAL tree on IBM's Triloka cluster. The speedup shown is based on the sequential performance of UTS, which is 2.104 million nodes per second. The parameter w indicates the number of random steals attempted before resorting to lifelines. The parameter z indicates the number of lifelines for each compute node. The UTS revision number used was 15277.

3.1 Experimental Platforms

We used three different experimental platforms for our empirical evaluation.

- Triloka: a small cluster of 16 IBM LS-22 blades connected by a 20Gb/sec IB network. Each node has 2 quad-core AMD 2.3Ghz Opteron processors, 16 GB of memory, and is running Red Hat Enterprise Linux 5.3.

- Blue Gene/P: We used the `surveyor` and `intrepid` systems located at the Argonne National Labratory and the `Watson4P` system located at the IBM T.J. Watson Research Center. Each compute node in a Blue Gene/P system has 2 GB of memory and 4 850 MHz PowerPC 450 processors each with a dual floating point unit.

- P7HV32: This is a 32-node Power7 cluster interconnected by Infiniband. Each compute node has 32 3.3 GHz processor cores, 128GB of physical memory and runs SuSE Linux Enterprise Server v 11.1 for ppc64.

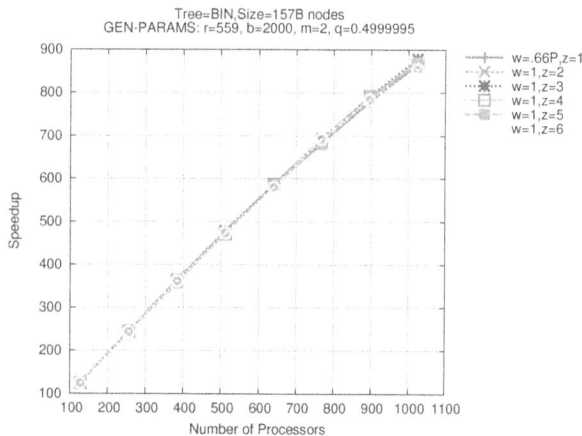

Figure 5. UTS speedup achieved for a 157 billion node BI-NOMIAL tree on IBM's P7HV32 cluster. The speedup shown is based on the sequential performance of UTS of the same problem, which is 2.7 million nodes per second. The parameter w indicates the number of random steals attempted before resorting to lifelines. The parameter z indicates the number of lifelines for each compute node. The UTS revision number used was 15294.

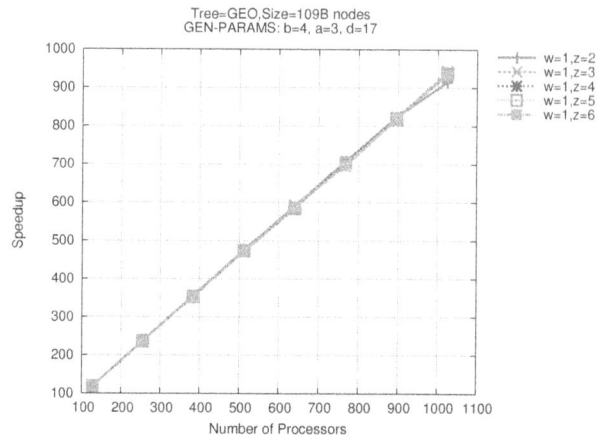

Figure 7. UTS speedup achieved for a 109 billion node GE-OMETRIC tree on IBM's Blue Gene/P cluster. The speedup shown is based on the sequential performance of UTS of the same problem, which is 0.37 million nodes per second. The parameter w indicates the number of random steals attempted before resorting to lifelines. The parameter z indicates the number of lifelines for each compute node. The UTS revision number used was 15290.

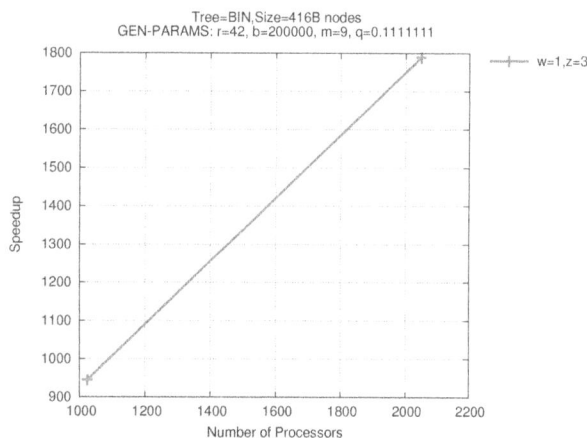

Figure 6. UTS speedup achieved for a 416 billion node BI-NOMIAL tree on Argonne National Lab's Blue Gene/P cluster. The speedup shown is based on the sequential performance of UTS, which is 0.54 million nodes per second. The parameter w indicates the number of random steals attempted before resorting to lifelines. The parameter z indicates the number of lifelines for each compute node. The UTS revision number used was 15277.

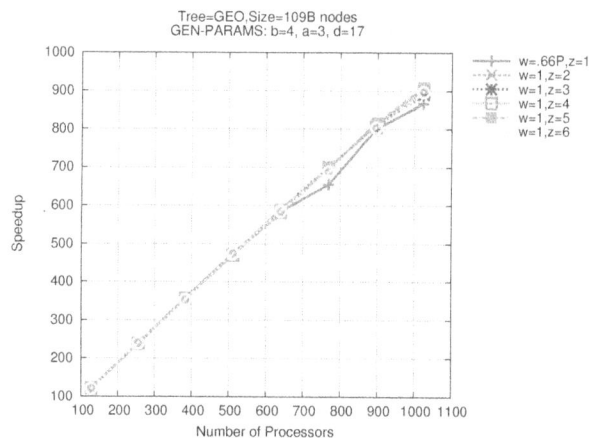

Figure 8. UTS speedup achieved for a 109 billion node GEOMETRIC tree on IBM's P7HV32 cluster. The speedup shown is based on the sequential performance of UTS of the same problem, which is 1.85 million nodes per second. The parameter w indicates the number of random steals attempted before resorting to lifelines. The parameter z indicates the number of lifelines for each compute node. The UTS revision number used was 15294.

On all platforms, we used X10 version 2.0.5. We used the C++ backend, which compiles[10] the X10 source code to C++ files which are then compiled into an executable using a standard C++ compiler. The generated C++ code was compiled with g++ v 4.3.2 on Triloka; g++ v 4.1.2 on Blue Gene/P and g++ v 4.3.4 (Power specific version) on P7HV32.

3.2 Discussion

Figure 1 and Figure 2 show the "lifestory" of a test run. We instrumented the application to record events corresponding to state transitions (i.e. transitions between *computing*, *stealing*, *distributing*, *probing* and *idle*) at each place. The start time for these lifestories was normalized to 0 to account for clock skew between the nodes. The histories were then merged in an order preserving way to determine the composite picture presented here. The picture shows at each instant the number of places that were computing, stealing, distributed or dead.

The two graphs are for different values of (w, z), viz. $(1, 3)$ and $(83, 1)$. Even though the throughput for both runs was the same, the graphs show variations in micro-structure. In particular, the computation with the high w value spends 22% more time stealing than the computation with the low w (not surprisingly) — the green area is substantially larger, and there is a visible dead area towards the end of the computation.[11] The graphs were fairly small and run on small number of cores; we expect the differences to be more pronounced with increase in number of cores.

Figure 3 shows speedup for the small x86 Triloka cluster. The implementation achieves 94% efficiency vs sequential execution for 128 cores. While not indicated here, similar performance curves were obtained for other combinations of w and z for this configuration. The speedups are measured with respect to sequential performance numbers. Since problem sizes run on large machines are typically large, it is impractical to obtain sequential performance numbers by running the same program in sequential mode. Therefore we compute sequential numbers by running the program on a smaller tree of the same basic shape. The actual parameters used to compute the sequential performance are given in Table 1.

Figure 4 presents the data for multiple executions of the 157B tree from [26] for different points in the (w, z) space. It can be seen that performance stays the same as w decreases dramatically, while z is increased modestly. At 1024 cores, the implementation delivers an efficiency of 87%. Figure 5 presents the data for this tree on the P7HV32 cluster, which also delivers 87% efficiency at 1024 cores. Note that the results for high-w $((w, z) = (0.66 \times P, 1))$ are starting to get marginally worse than results for high-z.[12]

Figure 6 shows that the efficiency is maintained, albeit at a bigger tree size, as the core count is doubled.

Finally, Figure 7 and Figure 8 show speedup for a geometric tree of 109B nodes on the Blue Gene/P and P7HV32 clusters respectively with varying values of w and z. The implementation achieves an efficiency of 92% and 89% respec-

tively. Again, high-w results tend to be slightly worse than high-z results.

4. Related and future work

A fundamental requirement for efficient parallel execution of a program is that work (both computational and otherwise) be evenly divided amongst the available computing resources; that is, the program's execution must be well load balancing. Many applications are *regular*; that is, these applications' computations and the related data can be partitioned *apriori*; regular programs can be efficiently load balanced statically. However, there are many applications which are irregular and dynamic; that is, the computations and the data sets in these applications cannot be partitioned *a priori*. Irregular applications are extremely sensitive to load balancing, and place unique requirements on parallel programming tools and runtimes that have not yet been satisfied. Till now, the best solutions for efficient execution of irregular applications on distributed-memory systems have heavily involved application-level dynamic load balancing.

Some of the early research on dynamic load balancing for shared-memory systems was carried out in the Mul-T Scheme [23] project; load balancing was achieved through lazy task creation wherein threads would steal work from one another when they ran out of work. Cilk [15], an extension to the C language, was the first system to provide efficient load balancing for a wide variety of irregular applications. Load balancing in Cilk applications is achieved by a scheduler that follows the *depth-first work, breadth-first steal* principle [5]. Cilk's scheduling policy, in which each thread of execution maintains its own set of tasks, and steals from other threads on a need-by basis, is often dubbed as *work-stealing*. Currently, there are many solutions for task parallelism that offer work-stealing schedulers. Of these, OpenMP 3.0 [27], Intel's Threading Building Blocks (TBB) [29], Microsoft's Parallel Patterns Library (PPL), and Task Parallel Library (TPL) are the most popular. The other variants of Cilk-like work-stealing in today's parallel frameworks include X10's *breadth-first* [7] work scheduling policy and Guo et al.'s [17] hybrid model for work stealing. Kambadur et al. [19] show that different work-stealing strategies are required for different irregular applications, and present a library framework to that allows easy customization of load balancing policies on shared memory. Berenbrink et al. [3] prove that work-stealing, by virtue of taking a distributed approach to load balancing processors, is stable.

The work-stealing approaches mentioned above efficiently and dynamically load balances applications in a shared-memory environment. However, these approaches are not directly applicable to distributed-memory machines because of a variety of issues such as network latency and bandwidth, and termination detection. Various bodies of work have addressed the problem of dynamic load balancing on distributed-memory machines. Grama et al. [16, 20] discuss various load balancing strategies for distributed parallel searches that are independent of the specific search technique. Blumofe et al. [6] adapt the Cilk work-stealing model to distributed shared memory by limiting the scope of the programs to be purely functional. ATLAS [1] and Satin [32] both use hierarchical work-steal to acheive global load balancing. Charm++ [18, 31] monitors the execution of its distributed programs for load imbalance and migrates computation objects to low-load places to correct the load imbalance. Global load balancing for message passing environ-

---

[10] The X10 compiler `x10c++` was given the command line arguments `-O -NO_CHECKS` to enable optimizations and disable array bounds and null pointer checking

[11] For $(w, z) = (83, 1)$, 1.835% of the total time was spent stealing, as opposed to 1.43% for $(w, z) = (1, 3)$.

[12] High w runs correspond to unrestricted random work-stealing. High z runs (with $w = 1$) correspond to more extensive use of lifelines.

ments has been researched for specific problems by Batoukov and Sorevik [2].

UTS, an excellent example of an irregular application, was first described by Prins et al. [28]. Although they tried various work-stealing strategies, they were unable to get good speedups on distributed-memory systems on their initial UPC [13] implementation; however, their implementation showed good performance on shared-memory machines. Later, Olivier et al. [24] formally introduced UTS as a benchmark to measure a parallel system's ability to dynamically load balance an application. Similar to [28], their OpenMP and UPC implementations showed good speedup on shared-memory systems, but not on distributed-memory systems. Dinan et al. [12] studied the ability of MPI [21, 22] to support dynamic load balancing required by UTS through application-level load balancing techniques. In this study, both centralized work-sharing and distributed work-stealing approaches were tried, and it was shown that work-stealing approaches with the right stealing granularity performed better on a wider variety of workloads than work-sharing. Olivier and Prins [26] provided the first scalable implementation of UTS on clusters that provided up to 80% efficiency on 1024 nodes. To this end, they employed a custom application-level load balancer along with optimizations such as one-sided communications and novel termination detection techniques. Finally, Dinan et al. [11] provide a framework for global load balancing, which was used to achieve speedups on 8196 processors. Global load balancing and termination detection facilities were provided to express irregular applications. By reserving one core per compute node on the cluster exclusively for lock and unlock operations, this framework allowed threads to steal work asynchronously without disrupting the victim threads. However, the cost paid was a static allocation (one core out of every eight) for communication. This results in lower throughput because the thread is not available for user-level computations.

4.1 Future work

Develop an analytical framework for lifeline graphs. It appears to us that random work-stealing and lifeline distribution graphs are two sides of the same coin. We believe that it should be possible to develop an analytical framework for lifeline graphs which can predict the performance (efficiency) of implementations with given values for parameters.

Some initial experimentation we have done leads to the possibility that high-z configurations deliver better performance at high processor counts with lower CPU utilization. Lower CPU utilization is of value in cloud-based multi-tenancy installations. For the 157B tree at 2048 cores, we observe 820 M Nodes/s for $(w, z) = (1024, 1)$, and 828 M Nodes/s for $(10, 10)$. (The $(10, 1)$ performance is 797 M nodes/s). Also as Figure 8 shows, at higher core counts high-w runs tend to be worse than high-z runs. We plan to run further experiments to investigate this phenomenon.

Implement adaptive stealing. [7] shows that the performance of graph algorithms can be improved in a shared memory context by using work-stealing with adaptive grain size. Workers add chunks of tasks to the deque; a thief steals one chunk at a time. The size of the chunk is determined by the worker based on the current size of the deque. A large deque means there is less demand for work, hence a larger chunk can be built. We believe these ideas can be adapted fruitfully to global load balancing.

Scaling out finish. We are interested in scaling computations to hundreds of thousands of cores. For this the current X10 implementation of `finish` must be restructured to use reduction trees and engineered to work at this scale.

Acknowledgements

We gratefully thank the many members of the X10 team who have contributed to several discussions related to these ideas, in particular David Cunningham, George Almasi, Olivier Tardieu and Igor Peshansky. The design and implementation of the `finish` scheme in the X10 implementation is due to Olivier Tardieu.

This research used resources of the Argonne Leadership Computing Facility at Argonne National Laboratory, which is supported by the Office of Science of the U.S. Department of Energy under contract DE-AC02-06CH11357.

This material is based upon work supported by the Defense Advanced Research Projects Agency under its Agreement No. HR0011-07-9-0002.

References

[1] J. E. Baldeschwieler, R. D. Blumofe, and E. A. Brewer. Atlas: an infrastructure for global computing. In *EW 7: Proceedings of the 7th workshop on ACM SIGOPS European workshop*, pages 165–172, New York, NY, USA, 1996. ACM.

[2] R. Batoukov and T. Sorevik. A Generic Parallel Branch and Bound Environment on a Network of Workstations. In *HiPer '99: Proceedings of High Performance Computing on Hewlett-Packard Systems*, pages 474–483, 1999.

[3] P. Berenbrink, T. Friedetzky, and L. A. Goldberg. The natural work-stealing algorithm is stable. *SIAM J. Comput.*, 32(5):1260–1279, 2003.

[4] S. M. Blackburn, R. L. Hudson, R. Morrison, J. E. B. Moss, D. S. Munro, and J. Zigman. Starting with termination: a methodology for building distributed garbage collection algorithms. *Aust. Comput. Sci. Commun.*, 23(1):20–28, 2001.

[5] R. D. Blumofe and C. E. Leiserson. Scheduling Multithreaded Computations by Work Stealing. In *Proceedings of the 35th Annual Symposium on Foundations of Computer Science (FOCS)*, pages 356–368, 1994.

[6] R. D. Blumofe and P. A. Lisiecki. Adaptive and reliable parallel computing on networks of workstations. In *ATEC '97: Proceedings of the annual conference on USENIX Annual Technical Conference*, pages 10–10, Berkeley, CA, USA, 1997. USENIX Association.

[7] G. Cong, S. Kodali, S. Krishnamoorthy, D. Lea, V. Saraswat, and T. Wen. Solving Large, Irregular Graph Problems Using Adaptive Work-Stealing. In *ICPP '08: Proceedings of the 2008 37th International Conference on Parallel Processing*, pages 536–545, Washington, DC, USA, 2008. IEEE Computer Society.

[8] J. Dean, S. Ghemawat, and G. Inc. Mapreduce: simplified data processing on large clusters. In *In OSDI'04: Proceedings of the 6th conference on Symposium on Opearting Systems Design and Implementation*, pages 137–150. USENIX Association, 2004.

[9] E. Dijkstra and C. Scholten. Termination detection for diffusing computations. In *Information Processing Letters*, volume 11, pages 1–4, 1980.

[10] E. W. Dijkstra. Derivation of a termination detection algorithm for distributed computations. pages 507–512, 1987.

[11] J. Dinan, D. B. Larkins, P. Sadayappan, S. Krishnamoorthy, and J. Nieplocha. Scalable work stealing. In *SC '09: Proceedings of the Conference on High Performance Computing Networking, Storage and Analysis*, pages 1–11, New York, NY, USA, 2009. ACM.

[12] J. Dinan, S. Olivier, G. Sabin, J. Prins, P. Sadayappan, and C.-W. Tseng. Dynamic Load Balancing of Unbalanced Computations

Using Message Passing. In *IPDPS 07: Parallel and Distributed Processing Symposium*, pages 1–8, Long Beach, CA, March 2007. IEEE International.

[13] T. A. El-Ghazawi, W. W. Carlson, and J. M. Draper. *UPC Language Specification*, 1.1 edition, May 2003. http://www.gwu.edu/~upc/downloads/upc_specs_1.1p2pre1.pdf.

[14] N. Francez and M. Rodeh. Achieving distributed termination without freezing. *IEEE Trans. Softw. Eng.*, 8(3):287–292, 1982.

[15] M. Frigo, C. E. Leiserson, and K. H. Randall. The implementation of the Cilk-5 multithreaded language. In *Proceedings of the ACM SIGPLAN '98 Conference on Programming Language Design and Implementation*, pages 212–223, Montreal, Quebec, Canada, June 1998. Proceedings published in ACM SIGPLAN Notices, Vol. 33, No. 5, May, 1998.

[16] A. Grama and V. Kumar. State of the Art in Parallel Search Techniques for Discrete Optimization Problems. *IEEE Trans. on Knowl. and Data Eng.*, 11(1):28–35, 1999.

[17] Y. Guo, R. Barik, R. Raman, and V. Sarkar. Work-First and Help-First Scheduling Policies for Async-Finish Task Parallelism. In *Proceedings of the 23rd IEEE International Parallel and Distributed Processing Symposium*, May 2009.

[18] L. V. Kalé and S. Krishnan. CHARM++: A portable concurrent object oriented system based on C++. In *Proceedings of Object Oriented Programming Systems, Languages and Applications, ACM Sigplan Notes*, volume 28, pages 91–108, 1993.

[19] P. Kambadur, A. Gupta, A. Ghoting, H. Avron, and A. Lumsdaine. PFunc: Modern task parallelism for modern high performance computing. In *Proceedings of the 2008 ACM/IEEE conference on Supercomputing (SC)*, Portland, Oregon, November 2009.

[20] V. Kumar, A. Y. Grama, and N. R. Vempaty. Scalable load balancing techniques for parallel computers. *J. Parallel Distrib. Comput.*, 22(1):60–79, 1994.

[21] Message Passing Interface Forum. MPI, June 1995. http://www.mpi-forum.org/.

[22] Message Passing Interface Forum. MPI-2, July 1997. http://www.mpi-forum.org/.

[23] E. Mohr, D. A. Kranz, and R. H. Halstead, Jr. Lazy Task Creation: A Technique for Increasing the Granularity of Parallel Programs. *IEEE Trans. Parallel Distrib. Syst.*, 2(3):264–280, 1991.

[24] S. Olivier, J. Huan, J. Liu, J. Prins, J. Dinan, P. Sadayappan, and C.-W. Tseng. UTS: an unbalanced tree search benchmark. In *LCPC'06: Proceedings of the 19th international conference on Languages and compilers for parallel computing*, pages 235–250, Berlin, Heidelberg, 2007. Springer-Verlag.

[25] S. Olivier, J. Huan, J. Liu, J. Prins, J. Dinan, P. Sadayappan, and C.-W. Tseng. Uts: an unbalanced tree search benchmark. In *Proceedings of the 19th international conference on Languages and compilers for parallel computing*, LCPC'06, pages 235–250, Berlin, Heidelberg, 2007. Springer-Verlag.

[26] S. Olivier and J. Prins. Scalable dynamic load balancing using UPC. In *ICPP '08: Proceedings of the 2008 37th International Conference on Parallel Processing*, pages 123–131, Washington, DC, USA, 2008. IEEE Computer Society.

[27] OpenMP Architecture Review Board. *OpenMP Application Program Interface, v3.0*. May 2008.

[28] J. Prins, J. Huan, B. Pugh, C.-W. Tseng, and P. Sadayappan. UPC Implementation of an Unbalanced Tree Search Benchmark. Technical Report 03-034, University of North Carolina at Chapel Hill, October 2003.

[29] J. Reinders. *Intel Threading Building Blocks*. O'Reilly, 2007.

[30] V. Saraswat, G. Almasi, G. Bikshandi, C. Cascaval, D. Cunningham, D. Grove, S. Kodali, I. Peshansky, and O. Tardieu. The asynchronous partitioned global address space model. In *AMP'10: Proceedings of The First Workshop on Advances in Message Passing*, June 2010.

[31] A. B. Sinha and L. V. Kalé. A load balancing strategy for prioritized execution of tasks. In *IIPS'93: Proceedings of International Parallel Processing Symposium*, pages 230–237, 1993.

[32] R. V. van Nieuwpoort, T. Kielmann, and H. E. Bal. Efficient load balancing for wide-area divide-and-conquer applications. In *PPoPP '01: Proceedings of the eighth ACM SIGPLAN symposium on Principles and practices of parallel programming*, pages 34–43, New York, NY, USA, 2001. ACM.

COREMU: A Scalable and Portable Parallel Full-system Emulator

Zhaoguo Wang   Ran Liu   Yufei Chen   Xi Wu   Haibo Chen   Weihua Zhang   Binyu Zang

Parallel Processing Institute, Fudan University

{zgwang, ranliu, chenyufei, wuxi, hbchen, zhangweihua, byzang}@fudan.edu.cn

Abstract

This paper presents the open-source COREMU, a scalable and portable parallel emulation framework that decouples the complexity of parallelizing full-system emulators from building a mature sequential one. The key observation is that CPU cores and devices in current (and likely future) multiprocessors are loosely-coupled and communicate through well-defined interfaces. Based on this observation, COREMU emulates multiple cores by creating multiple instances of existing sequential emulators, and uses a thin library layer to handle the inter-core and device communication and synchronization, to maintain a consistent view of system resources. COREMU also incorporates lightweight memory transactions, feedback-directed scheduling, lazy code invalidation and adaptive signal control to provide scalable performance. To make COREMU useful in practice, we also provide some preliminary tools and APIs that can help programmers to diagnose performance problems and (concurrency) bugs.

A working prototype, which reuses the widely-used QEMU as the sequential emulator, is with only 2500 lines of code (LOCs) changes to QEMU. It currently supports x64 and ARM platforms, and can emulates up to 255 [1] cores running commodity OSes with practical performance, while QEMU cannot scale above 32 cores. A set of performance evaluation against QEMU indicates that, COREMU has negligible uniprocessor emulation overhead, performs and scales significantly better than QEMU. We also show how COREMU could be used to diagnose performance problems and concurrency bugs of both OS kernel and parallel applications.

Categories and Subject Descriptors C.4 [*Performance of Systems*]: Modeling techniques; I.6.0 [*Simulation and Modelling*]: General; D.2.5 [*Testing and Debugging*]: Debugging aids

General Terms Design, Experimentation, Performance

Keywords Full-system Emulator, Parallel Emulator, Multicore

1. Introduction

The continuity of the Moore's Law has shifted the current computing to multicore or many-core eras. Currently, eight cores and twelve cores on a Chip are commercially available. It was predicated that tens to hundreds (and even thousands) of cores on a single chip would appear in the foreseeable future [31].

The advances of many-core hardware also make full-system emulation more important than before, due to the increasing need of pre-hardware development of system software, characterizing performance bottlenecks, exposing and analyzing software bugs (especially concurrent ones). Full-system emulation, which emulates the entire software stack including operating systems, libraries and user-level applications, is extremely useful in serving the above purposes. It is even claimed with evidence that simulators might be inaccurate or even useless if ignoring the system effects [7]. In light of the importance of full-system emulation, there has been a considerable amount of effort to build efficient full-system emulators. Examples include QEMU [21], Bochs [5], Simics [15] and Parallel Embra [14].

The many-core or multicore computing also creates tremendous challenges and opportunities to full-system emulation. On one hand, the rapid-increasing number of emulated cores requires full-system emulation to be scalable and be able to handle a reasonable scale of input. On the other hand, the abundant physical cores provide even more resources for full-system emulators to harness.

Unfortunately, most commodity full-system emulators are sequential and only time-slice emulated cores on a single physical core in a round-robin fashion [15, 16, 21, 23], or only support discontinued outdated host and guest processor pairs [14]. Hence, they cannot fully harness the power of likely abundant resources in current CMP architecture, resulting in poor performance *scalability* and *restricted parallelism*.

First, the sequential emulation design indicates linear slowdown when the number of emulated cores grows, thus scales poorly on current multicore platforms. Figure 1 shows the average execution time of processing 10 MB and 100MB input using *WordCount* in log scale, a MapReduce application for shared-memory multiprocessors in the Phoenix testsuite [22], running on an emulated Debian-Linux with kernel version 2.6.33-1 using the recent version of QEMU. The performance degrades linearly with the number of cores. When processing relative large input (e.g., 100MB), QEMU times out for only 32 emulated cores.

Second, the sequential design implies that there is limited parallelism exposed among emulated cores. This significantly restricts the use of full-system emulator to analyze software behaviors, thus sacrifices the fidelity of full-system emulation. This problem is critical as parallelism is crucial to exhibit bugs when running parallel workloads or debugging system software, which are especially important due to the pervasive existence of parallelism and the difficulty in writing correct parallel code.

Figure 2 shows the restricted parallelism problem using a simple *parallel counter* program. The program increases the *counter* using two parallel threads, with each thread increase it 500 times.

[1] The xAPIC specification in x86 supports up to 255 cores.

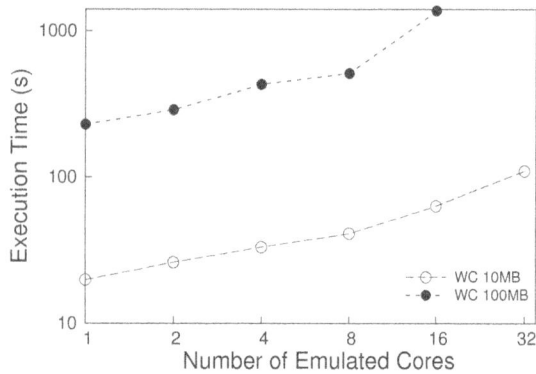

Figure 1: The execution time of WordCount processing 10 MB and 100MB input on QEMU running on a 16-core machine.

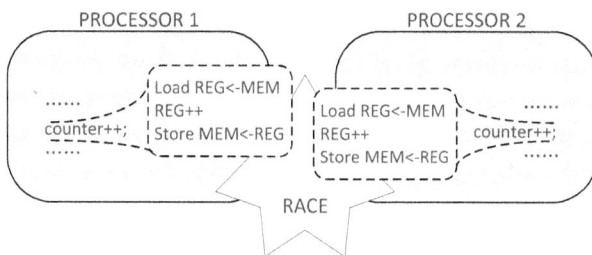

Figure 2: Bad Counter: the result will be incorrect as *INC* will not be executed atomically.

The expected output should be 1000 but it fails on a multicore system due to the data race between two threads. Unfortunately, *this program usually behaves correctly* on *full-system emulators that sequentially emulate multicore*. This is because the scheduling among cores only happens at a coarse-grained granularity (e.g., basic block) for the sake of performance, which naturally renders the *increment* atomic, resulting in no data race. In this example, a much subtler problem occurs on a CISC machine where the increment is translated to a single *INC* instruction *without lock prefix*. In such a case, the data race can only appear at *microinstruction* level, hence even scheduling at instruction granularity can hardly expose the data race bug.

Unfortunately, building a *parallel* full-system emulator is usually resource-intensive and requires years to be mature. Full-system emulators, unlike user-mode emulators, need to model the system aspects of a computing platform, including system-ISA, address translation, privilege levels, interrupts and a set of devices. Further, building a portable emulator is even harder because of the dramatic differences of both the user-ISA and system-ISA among diverse architectures. For example, QEMU becomes mature and widely adopted after years of active development and is currently still in active evolvement.

To address the difficulty of building a portable parallel emulator, this paper presents COREMU, a parallel emulation framework for CMP systems that decouples the complexity of supporting parallel emulation from maturing a sequential emulator. The key observation is that CPU cores and devices in current (and likely future) multiprocessors and multicore are loosely-coupled and these cores and devices communicate through well-defined interfaces. Based on this observation, COREMU emulates multiple cores by creating multiple instances of existing sequential emulators, and uses a thin

library layer to handle the inter-core and device communication and synchronization, to maintain a consistent view of system resources.

To ensure correctness and provide scalable performance, COREMU also incorporates several techniques to enable efficient parallel emulation. First, efficient and portable *core-to-core synchronization* is achieved through *lightweight memory transactions*, with the only assumption that the host architecture supports compare and swap (*CAS*) primitives [2], and allows the reuse of existing code generation for sequential emulation. Second, COREMU is built with a workload-aware feedback-directed scheduling that avoids situations such as lock-holder preemption and allows balanced scheduling of emulated cores. Third, to improve the scalability of code cache management, COREMU uses a private code cache scheme and addresses the issues with excessive inter-core cache eviction through *lazy cache invalidation*. Finally, efficient *core-to-core communication* is implemented through non-blocking data structures and real-time signals with *adaptive signal control*.

To make COREMU useful in practice, we also provide some preliminary tools and APIs to enable programmers to diagnose performance bottlenecks and bugs of both OS kernels and applications. First, COREMU provides a set of APIs including dynamically instrumenting programs and watching the accesses to user-specified addresses. Second, programmers could also use COREMU to collect memory traces of a program, which could be fed into a cache simulator (e.g., GEMS [17]) to study the cache behavior of a program.

We have built a working prototype that fully supports the x64 and ARM platform, in the form of a thin library composed of 2700 lines of code (LOCs) with only about 2500 LOCs changes to QEMU. Application benchmarks (such as MapReduce, PARSEC, dbench and Kernel Build) show that COREMU scales much better than QEMU: COREMU can emulate up to 255 cores of x64 architecture and 4 cores of ARM platform [3] while QEMU either fails to boot or times out when only emulating 32 cores. Compared to QEMU, the uniprocessor emulation overhead measured by SPECINT-2000 shows negligible performance penalty (within 1%) incurred by the parallel emulation. However, it achieves more than 20X speedup when emulating 16 cores compared to QEMU. The performance benefit is due to the fact that COREMU can leverage multiple available caches on multicore system and increased parallelism.

To demonstrate the usefulness of COREMU, we also use COREMU to debug both Linux kernel and user applications. Our study shows that COREMU can provide precise evidences to uncover several bugs. Cache simulation results using the typical matrix multiply show that COREMU can also accurately observe the cache behavior of a program.

In summary, this paper makes the following contributions:

1. A case for parallelizing full system emulators by reusing existing mature sequential emulator, which decouples the complexity of supporting parallel emulation from constructing and optimizing a sequential emulator.

2. A set of techniques to scale COREMU: lightweight memory transactions to achieve efficient synchronization among cores, feedback-directed scheduling, private code cache with lazy cache invalidation and adaptive signal control for scalable communication.

3. Implementation, evaluation and case studies of COREMU, which demonstrate the performance scalability and usefulness of COREMU.

---

[2] Other primitives such as *ll/sc* are similar to CAS.

[3] The Cortex-A9 MPCore supports a maximum of 4 cores

The rest of the paper is organized as follows: Section 2 provides background information on full-system emulation and relates COREMU to previous approaches. Section 3 and 4 presents the design and implementation of COREMU. Section 5 evaluates COREMU using various benchmarks. Section 6 demonstrates the usefulness of COREMU using several case studies. Finally, section 7 discusses future work and concludes.

2. Background and Related Work

In this section, we first use QEMU as an example to describe key techniques used in full-system emulation based on dynamic binary translation and then relate COREMU to previous work.

2.1 Full-System Emulation with Binary Translation

Binary translation: The main loop of QEMU translates and executes the emulated code based on basic blocks. Each block has one entry and one exit point and is sequentially executed. QEMU first translates the target machine code into common intermediate code, which is recognized by its *Tiny Code Generator* (*TCG*).

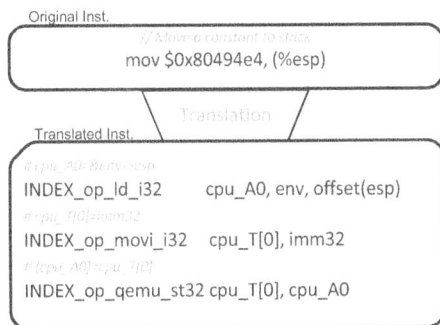

Figure 3: An example binary translation of a *mov* instruction in QEMU.

Figure 3 shows the generated operation code of each micro operation, along with its required parameters, when translating a *mov* instruction. The first item of each line represents the operation code (opcode), which is stored in gen_opc_ptr buffer. Other items give the parameters which are stored in gen_opparam_ptr buffer. The comment before each line shows the semantics of the line. Here, *cpu_A0* and *cpu_T[0]* are temporary registers allocated through *TCG*. The imm32 is $0x8049424 in this case, and QEMU gets the immediate when disassembling the binary code. After register allocation and machine code generation, the intermediate code will finally be emitted as binary code.

Multiprocessor emulation: QEMU emulates multiprocessor in a round-robin fashion: each emulated core has a time slice to execute, and yields the physical CPU to the next emulated core if the time slice has exhausted. Hence, there is no need to emulate atomic instructions, as the scheduling at basic blocks naturally guarantees the atomic execution of each instruction. Further, the time-slicing of cores will result in bad performance scalability due to the serialization of parallel code. For example, when a core holding a lock has exhausted its time slice, other cores waiting on such a lock will waste their time slices on spin-waiting the lock.

Full-system emulation support: Device emulation is done by providing port and memory mapped I/O callback functions. QEMU implements asynchronous I/O access, such as DMA, through signal mechanism and pipe. Interrupts are handled by setting vector bits in emulated interrupt controller. Before searching and executing translation blocks, QEMU peeks the interrupt controller to see if an interrupt presents, and emulates the interrupt handling procedure accordingly. This typically includes changing privilege level and

pointing the emulated program counter to the entry of the interrupt handler.

To support full-system emulation, QEMU implements a soft-MMU that translates the target virtual address to host virtual address. QEMU uses a soft-TLB to speedup target address translation. Soft-TLB caches address results in the same way as the hardware TLB. QEMU places look-up code before the code calling the soft-MMU callback.

Translation cache management: QEMU uses a single process to do system emulation and uses a single global translation cache. The central data structure used to manage translated code is TranslationBlock, which contains a pointer to the start of a translated block in the cache. Given an emulated program counter (target virtual address), QEMU checks whether its corresponding code has been translated and in the cache and translates the code and puts them into the cache upon a miss.

Physical pages containing translated code (code pages) are write-protected by QEMU to maintain code cache consistency. Specifically, the soft-TLB entries that point to code pages are marked as clean so that any modifications to the page will trap to a callback function, which invalidates the translation block by deleting the corresponding items from the virtual and physical tag hash tables.

2.2 Related Work

2.2.1 Full-system Emulation

The most related work with COREMU is Parallel Embra [14], which extends the original Embra emulator [29]. However, it was designed to support the SGI Origin 2000 with MIPS R10000 processors, which are out-of-date (15 years ago) and not commercially available now. In a contrast, COREMU runs current prevalent Chip-multiprocessors (e.g., x64) and supports emulation of multiple contemporary processors (e.g., x64 and ARM). To decouple the complexity of parallelism from binary translation, it adopts a layered structure and is likely to be easily re-targeted to new host-target architecture pairs. Further, COREMU uses a general and unified approach to handling atomic instruction emulation for weak ordering adopted by modern processors such as x64 and ARM, while Parallel Embra only emulates MIPS processor with a sequential consistency model. Finally, COREMU introduces several new techniques absent in Parallel Embra, such as synchronization with lightweight memory transactions, feedback-directed scheduling and thread-private cache with lazy invalidation. These techniques make COREMU able to run contemporary workloads with reasonable performance.

QEMU/KVM [2] is an accelerator that uses a virtualization layer to accelerate emulation on the same-ISA platform. However, the use of system virtualization loses both portability (e.g., only x86 to x86) and flexibility (e.g., no instrumentation support). Moreover, it requires hardware support.

Sulima [20] and Parallel Mambo [26] (which extends Mambo [6] for PowerPC) are two parallel full system emulators. They achieve parallel emulating through parallelizing the original sequential emulators. However, COREMU adopts a different, *core-per-thread*, organizing strategy and reuses mature sequential emulator for extensible cross-platform emulation. There are several user-level parallel emulators developed (for example, [19, 33]). Similar to COREMU, Graphite [19] provides user-level parallel functional simulation also using a multicore-on-multicore model. Instead of emulating only user-level applications, COREMU focuses on full-system emulation.

2.2.2 Simulation

There has been much research work devoted to fast and faithful simulation of multiprocessors. Broadly speaking, these work can be categorized to software approaches and hardware-assisted simulations. We discuss their relationships with COREMU in turn.

Software Approaches PTLsim [32] simulates x64 processor using a Virtual Machine Monitor (VMM). By contrast, COREMU supports cross-platform emulation, and uses binary translation for emulation, which provides flexibility such as instrumentation capability and statistics generation.

Most of the software approaches exploit tradeoff between speed and detail to achieve significant speedup, for example, *Statistical simulation* [28], *DiST* [30], AMD SimNow [3] and GEMS [17]. Compared to these systems, COREMU introduces non-determinism and leverages the true parallelism in the underlying processors to accelerate parallel full-system emulation.

Hardware-assisted Simulation The RAMP project from Berkeley investigates the use of FPGA to accelerate simulation of the CMP architecture. Specially, the RAMP Blue [27] models the future architectural features such as message-switching and transactional memory.

ProtoFlex [8, 9] is a hybrid functional emulator that uses FPGAs to accelerate performance-critical parts in emulation. The proposed technique, called transplanting, dynamically selects hot-traces to be emulated in FPGAs, while leaving uncommon traces being emulated in CPUs.

Recently, Chung et al. [10] proposed an approach to solve the emulation of atomic instruction using hardware support for transactional memory. In contrast, COREMU uses a more lightweight solution that only requires compare-and-swap support of the underlying processors, which is readily available on commodity processors.

Compared to these approaches, COREMU exploits abundant multicore resources for full-system emulation, which achieves reasonable performance without special hardware and is easy to deploy and use.

3. The COREMU Parallel Full-system Emulator

This section identifies the challenges in building a scalable parallel full-system emulator, shows the overall architecture of COREMU and presents the solutions to the identified challenges. Finally, we also present the preliminary support in COREMU for debugging and performance diagnosis.

3.1 Challenges in Building a Scalable Parallel Emulator

Compared to building a sequential emulator, there are several challenges in designing and implementing a scalable parallel emulator, due to the inherent differences during execution (i.e., time slicing vs. true parallelism). Here, we identify the key issues in building such an emulator for contemporary CMP architecture:

- *Atomic Instructions:* Unlike sequential emulators that inherently handles atomic instructions by scheduling at the basic-block level, a parallel emulator needs to efficiently emulate synchronization primitives to coordinate concurrent accesses to the emulated shared memory from each emulated core.

- *Scheduling Support:* To emulate a large number of cores with practical performance, it is critical to understand the workload behavior to schedule the emulated cores. For example, lock-holder preemption [25] can easily consume the available limited CPUs, resulting in extremely bad performance.

- *Scalable Code Cache Management:* There could be intensive contentions if adopting a shared code cache as that in sequential emulator when emulating a large number of virtual cores. Thus, an efficient code cache scheme is critical for the performance of parallel emulator.

- *Scalable Communications:* When emulating CPU cores in the scale of hundreds and even thousands, there could be easily excessive core-to-core and core-to-device messages, due to device interrupts (e.g., DMA, timer interrupts) and interprocessor interrupts (such as remote TLB shootdowns). Hence, it is likely that an emulated core could be frequently disturbed for processing messages, limiting its performance.

3.2 Overall Architecture

COREMU is designed based on the observation that cores in modern multicore or multiprocessor machines are loosely-coupled and communicated with well-defined interfaces. For example, each core has its own register file, control logic and separate cache. They independently execute instruction stream assigned to it and the communication channels between cores are *well defined*, such as Inter Processor Interrupt (IPI). Such an organization allows the separation of building fine-tuned sequential emulators from efficiently parallelizing it, thus decreases the complexity of building a parallel full-system emulator. It could be much easier to adapt the emulator to different host/target pairs to make such an emulator portable.

Figure 4 depicts the architecture of COREMU. Overall, COREMU is a multithreaded user program running on the hosted operating systems, emulating a cache-coherent shared memory multiprocessor to run operating systems and the applications. Each sequential emulator is essentially a threaded binary translator with its own translation cache holding already translated blocks (TBs). All devices are emulated using a separate thread. There is a thin library layer handling communications and synchronizations among emulated cores and devices through intercepting callouts. The library also maintains the coherence between each translation cache by coordinating the invalidation requests.

Atomic Instructions	Lightweight Memory Transactions
Scheduling	Feedback-Directed Scheduling
Code Cache	Private Cache w/ Lazy Inval.
Communication	Adaptive Signal Control

Table 1: Methodologies in COREMU.

Table 1 summarizes the underlying techniques in COREMU to enable a scalable parallel emulation of a large number of cores with practical performance, which will be presented in detail in the following sections.

3.2.1 Synchronization with Lightweight Memory Transactions

The fact that all emulated cores share a global, cache-coherent memory poses a challenge to scalable parallel emulation. Specifically, microprocessor exports a set of *atomic* instructions executed atomically, which are usually used to implement synchronization primitives. An efficient emulation of atomic instructions is critical to parallel emulation: (1) the emulation of atomic instruction should be fast and correct; (2) the emulation should be portable across a variety of architectures.

An intuitive solution is to perform an identical translation that maps the emulated atomic instruction to one on the host architecture, which is used in Parallel Embra [14]. This solution is fast and correct, but not portable, due to the idiosyncratic nature of different ISAs. For example, the ARM processor has only 2 atomic instructions, while x86 has around 20, which indicates that it is not always feasible for such a direct mapping. Furthermore, an atomic instruction in an emulated x86 core is usually decomposed into several non-atomic micro-operations on host architecture.

Another intuitive solution is to use *lock* to synchronize all parallel accesses, by associating each memory region with a lock to

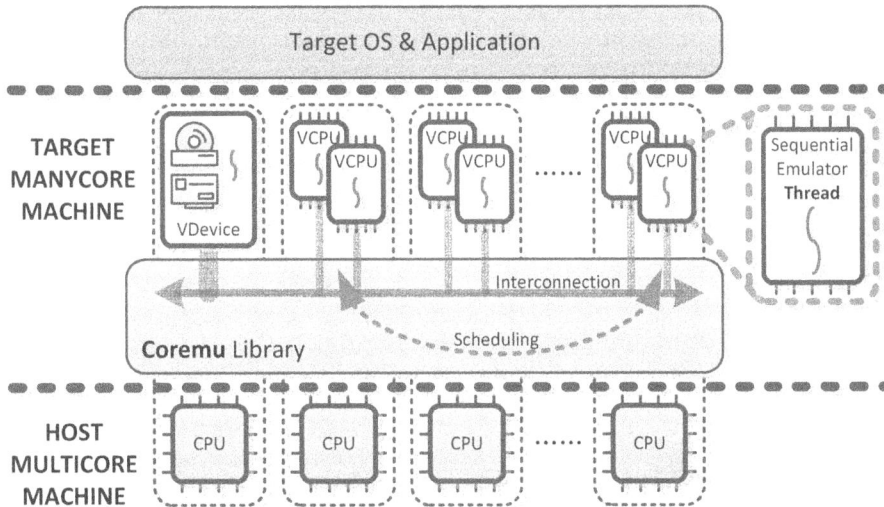

Figure 4: Overall architecture of COREMU, which uses a two-layer parallel emulation organization. COREMU library acts as the bonding agents between different emulated components.

serialize accesses to this region (in our initial implementation, each 64-byte region has a lock). Such a solution avoids a global lock so that parallel accesses to different memory regions are allowed. Unfortunately, while this solution seems plausible, it has correctness issues.

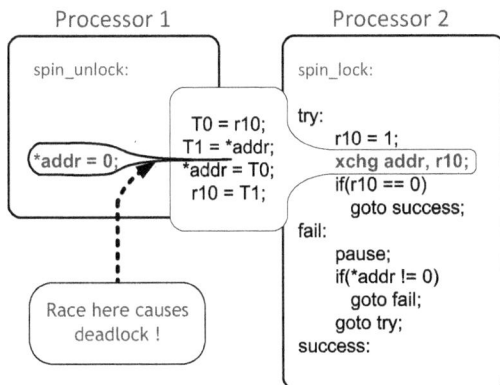

Figure 5: Weak atomicity problem due to partial locking.

For example, consider the deadlock illustrated in Figure 5. This example implements an efficient *spin_lock* and *spin_unlock* operations on Intel/AMD x64 machines. The *spin_unlock* operation simply stores a 0 into a lock. The *spin_lock* exchanges a 1 into the lock using atomic xchg, and checks whether the original value is 0. QEMU translates xchg by first reading out the two values into temporaries, and then storing them back with swapped order. If we partially protect the exchange with a lock, the store operation in *spin_unlock* can still happen during xchg, causing a deadlock afterwards.

Hence, to ensure *strong atomicity*, one must passively protect *all* atomic instructions using lock. However, this solution will incur prohibitive performance overhead as every memory access needs to acquire and release a lock.

COREMU solves the multiprocessor synchronization problem with *lightweight memory transactions* based on the well-known *Multi-Word Compare and Swap* (CASN) algorithm [12]. COREMU

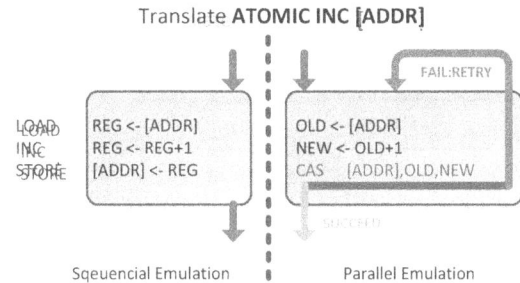

Figure 6: Example translation of an atomic INC

supports this operation with the only assumption that the underlying architecture supports CAS like synchronization primitives, which holds for most modern architectures. Figure 6 shows an example translation of INC instruction where host and target system uses the *same* word size.

Generally, the working flow is as follows: (1) Calculate the result into *tmp*; (2) Use CAS to store *tmp* into destination; (3) Proceed to the next instruction on success, or *re-execute* this instruction. Overall, our solution guarantees an efficient emulation of atomic instruction and allows the reuse of most sequential code generation. Further, our memory transactions are much more succinct compared to the general transactional memory due to the simple and clean semantics of instructions. These instructions usually only update a single memory location and the memory state only has one transition, hence very few states are needed to record during such transactions.

To illustrate the effectiveness of COREMU , we start two parallel threads to atomically update a shared counter one million times. The lock-based emulation only uses lock to *partially* protect the emulated INC. From our evaluation results COREMU emulation is 8X faster (6.82s vs. 47.69s) than a lock-based solution.

3.2.2 Feedback-Directed Scheduling

COREMU creates one thread for each emulated core or device. There might be more threads than physical cores with the number of emulated cores increasing. Hence, thread scheduling is crit-

217

ical to ensure practical performance when an excessive number of threads co-exist in the system. To address this problem, we propose a flexible feedback-directed scheduling mechanism to provide good scalability and reasonable fidelity for parallel emulation. The scheduling algorithm aims at utilizing the workload information in the emulated environments at the binary translation layer and uses such information as feedback to direct the scheduling among physical cores:

Lock-holder Preemption: Lock holder preemption is one of the limitations for performance scalability and fidelity for parallel emulating large scale virtual cores. The guest parallel workloads (including the operating system kernel) usually use spin-locks to guarantee exclusive accesses to shared data. Such spin-locks are, by design, only held for a short period of time and will be unlikely preempted until the lock is released.

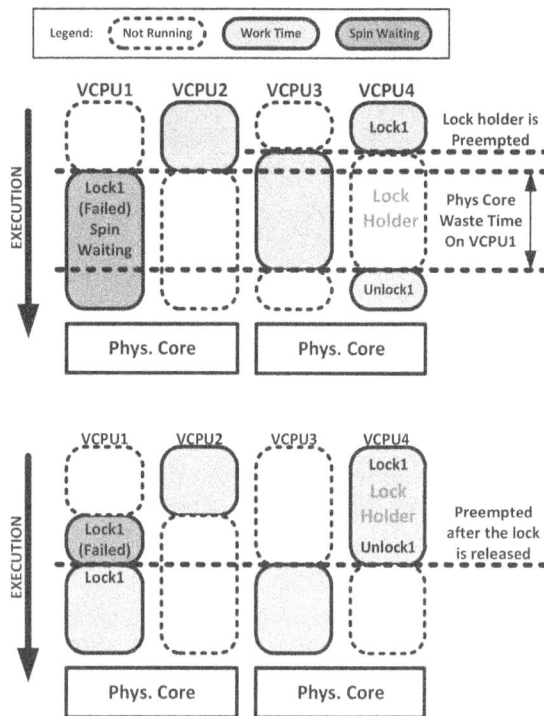

Figure 7: The problem of lock-holder preemption (top half) and the solution in COREMU to remedy the problem (bottom half).

However, when running a commodity operating system on a parallel emulator, the emulated environment may violate such a premise of using spin-locks. The emulated virtual core can be preempted even it is executing critical code protected by a spin-lock, as shown in the top half of Figure 7. Such lock holder preemption could result in a significant increase of the lock holding time. For workloads running on large-scale emulated cores, such a situation could be common and cause a serious performance degradation and poor fidelity.

Avoiding lock holder preemption can be achieved by either modifying (e.g., compiler instrumentation) the guest operating systems or workloads to give hints to the emulator (intrusive), or having the emulation layer to detect when the guest operating systems are not holding a lock (non-intrusive). To retain transparency, COREMU currently uses the latter approach to detecting the spin-locks.

Based on the observation that a spin-lock usually uses a *pause* instruction after the lock prefix instruction, we can pre-translate

more translation blocks when we find a lock prefix instruction has been translated. When COREMU detects a spin-lock, it tags the corresponding TBs. Afterwards, COREMU can detect if a virtual core has acquired a spin-lock successfully. To avoid lock holder preemption, COREMU feeds such hints to the underlying scheduler to avoid preemption when a virtual core is still executing a critical section. After the lock is released, COREMU also gives such a hint to the scheduler and the scheduler will decide if re-preempting the virtual cores. Finally, COREMU can also detect if a core is waiting on a lock and feed such a hint to the scheduler, which yields the virtual core until the lock release action is detected, as shown in the bottom half of Figure 7.

3.2.3 Thread-Private Cache with Lazy Invalidation

Like other binary translators, COREMU uses translation cache that caches translated code to improve emulation performance. For a parallel emulator that emulates a number of cores, as each core will access the translation cache, an efficient scheme is vitally important for the performance and scalability.

Basically, there are two design choices: thread-shared cache and thread-private cache. For thread-shared cache, all emulated cores share a single global cache and each piece of code has only one copy in the cache, which is efficient in memory space usage, yet would cause heavy contentions on the cache when emulating a relatively large number of cores or running workloads with poor code locality. For thread-private cache, where each emulated core has its own translation cache, which would result in fewer contentions, yet requires more memory spaces and excessive inter-core communications to maintain cache consistency.

To avoid possible contentions, COREMU uses a thread-private cache scheme because it naturally fits into COREMU's decoupled emulation model, where each core thread independently caches their executed code. However, this design leads to the *code eviction* problem, where a write to a code page must synchronize with other emulated cores to invalidate all cached translation blocks. A typical case for such an invalidation event corresponds to self-modifying code. In full system emulation, this happens more frequently when a code page owned by one process is reused as a data page by another process. For example, after a multi-threaded application exits and its memory pages have been reclaimed by the OS kernel, its pages could be used for holding program data. Unfortunately, such pages might still be in translation cache and other emulated cores are not aware of the status changes of these pages. Consequently, COREMU needs to issue *code eviction* events to other emulated cores to invalidate the code cache. According to our experience, there are typically hundreds of thousands of such events when booting Linux with 4 emulated cores. Furthermore, this number rapidly grows with the increase of emulated cores, which dramatically limits the performance scalability.

To address the scalability problem caused by excessive code evictions, COREMU uses a technique called *lazy invalidation*. Our key observation is: *the invalidated code pages are rarely re-executed later*. Hence, the invalidation could be postponed until the re-execution of stale cached-code (if such code is really self-modifying code or the page will again be used as code page). Specifically, on a code page write, all cached translation blocks are updated to return a value, which indicates that code eviction is needed. If such code is re-executed, COREMU removes the cached block from thread-private translation cache, re-translates and executes it. Lazy invalidation ensures the common case is fast, as the real re-execution of stale code cache implies self-modifying code or reused code, which is rare in practice.

Finally, to implement code page protection similar to QEMU, COREMU uses CAS to implement code page protection. Specifically, the core that maps the code should atomically replace the soft-TLB entries of other cores to protect the page so that any write afterwards traps into the lazy invalidation callback.

3.2.4 Communication with Adaptive Signal Control

In a sequential emulator, it is easy to handle core-to-core communication and core-to-device communication because it can process these asynchronous events in a synchronous way. For example, to emulate the IPI broadcasting, it simply sets the interrupt vector for each emulated core. However, for a parallel emulator, such a direct modification indicates concurrent or even parallel modifications to internal states of an emulated component. Using locks to provide safe concurrent modification is complicated and time-consuming. Further, it violates the design principle to decouple parallel emulation complexity from optimizing sequential ones.

Asynchronous communication in COREMU is handled using *Real Time Signal* (RT-Signal) [1] and non-blocking data structures. RT-Signal is used as communication primitive for its two useful properties. First, the delivering order is guaranteed to be FIFO, which ensures the fairness of handling the events. Second, the signals with the same type are buffered rather than ignored, thus all asynchronous events will not be lost. To handle asynchronous events from hardware and other cores, each core maintains a non-blocking FIFO queue to hold all these events.

However, naively sending all interrupts using RT-signals would result in excessive signals and cause significant overhead due to the high cost of trapping into and returning from signal handlers. Further, it limits system scalability as the number of interrupts increases rapidly with the increase of cores. For example, our tests indicates that a WordCount application with 10 MB input running on 8 emulated cores with 8 physical cores is even a bit slower than on 4 emulated cores on 4 physical cores (5.78s vs. 5.14s).

To solve this problem, COREMU uses a technique called *adaptive signal control* to reduce the signal-handling overhead by controlling the rate of signal sending. Specifically, COREMU only uses RT-signal to notify the target processor when the number of pending interrupts exceeds a threshold. The threshold is dynamically adjusted in the signal handler according to the frequency of received signals. Otherwise, each emulated core polls for pending interrupts. Using such an optimization, the execution time of WordCount on 8 emulated cores with 8 physical cores decreases from 5.78s to 2.47s.

3.3 Debugging and Diagnosis Support

COREMU is also built with some preliminary mechanisms to assist programmers to debug and diagnose the bugs and performance problems of parallel systems and applications:

Watchpoints: To assist programmers to find memory-related bugs effectively, COREMU is integrated with a watchpoint mechanism that can constantly monitor the accesses to a range of not only virtual addresses but also physical addresses. Programmers can also associate a callback function which will be triggered when a specific type of accesses to a watched address occur. A set of utility functions are also provided to be invoked by the callback function, including dumping the call stack, showing the execution context, showing the content of the stack, which helps programmers to understand the execution context. Programmers could control the execution of the monitoring by specifying the condition that triggers the monitoring, which could save the associated overhead.

Cache Simulation: Cache behavior is critical to program performance. Instead of writing a cache simulator to COREMU, we reuse a state-of-the-art simulator (i.e., GEMS [17]) by collecting memory traces using COREMU and feeding the traces to GEMS. This helps programmers to qualitatively identify the performance problems of some applications and system software.

4. Implementation

COREMU is implemented on x64 processors and currently uses QEMU as the sequential emulator. It is in the form of a multi-threaded application scheduled by the host operating systems. It supports the full system emulation of x64 and ARM processors. The COREMU library only requires around 2700 lines of C code, including the thin synchronization and communication layer and some well-known non-blocking data structures such as Michael and Scott's non-blocking FIFO queue [18].

Portability of COREMU: a Case Study using ARM Given the fully-fledged support for x64 platform, we found it quite easy to port it to other platforms. We chose ARM MPCore as the porting target given the popularity of ARM platform on mobile systems, as well as the readily support of sequential emulation of multiprocessors in QEMU. Two of our developers who are quite familiar with COREMU but are completely new to ARM platform, spend four days to port COREMU for ARM, adding only 150 LOCs.

Parallel Emulator Construction To construct a full-system emulator, we reuse all the high-level abstractions in QEMU, such as devices, processors and interrupt controllers. As we model each processor as a single thread, per-core objects need to be marked with __thread specifier. The marking is usually quite straight-forward since emulated processor objects are well defined.

The communication interfaces need slight adjustment which typically does not require deep understanding of the internal logic of QEMU. For example, we need to use COREMU interfaces to send I/O requests or interprocessor interrupts, and these interfaces are usually just wrapper functions for original QEMU interfaces. For device emulation, COREMU provides *debug mode* device emulation in case the driver is incorrect. Each emulated device has a lock and the lock is acquired at the entry of its I/O hook functions.

Atomic instruction emulation needs to be adjusted to be aware of their atomicity. This requires inserting calls to COREMU library to use memory transactions. Fortunately, most of the code can still be reused. For example, we can completely reuse all the code in QEMU that generates the decomposed micro operations.

Currently, COREMU allocates a fixed portion of memory for each emulated core as their translation cache. This strategy properly fits into the loose coupling nature of cores, except the disadvantage of linear space overhead with the number of cores. Fortunately, we found a 5 MB cache for each core is enough, even for some large parallel workloads. In future, we plan to implement a two-layer translation cache management scheme that combines the space efficiency of shared cache and the scalability of private cache, to support a larger scale many-core parallel emulation.

COREMU modifies the translated code invalidation callback. Every invalidated cached block is rewritten to just return a value, which indicates if code eviction is needed. Note that, while COREMU needs translated code modification, there is no need to modify the complicated internal states of the emulated core, such as translation block unlink or hash map invalidation. However, this requires a core to see the translation blocks produced by other cores. To achieve such a goal, COREMU maintains a data structure which records, across all cores, all translation blocks on a code page. Further, each translation block is provided with a lock and a flag to indicate whether the block has already been evicted. Upon getting the lock, COREMU checks the flag to see whether the rewriting has been done, hence avoids rewriting the code twice.

When emulating a large number of cores, the excessive time interrupts (i.e., signals) could easily exhaust most of the CPU cycles and starve the user programs. Hence, COREMU adaptively adjusts the rate of delivering time interrupt by emulating an time device (e.g., programmable interval time, PIT) according to the proportion of the number of emulated cores with the physical cores. To associate each emulated core with a signal, COREMU creates a per-thread local timer which signals the emulated processor based on the thread ID, which is retrieved using *gettid* system call.

5. Evaluation

This section evaluates COREMU by comparing it with QEMU when emulating x64 and ARM MPCore using various contemporary benchmarks that either require a relatively large input size and working set or require relatively long execution time.

5.1 Experimental Setup

All performance evaluation is performed on a 4 Quad-core (1.6 GHz) Intel x64 system running Debian-Linux with kernel version 2.6.26-2. The guest OS is also a Debian-Linux with kernel version 2.6.33-1 since the kernel version 2.6.26-2 cannot boot when emulated core exceeds 64. The host machine has 32GB memory and the guest is configured with 8 GB memory. We use several different types of applications to study their performance with regard to QEMU and COREMU: (1) SPECINT-2000 [13], a CPU-intensive benchmark; (2) the Canneal benchmark from PARSEC benchmark suite [4] using native input set, whose working set is around 2 GB; (3) WordCount benchmark included in Phoenix MapReduce testsuite for multicore [22], using a 100 MB word file; (4) dbench [24], a file system benchmark; (5) Parallel kernel build, which builds a compacted Linux kernel by specifying the currency level as the number of (emulated) cores.

We ported two MapReduce applications in the Phoenix testsuite to ARM platform to study the performance and scalability of emulated ARM MPCore: Matrix Multiply that multiply two 800 * 800 matrices; WordCount with a 10 MB file. The version of Linux used for emulated ARM is 2.6.28.

QEMU and the one used in COREMU are obtained from its Git repository on May, 4, 2010. COREMU and QEMU are configured with the same options. All these applications are compiled using gcc-4.3.2. As typical timing mechanism in emulated environments could be inaccurate on a large number of emulated cores, we use *rdtsc* instruction in such cases instead, since such an instruction will read the timestamp registers in the host platform directly in COREMU. For all the tests, we run the test program 5 times to get the average. In many cases, QEMU times out so we omit the results of QEMU.

5.2 Performance of Emulated x64

5.2.1 Uniprocessor Emulation Overhead

Figure 8 depicts the relative performance overhead to native Linux with 8 applications in SPECINT-2000 benchmark suite. As shown in the figure, COREMU incurs negligible performance overhead compared to QEMU, within 1% for all of these benchmarks. Compared to native execution, COREMU is 11X slower on average. The single core emulation overhead mainly comes from the communication among different components and the use of transactions to synchronize multiple cores. However, as the proportion of communications as well as memory transactions is relatively small in single-threaded applications, the incurred performance overhead is negligible.

5.2.2 Performance and Scalability of Emulated x64

We use four applications with diverse characteristics to evaluate the performance and scalability of COREMU on x64. The characteristics of those benchmarks are described as follows.

- *WordCount: Data-parallel applications:* The WordCount (wc) benchmark tries to demonstrate that COREMU can also run data-parallel applications with good performance.

- *Canneal: The case of handling large working set:* To demonstrate that COREMU can handle a large working set, we com-

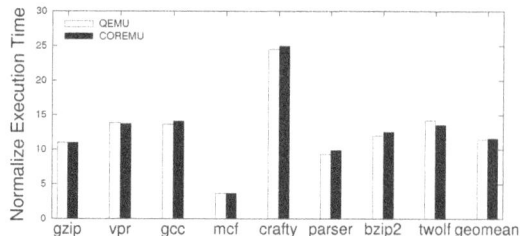

Figure 8: Uniprocessor emulation overhead with SPECINT-2000: the execution time is normalized to native execution time.

pared the performance and scalability of the Canneal benchmark from the PARSEC benchmark suites with 2GB input size.

- *dbench: Evaluating file system and I/O Performance:* We use dbench to evaluate file system and I/O performance and scalability of COREMU.

- *Parallel kernel build: Evaluating complex workload:* Building a Linux Kernel is a relatively complex workload as it involves creating a number of parallel processes to compile the source file.

To evaluate the performance and scalability, we compare the results of COREMU and those of QEMU with these benchmarks running on 1, 2, 4, 8, 16, 32, 64, 128 and 255 emulated cores. The results are shown in Figure 9, Figure 10, Figure 11 and Figure 12 in log scale. To illustrate the relative performance of COREMU, the native execution time of different applications are also presented.

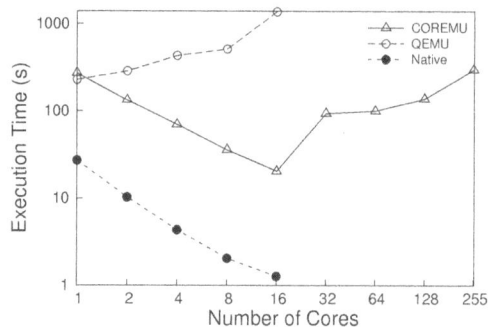

Figure 9: Performance and scalability of the WordCount benchmark with 100 MB input in log scale.

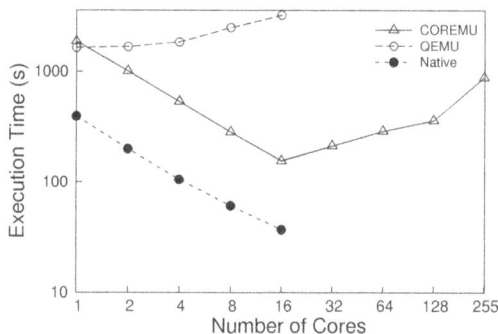

Figure 10: Performance and Scalability with Canneal benchmark from PARSEC testsuite in log scale.

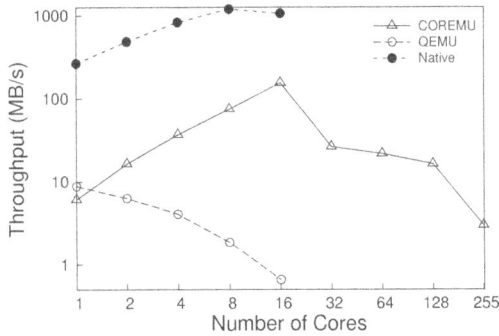

Figure 11: I/O performance results with dbench in log scale.

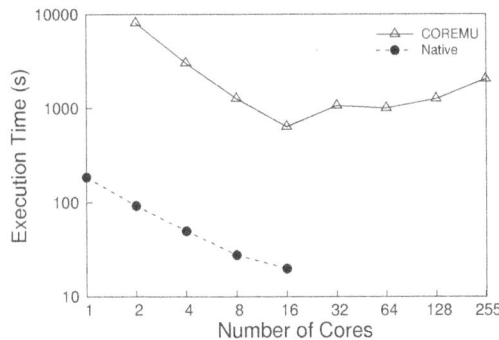

Figure 12: Performance and Scalability of the parallel kernel build benchmark in log scale.

As shown in the figures, COREMU achieves good performance scalability. It scales pretty well when the number of emulated cores increases from 1 to 16. When the emulated cores is larger than physical cores, the performance degradation is still acceptable. It can emulate up to 255 virtual cores with reasonable performance. In contrast, QEMU times out or crashes when emulating more than 16 cores due to cache thrashing or contentions. COREMU achieves a speedup from 20X to 67X when 16 virtual cores are emulated.

There are two reasons for the much better performance and scalability of COREMU. First, when emulating larger number of multiprocessors, there are a lot of synchronizations among threads, and threads frequently fall into spin-wait state. Sequential emulation can only exhaust the time slice of spin-wait. In COREMU, the feedback-directed scheduling can handle this case by detecting lock situation in emulated cores and yielding the control to another thread. Actually, during our process of development and optimization, COREMU can only emulate 32 cores without the feedback-directed scheduling optimization. Second, with the number of virtual core increasing, the implementation of COREMU can also lead to a good data locality and better usage of cache compared to that of QEMU.

As the four mentioned optimizations work together to make COREMU scale beyond 32 cores, we currently failed to identify the contribution of each optimization to the overall performance scalability, which will be our future work.

5.3 Performance of Emulated ARM

We use two applications, Matrix Multiply and WordCount to study the performance and scalability of emulated 1, 2, 3 and 4 ARM cores. Figure 13 shows the performance of the two applications running on QEMU and COREMU. As we currently do not have an ARM MPCore machine in hand, we omit the native data here. Like the performance trend of emulating x64, COREMU has similar performance with QEMU when emulating uniprocessor, but has better performance and scalability when emulating 2 to 4 cores, with the corresponding speedup of 1.67X (11.3s vs. 18.9s), 2.56X (7.2 vs. 16.25s) and 2.5X (6.1s vs. 15.5s) for WordCount and 1.96X (46s vs. 90.5s), 2.9X (30.96s vs. 90.85s) and 4.3X (22.9s vs. 91.17s) for Matrix Multiply accordingly.

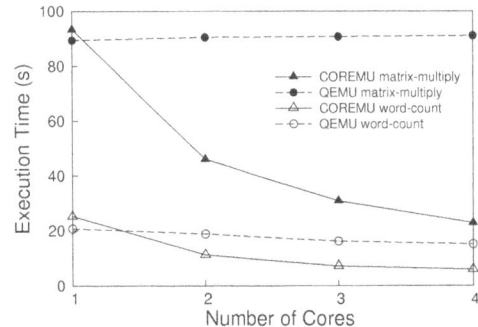

Figure 13: Performance results with Matrix Multiply and Word-Count on QEMU and COREMU.

6. Case Studies of COREMU

To demonstrate the usefulness of COREMU, we make several case studies by using COREMU to diagnose and debug the performance problems and (concurrency) bugs in both OS kernel and user applications.

Cache Simulation: We use the matrix multiply (mm) application from the Phoenix MapReduce framework [22], which is a parallel version of matrix multiply written using the MapReduce programming model. By collecting the memory traces using COREMU and replaying them in GEMS, we found that even when using 4 cores, the default version in COREMU incurs more than 26% L1 cache miss rate with the input size to be *500 X 500*. By transposing the input matrices before executing the MapReduce tasks, we observe that the L1 cache miss rate degrades to only 5%, leading to a performance speedup of more than 2X.

Debugging using Watchpoints: We use one kernel bug and one user bug to demonstrate how COREMU could be used for debugging. The kernel bug is a NULL pointer dereference bug caused by incorrect concurrent updates to the *inode->i_pipe* variable in Linux kernel version 2.6.21 [4]. After one thread has freed *inode->i_pipe* and set it to NULL, another thread tries to deference it. To detect such a bug, we inserted a watchpoint on updates to that variable and log accesses that write a NULL to that variable. Using COREMU, we quickly located the function and execution context nullifying that variable.

The user-level bug is from pbzip2 [5], which is an order violation concurrency bug. There are still accesses to the *fifo->mut* variable from the consumer threads after the variable has been freed by the main thread, which causes a segmentation fault. With COREMU, we diagnose the root cause of this bug similarly by inserting a watchpoint on *fifo->mut* and logging the accesses.

7. Conclusion and Future Work

We have presented the open-source COREMU, a scalable and portable full-system emulator for CMP systems. COREMU clusters multiple mature sequential emulators using a thin library layer,

---

[4] https://bugzilla.kernel.org/show_bug.cgi?id=14416

[5] http://www.eecs.umich.edu/ jieyu/bugs/pbzip2-094.html

hence decouples the complexity of supporting parallel emulation from building an optimizing sequential emulator. Experimental results show that COREMU has negligible uniprocessor performance overhead and scales much better than sequential emulators, and is orders of magnitude faster. From our experiences of building COREMU, we found that efficient emulation of synchronization primitives, efficient scheduling, scalable code cache management and efficient communication mechanism are the key to the performance and scalability of a parallel full-system emulator. We hope that our experiences could be useful for building other similar systems.

We plan to extend our work in several directions in future. First, while currently COREMU trade the determinism for performance by parallelizing the emulator, determinism is extremely useful to replay uncovered bugs. Hence, we plan to add record and replay support in COREMU, to support the execution replay of the full emulated multiprocessors [11]. Second, though there is no fundamental limitation to support other Host/Emulated processors pairs, we currently only tried a few. We are now trying to add more processors pairs to make it more portable. Finally, we are also providing more debugging and instrumentation support in COREMU to enable a more wide range of usages in performance debugging and diagnosis.

8. Acknowledgments and Availability

We thank the anonymous reviewers for their insightful comments. This work was funded by China National Natural Science Foundation under grant numbered 61003002 and 60903015, a grant from the Science and Technology Commission of Shanghai Municipality numbered 10511500100, China National 863 program numbered 2008AA01Z138, a research grant from Intel as well as a joint program between China Ministry of Education and Intel numbered MOE-INTEL-09-04, Fundamental Research Funds for the Central Universities in China and Shanghai Leading Academic Discipline Project (Project Number: B114).

The source code and OS images of COREMU can be downloaded from sourceforge (http://sourceforge.net/p/coremu/home/). They are distributed under the Lesser GNU General Public License.

References

[1] http://davmac.org/davpage/linux/rtsignals.html.

[2] Kvm/qemu. http://wiki.qemu.org/KVM.

[3] R. Bedichek. SimNow: Fast Platform Simulation Purely in Software. In *16th Hot Chips Symp*, 2004.

[4] C. Bienia, S. Kumar, J. Singh, and K. Li. The PARSEC benchmark suite: Characterization and architectural implications. In *Proc. PACT*, pages 72–81, 2008.

[5] Bochs. http://bochs.sourceforge.net/.

[6] P. Bohrer, J. Peterson, M. Elnozahy, R. Rajamony, A. Gheith, R. Rockhold, C. Lefurgy, H. Shafi, T. Nakra, R. Simpson, et al. Mambo: a full system simulator for the PowerPC architecture. *ACM SIGMETRICS Performance Evaluation Review*, 31(4):8–12, 2004.

[7] H. Cain, K. Lepak, B. Schwartz, and M. Lipasti. Precise and accurate processor simulation. In *Workshop on Computer Architecture Evaluation using Commercial Workload*, 2002.

[8] E. Chung, E. Nurvitadhi, J. Hoe, B. Falsafi, and K. Mai. A complexity-effective architecture for accelerating full-system multiprocessor simulations using FPGAs. In *Proc. FPGA*, pages 77–86, 2008.

[9] E. Chung, M. Papamichael, E. Nurvitadhi, J. Hoe, K. Mai, and B. Falsafi. ProtoFlex: Towards Scalable, Full-System Multiprocessor Simulations Using FPGAs. *ACM Transactions on Reconfigurable Technology and Systems (TRETS)*, 2009.

[10] J. Chung, M. Dalton, H. Kannan, and C. Kozyrakis. Thread-safe dynamic binary translation using transactional memory. In *IEEE HPCA*, 2008.

[11] G. W. Dunlap, D. G. Lucchetti, M. A. Fetterman, and P. M. Chen. Execution replay of multiprocessor virtual machines. In *VEE '08*, pages 121–130, 2008.

[12] T. L. Harris, K. Fraser, and I. A. Pratt. A practical multi-word compare-and-swap operation. In *Proc. DISC*, pages 265–279, 2002.

[13] J. Henning. SPEC CPU2000: Measuring CPU performance in the new millennium. *Computer*, 33(7):28–35, 2000.

[14] R. Lantz. *Parallel SimOS - Performance and Scalability for Large System*. PhD thesis, Computer Systems Laboratory, Stanford University, 2007.

[15] P. Magnusson, M. Christensson, J. Eskilson, D. Forsgren, G. Hllberg, J. Hgberg, F. Larsson, A. Moestedt, and B. Werner. Simics: A full system simulation platform. *Computer*, pages 50–58, 2002.

[16] P. Magnusson and B. Werner. Efficient memory simulation in SimICS. In *Proc. Annual Simulation Symposium*, pages 62–73, 1995.

[17] M. Martin, D. Sorin, B. Beckmann, M. Marty, M. Xu, A. Alameldeen, K. Moore, M. Hill, and D. Wood. Multifacet's general execution-driven multiprocessor simulator (GEMS) toolset. *ACM SIGARCH Computer Architecture News*, 33(4):99, 2005.

[18] M. Michael and M. L. Scott. Simple, fast, and practical non-blocking and blocking concurrent queue algorithms. In *Proc. PODC*, pages 267–275, 1996.

[19] J. Miller, H. Kasture, G. Kurian, C. Gruenwald III, N. Beckmann, C. Celio, J. Eastep, and A. Agarwal. Graphite: A Distributed Parallel Simulator for Multicores. In *Proc. HPCA*, 2010.

[20] A. Over, B. Clarke, and P. E. Strazdins. A comparison of two approaches to parallel simulation of multiprocessors. In *Proc. ISPASS*, pages 12–22, 2007.

[21] QEMU. http://qemu.org/.

[22] C. Ranger, R. Raghuraman, A. Penmetsa, G. R. Bradski, and C. Kozyrakis. Evaluating mapreduce for multi-core and multiprocessor systems. In *HPCA*, pages 13–24, 2007.

[23] M. Rosenblum, S. Herrod, E. Witchel, and A. Gupta. Complete computer system simulation: The SimOS approach. *IEEE Parallel & Distributed Technology: Systems & Applications*, 3(4):34–43, 1995.

[24] A. Tridgell. Dbench filesystem benchmark. http://dbench.samba.org/.

[25] V. Uhlig, J. LeVasseur, E. Skoglund, and U. Dannowski. Towards scalable multiprocessor virtual machines. In *Proceedings of the 3rd conference on Virtual Machine Research And Technology*. USENIX Association, 2004.

[26] K. Wang, Y. Zhang, H. Wang, and X. Shen. Parallelization of IBM mambo system simulator in functional modes. *SIGOPS Operating System Review*, 2008.

[27] S. Wee, J. Casper, N. Njoroge, Y. Tesylar, D. Ge, C. Kozyrakis, and K. Olukotun. A practical FPGA-based framework for novel CMP research. In *Proc. FPGA*, pages 116–125, 2007.

[28] T. F. Wenisch, R. E. Wunderlich, M. Ferdman, A. Ailamaki, B. Falsafi, and J. C. Hoe. Simflex: Statistical sampling of computer system simulation. *IEEE Micro*, 26(4):18–31, 2006.

[29] E. Witchel and M. Rosenblum. Embra: Fast and flexible machine simulation. *ACM SIGMETRICS Performance Evaluation Review*, 24(1):68–79, 1996.

[30] R. E. Wunderlich, T. F. Wenisch, B. Falsafi, and J. C. Hoe. Statistical sampling of microarchitecture simulation. *ACM Trans. Model. Comput. Simul.*, 16(3):197–224, 2006.

[31] D. Yeh, L.-S. Peh, S. Borkar, J. A. Darringer, A. Agarwal, and W. mei Hwu. Thousand-core chips [roundtable]. *IEEE Design & Test of Computers*, 25(3):272–278, 2008.

[32] M. Yourst. PTLsim: A cycle accurate full system x86-64 microarchitectural simulator. In *Proc. ISPASS*, pages 23–34, 2007.

[33] G. Zheng, G. Kakulapati, and L. V. Kalé. Bigsim: A parallel simulator for performance prediction of extremely large parallel machines. In *IPDPS*. IEEE Computer Society, 2004.

Wait-Free Queues With Multiple Enqueuers and Dequeuers *

Alex Kogan

Department of Computer Science
Technion, Israel
sakogan@cs.technion.ac.il

Erez Petrank

Department of Computer Science
Technion, Israel
erez@cs.technion.ac.il

Abstract

The queue data structure is fundamental and ubiquitous. Lock-free versions of the queue are well known. However, an important open question is whether practical wait-free queues exist. Until now, only versions with limited concurrency were proposed. In this paper we provide a design for a practical wait-free queue. Our construction is based on the highly efficient lock-free queue of Michael and Scott. To achieve wait-freedom, we employ a priority-based helping scheme in which faster threads help the slower peers to complete their pending operations. We have implemented our scheme on multicore machines and present performance measurements comparing our implementation with that of Michael and Scott in several system configurations.

Categories and Subject Descriptors   D.3.3 [*Programming Languages*]: Language Constructs and Features – Concurrent programming structures;   E.1 [*Data structures*]: Lists, stacks, and queues

General Terms   Algorithms, Performance

Keywords   concurrent queues, wait-free algorithms

1. Introduction

The proliferation of multicore systems motivates the research for efficient concurrent data structures. Being a fundamental and commonly used structure, first-in first-out (FIFO) queues[1] have been studied extensively, resulting in many highly concurrent algorithms (e.g., [14, 19, 21]). A concurrent queue algorithm supports linearizable `enqueue` and `dequeue` operations, which add and remove elements from the queue while observing the FIFO semantics.

A highly desired property of any concurrent data structure implementation, and queues in particular, is to ensure that a process (or a thread) completes its operations in a bounded number of steps, regardless of what other processes (or threads) are doing. This property is known in the literature as (bounded) *wait-freedom* [9, 11, 15]. It is particularly important in systems where

---

* This work was supported by the Israeli Science Foundation grant No. 283/10. The work of A. Kogan was also supported by the Technion Hasso Plattner Center.

[1] This paper deals with FIFO queues only, in the following referred simply as *queues*, for brevity.

strict deadlines for operation completion exist, e.g., in real-time applications or when operating under a service level agreement (SLA), or in heterogenous execution environments where some of the threads may perform much faster or slower than others. Yet, most previous queue implementations (e.g., [14, 17, 19, 21, 24, 25]) provide the weaker *lock-free* property; lock-freedom ensures that among all processes accessing a queue, at least one will succeed to finish its operation. Although such non-blocking implementations guarantee global progress, they allow scenarios in which all but one thread starve while trying to execute an operation on the queue. The few wait-free queue constructions that exist, as discussed later, are either stem from general transformations on sequential objects and are impractical due to significant performance drawbacks, or severely limit the number of threads that may perform one or both of the queue operations concurrently.

In fact, when considering concurrent data structures in general, one realizes that with only a few exceptions (e.g., [5, 22]), wait-free constructions are very rare in practice. A possible reason for this situation is that such constructions are hard to design in an efficient and practical way. This paper presents the first practical design of wait-free queues, which supports multiple concurrent dequeuers and enqueuers. Our idea is based on the lock-free queue implementation by Michael and Scott [19], considered to be one of the most efficient and scalable non-blocking algorithms in the literature [11, 14, 24]. Our design employs an efficient helping mechanism, which ensures that each operation is applied exactly once and in a bounded time. We achieve wait-freedom by assigning each operation a dynamic age-based priority and making threads with younger operations help older operations to complete. Moreover, we believe the scheme used to design the operations of our queue can be useful for other data structures as well. In addition to the base version of our wait-free algorithm, we propose several optimizations to boost the performance when the contention is low and/or the total number of threads in the system is high.

We have implemented our design in Java and compared it with an implementation of Michael and Scott's lock-free queue [19] using several benchmarks and various system configurations. Our performance evaluation shows that the wait-free algorithm is typically slower than the lock-free implementation, but the slowdown depends on the operating system configuration. Issues such as scheduling policy, memory management, policy of allocating threads to computing cores might have a crucial impact on the produced interleavings in thread executions. Interestingly, the wait-free queue is even faster than the lock-free one, in some realistic cases, in spite of its much stricter progress guarantee.

2. Related Work

Lock-free queue implementations are known for more than two decades, starting from works by Treiber [23], Massalin and Pu [17] and Valois [25]. The algorithm presented by Michael and Scott [19] almost 15 years ago is often considered the most scalable lock-free queue implementation to date [11, 14, 24]. Several recent works propose various optimizations over this implementation [14, 21].

Yet, until now, a practical wait-free implementation of the queue data structure remained an important open question. All previous proposals limited concurrency in queue operations. The first such implementation was introduced by Lamport [16] (also in [11]); it allows only one concurrent enqueuer and dequeuer. Also, the queue in [16] is based on a statically allocated array, which essentially bounds the number of elements that the queue may contain. More recently, David [8] proposed a wait-free queue that supports multiple dequeuers, but only one concurrent enqueuer. His queue is based on infinitely large arrays. The author states that he may get a bounded-array based implementation at the price of increased time complexity. Following David's work, Jayanti and Petrovic [13] proposed a wait-free queue implementation supporting multiple enqueuers, but only one concurrent dequeuer. The elements of their queue are stored in dynamically allocated nodes.

Thus, we are not aware of any previous implementation of a wait-free queue, which supports multiple concurrent enqueuers and multiple concurrent dequeuers. In particular, we are not familiar with an implementation that does not require such a queue to be statically allocated and does not use primitives stronger than compare-and-swap (CAS), widely available on modern processors.

In the context of non-blocking concurrent data structures, we should also mention *universal constructions* [10, 11]. These constructions are generic methods to transform any sequential object into lock-free (or wait-free) linearizable concurrent object. The first such construction was proposed by Herlihy [10]. His idea was to allow each concurrent process to create a private copy of the object, apply its changes locally and then attempt to modify the shared root pointer of the object to point the private copy. For the wait-free transformation, he employed a similar mechanism to ours, in which each process writes in a special array the details of the operation it is going to perform, while other processes may access this array and assist slower peers to complete their operations.

Herlihy's construction has two very significant performance drawbacks. First, the copying can be very costly, especially for large objects. Second, the construction precludes disjoint-access parallelism since it requires an atomic update of a single root pointer. Thus, even if concurrent operations modify different parts of the structure, as happens in queues, they still will contend. Although many optimizations were proposed to address one or both of these limitations [3, 4, 7, 20], universal constructions are hardly considered practical. It is worth mentioning that the recent work by Chuong et al. [7] gives a refined construction for queues, which allows concurrent enqueue and dequeue operations. Their queue, however, is implemented as a statically-allocated array, thus the upper bound on the total number of elements that can be inserted into the queue has to be set upfront. In addition, their work does not provide any performance evaluation.

3. Wait-Free Queue Algorithm

We start by presenting the idea of our wait-free queue, including the scheme by which the queue operations are implemented (Section 3.1). Following that, we provide the full implementation in Java of our base algorithm (Section 3.2). Preferring the simplicity of the presentation of principal ideas over performance optimality, we defer the discussion of potential optimizations of the base algorithm to Section 3.3. Utilizing the fact that Java is a garbage-collected language, in our base algorithm we do not deal with memory management and problems related to that. We elaborate on how our algorithm can be implemented in other runtime environments, such as C++, in Section 3.4. In our code, we follow the style of the lock-free algorithm by Michael and Scott [19] as it appears in [11].

For simplicity, we assume the queue stores integer values, though the extension for any generic type is trivial.

3.1 The idea in a nutshell

Similarly to the queue in [19], our wait-free implementation is based on the underlying singly-linked list and holds two references to the head and tail of the list, respectively called `head` and `tail`. Our implementation significantly extends the helping technique already employed by Michael and Scott in their original algorithm [19]. Every thread t_i starting an operation on the queue chooses a phase number, which is higher than phases of threads that have previously chosen phase numbers for their operations (we will explain later how the phase number is chosen). Then it records this number, along with some additional information on the operation it is going to execute on the queue, in a special `state` array.

Next, t_i traverses the `state` array and looks for threads with entries containing a phase number that is smaller or equal than the one chosen by t_i. Once such a thread t_j is found (it can be also t_i itself), t_i tries to help it execute its operation on the queue, i.e., to insert t_j's node into the queue (enqueue) or to remove the first node from the queue on behalf of t_j (dequeue). The thread t_i learns the details on t_j's operation from the `state` array. Finally, when t_i has tried to help all other threads with a phase number not larger than it has, it can safely return the execution to the caller of the (dequeue or enqueue) operation. That is, t_i can be confident that its own operation on the queue has been completed either by t_i or by some other concurrently running and helping thread.

Our algorithm is carefully designed to handle concurrent assistance correctly, and in particular, to avoid applying the same operation more than once. Essentially, this is the most sophisticated part of our design. The idea is to break each type of operation (i.e., dequeue and enqueue) into three atomic steps, so that steps belonging to the same operation can be executed by different threads, yet they cannot interleave with steps of other concurrent operations of the same type. These steps form the implementation scheme of the operations, and are presented hereby. (Under "internal structure of the queue" we mean the underlying linked list along with the `head` and `tail` references).

1. Initial change of the internal structure of the queue, such that all concurrent threads performing the operation of the same type realize that there is some operation-in-progress. At the end of this step, the operation-in-progress is linearized.

2. Updating the entry in the `state` array belonging to the thread that invoked the operation-in-progress with the fact that the thread's operation was linearized.

3. Finalizing the operation-in-progress, fixing the internal structure of the queue.

For the enqueue operation, we utilize the lazy nature of the original implementation [19], where this operation is done in two distinct phases. There, a thread tries first to append a new node to the end of the underlying linked list and then updates `tail` to refer the newly appended node. The important aspect of this lazy implementation is that other threads do not execute the first phase of their enqueue operation until the `tail` reference is updated, ensuring that at most one node can be beyond the node referenced by `tail` in the underlying linked list. (We refer to such a node as *dangling*). This lazy implementation fits nicely into the scheme presented above: The initial change of the queue in Step (1) is the appending of a new node to the end of the underlying linked list. Following this step, other threads cannot start their enqueue operations, but only can learn about the existence of an operation-in-progress and assist its completion with the next two steps of the scheme.

```
 1:  class Node {
 2:      int value;
 3:      AtomicReference<Node> next;
 4:      int enqTid;
 5:      AtomicInteger deqTid;
 6:      Node (int val, int etid) {
 7:          value = val;
 8:          next = new AtomicReference<Node>(null);
 9:          enqTid = etid;
10:          deqTid = new AtomicInteger(-1);
11:      }
12:  }

13:  class OpDesc {
14:      long phase;
15:      boolean pending;
16:      boolean enqueue;
17:      Node node;
18:      OpDesc (long ph, boolean pend, boolean enq, Node n) {
19:          phase = ph;
20:          pending = pend;
21:          enqueue = enq;
22:          node = n;
23:      }
24:  }
```

Figure 1. Internal structures.

```
25:  AtomicReference<Node> head, tail;
26:  AtomicReferenceArray<OpDesc> state;

27:  WFQueue () {
28:      Node sentinel = new Node(-1, -1);
29:      head = new AtomicReference<Node>(sentinel);
30:      tail = new AtomicReference<Node>(sentinel);

31:      state = new AtomicReferenceArray<OpDesc>(NUM_THRDS);

32:      for (int i = 0; i < state.length(); i++) {
33:          state.set(i, new OpDesc(-1, false, true, null));
34:      }
35:  }

36:  void help(long phase) {
37:      for (int i = 0; i < state.length(); i++) {
38:          OpDesc desc = state.get(i);
39:          if (desc.pending && desc.phase <= phase) {
40:              if (desc.enqueue) {
41:                  help_enq(i, phase);
42:              } else {
43:                  help_deq(i, phase);
44:              }
45:          }
46:      }
47:  }

48:  long maxPhase() {
49:      long maxPhase = -1;
50:      for (int i = 0; i < state.length(); i++) {
51:          long phase = state.get(i).phase;
52:          if (phase > maxPhase) {
53:              maxPhase = phase;
54:          }
55:      }
56:      return maxPhase;
57:  }

58:  boolean isStillPending(int tid, long ph) {
59:      return state.get(tid).pending && state.get(tid).phase <= ph;
60:  }
```

Figure 2. Auxiliary methods.

In the original implementation [19], the `dequeue` operation is implemented in one atomic step (the update of `head`), and thus its adaption for our scheme is more complicated. We solve it by adding a field to each node of the underlying linked list: A thread starts the `dequeue` operation by writing its ID into this field at the first node of the list. More precisely, a thread t_i executing the `dequeue` operation on behalf of t_j writes the ID of t_j. This is the first step of our scheme. Other threads cannot remove nodes from the list before they assist the thread whose ID is written in the first node to complete the next two steps of the scheme.

Special care should be given to the case of an empty queue. Since a `dequeue` operation on an empty queue can be executed by t_i on behalf of another thread t_j, t_i cannot simply throw an exception (or return a special "empty" value), as this will occur in a wrong execution context. Thus, t_i has to indicate this special situation in t_j's entry of the `state` array. Also, to avoid t_i from racing with another thread t_k that helps t_j's `dequeue` operation and thinks that the queue is actually non-empty, we require t_k to update t_j's entry in `state` with a reference to the first node in the underlying list. This update has to take place before t_k executes the first step of the scheme described above, i.e., before t_k puts t_j's ID into the special field of the first node in the list. All further details are elaborated and exemplified pictorially in Section 3.2.

It remains to describe how t_i chooses its phase number. To provide wait-freedom, we need to ensure that every time t_i chooses a number, it is greater than the number of any thread that has made its choice before t_i. For this purpose, we chose a simple implementation in which t_i calculates the value of the maximal phase stored in the `state` array and chooses this value plus one. The idea is inspired by the doorway mechanism proposed by Lamport in his famous Bakery algorithm for mutual exclusion [15]. Alternatively, one may use an atomic counter, which can be incremented and read atomically. This idea is described in Section 3.3.

3.2 Implementation

Internal structures and auxiliary methods

The code for internal structures used by our queue implementation is given in Figure 1, while auxiliary methods are in Figure 2. Our queue uses a singly-linked list with a sentinel node as an underlying representation, and relies on two inner classes: `Node` and `OpDesc`. The `Node` class (Lines 1–12) is intended to hold elements of the queue's underlying list. In addition to the common fields, i.e., a value and atomic reference to the next element (implemented with `AtomicReference` class of Java), `Node` contains two additional fields: `enqTid` and `deqTid`. As their names suggest, these fields hold the ID of the thread that performs or has already performed (probably, helped by another thread) the insertion or removal of the node to/from the queue. (In the following, we refer to ID of a thread as *tid*).

In more detail, when a node is created by a thread in the beginning of the `enqueue` operation, the thread records its tid in the `enqTid` field of the new node. This field will be used by other threads to identify the thread that tries to insert that particular node into the queue, and help it if needed. Similarly, during the `dequeue` operation, the tid of the node trying to remove the first node of the queue is recorded in the `deqTid` field of the first node in the underlying linked list. Again, this field is used to identify and help the thread performing a `dequeue` operation. Notice that while `enqTid` is set by only one thread (the one that wants to insert a node into the queue), `deqTid` may be modified by multiple threads concurrently performing a `dequeue` operation. As a result, while the former field is a regular (non-atomic) integer, the latter field is implemented as an atomic integer.

The `OpDesc` class (Lines 13–24) defines an operation descriptor record for each thread. This record contains information about

225

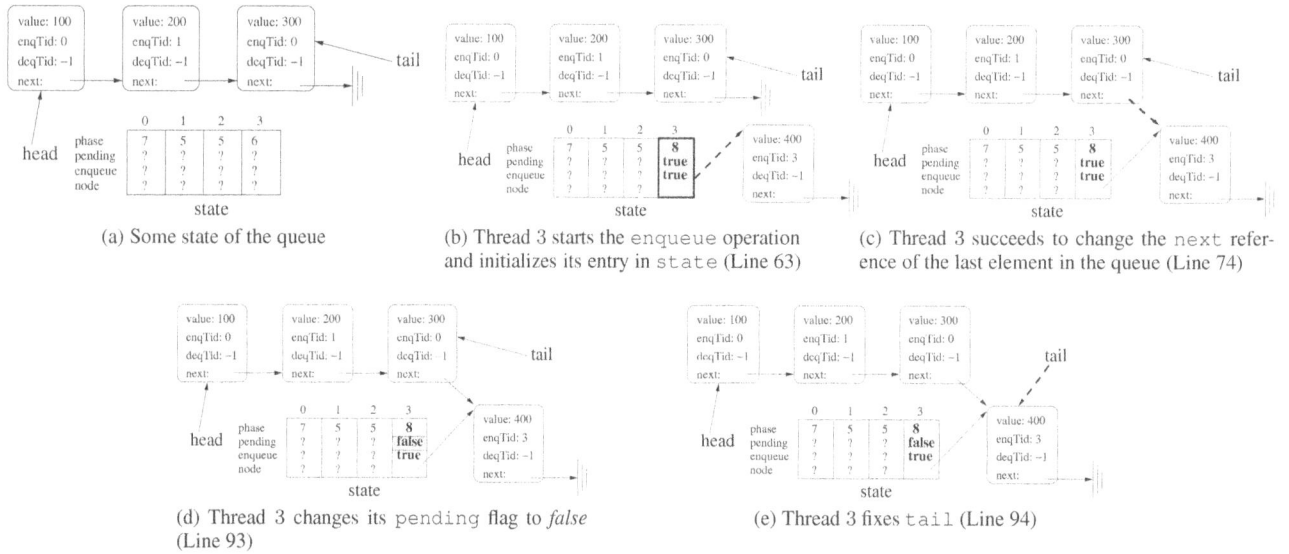

(a) Some state of the queue

(b) Thread 3 starts the `enqueue` operation and initializes its entry in `state` (Line 63)

(c) Thread 3 succeeds to change the `next` reference of the last element in the queue (Line 74)

(d) Thread 3 changes its `pending` flag to *false* (Line 93)

(e) Thread 3 fixes `tail` (Line 94)

Figure 3. The flow of the `enqueue` operation performed solely by Thread 3.

the phase at which the thread has performed (or is performing right now) its last operation on the queue (`phase` field), the type of the operation (`enqueue` field), the flag specifying whether the thread has a pending operation (`pending` field), and a reference to a node with a meaning specific to the type of the operation (`node` field). In case of the `enqueue` operation, the `node` field holds a reference to a node with a value that the considered thread tries to insert into the queue. In case of the `dequeue` operation, this field refers to a node preceding the one with a value that should be returned from the operation (this will be clarified later in this section when the `dequeue` operation is explained).

In addition to the definition of the inner classes, the `Queue` class contains several fields. Being based on a linked list, it has (atomic) references to the head and the tail of the list (Line 25). Additionally, it contains an array of atomic references to the `OpDesc` records of all threads, called `state` (Line 26). The size of the array, denoted as `NUM_THRDS`, is assumed to be known and equal to the number of threads that might perform operations on the queue[2]. In the following, where it is not ambiguous, we refer to the entry of a thread t_i in the `state` array as t_i's *state*.

The auxiliary methods are straight-forward. The queue constructor (Lines 27–35) initializes the underlying linked list with one sentinel (dummy) node. In addition, it initializes the `state` array appropriately. `help()` (Lines 36–47) accepts a phase number. It runs through all operation descriptors and calls `help_enq()` or `help_deq()` methods (detailed later in this section) according to the operation type recorded in the descriptor. Notice that `help_enq()` and `help_deq()` are invoked only for operations that are still pending and have a phase smaller or equal than the one passed as a parameter to `help()`. `maxPhase()` method (Lines 48–57) simply runs through the `state` array and calculates the maximal phase written in the operation descriptors. `isStillPending()` method (Lines 58–60) accepts tid and phase and checks whether the thread with ID equal to tid has a pending operation in a phase smaller or equal than the passed *phase* parameter.

enqueue operation

The flow of the operation is presented in Figure 3. For simplicity, Figure 3 considers the case in which a thread executes `enqueue` without interference from other threads. The implementation is given in Figure 4.

When a thread t_i calls the `enqueue` operation (i.e., `enq()` method of the queue), it first calculates the phase for the operation by adding 1 to the result returned from `maxPhase()` (Line 62). Then it creates a new node to hold the value to be enqueued and updates the corresponding entry in the `state` array with a new operation descriptor record (Line 63). We assume here that each thread can access its tid, while the tid is a number in the range $[0, \ldots, \text{NUM\_THRDS}-1]$. In Section 3.3 we discuss how the latter can be relaxed. Note also that the new node is created with `enqTid` field set to the tid of the thread (i in our example). Later in the code, this field will be used to locate the entry of t_i in the `state` array in order to complete t_i's `enqueue` operation.

Next, t_i calls `help()` (Line 64), which was explained above. When this call returns, all operations having phase smaller or equal than the one chosen by t_i in Line 62 are linearized, including the current `enqueue` operation of t_i. Finally, t_i calls the `help_finish_enq()` method (Line 65), which ensures that when t_i returns from the call to `enq()`, the `tail` reference of the queue does not refer a node before the one that was just enqueued by t_i. This is needed for correctness, as explained later in this section.

Next, we describe the implementation of the `help_enq()` method given in Lines 67–84. This method is called from `help()` for pending `enqueue` operations. It accepts two parameters, which are the ID of a thread t_x (i.e., x) who has a pending `enqueue` operation and the phase of the thread t_y actually calling `help_enq()`. Notice that these can be the same thread (i.e., $x = y$) or two different threads. Among other things, both parameters are used to verify that the `enqueue` operation of t_x for which `help_enq()` was called is still pending.

The actual implementation of `help_enq()` is a customized version of the `enq()` method in [19]. It checks whether the queue is in a state in which `tail` actually refers to the last node in the underlying linked list (Lines 69–72). If so, it tries to insert the new node just behind the last node in the list (Line 74). With respect to

---

[2] More precisely, `NUM_THRDS` can be an upper bound, not necessarily strict, on the number of threads that might access the queue.

```
61:  void enq(int value) {
62:     long phase = maxPhase() + 1;                      ▷ cf. Figure 3b
63:     state.set(TID, new
                OpDesc(phase, true, true, new Node(value, TID)));
64:     help(phase);
65:     help_finish_enq();
66:  }

67:  void help_enq(int tid, long phase) {
68:     while (isStillPending(tid, phase)) {
69:        Node last = tail.get();
70:        Node next = last.next.get();
71:        if (last == tail.get()) {
72:           if (next == null) {                         ▷ enqueue can be applied
73:              if (isStillPending(tid, phase)) {
74:                 if (last.next.compareAndSet(next, state.get(tid).node)) {
                                                          ▷ cf. Figure 3c
75:                    help_finish_enq();
76:                    return;
77:                 }
78:              }
79:           } else {                                    ▷ some enqueue is in progress
80:              help_finish_enq();                        ▷ help it first, then retry
81:           }
82:        }
83:     }
84:  }

85:  void help_finish_enq() {
86:     Node last = tail.get();
87:     Node next = last.next.get();
88:     if (next != null) {
89:        int tid = next.enqTid;                         ▷ read enqTid of the last element
90:        OpDesc curDesc = state.get(tid);
91:        if (last == tail.get() && state.get(tid).node == next) {
92:           OpDesc newDesc = new                         ▷ cf. Figure 3d
                OpDesc(state.get(tid).phase, false, true, next);
93:           state.compareAndSet(tid, curDesc, newDesc);
94:           tail.compareAndSet(last, next);             ▷ cf. Figure 3e
95:        }
96:     }
97:  }
```

Figure 4. enqueue operation

the scheme in Section 3.1, this is the first step of the scheme. The new node is located using the state array and tid parameter of help_enq() (Line 74). If succeeded, or if there is already some node after the one pointed by tail, help_finish_enq() is invoked (Line 75 or 80, respectively).

As its name suggests, help_finish_enq() is called to finish the progressing enqueue operation. In the original implementation of [19], this means to update the tail reference to refer to the newly added node. In our case, we need to update also the state of the thread whose node was just inserted to the list in Line 74. The entry of this thread in the state array is located by the enqTid field written in the newly added node (Line 89). After verifying that the corresponding entry in the state array still refers to the newly added node (Line 91), a new operation description record with the pending flag turned off is created and written in Lines 92–93. This is the second step of the scheme in Section 3.1. The verification in Line 91 is required for correctness to avoid races between threads running help_finish_enq() concurrently. Afterwards, the tail reference is updated to refer to the newly added (and the last) node in the list (Line 94), which is the third step of the scheme. Notice that the CAS operation in Line 93 may succeed more than once for the same newly added node. Yet, utilizing the fact that only one node can be dangling, our implementation ensures that

the state array remains consistent and the tail reference is updated only once per each node added to the list.

Having help_finish_enq() explained, we can argue why its invocation in Line 65 is necessary. Consider a thread t_i trying to apply an enqueue operation and being helped concurrently by another thread t_j. If t_j executes Line 93 and gets suspended, t_i might realize that its operation is already linearized (e.g., by checking the condition in Line 68), return to the caller of enq() and start another operation on a queue setting a new operation descriptor. In such a scenario, all further enqueue operations will be blocked (since the condition in Line 91 does not hold anymore) until t_j will resume and update the tail reference, breaking the wait-free progress property.

In addition, notice that both condition checks in Lines 68 and 73 are necessary for correctness. Removing the check in Line 68 (i.e., replacing this line with **while** (*true*) statement) will break the progress property, as a thread may always find some enqueue operation in progress and execute the call to help_finish_enq() at Line 80 infinitely many times. Along with that, removing the check in Line 73 will break the linearizability. This is because a thread t_i might pass the test in Line 68, get suspended, then resume and add an element to the queue, while at the same time, this element might have been already added to the queue by another concurrent thread during the time t_i was suspended.

dequeue operation

The flow of the operation is presented in Figure 5, while the code is given in Figure 6. As in the case of enqueue, a thread t_i starts the dequeue operation by choosing the phase number (Line 99), updating its entry in the state array (Line 100) and calling help() (Line 101). When the latter call returns, the current dequeue operation of t_i, as well as all operations having a phase not larger than t_i's phase, are linearized. Then t_i calls help_finish_deq() (Line 102), which ensures that when t_i returns from deq(), the head reference does not refer to a node with a deqTid field equal to i. Again, this is required for correctness. Finally, t_i examines the reference to a node recorded in its state (Lines 103–107). If it is null, then the operation was linearized when the queue was empty. Otherwise, t_i returns the value of the node following the one recorded in t_i's state in the underlying linked list. Intuitively, this is the value of the first real node in the queue at the instant t_i's dequeue operation linearizes, and the entry in the state array refers to the preceding sentinel at that time.

The code of help_deq(), called from help() for pending dequeue operations, is given in Lines 109–140. The parameters received by this method have the same meaning as in help_enq(). Similarly, its implementation is intended to be a customized version of the deq() method in [19]. Yet, although deq() in [19] is relatively simple, help_deq() appears to be slightly more complicated, carefully constructed to fit the scheme of Section 3.1.

For ease of explanation, let us assume first that the queue is not empty. In order to help t_i to complete the dequeue operation and remove an element from the queue, a thread t_j running help_deq() has to pass through four stages, illustrated in Figure 5: (1) place a reference from t_i's state to the first node in the underlying list, (2) update the deqTid field of the first node in the list with i, (3) update the pending field in the state of t_i to *false*, and (4) update head to refer to the next node in the underlying list. The first two stages are handled in help_deq(), while the last two are in the help_finish_deq() method. With respect to the scheme described in Section 3.1, Stages (2)–(4) implement the three steps of the scheme, while the additional Stage (1) is required to handle correctly the case of applying dequeue on an empty queue, as described later in this section.

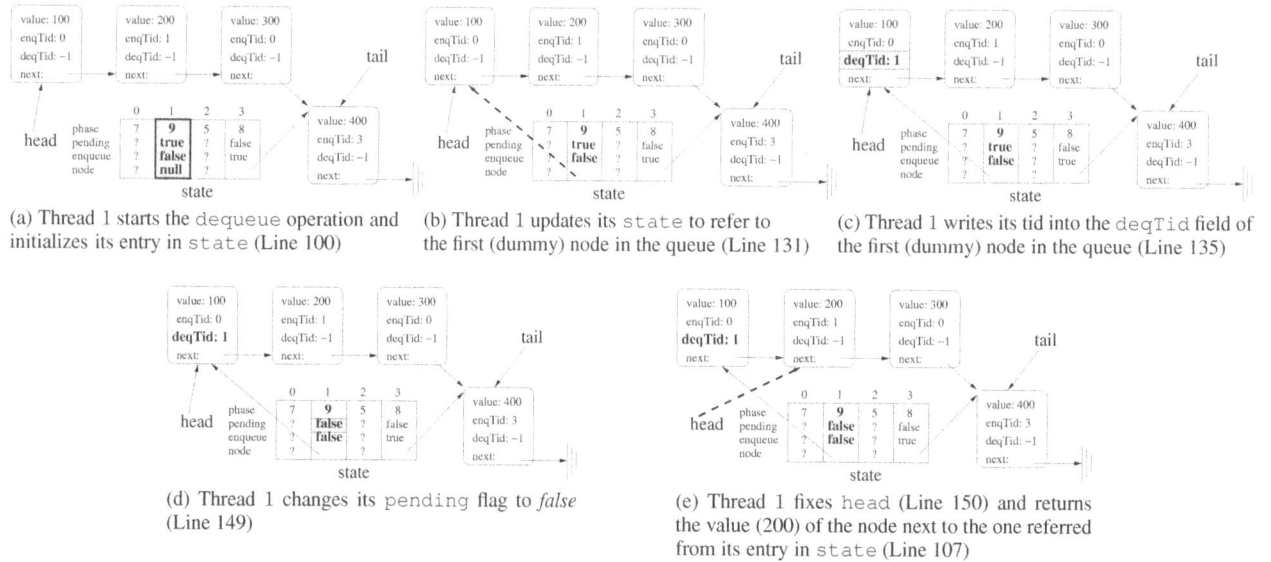

(a) Thread 1 starts the `dequeue` operation and initializes its entry in `state` (Line 100)

(b) Thread 1 updates its `state` to refer to the first (dummy) node in the queue (Line 131)

(c) Thread 1 writes its tid into the `deqTid` field of the first (dummy) node in the queue (Line 135)

(d) Thread 1 changes its `pending` flag to *false* (Line 149)

(e) Thread 1 fixes head (Line 150) and returns the value (200) of the node next to the one referred from its entry in `state` (Line 107)

Figure 5. The flow of the `dequeue` operation performed solely by Thread 1 after Thread 3 finishes its `enqueue` operation in Figure 3.

The `dequeue` operation of t_i is linearized at the instant t_j (or any other concurrent thread running `help_deq()` with *tid* parameter equal to i) succeeds to complete Stage (2). We say that at that time, t_j *locks* the sentinel referred by `head`. (To avoid any confusion, we emphasize that here the lock has only a logical meaning). Before that happens, t_j examines the node referred from t_i's `state` (Line 129). If it is different from the head of the queue as was read in Line 111, t_j tries to complete Stage (1) (Lines 130–131) (otherwise, some other thread has done it before). If failed, t_j realizes that some other thread has updated t_i's `state` and thus, t_j resets its operation, returning to the beginning of the **while** loop (Line 132). If succeeded, or if t_i's `state` already refers to the head of the queue, t_j tries to complete Stage (2) (Line 135). If succeeded again, then t_j locks the sentinel. Otherwise, some other thread did that (maybe even for the same `dequeue` operation). In any case, t_j calls `help_finish_deq()` (Line 136), which is supposed to complete the `dequeue` operation of the thread that locks the sentinel. Notice the condition checks in Lines 110 and 128. Similarly to the checks in `help_enq()`, the check in Line 110 is necessary to ensure the wait-freedom, while the check in Line 128 is required for the correct linearizability.

When t_j finds that the queue might be empty, i.e., when `head` and `tail` refer to the same node, it checks whether there is some `enqueue` operation in progress (Line 116). If so, it helps first to complete this operation (Line 123) and returns to the beginning of the **while** loop. Otherwise, t_j realizes that the queue is empty, and tries to update t_i's state accordingly (Lines 119–120). This is where Stage (1), i.e., putting a reference from t_i's `state` to the first node in the list, is required. Otherwise, a race between two helping threads, one looking at an empty queue and the other on a non-empty queue, is possible.

It remains to explain the details of `help_finish_deq()`. This method completes the `dequeue` operation in progress. First, it tries to update the `pending` field in the state of a thread t_k whose tid is written in the node referred by `head` (Lines 148–149). Notice that just like in `help_finish_enq()`, the CAS operation in Line 149 may succeed more than once for the same `dequeue` operation in progress. Finally, `head` is updated (Line 150), completing the final Stage (4) of the `dequeue` operation in progress.

3.3 Optimizations and enhancements

One of the shortcomings of the base implementation presented in Section 3.2 is that the number of steps executed by each thread when there is no contention still depends on n, the total number of threads that might perform an operation on the queue. This dependence appears in the calculation of the phase number in the `maxPhase()` method and in the `help()` method, where the `state` array is traversed.

It is possible, however, to resolve this drawback by changing the implementation in the following way. First, in order to calculate the phase number, a queue might have an internal `maxPh` field, which would be read by each thread initiating an operation on the queue and increased by an atomic operation, such as CAS or *Fetch-and-Add*[3]. Second, a thread may traverse only a chunk of the `state` array in a cyclic manner in the `help()` method. That is, in the first invocation of `help()`, it would traverse indexes 0 through $k - 1 \bmod n$ (in addition to its own index) for some $1 \le k < n$, in the second invocation – indexes $k \bmod n$ through $2k - 1 \bmod n$, and so on. Notice that this modification will preserve wait-freedom since a thread t_i may delay a particular operation of another thread t_j only a limited number of times, after which t_i will help to complete t_j's operation. Alternatively, each thread might traverse a random chunk of the array, achieving probabilistic wait-freedom. In any case, the running time of contention-free executions will be improved. In case of contention, however, when all n threads try to execute an operation on the queue concurrently, the operations may essentially take a number of steps dependent on n. Yet another option is to apply techniques of [2] to have the time complexity of the algorithm to depend on the number of threads concurrently accessing the queue rather than n.

In addition, our base implementation can be enhanced in several ways. First, notice that any update of `state` is preceded with an allocation of a new operation descriptor. These allocations might be wasteful (both from performance and memory consumptions aspects) if the following CAS operation fails while trying to update

---

[3] Notice that in the case of a CAS-based phase counter, a thread does not need to check the result of the CAS. A failure of its CAS operation would simply imply that another thread has chosen the same phase number.

```
98:  int deq() throws EmptyException {
99:      long phase = maxPhase() + 1;                              ▷ cf. Figure 5a
100:     state.set(TID, new OpDesc(phase, true, false, null));
101:     help(phase);
102:     help_finish_deq();
103:     Node node = state.get(TID).node;
104:     if (node == null) {
105:        throw new EmptyException();
106:     }
107:     return node.next.get().value;
108: }

109: void help_deq(int tid, long phase) {
110:     while (isStillPending(tid, phase)) {
111:         Node first = head.get();
112:         Node last = tail.get();
113:         Node next = first.next.get();
114:         if (first == head.get()) {
115:             if (first == last) {                               ▷ queue might be empty
116:                 if (next == null) {                            ▷ queue is empty
117:                     OpDesc curDesc = state.get(tid);
118:                     if (last == tail.get() && isStillPending(tid, phase)) {
119:                         OpDesc newDesc = new
                                OpDesc(state.get(tid).phase, false, false, null);
120:                         state.compareAndSet(tid, curDesc, newDesc);
121:                     }
122:                 } else {                                       ▷ some enqueue is in progress
123:                     help_finish_enq();                         ▷ help it first, then retry
124:                 }
125:             } else {                                           ▷ queue is not empty
126:                 OpDesc curDesc = state.get(tid);
127:                 Node node = curDesc.node;
128:                 if (!isStillPending(tid, phase)) break;
129:                 if (first == head.get() && node != first) {
130:                     OpDesc newDesc = new                       ▷ cf. Figure 5b
                                OpDesc(state.get(tid).phase, true, false, first);
131:                     if (!state.compareAndSet(tid, curDesc, newDesc)) {
132:                         continue;
133:                     }
134:                 }
135:                 first.deqTid.compareAndSet(-1, tid);           ▷ cf. Figure 5c
136:                 help_finish_deq();
137:             }
138:         }
139:     }
140: }

141: void help_finish_deq() {
142:     Node first = head.get();
143:     Node next = first.next.get();
144:     int tid = first.deqTid.get();          ▷ read deqTid of the first element
145:     if (tid != -1) {
146:         OpDesc curDesc = state.get(tid);
147:         if (first == head.get() && next != null) {
148:             OpDesc newDesc = new                               ▷ cf. Figure 5d
                        OpDesc(state.get(tid).phase, false, false,
                        state.get(tid).node);
149:             state.compareAndSet(tid, curDesc, newDesc);
150:             head.compareAndSet(first, next);                  ▷ cf. Figure 5e
151:         }
152:     }
153: }
```

Figure 6. dequeue operation

the state array (e.g., CAS in Lines 93 or 120). This issue can be easily solved by caching allocated descriptors used in unsuccessful CASes and reusing them when a new descriptor is required.

Second, when a thread finishes an operation on a queue, its operation descriptor remains to refer a node in the underlying linked list (unless it was a dequeue operation from an empty queue).

This node might be considered later by the garbage collector as a live object, even though it might have been removed from the queue a long time ago. This issue can be solved by setting a dummy operation descriptor record into the state of the thread just before it exits the deq() and enq() methods. This dummy record should have a null reference in its node field.

Third, our base implementation lacks validation checks that might be applied before executing (costly) CAS operations. For example, we might check whether the pending flag is already switched off before applying CAS in Lines 93 or 149. Although such checks might be helpful in performance tuning [14], they would definitely complicate the presentation of our algorithm. As stated before, we preferred simple presentation of principal ideas over optimality where possible, leaving (minor) performance tuning optimizations for future work.

In the base version of our algorithm, we assume threads to have unique IDs in a range between 0 and some known constant bound. However, the same thread can use different IDs in subsequent operations on the queue as long as they do not collide with IDs of other threads concurrently accessing the queue. As a result, the assumption above can be relaxed: To support applications in which threads are created and deleted dynamically and may have arbitrary IDs, threads can get and release (virtual) IDs from a small name space through one of the known long-lived wait-free renaming algorithms (e.g., [1, 6]). Also, our algorithm employs a phase counter, which theoretically may wrap and harm the wait-free progress property of our implementation. Since this counter is implemented as a 64-bit integer, this possibility is impractical.

3.4 Memory management and ABA issues

The algorithm presented in Section 3.2 relies on the existence of a garbage collector (GC) responsible for memory management, and in particular, for dynamic reclamation of objects not in use. Since a wait-free GC is not known to exist, the presentation of our algorithm would not be complete without discussing how the algorithm can manage its memory in a wait-free manner.

Also, another important benefit of GC is the elimination of all occurrences of the ABA problem [11] that originate from early reclamation of objects. The ABA problem denotes the situation where a thread may incorrectly succeed in applying a CAS operation even though the contents of the shared memory have changed between the instant it read the old value from the memory and the instant it applied the CAS with a new value. Such a situation may occur if a thread was suspended between the two instants, while many insertions and deletions executed on the queue in the interim period brought the contents of the location read by the thread into the identical state. In garbage-collected languages, such as Java, the problem does not exist, since an object referenced by some thread cannot be reallocated for any other use.

In order to adapt our algorithm for runtime environments in which GC is not implemented, we propose to use the Hazard Pointers [18] technique. The technique is based on associating *hazard pointers* with each thread. These pointers are single-writer multi-reader registers used by threads to mark (point on) objects that they may access later. When an object is removed from the data structure (in our case, by dequeue operation), the special RetireNode method is called, which recycles the object only if there are no hazard pointers pointing on it.

The integration of the Hazard Pointers technique into our algorithm requires a small modification of the latter. Specifically, we need to add a field into the operation descriptor records to hold a value removed from the queue (and not just a reference to the sentinel through which this value can be located). This is in order to be able to call RetireNode right at the end of help_deq(), even though the thread that actually invoked the corresponding dequeue operation might retrieve the value removed from the queue (e.g., execute Line 107) much later. Since our algorithm has a structure very similar to that of [19], further integration of the Hazard Pointers technique with our algorithm is very similar to the example in [18]. The exact details are out of scope of this short paper. We also notice that the same technique helps to prevent the ABA problem described above, and, since this technique is wait-free [18], our integrated solution remains wait-free.

4. Performance

We evaluated the performance of our wait-free queue comparing it to the lock-free queue by Michael and Scott [19], known as the most efficient lock-free dynamically allocated queue algorithm in the literature [11, 14, 24]. For the lock-free queue, we used the Java implementation exactly as it appears in [11]. We run our tests using three different system configurations: the first one consisted of an Intel blade server featuring two 2.5GHz quadcore Xeon E5420 processors operating under CentOS 5.5 Server Edition system, the second one is the same machine operating under Ubuntu 8.10 Server Edition system, while the third configuration consisted of a machine featuring two 1.6GHz quadcore Xeon E5310 processors operating under RedHat Enterprise 5.3 Linux Server. All machines were installed with 16GB RAM and were able to run concurrently 8 threads. All tests were run in Sun's Java SE Runtime version 1.6.0 update 22, using the HotSpot 64-Bit Server VM, with `-Xmx10G` `-Xms10G` flags.

In addition to the base version detailed in Section 3.2, we have also evaluated two optimizations mentioned in Section 3.3:

1. In each operation on the queue, a thread t_i tries to help only one thread, choosing the candidates in a cyclic order of the entries in the `state` array. As in the base version, the helping is actually done only if the candidate has a pending operation with a phase smaller or equal than t_i's.

2. The phase number is calculated using an atomic integer, i.e., each thread gets the value of that integer plus one and tries to increment it atomically using CAS, instead of traversing the `state` array in `maxPhase()`.

As mentioned in Section 3.3, these two modifications preserve wait-freedom. Following the methodology of Michael and Scott [19] and of Ladan-Mozes and Shavit [14], we evaluated the performance of the queue algorithms with the following two benchmarks:

- `enqueue-dequeue` pairs: the queue is initially empty, and at each iteration, each thread iteratively performs an `enqueue` operation followed by a `dequeue` operation.

- 50% `enqueues`: the queue is initialized with 1000 elements, and at each iteration, each thread decides uniformly at random and independently of other threads which operation it is going to execute on the queue, with equal odds for `enqueue` and `dequeue`.

We measured the completion time of each of the algorithms as a function of the number of concurrent threads. For this purpose, we varied the number of threads between 1 and 16 (i.e., up to twice the number of available cores). Each thread performed $1,000,000$ iterations. Thus, in the first benchmark, given the number of threads k, the number of operations is $2000000 \cdot k$, divided equally between `enqueue` and `dequeue`. In the second benchmark, the number of operations is $1000000 \cdot k$, with a random pattern of roughly 50% of `enqueues` and 50% of `dequeues`. Each data point presented in our graphs is the average of ten experiments run with the same set of parameters. The standard deviation of the results was negligible, and thus not shown for better readability.

The results for the first benchmark for each of the three system configurations we worked with are presented in Figure 7. The results reveal that the relative performance of the concurrent algorithms under test is intimately related to the system configuration. While in the RedHat and Ubuntu-operated machines, the lock-free algorithm is an unshakable winner, in the CentOS-operated machine its superiority ends when the number of threads approaches the number of available cores. After that point, the performance of the lock-free algorithm in the CentOS-operated machine falls behind the optimized wait-free version, even though our wait-free algorithms are expected for longer time needed for the bookkeeping of the `state` and trying to help slower threads. It is also worth noting that the relative performance of the concurrent algorithms in the other two system configurations is not identical. While on the RedHat-operated machine, the ratio of the optimized wait-free algorithm to the lock-free algorithm remains around 3, in the Ubuntu-operated machine this ratio continuously decreases with the number of threads, approaching 2.

Figure 8 presents results for the second benchmark for each of the three system configurations. The total completion time for all algorithms exhibits the similar behavior as in the first benchmark, but is roughly 2 times smaller. This is because this benchmark has only a half of the total number of operations of the first benchmark. The relative performance of the lock-free and wait-free algorithms is also similar. Interestingly, the CentOS-operated machine consistently exhibits better performance for the optimized wait-free algorithm when the number of threads increases.

When comparing the performance of the base wait-free algorithm with its optimized version, one can see that the latter behaves better as the number of threads increases (Figures 7 and 8). As discussed in Section 3.3, this happens since the optimized version does not have to traverse the `state` array, which increases in size with the increase in the number of threads. To evaluate which of the two optimizations has greater impact on the performance improvement, we implemented each of them separately and compared the performance of all four variations of our wait-free algorithm: the base (non-optimized) version, two versions with one of the optimizations each, and the version featuring both optimizations. Due to lack of space, we present only results for the `enqueue-dequeue` benchmark and only for the CentOS and RedHat-based configurations (Figure 9). We note that the relative performance in the other benchmark and in the third system configuration is the same.

As Figure 9 suggests, the performance gain is achieved mainly due to the first optimization, i.e., the modified helping mechanism in which a thread helps to at most one other thread when applying an operation on the queue. This is because this optimization reduces the possibility for scenarios in which all threads try to help the same (or a few) thread(s), wasting the total processing time. The impact of the second optimization (the maintenance of the phase number with CAS rather than by traversing `state`) is minor, yet it increases with the number of threads.

In addition to the total running time, we compared the space overhead of the algorithms, that is the amount of heap memory occupied by queues and by threads operating on them. For this purpose, we used the `--verbocegc` flag of Java, which forces Java to print statistics produced by its GC. These statistics include information on the size of live objects in the heap. We run the `enqueue-dequeue` benchmark with 8 threads, while one of the threads periodically invoked GC. To calculate the space overhead, we took the average of these samples (nine samples for each run). We varied the initial size of the queue between 1 and $10,000,000$ elements, in multiples of 10. To produce a data point, we run ten experiments with the same set of parameters and took the average.

Figure 10 shows the space overhead of the base and optimized versions of wait-free algorithms relatively to the lock-free one. The

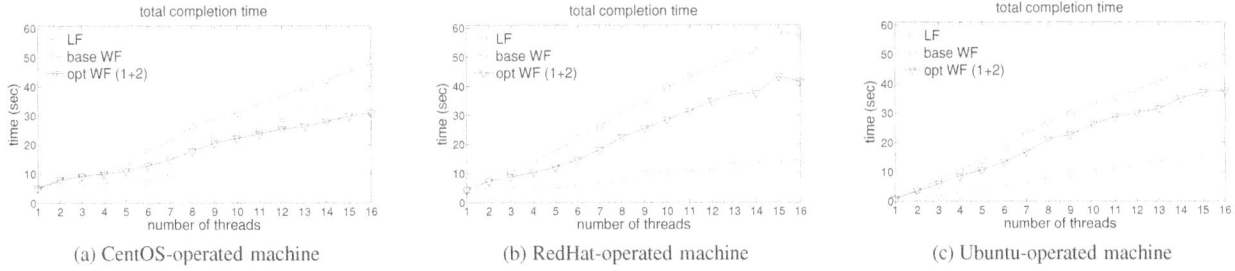

(a) CentOS-operated machine   (b) RedHat-operated machine   (c) Ubuntu-operated machine

Figure 7. Performance results of the `enqueue-dequeue` benchmark.

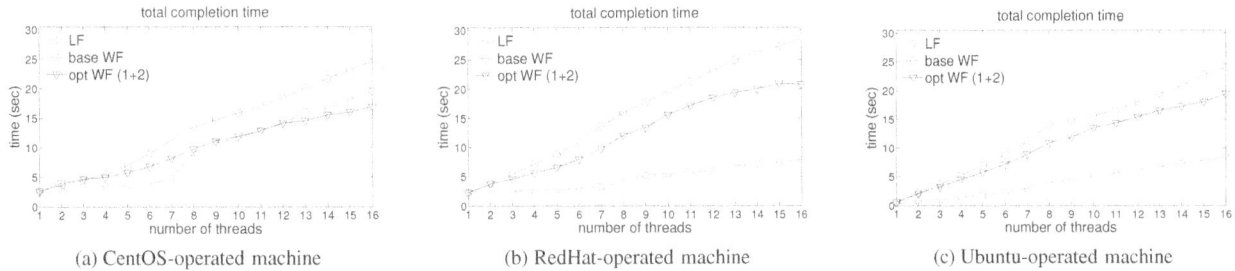

(a) CentOS-operated machine   (b) RedHat-operated machine   (c) Ubuntu-operated machine

Figure 8. Performance results of the 50% `enqueues` benchmark.

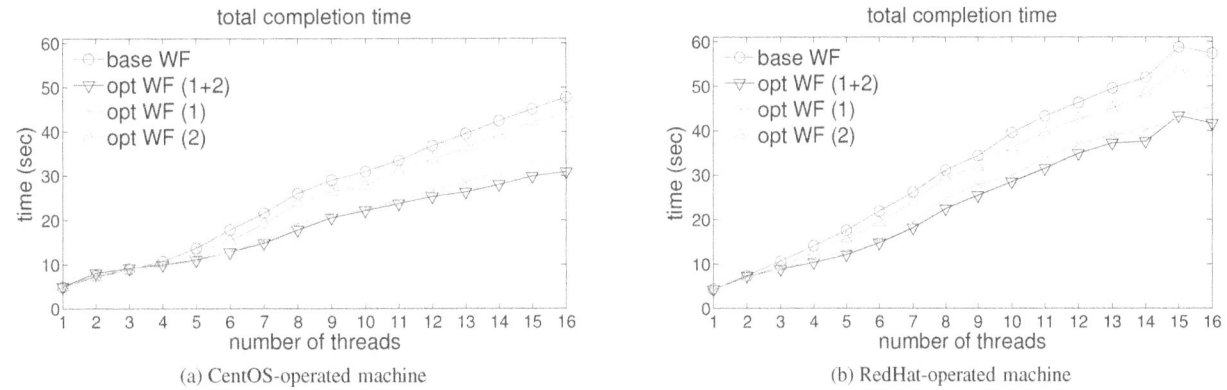

(a) CentOS-operated machine   (b) RedHat-operated machine

Figure 9. The impact of optimizations in the `enqueue-dequeue` benchmark.

shown results were produced on the RedHat-operated machine, while the results for the other two machines are similar. It follows that for small queues, the size of live objects maintained by wait-free algorithms is comparable to that of the lock-free implementation. This is because in these cases, the heap is dominated by objects, which are not part of queues. When the queue size increases, the ratio of sizes of maintained live objects reaches 1.5, meaning that our wait-free algorithms incur roughly 50% more space overhead over the lock-free one. This is because each node in the wait-free queue needs additional space for `deqTid` and `enqTid` fields.

5. Correctness

Due to lack of space, we provide only a sketch of a proof that our algorithm implements a concurrent wait-free queue. We start by describing the computational model assumed by our algorithm. Next, we briefly describe the proof of linearizability and wait-freedom property of our algorithm. In the process, we explain the

semantics of our queue and define the linearization points for its `enqueue` and `dequeue` operations.

5.1 Model

Our model of multithreaded concurrent system follows the linearizability model of [12] and assumes an asynchronous shared memory system, where programs are executed by n deterministic threads, which communicate by executing atomic operations on shared variables from some predefined, finite set. Threads are run on processors, and the decision of which thread will run on which processor is performed solely by a scheduler. It is very likely that the number of available processes is much smaller than n, and execution of any thread may be paused at any time and for arbitrary long due to page fault, cache miss, expired time quantum, etc. We assume that each thread has an ID, denoted as tid, which is a value between 0 and $n - 1$. In Section 3.3 we discuss how to relax this assumption. In addition, we assume each thread can access its tid and n.

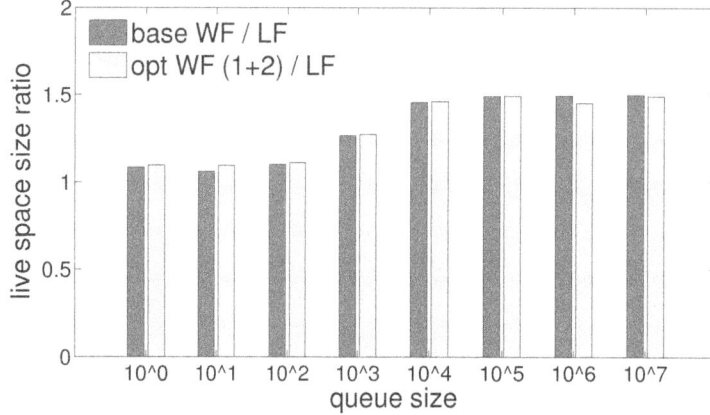

Figure 10. Space overhead evaluation as a function of the initial queue size.

When scheduled to run, a thread performs a sequence of computational steps. Each step may be either a local computation or an invocation of at most one atomic operation on a shared variable. We assume that our shared memory supports atomic reads, writes and compare-and-swap operations. The latter, abbreviated as CAS, is defined as follows: CAS(v, exp, new) changes the value of the shared variable v to new if and only if its value just before CAS is applied is equal to exp. In this case, CAS returns *true* and we say it was *successful*. Otherwise, the value of v is not changed, CAS returns *false* and we say it was *unsuccessful*.

A *configuration* of the system is a vector of a finite size that stores the states of n threads and the values of all shared variables. The state of a thread includes the values of thread's local variables, registers and the program counter. A (finite or infinite) sequence of steps, starting from an *initial configuration*, forms an *execution*. In the initial configuration, all shared variables have predefined initial values and all threads are in their initial states.

A concurrent queue is a data structure whose operations are linearizable [12] to those of a sequential queue. A sequential queue is a data structure that supports two operations: `enqueue` and `dequeue`. The first one accepts an element as an argument and inserts it into the queue. The second one does not accept arguments, removes and returns the oldest value from the queue. In the case of an empty queue, `dequeue` returns a special value (or throws an exception) and the queue remains unchanged.

5.2 Linearizability

We refer to a `dequeue` operation that returns a value as *successful*. If a `dequeue` operation ends by throwing an exception, we refer to it as *unsuccessful*. The `enqueue` operation is always successful. In the following, we define the linearization points for each of the queue operations. Notice that the source lines mentioned in the definition below can be executed either by the thread t_i that invoked the corresponding operation or by another concurrent thread t_j that tries to help t_i by running either `help_enq()` or `help_deq()` method with the tid parameter set to i.

DEFINITION 1. *The linearization points for each of the queue operations are as follows:*

- `Enqueue` *operation is linearized at the successful CAS in Line 74.*
- *Successful* `dequeue` *operation is linearized at the successful CAS in Line 135.*
- *Unsuccessful* `dequeue` *operation is linearized in Line 112.*

To prove the correctness of the linearization points defined above, we recall that our queue is based on a singly-linked list, represented by `head` and `tail` references, where the node referenced by `head` is called *dummy*. We define the state of the queue as a sequence of values of nodes in the list, starting from the node referenced by the `next` reference of the dummy node. (If such a node does not exist, that is the `next` reference of the dummy node is null, we say that the queue is empty).

In the full proof, we need to show that new nodes are always inserted at the end of the list (that is, after the last node reachable from `head` in the list), while the insertion order is consistent with the linearization order of `enqueue` operations. In addition, we need to show that nodes are always removed from the beginning of the list, while the order of removals is consistent with the linearization order of `dequeue` operations. This can be done in a way similar to [19] by careful inspection of the source lines that change the structure of the list .

In the second part of the proof, we need to show that each operation is linearized exactly once. In contrast to most lock-free implementations, including [19], in our case this statement is not trivial due to the concurrent assistance employed by our algorithm. Two central Lemmas in this part are stated below (their proof is omitted).

LEMMA 1. *In any execution and for any* `enqueue` *operation with value v_i invoked by thread t_j, the following steps occur in the stated order, and each of them occurs exactly once:*

1. *A node with value v_i is appended at the end of the linked list (Line 74).*
2. *The* `pending` *flag in the state of t_j is switched from* true *to* false *(Line 93).*
3. `Tail` *is updated to refer the node with value v_i (Line 94).*

LEMMA 2. *In any execution and for any successful* `dequeue` *operation invoked by thread t_j, the following steps occur in the stated order, and each of them occurs exactly once:*

1. *The* `deqTid` *field of a node referenced by* `head` *is updated with j (Line 135).*
2. *The* `pending` *flag in the state of t_j is switched from* true *to* false *(Line 149).*
3. `Head` *is updated to refer a node next to the one that has j in its* `deqTid` *field (Line 150).*

Notice that the steps in Lemmas 1 and 2 correspond to the steps in the scheme presented in Section 3.1

5.3 Wait-freedom

To prove wait-freedom property, we have to show that every call to either `enqueue` or `dequeue` returns in a bounded number of steps. In our implementation, both `enq()` and `deq()` call `help()`, which iterates a finite number of times (equal to the size of the `state` array), invoking `help_enq()` or `help_deq()` at most once in each iteration. Thus, in order to prove wait-freedom, we need to show that any invocation of `help_enq()` or `help_deq()` returns after a bounded number of steps.

We prove first that our implementation is lock-free. For this purpose, we need to show that every time a thread t_i executes an iteration of the **while** loop in either `help_enq()` or `help_deq()`, some thread t_j makes progress. That is, either one of the steps of Lemmas 1 or 2 occurs, or t_j finds the queue empty and executes a successful CAS in Line 120. This claim can be relatively easily concluded from the code.

To complete the proof of wait-freedom, we need to show that the number of operations that may linearize before any given operation is bounded. This follows directly from the way threads choose phase numbers, which is similar to the doorway mechanism in the Bakery algorithm [15]. This mechanism ensures that a thread t_i starting an `enq()` or a `deq()` method after t_j has chosen its phase number, will not finish the method before t_j's operation is linearized. Thus, after a bounded number of steps, a thread executing `help_enq()` or `help_deq()` will compete only with threads running the same method and helping the same operation.

6. Conclusions

FIFO queue is a fundamental data structure, found in many software system. Until now, no practical wait-free implementation of the queue was known. In this paper, we have shown the first such implementation that enables an arbitrary number of concurrent enqueuers and dequeuers. The significance of wait-freedom is in its ability to ensure a bounded execution time for each operation.

We have conducted performance evaluation of our implementation comparing it with a highly efficient lock-free algorithm [19]. The results reveal that the actual performance impact of wait-freedom is tightly coupled with the actual system configuration. In particular, we show that although our design requires more operations to provide the wait-free progress guarantee, it can beat the lock-free algorithm in certain system configurations and keep comparable performance ratios in others.

Acknowledgments

We would like to thank Roy Friedman for helpful discussions on the subject. Also, we would like to thank anonymous reviewers whose valuable comments helped to improve the presentation of this paper.

References

[1] Y. Afek and M. Merritt. Fast, wait-free (2k-1)-renaming. In *ACM Symposium on Principles of Distributed Computing (PODC)*, pages 105–112, 1999.

[2] Y. Afek, D. Dauber, and D. Touitou. Wait-free made fast. In *Proc. ACM Symposium on Theory of Computing (STOC)*, pages 538–547, 1995.

[3] J. Alemany and E. W. Felten. Performance issues in non-blocking synchronization on shared-memory multiprocessors. In *Proc. ACM Symposium on Principles of Distributed Computing (PODC)*, pages 125–134, 1992.

[4] J. H. Anderson and M. Moir. Universal constructions for large objects. *IEEE Trans. Parallel Distrib. Syst.*, 10(12):1317–1332, 1999.

[5] R. J. Anderson and H. Woll. Wait-free parallel algorithms for the union-find problem. In *Proc. ACM Symposium on Theory of Computing (STOC)*, pages 370–380, 1991.

[6] H. Attiya and A. Fouren. Adaptive and efficient algorithms for lattice agreement and renaming. *SIAM J. Comput.*, 31(2):642–664, 2001.

[7] P. Chuong, F. Ellen, and V. Ramachandran. A universal construction for wait-free transaction friendly data structures. In *Proc. ACM Symposium on Parallel Algorithms (SPAA)*, pages 335–344, 2010.

[8] M. David. A single-enqueuer wait-free queue implementation. In *Proc. Conf. on Distributed Computing (DISC)*, pages 132–143, 2004.

[9] M. Herlihy. Wait-free synchronization. *ACM Trans. Program. Lang. Syst.*, 13(1):124–149, 1991.

[10] M. Herlihy. A methodology for implementing highly concurrent objects. *ACM Trans. Program. Lang. Syst.*, 15(5):745–770, 1993.

[11] M. Herlihy and N. Shavit. *The Art of Multiprocessor Programming*. Morgan Kaufmann, 2008.

[12] M. Herlihy and J. M. Wing. Linearizability: A correctness condition for concurrent objects. *ACM Trans. Program. Lang. Syst.*, 12(3):463–492, 1990.

[13] P. Jayanti and S. Petrovic. Logarithmic-time single deleter, multiple inserter wait-free queues and stacks. In *Proc. Conf. on Found. of Soft. Technology and Theor. (FSTTCS)*, pages 408–419, 2005.

[14] E. Ladan-Mozes and N. Shavit. An optimistic approach to lock-free fifo queues. *Distributed Computing*, 20(5):323–341, 2008.

[15] L. Lamport. A new solution of Dijkstra's concurrent programming problem. *Commun. ACM*, 17(8):453–455, 1974.

[16] L. Lamport. Specifying concurrent program modules. *ACM Trans. Program. Lang. Syst.*, 5(2):190–222, 1983.

[17] H. Massalin and C. Pu. A lock-free multiprocessor OS kernel. Technical report CUCS-005-91, Computer Science Department, Columbia University, 1991.

[18] M. M. Michael. Hazard pointers: Safe memory reclamation for lock-free objects. *IEEE Trans. Parallel Distrib. Syst.*, 15(6):491–504, 2004.

[19] M. M. Michael and M. L. Scott. Simple, fast, and practical non-blocking and blocking concurrent queue algorithms. In *Proc. ACM Symposium on Principles of Distributed Computing (PODC)*, pages 267–275, 1996.

[20] M. Moir. Laziness pays! Using lazy synchronization mechanisms to improve non-blocking constructions. In *Proc. ACM Symposium on Principles of Distributed Computing (PODC)*, pages 61–70, 2000.

[21] M. Moir, D. Nussbaum, O. Shalev, and N. Shavit. Using elimination to implement scalable and lock-free FIFO queues. In *Proc. ACM Symposium on Parallel Algorithms (SPAA)*, pages 253–262, 2005.

[22] S. Moran, G. Taubenfeld, and I. Yadin. Concurrent counting. In *Proc. ACM Symposium on Principles of Distributed Computing (PODC)*, pages 59–70, 1992.

[23] K. R. Treiber. Systems programming: Coping with parallelism. Technical report RJ-5118, IBM Almaden Research Center, 1986.

[24] P. Tsigas and Y. Zhang. A simple, fast and scalable non-blocking concurrent FIFO queue for shared memory multiprocessor systems. In *Proc. ACM Symposium on Parallel Algorithms (SPAA)*, pages 134–143, 2001.

[25] J. D. Valois. Implementing lock-free queues. In *Proc. 7th Int. Conf. on Parallel and Distributed Computing Systems*, pages 64–69, 1994.

The STAPL Parallel Container Framework *

Gabriel Tanase   Antal Buss   Adam Fidel   Harshvardhan   Ioannis Papadopoulos   Olga Pearce
Timmie Smith   Nathan Thomas   Xiabing Xu   Nedal Mourad   Jeremy Vu   Mauro Bianco
Nancy M. Amato   Lawrence Rauchwerger

Parasol Lab, Dept. of Computer Science and Engineering
Texas A&M University, College Station, TX
stapl@cse.tamu.edu

Abstract

The Standard Template Adaptive Parallel Library (STAPL) is a parallel programming infrastructure that extends C++ with support for parallelism. It includes a collection of distributed data structures called pContainers that are thread-safe, concurrent objects, i.e., shared objects that provide parallel methods that can be invoked concurrently. In this work, we present the *STAPL Parallel Container Framework (PCF)*, that is designed to facilitate the development of generic parallel containers. We introduce a set of concepts and a methodology for assembling a pContainer from existing sequential or parallel containers, without requiring the programmer to deal with concurrency or data distribution issues. The PCF provides a large number of basic parallel data structures (e.g., pArray, pList, pVector, pMatrix, pGraph, pMap, pSet). The PCF provides a class hierarchy and a composition mechanism that allows users to extend and customize the current container base for improved application expressivity and performance. We evaluate STAPL pContainer performance on a CRAY XT4 massively parallel system and show that pContainer methods, generic pAlgorithms, and different applications provide good scalability on more than 16,000 processors.

Categories and Subject Descriptors   D.1.3 [*Concurrent Programming*]: Parallel Programming

General Terms   Languages, Design, Performance

Keywords   Parallel, Programming, Languages, Libraries, Data, Structures

---

* This research supported in part by NSF awards CRI-0551685, CCF-0833199, CCF-0830753, IIS-096053, IIS-0917266, NSF/DNDO award 2008-DN-077-ARI018-02, by the DOE NNSA under the Predictive Science Academic Alliances Program by grant DE-FC52-08NA28616, by THECB NHARP award 000512-0097-2009, by Chevron, IBM, Intel, Oracle/Sun and by Award KUS-C1-016-04, made by King Abdullah University of Science and Technology (KAUST). This research used resources of the National Energy Research Scientific Computing Center, which is supported by the Office of Science of the U.S. Department of Energy under Contract No. DE-AC02-05CH11231. Mourad is a masters student at KAUST who did an internship at the Parasol Lab. Tanase is currently a Research Staff Member at IBM T.J. Watson Research Center. Bianco is currently a scientist at the Swiss National Supercomputing Centre.

1. Introduction

Parallel programming is becoming mainstream due to the increased availability of multiprocessor and multicore architectures and the need to solve larger and more complex problems. The Standard Template Adaptive Parallel Library (STAPL) [3] is being developed to help programmers address the difficulties of parallel programming. STAPL is a parallel C++ library with functionality similar to STL, the ISO adopted C++ Standard Template Library [19]. STL is a collection of basic algorithms, containers and iterators that can be used as high-level building blocks for sequential applications. Similar to STL, STAPL provides building blocks for writing parallel programs – a collection of parallel algorithms (pAlgorithms), parallel and distributed containers (pContainers), and pViews to abstract data accesses to pContainers. pAlgorithms are represented in STAPL as task graphs called pRanges. The STAPL runtime system includes a communication library (ARMI) and an executor that executes pRanges. Sequential libraries such as STL [19], BGL [10], and MTL [9], provide the user with a collection of data structures that simplifies the application development process. Similarly, STAPL provides the Parallel Container Framework (PCF) which includes a set of elementary pContainers and tools to facilitate the customization and specialization of existing pContainers and the development of new ones.

pContainers are distributed, thread-safe, concurrent objects, i.e., shared objects that provide parallel methods that can be invoked concurrently. A large number of parallel data structures have been proposed in the literature. They are often complex, addressing issues related to data partitioning, distribution, communication, synchronization, load balancing, and thread safety. The complexity of building such structures for every parallel program is one of the main impediments to parallel program development. To alleviate this problem we are developing the *STAPL Parallel Container Framework (PCF)*. It consists of a collection of elementary pContainers and methods to specialize or compose them into pContainers of arbitrary complexity. Thus, instead of building distributed containers from scratch in an *ad-hoc* fashion, programmers can use inheritance to derive new specialized containers and composition to generate complex, hierarchical containers that naturally support hierarchical parallelism. Moreover, the PCF provides the mechanisms to enable any container, sequential or parallel, to be used in a distributed fashion without requiring the programmer to deal with concurrency issues such as data distribution.

The STAPL PCF makes several novel contributions.

- Object oriented design: Provides a set of classes and rules for using them to build new pContainers and customize existing ones.

- Composition: Supports composition of pContainers that allows the recursive development of complex pContainers that support nested parallelism.

- Interoperability: Provides mechanisms to generate a wrapper for any data structure, sequential or parallel, enabling it to be used in a distributed, concurrent environment.

- Library: It provides a library of basic pContainers constructed using the PCF as initial building blocks.

Some important properties of pContainers supported by the PCF are noted below.

Shared object view. Each pContainer instance is globally addressable. This supports ease of use, relieving the programmer from managing and dealing with the distribution explicitly, unless desired. This is accomplished using a generic software address translation mechanism that uses the same concepts for all pContainers in our framework.

Arbitrary degree and level of parallelism. For pContainers to provide scalable performance on shared and/or distributed memory systems they must support an arbitrary, tunable degree of parallelism, e.g., number of threads. Moreover, given the importance of hierarchical (nested) parallelism for current and foreseeable architectures, it is important for composed pContainers to allow concurrent access to each level of their hierarchy to better exploit locality.

Instance-specific customization. The pContainers in the PCF can be dynamic and irregular and can adapt (or be adapted by the user) to their environment. The PCF facilitates the design of pContainers that support advanced customizations so that they can easily be adapted to different parallel applications or even different computation phases of the same application. For example, a pContainer can dynamically change its data distribution or adjust its thread safety policy to optimize the access pattern of the algorithms accessing the elements. Alternatively, the user can request certain policies and implementations which can override the provided defaults or adaptive selections.

Previous STAPL publications present individual pContainers, focusing on their specific interfaces and performance (e.g., associative containers [25], pList [26], pArray [24]) or provide a high level description of the STAPL library as a whole, of which pContainers are only one component [3]. This paper presents for the first time the pContainer definition and composition formalism (Section 3), and the pContainer framework (PCF) base classes from which all pContainers derive (Section 4).

2. STAPL Overview

STAPL [2, 3, 22, 27] is a framework for parallel C++ code development (Fig. 1). Its core is a library of C++ components implementing parallel algorithms (pAlgorithms) and distributed data structures (pContainers) that have interfaces similar to the (sequential) C++ standard library (STL) [19]. Analogous to STL algorithms that use *iterators*, STAPL pAlgorithms are written in terms of pViews [2] so that the same algorithm can operate on multiple pContainers.

pAlgorithms are represented by pRanges. Briefly, a pRange is a task graph whose vertices are tasks and whose edges represent dependencies, if any, between tasks. A task includes both *work* (represented by *workfunctions*) and *data* (from pContainers, generically accessed through pViews). The executor, itself a distributed shared object, is responsible for the parallel execution of computations represented by pRanges. Nested parallelism can be created by invoking a pAlgorithm from within a task.

The runtime system (RTS) and its communication library ARMI (Adaptive Remote Method Invocation) provide the interface to the underlying operating system, native communication library and hardware architecture [22]. ARMI uses the remote method invocation (RMI) communication abstraction to hide the lower level implementations (e.g., MPI, OpenMP, etc.). A remote method invocation in STAPL can be blocking (sync_rmi) or nonblocking (async_rmi). ARMI provides the fence mechanism

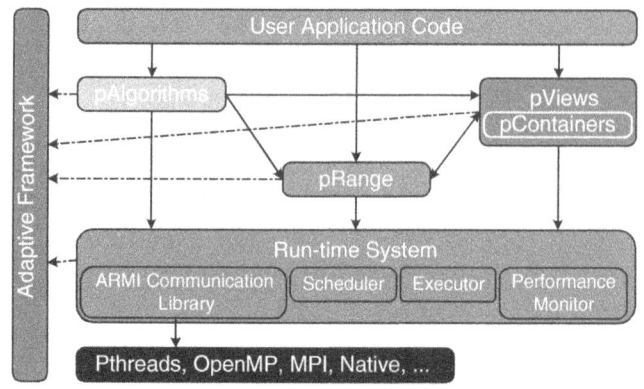

Figure 1. STAPL Overview

(rmi_fence) to ensure the completion of all previous RMI calls. The asynchronous calls can be aggregated by the RTS in an internal buffer to minimize communication overhead.

The RTS provides *locations* as an abstraction of processing elements in a system. A *location* is a component of a parallel machine that has a contiguous memory address space and has associated execution capabilities (e.g., threads). A location may be identified with a process address space. Different locations can communicate to each other only through RMIs. Internal STAPL mechanisms assure an automatic translation from one space to another, presenting to the less experienced user a unified data space. For more experienced users, the local/remote distinction of accesses can be exposed and performance enhanced for a specific application or application domain. STAPL allows for (recursive) nested parallelism.

3. The STAPL Parallel Container

Data structures are essential building blocks of any generic programming library. Sequential libraries such as STL [19], BGL [10], and MTL [9], provide data structures such as arrays, vectors, lists, maps, matrices, and graphs. A parallel container is an object oriented implementation of a data structure designed to be used efficiently in a parallel environment. Design requirements of the STAPL pContainer are listed below.

Scalable performance. pContainers must provide scalable performance on both shared and distributed memory systems. The performance of the pContainer methods must achieve the best known parallel complexity. This is obtained by efficient algorithms coupled with non-replicated, distributed data structures that allow a degree of concurrent access proportional to the degree of desired parallelism, e.g., the number of threads.

Thread safety and memory consistency model. When needed, the pContainer must be able to provide thread safe behavior and respect a memory consistency model. Currently, we support a relaxed consistency model. Due to space constraints, these issues are not addressed further in this paper; see [23] for details.

Shared object view. Each pContainer instance is globally addressable, i.e., it provides a shared memory address space. This supports ease of programming, allowing programmers to ignore the distributed aspects of the container if they so desire.

Composition. The capability to compose pContainers (i.e., pContainers of pContainers) provides a natural way to express and exploit nested parallelism while preserving locality. This feature is not supported by other general purpose parallel libraries.

Adaptivity. A design requirement of the STAPL pContainer is that it can easily be adapted to the data, the computation, and the system. For example, different storage options can be used for dense or sparse matrices or graphs or the data distribution may be modified during program execution if access patterns change.

3.1 `pContainer` definition

A STAPL *pContainer* is a distributed data structure that holds a finite *collection of typed elements* $\mathcal{C}$, each with a unique global identifier (GID), their associated storage $\mathcal{S}$, and an interface $\mathcal{O}$ (methods or operations) that can be applied to the collection. The interface $\mathcal{O}$ specifies an Abstract Data Type (ADT), and typically includes methods to read, write, insert or delete elements and methods that are specific to the individual container (e.g., `splice` for a `pList` or `out_degree` for a `pGraph` vertex).

The `pContainer` also includes meta information supporting data distribution: a *domain* $\mathcal{D}$, that is the union of the GIDs of the container's elements, and a mapping $\mathcal{F}$ from the container's domain $\mathcal{D}$ to the elements in $\mathcal{C}$. To support parallel use in a distributed setting, the collection $\mathcal{C}$ and the domain $\mathcal{D}$ are partitioned in a manner that is aligned with the storage of the container's elements.

Thus, a `pContainer` is defined as:

$$pC \stackrel{def}{=} (\mathcal{C}, \mathcal{D}, \mathcal{F}, \mathcal{O}, \mathcal{S}) \qquad (1)$$

The tuple $(\mathcal{C}, \mathcal{D}, \mathcal{F}, \mathcal{O})$ is known as the *native pView* of the `pContainer`. As described in [2], STAPL pViews generalize the iterator concept and enable parallelism by providing random access to collections of their elements. In pViews, the partition of $\mathcal{D}$ can be dynamically controlled and depends on the needs of the algorithm (e.g., a column-based partition of a `pMatrix` for an algorithm that processes the matrix by columns) and the desired degree of parallelism (e.g., one partition for each processor). The native pView associated with a `pContainer` is a special view in which the partitioned domain $\mathcal{D}$ is aligned with the distribution of the container's data. Performance is enhanced for algorithms that can use native pViews.

A `pContainer` stores its elements in a non-replicated fashion in a distributed collection of *base containers* (bContainers), each having a corresponding native pView. pContainers can be constructed from any base container, sequential or parallel, so long as it can support the required interface. The pContainers currently provided in STAPL use the corresponding STL containers (e.g., the STAPL pVector uses the STL vector), containers from other sequential libraries (e.g., MTL [9] for matrices), containers available in libraries developed for multicore (e.g., TBB [14] concurrent containers), or other pContainers. This flexibility allows for code reuse and supports interoperability with other libraries.

The `pContainer` provides a shared object view that enables programmers to ignore the distributed aspects of the container if they so desire. As described in more detail in Section 4.3, when a hardware mechanism is not available, the shared object view is provided by a software address resolution mechanism that first identifies the bContainer containing the required element and then invokes the bContainer methods in an appropriate manner to perform the desired operation.

3.2 `pContainer` composability

There are many common data structures that are naturally described as compositions of existing structures. For example, a `pVector` of `pLists` provides a natural adjacency list representation of a graph. To enable the construction and use of such data structures, we require that the composition of pContainers be a pContainer, i.e., that pContainers are closed under composition.

An important feature of composed pContainers is that they support hierarchical parallelism in a natural way – each level of the nested parallel constructs can work on a corresponding level of the pContainer hierarchy. If well matched by the machine hierarchy, this can preserve existing locality and improve scalability. Consider the example of a `pArray` of `pArrays`. This can be declared in STAPL using the following syntax:

```
p_array<p_array<int>> pApA(10);
```

Such a composed data structure can distribute both the top level and the nested pArrays in various ways across the machine. Accessing the elements of the nested pArrays is done naturally using a concatenation of the methods of the outer and inner pArrays. For example, `pApA.get_element(i).get_element(j)` returns a reference to the j-th element belonging to the i-th nested pArray. Moreover, data stored in a composed data structure can be efficiently exploited by nested pAlgorithms. In the pApA example, computing the minimum element of each of the nested pArrays can be done using a parallel `forall` on the outer pArray, and within each nested one, a reduction to compute the minimum value.

In the remainder of this section we formalize the pContainer composition definition. The *height* of a pContainer is the depth of the composition, i.e., the number of nested pContainers. Let $pC_1 = (\mathcal{C}_1, \mathcal{D}_1, \mathcal{F}_1, \mathcal{O}_1, \mathcal{S}_1)$ and $pC_2 = (\mathcal{C}_2, \mathcal{D}_2, \mathcal{F}_2, \mathcal{O}_2, \mathcal{S}_2)$ be pContainers of height H_1 and H_2, respectively. The composed pContainer $pC = pC_1 \circ pC_2$ is of height $H_1 + H_2$. In pC, each element of $pC_1[i]$, $i \in \mathcal{D}_1$, is an instance of pC_2, called $pC_{2i} = (\mathcal{C}_{2i}, \mathcal{D}_{2i}, \mathcal{F}_{2i}, \mathcal{O}_{2i}, \mathcal{S}_{2i})$. Each component of pC is derived appropriately from the corresponding components of pC_1 and pC_2. For example, in the special case when all the mapping functions $\mathcal{F}_{2i}$ and operations $\mathcal{O}_{2i}$ are the same, we have

$$\mathcal{D} = \bigcup_{i \in \mathcal{D}_1} (\{\mathcal{D}_1[i]\} \times \mathcal{D}_{2i})$$
$$\mathcal{F} = (\mathcal{F}_1, \mathcal{F}_2)$$
$$\mathcal{O} = (\mathcal{O}_1, \mathcal{O}_2)$$

where $\mathcal{F}(x, y) = (\mathcal{F}_1, \mathcal{F}_2)(x, y) = (\mathcal{F}_1(x), \mathcal{F}_2(y))$, $(x, y) \in \mathcal{D}$. The components $\mathcal{C}$ and $\mathcal{S}$ are isomorphic to $\mathcal{D}$ and defined similarly to it. With this formalism, arbitrarily deep hierarchies can be defined by recursively composing pContainers.

Given a composed pContainer $PC = (\mathcal{C}, \mathcal{D}, \mathcal{F}, \mathcal{O}, \mathcal{S})$, of height H, the GID of an element at level $h \leq H$ is a tuple $(x_1, \ldots, x_h)$. Similarly, the mapping function to access a pContainer at level h is a subsequence (prefix) of the tuple of functions $\mathcal{F}$, $\mathcal{F}^h(x_1, \ldots, x_h) = (\mathcal{F}_1(x_1), \mathcal{F}_2(x_2), \ldots, \mathcal{F}_h(x_h))$. The operations available at level h are $\mathcal{O}_h$. To invoke a method at level h, the appropriate element of the GID tuple has to be passed to each method invoked in the hierarchy, as shown in the example given at the beginning of this section.

`pContainer` composition is made without loss of information, preserving the meta information of its components in the same hierarchical manner. For example, if two distributed pContainers are composed, then the distribution information of the initial pContainers will be preserved in the new pContainer. A feature of our composition operation is that it allows for (static) specialization if machine mapping information is provided. For example, if the lower (bottom) level of the composed pContainer is distributed across a single shared memory node, then its mapping $\mathcal{F}$ can be specialized for this environment, e.g., some methods may turn into empty function calls.

4. The Parallel Container Framework (PCF)

An objective of the STAPL *Parallel Container Framework (PCF)* is to simplify the process of developing generic parallel containers. It is a collection of classes that can be used to construct new pContainers through inheritance and specialization that are customized for the programmer's needs while preserving the properties of the base container. In particular, the PCF can generate a wrapper for any standard data structure, sequential or parallel, that has the meta information necessary to use the data structure in a distributed, concurrent environment. This allows the programmer to concentrate on the semantics of the container instead of its concurrency and distribution management. Thus, the PCF makes developing a pContainer almost as easy as developing its sequential counterpart. Moreover, the PCF facilitates interoperability by

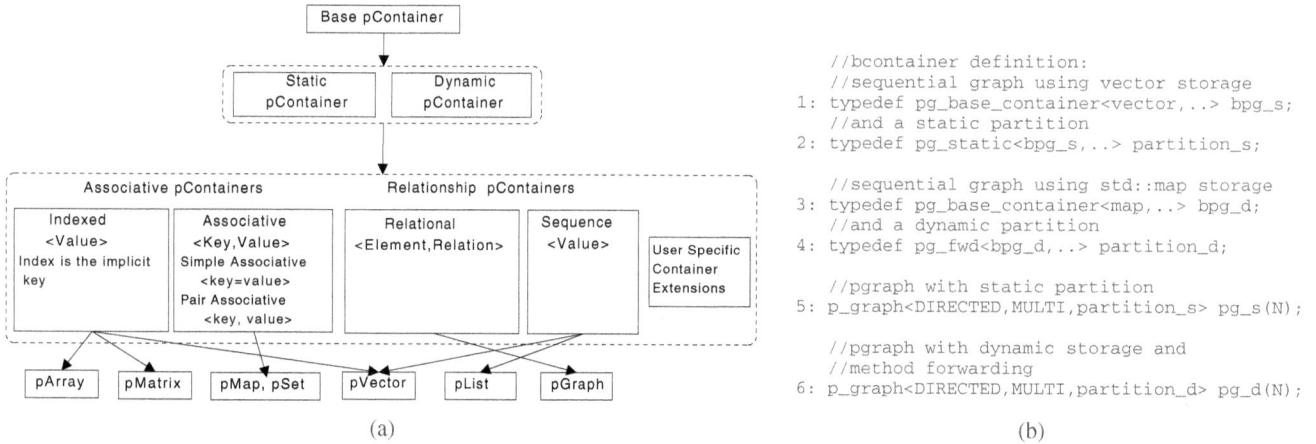

```
                                              //bcontainer definition:
                                              //sequential graph using vector storage
                                           1: typedef pg_base_container<vector,..> bpg_s;
                                              //and a static partition
                                           2: typedef pg_static<bpg_s,..> partition_s;

                                              //sequential graph using std::map storage
                                           3: typedef pg_base_container<map,..> bpg_d;
                                              //and a dynamic partition
                                           4: typedef pg_fwd<bpg_d,..> partition_d;

                                              //pgraph with static partition
                                           5: p_graph<DIRECTED,MULTI,partition_s> pg_s(N);

                                              //pgraph with dynamic storage and
                                              //method forwarding
                                           6: p_graph<DIRECTED,MULTI,partition_d> pg_d(N);
```

(a)   (b)

Figure 2. (a) PCF design. (b) pContainer customization.

enabling the use of parallel or sequential containers from other libraries, e.g., MTL [9], BGL [10] or TBB [14].

STAPL provides a library of pContainers constructed using the PCF. These include counterparts of STL containers (e.g., pVector, pList [26], and associative containers [25] such as pSet, pMap, pHashMap, pMultiSet, pMultiMap) and additional containers such as pArray [24], pMatrix, and pGraph.

Novice programmers can immediately use the available data structures with their default settings. More sophisticated parallel programmers can customize or extend the default behavior to further improve the performance of their applications. If desired, this customization can be modified by the programmer for every pContainer instance.

4.1 pContainer Framework design

The PCF is designed to allow users to easily build pContainers by inheriting from appropriate modules. It includes a set of base classes representing common data structure features and rules for how to use them to build pContainers. Figure 2(a) shows the main concepts and the derivation relations between them; also shown are the STAPL pContainers that are defined using those concepts. All STAPL pContainers are derived from the pContainer base class which is in charge of storing the data and distribution information. The remaining classes in the PCF provide minimal interfaces and specify different requirements about bContainers. First, the static and dynamic pContainers are classes that indicate if elements can be added to or removed from the pContainer. The next discrimination is between *associative* and *relational* pContainers. In associative containers, there is an implicit or explicit association between a key and a value. For example, in an array there is an implicit association between the index and the element corresponding to that index; we refer to such (multi-dimensional) arrays as indexed pContainers. In other cases, such as a hashmap, keys must be stored explicitly. The PCF provides an associative base pContainer for such cases. The relational pContainers include data structures that can be expressed as a collection of elements and relations between them. This includes graphs and trees, where the relations are explicit and may have values associated with them (e.g., weights on the edges of a graph), and lists where the relations between elements are implicit.

All classes of the PCF have default implementations that can be customized for each pContainer instance using template arguments called *traits*. This allows users to specialize various aspects, e.g., the bContainer or the data distribution, to improve the performance of their data structures. In Figure 2(b) we show an example of STAPL pseudocode illustrating how users can customize

an existing pGraph implementation. Users can select the storage by providing the type of an existing bContainer and similarly for the partition. Figure 2(b), line 5, shows the declaration of a directed pGraph allowing multiple edges between the same source and target vertices and using a static partition. With a static partition, users need to declare the size of the pGraph at construction time and subsequent invocations of the add_vertex method will trigger an assertion. Figure 2(b), line 6, shows the declaration of a pGraph using a dynamic partition that allows for addition and deletion of both vertices and edges. More details and performance results regarding the benefits of having different partitions and types of storage are discussed in Section 5.2.

4.2 pContainer Interfaces

For each concept in the PCF (Figure 2(a)) there is a corresponding interface consisting of various constructors and methods as described in [23]. pContainer methods can be grouped in three categories: synchronous, asynchronous and split phase. Synchronous methods have a return type and guarantee that the method is executed and the result available when they return. Asynchronous methods have no return value and return immediately to the calling thread. Split phase execution is similar to that in Charm++ [17]. The return type of a split phase method is a future that allocates space for the result. The invocation returns immediately to the user and the result can be retrieved by invoking the get method on the future which will return immediately if the result is available or block until the result arrives. Performance trade-offs between these three categories of methods are discussed in Section 5.5.

4.3 Shared Object View implementation

Recall that the elements of a pContainer are stored in non-replicated fashion in a distributed collection of bContainers. An important function of the PCF is to provide a shared object view that relieves the programmer from managing and dealing with the distribution explicitly, unless he desires to do so. In this section, we describe how this is done. Its performance is studied in Section 5.2.

The fundamental concept required to provide a shared object view is that each pContainer element has a unique global identifier (GID). The GID provides the shared object abstraction since all references to a given element will use the same GID. Examples of GIDs are indices for pArrays, keys for pMaps, and vertex identifiers for pGraphs.

The PCF supports the shared object view by providing an address translation mechanism that determines where an element with a particular GID is stored (or should be stored if it does not already exist). We now briefly review the PCF components involved in this address translation. As defined in Section 3.1, the set of GIDs of a

238

pContainer is called a *domain* $\mathcal{D}$. For example, the domain of a pArray is a finite set of indices while it is a set of keys for an associative pContainer. A pContainer's domain is partitioned into a set of non-intersecting *sub-domains* by a partition class, itself a distributed object that provides the map $\mathcal{F}$ from a GID to the sub-domain that contains it, i.e., a directory. There is a one-to-one correspondence between a sub-domain and a bContainer and in general, there can be multiple bContainers allocated in a *location*. Finally, a class called a partition-mapper maps a sub-domain (and its corresponding bContainer) to the location where it resides, and a location-manager manages the bContainers of a pContainer mapped to a given location.

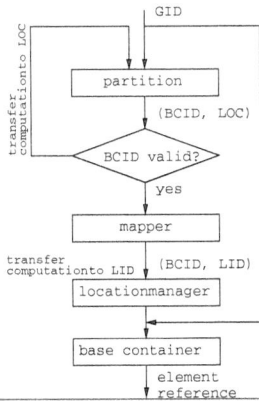

Figure 3. pContainer modules for performing address resolution to find the element reference corresponding to a given GID.

Figure 3 describes the address resolution procedure. Given the unique GID identifying a pContainer element, the partition class is queried about the sub-domain/bContainer associated with the requested GID. If the bContainer information (specified by a bContainer identifier, or BCID) is not available, the partition provides information about the location (LOC) where the bContainer information might be retrieved, and the process is restarted on that location. If the BCID is available and valid, then the partition-mapper returns information about the location where the bContainer resides (LID).

For static pContainers, i.e., containers that do not support the addition and deletion of elements, the domain does not change during execution. In this case, it is possible to optimize the address translation mechanism by employing a static partition that computes the mapping from a GID to a bContainer and a location in constant time by evaluating an expression or doing a table lookup. For example, a pArray with N elements can map the index i to the location $i\%P$, where P is the number of available locations. Or, for a pGraph where the number of vertices is fixed at construction, we can use a static partition that computes a vertex location in constant time using a hash table.

Dynamic pContainers, where elements can be added or deleted, need to employ dynamic partitions. Currently, we provide a dynamic partition implemented as a distributed directory. The directory statically associates a home for an individual GID that always knows the location where the respective GID is stored. If the element happens to migrate to a new location the home needs to be updated with information about the new location. With this directory implementation, accessing an element corresponding to a given GID involves two steps. First, find and query the home where the element lives and second, access the element on its location.

4.4 Method Forwarding

For a pContainer to operate on a non-local element, it must determine the element's location and invoke the method at that location. Hence, if the element's address cannot be determined locally,

then the address resolution process may add significantly to the critical path of the method's execution. To alleviate this problem, we combine the address resolution and the method execution into one operation. This mechanism, referred to as *method forwarding*, allows the method to be forwarded along with the address resolution process instead of first fetching the address from a remote location and then instantiating the remote method invocation.

As will be shown in Section 5.2, a partition using forwarding provides improved performance over a directory that determines the GID's location using synchronous communication.

5. pContainer **Performance Evaluation**

In this section, we evaluate the performance of representative pContainers developed using the PCF: pArray, pList, pMatrix, pGraph, pHashMap and composed pContainers. In Section 5.1, we study the scalability of parallel methods for pArray, pGraph and pList. We examine trade-offs for various address resolution mechanisms in Section 5.2 and for pContainer composition in Section 5.3. Sections 5.4, 5.5, and 5.6 analyze generic parallel algorithms, graph algorithms, and a MapReduce application, respectively.

With the exception of MapReduce, we conducted all our experimental studies on a 38,288 core Cray XT4 (CRAY4) available at NERSC. There are 9,572 compute nodes each with a quad core Opteron running at 2.3 GHz and a total of 8 GB of memory (2 GB of memory per core). The MapReduce study was performed on a Cray XT5 (CRAY5) with 664 compute nodes, each containing two 2.4 GHz AMD Opteron quad-core processors (5,312 total cores). In all experiments, a location contains a single processor core, and the terms can be used interchangeably.

All the experiments in this paper, with the exception of MapReduce, show standard weak scaling where the work per processor is kept constant. As we increase the number of cores the amount of work increases proportionally and the baseline for each experiment is the time on four cores which is the number of cores in a compute node on CRAY4. Confidence intervals are included in the plots. The machines used are very stable though and the variations for each experiment are small, so the confidence intervals are often not visible in the plots.

5.1 pContainer Methods

The performance of various STAPL pContainers has been studied in [4, 24–26]. In this section, we examine the performance of novel pContainer methods in the context of the pArray, pList and pGraph data structures.

To evaluate the scalability of the pContainer methods we designed a simple kernel in which all P available cores (locations) concurrently perform N/P invocations, for a given number of elements N. We report the time taken to perform all N operations globally. The measured time includes the cost of a fence to ensure the methods are globally finished. In Figure 4(a) we show the performance for pArray set_element, get_element and split_get_element. We performed a weak scaling study with 20M elements and 20M method invocations per location. In this experiment there are 1% remote accesses. We observe good scalability for the asynchronous invocations with only 5.8% increase in execution time as we scale the number of cores from 4 to 16384. For the synchronous methods, the execution time increases 237% relative to 4 cores and 29% relative to 8 cores. The big increase in execution time from 4 to 8 is due to the inter-node communication which negatively affects performance, especially for synchronous communication. For the split_get_element we performed two experiments where we invoke groups of 1000 or 5000 split phase operations before waiting for them to complete. The split phase methods have an inherent overhead for allocating the futures on the heap, but they do enable improved performance and scalability relative to the synchronous methods. Split phase execu-

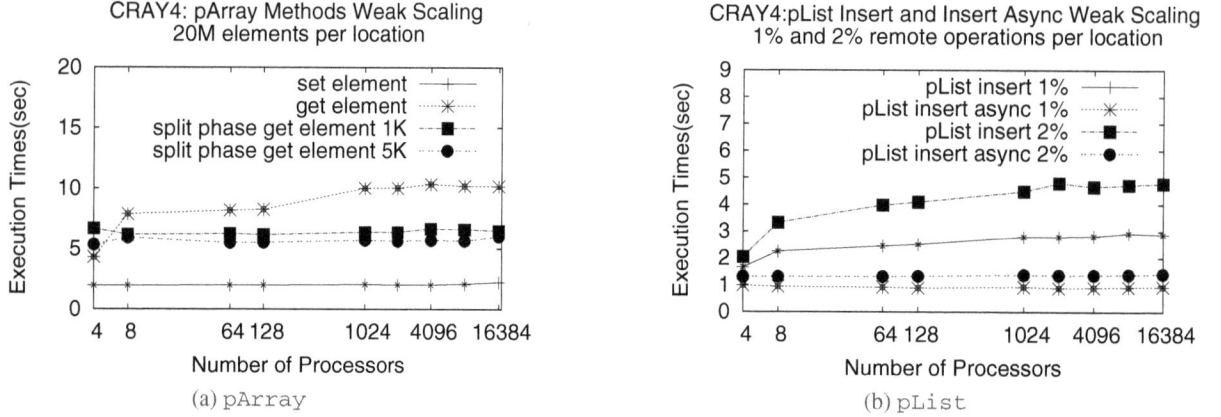

Figure 4. CRAY4: (a) pArray methods set_element, get_element and split phase get_element. 20M method invocations per location with 1% remote (b) 5M pList method invocations with 1% and 2% remote. The number of remote accesses is a variable that we can control as part of our experimental setup.

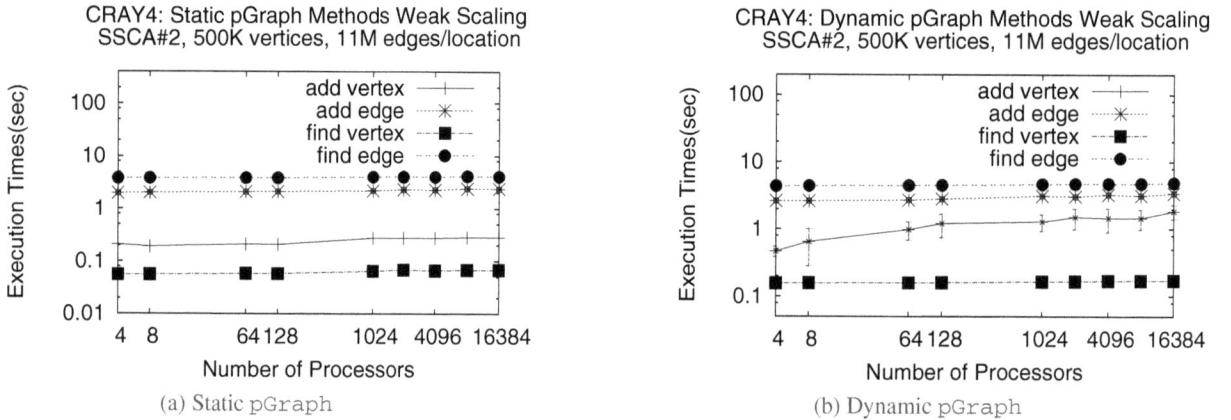

Figure 5. Evaluation of static and dynamic pGraph methods while using the SSCA2 graph generator; 500k vertices, 11.5M edges, ~40 remote edges per location; ~23 edges per vertex (a) For the static pGraph all vertices are built in the constructor; (b) The dynamic pGraph inserts vertices using add_vertex method.

tion enables the aggregation of the requests by the runtime system as well as allowing communication and computation overlap. For the split_get_element the overall execution time increases 4.5% as we scale the number of cores from 4 to 16384, when 5000 invocations are started before waiting the result.

In Figure 4(b), we show a weak scaling experiment on a pList using 5 million elements per core and up to 16384 cores (81.9 billion total method invocations performed). The synchronous insert adds an element at a given position and returns a reference to the newly inserted element. The insert_async inserts the element asynchronously and has no return value. In this experiment, the majority of the invocations are executed locally with 1% and 2%, respectively, being executed remotely. We observe good scalability of the two methods up to 16384 cores. The asynchronous versions of the pContainer methods are faster as they can overlap communication with computation and don't return information about the position where the element was added.

The pGraph is a relational data structure consisting of a collection of vertices and edges. The pGraph is represented as an adjacency list and depending on its properties, different bContainers can be used to optimize the data access. Here, we evaluate a static and a dynamic pGraph. The static pGraph allocates all its vertices in the constructor and subsequently only edges can be added or deleted. It uses a static partition that is implemented as an expression and has a bContainer that uses a std::vector to store the vertices, each of which uses a std::list to store edges. The dynamic pGraph uses a distributed directory to implement its partition and its bContainer uses std::hash_map for vertices and std::list for edges. We chose the std::hash_map in the dynamic case because it allows for fast insert and find operations. As shown in Figure 2(a), the static or dynamic behavior is achieved by passing the corresponding template arguments to the pGraph class.

We performed a weak scaling experiment on CRAY4 using a 2D torus where each core holds a stencil of 1500×1500 vertices and corresponding edges, and a random graph as specified in the SSCA2 benchmark [1]. SSCA2 generates a set of clusters where each cluster is densely connected and the inter cluster edges are sparse. We use the following parameters for SSCA2: cluster size = $(V/P)^{1/4}$, where V is the number of vertices of the graph, maximum number of parallel edges is 3, maximum edge weight is V, probability of intra clique edges is 0.5 and probability of an edge to be unidirectional 0.3. Figure 5 shows the execution time for add_vertex, add_edge, find_vertex and find_edges for

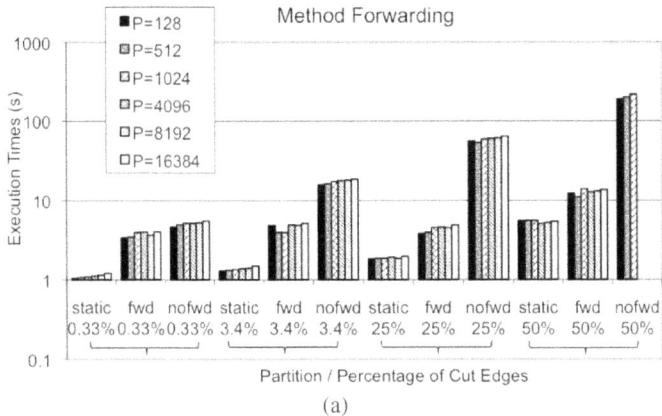

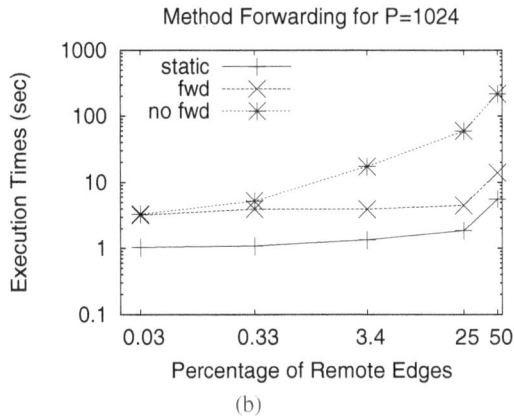

Figure 6. Find sources in a directed pGraph using static, dynamic with forwarding and dynamic with no forwarding partitions. Execution times for graphs with various percentages of remote edges for (a) various core counts and for (b) 1024 cores.

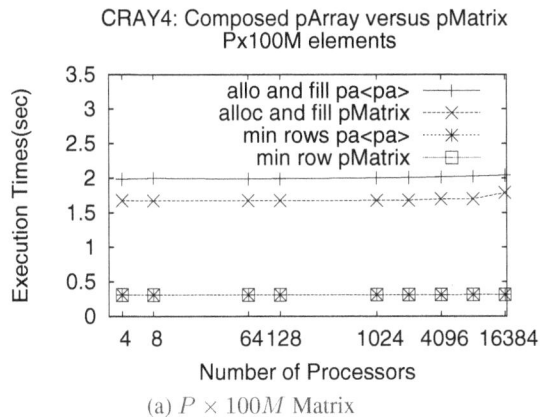

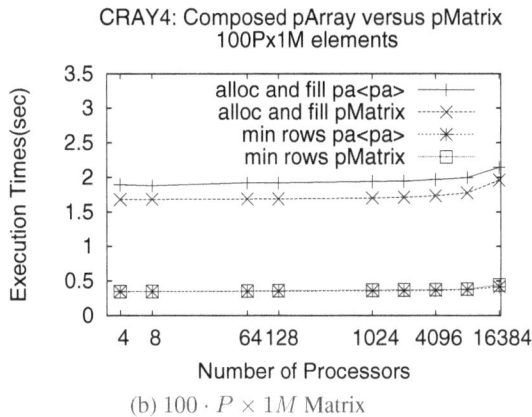

(a) $P \times 100M$ Matrix

(b) $100 \cdot P \times 1M$ Matrix

Figure 7. Comparison of parray<parray<>> ($pa < pa >$) and pMatrix on computing the minimum value for each row of a matrix. Weak scaling experiment with (a) $P \times 100M$ and (b) $100 \cdot P \times 1M$ elements. parray<parray<>> takes longer to initialize while the algorithm executions are very similar.

the SSCA2 input. For the dynamic pGraph the container is initially empty and vertices are added using add_vertex. As seen in the plots, the methods scale well up to 16384 cores. The addition of edges is a fully asynchronous parallel operation. Adding vertices in the dynamic pGraph causes additional asynchronous communication to update the directory information about where vertices are stored. The asynchronous communication overlaps well with the local computation of adding the vertices in the bContainer, thus providing good scalability up to a very large number of cores. The execution time increases 2.96 times for the add_vertex in the dynamic pGraph as we scale from 4 to 16384 cores. The mesh results are not included due to space limitations but they exhibit similar trends as the SSCA2 results.

5.2 Evaluation of address translation mechanisms

In this section, we evaluate the performance of the three types of address translation mechanisms introduced in Section 4.3: a static partition mapping GIDs to bContainers, and distributed dynamic partitions with and without method forwarding.

We evaluate the performance of the three partitions using a simple pGraph algorithm that finds source vertices (i.e., vertices with no incoming edges) in a directed graph. The algorithm traverses the adjacency list of each vertex and increments a counter on the

target vertex of each edge. The communication incurred by this algorithm depends on the number of remote edges, i.e., edges connecting vertices in two different bContainers. We considered four graphs, all 2D tori, which vary according to the percentage of remote edges: .33%, 3.4%, 25% and 50%. This was achieved by having each core hold a stencil of $150 \times 15,000$, $15 \times 150,000$, $2 \times 1,125,000$ and $1 \times 2,250,000$, respectively.

Figure 6(a) provides a summary of the execution times for the different percentages of remote edges and different numbers of cores, where scalability can be appreciated together with the increasing benefit of forwarding as the percentage of remote edges increases. In Figure 6(b) we include results for the three approaches on all four types of graphs for 1024 cores. As can be seen, for the methods with no forwarding and synchronous communication, the execution time increases as the percentage of remote edges increases. The static method and the method with forwarding track one another and do not suffer as badly as the percentage of remote edges increases. This indicates that the forwarding approach can scale similarly to the optimized static partition.

5.3 pContainer composition evaluation

So far we have made a case for the necessity of pContainer composition to increase programmer productivity. Instead of di-

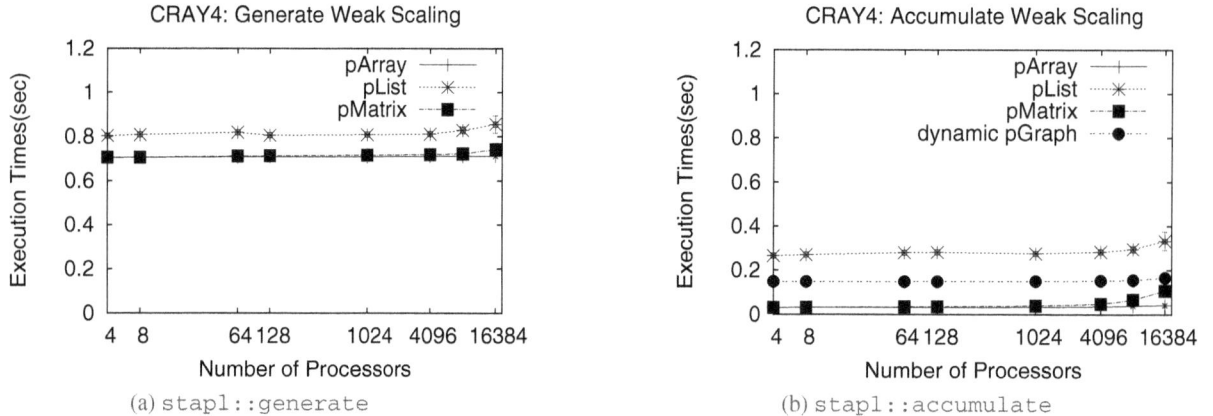

Figure 8. Execution times for `stapl::generate` and `stapl::accumulate` algorithms on CRAY4. Same algorithm applied to different data structures. The `pArray`, `pList` and `pMatrix` are with 20M elements per location. The input `pGraph` has a 1500x1500 mesh per location.

rectly building a complex `pContainer`, the programmer can compose one from the basic `pContainers` available in the PCF and shorten development and debugging time. The issue we study here is the impact of composition on performance.

For this comparative performance evaluation we compute the minimum element in each row of a matrix using both the `pMatrix` `pContainer` (which is available in the PCF library) and the composed `pArray` of `pArrays`. The algorithm code is the same for the two cases, due to the access abstraction mechanism provided by STAPL. It calls a parallel `forall` across the rows, and within each row, a reduction to compute the minimum value. We also measure the time to create and initialize the storage. The `pMatrix` allocates the entire structure in a single step, while the `pArray` of `pArrays` allocates the outer structure first and then allocates the single `pArray` elements individually. In Figure 7 we include, for CRAY4, the execution times for allocating and initializing the two data structures and the times to run the min-of-each-row algorithm, in a weak scaling experiment. Figure 7(a) shows the case of a $P \times 100M$ element matrix (P is the number of cores), while Figure 7(b) shows the case of a $100 \cdot P \times 1M$ element matrix. The aggregated input sizes are overall the same.

As expected, the `pArray` of `pArrays` initialization time is higher than that for a `pMatrix`. The time for executing the algorithm, however, is very similar for the two data structures and scales well to 16384 cores. While we cannot state with certainty that our PCF allows for efficient composition (negligible additional overhead) for any pair of `pContainers`, the obtained results are promising.

5.4 Generic pAlgorithms

Generic `pAlgorithms` can operate transparently on different data structures. We use `pViews` to abstract the data access and an algorithm can operate on any `pContainer` provided the corresponding `pViews` are available. We use the `stapl::generate` algorithm to produce random values and assign them to the elements in the container. It is a fully parallel operation with no communication for accessing the data. `stapl::accumulate` adds the values of all elements using a cross location reduction that incurs communication on the order of $O(\log P)$.

In Figure 8, we show the execution times for the `pAlgorithms` on `pArray`, `pList`, `pGraph`, and `pMatrix`. We performed a weak scaling experiment using 20M elements per location for `pArray`, `pList` and `pMatrix` and a torus with a 1500×1500 stencil per location for `pGraph`. The `pArray` and `pMatrix` are efficient static containers for accessing data based on indices and

linear traversals [4, 24]. For `pMatrix` the algorithms are applied to a linearization of the matrix. The `pList` is a dynamic `pContainer` optimized for fast insert and delete operations at the cost of a slower access time relative to static data structures such as `pArray`. `pGraph` is a relational data structure consisting of a collection of vertices and edges. Generic STL algorithms are used with `pGraph` to initialize the data in a `pGraph` or to retrieve values from vertices or edges. The `stapl::accumulate` adds the values of all the vertex properties.

The algorithms show good scalability as we scale the number of cores from 4 to 16384. There is less than 5% increase in execution time for `pArray` `stapl::generate` and about 33% for `stapl::accumulate` due to increased communication performed in the reduction ($O(\log P)$). All three algorithms on a `pList` with 20M elements per location provide good scaling. There is less than 6% increase in execution time for `stapl::generate` as we scale from 4 to 16384 cores and 26% for `stapl::accumulate`. The `pList` is generally slower than the other containers especially when the traversal cost dominates the computation performed. The `pMatrix` [4] considered was of size $P \times 20M$ where P is the number of locations, leading to a weak scaling experiment where each locations owns a row of size 20M. Similar to the `pArray`, there is less than 5% increase in execution time for `stapl::generate`, and less than 25% for `stapl::accumulate`.

This kind of analysis is useful to help users understand the performance benefits of various data structures. From all three plots we observe that the access time for a `pList` is higher than the access time for static `pContainers`, and this is due to the different behavior of the STL containers used as `bContainers`. The difference in performance is less for `stapl::generate` because it involves heavier computation (the random number generator).

5.5 `pGraph` algorithms

In this section, we analyze the performance of several `pGraph` algorithms for various input types and `pGraph` characteristics. `find_edges` collects all edges with maximum edge weight into an output `pList` (SSCA2 benchmark); `find_sources` collects all vertices with no incoming edges into an output `pList`. `find_sources` takes as input a collection of vertices and performs graph traversals in parallel. The traversal proceeds in a depth-first search style. When a remote edge is encountered, a new task is spawned to continue the traversal on the location owning the target. The current traversal will continue in parallel with the spawned one. This is useful, for example, when we want to com-

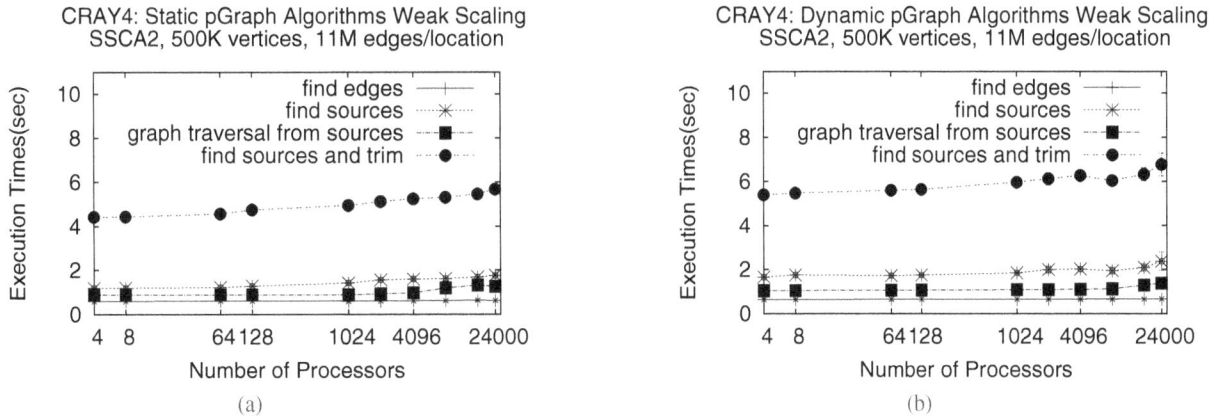

CRAY4: Static pGraph Algorithms Weak Scaling
SSCA2, 500K vertices, 11M edges/location

(a)

CRAY4: Dynamic pGraph Algorithms Weak Scaling
SSCA2, 500K vertices, 11M edges/location

(b)

Figure 9. Execution times for different `pGraph` algorithms on on CRAY4. Static versus dynamic `pGraph` comparison. The input is generated using the SSCA2 scalable generator with 500K vertices per core

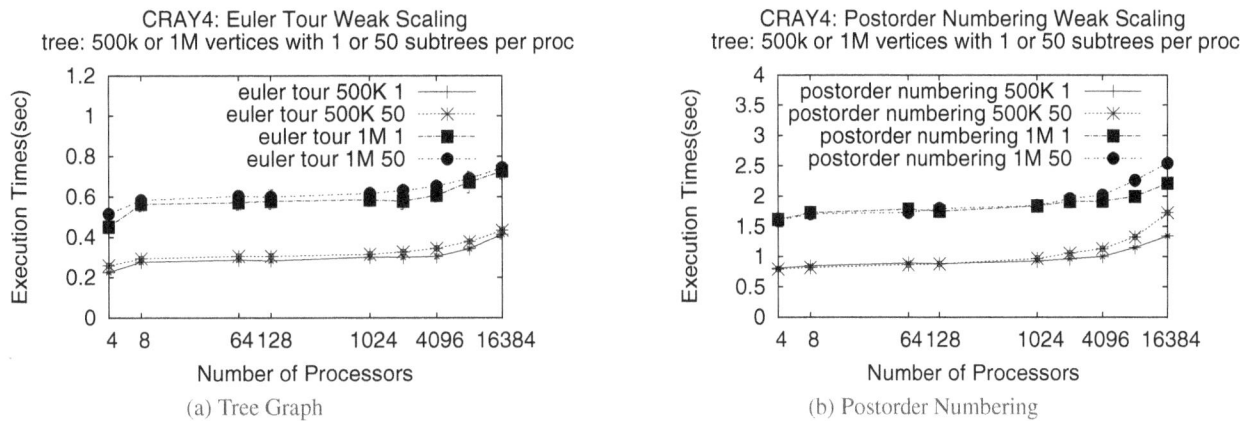

CRAY4: Euler Tour Weak Scaling
tree: 500k or 1M vertices with 1 or 50 subtrees per proc

(a) Tree Graph

CRAY4: Postorder Numbering Weak Scaling
tree: 500k or 1M vertices with 1 or 50 subtrees per proc

(b) Postorder Numbering

Figure 10. Execution times for Euler Tour and its post-order numbering applications using a tree made by a single binary tree with 500k or 1M subtrees per core.

pute all vertices and edges accessible from a set of starting points. `trim` is another useful computation when computing cycles or strongly connected components. It computes the set of sources for a directed graph and removes all their edges, recursively continuing with the newly created sources. The process will stop when there are no more sources.

We ran the algorithms on various input types including a torus, a sparse mesh and SSCA2 random graphs. In Figure 9, weak scaling results are shown for SSCA2 for both static and dynamic `pGraphs`. The number of cores is varied from 4 to 24000. For all algorithms considered, the static graph performed better due to the faster address resolution and `std::vector` storage for vertices versus `std::hash_map`. `find_edges`, a fully parallel algorithm, exhibits good scalability with less than 5% increase in execution time for both types of graphs. `find_sources` incurs communication proportional to the number of remote edges. The algorithms use two containers, traversing an input `pGraph` and generating an output `pList`. The traversal from sources and trim algorithm spawns new computation asynchronously as it reaches a remote edge. Additionally the `trim` algorithm removes `pGraph` edges, which negatively impacts performance. The increase in execution time for the trim algorithm is 28% for static and 25% for dynamic `pGraphs`. Figure 6 illustrates that the execution time of the `pGraph` algorithms increases with the number of remote edges.

The Euler Tour (ET) is an important representation of a graph for parallel processing. Since the ET represents a depth-first-search traversal, when it is applied to a tree it can be used to compute a number of tree functions such as rooting a tree, postorder numbering, vertex levels, and number of descendants [15]. The parallel ET algorithm [15] tested here uses a `pGraph` to represent the tree and a `pList` to store the final Euler Tour. In parallel, the algorithm executes traversals on the `pGraph` `pView` and generates Euler Tour segments that are stored in a temporary `pList`. Then, the segments are linked together to form the final `pList` containing the Euler Tour. The tree ET applications are computed using a generic algorithm which first initializes each edge in the tour with a corresponding weight, and then performs the partial sum algorithm. The partial sum result for each edge is copied back to the graph, and the final step computes the desired result.

Performance is evaluated by a weak scaling experiment on CRAY4 using as input a tree distributed across all locations. The tree is generated by first building a specified number of binary trees in each location and then linking the roots of these trees in a binary tree fashion. The number of remote edges is at most six times the number of subtrees for each location (for each subtree root, one to its root and two to its children in each location, with directed edges in both directions). Figure 10(a) and 10(b) show the execution time on CRAY4 for different sizes of the tree and

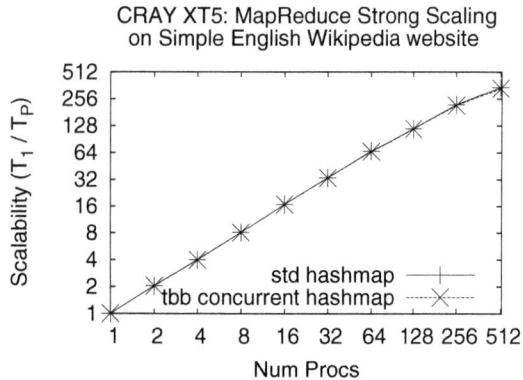

Figure 11. MapReduce used to count the number of occurrences of every word in Simple English Wikipedia website (1.5GB).

varying numbers of subtrees. The running time increases with the number of vertices per location because the number of edges in the computed ET increases correspondingly. When there are more subtrees specified in each location, there is more communication required to link them. Figure 10(b) shows the execution time for computing the postorder numbering. The running time increases with the number of vertices per location because the number of edges increases which are proportional to the computation. When more subtrees are specified in a location, more segments are formed in the pList and more communication is needed for the partial sum.

5.6 MapReduce

Here we examine the performance of a simple application implemented on top of a MapReduce framework developed in STAPL. The MapReduce uses the pHashMap, a dynamic associative pContainer[25]. The application splits the input data across the available cores and first applies the map and reduce functions locally. After the local MapReduce phase is finished, the processor asynchronously inserts its locally reduced data into a pHashMap. The asynchronous insert calls the user's reduce function if the key being inserted already exists in the pHashMap. The communication and data distribution is taken care of entirely by the pContainer. We ran a computation that computes the multiplicity of each word in a 1.5GB text input of the Simple-English Wikipedia website (simple.wikipedia.org). Because the input size was fixed, we include a strong scaling study where we measure the time taken to compute the multiplicity for all input words on CRAY5. In Figure 11 we show experiments corresponding to two different pHashMap storages, one using the STL std::hash_map and another using the TBB concurrent hash map. We observe that the application scales well up to 512 cores without noticeable differences for different storages. The slowdown on 256 and 512 cores is due to the small computation performed per core relative to the communication required to insert the data into the pHashMap.

6. Related Work

There is a large body of work in the area of parallel data structures with projects aiming at shared memory architectures, distributed memory architectures or both. Parallel programming languages [5–7, 29] typically provide built in arrays and provide minimal guidance to the user on how to develop their own specific parallel data structures. STAPL pContainers are generic data structures and this characteristic is shared by a number of existing projects such as PSTL [16], TBB [14], and POOMA [21]. The Parallel Standard Template Library (PSTL) provides vector, list, queue and associative containers as self contained implementations and without

emphasizing a common design. Intel Threading Building Blocks (TBB) provides generic data structures such as vectors, queues and hash maps adapted for shared memory systems. STAPL is distinguished from TBB in that it targets both shared and distributed systems and is explicitly designed for *extendibility*, providing the user with the means of developing new distributed data structures. A large number of projects provide individual parallel data structures such as Parallel Boost Graph Library [10], and Hierarchically Tiled Arrays [11] and Multiphase Specifically Shared Array in Charm++[17]. The STAPL PCF differs from them by providing a uniform design for all data structures provided.

There has been significant research in the area of concurrent data structures for shared memory architectures. Most of the related work [8, 12, 13, 18, 20, 28] is focused either on how to implement concurrent objects using different locking primitives or how to implement concurrent lock-free data structures. In contrast, the STAPL pContainers are designed to be used in both shared and distributed memory environments and address the additional complexity required to manage the data distribution. Ideas from these papers can be integrated in our framework at the level of bContainers for efficient concurrent access on one location.

The STAPL PCF differs from other languages and libraries by focusing on developing a generic infrastructure that will efficiently provide a shared memory abstraction for pContainers. The framework automates, in a very configurable way, aspects relating to data distribution and thread safety. We emphasize interoperability with other languages and libraries [4], and we use a compositional approach where existing data structures (sequential or concurrent, e.g., TBB containers) can be used as building blocks for implementing parallel containers.

7. Conclusion

In this paper, we presented the STAPL Parallel Container Framework (PCF), an infrastructure to facilitate the development of parallel and concurrent data structures. The salient features of this framework are: (a) a set of classes and rules to build new pContainers and customize existing ones, (b) mechanisms to generate wrappers around any sequential or parallel data structure, enabling its use in a distributed, concurrent environment and in cooperation with other libraries, and (c) support for the (recursive) composition of pContainers into nested, hierarchical pContainers that can support arbitrary degrees of nested parallelism. Furthermore, we have developed a library of basic pContainers constructed using the PCF as initial building blocks and demonstrated the scalability of its components on very large computer systems. We have shown how we have implemented a *shared object view* of the pContainers on distributed systems in order to relieve the programmer from managing and dealing with the distribution explicitly, unless so desired. The PCF allows users to customize its pContainers and adapt to dynamic and irregular environments, e.g., a pContainer can dynamically change its data distribution or adjust its thread safety policy to optimize the access pattern of the algorithms accessing the elements. Alternatively, the user can request certain policies and implementations that can override the provided defaults or adaptive selections. The PCF is an open ended project where users can add features as well as to the library and thus continuously improve the PCF's performance and utility. Our experimental results on a very large parallel machine available at NERSC show that pContainers provide good scalability for both static and dynamic pContainers.

References

[1] D. Bader and K. Madduri. Design and implementation of the hpcs graph analysis benchmark on symmetric multiprocessors. In *The 12th Int. Conf. on High Performance Computing*, Springer, 2005.

[2] A. Buss, A. Fidel, Harshvardhan, T. Smith, G. Tanase, N. Thomas, X. Xu, M. Bianco, N. M. Amato, and L. Rauchwerger, "The STAPL

pView," In *Int. Workshop on Languages and Compilers for Parallel Computing*, Houston, TX, 2010.

[3] A. Buss, Harshvardhan, I. Papadopoulos, O. Pearce, T. Smith, G. Tanase, N. Thomas, X. Xu, M. Bianco, N. M. Amato and L. Rauchwerger "STAPL: Standard template adaptive parallel library," In *Proc. of the 3rd Annual Haifa Experimental Systems Conf. (SYSTOR)*, pp. 1–10, 2010.

[4] A. Buss, T. Smith, G. Tanase, N. Thomas, M. Bianco, N. M. Amato, and L. Rauchwerger, "Design for interoperability in STAPL: pMatrices and linear algebra algorithms," In *Int. Workshop on Languages and Compilers for Parallel Computing, in Lecture Notes in Computer Science*, vol. 5335, pp. 304–315, July 2008.

[5] D. Callahan, B. L. Chamberlain, and H. P. Zima, "The cascade high productivity language," In *The Ninth Int. Workshop on High-Level Parallel Programming Models and Supportive Environments*, vol. 26, pp. 52–60, 2004.

[6] P. Charles, C. Grothoff, V. Saraswat, C. Donawa, A. Kielstra, K. Ebcioglu, C. Praun, and V. Sarkar, "X10: An object-oriented approach to non-uniform cluster computing," In *Proc. of the 20th annual ACM SIGPLAN Conf. on Object-Oriented Programming, Systems, Languages, and Applications*, New York, NY, 2005, pp. 519–538.

[7] D. Culler, A. Dusseau, S. C. Goldstein, A. Krishnamurthy, S. Lumetta, T. Eicken, and K. Yelick, "Parallel programming in Split-C," In *Int. Conf. on Supercomputing*, November 1993.

[8] M. Fomitchev and E. Ruppert, "Lock-free linked lists and skip lists," In *Proc. Symp. on Princ. of Distributed Programming*, New York, NY, 2004, pp. 50–59.

[9] P. Gottschling, D. S. Wise, and M. D. Adams, "Representation-transparent matrix algorithms with scalable performance," In *Proc. Int. Conf. on Supercomputing*, Seattle, Washington, 2007, pp. 116–125.

[10] D. Gregor and A. Lumsdaine, "The parallel BGL: A generic library for distributed graph computations," In *Proc. of Workshop on Parallel Object-Oriented Scientific Computing*, July 2005.

[11] J Guo, G. Bikshandi, B. B. Fraguela and D. Padua. Writing productive stencil codes with overlapped tiling. *Concurr. Comput. : Pract. Exper.*, 21(1):25–39, 2009.

[12] T. L. Harris, "A pragmatic implementation of non-blocking linked-lists," In *Proc. Int. Conf. Dist. Comput.*, London, UK, 2001, pp. 300–314.

[13] M. Herlihy, "A methodology for implementing highly concurrent data objects," *ACM Trans. Prog. Lang. Sys.*, vol. 15, no. 5, pp. 745–770, 1993.

[14] Intel. *Reference Manual for Intel Threading Building Blocks, version 1.0*. Intel Corp., Santa Clara, CA, 2006.

[15] J. JàJà, *An Introduction Parallel Algorithms*. Reading, MA: Addison–Wesley, 1992.

[16] E. Johnson, "Support for Parallel Generic Programming". PhD thesis, Indiana University, Indianapolis, 1998.

[17] L. V. Kale and S. Krishnan, "CHARM++: A portable concurrent object oriented system based on C++," *SIGPLAN Not.*, vol. 28, no. 10, pp. 91–108, 1993.

[18] M. M. Michael, "High performance dynamic lock-free hash tables and list-based sets," In *Proc. of the Fourteenth Annual ACM Symposium on Parallel Algorithms and Architectures*, Winnipeg, Manitoba, Canada, 2002, pp. 73–82.

[19] D. Musser, G. Derge, and A. Saini, *STL Tutorial and Reference Guide, Second Edition*. Reading, MA: Addison–Wesley, 2001.

[20] W. Pugh, "Concurrent maintenance of skip lists," Univ. of Maryland at College Park, Tech. Rep., UMIACS-TR-90-80, 1990.

[21] J. W. Reynders, P. J. Hinker, J. C. Cummings, S. R. Atlas, S. Banerjee, W. F. Humphrey, S. R. Karmesin, K. Keahey, M. Srikant, and M. D. Tholburn, "POOMA: A framework for scientific simulations of paralllel architectures," In Gregory V. Wilson and Paul Lu, editors, *Parallel Programming in C++* Cambridge, MA: MIT Press, 1996, pp. 547–588.

[22] S. Saunders and L. Rauchwerger, "ARMI: An adaptive, platform independent communication library," In *Proc. ACM SIGPLAN Symp. Prin. Prac. Par. Prog.*, San Diego, California, 2003, pp. 230–241.

[23] G. Tanase, "The STAPL Parallel Container Framework". PhD thesis, Texas A&M University, College Station, 2010.

[24] G. Tanase, M. Bianco, N. M. Amato, and L. Rauchwerger, "The STAPL pArray," In *Proc. of the 2007 Workshop on Memory Performance (MEDEA)*, Brasov, Romania, 2007, pp. 73–80.

[25] G. Tanase, C. Raman, M. Bianco, N. M. Amato, and L. Rauchwerger, "Associative parallel containers in STAPL," In *Int. Workshop on Languages and Compilers for Parallel Computing, in Lecture Notes in Computer Science*, vol. 5234, pp. 156–171, 2008.

[26] G. Tanase, X. Xu, A. Buss, Harshvardhan, I. Papadopoulos, O. Pearce, T. Smith, N. Thomas, M. Bianco, N. M. Amato, and L. Rauchwerger, "The STAPL pList," In *Int. Workshop on Languages and Compilers for Parallel Computing, in Lecture Notes in Computer Science*, vol. 5898, pp. 16–30, 2009.

[27] N. Thomas, G. Tanase, O. Tkachyshyn, J. Perdue, N. M. Amato, and L. Rauchwerger, A framework for adaptive algorithm selection in STAPL. In *Proc. ACM SIGPLAN Symp. Prin. Prac. Par.*, pp. 277–288, Chicago, IL, 2005.

[28] J. D. Valois, "Lock-free linked lists using compare-and-swap," In *Proc. ACM Symp. on Princ. of Dist. Proc. (PODC)*, New York, NY, 1995 , pp. 214–222.

[29] K. Yelick, L. Semenzato, G. Pike, C. Miyamoto, B. Liblit, A. Krishnamurthy, P. Hilfinger, S. Graham, D. Gay, P. Colella, and A. Aiken, "Titanium: A high-performance Java dialect," In ACM, editor, *ACM 1998 Workshop on Java for High-Performance Network Computing*, New York, NY, 1998.

CSX: An Extended Compression Format for SpMV on Shared Memory Systems

Kornilios Kourtis   Vasileios Karakasis   Georgios Goumas   Nectarios Koziris

National Technical University of Athens

{kkourt,bkk,goumas,nkoziris}@cslab.ece.ntua.gr

Abstract

The Sparse Matrix-Vector multiplication (SpMV) kernel scales poorly on shared memory systems with multiple processing units due to the streaming nature of its data access pattern. Previous research has demonstrated that an effective strategy to improve the kernel's performance is to drastically reduce the data volume involved in the computations. Since the storage formats for sparse matrices include metadata describing the structure of non-zero elements within the matrix, we propose a generalized approach to compress metadata by exploiting substructures within the matrix. We call the proposed storage format *Compressed Sparse eXtended (CSX)*. In our implementation we employ runtime code generation to construct specialized SpMV routines for each matrix. Experimental evaluation on two shared memory systems for 15 sparse matrices demonstrates significant performance gains as the number of participating cores increases. Regarding the cost of CSX construction, we propose several strategies which trade performance for preprocessing cost making CSX applicable both to online and offline preprocessing.

Categories and Subject Descriptors   J.2 [*Computer Applications*]: Physical Sciences and Engineering

General Terms   Algorithms, Performance

Keywords   Sparse Matrix-Vector Multiplication, Shared Memory, compression, SpMV, SMP

1. Introduction

Multicore processors have become the trend in all aspects of computing (commodity products, high performance systems, and future research directions). A factor that limits the ability of applications to scale on a large number of cores is the sharing of the memory hierarchy by the processing units. Applications with no data dependencies and good temporal locality tend to scale well, since each core can work independently using local data residing in its cache without interfering with the operation of other cores. On the other hand, applications with streaming access patterns tend to exhibit poor scaling due to contention on the memory subsystem. A technique to improve the multithreaded performance of these applications is to trade memory cycles for computation cycles via data compression. In other words, as core count increases, performing redundant computations to avoid memory accesses has the potential of increasing the scalability in applications with streaming memory accesses.

An important and ubiquitous computational kernel with streaming memory access pattern is the Sparse Matrix-Vector multiplication (SpMV). It is used in a large variety of applications in scientific computing and engineering. For example, it is the basic operation of iterative solvers, such as Conjugate Gradient (CG) and Generalized Minimum Residual (GMRES), which are extensively used to solve sparse linear systems resulting from the simulation of physical processes described by partial differential equations [21]. Furthermore, SpMV is a member of one of the "seven dwarfs", which are classes of applications that are believed to be important for at least the next decade [3].

The distinguishing characteristic of sparse matrices is that they are dominated by a large number of zeros, making it highly inefficient to perform operations using typical (dense) array structures. Special storage schemes are used instead, which target both the reduction of the storage requirements of the matrix and the efficient execution of various operations by performing only the necessary computations. Thus, the common approach is to store only the non-zero values of the matrix and employ additional indexing information representing the position of these values (*index data*).

Our previous work [2, 9] has identified the memory subsystem as the main performance bottleneck of the SpMV kernel. Obviously, this problem becomes more severe in a multithreaded environment, where multiple processing cores access the main memory. An approach for alleviating this problem is the reduction of the data volume accessed during the execution of the kernel (*working set*). In [15], we proposed the CSR-DU (CSR with Delta Units) storage format as a way to reduce the index data of non-zero elements across the same matrix row by applying compression. The approach is effective as it can significantly benefit the performance of the multithreaded SpMV kernel [14]. CSR-DU employs a coarse grain delta encoding technique; the sparse matrix is divided into areas, called *units*, with a variable number of elements, and for each of these areas the minimum size for representing the encoded delta values is selected. Following the same philosophy, Belgin et al. [5] proposed a storage scheme called PBR that exploits frequently repeated patterns within the matrix to reduce the working set and improve performance. However, both approaches are quite conservative in mining the regular patterns of sparse matrices, since CSR-DU scans patterns along a single row, while PBR scans patterns strictly row and column-aligned within specific block areas.

The work in this paper was motivated by two key observations: first, the utilization of regular patterns within matrices leads to significant performance improvements and, second, thorough inspection of the sparse matrix to mine as many patterns as possible can be a viable approach in a large class of applications, where the same matrix is used across numerous runs. For example, the typical linear system $Ax = b$ may be solved repeatedly for the same matrix A and different right-hand statements b. This second observation is also supported by the various preprocessing algorithms that are used to reorder a sparse matrix in order to reduce its bandwidth [21]. To this direction, we propose a generalized and elaborate storage format based on compression that aims at achieving more aggressive reduction in matrix metadata. We call this storage format *Compressed Sparse eXtended (CSX)*. In the proposed implementation, CSX is able to represent frequently occurring substructures along the same row, column, and diagonal, as well as dense two-dimensional blocks. To the best of our knowledge, this is the most general and flexible representation scheme for sparse matrices. We handle the above substructures in a unified way, by expressing each one of them as an appropriate transformation. We transform the initial matrix coordinates according to this transformation, partially sort the transformed coordinates lexicographically, and mine the non-zero elements that belong to the substructure.

Our experimental results indicate that CSX is able to provide significant performance improvements over a number of existing storage formats. Regarding the cost of preprocessing, the complexity is kept linear to the number of the non-zero elements of the input matrix. The total preprocessing time ranges from tens to a few thousands of serial CSR SpMV operations depending on the number of patterns being detected. The higher cost of preprocessing for CSX when trying to detect a large number of substructures makes it practical only for offline matrix preprocessing. However, by limiting the considered substructures, or searching for all substructures in a small part of the matrix using sampling, we manage to drop the preprocessing cost to a few hundreds of SpMV operations without severe loss in the final CSX performance. This makes CSX suitable also for online preprocessing of the input matrix.

The rest of the paper is organized as follows: Section 2 presents some relevant background information. Section 3 presents the CSX storage format together with its implementation details, while Section 4 presents the results of the performance evaluation. Section 5 discusses related work, and Section 6 concludes the paper and discusses directions for future work.

2. Background

2.1 Sparse matrix formats and the SpMV operation

The most commonly used storage format for sparse matrices is the Compressed Sparse Row (CSR) format [4, 21]. In CSR the matrix is stored in three arrays: `values`, `row_ptr`, and `col_ind`. The `values` array stores the non-zero elements of the matrix in row-major order, while the other two arrays store indexing information: `row_ptr` contains the location of the first (non-zero) element of each row within the `values` array and `col_ind` contains the column number for each non-zero element. An example of the CSR format for a 6×6 sparse matrix is presented in Figure 1. The size of the `values` and `col_ind` arrays are equal to the number of non-zero elements (`nnz`), while the `row_ptr` array size is equal to the number of rows (nrows) plus one. Other generic formats for sparse matrices are the Compressed Sparse Column (CSC), which is similar to CSR storing columns instead of rows, and the Coordinate format (COO), where each non-zero is stored as a triplet along with the coordinates of its location in the matrix.

The SpMV operation ($y = Ax$), is the multiplication of a sparse matrix A and a (dense) vector x, with the result stored in the (dense) output vector y. The operation is easily implemented for matrices stored in CSR form. The SpMV code for a matrix with N rows in CSR format is shown in Figure 2. The working set (`ws`) of the CSR SpMV operation consists of the matrix and vector data. Its size is

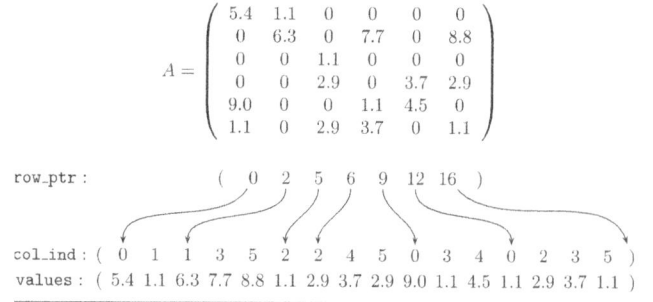

Figure 1. Example of the CSR storage format.

```
for (i=0; i<N; i++)
    for (j=row_ptr[i]; j<row_ptr[i+1]; j++)
        y[i] += values[j]*x[col_ind[j]];
```

Figure 2. SpMV code for the CSR format.

expressed by the following formula:

$$ws = \overbrace{(nnz \times (idx\_s + val\_s) + (nrows + 1) \times idx\_s)}^{\text{sparse matrix}}$$
$$+ \underbrace{(nrows + ncols) \times val\_s}_{\text{vectors}}$$

The idx_s and val_s terms represent the storage size required for an index and a value respectively. Since for most real-life sparse matrices it holds $nnz \gg nrows, ncols$, the most dominant terms of the working set is the size of the `col_ind` and `values` arrays, which have `nnz` elements. Commonly, vectors x and y have less than 2^{32} elements due to memory size restrictions and thus a 4-byte integer is used for index storage. Floating point values, however, normally require double precision, so the typical value for val_s is 8 bytes. Under these conditions, values constitute the larger portion of the working set by a factor of $2/3$, if we consider only the `col_ind` and `values` arrays. Hence, compression of index data after a point leads to diminishing returns because value data dominate the working set.

2.2 The CSR-DU storage format

Sophisticated sparse storage formats traditionally try to exploit contiguous elements, either in one or two dimensions. Examples include the BCSR format [20] and the variable length one-dimensional block format described in [19]. The index data compression approach of the CSR-DU storage format is based on the general premise that sparse matrices have dense areas, which do not necessarily contain contiguous non-zero elements. These areas can contribute significantly to index data size reduction, when delta encoding is used to reveal the highly redundant nature of the `col_ind` array [26]. In a delta encoding scheme the column indices are replaced with *deltas*, each of which is defined as the difference of the current index with the previous one. Since delta values are positive and less or equal than their corresponding column indices, they can be stored in smaller size integers, leading to index data size reduction. The CSR-DU storage format [15] is based on a coarse grain delta encoding scheme. The matrix is divided into areas called units, each of which is characterized by the minimum integer size able to represent the unit's delta-encoded column indices. For example, if for the delta values of the unit stands that $\delta_i \leq 2^8$, then only one byte is required for storing the delta values, while a unit with $2^8 < \delta_i \leq 2^{16}$ requires two-byte integers for storing the column index.

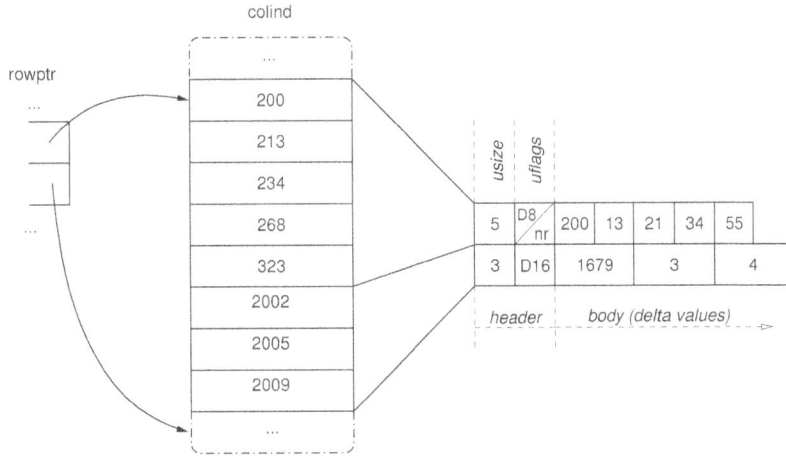

Figure 3. Example of the CSR-DU storage format, where a row is split into two units.

In the implementation of CSR-DU presented in [15], unit information is stored in a single byte-array called `ctl`, which consists of a *header* with the properties of the unit and the *main body* that includes the delta-encoded column indices. In the most simple form of CSR-DU, the header consists of two one-byte fields: `usize`, which is the number of elements the unit contains, and `uflags`, which encodes its characteristics. Since `usize` is stored in a single byte, the maximum possible number of elements per unit is $2^8 = 256$. The size in bytes (1, 2, 4 or 8 bytes) of the delta values stored in the main body can be extracted from the `uflags` field, along with a marker that designates the beginning of a new row. Figure 3 presents an example of the CSR-DU format. In this example a row with 8 elements is split into two units. The first unit has 5 elements, 1-byte delta sizes and a designator for a new row (`nr`), while the second unit has 3 elements and 2-byte delta sizes. The actual implementation of CSR-DU in [15] also includes a column index offset from the previous unit in the header. The offset is called `ujmp` and is stored as a (positive) variable-length integer at the end of the header.

3. Compressed Sparse eXtended (CSX)

3.1 Motivation and approach

Although the SpMV kernel is essentially simple, its actual and maximum performance depends strongly on the nature of the sparse matrix. A generalized storage format, like CSR, does not make any assumptions about the sparse matrix data, and thus it cannot exploit optimization opportunities that arise from special properties of the matrix. In the following paragraphs we describe a general optimization approach for the SpMV kernel based on a new storage format for sparse matrices, that targets the exploitation of regularities in the matrix. We call this storage format Compressed Sparse eXtended (CSX). We argue that this approach can be used for a wide range of optimizations that exploit matrix-specific knowledge. Our method is based on the extension of the concept of *units* introduced by CSR-DU to support different and arbitrary classes of regularities. Focusing on the generality and flexibility of our method, we employ a runtime code generation technique [13], where a specialized, matrix-specific SpMV operation is created, along with the encoded matrix data.

3.2 Exploiting substructures within the sparse matrix

Sparse matrices commonly represent physical structures of computational domains. For this reason, they carry repeated substructures of non-zero elements, expressing, for example, connectivity

Direction		Elements	
		y	x
Horizontal	$\rightarrow$	y_0	$x_0 + i\delta$
Vertical	$\downarrow$	$y_0 + i\delta$	x_0
Diagonal	$\searrow$	$y_0 + i\delta$	$x_0 + i\delta$
Anti-diagonal	$\swarrow$	$y_0 + i\delta$	$x_0 - i\delta$

Table 1. Directions for delta run-length encoding. The y and x columns contain an expression for generating the matrix elements for the specific direction given its delta value δ. Note that $0 \leq i < size$, where $size$ the number of elements in the unit.

between elements of a domain. To the best of our experience, the majority of the matrices expose these regularities along the same row, column, diagonal or may span multiple rows (columns or diagonals) in a two-dimensional structure. In the proposed storage format of CSX we consider the above kinds of substructures described in greater detail in the following paragraphs. Nevertheless, if necessary, other classes of regularities can be incorporated in the format to optimize matrices with different characteristics.

Horizontal substructures

In order to mine horizontal substructures within the sparse matrix, we extend the CSR-DU storage format to apply more aggressive index compression by employing run-length encoding in the delta values in multiple directions. Drawing inspiration from the variable length one-dimensional block format described in [19], we generalize the notion of sequential elements $(\alpha, \alpha + 1, \alpha + 2, \ldots)$, elements with a constant distance $(\alpha, \alpha + \delta, \alpha + 2\delta, \ldots)$ can be encoded using only the initial value, the constant distance, and their size. Since this technique essentially applies a run-length encoding on the delta values of the column indices, we will refer to it as *delta run-length encoding*.

Vertical and diagonal substructures

To further enhance index compression, we augment our approach to include multiple directions for the sparse matrix elements. The directions we consider are vertical, diagonal and anti-diagonal (see Tab. 1) with the same rationale as in the horizontal case.

Two-dimensional substructures

Two-dimensional substructures are common in sparse matrices, especially in those that arise from problems with underlying 2D/3D geometry [1, 11, 12]. Storage formats that exploit these structures, e.g., BCSR, can provide significant speedups over the standard CSR implementation in many cases, since apart from reducing the SpMV working set, they exhibit good computational characteristics [12, 24]. Therefore, we further extend our approach to support 2D-blocks.

Figure 4 presents the distribution of the most dominant substructures in the 15 matrices of our suite as discovered by CSX. Delta units are designated with DUx, where x is the number of bits used for the delta values. Dense blocks are either brow or bcol, depending on the alignment (see Section 3.3), with the numbers inside parenthesis indicating the block dimensions. Finally, the rest of the substructures are indicated with their literal name and the delta value inside parenthesis. We observe that there is a significant representation of the aforementioned substructures in our matrix suite, indicating that there is space for performance improvement by utilizing them. Interestingly enough, matrix rajat31 contains a rather uncommon substructure, since more than 20% of its non-zero elements lie along the same diagonal with step 11. Our approach is able to capture this substructure. How CSX discovers the different patterns inside a sparse matrix is discussed in the next section, while the matrix suite is detailed in Section 4.

3.3 CSX matrix construction

Our algorithm to construct the CSX matrix handles the supported substructures in a uniform way. The algorithm is based on a delta run-length encoding detector for the horizontal direction, which detects sequences (*runs*) of the same delta value. If the number of elements in a run is larger or equal than a specific configuration parameter, then the items are grouped together in a single unit. The detector can be easily implemented if we assume that the elements can be iterated in lexicographical order. To simplify the detection process, detection of overlapped runs is not supported. An example is presented in Figure 5, where the detector has been configured to detect runs of size larger than or equal to 4. Note that it does not detect the run of the indices $41, 61, 81$, since its size is 3, and it also does not detect the run of the indices $1, 21, 41, 61, 81$ since it overlaps with other elements. The algorithm for the detector of horizontal substructures is given in Alg. 1.

indices:	1	10	11	12	13	14	21	41	61	81
delta values:	1	9	1	1	1	1	7	20	20	20

1x4

Figure 5. Horizontal detection example.

Algorithm 1: Horizontal detector.

Input: $indices$: array of size n column indices
Input: lim: the minimum size for DRLE units

$deltas$ = deltaEncode($indices$)
$delta_{rle} \leftarrow deltas[0]$
$freq_{rle} \leftarrow 1$

for $i \leftarrow 1$ **to** n **do**
  if $deltas[i] == delta_{rle}$ **then**
    $\lfloor$ $freq_{rle} \leftarrow freq_{rle} + 1$
  else
      if $freq_{rle} \geq lim$ **then** encode in DRLE units
      else keep individual indices
      $delta_{rle} \leftarrow .deltas[i]$
      $freq_{rle} \leftarrow 1$

In order to detect the rest of the substructures discussed in the previous section, we use the horizontal detector and apply appropriate transformations on the matrix points coordinates. For example, to detect vertical runs we swap the coordinates of the elements. The transformations for the substructures implemented within CSX are shown in Table 2.

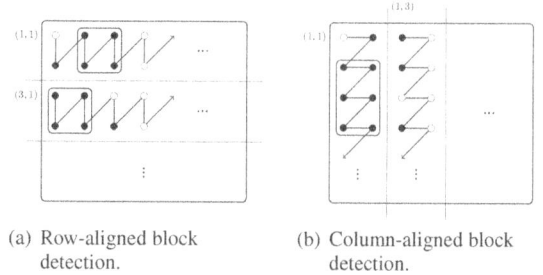

(a) Row-aligned block detection. (b) Column-aligned block detection.

Figure 6. Detection of two-dimensional dense substructures (black dots are non-zero elements).

For the 2D substructures, we need a non-linear transformation that will transform the 2D space into an 1D space. Since the input matrix is sparse, we chose not to map the 2D coordinate space of the whole matrix to 1D using a typical space-filling curve, e.g., Morton-order curve, because such an order (a) would require a linear space of $O(nrows^2)$ size, which is impractical for very large and sparse matrices, and (b) would imply a strict requirement on alignment and size of blocks, since such transformations are based on bit transformations. For that reason, we segment the matrix into horizontal (or vertical) bands of a specific width and apply a simple space-filling transformation inside that band. Figure 6 presents that schematically for bands of width 2, and Table 2 presents the exact formulas of the transformations, when segmenting the matrix horizontally or vertically. In a single detection phase, we are now able to detect all $r \times c$ blocks, with r or c constant, aligned at either r-rows or c-columns boundaries, respectively, depending on the orientation of the segmentation of the matrix. Although it is possible to detect totally unaligned blocks, this would induce additional space and time complexity. In detecting dense sub-blocks of the matrix, we instruct our detector to search only for substructures with $\delta = 1$.

Our generic substructure detector processes the input matrix in windows of w non-zero elements as it is depicted in Alg. 2. For each processing window, we transform the matrix elements and sort them lexicographically before passing them to the horizontal detector. After the detection phase completes, we transform back the window elements. The asymptotic complexity is determined by the complexity of sorting the elements of a window and the total number of processing windows. Assuming non-overlapping windows, the asymptotic complexity of the horizontal detector is $\lceil \frac{nnz}{w} \rceil O(w \log(w)) = O(nnz)$. Note that even when using overlapping windows, the asymptotic complexity does not change. Finally, increasing the processing window so that it approaches nnz lets us mine almost every substructure in the matrix, but increases considerably the preprocessing time.

In order to mine all the considered substructures/patterns from the matrix, we run the generic detector for each supported class of patterns (e.g., horizontal, diagonal, blocks with 2-row alignment, etc.) and record an estimate of the gain in the total size of the matrix (we ignore all patterns that cannot encode more than 10% of the non-zero elements of the matrix). The class of patterns that maximizes this estimate is selected for encoding and the procedure is repeated for the rest, unencoded, elements of the matrix until no other encoding can be applied. The remaining elements are

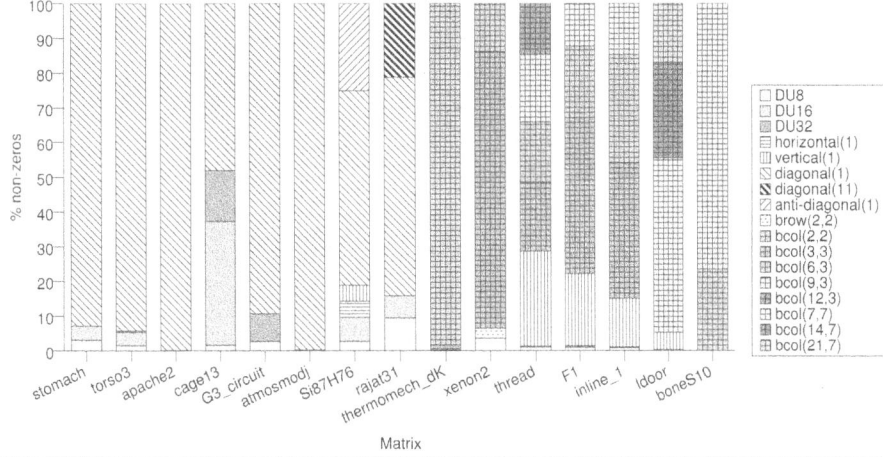

Figure 4. Distribution of substructures in the matrices of our suite.

Substructure	Transformation
Horizontal	$(i', j') = (i, j)$
Vertical	$(i', j') = (j, i)$
Diagonal	$(i', j') = (nrows + j - i, \min(i, j))$
Anti-diagonal	$(i', j') = \begin{cases} (nrows + j - i, j), & i < nrows \\ (j, i + j - nrows), & i \geq nrows \end{cases}$
Block (row aligned)	$(i', j') = (\lfloor \frac{i-1}{r} \rfloor + 1, \mod(i - 1, r) + r(j - 1) + 1)$
Block (column aligned)	$(i', j') = (\lfloor \frac{j-1}{c} \rfloor + 1, c(i - 1) + \mod(j - 1, c))$

Table 2. The transformations used to convert the different substructures to horizontal, in order to feed the CSX pattern detector. The number of rows of the matrix is denoted by $nrows$, and r and c are the required alignments for row- and column-aligned blocked substructures.

Algorithm 2: Generic detector.

Input: $elems$: array of size nnz of matrix elements
Input: w: size of processing window
Input: f: transformation function
Input: lim: the minimum size for DRLE units

$nw \leftarrow \lceil \frac{nnz}{w} \rceil$
for $i \leftarrow 1$ **to** nw **do**
$\quad welems \leftarrow \texttt{extract\_window}(elems, w)$
$\quad welems \leftarrow f(welems)$
$\quad \texttt{sort}(welems)$
$\quad \texttt{horizontal\_detector}(welems, lim)$
$\quad welems \leftarrow f^{-1}(welems)$

---

then stored in delta units in row-major order. The estimate used to score the different encodings is based on the idea that the major gain in the size of the matrix would come from the reduction of the `col_ind` structure. In order to keep our estimate simple, we assume that we keep one index for each pattern and one index for each unencoded element. So, if $npatt$ is the number of the encoded patterns and nnz_{enc} the number of the non-zeros encoded by this pattern, the selection criterion is

$$G = \overbrace{nnz}^{\text{initial}} - (\overbrace{npatt}^{\text{encoded}} + \overbrace{nnz - nnz_{enc}}^{\text{unencoded}}) \qquad (1)$$
$$= nnz_{enc} - npatt$$

3.4 Multiplication routines

After the matrix construction is complete, the `ctl` byte-array and the SpMV code needs to be generated. We use an encoding similar

to CSR-DU where, as depicted in Figure 3, each unit starts with two bytes: `uflags` and `usize`. In CSX, each unit represents an encoded pattern. The `usize` byte contains the number of elements for the specified unit and the `uflags` its type along with some book-keeping information. From the 8 bits of `uflags`, 6 are reserved for the encoding of the type, and 2 are used for a new row marker and a row offset marker. If the row offset bit is set, the header is followed by a variable-length integer equal to the number of empty rows. This is necessary, because the use of CSX units in directions other than the horizontal may lead to empty rows. For each unit type available, a unique 6-bit identifier is allocated for the type encoding, therefore limiting the maximum number of different unit types to 64. Different unit types may belong to the same class of patterns, e.g., horizontal(1) and horizontal(2) are different unit types, but belong to the horizontal class of patterns.

Our dynamic code generation approach uses the LLVM [16] compiler infrastructure. A core component of LLVM is its intermediate representation (IR), which resembles a RISC-like assembly, and it can be manipulated by optimization passes and used to produce native code for a number of different ISAs. The code for the SpMV operation is generated programmatically in LLVM's IR and is specific to each unit type. Subsequently, it is optimized and dynamically compiled into native code. An on-disk cache of generated versions can be used to reduce the overhead of compilation and optimization.

3.5 Restrictions and extensions

Overall, CSX is a very flexible storage format supporting several different substructures within the sparse matrix simultaneously. However, to simplify the implementation and reduce the run-time cost of preprocessing, a number of restrictions have been applied.

As discussed above, our implementation does not detect overlapping substructures and fully unaligned two-dimensional blocks (row or column alignment is required). Even with these restrictions, however, CSX is able to group the vast majority of the non-zero elements in our matrix suite (see Fig. 4) in utilizable substructures. Quite importantly, our detection approach based on transformations provides a straightforward mechanism to incorporate further meaningful substructures, provided they can be expressed as a coordinate transformation as well.

The preprocessing phase for CSX is broken down into two steps: substructure detection and matrix construction (encoding). Both steps require sorting of the processed elements. However, as discussed before, processing non-zero elements in windows keeps the overall complexity of the preprocessing phase linear to the number of non-zero elements of the matrix, without wasting a significant number of substructures. However, in the current implementation of CSX, processing in windows is performed only for the first step (detection) while the encoding step sorts all processed elements. This adds some additional cost to the preprocessing, which will be removed in future versions of the preprocessor.

The algorithm used by the detector to select the substructures to be encoded in the final CSX format is greedy in that it always selects the local optimal solution based on the criterion (1). This might lead to a suboptimal set of encoded substructures. Finally, our selection criterion considers only the reduction in the size of the encoded matrix and ignores any differences in the computational characteristics of the different substructures. We are also investigating improvements on these topics, such as faster search methods and more elaborate selection criteria.

4. Experimental evaluation

4.1 Experimental setup and methodology

We performed an experimental evaluation of the proposed storage format on two SMP platforms: (a) a 2-way quad-core system (totaling 8 cores) based on Intel Harpertown processors, and (b) a 4-way six-core system (totaling 24 cores) based on Intel Dunnington processors. Figure 7 and Table 3 present the cache hierarchies and the basic microarchitectural characteristics of our platforms.

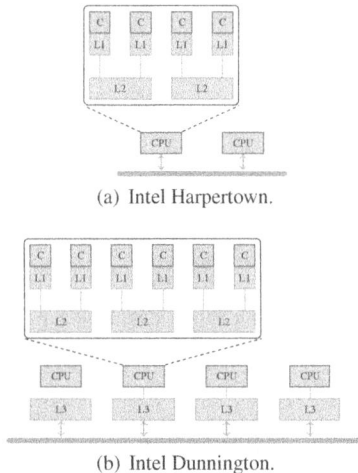

(a) Intel Harpertown.

(b) Intel Dunnington.

Figure 7. Cache hierarchies of used hardware platforms.

Both systems run a 64-bit version of the Linux OS (kernel version 2.6). We used version 2.5 of the LLVM compiler infrastructure and llvm-gcc 4.2.1 (a modified version of gcc that acts as a front-end for LLVM) as a static compiler. The parallelization of all versions of the SpMV kernel was done explicitly, using the POSIX

	Harpertown	**Dunnington**
Model	E5405	X7460
Frequency (GHz)	2.0	2.66
L1 (data/instr.)	32K/32K	32K/32K
L2 (unified)	6M (1/2 cores)	3M (1/2 cores)
L3 (unified)	–	16M
Number of cores	$2 \times 4 = 8$	$4 \times 6 = 24$

Table 3. System characteristics of used hardware platforms.

threads interface of the GNU C library (NPTL 2.7). Moreover, the sched_setaffinity() system call was used to bind the various threads to predefined cores.

The experiments were conducted by measuring the execution time of 128 consecutive SpMV operations with randomly created input vectors. We made no attempt to artificially pollute the cache after each iteration, in order to better simulate iterative scientific application behavior, where matrix data are present in the cache hierarchy, because either they have just been produced or they were recently accessed. By using multiple iterations, we induce temporal locality to our benchmark, and thus the streaming behavior of the SpMV kernel is maintained only if the working set, and more specifically the matrix data, are larger than the system's cache. For the multithreaded versions of the kernel, we used row partitioning and a static balancing scheme based on the non-zero elements, where each thread is assigned approximately the same number of non-zero elements and, thus, the same number of floating-point operations. The threads are always scheduled to run as "close" to the processors as possible, e.g., on Harpertown 2 threads are scheduled on the cores sharing the L2 cache, while 4 threads are scheduled on the same physical package (similarly for Dunnington). For the CSX matrix construction, we initially partition the data based on the number of non-zero elements and for each partition we perform the analysis and generate different SpMV versions for each thread.

We consider four different formats in our tests: CSR as the baseline standard format, BCSR as a state-of-the-art improvement over CSR, CSR-DU and CSX. The code for the CSR SpMV kernel was optimized to write the y[i] value at the end of each innermost loop, by keeping the intermediate result in a register. For BCSR we use block-specific optimized routines and report the best performing block shape out of a large number of candidates. Finally, we use a window of $w = 32K$ non-zero elements for the analysis of the matrix for CSX. We used 64-bit numerical values for all formats and 32-bit indices for CSR and BCSR.

The matrix suite that we used for the performance evaluation of our proposed technique consists of 15 matrices selected from the University of Florida sparse matrix collection [7]. We made an effort to include matrices that arise from different kind of problems. Table 4 presents our matrix suite and the characteristics of every matrix. For the sake of presentation, we have arranged the sparse matrices so that the first matrices are dominated by one-dimensional substructures while the latter from two-dimensional.

4.2 CSX SpMV performance

This section discusses the effect of the CSX storage format on the performance of the SpMV kernel. Figure 8 demonstrates the average speedup of the considered formats over serial CSR for all matrices on our platforms, while Fig. 9 presents the performance improvement of different versions of CSX over the multithreaded CSR.

The serial version of CSR-DU and BCSR on Harpertown lead to -8% and -2% performance degradation on average, respectively, while CSX manages to achieve a marginal 1% performance improvement. On Dunnington, CSR-DU almost matches the per-

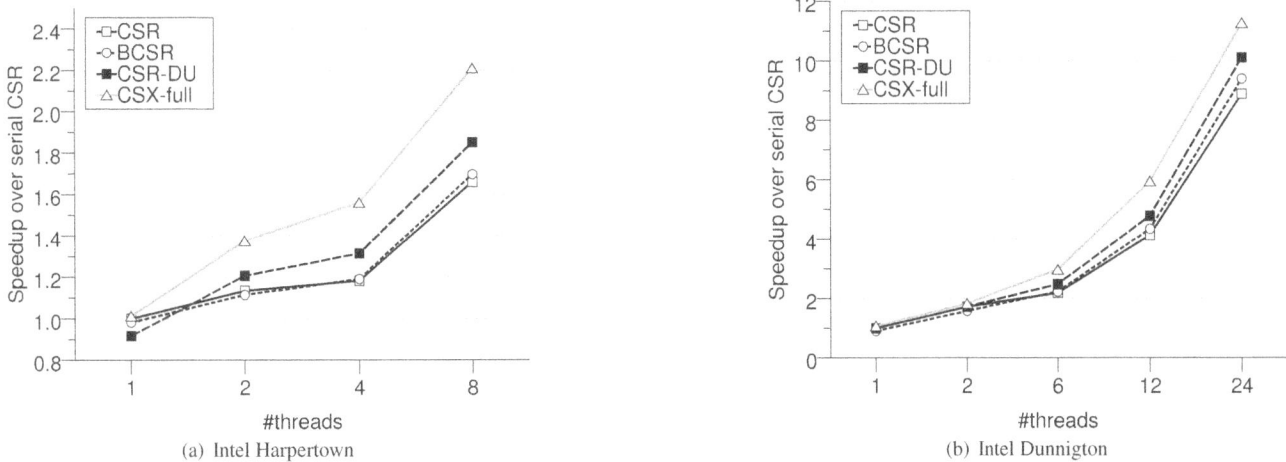

(a) Intel Harpertown

(b) Intel Dunnigton

Figure 8. Average speedup of SpMV execution time over the serial CSR version for all considered formats.

Matrix	rows	cols	nnz	size (MB)	Problem
stomach	213360	213360	3021648	35.39	2D/3D
torso3	259156	259156	4429042	51.67	2D/3D
apache2	715176	715176	4817870	57.86	Structural
cage13	445315	445315	7479343	87.29	Graph
G3_circuit	1585478	1585478	7660826	93.72	Circuit Sim.
atmosmodj	1270432	1270432	8814880	105.72	CFD
Si87H76	240369	240369	10661631	122.93	Chemistry
rajat31	4690002	4690002	20316253	250.39	Circuit Sim.
thermomech_dK	204316	204316	2846228	33.35	Thermal
xenon2	157464	157464	3866688	44.85	Materials
thread	29736	29736	4470048	51.27	Structural
F1	343791	343791	26837113	308.44	Structural
inline_1	503712	503712	36816342	423.25	Structural
ldoor	952203	952203	46522475	536.04	Structural
boneS10	914898	914898	55468422	638.28	Model Reduction

Table 4. The matrix suite used for the experimental evaluation. The size column displays the size of the matrix in MB when stored in the CSR format.

formance of CSR, BCSR falls further behind at −10%, and CSX gains 7% over CSR. When moving to multiple threads, however, the memory bandwidth problem becomes dominant and the compression formats show their potential. CSX achieves a 2.21 speedup on Harpertown (33% performance improvement over CSR) when all 8 cores are utilized and 11.27 speedup (25% improvement over CSR) on Dunnigton when all 24 cores are utilized. The speedups for CSR-DU are 1.85 (+11.6% over CSR) and 10.1 (+10.3% over CSR) for the Harpertown and Dunnigton platforms, respectively. BCSR cannot provide any speedup over CSR on average, since it suffers from excessive padding. However, BCSR can provide significant performance improvement over CSR for individual sparse matrices with a lot of dense sub-blocks (see Fig. 10). As depicted in Fig. 9, the best performance improvement over CSR on Dunnigton is achieved when using 12 threads and not 24, as it might be expected. This happens because 6 matrices of our suite, even in CSR format, fit into the platform's aggregate cache, which totals 64 MB. This also explains the superlinear speedup encountered when moving from 12 to 24 threads on Dunnigton for almost all the formats. For this reason, we will focus on the 12-thread configuration on Dunnigton in the following, where only two matrices (stomach and thermomech_dK) are close to the aggregate cache (32 MB). In the 12-thread configuration, when the memory bottle-

neck is the most apparent, the performance improvement of CSX over CSR reaches 42%.

Figure 10 presents also the performance improvement of two lighter versions of CSX, namely CSX-horiz and CSX-linear, which detect only horizontal or one-dimensional patterns. CSX-full is the full version of CSX, which also detects two-dimensional patterns. It is apparent that both these lightweight versions of CSX can provide considerable performance improvement over CSR and CSR-DU. Although Fig. 4 shows that horizontal patterns are not dominant in our suite, the block patterns are mined as horizontal when block detection is disabled. However, the diagonal patterns discovered by CSX-linear and CSX-all cannot be discovered by CSX-horiz and are encoded as CSR-DU delta units in this case. This explains the escalation in performance as we move from the pure CSR-DU to CSX-horiz and then to more elaborate pattern detection schemes.

Figure 10 presents a detailed per matrix view of the performance improvement achieved by BCSR, CSR-DU, and the different CSX variants when 8 cores are used on Harpertown and 12 cores on Dunnigton. CSX managed to achieve the best performance in all but one matrix, namely thermomech_dK, where BCSR achieved the best performance. This is not a surprise, since this matrix has almost all of its non-zero elements in 2×2 dense blocks (see Fig. 4), which, apparently, BCSR easily exploits without paying the cost of decompression performed by CSX. However, BCSR's performance is rather poor for the first 8 matrices of our suite, that exhibit mainly one-dimensional substructures, and are actually responsible for the poor average performance of BCSR.

As far as the different CSX variants are concerned, we observe that CSX-horiz falls back to CSR-DU performance for the first matrices of our suite, since these contain mainly diagonal structures. For the same reason, CSX-full cannot provide any additional speedup over CSX-linear. The last 7 matrices of the suite are block-dominated and CSX-all gives considerable improvements over the other two variants. The performance of CSX-horiz and CSX-linear is similar for these matrices, since they detect the same patterns (horizontal). Interestingly, these variants can detect the one-dimensional 'sub-patterns' comprising the blocks and provide considerable improvements over pure CSR-DU.

4.3 CSX preprocessing cost

The preprocessing time for CSX when detecting all available patterns (CSX-full variant) is comparable to a few thousands of serial CSR SpMV operations (the wall-clock time ranges from a few sec-

253

(a) Intel Harpertown

(b) Intel Dunnigton

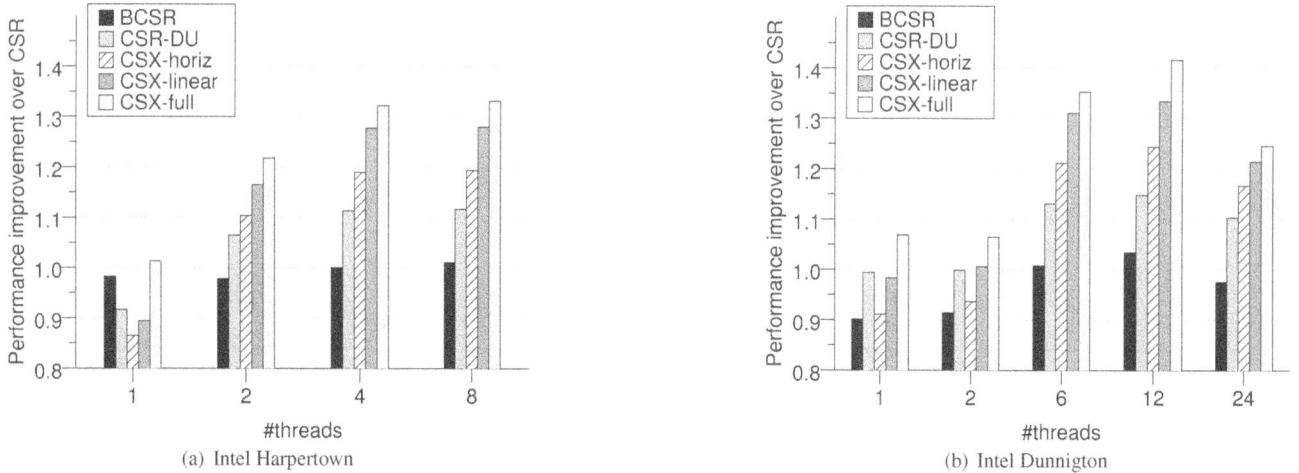

Figure 9. Average performance improvement over multithreaded CSR for different CSX detection schemes.

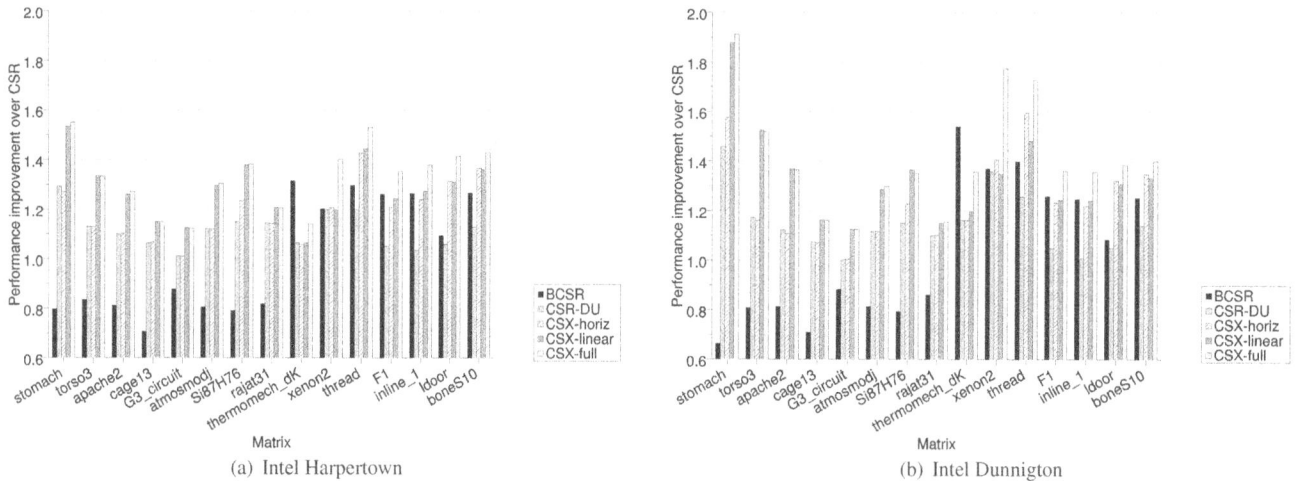

(a) Intel Harpertown

(b) Intel Dunnigton

Figure 10. Per matrix performance improvement over multithreaded CSR for Harpertown (8 threads) and Dunnington (12 threads).

ond to less than 10 minutes for the largest of our matrices). Since typical applications using SpMV may involve less than a thousand iterations, CSX preprocessing for all substructures is reasonable only for offline preprocessing. Even in this case, however, we argue that for real-life applications, where the sparse matrix is reused many times across numerous runs (e.g. solution of linear system $Ax = b$ with various values of b), this preprocessing cost is still practical.

However, for applications that require online CSX preprocessing and need to amortize this cost, we can trade performance for lower preprocessing time. An approach is to restrict the search to fewer substructures, as is the case of the CSX-horiz and CSX-linear variants discussed previously. Both these lightweight variants of CSX outperform significantly existing storage formats, although they do not reach the performance of the 'full' CSX. A second approach is to sample the input matrix, scanning only a representative part of it, in order to decide which substructures to encode in CSX. Figure 11 shows the preprocessing cost (in serial CSR SpMV operations) for CSR-DU and the aforementioned strategies. We applied uniform sampling over the whole matrix for CSX-linear and CSX-full (denoted as CSX-linear-s and CSX-full-s in Fig. 11).

Since the substructure detection phase of CSX is already performed using windows, sampling the matrix is rather straightforward: we scan only a certain number of preprocessing windows uniformly distributed all over the input matrix. Specifically, we searched for patterns in 5 windows of 32K non-zero elements, i.e., we sampled 160K of non-zero elements of the matrix, which is less than 6% of the non-zero elements of the smallest matrix in our suite (thermomech_dK). We observe in Fig. 11 that the preprocessing cost is drastically reduced, leading to practical preprocessing times even for online computations. Sampling the matrix is very effective, since it leads to a large reduction in the preprocessing cost with a minor effect on performance. We should also note that the current implementation of the CSX preprocessing can be further reduced with some additional implementation effort, e.g., avoiding the cost of sorting the matrix during the encoding (see Section 3.5) by using processing windows, and providing a multithreaded implementation of the preprocessing. We expect that these optimizations will further reduce the preprocessing cost to less than a hundred serial CSR SpMV operations, making CSX more suitable for online preprocessing of the matrix.

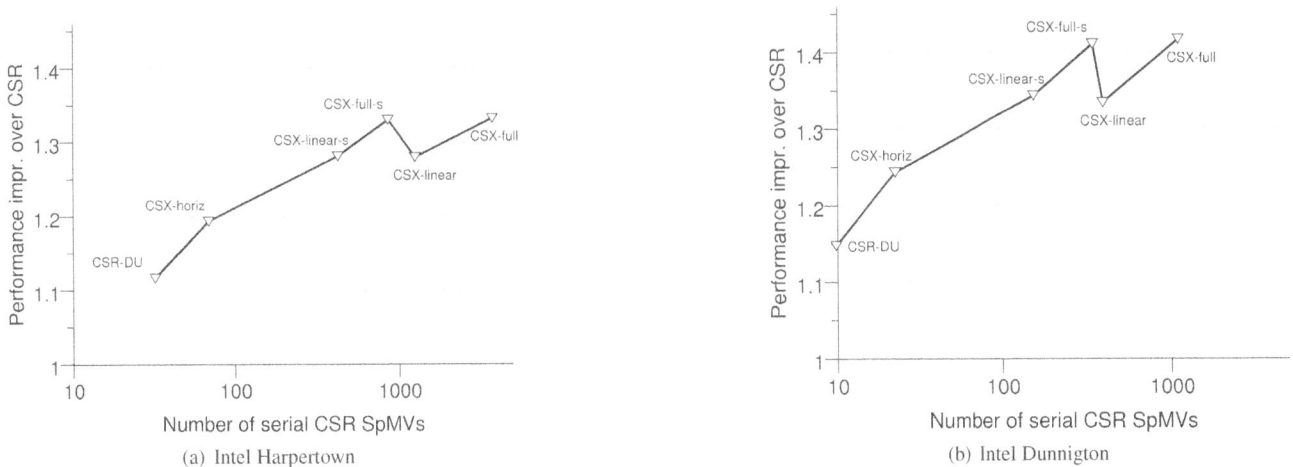

Figure 11. Tradeoff between preprocessing time and performance improvement over multithreaded CSR. The reported performance improvement is for 8 threads on Harpertown and 12 threads for Dunnington.

5. Related Work

Due to the importance of SpMV, there is an abundance of scientific work targeting the optimization of the serial version of the kernel. Several of these efforts [11,19,22–24] aim at the optimization of the irregular and indirect accesses on the input vector using methods such as matrix reordering, register blocking, and cache blocking. Other works [17,25] are concerned with the performance problems that arise in matrices with a large number of rows with small length.

A significant part of the SpMV optimization techniques reported in the related literature result in index data reduction. Typical examples are blocking methods such as BSCR [20] that store only per-block index information. A problem with these approaches is that, depending on the structure of the matrix, they may require appropriate padding with zero values. One of the first works that explicitly targets the compression of the index data is [26]. In this paper, Willcock and Lumsdaine propose two methods: *DCSR*, which compresses column indices using a byte-oriented delta encoding scheme to exploit the highly redundant nature of the `col_ind` array and *RPCSR*, which generates matrix-specific dynamic code by applying aggressive compression on column indices patterns for the whole matrix. In [15] we propose the CSR-DU format, which employs a delta encoding scheme to group areas of non-zero elements. CSR-DU is restricted to non-zero elements along the same row. Another recent work that targets performance improvement by reducing the index data volume is [5], where Belgin et al. propose a matrix representation that exploits repeated block patterns. The approach here divides the matrix into sub-blocks and searches for frequently encountered block patterns within these sub-blocks. The proposed storage format exhibits good serial performance, but is not so successful with multiple cores.

As far as the multithreaded version of the code is concerned, past work focuses mainly on SMP clusters, where researchers either apply and evaluate known uniprocessor optimization techniques (e.g., register and cache blocking) on SMPs or examine reordering techniques to improve locality of references and minimize communication cost [6,8,10,18]. Williams et. al [27] presented an evaluation of SpMV on a set of emerging multicore architectures. Their study covers a wide and diverse range of high-end chip multiprocessors, including recent multicores from AMD (Opteron X2) and Intel (Clovertown), Sun's Niagara2, and platforms comprised of one or two Cell processors. Their work includes a rich collection of optimizations, including some that are targeted specifically at

multithreading architectures, on a set of 14 matrices. Although this work focuses on a different class of optimizations, the authors state that they generate different kernel versions for different architectures. Hence this work, along with [5], conforms with our general approach and reveals the necessity for specialized SpMV routines, based on the execution environment (e.g., underlying architecture) or the matrix data for maximizing performance.

6. Conclusions – Future work

In this paper we present a new storage format for sparse matrices called Compressed Sparse eXtended (CSX) that targets the optimization of the SpMV kernel. CSX utilizes a variety of substructures within the sparse matrix, falling in two main categories: one-dimensional substructures across the same row, column or diagonal compressed using a delta run-length encoding scheme, and two-dimensional blocks. CSX is a very flexible storage format that can be further extended to incorporate other families of substructures if necessary. Experimental evaluation on 15 matrices and two multicore platforms has demonstrated that CSX can lead to significant and steady performance improvements over CSR and other, state-of-the-art storage formats. Regarding preprocessing, CSX incorporates a unified approach for the supported substructures based on transformations and exhibits a complexity linear to the number of non-zero elements of the input matrix. Thorough inspection of the matrix to collect the vast majority of substructures leads to a preprocessing cost that is practical for offline preprocessing. To extend the applicability of CSX to online preprocessing, we propose preprocessing strategies that scan a subset of the considered substructures or perform sampling of the matrix. In this way we are able to trade a small part of performance for a large part of preprocessing cost. Our view is that the above two characteristics of CSX (superior performance and low preprocessing cost) make this storage format the best approach for SpMV. For future work we intend to further reduce the preprocessing cost of CSX and report results from the incorporation of SpMV with CSX in applications like iterative solvers (CG, GMRES, etc.).

Acknowledgements

This paper is part of the 03ED255 research project, implemented within the framework of the 'Reinforcement Programme of Human Research Manpower' (PENED) and co-financed by National and

Community Funds (20% from the Greek Ministry of Development-General Secretariat of Research and Technology and 80% from E.U. – European Social Fund).

References

[1] R. C. Agarwal, F. G. Gustavson, and M. Zubair. A high performance algorithm using pre-processing for the sparse matrix-vector multiplication. In *Supercomputing'92*, pages 32–41, Minn., MN, November 1992. IEEE.

[2] W. K. Anderson, W. D. Gropp, D. K. Kaushik, D. E. Keyes, and B. F. Smith. Achieving high sustained performance in an unstructured mesh CFD application. In *SC '99: Proceedings of the 1999 ACM/IEEE Conference on Supercomputing*, page 69, New York, NY, USA, 1999. ACM.

[3] K. Asanovic, R. Bodik, B. C. Catanzaro, J. J. Gebis, P. Husbands, K. Keutzer, D. A. Patterson, W. L. Plishker, J. Shalf, S. W. Williams, and K. A. Yelick. The landscape of parallel computing research: A view from berkeley. Technical Report UCB/EECS-2006-183, EECS Department, University of California, Berkeley, December 18 2006.

[4] R. Barrett, M. Berry, T. F. Chan, J. Demmel, J. M. Donato, J. Dongarra, V. Eijkhout, R. Pozo, C. Romine, and H. V. der Vorst. *Templates for the Solution of Linear Systems: Building Blocks for Iterative Methods*. SIAM, Philadelphia, 1994.

[5] M. Belgin, G. Back, and C. J. Ribbens. Pattern-based sparse matrix representation for memory-efficient smvm kernels. In *ICS '09: Proceedings of the 23rd international conference on Supercomputing*, pages 100–109, New York, NY, USA, 2009. ACM.

[6] U. V. Catalyuerek and C. Aykanat. Decomposing irregularly sparse matrices for parallel matrix-vector multiplication. *Lecture Notes In Computer Science*, 1117:75–86, 1996.

[7] T. Davis. University of Florida sparse matrix collection. *NA Digest*, 97(23):7, 1997.

[8] R. Geus and S. Röllin. Towards a fast parallel sparse matrix-vector multiplication. In *Parallel Computing: Fundamentals and Applications, International Conference ParCo*, pages 308–315. Imperial College Press, 1999.

[9] G. Goumas, K. Kourtis, N. Anastopoulos, V. Karakasis, and N. Koziris. Performance evaluation of the sparse matrix-vector multiplication on modern architectures. *The Journal of Supercomputing*, 2008.

[10] E. Im and K. Yelick. Optimizing sparse matrix-vector multiplication on SMPs. In *9th SIAM Conference on Parallel Processing for Scientific Computing*. SIAM, March 1999.

[11] E. Im and K. Yelick. Optimizing sparse matrix computations for register reuse in SPARSITY. *Lecture Notes in Computer Science*, 2073:127–136, 2001.

[12] V. Karakasis, G. Goumas, and N. Koziris. A comparative study of blocking storage methods for sparse matrices on multicore architectures. In *12th IEEE International Conference on Computational Science and Engineering (CSE-09)*, Vancouver, Canada, 2009. IEEE Computer Society.

[13] D. Keppel, S. J. Eggers, and R. R. Henry. A case for runtime code generation. Technical Report UWCSE 91-11-04, University of Washington Department of Computer Science and Engineering, November 1991.

[14] K. Kourtis, G. Goumas, and N. Koziris. Improving the performance of multithreaded sparse matrix-vector multiplication using index and value compression. In *37th International Conference on Parallel Processing (ICPP'08)*, pages 511–519, Sept. 2008.

[15] K. Kourtis, G. Goumas, and N. Koziris. Optimizing sparse matrix-vector multiplication using index and value compression. In *CF '08: Proceedings of the 2008 conference on Computing frontiers*, pages 87–96, New York, NY, USA, 2008. ACM.

[16] C. Lattner and V. Adve. LLVM: A Compilation Framework for Lifelong Program Analysis & Transformation. In *Proceedings of the 2004 International Symposium on Code Generation and Optimization (CGO'04)*, Palo Alto, California, Mar 2004.

[17] J. Mellor-Crummey and J. Garvin. Optimizing sparse matrix-vector product computations using unroll and jam. *International Journal of High Performance Computing Applications*, 18(2):225, 2004.

[18] J. C. Pichel, D. B. Heras, J. C. Cabaleiro, and F. F. Rivera. Improving the locality of the sparse matrix-vector product on shared memory multiprocessors. In *PDP*, pages 66–71. IEEE Computer Society, 2004.

[19] A. Pinar and M. T. Heath. Improving performance of sparse matrix-vector multiplication. In *Supercomputing'99*, Portland, OR, November 1999. ACM SIGARCH and IEEE.

[20] Y. Saad. SPARSKIT: A basic tool kit for sparse matrix computations. Technical report, Computer Science Department, University of Minnesota, Minneapolis, MN 55455, June 1994. Version 2.

[21] Y. Saad. *Iterative Methods for Sparse Linear Systems*. SIAM, Philadelphia, PA, USA, 2003.

[22] S. Toledo. Improving the memory-system performance of sparse-matrix vector multiplication. *IBM Journal of Research and Development*, 41(6):711–725, 1997.

[23] R. Vuduc, J. Demmel, K. Yelick, S. Kamil, R. Nishtala, and B. Lee. Performance optimizations and bounds for sparse matrix-vector multiply. In *Supercomputing*, Baltimore, MD, November 2002.

[24] R. W. Vuduc and H. Moon. Fast sparse matrix-vector multiplication by exploiting variable block structure. In *High Performance Computing and Communications*, volume 3726 of *Lecture Notes in Computer Science*, pages 807–816. Springer, 2005.

[25] J. White and P. Sadayappan. On improving the performance of sparse matrix-vector multiplication. In *HiPC '97: 4th International Conference on High Performance Computing*, 1997.

[26] J. Willcock and A. Lumsdaine. Accelerating sparse matrix computations via data compression. In *ICS '06: Proceedings of the 20th annual International Conference on Supercomputing*, pages 307–316, New York, NY, USA, 2006. ACM Press.

[27] S. Williams, L. Oilker, R. Vuduc, J. Shalf, K. Yelick, and J. Demmel. Optimization of sparse matrix-vector multiplication on emerging multicore platforms. In *SC '07: Proceedings of the 2007 ACM/IEEE conference on Supercomputing*, Reno, NV, November 2007.

Auto-tuning of Fast Fourier Transform on Graphics Processors

Yuri Dotsenko†   Sara S. Baghsorkhi‡   Brandon Lloyd†   Naga K. Govindaraju†

†Microsoft Corporation   ‡University of Illinois at Urbana-Champaign
{yurido, dalloyd, nagag}@microsoft.com   bsadeghi@illinois.edu

Abstract

We present an auto-tuning framework for FFTs on graphics processors (GPUs). Due to complex design of the memory and compute subsystems on GPUs, the performance of FFT kernels over the range of possible input parameters can vary widely. We generate several variants for each component of the FFT kernel that, for different cases, are likely to perform well. Our auto-tuner composes variants to generate kernels and selects the best ones. We present heuristics to prune the search space and profile only a small fraction of all possible kernels. We compose optimized kernels to improve the performance of larger FFT computations. We implement the system using the NVIDIA CUDA API and compare its performance to the state-of-the-art FFT libraries. On a range of NVIDIA GPUs and input sizes, our auto-tuned FFTs outperform the NVIDIA CUFFT 3.0 library by up to $38\times$ and deliver up to $3\times$ higher performance compared to a manually-tuned FFT.

Categories and Subject Descriptors   D.2.2 [*SOFTWARE ENGI- NEERING*]: Design Tools and Techniques—Software libraries

General Terms   Performance, Algorithms

Keywords   Fast Fourier Transform, FFT, GPU, high performance, auto-tuning, performance analysis, performance tuning

1. Introduction

Graphics Processing Units (GPUs) are becoming increasingly popular in high-performance computing due to their low cost and high performance. Recent GPUs such as the NVIDIA Fermi GPUs have better support for double precision arithmetic widely used in scientific workloads and ECC memory for reliable computations. Over 0.5 Teraflop/s of double precision and a Teraflop of single precision performance combined with a peak memory bandwidth of over 150 GB/s, make GPUs ideal computing platforms for memory-intensive workloads such as Fast Fourier Transforms (FFTs).

FFTs are fundamental to many fields of science and engineering. They are widely applied in many high-performance problems including fluid mechanics, biomedical engineering, cryptography, wave simulations, etc. Recent research has demonstrated that GPUs can significantly accelerate performance of FFTs on GPUs as compared to CPUs [5, 11, 18]. With the increasing adoption of GPGPU

computing in commodity applications such as games and multimedia, hardware vendors are making significant improvements to each new generation of GPUs. Thus GPU capabilities are improving more rapidly than those of CPUs. Optimizing libraries to leverage these new capabilities is tedious and time consuming. Auto-tuning techniques are necessary to handle the increasing complexity in GPU compute and memory subsystems. Nukada and Matsuoka [10] use tuning for optimizing 3D FFT performance on GPUs, but their approach has limited search space and is unlikely to be efficient for arbitrary FFT configurations. In this paper, we present a complete FFT framework to optimize an FFT library for arbitrary dimensions and sizes.

Our main contributions are as follows:

- **FFT Kernel Generation:** We present an extensive analysis of factors affecting performance of an FFT kernel and design an FFT kernel generator to construct variants amenable to auto- tuning. These include algorithmic variants for FFT kernel generation such as Stockham or transposed Stockham formulations, accounting for the impact of the stride of concurrent memory accesses, padding for shared memory exchanges, twiddle factor optimizations, and I/O specializations.

- **Pruning Heuristics:** We present heuristics that significantly prune the auto-tuning search space. We account for the GPU computation and memory models to motivate our pruning heuristics in order to achieve high GPU resource utilization and memory performance.

- **Runtime Execution and Size:** We present profile-based techniques to reduce the number of variants that need to be stored in the FFT library.

We implemented an auto-tuning framework that automatically optimizes FFT kernel variants using the NVIDIA CUDA API and tested its performance on different NVIDIA GPU architectures. On a large distribution of sizes, the average performance of our auto-tuned libraries is 150, 125 and 50 Gigaflops/s for single precision on NVIDIA GTX280, GTX260 and 8800GTX GPUs, respectively. For double precision, we achieve an average performance of over 23 and 18 Gigaflops/s on NVIDIA GTX280 and GTX260 GPUs, respectively. Our algorithms achieve over $4\times$ higher performance than NVIDIA CUFFT 3.0 for the majority of the sizes and $> 30\%$ higher performance over the CUFFT best-case performance. Compared to Intel MKL performance on a high-end dual quad-core Xeon CPU, we achieve on average $12\times$ and $3.3\times$ higher performance for single and double precision for a wide range of 1D FFTs.

2. Related work

In this section, we provide a brief overview of the related work on auto-tuning techniques that particularly target FFTs on GPUs and CPUs. Van Loan [17] provides an overview of FFT algorithms and their variants.

The earliest FFT implementations on GPUs [9, 15, 8, 6, 16, 4] used graphics APIs such as DirectX or OpenGL to implement FFTs. The performance of these algorithms were limited by the restrictions present in these APIs such as lack of scatter support, access to local storage for data reuse and fine grain synchronization primitives. Recent research has focused on improving performance of FFTs on GPUs using computing languages such as CUDA [5, 11, 18]. These FFT algorithms achieve high performance on GPUs but require significant manual tuning to optimize the kernels. Because the hardware characteristics of GPUs varies widely with newer generation GPUs offering better memory hierarchy support, including larger local storage and register file sizes, memory bus widths, etc., it is non-trivial to optimize these algorithms for a range of GPUs.

Researchers have explored using auto-tuning algorithms on CPUs and FPGAs to optimize FFTs. Frigo and Johnson [3] presented an auto-tuning framework for optimizing FFT codelets on CPUs and Cell processors. Spiral [13] is a generator for optimized FFT libraries on FPGAs and CPUs. Chellappa et al. [1] later extended the algorithms to work well on Cell processors. These techniques are complimentary to ours. The factors that affect FFT performance on GPUs can be quite different than those on a CPU.

More recently, researchers have explored auto-tuning techniques for improving performance of algorithms such as GEMM and FFTs on GPUs. Ryoo et al. [14] used program optimization carving strategies to explore the optimization space and applied them to matrix multiplication. Li et al. [7] described auto-tuning techniques for optimizing GEMM on GPUs. Nukada and Matsuoka [10] presented an auto-tuning framework to optimize 3D FFT algorithms for mixed-radix sizes (the size of a dimension is $2^i 3^j 5^k$) on GPUs and demonstrated significant performance improvement against prior state-of-the-art FFT algorithms on GPUs. They efficiently optimize 1D FFTs of small sizes that are located contiguously in GPU memory and fit into shared memory; however, this set represents only a tiny subset of all FFT configurations. They perform a brute-force search on the entire space that is very large. We employ a similar approach for small 1D FFTs; however, we use a larger search space to utilize the GPU more efficiently and present space-pruning heuristics that reduce the auto-tuning time significantly. For other FFT configurations, our approaches are entirely different. Nukada and Matsuoka do not take advantage of fast on-chip shared memory, severely restricting the search space. This leads to sub-optimal performance, especially for FFTs of larger sizes (e.g., 1D FFTs) that require several passes over data located in GPU memory. In contrast, we exploit the shared memory to perform auto-tuning on a much larger space. This enables us to achieve higher performance for most FFT configurations due to reduction in the number of passes and more efficient GPU utilization. Another important difference is that we select the best performing FFT primitives taking into account input and output strides, which has significant impact on performance for most FFT configurations. We devise heuristics to reduce the auto-tuning time and to maintain reasonable profile size. While Nukada and Matsuoka's techniques can be applied to compute optimized FFTs for particular sizes, they may not be practical for optimizing an FFT library handling arbitrary dimensions and sizes. We present the first practical auto-tuning FFT framework on GPUs that can generate an optimized FFT library for arbitrary sizes and dimensions.

3. Overview

3.1 Graphics Processing Units

A GPU is made up of a number of multi-processors designed to handle a large number of threads. The execution model consists of many threads all running the same program called a *kernel*. All threads can access data stored in a high latency, high bandwidth global memory. The GPU schedules threads on each multiprocessor in groups of a fixed number of threads called *thread blocks*. Threads within a thread block can communicate with each other through a processor's low latency local storage, referred to as shared memory, and can synchronize using a barrier primitive. Thread blocks are further decomposed into small groups known on NVIDIA GPUs as *warps*. Threads within a warp share a common instruction counter and are processed in SIMD fashion on the multi-processor, with divergent branches handled by predication. Each thread is also allocated a fixed number of the private registers. Kernel performance on a GPU is affected by computational load, multi-processor resource utilization, and memory performance. AMD and NVIDIA GPU architectures are similar, but AMD uses different nomenclature (thread blocks/*groups*, shared memory/*local memory*, warps/*wavefronts*).

Each multi-processor has a limited amount of shared memory, registers, thread contexts, and thread block contexts. The number of threads that can be concurrently scheduled on the multi-processor, or *occupancy*, is constrained by these resources. Because the latency of global memory is handled by switching between active thread warps whenever a stall occurs, high occupancy is important to overlap memory accesses with computation. Multiple blocks can be scheduled on a multi-processor to provide additional warps. A kernel that uses too many registers, too much shared memory, or thread blocks that are too small may have low occupancy, which can lead to lower performance. Thread blocks with large number of threads can also degrade performance because fewer blocks are available to cover stalls caused by synchronization.

Memory performance can vary based on the memory access patterns in the kernel. On NVIDIA GPUs, when threads within the same half-warp access the same banks of the interleaved shared memory, a bank conflict occurs and the accesses are serialized. Bank conflicts should be avoided. When thread warps access contiguous locations in global memory, the accesses are coalesced into a smaller number of accesses and achieve higher performance. Global memory performance can also be affected by the access stride. Even coalesced accesses at large strides can exhibit poor performance due to "partition camping" where accesses are concentrated in just a few DRAM banks. The best memory performance comes by avoiding memory accesses altogether and storing the data in registers, but the number of registers available per thread is typically quite small.

3.2 Fast Fourier Transform

The Discrete Fourier Transform (DFT) of a sequence $x = x_0, \ldots, x_{N-1}$ and its inverse are defined as follows:

$$X_k = \sum_{n=0}^{N-1} x_n \omega_N^{kn}, \qquad x_n = 1/N \sum_{k=0}^{N-1} X_k \omega_N^{-kn},$$

where $k \in [0, N-1]$ and $\omega_N = e^{-2\pi i/N}$. A multi-dimensional DFT is computed by performing a multi-DFT independently along each dimension. To describe multi-dimensional sequences we will introduce some notation. We denote the dimensions of a multi-dimensional sequence by a tuple with the size of each dimension, represented by a capital letter, listed in reverse order, e.g. an $N_1 \times N_2 \times N_3$ sequence is denoted (N_3, N_2, N_1). We denote a specific element in the sequence by the tuple (n_3, n_2, n_1) with the corresponding small letter variables representing indices $n_i \in [0, N_i - 1]$. Assuming that the sequence is stored in a row-major array, the linear address of an element (n_3, n_2, n_1), denoted

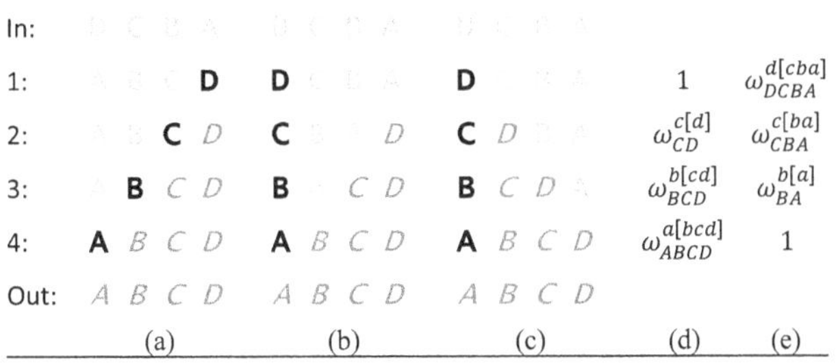

	(a)	(b)	(c)	(d)	(e)
In:	_D C B A_	_D C B A_	_D C B A_		
1:	_A B C_ **D**	**D** _D_ **D**	**D**	1	$\omega_{DCBA}^{d[cba]}$
2:	**C** _D_ **C** _D_	**C** _D_	**C** _D_	$\omega_{CD}^{c[d]}$	$\omega_{CBA}^{c[ba]}$
3:	**B** _C D_	**B** _C D_	**B** _C D_	$\omega_{BCD}^{b[cd]}$	$\omega_{BA}^{b[a]}$
4:	**A** _B C D_	**A** _B C D_	**A** _B C D_	$\omega_{ABCD}^{a[bcd]}$	1
Out:	_A B C D_	_A B C D_	_A B C D_		

Figure 1. (a) Cooley-Tukey, (b) Stockham, and (c) Transposed Stockham FFT algorithms using a 4-dimensional partitioning (D, C, B, A). The partition being transformed in each step is shown in bold. Untransformed partitions are shown in gray and transformed partitions in italicized blue. (d) Pre-twiddle and (e) post-twiddle factors.

$[n_3 n_2 n_1]$, is $((n_3 \cdot N_2 + n_2)N_1 + n_1$. Consider a multi-DFT on the second dimension. It is computed by performing $M = N_3 \cdot N_1$ DFTs of size N_2. The elements of the sequence in each DFT share a common DFT index $m = [n_3 n_1]$ and vary in the index n_2.

The term "Fast Fourier Transform" (FFT) refers to an entire family of algorithms for computing the DFT. An FFT factorizes the DFT to reduce the number of computations from $O(N^2)$ to $O(N \log N)$. An FFT of a single sequence can be computed by partitioning it into multiple dimensions and transforming each dimension, similar to multi-dimensional DFTs. Figure 1 shows several possible ways to arrange this computation. The Cooley-Tukey algorithm first reverses the partitions and then transforms each partition in-place. The Stockham and Transposed Stockham algorithms perform a multi-dimensional transpose in each step that results in the correct order for the output.

One difference from the multi-dimensional DFT is that each step requires that each element be scaled by a *twiddle factor* either before or after the DFT. We refer to this operation as *pre-twiddle* and *post-twiddle*, respectively. Pre-/post-twiddle correspond to what are commonly known in the FFT literature as decimation-in-time and decimation-in-frequency algorithms, respectively. The twiddle factor for each element is $\omega_{N_i L}^{n_i l}$, where n_i is the element's index in the partition being transformed N_i, L is the total number of elements in the untransformed partitions for post-twiddle or the transformed partitions for pre-twiddle, and l is the linearization of the partitions in L with indices in-order for pre-twiddle and reversed for post-twiddle (see Figure 1). Because L is empty for the first step of pre-twiddle and the last step of post-twiddle, the twiddle factors are 1.

If all of the partitions are the same size R, the algorithm is referred to as a *radix-R* FFT. When the partition size varies, the algorithm is referred to as a *mixed radix* FFT.

4. FFT kernels

To compute an $M \times N$ multi-FFT on the GPU, we partition the data, if necessary, and invoke a multi-FFT kernel to transform each partition. Each thread block of the kernel performs $M_b \leq M$ FFTs of size N_b, the size of the the current partition. We combine the FFT, the multi-dimensional transpose, and the multiplication by twiddle factors in a single kernel. For small partition sizes, each thread reads elements of a single FFT directly into registers and performs the computation. For larger partitions, the kernel applies an FFT recursively. In this case, each thread holds data for only

---

1. Read data from global memory into registers
2. Global pre-twiddle (if any)
3. Compute M_b FFTs. For each subpartition:
   (a) Local pre-twiddle
   (b) Compute FFT for data in registers
   (c) Exchange data through shared memory
4. Global post-twiddle (if any)
5. Scale and write data to global memory

Figure 2. Overall structure of an FFT kernel.

one subpartition at a time in registers and must exchange data with other threads through shared memory at each step. Finally, the data is scaled (for inverse) and written back to global memory. Figure 2 shows the overall structure of the FFT kernel.

There are many possible variations for an FFT kernel. Some of the variations depend on the precision and data type of the input, e.g., single or double, real or complex. Others are high level algorithmic variations that may have impact on performance, e.g., partitioning scheme, partition sizes, and pre- vs. post-twiddle. Finally, some variants differ by the low-level optimizations applied to the FFT kernel such as optimized memory access patterns for particular configurations or the number of FFTs to compute in a single thread block. These low-level optimizations are based on hardware characteristics that can significantly vary across different GPUs. Not all variations have impact on performance. An important contribution of this research was to determine factors that significantly affect performance and to express them in a form applicable to auto-tuning.

While it is possible to write a generic kernel that takes into account all possible variations, it would be quite slow. To achieve high performance it is critical to specialize the FFT kernel. For example, making certain variables constant may enable the compiler to produce more efficient code via loop unrolling, dead code elimination, and control flow simplification. Dead code elimination is particularly important on GPUs because eliminating a code block that utilizes a lot of registers may reduce the register count for the entire kernel, leading to higher occupancy and performance. Specializing a kernel for specific configurations can eliminate the costly branches required for a more general code. The downside of specialization is a larger space of parameters to tune the FFT kernel for and therefore, larger profile size and auto-tuning time. In this section, we will discuss the various components of the FFT kernel and the specializations that we use.

4.1 Framework

Global memory performance is not always uniform for reads and writes and tends to degrade at higher strides. To better conform to the memory performance of a particular GPU we include multiple variants for the high-level FFT algorithm that have different memory access patterns. We use both the Stockham and Transposed Stockham algorithms. The former reads with high stride and writes with lower strides while the latter reads from lower strides and writes to high stride. We specialize the kernel based on the algorithm type to make sure certain assumptions hold about the relative size of the input and output strides.

4.2 FFT size decomposition

Given a large FFT size, we decompose it into smaller partitions that can be computed within a thread block. Within a thread block, we decompose each partition further into subpartions that can be performed entirely in registers by a single thread. We refer to the size of these subpartitions as the FFT radices. We hand-optimized codelets to compute an $N_t \times M_t$ multi-FFT for $N_t \in \{2, 3, 4, 5, 8\}$. We also have routines for $N_t \in \{6, 9, 10, 12, 15, 16\}$ which simply apply the Stockham algorithm in registers using the optimized codelets.

The choice of the decomposition in a thread block can significantly affect the resources used such as the number of registers, the number of active threads and the amount of shared memory used. The smallest radix in a given decomposition defines the maximum number of threads necessary to execute. Larger radices require more registers to perform the FFT computation. Therefore, in a given decomposition, the largest radix defines the maximum number of registers that each thread requires for the FFT. The combination of these two factors can significantly vary the performance of the underlying kernel as it affects the occupancy on a GPU multiprocessor.

A thread block can be two-dimensional. Threads in one dimension cooperate to compute the FFT of a single sequence. Threads in the other dimension work on independent FFTs. We refer to the size of each dimension as T_n and T_m, respectively. Note that $T_m = M_b$. We define step i of kernel FFT by a triplet $\langle N_t^i, M_t^i, T_n^i \rangle$, where N_t^i is the register FFT radix, M_t^i is the number of FFTs batched together in registers, and T_n^i is the number of threads used for a single register FFT.

4.3 Shared memory exchange

When threads cooperate to compute the FFT kernel, they must exchange values between each register FFT. This is done to accomplish the subpartition shuffling. When performing the shared memory exchange, bank conflicts can occur. Bank conflicts can be alleviated with padding, as shown for powers-of-two [5] or for simple cases [10]. Our kernels exhibit more complex patterns due to register FFT batching and processing several FFTs in a block. Instead of deriving an analytical formula, we estimate the cost of each transpose using a machine model. Shared memory accesses and index computation contribute to transpose cost. We compute shared memory locations and corresponding banks that will be accessed during kernel generation. We calculate the degree of conflict D for each half-warp and assume that the cost of shared memory access is D. We estimate the cost of computing the padded index $Pad(i) = i + \lfloor \frac{i}{PadStride} \rfloor \times PadSize$, which is dependent on radix decomposition. We then simulate several padding strides and offsets and select the one that minimizes the transpose cost.

4.4 Twiddle computation

Multi-stage thread block FFT, shown in Figure 2, requires twiddle factors that can be computed in several ways: (1) computed on-the-fly as needed, (2) precomputed in the kernel and stored in registers, (3) precomputed in the kernel in and stored in shared memory, or (4) precomputed on the host and stored in constant memory. Each method presents tradeoff between cycles spent computing twiddle factors, access speed (constant and shared memories are slower than registers), and memory and registers used. Twiddle factors can be computed in the kernel using fast transcendental approximation instructions, higher precision routines that are slower and require many registers, iterative algorithms, or a combination of these. Because it is not always possible determine beforehand which twiddle factor mode will perform best in a given configuration we generate several kernel variants considering the above cases, and auto-tune them.

Modes (2) and (3) achieve the greatest benefit when using a *streaming FFT kernel*, which computes multiple sets of M_b FFTs by wrapping the steps in Figure 2 in a loop. We found that it is actually not necessary to explicitly precompute the twiddle factors outside of the loop because the compiler can hoist on-the-fly computations from inside the loop and cache the values in registers. We carefully choose the number of thread blocks to invoke so as to maximize GPU utilization. Using the formulas from the CUDA Occupancy Calculator [2] and the known shared memory usage and register and thread counts for a kernel, we compute the number of active thread blocks that can run across all the multiprocessors. We invoke this number of thread blocks and compute the number of loop iterations accordingly.

4.5 I/O specializations

FFT kernel performance strongly depends on efficient utilization of memory bandwidth. We support several I/O specializations that optimize common access patterns for FFT kernels. Let S_i and S_o denote the strides of FFT elements for kernel's read and write, respectively. We specialize for $S_i = S_o = 1$ case when the FFT can be computed in one pass. We call this kernel a *row* kernel, since FFTs are computed along the rows of the 2D matrix. The maximum size of row kernel is limited by the amount of available shared memory. The accesses are poorly coalesced for small N. We address this by additionally specializing the kernel to fetch a contiguous block of M_b FFTs into shared memory and perform a *coalesce transpose* [5] to properly rearrange data.

The *column* kernels, which operate along the columns of the 2D matrix, are additionally specialized to improve coalescing. First, we specialize kernels that operate at large strides (*LS* kernels) $\max(S_i, S_o) \geq M_b$; this optimizes memory accesses for the most common case. However, *LS* kernels do not coalesce memory accesses for the second important case when $S_i = 1$ or $S_o = 1$. We optimize I/O for this case by performing a coalesce transpose, and call these kernels *SSC* – small-stride coalesced. *SSC* kernels also coalesce data for small power-of-two strides $S \leq M_b$, since we always choose M_b to be a power-of-two. The remaining cases are hard to optimize efficiently due to complexity of the FFT memory access patterns. We handle them with the *SSN* (small-stride no-coalescing) kernels without coalescing specialization. *SSN* kernels are used rather infrequently, primarily to transform small-sized lower dimensions of multidimensional FFTs.

5. Auto-tuning of FFTs

Our FFT auto-tuning system performs offline tuning; *i.e.*, it collects a performance profile for a combination of the GPU, compiler and GPU driver. No new kernels are generated or profiled at runtime. The auto-tuner does a parameter sweep over the tuning space and creates a performance profile that, for each possible step of a global FFT, contains the runtime estimation and parameters of the best performing kernel variant. Profiling is done for a large data volume, e.g., 128 MB, since GPUs are typically used for large data sizes to fully leverage the available massive parallelism. The collected profile information is used at runtime to create the best partitioning and kernels to use for mixed radix FFT.

We split the space into three parts that we call the FFT space, stride space, and kernel space. The FFT space includes:

Precision type : single (SP), double (DP)
Data type : complex, real
Direction : forward or inverse

Radix : $N_b = 2^i 3^j 5^k$ of the FFT size decomposition
Algorithmic variants : Stockham, Transposed Stockham
Twiddle type : pre- or post-twiddle

The stride space represents pairs of input and output strides $\langle S_i, S_o \rangle$. A global FFT step corresponds to a combination of one FFT space point P_{FFT} and one stride pair.

A point P_K in the kernel space represents one specialized FFT kernel. The kernel space includes:

Kernel type : row or column
Decomposition of the kernel radix into $\langle N_t^i, M_t^i, T_n^i \rangle$
Number of FFTs in a thread block – M_b
Twiddle reuse type : single or streaming FFT kernel
Twiddle type : computed or table twiddle
Block type : full (M_b FFTs per block) or partial ($\leq M_b$ FFTs)
Row kernel I/O type : coalesced or uncoalesced
Column kernel I/O type : LS, SSC, SSN
Merging of global twiddle with I/O : yes or no
Pow2 global twiddle stride : use shifts instead of divisions
Iterative global twiddle : use trig. identities to apprx. sin/cos

We discussed most of the codelet specializations in Section 4.

Figure 3 gives an overview of our framework. We first generate the FFT space. For each P_{FFT}, we generate several variants of FFT kernels. Using similar variants with different M_b, we perform a preliminary step to prune slow-performing variants. The remaining variants are compiled in parallel to reduce compilation time. Row kernels require one profiling run; however, column kernels require many runs for different values of $\langle S_i, S_o \rangle$. Each new performance measurement updates the performance database that we use to prune slowly performing column kernels. We further reduce profile time and size by profiling only forward kernels and deriving profile of inverse-FFT kernels from the forward kernels. This approximation is reasonable since inverse FFT differs from forward FFT by only a few instructions. In the rest of the section, we present some of our pruning heuristics to reduce the tuning search space.

5.1 M_b pruning

M_b defines how many FFTs are batched in one thread block (TB) and has high impact on occupancy and coalescing. For example, if N_b is small, a kernel with $M_b = 1$ yields very low performance because the total number of FFTs that can run on one multi-processor is limited by the current maximum of 8 resident thread blocks per multi-processor (MP). Executing so few small FFTs per MP significantly under-utilizes the GPU. The inverse is also true: too many FFTs batched together may reduce overall performance because the cost of synchronization increases. In addition, GPU resources may be underutilized due to resource fragmentation, e.g. if a TB uses slightly more than a half of the shared memory, only one TB can be resident on a MP, and the remaining shared memory is not used. M_b value may also affect memory performance. For small N_b, we coalesce memory accesses in row kernels, but we cannot do so if M_b is very small, say 1. It is difficult to analytically determine the impact of M_b on performance for all combinations of N_b and M_b. Clearly, small radix and M_b combinations such as $N_b = 2$ and $M_b = 1$ can be pruned but it is unclear where the pruning boundary is. The decision is even harder because we do not know how many resources, such as registers, are required by a kernel until we compile the kernel. Instead of pruning M_b statically, we use a runtime "probe". We select matching variants, one per M_b, and compile and profile them. We sort M_b according to the probe performance. If probe's performance for a particular M_b is on average $\eta\%$ (say

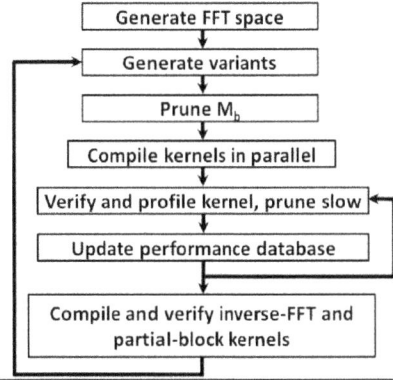

Figure 3. Scheme of our auto-tuning framework.

$\eta = 40\%$) slower than the best, we prune all kernels with this M_b, unless there was a run that yielded best performance. Pruning on M_b reduces the time required to compile and profile considerably. It also helps reduce the time to profile slow variants that may take long time to execute. Ranking M_b enhances column kernel pruning by increasing probability that fast variants run before slower ones.

5.2 Decomposition of FFT kernel radix

After $\langle N_t^i, M_t^i, T_n^i \rangle$ are computed, we prune some factorizations; we do not prune permutations of the same factorization because they may provide different number of I/O threads, padding, and code shapes. First, we prune configurations that require too many registers. We do not compile the kernel to reduce auto-tuning time; instead, we use the following heuristic. We prune a variant if the total register count $NumRegs = P \times (2 + TempRegThreshold) \times R \times T_n \times M_b$ exceeds the maximum register count per thread block, allowed by the architecture. P accounts for data precision: $P = 1$ for SP and $P = 2$ for DP. The factor of 2 is for real and imaginary components. $R = \max_i(N_t^i \times M_t^i)$ is the maximum number of FFT data elements held in registers. The $TempRegThreshold$ approximates how many additional, temporary registers are required to run FFTs; we chose $TempRegThreshold = 0.8$ so as to not prune too aggressively but to prune configurations that significantly exceed the machine register limit.

Second, we prune decompositions aggregating small radices. Small radices such as 2 and 3 lead to decomposition explosion – it is still fast to generate them, but compilation and profiling may be infeasible. Moreover, the number of shared-memory exchanges is large for decompositions with a lot of stages, and such decompositions are unlikely to perform well due to extra synchronization and instructions necessary to perform the exchanges. We prune a decomposition, if there are two factors N_t^i and N_t^j such that $N_t^k = N_t^i N_t^j$ and N_t^k is also a factor in the decomposition. This means that instead of two stages $\langle N_t^i, M_t^i, T_n^i \rangle$ with $M_t^i = N_t^j M_t^k$, and $\langle N_t^j, M_t^j, T_n^j \rangle$ with $M_t^j = N_t^i M_t^k$, we perform one stage $\langle N_t^k, M_t^k, T_n^k \rangle$ with a larger radix $N_t^k = N_t^i N_t^j$. One stage of a larger radix FFT is faster because there is no shared-memory transpose (an equivalent transpose happens in registers). Moreover, the composite radix N_t^k may be hand-optimized. Note that if there is no "assimilating" larger radix, we do not prune the decomposition. This lets us keep decompositions consisting of only small radices, e.g., $16 = 2 \times 2 \times 2 \times 2$.

5.3 Row and column kernel tuning

The kernel space for row kernels is relatively small, since they do not require algorithmic and twiddle specializations. The row kernels always operate at stride 1, and require only one performance sample per kernel, which takes very little time to collect. Almost all auto-tuning time is spent in compiling the variants. The variant generation time is negligible for both row and column kernels.

The tuning of column kernels is more time consuming. The kernel space is much larger. In addition, the performance of column kernels strongly depends on $\langle S_i, S_o \rangle$ stride values. The general trend is that performance decreases as strides increase, but the decrease is not monotonic or predictable. Therefore, we also perform the parameter sweep for each kernel at varying input and output strides to capture the behavior. However, the stride space is very large. We tune for a total data size of 2^{24} complex elements (SP), for which there are ≈ 115K legal stride pairs that are powers of 2, 3, and 5, which already makes the space too large. Moreover, there are many more legal stride pairs that are not powers of 2, 3, and 5, which may be induced by the lower dimensions of a multidimensional FFT. So, it is unrealistic to collect the exact performance profile for all legal stride combinations. Instead, we sample the stride space and approximate performance of a particular $\langle S_i, S_o \rangle$ pair by its closest stride sample from the same class.

We use a heuristic to identify sampling stride pairs $\langle S_i, S_o \rangle$. We classify $\langle S_i, S_o \rangle$ into five classes: $\langle Pow2, Pow2 \rangle$, $\langle CO, CO \rangle$, $\langle CO, NC \rangle$, $\langle NC, CO \rangle$, $\langle NC, NC \rangle$, where $Pow2$ denotes a power-of-two stride, CO denotes a stride for which most accesses are coalesced ($CO = CW \times k$, where CW is the coalesce width of the GPU, or CO is a small power-of-two for a SSC kernel), NC denotes other strides that make most accesses uncoalesced. The power-of-two stride pairs form a special class, rather than being a subset of $\langle CO, CO \rangle$, because on some GPUs performance of column kernels significantly degrades for large power-of-two strides, e.g. on the GTX280 that has 8 memory banks. This degradation is probably caused by partition camping and associativity effects.

We partition S_i and S_o dimensions into intervals; this induces a rectangular grid on the stride space. We select a sample pair for each stride pair class and for each block of the grid (if a legal stride pair exists). To keep the auto-tuning time manageable, it is desirable that the number of samples be relatively small. Based on this requirement and the observation that for large strides of the same class, the performance does not change as much as for smaller strides, we partition S_i and S_o dimensions into logarithmically-scaled intervals.

We measure runtime of a generated column kernel for each legal sample stride, and record t_e, time per element, in the performance database. The total number of samples is still very large and we use pruning to abort profiling of slow variants. We prune any kernel that exceeds shared memory or thread count limits. We allow kernels to exceed the maximum register limit by a small threshold, since registers can be spilled. After profiling, we record the best time per stride sample in performance database records. When profiling a column kernel, we count the number of slow samples that take more than $\eta\%$ (say $\eta = 20\%$) more time to run than the best recorded time. When the number of slow samples exceeds a certain threshold (say 20), we declare the kernel slow and do not profile it further. We reset the slow sample count each time the variant shows time that is better than the recorded best.

5.4 Schedule creation

After the tuning is done, we use the performance database to construct a partitioning and collection of kernel variants that delivers high-performance. A large FFT of length N is computed by partitioning the data into multiple dimensions and applying a kernel to each dimension. We refer to such a partitioning as a *schedule*. We take the estimated runtime per element t_e of each partition from the performance database. We collect performance profiles for several kernel radices, therefore there are several decompositions of N. We enumerate all schedules and select the schedule with minimum t_e. A schedule is created and cached before the FFT is executed; the overhead is on the order of milliseconds, which is negligible if the schedule is reused several times.

The performance database does not contain precise t_e for each stride pair. To get an estimated t_e for a given $\langle S_i, S_o \rangle$, we locate the closest sample pair within the same class; we use the Euclidean distance metric. The prediction is not perfect and introduces error. To estimate this error, we selected an FFT configuration for Stockham, pre-twiddle, radix-16 NS kernel and measured its performance for each legal stride pair $\langle S_i, S_o \rangle$, $S_i = 2^{i_1} 3^{j_1} 5^{k_1}$, $S_o = 2^{i_2} 3^{j_2} 5^{k_2}$, $S_o \leq S_i \leq 2^{20}$, and compared measured performance with the predicted. We observe that for roughly 50% of the stride pairs the prediction is less than 10% off and 80% of the stride pairs have a prediction error less than 20%. In the schedules where these stride pair kernels are used, the average prediction error due to our stride pair performance approximation is around 7% for 1D FFTs.

We construct four schedules corresponding to the profiled algorithmic variants: Stockham or Transposed Stockham and pre- or post-twiddle. We then measure runtime of each schedule. The measurement is done lazily, whenever the user code invokes the FFT library. After a few pilot runs, the library decides on the best performing schedule and uses it for all following invocations. Since schedules usually have comparable performance, the impact on overall performance is negligible and is further amortized by several consecutive invocations. Note that different algorithmic variants can be selected for forward and inverse FFT. The runtime selection of the variants allows our library to deliver higher performance, partially compensating for the misprediction error.

5.5 Performance profile size

The collected performance profile is quite large. Each sample includes best measured t_e and corresponding kernel *id*. The size of runtime sample information can be controlled by reducing the amount of specialization and the number of samples, e.g., we can use fewer radices and coarser sampling intervals.

Many specialized kernels must be included into the performance profile. The *cubin* representation for compiled kernels that we currently use leads to the kernel code being much larger than that of performance data. We performed an additional study to reduce the number of kernels in the final profile by reducing the amount of kernel specialization in two ways. (1) We combined corresponding forward and inverse FFT kernels into a single, less specialized kernel. To compute the inverse FFT, the input is conjugated before computing the forward FFT and the output is conjugated afterwards. (2) We merged corresponding full- and partial-block kernels. Instead of static full-block specialization we dynamically detect whether an instance of a thread block executes M_b FFTs (full block) and invoke specialized code for this case. Applying both techniques leads to a factor of ≈ 4 reduction in the number of kernels and the overall kernel profile size, but comes at a cost of $\approx 4.5\%$ performance loss on-average.

GPU	Core Clock (MHz)	Shader Clock (MHz)	MP	Peak Perf. (GFlops)	Memory Clock (MHz)	Memory (MB)	Bus Width (bits)	Peak BW (GiB/s)	Registers per MP	Shared memory	Driver
GTX280	650	1300	30	936	1150	1024	512	137	16K	16K	196.21
GTX260	575	1350	24	777	1000	1024	448	104	16K	16K	196.21
8800GTX	575	1350	16	518	900	768	384	80	8K	16K	196.21

Figure 4. GPUs used in experiments. MP is the number of multi-processors. The warp width for all the GPUs is 32.

We biased the set of kernels included into the final profile towards more frequently used kernels. We select a set of representative FFT configurations and mine the performance database to detect fast kernels that are to be selected during schedule construction. All kernels that were not selected are removed from the database and replaced by the equivalent selected kernels. We constructed the sample profiling set that corresponds to an FFT of size N residing in memory at stride s, which represents a dimension of a multidimensional FFT. $\forall s \in S$, where S is the set of sample strides, we construct schedules for the second dimension N, such that $N = 2^i 3^j 5^k$ and $N \leq \frac{E}{s}$, where E is the total number of data elements. Note that $s = 1$ represents all mixed radix 1D FFTs. To generate set S, we perform a logarithmic sampling of $[1, E)$ to bias sample density towards smaller strides as a kernel's performance varies more for smaller strides than for larger strides.

To further reduce the library size, we apply standard compression algorithms to compress the kernels. As the data flow for the different kernels can be similar, there is significant redundancy and the compression algorithms achieve a high compression ratio. At run-time, the kernels required by the schedules are decompressed and cached for later execution.

6. Implementation and profiling

We implemented an FFT kernel generator that supports all specializations described in Sections 4 and 5. Our generator is written in C++ and targets NVIDIA's CUDA API, but can easily be extended to support DirectX or OpenCL. FFT kernel specializations are expressed either via compile-time constants or via hand-optimized codelets. The generator enumerates the space and, for each point, creates a CUDA function that performs the specific FFT computation. The performance database includes *cubin* kernels and their estimated runtimes. We profiled using a large multi-FFT with as many FFT sequences as can fit into 2^{24} (2^{23}) single (double) precision elements. We collected performance profile for forward-FFT, full-block kernels that support both real and complex inputs.

We profiled all feasible row kernels. The total number of variants is ≈ 300 per GPU; the size of performance samples is negligible. The majority of the auto-tuning time is spent in compiling the kernels.

The FFT space for column kernels is much larger. We specialized kernel radix, FFT algorithm, global twiddle type, global twiddle stride, and kernel I/O. This alone already contributes a factor of $\approx 16\cdot$ (number of radices) to the auto-tuning time and profile size. The majority of auto-tuning time is spent running the kernels. To keep the time and space manageable, we selected 2^i points to partition the stride space and added a few points for smaller strides since performance is more sensitive for smaller stride values; this resulted in 2666 total sample stride pairs. To study the space, we collected data for 53 radices (SP). This results in ≈ 522K performance samples and ≈ 44K kernels that may be used to run any mixed-radix FFT. Each sample requires 6 bytes: 2 bytes for kernel id, 2 bytes for time estimation, and 2 bytes for kernel variant parameters, totaling to ≈ 3MB uncompressed. Kernels are kept in a *cubin* form and compress to ≈ 45MB.

We also collected a performance profile for less specialized kernels that do not have forward/inverse FFT and full-/partial-block specializations. We observed $\approx 4\times$ reduction in the profile size and $\approx 4.5\%$ performance loss for a large sample set of FFTs. We conclude that removing these specializations is pragmatic.

To evaluated the effect of biased kernel selection, we reduced the initial performance database using three sample profiling sets S (see 5.5) of size 1 ($s=1$ or only 1D FFTs), ≈ 500 and 1000 samples. To estimate performance loss, we constructed a larger randomly-generated evaluation set $\{S', N'_s\}$ such that a pair $\langle s', n'_s \rangle$ describes a mixed radix FFT computation of the second dimension n'_s of a 2D FFT $s' \times n'_s$. To our surprise, we found almost no difference in average performance among all four data bases (for both fully and less specialized profiles), indicating that it may be enough to collect only kernels used by the 1D FFTs to yield a good performance profile for all FFT sizes and dimensions. The biased selection for $|S| = 1$ resulted in $\approx 13\times$ reduction in the total number of kernels!

Auto-tuning time depends on parameters selected for tuning (radices, sampled strides, algorithm and twiddle types, etc.), speed of the CUDA compiler, and the GPU(s). For row kernels, compilation time dominates. For column kernels, performance sampling dominates. To obtain a high-performance library requires 2–3 days on a single PC/GPU. Beyond that performance gain diminishes rapidly. Auto-tuning time can be further reduced by using multiple PCs and GPUs.

7. Performance results

Experimental Methodology: We evaluate our approach on three different GPUs: GTX280, GTX260, and 8800GTX with specifications shown in Figure 4. The GPUs differ in memory configuration, the amount of memory bandwidth and compute power. An older 8800GTX has stricter coalescing requirements as discussed elsewhere [12]. We also observed that large-stride memory accesses show better performance on GTX260 than on GTX280 despite less available bandwidth, especially, for strides that are multiples of a large power-of-two.

We compare performance of our auto-tuned library, which uses CUDA 2.3, to that of NVIDIA's FFT library (CUFFT) version 3.0 and Intel's MKL version 10.2, which was run with 8 threads on a 2.27GHz Intel quad-core dual Xeon L5520 machine. We also compare performance of 1D and 3D FFTs with results published in [5, 10]. We measure performance in GFlops/s, which we compute as $\frac{\sum_{d=1}^{D} M_d(5N_d log_2 N_d)}{\text{execution time}}$, where D is the total number of dimensions, $M_d = E/N_d$ is the number of FFTs along each dimension and E is the total number of elements. We measure runtime of 100 runs on GPU using CUDA events [12], and use the median as the execution time. We do not measure data transfer times and assume the data is already present in GPU video memory. We measure accuracy by performing a forward transform followed by an inverse transform on complex data uniformly distributed in $[-0.5, 0.5]$. We then compare the result to the original data and divide the root mean squared error by 2.

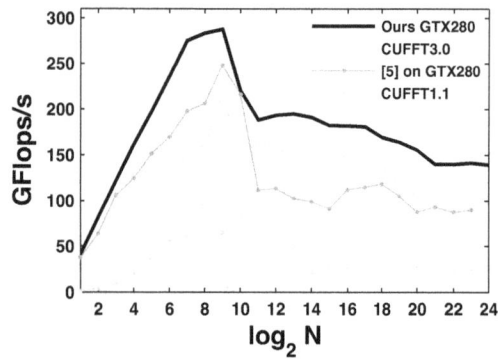

(a) SP power-of-two on GTX280

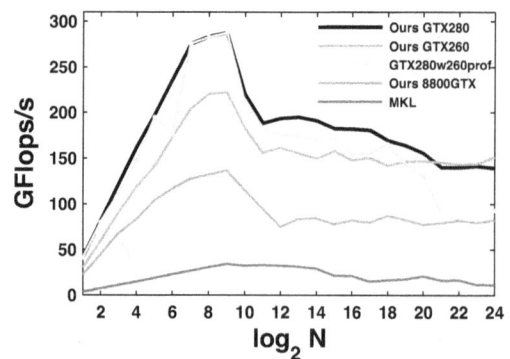

(b) SP power-of-two on GTX280, GTX260 and 8800GTX

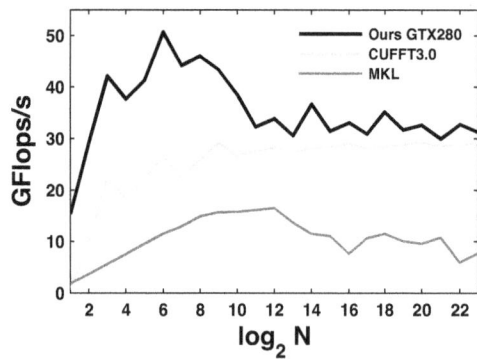

(c) DP power-of-two on GTX280

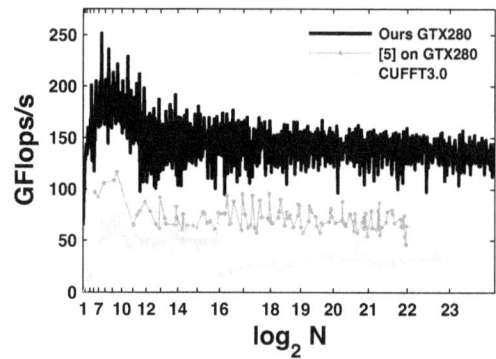

(d) SP mixed radix on GTX280

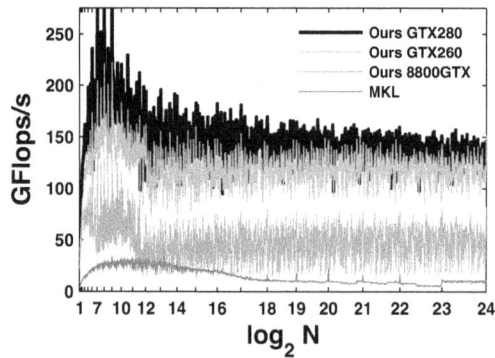

(e) SP mixed radix on GTX280, GTX260 and 8800GTX

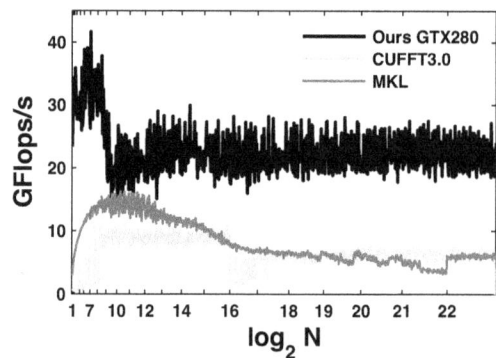

(f) DP mixed radix on GTX280

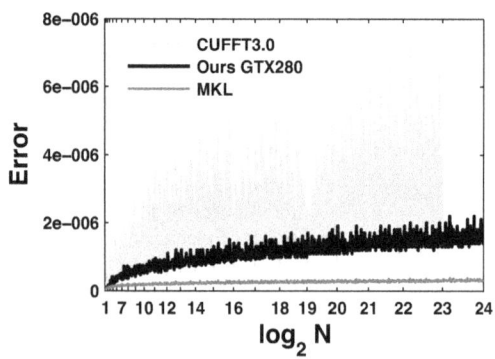

(g) Accuracy of single precision FFTs

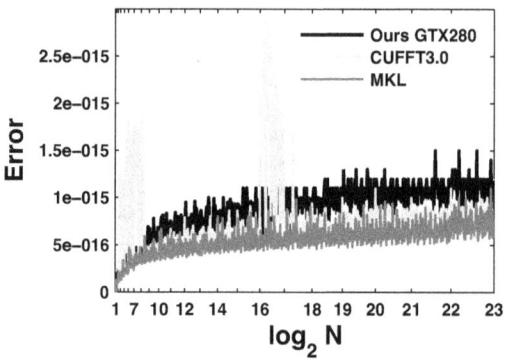

(h) Accuracy of double precision FFTs

Figure 5. Performance and accuracy of batched FFTs for single precision (SP) and double precision (DP)

Size	256x256x256	256x256x128	256x128x256	256x128x128	128x128x128	144x144x144	192x192x192	192x256x144
Ours	176	173	179	157	178	156	142	169
AT3dFFT	135	143	135	132	105	117	130	131
CUFFT3.0	failed	121	130	failed	failed	failed	failed	failed

Figure 6. Performance of 3D FFTs in GFlops/s

Power-of-two FFTs: Figure 5(a) shows performance of batched 1D power-of-two SP FFTs. We outperform CUFFT for all sizes by up to 90% for large N and up to 35x for small N. Such a high difference for small N is probably because CUFFT does not implement coalesce transpose. Our auto-tuned implementation outperforms a prior hand-optimized implementation [5] (curve *[5] on GTX280*) by up to 2x by automatically selecting the best-performing kernels and constructing efficient schedules. For $N \in [32, 2048]$, the improvement primarily comes from the optimization of thread block FFT twiddle, while for large N, efficient schedule construction wins over a hand-crafted schedule heuristic. For the previous implementation, there was a significant drop in performance when FFT does not fit into shared memory. This is not the case for the auto-tuned library, because our auto-tuned column kernels are much faster.

Figure 5(b) compares performance across GPUs. For all GPUs, sizes $N \in [2, 2048]$ are done in one pass using row kernels. The computation is bound by memory bandwidth for very small N, and the auto-tuner picks variants that coalesce loads and stores of several small FFTs and rearrange data using a coalesce transpose in shared-memory. Our auto-tuned libraries on GTX280 and GTX260 outperform 8800GTX due to higher compute capabilities and available memory bandwidth. For the same reason, our library on GTX280 outperforms GTX260 for most sizes; however, the performance becomes comparable for very large N. The performance on GTX280 drops faster as size increases due to degradation of effective memory bandwidth for accesses at larger power-of-two strides. The degradation is probably caused by associativity effects, because GTX280 has 8 memory banks, while GTX260 and 8800GTX have 7 and 6 memory banks, respectively. The performance curves are "flatter" for GTX260 and 8800GTX. Our library on GTX280 outperforms *MKL* by $9\times$ on average (up to $15.5\times$).

We also investigated the effect of using a profile from a different card. *GTX280w260prof* shows performance on a GTX280 using a profile obtained on a GTX260. The performance drops significantly for large N. We investigated the situation for $N = 2^{23}$ and found that the optimal schedule predicted for the GTX260 profile is $\langle 64, 64, 32, 64 \rangle$; however, radix-64 column kernel does not perform well for large strides on GTX280. The optimal schedule for the GTX280 profile is $\langle 32, 16, 32, 32, 16 \rangle$. Interestingly, it uses one more pass over the data, but still delivers higher performance by picking faster kernels.

Figure 5(c) compares the performance of power-of-two DP FFTs for our library, CUFFT and MKL. We outperform CUFFT by up to $25\times$ for very small N due to having better coalescing, $2\times$ for the mid-range due to using specialized row kernels, and 30% for large N. Compared to MKL, our library delivers on average $3.5\times$ higher performance (up to $8\times$).

Mixed Radix FFTs: Figures 5(d) and 5(e) show performance of our library on three GPUs, CUFFT on GTX280 and MKL for batched 1D mixed radix FFTs. On GTX280, our library outperforms CUFFT by up to $12\times$ for large N and by up to $38\times$ for small N. Even on an older-generation 8800GTX GPU, our library outperforms CUFFT3.0 on a GTX280. For CUFFT, mixed radix FFTs are $3\times$ slower than power-of-two FFTs and the performance

exhibits large variations. Our auto-tuned mixed radix FFTs perform comparably (within 20%) to power-of-two FFTs and performance curves are mostly flat for large N despite the fact that we approximate kernel performance for a particular stride pair $\langle S_i, S_o \rangle$ by using the closest suitable stride sample. Our library on GTX280 shows $12\times$ higher performance over MKL on average (up to $28\times$).

Figure 5(f) shows performance for mixed radix 1D DP FFTs on a GTX280. We outperform CUFFT by up to $4\times$ for large N and 100 times for small N. The bottleneck for DP FFTs is the performance of double precision arithmetic, especially transcendental functions for twiddle computation. The improvement comes primarily from the twiddle optimizations. We precompute thread block FFT twiddle factors, if any, on the CPU during the FFT schedule creation stage. The twiddle factors are retrieved from constant memory during kernel execution and may be cached in registers. The global twiddle is optimized via strength reduction of $\sin$ and $\cos$ using trigonometric identities. This improves performance by 2-3 times at the expense of slight decrease in accuracy. Compared to MKL, our library performs on average $3.3\times$ ($4\times$ for large N) times faster (up to $12.5\times$).

Figures 5(g) and 5(h) highlight the accuracy of the FFT algorithms. Our SP accuracy is in the order of 10^{-6} and is up to 6x better than the accuracy of CUFFT FFTs, which behaves erratically. The precision of MKL is in the order of 10^{-7} due to more precise $\sin$ and $\cos$. The DP accuracy is in the order of 10^{-16} to 10^{-15}. The DP accuracy of CUFFT is on average 23% higher than ours. We investigated the situation for $N = 900000$ that exhibits the highest difference. The error is introduced solely by the trigonometry strength reduction optimization in the global twiddle computation. If we use exact twiddle factors, the precision is slightly better than that of CUFFT's. However, using CUDA's DP $\sin$ and $\cos$ decreases performance by a factor of two. We believe that a slight loss of accuracy is an acceptable price to pay for 2-3$\times$ higher performance on GT200-generation GPUs. We expect that the performance of our DP routines will be higher on newer GPUs such as NVIDIA Fermi with better double precision support.

3D FFTs: We measured performance delivered by our auto-tuned library for several 3D FFT sizes to compare with CUFFT v3.0 and numbers published in [10] (AT3dFFT). The performance on an GTX280 is summarized in Figure 6. CUFFT executed correctly for only two sizes. We outperform AT3dFFT by up to 70% due to superior auto-tuning strategy for Y and Z dimensions. AT3dFFT column kernels perform computation entirely in registers, while we present the auto-tuner with an additional option to utilize shared memory. Using shared memory increases the radix and may save extra passes over the data. We investigated the schedule constructed by the library for $256 \times 256 \times 256$ and indeed saw that Y dimension was done in one pass, using radix-256 column kernel. The stride of the Z dimension is too large for radix-256 to perform well, and the library picks 16×16 decomposition. The performance of row kernels for the X dimension is roughly the same. Thus, our library saves one pass over the data resulting in 30% performance improvement.

Limitations: The size of the performance profile may be large because we have to use a lot of specialized precompiled kernels. Reducing the amount of specialization and selecting more frequently used kernels can significantly bring down the profile size at the expense of some performance loss; it is a trade-off. Perhaps, the best way to reduce the profile size is to encode kernel specializations in a few bytes and re-construct the kernel at runtime using a JIT or re-generate the kernel using the GPU compiler.

The performance estimation for a kernel may be inaccurate for the following reasons. First, we auto-tune for a particular data volume so it is possible that the prediction could be inaccurate for a different volumes, though we did not notice performance artifacts for different volumes. If this becomes an issue, it is possible to auto-tune for several representative data volumes. Second, we sparsely sample the stride space and assume that performance changes relatively smoothly. Third, we noticed that sometimes a sequence of kernels runs slower than the sum of runtime estimates for stand-alone kernel runs. Using the CUDA profiler, we found that performance of a kernel may be affected by another kernel executed earlier. This is quite unexpected and we attribute this to a bug in the GPU runtime.

Our FFT library assumes that data resides entirely within GPU memory. Our auto-tuning framework does not account for memory transfers and out-of-core FFT computations.

8. Conclusion and future directions

We presented an auto-tuning framework for automatically generating optimized FFT kernels on GPUs. Our pruning heuristics significantly reduce the optimization search space. Our runtime algorithm is used for efficient schedule execution. We demonstrated the performance improvements of our algorithms on three different GPUs on a wide range of size distributions in both single and double precision, and compared with prior state-of-the-art algorithms on CPUs and GPUs. Our algorithms achieve significant performance improvements while maintaining high accuracy.

There are several avenues for future work. We would like to extend our algorithms to other compute APIs and GPUs including the AMD 5800 series and the NVIDIA Fermi architecture. Another avenue for our work is to extend the auto-tuning framework to support DCT and DST transformations. Our current implementation does not account for data transfers and it would be interesting to extend our algorithms for data sets that do not fit in GPU memory.

References

[1] S. Chellappa, F. Franchetti, and M. Püeschel. Computer generation of fast Fourier transforms for the cell broadband engine. In *Proceedings of the 23rd international conference on Supercomputing*, 2009.

[2] N. Corp. CUDA occupancy calculator. http://developer.download.nvidia.com/compute/cuda/CUDA_Occupancy_calculator.xls, 2010.

[3] M. Frigo and S. G. Johnson. The design and implementation of FFTW3. *Proceedings of the IEEE*, 93(2):216–231, 2005.

[4] N. K. Govindaraju, S. Larsen, J. Gray, and D. Manocha. A memory model for scientific algorithms on graphics processors. In *Proceedings of the ACM/IEEE conference on Supercomputing*, 2006.

[5] N. K. Govindaraju, B. Lloyd, Y. Dotsenko, B. Smith, and J. Manferdelli. High performance discrete Fourier transforms on graphics processors. In *Proceedings of the ACM/IEEE conference on Supercomputing*, 2008.

[6] T. Jansen, B. von Rymon-Lipinski, N. Hanssen, and E. Keeve. Fourier volume rendering on the GPU using a split-stream-FFT. In *Proceedings of the Vision, Modeling, and Visualization Conference*, 2004.

[7] Y. Li, J. Dongarra, and S. Tomov. A note on auto-tuning GEMM for GPUs. Technical Report UT-CS-09-635, Massachusetts Institute of Technology, May 2009. LAPACK Working Note 212.

[8] J. L. Mitchell, M. Y. Ansari, and E. Hart. Advanced image processing with DirectX 9 pixel shaders. In W. Engel, editor, *ShaderX^2: Shader Programming Tips and Tricks with DirectX 9.0*. Wordware Publishing, Inc., 2003.

[9] K. Moreland and E. Angel. The FFT on a GPU. In *Proceedings of the ACM SIGGRAPH/EUROGRAPHICS Conference on Graphics Hardware*, 2003.

[10] A. Nukada and S. Matsuoka. Auto-tuning 3-D FFT library for CUDA GPUs. In *Proceedings of the Conference on High Performance Computing Networking, Storage and Analysis*, 2009.

[11] A. Nukada, Y. Ogata, T. Endo, and S. Matsuoka. Bandwidth intensive 3-D FFT kernel for GPUs using CUDA. In *Proceedings of the ACM/IEEE conference on Supercomputing*, 2008.

[12] NVIDIA Corp. *NVIDIA CUDA Programming Guide*, 2009.

[13] M. Pschel, J. M. F. Moura, B. Singer, J. Xiong, J. Johnson, D. Padua, M. Veloso, R. W. Johnson, M. Pschel, J. M. F. Moura, B. Singer, J. Xiong, J. Johnson, D. Padua, M. Veloso, and R. W. Johnson. Spiral: A generator for platform-adapted libraries of signal processing algorithms. *Journal of High Performance Computing and Applications*, 18:21–45, 2004.

[14] S. Ryoo, C. I. Rodrigues, S. S. Stone, S. S. Baghsorkhi, S.-Z. Ueng, J. A. Stratton, and W.-m. W. Hwu. Program optimization space pruning for a multithreaded GPU. In *Proceedings of the international symposium on Code generation and optimization*, 2008.

[15] J. Spitzer. Implementing a GPU-efficient FFT. *SIGGRAPH Course on Interactive Geometric and Scientific Computations with Graphics Hardware*, 2003.

[16] T. Sumanaweera and D. Liu. Medical image reconstruction with the FFT. In M. Pharr, editor, *GPU Gems 2*, pages 765–784. Addison-Wesley, 2005.

[17] C. Van Loan. *Computational Frameworks for the Fast Fourier Transform*. Society for Industrial Mathematics, 1992.

[18] V. Volkov and B. Kazian. Fitting FFT onto the G80 architecture, 2008. http:www.cs.berkeley.edu/~kubitron/courses/cs258-S08/projects/reports/project6_report.pdf.

Accelerating CUDA Graph Algorithms at Maximum Warp

Sungpack Hong   Sang Kyun Kim   Tayo Oguntebi   Kunle Olukotun

Computer Systems Laboratory
Stanford University
{hongsup, skkim38, tayo, kunle}@stanford.edu

Abstract

Graphs are powerful data representations favored in many computational domains. Modern GPUs have recently shown promising results in accelerating computationally challenging graph problems but their performance suffers heavily when the graph structure is highly irregular, as most real-world graphs tend to be. In this study, we first observe that the poor performance is caused by work imbalance and is an artifact of a discrepancy between the GPU programming model and the underlying GPU architecture. We then propose a novel virtual warp-centric programming method that exposes the traits of underlying GPU architectures to users. Our method significantly improves the performance of applications with heavily imbalanced workloads, and enables trade-offs between workload imbalance and ALU underutilization for fine-tuning the performance.

Our evaluation reveals that our method exhibits up to 9x speedup over previous GPU algorithms and 12x over single thread CPU execution on irregular graphs. When properly configured, it also yields up to 30% improvement over previous GPU algorithms on regular graphs. In addition to performance gains on graph algorithms, our programming method achieves 1.3x to 15.1x speedup on a set of GPU benchmark applications. Our study also confirms that the performance gap between GPUs and other multi-threaded CPU graph implementations is primarily due to the large difference in memory bandwidth.

Categories and Subject Descriptors D.1.3 [*Programming Techniques*]: Concurrent Programming – Parallel programming; D.3.3 [*Programming Languages*]: Language Constructs and Features – Patterns

General Terms Algorithms, Performance

Keywords Parallel graph algorithms, CUDA, GPGPU

1. Introduction

Graphs are widely-used data structures that describe a set of objects, referred to as *nodes*, and the connections between them, called *edges*. Certain graph algorithms, such as breadth-first search, minimum spanning tree, and shortest paths, serve as key components to a large number of applications [4, 5, 15–17, 22, 25] and have thus been heavily explored for potential improvement. Despite the considerable research conducted on making these algorithms

efficient, and the significant performance benefits they have reaped due to ever-increasing computational power, processing large irregular graphs quickly and effectively remains an immense challenge today. Unfortunately, many real-world applications involve large irregular graphs. It is therefore important to fully exploit the fine-grain parallelism in these algorithms, especially as parallel computation resources are abundant in modern CPUs and GPUs.

The Parallel Random Access Machine (PRAM) abstraction has often been used to investigate theoretical parallel performance of graph algorithms [18]. The PRAM abstraction assumes an infinite number of processors and unit latency to shared memory from any of the processors. Actual hardware approximations of PRAM, however, have been rare. Conventional CPUs lack in number of processors, and clusters of commodity general-purpose processors are poorly-suited as PRAM approximations due to their large internode communication latencies. In addition, clusters which span multiple address spaces impose the added difficulty of partitioning the graphs. In the supercomputer domain, several accurate approximations of the PRAM , such as the Cray XMT [13], have demonstrated impressive performance executing sophisticated graph algorithms [5, 17]. Unfortunately, such machines are prohibitively costly for many organizations.

GPUs have recently become popular as general computing devices due to their relatively low costs, massively parallel architectures, and improving accessibility provided by programming environments such as the Nvidia CUDA framework [23]. It has been observed that GPU architectures closely resemble supercomputers, as they implement the primary PRAM characteristic of utilizing a very large number of hardware threads with uniform memory latency. PRAM algorithms involving irregular graphs, however, fail to perform well on GPUs [15, 16] due to the workload imbalance between threads caused by the irregularity of the graph instance.

In this paper, we first observe that the significant performance drop of GPU programs from irregular workloads is an artifact of a discrepancy between the GPU hardware architecture and direct application of PRAM-based algorithms (Section 2). We propose a novel virtual warp-centric programming method that reduces the inefficiency in an intuitive but effective way (Section 3). We apply our programming method to graph algorithms, and show significant speedup against previous GPU implementations as well as a multi-threaded CPU implementation. We discuss why graph algorithms can execute faster on GPUs than on multi-threaded CPUs. We also demonstrate that our programming method can benefit other GPU applications which suffer from irregular workloads (Section 4).

This work makes the following contributions:

- We present a novel virtual warp-centric programming method which addresses the problem of workload imbalance, a general issue in GPU programming. Using our method, we improve upon previous implementations of GPU graph algorithms, by several factors in the case of irregular graphs.

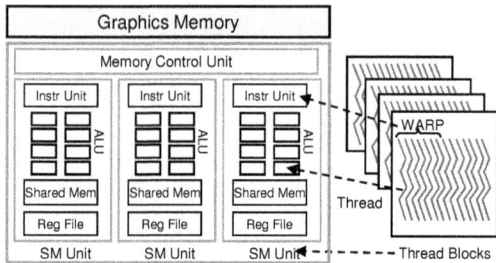

Figure 1. GPU architecture and thread execution model in CUDA.

- Our method provides a generalized, systematic scheme of warp-wise task allocation and improves the performance of GPU applications which feature heavy branch divergence or (unnecessary) scattering of memory accesses. Notably, it enables users to easily make the necessary trade-off between SIMD under-utilization and workload imbalance with a single parameter. Our method boosts the performance of a set of benchmark applications suffering from these issues by 1.3x – 15.1x.

- We provide a comparative analysis featuring a GPU and two different CPUs that examines which architectural traits are critical to the performance of graph algorithms. In doing so, we show that GPUs can outperform other architectures by providing sufficient random access memory bandwidth to exploit the abundant parallelism in the algorithm.

2. Background

2.1 GPU Architectures and the CUDA Programming Model

In this section, we briefly review the microarchitecture of modern graphics processors and the CUDA programming model approach to using them. We then provide a sample graph algorithm and illustrate how the conventional CUDA programming model can result in low performance despite abundant parallelism available in the graph algorithm. In this paper, we focus on Nvidia graphics architectures and terminology specific to their products. The concepts discussed here, however, are relatively general and apply to any similar GPU architecture.

2.2 Graph Algorithms on GPU

Figure 1 depicts a simplified block diagram of a modern GPU architecture, only displaying modules related to general purpose computation. As seen in the diagram, typical general-purpose graphics processors consist of multiple identical instances of computation units called Stream Multiprocessors (SM). An SM is the unit of computation to which a group of threads, called thread blocks, are assigned by the runtime for parallel execution. Each SM has one (or more) unit to fetch instructions, multiple ALUs (i.e., stream processors or CUDA cores) for parallel execution, a shared memory accessible by all threads in the SM, and a large register file which contains private register sets for each of the hardware threads. Each thread of a thread block is processed on an ALU in the SM. Since ALUs are grouped to share a single instruction unit, threads mapped on these ALUs execute the same instruction each cycle, but on different data. Each logical group of threads sharing instructions is called a warp. [1] Moreover, threads belonging to different warps can execute different instructions on the same ALUs, but in a different time slot. In effect, ALUs are time-shared between warps.

The following summarizes the discussion above: from the architectural standpoint, a group of threads in a warp performs as a SIMD(Single Instruction Multiple Data) unit, each warp in a thread block as a SMT(Simultaneous Multithreading) unit, and a thread block as a unit of multiprocessing.

That said, modern GPU architectures relax SIMD constraints by allowing threads in a given warp to execute different instructions. Since threads in a warp share an instruction unit, however, these varying instructions cannot be executed concurrently and are serialized in time, severely degrading performance. This advanced feature, so called SIMT (Single Instruction Multiple Threads), provides increased programming flexibility by deviating from SIMD at the cost of performance. Threads executing different instructions in a warp are said to diverge; if-then-else statements and loop-termination conditions are common sources of divergence.

Another characteristic of a graphics processor which greatly impacts performance is its handling of different simultaneous memory requests from multiple threads in a warp. Depending on the accessed addresses, the concurrent memory requests from a warp can exhibit three possible behaviors:

1. Requests targeting the same address are merged to be one unless they are atomic operations. In the case of write operations, the value actually written to memory is nondeterministically chosen from among merged requests.

2. Requests exhibiting spatial locality are maximally coalesced. For example, accesses to addresses i and $i + 1$ are served by a single memory fetch, as long as they are aligned.

3. All other memory requests (including atomic ones) are serialized in a nondeterministic order.

This last behavior, often called the scattering access pattern, greatly reduces memory throughput, since each memory request utilizes only a few bytes from each memory fetch.

To best utilize the aforementioned graphics processors for general purpose computation, the CUDA programming model was introduced recently by Nvidia [23]. CUDA has gained great popularity among developers, engineers, and scientists due to its easily accessible compiler and the familiar C-like constructs of its API extension. It provided a method of programming a graphics processor without thinking in the context of pixels or textures.

There is a direct mapping between CUDA's thread model and the PRAM abstraction; each thread is identified by its thread ID and is assigned to a different job. External memory access takes a unit amount of time in a massive threading environment, and no concept of memory coherence is enforced among executing threads. The CUDA programming model extends the PRAM abstraction to include the notion of shared memory and thread blocks, a reflection of the underlying hardware architecture as shown in Figure 1. All threads in a thread block can access the same shared memory, which provides lower latency and higher bandwidth access than global GPU memory but is limited in size. Threads in a thread block may also communicate with each other via this shared memory. This widely-used programming model efficiently maps computation kernels onto GPU hardware for numerous applications such as matrix multiplication.

The PRAM-like CUDA's thread model, however, exhibits certain discrepancies with the GPU microarchitecture that can significantly degrade performance. Especially, it provides no explicit notion of warps; they are transparent to the programmers due to the SIMT ability of the processors to handle divergent threads. As a result, applications written according to the PRAM paradigm will likely suffer from unnecessary path divergence, particularly when each *task* assigned to a thread is completely independent from other tasks. One example is parallel graph algorithms, where the irregular nature of real-world graph instances often induce extreme branch

---

[1] Note that the number of ALUs sharing an instruction unit (e.g. 8) can be smaller than the warp size. In such cases, the ALUs are time-shared between threads in a warp; this resembles vector processors whose vector length is larger than the number of vector lanes.

```
1   struct graph {
2     int nodes[N+1];//start index of edges from nth node
3     int edges[M];//destination node of mth edge
4     int levels[N]; // will contatin BFS level of nth node
5   };
6
7   void bfs_main(graph* g, int root) {
8     initialize_levels(g->levels, root);
9     curr = 0; finished = false;
10    do {
11      finished = true;
12      launch_gpu_bfs_kernel(g, curr++, &finished);
13    } while (!finished);
14  }

15  __kernel__
16  void baseline_bfs_kernel(int N, int curr, int *levels,
17      int *nodes, int *edges, bool* finished) {
18    int v = THREAD_ID;
19    if (levels[v] == curr) {
20  // iterate over neighbors
21      int num_nbr = nodes[v+1] - nodes[v];
22      int* nbrs = & edges[ nodes[v] ];
23      for(int i = 0; i < num_nbr; i++) {
24        int w = nbrs[i];
25        if (levels[w] == INF) { // if not visited yet
26          *finished = false;
27          levels[w] = curr + 1;
28  } } } }
```

Figure 2. The baseline GPU implementation of BFS algorithm.

divergence problems and scattering memory access patterns, as will be explained in the next section. In Section 3, we introduce a new generalized programming method that uses its awareness of the warp concept to address this problem.

Figure 2 is an example of a graph algorithm written in CUDA using the conventional PRAM-style programming from a previous work [15]. [2] This algorithm performs a breadth-first search (BFS) on the graph instance, starting from a given *root* node. More accurately, it assigns a "BFS level" to every (connected) vertex in the graph; the level represents the minimum number of hops to reach this node from the root node.

Figure 2 also describes the graph data structure used in the BFS, which is the same as the data structures used in other related work [6, 15, 16]. This data structure consists of an array of nodes and edges, where each element in the nodes array stores the start index (in the edges array) of the edges outgoing from each node. The edges array stores the destination nodes of each edge. The last element of the nodes array serves as a marker to indicate the length of the edges array. Figure 3.(a) visualizes the data structure. [3]

For this algorithm, the level of each node is set to ∞, except for the root which is set to zero. The kernel (code to be executed on the GPU) is called multiple times until all reachable nodes are visited, incrementing the current level by one upon each call. At each invocation, each thread visits a node which has the same current_level and marks all unvisited neighbors of the node with current_level+1. Nodes may be marked multiple time within a kernel invocation, since updates are not immediately visible to all threads. This does not affect correctness, as all updates will use the same correct value. This paper mainly focuses on the BFS algorithm, but our discussion can be applied to many similar parallel graph algorithms that process multiple nodes in parallel while exploring neighboring nodes from each. We will discuss some of these algorithms in Section 4.3.

The baseline BFS implementation shown in Figure 2 suffers a severe performance penalty when the graph is highly irregular, i.e. when the distribution of degrees (number of edges per node) is highly skewed. As we will show in Section 4, the baseline algorithm yields only a 1.5x speedup over a single-threaded CPU when the graph is very irregular. Performance degradation comes from execution path divergence at lines 19, 23, and 25 in Figure 2. Specifically, a thread that processes a high-degree node will iterate the loop at line 23 many more times than other threads, stalling other threads in its warp. Additional performance degradation comes from non-coalesced memory operations at lines 21, 22, 25, and 27 since their addresses exhibit no spatial locality across the threads. In addition, a repeated single-threaded access over con-

---

[2] The algorithm presented actually contains additional optimizations we made to the original version [15]; we eliminated unnecessary memory accesses and also eliminated an entire secondary kernel, which resulted in more than 20% improvement. We use this optimized version as our baseline.

[3] This data-structure is also known as compressed sparse row (CSR) in sparse-matrix computation domain [9].

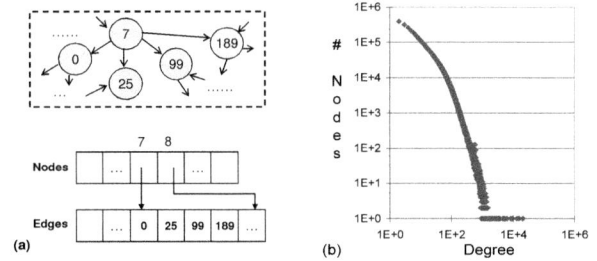

Figure 3. (a) A visualization of the graph data structure used in the BFS algorithm. (b) A degree distribution of a real-world graph instance (LiveJournal), which we used for our evaluation in Section 4.

secutive memory addresses (i.e., at line 21) actually wastes memory bandwidth by failing to exploit spatial locality in memory accesses.

Unfortunately, the nature of most real-world graph instances is known to be irregular [24]. Figure 3.(b) displays the degree distribution from one such example. Note that the plot is presented in log-log format. The distribution shows that although the average degree is small (about 17), there are many nodes which have degrees $10x \sim 100x$ (and some even 1000x) larger than the average.

3. Addressing Irregular Workloads using GPUs

3.1 Virtual Warp-centric Programming Method

We introduce a novel virtual warp-centric programming method which explicitly exposes the underlying SIMD nature of the GPU architecture to achieve better performance under irregular workloads.

Generalized warp-based task allocation

Instead of assigning a different task to each thread as is typical in PRAM-style programming, our approach allocates a chunk of tasks to each warp and executes distinct tasks as serial. We utilize multiple threads in a warp for explicit SIMD operations only, thereby preventing branch-divergence altogether. More specifically, the kernel in our programming model alternates between two phases: the SISD (Single Instruction Single Data) phase, which is the default serial execution mode, and the SIMD phase, the parallel execution mode. When the kernel is in the SISD phase, only a single stream of instructions is executed by each warp. In this phase, each warp is identified by a unique warp ID and works on an independent set of tasks. The degree of parallelism is thus maintained by utilizing multiple warps. In contrast, the SIMD phase begins by entering a special function explicitly invoked by the user. Once in the SIMD phase, each thread in the warp follows the same instruction sequence, but on different data based on its warp offset, or the lane ID within the given SIMD width. Unlike the classical (CPU-based) SIMD programming model, however, our SIMD threads are allowed more flexibility in executing instructions; they

```
29  template<int W_SZ> __device__
30  void memcpy_SIMD
31  (int W_OFF, int cnt, int* dest, int* src) {
32    for(int IDX = W_OFF; IDX < cnt; IDX += W_SZ)
33      dest[IDX] = src[IDX];
34    __threadfence_block(); }
35
36  template<int W_SZ> __device__
37  void expand_bfs_SIMD
38  (int W_SZ, int W_OFF, int cnt, int* edges,
39   int* levels, int curr, bool* finished) {
40    for(int IDX = W_OFF; IDX < cnt; IDX += W_SZ) {
41      int v = edges[IDX];
42      if (levels[v] == INF) {
43        levels[v] = curr + 1;
44        *finished = false;
45    } }
46    __threadfence_block();}
47
48  struct warpmem_t {
49    int levels[CHUNK_SZ];
50    int nodes[CHUNK_SZ + 1];
51    int scratch;
52  };
53  template<int W_SZ> __kernel__
```

```
54  void warp_bfs_kernel
55  (int N, int curr, int *levels,
56   int *nodes, int *edges, bool* finished) {
57    int W_OFF = THREAD_ID % W_SZ;
58    int W_ID = THREAD_ID / W_SZ;
59    int NUM_WARPS = NUM_THREADS / W_SZ;
60    extern __shared__ warp_mem_t SMEM[];
61    warpmem_t* MY = SMEM + (LOCAL_THREAD_ID / W_SZ);
62
63    // copy my work to local
64    int v_ = W_ID * CHUNK_SZ;
65    memcpy_SIMD<W_SZ> (W_OFF, CHUNK_SZ,
66      MY->levels, &levels[v_]);
67    memcpy_SIMD<W_SZ> (W_OFF, CHUNK_SZ+1,
68      MY->nodes, &nodes[v_]);
69
70    // iterate over my work
71    for(int v = 0; v < CHUNK_SZ; v++) {
72      if (MY->levels[v] == curr) {
73        int num_nbr = MY->nodes[v+1] - MY->nodes[v];
74        int* nbrs = &edges[ MY->nodes[v] ];
75        expand_bfs_SIMD<W_SZ> (W_OFF, num_nbr,
76          nbrs, levels, curr, finished)
77  } } }
```

Figure 4. BFS kernel written in virtual warp-centric programming model

can perform scattering/gathering memory accesses, execute conditional operations independently, and process dynamic data width. This is all done while taking advantage of the underlying hardware SIMT feature.

The proposed programming method has several advantages:

1. Unless explicitly intended by the user, this approach never encounters execution-path divergence issues. Intra-warp workload imbalance is therefore never unaware.

2. Memory access patterns can be more coalesced than the conventional thread-level task allocation in applications where concurrent memory accesses within a task exhibit much higher spatial locality than across different tasks.

3. Many developers are already familiar with our approach, since it resembles, in many ways, the traditional SIMD programming model for CPU architectures. However, the proposed approach is even simpler and more powerful than SIMD programming for CPU, since CUDA allows users to describe custom SIMD operations with C-like syntax.

4. This method allows for each task to allocate a substantial amount of privately-partitioned *shared memory* per task. This is because there are fewer warps than threads in a thread block.

In order to generally apply our programming method within current GPU hardware and compiler environments, we take simple means of replicated computation: during the SISD phase, every thread in a warp executes exactly the same instruction on exactly the same data. We enforce this by assigning the same warp ID to all threads in a warp. Note that this does not waste memory bandwidth since accesses from the same warp to the same destination address are merged into one by the underlying hardware.

Virtual Warp Size

Although naive warp-granular task allocation provides several merits aforementioned, it suffers from two potential drawbacks, where in both cases, unused ALUs within a warp limit the parallel performance of kernel execution:

1. If the native SIMD width of the user application is small, the underlying hardware will be under-utilized.

2. The ratio of the SIMD phase duration to the SISD phase duration imposes an Amdahl's limit on performance.

We address these issues by logically partitioning a warp into multiple virtual warps. Specifically, instead of setting the warp size parameter value to be the actual physical warp size of 32, we use a divisor (i.e. 4, 8, and 16). Multiple virtual warps are then co-located in one physical warp, with each virtual warp processing a different task. Note that all previous assumptions on a warp's execution behavior -- synchronized execution and merged memory accesses for the threads inside a warp -- are still valid within virtual warps. Thus, the parallelism of the SISD phase increases as a result of having multiple virtual warps for each physical warp, and the ALU utilization improves as well due to the logically narrower SIMD width.

Using virtual warps leads to the possibility of execution path divergence among different virtual warps, which in turn serializes different instruction streams among the warps. The degree of divergence among virtual warps, however, is most likely much less than among threads in a conventional PRAM warp. In essence, the virtual warp scheme can be viewed as a trade-off between execution-path divergence and ALU underutilization by varying a single parameter, the virtual warp size.

BFS in the Virtual Warp-centric Programming Method

Figure 4 displays the implementation of the BFS algorithm using our virtual warp-centric method. While the underlying BFS algorithm is fundamentally identical to the baseline implementation in Figure 2, the new implementation divides into SISD and SIMD phases. The main kernel (lines 54-77) executes the same instruction and data pattern for every thread in the warp, thus operating in the SISD phase. Functions in lines 30-46 operate in the SIMD phase, since distinct partitions of data are processed. Each warp also uses a private partition of shared memory; the data structure in lines 48-51 illustrates the layout of each private partition.

Lines 57-61 of the main kernel define several utility variables. The virtual-warp size (W_SZ) is given as a template parameter; the warp ID (W_ID) of the current warp and the warp offset (W_OFF) of each thread is computed using the warp size. Warp-private memory space is allocated by setting the pointer (MY) to the appropriate location in the shared memory space.

The virtual warp-centric implementation copies its portion of work to the private memory space (lines 64-68) before executing the main loop. As the function name implies, the memory copy operation is performed in a SIMD manner. After the memory copy operation finishes, the kernel executes the iterative BFS algorithm

```
78    BEGIN_SIMD_DEF(memcpy, int* dest, int* src)          92    USE_PRIV_MEM(warp_mem_t);
79    { dest[IDX] = src[IDX]; } END_SIMD_DEF                93    // copy my_work
80                                                          94    int v_ = N / NUM_WARPS * W_ID;
81    BEGIN_SIMD_DEF (expand_bfs, int* edges,               95    DO_SIMD(memcpy, CHUNK_SZ, MY->levels, &level[v_]);
82     int* level, int curr, bool*finished)                96    DO_SIMD(memcpy, CHUNK_SZ+1, MY->nodes, &nodes[v_]);
83    { int v = edges[IDX];                                 97
84     if (level[v] == INF) {                               98    // iterate over my_work
85        level[v] = curr + 1;                              99    for(int v = 0; v < CHUNK_SZ; v++) {
86        *finished = false;                                100      if (level[v] == curr) {
87     } } END_SIMD_DEF                                     101        int num_nbr = MY->nodes[v+1] - MY->nodes[v];
88                                                          102        int* nbrs = &edges[ MY->nodes[v] ];
89    BEGIN_WARP_KERNEL(warp_bfs_kernel,                    103        DO_SIMD(expand_bfs, num_nbr,
90       int N, int curr, int *level,                       104          nbrs, begin, level, curr, finished)
91       int *nodes, int * edges, bool* finished) {         105    } } } END_WARP_KERNEL
```

Figure 5. Same code as Figure 4 using macro-expansion. Type definition of `warp_mem_t` is same as before and omitted.

sequentially (lines 71-77), with the exception of explicitly-called SIMD functions. The expansion of BFS neighbors (line 75) is an explicit SIMD function call to the one defined at line 37, whose functionality is equivalent to lines 23-27 of the baseline algorithm Figure 2.

For a detailed explanation of how SIMD functions are implemented, consider the simple `memcpy` function in line 30. Each thread in a warp enters the function with a distinct warp offset (`W_OFF`), which leads to a different range of indices (`IDX`) of the data to be copied. The SIMT feature of CUDA enables the width of the SIMD operation to be determined dynamically. Although the SIMT feature guarantees synchronous execution of all threads at the end of the `memcpy` function, `__threadfence_block()` at line 34 is still required for intra-warp visibility of any pending writes before returning to SISD phase.[4] The second SIMD function, `expand_bfs` (line 37), is structured similarly to `memcpy`. The if-then-else statement in line 42 is an example of a conditional SIMD operation, automatically handled by SIMT hardware.

Using the virtual warp-centric method, the BFS code exhibits no execution-path divergence other than intended dynamic widths and conditional operations, as shown in Figure 4. Moreover, memory accesses are coalesced except the final scattering at line 42 and 43, which are inherent to the nature of the BFS algorithm.

Abstracting the Virtual Warp-centric Programming Method

As evident in the BFS example, the virtual warp-centric programming method is intuitive enough to be manually applied by GPU programmers. Closer inspection of the code in Figure 4, however, reveals some structural repetition in patterns that serve the programming method itself, rather than the user algorithm. Thus, providing an appropriate abstraction for the model can further reduce programmer effort as well as potential for error in the structural part of the program.

To this end, we introduce a small set of syntactic constructs intended to facilitate use of the programming model. Figure 5 illustrates how these constructs can simplify our previous warp-centric BFS implementation. For example, the SIMD function `memcpy` (line 30-33) in Figure 4 can be concisely expressed as line 78-79 in Figure 5. The constructs `BEGIN_SIMD_DEF` and `END_SIMD_DEF` automatically generate the function definition and outer-loop for work distribution. The user invokes the SIMD function using the `DO_SIMD` construct (line 95), where the function name, dynamic width, and other arguments are specified. Similarly, the `BEGIN_WARP_KERNEL` and `END_WARP_KERNEL` constructs indicate and generate the beginning and end of a warp-centric kernel, while the `USE_PRIV_MEM` construct allocates a private partition of shared memory.

The current set of constructs are implemented as C-macros, which is adequate to demonstrate how these constructs can generate desired routines and simplify programming. However, future compiler support of such virtual warp-centric constructs, or similar, could provide further benefits. For example, the compiler may choose to generate codes for SISD regions such that only a single thread in a warp is actually activated, rather than replicating computation. This eliminates unnecessary allocation of duplicated registers which are used only in the SISD phase and can also save power wasted by replicated computation.

3.2 Other Techniques

In this subsection, we discuss two other general techniques for addressing work imbalance. These techniques do not necessarily rely on the new programming model but can accompany it.

Deferring Outliers

The first technique is deferring execution of exceptionally large-sized tasks, which we term 'outliers'. Since there are a limited number of such tasks which induce load imbalance, we identify these tasks during main-kernel execution and defer their processing by placing them in a globally-shared queue, rather than processing them on-line. In subsequent kernel calls, each of the deferred tasks is executed individually, with its work parallelized across multiple threads. Figure 6 illustrates this idea.

In the BFS algorithm, the amount of work is proportional to the degree of each node, which is obtainable in $O(1)$ time given our data structure. For this technique, therefore, we simply defer processing of any node having degree greater than a predetermined threshold. Results in Section 4 explore the effects on performance when one varies this threshold.

This optimization technique requires the implementation of a global queue, a challenging task on a GPU in general. It is relatively simple, however, to implement a queue that always grows (or shrinks) during a kernel's execution. The code below exemplifies such an implementation using a single atomic operation:

```
AddQueue(int* q_idx, type_t* q, type_t item) {
   int old_idx = AtomicAdd(q_idx, 1);
   q[old_idx] = item; }
```

In our case, the overhead of the atomic operations is negligible compared to overall execution time, since queuing of deferred outliers is rare. However, this technique presents additional overhead via subsequent kernel invocations to process the deferred outliers.

Dynamic Workload Distribution

The virtual warp-centric programming method addresses the problem of workload imbalance inside a warp. However, there still exists the possibility of workload imbalance between warps: a single warp processing an exceptionally large task can stall the entire thread block (mapped to an SM), wasting computational resources. To solve this problem, we apply a dynamic workload distribution

---

[4] Although intra-warp visibility is attainable without the fence in some GPU generations (e.g. GT200), it is not guaranteed in general by the CUDA specification. Also note that the fence guarantees threadblock-wide visibility, which is larger than required; however, the performance impact of the overhead is negligible.

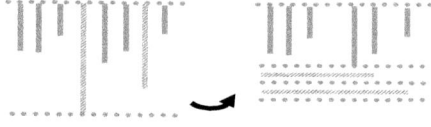

Figure 6. Visualization of deferring outliers: Each solid bar in the figure represents the amount of workload of each task. Tasks that have particularly large workload are deferred and later processed individually in parallel.

technique to our GPU graph algorithm. First, we instantiate only as many warps as there are physical resources. Second, each warp dynamically fetches a chunk of work from a shared work queue and processes it. All warps repeat this process until the work queue is emptied.

Note that this dynamic workload distribution technique is completely ineffective in the conventional PRAM-style programming; each thread in a warp cannot fetch another task until its fellow threads in the warp complete theirs. The same global queue implementation used for the deferring of outliers technique can be used for the work queue, since it only shrinks during a kernel execution. However, atomic operations during SISD phase should be handled with care as in following example:

```
if (WARP_OFFSET==0){
  MY->scratch = AtomicAdd(work_q, CHUNK_SZ);
  __threadfence_block();}
v_ = MY->scratch;
```

That is, since the GPU hardware does not merge, but serializes, atomic accesses that have the same destination address, only one thread should execute it for semantic correctness. The result of the single threaded atomic instruction can be propagated to all the other threads in the warp by means of shared memory without explicit synchronization.

For task parallelization, there is a well-known trade-off between static and dynamic workload distribution: Static distribution is vulnerable to load imbalance for tasks with varying workload, while dynamic distribution often imposes considerable overhead. In our case, the overhead is the atomic mutation of the work queue. The better scheme thus depends upon the size of the work chunk. Results in Section 4 will study this effect.

4. Experimental Results

In this section, we present experimental results in three categories. First, we explore the effectiveness of the methods we designed to address workload imbalance. Second, we study how different traits of various processor architectures affect the performance of graph algorithms. Third, we apply the virtual warp-centric programming method to other types of GPU applications, including two other graph algorithms.

4.1 Effect of Optimization Techniques

In the previous section, we introduced three techniques to avoid execution-path divergence and improve performance. In this section, we evaluate our proposed schemes by applying them in various combinations to the BFS algorithm with graph instances from different sources. Table 1 summarizes the experimental environments used for evaluation. For all results, speedup is measured against single-threaded execution time on the Out-of-Order (OOO) CPU machine described in the table, unless stated otherwise. The single-threaded execution used the same algorithm as the baseline in Figure 2, as it has been shown to be faster than other popular library such as Boost [16]. CPU and GPU BFS codes were compiled using gcc with the '-O3 -m32' flags and nvcc with the '-O3' flag, respectively.

Table 2 summarizes the properties of the graph instances used in the experiment. Of the four used, two of them are synthetically-generated graphs: RMAT and Random. RMAT [11] generates a scale-free graph which follows a power law degree distribution like many real world graphs [24], such as the world-wide web or a social networks. Random is a uniformly distributed graph instance created by randomly connecting m pairs of nodes out of a total n nodes. The average degree is set to 12 for both instances. Our experiment also includes two real world graph instances from a public large dataset collection [1]. LiveJournal exhibits a very irregular structure; its degree distribution was the example given in Figure 3.(b). Patents is relatively regular and has a smaller average degree.

Figure 7 illustrates the effectiveness of our proposed methods. Graph (a) compares five different configurations used on the GPU. The leftmost bar represents the speedup of the baseline GPU implementation (Figure 2). As evident in the graph, the performance of the baseline algorithm is particularly poor for irregular graph instances (RMAT, LiveJournal) due to the problem of workload imbalance. The next striped bar shows the performance when the deferring method is applied to the baseline. Deferring outliers produces a 1.9x improvement over the baseline implementation for RMAT, which features the worst workload imbalance, but does not provide significant speedup for any other graph instance.

The center solid bar represents the speedup of the BFS implementation using our virtual warp-centric programming method with virtual warp-size equal to physical warp-size (i.e. 32). RMAT and LiveJournal, in particular, exhibit dramatic performance improvements, as their workload imbalance is well-handled by this method The regular graph instance of Random, however, gained only minor improvements. This small speedup came from slightly better-coalesced memory access patterns in the warp-centric method (Section 3.1). For Patents, the warp-centric method resulted in performance degradation. This is not only because Patents is quite regular, but its average degree is small (~ 6). The naive warp-centric method therefore suffered from underutilization of warp resources, since the average SIMD width is determined by the average degree. A more detailed discussion follows shortly.

The two rightmost bars in Figure 7.(a) display the performance of the deferred outlier and dynamic workload distribution methods, when combined with the warp-centric method. Deferring outliers yields only a marginal performance gain since the warp-centric programming method already handles load imbalance reasonably well. In contrast, dynamic workload distribution allows for further speedup in severely imbalanced graphs such as RMAT. If the workload is evenly distributed, however, this method yields more overhead than benefit, as shown in the Random and Patent instances.

We now explore the trade-off between execution path divergence and ALU underutilization, by varying the virtual warp size. The result is shown in Figure 7.(b). The figure depicts the different optimal trade-off points for the graph instances. The regular graph instances (Random and Patents) achieve maximum average utilization of the SIMD lanes when the virtual warp size is set to approximately the average degree value. For RMAT, whose degree distribution is severely skewed, the best performance was achieved when avoiding execution path divergence as much as possible; a virtual warp size of 32 yielded optimal results. These results support the argument of having an intelligent runtime system that dynamically adjusts the virtual warp size according to the nature of the graph instance. With a properly selected virtual warp size, the virtual warp-centric method outperforms the baseline algorithm in all graph instances.

Figure 8 summarizes a sensitivity study of how performance was affected by the chosen parameter values and graph instance sizes. Figure 8.(a) shows the effect of changing the threshold value in the deferring outlier method; this value dictates the minimum

Architecture Name	Detailed Name	SMP sockets	Cores per chip	SMT per core	Last level cache size	Clock freq	Memory size, type
OOO CPU	Intel Xeon E5345	2	4	1	8 MB	2.3 Ghz	32GB, FB-DIMM DDR2
GPU	Nvidia Tesla GTX260	1	24	16	-	1.2 Ghz	1GB, GDDR3
SMT CPU	Sun UltraSPARC T2+	4	8	8	4 MB	1.6 Ghz	128GB, FB-DIMM DDR2
GPU2	Nvidia Tesla GTX275	1	30	16	-	1.4 Ghz	1GB, GDDR3

Table 1. Specifications of machines used in the experiments. GPU2 is only used to create Figure 10.

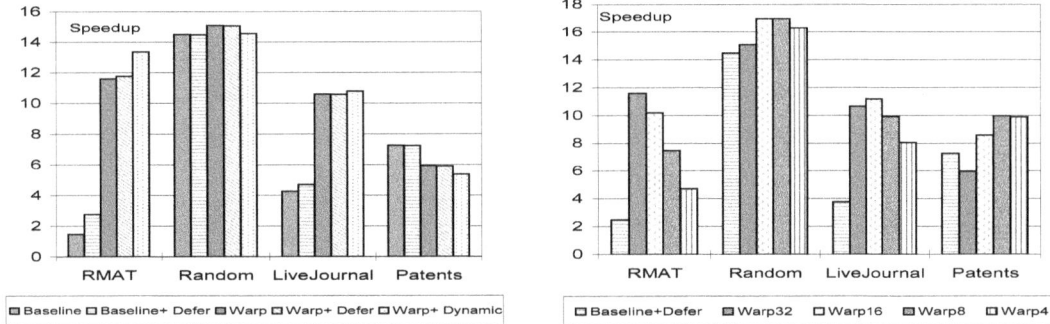

(a) Comparison of optimization techniques.

(b) Effect of virtual warp size.

Figure 7. Effect of optimizations with different graph instances.

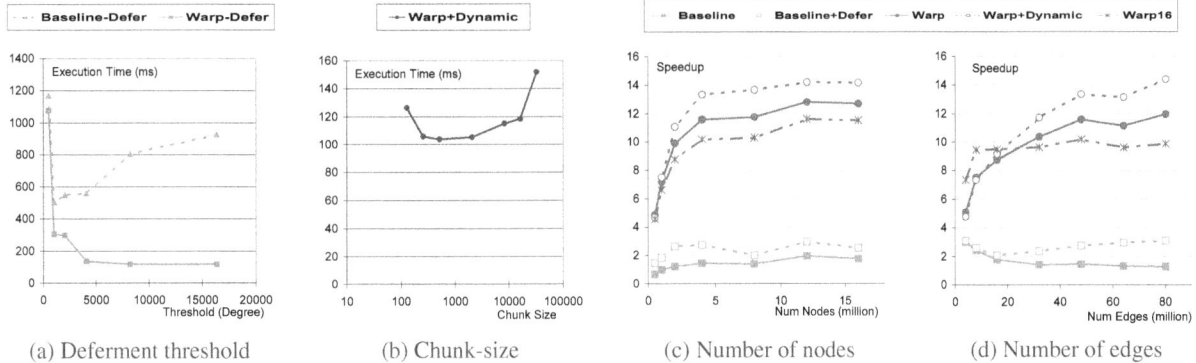

(a) Deferment threshold   (b) Chunk-size   (c) Number of nodes   (d) Number of edges

Figure 8. Sensitivity analysis on optimization parameters and input graph instance sizes: (a) and (b) used the same RMAT graph instance as in previous experiments and display the absolute execution time (lower is better) , while (c) and (d) used RMAT graph instances generated with different size parameters and display speedup against CPU execution (higher is better).

Name	Source	Nodes	Edges	Shape
RMAT	generate [7, 11]	$4 * 10^6$	$4.8 * 10^7$	irregular
Random	generate [7]	$4 * 10^6$	$4.8 * 10^7$	regular
LiveJournal	Real-world data [1]	4,308,451	68,993,773	irregular
Patents	Real-world data [1]	1,765,311	10,564,104	regular

Table 2. Characteristics of graph instances used in the experiments.

size of workload to be deferred. When applied to the baseline implementation (dashed line), the graphs shows that the resulting execution time is highly sensitive to the threshold value. Large values cause workload imbalance to persist; small ones result in too many additional kernel invocations for the deferred work. When combined with the virtual warp-centric method, however, the execution time is insensitive to the threshold value since our method adequately handles load imbalance already.

Figure 8.(b) shows the impact of workload chunk-size for the dynamic workload distribution method. This is a classical trade-off where small chunk-sizes increase the queue overhead, while large chunk-sizes tend to yield workload imbalance. Yet, the overall performance remains relatively insensitive to the chunk-size for a wide range (256 - 2048).

Finally, the plots in Figure 8.(c) and (d) show the scalability of each algorithm, as determined by the input size. Figure 8.(c) sweeps the number of nodes in the RMAT graph instance while fixing the average degree to 12. The relative speedup for the small graph instances in this GPU-based algorithm is low, because the CPU performed well due to increased cache hit rates. The plot clearly shows, however, that virtual warp-centric implementations provide superior speedup as the graph instances become large.

Figure 8.(d) varies the number of edges while keeping the number of nodes constant (4 million). This affects RMAT graph generation in two ways: (i) the average degree changes, and (ii) the graph instance becomes more skewed as the average degree increases. As a result, Figure 8.(d) confirms that when the average degree is small (especially when smaller than the warp size), the naive warp-centric implementations suffer from underutilization in the SIMD operations. In such cases, using a smaller virtual warp size (i.e. warp16) provides meaningful benefit. When the average degree is large, however, the load imbalance becomes more severe due to the increased level of degree skew; dynamic load balancing provides a larger benefit for such cases.

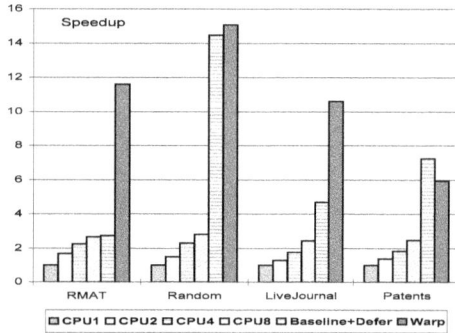

(a) Comparison against an out-of-order SMP.

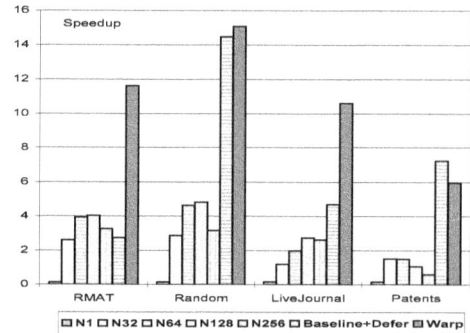

(b) Comparison against an SMT SMP.

Figure 9. Comparison against CPU execution.

4.2 Study of Architectural Effects

As seen in the previous subsection, the GPU implementations of our graph algorithm significantly outperform their CPU counterparts. We now explore which GPU architectural traits bring about this result and how.

In general, there are a few key architectural characteristics which account for whether performance improvements are delivered by GPU execution for a user application:

(1) GPU architectures enable massively parallel execution by providing many physical cores (SMs) and many ALUs per core.

(2) GPUs use a large number of warps to hide memory latency.

(3) GPU execution takes advantage of the directly-attached GDDR3 memory, which has higher bandwidth and lower latency than FB-DIMM based CPU main memory.

(4) GPUs do not spend bandwidth on coherence traffic.

To explore the effect of these traits on the graph algorithms, we first compared GPU performance to that of other multi-threaded processor architectures; we used the same BFS algorithm [5] on all the machines listed in Table 1 and measured performance.

Figure 9.(a) compares the speedup result on the OOO machine with the GPU results from Figure 7. The four leftmost bars represent the OOO machine execution with varying number of threads. The OOO execution results exhibit similar speedup values for every graph instance, since execution path divergence is not an issue for CPUs. However, the speedup was limited to around 2x with eight cores. Recall that there is no parallel overhead such as locks or atomic operations in our algorithm. Thus, the low speedup of OOO execution is due solely to a lack of memory bandwidth required to service the repeated last level cache misses caused by the random access memory pattern of the algorithm. The OOO performance for the Patents instance was particularly better than others, due to relatively higher cache hit rates resulting from the small graph size.

Figure 9.(b) shows the result of the same experiment on the SMT machine. The measured single thread performance (T1) was very poor compared to OOO execution, although the clock frequency of the SMT machine was more than half that of the OOO machine. This implies that the out-of-order execution successfully exploited the high degree of instruction level parallelism within the most time-consuming loop (line 23-27 in Figure 2). Once an adequate number of threads are used, however, the SMT machine soon outperforms the OOO machine due to higher throughput as shown in the 64-thread (T64) results. More interestingly, utilizing more sockets of the SMT machine (two sockets for T128 and four for

T256) does not necessarily result in better performance. This indicates that communication cost across chip boundaries, including bandwidth used for coherence traffic, is the major limiting factor for scalability on this machine.

Next, we explore the effect of bandwidth utilization and latency hiding in GPUs. Our experiment involves varying the number of warps and SMs when executing the dynamic load-balancing version of the warp-centric BFS. The result is shown in the two plots of Figure 10.(a); both plots are aligned to the number of active warps. The upper plot explores how latency hiding affects speedup by setting the number of SMs to the maximum (24) and changing the number of warps per SM. The performance gain from adding more than eight warps per SM is marginal, which indicates that performance is limited by the memory bandwidth after that point. The lower plot varies the number of SMs while fixing the number of warps per SM (to 16). Since each SM has limited internal memory bandwidth, more SMs performed better for the same number of warps.

Figure 10.(b) repeats the same experiment on a different GPU machine (GPU2 in Table 1). The plots also suggest that the performance is limited by the bandwidth, since GPU2, whose memory bandwidth is ∼10% larger than GPU1 [2], resulted in about 10% performance improvement. We also measured the memory bandwidth of random read accesses on these machines (omitted for brevity) and confirmed that the GPU has 3x ∼ 16x larger bandwidth than OOO and SMT CPUs, depending on the cache hit ratio.

To summarize, the graph algorithm has abundant parallelism, primarily in memory operations rather than computation; this parallelism can be exploited by using deep OOO execution, SMT hardware, or scattering SIMD operations as well as by using multiple cores and chips. Regardless of the hardware mechanism chosen, graph algorithms such as BFS are bound by memory bandwidth and require as much as possible in order to realize peak performance. The GPU had the largest memory bandwidth of all the machines we tested and therefore showed the best performance.

One common criticism of graph algorithm computation on GPUs is lack of support for very large graphs that do not fit in the GPU's limited memory. It would therefore be interesting to consider how the GPU would perform if the directly attached GDDR memory is replaced by FB-DIMM memory. This would allow GPUs to accommodate larger graph instances at the expense of a reduction in memory bandwidth. In such a case, the GPU performance should decrease, as per the reduced memory bandwidth, although the non-coherence and massive parallelism of the GPU enables it to utilize its bandwidth more efficiently. The merits of the CPU's cache will also diminish as data size grows.

Nevertheless, many real-world graphs (e.g. all instances in [1, 6]) still fit in GPU memory, and many interesting queries on these

---

[5] We also tried another multi-threaded CPU implementation [6] that uses spinlocks and private temporary work queues. However, the presented algorithm showed better performance in every configuration.

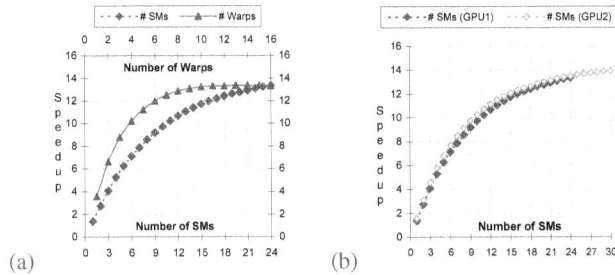

Figure 10. Effect of number of warps and number of SMs for GPU execution (Warp+Dynamic) with RMAT input.

graphs require a considerable amount of time, e.g calculating the average BFS number of all nodes from all other nodes requires O(N) repeated execution of single BFS number algorithm. Thus, fast GPU execution is practically very beneficial for many real-world problems.

4.3 Other Applications

In this subsection, we demonstrate that the virtual warp-centric programming method can be applied to other graph algorithms and provides the same merits as in the BFS algorithm. In addition, we apply our method to GPU applications other than graph algorithms to verify the benefits claimed in Section 3.1.

Figure 4.3 presents the speedup of our virtual warp-centric implementations. Note that in these graphs the baseline is the original PRAM-style GPU implementation, rather than any CPU version; our interest lies only in the effectiveness of our programming method rather than in the applications themselves.

The first two applications, SSSP (Single Source Shortest Path) and STCON(S-T Connectivity), are two other CUDA graph algorithms from [15, 16]. Although the detailed implementation of these algorithm differ from each other, they share a common algorithmic pattern as in the BFS algorithm to achieve parallelism: each node is visited in parallel to explore its neighbors. Thus analysis similar to the ones in the previous subsections can be made on these results. We used the RMAT graph instance as the input of these algorithms.

The next four applications are selective GPU benchmarks from the literature [8, 12, 20] that have some degree of branch path divergence and scattering memory access issues; however, they do not exhibit workload imbalance as severe as in the graph algorithms. Merge sort [20] recursively merges pairs of sorted sublists in parallel. After each merge operation, the size of sorted sublists doubles and the number of sublist halves. Thus, the application has no workload imbalance (except possibly at the end). However, memory divergence becomes an issue since each thread works on different sublists that are spaced apart. The warp-centric execution method eliminates memory divergence by assigning a pair of sublists to each warp. LU [20] implements a naive version of the LU decomposition. In this implementation, each thread computes one element in a KxK sub-matrix; thus, threads that handle boundary elements incur intra-warp memory divergence. Our programming method avoids this divergence by assigning a row partition to each warp. Backprop [12], a neural network application, performs vector-matrix multiplication in its first kernel. The original GPU implementation uses the entire thread block to compute the partial sum for a sub-matrix which requires column-wise reduction and synchronization. The warp centric method lets each warp independently accumulate partial sums from a chunk of rows, which obviates the synchronization and reduction. NN [8], another neural network application, processes separate data streams in each thread. Although the data streams are consecutive in memory, the start addresses are virtually randomized, causing memory divergence. The

warp-centric approach assigns a data stream to each warp, using the threads within a warp to fetch data in parallel.

Finally, Kmeans [12] represents applications where the conventional PRAM-style programming performs well. This application contains very little execution path divergence, and every memory access is well aligned across threads in a warp. Thus, the virtual warp-centric programming method yields only pure overhead: the SISD phase, SIMD width underutilization, as well as increased instruction count. This resulted in 40% overhead with warp-size 32, which has the worst resource utilization. Since our programming method does not require any change to the underlying hardware or compiler system, the user can simply choose not to use our method on non-suitable applications: applications without branch or memory divergence issues. Such applications are relatively easy to identify though code inspection, profiling, or simulation [8].

5. Related Work

There have been numerous implementations of parallel graph algorithms using various computer architectures, including distributed memory supercomputers [25], shared memory supercomputers [5, 17], multi-core SMP machines [6], and GPUs [15, 16]. Our work improves upon previous GPU implementations by several folds, introducing a new programming method that better considers the traits of modern GPU architectures.

Although naive warp-granular task allocation had been used ad hoc in some domains such as sparse-matrix multiplication [9], we proposed a generalized programming method for it using explicit SISD and SIMD phases as well as introduced the new concept of virtual-warp which enables trade-offs between underutilization and divergence.

Our programming method is a low-level construct that resides just on top of the GPU programming APIs. On the other side of the programming model spectrum are high-level approaches that abstract away architectural traits from the user; instead, the compiler/runtime system intelligently generates or selects proper execution codes based on high-level user description, targeting any processor architecture [10, 14]. Thus, these systems are actually complementary to our low-level method; they may decide when a virtual warp-centric method would be beneficial or what virtual warp-size should be utilized based on high-level information such as data access pattern analysis.

Unlike our virtual warp method, which prevents unnecessary divergence without hardware modification, Meng et al. proposed to modify the GPU architecture in order to address these issues [20]. When combined, these approaches complement our virtual warp method by allowing sub-warps to execute independently; thus, there is no need to pay the cost of divergence when using virtual warp sizes.

In this paper, we have not explored the effect of virtual warp-centric programming method with a GPU architecture that includes cache memory, e.g. Nvidia's Fermi [21]. Having cache memory may alleviate memory divergence issues for applications where each thread pursues an independent data stream, since the sequential locality is automatically exploited via cache. However, even with a cache, our warp-centric programming method still provides substantial benefits, since the cache pressure of having data streams per warp is considerably less than that of managing data per thread.

Very recently, Agarwal et al. [3] proposed a scalable BFS algorithm for multi-core CPU. Their optimization technique concurs with our observations in Section 4.2; they saved memory bandwidth by using bitmaps and intentionally avoided coherence traffic as much as possible. Note that there are still rooms to further improve GPU BFS algorithms through algorithmic enhancement. For example, we only applied a frontier-expansion method which maximizes sequential memory access; however it is better to apply

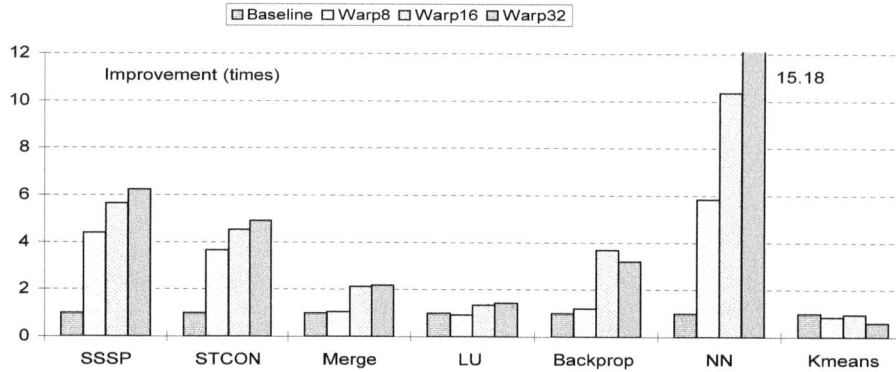

Figure 11. Performance improvement results of GPU applications using warp-centric programming method. Comparison is against original GPU implementation.

a fixed-point method, which manages a work-queue holding next-level nodes, for first and last few stages where only a few nodes are explored. It will also be interesting to apply the recent CPU techniques [3] for GPUs having last-level cache, which does not support coherence at all. We also refer interested readers to other studies on the impact of architectural traits on various applications [19, 21], other than graph algorithms.

6. Conclusion

Parallel execution of graph algorithms on GPUs suffered from workload imbalance for real-world graph instances. To address this issue, we proposed a novel virtual warp-centric programming method, a general strategy that prevents branch divergence and unnecessary scattering memory access. Users can also trade-off between SIMD utilization and branch divergence by varying the virtual warp size.

When applied to graph algorithms, our method resulted in up to 9x speedup over previous GPU implementations. In addition, a set of GPU benchmark applications that suffer from branch divergence and scattering memory accesses was accelerated by 1.3x to 15.1x over the baseline GPU implementations. Finally, we showed that the GPU executions of graph algorithms can outperform implementations on other architectures, mainly because of substantially larger memory bandwidth.

Acknowledgments

This work is supported by DOE contract, Sandia order 942017; Army contract AHPCRC W911NF-07-2-0027-1; DARPA contract, Oracle order 630003198; and Stanford PPL affiliates program, Pervasive Parallelism Lab: NVIDIA, Oracle/Sun, AMD, and NEC.

References

[1] Stanford large network dataset collection. http://snap.stanford.edu/data/index.html, 2009.

[2] http://en.wikipedia.org/wiki/GeForce_200_Series, 2010.

[3] V. Agarwal, F. Petrini, D. Pasetto, and D. Bada. Scalable Graph Exploration on Multicore Processors. In *ACM/IEEE SC*, 2010.

[4] D. Ajwani, R. Dementiev, and U. Meyer. A computational study of external-memory bfs algorithms. In *ACM-SIAM SODA*, 2006.

[5] D. Bader and K. Madduri. Designing multithreaded algorithms for breadth-first search and st-connectivity on the cray mta-2. In *IEEE ICPP*, 2006.

[6] D. Bader and K. Madduri. Snap, small-world network analysis and partitioning: An open-source parallel graph framework for the exploration of large-scale networks. In *IEEE IPDPS*, 2008.

[7] D. A. Bader and K. Madduri. Gtgraph: A synthetic graph generator suite. http://www.cc.gatech/edu/~kamesh/GTgraph/, 2006.

[8] A. Bakhoda, G. L. Yuan, W. W. L. Fung, H. Wong, and T. M. Aamodt. Analyzing cuda workloads using a detailed gpu simulator. In *IEEE ISPASS*, 2009.

[9] N. Bell and M. Garland. Efficient sparse matrix-vector multiplication on CUDA. In *Proc. Conf. Supercomputing (SC'09)*.

[10] H. Chafi, Z. DeVito, A. Moors, T. Rompf, A. K. Sujeeth, P. Hanrahan, M. Odersky, and K. Olukotun. Language virtualization for heterogeneous parallel computing. In *Proc. Conf. OOPSLA '10*, 2010.

[11] D. Chakrabarti, Y. Zhan, and C. Faloutsos. R-mat: A recursive model for graph mining. In *SDM*, 2004.

[12] S. Che, M. Boyer, J. Meng, D. Tarjan, J. Sheaffer, S.-H. Lee, and K. Skadron. Rodinia: A benchmark suite for heterogeneous computing. In *IEEE IISWC*, 2009.

[13] Cray, Inc. Cray xmt. http://www.cray.com/products/xmt/.

[14] K. Fatahalian, D. R. Horn, T. J. Knight, L. Leem, M. Houston, J. Y. Park, M. Erez, M. Ren, A. Aiken, W. J. Dally, and P. Hanrahan. Sequoia: programming the memory hierarchy. In *SC*, 2006.

[15] P. Harish and P. J. Narayanan. Accelerating large graph algorithms on the gpu using cuda. In *HiPC*, 2007.

[16] P. harish, V. Vineet, and P. Narayanan. Large graph algorithms for massively multithreaded architectures. Technical Report II-IT/TR/2009/74, International Institute of Information Technology Hyderabad, India, 2009.

[17] B. Hendrickson and J. Berry. Graph analysis with high-performance computing. *Computing in Science Engineering*, 10(2), march 2008.

[18] J. JáJá. *An introduction to parallel algorithms*. Addison Wesley, 1992.

[19] V. W. Lee, C. Kim, J. Chhugani, M. Deisher, D. Kim, A. D. Nguyen, N. Satish, M. Smelyanskiy, S. Chennupaty, P. Hammarlund, R. Singhal, and P. Dubey. Debunking the 100x gpu vs. cpu myth: an evaluation of throughput computing on cpu and gpu. In *ISCA*, 2010.

[20] J. Meng, D. Tarjan, and K. Skadron. Dynamic warp subdivision for integrated branch and memory divergence tolerance. In *ISCA*, 2010.

[21] J. Nickolls and W. J. Dally. The gpu computing era. *IEEE Micro*, 30(2), 2010.

[22] R. Niewiadomski, J. Amaral, and R. Holte. A parallel external-memory frontier breadth-first traversal algorithm for clusters of workstations. In *IEEE ICPP*, 2006.

[23] Nvidia. Cuda. http://www.nvidia.com/cuda/.

[24] D. J. Watts. *Small Worlds: the dynamics of Networks between Order and Randomness*, chapter 1–2. Princeton University Press, 1999.

[25] A. Yoo, E. Chow, K. Henderson, W. McLendon, B. Hendrickson, and U. Catalyurek. A scalable distributed parallel breadth-first search algorithm on bluegene/l. In *ACM/IEEE SC*, 2005.

Achieving a Single Compute Device Image in OpenCL for Multiple GPUs *

Jungwon Kim   Honggyu Kim   Joo Hwan Lee   Jaejin Lee

Center for Manycore Programming
School of Computer Science and Engineering
Seoul National University, Seoul 151-744, Korea
http://aces.snu.ac.kr
{jungwon, honggyu, joohwan}@aces.snu.ac.kr, jlee@cse.snu.ac.kr

Abstract

In this paper, we propose an OpenCL framework that treats multiple GPUs as a single compute device. Providing the single GPU image makes an OpenCL application written for a single GPU portable to the GPGPU systems with multiple GPUs. It also makes the application exploit the full computing power of the multiple GPUs and the entire amount of GPU memories available in the system. Our OpenCL framework automatically distributes at run time an OpenCL kernel written for a single GPU into multiple CUDA kernels that execute on the multiple GPUs. It applies a run-time memory access range analysis to the kernel by performing a sampling run and identifies an optimal workload distribution for the kernel. To achieve a single compute device image, the runtime maintains a virtual device memory that is allocated in the main memory of the GPGPU system. The OpenCL runtime treats the memory as if it were the memory of a single GPU device and keeps it consistent to the memories of the multiple GPUs. Our OpenCL-C-to-C translator generates the sampling code from the OpenCL kernel code and our OpenCL-C-to-CUDA-C translator generates the CUDA kernel code for the distributed OpenCL kernel. We show the effectiveness of our OpenCL framework by implementing the OpenCL runtime and the two source-to-source translators. We evaluate its performance with a GPGU system that contains eight GPUs using eleven OpenCL benchmark applications.

Categories and Subject Descriptors   D.1.3 [*PROGRAMMING TECHNIQUES*]: Concurrent Programming; D.3.4 [*PROGRAMMING LANGUAGES*]: Processors – Code generation, Compilers, Optimization, Run-time environments

General Terms   Algorithm, Design, Experimentation, Languages, Measurement, Performance

Keywords   OpenCL, Compilers, Runtime, Access range analysis, Workload distribution, Virtual device memory

---

* This work was supported by grant 2009-0081569 (Creative Research Initiatives: Center for Manycore Programming) from the National Research Foundation of Korea funded by the Korean government (Ministry of Education, Science and Technology). ICT at Seoul National University provided research facilities for this study.

1. Introduction

Open Computing Language (OpenCL)[7] is a standard for general-purpose, heterogeneous parallel programming. OpenCL provides a uniform programming environment for software developers to write portable code across heterogeneous parallel platforms, such as multicore CPUs, GPUs, Cell-BE processors, and DSPs. OpenCL consists of a programming language, called OpenCL C, and OpenCL runtime API functions. OpenCL C is a subset of C99 with some extensions and it is used to write computational kernels that execute on a compute device, such as a CPU and a GPU. OpenCL API functions are used to configure and manage OpenCL objects and to coordinate executions of the computational kernels. Since OpenCL has a strong CUDA[8, 15] heritage, a general-purpose GPU (GPGPU) system is a representative heterogeneous platform that OpenCL is targeting.

A recent GPU[18] contains more than 400 stream processors, capable of achieving more than 1 TFLOPS for single precision and more than 500 GFLOPS for double precision. A single GPU can deliver the supercomputing power at 1/20th of the power consumption and 1/10th of the cost when compared to the latest general-purpose, quad-core CPU. With the C-like CUDA or OpenCL language, software developers can develop GPU applications easily without using complex graphics programming APIs. High processing power, cost effectiveness, energy efficiency, and ease of programming provided by GPUs make them a natural choice for high performance computing.

Moreover, in support of this trend, many GPGPU systems start to have multiple GPU devices to solve large size problems[19, 20, 26, 28]. While GPGPU systems with multiple GPUs are widening their user base, the users still manually write code from scratch to exploit the multiple GPUs available in the system. In addition, converting an application written for a single GPU to run on multiple GPUs generally requires rewriting the code, and sometimes fairly extensive modifications are required. The programmer needs to insert code for distributing workload across multiple GPUs and managing data between the host main memory and multiple GPU device memories. Guaranteeing consistency between the multiple copies of data makes this process more difficult for the programmer.

In this paper, we propose an OpenCL framework that provides an illusion of a single compute device to the programmer for the multiple GPUs available in the system. It enables OpenCL applications written for a single compute device to run on the system with multiple GPUs without any modification. Moreover, our framework makes it possible to run the GPU applications that require a bigger size of data than the device memory size of a single GPU.

At run time, when the information about an OpenCL kernel index space is fully known to our OpenCL runtime, it distributes the kernel workload across multiple GPUs. To distribute the kernel workload across multiple GPU devices efficiently, our framework performs a sampling run just before the kernel is executed. The sampling run obtains the memory access range of each GPU for the kernel. The runtime distributes the kernel workload according to this memory access range information to minimize data transfer between the CPU and multiple GPUs.

To achieve a single compute device image, the OpenCL runtime maintains a virtual device memory that is allocated in the main memory of the GPGPU system. The runtime treats the virtual device memory as if it were the memory of a single GPU and keeps it consistent to the memories of the multiple GPUs. Our OpenCL-C-to-C translator generates the sampling code from the OpenCL kernel code and OpenCL-C-to-CUDA-C translator generates each GPU's CUDA kernel code for the distributed OpenCL kernel.

The major contributions of this paper are the following:

- We describe the design and implementation of our OpenCL framework for a GPGPU system with multiple GPU devices.

- We propose a run-time memory access range analysis technique. It detects efficiently the memory access ranges of each GPU for a given kernel work-group index space.

- We propose a run-time workload distribution technique that is optimal with regards to three optimality constraints: expressibility in a single grid of CUDA thread blocks (i.e., for the minimum number of kernel launches), workload balancing between multiple GPUs, and the minimum amount of data transfer.

- We describe translation techniques used in our two source-to-source translators: OpenCL-C-to-C and OpenCL-C-to-CUDA-C.

- We show the effectiveness of our OpenCL framework by implementing the OpenCL runtime and the two source-to-source translators. We evaluate its performance with a GPGPU system that contains 8 GPUs using 11 OpenCL benchmark applications.

The rest of the paper is organized as follows. Section 2 briefly describes OpenCL and its features. Section 3 explains the techniques of achieving a single compute device image in our OpenCL framework. Section 4 discusses and analyzes the evaluation result of our OpenCL framework. Section 5 describes related work. Finally, Section 6 concludes the paper.

2. Background

In this section, we briefly describe the OpenCL platform and its execution semantics. OpenCL inherited many features from CUDA[8, 15].

The OpenCL platform consists of a host processor connected to one or more *compute devices*, each of which contains one or more *compute units* (CUs). Each CU contains one or more *processing elements* (PEs). A PE is a *virtual* scalar processor. In addition, OpenCL defines four distinct memory regions: global, constant, local and private. *Compute device memory* consists of the global and constant memory regions. The local memory is shared by all PEs in the same compute unit. The private memory is local to a PE. Accesses to the global memory or the constant memory may be cached in the global/constant memory data cache if there is such a cache in the device. The OpenCL runtime maps each OpenCL platform component to a component in the target GPGPU system. The entire GPU card becomes an OpenCL compute device.

An OpenCL application consists of a *host program* and *kernels*. The host program executes on the host processor and submits *commands* to perform computations on the PEs within a compute

```
void matrixMul(float* C, float* A, float* B, int WA, int HA, int WB)
{
1:    for (int j = 0; j < HA; j++) {
2:        for (int i = 0; i < WB; i++) {
3:            float acc = 0.0f;
4:            for (int k = 0; k < WA; k++) {
5:                acc += A[k + j * WA] * B[i + k * WB];
6:            }
7:            C[i + j * WB] = acc;
8:        }
9:    }
}
```
(a)

```
__kernel void matrixMul( __global float* C, __global float* A,
                         __global float *B, int WA, int WB)
{
1:    int i = get_global_id(0);
2:    int j = get_global_id(1);
3:    float acc = 0.0f;
4:    for (int k = 0; k < WA; k++)
5:        acc += A[k + j * WA] * B[i + k * WB];
6:    C[i + j * WB] = acc;
}
```
(b)

```
#define BLOCK_SIZE 16
void main()
{
1:    ...
2:    cl_mem A_gpu, B_gpu, C_gpu;
3:    float *A_cpu, *B_cpu, *C_cpu;
4:    int WA, WB, WC;  // widths of matrices
5:    int HA, HB, HC;  // heights of matrices
6:                     // HB=WA, WC=WB, and HC=HA
7:    ...
8:    // Initialize the OpenCL runtime
9:    ...
10:   // Build and create the kernel
11:   ...
12:   // Allocate the main memory space for the matrices
13:   A_cpu = (float*) malloc(sizeA);
14:   B_cpu = (float*) malloc(sizeB);
15:   C_cpu = (float*) malloc(sizeC);
16:   // Initialize A_cpu, B_cpu, and C_cpu
17:   ...
18:   // Allocate the device memory for the matrices
19:   A_gpu = clCreateBuffer(context, CL_MEM_READ_ONLY,
20:                          sizeA, NULL, NULL);
21:   B_gpu = clCreateBuffer(context, CL_MEM_READ_ONLY,
22:                          sizeB, NULL, NULL);
23:   C_gpu = clCreateBuffer(context, CL_MEM_WRITE_ONLY,
24:                          sizeC, NULL, NULL);
25:   ...
26:   // Copy the matrices from the main memory to the device memory
27:   clEnqueueWriteBuffer(command_queue, A_gpu, CL_TRUE, 0, sizeA,
28:                        A_cpu, 0, NULL, NULL);
29:   clEnqueueWriteBuffer(command_queue, B_gpu, CL_TRUE, 0, sizeB,
30:                        B_cpu, 0, NULL, NULL);
31:   ...
32:   // Set up kernel arguments
33:   clSetKernelArg(kernel, 0, sizeof(cl_mem), &C_gpu);
34:   clSetKernelArg(kernel, 1, sizeof(cl_mem), &A_gpu);
35:   clSetKernelArg(kernel, 2, sizeof(cl_mem), &B_gpu);
36:   clSetKernelArg(kernel, 3, sizeof(int), &WA);
37:   clSetKernelArg(kernel, 4, sizeof(int), &WB);
38:   // Set the size of the global index space
39:   size_t globalWorkSize[] = {WC, HC};
40:   // Set the size of the local index space
41:   size_t localWorkSize[] = {BLOCK_SIZE, BLOCK_SIZE};
42:   // Execute the kernel
43:   clEnqueueNDRangeKernel(command_queue, kernel, 2, 0,
44:                          globalWorkSize, localWorkSize, 0, NULL, NULL);
45:   // Copy the result from the device memory to the main memory
46:   clEnqueueReadBuffer(command_queue, C_gpu, CL_TRUE, 0, sizeC,
47:                       C_cpu, 0, NULL, NULL);
}
```
(c)

Figure 1. (a) A C function for matrix multiplication. (b) The OpenCL kernel for the C function in (a). (c) The OpenCL host program for matrix multiplication.

device or to manipulate memory objects. There are three types of commands: kernel execution, memory, and synchronization. A kernel is a function and written in OpenCL C. It executes on a single compute device. It is submitted to a *command-queue* in the form of a kernel execution command by the host program. A compute device may have one or more command-queues. Commands in a command-queue are issued in-order or out-of-order depending on the queue type.

When the host program submit a kernel execution command to a command-queue, it defines an N-dimensional abstract index space for the kernel, where $1 \leq N \leq 3$. Each point in the index space is specified by an N-tuple of integers with each dimension starting at 0. Each point is associated with an execution instance of the kernel, which is called *work-item*. Thus, the N-tuple becomes the global ID of the associated work-item. Each work-item performs a different task based on its ID in an SPMD[4] manner. Before enqueueing a kernel command, the host program defines an integer array of length N (i.e., the dimension of the index space) that specifies the number of work-items in each dimension of the index space.

A *work-group* contains one or more work-items. Each work-group has a unique ID that is also an N-tuple. An integer array of length N specifies the number of work-groups in each dimension of the index space. A work-item in a work-group is assigned to a unique local ID within the work-group, treating the entire work-group as an index space. The index space is called a local index space. The global ID of a work-item can be computed with its local ID, work-group ID, and work-group size. Work-items in a work-group execute concurrently on the PEs of a single CU.

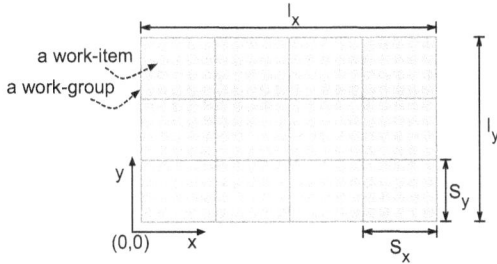

Figure 2. A two-dimensional index space.

For example, Figure 2 shows a two-dimensional index space whose sizes in dimensions x and y are I_x and I_y respectively. Suppose that the work-group size in dimension x is S_x and in dimension y is S_y. Let $(ID_x^{global}, ID_y^{global})$, $(ID_x^{local}, ID_y^{local})$, and $(ID_x^{group}, ID_y^{group})$ be the global ID, local ID, and work-group ID of a work-item in the index space, respectively. The number of work-groups in dimension x is computed by I_x/S_x and in dimension y is by I_y/S_y. Each work-group contains $S_x \times S_y$ work-items. The global ID is computed with the work-group size, work-group ID and local ID,

$$ID_x^{global} = S_x \cdot ID_x^{group} + ID_x^{local}$$

$$ID_y^{global} = S_y \cdot ID_y^{group} + ID_y^{local}$$

The host program enqueues memory commands that operate on memory objects in the device memory. Only the host program can dynamically create global or constant memory objects with OpenCL API functions. Pointers to the memory objects are passed as arguments to a kernel that accesses the objects. A memory object in the device memory is typically a *buffer object*, called in short as a *buffer*. A buffer stores a one-dimensional collection of elements that can be a scalar data type, a vector data type, or a user-defined structure.

For an example of the OpenCL kernel, consider a C function that performs matrix multiplication in Figure 1 (a). It computes $A \times B$ and stores the result in C. Figure 1 (b) shows an OpenCL kernel function that implements the C function. It is written in OpenCL C. OpenCL C has four address space qualifiers to distinguish different memory regions: `__global`, `__constant`, `__local` and `__private`. The `__global` qualifier is used in the argument declaration of the kernel. It tells the OpenCL C compiler that the buffers of matrices A, B, and C are allocated in the global memory. The kernel has a two-dimensional index space. OpenCL functions `get_global_id(0)` and `get_global_id(1)` return the first and

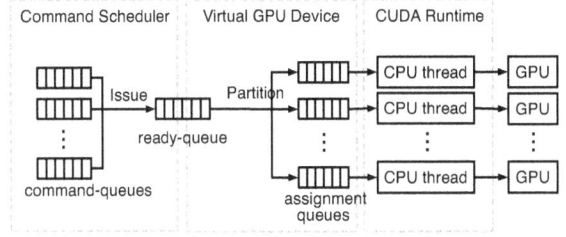

Figure 3. The organization of our OpenCL runtime

Actions taken by the host program	Tasks performed by our OpenCL runtime
1) Allocate buffers in the device memory for the input and output arrays by invoking **clCreateBuffer()**	• Allocate the requested buffers in the virtual device memory and record the information about the buffers
2) Copy the input arrays from the main memory to the buffers by invoking **clEnqueueWriteBuffer()**	• Copy the arrays to the virtual buffers
3) Set up kernel arguments by invoking **clSetKernelArg()**	• Record the information about the kernel arguments
4) Execute the kernel on the device by invoking **clEnqueueNDRangeKernel()**	• Perform a sampling run on the host to obtain access ranges of the virtual buffers by the kernel • Compute an optimal distribution of the workload in the kernel and the virtual buffers across multiple GPU devices • Allocate device buffers in each device memory based on the distribution • Copy the necessary chunks of the virtual buffers to the real buffers in each device • Execute the distributed kernel on the multiple devices
5) Copy the output arrays from the device to the host by invoking **clEnqueueReadBuffer()**	• Update the virtual buffers by comparing the updated device buffers with the twins of shared regions in the virtual buffers • Copy the requested buffers in the virtual device memory to the arrays in the host

Table 1. The tasks performed by our OpenCL runtime.

second elements of the global ID of the work-item that executes the kernel, respectively. Each work-item computes an element of C.

Figure 1 (C) shows the host program for the matrix multiplication. At the beginning, the host initializes the OpenCL runtime by creating an OpenCL context and a (in-order) command-queue for the compute device. Then, it builds and creates the kernel by invoking the OpenCL C compiler. The host allocates spaces for matrices A, B, and C (subscripted with _cpu) in the main memory (lines 12 – 15) and initializes them (lines 16 – 17). It also allocates buffer objects for matrices A, B, and C (subscripted with _gpu) in the device memory (lines 18 – 24). After allocating the buffers, the host copies matrices A and B from the main memory to the buffers by enqueueing memory commands to the command-queue (lines 26 – 30). After setting up kernel arguments to be passed to the kernel (lines 32 – 37), it specifies the dimension and size of the global and local index spaces (lines 38 – 41). The host executes the kernel by enqueueing a kernel command to the command-queue (lines 42 – 44). To copy matrix C from the buffer to the main memory, the host enqueues a memory command to the command-queue (lines 45 – 47). The command-queue is an in-order queue. Thus, the enqueued memory and kernel commands are issued to the compute device in order.

3. Achieving a Single Compute Device Image

In this section, we describe our technique that achieves a single compute device image from multiple GPUs.

3.1 Overview of Our OpenCL Runtime

Figure 3 shows the organization of our OpenCL runtime. It consists of a command scheduler thread, a virtual GPU device thread, and a CUDA runtime. The host program thread and the command scheduler thread share command-queues. The command scheduler dequeues each command-queue one by one and schedules the dequeued commands in the ready-queue. The command scheduler honors the type (in-order or out-of-order) of each command-queue and synchronization enforced by the host program. Our OpenCL runtime can handle OpenCL applications that have multiple host threads. In this case, each command-queue may contain commands from different host threads.

The virtual GPU device thread provides an illusion of a single GPU to the user. It dequeues the ready-queue. If the dequeued command is a kernel command, it partitions the work-group index space of the kernel into N *work-group assignments* to the N GPUs available in the system. A set of work-groups that is executed by a GPU is called a *work-group assignment*. The virtual GPU device thread encapsulates proper CUDA driver API functions[17] (e.g., cuLaunchGrid(), cuParamSetv(), cuMemcpyHtoD, cuMemAlloc(), etc.) and their arguments in an *assignment object* for each work-group assignment. Then it enqueues the objects in N *assignment queues* one by one.

An assignment queue is associated with a CUDA CPU thread. Each CUDA CPU thread is in charge of one GPU. Each CUDA CPU thread in the CUDA runtime dequeues its assignment queue. By extracting CUDA driver API functions and their arguments from the dequeued assignment object, the CUDA CPU thread sends appropriate CUDA commands to the associated GPU.

To achieve a single device image, the virtual GPU device maintains *virtual device memory* that is allocated in the main memory of the system. The virtual GPU device treats the memory as if it were the device memory of a single GPU and keeps it consistent to memories of the multiple GPUs. To distinguish a buffer object that is allocated in the virtual device memory from that allocated in a real GPU's memory, we call the former as a *virtual buffer object*, in short *virtual buffer*, and the latter as a *device buffer object*, in short *device buffer*.

In our OpenCL framework, an OpenCL kernel is translated into a parameterized CUDA kernel by our OpenCL-C-to-CUDA-C translator. When an OpenCL kernel is built in an OpenCL host program, our OpenCL-C-to-CUDA-C translator is invoked. When the work-group index space of the kernel is known at run time, our OpenCL runtime partitions the index space into N disjoint sets of work-groups (i.e., work-group assignments), where N is the number of GPUs available in the system. Then, each assignment is translated into a grid of CUDA thread blocks. Since CUDA does not allow a three-dimensional grid of thread blocks, our OpenCL runtime flattens a three-dimensional OpenCL work-group index space to a two-dimensional CUDA grid.

An overview of tasks performed by our OpenCL runtime is shown in Table 1. The first column in the table shows a typical sequence of actions taken by the host program to execute an OpenCL kernel on a single compute device (e.g., the sequence in the host program for matrix multiplication shown in Figure 1 (c)). The second column shows the tasks performed by our OpenCL runtime to enable each action taken by the host program.

3.2 Workload Distribution

Our OpenCL framework automatically distributes the workload contained in a kernel across multiple GPUs at run time when the associated kernel command is issued and the kernel index space is known. The unit of workload distribution is a work-group in the index space. Each buffer accessed by the kernel is also distributed over the multiple GPUs. Our workload distribution technique is based on the following two observations:

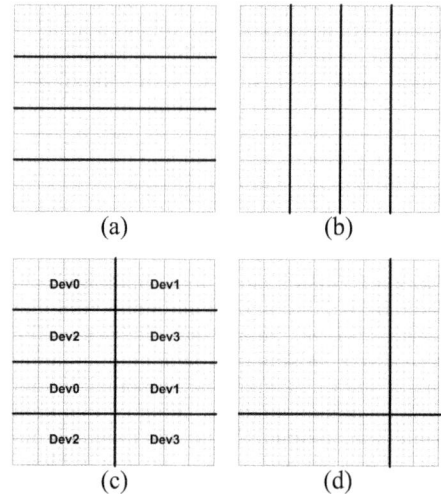

Figure 4. Different ways of partitioning the work-group index space for four GPUs.

Observation 1. *In OpenCL, there is no synchronization mechanism available between work-groups in the same kernel index space[7]. Thus, all work-groups in the same kernel index space are totally independent with each other.*

In other words, there is no dependence between work-groups in the same kernel index space. Moreover,

Observation 2. *According to the OpenCL memory consistency model[7], an update to a global memory location by a work-group does not need to be visible to other work-groups in the same kernel index space during the kernel execution.*

These two observations imply that we can freely distribute work-groups in the same index space across multiple GPUs and still preserve the original semantics of the OpenCL kernel.

We assume that there are enough work-items in a single work-group to make all processor (scalar) cores in the streaming multiprocessor of the GPU busy. We also assume that there are enough work-groups in the work-group index space to make all streaming multiprocessors in the GPU busy. There are three constraints on partitioning the work-group index space. One is about the expressibility of each work-group assignment in the partition with a single grid of CUDA thread blocks.

Constraint 1. *Each work-group assignment in the partition should be expressed in a single grid of CUDA thread blocks. In other words, the work-group IDs in each work-group assignment need to be contiguous in each dimension.*

For example, assume that there are four GPU devices and the kernel has a two-dimensional work-group index space. We can partition the work-group index space into disjoint work-group assignments in many ways. Figure 4 shows some of the partitions. A gray square in Figure 4 represents a work-group and a dot represents a work-item. There are four work-group assignments in the partition shown in Figure 4 (c). Since each assignment consists of two non-adjacent sets of eight work-groups, we cannot express the assignment with a single CUDA grid of thread blocks. For each set of eight work-groups in the work-group assignment, a single CUDA grid is required.

If a partition does not meet this constraint, the translated CUDA kernel needs to be launched multiple times to execute the work-group assignment. This introduces an unnecessary kernel launching overhead. Furthermore, a large number of thread blocks in a grid is a primary condition for keeping the entire GPU busy.

Another constraint is about the size balance between different work-group assignments in the partition. It is desirable to equally distribute all the work-groups in the index space across different work-group assignments.

Constraint 2. *The number of work-groups in each assignment should be well-balanced.*

Satisfying this condition makes all the available GPUs busy. For example, each assignment in the partition shown in Figure 4 (d) has a different number of work-groups. This is not desirable.

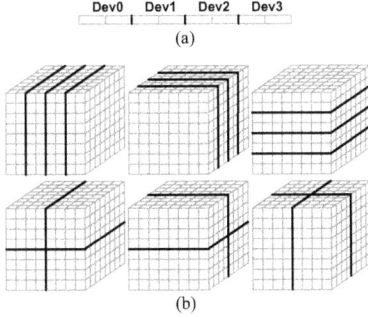

Figure 5. (a) The optimal partition with respect to Constraint 1 and Constraint 2 for one-dimensional index spaces with four GPUs. Each rectangle represents a work-group. (b) The optimal partitions with respect to Constraints 1 and Constraints 2 for three-dimensional index spaces with four GPUs. Each cube represents a work-group.

With respect to Constraint 1 and Constraint 2, the partitions in Figure 4 (a) and (b) are optimal for the two-dimensional index space. For one-dimensional index spaces, there is only one way of optimally partitioning the index space (Figure 5 (a)). For three-dimensional index spaces with four GPU devices, there are six different ways of optimally partitioning an index space as shown in Figure 5 (b).

Our OpenCL runtime has a built-in partition table. The table is indexed by a pair that consists of the dimension of the work-group index space and the number of available GPUs in the system. Each partition table entry records all optimal partitions with respect to Constraint 1 and Constraint 2. We call an optimal partition with respect to Constraint 1 and Constraint 2 as a *work-group optimal partition*.

The last constraint is about the data transfer overhead between the host memory and the GPU device memories.

Constraint 3. *The partition should guarantee a minimum amount of data transfer between the host memory and the GPU device memories.*

To find a partition that minimizes the data transfer overhead, our OpenCL runtime performs a buffer access range analysis (in the sampling run) for each candidate partition in the selected partition table entry.

3.3 Run-Time Buffer Access Range Analysis

An OpenCL kernel accesses the global memory in a compute device using a pointer (e.g., A_gpu, B_gpu, and C_gpu in Figure 1 (c)) that is passed by the host program. It typically refers to a buffer. That is, a global array in the kernel is contained in a buffer. After performing the buffer access range analysis on a buffer with a given partition, our runtime obtains the access range of the buffer by each work-group assignment in the partition. To do so, the runtime performs a sampling run on the host when the host enqueues a kernel execution command. At this point of time, the runtime has obtained

all the information about the kernel arguments and the kernel index space.

If the subscript of a reference to a global array is in an affine form of the global ID, work-group ID, and local ID of the work-item that accesses the array, then the address of the array reference can be computed with the value of the pointer to the global array and an affine function of the global ID, work-group ID, and local ID of the work-item. That is, the address of the array reference is an affine function of the global ID, work-group ID, and local ID. In addition, as mentioned in Section 2, the global ID of a work-item can be computed with its work-group ID and local ID. Thus, the address of the array reference can be represented with an affine function of the work-group ID and local ID only.

For example, suppose that we have a three-dimensional index space and the address of a reference to a global array in the kernel is an affine function of global ID, work-group ID (w_x, w_y, w_z), and local ID (l_x, l_y, l_z). Then, the function can be represented only with the work-group ID and local ID:

$$f(l_x, l_y, l_z, w_x, w_y, w_z) = \quad a_1 l_x + a_2 l_y + a_3 l_z + a_4 w_x \\ + a_5 w_y + a_6 w_z + a_7,$$

where a_i is a constant for all $i = 1, 2, ..., 7$.

The simplest way to figure out the access range of a buffer by a work-group assignment is obtaining the lower bound and upper bound of addresses accessed by each work-item in the assignment. However, performing this at run-time is a very time consuming process because a typical OpenCL kernel has a large index space that contains many work-items. Instead, we sample some representative work-items in the work-group assignment and use them to compute the assignment's buffer access range. To select the representative work-items, we use the following theorem:

Theorem 1. *Suppose that a function $f_N : [L_1, U_1] \times [L_2, U_2] \times ... \times [L_N, U_N] \to \mathbb{Z}$ is affine in N variables $x_1, x_2, ..., and x_N$, where $L_i, U_i \in \mathbb{Z}$ for all $i = 1, 2, ..., N$. Then the maximum and minimum of f_N occur among 2^N points $(x_1, x_2, ..., x_N)$ such that $x_i = L_i$ or $x_i = U_i$ for all $i = 1, 2, ..., N$.*

Proof. We prove this theorem using induction on N. When $N = 1$, either f_1 has the maximum at L_1 and the minimum at U_1 or *vice versa* because f_1 is a linear function. Assume that for some integer $k \geq 1$, the maximum and minimum of an affine function f_k occur among 2^k points $(x_1, x_2, ..., x_k)$ such that $x_i = L_i$ or $x_i = U_i$ for all $i = 1, 2, ..., k$. An affine function f_{k+1} can be represented with the sum of two affine function f_k and f_1,

$$f_{k+1}(x_1, x_2, ..., x_{k+1}) = \quad a_1 x_1 + a_2 x_2 + ... + a_k x_k \\ + a_{k+1} x_{k+1} + a_{k+2} \\ = \quad f_k(x_1, x_2, ..., x_k) + f_1(x_{k+1}),$$

where a_i is a constant for all $i = 1, 2, ..., k + 2$. Since f_k has the maximum, say max_k, and the minimum, say min_k, at some points among 2^k points $(x_1, x_2, ..., x_k)$, where $x_i = L_i$ or $x_i = U_i$ for all $i = 1, 2, ..., k$, and either f_1 has the maximum, say max_1, at L_1 and the minimum, say min_1, at U_1 or *vice versa*, f_{k+1} has the maximum $max_k + max_1$ and the minimum $min_k + min_1$ at some points among 2^{k+1} points $(x_1, x_2, ..., x_k, x_{k+1})$ such that $x_i = L_i$ or $x_i = U_i$ for all $i = 1, 2, ..., k, k + 1$. ∎

For example, consider Figure 6 (a). Assume that we have a one-dimensional index space and an array reference in the kernel whose subscripts are affine functions of the global ID, work-group ID, and local ID of a work-item. To find the access range of the array reference in a work-group, it is sufficient to check two work-items located in 0 and $S_x - 1$ in the work-group, where S_x is the size of the work-group. That is, the lower bound and upper bound of the addresses accessed by the reference in the work-group can be obtained by sampling $2^1 = 2$ work-items (the two black circles in Figure 6 (a)) in the work-group. Similarly, it is sufficient to

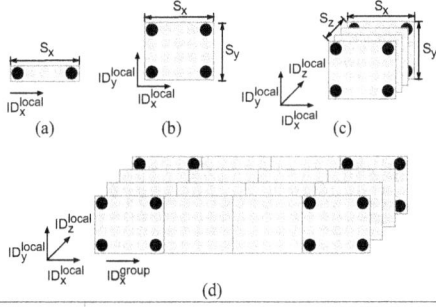

Figure 6. Representative work-items to measure the range of a buffer (array) that is accessed by a work-group assignment in the partition.

sample $2^2 = 4$ for a two-dimensional work-group (Figure 6 (b)) and $2^3 = 8$ for a three-dimensional work-group (Figure 6 (c)). An assignment in the given work-group partition typically consists of multiple work-groups as shown in Figure 6 (d). In this case, we have a three-dimensional local index space and a one-dimensional work-group index space. Thus, sampling $2^4 = 16$ work-items in the assignment is sufficient to find the access range of an affine array reference by all the work-items in the assignment.

In the worst case, it is sufficient to sample $2^6 = 64$ work-items for each work-group assignment in the partition when the assignment has a three-dimensional local index space and a three-dimensional work-group index space. The number of work-group assignments in the partition increases as the number of GPUs, say N_{device}, increases. In addition, the number of sampling is proportional to the number of work-group optimal partitions, say $N_{partition}$. Let D_{group} and D_{local} be the dimensions of the work-group index space and local index space. Then the number of work-items to be sampled by our runtime for each kernel is,

$$N_{partition} \cdot N_{device} \cdot 2^{(D_{group}+D_{local})}$$

However, to sample access ranges of a global array reference with our method, the reference needs to satisfy some more conditions with regards to the control flow. The conservative conditions that need to be simultaneously satisfied by a global array reference for sampling are as follows:

Sampling Condition

- Each index of the array reference is an affine function in global ID, work-group ID, and local ID.

- The array reference is not contained in a conditional statement.

- When the array reference is not contained in a loop, any variable used in its indices does not have more than one reaching definition.

- If the array reference is contained in well-behaved affine loops, each of its indices is an affine function in induction variables of the loops, global ID, work-group ID, and local ID.

A well-behaved loop[11] is a for loop in the form for(e1; e2; e3) stmt, in which e1 assigns a value to an integer variable i, e2 compares i to a loop invariant expression, e3 increments or decrements i by a loop invariant expression, and stmt contains no assignment to i. We say a well-behaved loop is *affine in the global ID, work-group ID, and local ID* if the expression assigned to i in e1 and the expression that is compared to i in e2 are some affine functions in the global ID, work-group ID, and local ID. That is, the lower bound and upper bound of the loop index variable of a well-behaved loop are affine functions in the global ID, work-group ID, and local ID.

If the array reference is contained in well-behaved affine loops and each of its indices is an affine function in induction variables

of the loops, global ID, work-group ID, and local ID, then the lower bound and upper bound of the index in the loop are also an affine function in the global ID, work-group ID, and local ID. This is because the lower bounds and upper bounds of the induction variables in the well-behaved affine loop are all an affine function in the global ID, work-group ID, and local ID. Based on Theorem 1, our runtime executes the loops with only the lower bounds and upper bounds of the loop indices.

After a sampling run, our runtime obtains buffer access ranges for each work-group assignment in all work-group optimal partitions. For an array reference that does not satisfy the sampling condition, our runtime conservatively assumes that every work-item accesses every element of the array. That is, the buffer access range of the array reference is the entire buffer. In this case, the runtime does not perform the sampling run for the array reference.

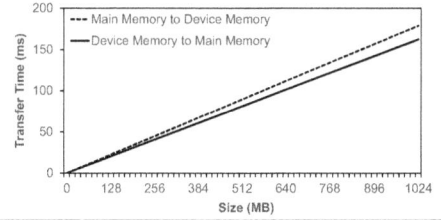

Figure 7. The data transfer time between the main memory and the GPU device memory through the PCI express bus.

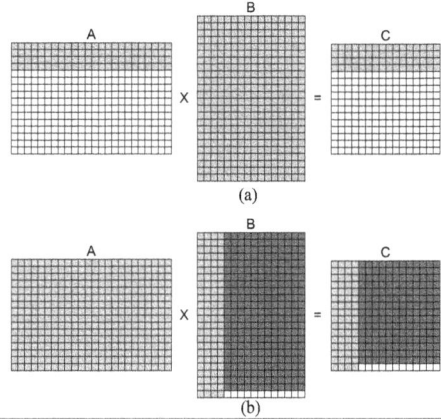

Figure 8. (a) The access range of arrays by a work-group assignment in the partition shown in Figure 4 (a) for the matrix multiplication kernel in Figure 1 (b). (b) The access range of arrays by a work-group assignment in the partition in Figure 4 (b).

3.4 Minimizing the Amount of Data Transfer

Figure 7 shows the data transfer time between the main memory (DDR3 72GB) and the GPU (NVIDIA GTX 480[13]) memory for different amounts of data transferred (from 16MB to 1024MB) through the PCI express bus. We see that the transfer time is strictly proportional to the amount of data transferred. In addition, if the OpenCL kernel accesses a buffer, then most probably all work-group assignments in a work-group optimal partition access the same buffer. This implies that the number of data transfers is most probably the same for all work-group optimal partitions. Thus, we can exclude the transfer initiation overhead of the PCI express bus from our consideration.

Since the data transfer time is strictly proportional to the amount of data transferred and the transfer is serialized by the PCI express bus, after the buffer access range analysis, the runtime computes the total amount of data transferred between the host and the devices for each work-group optimal partition that is recorded in the partition table entry. Then it chooses the partition that has the minimum amount of data transfer as an optimal partition with respect to Constraint 3.

```
void matrixMul(float *C, float *A, float *B, int WA, int WB)
{
    int i = get_global_id(0);
    int j = get_global_id(1);
    for ( int k = 0; k < WA; k += (WA-1) ) {
        GLOBAL_MEM_READ_float(&A[k + j * WA]);
        GLOBAL_MEM_READ_float(&B[i + k * WB]);
    }
    GLOBAL_MEM_WRITE_float(&C[i + j * WB]);
}
```
(a)

```
__global__ void matrixMul(float* C, float* A, float *B, int WA, int WB)
{
    int i = blockDim.x * blockIdx.x + threadIdx.x;
    int j = blockDim.y * blockIdx.y + threadIdx.y;
    float acc = 0.0f;
    for (int k = 0; k < WA; k++)
        acc += A[k + j * WA] * B[i + k * WB];
    C[i + j * WB] = acc;
}
```
(b)

```
__global__ void matrixMul(float* C, float* A, float *B, int WA, int WB,
                          uint memOffsetC, uint memOffsetA,
                          uint memOffsetB, uint3 blockOffset)
{
    int i = blockDim.x * (blockIdx.x + blockOffset.x) + threadIdx.x;
    int j = blockDim.y * (blockIdx.y + blockOffset.y) + threadIdx.y;
    float acc = 0.0f;
    for (int k = 0; k < WA; k++)
        acc += (A-memOffsetA)[k + j * WA]
             * (B-memOffsetB)[i + k * WB];
    (C-memOffsetC)[i + j * WB] = acc;
}
```
(c)

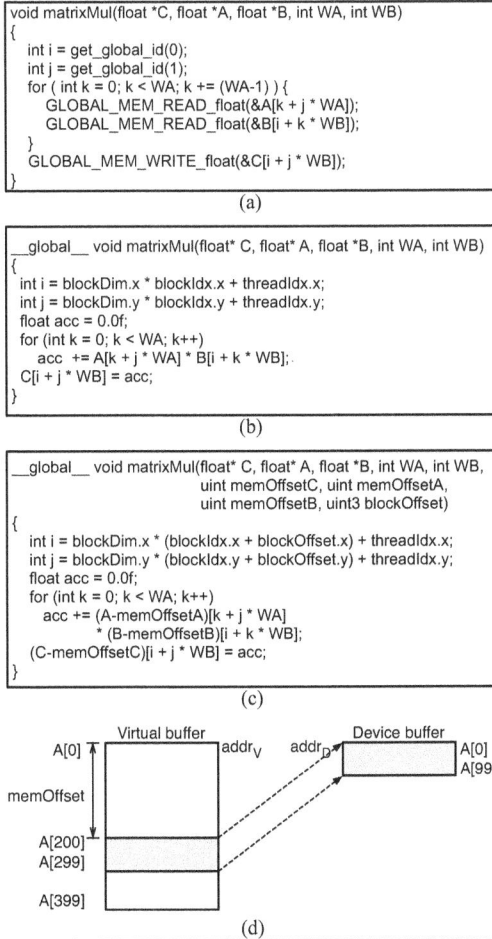
(d)

Figure 9. (a) The sampling code generated by our OpenCL-C-to-C translator for the matrix multiplication kernel in Figure 1 (b). (b) An equivalent CUDA kernel code to the matrix multiplication kernel in Figure 1 (b) for a single GPU. (c) The CUDA kernel code generated by our OpenCL-C-to-CUDA-C translator for multiple GPUs. (d) Address translation mechanism.

Figure 8 shows the buffer access ranges of the matrix multiplication kernel in Figure 1 (b). The ranges are found by our sampling run. Figure 8 (a) shows the ranges by a work-group assignment in the partition shown in Figure 4 (a). Figure 8 (b) shows the ranges by a work-group assignment in the partition shown in Figure 4 (b). Both of the partitions in Figure 8 (a) and Figure 8 (b) are work-group optimal. However, the partition in Figure 4 (b) requires more data transfer (the gray area in Figure 4 (b)) between the host and the devices. The elements in the darker gray areas in matrices B and C in Figure 8 (b) do not actually need to be transferred to the device buffer before the kernel execution or to the main memory after the kernel execution because they are not accessed by the device at all. Our method includes these areas because a buffer (array) is a one-dimensional collection of contiguous memory elements and it computes only the lower bound and upper bound of the buffer addresses accessed by each work-group assignment. Thus, the partition in Figure 4 (a) is better than that in Figure 4 (b).

3.5 Kernel Code Transformation

There are two source-to-source translators in our OpenCL framework. One is an OpenCL-C-to-CUDA-C translator that translates the OpenCL kernel code to the CUDA kernel code. The other is an OpenCL-C-to-C translator that translates the OpenCL kernel code to the sampling code.

Figure 9 (a) shows the sampling code generated by our OpenCL-C-to-C translator for the matrix multiplication kernel in Figure 1 (b). This code will be executed on the host by our runtime. In this code, the address of each affine global array reference is wrapped with a runtime API function. For example, GLOBAL_MEM_READ_float(&A[k+j*WA]); makes the runtime record the address of A[k+j*WA]. After recording the addresses for all work-items that are sampled, the runtime obtains the lower bound and upper bound of the addresses.

To generate the sampling code, our OpenCL-C-to-C translator uses program slicing techniques[25, 27]. First, it inlines user-defined function calls in the kernel. Then it performs constant propagation, loop invariant and induction variable recognition, and reaching definitions analysis for the kernel. The translator extracts the index computation slice for each array reference and iteratively applies forward substitution to the slice until there is no more forward-substitutable variable. The translator checks if it satisfies the sampling condition mentioned before. If the array reference satisfies the sampling condition, it replaces the reference in the slice with an appropriate API function (e.g., GLOBAL_MEM_READ_float()). The address of the reference (e.g., &A[k+j*WA]) is the argument to this function. After processing index computation slices of all affine array references that satisfy the sampling condition, the translator generate the sampling code. If the generated code contains a well-behaved affine loop, then the translator transforms the loop to iterate only for the lower bound and upper bound of the loop index (e.g., from for (int k = 0; k < WA; k++) to for (int k = 0; k < WA; k += (WA - 1)) in Figure 9 (a)).

An exception to the second item of the sampling condition is the case when an array reference is contained in a sole if statement with a condition of the form (e = 0), where e is a variable that becomes get_local_id(0). This case occurs when there is a reduction computation in the kernel, and the translator recognizes this idiom.

Figure 9 (b) shows an equivalent CUDA kernel code to the matrix multiplication kernel in Figure 1 (b). The CUDA reserved variable blockDim specifies the size of the local index space in OpenCL. Similarly, blockIdx and threadIdx are equivalent to the work-group ID and local ID in OpenCL, respectively. Figure 9 (c) shows the CUDA kernel code generated by our OpenCL-C-to-CUDA-C translator for the matrix multiplication kernel in Figure 1 (b) for multiple GPUs.

Since each dimension of blockIdx always starts with 0 in CUDA, we need to add an offset (blockOffset) to each dimension of blockIdx to preserve the original location of each work-item in the index space. In Figure 9 (d), the gray area in the virtual buffer is the access range of the work-group assignment that is assigned to a GPU. This portion of the virtual buffer is copied to the device buffer of the GPU. Then, an array reference A[200] in the virtual buffer becomes a reference A[0] in the device buffer. To make a reference A[200] in the CUDA kernel access the location of A[0] on the device, we need to shift the start address of the array in the CUDA kernel by -memOffset. Thus, a reference A[i] in the original OpenCL kernel becomes (A-memOffset)[i] in the CUDA kernel. Both of blockOffset and memOffset are passed to the CUDA kernel as arguments.

3.6 Managing the Virtual Device Memory

As mentioned before, our OpenCL runtime maintains the virtual device memory that is allocated in the host main memory. The

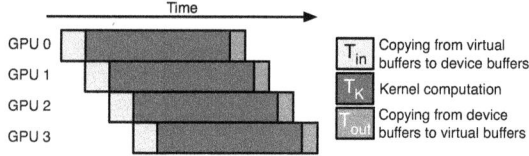

Figure 10. Overlapping the kernel computation and data transfer through the PCI express bus.

runtime treats it as if it were the device memory of a single GPU device and keeps it consistent to the memories of the multiple GPUs. Each buffer object is treated as a virtual buffer allocated in the virtual device memory. The virtual device memory is organized as a list of buffers. At the beginning, the list is empty.

When the host allocates a buffer object by invoking `clCreateBuffer()`, our virtual GPU device thread allocates the requested buffer in the virtual device memory. That is, it allocates a buffer in the host main memory and inserts the buffer into the list. When the host requests copying an array in the host program to a buffer object by invoking `clEnqueueWriteBuffer()`, it copies the array in the corresponding virtual buffer.

When the host enqueues a kernel execution command by invoking `clEnqueueNDRangeKernel()`, the runtime runs a sampling code to obtain virtual buffer access ranges and distributes the kernel workload. After obtaining the work-group optimal partition, the runtime assigns each work-group assignment in the partition to a GPU device. Using the access range information of each virtual buffer by the work-group assignment, the runtime allocates a device buffer, whose size is exactly the same as that of the access range, in the associated GPU device memory. Then, the runtime copies the virtual buffer area in the access range to the device buffer.

Our OpenCL runtime makes the virtual buffer consistent to the device buffers in the following two cases:

- When the host requests copying a buffer object to an array in the host program by invoking `clEnqueueReadBuffer()`.

- When a new kernel is launched and a GPU requires the data that has been modified by another GPU in the prior kernel execution.

The runtime creates in the main memory a twin (copy) of each shared and modified region of the virtual buffers between different GPUs. This sharing information is obtained from the buffer access range information. When a GPU has updated a device buffer and if the device buffer overlaps with one of the shared and modified regions, the runtime copies the device buffer to a temporary buffer space allocated in the main memory. The runtime updates the original virtual buffer with the result of comparison between the twin of the shared/modified region and the region in the temporary buffer. The non-shared regions in the temporary buffer are copied to the virtual buffer without any comparison. If the device buffer does not overlap with one of the shared/modified regions, the updated device buffer is directly copied to the corresponding area of the virtual buffer.

Sharing of virtual buffer access ranges between different GPU devices (i.e., between different work-group assignments in the partition) is mostly due to false sharing. Even though their access ranges overlap with each other, one GPU device typically does not modify the location that is modified by another device in the shared region.

3.7 Overlapping Data Transfer and Kernel Computation

Our method naturally overlaps data transfer and kernel computation as shown in Figure 10. Suppose that the work-group assignments and buffer access ranges are symmetric between N GPUs. Let T_K, T_{in}, and T_{out} be the kernel execution time on each GPU, the time taken to copy the virtual buffers to the device buffers before the

kernel execution, and the time taken to copy the device buffers to the virtual buffers after kernel execution on each GPU, respectively. Then, the overlap is maximized when $(N - 1) \cdot T_{in} \leq T_K$ and $T_{out} \leq T_{in}$. The total elapsed time will be $N \cdot T_{in} + T_K + T_{out}$.

4. Evaluation

In this section, we present the evaluation methodology and result for our OpenCL framework.

4.1 Methodology

Target machine. We evaluate the performance of our OpenCL framework using a system that consists of two Intel Xeon X5680 hexa-core CPUs, eight NVIDIA GeForce GTX 480 GPUs[13], and 72GB DDR3 main memory. It runs Ubuntu Linux 9.10. The CPU supports simultaneous multithreading (SMT) that enables two threads per core. The GPU has 1.6GB device memory and 15 streaming multiprocessors. Each streaming multiprocessor has 32 CUDA cores, and therefore each GPU has 480 CUDA cores. The GPUs communicate with the CPUs via a PCI-E Gen. 2 x16 bus that uses point-to-point serial links. The PCI-E Gen. 2 x16 bus has a data transfer rate of 8GBps (full duplex).

Benchmark applications. We run 11 OpenCL applications that are from various sources: AMD[1], PARSEC[3], CUDA Zone[16, 21], Parboil[24], NAS[12], and NVIDIA[17]. The applications from PARSEC, CUDA Zone, Parboil, and NAS are translated into OpenCL applications manually. Their details are described in Table 2. Column A shows the global memory size that is required to run each application, column B shows the number of kernels, column C shows the size of the work-group index space for each kernel in the application (separated by comma for each kernel, separated by a colon for the size in each dimension in the multi-dimensional work-group index space), column D shows the number of executions for each kernel (separated by comma), column E shows % execution time taken for the kernel to run on a single GPU in the total execution time, column F shows if inter-GPU communication through the main memory is required or not to run the application, column G indicates that if kernels in the application contains array references that do not satisfy the sampling condition as described in Section 3.3, column H shows if the references identified in column G are non-affine form of global ID, work-group ID, and local ID, and finally column I shows if the references identified in column G are contained in a conditional branch. Especially, all array references in Correlator and TPACF do not satisfy the sampling condition. This implies that we do not perform sampling runs for kernels in Correlator and TPACF and assume that each work-group assignment in the partition accesses the entire array.

Runtime and source-to-source translator. We have implemented our OpenCL runtime for multiple GPUs. We use NVIDIA CUDA Toolkit 3.1[17] to implement the runtime. We have implemented our OpenCL-C-to-C and OpenCL-C-to-CUDA-C translators by modifying **clang** that is a C front-end for the LLVM compiler infrastructure[9].

4.2 Results

Figure 11 shows the speedup numbers of the ideal case and our OpenCL framework over a single GPU for each application. We vary the number of GPUs (2, 4, and 8). The ideal speedup is obtained with the Amdahl's law[2]. We treat the OpenCL kernel execution time on a single GPU as the parallel fraction. The serial fraction is the time spent on a CPU by the application.

All applications but Correlator, EigenValue, MRI-Q, and RPES show a speedup that is close to the ideal speedup. Correlator has a single kernel in which each work-item has a different workload. Thus, for this kernel, an equal distribution of work-groups does not guarantee an equal distribution of workload in the kernel. Figure 12 shows the normalized average kernel execution time per GPU.

Application	Source	Description	Input	A	B	C	D	E	F	G	H	I
BinomialOption	AMD	Binomial option pricing	65520 samples, 100 iters.	2MB	1	65520	1	99.6%				
Blackscholes	PARSEC	Black-Scholes PDE	16773120 options, 1000 iters.	447.9MB	1	65520	1	92.7%				
Correlator	CUDA Zone	Radio astronomy signal correlator	512 stations, 128 channels	1282MB	1	512	1	83.3%		X	X	
CP	Parboil	Coulombic potential	8192x8192, 100000 atoms	256MB	1	512:512	25	99.7%				
EigenValue	AMD	Eigenvalue computation	65536x65536, 10 iters.	1.7MB	2	256, 256	6, 6	99.9%	X	X	X	
EP	NAS	Embarrassingly parallel	Class D	99MB	1	32768	1	99.9%		X		X
MatrixMul	NVIDIA	Matrix multiplication	8192x8192	768MB	1	512:512	1	68.7%				
MRI-Q	Parboil	Magnetic resonance imaging Q	Large	5MB	2	4, 1024	1, 2	50.3%		X		X
Nbody	NVIDIA	N-Body simulation	524288 bodies, 10 iters.	32MB	1	2048:1	1	99.5%		X		X
RPES	Parboil	Rys polynomial equation solver	Default	79.4MB	2	65528, 65528	54, 17	64.2%	X	X	X	X
TPACF	Parboil	Two-point angular correlation function	Default	9.5MB	1	201	1	63.8%		X		X

A: global memory size, B: # of kernels, C: the size of work-group index space, D: # of kernel executions, E: % execution time of kernels on a single GPU, F: inter-GPU communication, G: contains array references that do not satisfy the sampling condition, H: contains non-affine array references, I: contains array references in a conditional branch

Table 2. Applications used for the evaluation.

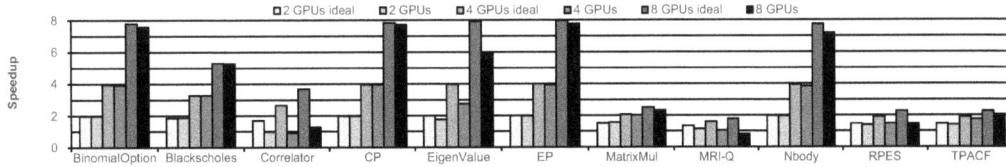

Figure 11. Speedup over a single GPU.

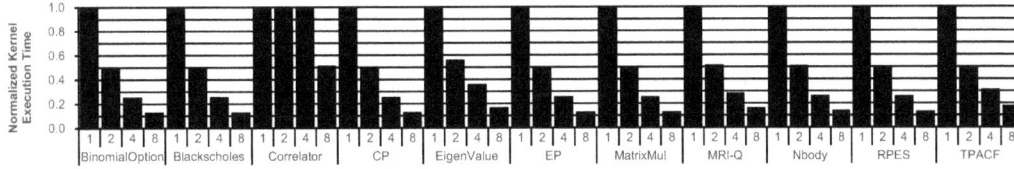

Figure 12. Average kernel execution time per GPU.

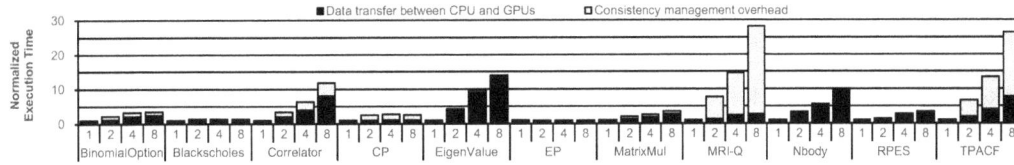

Figure 13. Data transfer time between the CPU and GPUs and consistency management overhead by the runtime.

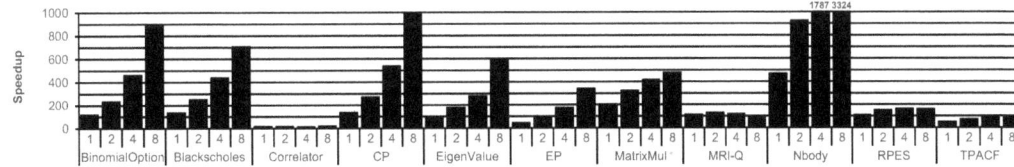

Figure 14. Speedup over a single CPU.

The average kernel execution time per GPU decreases linearly for all applications but Correlator. This accounts for the uneven distribution of the kernel workload in Correlator.

Another reason for the poor performance of Correlator is a high degree of read sharing and write sharing between buffer access ranges of different work-group assignments. Figure 13 shows the normalized data transfer time between the CPU and GPUs and consistency management overhead by the runtime for different numbers of GPUs. Data transfers are serialized by the PCI express bus. The consistency management overhead includes the overhead introduced by virtual buffer management (by the virtual GPU device thread), such as twin creation, CPU-to-CPU memory copy, and comparison for updates. The time is normalized to that of a single

GPU. Since the data transfer time with multiple GPUs increases when the number of GPUs increases, a high degree of sharing exists in buffer access ranges between different work-group assignments in Correlator. Moreover, increasing the number of GPUs also increases the consistency management overhead. This also means that Correlator has a high degree of overlap (i.e., false sharing) in buffer access ranges between different work-group assignments. There is no true sharing in Correlator.

EigenValue has large data transfer time between the CPU and GPUs for more than one GPU in Figure 13. It has two kernels that are consecutively executed. The second kernel reads data that has been written by the first. In addition, a GPU executing the second kernel reads data that has been written by another GPU in the first kernel (inter-GPU communication shown in Table 2). This accounts for the poor performance of EigenValue when compared with the ideal case. The case of RPES is similar to that of EigenValue. However, as the number of GPUs increases, RPES has a relatively small increment in the data transfer time between the CPU and GPUs in Figure 13. Since its kernel execution time is much smaller than its data transfer time, the data transfer time dominates the total execution time of RPES. TPACF has a significant amount of the consistency management overhead and data transfer time with more than one GPU. Unlike the case of RPES, the kernel execution time of TPACF is much bigger than the sum of data transfer time and consistency management time. Thus, the reduced kernel execution time due to multiple GPUs dominates TPACF's total execution time.

The poor performance of MRI-Q when compared with the ideal case is due to the high degree of false sharing between buffer access ranges from different work-group assignments. In Figure 13, it has a large amount of consistency management overhead due to the false sharing for more than one GPU. When the number of GPUs increases, the amount of overhead also increases.

Nbody has a relatively poor speedup with 8 GPUs. The reason is that the number of work-groups in Nbody is not big enough to make all streaming multiprocessors in the 8 GPUs busy. It also has data sharing between two consecutive execution instances of a single kernel (due to a loop that encloses the kernel) for more than one GPU. This results in a large amount of data transfer between the CPU and the GPUs in Figure 13. Not enough number of work-groups in the work-group index space (Table 2) also accounts for the poor performance of Correlator, EigenValue, MRI-Q, and TPACF with 8 GPUs.

As shown in Table 2, seven applications contain buffer references that do not satisfy the sampling condition. Our runtime conservatively assumes that the access range of these references is the entire buffer. The overheads of data transfer and consistent management in Correlator, RPES, and TPACF mainly come from the buffer references that do not satisfy the sampling condition.

Sampling overhead. The sampling overhead of our OpenCL runtime is negligible. The sampling overhead often increases as the number of GPUs, the dimension of the kernel index space, and the number of kernel executions increase. RPES has the biggest sampling overhead among the 11 benchmark applications. The work-group index space in RPES is two-dimensional and the number of total kernel executions is 71 as shown in Table 2. The sampling overhead in RPES with 8 GPUs accounts for 0.48% of its total execution time.

For your reference, Figure 14 shows the speedup of each application over a single CPU for different number of GPUs. The sequential CPU version of each application is obtained from the same source in Table 2. For MatrixMul, we optimize the CPU version using tiling; this is because the OpenCL version of MatrixMul exploits the same tiling optimization.

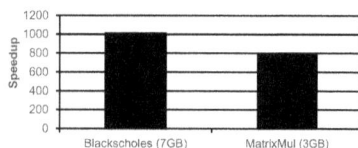

Figure 15. Speedup of applications that have a bigger data size than the memory size of a single GPU. The speedup is obtained with 8 GPUs over a single CPU.

Since our OpenCL runtime manages multiple device memories available in multiple GPUs through the virtual device memory, OpenCL applications with our OpenCL framework can process data whose size is much bigger than the size of the available memory in a single GPU. We choose some applications whose input is controllable to increase the size of data used. They are Blackscholes and MatrixMul. Figure 15 shows the speedups of Blackscholes and MatrixMul with 8 GPUs over a single CPU. Blackscholes processes 268,369,920 options and this requires 7GB of device memory. MatrixMul performs a matrix multiplication of two 16,384 x 16,384 floating point matrices. This requires a total of 3GB device memory. These two applications cannot be executed with a single GPU because the data size is bigger than the device memory size. For this reason, we obtain the speedup over a single CPU instead of a single GPU.

5. Related Work

Even though GPGPU systems with multiple GPUs are widening their user base, there have not been many proposals for exploiting those multiple GPUs. Most of the previous proposals require manual coding to exploit them. Unlike previous proposals, our approach is fully automatic and transparent to the user. With our approach, the unmodified OpenCL source code for a single GPU system runs directly on a multiple GPU system. To the best of our knowledge, our framework is the first OpenCL framework that automatically exploits multiple GPUs available in the system.

Schaa and Kaeli[22] categorize the GPU systems into distributed GPUs (a networked group of distributed systems each containing a single GPU) and shared-system GPUs (a single system containing multiple GPUs). They define performance estimation models to predict the performance of applications on these two categories. They show that their modeling framework works effectively on multiple GPUs. Quintana-Ortí et al.[20] propose a programming model and a runtime that solves dense linear algebra problems, such as matrix multiplication and Cholesky factorization, for multiple accelerators. Their approach is different from ours in that their runtime requires the detailed knowledge of an application before executing it, and the runtime schedules the tasks using a pre-built-in scheduling policy for the application. Phillips et al.[19] build a GPU-accelerated cluster for a molecular dynamics simulation of large bio-molecular systems and define API functions for programming the cluster. With 15 nodes (each node contains four GPUs), they achieve performance that nearly matches the performance of 330 CPU cores. Strengert et al.[23] introduce CUDASA, an extension to CUDA. CUDASA presents additional language elements that enable workload distribution capability for multiple GPUs. However, manual CUDASA coding is required to exploit multiple GPUs.

Data transfer between the CPU and GPUs can be a performance bottleneck for GPU applications[5, 8, 14, 29]. Thus, minimizing the data transfer overhead is a challenging problem. One solution is overlapping the data transfer and GPU computation. Gelado et al.[5] present a hardware support that overlaps the data transfer and GPU computation with a single GPU. It allows the CPU to transfer data for the next invocation of a CUDA kernel while the GPU is executing the current instance of the same kernel. Our framework enables overlapping the data transfer and GPU kernel computation for multiple GPUs without any hardware support.

There are some proposals for OpenCL frameworks[6, 10]. Gummaraju et al.[6] propose an OpenCL framework named Twin Peaks. It handles both CPUs and GPUs. Twin Peaks executes SPMD style OpenCL kernels on a CPU core by using routines that save/restore work-item contexts. They use their own light-weight `setjmp()` and `longjmp()` system calls for low overhead context switch. Lee et al.[10] propose an OpenCL framework for heterogeneous multicores with local memory, such as Cell BE processors. Their OpenCL framework has two optimization techniques for OpenCL programs running on the Cell BE architecture, namely work-item coalescing and preload-poststore buffering. Work-item coalescing is a technique that significantly reduces context switching overhead of executing an OpenCL kernel on multiple SPEs in the Cell BE processor. Preload-poststore buffering is a technique that hides memory latencies introduced by data transfers between the PPE and an SPE to execute the kernel.

6. Conclusions

We introduce the design and implementation of an OpenCL framework that provides an illusion of a single compute device to the programmer for multiple GPUs available in a GPGPU system. Providing a single virtual compute device image to the user makes an OpenCL application for a single GPU device portable to the system that has multiple GPUs. It also makes the application exploit full computing power of the multiple GPUs and all available GPU memories in the system.

Our OpenCL framework distributes the workload in an OpenCL kernel across multiple GPUs at run time when the information about the kernel work-group index space is known. To distribute the kernel workload across multiple GPUs efficiently, our framework performs a sampling run just before the kernel is executed. The sampling run obtains buffer access ranges of each affine array references for different GPUs. For non-affine array references, the runtime does not perform the sampling run and the access range becomes the entire buffer. Using this information, the runtime distributes the kernel work-group index space according to the three optimality constraints: expressibility in a single grid of CUDA thread blocks, load balancing between multiple GPUs, and the minimum amount of data transfer between the CPU and GPUs. To achieve a single compute device image, our runtime maintains the virtual device memory that is allocated in the main memory. The runtime treats the memory as if it were the memory of a single GPU and keeps it consistent to the memories of the multiple GPUs.

We have implemented our OpenCL runtime and compilers. Our OpenCL-C-to-C translator generates the sampling code from the OpenCL kernel code and OpenCL-C-to-CUDA-C translator generates the CUDA kernel code for the distributed OpenCL kernel. The experimental results with 11 OpenCL benchmark applications and a GPGPU system with 8 GPUs indicate that our approach is practical and promising.

References

[1] *ATI Stream Software Development Ket (SDK) v2.1.* AMD, 2010. http://developer.amd.com/gpu/atistreamsdk/pages/default.aspx.

[2] G. M. Amdahl. Validity of the single processor approach to achieving large scale computing capabilities. In *AFIPS '67 (Spring): Proceedings of the April 18-20, 1967, spring joint computer conference*, pages 483–485. ACM, 1967.

[3] C. Bienia, S. Kumar, J. P. Singh, and K. Li. The PARSEC benchmark suite: characterization and architectural implications. In *PACT '08: Proceedings of the 17th international conference on Parallel architectures and compilation techniques*, pages 72–81. ACM, October 2008.

[4] F. Darema. The SPMD Model: Past, Present and Future. *Lecture Notes in Computer Science*, 2131(1):1–1, January 2001.

[5] I. Gelado, J. H. Kelm, S. Ryoo, S. S. Lumetta, N. Navarro, and W.-m. W. Hwu. CUBA: an architecture for efficient CPU/co-processor data communication. In *ICS '08: Proceedings of the 22nd annual international conference on Supercomputing*, pages 299–308. ACM, June 2008.

[6] J. Gummaraju, L. Morichetti, M. Houston, B. Sander, B. R. Gaster, and B. Zheng. Twin peaks: a software platform for heterogeneous computing on general-purpose and graphics processors. In *PACT '10: Proceedings of the 19th international conference on Parallel architectures and compilation techniques*, pages 205–216. ACM, 2010.

[7] Khronos OpenCL Working Group. *The OpenCL Specification Version 1.0.* Khronos Group, 2009. http://www.khronos.org/opencl.

[8] D. B. Kirk and W.-m. W. Hwu. *Programming Massively Parallel Processors: A Hands-on Approach.* Morgan Kaufmann Publishers Inc., San Francisco, CA, USA, 2010. ISBN 0123814723, 9780123814722.

[9] C. Lattner and V. Adve. LLVM: A Compilation Framework for Lifelong Program Analysis & Transformation. In *CGO '04: Proceedings of the international symposium on Code generation and optimization*, pages 75–86, Washington, DC, USA, March 2004. IEEE Computer Society.

[10] J. Lee, J. Kim, S. Seo, S. Kim, J. Park, H. Kim, T. T. Dao, Y. Cho, S. J. Seo, S. H. Lee, S. M. Cho, H. J. Song, S.-B. Suh, and J.-D. Choi. An OpenCL framework for heterogeneous multicores with local memory. In *PACT '10: Proceedings of the 19th international conference on Parallel architectures and compilation techniques*, pages 193–204. ACM, 2010.

[11] S. S. Muchnick. *Advanced compiler design and implementation.* Morgan Kaufmann Publishers Inc., San Francisco, CA, USA, 1997. ISBN 1-55860-320-4.

[12] NASA Advanced Supercomputing Division. NAS Parallel Benchmarks. http://www.nas.nasa.gov/Resources/Software/npb.html.

[13] *NVIDIA Fermi Compute Architecture White Paper.* NVIDIA, 2009. http://www.nvidia.com/content/PDF/fermi_white_papers/NVIDIA_Fermi_Compute_Architecture_Whitepaper.pdf.

[14] *NVIDIA CUDA C Best Practices Guide 3.1.* NVIDIA, May 2010.

[15] *NVIDIA CUDA C Programming Guide 3.1.1.* NVIDIA, July 2010.

[16] *NVIDIA CUDA Zone.* NVIDIA, July 2010. http://www.nvidia.com/object/cuda_home_new.html.

[17] *NVIDIA GPU Computing Software Development Kit.* NVIDIA, June 2010. http://developer.nvidia.com/object/cuda_3_1_downloads.html.

[18] *Tesla M2050/M2070 GPU Computing Module.* NVIDIA, 2010. http://www.nvidia.com/object/product_tesla_M2050_M2070_us.html.

[19] J. C. Phillips, J. E. Stone, and K. Schulten. Adapting a message-driven parallel application to GPU-accelerated clusters. In *SC '08: Proceedings of the 2008 ACM/IEEE conference on Supercomputing*, pages 1–9, Piscataway, NJ, USA, November 2008. IEEE Press.

[20] G. Quintana-Ortí, F. D. Igual, E. S. Quintana-Ortí, and R. A. van de Geijn. Solving dense linear systems on platforms with multiple hardware accelerators. In *PPoPP '09: Proceedings of the 14th ACM SIGPLAN symposium on Principles and practice of parallel programming*, pages 121–130. ACM, 2009.

[21] J. W. Romein, P. C. Broekema, J. D. Mol, and R. V. van Nieuwpoort. The LOFAR correlator: implementation and performance analysis. In *PPoPP '10: Proceedings of the 15th ACM SIGPLAN symposium on Principles and practice of parallel programming*, pages 169–178. ACM, 2010.

[22] D. Schaa and D. Kaeli. Exploring the multiple-GPU design space. In *IPDPS '09: Proceedings of the 2009 IEEE International Symposium on Parallel&Distributed Processing*, pages 1–12, May 2009.

[23] M. Strengert, C. Müler, C. Dachsbacher, and T. Ertl. CUDASA: Compute Unified Device and Systems Architecture. In *Eurographics Symposium on Parallel Graphics and Visualization (EGPGV08)*, pages 49–56. Eurographics Association, April 2008.

[24] The IMPACT Research Group. Parboil Benchmark suite. http://impact.crhc.illinois.edu/parboil.php, 2009.

[25] F. Tip. A Survey of Program Slicing Techniques. Technical report, Amsterdam, The Netherlands, The Netherlands, 1994.

[26] V. Volkov and J. W. Demmel. Benchmarking gpus to tune dense linear algebra. In *SC '08: Proceedings of the 2008 ACM/IEEE conference on Supercomputing*, pages 1–11, Piscataway, NJ, USA, 2008. IEEE Press.

[27] M. Weiser. Program Slicing. In *ICSE '81: Proceedings of the 5th International Conference on Software Engineering*, pages 439–449, Piscataway, NJ, USA, 1981. IEEE Press.

[28] C. Yang, F. Wang, Y. Du, J. Chen, J. Liu, H. Yi, and K. Lu. Adaptive Optimization for Petascale Heterogeneous CPU/GPU Computing. In *IEEE Cluster '10: Proceedings of IEEE International Conference on Cluster Computing*, pages 19–28, Los Alamitos, CA, USA, 2010. IEEE Computer Society.

[29] Y. Yang, P. Xiang, J. Kong, and H. Zhou. A GPGPU compiler for memory optimization and parallelism management. In *PLDI '10: Proceedings of the 2010 ACM SIGPLAN conference on Programming language design and implementation*, pages 86–97. ACM, June 2010.

QoS Aware Storage Cache Management in Multi-Server Environments *

Ramya Prabhakar, Shekhar Srikantaiah, Rajat Garg, Mahmut Kandemir

Department of CSE, Pennsylvania State University

{rap244, srikanta, rgarg, kandemir}@cse.psu.edu

Abstract

In this paper, we propose a novel two-step approach to the management of the storage caches to provide predictable performance in multi-server storage architectures: (1) *An adaptive QoS decomposition and optimization* step uses max-flow algorithm to determine the best decomposition of application-level QoS to sub-QoSs such that the application performance is optimized, and (2) *A storage cache allocation* step uses feedback control theory to allocate shared storage cache space such that the specified QoSs are satisfied throughout the execution.

Categories and Subject Descriptors   D.4.2 [*Storage Management*]: Allocation/De-allocation Strategies

General Terms   Design, Experimentation, Performance

Keywords   Multi-server, Storage cache, QoS, I/O performance

1. Introduction

There have been recent studies [2, 5] on providing *quality of service (QoS)* in single-server storage systems, but there has been little research on coordinated schemes to regulate the effective performance provided by storage caches of multiple I/O servers. Clearly, *intra-server analysis* does not capture inter-server interactions, and as a result, cannot be used for satisfying QoS requirements from multiple servers. More specifically, an intra-server scheme has a local scope. It is oblivious to optimizations in resource allocations that can be performed by provisioning more storage cache on another under-utilized server. Current implementations of shared storage cache management do not provide mechanisms that accommodate multiserver-wide, application level QoS specification and management. We argue that a high level QoS specification needs to be mapped to sub-QoSs at different servers to handle resource allocation in each of the servers in a fine-grained manner. However, the question of how to determine an optimal decomposition of specified QoS into sub-QoSs is a challenging research issue because of the dynamic sharing of storage cache resources among simultaneously executing applications. Determining the best decomposition should consider the resource sharing patterns in the current phase of application execution. Also, once the sub-QoSs are determined, it is not trivial to determine how to best allocate storage cache resources within each I/O server to maximize a global (inter-application) metric. The key here is to identify which applications can make better use of available shared resources, as compared to others, once QoS requirements of all co-running applications are met.

Contributions: To address the above mentioned problems, we model the problem of finding the best QoS decomposition as an

* This work is supported in part by NSF grants #0937949, #0621402, #0724599, #0821527, and #0833126.

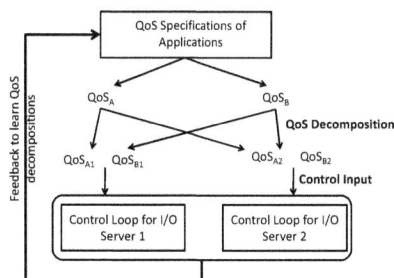

Figure 1. Two levels of adaptations in MSQoS scheme to allocate shared resources illustrated in a two server system.

adaptive max-flow problem in a network created by the QoS decomposition with QoS values as the capacities of the network flow. We then partition the shared storage cache space across applications using feedback control theory such that the specified QoSs are satisfied throughout the execution. We use a customized multiple-input multiple-output (MIMO) feedback controller to regulate the performance received by each application in each I/O server at the determined QoS component. Our experimental evaluation indicates that, on an average, our approach improves the I/O throughput of applications by 48.6%, 29.2%, and 20.7%, respectively, over the uncontrolled partitioning, fair share and uniform decomposition schemes.

2. Proposed MSQoS Cache Management Algorithm

MSQoS enables two levels of adaptations on available resources as shown in Figure 1 for a two-server system. At a finer granularity, the controller adapts to resource constraints by managing the resources dynamically to track the requested performance metric as closely as possible, and provides estimates of resources available at each server. At a coarse granularity, the adaptation module uses the feedback provided by controllers in each server, and adapts to the best QoS decomposition that reduces the stress on critical resources.

2.1 Controller Design for Automatic Feedback Control

Our proposed customized control architecture is based on a MIMO model that can track reference inputs for multiple applications with reasonable accuracy. Our proposed controller consists of three major components: (i) *per-application controllers (PAC)*; (ii) *conflict manager (CM)*; and (iii) *a target revision component (TRC)*. PAC is responsible for accurately predicting the amount of storage cache space required for achieving the target QoS components (I/O throughput). It is based on a per-application I/O throughput vs. cache size *regression* model that it maintains and updates dynamically to adapt to phase behavior of applications. The output

Parameter	Value
Number of Storage Servers	4
Number of Applications	4
Storage Server Cache Size	1 GB
Disk RPM	10,045
Disk Seek Time	5 msec
Controller invocation interval	3 sec
QoS decomposition interval	30 sec
Cache Block Size	16 KB
Replacement Policy in Storage Server Cache	LRFU

Table 1. Important experimental parameters.

of this component is a storage cache size which can achieve the required QoS component for that application. The main job of **CM** is to provide a *feasible allocation* by recovering the excess cache capacity in a manner proportional to the application priorities. When the storage cache space requested is less than what is available, **TRC** could increase the utilization of the storage cache by allocating cache space to applications based on their priorities.

2.2 Adaptive QoS Decomposition using Max-flow Algorithm

We model the QoS decomposition of application specifications as a *network* where the applications and I/O servers form the nodes and the QoS component of a particular application's QoS specification to a specific I/O server forms an edge between the application and that I/O server. We add a virtual source node and a virtual sink node such that all application nodes are connected to the virtual source and all server nodes are connected to the virtual sink node. Each edge in this network has an associated capacity. Since QoS specifications are represented as the capacities of the edges from the source to applications, finding a QoS decomposition that is satisfiable by the servers is equivalent to finding *maximum flows* on the network from the source to the sink. In the Ford-Fulkerson method, we start with a flow, $f(u, v) = 0$ for all $u, v \in V$, giving an initial flow of value 0. At each iteration, we increase the flow value by finding an augmenting path and then augmenting the flow along this path. We repeat this process until no augmenting path can be found. It has been shown that this algorithm terminates with the maximum flow solution in polynomial time if the augmentation paths are selected in breadth-first order. The weights of the edges between application nodes and server nodes in the solution to the maximum flow problem represent a valid QoS decomposition which is expected to satisfy the QoS specification to the greatest extent possible.

3. Experimental Setup

We built a storage cache simulator that supports multiple applications accessing different storage servers. Our simulator simulates shared storage caches in the multiple storage servers, and is interfaced with DiskSim 3.0, an accurate time-aware disk simulator, that simulates the Seagate ST39102LW disk model for measuring I/O performance. The important experimental parameters are described in Table 1. We used traces of the following four I/O intensive benchmarks: **BTIO** [6] is a NAS Parallel Benchmark that is an I/O version of BT (Block Tridiagonal) benchmark. **IOR** is a flexible I/O benchmark developed by the Scalable I/O Project (SIOP) at LLNL that performs Interleaved or Random (IOR) reads and writes to/from a single file [4]. **HP-IO** [1] is a high-performance I/O benchmark that manipulates regular data types characterized by region size, count and spacing. Finally, **MPI-tile-I/O** [3] is a benchmark that tests the performance of MPI-I/O for non-contiguous access workload.

4. Experimental Results

We first describe the *base schemes* against which we compare the performance of our proposed MSQoS scheme. In *uncontrolled*

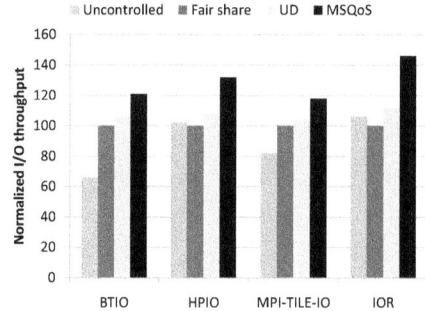

Figure 2. Comparison of throughputs obtained with MSQoS against the base schemes.

partitioning scheme, the system does not enforce any partitioning of the shared storage cache space. In *Fair Share* this scheme, the storage cache space in each server is divided equally among applications that access that server. In *Uniform Decomposition (UD)* scheme, the server caches are controlled by the feedback controller described earlier. However, it contrasts with MSQoS in that it does not have an adaptive QoS decomposition scheme.

Figure 2 plots the results of the comparison to base schemes normalized to the throughput obtained in the fair share case. We can see from Figure 2 that MSQoS achieves much higher throughput than the specified QoS. While the uniform decomposition performs better than the uncontrolled partitioning and the fair share case, it is unable to achieve the requested throughput guarantee in case of MPI-Tile-IO. We observed that it is due to excessive inter-application interference with the cache-intensive applications like IOR in servers 1 and 2 and with HPIO in servers 1 and 3. The benefits obtained by MSQoS over the uniform decomposition scheme are significant. A reason for this improvement in throughput is the ability of adaptive QoS decomposition scheme to dynamically vary the QoS components of an application among the different servers it accesses. In addition to the dynamic QoS decomposition, it is also important that the controllers give the right feedback about server capacity in response to the specified QoS components whenever possible. MSQoS is able to achieve significant throughput benefits in case of MPI-Tile-IO. On an average, MSQoS improves the throughput of our applications by 48.6%, 29.2%, and 20.7%, respectively, over the uncontrolled partitioning, fair share and uniform decomposition schemes.

5. Conclusions

In this work, we propose MSQoS, a multiserver QoS architecture, that first determines the best decomposition of application-level QoS to sub-QoSs (per-I/O server) in the adaptive QoS decomposition and optimization step using a max-flow formulation of the problem, and then allocates the shared storage cache such that the specified sub-QoSs are satisfied using feedback control theory.

References

[1] A. Ching. Evaluating I/O characteristics and methods for storing structured scientific data. In *IPDPS*, 2006.

[2] P. Goyal et al. Cachecow: Providing QoS for storage system caches. In *SIGMETRICS*, 2003.

[3] A. N. Laboratories. Parallel I/O benchmarking consortium. http://www.mcs.anl.gov/research/projects/pio-benchmark/.

[4] H. Shan et al. Using IOR to analyze the I/O performance for HPC platforms. In *Technical Report, National Energy Research Scientific Computing Center (NERSC), Computational Research Division, Lawrence Berkeley National Laboratory*, 2003.

[5] S. Uttamchandani et al. Polus: Growing storage QoS management beyond a "4-year old kid". In *FAST*, 2004.

[6] P. Wong and R. F. V. Wijngaart. NAS parallel benchmarks I/O version 2.4. NASA Technical Report, 2003.

Weak Atomicity Under the x86 Memory Consistency Model

Amitabha Roy
University of Cambridge
amitabha.roy@cl.cam.ac.uk

Steven Hand
University of Cambridge
steven.hand@cl.cam.ac.uk

Tim Harris
Microsoft Research, Cambridge
tharris@microsoft.com

Abstract

We consider the problem of building a weakly atomic Software Transactional Memory (STM), that provides Single (Global) Lock Atomicity (SLA) while adhering to the x86 memory consistency model (x86-MM).

Categories and Subject Descriptors D.1.3 [*Software*]: Programming Techniques Concurrent Programming

General Terms Algorithms, Theory, Performance

Keywords Software Transactional Memory, x86 Memory Model

1. Introduction

Single Lock Atomicity semantics require that "atomic" blocks behave as if they all acquire a single process-wide lock at the beginning and release it at the end. There has been considerable work on providing SLA for the Java memory model [3] and some on C/C++ [6]. In contrast to SLA work in these *language* level memory models, there has been no work on providing SLA at the level of a processor memory consistency model. The simple example below illustrates how the memory models differ greatly.

```
// Thread 1        | // Thread 2
atomic {           |
   X = 10;         | t1 = Y;
   Y = 10; }       | t2 = X;
```
C++: Catch fire due to data race, any result allowed
Java: Intra-thread reordering allowed
x86: No intra-thread reordering

In the example, the result `t1 == 10` and `t2 == 0` is allowed by the C++ and Java memory models but forbidden by the x86 one. An STM used to implement SLA and the x86 memory model must ensure that the forbidden result does not occur. A practical application of such an STM would be as the last stage in compilation (after machine code is generated) or through a dynamic binary rewriting engine [4]. The natural consequence of the lack of such an STM is that work needing it suffers from caveats in general applicability, requiring the user to be aware of the internals of the underlying STM implementation.

We have designed an STM algorithm that provides SLA and x86-MM to the most general class of programs possible. We exclude only programs with Transactional Reads Unprotected Writes

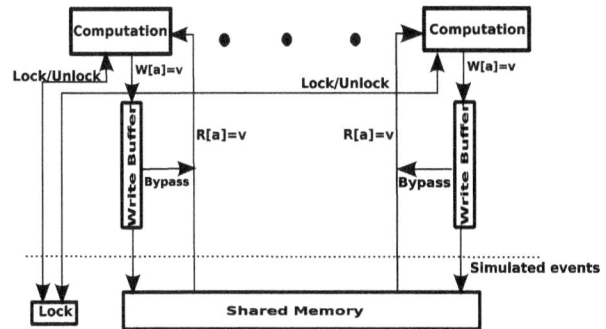

Figure 1. TSO state machine with per processor private memory

```
int X = 0, Y = 0, Z = 0; bool done1 = false, done2 = false;
// Thread 1    | // Thread 2   | // Thread 3  | // Thread 4
atomic {       | atomic {      | Y = 300;     | t1 = done1;
   X = 100;    |    if(Y == 0) | X = 300;     | t2 = done2;
   done1 = true; |    Z = 1;   |              |
}              |    done2 = true; |           |
               | }             |              |
       // Not allowed by x86-MM and SLA:
  // X == 100 and t1 == true and t2 == false and Z == 1
```

Figure 2. Loads must be ordered across atomic blocks

(TRUW) races, which is a race between a read in a transaction and a write outside any transaction. Crucially however, we use weak atomicity and ensure that ad-hoc synchronisation [2] done by the program is preserved.

2. Memory Consistency

We use the memory consistency model of Owens et al. as reference [5] (Figure 1). This casts the x86 as a sequential machine except for a write buffer that delays the visibility of stores to other processors. Each processor can acquire a lock to gain exclusive access to memory (modelling locked instructions). Interestingly, under the write-back memory type in x86, load fences and store fences become no-ops (since loads and stores are already ordered). On the other hand, locked instructions and memory fences (`mfence`) need to flush the write buffer on the executing processor.

3. x86-MM + SLA = Impossible

We prove by example that any STM that aims to provide x86-MM and SLA for transactions in *any* program must execute transactions serially (and hence can provide no scalability).

Consider the program fragments in Figure 2. When executing on the state machine of Figure 1, we have the following reasoning: `Thread 4` is the 'witness' to `Thread 1` acquiring the global lock

PPoPP'11, February 12–16, 2011, San Antonio, Texas, USA.
ACM 978-1-4503-0119-0/11/02.

```
                int X = 0, Y = 0, Z = 0, W = 0;
    // Thread 1          // Thread 2          // Thread 3
    atomic {             atomic {             t1 = X ;
       X = 100;             Z = 100;          t2 = Z;
       Y = 100;             W = 100;          t3 = W;
    }                    }                    t4 = Y;
            // Not allowed by x86-MM and SLA:
       t1 == 100 and t2 == 0 and t3 == 100 and t4 == 0
```

Figure 3. Stores must be ordered across atomic blocks

before `Thread` 2. Since the final value of X is 100, `Thread` 3 must have flushed its write to X from its write buffer to main-memory before `Thread` 1. This also means that it must have flushed its write to Y before `Thread` 1 flushed its write to X. `Thread` 2 cannot acquire the lock until thread 1 has flushed its write buffer (in order for the unlock to be visible to it) and hence when it acquires the lock the writes by thread 3 are already in memory. Hence it cannot read Y == 0 and thus cannot set Z = 1. Finally, note that the program fragment is also an example of a TRUW race, between the stores to Y on `Thread` 3 and the load from Y on `Thread` 2.

A weakly atomic STM will not see any conflicts from `Thread` 3 or `Thread` 4, which means that it cannot detect the departure from x86-MM by solely depending on conflict detection. Instead it must always serialise the loads in a transaction after all stores in a previous transaction.

In Figure 3, on the other hand, stores from the transaction in `Thread` 2 must be ordered after all stores in the transaction on `Thread` 1. Interleaving leads to the disallowed result. Interleaving however does not cause any conflicts and hence a weakly atomic STM is forced to serialise all stores in a transaction after all stores in a previous transaction.

One also needs to consider the fact that buffering of writes (lazy update) is essential for the STM not to expose speculative writes to non-transactional reads. This means reads must always precede and complete before transaction linearisation, followed by writeback. Coupled with the intra-thread ordering requirements illustrated by the two examples above, one concludes that that the only way to preserve SLA under x86-MM for all programs is to ensure that transactions execute all their operation serially with no overlap. It is thus not possible to build a weakly atomic STM with any kind of scalability optimisations while still providing SLA on x86-MM for *all programs*. This is in contrast to work that strives to provide SLA in Java [3]. This is because the language level memory models are more permissive. For example, the language level memory models for C++ and Java *allow* the results in the examples by virtue of allowing reordering of operations on the same thread (within the transaction).

4. x86-MM + SLA − TRUW Races = Possible

We have designed and implemented an STM (without complete serialisation) that provides SLA + x86 MM to all programs excluding those with TRUW races. The salient points of the algorithm are listed below.

4.1 Speculation Phase

During the speculation phase we depend on STM read and write barriers to log all loads and stores. We use as a basis a lazy weakly atomic STM similar to TL2 [1]. However we log every read and write into software read and write buffers with no merging of adjacent reads and writes (unlike STMs that use larger granularities such as a cache line). This is critical to preserving the x86-MM. Further, we handle accesses of any size including overlapping accesses. We fall back to irrevocability on encountering any memory

access originating from a locked instruction or on encountering an `mfence`. Both of these instructions require flushing the write buffer and hence would lead to a departure from the x86-MM when executing with the STM.

4.2 Commit Phase

We use a two phase commit. The first phase of the commit acquires metadata locks on modified locations. The second phase verifies every read from the read buffer in addition to checking STM metadata. At this point the transaction succeeds and the write logs are played back into shared memory.

We introduce additional synchronisation between threads in the commit phase. Each commit acquires a unique commit ticket from a global counter. Threads with a later commit ticket must execute their write back phase after threads with an earlier commit ticket have finished their write back phase. The read checks are performed in parallel, the departure from total serialisation costs us the capability to handle TRUW races. The commit phase includes a dynamic race detector (false negatives but no false positives) for the TRUW races we cannot handle for no additional performance penalty.

4.3 Speculation Safety

Our focus for the STM has been safety. In addition to preserving the x86 memory consistency model for any program not including a TRUW race, we also provide the same guarantee to *speculating* threads. A speculating thread is not allowed to execute with a read set that it could not have seen when executing with SLA. Further, since we buffer writes, no uncommitted values are allowed to leak out of speculating transactions.

5. Conclusion

We have designed and implemented an STM algorithm to provide SLA and the x86 memory consistency model to transactions. This is not merely an academic exercise and the STM we have designed is integrated with an efficient instrumentation system for x86 binaries that we have built. The two together provide SLA for atomic blocks delimited by a single global lock in the binary, provided the program is free of TRUW races.

References

[1] D. Dice, O. Shalev, and N. Shavit. Transactional locking II. In *DISC '06: Proc. 20th International Symposium on Distributed Computing*, pages 194–208, Sept. 2006.

[2] A. Jannesari and W. Tichy. Identifying ad-hoc synchronization for enhanced race detection. In *IPDPS '10: Proc. 25th IEEE International Symposium on Parallel Distributed Processing (IPDPS)*, pages 1–10, April 2010.

[3] V. Menon, S. Balensiefer, T. Shpeisman, A.-R. Adl-Tabatabai, R. Hudson, B. Saha, and A. Welc. Single global lock semantics in a weakly atomic STM. In *TRANSACT '08, 3rd ACM SIGPLAN Workshop on Languages, Compilers, and Hardware Support for Transactional Computing*, Feb. 2008.

[4] M. Olszewski, J. Cutler, and J. G. Steffan. JudoSTM: A dynamic binary-rewriting approach to software transactional memory. In *PACT '07: Proc. 16th International Conference on Parallel Architecture and Compilation Techniques*, pages 365–375, Sept. 2007.

[5] S. Owens, S. Sarkar, and P. Sewell. A better x86 memory model: x86-TSO. In *TPHOLs: 22nd Annual Conference on Theorem Proving in Higher Order Logics*, 2009.

[6] C. Wang, W.-Y. Chen, Y. Wu, B. Saha, and A.-R. Adl-Tabatabai. Code generation and optimization for transactional memory constructs in an unmanaged language. In *CGO '07: Proc. 2007 International Symposium on Code Generation and Optimization*, pages 34–48, Mar. 2007.

Kremlin: Like gprof, but for Parallelization

Donghwan Jeon   Saturnino Garcia   Chris Louie   Sravanthi Kota Venkata   Michael Bedford Taylor

University of California, San Diego

{djeon, sat, cmlouie, skotavenkata, mbtaylor}@cs.ucsd.edu

Abstract

This paper overviews Kremlin, a software profiling tool designed to assist the parallelization of serial programs. Kremlin accepts a serial source code, profiles it, and provides a list of regions that should be considered in parallelization. Unlike a typical profiler, Kremlin profiles not only work but also parallelism, which is accomplished via a novel technique called *hierarchical critical path analysis*. Our evaluation demonstrates that Kremlin is highly effective, resulting in a parallelized program whose performance sometimes outperforms, and is mostly comparable to, manual parallelization. At the same time, Kremlin would require that the user parallelize significantly fewer regions of the program. Finally, a user study suggests Kremlin is effective in improving the productivity of programmers.

Categories and Subject Descriptors D.2.2 [*Software Engineering*]: Design Tools and Techniques; D.1.3 [*Programming Techniques*]: Concurrent Programming—parallel programming

General Terms Measurement, Performance

1. Introduction

As multicore processors dominate mainstream computing, more programmers are forced to parallelize their serial programs. Although tools such as OpenMP and Cilk++[4] have been proposed to help programmers with this task, one important question has been largely overlooked: "which parts of the program should I spend time parallelizing?"

`gprof` and similar profilers provide a solution to a similar problem in serial optimization. A conventional profiler models a program as a hierarchical region where a region typically represents a loop or a function and possibly contains other subregions. The profiler produces a list of regions ordered by their work coverage. We call this ordered list a "plan" because it focuses the programmer's efforts on the regions where optimization is likely the most fertile: those regions with the largest percentage of work. Unfortunately, traditional profilers have limited value during parallelization because they do not profile parallelism, leaving the programmer to manually determine if a region has any parallelism.

In this paper, we overview Kremlin, a profiling tool that is designed to help during the parallelization of a serial program. Kremlin produces a plan based on not only work but also parallelism. In accordance with Amdahl's Law, Kremlin calculates the speedup

PPoPP'11, February 12–16, 2011, San Antonio, Texas, USA.
ACM 978-1-4503-0119-0/11/02.

```
$> make CC=kremlin-cc
$> ./tracking data
$> kremlin tracking --openmp

    File (lines)        Parallelism   Cov.(%)
1   imageBlur.c (49-58)    145.3        9.7
2   imageBlur.c (37-45)    145.3        8.7
3   getIPatch.c (26-35)     25.3        8.86
... ...                     ...          ...
```

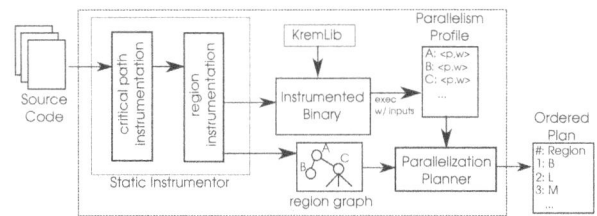

Figure 1. (top) Kremlin Usage Model and (bottom) the Overview of Kremlin System Architecture

from parallelizing a region by using both its parallelism and its work, ordering regions by their calculated speedup.

The major challenge in a profiler for parallelization is to extract the region-localized parallelism for each region. The region-localized parallelism represents the maximum speedup in a region when only that region–not its subregions–are parallelized. Previous work in critical path analysis (CPA) [3] measured the amount of parallelism in a program but did not localize parallelism to specific regions. Kremlin overcomes this problem by employing a novel technique called *hierarchical critical path analysis, or HCPA*. Based on the program's region hierarchy and CPA results for each region, *HCPA* extracts region-localized parallelism.

From our preliminary evaluation with NAS Parallel Bench (NPB) [2], Kremlin turns out to be very effective. Kremlin reduces the number of regions parallelized by 1.59X on average compared to a third-party parallelization, while outperforming the third-party's performance by as high as 1.85X, with a geometric mean of 1.08X. A user study shows that Kremlin greatly reduces the amount of time that users waste on trying to parallelizing regions that offer little-to-no benefit.

2. Kremlin Overview

Figure 1 illustrates the Kremlin system. Kremlin's usage model is similar to `gprof` (see Figure 1-top). The user compiles input code with a drop-in replacement compiler called `kremlin-cc` to generate an instrumented binary. After the user executes the generated binary, Kremlin outputs a plan consisting of the regions that should be parallelized based on the parallelism profile gathered at runtime. Internally, Kremlin consists of two major modules: the static instrumentor and the parallelization planner (see Figure 1-bottom).

Benchmark	Total	Third-Party	Kremlin	Reduction
bt	447	54	27	**2.00x**
cg	135	22	9	**2.44x**
ep	41	1	1	**1.00x**
ft	447	6	6	**1.00x**
is	59	1	1	**1.00x**
lu	509	28	11	**2.55x**
mg	653	10	8	**1.25x**
sp	1366	70	58	**1.21x**
Overall	3657	192	121	**1.59x**

(a) Plan Size Comparison

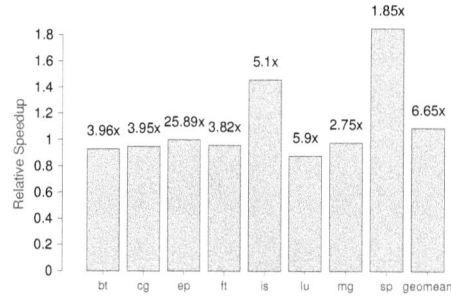

(b) Relative (bar) and Absolute (number) Speedup of Kremlin

Figure 2. Evaluation of Kremlin based Parallelization. Compared to a third-party manual parallelization [1], Kremlin-based parallelization achieves comparable or better speedups with less regions parallelized.

Static Instrumentor The instrumentor inserts function calls in the source code so that Kremlin correctly captures the regions hierarchy and gathers parallelism-relevant information. The instrumented code is linked to KremLib, which implements the instrumentation functions. HCPA specially treats false dependences and easy-to-break dependences as they can create a false impression of seriality in the region. Although the overhead of HCPA instrumentation could be high, the use of a compression technique significantly lowers the overhead. In NPB, the compression technique reduces the average log file size from 17.9GB to 150KB.

Parallelization Planner The parallelization planner produces a plan based on the information gathered from instrumentation. From localized parallelism and work, the planner can calculate the impact on application speedup when a region is parallelized. However, parallelizing a region could affect the potential parallelization benefit in other regions, complicating the design of the planner. For example, consider a doubly-nested loop where both inner and outer loops are parallel. Parallelizing the outer loop directly impacts the benefit of parallelizing the inner loop as the work coverage of the loop nest in the program has already shrunk when the outer region is parallelized. The planner iteratively selects the region with the maximum application speedup, updating the speedup of other regions based on the region hierarchy and the parallelization status of each region. This greedy algorithm finishes when the calculated speedup does not meet a minimum threshold value.

3. Preliminary Results

Our preliminary results examine three key aspects of Kremlin: its plan size, the speedup gained from following it, and its impact on a programmer's productivity. We examined NPB because a third-party OpenMP parallelization is available [1]. We ran Kremlin on the serial run of each benchmark to get a parallelism plan, and created a Kremlin-based parallel implementation. All results were gathered on a 32-core system (8x AMD Opteron 8380 processors).

Kremlin Plan Size To determine Kremlin's ability to reduce the number of regions considered during parallelization, we measured the number of parallelized regions in the third-party parallel version and compared it to Kremlin's plans. Figure 2(a) shows this information. Kremlin recommends 1.59X fewer regions on average compared to the third-party version. Furthermore, Kremlin never recommends more regions than the third-party version, suggesting its value in reducing a programmer's effort.

Kremlin Plan Performance While the smaller plan produced by Kremlin can reduce the effort to parallelize a program, the plan would be of limited utility if it leads to poor performance. To determine the performance of Kremlin based parallelization, we com-

pared it with the performance of the third-party parallel version. Figure 2(b) shows Kremlin significantly outperforms the manual parallelization in is (1.46X) and sp (1.85X) while offering competitive performance in remaining benchmarks, resulting in 1.08X geometric mean speedup against the third-party. The improved performance in is and sp resulted from Kremlin uncovering parallelism at a coarser-grain than was exploited by the third-party.

Impact on the Productivity of Programmers In order to see Kremlin's impact on the productivity of programmers, we performed a user study involving seven students in a graduate-level course at UCSD. Students were split into two groups (A and B) and asked to parallelize two programs. For program 1, group A had access to both gprof *and* Kremlin while group B had access to only gprof. For program 2, the tool access was alternated to normalize group differences in the study. We identified the critical regions, those that bring a speedup over 5%, of the two programs via extensive manual parallelization before the experiment. We measured the time students spent in parallelizing these critical regions as opposed to other regions. In both programs, the group who had access to Kremlin spent a much larger percentage of time on critical regions (84% vs 56% in program 1, 92% vs 49% in program 2). Although the sample size is admittedly small, this result suggests that Kremlin improves programmer productivity by reducing the time spent on regions that do not have a large benefit.

4. Conclusion and Future Work

Kremlin helps parallelization by providing a parallelism plan that ranks regions in the order of importance in parallelization. From our experiments with NPB, Kremlin was able to significantly reduce the number of regions parallelized compared to a manual parallelization, without sacrificing the performance. Also, our user study demonstrates a programmer with Kremlin tends to focus on regions that actually bring a speedup from parallelization, suggesting Kremlin would improve a programmer's productivity. We are currently striving to improve the quality of the parallelization planner by incorporating a wider range of information such as program structure, parallelization platforms, and target machine parameters. *This work was funded in part by NSF Award 0725357.*

References

[1] "NAS Parallel Benchmarks 2.3; OpenMP C." www.hpcc.jp/Omni/.

[2] Bailey et al. "The NAS parallel benchmarks." In *SC*, 1991.

[3] M. Kumar. "Measuring parallelism in computation-intensive scientific/engineering applications." *IEEE TOC*, Sep 1988.

[4] C. E. Leiserson. "The Cilk++ concurrency platform." In *DAC*, 2009.

Time Skewing Made Simple

Robert Strzodka   Mohammed Shaheen

Max Planck Institut Informatik, Saarbrücken, Germany
{strzodka,mshaheen}@mpi-inf.mpg.de

Dawid Pająk

Pomeranian University of Technology, Szczecin, Poland
dpajak@mpi-inf.mpg.de

Abstract

Time skewing and loop tiling has been known for a long time to be a highly beneficial acceleration technique for nested loops especially on bandwidth hungry multi-core processors, but it is little used in practice because efficient implementations utilize complicated code and simple or abstract ones show much smaller gains over naive nested loops. We break this dilemma with an essential time skewing scheme that is both compact and fast.

Categories and Subject Descriptors   D.1.3 [*Programming Techniques*]: Concurrent Programming—parallel programming

General Terms   Algorithms, Performance

Keywords   time skewing, loop tiling, temporal blocking, data locality, bandwidth, memory wall, memory bound, stencil

1. Introduction

Time skewing [12] is a successful technique to accelerate multiple iterations of a memory-bound stencil computation. If we do not exploit the temporal locality between iterations, then the performance is necessarily limited by the system bandwidth. In this case, Kamil et al. [7] show that after careful code optimization 0.49 Gkernels/s (giga kernel executions per sec) can be achieved with a Laplace stencil kernel (8 flops) on a $256^3 \times 100$ domain on a quad-core Xeon X5550. With time skewing, Wittmann et al. [11] achieve already 1.75 Gkernels/s on a similar system with a Jacobi kernel (6 flops) on a $600^3 \times 100$ domain. So there is a large benefit to this technique, however, the authors admit that the code used to obtain this result is complicated, specific to this type of kernel and multiple parameters had to be tuned manually.

Frigo and Strumpen [3] introduced a *cache oblivious* time skewing scheme that can be cast into few lines of code and adapts automatically to the memory hierarchy without the need for parameter tuning. However, practical implementations do require some adaptation to hardware and even then it is difficult to beat an optimized naive scheme in case of constant boundary conditions [6]. Strzodka et al. [10] offer a high performance implementation of cache oblivious stencils but at the expense of more complicated code.

If we want to exploit the power of time skewing without the programming complexity, then PluTo [2] is a great tool that offers easy-to-use source-to-source transformations. Given a source file it generates the optimized transformed code that can be compiled in-stead of the original source, so the complexity of time skewing and other transformations is hidden from the programmer. Other state-of-art tiling schemes for (partially) nested loops are HiTLoG [8], PrimeTile [5], and PTile [1]. Unfortunately, the abstraction has its price in performance as Fig. 1 demonstrates in comparison to PluTo, and the newest results of PTile being up to 30% faster on such kernels do not change the picture significantly.

So the current dilemma is that efficient time skewing implementations operate with complicated code and simple or abstract ones show much smaller gains over naive nested loops that are highly optimized by compilers. We resolve this problem by selecting only few time skewing and tiling transformations based on their impact on performance and create a compact time skewing scheme that maintains high performance.

2. Essential Time Skewing (EssTS)

We go back to the essence of time skewing and rather than outlining all possible options identify few crucial transformations that have the largest impact on performance. In this way, the transformed code is not much longer than the naive implementation but performs much better.

Alg. 1 shows the transformation of a naive iterative stencil computation in 3D to a time-skewed, tiled and parallelized scheme. The transformation can be applied to any stencil computation as long as the slopes of the stencil are known a-priori. It occurs in three steps.

- Time-skewing: the t-loop and the z-loop change order, thus access to the z-coordinate has to be offset by s*t, where s is the slope of the stencil in the z-direction.
- Tiling: The inner t,y-loops are tiled to enable in-cache processing. This introduces an outer loop over all tiles.
- Parallelization: The tileSet is split into disjoint subsets such that each thread executes one subset.

The parallelization step is responsible for a big complication of the code if locally dependent tiles are chosen. Wittmann et al. [11] employ thread parallelization in time, which introduces multiple delay parameters and gives asymmetric roles to different thread functions. Strzodka et al. [10] use a hierarchical thread distribution that requires complex load-balancing. Liu and Li [9] use simple dependent tiles and then either the parallelization has to move into the tiles restricting its impact or the synchronization has to be relaxed restricting the applicability of the scheme.

A largely overlooked solution that produces much simpler code is to use tiles that are locally independent. Clearly, large subsets of tiles cannot be completely independent, since the stencil computation couples all values in the domain. However, the space dimensions are large (otherwise the domain would fit into the cache), so it suffices to make them spatially independent, e.g. Frigo and Strumpen [4] use trapezoidal cuts. For highest code simplicity we recommend the diamond shape, because a diamond has exactly two

PPoPP'11,   February 12–16, 2011, San Antonio, Texas, USA.
ACM 978-1-4503-0119-0/11/02.

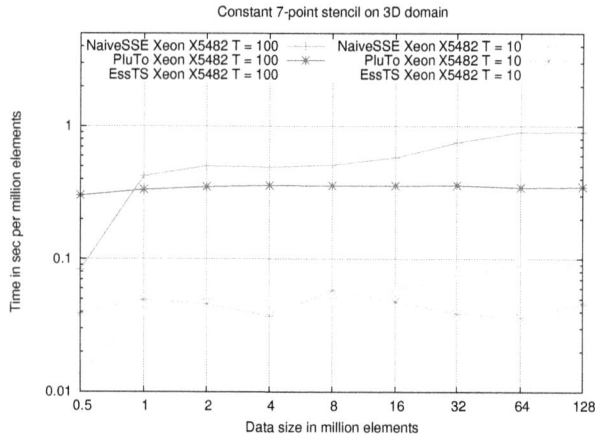

Figure 1. Performance of the Xeon X5482 on a constant 7-point stencil in 3D (13 flops). GFLOPS for 128 million elements with $T = 100$: NaiveSSE Xeon 1.4, PluTo Xeon 3.7, EssTS Xeon 13.

predecessors in time, so wait_on_dependencies() consists of two simple checks without the need to distinguish differently shaped trapezoids. In either case, it is easy to specify the tile boundaries in tstart(), tend(), ystart(), yend(). In the cache oblivious version tile sizes are determined through a series of hierarchical cuts, in the simplest version tile sizes correspond directly to the cache size available to each thread. In summary, the code from Alg. 1 concentrates in its simplicity on the most essential parts of an effective time skewing scheme and this suffices to obtain high performance.

Fig. 1 compares the vectorized naive scheme (NaiveSSE) with the automatic parallelizer and locality optimizer PluTo [2] and our essential time skewing code (EssTS) in the simplest variant. The timings have been obtained on a quad-core Xeon X5482 (Harpertown) 3.2 GHz system, benchmarked with 6.2 GB/s system and 64.2 GB/s L2 cache bandwidth (12 MiB) and 40.8 GFLOPS peak, running a 64-bit Linux and icpc-11.1 compiler with 4 pthreads in double precision. The naive scheme is only strong for the 0.5 mil. elements domain which is processed in-cache. PluTo compares well against the naive scheme, however, there is still much opportunity for improvement. EssTS performs on all domains similarly, as though the entire data could always fit into the cache.

3. Conclusions

Effective time skewing does not require complex code. With only three essential transformations we can turn a naive stencil computation into a parallel bandwidth optimized scheme of only slightly longer code but far superior performance.

References

[1] M. M. Baskaran, A. Hartono, S. Tavarageri, T. Henretty, J. Ramanujam, and P. Sadayappan. Parametrized tiling revisited. In *Proc. of the International Symposium on Code Generation and Optimization (CGO'10)*, 2010.

[2] U. Bondhugula, A. Hartono, J. Ramanujam, and P. Sadayappan. A practical automatic polyhedral parallelizer and locality optimizer. *SIGPLAN Not.*, 43(6):101–113, 2008.

[3] M. Frigo and V. Strumpen. Cache oblivious stencil computations. In *ICS '05: Proceedings of the 19th annual international conference on Supercomputing*, pages 361–366. ACM, 2005.

[4] M. Frigo and V. Strumpen. The cache complexity of multithreaded cache oblivious algorithms. In *SPAA '06: Proceedings of the eighteenth annual ACM symposium on Parallelism in algorithms and architectures*, pages 271–280, New York, NY, USA, 2006. ACM.

Alg. 1 Essential time skewing example in 3D. Only few transformations are necessary to obtain much faster parallel C++ code from the naive implementation. Function stencil_SSE() contains the stencil computation vectorized along the x-axis from 0 to WIDTH. The remaining freedom lies in choosing the tile form and thus defining the tileSet, its dependencies in wait_on_dependencies() and the tile boundary functions tstart(), tend(), ystart(), yend().

```
void NaiveSSE_3D ()
{
    for(int t = 0; t < T; t++) {
        for(int z = 0; z < DEPTH; z++) {
            for(int y = 0; y < HEIGHT; y++) {
                stencil_SSE(t, z, y, 0, WIDTH);
            }//y
        }//z
    }//t
}
```

```
void EssTS_3D (int threadID)
{
    for( TileIt tile = tileSet[threadID].begin();
         tile != tileSet[threadID].end(); ++tile) {
    wait_on_dependencies(tile);

    for(int z = 0; z < DEPTH; z++) {
        for(int t = tstart(tile,z); t < tend(tile,z); t++) {
        for(int y = ystart(tile,z,t); y < yend(tile,z,t); y++) {
            stencil_SSE(t, z-s*t, y, 0, WIDTH);
        }}//t,y
    }//z

    }//tile
}
```

[5] A. Hartono, M. M. Baskaran, C. Bastoul, A. Cohen, S. Krishnamoorthy, B. Norris, J. Ramanujam, and P. Sadayappan. Parametric multi-level tiling of imperfectly nested loops. In *Proceedings of the 23rd International Conference on Supercomputing*, pages 147–157, 2009.

[6] S. Kamil, K. Datta, S. Williams, L. Oliker, J. Shalf, and K. Yelick. Implicit and explicit optimizations for stencil computations. In *MSPC '06: Proceedings of the 2006 workshop on Memory system performance and correctness*, pages 51–60. ACM, 2006.

[7] S. Kamil, C. Chan, L. Oliker, J. Shalf, and S. Williams. An auto-tuning framework for parallel multicore stencil computations. In *International Parallel & Distributed Processing Symposium (IPDPS)*, 2010.

[8] D. Kim, L. Renganarayanan, D. Rostron, S. V. Rajopadhye, and M. M. Strout. Multi-level tiling: M for the price of one. In *Proceedings of the ACM/IEEE Conference on Supercomputing*, page 51, 2007.

[9] L. Liu and Z. Li. Improving parallelism and locality with asynchronous algorithms. In *Proceedings ACM symposium on Principles and practice of parallel programming*, PPoPP '10, pages 213–222, 2010.

[10] R. Strzodka, M. Shaheen, D. Pajak, and H.-P. Seidel. Cache oblivious parallelograms in iterative stencil computations. In *ICS '10: Proceedings of the 24th ACM International Conference on Supercomputing*, pages 49–59. ACM, 2010.

[11] M. Wittmann, G. Hager, and G. Wellein. Multicore-aware parallel temporal blocking of stencil codes for shared and distributed memory. In *Proc. Workshop on Large-Scale Parallel Processing (LSPP'10) at IPDPS'10*, 2010.

[12] D. Wonnacott. Using time skewing to eliminate idle time due to memory bandwidth and network limitations. In *Proceedings of International Parallel and Distributed Processing Symposium*, 2000.

Evaluating Graph Coloring on GPUs

A.V. Pascal Grosset, Peihong Zhu, Shusen Liu, Suresh Venkatasubramanian, Mary Hall

School of Computing, University of Utah, Salt Lake City, Utah, USA

zetwal@cs.utah.edu, peihong.zhu@utah.edu, shusen.liu@utah.edu, suresh@cs.utah.edu, mhall@cs.utah.edu

Abstract

This paper evaluates features of graph coloring algorithms implemented on graphics processing units (GPUs), comparing coloring heuristics and thread decompositions. As compared to prior work on graph coloring for other parallel architectures, we find that the large number of cores and relatively high global memory bandwidth of a GPU lead to different strategies for the parallel implementation. Specifically, we find that a simple uniform block partitioning is very effective on GPUs and our parallel coloring heuristics lead to the same or fewer colors than prior approaches for distributed-memory cluster architecture. Our algorithm resolves many coloring conflicts across partitioned blocks on the GPU by iterating through the coloring process, before returning to the CPU to resolve remaining conflicts. With this approach we get as few color (if not fewer) than the best sequential graph coloring algorithm and performance is close to the fastest sequential graph coloring algorithms which have poor color quality.

Categories and Subject Descriptors D.1.3 [*Programming Techniques*]: Concurrent Programming

General Terms Algorithms, Performance

Keywords Graph coloring, Parallel algorithm, GPU, CUDA

1. Introduction

Graph coloring refers to the assignment of labels or colors to elements of a graph (vertices or edges) subject to certain constraints. In this paper, we consider the specific problem of assigning colors to vertices so that no two neighboring vertices (vertices connected by an edge) have the same color. There are several known applications of graph coloring like assigning frequencies to wireless access points, time-tabling and scheduling, register allocation and printed circuit testing among others. The aim is usually to have as few colors as possible as quickly as possible.

Graph coloring is NP-hard, and even computing a $n^{1-\epsilon}$-approximation of the chromatic number of a graph is NP-hard [5]. Therefore, a number of heuristics have been developed to assign colors to vertices; some commonly used heuristics include First Fit(FF), Largest Degree Order(LDO) and Saturation Degree Order(SDO) [2]. These heuristics tend to trade off minimizing the number of colors and execution time but generally the faster algorithms have poor coloring quality while the slow ones tend to yield

fewer colors. Combinations of these algorithms have also been used to create better heuristics like the combined SDO & LDO [2].

This paper examines a graphics processing unit (GPU) mapping of parallel graph coloring. Prior parallel graph coloring algorithms have been evaluated on conventional shared-memory multiprocessors [4] or distributed systems [3] but to the best of our knowledge, this is the first study of how GPU architectures affect performance gains and number of assigned colors in a parallel implementation. Our study demonstrates that features of the GPU architecture significantly impact the algorithms selected. Specifically, the support for efficient fine-grain multithreading facilitates strong performance gains over CPU implementations. Because hundreds or even thousands of threads can be applied to the parallel coloring, we can obtain as few colors as the best sequential algorithm while operating nearly as fast as the fastest sequential algorithms.

GPUs have different architectures compared to parallel computers where most of the parallel graph-coloring algorithms are run. The main differences is that they have many processors, for example, a Tesla S1070 processor has 240 cores, but each of the cores is slower than a state-of-the-art CPU. Also, a GPU stores the data in the global memory which all the cores can readily access.

2. Algorithm

In this paper, we propose a framework based on the G-M algorithm [4], which is adapted for an NVIDIA GPU platform. In addition, two new heuristics are proposed to match the parallelism exploited by the GPU, which are shown to give better coloring quality than FF that is comparable to Sequential FF running time.

2.1 The Graph Coloring Framework

Algorithm 1 Graph Coloring Framework

Phase 1 : *Graph Partitioning − CPU*
    Logically partition graph into subgraphs
    Identify boundary nodes
    Count neighbors outside the subgraph for each vertex

Phase 2 : *Graph Coloring* & *Conflict Solving − GPU*
    while Number of color conflicts is high **do**
        Color graph using the specified heuristic
        Identify color conflicts

Phase 3 : *Sequential Conflicts Resolution − CPU*
    Residual conflicts are eliminated

Phase 1: Graph Partitioning: The graph is initially padded with empty nodes so that it is exactly divisible by the total number of threads (p). Each thread equally takes n/p vertices, which is a load-balanced approach.

Phase 2: Graph Coloring & **Conflicts detection:** Each thread assigns colors to its subgraph but checks the whole graph before al-

PPoPP'11, February 12–16, 2011, San Antonio, Texas, USA.
ACM 978-1-4503-0119-0/11/02.

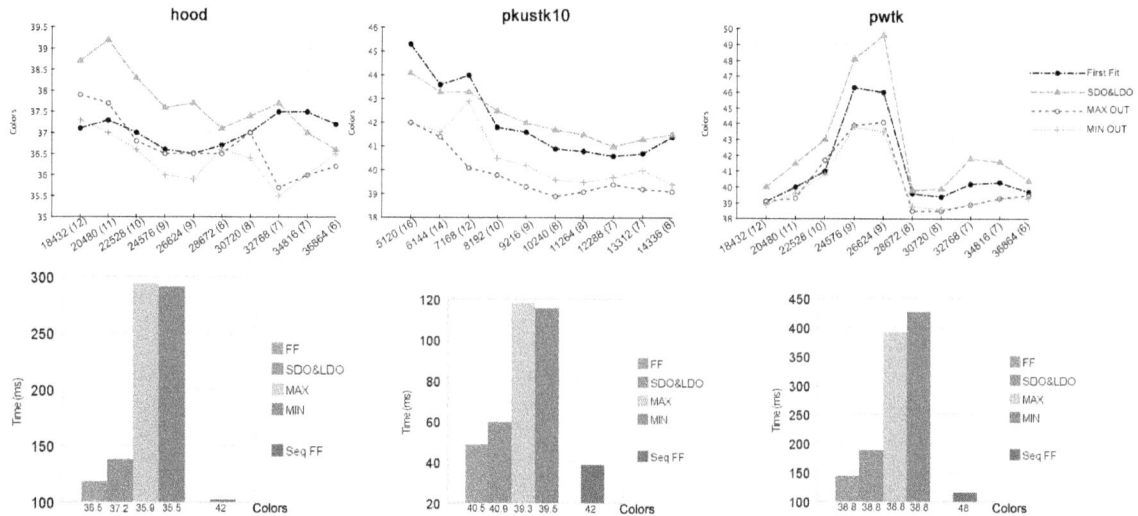

Figure 1. First row: Average Colors vs Threads (Subgraph size) - Second row: Value below each bar shows the best average color and their matching time is indicated on the y-axis.

locating colors. We tried four heuristics including two new heuristics (MAX OUT and MIN OUT) for color allocation:

i) First Fit: Allocate the smallest possible color to each vertex - no specific criteria is used to choose which vertex to color first.

ii) SDO & LDO: Color is allocated to the vertex having the highest saturation and then highest degree.

iii) MAX OUT: Color is allocated to the vertex having most neighbors out of the subgraph and then highest degree.

iv) MIN OUT: Color is allocated to the vertex having fewest neighbors out of the subgraph and then highest degree.

Conflicts occurring between vertices in different subgraphs are identified by assigning one thread per boundary node which checks for color conflicts and reset the color of these nodes to null.

Phase 3: Sequential Conflicts Resolution Dropping to the CPU to solve the conflicts is common in many approaches but given that we have many small partitions, we tend to have lots of conflicts and resolving that on the CPU can be quite slow. So we do multiple passes of step 2 on GPU until the number of conflicts become very small and can be quickly solved sequentially on the CPU.

3. Experiments and Results

The algorithm has been implemented using the CUDA API and the tests were carried out on a Tesla S1070 with real graphs from the University of Florida Sparse Matrix Collection[1]. In this paper we will focus on 3 different graphs shown in Table 1.

Name				Colors		Time(ms)
	n	m	Δ	FF	SDO & LDO	FF
hood	220,542	5,273,947	76	42	36	104
pkustk10	81,920	2,114,154	89	42	42	39
pwtk	217,918	5,926,171	179	57	48	48

Table 1. Graph properties and sequential coloring baselines: n- number of vertices, m -number of edges, Δ- max degree.

To investigate the impact of parallel graph coloring algorithms on both performance and number of colors obtained, the number of threads is linearly incremented and the timing and color obtained is compared and the results are shown in Figure 1.

The results (average of 10 runs) show that MAX and MIN generally yield fewer colors and we also notice that good coloration

is obtained at relatively small subgraph sizes. For pwtk, coloring gets worse at subgraph sizes of around 9. We believe that this is due to unfortunate partitioning as if the vertices are shuffled and then colored, we do not see that peak. [2] explains why SDO & LDO is better than FF. MAX and MIN substitute choice based on saturation for SDO & LDO for vertices in or out of the subgraph. This favors vertices which have more connection to the other vertices.

In terms of speed among the parallel graph coloring algorithms, First Fit is the fastest followed by SDO & LDO, MIN and MAX which take roughly the same amount of time. MIN and MAX are at least twice as slow as they require twice as much memory access compared to SDO & LDO.

The best combination of good coloring and high performance is given by Parallel SDO & LDO; its running time is within a factor of 2 of sequential First Fit.

4. Conclusion

The proposed GPU implementation provides much better coloring quality in terms of number of colors used, and the running time is comparable to sequential FF (known as the fastest sequential coloring algorithm). Running on GPU introduces overheads but the hundreds of cores allows for extreme parallelism and the nondeterminism makes initial bad choices less damaging allowing Parallel First Fit to give better colors than the Sequential one. In many cases, it can even beat colors reported in [3].

References

[1] The university of florida sparse matrix collection. URL http://www.cise.ufl.edu/research/sparse/matrices/.

[2] H. Al-Omari and K. Sabri. New graph coloring algorithms. *Am. J. Math. & Stat*, 2(4):739–741, 2006.

[3] A. M. F. B. E. C. Bozdag, D Gebremedhin. A framework for scalable greedy coloring on distributed-memory parallel computers. *Journal of Parallel and Distributed Computing*, 68(4):515–535, 2008.

[4] A. Gebremedhin and F. Manne. Scalable parallel graph coloring algorithms. *Concurrency: Practice and Experience*, 12(12):1131–1146, 2000.

[5] D. Zuckerman. Linear degree extractors and the inapproximability of max clique and chromatic number. *Theory of Computing*, 3(1):103–128, 2007. doi: 10.4086/toc.2007.v003a006. URL http://www.theoryofcomputing.org/articles/v003a006.

Two Examples of Parallel Programming without Concurrency Constructs (PP-CC)

Chen Ding

University of Rochester
cding@cs.rochester.edu

Categories and Subject Descriptors   D.1.3 [*Concurrent programming*]: Parallel programming

General Terms   Languages, Performance

1. Introduction

Speculative parallelization divides a program into possibly parallel tasks. Parallel execution succeeds if it produces the same output as the original program; otherwise, it is reverted to sequential execution. Previous studies have developed various programming primitives [1,3,6,8–11,13]. Many of these new primitives are *hints* and do not change program output even if they are wrong.

Consider the two hints below. In each case, a hint annotates a code block and suggests the presence or absence of parallelism in the execution of the code block. They are developed as part of the *BOP* system and hence bear a common prefix [3].

- A *possibly parallel region bop_ppr* suggests that run-time instances of the code block are parallel. A *PPR* block is similar to a safe future [11] or an ordered transaction [10].

- A *likely serial region bop_ordered* suggests that run-time instances of the code block should be executed sequentially in program order. The meaning is similar to the ordered directive in OpenMP except that bop_ordered is a hint (implemented using speculative post-wait [4], which is an extension of Cytron's *do-across* construct [2]).

The two hints do not change the program output. They are more appropriately called a *parallelization interface* rather than a parallel programming interface. While a parallel language controls both parallelism and its semantics, a parallelization interface affects only parallelism but not the program result.

A parallelization interface cannot use concurrency constructs. In this paper, a *concurrency construct* is defined as a synchronization primitive that permits out-of-order access to shared data. Common examples are locks, barriers, critical and atomic sections, and transactions. Concurrency constructs allow a program, when given the same input, to produce one of several possible results that are all correct. Parallelization hints are limited to producing a single outcome—the sequential result—and have to enforce in-order up-

```
while q.has_work          while q.has_work
  w = q.get_work            w = q.get_work
                            bop_ppr {
  t = w.do_lots_work          t = w.do_lots_work
                              bop_ordered {
  result_tree.add(t)            result_tree.add(t)
                              }
                            }
end while                 end while
```

Figure 1. A work loop

dates of shared data in general (except when out-of-order access does not change the result).

The benefit of hints is safe parallel programming. Many issues affect safety. A program may call third-party code that is not thread safe. It may not be completely parallel, and the degree of parallelism may change from input to input. In addition, the granularity may be unknown or input dependent. Some tasks may be so short that sequential execution is fastest. Traditionally, a user should resolve all these issues in order to parallelize a program. With hints, the parallelism can always be suggested. Furthermore, no parallel debugging is needed. The parallel execution is correct if the sequential one is.

Concurrency constructs have been a mainstay of parallel programming, a question naturally arises as to how expressive and usable a parallelization interface can be without them. It is difficult to quantify usability. This short paper tries to answer the question through two examples of parallel programming without concurrency constructs.

2. A While Loop

Information processing is often implemented by a while loop, as shown in Figure 1. The loop body has three steps: dequeue the next work, process it, and insert the output into result_tree. The parallelized version encloses the last two steps in a *PPR* block, suggesting that the work can be done in parallel once it is dequeued.

Consider the step of tree insertion. On the one hand, it is part of the *PPR* block so it obtains the result of parallel processing. On the other hand, the tree is shared, so the insertion is serialized by the bop_ordered hint. The resulting tree is identical to one from sequential execution.

As a comparison, consider parallelizing the work loop using OpenMP. The step of tree insertion is marked as a critical section. As a concurrency construct, the critical section allows tree insertions to happen in any order—a later iteration may insert first if it finishes earlier. Out-of-order insertion improves parallelism—a later task does not have to wait—but it leads to non-determinism—

PPoPP'11,   February 12–16, 2011, San Antonio, Texas, USA.
ACM 978-1-4503-0119-0/11/02.

the shape of the tree may differ from run to run. Non-determinism complicates debugging. Suppose the implementation has an infrequent error that manifests once every hundred executions. A user will have difficulty reproducing it in a debugger.

An ordered block requires in-order tree insertion and loses parallelism. However, the loss may be compensated by starting future *PPR* tasks when processors are idle [14]. As a hint, a *PPR* block does not have to finish before starting the subsequent *PPR* blocks (if they exist). In comparison, it is unsafe for OpenMP to overlap the execution of consecutive loops.

Next we show that hints may increase the amount of parallelism without complex programming.

3. Time Skewing

Iterative solvers are widely used to compute fixed-point or equilibrium solutions. Figure 2 shows the structure of a typical solver as a two-nested loop. The outer level is the time-step loop. In each time step, the inner loop computes on some domain data. The inner loop is usually data parallel. The time steps, however, have three types of dependences: the convergence check, which depends on the entire time step; the continuation check, which depends on the convergence result of the last step; and the cross time-step data conflict, since time steps use and modify the same domain data.

In manual parallelization, a barrier is inserted between successive time steps to preserve all three dependences. Although simple to implement, the solution precludes parallelism between time steps. Previous literature shows that by overlapping time steps, one may obtain large performance improvements for both sequential [7, 12] and parallel [5] executions. Wonnacott termed the transformation *time skewing* [12].

Parallelization hints can express time skewing with four annotations shown in Figure 2. It uses two parallel blocks. The first block allows each time step to be parallelized. The second allows consecutive time steps to overlap. In addition, it uses two ordered blocks. The first serialize data updates in the inner loop. The second delays the convergence check after all data updates are completed.

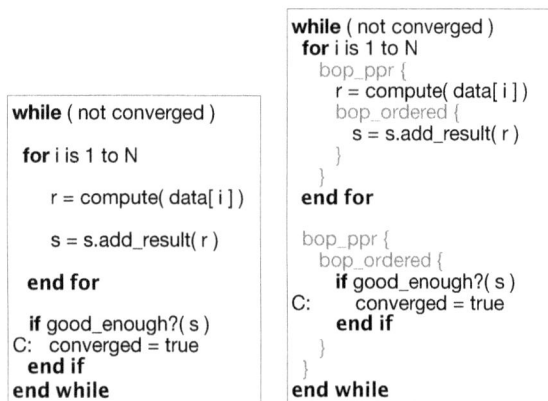

```
while ( not converged )

  for i is 1 to N

    r = compute( data[ i ] )

    s = s.add_result( r )

  end for

  if good_enough?( s )
C:  converged = true
  end if
end while
```

```
while ( not converged )
  for i is 1 to N
    bop_ppr {
      r = compute( data[ i ] )
      bop_ordered {
        s = s.add_result( r )
      }
    }
  end for

  bop_ppr {
    bop_ordered {
      if good_enough?( s )
C:      converged = true
      end if
    }
  }
end while
```

Figure 2. Time skewing—successive time steps may overlap

The hints ignore the continuation dependence and cross time-step conflicts since they happen infrequently. The continuation check fails only at the last iteration. Cross-iteration conflicts usually do not happen immediately if the inner loop processes domain data in a fixed order. The *BOP* speculation support will detect and correct these errors when they happen. In other times, the parallelism between time steps is profitably exploited. We have tested a case in which the *BOP* version was 18% faster than the OpenMP

version on 7 processors, thanks to time skewing. In this case, parallelization hints outperformed critical section and barrier synchronization while still maintaining the sequential result.

4. Summary

The two examples show the limitation and benefits of parallel programming without concurrency constructs:

- *No concurrency constructs.* No out-of-order updates as permitted by locks, barriers, atomic sections, and transactions.

- *Speculation support.* The cost limits the efficiency and scalability.

- *Ease of parallel programming.* Hints relieve a user from correctness considerations and may be inserted by hand or automatically.

- *Speculative parallelism.* A user may parallel code that is often but not always parallel.

The first two mean less parallelism and more overhead. The next two, however, mean easier, safe parallelization. Ease of programming may mean faster speed, as shown by the second example.

References

[1] E. D. Berger, T. Yang, T. Liu, and G. Novark. Grace: Safe multithreaded programming for C/C++. In *Proceedings of OOPSLA*, 2009.

[2] R. Cytron. Doacross: Beyond vectorization for multiprocessors. In *Proceedings of the 1986 International Conference on Parallel Processing*, pages 836–844, St. Charles, IL, Aug. 1986.

[3] C. Ding, X. Shen, K. Kelsey, C. Tice, R. Huang, and C. Zhang. Software behavior oriented parallelization. In *Proceedings of PLDI*, pages 223–234, 2007.

[4] B. Jacobs, T. Bai, and C. Ding. Distributive program parallelization using a suggestion language. Technical Report URCS #952, Department of Computer Science, University of Rochester, 2009.

[5] L. Liu and Z. Li. Improving parallelism and locality with asynchronous algorithms. In *Proceedings of PPOPP*, pages 213–222, 2010.

[6] A. Raman, H. Kim, T. R. Mason, T. B. Jablin, and D. I. August. Speculative parallelization using software multi-threaded transactions. In *Proceedings of ASPLOS*, pages 65–76, 2010.

[7] Y. Song and Z. Li. New tiling techniques to improve cache temporal locality. In *Proceedings of PLDI*, pages 215–228, Atlanta, Georgia, May 1999.

[8] C. Tian, M. Feng, and R. Gupta. Supporting speculative parallelization in the presence of dynamic data structures. In *Proceedings of PLDI*, pages 62–73, 2010.

[9] C. Tian, M. Feng, V. Nagarajan, and R. Gupta. Copy or Discard execution model for speculative parallelization on multicores. In *Proceedings of ACM/IEEE MICRO*, pages 330–341, 2008.

[10] C. von Praun, L. Ceze, and C. Cascaval. Implicit parallelism with ordered transactions. In *Proceedings of PPOPP*, Mar. 2007.

[11] A. Welc, S. Jagannathan, and A. L. Hosking. Safe futures for Java. In *Proceedings of OOPSLA*, pages 439–453, 2005.

[12] D. Wonnacott. Achieving scalable locality with time skewing. *International Journal of Parallel Programming*, 30(3), June 2002.

[13] A. Zhai, J. G. Steffan, C. B. Colohan, and T. C. Mowry. Compiler and hardware support for reducing the synchronization of speculative threads. *ACM Transactions on Architecture and Code Optimization*, 5(1):1–33, 2008.

[14] C. Zhang, C. Ding, X. Gu, K. Kelsey, T. Bai, and X. Feng. Continuous speculative program parallelization in software. In *Proceedings of PPOPP*, pages 335–336, 2010.

A Wait-Free NCAS Library for Parallel Applications with Timing Constraints

Philippe Stellwag, Fabian Scheler, Jakob Krainz, Wolfgang Schröder-Preikschat

Friedrich-Alexander University Erlangen-Nuremberg
Computer Science 4
Martensstr. 1, Erlangen, Germany
{stellwag,scheler,krainz,wosch}@cs.fau.de

Abstract

We introduce our major ideas of a wait-free, linearizable, and disjoint-access parallel NCAS library, called RTNCAS. It focuses the construction of wait-free data structure operations (DSO) in real-time circumstances. RTNCAS is able to conditionally swap multiple independent words (NCAS) in an atomic manner. It allows us, furthermore, to implement arbitrary DSO by means of their sequential specification.

Categories and Subject Descriptors D.1.3 [*Programming Techniques*]: Concurrent Programming

General Terms Algorithms, Design

1. Introduction

Sequential DSO usually rely on exclusive access to the parts of the data structure (DS). Their methods are typically implemented using reads and writes to single words spread out over the whole critical region to manipulate the state of a DS. This induces convoy effects and other timing drawbacks. Also prior universal constructions, such as Herlihy's work [1], serialize all DSO; this induces priority inversion in real-time circumstances.

Our Contribution

RTNCAS guarantees that DSO built on top of it are linearizable [2] and offer the following properties: **1. Lock freedom** offers interrupt transparency, and neither depends on system libraries nor induces restrictions to the scheduler (we do not consider backoff algorithms here). Under concurrent usage they also frequently yield better performance than blocking counterparts. As no local progress guarantees can be given for such operations, it is usually not possible to determine an upper bound for the worst-case execution time (WCET) of such DSO. We use lock-free DSO in RTNCAS to gain a stronger progress guarantee later on. **2. Wait freedom** [1] is similar to lock freedom, but additionally guarantees a definable and bounded WCET. Hereby, the temporal progress requirements of real-time applications can be satisfied. Note that correctness in real-time systems is both, functional correctness as well as timeliness. **3. Disjoint-access parallelism** [3] enables parallel executions of

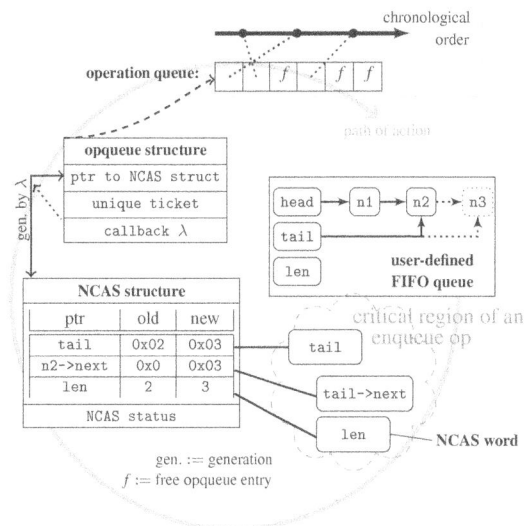

gen. := generation
f := free opqueue entry

operations accessing disjointed memory locations. This yields additional benefits in terms of parallel performance and minimal priority inversions.

Starting with a sequential implementation of a DSO, we apply several transformations to it. Each transformation ensures the next stronger progress property (from 1. to 3.) and finally, a wait-free and disjoint-access-parallel DSO is reached.

Our work was inspired by Ramamurthy [4, pp. 138 ff.]. His NCAS, however, only focuses priority-based real-time systems on uni-processors. To the best of our knowledge, RTNCAS is the first generic approach to build interrupt-transparent DSO even in parallel real-time systems, and also considers disjoint-access parallelism. It is, furthermore, not restricted to priority-based real-time systems.

2. Design of RTNCAS

The construction of an NCAS library that satisfies the above stated properties is a rather complex task. Thereby many serious problems arise on the implementation level that we cannot discuss completely within these two pages. Thus, we only adumbrate the design of RTNCAS, and point to some interesting problems and results.

The figure shows the major idea and all data structures involved in RTNCAS. It illustrates an example of adding a node n3 to a FIFO queue by using RTNCAS. An enqueue operation implemented via locks would modify `tail`, `tail->next`, `len` inside a critical region to ensure atomicity. To add n3 to the queue using RTNCAS, all words of the data structure are encapsulated into NCAS words. The thread performing the enqueue operation has to create an

PPoPP '11, February 12–16, 2011, San Antonio, Texas, USA.
ACM 978-1-4503-0119-0/11/02.

opqueue structure containing a unique ticket to be able to deduce a chronological order and a user-defined callback λ to create an NCAS structure describing the atomic state transformation to enqueue n3. This opqueue structure is enqueued to the operation queue providing a wait-free helping scheme, where concurrent threads help each other to perform those stalled operations.

2.1 Lock-Free Operations

In a first step the formerly sequential DSO has to be transformed into a lock-free operation. This is accomplished by reading the old state of the DS via a *read method*, computing a new state, and, finally, atomically exchanging the old state with the new one by an NCAS operation. In case of concurrent interference the NCAS operation may fail and the complete operation including reading the old state and computing the new state has to be repeated.

The usage of the NCAS operation as described above is both lock-free and linearizable. We have implemented a NCAS method to support lock-free DSO and a read method to retrieve the actual value from the DS. Both are weakly wait-free, i.e. they respond within finite time, but may fail due to concurrent interferences and then have to be repeated.

2.2 Wait-Free Operations

The usage of the NCAS operation within such a retry-loop prevents the estimation of a WCET in the presence of contention. This is due to the unknown number of retries needed to successfully complete the DSO; under hard real-time conditions this is unacceptable. To overcome this, we transform the lock-free DSO into a wait-free one by means of a helping scheme implemented via an *operation queue*. This helping scheme facilitates the implementation of wait-free DSO. Thereby, wait freedom allows to determine the WCET that is essential in real-time circumstances.

The operation queue is implemented by a wait-free FIFO and works as follows: Every thread encapsulates its DSO into a so-called *opqueue structure*. This structure contains a pointer to a *callback* λ, a pointer to the *NCAS structure* (which contains the addresses of the words to be changed, and the corresponding old/new values) generated by the callback λ, and a unique ticket to establish a chronological order among all elements within the operation queue. λ is a user-defined callback that uses the sequential DSO to build the NCAS structure with old and new values.

After inserting its own DSO to the operation queue, each thread performs the following steps until its own DSO is completed: Get the oldest opqueue structure from the operation queue and try to perform the encapsulated operation. The latter is done as follows: **1.** The opqueue structure is checked for an active NCAS structure, i.e. a structure whose associated NCAS operation might still be executed. If one is found, the second step is skipped. **2.** λ is used to create a new NCAS structure. A thread then tries to atomically replace the reference to the NCAS structure in the opqueue structure with a reference to the newly created one by means of a CAS instruction. **3.** The NCAS structure is then executed in a cooperative manner. Thereby all threads always working on the same active NCAS structure (consensus object). Finally, in case of a successful execution, the opqueue structure is dequeued.

The operation queue, however, requires (1) a wait-free FIFO that allows us to find and use the oldest entry, and (2) the NCAS implementation has to support cooperation: If all active threads work on the same NCAS operation (using the same NCAS structure), the described NCAS operation must be completed successfully.

2.3 Disjoint-Access-Parallel Operations

The helping scheme implemented by the operation queue has one disadvantage: All DSO are performed sequentially as be known from previous approaches that may results in convoy effects, and may cause poor performance. To avoid this, we introduce the concept of *speculative execution*.

Before inserting an opqueue structure into the operation queue, each thread tries to execute the DSO speculatively by the corresponding lock-free operation. If the speculative execution fails, an opqueue structure will be enqueued into the operation queue and the thread carries on as described in the previous section. If the speculative execution is successful, the thread still works on the oldest entry of the operation queue. This is required to guarantee progress for the oldest entry in the operation queue. Otherwise, the oldest entry might starve due to continuously interfering speculative executions. By forcing every thread to execute at least one opqueue structure from the operation queue, it can be guaranteed that the oldest entry in the operation queue is completed in finite time.

Using speculative execution, finally, we support the implementation of wait-free and disjoint-access-parallel DSO based on top of the wait-free operations provided by the helping scheme introduced in Sec. 2.2. Furthermore, the degree of disjoint-parallel accesses can be chosen with respect to the number of speculative executions that can take place concurrently.

3. Preliminary Results

We have implemented several DSO, such as push/pop on a stack or enqueue/dequeue on a queue, by means of spinlocks as well as RTNCAS. Numerous benchmarks that perform DSO (a) with increasing concurrency, and (b) with an increasing number of words to be touched simultaneously show very encouraging results: On the one hand and without speculative executions, RTNCAS operations show at average four times less jitter than operations with spinlocks. Moreover, RTNCAS-based operations show about ten times higher average times; however, the throughput of RTNCAS-based operations per time unit are slightly higher compared to the spinlock case. This is due to our helping scheme and is the crucial factor for our significant low execution jitter. On the other hand, these advantages go along with comparable maximal response times of operations built on top of RTNCAS.

Furthermore, with an increasing number of speculative executions, we are able to trade a higher degree of disjoint-access parallelism to a higher jitter. This allows us to achieve a higher average-case performance for appropriate (e.g., soft real-time) use cases.

4. Conclusion and Further Work

We have sketched the design of RTNCAS, a library offering linearizable, lock-free, wait-free and disjoint-access-parallel interfaces for reading and conditionally swapping multiple words in an atomic manner. Developers of shared data structures now have an easy way to achieve full interrupt-transparency with a strong progress guarantee. With RTNCAS, developers can, furthermore, use their sequential algorithms on top of it without modifications. Currently, we are still working on several optimizations to reduce the WCET of RTNCAS-based DSO. Moreover, we are also close to complete a formal proof of correctness for RTNCAS and its components.

References

[1] M. P. Herlihy. Wait-free synchronization. *in ACM Transactions on Programming Languages and Systems*, 11(1):124–149, January 1991.

[2] M. P. Herlihy and J. M. Wing. Linearizability: A correctness condition for concurrent objects. *in ACM Transactions on Programming Languages and Systems*, 12(3):463–492, 1990.

[3] A. Israeli and L. Rappoport. Disjoint-access-parallel implementations of strong shared memory primitives. *in Proc. of the Symp. on Principles of Distributed Computing*, pages 151–160, 1994.

[4] S. Ramamurthy. A lock-free approach to object sharing in real-time systems. *PhD thesis, Univ. of North Carolina at Chapel Hill*, 1997.

Algorithm-Based Recovery for HPL

Teresa Davies, Zizhong Chen, Christer Karlsson, Hui Liu

Colorado School of Mines

tdavies@mines.edu, zchen@mines.edu, ckarlsso@mines.edu, huliu@mines.edu

Abstract

When more processors are used for a calculation, the probability that one will fail during the calculation increases. Fault tolerance is a technique for allowing a calculation to survive a failure, and includes recovering lost data. A common method of recovery is diskless checkpointing. However, it has high overhead when a large amount of data is involved, as is the case with matrix operations. A checksum-based method allows fault tolerance of matrix operations with lower overhead. This technique is applicable to the LU decomposition in the benchmark HPL.

Categories and Subject Descriptors C.4 [*Performance of Systems*]: Fault tolerance

General Terms Algorithms, Performance

1. Introduction

Fault tolerance is becoming more important as the number of processors used for a single calculation increases [9]. When more processors are used, the probability that one will fail increases [2]. Therefore, it is necessary, especially for long-running calculations, that they be able to survive the failure of one or more processors. One critical part of recovery from failure is recovering the lost data. There is always overhead associated with preparing for a failure, even during the runs when no failure occurs, so it is important to choose the method with the lowest possible overhead. There are various approaches to the problem of recovering lost data involving saving the processor state periodically in different ways, either by saving the data directly [5, 8] or by maintaining some sort of checksum of the data [1, 3, 6] from which it can be recovered.

One approach to fault tolerance is to save the data to disk periodically [10], at set checkpoints. In the event of a failure, all processes are rolled back to the time of the previous checkpoint. Unfortunately, this method does not scale well. Often all processes make a checkpoint at the same time, so that all of the processes will simultaneously attempt to write to the disk. This is a serious bottleneck, made worse by the fact that disk accesses are slow.

In response to this issue diskless checkpointing [8] was introduced. This technique has each processor save its own checkpoint state in the memory of another processor, thereby eliminating the need for a slow write to disk. A key factor in the performance of diskless checkpointing is the size of the checkpoint, since it requires that all of the data to be saved be sent to another processor. The overhead is reduced when only changed values are saved. However, matrix operations are not susceptible to this optimization [5], since many elements, up to the entire matrix, could be changed at each step of the algorithm.

Algorithm-based fault tolerance [4, 6] is a technique that has been used to detect miscalculations in matrix operations. This technique consists of adding a checksum row or column to the matrices being operated on. For many matrix operations, a checksum can be shown to be correct at the end of the calculation, and can be used to find errors after the fact. Just as some matrix operations maintain a checksum at the end, some algorithms for matrix operations maintain a checksum during the calculation. It has been shown in [1] how a checksum is maintained in the outer product matrix-matrix multiply. It is also made clear that not all algorithms will maintain the checksum in the middle of the calculation. In [3], a checksum is used to recover from a failure during the ScaLAPACK Cholesky decomposition. In this paper, we apply the checksum technique to the LU decomposition used by High Performance Linpack (HPL) [7].

2. Method

For many parallel matrix operations, the matrix involved is very large. Since the entire matrix cannot fit on one processor, it may be stored in 2D block cyclic fashion [1, 3, 5]. Block cyclic distribution is used in HPL. Adding checksums to a matrix stored in block cyclic fashion can be done by adding extra processors, which hold an element by element sum of the local matrices on processors in the same row or the same column of the processor grid. Because of the block cyclic distribution, checksum elements are encountered periodically during the calculation, and may need to be treated differently from normal elements. In the case of the LU factorization, iterations involving checksum elements on the main diagonal are skipped because they are not necessary for a correct checksum. The type of failure that we can recover from with this technique is a fail-stop failure, which means that a process stops and loses all of its data. The main task that we are able to perform is to recover the lost data using the checksums stored in other processors.

There are different algorithms for the LU decomposition, not all of which will necessarily maintain a checksum at each step. However, the right looking algorithm, which is used by HPL, maintains a checksum at each step as is required because each iteration updates the entire matrix. Other algorithms do the update just before factoring that part of the matrix, so that a checksum of the matrix is not maintained. Pivoting is part of the LU decomposition, and makes column checksums incorrect by swapping rows that go into different checksums. Column checksums would be needed to recover the L matrix. However, in HPL the L matrix is not needed for the solution to the equation because it is applied to the right hand side during the calculation. Therefore, we do not add column checksums, and in the event of a failure we do not recover L because it is not needed for the solution of the equation.

PPoPP'11, February 12–16, 2011, San Antonio, Texas, USA.
ACM 978-1-4503-0119-0/11/02.

Right-looking LU factorization maintains a checksum at each step, as shown below.

The right-looking algorithm is:

```
for i = 1 to n-1
    A(i+1:n,i) = A(i+1:n,i)/A(i,i)
    A(i+1:n,i+1:n) = A(i+1:n,i+1:n)
                   - A(i+1:n,i)*A(i,i+1:n)
```

In an iteration of the loop, the original matrix is:

$$
\begin{pmatrix}
a_{11} & a_{12} & \ldots & a_{1n} & \sum_{j=1}^{n} a_{1j} \\
a_{21} & a_{22} & \ldots & a_{2n} & \sum_{j=1}^{n} a_{2j} \\
\vdots & \vdots & & \vdots & \vdots \\
a_{n1} & a_{n2} & \ldots & a_{nn} & \sum_{j=1}^{n} a_{nj}
\end{pmatrix}
$$

It can be written as

$$
\begin{pmatrix}
a_{11} & A_{12} & \sum A_{12} \\
A_{21} & A_{22} & \sum A_{22}
\end{pmatrix}
$$

The first step of the iteration makes the matrix into

$$
\begin{pmatrix}
a_{11} & A_{12} & \sum A_{12} \\
A_{21}/a_{11} & A_{22} & \sum A_{22}
\end{pmatrix}
$$

The second step modifies the trailing matrix as follows:

$$
\begin{aligned}
& \begin{pmatrix} A_{22} & \sum A_{22} \end{pmatrix} - \begin{pmatrix} A_{21}/a_{11} \end{pmatrix} \begin{pmatrix} A_{12} & \sum A_{12} \end{pmatrix} \\
= & \begin{pmatrix} A_{22} & \sum A_{22} \end{pmatrix} - \begin{pmatrix} A_{21}A_{12}/a_{11} & A_{21}/a_{11} \sum A_{12} \end{pmatrix} \\
= & \begin{pmatrix} A_{22} - A_{21}A_{12}/a_{11} & \sum A_{22} - A_{21}/a_{11} \sum A_{12} \end{pmatrix}
\end{aligned}
$$

Note that $A_{22} - A_{21}A_{12}/a_{11} = a_{ij} - a_{i1}a_{1j}/a_{11}$ for $i = 2, \ldots n$ and $j = 2, \ldots n$.

The first term of each sum is zero. Therefore they become sums of the elements in the trailing matrix only. The trailing matrix contains correct checksums at the end of the iteration. The row that became part of U has a checksum for itself. The column that is part of L no longer has a checksum that it is part of, but it is also no longer needed for the final result.

3. Performance

Even when there is no failure, preparing for one has a cost. For this method, the time overhead is performing the checksum at the beginning. The extra processors required to hold the checksums are another type of overhead. One extra column of processors is added to the processor grid. The number of iterations is not increased; the checksum rows are skipped because performing the factorization on checksum blocks is not necessary for maintaining a correct checksum.

This method performs better than diskless checkpointing in that it has lower overhead. Because the extra processors do the same tasks as the normal processors in the same row, the time to do an iteration is not significantly increased by adding the checksums. In contrast, performing a checkpoint requires extra work periodically to update it. If the checkpoint is done every iteration, then the cost of recovery is the same as with a checksum, but the cost during the calculation is clearly higher.

For checkpointing, the optimum interval depends on the failure rate and the time it takes to do a checkpoint. The more frequently failures are likely to occur, the smaller the interval must be. The longer the checkpoint itself takes, the fewer checkpoints there should be in the total running time, so the interval is longer for a larger checkpoint. The checksum technique, in contrast, does not take any extra time to keep the sum up to date.

N	P	Total time (s)	Checksum time (s)	Overhead (%)	Performance (Gflops)
384000	96	913.16	5.72	0.630	41340
432000	108	995.98	5.70	0.576	53960
480000	120	1137.26	5.69	0.503	64830
528000	132	1254.81	5.91	0.473	78200

Table 1. $N \times N$ matrix on $P \times P$ processor grid: overhead and performance

Both checkpoint and checksum recoveries use a reduce of some sort to calculate the lost values, so that the recovery time is comparable for the two methods. In addition to the time to recover, the overhead includes the length of the repeated work. This overhead is less when the interval between checkpoints is shorter. However, an important point about matrix operations is that the time to perform a checkpoint is long, so that the optimum interval will also be longer. It is unlikely that the interval can be as short as one iteration, so the checksum method has lower overhead in terms of repeated work.

4. Conclusion

We have shown that a checksum can be used for recovery in HPL. There are two ways in which the overhead of the checksum method is less than that of checkpointing: the time added when there is no failure, and the time lost when a failure occurs. Therefore the performance with our technique is expected to be better than the performance with checkpointing for nearly all cases.

References

[1] Z. Chen and J. Dongarra. Algorithm-based fault tolerance for fail-stop failures. *IEEE Transactions on Parallel and Distributed Systems*, 19 (12), 2008.

[2] G. A. Gibson, B. Schroeder, and J. Digney. Failure tolerance in petascale computers. *CTWatchQuarterly*, 3(4), November 2007.

[3] D. Hakkarinen and Z. Chen. Algorithmic cholesky factorization fault recovery. In *Proceedings of the 24th IEEE International Parallel and Distributed Processing Symposium*, Atlanta, GA, USA, April 2010.

[4] K.-H. Huang and J. A. Abraham. Algorithm-based fault tolerance for matrix operations. *IEEE Transactions on Computers*, C-33:518–528, 1984.

[5] Y. Kim. *Fault Tolerant Matrix Operations for Parallel and Distributed Systems*. PhD thesis, University of Tennessee, Knoxville, June 1996.

[6] F. T. Luk and H. Park. An analysis of algorithm-based fault tolerance techniques. *Journal of Parallel and Distributed Computing*, 5(2):172–184, 1988.

[7] A. Petitet, R. C. Whaley, J. Dongarra, and A. Cleary. HPL - a portable implementation of the high-performance linpack benchmark for distributed-memory computers. http://www.netlib.org/benchmark/hpl, September 2008.

[8] J. S. Plank, K. Li, and M. A. Puening. Diskless checkpointing. *IEEE Transactions on Parallel and Distributed Systems*, 9(10):972–986, 1998.

[9] B. Schroeder and G. A. Gibson. A large-scale study of failures in high-performance computing systems. In *Proceedings of the International Conference on Dependable Systems and Networks*, Philadelphia, PA, USA, June 2006.

[10] C. Wang, F. Mueller, C. Engelmann, and S. Scot. Job pause service under LAM/MPI+BLCR for transparent fault tolerance. In *Proceedings of the 21st IEEE International Parallel and Distributed Processing Symposium*, Long Beach, CA, USA, March 2007.

Active Pebbles: A Programming Model For Highly Parallel Fine-Grained Data-Driven Computations

Jeremiah Willcock

Indiana University
150 S. Woodlawn Ave
Bloomington, IN 47405, USA
jewillco@cs.indiana.edu

Torsten Hoefler

University of Illinois at
Urbana-Champaign
1205 W. Clark St.
Urbana, IL 61801, USA
htor@illinois.edu

Nicholas Edmonds
Andrew Lumsdaine

Indiana University
150 S. Woodlawn Ave
Bloomington, IN 47405, USA
{ngedmond,lums}@cs.indiana.edu

Abstract

A variety of programming models exist to support large-scale, distributed memory, parallel computation. These programming models have historically targeted coarse-grained applications with natural locality such as those found in a variety of scientific simulations of the physical world. Fine-grained, irregular, and unstructured applications such as those found in biology, social network analysis, and graph theory are less well supported. We propose Active Pebbles, a programming model which allows these applications to be expressed naturally; an accompanying execution model ensures performance and scalability.

Categories and Subject Descriptors D.1.3 [*Programming Techniques*]: Concurrent Programming—Parallel Programming

General Terms Performance, Design

Keywords Irregular applications, programming models, active messages

1. Introduction

High-performance computing (HPC) traditionally focuses on problems with a static communication and computation schedule. This is reflected in today's de facto benchmark (HPL, High-Performance Linpack) and programming model (MPI, Message Passing Interface). Many problems, such as the solution of partial differential equations as used in numerous simulation techniques, fit this category. Less regular computations, such as adaptive mesh refinement, often use unstructured meshes to better represent physical phenomena. The resulting unstructured grids require more dynamic communication and computation schemes. However, such physical models still have a natural locality related to the properties of the modeled systems. Recently, a new class of dynamic and unstructured problems has emerged from areas such as biology, social network modeling, and graph theory. The most difficult instances of these problems require fine-grained, unstructured, data-driven accesses, as can be found in the solution of many graph problems such as betweenness centrality [3] or parallel shortest path search [5].

Traditional coarse-grained HPC applications can be expressed efficiently in the bulk synchronous parallel (BSP) model. However, the irregular, data-driven structure of graph applications prevents them from being statically coarsened to fit the BSP model well. Approaches which perform coarsening at run-time group operations based on concurrent execution and not necessarily actual

computational dependencies. The fine-grained computational dependencies of these irregular, data-driven problems necessitate a data-driven programming model. We propose Active Pebbles (AP), a flexible programming model for fine-grained data-driven computations. AP allows the programmer to implement algorithms at their *natural* granularities (e.g., with billions of vertices, each of only a few bytes).

The AP programming model is related to Active Messages (AM) in that it utilizes fine-grained method invocation targeting globally-addressable objects. The two main differences between AP and AM are that AP implements transparent object addressing (and allows various object distribution schemes) and that objects are handled in bulk, i.e., they have no individual identity and may be processed in parallel. This enables the implementation of fine-grained algorithms at their natural levels of granularity and allows AP to fully capture their fine-grained dependency structures.

We also specify an execution model for AP which is crucial to achieving high performance at large process counts. In order to achieve this, AP exploits four main techniques:

1. Message Coalescing
2. Active Routing
3. Message Reductions
4. Termination Detection

The programming model ensures easy and abstract specification of parallel algorithms and is independent of the underlying execution architecture. However, the flexible execution model ensures the performance and scalability of the final AP application. The philosophy of the execution model is to transform the fine-grained unstructured specification into a representation that efficiently leverages the underlying architecture. Message coalescing can be used to adapt the message size to the network, active routing can transform all-to-all communication patterns into optimized collective patterns (similar to MPI collective operations), and message reductions can be used to spread the computational load and reduce network traffic.

2. Related Work

Several parallel programming models and languages have been designed in the recent past to address the challenges of data-intensive computing. PGAS languages such as Unified Parallel C [7] and Co-Array Fortran [6] allow shared access to distributed data, but they provide no method for invoking remote computations. Charm++ allows message-driven programming of relatively coarse-grained objects and supports advanced techniques such as redistribution and migration. Recently developed HPCS languages like Chapel [1] and X10 [2] allow the expression of distributed computations. However, it is unclear if these languages readily support fine-grained applications, e.g., billions of "places" in X10. We claim that if they were to support a similar fine-grained model

PPoPP'11, February 12–16, 2011, San Antonio, Texas, USA.
ACM 978-1-4503-0119-0/11/02.

then they would need to use the same techniques as we define in our execution model.

3. The Active Pebble Model

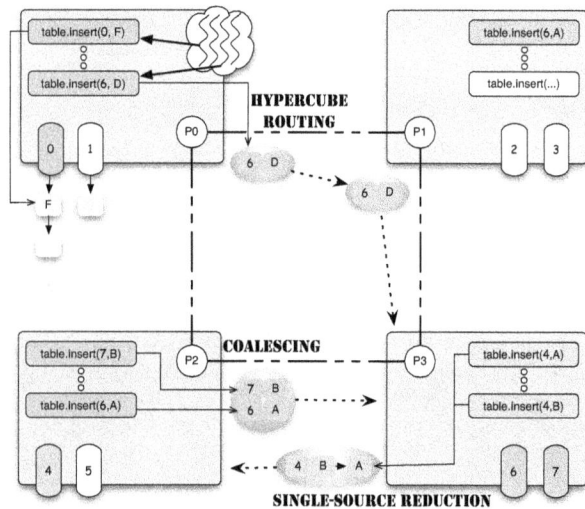

Figure 1. Overview of the Active Pebbles programming model.

3.1 Active Pebble Terminology

The primary abstractions in the AP model are pebbles and targets. Pebbles are light-weight active messages that operate on targets (which can, transparently, be local or remote). Targets are created by binding together a data object with a message handler, through the use of a distribution object. In Figure 1, targets are the destination buckets of a hash table, and hash values are used directly as destination addresses. The distribution object in this example would map each key i to process $\lfloor i/2 \rfloor$. Each pebble flows through the network from its source rank to its destination rank (determined by the distribution object). Handler functions can be multi-threaded and process incoming pebbles in any order; thus, the Active Pebbles model allows for an optimized implementation on multi-core nodes and accelerators. The techniques for optimized pebble transport and processing are discussed in detail in the following sections.

3.2 Fine-grained Pebble Addressing

Because AP is intended for problems with unstructured data, fine-grained addressing of pebbles based on their targets is essential. By making this addressing transparent to the user, local data can be treated similarly to remote data, avoiding special-casing for local and remote data. The method by which addressing is performed can be specified by the application programmer; both static and dynamic addressing is supported.

3.3 Message Coalescing

Modern networks are poorly suited for sending large numbers of small messages. They become injection-rate-limited before becoming bandwidth-limited. In order to overcome the injection rate limitation and achieve higher bandwidth utilization, message coalescing is necessary. By performing message coalescing at run-time, AP increases both message latency and network bandwidth utilization. The degree of message coalescing is selectable by the application programmer. This in effect coarsens the application at run time to better fit the parameters of the network. Taking the fine-grained application specification provided by the programmer and performing the minimal level of coarsening necessary to achieve good network bandwidth utilization minimizes the increase in message latency as well as enabling the application specification to be portable across hardware platforms.

3.4 Active Routing

In applications with good locality, the communication pattern (which processes communicate with which others) is generally sparse. By contrast, because data-driven applications are fine-grained and unstructured, the communication patterns are often dense. As process counts become large, maintaining $\mathcal{O}(P)$ communication buffers and their associated channels per process becomes infeasible. Active Routing simulates a virtual topology on top of the physical network topology and reduces the number of peers each process communicates with to $\mathcal{O}(\log P)$ or even $\mathcal{O}(1)$.

3.5 Message Reductions

It is often the case that multiple messages are sent to the same target by a single process. In some cases these messages may be redundant, while in other cases they may able to be combined via some reduction operation. Performing these reductions at the sender reduces network bandwidth utilization, as well as processing time at the target. Duplicate message elimination and message reductions are transparent to the application programmer, while the reduction operation to utilize for a given message type is user-specified. The effectiveness of message reductions is directly proportional to the number of messages they operate on, with higher degrees of coalescing increasing the effectiveness of reductions.

3.6 Termination Detection

Because AP utilizes a fully-general messaging model which supports sending messages from message handlers, it is not necessarily the case that the length of the longest chain of recursive messages is known at compile-time. Detecting delivery of all outstanding messages requires distributed termination detection [4]. The most efficient termination detection algorithm depends on whether dependent messages are known to be of a fixed-depth or may be of unbounded depth, as well as available features of the underlying network such as message counting or acknowledgment.

4. Conclusion

Active Pebbles consists of two parts, a *programming model* which allows fine-grained, unstructured, data-driven applications to be expressed at their natural level of granularity, and an *execution model* which maps this fine-grained expression to an efficient implementation. Separating expression from implementation allows the application specification to be portable across hardware platforms. Utilizing the four techniques described, the execution model allows the application specification to be adapted to the properties of the underlying physical network to enable maximum performance.

References

[1] D. Callahan, B. L. Chamberlain, and H. P. Zima. The Cascade High Productivity Language. In *Ninth Intl. Workshop on High-Level Par. Prog. Models and Supportive Environments*, pages 52–60, April 2004.

[2] P. Charles, C. Grothoff, V. A. Saraswat, et al. X10: An object-oriented approach to non-uniform cluster computing. In *Object-Oriented Programming, Systems, Languages and Apps.*, pages 519–538, 2005.

[3] N. Edmonds, T. Hoefler, and A. Lumsdaine. A space-efficient parallel algorithm for computing betweenness centrality in distributed memory. In *Int.l Conf. on High Performance Computing*, Goa, India, Dec. 2010.

[4] F. Mattern. Algorithms for distributed termination detection. *Distributed Computing*, 2(3):161–175, 1987.

[5] U. Meyer and P. Sanders. Δ-stepping: A parallelizable shortest path algorithm. *J. Algorithms*, 49(1):114–152, 2003. ISSN 0196-6774.

[6] R. W. Numrich and J. Reid. Co-array Fortran for parallel programming. *SIGPLAN Fortran Forum*, 17(2):1–31, 1998.

[7] UPC Consortium. UPC Language Specifications, v1.2. Technical report, Lawrence Berkeley National Laboratory, 2005. LBNL-59208.

Symbolically Modeling Concurrent MCAPI Executions *

Topher Fischer

Brigham Young University

javert42@cs.byu.edu

Eric Mercer

Brigham Young University

egm@cs.byu.edu

Neha Rungta

NASA Ames Research Center

neha.s.rungta@nasa.gov

Abstract

Improper use of Inter-Process Communication (IPC) within concurrent systems often creates data races which can lead to bugs that are challenging to discover. Techniques that use Satisfiability Modulo Theories (SMT) problems to symbolically model possible executions of concurrent software have recently been proposed for use in the formal verification of software. In this work we describe a new technique for modeling executions of concurrent software that use a message passing API called MCAPI. Our technique uses an execution trace to create an SMT problem that symbolically models all possible concurrent executions and follows the same sequence of conditional branch outcomes as the provided execution trace. We check if there exists a satisfying assignment to the SMT problem with respect to specific safety properties. If such an assignment exists, it provides the conditions that lead to the violation of the property. We show how our method models behaviors of MCAPI applications that are ignored in previously published techniques.

Categories and Subject Descriptors D.2.4 [*Software Engineering*]: Software/Program Verification—Model checking

General Terms Languages, Verification

Keywords MCAPI, Symbolic Analysis, Multicore, SMT

1. Introduction

With the growing availability of multicore processors has come an increase in the amount and complexity of concurrent software. The non-deterministic interleaving of threads within a concurrent program can lead to bugs that are very difficult to discover. Misuse of Inter-Process Communication (IPC) within concurrent software creates data races that can then lead to errors within a system. Because the manifestations of the data races depend on the whims of the operating system's scheduler and delays in message transmission, error states that are the result of data races can be very difficult to produce, reproduce, and identify with ad-hoc testing methods.

Message passing is a form of IPC that involves defining message endpoints that provide different threads the ability to send data to specific endpoints. The Multicore Communications API (MCAPI) is a new message passing API that was released by an organization known as the Multicore Association [4]. MCAPI provides an interface designed for embedded systems that allows communication at different system levels. For example, MCAPI can be implemented in both hardware and software so that an application running in a Linux environment can communicate directly with a graphics processing unit (GPU) and a digital signal processor (DSP).

The semantics of message passing applications are difficult to model. Data non-determinism in message passing applications is expressed in instances where a single receive operation could receive a message from any number of send operations. Which message is received depends on process scheduling and the length of delays in message transmission. The two previously proposed methods for formal MCAPI application verification do not correctly model all the possible behaviors of MCAPI applications. This work specifically overcomes those limitations.

MCC (MCAPI Checker) is a model checker specifically written to verify MCAPI applications [5]. Although MCC represents important progress in the verification of MCAPI applications, it ignores certain behaviors of MCAPI applications because it is not able to consider non-deterministic delays in the communication network when sending messages from two different threads to a common endpoint. Ignoring these behaviors prevents MCC from performing a complete verification of MCAPI applications.

Wang et al. recently described an SMT-based model checking framework called Fusion [6]. Fusion employs a property-driven reduction technique for the verification of concurrent applications that used shared memory. In a series of benchmark tests it was shown that Fusion had significantly shorter runtimes than a comparable tool, Inspect, that uses dynamic partial-order reduction (DPOR) [3, 7]. The impressive results of Fusion were the inspiration for this work to generate SMT problems to model MCAPI applications.

A very closely related work attempts to model MCAPI application executions as SMT problems [2]. To the best of our knowledge this work ignores potential delays in the MCAPI communication network. By ignoring these possible delays this work does not properly model certain MCAPI application behaviors. As with MCC, by ignoring these possible behaviors the method defined in [2] cannot perform a complete verification of MCAPI applications.

We have defined a new method for modeling MCAPI application executions as SMT problems in a manner that symbolically models all possible concurrent executions and follow the same sequence of conditional branch outcomes as the provided execution trace. Our method captures all possible behaviors of the system, and it is much simpler than the method presented in [2]. We briefly describe our method in the following section.

2. Modeling MCAPI Executions

As an illustration we present an abstraction of a very simple MCAPI application in Figure 1. The *send* calls are used to send messages to specified threads. A thread can obtain the message by calling *recv*. When multiple threads send messages to a single endpoint no order of messages is guaranteed when the receiving thread calls the *recv* function. For example, since both *send* calls

* This work is supported by NSF CCF-0903491 and SRC 2009-TJ-1994.

Thread t_0	Thread t_1	Thread t_2
1: recv(A)	recv(C)	send(Y):t_0
2: recv(B)	send(X):t_0	send(Z):t_1

Figure 1: Simplified MCAPI program.

sending to thread t_0 can occur before thread t_0 is executed, either message could be received when thread t_0 calls $recv$ on line 1.

The process of creating an SMT problem to model an MCAPI application execution is started by generating an arbitrary execution trace through the program and then analyzing the trace to generate a set of possible matching send operations for each receive operation in the trace. A pair of send and receive operations *match* when the receive operation receives the message that was sent by the send operation. We call this pair of operations a "match pair".

```
1: 𝒫_MatchPairs = true
2: for each recv ∈ MatchPairs do
3:    tmp := false
4:    for each send ∈ getSends(recv) do
5:       tmp := tmp ∨ match(recv, send)
6:    𝒫_MatchPairs := 𝒫_MatchPairs ∧ (tmp)
```

Figure 2: Match pair encoding algorithm.

Our trace analysis generates a set $MatchPairs$ that contains every receive operation in the trace, and it also provides a function getSends that maps each receive operation to the set of all the send operations that it could match with. This set and function are used in the simple algorithm shown in Figure 2 that encodes all possible match pairs in the execution trace being modeled. The inner loop of this algorithm constructs a disjunction, in the variable tmp, of all the send operations that a specific receive operation could pair with. The outer loop forms a conjunction of the disjunctions created for each of the receive operations in the trace. The result is a boolean representation of every possible match pair discovered in the trace analysis. The trace analysis also assigns each send operation a unique identifier for use in the SMT problem. Each receive operation is associated with an unbound identifier variable that an SMT solver will attempt to assign with the value of a single send operation's identifier. If such an assignment can occur, given the constraints of the problem, it signifies a match between the send and receive operations.

```
1: 𝒫_Unique = true
2: for each recv_i ∈ {0 … |Recvs|} do
3:    for each recv_j ∈ {i + 1 … |Recvs|} do
4:       𝒫_Unique := 𝒫_Unique ∧ isDiffSend(recv_i, recv_j)
```

Figure 3: Uniqueness assertion algorithm.

The match function on line 5 of Figure 2 is a simple function for use in the SMT model. Given a receive and a send operation the match function asserts that the call to send occurs before the call to receive, the message sent is the same message that is being received, and that the identifiers of the two operations are equal. MCAPI also provides a non-blocking receive operation along with a wait operation that blocks until the associated non-blocking call has completed. In the case of a non-blocking receive, the match function asserts that the call to send occurs before the call to the wait operation that is associated with the receive. Checking the identifiers assures that a specific receive operation is matched with

$t_2 : send(Y) \rightarrow t_0 : recv(A)$	$t_2 : send(Z) \rightarrow t_1 : recv(C)$
$t_2 : send(Z) \rightarrow t_1 : recv(C)$	$t_1 : send(X) \rightarrow t_0 : recv(A)$
$t_1 : send(X) \rightarrow t_0 : recv(B)$	$t_2 : send(Y) \rightarrow t_0 : recv(B)$
(a) Possible send/recv Pairings.	(b) Possible send/recv Pairings.

Figure 4: Possible Pairings of send/recv calls from Figure 1.

a specific send operation, and that each receive operation is paired with a different send operation. To assert this we use the algorithm in Figure 3. The results from the two algorithms are conjuncted with assertions on program order ($\mathcal{P}_{Order}$), negated properties that define a correct system ($\neg\mathcal{P}_{Prop}$), and other events in the execution ($\mathcal{P}_{Events}$). The result is an SMT problem that models possible executions of an MCAPI application.

$$\mathcal{P} = \mathcal{P}_{Order} \wedge \mathcal{P}_{MatchPairs} \wedge \mathcal{P}_{Unique} \wedge \neg\mathcal{P}_{Prop} \wedge \mathcal{P}_{Events}$$

The SMT problem can be solved by a constraint solver such as Yices [1]. As the system properties are negated, if the SMT problem is found to be satisfiable then a property violation is possible in the application under test. A simple analysis of the set of satisfying assignments provides a description of the path to the error state.

As stated previously, the technique used in MCC does not consider non-deterministic delays that can occur when two messages are sent from different threads to a common endpoint. If applied to the scenario in Figure 1, MCC would only explore the behavior shown in Figure 4a. It would not consider that the message from send(Y) in thread t_2 could delay so long that the recv(A) operation would receive its message from send(X) in thread t_1. Besides presenting an unnecessarily complicated encoding method, the method presented in [2] also ignores the behavior represented in Figure 4b.

3. Results and Future Work

We have formally defined the semantics of a relevant subset of the MCAPI API in the Redex rewrite language. Based on these semantics we have created a tool that takes as input a trace, a set of match pairs, and a set of correctness properties. The output is an SMT problem that accurately models all possible executions of the trace. A precise set of match pairs can be generated through a depth-first abstract execution of the trace. Though precise, this method can be prohibitively expensive in computation time. As future work we plan to define a method for generating a reasonable over-approximation of the match-pair set, and to define a method for using the over-approximated set of match pairs to generate an SMT problem that models all possible behaviors of the trace.

References

[1] B. Dutertre and L. de Moura. A Fast Linear-Arithmetic Solver for DPLL(T). In *CAV*, volume 4144 of *LNCS*, pages 81–94, 2006.

[2] M. Elwakil and Z. Yang. Debugging support tool for mcapi applications. In *PADTAD*, 2010.

[3] C. Flanagan and P. Godefroid. Dynamic partial-order reduction for model checking software. In *POPL*, pages 110–121. ACM, 2005.

[4] http://www.multicore association.org/workgroup/mcapi.php.

[5] S. Sharma, G. Gopalakrishanan, E. Mercer, and J. Holt. Mcc - a runtime verification tool for mcapi user applications. In *FMCAD*, 2009.

[6] C. Wang, S. Chaudhuri, A. Gupta, and Y. Yang. Symbolic pruning of concurrent program executions. In *ESEC/FSE*, pages 23–32, New York, NY, USA, 2009. ACM.

[7] Y. Yang, X. Chen, and G. Gopalakrishnan. Inspect: A runtime model checker for multithreaded c programs. Technical report, 2008.

Automatic Formal Verification of MPI-Based Parallel Programs

Stephen F. Siegel

Verified Software Laboratory, Department of Computer
and Information Sciences, University of Delaware
siegel@cis.udel.edu

Timothy K. Zirkel

Verified Software Laboratory, Department of Computer
and Information Sciences, University of Delaware
zirkeltk@udel.edu

Abstract

The Toolkit for Accurate Scientific Software (TASS) is a suite of tools for the formal verification of MPI-based parallel programs used in computational science. TASS can verify various safety properties as well as compare two programs for functional equivalence. The TASS front end takes an integer $n \geq 1$ and a C/MPI program, and constructs an abstract model of the program with n processes. Procedures, structs, (multi-dimensional) arrays, heap-allocated data, pointers, and pointer arithmetic are all representable in a TASS model. The model is then explored using symbolic execution and explicit state space enumeration. A number of techniques are used to reduce the time and memory consumed. A variety of realistic MPI programs have been verified with TASS, including Jacobi iteration and manager-worker type programs, and some subtle defects have been discovered. TASS is written in Java and is available from http://vsl.cis.udel.edu/tass under the Gnu Public License.

Categories and Subject Descriptors D.2.4 [*Software Engineering*]: Software/Program Verification—Formal methods

General Terms Verification

Keywords Symbolic execution, MPI, message-passing, debugging, verification

1. Motivation. Developing correct, portable MPI-based parallel programs is difficult for several reasons. First, traditional testing methods can only sample a small portion of a program's parameter and input space. Second, there are many sources of nondeterminism arising from MPI, e.g., how statements from different processes are interleaved in time, the buffering policy of the MPI implementation, and the use of "wildcard" receives. Often, a program may appear to run correctly on one machine, but when ported to a new platform which resolves the nondeterminism differently, a defect is revealed. These defects may manifest themselves as deadlocks or as results which are incorrect or differ unexpectedly from execution to execution. Such defects are often difficult to identify and isolate.

2. Symbolic Execution. TASS uses *symbolic execution* [3, 4] to deal with the issue of the input space. The user may insert pragmas into the C source to identify input variables, e.g.,

```
#pragma TASS input { N > 1 && N <= 10 }
int N;
```

(This pragma is accompanied by a predicate which restricts the input space.) TASS initially assigns a unique *symbolic constant* $(X_1, X_2, \ldots)$ to each such variable. As TASS "executes" the program, operations on these values result in more complex symbolic expressions.

A branch is treated as a nondeterministic choice, and a boolean-valued *path condition* variable pc is used to record the choices made. For example, if the *true* branch is chosen at a branch on condition a>0, when the value of a is the symbolic expression $X_1 + 1$ and the value of pc is $X_2 < 0$, then the value of pc becomes $X_2 < 0 \land X_1 + 1 > 0$. Automated theorem proving techniques are used to determine if pc becomes unsatisfiable, which indicates the current path is infeasible and need not be explored. TASS dispatches most of the proofs itself, but when it cannot, it invokes CVC3 [1]. If CVC3 cannot produce a definitive answer, TASS logs a *possible* violation. TASS analysis is *safe*: if it says a property holds, the property holds (within the specified bounds). Spurious error reports are possible, but rare, in our experience.

The ability to reason about the infinite input space is one of the main advantages over traditional testing and dynamic verifiers such as ISP [10], which analyze executions for one input vector at a time.

3. State enumeration. A *symbolic state* assigns a symbolic expression to each variable in the program, including pc. It represents a set of concrete states: any assignment of concrete values to symbolic constants that satisfies pc results in a concrete state in the set.

TASS uses explicit state enumeration techniques to deal with the nondeterminism arising from MPI (as well as from symbolic execution branches described above). An explicit representation of the state is used, and the set of all reachable states is explored with a depth-first search. Typically, the user places bounds on certain variables to ensure the state space is finite (or reasonably small).

A number of techniques are used to reduce the memory footprint. The state is represented hierarchically: at the highest level there are components for the input and output variables, the state of each process, and the set of buffered messages. A process state consists of the state of each global variable and a call stack. The call stack is a sequence of frames. Each frame has the value of all local variables and the current location within a function body. The life-cycle of a state component has three phases: mutable, immutable, and canonic (flyweighted). These design choices facilitate maximal sharing between states on the stack or seen set, while still allowing fast modifications when a component is not shared.

4. Properties checked. TASS checks a number of safety properties as it explores the state space: absence of (absolute or potential) deadlocks, buffer overflows (from pointer arithmetic, array indexing, etc.), reading uninitialized variables, division by zero, memory leaks, and assertion violations; the type and size of a message received with MPI_Recv are compatible with the receive buffer/type; proper use of malloc and free, MPI_Init, MPI_Finalize, and so on. In all cases, violations are logged and the search continues

program	bounds	nprocs	time (s)	states
adder	$n \leq 200$	30	443	411044
diffusion	$n_x \leq 100 \wedge n_t \leq 2$	50	4653	5788608
matmat	$l \leq 2 \wedge m \leq 2 \wedge n \leq 10$	7	13157	151752013
matmat	$l \leq 2 \wedge m \leq 2 \wedge n \leq 10$	11	242	10543295
integrate	$intervals = 12 \wedge tol = 0.01$	6	3788	3511123
laplace	$n_x \leq 4 \wedge n_y \leq 12 \wedge n_t \leq 30$	5	30911	3384271
laplace	$n_x \leq 4 \wedge n_y \leq 30 \wedge n_t \leq 3$	20	1787	875577

Figure 1. TASS performance verifying functional equivalence

after adjustments to the path condition, in order to report as many errors as possible from a single search. If no errors are reported then it is guaranteed that all the safety properties hold on all executions with the given processor count and within the specified bounds.

5. Simplification. Two symbolic states are *equivalent* if they represent the same set of concrete states. The ability to recognize equivalence can greatly reduce the search space. This can often be accomplished by transforming symbolic expressions into a canonical form. For example, TASS transforms every real-valued expression into a quotient p/q, where p and q are polynomials in *primitive* expressions. (A *primitive expression* is any non-concrete expression that is not the result of +, -, *, or /; symbolic constants and array-read and array-write expressions are examples.)

TASS performs other equivalence-preserving state transformations. For example, each equation occurring as a clause in pc may be considered a linear expression $\sum_i a_i x_i$, where a_i is a concrete real and x_i is a monomial in the primitives. Gaussian elimination is performed on the matrix of coefficients resulting from these equations to determine if any monomials can be reduced to concrete values. For example if pc is $X_1 + X_2 = 3 \wedge X_1 - X_2 = 1$, then 2 will be substituted for X_1 wherever X_1 occurs in the state, 1 will be substituted for X_2, and pc will become *true*.

6. Reduction. Exploring every possible interleaving is not necessary to verify the properties in our list. For example, for programs which restrict their use of MPI to a certain safe subset (which excludes `MPI_ANY_SOURCE`), it can be shown that it is safe to consider a single interleaving [6, 7]. TASS uses the "urgent" partial order reduction algorithm, an optimization which is safe even in the presence of `MPI_ANY_SOURCE` [5]. For programs in the safe set, it still explores only a single interleaving; otherwise, whenever some process is at an any-source receive, some subset of the possible interleavings must be explored. This can reduce the number of states explored dramatically.

7. Comparative symbolic execution. Pragmas can be inserted into the source code to identify output as well as input variables. Together, these annotations specify an input set X and output set Y, and the program may be considered a function $f: X \rightarrow Y$. Two programs with the same X and Y may be compared to see if they define the same function. This is extremely useful in computational science, where developers often start with a simple sequential version of an algorithm, and transform it by hand by adding layers of optimizations and parallelism before arriving at the production code. TASS gives the developers the ability to check that the original and final codes are functionally equivalent. The technique used is *comparative symbolic execution* [9]. TASS constructs a model in which the two programs read the same input and run concurrently, and checks the assertion that the outputs agree at termination. (KLEE [2] is another symbolic execution tool which has been used to verify functional equivalence in some cases; however it does not apply to parallel programs.)

8. Collective assertions. Assertions are an important tool for developing reliable sequential programs. However, assertions within

a single process are unable to capture important properties of the interactions between different processes. To remedy this, TASS gives users the ability to use *collective assertions* [8]. A single collective assertion comprises a set of locations in each process and an expression on the global state. The semantics are defined as follows: whenever control in a process reaches one of the locations, a "snapshot" of the local state of that process is sent to a coordinator; once a snapshot has been received from each process, the expression is evaluated on the global state formed by uniting the snapshots.

9. Collective loop invariants. The infinite-state problem arising from loops can be surmounted in some cases using an invariant, which the user can associate to a loop using another pragma. The invariant is a form of collective assertion which is not only checked by TASS, but is used to simplify the state of a process after each loop iteration. This results in a possible loss of precision (i.e., possible spurious error reports) but is still safe. This technique applies to loops that cut across multiple processes, and even to comparative symbolic execution.

10. Experiments. We have applied TASS to small but non-trivial MPI programs. Examples include (1) a program to sum the elements of a block-distributed array, (2) a block-distributed solver for the 1d-diffusion equation, (3) a manager-worker matrix multiplication routine, (4) a 1d adaptive mesh numerical integrator, and (5) a column-distributed 2d-Laplace solver using Jacobi iteration. Results for verifying the equivalence of various configurations of these with the corresponding sequential/specification program are shown in Fig. 1. More extensive case studies, and further extensions and optimizations, are in progress.

Acknowledgments

Supported by NSF grants CCF-0953210 and CCF-0733035 and the University of Delaware Research Foundation.

References

[1] C. Barrett and C. Tinelli. CVC3. In W. Damm and H. Hermanns, editors, *CAV 2007*, volume 4590 of *LNCS*, pages 298–302. Springer.

[2] C. Cadar, D. Dunbar, and D. Engler. KLEE: Unassisted and automatic generation of high-coverage tests for complex systems programs. *Proc. 8th USENIX Symposium on Operating Systems Design and Implementation*, 2008.

[3] S. Khurshid, C. S. Păsăreanu, and W. Visser. Generalized symbolic execution for model checking and testing. In H. Garavel and J. Hatcliff, editors, *TACAS 2003*, volume 2619 of *LNCS*, pages 553–568.

[4] J. C. King. Symbolic execution and program testing. *Communications of the ACM*, 19(7):385–394, 1976.

[5] S. F. Siegel. Efficient verification of halting properties for MPI programs with wildcard receives. In R. Cousot, editor, *VMCAI 2005*, volume 3385 of *LNCS*, pages 413–429.

[6] S. F. Siegel and G. S. Avrunin. Modeling wildcard-free MPI programs for verification. In *PPoPP '05*, pages 95–106. ACM, 2005.

[7] S. F. Siegel and G. S. Avrunin. Verification of halting properties for MPI programs using nonblocking operations. In F. Cappello, T. Hérault, and J. Dongarra, editors, *Euro PVM/MPI 2007*, volume 4757 of *LNCS*, pages 326–334. Springer, 2007.

[8] S. F. Siegel and T. K. Zirkel. Collective assertions. In R. Jhala and D. Schmidt, editors, *VMCAI 2011*, volume 6538 of *LNCS*, pages 387–402.

[9] S. F. Siegel, A. Mironova, G. S. Avrunin, and L. A. Clarke. Combining symbolic execution with model checking to verify parallel numerical programs. *ACM TOSEM*, 17(2):Article 10, 1–34, 2008.

[10] A. Vo, S. Vakkalanka, M. DeLisi, G. Gopalakrishnan, R. M. Kirby, and R. Thakur. Formal verification of practical MPI programs. In *PPoPP 2009*, pages 261–270. ACM.

SCRATCH: a Tool for Automatic Analysis of DMA Races *

Alastair F. Donaldson   Daniel Kroening   Philipp Rümmer

Oxford University Computing Laboratory, Oxford, UK

{Alastair.Donaldson,Daniel.Kroening,Philipp.Ruemmer}@comlab.ox.ac.uk

Abstract

We present the SCRATCH tool, which uses bounded model checking and k-induction to automatically analyse software for multicore processors such as the Cell BE, in order to detect DMA races.

Categories and Subject Descriptors F.3.1 [*Logics and Meanings of Programs*]: Specifying, Verifying & Reasoning about Programs

General Terms Languages, Theory, Verification

Keywords Model checking, k-induction, Cell BE, DMA

1. Introduction

Multicore processors such as the Cell BE avoid the memory wall problem by equipping cores with local, "scratch-pad" memories. Direct Memory Access (DMA) is the mechanism used to transfer data between main and scratch-pad memories. A DMA operation requests that a contiguous chunk of memory be copied between memory spaces *asynchronously*: program execution can continue while the DMA operation is pending. This allows the latency associated with data movement to be hidden, by overlapping computation with communication using double- or triple-buffering. Correct programming of DMAs is notoriously difficult. *DMA races*, where two DMAs operate on the same region of memory and at least one modifies the memory, are easily introduced due to missing synchronization commands, and lead to nondeterministically occurring bugs that are hard to reproduce and fix.

We present SCRATCH,[1] a formal verification tool for automatic, static analysis of DMA races on scratchpad memory. SCRATCH operates on a C program for one of the Synergistic Processor Element (SPE) cores of the Cell BE processor, and uses a combination of SAT-based bounded model checking [2, 3] and k-induction [6] to detect, or prove absence of, DMA races on SPE local store. The tool uses a novel, implicit encoding of DMA operations, drawing on the notion of *prophecy* variables [1]. We describe this encoding and our use of k-induction, and show experimentally that SCRATCH is effective in DMA race analysis for a range of benchmarks.

Although implemented for the Cell platform, the techniques behind SCRATCH are general, and could easily be adapted to other multicore systems that use DMA.

---

* Supported by EPSRC grants EP/G051100 and EP/G026254/1, the EU FP7 STREP MOGENTES, and the EU ARTEMIS CESAR project.

[1] Tool and benchmarks available at http://www.cprover.org/scratch.

2. An implicit encoding of DMAs

SCRATCH uses four tracker variables to collaboratively track a single, *arbitrary* DMA operation. DMA races are detected by instrumenting the program so that on issue, a DMA is compared with the DMA currently tracked by the variables (if any). Because the tracked DMA is chosen arbitrarily from the set of previously issued DMAs, any potential DMA race will be detected by symbolic execution of the instrumented program up to a sufficient depth. We call this encoding *implicit*: a DMA is implicitly compared with all prior DMAs; no explicit history of active DMAs is required. The tracker variables are: `valid`, a flag which is *false* if no DMA operation is tracked, and *true* otherwise; `addr`, `sz` and `tag`, which record the local store address, size and identifying tag for a pending DMA operation if `valid`=*true*, and whose values are irrelevant if `valid`=*false*. Initially, `valid` is set to *false*, and the other tracker variables are nondeterministically assigned.

A DMA `get` operation has the form `get`(l,h,s,t), and requests a data transfer of s contiguous bytes from host memory region $[h, h + s)$ to local memory region $[l, l + s)$. The operation is identified by tag t (a value in the range $[0..ws - 1]$, where ws is the processor word-size); this tag can be used subsequently to synchronize with the `get` operation. The size parameter s must be less than max, a hardware-imposed maximum transfer size. The SCRATCH instrumenter replaces a `get` operation with the following code:

```
(1)    assert((unsigned)t < ws && (unsigned)s < max);
(2)    assert(!valid || l+s <= addr || addr+sz <= s);
(3)    memset(l,*,s);
(4)    if(*){ valid = true; addr = l; sz = s; tag = t; }
```

Statement (1) ensures that the size and tag associated with the operation are within the range permitted by the hardware. Statement (2) checks that if the tracker variables are tracking a DMA operation d, the new DMA operation does not locally race with d. Statement (3) over-approximates the effect of the DMA by modelling transfer of *arbitrary* data from host memory. Here $*$ denotes a nondeterministic value, and the intended semantics is that $*$ is evaluated separately for each byte in the region $[l, l + s)$. The statements labelled (4) assign details of the new DMA operation to the tracker variables, setting `valid` to *true*. By nondeterministically guarding these statements, we ensure that an *arbitrary* DMA operation is tracked in the instrumented program. A DMA `put` operation is dual to a `get` operation and is encoded similarly.

A DMA `wait` operation has the form `wait`$(mask)$, and causes execution to block until all DMA operations identified by tag i have completed, for each $0 \le i < ws$ such that $mask[i] = 1$. A `wait` operation is encoded by SCRATCH as follows:

```
assume( ((1<<tag)&mask ) == 0 );
```

If `assume`(e) is executable with e=*false*, the current execution trace is discarded; otherwise the statement is a no-op. Rather than handling a `wait` by explicitly erasing details of a DMA if it is identified by a tag whose bit is set in $mask$, the encoding simply decides that no DMA with this property was tracked in the first place! The instrumentation variables can be regarded as *prophetic* [1] since the future program execution determines whether a DMA operation should be tracked.

SCRATCH handles the full range of DMA operations supported by the Cell architecture, including fence, barrier and list operations, via appropriate adaptations of the above instrumentation.

Comparison with an existing, explicit encoding. An alternative encoding of DMA operations for race analysis has been presented [4]. This *explicit* encoding mirrors the runtime monitoring approach employed by the IBM Race Check library [5], recording a bounded history of D pending DMA operations (for some $D > 0$), and checking new DMA operations against the history log. Although more intuitive than our new implicit encoding, the explicit encoding is less efficient when SAT-based symbolic model checking is used for analysis, since the size of the representation is proportional to the parameter D, which may be large for complex examples. Furthermore, the explicit encoding cannot handle programs where the number of DMA operations that may be issued simultaneously is unbounded; our new encoding does not suffer from this restriction.

3. SAT-based model checking with k-induction

SCRATCH builds on the SAT-based model checker CBMC [3], which allows instrumented programs to be symbolically executed up to a given depth, and bit-blasted to yield a SAT representation for which satisfying assignments correspond to DMA races. This facilitates bug-finding, but cannot prove *absence* of DMA races. To achieve this latter goal, SCRATCH combines SAT-based analysis with k-induction [6], applying k-induction directly to program loops. To verify unbounded absence of DMA races for an instrumented program of the form α; `while`(c) $\{\beta\}$ γ, SCRATCH solves a series of verification problems using bounded model checking. For increasing values of k, starting with $k = 0$, a base case and a step case are checked:

Base case: $\alpha;$ $\underbrace{\texttt{if}(c)\,\{\beta\}\dots\texttt{if}(c)\,\{\beta\}}_{k\text{ times}}$ $\texttt{if}(!c)\,\{\gamma\}$

Step case:
$\texttt{havoc};$ $\underbrace{\texttt{assume}(c);\ \overline{\beta};\dots;\ \texttt{assume}(c);\ \overline{\beta};}_{k\text{ times}}$ $\texttt{if}(c)\,\{\beta\}\ \texttt{else}\,\{\gamma\}$

The base case consists of the loop unwound k times. A base case failure yields a counterexample exposing a DMA race; otherwise we know that a DMA race cannot occur within k loop iterations.

In the step case, `havoc` sets every program variable to a nondeterministic value, and $\overline{\beta}$ denotes the sequence β with `assert` replaced by `assume` throughout. The step case succeeds when, from *any* potential state, if k loop iterations can be executed without encountering a DMA race then a further iteration can be executed (if c still holds), or the loop epilogue can be executed (if c does not hold), without a DMA race occurring. If there is some k for which both the base case and step case hold, the theory of k-induction guarantees that a DMA race can never occur. SCRATCH tries k-induction with increasing values for k until a result is obtained, or a "give up" value for k is reached. Nested loops are handled via translation to a single, monolithic loop.

We find k-induction works well in our application domain because DMA operations in loops are typically designed to be pending for only a bounded number of loop iterations. This often allows k-induction to succeed with a value of k proportional to the bound.

4. Experimental evaluation

Benchmarks. We evaluate SCRATCH using a set of 22 benchmarks adapted from examples supplied with the IBM Cell SDK [5]. The benchmarks include a variety of data processing programs, using single-, double- or triple-buffering for data-movement; two audio

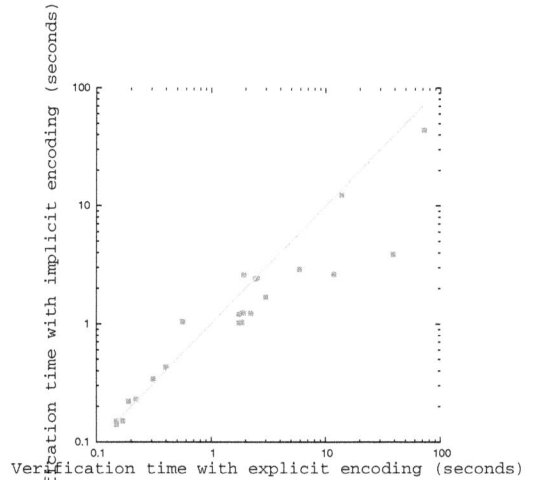

Figure 1. Verification times for correct benchmarks using an explicit encoding of DMAs [4] and our new, implicit encoding

processing applications; two particle simulations using Euler integration; and quaternion Julia set ray-tracing.

We apply SCRATCH to correct and buggy versions of the benchmarks. In two cases we found genuine bugs. For the remaining benchmarks, bugs are injected into the examples, either by removing a `wait` operation, changing the tag used to identify a DMA, or switching an operation between `get` and `put`. Experiments are performed on a 3GHz Intel Xeon platform with 48Gb RAM, running Ubuntu. MiniSat 2.0 is used as a back-end SAT solver.

Bug-finding. Bounded model checking proves extremely effective for detecting DMA races in buggy versions of our benchmarks. With our new encoding, the maximum verification time across all benchmarks (averaged over multiple runs) is 0.87s. Performance is slightly better than with the explicit encoding of [4], a speedup of $1.52\times$ is achieved using our new encoding in the best case.

Proving race freedom. Each point in the scatter plot of Figure 1 represents one of our benchmarks; its x- and y-coordinates show the time (in seconds) taken to verify the correct version of this benchmark using the explicit and implicit encoding of DMA operations, respectively. Points appearing below the diagonal line correspond to benchmarks where our new encoding is faster. The results show that k-induction provides a tractable method for proving absence of races. Sometimes the implicit encoding significantly outperforms the explicit encoding: verification with the implicit encoding is 10 times faster for one of the *Euler* examples. In this benchmark, an SPE can issue 10 concurrent DMAs. The explicit encoding tracks all these DMAs, leading to a large SAT instance, while the largest SAT instance for the implicit encoding, which is independent of the number of issued DMAs, is almost $10\times$ smaller.

References

[1] M. Abadi and L. Lamport. The existence of refinement mappings. *Theor. Comput. Sci.*, 82(2):253–284, 1991.

[2] A. Biere, A. Cimatti, E. M. Clarke, O. Strichman, and Y. Zhu. Bounded model checking. *Advances in Computers*, 58:118–149, 2003.

[3] E. Clarke, D. Kroening, and F. Lerda. A tool for checking ANSI-C programs. In *TACAS*, pages 168–176, 2004.

[4] A. F. Donaldson, D. Kroening, and P. Rümmer. Automatic analysis of scratch-pad memory code for heterogeneous multicore processors. In *TACAS*, pages 280–295, 2010.

[5] IBM. Cell BE resource center, October 2009. http://www.ibm.com/developerworks/power/cell/.

[6] M. Sheeran, S. Singh, and G. Stålmarck. Checking safety properties using induction and a SAT-solver. In *FMCAD*, pages 108–125, 2000.

Automatic Safety Proofs for Asynchronous Memory Operations *

Matko Botinčan   Mike Dodds

University of Cambridge, UK

{matko.botincan,mike.dodds}@cl.cam.ac.uk

Alastair F. Donaldson

University of Oxford, UK

alastair.donaldson@comlab.ox.ac.uk

Matthew J. Parkinson

Microsoft Research Cambridge, UK

mattpark@microsoft.com

Abstract

We present a work-in-progress proof system and tool, based on separation logic, for analysing memory safety of multicore programs that use asynchronous memory operations.

Categories and Subject Descriptors   F.3.1 [*Logics and Meanings of Programs*]: Specifying, Verifying & Reasoning about Programs

General Terms   Languages, Theory, Verification

Keywords   Separation logic, memory safety, concurrency

1. Introduction

Asynchronous memory operations are an important feature of modern multicore systems. They provide a means for coping with the high cost of shared memory access: cores can delegate data-movement to dedicated hardware, and continue processing on fast, private memory, without contention. Asynchronous memory operations are widely available, e.g. DMA operations in the Cell BE, I/O Acceleration Technology in Intel Xeon cores, and asynchronous memory copying in CUDA/OpenCL.

The high performance permitted by asynchronous memory operations comes at a price: increased programming complexity. Erroneous synchronisation within a thread can lead to data races, for example when copying a section of memory by an asynchronous operation and then writing to it before the operation completes. If a function returns while an asynchronous operation on a local variable is still pending (perhaps as a part of a speculative pre-fetch), the operation may corrupt the stack frame of subsequently called functions. These problems are compounded in a multithreaded setting: incorrectly managed asynchronous operations can lead to inter-core data races. Asynchronous operations run concurrently with other threads, and they have undefined behaviour over written memory until synchronised. The defects described above thus lead to highly nondeterministic behaviour, thus buggy programs may behave entirely correctly on some implementations, while failing dramatically on others.

We report work in progress on a methodology and tool for automatically proving safety of multicore programs that use asyn-

---

* This work was supported by the EPSRC, RAEng and the Gates trust.

```
void master(char src[length], char dst[length]) {
    tid* t[N]; int i;            // 'master' runs on host core.
    for (i=0; i<N; i++)
        { t[i] = fork(slave, src+i*M*L, dst+i*M*L, M, i); }
    for (i=0; i<N; i++) { join(t[i]); }
}
void slave(char* in, char* out, int M, int t) {
    char buf[L]; int i = 0;
    while (i < M) {
        get(buf, in, L, t);    // 'slave' runs on accelerator cores, e.g. SPEs
        wait(t);               // 'in' and 'out' point to host memory
        in = in + L;           // 'buf' allocated in scratch-pad memory
        // Process data in the array
        put(buf, out, L, t);
        wait(t);
        out = out + L; i = i + 1;
    } }
```

Figure 1. Data processing example using single buffering.

chronous memory operations. Reasoning about such operations involves complex flow-, path- and context-sensitive analysis of accesses to possibly overlapping regions of memory. We propose a deductive, proof-based approach that enables automation of this analysis. If a proof can be found via our method then the program is guaranteed to be race-free and memory-safe. We show how proofs are performed with an example drawn from the IBM Cell SDK [4]. We then outline our approach to automating this proof strategy.

2. Proving safety: a worked example

Single buffering. In the example of Fig. 1, a master thread divides array processing among several slave threads. The master thread runs on the host core, while slave threads run on accelerator cores equipped with scratch-pad memory, e.g. SPEs in the Cell BE architecture. In the slave function, operation **get/put** initiates an asynchronous copy to/from the thread's private memory, respectively. Operations are parameterised by associated tags; calling **wait** on a tag t blocks until all operations associated with t have completed. The function slave uses these operations to implement single buffering. An internal buffer of size L is used to store chunks of the shared array. Operations **get** and **put** are used to fill the buffer and push the results of processing (details of which are omitted) back to the main program. More complex algorithms, using double- or triple-buffering, exploit asynchrony to improve performance by overlapping computation with communication.

Proving safety. Our system is based on separation logic [5], which extends Hoare logic to permit reasoning about dynamically allocated data structures. This is achieved via a new *spatial conjunction* logical connective: $P_1 * P_2$ means that there exists a splitting of the memory into two disjoint parts, one satisfying P_1 and the other P_2. Separation logic also has a new rule, the frame rule, which allows us just consider the memory that a command changes, and know that the rest is unchanged implicitly.

To reason about the single-buffer example, we introduce two new assertions: $\mathsf{arr}(x, l)$ denotes that x is the address of the first element of an array segment of length l; $\mathsf{MFC}(\mathsf{t}, \mathcal{O})$ (for '*memory flow controller*'), denotes pending asynchronous memory operations. The argument t is the tag controlling the operations, while $\mathcal{O}$ is the set of pending operations. When a thread calls **get** or **put**, the arguments of the operation are added to the set, as follows:

$$\left\{ \begin{array}{c} \mathsf{arr}(\mathsf{l}, \mathsf{s}) * \mathsf{arr}(\mathsf{h}, \mathsf{s}) \\ * \, \mathsf{MFC}(\mathsf{t}, \mathcal{O}) \end{array} \right\} \mathbf{get}/\mathbf{put}(\mathsf{l}, \mathsf{h}, \mathsf{s}, \mathsf{t}) \left\{ \mathsf{MFC}\left(\mathsf{t}, \{\langle \mathsf{l}, \mathsf{h}, \mathsf{s}\rangle\} \cup \mathcal{O}\right) \right\}$$

Note that the source and target arrays disappear in the operation post-conditions. Intuitively, these resources are given away to the memory flow controller until the operation finishes. This transfer of resource is essential to ensure race-freedom of the client program.

The above specifications require that each operation can write to both local and shared arrays. In our real proof system, we additionally parameterise arrays by a permission level π, controlling read and write access. If $\pi \in (0..1)$ then the elements of the array can only be read by the thread, while if $\pi = 1$ then the elements can also be written to. The specification for **get** is then as follows (the specification for **put** is dual):

$$\left\{ \begin{array}{c} \mathsf{arr}(\mathbf{1}, \mathsf{l}, \mathsf{s}) * \mathsf{arr}(\pi, \mathsf{h}, \mathsf{s}) \\ * \, \mathsf{MFC}(\mathsf{t}, \mathcal{O}) \end{array} \right\} \ \mathbf{get}(\mathsf{l}, \mathsf{h}, \mathsf{s}, \mathsf{t}) \ \left\{ \mathsf{MFC}\left(\mathsf{t}, \{\langle \mathsf{l}, \mathsf{h}, \mathsf{s}\rangle\} \cup \mathcal{O}\right) \right\}$$

When a thread calls **wait()**, the resources held by the memory flow controller are returned. Here $\circledast$ is the iterated version of $*$:

$$\left\{ \mathsf{MFC}(t, \mathcal{O}) \right\} \quad \mathbf{wait}(\mathsf{t}) \quad \left\{ \begin{array}{c} \mathsf{MFC}(t, \emptyset) \, * \\ \circledast_{\langle \mathsf{l}, \mathsf{h}, \mathsf{s}\rangle \in \mathcal{O}} . \, \mathsf{arr}(\mathsf{l}, \mathsf{s}) * \mathsf{arr}(\mathsf{h}, \mathsf{s}) \end{array} \right\}$$

The precondition to slave must ensure that the function can read elements of the in array and write to elements of the out array:

$$\mathsf{arr}(\mathsf{in}, \mathsf{M} \cdot \mathsf{L}) * \mathsf{arr}(\mathsf{out}, \mathsf{M} \cdot \mathsf{L}) \tag{1}$$

The proof for the body of the **while** loop in slave is given in Fig. 2; it uses the array segment splitting rule that allows $\mathsf{arr}(x, l)$ to be split as $\mathsf{arr}(x, i) * \mathsf{arr}(x+i, l-i)$ for $0 < i < l$. This rule is also applied backwards to combine smaller array segments into a bigger one. At slave's exit point we end up with the postcondition having the same symbolic representation as the precondition.

Verifying master (Fig. 3) requires rules for **fork** and **join**. Here Γ is an environment associating threads with specifications.

$$\frac{\mathsf{f}(\bar{\mathsf{x}}) \colon \{P\}\_\{Q\} \in \Gamma}{\Gamma \vdash \{P[\bar{\mathsf{e}}/\bar{\mathsf{x}}]\} \ \mathsf{t} = \mathbf{fork}(\mathsf{f}, \bar{\mathsf{e}}) \ \{\mathsf{thread}(\mathsf{t}, \mathsf{f}, \bar{\mathsf{e}})\}} \ \text{FORK}$$

$$\frac{\mathsf{f}(\bar{\mathsf{x}}) \colon \{P\}\_\{Q\} \in \Gamma}{\Gamma \vdash \{\mathsf{thread}(\mathsf{t}, \mathsf{f}, \bar{\mathsf{e}})\} \ \mathsf{v} = \mathbf{join}(\mathsf{t}) \ \{Q[\bar{\mathsf{e}}; \mathsf{v}/\bar{\mathsf{x}}; \mathsf{ret}]\}} \ \text{JOIN}$$

Upon forking a new thread, the parent thread obtains the assertion thread that stores information about passed arguments for program variables and gives up ownership of the precondition of the function. Joining requires that the executing thread owns the thread handle which it then exchanges for the function's postcondition.

3. Automating the proof system

We have built a prototype tool for automating proofs of the kind illustrated in §2; the proof annotations in Figs. 2 and 3, marked in blue, were synthesized by our tool. The tool accepts Cell BE programs written in a C fragment, where asynchronous memory operations correspond to DMA requests. An input program is translated

```
while (i < M) {
  { arr(in − (i · L), L·M) ∗ arr(out − (i · L), L·M)
      ∗ arr(buf, L) ∗ MFC(t, ∅) ∧ i < M }
  get(in, buf, L, t);
  { arr(in − (i·L), i·L) ∗ arr(in + L, L·(M−i−1)) ∗
    arr(out − (i · L), L·M) ∗ MFC(t, {⟨in, buf, L⟩}) ∧ i < M }
  wait(t);
  { arr(in − (i · L), L·M) ∗ arr(out − (i · L), L·M)
      ∗ arr(buf, L) ∗ MFC(t, ∅) ∧ i < M }
  in = in + L;
  // Process data in the array.
  put(buf, out, L, t);
  { arr(out − (i·L), i·L) ∗ arr(out + L, L·(M−i−1)) ∗
    arr(in − ((i+1)·L), L·M) ∗ MFC(t, {⟨buf, out, L⟩}) ∧ i < M }
  wait(t);
  { arr(in − ((i+1)·L), L·M) ∗ arr(out − (i·L), L·M) ∗
      arr(buf, L) ∗ MFC(t, {⟨buf, out, L⟩}) ∧ i < M }
  out = out + L; i = i + 1;
}
```

Figure 2. Proof of the main loop of the slave function.

```
{ arr(src, N·M·L) ∗ arr(dst, N·M·L) }
for(i=0; i<N; i++){ t[i] = fork(slave, src+i∗M∗L, dst+i∗M∗L, M, i)}
{ ⊛₀≤i<N . thread(t[i], slave, ⟨src+i·M·L, dst+i·M·L, M, i⟩) }
for(i=0; i<N; i++){ join(t[i]) }
{ arr(src, N·M·L) ∗ arr(dst, N·M·L) }
```

Figure 3. Proof of the master's body.

into the internal representation of jStar, a theorem prover for separation logic [2]. Using jStar, we have built a fully-fledged proof system for race-freedom and memory safety in presence of thread concurrency, incorporating the proof rules of §2. Asynchronous memory operations are defined at the byte level but are usually applied to structured data. Our logic uses rewrite rules to marshal data between structured and byte-level representations, according to the C memory model and Cell alignment rules. Arithmetic obligations are discharged to an SMT solver. Currently, the user is required to manually specify pre- and post-conditions for functions (e.g., like the one in Eq. 1 for the slave function). To avoid this, we plan to use *abduction* [1]. Abduction automatically generates (approximations of) resources needed for an operation to execute without error. They can be pushed to the start of a function, automatically generating (partial) preconditions, and from that function specifications.

Unlike an approach to solving this problem based on model checking [3], our method applies to concurrent programs that use dynamic thread creation. Our implementation focuses on Cell BE programs, but could be applied to other platforms (e.g., CUDA and OpenCL). We are intentionally building our logic and our tools to be generic and modular, thus adaptable to these other settings.

References

[1] C. Calcagno, D. Distefano, P. W. O'Hearn, and H. Yang. Compositional shape analysis by means of bi-abduction. In *POPL*, 2009.

[2] D. Distefano and M. J. Parkinson. jStar: towards practical verification for Java. In *OOPSLA*, 2008.

[3] A. F. Donaldson, D. Kroening, and P. Rümmer. Automatic analysis of scratch-pad memory code for heterogeneous multicore processors. In *TACAS*, 2010.

[4] IBM. Cell BE, 2009. http://ibm.com/developerworks/power/cell.

[5] J. C. Reynolds. Separation logic: A logic for shared mutable data structures. In *LICS*, 2002.

Author Index

www.ingramcontent.com/pod-product-compliance
Lightning Source LLC
Chambersburg PA
CBHW080925220326
41598CB00034B/5684